Lecture Notes in Computer Science   14933

Formal Methods

Subline of Lecture Notes in Computer Science

More information about this series at https://link.springer.com/bookseries/558

André Platzer · Kristin Yvonne Rozier ·
Matteo Pradella · Matteo Rossi
Editors

Formal Methods

26th International Symposium, FM 2024
Milan, Italy, September 9–13, 2024
Proceedings, Part I

 Springer

Editors
André Platzer
Karlsruhe Institute of Technology
Karlsruhe, Germany

Kristin Yvonne Rozier
Iowa State University
Ames, IA, USA

Matteo Pradella
Politecnico di Milano
Milan, Italy

Matteo Rossi
Politecnico di Milano
Milan, Italy

ISSN 0302-9743   ISSN 1611-3349 (electronic)
Lecture Notes in Computer Science
ISBN 978-3-031-71161-9   ISBN 978-3-031-71162-6   (eBook)
https://doi.org/10.1007/978-3-031-71162-6

This Springer imprint is published by the registered company Springer Nature Switzerland AG
The registered company address is: Gewerbestrasse 11, 6330 Cham, Switzerland

If disposing of this product, please recycle the paper.

Preface

These volumes contain the papers presented for publication at the 26th International Symposium on Formal Methods (FM 2024), held in Milano, Italy, during September 9–13, 2024.

FM 2024 is the 26th event in the series of symposia organized by Formal Methods Europe (FME), an independent association whose aim is to stimulate the use of, and research on, formal methods for software development. The FM symposia have been successful in bringing together participants from academia, industry, and governments around a program of original papers on research and industrial experience, workshops, tutorials, reports on tools, projects, and ongoing doctoral research. FM 2024 is both an occasion to celebrate and a platform for enthusiastic researchers and practitioners from a diversity of backgrounds to exchange their ideas and share their experiences.

In addition to the main research track, FM 2024 included an Embedded Systems track, an Industry Day (I-Day) track, a Tutorial Paper track, a Journal First track, and a Doctoral Symposium. Also, 5 conferences and 6 workshops were co-located with FM 2024.

FM 2024 featured keynotes by David Basin (ETH Zürich), Hadas Kress-Gazit (Cornell University) and Marta Kwiatkowska (University of Oxford) with Byron Cook (University College London and AWS) as joint speaker for I-Day and the co-located conference on Formal Methods for Industrial Critical Systems (FMICS).

One main innovation of FM 2024 is the addition of a tutorial paper category. Tutorial papers present ideas with a focus on pedagogy over technical advances. By being written in a broadly-accessible way, tutorials clarify important ideas, bring new researchers into the community, and serve as a bridge to practitioners.

With 219 submissions, FM 2024 received a record-breaking number of paper submissions, which made it possible to select a particularly strong program. The main FM 2024 track received 178 submissions (143 regular research submissions, 8 case study submissions, 21 long tool paper submissions, 6 short tool demonstration submissions). The special embedded systems track of FM 2024 received 17 embedded submissions, the new tutorial paper track received 14 tutorial submissions, and the I-Day track received 10 industry report submissions. All paper submissions complying with the submission guidelines were reviewed by at least 3 reviewers, with a short author feedback period for a subset of the submissions selected for clarification and feedback by the 48 PC members. The main FM track accepted 44 papers (31 regular research papers, 1 case study paper, 8 long tool papers, 4 short tool demonstration papers) giving a 25% acceptance rate. The embedded systems track accepted 6 papers, the tutorial paper track accepted 10 papers, and the I-day track accepted 6 papers (3 regular papers, 2 case study papers, 1 extended abstract). Finally, 5 papers were selected for the Journal First track, and the Doctoral Symposium received 15 submissions (neither the journal first track papers nor the doctoral symposium ones appear in these proceedings).

FM 2024 invited the authors of all accepted papers to optionally submit an *artifact* —i.e., any additional material such as software, data sets, log files, machine-checkable proofs, etc., that substantiates the claims made in the paper—to the FM 2024 Artifact Evaluation Committee (AEC). After a short quick-check phase three AEC members reviewed each artifact in terms of consistency with and reproducibility of results presented in the paper, completeness, documentation and ease of (re-)use, and availability in an online repository with a DOI. Based on these reviews, and strictly following the EAPLS guidelines for artifact badging,[1] every artifact was awarded up to two badges:

Available. Artifacts that are publicly archived in a permanent way with a DOI that are in some way "relevant to" and "add value beyond the text in the article" are awarded the *available* badge.

Functional. Artifacts that are documented (containing at least an inventory and "sufficient description to enable the artifacts to be exercised"), consistent (i.e., "relevant to the associated paper, and significantly contribute to the generation of its main results"), complete ("as far as possible"), and exercisable, receive the *functional* badge.

Reusable. *Functional* and *available* artifacts that are "very carefully documented and well-structured to the extent that reuse and repurposing is facilitated" receive the *reusable* badge instead of the *functional* one.

Of the 45 submitted artifacts, 42 received the *available* badge, 18 were *functional*, and 14 were awarded the (*functional* and) *reusable* badge.

We are exceedingly grateful to everyone involved in making FM 2024 a success. We appreciate, in particular, the support by the FME board in all difficult decisions and are grateful to all PC members, Artifact Evaluation Commitee members, and subreviewers for volunteering their time in reviewing the submissions to FM, which was particularly challenging in light of the record high number of submissions, and for discussing papers thoroughly toward reaching consensus decisions. We also thank the other committees responsible for the Tutorial Paper track, Embedded Systems track, I-Day track, Journal First track, Doctoral Symposium, and workshops.

Finally we thank Springer for publishing these proceedings in the FM subline of LNCS and appreciate EasyChair in managing the paper submissions, reviewing, and proceedings compilation process.

July 2024

André Platzer
Kristin Yvonne Rozier
Matteo Pradella
Matteo Rossi

---

[1] https://eapls.org/pages/artifact_badges/eapls.org/pages/artifact_badges.

Organization

Program Committees

Research Track

André Platzer (Co-chair)	Karlsruhe Institute of Technology, Germany
Kristin Yvonne Rozier (Co-chair)	Iowa State University, USA
Erika Abraham	RWTH Aachen University, Germany
Wolfgang Ahrendt	Chalmers University of Technology, Sweden
Dalal Alrajeh	Imperial College London, UK
Luís Soares Barbosa	University of Minho, Portugal
Gilles Barthe	MPI-SP/IMDEA Software Institute, Spain
Dirk Beyer	LMU Munich, Germany
Pablo Castro	Universidad Nacional de Rio Cuarto, Argentina
Ana Cavalcanti	University of York, UK
Milan Ceska	Brno University of Technology, Czech Republic
Marsha Chechik	University of Toronto, Canada
Alessandro Cimatti	Fondazione Bruno Kessler, Italy
Alexandre Duret-Lutz	EPITA Research Laboratory (LRE), France
Marie Farrell	University of Manchester, UK
Orna Grumberg	Technion - Israel Institute of Technology, Israel
Arie Gurfinkel	University of Waterloo, Canada
Anne E. Haxthausen	Technical University of Denmark, Denmark
Marieke Huisman	University of Twente, The Netherlands
Reiner Hähnle	TU Darmstadt, Germany
Peter Höfner	Australian National University, Australia
Einar Broch Johnsen	University of Oslo, Norway
Joost-Pieter Katoen	RWTH Aachen University, Germany
Nikolai Kosmatov	Thales Research & Technology, France
Orna Kupferman	Hebrew University, Israel
Peter Lammich	University of Twente, The Netherlands
Martin Leucker	University of Lübeck, Germany
Jianwen Li	East China Normal University, China
Ravi Mangal	Colorado State University, USA
Mieke Massink	CNR, Italy
Anastasia Mavridou	KBR/NASA, USA
Annabelle McIver	Macquarie University, Australia
Claudio Menghi	University of Bergamo, Italy
Stefan Mitsch	DePaul University, USA
Cesar Munoz	NASA, USA
Aniello Murano	University of Naples Federico II, Italy

Violet Ka I Pun	Western Norway University of Applied Sciences, Norway
Zvonimir Rakamaric	Amazon Web Services, USA
Philipp Rümmer	University of Regensburg, Germany
Cristina Seceleanu	Mälardalen University, Sweden
Natasha Sharygina	Università della Svizzera italiana, Switzerland
Jun Sun	Singapore Management University, Singapore
Lucas Martinelli Tabajara	Rice University, USA
Yong Kiam Tan	A*STAR, Singapore
Stefano Tonetta	Fondazione Bruno Kessler, Italy
Georg Weissenbacher	TU Wien, Austria
Virginie Wiels	ONERA/DTIS, France
Huan Xu	University of Maryland, USA
Naijun Zhan	Chinese Academy of Sciences, China
Shufang Zhu	University of Oxford, UK

Embedded Systems Track

Alessandro Cimatti (Chair)	Fondazione Bruno Kessler, Italy
Frédéric Boulanger	CentraleSupélec, France
Lei Bu	Nanjing University, China
Qinxiang Cao	Shanghai Jiao Tong University, China
Liqian Chen	National University of Defense Technology, China
Martin Fränzle	Carl von Ossietzky Universität Oldenburg, Germany
Paula Herber	University of Münster, Germany
Inigo Incer	California Institute of Technology, USA
Ahmed Irfan	SRI International, USA
Eunsuk Kang	Carnegie Mellon University, USA
Sergio Mover	École Polytechnique, France
Dejan Nickovic	AIT Austrian Institute of Technology, Austria
Pierluigi Nuzzo	University of Southern California, USA
Roberto Passerone	University of Trento, Italy
Heyuan Shi	Central South University, China
Fu Song	Chinese Academy of Sciences, China
Cong Tian	Xidian University, China
Stavros Tripakis	Northeastern University, USA

Tutorial Papers Track

Shriram Krishnamurthi (Co-chair)	Brown University, USA
Luigia Petre (Co-chair)	Åbo Akademi University, Finland
Anindya Banerjee	IMDEA Software Institute, Spain
Nikolaj Bjørner	Microsoft, USA
Marcello Bonsangue	Leiden University, The Netherlands
David Thrane Christiansen	Lean FRO, LLC, Denmark
Brijesh Dongol	University of Surrey, UK

Jan Friso Groote   TU Eindhoven, The Netherlands
Stefan Hallerstede   Aarhus University, Denmark
Daniel Jackson   Massachusetts Institute of Technology, USA
Jeroen Keiren   TU Eindhoven, The Netherlands
Markus Alexander Kuppe   Microsoft, USA
Thierry Lecomte   CLEARSY, France
Jannis Limperg   LMU Munich, Germany
Rosemary Monahan   Maynooth University, Ireland
Tim Nelson   Brown University, USA
Maurice ter Beek   CNR, Italy

Industry Day Track

Oksana Tkachuk (Co-chair)   Amazon Web Services, USA
Tim Willemse (Co-chair)   TU Eindhoven, The Netherlands
Nikolaj Bjørner   Microsoft, USA
Jennifer Davis   Collins Aerospace, USA
Leo Freitas   Newcastle University, UK
Dimitra Giannakopoulou   Amazon Web Services, USA
Mario Gleirscher   University of Bremen, Germany
Cláudio Gomes   Aarhus University, Denmark
Klaus Havelund   California Institute of Technology, USA
Nikolai Kosmatov   Thales Research & Technology, France

Artifact Evaluation

Carlos E. Budde (Co-chair)   Università di Trento, Italy
Arnd Hartmanns (Co-chair)   University of Twente, The Netherlands
Jie An   Chinese Academy of Sciences (ISCAS), China
Alberto Bombardelli   Fondazione Bruno Kessler, Italy
Konstantin Britikov   Università della Svizzera italiana, Switzerland
Laura Bussi   CNR, Italy
Julie Cailler   LIRMM, France
Emily Clement   Université Paris Cité, CNRS, IRIF, France
César Cornejo   Universidad Nacional de Rio Cuarto, Argentina
Yanni Dong   University of Twente, The Netherlands
Daniel Drodt   TU Darmstadt, Germany
Federico Formica   McMaster University, Canada
Fabrizio Fornari   University of Camerino, Italy
Laura P. Gamboa Guzman   Iowa State University, USA
Rong Gu   Mälardalen University, Sweden
Long H. Pham   Singapore Management University, Singapore
Tobias John   University of Oslo, Norway
Aditi Kabra   Carnegie Mellon University, USA
Mehrdad Karrabi   Institute of Science and Technology Austria, Austria
Paul Kobialka   University of Oslo, Norway
Marian Lingsch-Rosenfeld   LMU Munich, Germany

Alexander Mackay	Australian National University, Australia
Andrea Manini	Politecnico di Milano, Italy
Antoine Martin	EPITA Research Laboratory (LRE), France
Lucas Martinelli Tabajara	Rice University, USA
Tobias Nießen	TU Wien, Austria
Tommaso Oss	University of Trento, Italy
Quentin Peyras	ONERA, France
Andrea Pferscher	University of Oslo, Norway
Roberto Pizziol	IMT School for Advanced Studies Lucca, Italy
Francesco Pontiggia	TU Wien, Austria
Edoardo Putti	University of Twente, The Netherlands
Florian Renkin	Université Paris Cité, IRIF, France
Guillermo Román-Díez	Universidad Politécnica de Madrid, Spain
Alec Rosentrater	Iowa State University, USA
Lorenzo Rossi	University of Camerino, Italy
Ömer Sayilir	University of Twente, The Netherlands
Philipp Schlehuber-Caissier	EPITA Research Laboratory (LRE), France
Riccardo Sieve	University of Oslo, Norway
Reza Soltani	University of Twente, The Netherlands
Alexander Stekelenburg	University of Twente, The Netherlands
Jack Stodart	Australian National University, Australia
Emily Yu	Institute of Science and Technology Austria, Austria

Journal First Track

Michael Butler (Chair)	University of Southampton, UK
Dines Bjørner	Technical University of Denmark, Denmark
Eerke Boiten	De Montfort University, UK
Maurice ter Beek	CNR, Italy

Doctoral Symposium

Carlo A. Furia (Co-chair)	Università della Svizzera italiana, Switzerland
Laura Kovács (Co-chair)	TU Wien, Austria
Wolfgang Ahrendt	Chalmers University of Technology, Sweden
Marcello M. Bersani	Politecnico di Milano, Italy
Nikolaj Bjørner	Microsoft, USA
Paula Herber	University of Münster, Germany
Marieke Huisman	University of Twente, The Netherlands
Alexandra Mendes	University of Porto, Portugal
Rosemary Monahan	Maynooth University, Ireland
Raúl Pardo	IT University of Copenhagen, Denmark
Simon Robillard	Université de Montpellier, France
Silvia Lizeth Tapia Tarifa	University of Oslo, Norway
Stefano Tonetta	Fondazione Bruno Kessler, Italy
Mattias Ulbrich	Karlsruhe Institute of Technology, Germany

FME Board

Ana Cavalcanti   University of York, UK
Maurice ter Beek   CNR, Italy
Nico Plat   Thanos, The Netherlands
Lars-Henrik Eriksson   Uppsala University, Sweden
Einar Broch Johnsen   University of Oslo, Norway

Organization Committee

General Chairs

Matteo Pradella   Politecnico di Milano, Italy
Matteo Rossi   Politecnico di Milano, Italy

Sponsorship and Exhibition Chairs

Marcello M. Bersani   Politecnico di Milano, Italy
Michele Chiari   TU Wien, Austria

Social Media Chair

Livia Lestingi   Politecnico di Milano, Italy

Workshop Chairs

Stefania Gnesi   CNR, Italy
Marieke Huisman   University of Twente, The Netherlands

Additional Reviewers

Yehia Abd Alrahman
Emma Ahrens
Aliyu Tanko Ali
Shaull Almagor
José Bacelar Almeida
Roman Andriushchenko
Santiago Arranz-Olmos
Anagha Athavale
Ziggy Attala
Giorgio Audrito
Peter Backeman
Daniel Baier
Jialu Bao
Chinmayi Prabhu Baramashetru
Davide Basile
Ludovico Battista
Kevin Batz
Anna Becchi

Valeria Bengolea
Raphaël Berthon
Lionel Blatter
Martin Blicha
Alberto Bombardelli
Frédéric Boniol
Alexander Bork
Konstantin Britikov
Christopher Brix
Julien Brunel
Richard Bubel
Julie Cailler
Georgiana Caltais
Mishel Carelli
Valentin Cassano
Valentina Castiglioni
Davide Catta
Claudia Cauli

David Chemouil
Mingshuai Chen
Xin Chen
Felix Cherubini
Po-Chun Chien
Vincenzo Ciancia
Davide Davoli
André De Matos Pedro
Erik De Vink
Ramiro Demasi
Daniel Drodt
Manuel Eberl
Zafer Esen
Grigory Fedyukovich
Marco A. Feliu
Nick Feng
Shenghua Feng
Anthony Fernandes Pires
Angelo Ferrando
Carla Ferreira
Joao F. Ferreira
Ira Fesefeldt
Paul Fiterau-Brostean
Simon Foster
Luis Garcia
Christina Gehnen
Tiberiu A. Georgescu
Marcus Gerhold
Roland Glück
Michał Tomasz Godziszewski
R. Govind
Srajan Goyal
Lukas Graussam
Alberto Griggio
Lukas Grätz
Rong Gu
Vojtěch Havlena
Holly Hendry
Paula Herber
Roland Herrmann
Hans-Dieter Hiep
Raik Hipler
Sebastian Holler
Lukáš Holík
Jacob Howe
Aditi Kabra

Hannes Kallwies
Eduard Kamburjan
Emin Karayel
Jeroen J. A. Keiren
Ata Keskin
Matthias Kettl
Karam Kharraz
Bram Kohlen
Tomáš Kolárik
Katherine Kosaian
József Kovács
Gereon Kremer
Harald König
Faezeh Labbaf
Martin Lange
Jonathan Laurent
Tristan Le Gall
Nham Le
Thomas Lemberger
Ondrej Lengal
Yong Li
Chencheng Liang
Marian Lingsch-Rosenfeld
Debasmita Lohar
Delphine Longuet
Michele Loreti
Andreas Lööw
Filip Macák
Alexandre Madeira
Vadim Malvone
Lina Marsso
Manuel A. Martins
Alexandra Mendes
Robert Mensing
Hannah Mertens
Munyque Mittelmann
Alvaro Miyazawa
Mariano Moscato
Mohammadreza Mousavi
Sergio Mover
Logan Murphy
Muhammad Naeem
Jasper Nalbach
Renato Neves
Kim Nguyen
Thomas Noll

Jose Oliveira
Rodrigo Otoni
Gianmarco Parretti
Mário Pereira
Quentin Peyras
Adrien Pommellet
Siddharth Priya
José Proença
Valentin Promies
Edoardo Putti
Tim Quatmann
Willard Rafnsson
Itsaka Rakotonirina
Omer Rappoport
António Ravara
Gianluca Redondi
Germán Regis
Andrew Reynolds
Pedro Ribeiro
Martin Sachenbacher
Augusto Sampaio
Abhiroop Sarkar
Jonas Schiffl
Philipp Schlehuber-Caissier
Philipp Schröer
Roberto Sebastiani
Filipo Sharevski
Xujie Si
Teofil Sidoruk
Julien Signoles
Joseph Slagel
Jorge Sousa Pinto
Francesco Spegni
Daniel Stan
Martin Steffen
Alexander Stekelenburg
Volker Stolz

Han Su
Roger Su
Yusen Su
Silvia Lizeth Tapia Tarifa
Philip Tasche
Samuel Teuber
Daniel Thoma
Chun Tian
Gan Ting
Laura Titolo
Noriko Tomuro
Dmitriy Traytel
Mattias Ulbrich
Tom van Dijk
Andrea Vandin
Mahsa Varshosaz
Hari Govind Vediramana Krishnan
Franck Vedrine
Adele Veschetti
Henrik Wachowitz
Philipp Wendler
Hao Wu
Yechuan Xia
Shengping Xiao
Norihiro Yamada
Fang Yan
Tengshun Yang
Kangfeng Ye
Lina Ye
Bohua Zhan
Zhi Zhang
Hengjun Zhao
Xingyu Zhao
Ghiles Ziat
Martin Zimmermann
Paolo Zuliani

Contents – Part I

Programming Languages

Logic and Automata

Contents – Part II

Embedded Systems Track

Industry Day Track

Tutorial Papers

Invited Papers

Adversarial Robustness Certification for Bayesian Neural Networks

Matthew Wicker[1], Andrea Patane[2], Luca Laurenti[3],
and Marta Kwiatkowska[4](✉)

[1] Imperial College, London, UK
m.wicker@imperial.ac.uk
[2] School of Computer Science and Statistics, Trinity College Dublin, Dublin, Ireland
apatane@tcd.ie
[3] Delft Center for Systems and Control (DCSC), TU Delft, Delft, The Netherlands
l.laurenti@tudelft.nl
[4] Department of Computer Science, University of Oxford, Oxford, UK
marta.kwiatkowska@cs.ox.ac.uk

Abstract. We study the problem of certifying the robustness of Bayesian neural networks (BNNs) to adversarial input perturbations. Specifically, we define two notions of robustness for BNNs in an adversarial setting: probabilistic robustness and decision robustness. The former deals with the probabilistic behaviour of the network, that is, it ensures robustness across different stochastic realisations of the network, while the latter provides guarantees for the overall (output) decision of the BNN. Although these robustness properties cannot be computed analytically, we present a unified computational framework for efficiently and formally bounding them. Our approach is based on weight interval sampling, integration and bound propagation techniques, and can be applied to BNNs with a large number of parameters independently of the (approximate) inference method employed to train the BNN. We evaluate the effectiveness of our method on tasks including airborne collision avoidance, medical imaging and autonomous driving, demonstrating that it can compute non-trivial guarantees on medium size images (i.e., over 16 thousand input parameters).

Keywords: Certification · Bayesian Neural Networks · Adversarial Robustness · Classification · Regression · Uncertainty

1 Introduction

While neural networks (NNs) regularly obtain state-of-the-art performance in many supervised machine learning problems [2,15], they are vulnerable to adversarial attacks, i.e., imperceptible modifications of their inputs that result in an incorrect prediction [42]. Along with several other vulnerabilities [8], the discovery of adversarial examples has made the deployment of NNs in real-world, safety-critical applications increasingly challenging. The design and analysis of

© The Author(s) 2025
A. Platzer et al. (Eds.): FM 2024, LNCS 14933, pp. 3–28, 2025.
https://doi.org/10.1007/978-3-031-71162-6_1

methods that can mitigate such vulnerabilities, or compute provable guarantees on their worst-case behaviour in adversarial conditions, is therefore of utmost importance [44].

While retaining the advantages intrinsic to deep learning, Bayesian neural networks (BNNs), i.e., NNs with a probability distribution placed over their weights and biases [33], enable probabilistically principled evaluation of *model uncertainty*. Because of their ability to model uncertainty [27], the application of BNNs is particularly appealing in safety-critical scenarios, where uncertainty could be taken into account at prediction time to enable safe decision-making [4,11,32,57]. To this end, various techniques have been proposed for the evaluation of BNNs' robustness, including generalisation of gradient-based adversarial attacks [31], statistical verification techniques [12], and formal verification approaches aimed at verifying that the decisions made by a BNN are safe [1,7] or checking the robustness of the neural networks sampled from the BNN posterior [7,12,29]. The increasingly diverse techniques for analysing robustness of Bayesian neural networks have resulted in divergent robustness properties, some directly analysing the stochasticity of the system [12] and others directly adapting robustness specifications from deterministic systems [7]. To the best of our knowledge, there is a lack of systematic, unified approaches for computing formal (i.e., with certified bounds) guarantees on the range of emergent quantitative robustness properties against adversarial input perturbations for BNNs.

In this work, we develop a probabilistic verification framework to quantify the adversarial robustness of BNNs. In particular, we model adversarial robustness as an *input-output specification* defined by a given compact set of input points, $T \subseteq \mathbb{R}^m$, and a given convex polytope output set, $S \subseteq \mathbb{R}^n$ (called a safe set). A neural network satisfies this specification if all points in T are mapped into S. For a particular specification, we focus on two main properties of a BNN of interest for adversarial prediction settings: *probabilistic robustness* [12,50] and *decision robustness* [7,23]. The former is defined as the probability that a network sampled from the posterior distribution is robust, which thus provides a general measure of the robustness of a BNN. In contrast, *decision robustness* focuses on the decision step, and evaluates the robustness of the optimal decision of a BNN. That is, a BNN satisfies decision robustness if, for all points in T, the expectation of the output of the BNN in the case of regression, or the argmax of the expectation of the softmax for classification, are contained in S.

Unfortunately, evaluating probabilistic and decision robustness for a BNN is not trivial, as it involves computing distributions and expectations of high-dimensional random variables passed through a non-convex function. Nevertheless, we derive a unified algorithmic framework based on computations over the BNN weight space that yields *certified lower* and *upper bounds* for both properties. Specifically, we show that probabilistic robustness is equivalent to the measure, w.r.t. the BNN posterior, of the set of weights for which the resulting deterministic NN is robust. Computing upper and lower bounds for the probability involves sampling compact sets of weights according to the BNN posterior, and propagating each of these weight sets, H, through the neural network architecture, jointly with the input region T, to check whether all the networks instantiated by weights in H are safe. To do so, we generalise bound propagation techniques developed for deterministic neural networks to the Bayesian setting and instantiate explicit schemes for Interval Bound Propagation (IBP) and Linear Bound Propagation (LBP) [20]. Similarly, in the case of decision robustness, we show that formal bounds can be obtained by partitioning the weight space into different weight sets, and for each weight set J we employ bound propagation techniques to compute the maximum and minimum of the decision of the NN for any input point in T and any weight in the set J. The resulting extrema are then averaged w.r.t. posterior measure to obtain sound lower and upper bounds on decision robustness.

We empirically validate our framework using case studies from airborne collision avoidance [25], medical image recognition [56], and autonomous driving [40]. We demonstrate that our framework is able to compute sound upper and lower bounds for both notions of robustness for Bayesian neural networks. Moreover, we study the effect of approximate inference, as well as depth and width of the neural network classifier, on our guarantees. We find that our approach, even when using simple interval bound propagation, is able to provide non-trivial certificates of adversarial robustness and predictive uncertainty properties for Bayesian neural networks with four hidden layers and more than 16,000 input dimensions. We additionally use our approach to show how approximate Bayesian posteriors may provide provably robust uncertainty estimation for random noise inputs while failing to provide the same guarantees for more structured classes of out-of-distribution inputs[1].

In summary, this paper makes the following contributions[2]

- We present an algorithmic framework based on convex relaxation techniques for the robustness analysis of BNNs in adversarial settings.
- We derive explicit lower- and upper-bounding procedures based on IBP and LBP for the propagation of input and weight intervals through the BNN posterior function.
- We empirically show that our method can be used to certify BNNs consisting of multiple hidden layers and with hundreds of neurons per layer.

Probabilistic robustness was introduced in [50]. This work extends [50] in several aspects. In contrast to [50], which focused only on probabilistic robustness, here we also tackle decision robustness and embed the calculations for the two properties in a common computational framework. Furthermore, while the method in [50] only computes lower bounds, in this paper we also develop a technique for upper bound computation. Finally, we extend the empirical analysis to include additional datasets, evaluation of convolutional architectures, scalability analysis, as well as certification of out-of-distribution (OOD) uncertainty.

---

[1] An implementation to reproduce all the experiments can be found at: https://github.com/matthewwicker/AdversarialRobustnessCertificationForBNNs.

[2] In view of space constraints, additional details are available in Appendix at https://arxiv.org/abs/2306.13614.

Related Works. The vast majority of existing NN verification methods have been developed specifically for deterministic NNs, with approaches including abstract interpretation [20], mixed integer linear programming [19,36,43,54,60], Monte Carlo search-based frameworks [24,48,55], convex relaxation [23,45,59] and SAT/SMT [25,26]. However, these methods cannot be directly applied to BNNs because they all assume that the weights of the network are deterministic, i.e., fixed to a given value, while in the Bayesian setting weights are not fixed, but distributed according to the BNN posterior. Statistical approaches to quantify the robustness of BNNs that are ϵ approximately correct up to a confidence/probability of error bounded by $1 - \delta$, for $\delta > 0$, have been developed in [12,32]. In contrast, the methods in this paper do not rely on confidence intervals and return guaranteed upper and lower bounds on the true probability that a BNN satisfies a specific property.

Since the publication of our preliminary work [50], other papers have studied the problem of verifying BNN robustness [1,3,7,29,51,52]. However, [7] only considers verification of BNNs with weight distributions of bounded support, and consequently does not include Gaussian posterior distributions, which are commonly employed in practice. [1] develops an approach based on dynamic programming to certify decision robustness for BNNs, which improves the precision of BNN verification by performing bound propagation in the latent space of BNNs, rather than working on the space of weights. However, this approach is restricted to decision robustness. Further, [3] develops an approach based on mixed integer linear programming (MILP), which is specific for probabilistic robustness. It is unclear how these approaches could be extended to encompass both probabilistic and decision robustness. In contrast, in this paper we propose a simple and general framework that encompasses both decision and probabilistic robustness, and can be applied to both fully-connected and convolutional neural network architectures. Another related method is [29], which takes a distribution-free approach and considers a dynamical system whose one-step dynamics includes a neural network, and computes the set of weights that satisfy an infinite-horizon safety property. Note that, as the support of a Gaussian distribution is unbounded, similarly to [7], this approach does not support Gaussian posterior distributions over the weights. We also mention [52], which builds on the results of [51] to develop certification for reach-avoid properties of dynamical systems described by BNNs. Finally, [49] considers certifiable robust training and introduces the concept of robust likelihood that we employ in our experimental evaluation.

In the context of Bayesian learning, methods to compute adversarial robustness measures have been explored for Gaussian processes (GPs), both for regression [13] and classification tasks [35,38]. However, because of the non-linearity in NN architectures, GP-based approaches cannot be directly employed for BNNs. Furthermore, the vast majority of approximate Bayesian inference methods for BNNs do not utilise Gaussian approximations over the latent space [10]. In contrast, our method is specifically tailored to take into account the non-linear nature of BNNs and can be directly applied to a range of approximate Bayesian inference techniques used in the literature.

2 Background on Bayesian Deep Learning

We consider a dataset of $n_\mathcal{D}$ independent pairs of inputs and labels, $\mathcal{D} = \{(x_i, y_i)\}_{i=1}^{n_\mathcal{D}}$, with $x_i \in \mathbb{R}^m$, where each output $y \in \mathbb{R}^n$ is either a one-hot class vector for classification or a real-valued vector for regression. The aim of Bayesian learning is to learn the function generating $\mathcal{D}$ via a feed forward-neural network $f^w : \mathbb{R}^m \to \mathbb{R}^n$, parameterised by a vector $w \in \mathbb{R}^{n_w}$ containing all its weights and biases. We denote with $f^{w,1}, ..., f^{w,K}$ the K layers of f^w and take the activation function of the ith layer to be $\sigma^{(i)}$, abbreviated to just σ in the case of the output activation.[3] Throughout this paper, we will use $f^w(x)$ to represent pre-activation of the last layer.

Bayesian deep learning starts with a prior distribution, $p(w)$, over the vector $\mathbf{w}$ of random variables associated to the weights. Placing a distribution over the weights defines a stochastic process indexed by the input space, which we denote as $f^{\mathbf{w}}$. Note that we use bold to distinguish the stochastic process parameterised by a random variable, $f^{\mathbf{w}}$, and the deterministic function that results from sampling a single parameter value, f^w. To obtain the posterior distribution, the BNN prior is updated according to the likelihood, $p(\mathcal{D}|w)$, via the Bayes rule, i.e., $p(w|\mathcal{D}) \propto p(\mathcal{D}|w)p(w)$ [9]. The cumulative distribution of $p(w|\mathcal{D})$, which we denote as $P(\cdot)$, is such that for $R \subseteq \mathbb{R}^{n_w}$ we have:

$$P(R) := \int_R p(w|\mathcal{D})dw. \tag{1}$$

The posterior $p(w|\mathcal{D})$ is in turn used to calculate the output of a BNN on an unseen point, x^*. The distribution over outputs is called the posterior predictive distribution and is defined as:

$$p(y^*|x^*, \mathcal{D}) = \int p(y^*|x^*, w)p(w|\mathcal{D})dw. \tag{2}$$

When employing a Bayesian model, the overall final prediction is taken to be a single value, $\hat{y}$, that minimizes the Bayesian risk of an incorrect prediction according to the posterior predictive distribution and a loss function $\mathcal{L}$. Formally, the final decision of a BNN is computed as

$$\hat{y} = \arg\min_{y^*} \int_{\mathbb{R}^n} \mathcal{L}(y, y^*)p(y^*|x^*, \mathcal{D})dy^*. \tag{3}$$

This minimization is the subject of Bayesian decision theory [6], and the final form of $\hat{y}$ depends on the specific loss function $\mathcal{L}$ employed in practice. In this

---

[3] We assume, for the purposes of linear bound propagation in Appendix D.4, that the activation functions have a finite number of inflection points, which holds for activation functions commonly used in practice [21].

paper, we focus on two standard loss functions widely employed for classification and regression problems[4], described in more detail below.

Classification. For classification problems, the 0–1 loss, denoted ℓ_{0-1}, is commonly employed. ℓ_{0-1} assigns a penalty of 0 to the correct prediction, and 1 otherwise. It can be shown that the optimal decision in this case is given by the class for which the predictive distribution obtains its maximum, i.e.:

$$\hat{y} = \arg\max_{i=1,\ldots,n} p_i(y^*|x^*, \mathcal{D}) = \arg\max_{i=1,\ldots,n} \mathbb{E}_{w \sim p(w|\mathcal{D})} \left[\sigma_i(f^w(x)) \right],$$

where σ_i represents the ith output component of the softmax function.

Regression. For regression problems, the ℓ_2 loss is generally employed. ℓ_2 assigns a penalty to a prediction according to its ℓ_2 distance from the ground truth. It can be shown that the optimal decision in this case is given by the expected value of the BNN output over the posterior distribution, i.e., $\hat{y} = \mathbb{E}_{w \sim p(w|\mathcal{D})} [f^w(x)]$. Unfortunately, because of the non-linearity of neural network architectures, the computation of the posterior distribution over the weights, $p(w|\mathcal{D})$, is generally intractable [33]. Hence, various approximation methods have been studied to perform inference with BNNs in practice. Among these, we will consider Hamiltonian Monte Carlo (HMC) [33] and Variational Inference (VI) [10]. While HMC is a sample-based method that involves defining a Markov chain whose invariant distribution is $p_{\mathbf{w}}(w|\mathcal{D})$ [33], VI proceeds by finding a Gaussian approximating distribution over the weight space $q(w) \sim p_{\mathbf{w}}(w|\mathcal{D})$ in a trade-off between approximation accuracy and scalability. For simplicity of notation, in the rest of the paper we will indicate with $p(w|\mathcal{D})$ the posterior distribution estimated by either of the two methods, and clarify the methodological differences when they arise.

3   Problem Statement

We focus on local specifications defined over an input compact set $T \subseteq \mathbb{R}^m$, which we assume to be a box (axis-aligned linear constraints), and output set $S \subseteq \mathbb{R}^n$ in the form of a convex polytope:

$$S = \{y \in \mathbb{R}^n \mid C_S y + d_S \geq 0\}, \tag{4}$$

where $C_S \in \mathbb{R}^{n_S \times n}$ and $d_S \in \mathbb{R}^{n_S}$ are the matrix and vector encoding the polytope constraints, with n_S being the number of output constraints. Throughout the paper we will refer to an input-output set pair, T and S, as defined above, as a *robustness specification*. We note that our formulation of robustness specification captures various important properties used in practice, such as classifier

---

[4] In Appendix B we discuss how our method can be generalised to other losses commonly employed in practice.

monotonicity [41], adversarial robustness [22,24], and individual fairness [5]. For instance, targeted adversarial robustness for classification, which aims to find an adversarial example belonging to a specified class, can be captured by setting C_S to an $n_S \times n$ matrix of all zeros with a -1 in the diagonal entry corresponding to the true class and a 1 on the diagonal entry corresponding to the target class. Similarly, for regression, one uses C_S to encode the absolute deviation from the target value and d_S to encode the maximum tolerable deviation.

Probabilistic robustness accounts for the probabilistic behaviour of a BNN with respect to a robustness specification.

Definition 1 (Probabilistic robustness). *Given a Bayesian neural network* $f^{\mathbf{w}}$, *an input set* $T \subseteq \mathbb{R}^m$ *and an output set* $S \subseteq \mathbb{R}^n$, *also called safe set of outputs, define probabilistic robustness as*

$$P_{safe}(T, S) := Prob_{w \sim p(w|\mathcal{D})}(\forall x \in T, f^w(x) \in S). \tag{5}$$

Given $\eta \in [0,1]$, *we then say that* $f^{\mathbf{w}}$ *is probabilistically robust, or safe, for robustness specifications* (T, S) *with probability at least* η *iff* $P_{safe}(T, S) \geq \eta$.

Probabilistic robustness considers the adversarial behaviour of the model while accounting for the uncertainty arising from the posterior distribution. In particular, $P_{\text{safe}}(T, S)$ quantifies *the proportion* of networks sampled from $f^{\mathbf{w}}$ that satisfy a given input-output specification, and can be used directly as a measure of compliance for Bayesian neural networks [7,16,32]. Exact computation of $P_{\text{safe}}(T, S)$ is hindered by the size and non-linearity of neural networks. Therefore, in this work, we aim to compute provable bounds on probabilistic robustness.

Problem 1 (Bounding probabilistic robustness). Given a Bayesian neural network $f^{\mathbf{w}}$, an input set $T \subseteq \mathbb{R}^m$ and a set $S \subseteq \mathbb{R}^n$ of safe outputs, compute (non-trivial) lower and upper bounds P^L_{safe} and P^U_{safe} such that

$$P^L_{\text{safe}} \leq P_{\text{safe}}(T, S) \leq P^U_{\text{safe}}. \tag{6}$$

3.1   Decision Robustness

While P_{safe} attempts to measure the probability of robustness of neural networks sampled from the BNN posterior, we are often interested in evaluating robustness w.r.t. a specific decision. In order to do so, we consider *decision robustness*, which is computed over the final decision of the BNN. In particular, given a loss function and a decision $\hat{y}$ we have the following.

Definition 2 (Decision robustness). *Consider a Bayesian neural network* $f^{\mathbf{w}}$, *an input set* $T \subseteq \mathbb{R}^m$ *and an output set* $S \subseteq \mathbb{R}^n$. *Assume that the decision for a loss* $\mathcal{L}$ *for* $x \in \mathbb{R}^m$ *is given by* $\hat{y}(x)$ *(Eq. 3). Then, the Bayesian decision is considered to be robust if* $\forall x \in T, \hat{y}(x) \in S$.

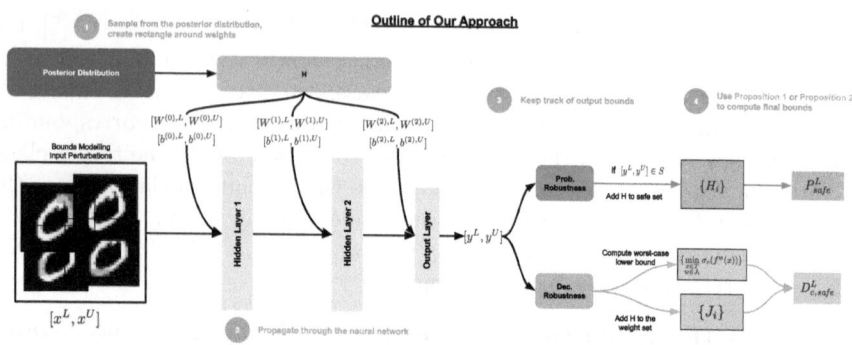

Fig. 1. A diagram illustrating a single iteration of the computational flow for the certification process of a BNN w.r.t. decision robustness (green) and probabilistic robustness (purple). This process is summarised in Algorithm 1 (Color figure online).

As discussed in Sect. 2, since the specific form of the decision depends on the loss function, the definition of decision robustness takes different form depending on whether the BNN is used for classification or for regression. We thus arrive at the following problem.

Problem 2 (Bounding decision robustness). Let $f^{\mathbf{w}}$ be a BNN with posterior distribution $p(w|\mathcal{D})$. Consider a robustness specification (T, S) and assume $\mathcal{L} = \ell_{0-1}$ for classification or $\mathcal{L} = \ell_2$ for regression. We aim at computing (non-trivial) lower and upper bounds D_{safe}^L and D_{safe}^U such that:

$$D_{\text{safe}}^L \leq \mathbb{E}[s(f^w(x))] \leq D_{\text{safe}}^U \quad \forall x \in T,$$

where s corresponds to the likelihood function σ in the case of classification (e.g., the softmax) and simply denotes the identity function in the case of regression.

Problem 2 suggests that, while for regression we can simply bound the expected output of the BNN, for classification we need to bound the predictive posterior to compute bounds on the final decision, i.e., we need to propagate these inside the softmax. This is similar to what is done for deterministic neural networks, where, in the case of classification, the bounds are often computed over the logits, and then used to provide guarantees for the final decision [23].

3.2   Approach Outline

We design an algorithmic framework for computing worst- and best-case bounds (lower and upper bounds, respectively) on local robustness properties for Bayesian neural networks, taking account of both the posterior distribution (P_{safe}^L and P_{safe}^U) and the overall model decision (D_{safe}^L and D_{safe}^U). First, we show how the two robustness properties of Definitions 1 and 2 can be reformulated in terms of computation over weight intervals. This allows us to derive a unified approach, which enables bounding of the robustness of the BNN posterior (i.e., probabilistic robustness) and that of the overall model decision (i.e., decision robustness) by means of *bound propagation* and *posterior integral* computation over hyperrectangles. For a discussion of when each bound may be useful see Appendix A.

A visual outline for our framework is presented in Fig. 1. The presentation of the framework is organised as follows. We first introduce a general theoretical schema for bounding the robustness quantities of interest (Sect. 4). We then show how the required integral computations can be achieved for practical Bayesian posterior inference techniques (Sect. 5.1). This allows us to extend bound propagation techniques to deal with both input variable intervals and intervals over the weight space, which we rely on to instantiate approaches respectively based on Interval Bound Propagation (Sect. 5.2) and Linear Bound Propagation techniques (Appendix C.). Finally, in Sect. 6, we present an overall algorithm that produces the desired bounds.

4   BNN Adversarial Robustness via Weight Sets

We show how a single computational framework can be leveraged to compute bounds on both definitions of BNN robustness. We start by converting the computation of robustness into the weight space and then define a family of weight intervals that we utilise to bound the integrations required by both definitions. Proofs for the main results in this section are presented in Appendix D.

4.1   Bounding Probabilistic Robustness

We first show that the computation of $P_{\text{safe}}(T, S)$ is equivalent to computing a *maximal* set of safe weights H such that each network associated to weights in H is safe w.r.t. the robustness specification at hand.

Definition 3 (Maximal safe and unsafe sets). *We say that $H \subseteq \mathbb{R}^{n_w}$ is the maximal safe set of weights from T to S, or simply the maximal safe set of weights, iff $H = \{w \in \mathbb{R}^{n_w} \mid \forall x \in T, f^w(x) \in S\}$. Similarly, we say that $K \subseteq \mathbb{R}^{n_w}$ is the maximal unsafe set of weights from T to S, or simply the maximal unsafe set of weights, iff $K = \{w \in \mathbb{R}^{n_w} \mid \exists x \in T, f^w(x) \notin S\}$.*

Intuitively, H and K simply encode the input-output specifications S and T in the BNN weight space. The following lemma, which follows from Eq. 5, allows us to relate the maximal sets of weights to probabilistic robustness.

Lemma 1. *Let H and K be the maximal safe and unsafe sets of weights from T to S. Assume that $w \sim p(w|\mathcal{D})$. Then, it holds that*

$$P(H) = \int_H p(w|\mathcal{D})dw = P_{safe}(T, S) = 1 - \int_K p(w|\mathcal{D})dw = 1 - P(K). \quad (7)$$

Unfortunately, an exact computation of sets H and K is infeasible in general and may not be possible to capture using any finite number of sets. However, we can compute subsets of H and K. Such subsets can then be used to compute upper and lower bounds on the value of $P_{\text{safe}}(T, S)$ by considering subsets of the maximal safe and unsafe weights.

Definition 4 (Safe and unsafe sets). *Given a maximal safe set H or a maximal unsafe set K of weights, we say that $\hat{H}$ and $\hat{K}$ are a safe and unsafe set of weights from T to S iff $\hat{H} \subseteq H$ and $\hat{K} \subseteq K$, respectively.*

Without maximality, we no longer have strict equality in Lemma 1, but we can use $\hat{H}$ and $\hat{K}$ to arrive at bounds on the value of probabilistic robustness. Specifically, we proceed by defining $\hat{H}$ and $\hat{K}$ as the union of a family of disjoint weight intervals, as these can provide flexible approximations of H and K. That is, we consider $\mathcal{H} = \{H_i\}_{i=1}^{n_H}$, with $H_i = [w_i^{L,H}, w_i^{U,H}]$ and $\mathcal{K} = \{K_i\}_{i=1}^{n_K}$, with $K_i = [w_i^{L,K}, w_i^{U,K}]$, such that $H_i \subset H$ and $K_i \subset K$, $\hat{H} = \bigcup_{i=1}^{n_H} H_i$, $\hat{K} = \bigcup_{i=1}^{n_K} K_i$, and $H_i \cap H_j = \emptyset$ and $K_i \cap K_j = \emptyset$, for any $i \neq j$. Hence, as a consequence of Lemma 1, and by the fact that $\hat{H} \subseteq H$ and $\hat{K} \subseteq K$, we obtain the following.

Proposition 1 (Bounds on probabilistic robustness). *Let H and K be the maximal safe and unsafe sets of weights from T to S. Consider two families of pairwise disjoint weight intervals $\mathcal{H} = \{H_i\}_{i=1}^{n_H}$, $\mathcal{K} = \{K_i\}_{i=1}^{n_K}$, where for all i it holds that $H_i \subseteq H$ and $K_i \subseteq K$. Let $\hat{H} \subseteq H$ and $\hat{K} \subseteq K$ be non-maximal safe and unsafe sets of weights, with $\hat{H} = \bigcup_{i=1}^{n_H} H_i$ and $\hat{K} = \bigcup_{i=1}^{n_K} K_i$. Assume that $w \sim p(w|\mathcal{D})$. Then, it holds that*

$$P_{safe}^L := \sum_{i=1}^{n_H} P(H_i) \leq P_{safe}(T, S) \leq 1 - \sum_{i=1}^{n_K} P(K_i) =: P_{safe}^U, \tag{8}$$

that is, P_{safe}^L and P_{safe}^U are lower and upper bounds on probabilistic robustness.

Through the use of Proposition 1, we can thus bound probabilistic robustness by performing computation over sets of safe and unsafe intervals.[5] Before explaining in detail how such bounds can be explicitly computed, we first show, in the next section, how a similar derivation leads us to analogous bounds and computations for decision robustness.

4.2   Bounding Decision Robustness

The key difference between our formulation of probabilistic robustness and that of decision robustness is that, for the former, we are only interested in the behaviour of neural networks extracted from the BNN posterior that satisfy the robustness requirements (hence the distinction between H- and K-weight intervals), whereas to compute sound bounds on decision robustness we need to

---

[5] In Appendix E.4. we extend the results to general hyper-rectangles by using the Bonferroni bound.

take into account the overall worst-case behaviour of an expected value computed for the BNN predictive distribution. As such, rather than computing safe and unsafe sets, we only need a family of weight sets, $\mathcal{J} = \{J_i\}_{i=1}^{n_J}$, which we can rely on for bounding $D_{\text{safe}}(T, S)$. In the following, we explicitly show how to do this for classification with likelihood σ. The bound for regression follows similarly by using the identity function as σ.

Proposition 2 (Bounding decision robustness). *Let $\mathcal{J} = \{J_i\}_{i=1}^{n_J}$, with $J_i \subset \mathbb{R}^{n_w}$, be a family of disjoint weight intervals. Let σ^L and σ^U be vectors that lower- and upper-bound the co-domain of the final activation function, and $c \in \{1, \ldots, m\}$ an index spanning the BNN output dimension. Define:*

$$D_{safe,c}^{L} := \sum_{i=1}^{n_J} P(J_i) \min_{\substack{x \in T \\ w \in J_i}} \sigma_c(f^w(x)) + \sigma^L \left(1 - \sum_{i=1}^{n_J} P(J_i) \right) \tag{9}$$

$$D_{safe,c}^{U} := \sum_{i=1}^{n_J} P(J_i) \max_{\substack{x \in T \\ w \in J_i}} \sigma_c(f^w(x)) + \sigma^U \left(1 - \sum_{i=1}^{n_J} P(J_i) \right). \tag{10}$$

Consider $D_{safe}^{L} = [D_{safe,1}^{L}, \ldots, D_{safe,m}^{L}]$ and $D_{safe}^{U} = [D_{safe,1}^{U}, \ldots, D_{safe,m}^{U}]$, then:

$$D_{safe}^{L} \leq \mathbb{E}_{p(w|\mathcal{D})}[\sigma(f^w(x))] \leq D_{safe}^{U} \quad \forall x \in T,$$

that is, D_{safe}^{L} and D_{safe}^{U} bound the predictive posterior in T.

Intuitively, the first term in the bounds of Eqs. (9) (and similarly (10)) considers the worst-case output for the input set T and each interval J_i, while the second term accounts for the worst-case value of the posterior mass not captured by the family of intervals $\mathcal{J}$. The bound is valid for any family of intervals $\mathcal{J}$. Ideally, however, the partition should be finer around regions of high probability mass of the posterior distribution, as these make up the dominant term in the computation of the posterior predictive. We discuss in Sect. 5 how we select these intervals in practice so as to empirically obtain non-vacuous bounds.

4.3 Computation of the Lower and Upper Bounds

We now propose a unified approach to computing the lower and upper bounds. We observe that Eqs. (8), (9) and (10) require the integration of the posterior distribution over weight intervals. While this is in general intractable, we have built the bounds so that H_i, K_i and J_i are axis-aligned hyper-rectangles, and so the computation can be done exactly for commonly used approximate Bayesian inference methods (discussed in detail in Sect. 5.1).

For the explicit computation of decision robustness, the only missing ingredient is then the computation of the minimum and maximum of $\sigma(f^w(x))$ for $x \in T$ and $w \in J_i$. We do this by bounding the BNN output for any given rectangle, R, in the weight space. That is, we will compute upper and lower bounds

y^L and y^U such that:

$$y^L \leq \min_{\substack{x \in T \\ w \in R}} f^w(x) \quad y^U \geq \max_{\substack{x \in T \\ w \in R}} f^w(x), \tag{11}$$

which can then be used to bound $\sigma(f^w(x))$ by simple propagation over the softmax. The derivation of such bounds will be the subject of Sect. 5.2.

Finally, observe that, whereas for decision robustness we can simply select any weight interval J_i, for probabilistic robustness one needs to make a distinction between safe sets (H_i) and unsafe sets (K_i). It turns out that this can be done by bounding the output of the BNN in each of these intervals. For example, in the case of the safe sets, by definition we have that $\forall w \in H_i, \forall x' \in T$ it follows that $f^w(x') \in S$. By defining y^L and y^U as in Eq. (11), we can see that it suffices to check whether $[y^L, y^U] \subseteq S$. Hence, the computation of probabilistic robustness also depends on the computation of such bounds.

Therefore, once we have shown how to compute $P(R)$ for any weight interval and y^L and y^U, the bounds in Proposition 1 and Proposition 2 can be computed explicitly, and we can thus bound probabilistic and decision robustness.

5   Explicit Bound Computation

In this section, we provide details of the computational schema needed to calculate the theoretical bounds presented in Sect. 4.

5.1   Integral Computation over Weight Intervals

Key to the bound computation is the ability to compute the integral of the posterior distribution over a combined set of weight intervals. Crucially, the shape of the weight sets $\mathcal{H} = \{H_i\}_{i=1}^{n_H}$, $\mathcal{K} = \{K_i\}_{i=1}^{n_K}$ and $\mathcal{J} = \{J_i\}_{i=1}^{n_J}$ is a parameter of the method, which can be leveraged to simplify the integral computation depending on the particular form of the approximate posterior distribution. We build each weight interval as an axis-aligned hyper-rectangle of the form $R = [w^L, w^U]$ for w^L and $w^U \in \mathbb{R}^{n_w}$.

Weight Intervals for Decision Robustness. In the case of decision robustness, it suffices to sample any weight interval J_i to compute the bounds we derived in Proposition 2. Clearly, the bound is tighter if the $\mathcal{J}$ family is finer around the area of high probability mass for $p(w|\mathcal{D})$. In order to obtain such a family we proceed as follows. First, we define a *weight margin* $\gamma > 0$, whose role is to parameterise the radius of the weight intervals. We then iteratively sample weight vectors w_i from $p(w|\mathcal{D})$, for $i = 1, \ldots, n_J$, and define $J_i = [w_i^L, w_i^U] = [w_i - \gamma, w_i + \gamma]$. Thus defined weight intervals naturally concentrate around the area of greater density for $p(w|\mathcal{D})$, while asymptotically covering the whole support of the distribution.

Weight Intervals for Probabilistic Robustness. On the other hand, for the computation of probabilistic robustness one has to make a distinction between safe and unsafe weight intervals, H_i and K_i. As explained in Sect. 4.3, this can be done by bounding the output of the BNN in each of these intervals. For example, in the case of the safe sets, by definition, H_i is safe if and only if $\forall w \in H_i, \forall x' \in T$ we have that $f^w(x') \in S$. Thus, in order to build a family of safe (respectively unsafe) weight intervals H_i (resp. K_i), we proceed as follows. As for decision robustness, we iteratively sample weights w_i from the posterior used to build hyper-rectangles of the form $R_i = [w_i - \gamma, w_i + \gamma]$. We then propagate R_i through the BNN and check whether the output is (resp. is not) a subset of S. The derivation of such bounds on propagation will be the subject of Sect. 5.2.

Once the family of weights is computed, it remains to compute the cumulative distribution over such sets. The specific computations depend on the particular form of Bayesian approximate inference that is employed. We discuss explicitly the case of Gaussian variational approaches, and of sample-based posterior approximation (e.g., HMC).

Variational Inference. For variational approximations, $p(w|\mathcal{D})$ takes the form of a multi-variate Gaussian distribution over the weight space. The resulting computations reduce to the integral of a multi-variate Gaussian distribution over a finite-sized axis-aligned rectangle, which can be computed using standard methods from statistics [14]. In particular, under the common assumption of variational inference with a Gaussian distribution with diagonal covariance matrix [28], i.e., $p(w|\mathcal{D}) = \mathcal{N}(\mu, \Sigma)$, with $\Sigma = \text{diag}(\Sigma_1, \ldots, \Sigma_{n_w})$, we obtain the following result for the posterior integration:

$$P(R) = \int_R p(w|\mathcal{D})dw = \prod_{j=1}^{n_w} \frac{1}{2}\left(\text{erf}\left(\frac{\mu_j - w_i^L}{\sqrt{2\Sigma_j}}\right) - \text{erf}\left(\frac{\mu_j - w_i^u}{\sqrt{2\Sigma_j}}\right)\right). \quad (12)$$

By plugging this into the bound equations for probabilistic robustness and for decision robustness, one obtains a closed-form formula for the bounds given weight set interval families $\mathcal{H}$, $\mathcal{K}$ and $\mathcal{J}$.

Sample-Based Approximations. In the case of sample-based posterior approximation (e.g., HMC), we have that $p(w|\mathcal{D})$ defines a distribution over a finite set of weights. In this case we can simplify the computations by selecting the weight margin $\gamma = 0$, so that each sampled interval is of the form $R = [w_i, w_i]$ and its probability under the discrete posterior will trivially be:

$$P(R_i) = p(w_i|\mathcal{D}). \quad (13)$$

5.2   Bounding Bayesian Neural Network Output

Given an input set, T, and a weight interval, $R = [w^L, w^U]$, the second key step in computing probabilistic and decision robustness is the bounding of the output of the BNN over R given T. That is, we need to derive methods to compute $[y^L, y^U]$ such that $\forall w \in [w^L, w^U], \forall x' \in T$ it follows that $f^w(x') \in [y^L, y^U]$.

In this section, we consider Interval Bound Propagation (IBP) as a method for computing the desired output set over-approximations, and defer the discussion of Linear Bound Propagation (LBP) to Appendix C. Before discussing IBP in more detail, we first introduce common notation for the rest of the section. We consider feed-forward neural networks of the form:

$$z^{(0)} = x, \quad \zeta_i^{(k+1)} = \sum_{j=1}^{n_k} W_{ij}^{(k)} z_j^{(k)} + b_i^{(k)}, \quad z_i^{(k)} = \sigma(\zeta_i^{(k)}) \qquad (14)$$

for $k = 1, \ldots, K$ and $i = 0, \ldots, n_k$, where K is the number of hidden layers, $\sigma(\cdot)$ is a pointwise activation function, $W^{(k)} \in \mathbb{R}^{n_k \times n_{k-1}}$ and $b^{(k)} \in \mathbb{R}^{n_k}$ are the matrix of weights and vector of biases that correspond to the kth layer of the network, and n_k is the number of neurons in the kth hidden layer. Note that, while Eq. (14) is written explicitly for fully-connected layers, convolutional layers can be accounted for by embedding them in fully-connected form [59].

We write $W_{i:}^{(k)}$ for the vector comprising the elements from the ith row of $W^{(k)}$, and similarly $W_{:j}^{(k)}$ for that comprising the elements from the jth column. $\zeta^{(K+1)}$ represents the final output of the network (or the logit in the case of classification networks), that is, $\zeta^{(K+1)} = f^w(x)$. We write $W^{(k),L}$ and $W^{(k),U}$ for the lower and upper bound induced by R for $W^{(k)}$, and $b^{(k),L}$ and $b^{(k),U}$ for the bounds of $b^{(k)}$, for $k = 0, \ldots, K$. Observe that $z^{(0)}$, $\zeta_i^{(k+1)}$ and $z_i^{(k)}$ are all functions of the input point x and of the combined vector of weights $w = [W^{(0)}, b^{(0)}, \ldots, W^{(K)}, b^{(K)}]$. We omit the explicit dependency for simplicity of notation. Finally, we remark that, as both the weights and the input vary in a given set, the middle expression of Eq. (14) defines a quadratic form.

Interval Bound Propagation (IBP). IBP has already been employed for fast certification of deterministic neural networks [23]. The only adjustment needed in our setting is that, at each layer, we also need to propagate the interval of the weight matrix $[W^{(k),L}, W^{(k),U}]$ and that of the bias vector $[b^{(k),L}, b^{(k),U}]$. This can be done by noticing that the minimum and maximum of each term of the bi-linear form of Eq. (14), that is, of each monomial $W_{ij}^{(k)} z_j^{(k)}$, lies in one of the four corners of the interval $[W_{ij}^{(k),L}, W_{ij}^{(k),U}] \times [z_j^{(k),L}, z_j^{(k),U}]$, and by adding the minimum and maximum values respectively attained by $b_i^{(k)}$. As in the deterministic case, interval propagation through the activation function proceeds by observing that generally employed activation functions are monotonic. This is summarised in the following proposition.

Proposition 3. *Let $f^w(x)$ be the network defined by Eq. (14), let for $k = 0, \ldots, K$:*

$$t_{ij}^{(k),L} = \min\{W_{ij}^{(k),L} z_j^{(k),L}, W_{ij}^{(k),U} z_j^{(k),L}, W_{ij}^{(k),L} z_j^{(k),U}, W_{ij}^{(k),U} z_j^{(k),U}\} \qquad (15)$$

$$t_{ij}^{(k),U} = \max\{W_{ij}^{(k),L} z_j^{(k),L}, W_{ij}^{(k),U} z_j^{(k),L}, W_{ij}^{(k),L} z_j^{(k),U}, W_{ij}^{(k),U} z_j^{(k),U}\} \qquad (16)$$

where $i = 1, \ldots, n_{k+1}$, $j = 1, \ldots, n_k$, $z^{(k),L} = \sigma(\zeta^{(k),L})$, $z^{(k),U} = \sigma(\zeta^{(k),U})$ and

$$\zeta^{(k+1),L} = \sum_j t^{(k),L}_{:j} + b^{(k),L}, \quad \zeta^{(k+1),U} = \sum_j t^{(k),U}_{:j} + b^{(k),U}. \qquad (17)$$

Then we have that $\forall x \in T$ and $\forall w \in R$: $f^w(x) = \zeta^{(K+1)} \in \left[\zeta^{(K+1),L}, \zeta^{(K+1),U}\right]$.

The minima and maxima in Proposition 3 are the tightest possible bounds one can compute on matrix multiplication. A more efficient scheme for this propagation is detailed in [46], which can be seen as an adaptation of [37] to NN operations. Additionally, our approach can be linked to abstract interpretation with simultaneous abstract sets (in our case from the orthotope domain) over inputs and weights [20]. Regardless, [34] shows that both have an over-approximation factor of 1.5. Similar bound formulations have been employed across the deterministic NN certification literature [18,39,47,53]. In Appendix C, we employ linear bounds on Eq. 17, which can tighten the bounds computed by our method as shown initially in [50]. In [1] dynamic programming is used to tighten these bounds further, and in [39], outside the context of BNNs, an extension of CROWN is developed for the same problem. We emphasise that, regardless of the propagation or tightening employed, each of these approaches can be seen as an instantiation of the framework provided in this work.

Algorithm 1. Lower Bounds for BNN Probabilistic Robustness

Input: T – Input Region, $f^{\mathbf{w}}$ – Bayesian Neural Network, $p(w|\mathcal{D})$ – Posterior Distribution with variance Σ, N – Number of Samples, γ – Weight margin.
Output: A sound lower bound on $P_{\text{safe}}(T, S)$.

1: $\mathcal{H} \leftarrow \emptyset$ # $\mathcal{H}$ is a set of known safe weight intervals
2: $v \leftarrow \gamma \cdot I \cdot \Sigma$ # Elementwise product to obtain width of weight margin
3: **for** $i \leftarrow 0$ to N **do**
4:     $w^{(i)} \sim p(w|\mathcal{D})$
5:     # Assume weight intervals are built to be disjoint
6:     $[w^{(i),L}, w^{(i),U}] \leftarrow [w_i - v, w_i + v]$
7:     # Interval/Linear Bound Propagation, Section 5.2
8:     $y^L, y^U \leftarrow \mathbf{Propagate}(f, T, [w^{(i),L}, w^{(i),U}])$
9:     **if** $[y^L, y^U] \subset S$ **then**
10:         $\mathcal{H} \leftarrow \mathcal{H} \bigcup \{[w^{(i),L}, w^{(i),U}]\}$
11:     **end if**
12: **end for**
13: $P^L_{\text{safe}} \leftarrow 0.0$
14: **for** $[w^{(i),L}, w^{(i),U}] \in \mathcal{H}$ **do**
15:     $P^L_{\text{safe}} = P^L_{\text{safe}} + P([w^{(i),L}, w^{(i),U}])$ # Compute safe weight probs, Section 5.1
16: **end for**
17: **return** P^L_{safe}

6   Complete Bounding Algorithm

In this section, we assemble complete algorithms for the computation of bounds on $P_{\text{safe}}(T, S)$ and $D_{\text{safe}}(T, S)$ based on the results discussed so far, leaving the detailed algorithms to Appendix D. Appendix A discusses further use cases for the bounds. The computational complexity of the algorithm is discussed in Appendix F.

6.1   Lower-Bounding Algorithm

We provide a step-by-step outline for how to compute lower bounds on $P_{\text{safe}}(T, S)$ in Algorithm 1. We start (line 1) by initialising the family of safe weight sets $\mathcal{H}$ to be the empty set and by scaling the weight margin with the posterior weight scale (line 2). We then iteratively (line 3) proceed by sampling weights from the posterior distribution (line 4), building candidate weight boxes (line 6), and propagating the input and weight box through the BNN (line 8). We next check whether the propagated output set is inside the safe output region S, and, if so, update the family of weights $\mathcal{H}$ to include the weight box currently under consideration (lines 9 and 10). Finally, we rely on the results in Sect. 5.1 to compute the overall probabilities over all the weight sets in $\mathcal{H}$, yielding a valid lower bound for $P_{\text{safe}}(T, S)$. For clarity of presentation, we assume that all the weight boxes that we sample in lines 4–6 are pairwise disjoint, as this simplifies the probability computation. The general case with overlapping weight boxes relies on the Bonferroni bound and is given in Appendix E.4.

The algorithm for the computation of a lower bound on $D_{\text{safe}}(T, S)$ (listed in the Appendix E as Algorithm 2) proceeds in an analogous way, but without the need to perform the check in line 9, and by adjusting line 15 to the formula from Proposition 2.

6.2   Upper-Bounding Algorithm

Upper-bounding $P_{\text{safe}}(T, S)$ and $D_{\text{safe}}(T, S)$ follows the same computational flow as Algorithm 1. The algorithms for the computation of upper bounds on probabilistic and decision robustness are listed respectively as Algorithm 3 and 4 in Appendix E. We again proceed by sampling a rectangle around the weights, propagate bounds through the NN, and compute the probabilities of weight intervals. The key change to the algorithm to allow upper bound computation involves computing the best case, rather than the worst case, for y for decision robustness (line 12 in Algorithm 3) and ensuring that the entire interval $[y^L, y^U] \notin S$ (line 18) for probabilistic robustness.

7   Experiments

In this section we experimentally validate our framework on a variety of tasks, including airborne collision avoidance, medical imaging, and autonomous driving applications. We mainly focus on verifying the adversarial robustness and

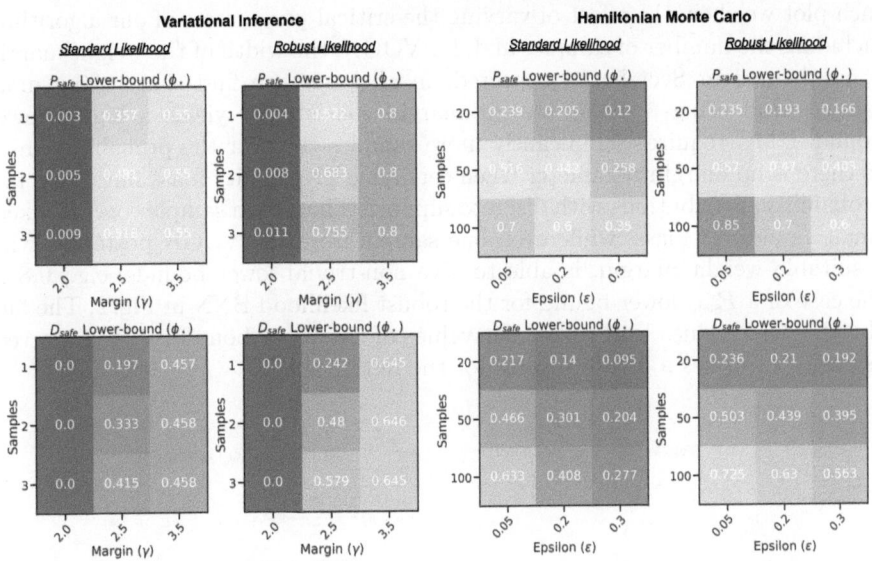

Fig. 2. Top Row: Lower bounds on P_{safe}. **Bottom Row:** Lower bounds on D_{safe}. **Left Two Columns:** Bound values for VI-inferred BNN averaged over 1000 test-set examples using various likelihoods, number of samples, and weight-margin values. **Right Two Columns:** Bound values for HMC-inferred BNN averaged over 1000 test-set examples using various likelihoods, number of samples, and values of ϵ.

uncertainty of classification problems that use the 0–1 loss. For a discussion of how our framework applies to a wider class of specifications see Appendix A, and Appendix B for an extension to other decision rules. In each case study, we take the input set to be the interval $T_{\epsilon}(x) := [x - \epsilon, x + \epsilon]$, where $\epsilon \geq 0$ is a parameter that we vary in our experiments. For all experiments, S is the set of all vectors where the true class is returned. Experiments are run on a server equipped with 2x AMD EPYC 9334 CPUs and 2x NVIDIA L40 GPUs. Details on training hyper-parameters can be found in Appendix G.

7.1 Airborne Collision Avoidance

We start with the airborne collision avoidance benchmark, which is commonly used to evaluate the robustness of neural network controllers in a safety-critical scenario [25,26]. In particular, we consider the horizontal collision avoidance scenario (HCAS) from [25], and work with a single hidden layer neural network with 125 hidden neurons trained both using Variational Online Gauss Newton (VOGN) [28] and Hamiltonian Monte Carlo (HMC) [33]. We infer posteriors using both the standard likelihood and the robust likelihood proposed in [49]. In Fig. 2 we study the guarantees that our method is able to provide for each combination of the inference method and likelihood. We plot the lower bound on P_{safe} and D_{safe} resulting from Algorithm 1 averaged over 1000 test-set samples. In each plot we show the effect of varying the critical parameters of our algorithm, including the number of samples and, for VOGN, the width of the weight margin γ, as defined in Sect. 5. As expected, in all cases, we find that taking more samples and using a higher weight margin consistently yields a higher lower bound. HMC requires significantly more samples to cover the probability mass as there is no margin parameter when certifying probability mass functions, i.e., probability distributions with discrete support. Thus, each sample covers a fixed, small amount of mass, while even one sample from the VOGN posterior, with a suitable weight margin, is able to give non-trivial lower bounds, e.g., 0.8 in the case of a P_{safe} lower bound for the robust likelihood BNN in Fig. 2. The fact that higher ϵ values lead to smaller values of the lower bound is also expected, as larger ϵ implies a greater radius for the initial set T.

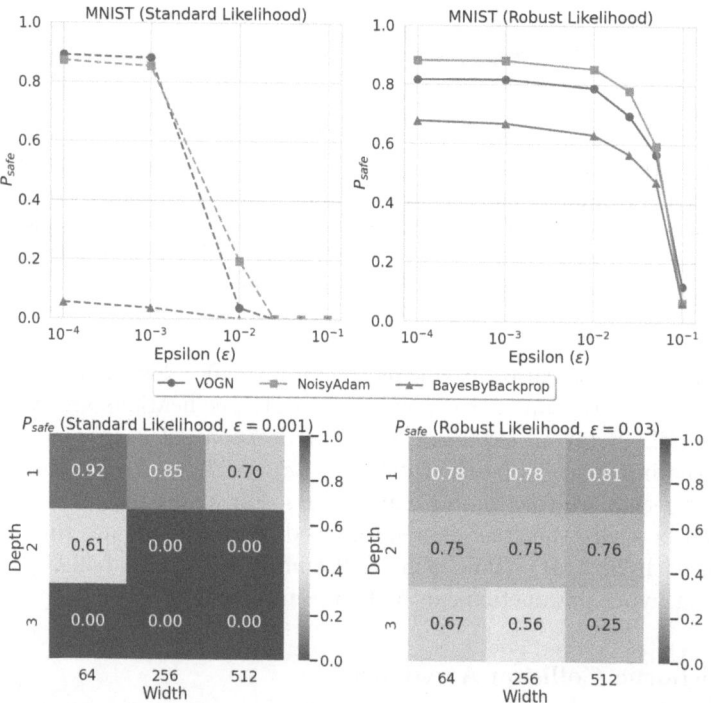

Fig. 3. Top Row: Computed lower bound values on P_{safe} for robust-likelihood VOGN posterior (right) and standard VOGN posterior (left). **Bottom Row:** Computed lower bound P_{safe} values for the VOGN posterior while varying depth and width parameters of the BNN architecture.

7.2   Image Classification

We now turn our attention to image classification, considering first the widely used MNIST benchmark with 28 by 28 pixel grey-scale images [30] and then two safety-critical tasks from medical image classification and autonomous driving.

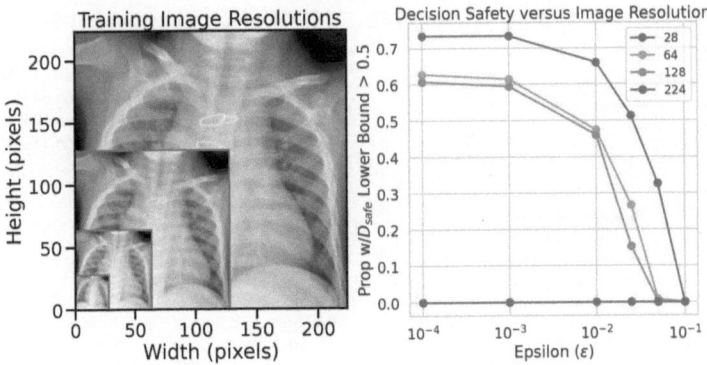

Fig. 4. Left: Different training image resolutions on a training image sample from PneumoniaMNIST. **Right:** Our computed lower bounds on D_{safe}, which correspond to adversarial robustness certificates as we vary the resolution fed into a VOGN-inferred BNN.

MNIST Digit Recognition. In Fig. 3, we present two plots certifying (via lower bounds on P_{safe}) a single hidden layer neural network with 100 hidden neurons with parameters inferred using VOGN [28], BayesByBackprop [10] and NoisyAdam [58], using both robust and standard likelihoods as for the airborne collision avoidance case study. In the top row of Fig. 3, we plot the computed lower bounds as we increase the value of ϵ. For the posterior inferred by each inference method using the standard likelihood, we observe that our method is only able to certify low values of P_{safe}, even for small values of ϵ, e.g., 0.001. However, for the robust likelihood posteriors, we are able to certify non-trivial robustness guarantees even at $\epsilon = 0.1$. Additionally, we observe that Bayes-ByBackprop [10] has consistently lower certified values of P_{safe}. We hypothesis that this is due to BayesByBackprop having a higher variance posterior, which in turn results in the propagation of wider weight intervals that can introduce significant approximation.

In the bottom half of Fig. 3, we study how our lower bounds on P_{safe} change as we increase the depth and width of the neural network architecture. For this study we exclusively employ VOGN, but, as previously, still utilise the standard (left) and robust (right) likelihoods. We find that, for the standard likelihood, we are able to obtain high lower bounds (greater than 0.7) for all one-layer networks regardless of width, but struggle with increasing depths. For the posteriors inferred using the robust likelihood, we observe that the lower bounds produced by our approach only begin to decrease when the depth reaches three layers with significant width. We additionally highlight that, for the posteriors inferred using the robust likelihood, we use a much larger ϵ (=0.03) compared to what is used to get non-trivial bounds in the standard training case ($\epsilon = 0.001$).

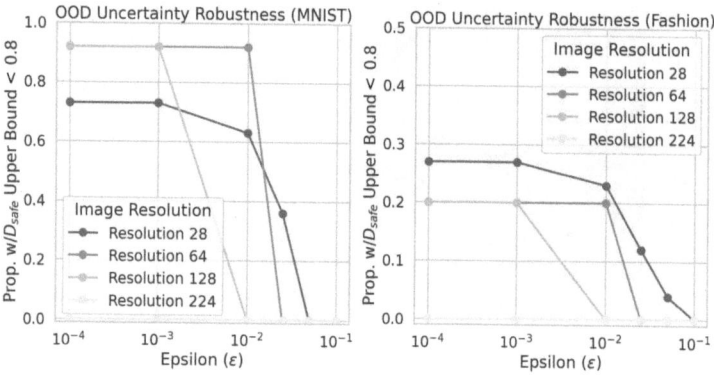

Fig. 5. Computing upper bounds on D_{safe} to certify robust uncertainty estimates from posteriors inferred on PneumoniaMNIST. **Left:** Uncertainty certificates for PneumoniaMNIST posterior on MNIST dataset. **Right:** Uncertainty certificates for PneumoniaMNIST posterior on FashionMNIST dataset.

Medical Image Classification. We now turn our attention to a more realistic safety-critical application from the medical image classification domain. In particular, we study the PneumoniaMNIST dataset from the MedMNIST suite of benchmarks [56]. PneumoniaMNIST is a dataset of greyscale images of chest X-rays that pose a binary classification problem, with one class representing normal chest X-rays and the other class presenting with pneumonia. In the most recent iteration of the MedMNIST benchmark, an option for different resolutions is provided ranging from 28 by 28, the same resolution as MNIST, up to 224 by 224, the same resolution as the popular, large-scale ImageNet dataset [17]. In the left-hand-side plot of Fig. 4, we visualize the significant differences between these input dimensionalities. We use these datasets to study how well our certification approaches scale with increasing input dimensionality. We work with a four-layer convolutional architecture with two 2D convolution layers, an average pooling layer, and a final fully-connected layer consisting of 50 neurons. For each network studied in this section, we use the robust likelihood of [49] in order to obtain non-trivial certifications. Additionally, we turn our attention to bounding decision robustness, D_{safe}, rather than probabilistic robustness, P_{safe}, employed for MNIST evaluation. Decision robustness is more appropriate here due to the safety-critical nature of pneumonia classification, compared to handwritten digit classification. In particular, we begin by computing lower bounds on D_{safe}, which in turn allows us to compute adversarial robustness certificates commensurate with those computed for deterministic neural networks. We find (see the right-hand-side plot of Fig. 4) that an increase in resolution corresponds to a significant decrease in the lower bounds computed by our approach, which is a result of greater approximation introduced by bound propagation techniques. Nevertheless, on images with 128 by 128 resolution, our guarantees continue to provide non-trivial bounds.

In addition to computing lower bounds on D_{safe} to certify the adversarial robustness of our trained posteriors, we also compute upper bounds on D_{safe} to provide certificates that our posterior is provably, robustly uncertain on given out-of-distribution inputs. To study this, we use the MNIST dataset as well as the FashionMNIST dataset (consisting of greyscale, 28 by 28, images of clothing items) as out-of-distribution examples for pneumonia classification. We then consider an example *uncertain* if the maximum value of the posterior predictive distribution is less than 0.8 (an arbitrary, user-definable threshold, which may require calibration to the specific setting). In Fig. 5 we plot the proportion of test-set inputs for which the inferred posterior is robustly uncertain on MNIST (left plot) and FashionMNIST (right plot). For very small values of ϵ, we notice that the network is much more robustly uncertain on MNIST examples then on FashionMNIST examples. Further, we find that, similarly to robustness certification, we are unable to certify any non-trivial uncertainty properties for images with 224 by 224 resolution.

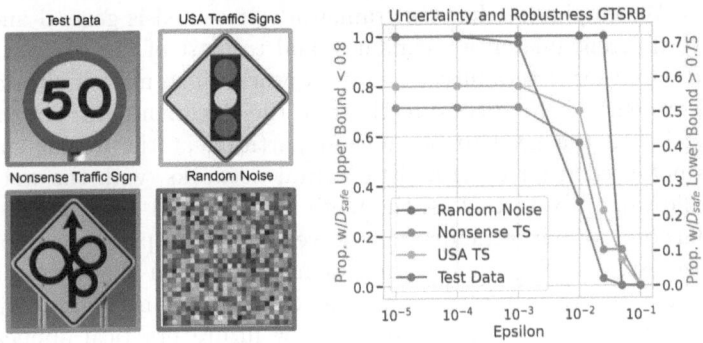

Fig. 6. Analysis of BNN inferred on GTSRB dataset. **Left:** Example in-distribution image (top left) and out-of-distribution images. **Right:** Adversarial robustness certificates (red) and uncertainty certificates (shades of green) using lower and upper bounds on D_{safe} respectively for different levels of ϵ. (Color figure online)

Traffic Sign Recognition Classification. Our final safety-critical case study comes from autonomous navigation using the German Traffic Sign Recognition Benchmark (GTSRB) [40]. In particular, we study a three-class subset of the

GTSRB dataset with a three-layer CNN model with parameters inferred using the robust likelihood and VOGN. In Fig. 6 we plot an example of the 50 km/h sign (an in-distribution image) and different examples from three different out-of-distribution datasets: United States Traffic Signs, Nonsense Traffic Signs, and random noise. The first two are small sets of images curated from royalty free image databases online and the third is sampled from a unit normal distribution. Using each of these datasets, we study both adversarial robustness (ensuring a sufficiently high D_{safe} lower bound) and uncertainty properties (ensuring sufficiently low D_{safe} upper bound) of the trained network that achieves 96% test-set accuracy. In the right-hand-side plot of Fig. 6 (in red), we show that our method is able to compute non-trivial adversarial robustness guarantees up to $\epsilon = 0.001$. In various shades of green, we show that the uncertainty guarantees we compute are also non-trivial for similar values of ϵ.

8   Conclusion

In this work, we introduced a computational framework for evaluating robustness properties of BNNs operating under adversarial settings. In particular, we have discussed how probabilistic robustness and decision robustness can be upper- and lower-bounded via a combination of posterior sampling, integral computation over boxes and bound propagation techniques. We have detailed how to compute these properties for the case of HMC and VI posterior approximation, and how to instantiate the bounds for interval and linear bound propagation techniques. We emphasise that the framework presented is general and can be adapted to different inference techniques, and to most of the verification techniques employed for deterministic neural networks. The main limitation of the approach presented here arises directly from the Bayesian nature of the underlying model, i.e., the need to bound and partition at the weight space level (which is not needed for deterministic neural networks, with the weight fixed to a specific value). Nevertheless, the methods presented here provide the first general-purpose, formal technique for the verification of probabilistic and decision robustness, as well as uncertainty quantification, in Bayesian neural networks, systematically evaluated on a range of tasks and network architectures. We hope this can serve as a sound basis for future practical applications in safety-critical scenarios.

Acknowledgments. This project received funding from the ERC under the European Union's Horizon 2020 research and innovation programme (FUN2MODEL, grant agreement No. 834115). MK further acknowledges funding from ELSA: European Lighthouse on Secure and Safe AI project (grant agreement No. 101070617 under UK guarantee). Preliminary work on this paper was done while Matthew Wicker, Andrea Patane and Luca Laurenti were at the University of Oxford funded by FUN2MODEL.

Disclosure of Interests. The authors have no competing interests to declare that are relevant to the content of this article.

References

1. Adams, S., Patane, A., Lahijanian, M., Laurenti, L.: BNN-DP: robustness certification of Bayesian neural networks via dynamic programming. In: ICML, pp. 133–151. PMLR (2023)
2. Aggarwal, R., et al.: Diagnostic accuracy of deep learning in medical imaging: a systematic review and meta-analysis. NPJ Digit. Med. **4**(1), 1–23 (2021)
3. Batten, B., Hosseini, M., Lomuscio, A.: Tight verification of probabilistic robustness in Bayesian neural networks. In: AISTATS (2024)
4. Bekasov, A., Murray, I.: Bayesian adversarial spheres: Bayesian inference and adversarial examples in a noiseless setting. arXiv preprint arXiv:1811.12335 (2018)
5. Benussi, E., Patane, A., Wicker, M., Laurenti, L., Kwiatkowska, M.: Individual fairness guarantees for neural networks. In: IJCAI (2022)
6. Berger, J.O.: Statistical Decision Theory and Bayesian Analysis. Springer, Heidelberg (2013). https://doi.org/10.1007/978-1-4757-4286-2
7. Berrada, L., et al.: Make sure you're unsure: a framework for verifying probabilistic specifications. In: NeurIPS, vol. 34 (2021)
8. Biggio, B., Roli, F.: Wild patterns: ten years after the rise of adversarial machine learning. Pattern Recogn. **84**, 317–331 (2018)
9. Bishop, C.: Neural Networks for Pattern Recognition. Oxford University Press, Oxford (1995)
10. Blundell, C., Cornebise, J., Kavukcuoglu, K., Wierstra, D.: Weight uncertainty in neural networks. In: ICML (2015)
11. Carbone, G., Wicker, M., Laurenti, L., Patane, A., Bortolussi, L., Sanguinetti, G.: Robustness of Bayesian neural networks to gradient-based attacks. In: NeurIPS, vol. 33, pp. 15602–15613 (2020)
12. Cardelli, L., Kwiatkowska, M., Laurenti, L., Paoletti, N., Patane, A., Wicker, M.: Statistical guarantees for the robustness of Bayesian neural networks. In: IJCAI (2019)
13. Cardelli, L., Kwiatkowska, M., Laurenti, L., Patane, A.: Robustness guarantees for Bayesian inference with Gaussian processes. In: AAAI (2018)
14. Chang, S.H., Cosman, P.C., Milstein, L.B.: Chernoff-type bounds for the Gaussian error function. IEEE Trans. Commun. **59**(11), 2939–2944 (2011)
15. Chen, L., et al.: Deep neural network based vehicle and pedestrian detection for autonomous driving: a survey. IEEE Trans. Intell. Transp. Syst. **22**(6), 3234–3246 (2021)
16. De Palma, G., Kiani, B., Lloyd, S.: Adversarial robustness guarantees for random deep neural networks. In: ICML, pp. 2522–2534. PMLR (2021)
17. Deng, J., Dong, W., Socher, R., Li, L.J., Li, K., Fei-Fei, L.: Imagenet: a large-scale hierarchical image database. In: CVPR, pp. 248–255 (2009)
18. Doherty, A., Wicker, M., Laurenti, L., Patane, A.: Individual fairness in Bayesian neural networks. arXiv preprint arXiv:2304.10828 (2023)
19. Dvijotham, K., Garnelo, M., Fawzi, A., Kohli, P.: Verification of deep probabilistic models. arXiv preprint arXiv:1812.02795 (2018)
20. Gehr, T., Mirman, M., Drachsler-Cohen, D., Tsankov, P., Chaudhuri, S., Vechev, M.: Ai2: safety and robustness certification of neural networks with abstract interpretation. In: 2018 IEEE S&P, pp. 3–18. IEEE (2018)
21. Goodfellow, I., Bengio, Y., Courville, A.: Deep Learning. MIT Press, Cambridge (2016)

22. Goodfellow, I.J., Shlens, J., Szegedy, C.: Explaining and harnessing adversarial examples. arXiv preprint arXiv:1412.6572 (2014)
23. Gowal, S., et al.: On the effectiveness of interval bound propagation for training verifiably robust models. In: SecML 2018 (2018)
24. Huang, X., Kwiatkowska, M., Wang, S., Wu, M.: Safety verification of deep neural networks. In: Majumdar, R., Kunčak, V. (eds.) CAV 2017. LNCS, vol. 10426, pp. 3–29. Springer, Cham (2017). https://doi.org/10.1007/978-3-319-63387-9_1
25. Julian, K.D., Kochenderfer, M.J.: Guaranteeing safety for neural network-based aircraft collision avoidance systems. In: DASC (2019)
26. Katz, G., Barrett, C., Dill, D.L., Julian, K., Kochenderfer, M.J.: Reluplex: an efficient SMT solver for verifying deep neural networks. In: Majumdar, R., Kunčak, V. (eds.) CAV 2017. LNCS, vol. 10426, pp. 97–117. Springer, Cham (2017). https://doi.org/10.1007/978-3-319-63387-9_5
27. Kendall, A., Gal, Y.: What uncertainties do we need in Bayesian deep learning for computer vision? In: NeurIPS (2017)
28. Khan, M., Nielsen, D., Tangkaratt, V., Lin, W., Gal, Y., Srivastava, A.: Fast and scalable Bayesian deep learning by weight-perturbation in Adam. In: ICML, pp. 2611–2620. PMLR (2018)
29. Lechner, M., Žikelić, D., Chatterjee, K., Henzinger, T.: Infinite time horizon safety of Bayesian neural networks. In: NeurIPS, vol. 34, pp. 10171–10185 (2021)
30. LeCun, Y.: The MNIST database of handwritten digits (1998)
31. Liu, X., Li, Y., Wu, C., Hsieh, C.J.: Adv-BNN: improved adversarial defense through robust Bayesian neural network. In: ICLR (2019)
32. Michelmore, R., Wicker, M., Laurenti, L., Cardelli, L., Gal, Y., Kwiatkowska, M.: Uncertainty quantification with statistical guarantees in end-to-end autonomous driving control. In: ICRA (2019)
33. Neal, R.M.: Bayesian Learning for Neural Networks. Springer, New York (2012). https://doi.org/10.1007/978-1-4612-0745-0
34. Diep, N.H.: Efficient implementation of interval matrix multiplication. In: Jónasson, K. (ed.) PARA 2010. LNCS, vol. 7134, pp. 179–188. Springer, Heidelberg (2012). https://doi.org/10.1007/978-3-642-28145-7_18
35. Patane, A., Blaas, A., Laurenti, L., Cardelli, L., Roberts, S., Kwiatkowska, M.: Adversarial robustness guarantees for Gaussian processes. J. Mach. Learn. Res. **23** (2022)
36. Raghunathan, A., Steinhardt, J., Liang, P.S.: Semidefinite relaxations for certifying robustness to adversarial examples. In: NeurIPS, vol. 31 (2018)
37. Rump, S.M.: Fast and parallel interval arithmetic. BIT Numer. Math. **39**, 534–554 (1999)
38. Smith, M.T., Grosse, K., Backes, M., Alvarez, M.A.: Adversarial vulnerability bounds for Gaussian process classification. arXiv preprint arXiv:1909.08864 (2019)
39. Sosnin, P., Müller, M., Baader, M., Tsay, C., Wicker, M.: Certified robustness to data poisoning in gradient-based training. arXiv preprint arXiv:2406.05670 (2024)
40. Stallkamp, J., Schlipsing, M., Salmen, J., Igel, C.: Man vs. computer: benchmarking machine learning algorithms for traffic sign recognition. Neural Netw. **32**, 323–332 (2012)
41. Stanforth, R., Gowal, S., Mann, T., Kohli, P., et al.: A dual approach to scalable verification of deep networks. arXiv preprint arXiv:1803.06567 (2018)
42. Szegedy, C., et al.: Intriguing properties of neural networks. In: ICLR (2014)
43. Tjeng, V., Xiao, K., Tedrake, R.: Evaluating robustness of neural networks with mixed integer programming. arXiv preprint arXiv:1711.07356 (2017)

44. Wei, T., Liu, C.: Safe control with neural network dynamic models. In: Learning for Dynamics and Control Conference, pp. 739–750. PMLR (2022)

45. Weng, T.W., et al.: Towards fast computation of certified robustness for ReLU networks. In: ICML (2018)

46. Wicker, M.: Adversarial robustness of Bayesian neural networks. Ph.D. thesis, University of Oxford (2021)

47. Wicker, M., Heo, J., Costabello, L., Weller, A.: Robust explanation constraints for neural networks. arXiv preprint arXiv:2212.08507 (2022)

48. Wicker, M., Huang, X., Kwiatkowska, M.: Feature-guided black-box safety testing of deep neural networks. In: Beyer, D., Huisman, M. (eds.) TACAS 2018. LNCS, vol. 10805, pp. 408–426. Springer, Cham (2018). https://doi.org/10.1007/978-3-319-89960-2_22

49. Wicker, M., Laurenti, L., Patane, A., Chen, Z., Zhang, Z., Kwiatkowska, M.: Bayesian inference with certifiable adversarial robustness. In: AISTATS, pp. 2431–2439. PMLR (2021)

50. Wicker, M., Laurenti, L., Patane, A., Kwiatkowska, M.: Probabilistic safety for Bayesian neural networks. In: UAI, pp. 1198–1207. PMLR (2020)

51. Wicker, M., Laurenti, L., Patane, A., Paoletti, N., Abate, A., Kwiatkowska, M.: Certification of iterative predictions in Bayesian neural networks. In: UAI, pp. 1713–1723. PMLR (2021)

52. Wicker, M., Laurenti, L., Patane, A., Paoletti, N., Abate, A., Kwiatkowska, M.: Probabilistic reach-avoid for Bayesian neural networks. Artif. Intell. (2024)

53. Wicker, M., et al.: Certificates of differential privacy and unlearning for gradient-based training. arXiv preprint arXiv:2406.13433 (2024)

54. Wong, E., Kolter, Z.: Provable defenses against adversarial examples via the convex outer adversarial polytope. In: ICML, pp. 5286–5295. PMLR (2018)

55. Wu, M., Wicker, M., Ruan, W., Huang, X., Kwiatkowska, M.: A game-based approximate verification of deep neural networks with provable guarantees. Theoret. Comput. Sci. **807**, 298–329 (2020)

56. Yang, J., et al.: MedMNIST v2-a large-scale lightweight benchmark for 2D and 3D biomedical image classification. Sci. Data **10**(1), 41 (2023)

57. Yuan, M., Wicker, M., Laurenti, L.: Gradient-free adversarial attacks for Bayesian neural networks. In: AABI (2020)

58. Zhang, G., Sun, S., Duvenaud, D., Grosse, R.: Noisy natural gradient as variational inference. In: ICML, pp. 5852–5861. PMLR (2018)

59. Zhang, H., Weng, T.W., Chen, P.Y., Hsieh, C.J., Daniel, L.: Efficient neural network robustness certification with general activation functions. In: NeurIPS, pp. 4939–4948 (2018)

60. Zhang, X., Wang, B., Kwiatkowska, M.: Provable preimage under-approximation for neural networks. In: Finkbeiner, B., Kovács, L. (eds.) TACAS 2024. LNCS, vol. 14572, pp. 3–23. Springer, Cham (2024). https://doi.org/10.1007/978-3-031-57256-2_1

Getting Chip Card Payments Right

David Basin[1]($\boxtimes$) , Xenia Hofmeier[1] , Ralf Sasse[1] , and Jorge Toro-Pozo[2]

[1] Department of Computer Science, ETH Zurich, Zurich, Switzerland
{basin,xenia.hofmeier,ralf.sasse}@inf.ethz.ch
[2] SIX Digital Exchange, Zurich, Switzerland
jorge.toro@sdx.com

Abstract. EMV is the international protocol standard for smart card payments and is used in billions of payment cards worldwide. Despite the standard's advertised security, various issues have been previously uncovered, deriving from logical flaws that are hard to spot in EMV's lengthy and complex specification. We have formalized various models of EMV in Tamarin, a symbolic model checker for cryptographic protocols. Tamarin was extremely effective in finding critical flaws, both known and new, and in many cases exploitable on actual cards. We report on these past problems as well as followup work where we verified the latest, improved version of the protocol, the EMV kernel C8. This work puts C8's correctness on a firm, formal basis, and clarifies which guarantees hold for C8 and under which assumptions. Overall our work supports the thesis that cryptographic protocol model checkers like Tamarin have an essential role to play in improving the security of real-world payment protocols and that they are up to this challenge.

Keywords: Formal Methods · Security · Model Checking · EMV

1 Introduction

EMV is the de facto standard for smart card payments. It is named after Europay, Mastercard, and Visa, the three founding companies that initiated this standard, which is now managed by EMVCo. With 12.9 billion EMV cards in circulation and over 90% of card payments using EMV, the EMV protocol is by far the most prominent in-person payment protocol used worldwide [11].

EMVCo provides specifications for the different technologies used for card, mobile, and online payment. The card payment standards include specifications for *contact* transactions, where the payment card must be inserted into the payment terminal, and *contactless* transactions, where the card and terminal communicate wirelessly over NFC. The contactless protocol has numerous variants called *kernels*, associated with the different EMVCo members.

We thank Mastercard for their past support. All opinions and conclusions expressed in this paper are those of the authors.

A. Platzer et al. (Eds.): FM 2024, LNCS 14933, pp. 29–51, 2025.
https://doi.org/10.1007/978-3-031-71162-6_2

1.1   Attacks on EMV

Security is central to the proper functioning and acceptance of electronic payments. Unfortunately, there has been a long history of attacks on EMV cards and protocols. These range from cloning attacks [17], where a functioning card clone is produced, to PIN-bypass attacks where transactions that should require a PIN are performed without it. Early PIN-bypass attacks targeted contact transactions. For example, the attack of Murdoch et al. [15] uses a wired machine-in-the-middle (MITM) infrastructure between the card and the terminal. While effective, such attacks are not practically relevant as the MITM infrastructure is difficult to conceal. In contrast, MITM attacks on the NFC channel are a serious threat as the attack infrastructure is inconspicuous. Such attacks can be carried out, for example, using two smart phones that forward and modify the communication between the card and the terminal. Examples of this are the recent PIN-bypass attacks on EMV contactless [5–7,16].

Given EMV's lengthy and complex specification, running over 2,000 pages, it is not surprising that many weaknesses went undiscovered for quite some time, even long after the protocol became widely used. The weaknesses exploited were manifold and included issues in EMV's legacy modes, like the magstripe mode exploited by the cloning attack of Roland and Langer [17], the interoperability of the different kernels, as exploited by our previous card brand mixup attack [5], and most importantly weaknesses in EMV's options for different authentication methods that authenticate different data, as highlighted by our previous analysis of the EMV protocol [6].

To address weaknesses like those above, and to improve overall payment security, EMVCo recently developed its new, eighth, contactless kernel called C8. This new kernel reduces the protocol's complexity, introduces new security features, and removes known insecure features such as magstripe mode. Its new security features include modern cryptographic algorithms, privacy protection mechanisms, relay protection, and new authentication methods.

1.2   Applying Formal Methods

In this paper, we focus on the use of the Tamarin prover [3,14,18], a robust verification tool for cryptographic protocols, to uncover weaknesses in EMV and validate recently deployed countermeasures and other protocol improvements. We will explain Tamarin in Sect. 2.2 and we provide a brief survey here on how it has been used in the past to analyze EMV.

As mentioned above, we analyzed the EMV contact and contactless protocol in our previous work [6] using Tamarin. Our analysis revealed known attacks, such as the PIN-bypass attack on contact transactions by Murdoch et al. [15], as well as new attacks on EMV contactless. These new attacks include a PIN-bypass attack on the Visa kernel that was demonstrated on live systems and a separate attack that targets merchants. In the latter attack, the adversary pays for some goods, the terminal accepts the transaction, the adversary walks out of the store with the goods, and the bank later declines the transaction. This attack leaves the merchant "holding the bag" in that the adversary gets the goods but the merchant is cheated out of payment. These attacks target EMV transactions with weak authentication methods. By evaluating the security properties of transactions with different authentication methods, we could not only identify such attacks but also identify secure methods and prove that the security properties hold for our model of transactions with these methods. In this way, we could prove the security of the most common contactless Mastercard transactions.

Subsequent work of ours extended our EMV model to also specify the routing of transaction information between the terminal and bank [5]. As this communication is not described by the public specification of EMV, our initial models made assumptions about this communication. These assumptions included that transactions between a Mastercard card and a terminal running the Visa kernel would not be accepted by the bank. However, our experiments showed that this was not the case. After adapting our model to account for such transactions, Tamarin found an attack that we named the "card brand mixup attack." The attack is quite surprising: the terminal is tricked into running the Visa kernel with a Mastercard card, which in turn allows the adversary to perform the PIN-bypass attack targeting the Visa kernel. This attack was also successfully tested on live systems. Mastercard implemented countermeasures against this attacks, which we verified by attempting, and failing, to reproduce the attacks after their countermeasures were in place.

Over time, we found many different kinds of attacks using Tamarin. This reflects the multiple models we made, at increasing levels of precision, which allowed us to produce stronger verification results or, alternatively, find increasingly subtle problems in the design of the different EMV kernels. This was the case for our initial models, which were unable to capture the card brand mixup attack as routing aspects were initially omitted. Another example of this was that our initial models of EMV employed certain abstractions to aid Tamarin's termination. In particular, we abstracted away from certain failure modes that were part of the complex decision tree used to determine when the terminal rejects or accepts transactions. As a result, our original models were too abstract to capture our latest attack on the Mastercard kernel, which exploits failure modes associated with certificate lookup failures [7].

Tamarin however is a verification tool, not just a tool for attack finding. In all our previous work, after discovering attacks, we used Tamarin to verify proposed countermeasures. In addition to our own work, Tamarin has also been used by other researchers to verify EMV protocol extensions for relay protection, as done by Radu et al. [16] and Coppola et al. [8].

1.3 Contributions

In this work, we analyze the security of the new C8 kernel using Tamarin. In contrast to past work on formally modeling EMV, which occurred after the kernels analyzed were implemented and released, we report here on the analysis of C8 during its standardization. This provides confidence in the protocol's design before its deployment and provides an alternative to the many iterations of penetrate-and-patch, caused by the design errors discovered and exploited in the past.[1]

Our model of C8 includes its new security features, including its new authentication methods, its relay resistance protocol, and its new privacy features. As C8 is based on the other EMV protocols, we could reuse parts of the Tamarin models from our previous verification efforts [5,6], which sped up the modeling process significantly. After modeling, we analyzed C8's different configurations individually, each configuration consisting of different supported authentication methods for the card and cardholder.

Our analysis shows that C8 is a well-designed protocol that can be used securely, although not with all configurations. Specifically, we use Tamarin to identify both secure and insecure configurations, prove the security properties of the transactions with secure configurations, and find potential attacks on transactions with insecure configurations. We find, for example, that at least one of the available authentication methods must be used in each transaction to prevent attacks. Moreover, offline accepted transactions specifically require the terminal to verify the card's certificate. Overall, our analysis puts the security of this new EMV kernel on a firm, formal basis by highlighting assumptions on its configuration and implementation that are necessary and sufficient for its secure usage.

Outline. In Sect. 2 we provide background on C8 and Tamarin. In Sect. 3 we describe our Tamarin model of C8, including its desired security properties. In Sect. 4, we present our results and in Sect. 5 we draw conclusions.

2   Background

2.1   The C8 Protocol

The EMV specification describes the communication between a payment card and a payment terminal consisting of the terminal's commands followed by the card's responses. At the end of such a transaction, the terminal sends the transaction data to the bank that issued the card.

As observed in the introduction, EMV offers two protocol variants: contact and contactless. Moreover, there are variants of the contactless protocol called kernels and further complexity is introduced by the kernels' different configuration options. We first provide a general overview of EMV transactions that apply to all protocol variants and configurations.

---

[1] Note that our work is unlikely to be the final word on C8's security as it focuses on an abstract model of the design and we cannot rule out other weaknesses that adversaries may exploit, such as errors in the implementation. Moreover, adversaries may have capabilities not captured by our models, such as the ability to carry out side-channel attacks on the cryptography used.

To prevent fraud, the payment card authenticates transaction data to two different parties and in two different ways: once to the bank and once to the terminal. The card authenticates to the bank using a message authentication code (MAC) that is calculated using a session key derived from a symmetric long-term key shared between the card and the bank. The authentication to the terminal is signature based, and the asymmetric public key associated to the card's private signing key is authenticated using a certificate chain. The authenticated transaction data may differ for the two authentication methods and it also depends on the protocol variant and the configuration. It generally contains static data such as the card number (also called Primary Account Number (**PAN**)), payment details such as the amount and currency, and transaction specific data, for example, identifying the configuration.

In addition to the card authenticating the transaction data, the cardholder's presence is ensured using a Cardholder Verification Method (CVM). The CVMs include providing a PIN to the terminal, providing a paper signature, and Consumer Device CVM (CDCVM) where the card authenticates the cardholder, usually using a mobile device such as a smart phone. The PIN can either be verified offline by the terminal or online by the bank. Offline PIN is only offered by contact transactions, whereas contactless transactions require online PIN. Transactions with a value above the *CVM Required Limit* require some CVM, whereas transactions below this limit allow for no CVM.

At the end of a transaction, the terminal chooses to either decline the transaction offline, authorize the transaction offline, or send the transaction to the bank for online authorization. Note that transactions with online PIN also require online authorization.

The new C8 kernel is described in Book C8 [9] and Book E [10]. It offers many improved security features over past kernels. These include new methods to authenticate the transaction to the terminal and bank, modern cryptographic algorithms, privacy protection mechanisms, and a relay resistance protocol. Known insecure features such as the contactless magstripe mode were removed from the specification. The CVM performed is now chosen by the card and cards support Elliptic Curve Cryptography (ECC), AES, and RSA. Figure 1 shows a simplified C8 transaction. In what follows, we describe the abstraction of C8 that we modeled in Tamarin.

In C8, the card authenticates the transaction to the bank as with other EMV kernels using an Application Cryptogram (**AC**). The **AC** is a MAC computed over transaction data using a session key derived from the symmetric long-term key **mk** shared between the card and the bank and the Application Transaction Counter (**ATC**), which is increased for each transaction.

The signature-based authentication to the terminal used in prior EMV kernels is replaced by a MAC-based authentication. The card constructs the Enhanced Data Authentication (**EDA**)-**MAC** using a session key. The **EDA-MAC** authenticates the **AC** and the new Issuer Application Data (**IAD**)-**MAC**. The **IAD-MAC** is calculated over transaction data including the transaction amount, a terminal-sourced nonce, and a card-sourced nonce.

For the card to create these two MACs, the card and terminal establish symmetric session keys using a *blinded Diffie-Hellman* key exchange. The card has a static private-public key pair $(\mathbf{d_C}, \mathbf{Q_C})$ while the terminal generates a fresh ephemeral key pair $(\mathbf{d_T}, \mathbf{Q_T})$ for each transaction. The key exchange starts with the terminal sending its ephemeral public key $\mathbf{Q_T}$ to the card. The card generates a random *blinding factor* $\mathbf{r}$ and calculates a blinded public key $\mathbf{R}$ from its secret key $\mathbf{d_C}$ and $\mathbf{r}$. The card also calculates a shared secret $\mathbf{z} = \mathbf{Q_T}^{\mathbf{r} \times \mathbf{d_C}}$ from its secret key $\mathbf{d_C}$, the blinding factor $\mathbf{r}$, and the terminal's ephemeral public key $\mathbf{Q_T}$. From this shared secret $\mathbf{z}$, it derives two symmetric session keys, one for confidentiality $\mathbf{sk_c}$ and one for integrity $\mathbf{sk_i}$, using two Key Derivation Functions (KDF_c and KDF_i). The card then encrypts $\mathbf{r}$ with the session key for confidentiality $\mathbf{sk_c}$ and sends it together with the blinded public key $\mathbf{R}$ to the terminal. The terminal can derive the shared secret $\mathbf{z}$ from the blinded public key $\mathbf{R}$ and its ephemeral secret key $\mathbf{d_T}$ and recover $\mathbf{r}$.

To protect this key exchange from a machine-in-the-middle (MITM) attack, there are two options: *local authentication* or *copying the **IAD-MAC** into **IAD***. During local authentication, the terminal authenticates the card's public key $\mathbf{Q_C}$ by validating the card's certificates and the blinding factor $\mathbf{r}$. This verification is only performed if the terminal and card support local authentication. The second option of copying the **IAD-MAC** to the **IAD** lets the bank detect a MITM attack through the **IAD-MAC**. Namely, the card authenticates the **IAD-MAC** to the bank by including it in the **AC** and the terminal recalculates the **IAD-MAC** with its view of the session key and sends it to the bank as part of the **IAD**. The bank then verifies that the **IAD-MAC** received from the card in the **AC** is the same as the **IAD-MAC** received from the terminal in the **IAD**. Including the **IAD-MAC** in the **AC** is optional for the card. If the card performs this action, it indicates to the terminal that it must include the **IAD-MAC** in the **IAD**. We thus call this authentication method *copy **IAD-MAC** into **IAD***.

The use of blinding provides privacy protection against eavesdroppers by protecting sensitive data. Namely, data that identifies the card, like the card number (**PAN**), is encrypted with the session key for confidentiality $\mathbf{sk_c}$.

C8 also supports the Relay Resistance Protocol (RRP), which protects against relay attacks. In a relay attack, messages between a terminal and a remote card are forwarded and potentially modified. The RRP prevents such attacks by requiring the card to be close to the terminal. The RRP includes the exchange of two nonces, the terminal-sourced Terminal Relay Resistance Entropy (**TRRE**) and the card-sourced Device Relay Resistance Entropy (**DRRE**). The terminal's **TRRE** is included in the **AC** and **IAD-MAC** and the card's **DRRE** is included in the **IAD-MAC**. The terminal times this exchange to determine the distance between the card and terminal. If the estimated distance exceeds a given limit, the terminal may decline the transaction.

2.2   The Tamarin Prover

Tamarin is an automated tool for modeling and analyzing cryptographic protocols. Given a protocol model, security properties, and adversary capabilities, Tamarin can prove that the property holds for the protocol and adversary model, or provide an attack violating the property. Due to the undecidable nature of the underlying verification problem, Tamarin may sometimes fail to terminate.

Tamarin analyzes designs, not code, and cryptographic functionality is handled not by considering its implementation, but rather its abstract properties. In particular, Tamarin works with a symbolic model of protocols where bitstring messages are represented as terms, cryptographic operators are mod-

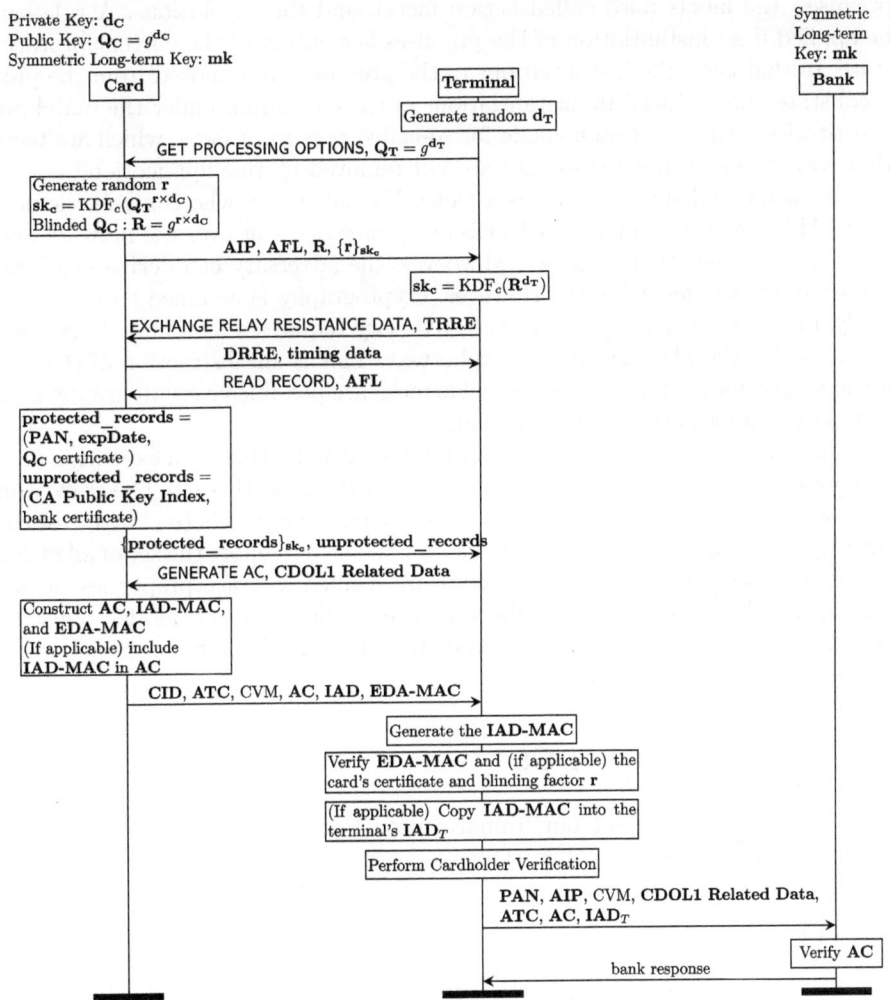

Fig. 1. Message sequence chart of our C8 protocol model abstraction.

eled as function symbols, and their properties are expressed with equational theories. For example, symmetric encryption is modeled by a function senc of arity two and the symmetric decryption is modeled using the function sdec also of arity two. The properties of these functions are modeled by the equation $\mathrm{sdec}(\mathrm{senc}(m, k), k) = m$, expressing that the decryption of a ciphertext with the correct key results in the original plaintext.

In Tamarin, *facts* are used to represent agents' local states and messages on the network. A fact has the form $\mathsf{F}(t_1, ..., t_n)$, consisting of the fact's name F applied to terms t_i. The protocol's state consists of the agents' local states and the messages on the network and thus is represented by a multiset of facts.

The protocol's state makes a transition to a new state by the application of a labeled multiset-rewrite rule. A rule consists of three multisets of facts: the premises, the labels (also called action facts), and the conclusions. A rule can be applied if an instantiation of the premises is a subset of the current protocol state. In that case, the instantiations of the premises are removed from the protocol state and replaced by instantiations of the conclusion under the matching substitution. An exception is made for so-called *persistent* facts, which are facts that stay in the protocol state and are not removed by rule application.

Tamarin's built-in adversary is a Dolev-Yao adversary who controls the network. This means the adversary learns every message sent over the network and can send messages that it knows. Moreover, the adversary can derive messages from those messages it knows. However, cryptography is assumed to work perfectly, meaning, for example, that the adversary requires a matching decryption key to derive the plaintext from a ciphertext. This is an abstraction of the real world where, for example, side-channel attacks are possible or cryptography may leak partial information about the plaintext.

A protocol P is modeled by a set of multiset rewrite rules. An execution of P is represented by a sequence of applications of rules from this set. The trace α of such an execution consists of the associated sequence of labels $(\alpha_1, ..., \alpha_n)$ of the rules applied, where α_i is a multiset of action facts. We denote the set of all of P's traces by $\mathrm{traces}(P)$. Security properties are defined as trace properties, which are expressed as first-order formulas on traces, called *lemmas* (as they must be proven), and Tamarin analyzes whether they hold for all (or, in special cases, some) of the protocol's traces.

3   Tamarin Model of C8

In this section, we present our Tamarin model of C8, the formalized security properties, and our methodology. Our model is available at [4].

3.1   Protocol Model

We model the actions of three parties: the card, the terminal, and the bank. The channel between the terminal and the bank is modeled as a secure channel, which provides confidentiality and authenticity. The NFC channel between the card and the terminal is modeled as being controlled by a Dolev-Yao adversary since the adversary can tamper with the NFC channel as it is not cryptographically protected. That protection is what the C8 protocol should achieve.

All EMV kernels rely on a public key infrastructure so that the terminal can authenticate the card's public key Q_C. We abstractly model this as the CA's self-signed certificate, which can be accessed by the terminal, the bank's certificate signed by the CA, and the card's public key certificate signed by the bank, which the card stores and sends to the terminal. The CA's certificate and the card's records are modeled as persistent facts, accessed by the bank and card respectively. The symmetric long-term key **mk** shared between the card and the bank is also modeled as a persistent fact that the card and bank can access.

EMV requires cardholder verification for high value transactions. In practice, terminals should reject high value transactions with a card that apparently does not support cardholder verification and instruct the cardholder to use the contact interface. Thus, our model does not allow a terminal to complete high value transactions without cardholder verification.

As previously mentioned, the C8 protocol is quite complex. In addition to those abstractions that are standard in symbolic models, we incorporated further abstractions and simplifications where required to aid proof termination. This includes omitting some configuration options, such as only modeling Version 2, which we described in Sect. 2.1, requiring the optional RRP, omitting some features such as Data Storage or the Select phase, and omitting some data objects, such as the **PDOL**.

As the C8 kernel is based on the other EMV kernels, we were able to reuse substantial parts of our previous EMV models [5,6] for our new model of C8. While a public specification of C8 was available for our work, this specification only covers the communication between the card and the terminal and not the actions of the bank. In addition, some proprietary data such as the **CDOL1 Related Data** is not part of the specification. In our previous works, we clarified underspecified protocol aspects by inspecting actual transaction transcripts that were collected using our MITM infrastructure. However, this was not possible for C8, as it is not yet implemented on publicly available cards. Fortunately, we were able to discuss the protocol with one of the EMVCo partners to resolve ambiguities or missing information.

3.2 Security Properties

The EMV protocol should provide guarantees to the cardholder, the merchant, and the bank. We express these guarantees as security properties that hold from the perspective of these three parties. We formulate the same properties as in our previous work [6] plus additional ones, which we explain next.

Authentication. After a successful transaction, the card's bank transfers funds from the cardholder's account to the merchant's account. The C8 protocol should provide the bank the information needed for this transfer. This includes the card's **PAN**, which identifies the cardholder's account, the terminal's identity, which identifies the merchant's account, the amount, and the currency. Providing the correct information means that the card, the terminal, and the bank should agree on this data. Situations (which likely are attacks) should be avoided where the card sees some low value while the terminal and bank agree on a different high value, or where a card sees its own **PAN** whereas the terminal sees a different card's **PAN** that was not involved in the transaction.

We formalize such agreement as authentication properties. Namely, we formalize two injective agreement properties [12], one for the authentication of the card and bank to the terminal and one for the card and terminal to the bank. Injective agreement states that whenever agent A in role r_A finished the protocol apparently with agent B in role r_B, then B was running the protocol with A and both agree on the data t. In addition, injective agreement rules out replay attacks by enforcing unique protocol runs with the data t.

The views of the protocol participants are expressed with the action facts Commit and Running, where $\mathsf{Commit}(A, B, \langle r_B, r_A, t \rangle)$ states that agent A in role r_A finished the protocol apparently with agent B in role r_B with data t and $\mathsf{Running}(B, A, \langle r_B, r_A, t \rangle)$ states that agent B in role r_B is running the protocol with agent A in role r_A and data t. Note that the order of the arguments A and B, which are the agents in Commit and Running, is intentionally swapped as the first argument represents the agent doing that action. Additionally, we mark agents as being expected to be non-compromised, also called honest, with Honest. We also track when agents have been compromised with Compromised. When an agent that should not be compromised has been compromised, then the property holds vacuously, which we explain in more detail shortly. Using these action facts, we formalize injective agreement to the terminal in the following lemma, which we subsequently check with Tamarin.

Lemma 1 (Authentication to the Terminal). *A protocol P satisfies authentication to the terminal if for every trace $\alpha \in traces(P)$:*

$$\forall T, P, r, t, i. \mathsf{Commit}(T, P, \langle r, \mathsf{'Terminal'}, t \rangle) \in \alpha_i \implies$$
$$(\exists j.\ \mathsf{Running}(P, T, \langle r, \mathsf{'Terminal'}, t \rangle) \in \alpha_j\ \wedge$$
$$\nexists i_2, T_2, P_2.\ \mathsf{Commit}(P_2, T_2, \langle r, \mathsf{'Terminal'}, t \rangle) \in \alpha_{i_2} \wedge i_2 \neq i)\ \vee$$
$$\exists A, k.\ \mathsf{Honest}(A) \in \alpha_i \wedge \mathsf{Compromise}(A) \in \alpha_k.$$

The first two lines of this lemma express that whenever the terminal T finished the protocol with the apparent communication partner P in role $r \in \{\mathsf{'Card'}, \mathsf{'Bank'}\}$, then P was running the protocol with T and both agree on the transaction data t. The third line specifies unique protocol runs with transaction data t by forbidding any terminals to finish the protocol with t apart from the above terminal that committed at time point i. In other words, should such a replay be possible in the protocol, it would violate this property.

In our model, we consider the security of the protocol in the presence of compromised agents. Compromise means that an agent's key material has been revealed and the adversary can thereby impersonate that agent. The compromisable key material includes the private keys of the CA, bank, and card, as well as the symmetric long-term key $\mathbf{mk}$ shared between the card and the terminal, and the terminal's ephemeral secret key $\mathbf{d_T}$. While a protocol cannot provide authentication guarantees when run with compromised agents, it should for sessions involving non-compromised agents, even when other agents (not involved in the session) are compromised. This is expressed in the last line of the above lemma. Agents involved in the session are named with the action fact Honest. The property does not have to hold if these agents were compromised, indicated by Compromise.

In addition to agreeing on the **PAN**, terminal identity, amount, and currency, the parties should agree on control data to ensure the correct transaction flow. This ensures that the parties have the same view of the performed transaction. This guarantees, for example, that if the card expects the terminal to perform online PIN, then the terminal did so. Thus, we consider the following transaction data to be agreed upon (i.e., the term t in Lemma 1): the **PAN**, the **AIP**, the CVM, the **ATC**, the **CDOL1**, the **AC**, the **IAD**, and the **AID**.

The authentication to the bank is expressed in a lemma very similar to the one above. The only differences is that the ground term 'Terminal' is replaced by 'bank'. Moreover, we formulated additional security properties, which we discuss next and formalize in Appendix A.

Bank Accepts. The merchant not only requires that the correct information for the fund transfer is provided, but also that the merchant receives their funds after a successful transaction. In other words, the bank should not decline transactions that were previously accepted by the terminal. This prevents the scenario described in the introduction where the adversary pays with a card for goods, the terminal accepts, the adversary walks out with the goods, and afterwards, the bank declines the transaction. Thus the merchant does not receive the funds for the purchase. This is especially relevant for offline-capable terminals that do not request online authorization.

Secrecy. The third property concerns the secrecy of critical data, i.e., the adversary cannot learn this data. This data includes the card's PIN and key material, consisting of the symmetric long-term key $\mathbf{mk}$ and the asymmetric secret key $\mathbf{d_C}$. The PIN should stay secret as criminals could otherwise steal the card and use the PIN and the card to pay for high amounts or withdraw money. The key material should stay secret as the adversary could misuse it to forge transactions.

Privacy. The C8 kernel introduces the blinded Diffie-Hellman key exchange to encrypt sensitive card-sourced data. This sensitive data includes the blinding factor $\mathbf{r}$ and any data returned by the READ RECORD response that uniquely identifies the card, for example, the card's **PAN**, certificate, and public key $\mathbf{Q_C}$. The encryption of this data protects the cardholder's privacy as, without it, an adversary observing data such as the **PAN** could track the cardholder's movement. We used Tamarin to prove the secrecy of the card's **PAN**.

Relay Resistance. For the C8 kernel, we verify properties of C8's Relay Resistance Protocol (RRP). We specify *relay resistance* using the formalism defined by Mauw et al. [13]. They reduce the correctness of distance-bounding protocols, such as RRP, to the order of messages being sent and received and they abstract away time. For C8's RRP, this means that the following actions must be performed sequentially in the following order: first, the terminal sends the EXCHANGE RELAY RESISTANCE DATA command with its nonce **TRRE**, then the card receives this message and responds with the **DRRE**, and finally the terminal receives this message. If these actions were not performed in this order, an adversarial card could send the response before the card sent the command. This would reduce the terminal's time measurements and thus reduce the estimated distance.

Note that our symbolic abstraction of relay resistance does not cover timing and physical layer attacks on RRP. Thus, our model does not capture relay attacks exploiting inaccurate timings, or exploiting properties of the physical layer. As a result, attacks like Radu et al.'s. [16] that exploit inaccurate timings and the Early-Detect and Late-Commit attacks targeting the NFC layer pointed out by Coppola et al. [8] fall outside of our analysis.

Executability. As a sanity check, we prove *executability* lemmas. These lemmas describe an expected protocol execution without adversary interference and provide a sanity check that the protocol is not inoperable due to modeling errors.

3.3   Analysis Approach

As mentioned, C8 offers multiple configuration options. As depicted in Table 1, we model the options to perform local authentication, copying the **IAD-MAC** into the **IAD**, performing online PIN or no CVM, and high or low value transactions. Each transaction has a fixed combination of configuration options, corresponding to instances of these four parameters, which we call a *configuration*. In our analysis of C8, we follow the approach taken in [5,6]: we model transactions arising from all configurations running and interacting in parallel. In our formalization of the security properties though, we consider each configuration separately. To do this, for each configuration we generate a so-called *target model* that we analyze with Tamarin. This allows us to determine which configurations are secure or insecure. Details on this approach can be found in [6].

Our previous models considered offline and online authorized transactions in the same model. An attack discovered for this model might only be possible for offline authorized transactions, but not for online authorized transactions, and this would not be apparent from the verification results. The C8 specification has the option for online and offline authorized transactions. However, since there is an industry push for online transactions, we additionally analyze online

Table 1. The four parameters comprising a configuration

Parameter	Instances	Determines
LocalAuth	- Yes	Whether local authentication is performed, i.e. whether the terminal verified the certificates and the blinding factor (note that the **EDA-MAC** is always validated).
	- No	
CopyIAD	-Yes	Whether the **IAD-MAC** is copied into the **IAD** itself and whether the **IAD-MAC** is included in the **AC**.
	- No	
CVM	- NoCVM	The CVM used in the transaction.
	- OnlinePIN	
Value	- Low	Whether the transaction amount is below (low) or above (high) the CVM Required Limit.
	- High	

authorized transactions separately. Thus, we analyze the 16 configurations twice: first we consider just online authorized transactions and second we allow for both offline and online authorization. Note that the second model includes all the online traces from the first model and also traces from offline transactions.

4   Results

In this section, we present the results of our analysis of the C8 protocol. In Table 2 we summarize the results for transactions requiring online authorization and in Table 3 we show the results for transactions supporting both offline and online authorization. The tables show for each configuration which lemmas were verified ($\checkmark$) or falsified ($\times$), the lines of code of the target model, and the time Tamarin required for analyzing the model. For our analysis, we used Tamarin version 1.9.0 [1] on a compute server running Ubuntu 20.04.3 with two Intel(R) Xeon(R) E5-2650 v4 @ 2.20 GHz CPUs, with 12 cores each. We used 14 threads and at most 32 GB of RAM per configuration.

The analysis of some of the models required hours due to their size and complexity. Moreover, to achieve termination, we needed to write so-called oracles, which are Python scripts that guide Tamarin's proof search. Also note that some of the models supporting offline (and as always online) authorization have longer proof times than the models requiring strictly online authorization. This is because the models supporting offline and online authorization have a larger search space than the models with only online authorization. Additionally, the proofs for the relay resistance lemma did not terminate within a few days for some of the configurations supporting offline authorization, namely Models 3.11 and 3.15 in Table 3, marked with 🌐. Hence, in these cases, we cannot draw conclusions with Tamarin about whether the respective statement holds.

As our model does not allow for high value transactions without CVM, the models with NoCVM and High are not executable. Thus, we did not analyze these configurations. Since security properties for non-executable protocols hold trivially, these lemmas are marked with NA.

Table 2. Results for lemmas for configurations requiring online authorization.

No.	Configuration				Exec.	Bank Acc.	Auth. to Term.	Auth. to Bank	Relay Resist.	Lines of code	Analysis time
	LocalAuth	CopyIAD	CVM	Value							
2.1	No	No	OnlinePIN	Low	✓	✓	×	×	×	610	3h29m45s
2.2	No	No	OnlinePIN	High	✓	✓	×	×	×	610	3h26m37s
2.3	No	No	NoCVM	Low	✓	✓	×	×	×	603	2h42m23s
2.4	No	No	NoCVM	High	×	NA	NA	NA	NA	561	4m08s
2.5	No	Yes	OnlinePIN	Low	✓	✓	✓	✓	✓	628	6m35s
2.6	No	Yes	OnlinePIN	High	✓	✓	✓	✓	✓	628	6m02s
2.7	No	Yes	NoCVM	Low	✓	✓	✓	✓	✓	621	7m13s
2.8	No	Yes	NoCVM	High	×	NA	NA	NA	NA	561	4m05s
2.9	Yes	No	OnlinePIN	Low	✓	✓	✓	✓	✓	628	1h18m33s
2.10	Yes	No	OnlinePIN	High	✓	✓	✓	✓	✓	628	1h16m38s
2.11	Yes	No	NoCVM	Low	✓	✓	✓	✓	✓	621	3h31m35s
2.12	Yes	No	NoCVM	High	×	NA	NA	NA	NA	561	4m03s
2.13	Yes	Yes	OnlinePIN	Low	✓	✓	✓	✓	✓	628	7m30s
2.14	Yes	Yes	OnlinePIN	High	✓	✓	✓	✓	✓	628	8m12s
2.15	Yes	Yes	NoCVM	Low	✓	✓	✓	✓	✓	621	8m01s
2.16	Yes	Yes	NoCVM	High	×	NA	NA	NA	NA	561	4m19s

4.1 Secure Configurations

To begin with, the secrecy of the PIN, the symmetric long-term key **mk**, and the card's secret key d_C, not included in Tables 2 and 3, hold for all configurations. We cover the secrecy of the **PAN** in Sect. 4.3. Note that the lemma *bank accepts* is verified for all the configurations that require online authorization, shown in Table 2, as the bank can only reject offline authorized transactions but not online authorized transactions (as the bank was already involved in an online transaction and has agreed).

Tamarin verified that most configurations requiring online authorization are secure, namely, the configurations with one or both of the authentication methods *local authentication* and *copy **IAD-MAC** into **IAD*** (Configurations 2.5–2.16 in Table 2). For the configurations supporting offline and online authorization, Tamarin verified the same secure configurations with two exceptions. First, Tamarin found attacks for the configuration without local authentication, with copying the **IAD-MAC** into the **IAD**, with no CVM, and a low value, i.e., Configuration 3.7 in Table 3. These attacks violate the lemmas *bank accepts*, *authentication to the terminal*, and *relay resistance*. We present these attacks in Sect. 4.2. The second exception was already mentioned above: Tamarin did not terminate for the relay resistance lemma for two configurations supporting offline authorization. However, Tamarin verified the other lemmas for these configurations.

Table 3. Results for lemmas for configurations supporting offline and online authorization.

No.	Configuration				Exec.	Bank Acc.	Auth. to Term.	Auth. to Bank	Relay Resist.	Lines of code	Analysis time
	LocalAuth	CopyIAD	CVM	Value							
3.1	No	No	OnlinePIN	Low	✓	✓	×	×	×	641	3h01m30s
3.2	No	No	OnlinePIN	High	✓	✓	×	×	×	641	3h00m31s
3.3	No	No	NoCVM	Low	✓	×	×	×	×	633	4h37m23s
3.4	No	No	NoCVM	High	×	NA	NA	NA	NA	591	7m49s
3.5	No	Yes	OnlinePIN	Low	✓	✓	✓	✓	✓	659	11m41s
3.6	No	Yes	OnlinePIN	High	✓	✓	✓	✓	✓	659	11m29s
3.7	No	Yes	NoCVM	Low	✓	×	×	✓	×	651	4h29m14s
3.8	No	Yes	NoCVM	High	×	NA	NA	NA	NA	591	9m45s
3.9	Yes	No	OnlinePIN	Low	✓	✓	✓	✓	✓	659	1h18m46s
3.10	Yes	No	OnlinePIN	High	✓	✓	✓	✓	✓	659	1h14m59s
3.11	Yes	No	NoCVM	Low	✓	✓	✓	✓	🕗	640	4h14m22s
3.12	Yes	No	NoCVM	High	×	NA	NA	NA	NA	591	10m47s
3.13	Yes	Yes	OnlinePIN	Low	✓	✓	✓	✓	✓	659	13m42s
3.14	Yes	Yes	OnlinePIN	High	✓	✓	✓	✓	✓	659	12m25s
3.15	Yes	Yes	NoCVM	Low	✓	✓	✓	✓	🕗	640	1h16m21s
3.16	Yes	Yes	NoCVM	High	×	NA	NA	NA	NA	591	12m31s

4.2 Insecure Configurations

Tamarin found attacks on two sets of configurations: a MITM attack on blinded Diffie-Hellman that targets configurations without local authentication and without copying the **IAD-MAC** into the **IAD** (Configurations 2.1–2.3 and 3.1–3.3) and an attack targeting configurations with offline authorization and without local authentication and without Online PIN (Configuration 3.7). We describe these attacks next.

MITM Attack on Blinded Diffie-Hellman. The Blinded Diffie-Hellman key exchange is vulnerable to the same MITM attack as the naive Diffie-Hellman key exchange without authentication. The C8 protocol prevents this attack by the two authentication methods of local authentication and copying the **IAD-MAC** into the **IAD**. Moreover, this should not be a problem in practice as C8 is designed to be used with these authentication methods. Nevertheless, our formal analysis highlights why these authentication methods are essential and that the protocol must be used as intended: Configurations with neither of these authentication methods, namely Configurations 2.1–2.3 and 3.1–3.3, are vulnerable to this MITM attack. Variations of this attack violate the lemmas *bank accepts*, *authentication to the terminal*, *authentication to the bank*, and *relay resistance*.

We present the MITM attack on the authentication to the terminal in Fig. 2. The adversary injects their own public keys $\mathbf{Q_{T\,adv.}} = g^{\mathbf{d_{T\,adv.}}}$, $\mathbf{R_{adv.}} = g^{\mathbf{r_{adv.}} \times \mathbf{d_{C\,adv.}}}$ and thus shares the secret $\mathbf{z}_T = g^{\mathbf{r_{adv.}} \times \mathbf{d_{C\,adv.}} \times \mathbf{d_T}}$ with the termi-

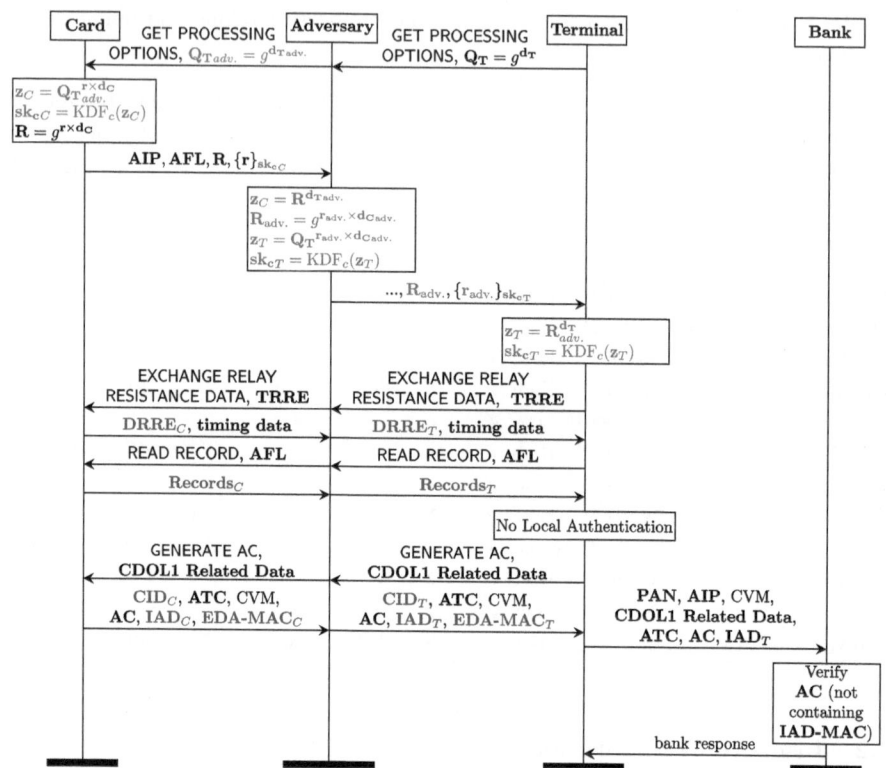

Fig. 2. MITM attack on blinded Diffie–Hellman violating the authenticity property for transactions with configurations without local authentication and without copying the **IAD-MAC** into the **IAD**. The keys injected by the adversary are highlighted in red and the terms that the terminal and the card disagree on are highlighted in blue. (Color figure online)

nal and the secret $\mathbf{z}_C = g^{\mathbf{r} \times \mathbf{d_C} \times \mathbf{d_{Tadv.}}}$ with the card. The adversary can then modify messages that are authenticated using the malicious Diffie–Hellman keys. Our analysis showed that this attack results in a disagreement on the **IAD**, the card's nonce **DRRE**, and the **CID**, which encodes if and how the transaction is authorized. The rest of the (dynamic) transaction data objects are agreed upon by the parties. The disagreement on the **DRRE** leads to the attack on the relay resistance property that we present in Sect. 4.4. Disagreement on the **IAD** and **CID** means that these data objects are vulnerable to adversarial modification; however we have not identified a real-world exploit that is possible using such a modification.

This attack is only possible if local authentication is not performed and the **IAD-MAC** is not included in the **IAD**. Both local authentication and copying the **IAD-MAC** into the **IAD** are in principle optional. However, clearly transactions with neither authentication method should be prevented. We now describe the mechanisms with which the terminal and card decide if they perform these authentication methods, starting with copying the **IAD-MAC** into the **IAD**.

According to Book E [10], each payment system may choose how to generate the **AC** and thus including the **IAD-MAC** in the **AC** input is optional, however it is recommended. If the **AC** authenticates the **IAD-MAC**, the card indicates in the Application Interchange Profile (**AIP**) to the terminal that it must include the **IAD-MAC** in the **IAD**. The terminal follows the instructions to include or not include the **IAD-MAC** inside the **IAD**, but does not perform additional checks regarding this authentication method. Thus, the decision to include or not include the **IAD-MAC** inside the **IAD** lies with the card's payment system.

In contrast, local authentication is only performed if the card and terminal support it. This is indicated by the **AIP** and **kernel qualifier**. In addition, the terminal may choose to decline or request online authorization for transactions where local authentication is not performed or failed. This is configured for each terminal in the Terminal Action Code-Denial (**TAC-Denial**) and Terminal Action Code-Online (**TAC-Online**).

From the discussion above, it follows that terminals could generally require local authentication and cards could generally require including the **IAD-MAC** in the **IAD**. Thus, both the card and the terminal could require an authentication method that prevents this attack. However, we could not verify that this holds in practice as cards and terminals supporting C8 are not yet publicly available.

Exploiting Offline Authorization. In offline authorized transactions, the terminal accepts the transaction and later sends the transaction data to the bank for processing. Tamarin found an attack for offline authorized transactions for the configurations without local authentication, with copying the **IAD-MAC** into the **IAD**, and without CVM (Configuration 3.7). Note that the configurations with online PIN (Configurations 3.5 and 3.6) are not vulnerable to this attack, as this attack targets offline authorized transactions and online PIN requires the transaction to be authorized online. The attack also does not violate the lemma *authentication to the bank*, as this lemma only considers online authorized transactions. The attack is similar to the above MITM attack. However, it also targets the configurations with copying the **IAD-MAC** into the **IAD** that are secure for transactions without offline authorization. Copying the **IAD-MAC** into the **IAD** does not prevent the attack because the transaction is authorized offline and the terminal cannot verify the **IAD-MAC** inside the **AC**. However, the bank will decline the transaction after the terminal accepted offline, which violates the *bank accepts* lemma and represents a *merchant holding the bag* attack as presented in our previous work [6] and explained in the introduction.

The above discussion shows that offline authorized transactions must perform local authentication. This is also stated by the specification regarding the RRP: the RRP requires local authentication for offline transactions. As stated above, the terminal can be configured to decline transactions without local authentication or request online authorization for such transactions.

4.3 Privacy

The blinded Diffie-Hellman key exchange was incorporated into C8 to provide privacy protection against a passive adversary by encrypting the **PAN** with the session key $\mathbf{sk_c}$ to ensure its confidentiality. In our analysis, we consider an active adversary on the NFC channel between the card and the terminal. Tamarin finds a trivial MITM attack on the secrecy of the **PAN**: since the terminal is not authenticated to the card, an active adversary can start a protocol run with a card, establish a session key, and learn the **PAN** since the card sends it encrypted with the established, adversary-known session key. Thus, C8's privacy protection mechanisms are not effective against an active MITM adversary.

This attack is not, however, unexpected. The specification explicitly states that the blinded Diffie-Hellman key exchange only provides privacy protection for a *passive* adversary, not an *active* one. An active adversary can send, receive, and modify messages on the NFC channel and thus communicate with both the card and the terminal. In contrast, a passive adversary can only listen in on the communication between a legitimate card and terminal.

We observe that in situations where a malicious device listens in on such communication, the adversary could just as easily install an active device. For example, an adversary could cooperate with a merchant that presents the cardholder with a terminal emulator that reads card data, including the **PAN**. To avoid raising the cardholder's suspicion, this emulator could first perform the attack, abort the transaction, and afterwards start a new, legitimate transaction and relay this transaction to a legitimate terminal. Due to the large number of different terminal providers and soon also phone-based terminals [2], such a terminal emulator would not raise any suspicions. Moreover, as the terminal emulator is not connected to a bank, such an attack would not be detected by the bank.

4.4 Relay Resistance

Our analysis shows that relay resistance holds for the secure configurations, namely Configurations 2.5–2.16, 3.5–3.6, and 3.9–3.16. For the insecure configurations, namely Configurations 2.1–2.3, 3.1–3.3, and 3.7, Tamarin identified an attack. Thus, for the RRP to be effective, offline authorized transactions require local authentication and online authorized transactions require either local authentication or copying the **IAD-MAC** into the **IAD**. This attack should not be possible for specification-conform implementations, as the specification also states these requirements. Namely, it states that the RRP requires local authentication for offline transactions and for online transactions the RRP relies on "**IAD-MAC** combined with online card authentication" ([9], page 49), which we understand as a requirement to include the **IAD-MAC** in the **IAD**.

The attack targeting these insecure configurations is a variant of the MITM attack described in Sect. 4.2, targeting the relay resistance property. After this attack, the adversary and terminal share a session key for integrity $\mathbf{sk}_{iT} = KDF_c(\mathbf{z}_T)$ with which the adversary can forge the **IAD-MAC**. And as the card's **DRRE** is only authenticated by the **IAD-MAC**, the adversary can send the terminal its own **DRRE**, authenticating it with its forged **IAD-MAC**. Thus, the adversary can send the **DRRE** before the card received the terminal's **TRRE**, thereby violating the relay resistance property.

5   Conclusion

EMV has been wildly successful as a payment standard, but unfortunately it has also witnessed years of penetrate-and-patch as weaknesses have been discovered. This experience is not unique to electronic payments: testing, code review, and other forms of scrutiny, while helpful for quality assurance, ultimately fall short given a highly complex protocol whose failures can have enormous consequences. Over the past years, our experience analyzing EMV has shown that building formal models and constructing proofs is essential both in finding attacks and sharpening the assumptions needed (on the adversary or the security properties) for security proofs.

Concretely, in past work we found numerous weaknesses that lead to direct attacks on Visa and Mastercard cards that we could demonstrate in the wild. EMVCo has developed a new kernel, C8, that incorporates many of our suggested improvements. In the work reported here, we were able to construct correctness proofs for most of C8's configurations. For those configurations where we had counterexamples (i.e., attacks), we were unable to validate them in reality as cards supporting C8 have not yet been released. Overall our results here show that EMV's security has indeed been improved. They also highlight the importance of EMVCo's requirements on which configurations may be safely used, which must be carefully followed through into the implementation.

A   Lemmas

In this section, we state the lemmas formalizing the security properties presented in Sect. 3.2.

The lemma *bank accepts* states that if the terminal accepts a transaction t at some time point i, there cannot be a time point j at which the bank declines the transaction or an agent claimed to be honest at time point i is compromised.

Lemma 2 (Bank Accepts). *A protocol P satisfies the property that the bank accepts terminal-accepted transactions if for every $\alpha \in traces(P)$:*

$$\forall t,i.\ \mathsf{TerminalAccepts}(t) \in \alpha_i \implies$$
$$\nexists j.\ \mathsf{BankDeclines}(t) \in \alpha_j \vee$$
$$\exists A,k.\ \mathsf{Honest}(A) \in \alpha_i \wedge \mathsf{Compromise}(A) \in \alpha_k.$$

Secrecy states that a term x claimed to be secret at time point i is not known by the adversary at any time point j or an agent claimed to be honest at time point i is compromised. The adversary's knowledge of x is expressed by the action fact $\mathsf{KU}(x)$, which is part of Tamarin's built-in adversary rules.[2] By proving the lemma with Tamarin we establish there is no scenario whatsoever in which the adversary can learn x, which was claimed secret, unless the compromise has happened.

Lemma 3 (Secrecy). *A protocol P satisfies* secrecy *if for every $\alpha \in$ traces(P):*

$$\forall x, i.\ \mathsf{Secret}(x) \in \alpha_i \implies$$
$$\nexists j.\ \mathsf{KU}(x) \in \alpha_j\ \vee$$
$$\exists A, k.\ \mathsf{Honest}(A) \in \alpha_i \wedge \mathsf{Compromise}(A) \in \alpha_k.$$

The relay resistance property, adapted from [13], states that if the terminal reaches the end of a transaction with a card C, the terminal's nonce x, and the card's nonce y, at time point i, indicated by $\mathsf{CheckRelayResistance}(C, x, y) \in \alpha_i$, then the following actions were performed in the given order: first, the terminal started the RRP by sending the **EXCHANGE RELAY RESISTANCE DATA** with its nonce x; second, the card C received this command and responds; and third, the terminal receives the card's nonce y or an agent claimed to be honest at time point i is compromised.

Lemma 4 (Relay Resistance). *A protocol P satisfies* relay resistance *if for every $\alpha \in$ traces(P):*

$$\forall C, x, y, i.$$
$$\mathsf{CheckRelayResistance}(C, x, y) \in \alpha_i \implies$$
$$\big(\exists s, a, e.\ s < a\ \wedge\ a < e\ \wedge\ \mathsf{FastPhaseStarts}(x) \in \alpha_s\ \wedge$$
$$\mathsf{FastPhaseAction}(C) \in \alpha_a\ \wedge\ \mathsf{FastPhaseEnds}(y) \in \alpha_e\big)\ \vee$$
$$\exists A, k.\ \mathsf{Honest}(A) \in \alpha_i \wedge \mathsf{Compromise}(A) \in \alpha_k.$$

The executability lemma requires a trace, where both the card and terminal and the card and bank have matching Running and Commit facts and where no agent was compromised. The Running and Commit facts are also used to express the authentication property, see Sect. 3.2.

---

[2] Note that there are different ways to represent the adversary's knowledge in Tamarin. $\mathsf{K}(x)$ means that the adversary has sent the value as input to the protocol, whereas $\mathsf{KU}(x)$ states that the adversary has the ability to construct the value. Thus, we use $\mathsf{KU}(x)$ here to formalize that the adversary cannot construct the value x.

Lemma 5 (Executability). *A protocol P is* executable *if $\alpha \in traces(P)$ exists such that:*

$$\exists t, C, B, nc, i, j, k, l.$$
$$\mathsf{Running}(C, nc, \langle \mathsf{'Card'}, \mathsf{'Terminal'}, t \rangle) \in \alpha_i \wedge$$
$$\mathsf{Commit}(nc, C, \langle \mathsf{'Card'}, \mathsf{'Terminal'}, t \rangle) \in \alpha_j \wedge$$
$$\mathsf{Running}(C, B, \langle \mathsf{'Card'}, \mathsf{'Bank'}, t \rangle) \in \alpha_k \wedge$$
$$\mathsf{Commit}(B, C, \langle \mathsf{'Card'}, \mathsf{'Bank'}, t \rangle) \in \alpha_l \wedge$$
$$\nexists A, a.\ \mathsf{Compromise}(A) \in \alpha_a.$$

B Acronyms

AC	Application Cryptogram	The MAC authenticating the card to the terminal
AFL	Application File Locator	Used by the terminal to request the card's static data
AID	Application Identifier	Identifies the supported kernels
AIP	Application Interchange Profile	Informs the terminal of the card's capabilities
ATC	Application Transaction Counter	Counter used to derive the session key for the AC
CA	Certificate Authority	Issues certificates
CDCVM	Consumer Device CVM	The card (usually a smart phone) authenticates the cardholder
CDOL1	Card Risk Management Data Object List	List of data that the terminal must provide to the card
CID	Cryptogram Information Data	Encodes if and how the transaction is authorized
CVM	Cardholder Verification Method	Method of cardholder authentication
DRRE	Device Relay Resistance Entropy	Card-sourced nonce exchanged during the RRP
ECC	Elliptic Curve Cryptography	Asymmetric cryptographic technique
EDA-MAC	Enhanced Data Authentication-MAC	MAC authenticating the card to the terminal
IAD	Issuer Application Data	Contains proprietary application data
IAD-MAC	Issuer Application Data-MAC	MAC authenticating the card to the terminal
KDF	Key Derivation Function	Used to establish a key from some input
MAC	Message Authentication Code	Symmetric authentication technique
MITM	machine-in-the-middle	Also known as man-in-the-middle
NFC	Near Field Communication	Standard for wireless communication
PAN	Primary Account Number	Card number
PDOL	Processing Data Object List	List of data that the terminal must provide to the card
PIN	Personal Identification Number	Short number authenticating the card holder
RRP	Relay Resistance Protocol	Protocol protecting against relay attacks
TAC	Terminal Action Code	Configures under which conditions the terminal should take certain actions
TRRE	Terminal Relay Resistance Entropy	Terminal-sourced nonce exchanged during the RRP

References

1. Tamarin Version 1.9.0, Git Revision: 57e619fef32033293e4a83c0be67cc6e296bf166, branch: develop
2. Apple Inc.: Tap to Pay on iPhone. https://developer.apple.com/tap-to-pay/
3. Basin, D., Cremers, C., Jannik, D., Sasse, R.: Modeling and analyzing security protocols with Tamarin: a comprehensive guide. In: Information Security and Cryptography. Springer (2024). To appear
4. Basin, D., Hofmeier, X., Sasse, R., Toro-Pozo, J.: Tamarin models of C8. https://github.com/tamarin-prover/tamarin-prover/tree/develop/examples/fm24-cardpayments
5. Basin, D., Sasse, R., Toro-Pozo, J.: Card brand mixup attack: bypassing the PIN in non-visa cards by using them for visa transactions. In: 30th USENIX Security Symposium (USENIX Security 21), pp. 179–194. USENIX Association (2021)
6. Basin, D., Sasse, R., Toro-Pozo, J.: The EMV standard: break, fix, verify. In: 2021 IEEE Symposium on Security and Privacy (SP), pp. 1766–1781. IEEE, San Francisco (2021)
7. Basin, D., Schaller, P., Toro-Pozo, J.: Inducing authentication failures to bypass credit card PINs. In: 32nd USENIX Security Symposium, p. 15. USENIX Association (2023)
8. Coppola, D., et al.: PURE: payments with UWB RElay-protection. In: 33rd USENIX Security Symposium (USENIX Security 2024) (2024)
9. EMVCo. EMV Contactless Specifications for Payment Systems, Book C-8, Kernel 8 Specification, Version 1.1 (2023). https://www.emvco.com/specifications
10. EMVCo. EMV Contactless Specifications for Payment Systems, Book E, Security and Key Management, Version 1.0 (2023). https://www.emvco.com/specifications/
11. Ferro, C.: Annual Report 2023: Enhancing EMV Technologies to Supporting Emerging Payments. https://www.emvco.com/knowledge-hub/annual-report-2023-enhancing-emv-technologies-to-supporting-emerging-payments/
12. Lowe, G.: A hierarchy of authentication specifications. In: Proceedings 10th Computer Security Foundations Workshop, pp. 31–43 (1997)
13. Mauw, S., Smith, Z., Toro-Pozo, J., Trujillo-Rasua, R.: Distance-bounding protocols: verification without time and location. In: 2018 IEEE Symposium on Security and Privacy (SP), pp. 549–566 (2018)
14. Meier, S., Schmidt, B., Cremers, C., Basin, D.: The TAMARIN prover for the symbolic analysis of security protocols. In: Sharygina, N., Veith, H. (eds.) CAV 2013. LNCS, vol. 8044, pp. 696–701. Springer, Heidelberg (2013). https://doi.org/10.1007/978-3-642-39799-8_48
15. Murdoch, S.J., Drimer, S., Anderson, R., Bond, M.: Chip and PIN is broken. In: 2010 IEEE Symposium on Security and Privacy, pp. 433–446. IEEE, Oakland (2010)
16. Radu, A.I., Chothia, T., Newton, C.J., Boureanu, I., Chen, L.: Practical EMV relay protection. In: 2022 IEEE Symposium on Security and Privacy (SP), pp. 1737–1756. IEEE, San Francisco (2022)
17. Roland, M., Langer, J.: Cloning credit cards: a combined pre-play and downgrade attack on EMV contactless. In: 7th USENIX Workshop on Offensive Technologies (WOOT 13) (2013)
18. Schmidt, B., Meier, S., Cremers, C., Basin, D.: Automated analysis of Diffie-Hellman protocols and advanced security properties. In: 2012 IEEE 25th Computer Security Foundations Symposium, pp. 78–94. IEEE, Cambridge (2012)

Fundamentals of Formal Verification

A Local Search Algorithm
for MaxSMT(LIA)

Xiang He[1,2], Bohan Li[1,2], Mengyu Zhao[1,2], and Shaowei Cai[1,2(✉)]

[1] Key Laboratory of System Software (Chinese Academy of Sciences) and State Key Laboratory of Computer Science, Institute of Software, Chinese Academy of Sciences, Beijing, China
{hexiang,libh,zhaomy,caisw}@ios.ac.cn
[2] School of Computer Science and Technology University of Chinese Academy of Sciences, Beijing, China

Abstract. MaxSAT modulo theories (MaxSMT) is an important generalization of Satisfiability modulo theories (SMT) with various applications. In this paper, we focus on MaxSMT with the background theory of Linear Integer Arithmetic, denoted as MaxSMT(LIA). We design the first local search algorithm for MaxSMT(LIA) called PairLS, based on the following novel ideas. A novel operator called *pairwise* operator is proposed for integer variables. It extends the original local search operator by simultaneously operating on two variables, enriching the search space. Moreover, a compensation-based picking heuristic is proposed to determine and distinguish the *pairwise* operations. Experiments are conducted to evaluate our algorithm on massive benchmarks. The results show that our solver is competitive with state-of-the-art MaxSMT solvers. Furthermore, we also apply the *pairwise* operation to enhance the local search algorithm of SMT, which shows its extensibility.

Keywords: MaxSMT · Linear Integer Arithmetics · Local Search

1 Introduction

The maximum satisfiability problem (MaxSAT) is an optimization version of the satisfiability problem (SAT), aiming to minimize the number of falsified clauses, and it has various applications [23]. A generalization of MaxSAT is the weighted Partial MaxSAT problem, where clauses are divided into hard and soft clauses with weights (positive numbers). The goal is to find an assignment that satisfies all hard clauses and minimizes the total weight of falsified soft clauses. MaxSAT solvers have made substantial progress in recent years [2,18,20,24,26].

However, MaxSAT has limited expressiveness, and it can be generalized from the Boolean case to Satisfiability Modulo Theories (SMT), deciding the satisfiability of a first-order logic formula with respect to certain background theories,

---

X. He and B. Li—These two authors are co-first authors, as they contribute equally.

© The Author(s) 2025
A. Platzer et al. (Eds.): FM 2024, LNCS 14933, pp. 55–72, 2025.
https://doi.org/10.1007/978-3-031-71162-6_3

leading to a generalization called MaxSAT Modulo Theories (MaxSMT) [30]. With its enhanced expressive power, MaxSMT has various practical applications, such as safety verification [6], concurrency debugging [34], non-termination analysis [19] and superoptimization [1].

Compared to MaxSAT and SMT solving, the research on MaxSMT solving is still in its preliminary stage. Cimatti et al. [13] introduced the concept of "Theory of Costs" and developed a method to manage SMT with Pseudo-Boolean (PB) constraints and minimize PB cost functions. Sebastiani et al. [31,32] proposed an approach to solve MaxSMT problem by encoding it into SMT with PB functions. A modular approach for MaxSMT called Lemma-Lifting was proposed by Cimatti et al. [14], which involves the iterative exchange of information between a lazy SMT solver and a purely propositional MaxSAT solver. The implicit hitting set approach was lifted from the propositional level to SMT [15]. Two well-known MaxSMT solvers are OptiMathSAT [33] and νZ [5], which are currently the state-of-the-art MaxSMT solvers. In this paper, we focus on the MaxSMT problem with the background theory of Linear Integer Arithmetic (LIA), denoted as MaxSMT(LIA), which consists of arithmetic atomic formulas in the form of linear equalities or inequalities over integer variables.

We apply the local search method to solve MaxSMT(LIA). Although local search has been successfully used to solve SAT [3,4,11,12,22] and recently to SMT on the theory of bit-vector theory [16,27–29], integer arithmetic [9,10] and real arithmetic [21,25], this is the first time that it is applied to MaxSMT.

First, we propose a novel operator for integer variables, named *pairwise operator*, to enrich the search space by simultaneously operating on two variables. When the algorithm falls into a local optimum w.r.t. operations on a single variable, further exploring the neighborhood structure of the *pairwise operator* can help it escape from the local optimum.

Moreover, a novel method based on the concept of *compensation* is proposed to determine the *pairwise operation*. Specifically, the *pairwise operation* is determined as a pair of simultaneous modifications, one to satisfy a falsified clause, and the other to minimize the disruptions the first operation might wreak on the already satisfied clauses. Then, a two-level picking heuristic is proposed to distinguish these *pairwise operations*, by considering the potential of a literal becoming falsified.

Based on the above novel ideas, we design the first local search solver for MaxSMT(LIA) called PairLS, prioritizing hard clauses over soft clauses. Experiments are conducted on massive benchmarks. New instances based on SMT-LIB are generated to enrich the benchmarks for MaxSMT(LIA). We compare our solver with 2 state-of-the-art MaxSMT(LIA) solvers, OptiMathSAT and νZ. Experimental results show that our solver is competitive with these state-of-the-art solvers. We also present the evolution of solution quality over time, showing that PairLS can efficiently find a promising solution within a short cutoff time. Ablation experiments are also conducted to confirm the effectiveness of proposed strategies. Moreover, we apply the *pairwise* operator to enhance the local search algorithm of Satisfiability Modulo Theories, demonstrating its extensibility.

2 Preliminary

2.1 MaxSMT on Linear Integer Arithmetics

The Satisfiability modulo theories (SMT) problem determines the satisfiability of a given quantifier-free first-order formula with respect to certain background theories. Here we consider the theory of Linear Integer Arithmetic (LIA), consisting of arithmetic formulae in the form of linear equalities or inequalities over integer variables ($\sum_{i=0}^{n} a_i x_i \leq k$ or $\sum_{i=0}^{n} a_i x_i = k$)[1]. An atomic formula can be a propositional variable or an arithmetic formula. A *literal* is an atomic formula, or the negation of an atomic formula. A *clause* is the disjunction of a set of literals, and a formula in *conjunctive normal form (CNF)* is the conjunction of a set of clauses. Given the sets of propositional variables and integer variables, denoted as P and X respectively, an assignment α is a mapping $X \rightarrow Z$ and $P \rightarrow \{false, true\}$, and $\alpha(x)$ denotes the value of a variable x under α.

The (weighted partial) MaxSAT Modulo Theories problem (MaxSMT for short) is generated from SMT. The clauses are divided into *hard* clauses and *soft* clauses with positive weight.

Definition 1. *For a MaxSMT instance F, given the current assignment α, if it satisfies all hard clauses, then α is a feasible solution, and the cost is defined as the total weight of all falsified soft clauses, denoted as $cost(\alpha)$.*

MaxSMT aims to find a feasible solution with minimal *cost*, that is, to find an assignment satisfying all hard clauses and minimizing the sum of the weights of the falsified soft clauses. The MaxSMT problem with the background theory of LIA is denoted as MaxSMT(LIA).

Example 1. Given a MaxSMT(LIA) formula $F = c_1 \wedge c_2 \wedge c_3 \wedge c_4 = (a - b \leq 1 \vee a - c \leq 0) \wedge (b - c \leq -1) \wedge (a - d \leq 1) \wedge (A)$, let c_1 and c_4 be hard clauses, c_2 and c_3 be soft clauses with weight 1 and 2. Given the current assignment $\alpha = \{a = 0, b = 0, c = 0, d = 0, A = true\}$, $cost(\alpha) = 1$, since only c_2 is falsified.

2.2 Local Search Components

The *clause weighting scheme* is a popular local search method that associates an additional property (which is an integer number) called *penalty weight* to clauses and dynamically adjusts them to prevent the search from getting stuck in a local optimum. We adopt the weighting scheme called Weighting-PMS [20] to instruct the search. Weighting-PMS has been applied in state-of-the-art local search solvers for MaxSAT, such as SATLIKE [20] and SATLIKE3.0 [8]. When the algorithm falls into a local optimum, the Weighting-PMS dynamically adjusts the *penalty weights* of hard and soft clauses to guide the search direction.

Note that the *penalty weight* and the original weight of soft clauses are different. The goal of MaxSMT is to minimize the total original weight of unsatisfied

---

[1] strict linear equalities in the form of ($\sum_{i=0}^{n} a_i x_i < k$) can be transformed to ($\sum_{i=0}^{n} a_i x_i \leq k - 1$).

soft clauses, while the *penalty weight* is updated during the search process, guiding the search in a promising direction.

Another key component of a local search algorithm is the *operator*, defining how to modify the current solution. When an operator is instantiated by specifying the variable to operate and the value to assign, an *operation* is obtained.

Definition 2. *The score of an operation op, denoted by score(op), is the decrease of the total penalty weight of falsified clauses caused by applying op.*

An operation is *decreasing* if its *score* is greater than 0. Note that given a set of clauses, denoted as C, the *score* of operation op on the subformula composed of C is denoted as $score_C(op)$.

3   Review of LS-LIA

As our algorithm adopts the two-mode framework of LS-LIA, which is the first local search algorithm for SMT(LIA) [9], we briefly review it in this section.

After the initialization, the algorithm switches between Integer mode and Boolean mode. In each mode, an operation on a variable of the corresponding data type is selected to modify the current assignment. The two modes switch to each other when the number of non-improving steps of the current mode reaches a threshold. The threshold is set to $L \times P_b$ for the Boolean mode and $L \times P_i$ for the Integer mode, where P_b and P_i denote the proportion of Boolean and integer literals to all literals in falsified clauses, and L is a parameter.

In the Boolean mode, the *flip* operator is adopted to modify a Boolean variable to the opposite of its current value. In the Integer mode as in Algorithm 1, a novel operator called **critical move** (*cm* for short) is proposed by considering the literal-level information.

Definition 3. *The critical move operator, denoted as $cm(x, \ell)$, assigns an integer variable x to the threshold value making literal ℓ true, where ℓ is a falsified literal containing x.*

Specifically, the *threshold value* refers to the minimum modification to x that can make ℓ true. Example 2 is given to help readers understand the definition.

Example 2. Given two falsified literals $\ell_1 : (2a - b \leq -3)$ and $\ell_2 : (5c - d = 5)$, and the current assignment is $\alpha = \{a = 0, b = 0, c = 0, d = 0\}$. Then $cm(a, \ell_1)$, $cm(b, \ell_1)$, $cm(c, \ell_2)$, and $cm(d, \ell_2)$ refers to assigning a to -2, assigning b to 3, assigning c to 1 and assigning d to -5 respectively.

An important property of the *critical move* operator is that after the execution, the corresponding literal must be true. Therefore, by picking a falsified literal and performing a *cm* operation on it, we can make the literal true.

In our algorithm for MaxSMT(LIA), the *critical move* operator is also adopted to make a falsified literal become true.

Algorithm 1: Integer Mode of LS-LIA

---

1 **while** *non-improving steps* $\leq L \times P_i$ **do**
2   **if** *all clauses are satisfied* **then** return **if** $\exists$ *decreasing cm operation* **then**
3         $op :=$ such an operation with the greatest *score*

4   **else**
5   update penalty weights;
6         $c :=$ a random falsified clause with integer variables;
7         $op :=$ a *cm* operation in c with *score*;

8   perform op ;

---

4   Pairwise Operator

In this section, we introduce a novel operator for integer variables, denoted as *pairwise operator*. It extends the original *critical move* operator to enrich the search space, serving as an extended neighborhood structure. We first introduce the motivation for the pairwise operator. Then, based on pairwise operator, the framework of our algorithm in Integer mode is proposed.

4.1   Motivation

The original *critical move* operator only considers one single variable each time. However, it may miss potential decreasing operations. Specifically, when there exists no decreasing *critical move* operation, operations that simultaneously modify two variables may be decreasing, which are not considered by *critical move*.

Example 3. Given a formula $F = c_1 \wedge c_2 \wedge c_3 = (a - b \leq -2) \wedge (b - c \leq 1) \wedge (c - a \leq 1)$ where the penalty weight of each clause is 1. and the current assignment is $\alpha = \{a = 0, b = 0, c = 0\}$. There exist two *critical move* operations: $cm(a, a - b \leq -2)$ and $cm(b, a - b \leq -2)$, referring to assigning a to -2 and b to 2, respectively. Both operations are not decreasing, since these two operations will respectively falsify c_3 and c_2. However, simultaneously assigning b to 2 and c to 1 can be decreasing, since after the operation, all clauses become satisfied.

Thus, the *pairwise operator* simultaneously modifying two variables is proposed to find a decreasing operation when there is no decreasing *cm* operation.

Definition 4. *Pairwise operator, denoted as* $p(v_1, v_2, val_1, val_2)$, *will simultaneously modify* v_1 *to* val_1 *and* v_2 *to* val_2 *respectively, where* v_1 *and* v_2 *are integer variables, and* val_1 *and* val_2 *are integer parameters.*

The *pairwise operator* can be regarded as an extended neighborhood. When there exists no decreasing *critical move* operation, indicating that the local optimum of modifying individual variables is found, the search space can be expanded by simultaneously modifying two variables, and the solution may be further improved, thanks to the following property:

Proposition 1. *Given a pairwise operation $op_1 = p(v_1, v_2, val_1, val_2)$, and two operations individually assigning v_1 to val_1 and v_2 to val_2, denoted as op_2 and op_3 respectively. op_1 is decreasing while neither op_2 nor op_3 is decreasing, only if there exists a clause c containing both v_1 and v_2, and on clause c, $score_{\{c\}}(op_1) > score_{\{c\}}(op_2) + score_{\{c\}}(op_3)$.*

The proof can be found in Appendix A in [17]. Recall the Example 3, the *pairwise operation* that simultaneously assigns b to 2 and c to 1, denoted as op_1, is decreasing, while none of the operations that individually assign b to 2 and c to 1, denoted as op_2 and op_3, is decreasing. The reason lies in that b and c both appear in the clause c_2, and $score_{\{c_2\}}(op_1) > score_{\{c_2\}}(op_2) + score_{\{c_2\}}(op_3)$.

5   Compensation-Based Picking Heuristic

To find a decreasing *pairwise operation* when there is no decreasing *cm* operation, we first introduce a method based on the concept of *compensation* to determine *pairwise operations*, which can satisfy the necessary condition in Proposition 1 (Details can be found in Lemma 1 of Appendix B in [17]). Then, among these *pairwise operations*, we propose a two-level heuristic to distinguish them, by considering the potential of the compensated literals becoming falsified.

5.1   Pairwise Operation Candidates for Compensation

Motivation for compensation: Since one variable may exist in multiple literals, changing a variable will affect all literals containing the variable, and may make some originally true literals become false. Moreover, if the literal is the reason for some clauses being satisfied, i.e., it is the only true literal in the clause, then falsifying the literal also falsifies the clause.

Formally, for an operation op, we define a special set of literals $CL(op) = \{\ell | \ell$ is true and is the only true literal for some clauses, but ℓ would become false after individually performing $op\}$. After performing an operation op, the literals in the set $CL(op)$ are of special interest since some clauses containing such a literal would become falsified.

Concept of compensation: Let op_1 and op_2 denote two operations modifying individual variables. To minimize the disruptions that op_1 might wreak on the already satisfied clauses, another operation op_2 is simultaneously executed to make a literal $\ell \in CL(op_1)$ remain true under the assignment after operating op_1. op_2 is denoted as *compensation* for ℓ, and literals in the set CL are denoted as **C**ompensated **L**iterals.

Compensation-based pairwise operation: A pairwise operation $p(v_1, v_2, val_1, val_2)$ can be regarded as simultaneously performing a pair of operations modifying individual variables, op_1 assigning v_1 to val_1 and op_2 assigning v_2 to val_2. The procedure to determine op_1 and op_2 is described as follows.

First, a candidate op_1 is chosen to satisfy a falsified clause. To this end, we pick a variable v_1 from a false literal ℓ_1 in a random falsified clause, and op_1 is the corresponding cm operation, $cm(v_1, \ell_1)$. It prioritizes literals from **hard** clauses and soft clauses are considered only when all hard clauses are satisfied. To obtain sufficient candidates of op_1, K (a parameter) literals are randomly selected from overall falsified clauses, and all variables in these literals are considered. The set of all candidate op_1 found in this stage is denoted as $CandOp$.

Second, given a literal $\ell_2 \in CL(op_1)$, the op_2 w.r.t $op_1 \in CandOp$ is determined to guarantee that ℓ_2 remains true after simultaneously performing op_1 and op_2, meaning that op_2 is selected to *compensate* for ℓ_2. Specifically, to determine op_2, we pick a variable v_2 appearing in a literal $\ell_2 \in CL(op_1)$, and calculate the value val_2 according to $cm(v_2, \ell_2)$ assuming op_1 performed.

Example 4. Let us consider the formula presented in Example 3: $F = c_1 \wedge c_2 \wedge c_3 = (a - b \leq -2) \wedge (b - c \leq 1) \wedge (c - a \leq 1)$ where the penalty weight of each clause is 1, and the current assignment is $\alpha = \{a = 0, b = 0, c = 0\}$. There is no decreasing *critical move* operation. As shown in Fig. 1, performing $op_1 = cm(b, a - b \leq -2)$ that assigns b to 2 would falsify the literal $\ell = (b - c \leq 1)$, the only true literal in c_2. To compensate for ℓ, the operation op_2 that assigns c to 1 is determined according to $cm(c, \ell)$, assuming that op_1 has been performed. All clauses become satisfied after simultaneously performing op_1 and op_2, and thus a decreasing pairwise operation $p(b, c, 2, 1)$ is found.

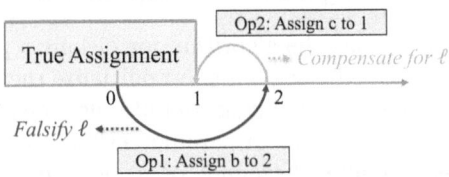

Fig. 1. Given the literal $\ell = (b - c \leq 1)$, the axis refers to the value of $(b - c)$. Individually performing op_1 will falsify ℓ, while op_2 can compensate for ℓ.

Note that there may exist multiple variables in the literal $\ell_2 \in CL(op_1)$, and thus given the operation op_1, and the literal ℓ_2 selected in the second step, a set of pairwise operations is determined by considering all variables in ℓ_2 except the variable in op_1, denoted as **pair_set**(ℓ_2, op_1).

5.2   Two-Level Heuristic

Among the literals selected in the second step of determining a *pairwise operation*, we consider that some literals are more likely to become false, and should be given higher priority. Thus, we distinguish such literals from others. They are formally defined as follows.

Definition 5. *Given an assignment α, and a literal in the form of $\sum_{i=0}^{n} a_i x_i \leq k$, we denote $\Delta = \sum_{i=0}^{n} a_i \alpha(x_i) - k$. The literal is a **fragile** literal if $\Delta = 0$ holds. Any true literal with $\Delta < 0$ is **safe**.*

A *fragile* literal with $\Delta = 0$ is true as the inequality $\Delta \leq 0$ holds, but it can be falsified by any little disturbance that enlarges Δ of the corresponding *fragile* literal. Comparatively, a literal is *safe* means that even if the value of a variable in the literal changes comparatively larger (as long as $\Delta \leq 0$ after the modification), it remains true.

Example 5. Consider the formula: $F = l_1 \wedge l_2 \wedge l_3 = (b - a \leq -1) \wedge (a - c \leq 0) \wedge (a - d \leq 3)$, where the current assignment is $\alpha = \{a = 0, b = 0, c = 0, d = 0\}$. l_2 and l_3 are two true literals. l_2 is a *fragile* literal since its $\Delta = 0$, while l_3 is a *safe* literal since its $\Delta < 0$. We consider that l_2 is more fragile than l_3, since a small disturbance, $cm(a, l_1)$ that assigns a to 1, can falsify l_2 but not l_3.

In the second step of determining a pairwise operation, among those *compensated literals*, we prefer *fragile* literals and prioritize the corresponding pairwise operations. Based on the intuition above, a two-level picking heuristic is defined:

- We first choose the decreasing pairwise operation involving a *fragile* compensated literal.
- If there exists no such decreasing pairwise operation, we further select the pairwise operation involving *safe* compensated literals.

5.3   Algorithm for Picking a Pairwise Operation

Based on the picking heuristic, the algorithm for picking a pairwise operation is described in Algorithm 2. In the beginning, we initialize the set of pairwise operations involving *fragile* and *safe* compensated literals, denoted as *FragilePairs* and *SafePairs* (line 1). Firstly, K (a parameter) false literals are picked from overall falsified clauses, and all *critical move* operations in these literals are added into *CandOp* (lines 2–7). Note that it prioritizes hard clauses over soft clauses.

Then, for each operation $op_1 \in CandOp$, we go through each compensated literal $\ell_2 \in CL(op_1)$. If ℓ_2 is *fragile* (resp. *safe*), the set of corresponding *pairwise operations* determined by $pair\_set(\ell_2, op_1)$ are added to the *FragilePairs* (resp. *SafePairs*) (line 8–13).

According to the two-level picking heuristic, if there exist decreasing operations in *FragilePairs*, we pick the one with the greatest *score* (lines 14–15). Otherwise, we pick a decreasing operation in *SafePairs* if it exists (lines 16–17). An operation with the greatest *score* is selected via the BMS heuristic [7]. Specifically, the BMS heuristic samples t pairwise operations (a parameter), and selects the decreasing one with the greatest *score*.

6 Local Search Algorithm

Based on the above novel components, we propose our algorithm for MaxSMT(L IA) called PairLS, prioritizing hard clauses over soft clauses. PairLS initializes the complete current solution α by assigning all Integer variables to 0 and all Boolean variables to $false$. Then, PairLS switches between Integer mode and Boolean mode. When the time limit is reached, the best solution α^* and the corresponding best cost $cost^*$ are reported if a feasible solution can be found. Otherwise, "No solution found" is reported.

The Integer mode of PairLS is described in Algorithm 3. The current solution α is iteratively modified until the number of non-improving steps non_impr_step exceeds the threshold $bounds$ (line 1). If a feasible solution with a smaller $cost$ is found, then the best solution α^* and the best cost $cost^*$ are updated (lines 2–3). In each iteration, the algorithm first tries to find a decreasing $critical\ move$ operation with the greatest score via BMS heuristic [7] (line 4–7). Note that it prefers to pick operations from falsified hard clauses, and falsified soft clauses are picked only if all hard clauses are satisfied. If it fails to find any decreasing $critical\ move$ operation, indicating that it falls into the local optimum of modifying individual variables, then it continues to search the neighborhood of $pairwise\ operation$ (line 8). If there exists no decreasing operation in both neighborhoods, the algorithm further escapes from the local optimum by updating the

---

Algorithm 2: pick_pairwise_op

Output: a decreasing pairwise operation if found

1 $FragilePairs := \emptyset, SafePairs := \emptyset,\ CandOp := \emptyset\ BestPair := null$;
2 **for** $i = 1\ to\ K$ **do**
3   **if** $\exists$ *hard falsified clauses* **then**
4          $\ell_1 :=$ a random literal in a falsified hard clause ;
5   **else if** $\exists$ *soft falsified clauses* **then**
6          $\ell_1 :=$ a random literal in a falsified soft clause ;
7      $CandOp := CandOp \bigcup \{cm(x, \ell_1) | x\ appears\ in\ \ell_1\}$;
8 **foreach** op_1 *in* $CandOp$ **do**
9   **foreach** *literal* $\ell_2 \in CL(op_1)$ **do**
10   **if** ℓ_2 *is fragile* **then**
11             $FragilePairs := FragilePairs \cup pair\_set(\ell_2, op_1)$;
12   **else if** ℓ_2 *is safe* **then**
13             $SafePairs := SafePairs \cup pair\_set(\ell_2, op_1)$;

14 **if** $\exists$ *decreasing operation in* $FragilePairs$ **then**
15     $BestPair :=$ the operation with the greatest score picked by BMS;
16 **else if** $\exists$ *decreasing operation in* $SafePairs$ **then**
17     $BestPair :=$ the operation with the greatest score picked by BMS;
18 **return** $BestPair$;

Algorithm 3: Integer Mode of PairLS

---

1 **while** *non_imp_steps < MaxSteps* **do**

2   **if** $\nexists$ *falsified hard clauses AND cost(α) < cost** **then**

3      $\lfloor$ $\alpha^* := \alpha,\ cost^* := cost(\alpha)$;

4   **if** $\exists$ *decreasing critical move in hard falsified clauses* **then**

5      $\lfloor$ *op* := a decreasing critical move with the greatest score picked by BMS;

6   **else if** $\exists$ *decreasing critical move in soft falsified clauses* **then**

7      $\lfloor$ *op* := a decreasing critical move with the greatest score picked by BMS;

8   **else** *op* := *pick_pairwise_op()* **if** *op == null* **then**

9   update penalty weights by Weighting-PMS;

10   **if** $\exists$ *falsified hard clauses* **then** *c* := a random falsified hard clause

         else *c* := a random falsified soft clause *op* := the critical move with the
         $\lfloor$ greatest *score* in c;

11   $\lfloor$ perform *op* to modify α;

---

penalty weight (line 10), and satisfying a random clause by performing a *critical move* operation in it, preferring the one with the greatest *score* (lines 11–13). Specifically, it also prioritizes hard clauses over soft clauses.

In the Boolean mode, the formula is reduced to a subformula that purely contains Boolean variables, which is indeed a MaxSAT instance. Thus, our algorithm performs in the same way as SATLike3.0[2], a state-of-the-art local search algorithm for MaxSAT [20].

7   Experiments

Experiments are conducted on 3 benchmarks to evaluate PairLS, comparing it with state-of-the-art MaxSMT solvers. The promising experimental result indicates that our algorithm is efficient and effective in most instances. We also present the evolution of solution quality over time, showing that PairLS can efficiently find promising solutions within a short time limit. Moreover, the ablation experiment is carried out to confirm the effectiveness of our proposed strategies.

7.1   Experiment Preliminaries

Implementation: PairLS is implemented in C++ and compiled by g++ with the '-O3' option enabled. There are 3 parameters in the solver: L for switching modes; t (the number of samples) for the BMS heuristic; K denotes the size of *CandOp*. The parameters are tuned according to our preliminary experiments and suggestions from the previous literature. They are set as follows: $L = 20$, $t = 100$, $K = 10$.

---

[2] https://lcs.ios.ac.cn/~caisw/Code/maxsat/SATLike3.0.zip.

Competitors: We compare PairLS with 2 state-of-the-art MaxSMT solvers, namely OptiMathSAT(version 1.7.3) and νZ(version 4.11.2). OptiMathSAT applies MaxRes as the MaxSAT engine, denoted as Opt_res, while the default configuration encodes the MaxSMT problem as an optimization problem, denoted as Opt_omt. νZ also has 2 configurations based on the MaxSAT engines MaxRes and WMax, denoted as νZ_res and νZ_wmax, respectively. The binary code of OptiMathSAT and νZ is downloaded from their websites.

Benchmarks: Our experiments are conducted on 3 benchmarks. Those instances where the hard constraints are unsatisfiable are excluded, as they do not have feasible solutions.

Benchmark MaxSMT-LIA: This benchmark consists of 5520 instances generated based on SMT(LIA) instances from SMT-LIB[3]. The original SMT(LIA) benchmark consists of 690 instances from 3 families, namely bofill, convert, and wisa[4]. We adopt the same method to generate instances as in previous literature [15]: adding randomly chosen arithmetic atoms in the original problem with a certain proportion as unit soft assertions. 4 proportions of soft clauses (denoted as SR) are applied, namely 10%, 25%, 50% and 100%. 2 MaxSMT instances can be generated from each original SMT instance, based on different ways to associate soft clauses with weights: one associates each soft clause with a unit weight of 1, and the other associates each soft clause with a random weight between 1 and the total number of atoms. Instances with unit weights and random weights are not distinguished as in [15]. The total number of instances is $690 \times 2 \times 4 = 5520$, where 690 denotes the number of original SMT(LIA) instances, 2 denotes 2 kinds of weights associated with soft clauses, and 4 denotes the 4 proportions of soft clauses. Note that the "bofill" family was adopted in [15], while the family of "convert" and "wisa" are new instances.

Benchmark MaxSMT-IDL: This benchmark contains 12888 new MaxSM-T instances generated by the above method, based on 1611 SMT(IDL) instances including all families from SMT-LIB[5] (similar to MaxSMT-LIA benchmark, the total number of instances is $1611 \times 2 \times 4 = 12888$). Instances with unit weights and random weights are also not distinguished when reporting results.

Benchmark LL: The benchmark was proposed in [14]. Unsatisfiable instances and instances over linear real arithmetic are excluded, resulting in 114 instances in total. 56 instances contain soft clauses with unit weights of 1, and 58 instances contain soft clauses with random weights ranging from 1 to 100. Instances with *Unit* weights and *Random* weights are distinguished as in [14].

Experiment Setup: All experiments are conducted on a server with Intel Xeon Platinum 8153 2.00GHz and 2048G RAM under the system CentOS 7.7.1908.

---

[3] https://clc-gitlab.cs.uiowa.edu:2443/SMT-LIB-benchmarks/QF_LIA.

[4] SMT(LIA) instances from other families are excluded because most of them are in the form of a conjunction of unit clauses, and thus the generation method is not applicable, since each produced soft assertion is also a hard assertion.

[5] https://clc-gitlab.cs.uiowa.edu:2443/SMT-LIB-benchmarks/QF_IDL.

Each solver executes one run for each instance in these benchmarks, as they contain sufficient instances. The cutoff time is set to 300 s for the MaxSMT-LIA and MaxSMT-IDL benchmarks as previous work [15], and 1200 s for the LL benchmark as previous work [14]. The source code and generated benchmarks can be found in the repository[6].

For each family of instances, we report the number of instances where the corresponding solver can find the best solution with the smallest *cost* among all solvers, denoted by #*win*, and the average running time to yield those best solutions, denoted as *time*. Note that when multiple solvers find the best solution with the same *cost* within the cutoff time, they are all considered to be winners. The solvers with the most #*win* in the table are emphasized with **bold** value.

The *solution* found by solvers and the corresponding time are defined as follows: As for complete solvers, νZ and OptiMathSAT, we take the best upper bound found within the cutoff time as their *solution*, and the time to find such upper bound is recorded by referring to the log file. Note that the proving time for complete solvers is excluded. As for PairLS, the best *solution* found so far within the cutoff time and the time to find such a solution are recorded.

7.2 Comparison to Other MaxSMT Solvers

Results on benchmark MaxSMT-LIA: As presented in Table 1, PairLS shows competitive and complementary performance on this benchmark. Except for the 25% category, PairLS always leads in the total number of winning instances regardless of the proportion of soft clauses SR. On the "bofill" family, PairLS performs better on instances with larger SR, confirming that PairLS is good at solving hard instances. On the "convert" family, PairLS outperforms all competitors regardless of SR. On the "wisa" family, PairLS cannot rival its competitors. In Fig. 3 of Appendix C in [17], we also present the run time comparison between PairLS and the best configuration of competitors, namely νZ_res and Opt_res. The run time comparison indicates that PairLS is more efficient than Opt_res and is complementary to νZ_res.

Results on benchmark MaxSMT-IDL: As presented in Table 2, PairLS can significantly outperform all competitors regardless of the proportion of soft clauses. In the overall benchmark, PairLS can find a better solution than all competitors on 53.5% of total instances, and it can lead the best competitor by 1224 "winning" instances, confirming its dominating performance. In Fig. 4 of Appendix C in [17], we also present the run time comparison between PairLS and the best configuration of competitors, namely νZ_res and Opt_omt, indicating that PairLS is more efficient than competitors in instances with small SR.

Results on LL benchmark: The results are shown in Table 3. PairLS shows comparable but overall poor performance compared to its competitors on this benchmark. One possible reason is that the front-end encoding for these benchmarks would generate many auxiliary Boolean variables, while PairLS cannot

---

[6] https://github.com/PairLS/PairLS/releases/download/PairLS/PairLS.rar

effectively explore the Boolean structure as LS-LIA [9]. Specifically, the average number of auxiliary variables in this benchmark is 1220, while the counterparts in MaxSMT-LIA and MaxSMT-IDL are 327 and 528.

Table 1. Results on benchmark MaxSMT-LIA. The results are classified according to the proportion of soft clauses, SR. Sum presents the overall performance.

SR	family	#inst	Opt_omt #win(time)	Opt_res #win(time)	νZ_res #win(time)	νZ_wmax #win(time)	PairLS #win(time)
10%	bofill	814	773(17.1)	777(7.1)	758(7.9)	**797**(7.6)	762(10.9)
	convert	560	445(21.1)	495(1.2)	228(18.4)	8(103.1)	**558**(1.1)
	wisa	6	4(27.4)	3 (33.3)	**6** (11.3)	0(0)	0(0)
	Total	1380	1222(18.6)	1275(4.9)	992(10.3)	805(8.5)	**1320**(6.7)
25%	bofill	814	736(59.2)	720 (17.1)	677(21.9)	**776**(21.8)	641(35.4)
	convert	560	415(16.3)	493(12.7)	205(13.3)	5(125.6)	**558**(1.4)
	wisa	6	**4**(14.5)	1(11.3)	**4**(73.2)	0(0)	0(0)
	Total	1380	1155(43.6)	**1214**(16.1)	886(20.1)	781(22.5)	1199(19.6)
50%	bofill	814	82(231.0)	489(12.1)	515(33.1)	217(35.8)	**542**(66.7)
	convert	560	405(22.3)	508(9.1)	177(19.8)	0(0)	**558**(1.2)
	wisa	6	3(36.6)	1(11.3)	**5**(39.2)	0(0)	0(0)
	Total	1380	490(57.3)	998(10.8)	697(29.8)	217(39.7)	**1100**(33.4)
100%	bofill	814	0(0)	0(0)	402(75.6)	15(20.7)	**601**(128.8)
	convert	560	399(27.3)	503(14.7)	185(19.3)	19(55.0)	**558**(1.2)
	wisa	6	1(162.2)	1(193.3)	**6**(38.3)	0(0)	0(0)
	Total	1380	400(27.7)	504(15.0)	593(57.6)	34(39.9)	**1159**(67.3)
Sum		5520	3267(34.3)	3937(10.9)	3168(26.1)	1837(18.7)	**4778**(30.7)

7.3 Evolution of Solution Quality

To be more informative in understanding how the solvers compare in practice, the evolution of the solution quality over time is presented. Specifically, we evaluate the overall performance on the MaxSMT-LIA and MaxSMT-IDL benchmark with 4 cutoff times, denoted as *cutoff*: 50, 100, 200, 300 s. Given an instance, the proportion of the *cost* to the sum of soft clause weights is denoted as $cost_P$[7]. The average $cost_P$ over time is presented in Fig. 2, showing that PairLS can efficiently find high-quality solutions within a short time. Moreover, we also report the "winning" instances over time. As shown in Appendix D in [17], on

---

[7] If no feasible solution is found, then $cost_P$ is set as 1. Note that we present the average $cost_P$ rather than the average *cost*, since the *cost* of certain instances can be quite large, dominating the average *cost*.

Table 2. Results on MaxSMT-IDL benchmark. The results are classified according to the proportion of soft clauses, SR. Sum presents the overall performance.

SR	#inst	Opt_omt #win(time)	Opt_res #win(time)	νZ_res #win(time)	νZ_wmax #win(time)	PairLS #win(time)
10%	3222	1086(248.1)	873(201.6)	1151(238.4)	839(221.5)	**1542**(159.9)
25%	3222	1171(195.2)	934(178.6)	1502(192.7)	722(292.1)	**1744**(148.0)
50%	3222	1094(195.8)	890(183.2)	1461(198.2)	758(290.9)	**1829**(149.3)
100%	3222	1061(204.1)	880(198.3)	1559(201.6)	934(260.4)	**1782**(157.1)
Sum	12888	4412(210.5)	3577(190.2)	5673(205.8)	3253(264.5)	**6897**(153.3)

Table 3. Results on LL benchmark. Instances with $Unit$ weights and $Random$ weights are distinguished. Sum presents the overall performance.

Category	#inst	Opt_omt #win(time)	Opt_res #win(time)	νZ_res #win(time)	νZ_wmax #win(time)	PairLS #win(time)
$Unit$	56	41(117.3)	32(130.3)	**49**(183.2)	15(40.0)	23(0.4)
$Random$	58	45(117.9)	37(120.3)	**53**(100.1)	17(39.0)	22(0.4)
Sum	114	86(117.6)	69(124.9)	**102**(140.0)	32(39.5)	45(0.4)

each benchmark, PairLS leads the best competitor by at least 645 "winning" instances regardless of the cutoff time, confirming its dominating performance.

7.4   Effectiveness of Proposed Strategies

To analyze the effectiveness of our proposed strategies, two modified versions of PairLS are proposed as follows.

- To analyze the effectiveness of *pairwise operation*, we modify PairLS by only using the *critical move* operator, leading to the version v_{no_pair}.
- To analyze the effectiveness of two-level heuristic in *compensation-based picking heuristic* for picking a pairwise operation, PairLS is modified by selecting pairwise operation without distinguishing the *fragile* and *safe* compensated literals, leading to the version v_{one_level}.

We compare PairLS with these modified versions on 3 benchmarks. The results of this ablation experiment are presented in Table 4, confirming the effectiveness of the proposed strategies.

Moreover, we also analyze the extension for simultaneously operating on more variables. PairLS is modified by simultaneously modifying three variables, where the third variable is modified to compensate for the second one, leading to the version v_{tuple}. We conduct our experiments on MaxSMT-LIA. The results are in Appendix E in [17]. When $N = 3$, the number of possible operations increases from $O(k^2)$ to $O(k^3)$, where k is the number of variables in unsatisfied clauses. This might significantly slow down the searching process, indicating that modifying 2 variables simultaneously is the best choice of trade-off between cost and effectiveness.

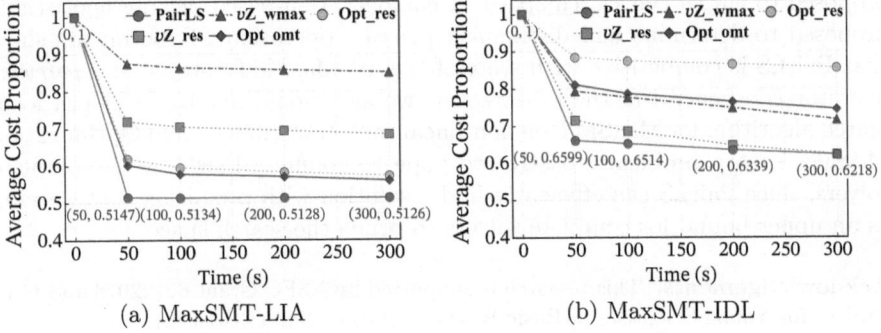

(a) MaxSMT-LIA   (b) MaxSMT-IDL

Fig. 2. Evolution of average $cost_P$

Table 4. Comparing PairLS with its modified versions. The number of instances where PairLS performs better and worse are presented, denoted as #better and #worse respectively. An algorithm is better than its competitor on a certain instance if it can find a solution with a lower *cost*.

	#inst	v_{no_pair}		v_{one_level}	
		#better	#worse	#better	#worse
MaxSMT-LIA	5520	**1834**	65	**705**	457
MaxSMT-IDL	12888	**3242**	1962	**3005**	1826
LL		114	**27**	0	**5**	0

8 Discussion on the Extension of Pairwise Operation

Since *pairwise* operator can be adapted to SMT(LIA) instances without additional modifications, a potential extension is incorporating it into the local search algorithm for SMT(LIA). When there is no decreasing *cm* operation in the integer mode of LS-LIA (Algorithm 1 in Page 5), we apply the *pairwise* operator to LS-LIA to enrich the search space as in PairLS, resulting in the corresponding version called LS-LIA-Pair. We compare LS-LIA-Pair with LS-LIA and other complete SMT solvers on SMT(LIA) instances, reporting the number of **unsolved instances** for each solver (Details are in Appendix F in [17]). Without any **specific customization** tailored for SMT, in both categories, LS-LIA-Pair can solve 20 more instances compared to LS-LIA, which demonstrates that *pairwise* operator is an extensible method and could be further explored to enhance the local search algorithm for SMT.

9   Conclusion and Future Work

In this paper, we propose the first local search algorithm for MaxSMT(LIA), called PairLS, based on the following components. A novel *pairwise* operator is proposed to enrich the search space. A compensation-based picking heuristic is proposed to determine and distinguish *pairwise* operations. Experiments show that PairLS is competitive with state-of-the-art MaxSMT solvers, and *pairwise* operator is a general method. Moreover, we also would like to develop a local search algorithm for MaxSMT on non-linear integer arithmetic and Optimization Modulo Theory problems. Lastly, we hope to combine PairLS with complete solvers, since PairLS can efficiently find a solution with promising *cost*, serving as an upper bound for complete solvers to prune the search space.

Acknowledgements. This research is supported by NSFC Grant 62122078 and CAS Project for Young Scientists in Basic Research (Grant No. YSBR-040).

References

1. Albert, E., Gordillo, P., Rubio, A., Schett, M.A.: Synthesis of super-optimized smart contracts using Max-SMT. In: Lahiri, S.K., Wang, C. (eds.) Computer Aided Verification: 32nd International Conference, CAV 2020, Los Angeles, CA, USA, July 21–24, 2020, Proceedings, Part I, pp. 177–200. Springer International Publishing, Cham (2020). https://doi.org/10.1007/978-3-030-53288-8_10

2. Ansótegui, C., Bonet, M.L., Levy, J.: Sat-based MaxSAT algorithms. Artif. Intell. **196**, 77–105 (2013)

3. Balint, A., Schöning, U.: Choosing probability distributions for stochastic local search and the role of make versus break. In: Proceedings of SAT 2012, pp. 16–29 (2012)

4. Biere, A., Splatz, L., Plingeling, T.: YalSAT entering the SAT competition 2016. In: Proceedings of SAT Competition 2016, pp. 44–45 (2016)

5. Bjørner, N.S., Phan, A.D.: νz-maximal satisfaction with z3. Scss **30**, 1–9 (2014)

6. Brockschmidt, M., Larra, D., Oliveras, A., Rodrıguez-Carbonell, E., Rubio, A.: Compositional safety verification with Max-SMT. In: 2015 Formal Methods in Computer-Aided Design (FMCAD), pp. 33–40. IEEE (2015)

7. Cai, S.: Balance between complexity and quality: Local search for minimum vertex cover in massive graphs. In: Twenty-Fourth International Joint Conference on Artificial Intelligence, pp. 747–753 (2015)

8. Cai, S., Lei, Z.: Old techniques in new ways: clause weighting, unit propagation and hybridization for maximum satisfiability. Artif. Intell. **287**, 103354 (2020)

9. Cai, S., Li, B., Zhang, X.: Local search for SMT on linear integer arithmetic. In: Shoham, S., Vizel, Y. (eds.) Computer Aided Verification: 34th International Conference, CAV 2022, Haifa, Israel, August 7–10, 2022, Proceedings, Part II, pp. 227–248. Springer International Publishing, Cham (2022). https://doi.org/10.1007/978-3-031-13188-2_12

10. Cai, S., Li, B., Zhang, X.: Local search for satisfiability modulo integer arithmetic theories. ACM Trans. Comput. Log. **24**(4), 1–26 (2023)

11. Cai, S., Luo, C., Su, K.: CCAnr: a configuration checking based local search solver for non-random satisfiability. In: Heule, M., Weaver, S. (eds.) Theory and Applications of Satisfiability Testing – SAT 2015, pp. 1–8. Springer International Publishing, Cham (2015). https://doi.org/10.1007/978-3-319-24318-4_1

12. Cai, S., Su, K.: Local search for Boolean satisfiability with configuration checking and subscore. Artif. Intell. **204**, 75–98 (2013)

13. Cimatti, A., Franzén, A., Griggio, A., Sebastiani, R., Stenico, C.: Satisfiability modulo the theory of costs: foundations and applications. In: International Conference on Tools and Algorithms for the Construction and Analysis of Systems, pp. 99–113. Springer (2010)

14. Cimatti, A., Griggio, A., Schaafsma, B.J., Sebastiani, R.: A modular approach to MaxSAT modulo theories. In: Järvisalo, M., Van Gelder, A. (eds.) Theory and Applications of Satisfiability Testing – SAT 2013, pp. 150–165. Springer, Berlin, Heidelberg (2013). https://doi.org/10.1007/978-3-642-39071-5_12

15. Fazekas, K., Bacchus, F., Biere, A.: Implicit hitting set algorithms for maximum satisfiability modulo theories. In: Galmiche, D., Schulz, S., Sebastiani, R. (eds.) Automated Reasoning, pp. 134–151. Springer International Publishing, Cham (2018). https://doi.org/10.1007/978-3-319-94205-6_10

16. Fröhlich, A., Biere, A., Wintersteiger, C., Hamadi, Y.: Stochastic local search for satisfiability modulo theories. In: Proceedings of AAAI 2015, vol. 29 (2015)

17. He, X., Li, B., Zhao, M., Cai, S.: A local search algorithm for MaxSMT(LIA) (2024). https://arxiv.org/abs/2406.15782

18. Ignatiev, A., Morgado, A., Marques-Silva, J.: RC2: an efficient MaxSAT solver. J. Satisfiability, Boolean Model. Comput. **11**(1), 53–64 (2019)

19. Larraz, D., Nimkar, K., Oliveras, A., Rodríguez-Carbonell, E., Rubio, A.: Proving non-termination using Max-SMT. In: Computer Aided Verification: 26th International Conference, CAV 2014, Held as Part of the Vienna Summer of Logic, VSL 2014, Vienna, Austria, July 18–22, 2014. Proceedings 26, pp. 779–796. Springer (2014). https://doi.org/10.1007/978-3-319-08867-9_52

20. Lei, Z., Cai, S.: Solving (weighted) partial MaxSAT by dynamic local search for sat. In: IJCAI, vol. 7, pp. 1346–52 (2018)

21. Li, B., Cai, S.: Local search for SMT on linear and multilinear real arithmetic. arXiv preprint arXiv:2303.06676 (2023)

22. Li, C.M., Li, Y.: Satisfying versus falsifying in local search for satisfiability. In: Proceedings of SAT 2012, pp. 477–478 (2012)

23. Li, C.M., Manya, F.: MaxSAT, hard and soft constraints. In: Handbook of satisfiability, pp. 903–927. IOS Press (2021)

24. Li, C.M., Xu, Z., Coll, J., Manyà, F., Habet, D., He, K.: Combining clause learning and branch and bound for MaxSAT. In: 27th International Conference on Principles and Practice of Constraint Programming (CP 2021). Schloss Dagstuhl-Leibniz-Zentrum für Informatik (2021)

25. Li, H., Xia, B., Zhao, T.: Local search for solving satisfiability of polynomial formulas. arXiv preprint arXiv:2303.09072 (2023)

26. Martins, R., Manquinho, V., Lynce, I.: Open-WBO: a modular MaxSAT solver'. In: Sinz, C., Egly, U. (eds.) SAT 2014. LNCS, vol. 8561, pp. 438–445. Springer, Cham (2014). https://doi.org/10.1007/978-3-319-09284-3_33

27. Niemetz, A., Preiner, M.: Ternary propagation-based local search for more bit-precise reasoning. In: 2020 Formal Methods in Computer Aided Design (FMCAD), pp. 214–224 (2020)

28. Niemetz, A., Preiner, M., Biere, A.: Precise and complete propagation based local search for satisfiability modulo theories. In: Chaudhuri, S., Farzan, A. (eds.) Computer Aided Verification: 28th International Conference, CAV 2016, Toronto, ON, Canada, July 17-23, 2016, Proceedings, Part I, pp. 199–217. Springer International Publishing, Cham (2016). https://doi.org/10.1007/978-3-319-41528-4_11

29. Niemetz, A., Preiner, M., Biere, A.: Propagation based local search for bit-precise reasoning. Formal Methods Syst. Design **51**(3), 608–636 (2017)

30. Nieuwenhuis, R., Oliveras, A.: On sat modulo theories and optimization problems. In: Theory and Applications of Satisfiability Testing-SAT 2006: 9th International Conference, Seattle, WA, USA, August 12-15, 2006. Proceedings 9, pp. 156–169. Springer (2006). https://doi.org/10.1007/11814948_18

31. Sebastiani, R., Tomasi, S.: Optimization in SMT with ($\mathbb{Q}$) cost functions. In: International Joint Conference on Automated Reasoning, pp. 484–498. Springer (2012). https://doi.org/10.1007/978-3-642-31365-3_38

32. Sebastiani, R., Tomasi, S.: Optimization modulo theories with linear rational costs. ACM Trans. Comput. Logic (TOCL) **16**(2), 1–43 (2015)

33. Sebastiani, R., Trentin, P.: OptiMathSAT: a tool for optimization modulo theories. J. Autom. Reason. **64**(3), 423–460 (2020)

34. Terra-Neves, M., Machado, N., Lynce, I., Manquinho, V.: Concurrency debugging with MaxSMT. In: Proceedings of the AAAI Conference on Artificial Intelligence, vol. 33, pp. 1608–1616 (2019)

Integrating Loop Acceleration Into Bounded Model Checking

Florian Frohn$^{(\boxtimes)}$ and Jürgen Giesl$^{(\boxtimes)}$

RWTH Aachen University, Aachen, Germany
{florian.frohn,giesl}@informatik.rwth-aachen.de

Abstract. *Bounded Model Checking* (BMC) is a powerful technique for proving unsafety. However, finding *deep counterexamples* that require a large bound is challenging for BMC. On the other hand, *acceleration techniques* compute "shortcuts" that "compress" many execution steps into a single one. In this paper, we tightly integrate acceleration techniques into SMT-based bounded model checking. By adding suitable "shortcuts" on the fly, our approach can quickly detect deep counterexamples. Moreover, using so-called *blocking clauses*, our approach can prove safety of examples where BMC diverges. An empirical comparison with other state-of-the-art techniques shows that our approach is highly competitive for proving unsafety, and orthogonal to existing techniques for proving safety.

1 Introduction

Bounded Model Checking (BMC) is a powerful technique for disproving safety properties of, e.g., software or hardware systems. However, as it uses breadth-first search to find counterexamples, the search space grows exponentially w.r.t. the *bound*, i.e., the limit on the length of potential counterexamples. Thus, finding *deep counterexamples* that require large bounds is challenging for BMC. On the other hand, *acceleration techniques* can compute a first-order formula that characterizes the transitive closure of the transition relation induced by a loop. Intuitively, such a formula corresponds to a "shortcut" that "compresses" many execution steps into a single one. In this paper, we consider relations defined by quantifier-free first-order formulas over some background theory like non-linear integer arithmetic and two disjoint vectors of variables $\vec{x}$ and $\vec{x}'$, called the *pre-* and *post-variables*. Such *transition formulas* can easily represent, e.g., *transition systems* (TSs), linear *Constrained Horn Clauses* (CHCs), and *control-flow automata* (CFAs).[1] Thus, they subsume many popular intermediate representations used for verification of systems specified in more expressive languages.

---

funded by the Deutsche Forschungsgemeinschaft (DFG, German Research Foundation) - 235950644 (Project GI 274/6-2).

[1] To this end, it suffices to introduce one additional variable that represents the control-flow location (for TSs and CFAs) or the predicate (for linear CHCs).

© The Author(s) 2025
A. Platzer et al. (Eds.): FM 2024, LNCS 14933, pp. 73–91, 2025.
https://doi.org/10.1007/978-3-031-71162-6_4

In contrast to, e.g., source code, transition formulas are completely unstructured. However, source code may be unstructured, too (e.g., due to $\texttt{gotos}$), i.e., one cannot rely on the input being well structured. So the fact that our approach is independent from the structure of the input makes it broadly applicable.

Example 1. Consider the transition formula $\tau := \tau_{x<100} \vee \tau_{x=100}$ where

$\tau_{x<100} := x < 100 \wedge x' = x + 1 \wedge y' = y$ and

$\tau_{x=100} := x = 100 \wedge x' = 0 \wedge y' = y + 1.$

```
while (x <= 100) {
    while (x < 100) x++;
    x = 0, y++;
}
```

Listing 1. Implementation of τ

It defines a relation $\rightarrow_\tau$ on $\mathbb{Z} \times \mathbb{Z}$ by relating the pre-variables x and y with the post-variables x' and y'. So for all $c_x, c_y, c'_x, c'_y \in \mathbb{Z}$, we have $(c_x, c_y) \rightarrow_\tau (c'_x, c'_y)$ iff $[x/c_x, y/c_y, x'/c'_x, y'/c'_y]$ is a model of τ, i.e., iff there is a step from a state with $x = c_x \wedge y = c_y$ to a state with $x = c'_x \wedge y = c'_y$ in Listing 1. To prove that an *error state* satisfying $\psi_{\text{err}} := y \geq 100$ is reachable from an *initial state* which satisfies $\psi_{\text{init}} := x \leq 0 \wedge y \leq 0$, BMC has to unroll τ 10100 times.

Our new technique *Accelerated* BMC (ABMC) uses the following *acceleration*

$$n > 0 \wedge x + n \leq 100 \wedge x' = x + n \wedge y' = y \qquad (\tau_i^+)$$

of $\tau_{x<100}$: As we have $(c_x, c_y) \rightarrow^+_{\tau_{x<100}} (c'_x, c'_y)$ iff $\tau_i^+[x/c_x, y/c_y, x'/c'_x, y'/c'_y]$ is satisfiable, τ_i^+ is a "shortcut" for many $\rightarrow_{\tau_{x<100}}$-steps.

To compute such a shortcut τ_i^+ from the formula $\tau_{x<100}$, we use existing acceleration techniques [18]. In the example above, n serves as loop counter. Then the literal $x' = x + 1$ of $\tau_{x<100}$ gives rise to the recurrence equations $x^{(0)} = x$ and $x^{(n)} = x^{(n-1)} + 1$, which yield the closed form $x^{(n)} = x + n$, resulting in the literal $x' = x + n$ of τ_i^+. Thus, the literal $x + n \leq 100$ of τ_i^+ is equivalent to $x^{(n-1)} < 100$. As x is monotonically increasing (i.e., $\tau_{x<100}$ implies $x < x'$), $x^{(n-1)} < 100$ implies $x^{(n-2)} < 100$, $x^{(n-3)} < 100$, ..., $x^{(0)} < 100$, i.e., the loop $\tau_{x<100}$ can indeed be executed n times.

So τ_i^+ can simulate arbitrarily many steps with τ in a single step, as long as x does not exceed 100. Here, acceleration was applied to $\tau_{x<100}$, i.e., the projection of τ to the case $x < 100$, which corresponds to the inner loop of Listing 1. We also call such projections *transitions*. Later, ABMC also accelerates the outer loop (consisting of $\tau_{x=100}$, $\tau_{x<100}$, and τ_i^+), resulting in

$$n > 0 \wedge x = 100 \wedge 1 < x' \leq 100 \wedge y' = y + n. \qquad (\tau_o^+)$$

For technical reasons, our algorithm accelerates $[\tau_{x=100}, \tau_{x<100}, \tau_i^+]$ instead of just $[\tau_{x=100}, \tau_i^+]$, so that τ_o^+ requires $1 < x'$, i.e., it only covers cases where $\tau_{x<100}$ is applied at least twice after $\tau_{x=100}$. Details will be clarified in Sect. 3.2, see in particular Fig. 1. Using these shortcuts, ABMC can prove unsafety with bound 7.

While our main goal is to improve BMC's capability to find deep counterexamples, the following straightforward observations can be used to *block* certain parts of the transition relation in ABMC:

1. After accelerating a sequence of transitions, the resulting accelerated transition should be preferred over that sequence of transitions.
2. If an accelerated transition has been used, then the corresponding sequence of transitions should not be used immediately afterwards.

Both observations exploit that an accelerated transition describes the transitive closure of the relation induced by the corresponding sequence of transitions. Due to its ability to block parts of the transition relation, ABMC is able to prove safety in cases where BMC would unroll the transition relation indefinitely.

Outline. After introducing preliminaries in Sect. 2, we show how to use acceleration in order to improve the BMC algorithm to ABMC in Sect. 3. To increase ABMCs capabilities for proving safety, Sect. 4 refines ABMC by integrating blocking clauses. In Sect. 5, we discuss related work, and in Sect. 6, we evaluate our implementation of ABMC in our tool LoAT.

2 Preliminaries

We assume familiarity with basics from many-sorted first-order logic [15]. Without loss of generality, we assume that all formulas are in negation normal form (NNF). $\mathcal{V}$ is a countably infinite set of variables and $\mathcal{A}$ is a first-order theory over a k-sorted signature Σ with carrier $\mathcal{C} = (\mathcal{C}_1, \ldots, \mathcal{C}_k)$. For each entity e, $\mathcal{V}(e)$ is the set of variables that occur in e. $\mathsf{QF}(\Sigma)$ denotes the set of all quantifier-free first-order formulas over Σ, and $\mathsf{QF}_\wedge(\Sigma)$ only contains conjunctions of Σ-literals. We let $\top$ and $\bot$ stand for "true" and "false", respectively.

Given $\psi \in \mathsf{QF}(\Sigma)$ with $\mathcal{V}(\psi) = \vec{y}$, we say that ψ is $\mathcal{A}$-*valid* (written $\models_\mathcal{A} \psi$) if every model of $\mathcal{A}$ satisfies the universal closure $\forall \vec{y}. \psi$ of ψ. Moreover, $\sigma : \mathcal{V}(\psi) \rightarrow \mathcal{C}$ is an $\mathcal{A}$-*model* of ψ (written $\sigma \models_\mathcal{A} \psi$) if $\models_\mathcal{A} \sigma(\psi)$, where $\sigma(\psi)$ results from ψ by instantiating all variables according to σ. If ψ has an $\mathcal{A}$-model, then ψ is $\mathcal{A}$-*satisfiable*. We write $\psi \models_\mathcal{A} \psi'$ for $\models_\mathcal{A} (\psi \implies \psi')$, and $\psi \equiv_\mathcal{A} \psi'$ means $\models_\mathcal{A} (\psi \iff \psi')$. In the sequel, we omit the subscript $\mathcal{A}$, and we just say "valid", "model", and "satisfiable". We assume that $\mathcal{A}$ is complete, i.e., we either have $\models \psi$ or $\models \neg\psi$ for every closed formula over Σ.

We write $\vec{x}$ for sequences and x_i is the ith element of $\vec{x}$. We use "::" for concatenation of sequences, where we identify sequences of length 1 with their elements, so we may write, e.g., $x :: xs$ instead of $[x] :: xs$.

Let $d \in \mathbb{N}$ be fixed, and let $\vec{x}, \vec{x}' \in \mathcal{V}^d$ be disjoint vectors of pairwise different variables, called the *pre-* and *post-variables*. Each $\tau \in \mathsf{QF}(\Sigma)$ induces a *transition relation* $\rightarrow_\tau$ on $\mathcal{C}^d$ where $\vec{s} \rightarrow_\tau \vec{t}$ iff $\tau[\vec{x}/\vec{s}, \vec{x}'/\vec{t}]$ is satisfiable. Here, $[\vec{x}/\vec{s}, \vec{x}'/\vec{t}]$ denotes the substitution θ with $\theta(x_i) = s_i$ and $\theta(x_i') = t_i$ for all $1 \leq i \leq d$. We refer to elements of $\mathsf{QF}(\Sigma)$ as *transition formulas* whenever we are interested in

---

Algorithm 1: BMC – Input: a safety problem $\mathcal{T} = (\psi_{\text{init}}, \tau, \psi_{\text{err}})$

---

1 $b \leftarrow 0$; $\text{add}(\mu_b(\psi_{\text{init}}))$
2 **while** $\top$ **do**
3 │ $\text{push}()$; $\text{add}(\mu_b(\psi_{\text{err}}))$
4 │ **if** $\text{check\_sat}()$ **do return** unsafe **else** $\text{pop}()$; $\text{add}(\mu_b(\tau))$
5 │ **if** $\neg\text{check\_sat}()$ **do return** safe **else** $b \leftarrow b+1$

---

their induced transition relation. Moreover, we also refer to *conjunctive* transition formulas (i.e., elements of $\text{QF}_\wedge(\Sigma)$) as *transitions*. A *safety problem* $\mathcal{T}$ is a triple $(\psi_{\text{init}}, \tau, \psi_{\text{err}}) \in \text{QF}(\Sigma) \times \text{QF}(\Sigma) \times \text{QF}(\Sigma)$ where $\mathcal{V}(\psi_{\text{init}}) \cup \mathcal{V}(\psi_{\text{err}}) \subseteq \vec{x}$. It is *unsafe* if there are $\vec{s}, \vec{t} \in \mathcal{C}^d$ such that $[\vec{x}/\vec{s}] \models \psi_{\text{init}}$, $\vec{s} \rightarrow^*_\tau \vec{t}$, and $[\vec{x}/\vec{t}] \models \psi_{\text{err}}$.

The *composition* of τ and τ' is $\odot(\tau, \tau') := \tau[\vec{x}'/\vec{x}''] \wedge \tau'[\vec{x}/\vec{x}'']$ where $\vec{x}'' \in \mathcal{V}^d$ is fresh. Here, we assume $\mathcal{V}(\tau) \cap \mathcal{V}(\tau') \subseteq \vec{x} \cup \vec{x}'$ (which can be ensured by renaming other variables correspondingly). So $\rightarrow_{\odot(\tau,\tau')} = \rightarrow_\tau \circ \rightarrow_{\tau'}$ (where $\circ$ denotes relational composition). For finite sequences of transition formulas we define $\odot([]) := (\vec{x} = \vec{x}')$ (i.e., $\rightarrow_{\odot([])}$ is the identity relation) and $\odot(\tau :: \vec{\tau}) := \odot(\tau, \odot(\vec{\tau}))$. We abbreviate $\rightarrow_{\odot(\vec{\tau})}$ by $\rightarrow_{\vec{\tau}}$.

Acceleration techniques compute the transitive closure of relations. In the following definition, we only consider conjunctive transition formulas, since many existing acceleration techniques do not support disjunctions [8], or approximate in the presence of disjunctions [18]. So the restriction to conjunctive formulas ensures that our approach works with arbitrary existing acceleration techniques.

Definition 2 (Acceleration). *An acceleration technique is a function* accel : $\text{QF}_\wedge(\Sigma) \rightarrow \text{QF}_\wedge(\Sigma')$ *such that* $\rightarrow_{\text{accel}(\tau)} \subseteq \rightarrow^+_\tau$, *where Σ' is the signature of a first-order theory $\mathcal{A}'$.*

We abbreviate $\text{accel}(\odot(\vec{\tau}))$ by $\text{accel}(\vec{\tau})$. So as we aim at finding counterexamples, we allow under-approximating acceleration techniques, i.e., we do not require $\rightarrow_{\text{accel}(\tau)} = \rightarrow^+_\tau$. Definition 2 allows $\mathcal{A}' \neq \mathcal{A}$, as most theories are not "closed under acceleration". For example, accelerating the following Presburger formula on the left may yield the non-linear formula on the right:

$$x' = x + y \wedge y' = y \qquad\qquad n > 0 \wedge x' = x + n \cdot y \wedge y' = y.$$

3   From BMC to ABMC

In this section, we introduce accelerated bounded model checking. To this end, we first recapitulate bounded model checking in Sect. 3.1. Then we present ABMC in Sect. 3.2. To implement ABMC efficiently, heuristics to decide when to perform acceleration are needed. Thus, we present such a heuristic in Sect. 3.3.

3.1   Bounded Model Checking

Algorithm 1 shows how to implement BMC on top of an incremental SMT solver. In Line 1, the description of the initial states is added to the SMT problem.

Here and in the following, for all $i \in \mathbb{N}$ we define $\mu_i(x) := x^{(i)}$ if $x \in \mathcal{V} \setminus \vec{x}'$, and $\mu_i(x') = x^{(i+1)}$ if $x' \in \vec{x}'$. So in particular, we have $\mu_i(\vec{x}) = \vec{x}^{(i)}$ and $\mu_i(\vec{x}') = \vec{x}^{(i+1)}$, where we assume that $\vec{x}^{(0)}, \vec{x}^{(1)}, \ldots \in \mathcal{V}^d$ are disjoint vectors of pairwise different variables. In the loop, we set a backtracking point with the "push()" command and add a suitably variable-renamed version of the description of the error states to the SMT problem in Line 3. Then we check for satisfiability to see if an error state is reachable with the current bound in Line 4. If this is not the case, the description of the error states is removed with the "pop()" command that deletes all formulas from the SMT problem that have been added since the last backtracking point. Then a variable-renamed version of the transition formula τ is added to the SMT problem. If this results in an unsatisfiable problem in Line 5, then the whole search space has been exhausted, i.e., then $\mathcal{T}$ is safe. Otherwise, we enter the next iteration.

Example 3 (BMC). For the first 100 iterations of Algorithm 1 on Example 1, all models found in Line 5 satisfy the 1st disjunct $\mu_b(\tau_{x<100})$ of $\mu_b(\tau)$. Then we may have $x^{(100)} = 100$, so that the 2nd disjunct $\mu_b(\tau_{x=100})$ of $\mu_b(\tau)$ applies once and we get $y^{(101)} = y^{(100)} + 1$. After another 100 iterations, the 2nd disjunct $\mu_b(\tau_{x=100})$ may apply again, etc. After 100 applications of the 2nd disjunct (and thus a total of 10100 steps), there is a model with $y^{(10100)} = 100$, so that unsafety is proven.

3.2   Accelerated Bounded Model Checking

To incorporate acceleration into BMC, we have to bridge the gap between (disjunctive) transition formulas and acceleration techniques, which require conjunctive transition formulas. To this end, we use *syntactic implicants*.

Definition 4 (Syntactic Implicant Projection [22]). *Let $\tau \in \mathsf{QF}(\Sigma)$ be in NNF and assume $\sigma \models \tau$. We define the syntactic implicants $\mathsf{sip}(\tau)$ of τ as follows:*

$$\mathsf{sip}(\tau, \sigma) := \bigwedge \{\lambda \mid \lambda \text{ is a literal of } \tau, \sigma \models \lambda\} \qquad \mathsf{sip}(\tau) := \{\mathsf{sip}(\tau, \sigma) \mid \sigma \models \tau\}$$

Since τ is in NNF, $\mathsf{sip}(\tau, \sigma)$ implies τ, and it is easy to see that $\tau \equiv \bigvee \mathsf{sip}(\tau)$. Whenever the call to the SMT solver in Line 5 of Algorithm 1 yields sat, the resulting model gives rise to a sequence of syntactic implicants, called the *trace*. To define the trace formally, note that when we integrate acceleration into BMC, we may not only add τ to the SMT formula as in Line 4, but also *learned transitions* that result from acceleration. Thus, the following definition allows for changing the transition formula. In the sequel, $\circ$ also denotes composition of substitutions, i.e., $\theta' \circ \theta := [x/\theta'(\theta(x)) \mid x \in \mathsf{dom}(\theta') \cup \mathsf{dom}(\theta)]$.

Algorithm 2: ABMC – Input: a safety problem $\mathcal{T} = (\psi_{\text{init}}, \tau, \psi_{\text{err}})$

1 $b \leftarrow 0$; $V \leftarrow \varnothing$; $E \leftarrow \varnothing$;   add($\mu_b(\psi_{\text{init}})$)
2 **if** ¬check_sat() **do return** safe **else** $\sigma \leftarrow$ get_model()
3 **while** ⊤ **do**
4 $\quad$ push(); add($\mu_b(\psi_{\text{err}})$)
5 $\quad$ **if** check_sat() **do return** unsafe **else** pop()
6 $\quad$ $\vec{\tau} \leftarrow$ trace$_b(\sigma)$; $V \leftarrow V \cup \vec{\tau}$; $E \leftarrow E \cup \{(\tau_1, \tau_2) \mid [\tau_1, \tau_2]$ is an infix of $\vec{\tau}\}$
7 $\quad$ **if** $\vec{\tau} = \vec{\pi} :: \vec{\pi}^{\circlearrowright} \wedge \vec{\pi}^{\circlearrowright}$ is cyclic $\wedge$ should_accel($\vec{\pi}^{\circlearrowright}$) **do** add($\mu_b(\tau \vee \text{accel}(\vec{\pi}^{\circlearrowright}))$)
8 $\quad$ **else** add($\mu_b(\tau)$)
9 $\quad$ **if** ¬check_sat() **do return** safe **else** $\sigma \leftarrow$ get_model(); $b \leftarrow b + 1$

Definition 5 (Trace). *Let* $[\tau_i]_{i=0}^{b-1}$ *be a sequence of transition formulas and let* σ *be a model of* $\bigwedge_{i=0}^{b-1} \mu_i(\tau_i)$. *Then the* trace *induced by* σ *is*

$$\text{trace}_b(\sigma, [\tau_i]_{i=0}^{b-1}) := [\text{sip}(\tau_i, \sigma \circ \mu_i)]_{i=0}^{b-1}.$$

We write trace$_b(\sigma)$ *instead of* trace$_b(\sigma, [\tau_i]_{i=0}^{b-1})$ *if* $[\tau_i]_{i=0}^{b-1}$ *is clear from the context.*

So each model σ of $\bigwedge_{i=0}^{b-1} \mu_i(\tau_i)$ corresponds to a sequence of steps with the relations $\rightarrow_{\tau_0}, \rightarrow_{\tau_1}, \ldots, \rightarrow_{\tau_{b-1}}$, and the trace induced by σ contains the syntactic implicants of the formulas τ_i that were used in this sequence.

Example 6 (Trace). Reconsider Example 3. After two iterations of the loop of Algorithm 1, the SMT problem consists of the following formulas:

$$x^{(0)} \leq 0 \wedge y^{(0)} \leq 0 \tag{ψ_{init}}$$
$$(x^{(0)} < 100 \wedge x^{(1)} = x^{(0)} + 1 \wedge y^{(1)} = y^{(0)}) \vee (x^{(0)} = 100 \wedge x^{(1)} = 0 \wedge y^{(1)} = y^{(0)} + 1) \tag{τ}$$
$$(x^{(1)} < 100 \wedge x^{(2)} = x^{(1)} + 1 \wedge y^{(2)} = y^{(1)}) \vee (x^{(1)} = 100 \wedge x^{(2)} = 0 \wedge y^{(2)} = y^{(1)} + 1) \tag{τ}$$

With $\sigma = [x^{(i)}/i, y^{(i)}/0 \mid 0 \leq i \leq 2]$, we get trace$_2(\sigma) = [\tau_{x<100}, \tau_{x<100}]$, as:

$$\text{sip}(\tau, \sigma \circ \mu_0) = \text{sip}(\tau, [x/0, y/0, x'/1, y'/0]) = \tau_{x<100}$$
$$\text{sip}(\tau, \sigma \circ \mu_1) = \text{sip}(\tau, [x/1, y/0, x'/2, y'/0]) = \tau_{x<100}$$

To detect situations where applying acceleration techniques pays off, we need to distinguish traces that contain loops from non-looping ones. Since transition formulas are unstructured, the usual techniques for detecting loops (based on, e.g., program syntax or control flow graphs) do not apply in our setting. Instead, we rely on the *dependency graph* of the transition formula.

Definition 7 (Dependency Graph). *Let* τ *be a transition formula. Its dependency graph* $\mathcal{DG} = (V, E)$ *is a directed graph whose vertices* $V := \text{sip}(\tau)$ *are* τ's *syntactic implicants, and* $\tau_1 \rightarrow \tau_2 \in E$ *if* $\odot(\tau_1, \tau_2)$ *is satisfiable. We say that* $\vec{\tau} \in \text{sip}(\tau)^c$ *is* $\mathcal{DG}$-cyclic *if* $c > 0$ *and* $(\tau_1 \rightarrow \tau_2), \ldots, (\tau_{c-1} \rightarrow \tau_c), (\tau_c \rightarrow \tau_1) \in E$.

So intuitively, the syntactic implicants corre-
spond to the different cases of $\rightarrow_\tau$, and τ's
dependency graph corresponds to the control
flow graph of $\rightarrow_\tau$. The dependency graph for Example 1 is on the side.

However, as the size of $\mathsf{sip}(\tau)$ is worst-case exponential in the number of disjunctions in τ, we do not compute τ's dependency graph eagerly. Instead, ABMC maintains an under-approximation, i.e., a subgraph $\mathcal{G}$ of the dependency graph, which is extended whenever two transitions that are not yet connected by an edge occur consecutively on the trace. As soon as a $\mathcal{G}$-cyclic suffix $\vec{\pi}^\circlearrowleft$ is detected on the trace, we may accelerate it. Therefore, the trace may also contain the learned transition $\mathsf{accel}(\vec{\pi}^\circlearrowleft)$ in subsequent iterations. Hence, to detect cyclic suffixes that contain learned transitions, they have to be represented in $\mathcal{G}$ as well. Thus, $\mathcal{G}$ is in fact a subgraph of the dependency graph of $\tau \vee \bigvee \mathcal{L}$, where $\mathcal{L}$ is the set of all transitions that have been learned so far.

This gives rise to the ABMC algorithm, which is shown in Algorithm 2. Here, we just write "cyclic" instead of (V, E)-cyclic. The difference to Algorithm 1 can be seen in Lines 6 and 7. In Line 6, the trace is constructed from the current model. Then, the approximation of the dependency graph is refined such that it contains vertices for all elements of the trace, and edges for consecutive elements of the trace. In Line 7, a cyclic suffix of the trace may get accelerated, provided that the call to should_accel (which will be discussed in detail in Sect. 3.3) returns $\top$. In this way, in the next iteration the SMT solver can choose a model that satisfies $\mathsf{accel}(\vec{\pi}^\circlearrowleft)$ and thus simulates several instead of just one $\rightarrow_\tau$-step. Note, however, that we do *not* update τ with $\tau \vee \mathsf{accel}(\vec{\pi}^\circlearrowleft)$. So in every iteration, at most one learned transition is added to the SMT problem. In this way, we avoid blowing up τ unnecessarily. Note that we only accelerate "real" cycles $\vec{\pi}^\circlearrowleft$ where $\odot(\vec{\pi}^\circlearrowleft)$ is satisfiable, since $\vec{\pi}^\circlearrowleft$ is a suffix of the trace, whose satisfiability is witnessed by σ.

As we rely on syntactic implicants and dependency graphs to detect cycles, ABMC is decoupled from the specific encoding of the input. So for example, transition formulas may be represented in CNF, DNF, or any other structure.

Figure 1 shows a run of Algorithm 2 on Example 1, where the formulas that are added to the SMT problem are highlighted in gray , and $x^{(i)} \mapsto c$ abbreviates $\sigma(x^{(i)}) = c$. For simplicity, we assume that should_accel always returns $\top$, and the model σ is only extended in each step, i.e., $\sigma(x^{(i)})$ and $\sigma(y^{(i)})$ remain unchanged for all $0 \leq i < b$. In general, the SMT solver can choose different values for $\sigma(x^{(i)})$ and $\sigma(y^{(i)})$ in every iteration. On the right, we show the current bound b, and the formulas that give rise to the formulas on the left when renaming their variables suitably with μ_b. Initially, the approximation $\mathcal{G} = (V, E)$ of the dependency graph is empty. When $b = 2$, the trace is $[\tau_{x<100}, \tau_{x<100}]$, and the corresponding edge is added to $\mathcal{G}$. Thus, the trace has the cyclic suffix $\tau_{x<100}$ and we accelerate it, resulting in τ_i^+, which is added to the SMT problem. Then we obtain the trace $[\tau_{x<100}, \tau_{x<100}, \tau_i^+]$, and the edge $\tau_{x<100} \rightarrow \tau_i^+$ is added to $\mathcal{G}$. Note that Algorithm 2 does not enforce the use of τ_i^+, so τ might still be unrolled instead, depending on the models found by the SMT solver. We will address this issue in Sect. 4.

ABMC($\mathcal{T}$)

1: $x^{(0)} \leq 0 \land y^{(0)} \leq 0$ $\psi_{\text{init}}, b = 0$

2 & 6: $x^{(0)} \mapsto 0, y^{(0)} \mapsto 0$ $\| \vec{\tau} \leftarrow []$ $\| E \leftarrow \varnothing$

8: $(x^{(0)} < 100 \land x^{(1)} = x^{(0)} + 1 \land y^{(1)} = y^{(0)}) \lor \ldots$ τ

6 & 9: $x^{(1)} \mapsto 1, y^{(1)} \mapsto 0$ $\| \vec{\tau} \leftarrow [\tau_{x<100}]$ $\| E \leftarrow \varnothing$ $b = 1$

8: $(x^{(1)} < 100 \land x^{(2)} = x^{(1)} + 1 \land y^{(2)} = y^{(1)}) \lor \ldots$ τ

6 & 9: $x^{(2)} \mapsto 2, y^{(2)} \mapsto 0$ $\| \vec{\tau} \leftarrow \vec{\tau} :: \tau_{x<100}$ $\| E \leftarrow \{\tau_{x<100} \to \tau_{x<100}\}$ $b = 2$

7: $\ldots \lor (n^{(2)} > 0 \land x^{(2)} + n^{(2)} \leq 100 \land x^{(3)} = x^{(2)} + n^{(2)} \land y^{(3)} = y^{(2)})$ $\tau \lor \tau_i^+$

6 & 9: $x^{(3)} \mapsto 100, y^{(3)} \mapsto 0 \| \vec{\tau} \leftarrow \vec{\tau} :: \tau_i^+$ $\| E \leftarrow E \cup \{\tau_{x<100} \to \tau_i^+\}$ $b = 3$

8: $\ldots \lor (x^{(3)} = 100 \land x^{(4)} = 0 \land y^{(4)} = y^{(3)} + 1)$ τ

6 & 9: $x^{(4)} \mapsto 0, y^{(4)} \mapsto 1$ $\| \vec{\tau} \leftarrow \vec{\tau} :: \tau_{x=100}$ $\| E \leftarrow E \cup \{\tau_i^+ \to \tau_{x=100}\}$ $b = 4$

8: $(x^{(4)} < 100 \land x^{(5)} = x^{(4)} + 1 \land y^{(5)} = y^{(4)}) \lor \ldots$ τ

6 & 9: $x^{(5)} \mapsto 1, y^{(5)} \mapsto 1$ $\| \vec{\tau} \leftarrow \vec{\tau} :: \tau_{x<100}$ $\| E \leftarrow E \cup \{\tau_{x=100} \to \tau_{x<100}\}$ $b = 5$

7: $\ldots \lor (n^{(5)} > 0 \land x^{(5)} + n^{(5)} \leq 100 \land x^{(6)} = x^{(5)} + n^{(5)} \land y^{(6)} = y^{(5)})$ $\tau \lor \tau_i^+$

6 & 9: $x^{(6)} \mapsto 100, y^{(6)} \mapsto 1 \| \vec{\tau} \leftarrow \vec{\tau} :: \tau_i^+$ $\| E \leftarrow E$ $b = 6$

7: $\ldots \lor (n^{(6)} > 0 \land x^{(6)} = 100 \land 1 < x^{(7)} \leq 100 \land y^{(7)} = y^{(6)} + n^{(6)})$ $\tau \lor \tau_o^+$

4: $y^{(7)} \geq 100$ $b = 7$

5: **unsafe**

Fig. 1. Running ABMC on Example 1

Next, $\tau_{x=100}$ already applies with $b = 4$ (whereas it only applied with $b = 100$ in Example 3). So the trace is $[\tau_{x<100}, \tau_{x<100}, \tau_i^+, \tau_{x=100}]$, and the edge $\tau_i^+ \to \tau_{x=100}$ is added to $\mathcal{G}$. Then we obtain the trace $[\tau_{x<100}, \tau_{x<100}, \tau_i^+, \tau_{x=100}, \tau_{x<100}]$, and add $\tau_{x=100} \to \tau_{x<100}$ to $\mathcal{G}$. Since the suffix $\tau_{x<100}$ is again cyclic, we accelerate it and add τ_i^+ to the SMT problem. After one more step, the trace $[\tau_{x<100}, \tau_{x<100}, \tau_i^+, \tau_{x=100}, \tau_{x<100}, \tau_i^+]$ has the cyclic suffix $[\tau_{x=100}, \tau_{x<100}, \tau_i^+]$. Accelerating it yields τ_o^+, which is added to the SMT problem. Afterwards, unsafety can be proven with $b = 7$.

Since using acceleration is just a heuristic to speed up BMC, all basic properties of BMC immediately carry over to ABMC.

Theorem 8 (Properties of ABMC). *ABMC is*

Sound: *If* $\mathsf{ABMC}(\mathcal{T})$ *returns* (un)safe, *then* $\mathcal{T}$ *is (un)safe.*
Refutationally Complete: *If* $\mathcal{T}$ *is unsafe, then* $\mathsf{ABMC}(\mathcal{T})$ *returns* unsafe.
Non-Terminating: *If* $\mathcal{T}$ *is safe, then* $\mathsf{ABMC}(\mathcal{T})$ *may not terminate.*

3.3   Fine Tuning Acceleration

We now discuss should_accel, our heuristic for applying acceleration. To explain the intuition of our heuristic, we assume that acceleration does not approximate and thus $\rightarrow_{\mathsf{accel}(\vec{\tau})} = \rightarrow_{\vec{\tau}}^{+}$, but in our implementation, we also use it if $\rightarrow_{\mathsf{accel}(\vec{\tau})} \subseteq \rightarrow_{\vec{\tau}}^{+}$. This is uncritical for correctness, as using acceleration in Algorithm 2 is *always* sound.

First, acceleration should be applied to cyclic suffixes consisting of a single *original* (i.e., non-learned) transition. However, applying acceleration to a single learned transition is pointless, as

$$\rightarrow_{\mathsf{accel}(\mathsf{accel}(\tau))} = \rightarrow_{\mathsf{accel}(\tau)}^{+} = (\rightarrow_{\tau}^{+})^{+} = \rightarrow_{\tau}^{+} = \rightarrow_{\mathsf{accel}(\tau)}.$$

Requirement 1. should_accel$([\pi]) = \top$ *iff* $\pi \in \mathsf{sip}(\tau)$.

Next, for every cyclic sequence $\vec{\pi}$, we have

$$\rightarrow_{\mathsf{accel}(\vec{\pi}::\mathsf{accel}(\vec{\pi}))} = \rightarrow_{\vec{\pi}::\mathsf{accel}(\vec{\pi})}^{+} = (\rightarrow_{\vec{\pi}} \circ \rightarrow_{\vec{\pi}}^{+})^{+} = \rightarrow_{\vec{\pi}} \circ \rightarrow_{\vec{\pi}}^{+} = \rightarrow_{\vec{\pi}::\mathsf{accel}(\vec{\pi})},$$

and thus accelerating $\vec{\pi} :: \mathsf{accel}(\vec{\pi})$ is pointless, too. More generally, we want to prevent acceleration of sequences $\vec{\pi}_2 :: \mathsf{accel}(\vec{\pi}) :: \vec{\pi}_1$ where $\vec{\pi} = \vec{\pi}_1 :: \vec{\pi}_2$ as

$$\rightarrow_{\vec{\pi}_2::\mathsf{accel}(\vec{\pi})::\vec{\pi}_1}^{2} = \rightarrow_{\vec{\pi}_2::\mathsf{accel}(\vec{\pi})::\vec{\pi}::\mathsf{accel}(\vec{\pi})::\vec{\pi}_1} \subseteq \rightarrow_{\vec{\pi}_2::\mathsf{accel}(\vec{\pi})::\vec{\pi}_1}$$

and thus $\rightarrow_{\mathsf{accel}(\vec{\pi}_2::\mathsf{accel}(\vec{\pi})::\vec{\pi}_1)} = \rightarrow_{\vec{\pi}_2::\mathsf{accel}(\vec{\pi})::\vec{\pi}_1}^{+} = \rightarrow_{\vec{\pi}_2::\mathsf{accel}(\vec{\pi})::\vec{\pi}_1}$. So in general, the cyclic suffix of such a trace consists of a cycle $\vec{\pi}$ and $\mathsf{accel}(\vec{\pi})$, but it does not necessarily start with either of them. To take this into account, we rely on the notion of *conjugates*.

Definition 9 (Conjugate). *We say that two vectors* $\vec{v}, \vec{w}$ *are conjugates (denoted* $\vec{v} \equiv_{\circ} \vec{w}$*) if* $\vec{v} = \vec{v}_1 :: \vec{v}_2$ *and* $\vec{w} = \vec{v}_2 :: \vec{v}_1$*.*

So a conjugate of a cycle corresponds to the same cycle with another entry point.

Requirement 2. should_accel$(\vec{\pi}') = \bot$ *if* $\vec{\pi}' \equiv_{\circ} \vec{\pi} :: \mathsf{accel}(\vec{\pi})$ *for some* $\vec{\pi}$.

In general, however, we also want to accelerate cyclic suffixes that contain learned transitions to deal with nested loops, as in the last acceleration step of Fig. 1.

Requirement 3. should_accel$(\vec{\pi}') = \top$ *if* $\vec{\pi}' \not\equiv_{\circ} \vec{\pi} :: \mathsf{accel}(\vec{\pi})$ *for all* $\vec{\pi}$.

Requirements 1 to 3 give rise to a complete specification for should_accel: If the cyclic suffix is a singleton, the decision is made based on Requirement 1, and otherwise the decision is made based on Requirements 2 and 3. However, this specification misses one important case: Recall that the trace was $[\tau_{x<100}, \tau_{x<100}]$ before acceleration was applied for the first time in Fig. 1. While both $[\tau_{x<100}]$ and $[\tau_{x<100}, \tau_{x<100}]$ are cyclic, the latter should not be accelerated, since accel($[\tau_{x<100}, \tau_{x<100}]$) is a special case of τ_i^+ that only represents an even number of steps with $\tau_{x<100}$. Here, the problem is that the cyclic suffix contains a *square*, i.e., two adjacent repetitions of the same non-empty sub-sequence.

Requirement 4. should_accel($\vec{\pi}$) = $\bot$ *if* $\vec{\pi}$ *contains a square.*

Thus, should_accel($\vec{\pi}'$) yields $\top$ iff the following holds:

$$(|\vec{\pi}'| = 1 \wedge \vec{\pi}' \in \mathsf{sip}(\tau)) \vee (|\vec{\pi}'| > 1 \wedge \vec{\pi}' \text{ is square-free} \wedge \forall \vec{\pi}. \, (\vec{\pi}' \not\equiv_{\circ} \vec{\pi} :: \mathsf{accel}(\vec{\pi})))$$

All properties that are required to implement should_accel can easily be checked automatically. To check $\vec{\pi}' \not\equiv_{\circ} \vec{\pi} :: \mathsf{accel}(\vec{\pi})$, our implementation maintains a map from learned transitions to the corresponding cycles that have been accelerated.

However, to implement Algorithm 2, there is one more missing piece: As the choice of the cyclic suffix in Line 7 is non-deterministic, a heuristic for choosing it is required. In our implementation, we choose the *shortest* cyclic suffix such that should_accel returns $\top$. The reason is that, as observed in [22], accelerating short cyclic suffixes before longer ones allows for learning more general transitions.

4   Guiding ABMC with Blocking Clauses

As mentioned in Sect. 3.2, Algorithm 2 does not enforce the use of learned transitions. Thus, depending on the models found by the SMT solver, ABMC may behave just like BMC. We now improve ABMC by integrating *blocking clauses* that prevent it from unrolling loops instead of using learned transitions. Here, we again assume $\rightarrow_{\mathsf{accel}(\vec{\tau})} = \rightarrow_{\vec{\tau}}^+$, i.e., that acceleration does not approximate. Otherwise, blocking clauses are only sound for proving unsafety, but not for proving safety.

Blocking clauses exploit the following straightforward observation: If the learned transition $\tau_\ell = \mathsf{accel}(\vec{\pi}^{\circlearrowright})$ has been added to the SMT problem with bound b and an error state can be reached via a trace with prefix

$$\vec{\pi} = [\tau_0, \ldots, \tau_{b-1}] :: \vec{\pi}^{\circlearrowright} \qquad \text{or} \qquad \vec{\pi}' = [\tau_0, \ldots, \tau_{b-1}, \tau_\ell] :: \vec{\pi}^{\circlearrowright},$$

then an error state can also be reached via a trace with the prefix $[\tau_0, \ldots, \tau_{b-1}, \tau_\ell]$, which is not continued with $\vec{\pi}^{\circlearrowright}$. Thus, we may remove traces of the form $\vec{\pi}$ and $\vec{\pi}'$ from the search space by modifying the SMT problem accordingly.

To do so, we assign a unique identifier to each learned transition, and we introduce a fresh integer-valued variable ℓ which is set to the corresponding identifier whenever a learned transition is used, and to 0, otherwise.

Algorithm 3: ABMC$_b$ – Input: a safety problem $\mathcal{T} = (\psi_{\mathsf{init}}, \tau, \psi_{\mathsf{err}})$

1 $b \leftarrow 0;\ V \leftarrow \varnothing;\ E \leftarrow \varnothing;\ \mathsf{id} \leftarrow 0;\ \tau \leftarrow \tau \wedge \ell = 0;\ \mathsf{cache} \leftarrow \varnothing;\ \mathsf{add}(\mu_b(\psi_{\mathsf{init}}))$

2 **if** $\neg\mathsf{check\_sat}()$ **do return** safe **else** $\sigma \leftarrow \mathsf{get\_model}()$

3 **while** $\top$ **do**

4 $\quad$ $\mathsf{push}();\quad \mathsf{add}(\mu_b(\psi_{\mathsf{err}}))$

5 $\quad$ **if** $\mathsf{check\_sat}()$ **do return** unsafe **else** $\mathsf{pop}()$

6 $\quad$ $\vec{\tau} \leftarrow \mathsf{trace}_b(\sigma);\quad V \leftarrow V \cup \vec{\tau};\quad E \leftarrow E \cup \{(\tau_1, \tau_2) \mid [\tau_1, \tau_2]\ \text{is an infix of } \vec{\tau}\}$

7 $\quad$ **if** $\vec{\tau} = \vec{\pi} :: \vec{\pi}^{\circlearrowleft} \wedge \vec{\pi}^{\circlearrowleft}\ is\ (V, E)\text{-}cyclic \wedge \mathsf{should\_accel}(\vec{\pi}^{\circlearrowleft})$ **do**

8 $\quad\quad$ **if** $\exists\tau_c.\ (\vec{\pi}^{\circlearrowleft}, \tau_c) \in \mathsf{cache}$ **do**

9 $\quad\quad\quad$ $\tau_\ell \leftarrow \tau_c$ $\qquad\qquad\qquad\qquad$ // the result of accelerating $\vec{\pi}^{\circlearrowleft}$ was cached

10 $\quad\quad$ **else**

11 $\quad\quad\quad$ $\mathsf{id} \leftarrow \mathsf{id} + 1;\ \tau_\ell \leftarrow \mathsf{accel}(\vec{\pi}^{\circlearrowleft}) \wedge \ell = \mathsf{id}$ $\quad$ // generate new ID and accelerate

12 $\quad\quad\quad$ $\mathsf{cache} \leftarrow \mathsf{cache} \cup \{(\vec{\pi}^{\circlearrowleft}, \tau_\ell)\}$ $\qquad\qquad\qquad\qquad$ // update cache

13 $\quad\quad$ $\beta_1 \leftarrow \neg\left(\bigwedge_{i=0}^{|\vec{\pi}^{\circlearrowleft}|-1} \mu_{b+i}(\pi_i^{\circlearrowleft})\right)$ $\qquad\qquad$ // neither unroll $\vec{\tau}^{\circlearrowleft}$ right now...

14 $\quad\quad$ $\beta_2 \leftarrow \ell^{(b)} \neq \mathsf{id} \vee \neg\left(\bigwedge_{i=0}^{|\vec{\pi}^{\circlearrowleft}|-1} \mu_{b+i+1}(\pi_i^{\circlearrowleft})\right)$ $\qquad$ // ...nor after using the

15 $\quad\quad$ $\mathsf{add}(\mu_b(\tau \vee \tau_\ell) \wedge \beta_1 \wedge \beta_2)$ $\qquad\qquad\qquad$ // accelerated transition

16 $\quad$ **else** $\mathsf{add}(\mu_b(\tau))$

17 $\quad$ **if** $\neg\mathsf{check\_sat}()$ **do return** safe **else** $\sigma \leftarrow \mathsf{get\_model}();\quad b \leftarrow b + 1$

Example 10 (Blocking Clauses). Reconsider Fig. 1 and assume that we modify τ by conjoining $\ell = 0$, and τ_i^+ by conjoining $\ell = 1$. Thus, we now have

$$\tau_{x<100} \equiv x < 100 \wedge x' = x + 1 \wedge y' = y \wedge \ell = 0 \qquad\qquad \text{and}$$
$$\tau_i^+ \equiv n > 0 \wedge x + n \leq 100 \wedge x' = x + n \wedge y' = y \wedge \ell = 1.$$

When $b = 2$, the trace is $[\tau_{x<100}, \tau_{x<100}]$, and in the next iteration, it may be extended to either $\vec{\pi} = [\tau_{x<100}, \tau_{x<100}, \tau_{x<100}]$ or $\vec{\tau} = [\tau_{x<100}, \tau_{x<100}, \tau_i^+]$. However, as $\rightarrow_{\tau_i^+} = \rightarrow_{\tau_{x<100}}^+$, we have $\rightarrow_{\vec{\pi}} \subseteq \rightarrow_{\vec{\tau}}$, so the entire search space can be covered without considering the trace $\vec{\pi}$. Thus, we add the blocking clause

$$\neg\mu_2(\tau_{x<100}) \qquad\qquad\qquad\qquad\qquad (\beta_1)$$

to the SMT problem to prevent ABMC from finding a model that gives rise to the trace $\vec{\pi}$. Note that we have $\mu_2(\tau_i^+) \models \beta_1$, as $\tau_{x<100} \models \ell = 0$ and $\tau_i^+ \models \ell \neq 0$. Thus, β_1 blocks $\tau_{x<100}$ for the third step, but τ_i^+ can still be used without restrictions. Therefore, adding β_1 to the SMT problem does not prevent us from covering the entire search space.

Similarly, we have $\rightarrow_{\vec{\pi}'} \subseteq \rightarrow_{\vec{\tau}}$ for $\vec{\pi}' = [\tau_{x<100}, \tau_{x<100}, \tau_i^+, \tau_{x<100}]$. Thus, we also add the following blocking clause to the SMT problem:

$$\ell^{(2)} \neq 1 \vee \neg\mu_3(\tau_{x<100}) \qquad\qquad\qquad\qquad (\beta_2)$$

ABMC with blocking clauses can be seen in Algorithm 3. The counter id is used to obtain unique identifiers for learned transitions. Thus, it is initialized with 0 (Line 1) and incremented whenever a new transition is learned (Line 11).

Moreover, as explained above, $\ell = 0$ is conjoined to τ (Line 1), and $\ell = $ id is conjoined to each learned transition (Line 11).

In Lines 13 and 14, the blocking clauses β_1 and β_2 which correspond to the superfluous traces $\vec{\pi}$ and $\vec{\pi}'$ above are created, and they are added to the SMT problem in Line 15. Here, $\pi_i^{\circlearrowleft}$ denotes the ith transition in the sequence $\vec{\pi}^{\circlearrowleft}$.

Importantly, Algorithm 3 caches (Line 12) and reuses (Line 9) learned transitions. In this way, the learned transitions that are conjoined to the SMT problem have the same id if they stem from the same cycle, and thus the blocking clauses β_1 and β_2 can also block sequences $\vec{\pi}^{\circlearrowleft}$ that contain learned transitions, as shown in the following example.

Example 11 (Caching). Let τ have the dependency graph given below. As Alg. 3 conjoins $\ell = 0$ to τ, assume $\tau_i \models \ell = 0$ for all $i \in \{1, 2, 3\}$. Moreover, assume that accelerating τ_2 yields τ_2^+ with $\tau_2^+ \models \ell = 1$. If we obtain the trace $[\tau_1, \tau_2^+, \tau_3]$, it can be accelerated. Thus, Alg. 3 would add

$$\beta_1 \equiv \neg\left(\mu_3(\tau_1) \wedge \mu_4(\tau_2^+) \wedge \mu_5(\tau_3)\right)$$

to the SMT problem. If the next step yields the trace $[\tau_1, \tau_2^+, \tau_3, \tau_2]$, then τ_2 is accelerated again. Without caching, acceleration may yield a new transition $\tau_{2'}^+$ with $\tau_{2'}^+ \models \ell = 2$. As the SMT solver may choose a different model in every iteration, the trace may also change in every iteration. So after two more steps, we could get the trace $[\tau_1, \tau_2^+, \tau_3, \tau_1, \tau_{2'}^+, \tau_3]$. At this point, the "outer" loop consisting of τ_1, arbitrarily many repetitions of τ_2, and τ_3, has been unrolled a second time, which should have been prevented by β_1. The reason is that $\tau_2^+ \models \ell = 1$, whereas $\tau_{2'}^+ \models \ell = 2$, and thus $\tau_{2'}^+ \models \neg\tau_2^+$. With caching, we again obtain τ_2^+ when τ_2 is accelerated for the second time, such that this problem is avoided.

Remarkably, blocking clauses allow us to prove safety in cases where BMC fails.

Example 12 (Proving Safety with Blocking Clauses). Consider the safety problem $(x \leq 0, \tau, x > 100)$ with $\tau \equiv x < 100 \wedge x' = x + 1$. Algorithm 1 cannot prove its safety, as τ can be unrolled arbitrarily often (by choosing smaller and smaller initial values for x). With Algorithm 3, we obtain the following SMT problem with $b = 3$.

$$\mu_0(x \leq 0) \qquad \text{(initial states)}$$
$$\mu_0(\tau \wedge \ell = 0) \qquad (\tau)$$
$$\mu_1(\tau \wedge \ell = 0) \qquad (\tau)$$
$$\neg\mu_2(\tau \wedge \ell = 0) \qquad (\beta_1)$$
$$\ell^{(2)} \neq 1 \vee \neg\mu_3(\tau \wedge \ell = 0) \qquad (\beta_2)$$
$$\mu_2((\tau \wedge \ell = 0) \vee (n > 0 \wedge x + n \leq 100 \wedge x' = x + n \wedge \ell = 1)) \quad (\tau \vee \mathsf{accel}(\tau))$$
$$\mu_3(\tau \wedge \ell = 0) \qquad (\tau)$$

From the last formula and β_2, we get $\ell^{(2)} \neq 1$, but the formula labeled with $(\tau \vee \mathsf{accel}(\tau))$ and β_1 imply $\mu_2(\ell = 1) \equiv \ell^{(2)} = 1$, resulting in a contradiction. Thus, due to the blocking clauses, $\mathsf{ABMC_b}$ can prove safety with the bound $b = 3$.

Like ABMC, $\mathsf{ABMC_b}$ preserves BMC's main properties (see [23] for a proof).

Theorem 13. $\mathsf{ABMC_b}$ *is sound and refutationally complete, but non-terminating.*

5   Related Work

There is a large body of literature on bounded model checking that is concerned with encoding temporal logic specifications into propositional logic, see [5,6] as starting points. This line of work is clearly orthogonal to ours.

Moreover, numerous techniques focus on proving *safety* or *satisfiability* of transition systems or CHCs, respectively (e.g., [13,17,25,27,29,36]). A comprehensive overview is beyond the scope of this paper. Instead, we focus on techniques that, like ABMC, aim to prove unsafety by finding long counterexamples.

The most closely related approach is *Acceleration Driven Clause Learning* [21,22], a calculus that uses depth-first search and acceleration to find counterexamples. So one major difference between ABMC and ADCL is that ABMC performs breadth-first search, whereas ADCL performs depth-first search. Thus, ADCL requires a mechanism for backtracking to avoid getting stuck. To this end, it relies on a notion of *redundancy*, which is difficult to automate. Thus, in practice, approximations are used [22, Sect. 4]. However, even with a complete redundancy check, ADCL might get stuck in a safe part of the search space [22, Thm. 18]. ABMC does not suffer from such deficits.

Like ADCL, ABMC also tries to avoid redundant work (see Sects. 3.3 and 4). However, doing so is crucial for ADCL due to its depth-first strategy, whereas it is a mere optimization for ABMC.

On the other hand, ADCL applies acceleration in a very systematic way, whereas ABMC decides whether to apply acceleration or not based on the model that is found by the underlying SMT solver. Therefore, ADCL is advantageous for examples with deeply nested loops, where ABMC may require many steps until the SMT solver yields models that allow for accelerating the nested loops one after the other. Furthermore, ADCL has successfully been adapted for proving non-termination [21], and it is unclear whether a corresponding adaption of ABMC would be competitive. Thus, both techniques are orthogonal. See Sect. 6 for an experimental comparison of ADCL with ABMC.

Other acceleration-based approaches [4,9,19] can be seen as generalizations of the classical state elimination method for finite automata: Instead of transforming finite automata to regular expressions, they transform transition systems to formulas that represent the runs of the transition system. During this transformation, acceleration is the counterpart to the Kleene star in the state elimination method. Clearly, these approaches differ fundamentally from ours.

In [30], under-approximating acceleration techniques are used to enrich the control-flow graph of C programs. Then an external model checker is used to find counterexamples. In contrast, ABMC tightly integrates acceleration into BMC, and thus enables an interplay of both techniques: Acceleration changes the state of the bounded model checker by adding learned transitions to the SMT problem. Vice versa, the state of the bounded model checker triggers acceleration. Doing so is impossible if the bounded model checker is used as an external black box.

In [31], the approach from [30] is extended by a program transformation that, like our blocking clauses, rules out superfluous traces. For structured programs, program transformations are quite natural. However, as we analyze unstructured transition formulas, such a transformation would be very expensive in our setting. More precisely, [31] represents programs as CFAs. To transform them, the edges of the CFA are inspected. In our setting, the syntactic implicants correspond to these edges. An important goal of ABMC is to avoid computing them explicitly. Hence, it is unclear how to apply the approach from [31] in our setting.

Another related approach is described in [26], where acceleration is integrated into a CEGAR loop in two ways: (1) as preprocessing and (2) to generalize interpolants. In contrast to (1), we use acceleration "on the fly". In contrast to (2), we do not use abstractions, so our learned transitions can directly be used in counterexamples. Moreover, [26] only applies acceleration to conjunctive transition formulas, whereas we accelerate conjunctive variants of arbitrary transition formulas. So in our approach, acceleration techniques are applicable more often, which is particularly useful for finding long counterexamples.

Finally, *transition power abstraction* (TPA) [7] computes a sequence of over-approximations for transition systems where the nth element captures 2^n instead of just n steps of the transition relation. So like ABMC, TPA can help to find long refutations quickly, but in contrast to ABMC, TPA relies on over-approximations.

6   Experiments and Conclusion

We presented ABMC, which integrates acceleration techniques into bounded model checking. By enabling BMC to find deep counterexamples, it targets a major limitation of BMC. However, whether ABMC makes use of transitions that result from acceleration depends on the models found by the underlying SMT solver. Hence, we introduced *blocking clauses* to enforce the use of accelerated transitions, which also enable ABMC to prove safety in cases where BMC fails.

We implemented ABMC in our tool LoAT [20]. It uses the SMT solvers Z3 [33] and Yices [14]. Currently, our implementation is restricted to integer arithmetic. It uses the acceleration technique from [18] which, in our experience, is precise in most cases where the values of the variables after executing the loop can be expressed by polynomials of degree ≤ 2 (i.e., here we have $\to_{\mathsf{accel}(\tau)} = \to_\tau^+$). If acceleration yields a non-polynomial formula, then this formula is discarded by our implementation, since Z3 and Yices only support polynomials. We evaluate our approach on the examples from the category LIA-Lin (linear CHCs with linear integer arithmetic)[2] from the CHC competition '23 [11], which contain problems from numerous applications like verification of C, Rust, Java, and higher-order programs, and regression verification of LLVM programs, see [12] for details. By using CHCs as input format, our approach can be used by any CHC-based tool like Korn [16] and SeaHorn [24] for C and C++ programs, JayHorn for Java programs [28], HornDroid for Android [10], RustHorn for Rust programs [32], and SmartACE [35] and SolCMC [3] for Solidity.

We compared several configurations of LoAT with the techniques of other leading CHC solvers. More precisely, we evaluated the following configurations:

LoAT We used LoAT's implementations of Algorithm 1 (LoAT BMC), Algorithm 2 (LoAT ABMC), Algorithm 3 (LoAT ABMC$_b$), and ADCL (LoAT ADCL).

Z3 [33] We used Z3 4.13.0, where we evaluated its implementations of the Spacer algorithm (Spacer [29]) and BMC (Z3 BMC).

Golem [7] We used Golem 0.5.0, where we evaluated its implementations of *transition power abstraction* (Golem TPA [7]) and BMC (Golem BMC).

Eldarica [27] We used Eldarica 2.1.0. We tested all five configurations that are used in parallel in its portfolio mode (-portfolio), and included the two that found the most counterexamples: CEGAR with acceleration as preprocessing (Eldarica CEGAR, eld -splitClauses:1 -abstract:off -stac) and symbolic execution (Eldarica SYM, eld -splitClauses:1 -sym).

Note that all configurations except Spacer and Eldarica CEGAR are specifically designed for finding counterexamples. We did not include further techniques for proving safety in our evaluation, as our focus is on *dis*proving safety. We ran our experiments on StarExec [34] with a wallclock timeout of 300s, a cpu timeout of 1200s, and a memory limit of 128 GB per example.

2023	unsafe		safe	
	✓	!	✓	!
LoAT ABMC	73	–	31	–
LoAT ABMC$_b$	72	0	75	11
Golem TPA	64	0	83	5
LoAT BMC	60	0	36	0
Z3 BMC	57	–	21	–
LoAT ADCL	56	1	0	–
Golem BMC	55	–	20	–
Spacer	51	4	151	53
Eldarica CEGAR	46	1	107	13
Eldarica SYM	46	1	68	15

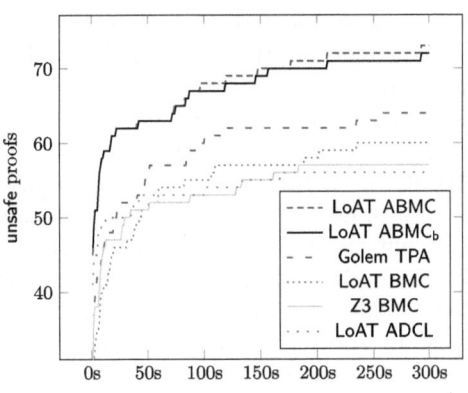

---

[2] The restriction of our approach to linear clauses (with at most one negative literal) is "inherited" from BMC. In contrast, our approach also supports non-linear arithmetic, but we are not aware of corresponding benchmark collections.

The results can be seen in the table above. The columns with ! show the number of unique proofs, i.e., the number of examples that could only be solved by the corresponding configuration. Such a comparison only makes sense if just one implementation of each algorithm is considered. For instance, LoAT's, Z3's, and Golem's implementations of the BMC algorithm work well on the same class of examples, so that none of them finds unique proofs if all of them are taken into account. Thus, for ! we disregarded LoAT ABMC, Z3 BMC, and Golem BMC.

The table shows that our implementation of ABMC is very powerful for proving unsafety. In particular, it shows a significant improvement over LoAT BMC, which is implemented very similarly, but does not make use of acceleration.

Note that all unsafe instances that can be solved by ABMC can also be solved by other configurations. This is not surprising, as LoAT ADCL is also based on acceleration techniques. Hence, ABMC combines the strengths of ADCL and BMC, and conversely, unsafe examples that can be solved with ABMC can usually also be solved by one of these techniques. So for unsafe instances, the main contribution of ABMC is to have *one* technique that performs well both on instances with shallow counterexamples (which can be solved by BMC) as well as instances with deep counterexamples only (which can often be solved by ADCL).

On the instance that can only be solved by ADCL, our (A)BMC implementation spends most of the time with applying substitutions, which clearly shows potential for further optimizations. Due to ADCL's depth-first strategy, it produces smaller formulas, so that applying substitutions is cheaper.

Regarding safe examples, the table shows that our implementation of ABMC is not competitive with state-of-the-art techniques.[3] However, it finds several unique proofs. This is remarkable, as LoAT is not at all fine-tuned for proving safety. For example, we expect that LoAT's results on safe instances can easily be improved by integrating over-approximating acceleration techniques. While such a variant of ABMC could not prove unsafety, it would presumably be much more powerful for proving safety. We leave that to future work.

The plot on the previous page shows how many unsafety proofs were found within 300 s, where we only include the six best configurations for readability. It shows that ABMC is highly competitive on unsafe instances, not only in terms of solved examples, but also in terms of runtime. The plot on the right compares the length of the counterexamples found by LoAT $ABMC_b$ and BMC to show the impact of acceleration. Here, only examples where both techniques disprove safety are considered, and the counterexamples found by $ABMC_b$ may contain accelerated transitions. There are no

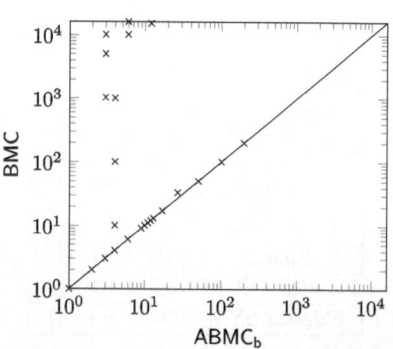

---

[3] LoAT ABMC finds fewer safety proofs than LoAT BMC since acceleration sometimes yields transitions with non-linear arithmetic that make the SMT problem harder.

points below the diagonal, i.e., the counterexamples found by $ABMC_b$ are at most as long as those found by BMC. The points above the diagonal indicate that the counterexamples found by $ABMC_b$ are sometimes shorter by orders of magnitude (note that the axes are log-scaled).

Our results also show that blocking clauses have no significant impact on ABMC's performance on unsafe instances, neither regarding the number of solved examples, nor regarding the runtime. In fact, $ABMC_b$ solved one instance less than ABMC (which can, however, also be solved by $ABMC_b$ with a larger timeout). On the other hand, blocking clauses are clearly useful for proving safety, where they even allow LoAT to find several unique proofs.

In future work, we plan to support other theories like reals, bitvectors, and arrays, and we will investigate an extension to non-linear CHCs. Our implementation is open-source and available on Github. For the sources, a pre-compiled binary, and more information on our evaluation, we refer to [2].

Data Availability Statement. An artifact containing LoAT which allows to replicate our experiments is available at [1].

References

1. Artifact for "Integrating Loop Acceleration into Bounded Model Checking" (2024). https://doi.org/10.5281/zenodo.11954015
2. Evaluation of "Integrating Loop Acceleration into Bounded Model Checking" (2024). https://loat-developers.github.io/abmc-eval/
3. Alt, L., Blicha, M., Hyvärinen, A.E.J., Sharygina, N.: SolCMC: Solidity compiler's model checker. In: CAV 2022. LNCS, vol. 13371, pp. 325–338. Springer, Heidelberg (2022). https://doi.org/10.1007/978-3-031-13185-1_16
4. Bardin, S., Finkel, A., Leroux, J., Petrucci, L.: FAST: acceleration from theory to practice. Int. J. Softw. Tools Technol. Transf. **10**(5), 401–424 (2008). https://doi.org/10.1007/s10009-008-0064-3
5. Biere, A., Cimatti, A., Clarke, E.M., Strichman, O., Zhu, Y.: Bounded model checking. Adv. Comput. **58**, 117–148 (2003). https://doi.org/10.1016/S0065-2458(03)58003-2
6. Biere, A.: Bounded model checking. In: Handbook of Satisfiability - Second Edition. Frontiers in Artificial Intelligence and Applications, vol. 336, pp. 739–764. IOS Press (2021). https://doi.org/10.3233/FAIA201002
7. Blicha, M., Fedyukovich, G., Hyvärinen, A.E.J., Sharygina, N.: Transition power abstractions for deep counterexample detection. In: TACAS 2022. LNCS, vol. 13243, pp. 524–542. Springer, Heidelberg (2022). https://doi.org/10.1007/978-3-030-99524-9_29
8. Bozga, M., Gîrlea, C., Iosif, R.: Iterating octagons. In: TACAS 2009. LNCS, vol. 5505, pp. 337–351. Springer, Heidelberg (2009). https://doi.org/10.1007/978-3-642-00768-2_29
9. Bozga, M., Iosif, R., Konečný, F.: Relational analysis of integer programs. Technical Report TR-2012-10, VERIMAG (2012). https://www-verimag.imag.fr/TR/TR-2012-10.pdf
10. Calzavara, S., Grishchenko, I., Maffei, M.: HornDroid: practical and sound static analysis of Android applications by SMT solving. In: EuroS&P 2016, pp. 47–62. IEEE (2016). https://doi.org/10.1109/EuroSP.2016.16

11. CHC Competition. https://chc-comp.github.io
12. De Angelis, E., Govind V. K., H.: CHC-COMP 2023: Competition report (2023). https://chc-comp.github.io/2023/CHC_COMP_2023_Competition_Report.pdf
13. Dietsch, D., Heizmann, M., Hoenicke, J., Nutz, A., Podelski, A.: Ultimate TreeAutomizer (CHC-COMP tool description). In: HCVS/PERR@ETAPS 2019. EPTCS, vol. 296, pp. 42–47 (2019). https://doi.org/10.4204/EPTCS.296.7
14. Dutertre, B.: Yices 2.2. In: CAV 2014. LNCS, vol. 8559, pp. 737–744. Springer, Heidelberg (2014). https://doi.org/10.1007/978-3-319-08867-9_49
15. Enderton, H.B.: A Mathematical Introduction to Logic. Academic Press, New York (1972)
16. Ernst, G.: Loop verification with invariants and contracts. In: VMCAI 2022 [2], pp. 69–92 (2022). https://doi.org/10.1007/978-3-030-94583-1_4
17. Fedyukovich, G., Prabhu, S., Madhukar, K., Gupta, A.: Solving constrained Horn clauses using syntax and data. In: FMCAD 2018 [1], pp. 1–9 (2018). https://doi.org/10.23919/FMCAD.2018.8603011
18. Frohn, F.: A calculus for modular loop acceleration. In: TACAS 2020. LNCS, vol. 12078, pp. 58–76. Springer, Heidelberg (2020). https://doi.org/10.1007/978-3-030-45190-5_4
19. Frohn, F., Naaf, M., Brockschmidt, M., Giesl, J.: Inferring lower runtime bounds for integer programs. ACM Trans. Program. Lang. Syst. **42**(3), 13:1–13:50 (2020). https://doi.org/10.1145/3410331
20. Frohn, F., Giesl, J.: Proving non-termination and lower runtime bounds with LoAT (system description). In: IJCAR 2022. LNCS, vol. 13385, pp. 712–722. Springer, Heidelberg (2022). https://doi.org/10.1007/978-3-031-10769-6_41
21. Frohn, F., Giesl, J.: Proving non-termination by acceleration driven clause learning. In: CADE 2023. LNCS, vol. 14132, pp. 220–233. Springer, Heidelberg (2023). https://doi.org/10.1007/978-3-031-38499-8_13
22. Frohn, F., Giesl, J.: ADCL: Acceleration driven clause learning for constrained Horn clauses. In: SAS 2023. LNCS, vol. 14284, pp. 259–285. Springer, Heidelberg (2023). https://doi.org/10.1007/978-3-031-44245-2_13
23. Frohn, F., Giesl, J.: Integrating loop acceleration into bounded model checking. CoRR abs/2401.09973 (2024). https://doi.org/10.48550/arXiv.2401.09973
24. Gurfinkel, A., Kahsai, T., Komuravelli, A., Navas, J.A.: The SeaHorn verification framework. In: CAV 2015. LNCS, vol. 9206, pp. 343–361. Springer, Heidelberg (2015). https://doi.org/10.1007/978-3-319-21690-4_20
25. Hoder, K., Bjørner, N.S.: Generalized property directed reachability. In: SAT 2012. LNCS, vol. 7317, pp. 157–171. Springer, Heidelberg (2012). https://doi.org/10.1007/978-3-642-31612-8_13
26. Hojjat, H., Iosif, R., Konečný, F., Kuncak, V., Rümmer, P.: Accelerating interpolants. In: ATVA 2012. LNCS, vol. 7561, pp. 187–202. Springer, Heidelberg (2012). https://doi.org/10.1007/978-3-642-33386-6_16
27. Hojjat, H., Rümmer, P.: The Eldarica Horn solver. In: FMCAD 2018 [1], pp. 1–7. https://doi.org/10.23919/FMCAD.2018.8603013
28. Kahsai, T., Rümmer, P., Sanchez, H., Schäf, M.: JayHorn: a framework for verifying Java programs. In: CAV 2016. LNCS, vol. 9779, pp. 352–358. Springer, Heidelberg (2016). https://doi.org/10.1007/978-3-319-41528-4_19
29. Komuravelli, A., Gurfinkel, A., Chaki, S.: SMT-based model checking for recursive programs. Formal Methods Syst. Des. **48**(3), 175–205 (2016). https://doi.org/10.1007/s10703-016-0249-4

30. Kroening, D., Lewis, M., Weissenbacher, G.: Under-approximating loops in C programs for fast counterexample detection. Formal Methods Syst. Des. **47**(1), 75–92 (2015). https://doi.org/10.1007/s10703-015-0228-1
31. Kroening, D., Lewis, M., Weissenbacher, G.: Proving safety with trace automata and bounded model checking. In: FM 2015. LNCS, vol. 9109, pp. 325–341. Springer, Heidelberg (2015). https://doi.org/10.1007/978-3-319-19249-9_21
32. Matsushita, Y., Tsukada, T., Kobayashi, N.: RustHorn: CHC-based verification for Rust programs. ACM Trans. Program. Lang. Syst. **43**(4), 15:1–15:54 (2021). https://doi.org/10.1145/3462205
33. de Moura, L., Bjørner, N.: Z3: An efficient SMT solver. In: TACAS 2008. LNCS, vol. 4963, pp. 337–340. Springer, Heidelberg (2008). https://doi.org/10.1007/978-3-540-78800-3_24
34. Stump, A., Sutcliffe, G., Tinelli, C.: StarExec: a cross-community infrastructure for logic solving. In: IJCAR 2014. LNCS, vol. 8562, pp. 367–373. Springer, Heidelberg (2014). https://doi.org/10.1007/978-3-319-08587-6_28
35. Wesley, S., Christakis, M., Navas, J.A., Trefler, R.J., Wüstholz, V., Gurfinkel, A.: Verifying Solidity smart contracts via communication abstraction in SmartACE. In: VMCAI 2022 [2], pp. 425–449. https://doi.org/10.1007/978-3-030-94583-1_21
36. Zhu, H., Magill, S., Jagannathan, S.: A data-driven CHC solver. In: PLDI 2018, pp. 707–721 (2018). https://doi.org/10.1145/3192366.3192416

Nonlinear Craig Interpolant Generation Over Unbounded Domains by Separating Semialgebraic Sets

Hao Wu[1] , Jie Wang[2] , Bican Xia[3] , Xiakun Li[3] , Naijun Zhan[1,4] , and Ting Gan[5](✉)

[1] SKLCS, Institute of Software, University of CAS,
Beijing, China
{znj,wuhao}@ios.ac.cn
[2] Academy of Mathematics and Systems Science, CAS,
Beijing, China
wangjie212@amss.ac.cn
[3] School of Mathematical Sciences, Peking University, Beijing, China
xbc@math.pku.edu.cn, 2301110072@stu.pku.edu.cn
[4] School of Computer Science, Peking University, Beijing, China
[5] School of Computer Science, Wuhan University, Wuhan, China
ganting@whu.edu.cn

Abstract. Interpolation-based techniques become popular in recent years, as they can improve the scalability of existing verification techniques due to their inherent modularity and local reasoning capabilities. Synthesizing Craig interpolants is the cornerstone of these techniques. In this paper, we investigate nonlinear Craig interpolant synthesis for two polynomial formulas of the general form, essentially corresponding to the underlying mathematical problem to separate two disjoint semialgebraic sets. By combining the homogenization approach with existing techniques, we prove the existence of a novel class of non-polynomial interpolants called semialgebraic interpolants. These semialgebraic interpolants subsume polynomial interpolants as a special case. To the best of our knowledge, this is the first existence result of this kind. Furthermore, we provide complete sum-of-squares characterizations for both polynomial and semialgebraic interpolants, which can be efficiently solved as semidefinite programs. Examples are provided to demonstrate the effectiveness and efficiency of our approach.

Keywords: Craig interpolation · Separating semialgebraic sets · Homogenization · Sum-of-squares · Semidefinite programming

H. Wu and J. Wang—The first two authors contributed equally to this work and should be considered co-first authors. This work has been partially funded by the National Key R&D Program of China under grant No. 2022YFA1005101 and 2022YFA1005102, by the NSFC under grant No. 62192732, 62032024, and 12201618, by the CAS Project for Young Scientists in Basic Research under grant No. YSBR-040, by the Key R&D Program of Hubei Province (2023BAB170), and by the Fundamental Research Funds for the Central Universities.

A. Platzer et al. (Eds.): FM 2024, LNCS 14933, pp. 92–110, 2025.
https://doi.org/10.1007/978-3-031-71162-6_5

1   Introduction

Background. Craig interpolant is a fundamental concept in formal verification and automated theorem proving. It was introduced by William Craig in the 1950s as a tool for reasoning about logical formulas and their satisfiability. Craig interpolation techniques possess excellent modularity and local reasoning capabilities, making them effective tools for enhancing the scalability of formal verification methods, like theorem proving [23,35], model-checking [31], abstract interpretation [14,32], program verification [19,26] and so on.

Efficient generation of Craig interpolants is crucial in interpolation-based techniques, and therefore has garnered increasing attention. Formally, a formula I is called a Craig interpolant for two mutually exclusive formulae ϕ and ψ in a background theory $\mathcal{T}$, if it is defined on the common symbols of ϕ and ψ, implied by ϕ in the theory $\mathcal{T}$, and inconsistent with ψ in the theory $\mathcal{T}$. Due to the diversity of background theories and their integration, researchers have been dedicated to developing efficient interpolation synthesis algorithms. Currently, numerous effective algorithms for automatic synthesis of interpolants have been proposed for various fragments of first-order logic, e.g., linear arithmetic [14], logic with arrays [15,33], logic with sets [20], equality logic with uninterpreted functions (EUF) [5,32], etc., and their combinations [22,38,43]. Moreover, D'Silva et al. [9] explored how to compare the strength of various interpolants.

However, interpolant generation for nonlinear arithmetic and its combination with the aforementioned theories is still in infancy, although nonlinear polynomial inequalities are quite common in software involving number theoretic functions as well as hybrid systems [44,45]. In addition, when the formulas ϕ and ψ are defined by polynomial inequalities, generating an interpolant is essentially equivalent to the mathematical problem of separating two disjoint semialgebraic sets, which has a long history and is a challenging mathematical problem [1].

In [7], Dai et al. attempted to generate interpolants for conjunctions of mutually contradictory nonlinear polynomial inequalities without unshared variables. They proposed an algorithm based on Stengle's Positivstellensatz [41], which guarantees the existence of a witness and can be computed using semidefinite programming (SDP). While their algorithm is generally incomplete, it becomes complete when all variables are bounded, known as the Archimedean condition (see in Sect. 2.1).

In [10], Gan et al. introduced an algorithm for generating interpolants specifically for quadratic polynomial inequalities. Their approach is based on the insight that analyzing the solution space of concave quadratic polynomial inequalities can be achieved by linearizing them, using a generalization of Motzkin's transposition theorem. Additionally, they discussed generating interpolants for a combination of the theory of quadratic concave polynomial inequalities and EUF using a hierarchical calculus proposed in [39] and employed in [38].

In [11], Gan et al. further extended the problem from the case of quadratic concave inequalities to the more general Archimedean case. To accomplish this, they utilized Putinar's Positivstellensatz and proposed a Craig interpolation generation method based on SDP. This method allows to generate interpolants in a broader class of situations involving nonlinear polynomial inequalities. However, the Archimedean condition still imposes a limitation on the method, as it requires bounded domains.

In [4], Chen et al. proposed a counterexample-guided framework based on support vector machines for synthesizing nonlinear interpolants. Later in [27], Lin et al. combined this framework and deep learning for synthesizing neural interpolants. In [18], Jovanović and Dutertre also designed a counterexample-guided framework based on cylindrical algebraic decomposition (CAD) for synthesizing interpolants as boolean combinations of constraints. However, these approaches rely on quantifier elimination to ensure completeness and convergence, which terribly affects their efficiency due to its doubly exponential time complexity [8].

For theories including non-polynomial expressions, the general idea is to abstract non-polynomial expressions into polynomial or linear expressions. In [13], Gao and Zufferey presented an approach for extracting interpolants for nonlinear formulas that may contain transcendental functions and differential equations. They accomplished this by transforming proof traces from a δ-decision procedure [12] based on interval constraint propagation (ICP) [3]. Like the Archimedean condition, δ-decidability also imposes the restriction that variables are bounded (in a hyper-rectangle). A similar idea was also reported in [24]. In [6,40], Srikanth et al. and Cimatti et al. proposed approaches to abstract nonlinear formulas into the theory of linear arithmetic with uninterpreted functions.

Contributions. In this paper, we consider how to synthesize an interpolant function $h(\mathbf{x})$ for two polynomial formulas $\phi(\mathbf{x}, \mathbf{y})$ and $\psi(\mathbf{x}, \mathbf{z})$ such that $\phi(\mathbf{x}, \mathbf{y}) \models h(\mathbf{x}) > 0$ and $\psi(\mathbf{x}, \mathbf{z}) \models h(\mathbf{x}) < 0$ without assuming the Archimedean condition, i.e., the variables in ϕ and ψ can have an unbounded range of values. Here, uncommon variables of ϕ and ψ are allowed, and the description of formulas may involve any polynomial of any degree. Hence the problem is more general than the ones discussed in [7,10,11], and is also more difficult as polynomial interpolants may not exist [1]. To address this problem, we first utilize homogenization techniques to elevate the descriptions of ϕ and ψ to the homogeneous space. In this homogeneous space, we can impose the constraint that the variables lie on a unit sphere, thus reviving the Archimedean condition. Combining this idea with the work in [11], we can prove the existence of a semialgebraic function $h(\mathbf{x}) = h_1(\mathbf{x}) + h_2(\mathbf{x})\sqrt{\|\mathbf{x}\|^2 + 1}$ such that $h(\mathbf{x}) > 0$ serves as an interpolant, where h_1, h_2 are polynomials (h becomes a polynomial when $h_2 = 0$). Furthermore, we provide sum-of-squares (SOS) programming procedures for finding such semialgebraic interpolants as well as polynomial interpolants. Under certain assumptions, we prove that the SOS procedures are sound and complete.

Organization. The rest of the paper is organized as follows. Preliminaries are introduced in Sect. 2. Section 3 proves the existence of an interpolant for two mutually contradictory polynomial formulas. Section 4 derives an SOS characterization for the interpolant. Section 5 presents an SDP-based method for computation and provides examples. Finally, Sect. 6, we conclude this paper and discuss some future works. Omitted proofs and portraits for examples can be found in the extended version [42].

2   Preliminaries

We first fix some basic notations. Let $\mathbb{N}$ and $\mathbb{R}$ be the sets of integers and real numbers, respectively. By convention, we use boldface letters to denote vectors. Fixing a vector of indeterminates $\mathbf{x} := (x_1, \ldots, x_r)$, let $\mathbb{R}[\mathbf{x}]$ denote the polynomial ring in variables $\mathbf{x}$ over real numbers. We use $\Sigma[\mathbf{x}] := \{\sum_{i=1}^m p_i^2 \mid p_i \in \mathbb{R}[\mathbf{x}], m \in \mathbb{N}\}$ to denote the set of SOS polynomials in variables $\mathbf{x}$. A basic semialgebraic set $S \subseteq \mathbb{R}^r$ is of the form $\{\mathbf{x} \in \mathbb{R}^r \mid p_1(\mathbf{x}) \rhd 0, \ldots, p_m(\mathbf{x}) \rhd 0\}$, where $p_i(\mathbf{x}) \in \mathbb{R}[\mathbf{x}]$ and $\rhd \in \{\geq, >\}$ (each of the inequalities can be either strict or non-strict). A basic semialgebraic set is said to be *closed* if it is defined by non-strict inequalities. Semialgebraic sets are formed as unions of basic semialgebraic sets. i.e., $T = \bigcup_{i=1}^n S_i$ is a semialgebraic set, where each S_i is a basic semialgebraic set. For any (semialgebraic) set $S \subseteq \mathbb{R}^r$, let $\mathrm{cl}(S)$ denote the closure of S. Let $\bot$ and $\top$ stand for **false** and **true**, respectively. For a vector $\mathbf{x} \in \mathbb{R}^r$, let $\|\mathbf{x}\| := \sqrt{\sum_{i=1}^r x_i^2}$ denote the standard Euclidean norm.

In the following, we give a brief introduction on important notions used throughout the rest of this paper and then describe the problem of interest.

2.1   Quadratic Module

Definition 1 (Quadratic Module [30]). *A subset $\mathcal{M}$ of $\mathbb{R}[\mathbf{x}]$ is called a quadratic module if it contains 1 and is closed under addition and multiplication with squares, i.e.,*

$$1 \in \mathcal{M}, \mathcal{M} + \mathcal{M} \subseteq \mathcal{M}, \text{ and } p^2 \mathcal{M} \subseteq \mathcal{M} \text{ for all } p \in \mathbb{R}[\mathbf{x}].$$

Definition 2. *Let $\overline{p} := \{p_1, \ldots, p_m\}$ be a finite subset of $\mathbb{R}[\mathbf{x}]$. The quadratic module $\mathcal{M}_{\mathbf{x}}(\overline{p})$, or simply $\mathcal{M}(\overline{p})$, generated by $\overline{p}$ is the smallest quadratic module containing all p_i, i.e.,*

$$\mathcal{M}_{\mathbf{x}}(\overline{p}) := \{\sigma_0 + \sum_{i=1}^m \sigma_i p_i \mid \sigma_0, \sigma_i \in \Sigma[\mathbf{x}]\}.$$

Let S be a closed basic semialgebraic set described by $\overline{p} \geq \mathbf{0}$, i.e.,

$$S := \{\mathbf{x} \in \mathbb{R}^r \mid p_1(\mathbf{x}) \geq 0, \ldots, p_m(\mathbf{x}) \geq 0\}. \tag{1}$$

Since SOS polynomials are non-negative, it is easy to verify that the quadratic module $\mathcal{M}(\overline{p})$ is a subset of polynomials that are nonnegative on S. In fact, under the so-called the Archimedean condition, the quadratic module $\mathcal{M}(\overline{p})$ contains all polynomials that are strictly positive over S. Both the condition and the statement are formalized as follows.

Definition 3 (Archimedean [30]). *Let $\mathcal{M}$ be a quadratic module of $\mathbb{R}[\mathbf{x}]$. $\mathcal{M}$ is said to be Archimedean if there exists some $a > 0$ such that $a - \|\mathbf{x}\|^2 \in \mathcal{M}$. Furthermore, if $\mathcal{M}(\overline{p})$ is Archimedean, we say that the semialgebraic set S as defined in Eq. (1) is of the Archimedean form.*

Theorem 1 (Putinar's Positivstellensatz [36]). *Let $\overline{p} := \{p_1, \ldots, p_m\}$ and S be defined in Eq. (1). Assume that the quadratic module $\mathcal{M}(\overline{p})$ is Archimedean. If $f(\mathbf{x}) > 0$ over S, then $f \in \mathcal{M}(\overline{p})$.*

The above theorem serves as a key result in real algebraic geometry, as it provides a simple characterization of polynomials that are locally positive on closed basic semialgebraic sets. Because of this, Theorem 1 is widely used in the field of polynomial optimization, referring to [25,30] for an in-depth treatment of this topic.

Though powerful, Theorem 1 relies on the Archimedean condition. Note that the inclusion $a - \|\mathbf{x}\|^2 \in \mathcal{M}$ implies that $a - \|\mathbf{x}\|^2 \geq 0$ over S, deducing that S is contained in a ball with radius $\sqrt{a}$. As a result, in case that the set S is unbounded, Theorem 1 is not directly applicable.

2.2 Homogenization

Let $\mathbf{x} = (x_1, \ldots, x_r) \in \mathbb{R}^r$ be an r-tuple of variables and x_0 a fresh variable. Suppose that $f(\mathbf{x}) \in \mathbb{R}[\mathbf{x}]$ is a polynomial of degree d_f. We denote by $\tilde{f}(x_0, \mathbf{x}) \in \mathbb{R}[x_0, \mathbf{x}]$ the homogenization of $f(\mathbf{x})$ which is obtained by substituting $\frac{x_1}{x_0}$ for x_1, ..., $\frac{x_r}{x_0}$ for x_r in $f(\mathbf{x})$ and then multiplying with $x_0^{d_f}$, that is,

$$\tilde{f}(x_0, \mathbf{x}) := x_0^{d_f} f(\frac{x_1}{x_0}, \ldots, \frac{x_r}{x_0}). \tag{2}$$

For example, if $f(\mathbf{x}) = x_1^3 + 2x_1x_2 + 3x_2 + 4$, then $\tilde{f}(x_0, \mathbf{x}) = x_1^3 + 2x_0x_1x_2 + 3x_0^2x_2 + 4x_0^3$. In what follows, we always use the variable x_0 as the homogenizing variable.

Let S be defined as in Eq. (1). We define the following set related to S by homogenizing polynomials in the description of S:

$$\tilde{S}^h := \{(x_0, \mathbf{x}) \in \mathbb{R}^{r+1} \mid \tilde{p}_1(x_0, \mathbf{x}) \geq 0, \ldots, \tilde{p}_m(x_0, \mathbf{x}) \geq 0, x_0 > 0, x_0^2 + \|\mathbf{x}\|^2 = 1\}. \tag{3}$$

Obviously, the following property holds.

Property 1. *Let S be as in Eq. (1) and $\tilde{S}^h$ be defined as above. Then, $\mathbf{x} \in S$ if and only if*

$$\left(\frac{1}{\sqrt{1 + \|\mathbf{x}\|^2}}, \frac{x_1}{\sqrt{1 + \|\mathbf{x}\|^2}}, \ldots, \frac{x_r}{\sqrt{1 + \|\mathbf{x}\|^2}} \right) \in \tilde{S}^h.$$

Moreover, $(x_0, \mathbf{x}) \in \tilde{S}^h$ if and only if $(\frac{x_1}{\sqrt{1-\|\mathbf{x}\|^2}}, \ldots, \frac{x_r}{\sqrt{1-\|\mathbf{x}\|^2}}) \in S$.

Property 1 shows that there exists a one-to-one correspondence between points in $S \in \mathbb{R}^n$ and those in $\tilde{S}^h \in \mathbb{R}^{n+1}$.

We also define the set $\tilde{S}$ by replacing $x_0 > 0$ in Eq. (3) with $x_0 \geq 0$:

$$\tilde{S} := \{(x_0, \mathbf{x}) \in \mathbb{R}^{r+1} \mid \tilde{p}_1(x_0, \mathbf{x}) \geq 0, \ldots, \tilde{p}_m(x_0, \mathbf{x}) \geq 0, x_0 \geq 0, x_0^2 + \|\mathbf{x}\|^2 = 1\}. \tag{4}$$

To capture the relation between $\tilde{S}^h$ and $\tilde{S}$, we introduce the following definition and a related useful lemma.

Definition 4. *A closed basic semialgebraic set S is closed at ∞ if* $\mathrm{cl}(\tilde{S}^h) = \tilde{S}$.

Lemma 1 ([17])**.** *Let $f \in \mathbb{R}[\mathbf{x}]$ and S be a closed basic semialgebraic set. Then $f \geq 0$ on S if and only if $\tilde{f} \geq 0$ on $\mathrm{cl}(\tilde{S}^h)$. Moreover, assuming that S is closed at ∞, then $f \geq 0$ on S if and only if $\tilde{f} \geq 0$ on $\tilde{S}$.*

Let us define

$$S^{(\infty)} := \{\mathbf{x} \in \mathbb{R}^r \mid p_1^{(\infty)}(\mathbf{x}) \geq 0, \ldots, p_m^{(\infty)}(\mathbf{x}) \geq 0, \|\mathbf{x}\|^2 = 1\}, \tag{5}$$

where $p^{(\infty)}(\mathbf{x})$ denotes the highest degree homogeneous part of a polynomial $p(\mathbf{x}) \in \mathbb{R}[\mathbf{x}]$, e.g., if $p = x_1^2 + 2x_1 x_2 + 3x_2^2 + 4x_1 + 5x_2$, then $p^{(\infty)} = x_1^2 + 2x_1 x_2 + 3x_2^2$.

Property 2. *Let $\tilde{S}^h$, $\tilde{S}$ and $S^{(\infty)}$ be defined as above. If $S^{(\infty)}$ is empty, then $\tilde{S}^h = \tilde{S}$.*

2.3   Problem Description

Given two formulas ϕ and ψ in a first-order theory $\mathcal{T}$ s.t. $\phi \models \psi$, Craig showed that there always exists an *interpolant* I over the common symbols of ϕ and ψ s.t. $\phi \models I$ and $I \models \psi$. In the context of verification, we slightly abuse the terminology following [32]: A *reverse interpolant* (as coined in [22]) I over the common symbols of ϕ and ψ is defined as follows.

Definition 5 (Interpolant). *Given two formulas ϕ and ψ in a theory $\mathcal{T}$ s.t. $\phi \wedge \psi \models_{\mathcal{T}} \perp$, a formula I is an interpolant of ϕ and ψ if (1) $\phi \models_{\mathcal{T}} I$; (2) $I \wedge \psi \models_{\mathcal{T}} \perp$; and (3) I only contains common symbols and free variables shared by ϕ and ψ.*

The interpolant synthesis problem of interest in this paper is formulated as follows.

Problem 1. Let $\phi(\mathbf{x}, \mathbf{y})$ and $\psi(\mathbf{x}, \mathbf{z})$ be two polynomial formulas of the form

$$\phi(\mathbf{x}, \mathbf{y}) := \bigvee_{k=1}^{K_\phi} \bigwedge_{i=1}^{m_k} f_{k,i}(\mathbf{x}, \mathbf{y}) \geq 0, \tag{6}$$

$$\psi(\mathbf{x}, \mathbf{z}) := \bigvee_{k'=1}^{K_\psi} \bigwedge_{j=1}^{n_{k'}} g_{k',j}(\mathbf{x}, \mathbf{z}) \geq 0, \tag{7}$$

where $\mathbf{x} \in \mathbb{R}^{r_1}$, $\mathbf{y} \in \mathbb{R}^{r_2}$, $\mathbf{z} \in \mathbb{R}^{r_3}$ are variable vectors, $r_1, r_2, r_3 \in \mathbb{N}$, and $f_{k,i}, g_{k',j}$ are polynomials in the corresponding variables. We aim to find a function $h(\mathbf{x})$ such that $h(\mathbf{x}) > 0$ is an interpolant for ϕ and ψ, i.e.,

$$\phi(\mathbf{x}, \mathbf{y}) \models h(\mathbf{x}) > 0 \text{ and } \psi(\mathbf{x}, \mathbf{z}) \models h(\mathbf{x}) < 0.$$

Here $h(\mathbf{x})$ is called an interpolant function. Specifically, we are interested in two scenarios where

1. **Polynomial interpolants**: the function $h(\mathbf{x})$ is a polynomial in $\mathbb{R}[\mathbf{x}]$;
2. **Semialgebraic interpolants**[1]: the function $h(\mathbf{x})$ can be expressed as

$$h(\mathbf{x}) = h_1(\mathbf{x}) + \sqrt{\|\mathbf{x}\|^2 + 1} \cdot h_2(\mathbf{x}), \tag{8}$$

with $h_1(\mathbf{x}), h_2(\mathbf{x}) \in \mathbb{R}[\mathbf{x}]$.

Obviously, the second case degenerates to the first case when $h_2(\mathbf{x}) = 0$.

Remark 1. Like in [11,12], we require ϕ and ψ to be defined by *non-strict* polynomial inequalities, mainly for two reasons: (1) Theoretically, our approach relies on Theorem 1, which necessitates a closed underlying basic semialgebraic set. (2) Numerically, we employ numerical solvers incapable of distinguishing $\geq$ from $>$. In the coming sections, we will see the significance of both closedness and closedness at ∞ for the existence of interpolants.

3   Existence of Interpolant

In this section, we prove the existence of a semialgebraic interpolant function $h(\mathbf{x})$ of the form Eq. (8), under certain conditions on ϕ and ψ. In Sect. 3.1, we begin by focusing on the scenario where both ϕ and ψ exclusively involve the variable $\mathbf{x}$. Subsequently, in Sect. 3.2, we expand our scope to the case where unshared variables, $\mathbf{y}$ and $\mathbf{z}$, emerge.

3.1   Interpolant Between $\phi(\mathbf{x})$ and $\psi(\mathbf{x})$

In this part, we prove the existence of a semialgebraic interpolant function of the form in Eq. (8) that separates the two closed semialgebraic sets in $\mathbb{R}^r$ corresponding to $\phi(\mathbf{x})$ and $\psi(\mathbf{x})$. The basic idea goes as follows: First, we consider the problem of finding a semialgebraic function $h(\mathbf{x})$ such that $h(\mathbf{x}) = 0$ separates two closed basic semialgebraic sets S_1 and S_2 in $\mathbb{R}^r$. Using the homogenization technique, we prove that there exists a polynomial $g \in \mathbb{R}[x_0, \mathbf{x}]$ with $g(x_0, \mathbf{x}) = 0$ separating $\tilde{S}_1$ and $\tilde{S}_2$, and the existence of $h(\mathbf{x})$ is directly induced by that of g (see Proposition 2). After that, we extend the result to the case where S_1 becomes a closed semialgebraic set (see Lemma 3) and when both S_1 and S_2 are closed semialgebraic sets (see Theorem 2).

We begin by recapping an existing result from [11].

---

[1] A function $f(\mathbf{x})$ is called semialgebraic if its graph $\{(\mathbf{x}, f(\mathbf{x})) \mid \mathbf{x} \in \mathbb{R}^r\}$ is a semialgebraic set. The graph of $h(\mathbf{x})$ is $\{\mathbf{x} \in \mathbb{R}^r \mid \exists w. \, h(\mathbf{x}) = h_1(\mathbf{x}) + w \cdot h_2(\mathbf{x}) \wedge w^2 = 1 + \|\mathbf{x}\|^2 \wedge w \geq 0\}$.

Proposition 1 ([11, **Lemma 2**]). *Let* $S_1 = \{\mathbf{x} \in \mathbb{R}^r \mid p_1(\mathbf{x}) \geq 0, \ldots, p_m(\mathbf{x}) \geq 0\}$, $S_2 = \{\mathbf{x} \in \mathbb{R}^r \mid q_1(\mathbf{x}) \geq 0, \ldots, q_n(\mathbf{x}) \geq 0\}$ *be two closed basic semialgebraic sets of the Archimedean form. Assuming that $S_1 \cap S_2 = \emptyset$, then there exists a polynomial $h(\mathbf{x}) \in \mathbb{R}[\mathbf{x}]$ such that*

$$\forall \mathbf{x} \in S_1. \ h(\mathbf{x}) > 0 \ and \ \forall \mathbf{x} \in S_2. \ -h(\mathbf{x}) > 0. \tag{9}$$

It is important to emphasize that the proof of Proposition 1 relies on Theorem 1 and hence is limited to the case where the sets S_1 and S_2 are of the Archimedean form. In the following Proposition 2, we show how to remove this restriction.

Proposition 2. *Let* $S_1 = \{\mathbf{x} \in \mathbb{R}^r \mid p_1(\mathbf{x}) \geq 0, \ldots, p_m(\mathbf{x}) \geq 0\}$, $S_2 = \{\mathbf{x} \in \mathbb{R}^r \mid q_1(\mathbf{x}) \geq 0, \ldots, q_n(\mathbf{x}) \geq 0\}$ *be closed basic semialgebraic sets. Assuming that $\tilde{S}_1 \cap \tilde{S}_2 = \emptyset$, then there exists a semialgebraic function $h(\mathbf{x})$ of the form in Eq. (8) such that*

$$\forall \mathbf{x} \in S_1. \ h(\mathbf{x}) > 0 \ and \ \forall \mathbf{x} \in S_2. \ -h(\mathbf{x}) > 0. \tag{10}$$

Proof. By the definition of $\tilde{S}$ in Eq. (4), we know that $\tilde{S}_1$ and $\tilde{S}_2$ are two basic semialgebraic sets of the Archimedean form (as $1 - x_0^2 - \|\mathbf{x}\|^2$ belongs to the corresponding quadratic modules). Since $\tilde{S}_1 \cap \tilde{S}_2 = \emptyset$, by invoking Proposition 1, there exists a polynomial $g \in \mathbb{R}[x_0, \mathbf{x}]$ such that

$$\forall (x_0, \mathbf{x}) \in \tilde{S}_1. \ g(x_0, \mathbf{x}) > 0 \ and \ \forall (x_0, \mathbf{x}) \in \tilde{S}_2. \ -g(x_0, \mathbf{x}) > 0. \tag{11}$$

Note that for any $\mathbf{x} \in S_1$ (resp. S_2), by Property 1 we have $\left(\frac{1}{\sqrt{\|\mathbf{x}\|^2+1}}, \frac{\mathbf{x}}{\sqrt{\|\mathbf{x}\|^2+1}}\right) \in \tilde{S}_1$ (resp. $\tilde{S}_2$). Let

$$h(\mathbf{x}) := (\sqrt{\|\mathbf{x}\|^2 + 1})^{\deg(g)} g\left(\frac{1}{\sqrt{\|\mathbf{x}\|^2 + 1}}, \frac{\mathbf{x}}{\sqrt{\|\mathbf{x}\|^2 + 1}}\right). \tag{12}$$

Since $(\sqrt{\|\mathbf{x}\|^2 + 1})^{\deg(g)} \geq 1$, combining with Eq. (11), we have that $h(\mathbf{x})$ satisfies Eq. (10).

To see that $h(\mathbf{x})$ admits the form in Eq. (8), we expand the right-hand side of Eq. (12) and simplify the terms with power of $\sqrt{\|\mathbf{x}\|^2 + 1}$ greater than or equal to 2. After simplification, we collect the terms with and without $\sqrt{\|\mathbf{x}\|^2 + 1}$ into two groups so that $h(\mathbf{x})$ can be expressed as $h_1(\mathbf{x}) + \sqrt{\|\mathbf{x}\|^2 + 1} \cdot h_2(\mathbf{x})$ for $h_1(\mathbf{x}), h_2(\mathbf{x}) \in \mathbb{R}[\mathbf{x}]$. $\square$

In order to check whether the condition $\tilde{S}_1 \cap \tilde{S}_2 = \emptyset$ in Proposition 2 holds, one can use the following lemma.

Lemma 2. *Given two closed basic semialgebraic set S_1 and S_2, if $S_1 \cap S_2 = \emptyset$ and $S_1^{(\infty)} \cap S_2^{(\infty)} = \emptyset$, then $\tilde{S}_1 \cap \tilde{S}_2 = \emptyset$.*

Now, we extend the result in Proposition 2 to the case when S_1 and S_2 are two closed semialgebraic sets. A closed semialgebraic set, say T, is a union of some closed basic semialgebraic sets, i.e., $T = \cup_{i=1}^a S_i$ with

$$S_i = \{\mathbf{x} \in \mathbb{R}^r \mid p_{i1}(\mathbf{x}) \geq 0, \ldots, p_{im_i}(\mathbf{x}) \geq 0\}, \quad i = 1, \ldots, a,$$

where $p_{ik}(\mathbf{x}) \in \mathbb{R}[\mathbf{x}]$, $m_i \in \mathbb{N}$, $k = 1, ..., m_i$, $i = 1, ..., a$. Mirroring the definition of $S^{(\infty)}$ and $\tilde{S}$, we define $T^{(\infty)} := \bigcup_{i=1}^{a} S_i^{(\infty)}$ and $\tilde{T} := \bigcup_{i=1}^{a} \tilde{S}_i$. In the following lemma, we deal with the case when S_1 in Proposition 2 becomes a union of closed basic semialgebraic sets.

Lemma 3. *Let* $T_1 = \cup_{i=1}^{a} S_i$ *be a closed semialgebraic set with* $S_i = \{\mathbf{x} \in \mathbb{R}^r \mid p_{i1}(\mathbf{x}) \geq 0, ..., p_{im_i}(\mathbf{x}) \geq 0\}$, *and let* $T_2 = \{\mathbf{x} \in \mathbb{R}^r \mid q_1(\mathbf{x}) \geq 0, ..., q_n(\mathbf{x}) \geq 0\}$ *be a closed basic semialgebraic set. Assume that* $\tilde{T}_1 \cap \tilde{T}_2 = \emptyset$. *Then there exists a polynomial* $g \in \mathbb{R}[x_0, \mathbf{x}]$ *such that*

$$\forall (x_0, \mathbf{x}) \in \tilde{T}_1. \; g(x_0, \mathbf{x}) > 0 \; and \; \forall (x_0, \mathbf{x}) \in \tilde{T}_2. \; -g(x_0, \mathbf{x}) > 0. \tag{13}$$

Then, we use Lemma 3 to prove the case where both sets are unions of closed basic semialgebraic sets.

Theorem 2. *Let* $T_1 = \cup_{i=1}^{a} S_i$ *and* $T_2 = \cup_{j=1}^{b} S_j'$ *be closed semialgebraic sets, where* S_i *and* S_j' *are closed basic semialgebraic sets for* $i = 1, ..., a, j = 1, ..., b$. *Assume* $\tilde{T}_1 \cap \tilde{T}_2 = \emptyset$. *Then there exists a semialgebraic function* $h(\mathbf{x})$ *of the form in Eq.* (8) *such that*

$$\forall \mathbf{x} \in T_1. \; h(\mathbf{x}) > 0 \; and \; \forall \mathbf{x} \in T_2. \; -h(\mathbf{x}) > 0. \tag{14}$$

Similarly to Lemma 2, the condition $\tilde{T}_1 \cap \tilde{T}_2 = \emptyset$ can be verified by checking whether $T_1 \cap T_2 = \emptyset$ and $T_1^{(\infty)} \cap T_2^{(\infty)} = \emptyset$. As a direct inference of Theorem 2, we know that there exists a semialgebraic function $h(\mathbf{x})$ of the form in Eq. (8) such that $h(\mathbf{x}) > 0$ is an interpolant of $\phi(\mathbf{x})$ and $\psi(\mathbf{x})$.

3.2   Interpolant Between $\phi(\mathbf{x}, \mathbf{y})$ and $\psi(\mathbf{x}, \mathbf{z})$

Let $\phi(\mathbf{x}, \mathbf{y})$ and $\psi(\mathbf{x}, \mathbf{z})$ be given in Problem 1. We denote by $T_\phi \subseteq \mathbb{R}^{r_1 + r_2}$ and $T_\psi \subseteq \mathbb{R}^{r_1 + r_3}$ the semialgebraic sets corresponding to ϕ and ψ, i.e.,

$$T_\phi := \bigcup_{k=1}^{K_\phi} S_k, \; \text{with} \; S_k := \{(\mathbf{x}, \mathbf{y}) \in \mathbb{R}^{r_1 + r_2} \mid \bigwedge_{i=1}^{m_k} f_{k,i}(\mathbf{x}, \mathbf{y}) \geq 0\}, \tag{15}$$

$$T_\psi := \bigcup_{k'=1}^{K_\psi} S_{k'}', \; \text{with} \; S_{k'}' := \{(\mathbf{x}, \mathbf{z}) \in \mathbb{R}^{r_1 + r_3} \mid \bigwedge_{j=1}^{n_{k'}} g_{k',j}(\mathbf{x}, \mathbf{z}) \geq 0\}. \tag{16}$$

Since an interpolant contains only common symbols of ϕ and ψ, Problem 1 can be reduced to finding a function $h(\mathbf{x})$ such that $h(\mathbf{x}) = 0$ separates the two projection sets $P_\mathbf{x}(T_\phi) := \{\mathbf{x} \in \mathbb{R}^{r_1} \mid \exists \mathbf{y}. (\mathbf{x}, \mathbf{y}) \in T_\phi\}$ and $P_\mathbf{x}(T_\psi) := \{\mathbf{x} \in \mathbb{R}^{r_1} \mid \exists \mathbf{z}. (\mathbf{x}, \mathbf{z}) \in T_\psi\}$. We have the following theorem as a direct consequence of Theorem 2.

Theorem 3. *Let $\phi(\mathbf{x}, \mathbf{y})$ and $\psi(\mathbf{x}, \mathbf{z})$ be defined in Problem 1, and let $P_{\mathbf{x}}(T_\phi)$ and $P_{\mathbf{x}}(T_\psi)$ be defined above. Let $T_1 = \mathrm{cl}(P_{\mathbf{x}}(T_\phi))$ and $T_2 = \mathrm{cl}(P_{\mathbf{x}}(T_\psi))$. Assume $\tilde{T}_1 \cap \tilde{T}_2 = \emptyset$. Then there exists a semialgebraic function $h(\mathbf{x})$ of the form in Eq. (8) such that*

$$\forall \mathbf{x} \in P_{\mathbf{x}}(T_\phi).\ h(\mathbf{x}) > 0 \ and \ \forall \mathbf{x} \in P_{\mathbf{x}}(T_\psi).\ -h(\mathbf{x}) > 0. \tag{17}$$

As a consequence, $h(\mathbf{x}) > 0$ is a semialgebraic interpolant of $\phi(\mathbf{x}, \mathbf{y})$ and $\psi(\mathbf{x}, \mathbf{z})$.

Remark 2. Note that in Theorem 3, we need to consider the closures $\mathrm{cl}(P_{\mathbf{x}}(T_\phi))$ and $\mathrm{cl}(P_{\mathbf{x}}(T_\psi))$ rather than $P_{\mathbf{x}}(T_\phi)$ and $P_{\mathbf{x}}(T_\psi)$ themselves. The reason lies in that the projections of closed semialgebraic sets are not necessarily closed. For example, consider $\phi(\mathbf{x}, \mathbf{y}) := x_1 x_2 - 1 \geq 0 \wedge x_2 \geq 0$ with $\mathbf{x} = x_1$ and $\mathbf{y} = x_2$. Then $P_{\mathbf{x}}(T_\phi) = \{x_1 \mid x_1 > 0\}$ is an open set.

4 Sum-of-Squares Formulation

In this section, we provide SOS characterizations for polynomial and semialgebraic interpolants. For simplicity, we will focus on the case where ϕ and ψ are conjunctions of polynomial inequalities given by

$$\phi(\mathbf{x}, \mathbf{y}) := \bigwedge_{i=1}^{m} f_i(\mathbf{x}, \mathbf{y}) \geq 0 \ and \ \psi(\mathbf{x}, \mathbf{z}) := \bigwedge_{j=1}^{n} g_j(\mathbf{x}, \mathbf{z}) \geq 0, \tag{18}$$

where $\mathbf{x} \in \mathbb{R}^{r_1}$, $\mathbf{y} \in \mathbb{R}^{r_2}$, and $\mathbf{z} \in \mathbb{R}^{r_3}$. Extending to the general case is straightforward.

4.1 SOS Characterization for Polynomial Interpolants

In this part, we provide an SOS characterization for polynomial interpolants based on homogenization. We prove that the characterization is sound and weakly complete. Furthermore, we provide a concrete example to show that our new characterization is strictly more expressive than the one in [11].

Theorem 4 (Weak Completeness). *Let ϕ, ψ be defined as in Eq. (18) and let S_ϕ, and S_ψ be the basic semialgebraic sets corresponding to ϕ and ψ. Let $\tilde{f}_{m+1} = x_0$, $\tilde{g}_{n+1} = x_0$, $\tilde{f}_{m+2} = x_0^2 + \|\mathbf{x}\|^2 + \|\mathbf{y}\|^2 - 1$, and $\tilde{g}_{n+2} = x_0^2 + \|\mathbf{x}\|^2 + \|\mathbf{z}\|^2 - 1$. If $h(\mathbf{x}) \in \mathbb{R}[\mathbf{x}]$ is a polynomial interpolant function of ϕ and ψ, then the homogenized polynomial $\tilde{h}(x_0, \mathbf{x})$ satisfies, for arbitrarily small $\epsilon > 0$,*

$$\tilde{h}(x_0, \mathbf{x}) + \epsilon = \sigma_0 + \sum_{i=1}^{m+2} \sigma_i \tilde{f}_i(x_0, \mathbf{x}, \mathbf{y}),$$

$$-\tilde{h}(x_0, \mathbf{x}) + \epsilon = \tau_0 + \sum_{j=1}^{n+2} \tau_j \tilde{g}_j(x_0, \mathbf{x}, \mathbf{z}), \tag{19}$$

for some $\sigma_i \in \Sigma[x_0, \mathbf{x}, \mathbf{y}]$, $i = 0, \ldots, m+1$, $\sigma_{m+2} \in \mathbb{R}[x_0, \mathbf{x}, \mathbf{y}]$, $\tau_i \in \Sigma[x_0, \mathbf{x}, \mathbf{z}]$, $i = 0, \ldots, n+1$, $\tau_{n+2} \in \mathbb{R}[x_0, \mathbf{x}, \mathbf{z}]$.

Remark 3. In Eq. (19), we add a small quantity $\epsilon > 0$ to the left-hand sides in order to invoke Theorem 1. The ideal case is $\epsilon = 0$. Fortunately, in most practice circumstances, we can safely set $\epsilon = 0$ when the *finite convergence property* [34, Theorem 1.1] holds. Indeed, the finite convergence property is generically true and is violated only when h and S_ϕ (or S_ψ) are of certain singular forms.

Theorem 5 (Soundness). *Let ϕ and ψ be defined as in Eq. (18). Suppose that $h(\mathbf{x})$ is a polynomial such that its homogenization $\tilde{h}(x_0, \mathbf{x})$ satisfies Eq. (19) with $\epsilon = 0$. Assume $\phi \wedge h(\mathbf{x}) = 0 \models \bot$ and $\psi \wedge h(\mathbf{x}) = 0 \models \bot$. Then $h(\mathbf{x})$ is an interpolant function of ϕ and ψ.*

Now we compare our characterization Eq. (19) with [11, Theorem 5] which states that if S_ϕ and S_ψ are of the Archimedean form, then a polynomial interpolant function $h(\mathbf{x})$ can be expressed as

$$
\begin{aligned}
h(\mathbf{x}) - 1 &= \sigma_0 + \sum_{i=0}^{m} \sigma_i f_i(\mathbf{x}, \mathbf{y}), \\
-h(\mathbf{x}) - 1 &= \tau_0 + \sum_{j=0}^{n} \tau_j g_j(\mathbf{x}, \mathbf{z}),
\end{aligned}
\tag{20}
$$

for some $\sigma_i \in \Sigma[\mathbf{x}, \mathbf{y}]$, $i = 0, \ldots, m$ and $\tau_j \in \Sigma[\mathbf{x}, \mathbf{z}]$, $j = 0, \ldots, n$. Clearly, since Theorem 4 removes the restriction of the Archimedean condition, our characterization is *strictly* more expressive.

Let $M(x_1, x_2) := x_1^4 x_2^2 + x_1^2 x_2^4 - 3x_1^2 x_2^2 + 1$ be the Motzkin polynomial. It is well known that $M(x_1, x_2)$ is nonnegative but is not an SOS.

Proposition 3. *The polynomial $M(x_1, x_2) + 1$ is positive but is not an SOS.*

Example 1. Let $\phi := 1 \geq 0 (= \top)$ and $\psi := -1 \geq 0 (= \bot)$. By Proposition 3, the polynomial $M(x_1, x_2) + 1$ is an interpolant function of ϕ and ψ but does not admit a representation as in Eq. (20), i.e., the program

$$
\begin{aligned}
&\text{find} \quad \sigma_0 \in \Sigma[x_1, x_2] \\
&\text{s.t.} \quad x_1^4 x_2^2 + x_1^2 x_2^4 - 3x_1^2 x_2^2 + 2 = \sigma_0
\end{aligned}
$$

is not feasible. However, a numerical solution to the following program:

$$
\begin{aligned}
&\text{find} \quad \sigma_0, \sigma_1 \in \Sigma[x_0, x_1, x_2], \sigma_2 \in \mathbb{R}[x_0, x_1, x_2] \\
&\text{s.t.} \quad x_1^4 x_2^2 + x_1^2 x_2^4 - 3x_1^2 x_2^2 x_0^2 + 2x_0^6 = \sigma_0 + \sigma_1 x_0 + \sigma_2 (1 - x_0^2 - x_1^2 - x_2^2).
\end{aligned}
$$

can be obtained by employing the Julia package TSSOS [28] and the SDP solver MOSEK [2]. Therefore, the polynomial $M(x_1, x_2) + 1$ admits a representation as in Eq. (19) with $\epsilon = 0$.

4.2   SOS Characterization for Semialgebraic Interpolants

Let $h(\mathbf{x})$ be a semialgebraic interpolant function of the form in Eq. (8) and let w be a fresh variable. Though $h(\mathbf{x})$ is not a polynomial, it can be equivalently represented by a polynomial $l(\mathbf{x}, w) = h_1(\mathbf{x}) + w \cdot h_2(\mathbf{x}) \in \mathbb{R}[\mathbf{x}, w]$ with additional polynomial constraints $w^2 = 1 + \|\mathbf{x}\|^2$ and $w \geq 0$. Adopting this idea, we have the following completeness theorem. The soundness result for the semialgebraic case is omitted, as it is essentially the same as Theorem 5.

Theorem 6 (Completeness). *Let ϕ, ψ be defined as in Eq. (18) and let S_ϕ, and S_ψ be the basic semialgebraic sets corresponding to ϕ and ψ. Let $S_1 = \mathrm{cl}(\mathrm{P}_\mathbf{x}(S_\phi))$, $S_2 = \mathrm{cl}(\mathrm{P}_\mathbf{x}(S_\psi))$, $\tilde{f}_{m+1} = \tilde{g}_{n+1} = x_0$, $\tilde{f}_{m+2} = \tilde{g}_{m+2} = w$, $\tilde{f}_{m+3} = x_0^2 + \|\mathbf{x}\|^2 + w^2 + \|\mathbf{y}\|^2 - 1$, and $\tilde{g}_{n+3} = x_0^2 + \|\mathbf{x}\|^2 + w^2 + \|\mathbf{z}\|^2 - 1$, $\tilde{f}_{m+4} = \tilde{g}_{n+4} = x_0^2 + \|\mathbf{x}\|^2 - w^2$. Assume that the following two conditions hold: (1) $\tilde{S}_1 \cap \tilde{S}_2 = \emptyset$; (2) S_ϕ and S_ψ are closed at ∞. Then there exists a semialgebraic interpolant function $h(\mathbf{x})$ of the form in Eq. (8) such that the polynomial $l(\mathbf{x}, w) = h_1(\mathbf{x}) + w \cdot h_2(\mathbf{x}) \in \mathbb{R}[\mathbf{x}, w]$ satisfies, for arbitrarily small $\epsilon > 0$,*

$$
\begin{aligned}
\tilde{l}(x_0, \mathbf{x}, w) + \epsilon &= \sigma_0 + \sum_{i=1}^{m+4} \sigma_i \tilde{f}_i(x_0, \mathbf{x}, \mathbf{y}), \\
-\tilde{l}(x_0, \mathbf{x}, w) + \epsilon &= \tau_0 + \sum_{j=1}^{n+4} \tau_j \tilde{g}_j(x_0, \mathbf{x}, \mathbf{z}),
\end{aligned}
\tag{21}
$$

for some $\sigma_i \in \Sigma[x_0, \mathbf{x}, \mathbf{y}, w]$, $i = 0, \ldots, m+2$, $\sigma_{m+3}, \sigma_{m+4} \in \mathbb{R}[x_0, \mathbf{x}, \mathbf{y}, w]$, $\tau_i \in \Sigma[x_0, \mathbf{x}, \mathbf{z}, w]$, $i = 0, \ldots, n+2$, $\tau_{n+3}, \tau_{n+4} \in \mathbb{R}[x_0, \mathbf{x}, \mathbf{z}, w]$.

We want to emphasize that Theorem 6 is a stronger result than Theorem 4, in the sense that Theorem 6 guarantees the existence of a semialgebraic interpolant (as per Theorem 3), which is not the case for polynomial interpolants in Theorem 4.

5   Synthesizing Interpolant via SOS Programming

In this section, we propose an SOS programming procedure to synthesize polynomial and semialgebraic interpolants. Concrete examples are provided to demonstrate the effectiveness and efficiency of our method. For all examples, existing approaches [7,10,12] are not applicable due to their restrictions on formulas, and the method in [11] also fails to produce interpolants of specified degrees.

Synthesizing Polynomial Interpolants: Let T_ϕ, T_ψ, S_k, and $S_{k'}$ be defined as in Eq. (15) and Eq. (16). By treating S_k and S'_k respectively as S_ϕ and S_ψ in Theorem 4, the problem of synthesizing a polynomial interpolant for ϕ and ψ is reduced to solving the following SOS program:

$$
\begin{cases}
\text{find} \quad h(\mathbf{x}) \\
\text{s.t.} \quad \tilde{h}(x_0, \mathbf{x}) = \sigma_{k,0} + \sum_{i=1}^{m_k+2} \sigma_{k,i} \tilde{f}_{k,i} \quad \text{for } k = 1, \dots, K_\phi, \\
\qquad -\tilde{h}(x_0, \mathbf{x}) = \tau_{k',0} + \sum_{j=1}^{n_{k'}+2} \tau_{k',j} \tilde{g}_{k',j} \quad \text{for } k' = 1, \dots, K_\psi, \\
\qquad \sigma_{k,0}, \dots, \sigma_{k,m+1} \in \Sigma[x_0, \mathbf{x}, \mathbf{y}], \sigma_{k,m+2} \in \mathbb{R}[x_0, \mathbf{x}, \mathbf{y}], \\
\qquad\quad \text{for } k = 1, \dots, K_\phi, \\
\qquad \tau_{k',0}, \dots, \tau_{k',n+1} \in \Sigma[x_0, \mathbf{x}, \mathbf{z}], \tau_{k',n+2} \in \mathbb{R}[x_0, \mathbf{x}, \mathbf{y}], \\
\qquad\quad \text{for } k = 1, \dots, K_\psi,
\end{cases}
\tag{22}
$$

where $\tilde{f}_{k,m+1} = \tilde{g}_{k',n+1} = x_0$, $\tilde{f}_{k,m+2} = x_0^2 + \|\mathbf{x}\|^2 + \|\mathbf{y}\|^2 - 1$, $\tilde{g}_{k',n+2} = x_0^2 + \|\mathbf{x}\|^2 + \|\mathbf{z}\|^2 - 1$ for $k = 1, \dots, K_\phi$ and $k' = 1, \dots, K_\psi$.

As Theorem 5 suggests, a solution $h(\mathbf{x})$ to the above program only ensures that $\phi \models h(\mathbf{x}) \geq 0$ and $\psi \models -h(\mathbf{x}) \leq 0$. Nevertheless, since numerical solvers are unable to distinguish $\geq$ from $>$, the equalities are usually not attainable for a numerical solution[2]. Therefore, we can view the SOS program Eq. (22) as a sound approach for computing $h(\mathbf{x})$, while completeness follows from verifying the conditions discussed in Remark 3.

In practice, we solve the program Eq. (22) by solving a sequence of SDP relaxations which are obtained by restricting the highest degree of involved polynomials. Concretely speaking, suppose that we would like to find a polynomial interpolant function $h(\mathbf{x})$ of degree d, we set the template of $h(\mathbf{x})$ to be $h(\mathbf{x}) = \sum_{|\alpha| \leq d} c_\alpha \mathbf{x}^\alpha$, where $\alpha = (\alpha_1, \dots, \alpha_{r_1}) \in \mathbb{N}^{r_1}$, $|\alpha| = \alpha_1 + \cdots \alpha_{r_1}$, and $c_\alpha \in \mathbb{R}$ are coefficients to be determined. Then, the homogenization of $h(\mathbf{x})$ is $\tilde{h}(x_0, \mathbf{x}) = \sum_{|\alpha| \leq d} c_\alpha x_0^{d-|\alpha|} \mathbf{x}^\alpha$.

Given a relaxation order $s \in \mathbb{N}$ with $2s \geq d$, we set the degrees of the remaining unknown polynomials σ_i, τ_j appropriately to ensure that the maximum degree of polynomials involved in Eq. (22) equals $2s$. We refer to the resulting program as the s-th relaxation of Eq. (22), which can be translated into an SDP and can be numerically solved in polynomial time. If the s-th relaxation is solvable, it yields a solution $h(\mathbf{x})$ that serves as a polynomial interpolant function of ϕ and ψ. If it is not solvable, we then increase the relaxation order s to obtain a tighter relaxation, or alternatively, we can increase the degree d of $h(\mathbf{x})$ to search for interpolants of higher degree.

In the following, all experiments were conducted on a Mac lap-top with Apple M2 chip and 8GB memory. We use the Julia package TSSOS [28] to formulate SOS programs and rely on the SDP solver MOSEK [2] to solve them. All numerical results are symbolically verified using MATHEMATICA to be real interpolants.

---

[2] For example, SDP solvers based on interior-point methods typically return strictly feasible solutions.

Example 2 (adapted from [4]). Let $\mathbf{x} = (x, y)$ and $\mathbf{y} = \mathbf{z} = \emptyset$, i.e., there is no uncommon variables. We define the following polynomials:

$$f_1 = 11 - x^4 + 0.1y^4, \qquad\qquad f_2 = y^3,$$
$$f_3 = 0.9025 - (x - 1)^4 - y^4, \qquad f_4 = (x - 1)^4 + y^4 - 0.09,$$
$$f_5 = (x + 1)^4 + y^4 - 1.1025, \qquad f_6 = 0.04 - (x + 1)^4 - y^4,$$
$$g_1 = 11 - x^4 + 0.1y^4, \qquad\qquad g_2 = -y^3,$$
$$g_3 = 0.9025 - (x + 1)^4 - y^4, \qquad g_4 = (x + 1)^4 + y^4 - 0.09,$$
$$g_5 = (x - 1)^4 + y^4 - 1.1025, \qquad g_6 = 0.04 - (x - 1)^4 - y^4.$$

Let ϕ and ψ be defined by

$$\phi := (f_1 \geq 0 \wedge f_2 \geq 0 \wedge f_4 \geq 0 \wedge f_5 \geq 0) \vee (f_3 \geq 0 \wedge f_4 \geq 0 \wedge f_5 \geq 0) \vee (f_6 \geq 0),$$
$$\psi := (g_1 \geq 0 \wedge g_2 \geq 0 \wedge g_4 \geq 0 \wedge g_5 \geq 0) \vee (g_3 \geq 0 \wedge g_4 \geq 0 \wedge g_5 \geq 0) \vee (g_6 \geq 0).$$

Set the degree of the polynomial interpolation function $h(x, y)$ to 7. It takes 0.16 s to solve the 4-th relaxation Eq. (22), yielding the solution

$$h(x, y) = -0.00153942y + 0.03053692x + \cdots + 0.06109453x^6y + 0.01643640x^7,$$

where the coefficients have been scaled so that the largest absolute value is 1.

Synthesizing Semialgebraic Interpolants: Similarly, the synthesis of a semialgebraic interpolant is reduced to solving the following SOS program:

$$\begin{cases} \text{find} \quad h_1(\mathbf{x}), h_2(\mathbf{x}) \\ \text{s.t.} \quad l(\mathbf{x}, w) = h_1(\mathbf{x}) + w \cdot h_2(\mathbf{x}), \\ \qquad \tilde{l}(x_0, \mathbf{x}, w) = \sigma_{k,0} + \sum_{i=1}^{m_k+4} \sigma_{k,i} \tilde{f}_{k,i} \quad \text{for } k = 1, \ldots, K_\phi, \\ \qquad -\tilde{l}(x_0, \mathbf{x}, w) = \tau_{k',0} + \sum_{j=1}^{n_{k'}+4} \tau_{k',j} \tilde{g}_{k',j} \quad \text{for } k' = 1, \ldots, K_\psi, \qquad (23) \\ \qquad \sigma_{k,0}, \ldots, \sigma_{k,m+2} \in \Sigma[x_0, \mathbf{x}, \mathbf{y}], \sigma_{k,m+3}, \sigma_{k,m+4} \in \mathbb{R}[x_0, \mathbf{x}, \mathbf{y}], \\ \qquad\qquad \text{for } k = 1, \ldots, K_\phi, \\ \qquad \tau_{k',0}, \ldots, \tau_{k',n+2} \in \Sigma[x_0, \mathbf{x}, \mathbf{z}], \tau_{k',n+3}, \tau_{k',n+4} \in \mathbb{R}[x_0, \mathbf{x}, \mathbf{y}], \\ \qquad\qquad \text{for } k = 1, \ldots, K_\psi, \end{cases}$$

where $\tilde{f}_{k,m+1} = \tilde{g}_{k',n+1} = x_0$, $\tilde{f}_{k,m+2} = \tilde{g}_{k',n+2} = w$, $\tilde{f}_{k,m+3} = x_0^2 + \|\mathbf{x}\|^2 + w^2 + \|\mathbf{y}\|^2 - 1$, $\tilde{g}_{k',n+3} = x_0^2 + \|\mathbf{x}\|^2 + w^2 + \|\mathbf{z}\|^2 - 1$, $\tilde{f}_{k,m+4} = \tilde{g}_{k',n+4} = x_0^2 + \|\mathbf{x}\|^2 - w^2$, for $k = 1, \ldots, K_\phi$ and $k' = 1, \ldots, K_\psi$.

By Theorem 6, if a feasible solution (h_1, h_2) of Eq. (23) is found, then $h(\mathbf{x}) = h_1(\mathbf{x}) + \sqrt{\|\mathbf{x}\|^2 + 1} \cdot h_2(\mathbf{x})$ is a semialgebraic interpolant function for ϕ and ψ. In practice, w.l.o.g., we can assume that h_1 and h_2 are of the same degree d and solve SDP relaxations of Eq. (23). The soundness result is similar to that of Eq. (22), requiring that $h(\mathbf{x}) = 0$ is not attainable over T_ϕ and T_ψ.

Example 3. Let $\mathbf{x} = (x, y)$, $\mathbf{y} = \mathbf{z} = \emptyset$. We define

$$\phi(x,y) = 8xy - (x^2 - y^3)^2 \geq 0 \wedge x^2 + y^2 - 1 \geq 0,$$
$$\psi(x,y) = -12.5xy - (x^2 + y^2)^2 \geq 0 \wedge x^2 + y^2 - 1 \geq 0.$$

Let the degree of $h_1(\mathbf{x})$ and $h_2(\mathbf{x})$ to be 3, a solution to the 2-th relaxation of Eq. (23) is found in 0.02 s:

$$h_1 = -0.04402209 - 0.00093184y + 0.01446436x + \cdots - 0.03703461x^3,$$
$$h_2 = 0.05644318 - 0.01305178y + 0.02407258x + \cdots + 0.23199837x^2.$$

As a comparison, solving Eq. (22) fails to produce a polynomial interpolant function of degree 3, but succeeds at degree 4.

Example 4. Let $\mathbf{x} = (x, y, z)$, $\mathbf{y} = \emptyset$, and $\mathbf{z} = (r, R)$. We define

$$\phi(x,y,z) := 1 + 0.1z^4 - x^4 - y^4 \geq 0 \wedge 10z^4 - x^4 - y^4 \geq 0,$$
$$\psi(x,y,z,r,R) := 4R^2(x^2 + y^2) - (x^2 + y^2 + z^2 + R^2 - r^2)^2 \geq 0$$
$$\wedge\, 6 \geq R \geq 4 \wedge 1 \geq r \geq 0.5,$$

where $\exists r, \exists R.\ \psi(x, y, z, r, R)$ describes the set of interior points of a 3-dimensional torus with unknown minor radius $r \in [0.5, 1]$ and major radius $R \in [4, 6]$. By solving Eq. (22) and Eq. (23), we obtain a polynomial interpolant

$$h_p(x,y,z) = 1.0 - 0.35507338x^2 - 0.35507338y^2 + 0.45264895z^2,$$

and a semialgebraic interpolant function with

$$h_1(x,y,z) = 0.98004189 - 0.26291972x^2 - 0.26291978y^2 + 0.417581644z^2,$$
$$h_2(x,y,z) = 1.0 - 0.51670759x^2 - 0.51670759y^2 + 0.60569150z^2.$$

As a comparison, [11] fails to produce an interpolant of degree less than 4.

6   Conclusions and Future Work

In this paper, we have addressed the problem of synthesizing Craig interpolants for two general polynomial formulas. By combining the polynomial homogenization techniques with the approach from [11], we have presented a complete SOS characterization of semialgebraic (and polynomial) interpolants. Compared with existing works, our approach removes the restrictions on the form of formulas and is applicable to any polynomial formulas, especially when variables have unbound domains. Moreover, sparsity of polynomial formulas can be exploited to improve the scalability of our approach [16, 29].

Our Craig interpolation synthesis technique offers broad applicability in various verification tasks. It can be used as a sub-procedure, for example, in CEGAR-based model checking for identifying counterexamples [32], in bounded model checking for generating proofs [21], in program verification for squeezing invariants [26], and in SMT for reasoning about nonlinear arithmetic [18]. Compared with existing algorithms, our SDP-based algorithm is efficient and provides a relative completeness guarantee. However, the practical implementation is not a trivial undertaking, as it requires suitable strategies for storing numerical interpolants and taming numerical errors [37]. This remains an ongoing work of our research.

Data Availability Statement. The experimental results of this paper may be reproduced using the artifact on Figshare https://doi.org/10.6084/m9.figshare.26131378, or via GitHub link https://github.com/EcstasyH/Interpolation.

References

1. Acquistapace, F., Andradas, C., Broglia, F.: Separation of semialgebraic sets. J. Am. Math. Soc. **12**(3), 703–728 (1999). https://doi.org/10.1090/S0894-0347-99-00302-1
2. Andersen, E.D., Andersen, K.D.: The Mosek interior point optimizer for linear programming: an implementation of the homogeneous algorithm. In: Frenk, H., Roos, K., Terlaky, T., Zhang, S. (eds.) High Performance Optimization, pp. 197–232. Springer US, Boston, MA (2000). https://doi.org/10.1007/978-1-4757-3216-0_8
3. Benhamou, F., Granvilliers, L.: Continuous and interval constraints. In: Handbook of Constraint Programming, Foundations of Artificial Intelligence, vol. 2, pp. 571–603 (2006). https://doi.org/10.1016/S1574-6526(06)80020-9
4. Chen, M., Wang, J., An, J., Zhan, B., Kapur, D., Zhan, N.: NIL: learning nonlinear interpolants. In: Fontaine, P. (ed.) Automated Deduction – CADE 27: 27th International Conference on Automated Deduction, Natal, Brazil, August 27–30, 2019, Proceedings, pp. 178–196. Springer International Publishing, Cham (2019). https://doi.org/10.1007/978-3-030-29436-6_11
5. Cimatti, A., Griggio, A., Sebastiani, R.: Efficient interpolation generation in satisfiability modulo theories. In: Tools and Algorithms for the Construction and Analysis of Systems, TACAS 2008. Lecture Notes in Computer Science, vol. 4963, pp. 397–412 (2008). https://doi.org/10.1007/978-3-540-78800-3_30
6. Cimatti, A., Griggio, A., Irfan, A., Roveri, M., Sebastiani, R.: Incremental linearization for satisfiability and verification modulo nonlinear arithmetic and transcendental functions. ACM Trans. Comput. Log. **19**(3), 19:1–19:52 (2018). https://doi.org/10.1145/3230639
7. Dai, L., Xia, B., Zhan, N.: Generating non-linear interpolants by semidefinite programming. In: Sharygina, N., Veith, H. (eds.) Computer Aided Verification - 25th International Conference, CAV 2013. Lecture Notes in Computer Science, vol. 8044, pp. 364–380. Springer (2013). https://doi.org/10.1007/978-3-642-39799-8_25
8. Davenport, J.H., Heintz, J.: Real quantifier elimination is doubly exponential. J. Symb. Comput. **5**(1–2), 29–35 (1988). https://doi.org/10.1016/S0747-7171(88)80004-X
9. D'Silva, V.V., Kroening, D., Purandare, M., Weissenbacher, G.: Interpolant strength. In: Verification, Model Checking, and Abstract Interpretation, 11th International Conference, VMCAI 2010. Lecture Notes in Computer Science, vol. 5944, pp. 129–145. Springer (2010). https://doi.org/10.1007/978-3-642-11319-2_12

10. Gan, T., Dai, L., Xia, B., Zhan, N., Kapur, D., Chen, M.: Interpolant synthesis for quadratic polynomial inequalities and combination with EUF. In: Automated Reasoning: 8th International Joint Conference, IJCAR 2016, pp. 195–212. Springer (2016). https://doi.org/10.1007/978-3-319-40229-1_14

11. Gan, T., Xia, B., Xue, B., Zhan, N., Dai, L.: Nonlinear Craig interpolant generation. In: Computer Aided Verification - 32nd International Conference, CAV 2020. Lecture Notes in Computer Science, vol. 12224, pp. 415–438. Springer (2020). https://doi.org/10.1007/978-3-030-53288-8_20

12. Gao, S., Kong, S., Clarke, E.M.: Proof generation from delta-decisions. In: 16th International Symposium on Symbolic and Numeric Algorithms for Scientific Computing, SYNASC 2014, pp. 156–163. IEEE Computer Society (2014). https://doi.org/10.1109/SYNASC.2014.29

13. Gao, S., Zufferey, D.: Interpolants in nonlinear theories over the reals. In: Tools and Algorithms for the Construction and Analysis of Systems - 22nd International Conference, TACAS 2016. Lecture Notes in Computer Science, vol. 9636, pp. 625–641. Springer (2016). https://doi.org/10.1007/978-3-662-49674-9_41

14. Henzinger, T.A., Jhala, R., Majumdar, R., McMillan, K.L.: Abstractions from proofs. In: Proceedings of the 31st ACM SIGPLAN-SIGACT Symposium on Principles of Programming Languages, POPL 2004, pp. 232–244. ACM (2004). https://doi.org/10.1145/964001.964021

15. Hoenicke, J., Schindler, T.: Efficient interpolation for the theory of arrays. In: Automated Reasoning - 9th International Joint Conference, IJCAR 2018. Lecture Notes in Computer Science, vol. 10900, pp. 549–565. Springer (2018). https://doi.org/10.1007/978-3-319-94205-6_36

16. Huang, L., Kang, S., Wang, J., Yang, H.: Sparse polynomial optimization with unbounded sets (2024). https://arxiv.org/abs/2401.15837

17. Huang, L., Nie, J., Yuan, Y.: Homogenization for polynomial optimization with unbounded sets. Math. Program. **200**(1), 105–145 (2023). https://doi.org/10.1007/S10107-022-01878-5

18. Jovanovic, D., Dutertre, B.: Interpolation and model checking for nonlinear arithmetic. In: Computer Aided Verification - 33rd International Conference, CAV 2021. Lecture Notes in Computer Science, vol. 12760, pp. 266–288. Springer (2021). https://doi.org/10.1007/978-3-030-81688-9_13

19. Jung, Y., Lee, W., Wang, B., Yi, K.: Predicate generation for learning-based quantifier-free loop invariant inference. In: Tools and Algorithms for the Construction and Analysis of Systems - 17th International Conference, TACAS 2011. Lecture Notes in Computer Science, vol. 6605, pp. 205–219. Springer (2011). https://doi.org/10.1007/978-3-642-19835-9_17

20. Kapur, D., Majumdar, R., Zarba, C.G.: Interpolation for data structures. In: Proceedings of the 14th ACM SIGSOFT International Symposium on Foundations of Software Engineering, FSE 2006, pp. 105–116. ACM (2006). https://doi.org/10.1145/1181775.1181789

21. Komuravelli, A., Gurfinkel, A., Chaki, S.: SMT-based model checking for recursive programs. In: Computer Aided Verification - 26th International Conference, CAV 2014. Lecture Notes in Computer Science, vol. 8559, pp. 17–34. Springer (2014). https://doi.org/10.1007/978-3-319-08867-9_2

22. Kovács, L., Voronkov, A.: Interpolation and symbol elimination. In: 22nd International Conference on Automated Deduction, CADE'22. Lecture Notes in Computer Science, vol. 5663, pp. 199–213. Springer (2009). https://doi.org/10.1007/978-3-642-02959-2_17

23. Krajíček, J.: Interpolation theorems, lower bounds for proof systems, and independence results for bounded arithmetic. J. Symb. Log. **62**(2), 457–486 (1997). https://doi.org/10.2307/2275541

24. Kupferschmid, S., Becker, B.: Craig interpolation in the presence of non-linear constraints. In: Fahrenberg, U., Tripakis, S. (eds.) Formal Modeling and Analysis of Timed Systems - 9th International Conference, FORMATS 2011. Lecture Notes in Computer Science, vol. 6919, pp. 240–255. Springer (2011). https://doi.org/10.1007/978-3-642-24310-3_17

25. Lasserre, J.B.: Moments, positive polynomials and their applications, vol. 1. World Scientific (2009). https://doi.org/10.1142/p665

26. Lin, S., Sun, J., Xiao, H., Sanán, D., Hansen, H.: Fib: Squeezing loop invariants by interpolation between forward/backward predicate transformers. In: Proceedings of the 32nd IEEE/ACM International Conference on Automated Software Engineering, ASE 2017, pp. 793–803. IEEE Computer Society (2017). https://doi.org/10.1109/ASE.2017.8115690

27. Lin, W., Ding, M., Lin, K., Mei, G., Ding, Z.: Formal synthesis of neural Craig interpolant via counterexample guided deep learning. In: 9th International Conference on Dependable Systems and Their Applications, DSA 2022, pp. 116–125. IEEE (2022). https://doi.org/10.1109/DSA56465.2022.00023

28. Magron, V., Wang, J.: TSSOS: a Julia library to exploit sparsity for large-scale polynomial optimization. CoRR **abs/2103.00915** (2021). https://arxiv.org/abs/2103.00915

29. Magron, V., Wang, J.: Sparse Polynomial Optimization - Theory and Practice, Series on Optimization and its Applications, vol. 5. WorldScientific (2023). https://doi.org/10.1142/Q0382

30. Marshall, M.: Positive polynomials and sums of squares. Am. Math. Soc., 146 (2008)

31. McMillan, K.L.: Interpolation and sat-based model checking. In: Computer Aided Verification, 15th International Conference, CAV 2003. Lecture Notes in Computer Science, vol. 2725, pp. 1–13. Springer (2003). https://doi.org/10.1007/978-3-540-45069-6_1

32. McMillan, K.L.: An interpolating theorem prover. Theor. Comput. Sci. **345**(1), 101–121 (2005). https://doi.org/10.1016/J.TCS.2005.07.003

33. McMillan, K.L.: Quantified invariant generation using an interpolating saturation prover. In: Tools and Algorithms for the Construction and Analysis of Systems, 14th International Conference, TACAS 2008. Lecture Notes in Computer Science, vol. 4963, pp. 413–427. Springer (2008). https://doi.org/10.1007/978-3-540-78800-3_31

34. Nie, J.: Optimality conditions and finite convergence of Lasserre's hierarchy. Math. Program. **146**(1–2), 97–121 (2014). https://doi.org/10.1007/S10107-013-0680-X

35. Pudlák, P.: Lower bounds for resolution and cutting plane proofs and monotone computations. J. Symb. Log. **62**(3), 981–998 (1997). https://doi.org/10.2307/2275583

36. Putinar, M.: Positive polynomials on compact semi-algebraic sets. Indiana Univ. Math. J. **42**(3), 969–984 (1993). https://www.jstor.org/stable/24897130

37. Roux, P., Voronin, Y., Sankaranarayanan, S.: Validating numerical semidefinite programming solvers for polynomial invariants. Formal Methods Syst. Design **53**(2), 286–312 (2018). https://doi.org/10.1007/s10703-017-0302-y

38. Rybalchenko, A., Sofronie-Stokkermans, V.: Constraint solving for interpolation. J. Symb. Comput. **45**(11), 1212–1233 (2010). https://doi.org/10.1016/J.JSC.2010.06.005

39. Sofronie-Stokkermans, V.: Interpolation in local theory extensions. Log. Methods Comput. Sci. **4**(4) (2008). https://doi.org/10.2168/LMCS-4(4:1)2008
40. Srikanth, A., Sahin, B., Harris, W.R.: Complexity verification using guided theorem enumeration, pp. 639–652 (2017). https://doi.org/10.1145/3009837.3009864
41. Stengle, G.: A nullstellensatz and a positivstellensatz in semialgebraic geometry. Ann. Math. **207**, 87–97 (1974). https://doi.org/10.1007/BF01362149
42. Wu, H., Wang, J., Xia, B., Li, X., Zhan, N., Gan, T.: Nonlinear Craig interpolant generation over unbounded domains by separating semialgebraic sets (2024). https://arxiv.org/abs/2407.00625
43. Yorsh, G., Musuvathi, M.: A combination method for generating interpolants. In: 20th International Conference on Automated Deduction, CADE'20. Lecture Notes in Computer Science, vol. 3632, pp. 353–368. Springer (2005). https://doi.org/10.1007/11532231_26
44. Zhan, N., Wang, S., Zhao, H.: Formal Verification of Simulink/Stateflow Diagrams. A Deductive Approach. Springer (2017). https://doi.org/10.1007/978-3-319-47016-0
45. Zhao, H., Zhan, N., Kapur, D., Larsen, K.G.: A "hybrid" approach for synthesizing optimal controllers of hybrid systems: a case study of the oil pump industrial example. In: Formal Methods - 18th International Symposium, FM 2012, Lecture Notes in Computer Science, vol. 7436, pp. 471–485. Springer (2012). https://doi.org/10.1007/978-3-642-32759-9_38

Practical Approximate Quantifier Elimination for Non-linear Real Arithmetic

S. Akshay[1], Supratik Chakraborty[1], Amir Kafshdar Goharshady[2(✉)],
R. Govind[3], Harshit Jitendra Motwani[2], and Sai Teja Varanasi[1]

[1] IIT Bombay, Mumbai, India
{akshayss,supratik,200050152}@cse.iitb.ac.in
[2] HKUST, Hong Kong, China
{goharshady,csemotwani}@ust.hk
[3] Uppsala University, Uppsala, Sweden
govind.rajanbabu@it.uu.se

Abstract. Quantifier Elimination (QE) concerns finding a quantifier-free formula that is semantically equivalent to a quantified formula in a given logic. For the theory of non-linear arithmetic over reals (NRA), QE is known to be computationally challenging. In this paper, we show how QE over NRA can be solved approximately and efficiently in practice using a Boolean combination of constraints in the linear arithmetic over reals (LRA). Our approach works by approximating the solution space of a set of NRA constraints when all real variables are bounded. It combines adaptive dynamic gridding with application of Handelman's Theorem to obtain the approximation efficiently via a sequence of linear programs (LP). We provide rigorous approximation guarantees, and also proofs of soundness and completeness (under mild assumptions) of our algorithm. Interestingly, our work allows us to bootstrap on earlier work (viz. [38]) and solve quantified SMT problems over a combination of NRA and other theories, that are beyond the reach of state-of-the-art solvers. We have implemented our approach in a preprocessor for Z3 called POQER. Our experiments show that POQER+Z3EG outperforms state-of-the-art SMT solvers on non-trivial problems, adapted from a suite of benchmarks.

1 Introduction

Given a first-order logic formula with quantifiers, quantifier elimination (or QE) requires us to find a quantifier-free formula that is semantically equivalent to the given quantified formula. Not every first-order theory admits QE; however, several important ones do, and QE for several such theories are implemented in modern Satisfiability Modulo Theories (SMT) solvers (viz. [1,9,27,31,36]). QE in combinations of first-order theories is particularly challenging, and algorithms that achieve this for some theories used in practical applications have been reported in earlier works (e.g. [11,38,51]). However, QE (even approximate versions) in combinations of theories including non-linear real arithmetic (NRA)

© The Author(s) 2025
A. Platzer et al. (Eds.): FM 2024, LNCS 14933, pp. 111–130, 2025.
https://doi.org/10.1007/978-3-031-71162-6_6

has proved more difficult. This is not surprising since QE over NRA is computationally challenging by itself [29]. In this paper, we add to the repertoire of practically efficient techniques for reasoning about NRA constraints by showing how NRA constraints over bounded variables can be approximated efficiently using a Boolean combination of real interval constraints. This yields a practical algorithm for approximately solving QE over NRA, and also allows us to bootstrap on existing QE techniques that work well for combinations of LRA and other theories (viz. [38]) to solve QE in combinations of theories including NRA.

At the heart of our approach lies a practically efficient technique for approximating a Boolean combination of polynomial inequalities over bounded reals with a Boolean combination of real interval constraints. This immediately yields a practically efficient approximate QE algorithm for NRA. This problem is also popularly called QE over reals (henceforth called QER). QER is a central problem in computer algebra and real algebraic geometry, with many practical applications, including control system design [35,42,46], program verification [14,50,62,64,66], analysis of hybrid systems [7,79] and robot motion planning [53,56,77]. The study of QER has a long and storied history. Tarski first showed the decidability of QER in [71]. By the Tarski-Seidenberg theorem, the projection of a semi-algebraic set (i.e. solutions of a Boolean combination of polynomial inequalities) is always semi-algebraic [67,71]. Hence, it suffices to eliminate existentially quantified variables from a conjunction of polynomial inequalities. A landmark result in this area was the development of the *cylindrical algebraic decomposition (CAD)* algorithm by Collins [28] in 1975. Over the past half century, CAD has remained one of the most important algorithms for QER, although several improvements have been proposed over the years. An excellent, albeit dated, survey of these algorithms can be found in [16,29], while more recent works have been reported in [3,12,26,49,52,57,58,65,68]. The book by Basu, Pollack and Roy [10] is a definitive treatise on exact algorithms for QER and related problems. Over the years, practical scalability concerns have also motivated researchers to investigate versions of QER for special cases [32,47,48,54,59,63,75,76]. Advances resulting from these efforts have been implemented in state-of-the-art tools, including open-source academic tools such as QEPCAD [13,30], REDLOG [34], SMT-RAT [31] and SageMath [72], as well as commercial tools such as Mathematica [44,68,69] and Maple [25,45].

The verification community has long been interested in QER, thanks to its many applications in problems related to automated reasoning. For example, QER for polynomial equalities and disequalities has been used to compute strongest post- and weakest pre-conditions of programs [14,62], to compute abstract transformers for program statements [60], and for inductive assertion and program invariant generation [50,66]. In hybrid systems verification, reach set computation has been shown to reduce to QER [7,79]. In [78], QER has been used to find parametric optimal strategies for Markov decision processes. Quantifier elimination in mixed theories including the theory of linear real arithmetic (LRA) has been reported in several earlier works (see e.g. [11,38,51]). For example, [11] gives model based projection techniques for several combinations of theories and [38] gives e-graph based techniques for similar combinations. However, quantifier elimination (even approximate versions) in combinations of theories including NRA has remained elusive in practice, primarily because of the high-degree polynomials that result in general from QER.

Our algorithm provides strong guarantees of approximation and allows the user to trade off precision for performance. It builds upon the well-known theorem of Handelman [41] which characterizes positive polynomials over polytopes. This theorem has previously been used in developing static analysis methods for termination and runtime analysis [17–19,43], cost analysis [15,21,23,24,70,74], invariant generation [20], reachability [8,73] and LTL verification [22], as well as program synthesis [4,39]. See [6] for a comparison between the current work and [4]. Most of these approaches are template-based and use Handelman's theorem to solve for unknown variables in their templates. In contrast, our approach is gridding-based and uses techniques similar to PROPhESY [33] but combines them with Handelman-based reasoning. The primary workhorse we use at the backend is a linear-programming (LP) solver, with occasional invocations of an SMT solver. This allows our method to scale well on many non-trivial examples. Our primary contributions are as follows:

1. We formalize two notions of approximation for QER, called ϵ-*approximation* and (ϵ, δ)-*approximation*, that are motivated by practical applications and introduce union of (adaptively sized) hyperrectangles as a knowledge representation form for approximate QER. This allows us to compute ϵ- and (ϵ, δ)-approximations of QER, for every $\epsilon, \delta > 0$, efficiently in practice.

2. We present an approach to over- and under-approximate NRA constraints with a Boolean combination of LRA constraints, where each dimension is bounded. Specifically, we use Handelman's Theorem in combination with dynamic adaptive gridding to reduce the approximation problem to multiple linear programming (LP) instances, that are then discharged by a state-of-the-art LP solver.

3. We prove the soundness of our algorithm, and its completeness under two different settings. Assuming access to a sound and complete satisfiability oracle for polynomial inequalities (in practice, an SMT solver), we show that our algorithm produces an ϵ-approximation of QER. Without access to the above oracle, and relying only on linear programming, we can obtain (ϵ, δ)-approximations of QER. Our notions of approximation for the original semialgebraic set are closely related to those of [37]. Due to the special format of our approximation as a union of hyperrectangles, we obtain approximations of the projection set easily. Our approach extends the results of [55] which directly approximate the projection.

4. We apply this new algorithm to show how QE over theories involving Non-linear Real Arithmetic (NRA) can be reduced to QE over LRA and other theories, thereby making it possible to solve problems beyond the reach of state-of-the-art solvers.
5. We show the practical effectiveness of our algorithm through two sets of experiments with POQER – a tool that implements our algorithm. First, a comparison with state-of-the-art tools shows that POQER significantly out-performs available open-source tools that perform exact QER, even with small values of ϵ and δ. Comparison with Mathematica, a commercial tool, shows that our tool almost always generates solutions (unions of hyperrectangles) that are easier to process subsequently than solutions generated by Mathematica. Second, we demonstrate how POQER can find approximate solutions for NRA+ADT benchmarks well beyond the reach of state-of-the-art SMT-solvers like Z3 and Z3EG.

2   Algorithm

In this section, we start by formalizing our quantifier elimination problem as computing a projection $\pi(S)$ of a semialgebraic set S. We then present the concept of ϵ-inflations to overapproximate semialgebraic sets, in our case the projection $\pi(S)$, to a desired level ϵ of precision. This is followed by our algorithm which computes an ϵ-approximation of $\pi(S)$.

2.1   Problem Definition

Input Format. We are given a positive real number ϵ and a finite set $\mathcal{V} = \{v_1, v_2, \ldots, v_n\}$ of real-valued variables partitioned into two sets $\mathcal{V}_1$ and $\mathcal{V}_2$. Throughout this paper, we use the standard vector notation for valuations to variables and assume that $\mathcal{V}_1$ comes before $\mathcal{V}_2$ lexicographically. Our input also contains a formula φ from the grammar below:

$$
\begin{aligned}
\varphi &:= \ell \mid \neg\varphi \mid \varphi \wedge \varphi \mid \varphi \vee \varphi \quad \text{formulas} \\
\ell &:= f \geq 0 \mid f > 0 \quad\quad\quad\quad \text{literals} \\
f &\in \mathbb{R}[\mathcal{V}] \quad\quad\quad\quad\quad\quad \text{polynomials}
\end{aligned}
$$

The input formula φ naturally defines the semialgebraic set

$$
S := SAT(\varphi) := \{\mathbf{x} \in \mathbb{R}^n \mid \mathbf{x} \models \varphi\}.
$$

We assume the set S is bounded, i.e. there is a positive real number B given in the input such that for all $\mathbf{x} \in S$, we have $\|\mathbf{x}\| < B$.

Projection. Given a set $S \subseteq \mathbb{R}^n$, its projection $\pi(S)$ onto $\mathcal{V}_1$ is defined as

$$
\pi(S) := \{\mathbf{x_1} \in \mathbb{R}^{|\mathcal{V}_1|} \mid \exists \mathbf{x_2} \in \mathbb{R}^{|\mathcal{V}_2|} \ (\mathbf{x_1}, \mathbf{x_2}) \in S\}.
$$

Our goal is to approximate $\pi(S)$. We now formalize this.

ϵ-inflations and ϵ-approximations. Given $\epsilon > 0$ and a set $T \subseteq \mathbb{R}^n$, we define the ϵ-*inflation* of T as

$$\mathcal{I}_\epsilon(T) := \{\mathbf{x} \in \mathbb{R}^n \mid \exists \mathbf{x}' \in T \;\; ||\mathbf{x} - \mathbf{x}'|| < \epsilon\}.$$

In other words, $\mathcal{I}_\epsilon(T)$ consists of all the points in T as well as points that are within a distance ϵ to T. We say $O \subseteq \mathbb{R}^n$ is an ϵ-*approximation* of T iff $T \subseteq O \subseteq \mathcal{I}_\epsilon(T)$. Intuitively, an ϵ-approximation includes everything in the original set T and may also include some extra points, but these points are guaranteed to be within ϵ distance to the boundary of T. In this work, we use the Euclidean norm, but our results are independent of the distance metric used and can be straightforwardly extended to other norms.

Output. Our algorithm outputs an ϵ-approximation of $\pi(S)$.

Example. Figure 1 shows a semi-algebraic set in black and its ϵ-inflation in red.

Hyperrectangles. A *hyperrectangle* $H \subseteq \mathbb{R}^n$ is the set of points that satisfy the inequalities

$$\psi_H := \begin{cases} \alpha_1 \leq v_1 \leq \beta_1 \\ \alpha_2 \leq v_2 \leq \beta_2 \\ \quad \vdots \\ \alpha_n \leq v_n \leq \beta_n \end{cases}$$

Fig. 1. A semi-algebraic set S (black) and its ϵ-inflation (red) (Color figure online)

where the α_i and β_i's are real constants and we have $\beta_i > \alpha_i$ for every $1 \leq i \leq n$.

Literal Complements. Let ℓ be a literal. We define its complement $\overline{\ell}$ as follows:

$$\overline{\ell} := \begin{cases} -f > 0 & \ell = (f \geq 0) \\ -f \geq 0 & \ell = (f > 0) \end{cases}$$

It is easy to see that $\overline{\ell} \equiv \neg\ell$.

Ternary Evaluation. Let φ be a Boolean formula and L the set of literals appearing in φ. Consider a function $\theta : L \to \{0, 1, ?\}$ that assigns a truth value to each literal. Here, ? models uncertainty. Based on the function θ, we define the evaluation of φ recursively as follows:

$$[\![\ell]\!]_\theta = \theta(\ell) \qquad\qquad [\![\varphi_1 \vee \varphi_2]\!]_\theta = \begin{cases} 1 & [\![\varphi_1]\!]_\theta = 1 \vee [\![\varphi_2]\!]_\theta = 1 \\ 0 & [\![\varphi_1]\!]_\theta = 0 \wedge [\![\varphi_2]\!]_\theta = 0 \\ ? & \text{otherwise} \end{cases}$$

$$[\![\neg\varphi]\!]_\theta = \begin{cases} ? & [\![\varphi]\!]_\theta = ? \\ \neg[\![\varphi]\!]_\theta & \text{otherwise} \end{cases} \qquad [\![\varphi_1 \wedge \varphi_2]\!]_\theta = \begin{cases} 1 & [\![\varphi_1]\!]_\theta = 1 \wedge [\![\varphi_2]\!]_\theta = 1 \\ 0 & [\![\varphi_1]\!]_\theta = 0 \vee [\![\varphi_2]\!]_\theta = 0 \\ ? & \text{otherwise} \end{cases}$$

Informally, we are going to use this kind of evaluation when we want to check whether a given φ holds over all points in a set (1), none of the points in the set (0) or potentially some of them (?). We say we are *uncertain* about φ when $[\![\varphi]\!]_\theta = ?$.

2.2   Our Overapproximation Algorithm

Oracles. Our algorithm is modular and relies on two oracles:

- *Implication Oracle:* Given a hyperrectangle $H \subseteq \mathbb{R}^n$ and a literal ℓ, this oracle checks whether ℓ holds at every point in H. Equivalently, as ψ_H is the formula defining H, it checks whether $\forall \mathbf{x} \in \mathbb{R}^n \ \psi_H \Rightarrow \ell$.
- *Satisfiability Oracle:* This oracle decides whether a given semialgebraic set is non-empty, i.e., it checks the satisfiability of a given formula φ.

We say that an oracle is *sound* if whenever it returns true, the implication (resp. satisfiability) holds. Conversely, an oracle is *complete* if whenever the implication (resp. satisfiability) holds, it returns true.

In this section, we provide the main procedure of our algorithm, assuming that the two oracles above are available. In Sect. 2.3, we will provide an LP-based implication oracle. Thus, calls to the implication oracle are relatively cheap in practice. In contrast, we rely on SMT solvers as satisfiability oracles. Thus, for practical scalability, our approach calls this oracle as late as possible and only in ϵ-diameter subsets of $\mathbb{R}^n$. Finally, in Sect. 2.4 we show that our over-approximation remains sound even in the absence of a satisfiability oracle but can only provide a weaker guarantee of approximation quality.

Our Algorithm. We are now ready to present our algorithm that finds an ϵ-approximation of $\pi(S)$. See [6] for a discussion of the intuition. Our algorithm consists of three steps and is provided in Algorithm 1.

Step 1. Literal Extraction. In the first step, our algorithm generates a set L consisting of all literals ℓ that appear in the formula φ. This is done by a standard parsing of φ.

Step 2. Dynamic Gridding. In this step, our initial goal is to produce an ϵ-approximation O of S itself, rather than its projection. Given that S is bounded, we can apply the idea of gridding. However, we do this in a dynamic and recursive manner, creating smaller grid cells only when necessary.

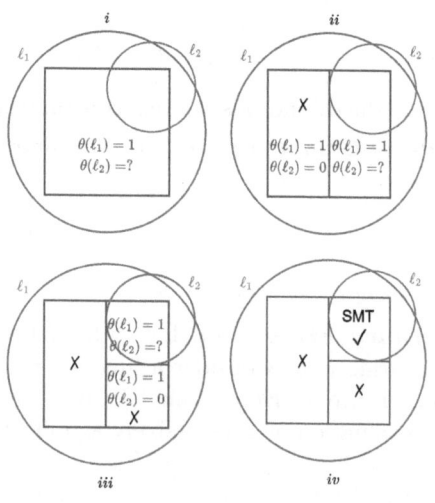

Fig. 2. An example of our gridding algorithm with memoization

We keep a set A of hyperrectangles whose union forms our answer. Initially $A = \emptyset$. We start with a hyperrectangle H_0 which covers all of S as the initial grid cell. For example, we can set $H_0 = \{(x_1, x_2, \ldots, x_n) \mid -B \leq x_i \leq B\}$. When processing each grid cell H, our algorithm does the following:

(a) For every literal $\ell \in L$, use the implication oracle to decide whether ℓ holds at every point in H, i.e. check $\forall \mathbf{x} \in \mathbb{R}^n \ \psi_H \Rightarrow \ell$.

(b) For every literal $\ell \in L$, use implication oracle to decide whether its complement $\bar{\ell}$ holds at every point in H, i.e. query the oracle for $\forall \mathbf{x} \in \mathbb{R}^n \ \psi_H \Rightarrow \bar{\ell}$.

(c) Create a ternary valuation $\theta : L \to \{0, 1, ?\}$ in which $\theta(\ell) = 1$ if the check in (a) passes, $\theta(\ell) = 0$ if the check in (b) passes and otherwise $\theta(\ell) = ?$. Use this valuation to evaluate $[|\varphi|]_\theta$, thus deciding whether φ holds at every point in H.

(d) If $[|\varphi|]_\theta = 1$, then add the grid cell H to the answer A. Conversely, if $[|\varphi|]_\theta = 0$, exclude H from A. The only remaining case is if we are uncertain about φ. We break this down into two further cases:

  (i) If the diameter of H is more than ϵ, cut H into two halves H' and H'' by bisecting its longest edge. Apply the algorithm recursively on both.

  (ii) If the diameter of H is at most ϵ, then use the satisfiability oracle on $\psi_H \wedge \varphi$. This will tell us whether there exists at least one point in H that satisfies φ. If such a point exists, include H in A. Else, exclude H.

Memoization. If one of the checks in (a) or (b) above succeed, then the corresponding (complement) literal holds at every point in H. Thus, if the algorithm later divides H in (d), we do not need to check the same literals again in H' and H''. Hence, our algorithm memoizes the set of literals that are known to hold or not hold at every point in H. This is shown as L_1 and L_0 in the pseudocode.

Example. Figure 2 shows a simple example of our dynamic gridding. Our goal is to approximate the intersection $\varphi = \ell_1 \wedge \ell_2$ of the two red circles, i.e. each circle corresponds to a literal ℓ_i. A grid cell is shown in blue in part (i). Initially, our algorithm finds out that ℓ_1 holds at every point in the cell, but ℓ_2 is uncertain. Thus, in part (ii), we divide our cell in two. At this point we already know that ℓ_1 holds in both halves. This is memoized (shown in green) and not recomputed. In the left half, ℓ_2 does not hold at any point. Thus, we have $\theta(\ell_2) = 0$ and exclude this half from the solution. In part (iii), we cut the right half in two. The bottom part is excluded from the solution since no point in it satisfies ℓ_2. In the top right part, ℓ_1 is known to hold everywhere (memoized) and ℓ_2 is uncertain. However, at this point the diameter of the cell is less than ϵ. Thus, our approach makes an SMT call in part (iv) and realizes that there is a point in this cell that satisfies φ. Hence, the top right cell is included in the answer.

Step 3. Projection. Let $O = \bigcup_{H \in A} H$. We will prove further below that O is an ϵ-approximation of S. However, we would like an ϵ-approximation of $\pi(S)$. In this step, the algorithm computes $\pi(O) = \bigcup_{H \in A} \pi(H)$ and outputs it as the answer. We note that projecting each hyperrectangle $H \in A$ is a simple matter of dropping some constraints. Specifically, we have:

$$\psi_H = \begin{cases} \alpha_1 \leq v_1 \leq \beta_1 \\ \quad \vdots \\ \alpha_n \leq v_n \leq \beta_n \end{cases} \Rightarrow \psi_{\pi(H)} = \begin{cases} \alpha_1 \leq v_1 \leq \beta_1 \\ \quad \vdots \\ \alpha_{|\mathcal{V}_1|} \leq v_{|\mathcal{V}_1|} \leq \beta_{|\mathcal{V}_1|} \end{cases}.$$

Theorem 1 (Correctness, Proof in [6]). *Assume that we have a sound implication oracle and a sound and complete satisfiability oracle. Given*

Algorithm 1. POQER

```
 1: A ← ∅
 2: L ← ∅
 3: procedure MAIN(φ, ε, n, 𝒱, 𝒱₁, 𝒱₂, B)
 4:     L ← literals in φ                                                    ▷ Step 1
 5:     ψ_{H₀} ← ⋀_{i=1}^{n} −B ≤ v_i ≤ B
 6:     GRID(H₀, ∅, ∅, φ, ε, n, 𝒱)                                          ▷ Step 2
 7:     X ← ∅
 8:     for all H ∈ A do                                                     ▷ Step 3
 9:         X ← X ∪ PROJECT(H, 𝒱₁)
10:     return X
11: procedure GRID(H, L₀, L₁, φ, ε, n, 𝒱)
12:     θ ← ∅
13:     for all ℓ ∈ L do
14:         if ℓ ∈ L₁ ∨ IMPLICATIONORACLE(H, ℓ, n, 𝒱) then                   ▷ Step 2 (a)
15:             θ[ℓ] ← 1
16:             L₁ = L₁ ∪ {ℓ}                                                ▷ Memoization
17:         else if ℓ ∈ L₀ ∨ IMPLICATIONORACLE(H, ℓ̄, n, 𝒱) then             ▷ Step 2 (b)
18:             θ[ℓ] ← 0
19:             L₀ = L₀ ∪ {ℓ}                                                ▷ Memoization
20:         else
21:             θ[ℓ] ←?
22:     if [|φ|]_θ = 1 then                                                  ▷ Step 2 (d), Ternary Evaluation
23:         A ← A ∪ {H}                                                      ▷ Adding H to the overapproximation
24:     else if [|φ|]_θ =? then
25:         if DIAMETER(H) ≥ ε then
26:             H', H'' ← CUTINHALVES(H)
27:             GRID(H', L₀, L₁, φ, ε, n, 𝒱)                                 ▷ Recursive Calls on Halves of H
28:             GRID(H'', L₀, L₁, φ, ε, n, 𝒱)
29:         else if SATISFIABILITYORACLE(ψ_H ∧ φ, n, 𝒱) then
30:             A ← A ∪ {H}                                                  ▷ Adding H to the overapproximation
```

$\varphi, \epsilon, n, \mathcal{V}, \mathcal{V}_1, \mathcal{V}_2,$ and B as input, let $S := \{\mathbf{x} \in \mathbb{R}^n \ \ x \models \varphi\}$ be bounded by a ball of radius B around the origin. Then, Algorithm 1 (POQER), outputs an ϵ-approximation of $\pi(S)$, i.e. the projection of S onto $\mathcal{V}_1$, as desired.

2.3 Our Implication Oracle

As mentioned in the previous section, our algorithm depends on a sound oracle to check whether a given polynomial inequality (literal) ℓ of the form $f \geq 0$ or $f > 0$ holds over the entirety of a hyperrectangle H. In this section, we provide such an oracle. Specifically, given the inequalities ψ_H that define the hyperrectangle H, our goal is to check whether $\forall \mathbf{x} \in \mathbb{R}^n \ \ \psi_H \Rightarrow \ell$ holds. Our algorithm is sound and can also provide semi-completeness guarantees for *strict* literals, i.e. literals of the form $f > 0$.

Semi-group generated by Φ. Consider the set $\mathcal{V} = \{v_1, \dots v_n\}$ of real-valued variables and the following system of linear inequalities over $\mathcal{V}$:

$$\Phi := \begin{cases} a_{1,0} + a_{1,1} \cdot v_1 + \dots + a_{1,n} \cdot v_n \bowtie_1 0 \\ \quad \vdots \\ a_{m,0} + a_{m,1} \cdot v_1 + \dots + a_{m,n} \cdot v_n \bowtie_m 0 \end{cases}$$

where $\bowtie_i \in \{>, \geq\}$ for all $1 \leq i \leq m$. Let g_i be the left hand side of the i-th inequality, i.e. $g_i(v_1, \dots, v_n) := a_{i,0} + a_{i,1} \cdot v_1 + \dots a_{i,n} \cdot v_n$. The *semi-group* of Φ is defined as: $SG(\Phi) := \left\{ \prod_{i=1}^{m} g_i^{k_i} \mid m \in \mathbb{N} \wedge \forall i \ k_i \in \mathbb{N} \cup \{0\} \right\}$. In other words, this semi-group contains all polynomials that can be obtained as a multiplication of the g_i's. Note that $1 \in SG(\Phi)$. We define $SG_d(\Phi)$ as the subset of polynomials in $SG(\Phi)$ of degree at most d.

Theorem 2 (Handelman's Theorem [41]). *Consider the following system of equations over $\mathcal{V}$:*

$$\Phi := \begin{cases} a_{1,0} + a_{1,1} \cdot v_1 + \ldots + a_{1,n} \cdot v_n \geq 0 \\ \qquad\qquad\vdots \\ a_{m,0} + a_{m,1} \cdot v_1 + \ldots + a_{m,n} \cdot v_n \geq 0 \end{cases}.$$

If Φ is satisfiable, its solution set is compact, $f \in \mathbb{R}[\mathcal{V}]$ and we have $\forall \boldsymbol{x} \in \mathbb{R}^n \ \Phi \Rightarrow f > 0$, then there exist non-negative real numbers $\lambda_0, \ldots \lambda_k$ and semigroup elements $h_1, \ldots, h_k \in SG(\Phi)$ such that $f = \lambda_0 + \lambda_1 \cdot h_1 + \cdots + \lambda_k \cdot h_k$.

Basic Idea of Our Implication Oracle. Consider the hyperrectangle H and its defining inequalities ψ_H which can be rewritten in the following form:

$$\psi_H = \begin{cases} g_1 := v_1 - \alpha_1 \geq 0 \\ g_2 := \beta_1 - v_1 \geq 0 \\ \qquad\vdots \\ g_{2 \cdot n - 1} := v_n - \alpha_n \geq 0 \\ g_{2 \cdot n} := \beta_n - v_n \geq 0 \end{cases}$$

It is clear by definition that every g_i is non-negative at every point in H. Thus, any multiplication $h \in SG_d(\psi_H)$ of the g_i's will also be non-negative throughout H. Finally, we can take any linear combination of such polynomials with non-negative coefficients, i.e.

$$f = \lambda_0 + \lambda_1 \cdot h_1 + \cdots + \lambda_k \cdot h_k \tag{1}$$

$h_i \in SG_d(\psi_H)$ $\lambda_i \geq 0$, and such an f will be non-negative at every point in H. Moreover, if $\lambda_0 > 0$, then f will be strictly positive at every point in H.

The Oracle. Our implication oracle is provided in Algorithm 2. Given a fixed degree $d \in \mathbb{N}$, it first generates $SG_d(\psi_H)$. It then symbolically computes a linear combination of the polynomials in $SG_d(\psi_H)$ by creating fresh variables for each λ_i as in the RHS of Eq. (1). This allows us to write Eq. (1) symbolically. Note that both sides of this equation are polynomials in $\mathbb{R}[\mathcal{V}]$, thus they are equal if and only if each monomial has the same coefficient on both sides. The algorithm computes the coefficient of each monomial on both sides and equates them. This leads to a linear programming instance over the λ_i's, which is in turn handled by an external solver.

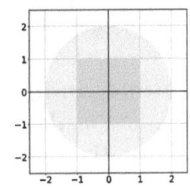

Fig. 3. The hyperrectangle H defined by ψ_H lying inside the region $f > 0$.

Example. Consider the literal $\ell = (f > 0)$ where $f = 4 - x^2 - y^2$. Let H be the hyperrectangle defined by the inequalities $-1 \le x \le 1$ and $-1 \le y \le 1$. We have $\psi_H = \{x + 1 \ge 0, -x + 1 \ge 0, y + 1 \ge 0, -y + 1 \ge 0\}$. Let $d = 2$. Then, $SG_d(\psi_H)$ contains all polynomials of degree at most 2 that can be obtained as a multiplication of the g_i's. This includes $g_1^2, g_1 \cdot g_2, g_1 \cdot g_3, g_1 \cdot g_4, g_2^2, g_2 \cdot g_3, g_2 \cdot g_4, g_3^2, g_3 \cdot g_4, g_4^2, g_1, g_2, g_3, g_4, 1$. Since ℓ holds at every point in the hyperrectangle H, we can write f as a linear combination of these polynomials as follows: $4 - x^2 - y^2 = 1 \cdot (1 - x^2) + 1 \cdot (1 - y^2) + 2 \cdot 1 = 1 \cdot g_1 \cdot g_2 + 1 \cdot g_3 \cdot g_4 + 2 \cdot 1$ (Fig. 3).

Algorithm 2. Our Implication Oracle

1: **procedure** IMPLICATIONORACLE($H, \ell, n, \mathcal{V}, d$)
2:      $LP \leftarrow \emptyset$
3:      $SG \leftarrow \{1\}$ ▷ SG will become $SG_d(\psi_H)$
4:      $M \leftarrow \{1\}$ ▷ M will become the set of all monomials of degree $\le d$
5:      **for** $1 \le i \le d$ **do**
6:          $SG \leftarrow SG \cup \{g \cdot h \mid g \in \psi_H \wedge h \in SG\}$
7:          $M \leftarrow M \cup \{v_i \cdot h \mid v_i \in \mathcal{V} \wedge h \in M\}$
8:      $k \leftarrow |SG|$
9:      Create $k + 1$ fresh variables $\lambda_0, \lambda_1, \ldots, \lambda_k$ in LP
10:     **if** $\ell = (f > 0)$ **then**
11:         Add the constraint $\lambda_0 > 0$ to LP
12:     **else if** $\ell = (f \ge 0)$ **then**
13:         Add the constraint $\lambda_0 \ge 0$ to LP
14:     **for** $1 \le i \le k$ **do**
15:         Add the constraint $\lambda_i \ge 0$ to LP
16:     $LHS \leftarrow f$ where $\ell = (f > 0)$ or $\ell = (f \ge 0)$
17:     $RHS \leftarrow \sum_{i=0}^{k} \lambda_i \cdot SG[i]$
18:     **for all** $m \in M$ **do**
19:         $l =$ coefficient of m in LHS
20:         $r =$ coefficient of m in RHS
21:         Add the constraint $l = r$ to LP
22:     **if** LP has a solution **then**
23:         **return true**
24:     **else**
25:         **return false**

Theorem 3 (Soundness and Semi-completeness, Proof in [6]). *Given a hyperrectangle H and a literal ℓ in the input, and a degree bound d, Algorithm 2 is sound in deciding whether $\forall \boldsymbol{x} \in \mathbb{R}^n$ $\psi_H \Rightarrow \ell$. Moreover, if ℓ is of the form $f > 0$, then there exists a degree bound d, depending on both H and ℓ, for which the algorithm is complete in deciding $\forall \boldsymbol{x} \in \mathbb{R}^n$ $\psi_H \Rightarrow \ell$.*

Runtime Analysis. In Algorithm 2, let d be the degree, n the number of variables, and m the number of linear inequalities in our hypothesis hyperrectangle H. Then, the size of $|M| = \binom{n+d}{d}$ and $|SG| = \binom{m+d}{d}$. For each element of SG, we add a λ_i to our linear programming instance. Similarly, for each monomial in M, we add a constraint equating its coefficients on the two sides. Thus, we have an LP instance with $O\left(\binom{m+d}{d}\right)$ variables and $O\left(\binom{n+d}{d}\right)$ constraints. We note that current state-of-the-art LP-solving algorithms work in polynomial-time $O(N^\omega)$ where N is their input size and ω is the matrix multiplication constant.

2.4   Removing the Satisfiability Oracle

Our approximate quantifier elimination algorithm in Sect. 2.2 requires two oracles: one for implication and another for satisfiability. As mentioned above, we use SMT calls for the satisfiability oracle, but the implication oracle (Sect. 2.3) is much more practical and relies only on linear programming. Moreover, it provides a semi-completeness guarantee (Theorem 3) which is not used in the main algorithm (Theorem 1). So, a natural question is whether we can remove the satisfiability oracle altogether. We first argue that this is unlikely to lead to an efficient algorithm with our notion of ϵ-approximation, since it is an ETR-hard problem. However, we can provide a weaker guarantee for positive formulas.

ETR-Hardness. Let $\psi := (\exists v_1, v_2, \ldots, v_n \; \varphi)$ be a formula in the existential theory of the reals. ψ holds if and only if $SAT(\varphi) \neq \emptyset$, but we have

$$SAT(\varphi) \neq \emptyset \Leftrightarrow \pi(SAT(\varphi)) \neq \emptyset \Leftrightarrow \mathcal{I}_\epsilon(\pi(SAT(\varphi))) \neq \emptyset.$$

Thus, to decide ψ, we can simply find an ϵ-approximation of $\pi(SAT(\varphi))$ and check its non-emptiness.

Positive Formulas. A formula φ is called *positive* if it is generated from the grammar below:

$$\begin{aligned} \varphi &:= \ell \mid \varphi \wedge \varphi \mid \varphi \vee \varphi & \text{positive formulas} \\ \ell &:= f \geq 0 \mid f > 0 & \text{literals} \\ f &\in \mathbb{R}[\mathcal{V}] & \text{polynomials} \end{aligned}$$

The only difference between this grammar and that of Sect. 2.1 is the absence of the negation operator. We note that any formula can be written as an equivalent positive formula since the complement of each literal is itself a literal. Thus, in the remainder of this section, we assume that the formula φ is positive.

(ϵ, δ)***-perturbation.*** Let $\epsilon, \delta > 0$ and φ be a positive formula. We define the (ϵ, δ)-perturbation $SAT_{\epsilon,\delta}(\varphi)$ of $SAT(\varphi)$ recursively as follows:

– For every literal $\ell = (f > 0)$ or $\ell = (f \geq 0)$ we have

$$SAT_{\epsilon,\delta}(\ell) = \mathcal{I}_\epsilon(SAT(f + \delta \geq 0)).$$

Intuitively, we are overapproximating $SAT(\ell)$ in two ways: (i) we are allowing the value of f to decrease to $-\delta$ instead of just 0, and (ii) we are taking an ϵ-inflation of the resulting solutions. In other words, we are considering that our evaluation of f might have a numerical error of up to δ and that our approximation of the solution set might contain some extra points which are within ϵ distance to the original set.

– If $\varphi = \varphi_1 \wedge \varphi_2$, then $SAT_{\epsilon,\delta}(\varphi) := SAT_{\epsilon,\delta}(\varphi_1) \cap SAT_{\epsilon,\delta}(\varphi_2)$.
– If $\varphi = \varphi_1 \vee \varphi_2$, then $SAT_{\epsilon,\delta}(\varphi) := SAT_{\epsilon,\delta}(\varphi_1) \cup SAT_{\epsilon,\delta}(\varphi_2)$.

We remark that we always have $SAT(\varphi) \subseteq \mathcal{I}_\epsilon(SAT(\varphi)) \subseteq SAT_{\epsilon,\delta}(\varphi)$. We say that a set O is an (ϵ, δ)-*approximation* of $SAT(\varphi)$ if $SAT(\varphi) \subseteq O \subseteq SAT_{\epsilon,\delta}(\varphi)$.

We note that there are subtle yet important differences in the definitions of ϵ-approximation and (ϵ, δ)-approximation, thus an $(\epsilon, 0)$-approximation is not the same as an ϵ-approximation as defined in Sect. 2.1.

Modified Algorithm. We take the exact same algorithm as in Sect. 2.2 (Algorithm 1), but only change Step 2 (d)(ii) as follows:

- If the diameter of H is at most ϵ, for every literal $\ell \in L$ of the form $f > 0$ or $f \geq 0$, use the implication oracle to decide the following formula:
  - $\forall \mathbf{x} \in \mathbb{R}^n \ \psi_H \Rightarrow -f - \delta > 0$

  If the check passes, update $\theta(\ell)$ to 0. Otherwise, update it to 1. Finally, compute $[|\varphi|]_\theta$ and if it is 1 then include H in the answer A.

Algorithm 3 in [6] provides a psuedocode of this variant. See [6] for a discussion of the intuition behind this approach.

Theorem 4 (Proof in [6]). *Assume that we have a sound and complete implication oracle. Given $\varphi, \epsilon, \delta, n, \mathcal{V}, \mathcal{V}_1, \mathcal{V}_2$ and B as input, let $SAT(\varphi)$ be bounded by a ball of radius B around the origin. Then, Algorithm 3 of [6] (Modified POQER), outputs a set X such that $\pi(SAT(\varphi)) \subseteq X \subseteq \pi(SAT_{\epsilon,\delta}(\varphi))$. In other words, it outputs an (ϵ, δ)-approximation of $SAT(\varphi)$.*

3   Experimental Results

We implemented our approach in a tool called POQER (Practical Overapproximate Quantifier Elimination for Reals) and performed two experiments:

- Our first experiment considers QER over formulas in Non-linear Real Arithmetic (NRA). To the best of our knowledge, we are providing the first approximate solution for quantifier elimination over NRA. Thus, we had to compare our scalability with previous *exact* solutions. Note that under-approximating the result of applying QER to a polynomial constraint φ is equivalent to complementing the over-approximation of QER applied to $\neg\varphi$. Hence, we focus only on over-approximating QER in this experiment. Moreover, since every Boolean combination of polynomial constraints can be equivalently expressed in disjunctive normal form, and since existential quantification distributes over disjunction, we focus only on conjunctions of polynomial constraints.
- In our second experiment, we considered the problem of satisfiability checking for mixed formulas in NRA+ADT, i.e. theories of Non-linear Real Arithmetic and Algebraic Data Types. We first used POQER to eliminate quantifiers in the NRA part of the formula, obtaining both over- and under-approximations, and writing it as a union of hyperrectangles. We then combined this approximation with the ADT part and passed it to a state-of-the-art tool for LRA+ADT, namely Z3EG. As baselines, we compared our performance with state-of-the-art SMT solvers Z3 and Z3EG.

Implementation and Environment Details. We implemented POQER (Algorithm 1) in C++, with Z3 as the satisfiability oracle (see Sect. 2). We used Gurobi [40] as our LP-solver. The results were obtained on a 3.5GHz Intel Core i5 1030NG7 Machine with 8 GB of RAM running MacOS. We will submit our tool (POQER) for artifact evaluation and make it publicly available as free and open-source software.

First Experiment (QER). Due to the lack of publicly-available tools performing *approximate* quantifier elimination in NRA (non-linear real arithmetic), we are unable to present an apples-to-apples comparison. However, we report comparisons with several tools that perform exact QER. There are several (academic and commercial) tools implementing CAD and its variants, but we observe that the result of QER given by them is often as high-degree polynomials or their radicals. This makes it practically impossible to use these results in downstream processing using modern SMT solvers. Hence, we study not only whether these tools are able to solve a QER problem within a time budget, but also the format in which they provide the answer. Although our algorithm is parallel, we only compare using a sequential variant to be as fair as possible.

CAD (and variant algorithms for QER) are reported to be implemented in publicly available SMT solvers such as SMT-RAT [31], Yices2 [36], Z3 [61] and cvc5 [9]. However, SMT solvers are decision procedures for checking satisfaction of (possibly quantified) formulas in a combination of theories. Hence, they do not provide the result of quantifying a subset of variables in a formula. While this suffices in applications where the goal is to check if a formula is satisfiable, it falls short of the requirements in other applications, viz. weakest pre-condition computation, where we genuinely require the result of quantifying a subset of variables from NRA constraints. SMT-RAT [31] appears to have had a soundness issue in the quantifier elimination for QER (as noted in [2]) which we were unable to circumvent. Therefore, we compare our approach to two state-of-the-art methods: (a) SageMath [72], a versatile open-source computer algebra system, that includes an implementation of QEPCAD [13,30], and (b) Mathematica [44], a widely-used and highly-optimized commercial computer algebra system, that employs a portfolio of powerful algorithms and heuristics for QER. We aim to answer the following research questions through our first experiment:

RQ1: Given a time of 30 min, how many QER tasks from our benchmark suite are solved by SageMath, Mathematica and POQER? We use the `Reduce` function in Mathematica and `qepcad` in SageMath.

RQ2: For each of the above three tools, is the output of a QER problem free of further NRA constraints?

RQ3: Does using Handelman's Theorem and linear programming in POQER help achieve better performance compared to the use of a state-of-the-art SMT solver (Z3)? To answer this, we performed an ablation study by removing our Handelman-based implication oracle and instead directly applying Z3 as both implication and satisfiability oracles.

Benchmarks. Given the lack of standard benchmarks for QER, we designed a suite of benchmarks, each of which is a conjunction of polynomial inequalities, with range constraints on each dimension. Our benchmarks (see [6] for details) have 2–8 variables, degrees 2–6, and between 2 to 10 polynomials each.

Results. Our results are summarized in Table 1. We computed ϵ-approximations using POQER for three different values of ϵ to understand how POQER's performance scales with decreasing values of ϵ. We observe that SageMath failed to complete the QER task within the timeout in all but four cases, where it provided a solution in NRA, as indicated by the asterisks. Mathematica performed significantly better, generating solutions in NRA in most instances. In 4 instances, the solutions are generated in a form that would require NRA with quantifiers, if we were to encode them in SMT. We show these solutions in [6]. Clearly, these solutions are intractably complicated and pose serious challenges for downstream automated reasoning tasks. Since SageMath and Mathematica implement exact QER, it is not possible to circumvent these complicated solution forms in general. POQER with $\epsilon = 0.1$ successfully solved all benchmarks within the 30-minute timeframe, showcasing the effectiveness of our tool. POQER with $\epsilon = 0.05$ and 0.01, fell short only in two and three instances respectively. Thus, our experiments answer research question RQ1 in favor of POQER for all three values of ϵ considered, when compared to SageMath or Mathematica. RQ2 is answered in the positive for POQER in all cases, while it is mostly in the negative for SageMath and Mathematica, since they compute exact solutions which are often non-linear (in NRA) and sometimes even quantified. Finally, for RQ3, from columns Z3dir.05 and PQ.05 of Table 1, we can conclude that using Handelman's Theorem and LP-solving significantly improves the performance of POQER vis-a-vis using a state-of-the-art SMT solver (Z3) in all but one example. On Benchmark Ex11, the Z3 approach is unusually fast, which is presumably due to its internal heuristics. We also report the number of hyperrectangles that we generate as well as number of hyperrectangles after the projection of variables (shown in last two columns of Table 1). Finally, more details are reported in [6]. Looking deeper into the results, we observe that Mathematica tends to solve most benchmarks efficiently, but has difficulty in solving problems with a larger number of eliminations, as each quantifier elimination results in increasingly complex solutions. In contrast, our approach benefits from the simpler structure of our solutions, enabling us to deliver faster results even when multiple quantifiers must be eliminated. Furthermore, Mathematica produces solutions in a complicated format, i.e. as degree polynomial inequalities in multiple variables. See [6] for more details.

Second Experiment: NRA+ADT. The last observation above enables the use of approximate quantifier elimination in a combination of NRA and other theories, such as ADT (theory of algebraic data types), by reducing it to LRA+ADT. NRA+ADT formulas are often highly intractable and beyond the reach of modern SMT solvers. To the best of our knowledge, there are no approximate solutions for NRA+ADT in the literature, either. In contrast, an effective tool for LRA+ADT, called Z3EG, has recently been developed in [38].

Benchmarks. We took the Z3EG benchmarks which are in LRA+ADT and added a single NRA constraint to each of them, thus obtaining NRA+ADT

Table 1. Results of our First Experiment. **SM** refers to Sagemath, **MA** refers to Mathematica, **PQ.1, PQ.05, PQ.01** refer respectively to POQER with $\epsilon = 0.1, 0.05, 0.01$. ✓ indicates that the method terminates within 30 min, ✗ indicates a timeout. ♦ indicates that the solution is in QF-NRA. ▲ indicates NRA (with quantifiers). The columns **PQ.05** and **Z3dir.05** respectively refer to time taken in seconds by POQER and POQER where the Implication Oracle is replaced by Z3. **#H** is the number of hyperrectangles computed by POQER while **#PH** is the number of hyperrectangles after the projection.

#B	SM	MA	PQ.1	PQ.05	PQ.01	Z3dir.05	PQ.05	#H	#PH
Ex1	✗	♦	✓	✗	✗	1100	233	526	103
Ex2	✗	✗	✓	✗	✗	TO	TO	–	–
Ex3	✗	▲	✓	✓	✓	370	199	1144	256
Ex4	✗	✗	✓	✓	✓	TO	31	334	76
Ex5	♦	✓	✓	✓	✓	5	3	35	6
Ex6	✗	♦	✓	✓	✓	71	14	151	33
Ex7	♦	♦	✓	✓	✓	8	3	20	5
Ex8	♦	♦	✓	✓	✓	97	19	426	148
Ex9	✗	▲	✓	✓	✓	321	223	1144	256
Ex10	♦	✓	✓	✓	✓	17	7	46	6
Ex11	✗	▲	✓	✓	✓	191	340	695	140
Ex12	✗	✗	✓	✓	✓	212	46	16	8
Ex13	✗	✗	✓	✓	✗	409	91	89	26
Ex14	✗	✗	✓	✓	✓	204	40	16	8
Ex15	✗	▲	✓	✓	✓	231	97	687	140

formulas. The added NRA constraint is $\forall x \ \ x \in [-10, 10] \Rightarrow \exists y \in [-10, 10] \ \ x^3 + x \geq y^3 + 3 \cdot y + 4$, in which x is a variable already present in the original ADT formula and y is a fresh variable. Thus, our formulas combine NRA and ADT and are particularly challenging for modern SMT solvers. To each NRA+ADT benchmark, we first applied POQER to obtain over- and under-approximations in LRA+ADT. We then passed the resulting approximate formulas to Z3EG. As baseline comparisons, we also passed the same NRA+ADT benchmarks to Z3 and Z3EG. We observed that POQER significantly outperforms other tools on these SMT benchmarks. The results are summarized in Table 2.

Table 2. Results of our Second Experiment. TO stands for timeout > 2 mins.

Z3EG			Z3			POQER		
SAT	UNSAT	TO	SAT	UNSAT	TO	SAT	UNSAT	TO
1833	1489	1518	2096	836	1908	3262	1550	28

4   Conclusion

We presented an algorithm that computes ϵ- and (ϵ, δ)-approximations of QER, for every $\epsilon, \delta > 0$. Our approach combines adaptive dynamic gridding with application of Handelman's Theorem to solve the approximation problem via a sequence of linear programs (LP). We provide formal guarantees of soundness, and guarantee completeness under mild assumptions. Our approach also allows us to solve quantified SMT problems over mixed theories including NRA, such as NRA+ADT.

Acknowledgments. A longer version of this work, including appendices and proofs, is available at [6]. The research was supported by the SERB MATRICS grant MTR/2023/001167 of the Government of India, the Asian Universities Alliance Scholars Award Program (AUASAP), which financed a visit by S. Akshay to HKUST and another visit by A.K. Goharshady to IIT Bombay, as well as the Hong Kong Research Grants Council (RGC) ECS Project Number 26208122. The authors are grateful to the Schloss Dagstuhl – Leibniz Center for Informatics. This collaboration started at the Dagstuhl Seminar 23241: "Scalable Analysis of Probabilistic Models and Programs". Author names are ordered alphabetically.

Data Availability Statement. The artifact used to generate the experimental results, as well as its source code, are publicly available at GitHub. The artifact is also archived on Zenodo [5].

References

1. Z3. https://github.com/z3prover/z3
2. Github issue for QF_NRA formula (mcsat) (2020). https://github.com/ths-rwth/smtrat/issues/91
3. Ábrahám, E., Davenport, J.H., England, M., Kremer, G.: Deciding the consistency of non-linear real arithmetic constraints with a conflict driven search using cylindrical algebraic coverings. J. Log. Algebraic Methods Program. **119** (2021)
4. Akshay, S., Chakraborty, S., Goharshady, A.K., Govind, R., Motwani, H.J., Varanasi, S.T.: Automated synthesis of decision lists for polynomial specifications over integers. In: LPAR, vol. 100, pp. 484–502 (2024)
5. Akshay, S., Chakraborty, S., Goharshady, A.K., Govind, R., Motwani, H.J., Varanasi, S.T.: Practical approximate quantifier elimination for non-linear real arithmetic (artifact) (2024). https://doi.org/10.5281/zenodo.12600106
6. Akshay, S., Chakraborty, S., Goharshady, A.K., Govind, R., Motwani, H.J., Varanasi, S.T.: Practical approximate quantifier elimination for non-linear real arithmetic (long version). https://hal.science/hal-04629011 (2024)
7. Anai, H., Weispfenning, V.: Reach set computations using real quantifier elimination. In: HSCC, pp. 63–76 (2001)
8. Asadi, A., Chatterjee, K., Fu, H., Goharshady, A.K., Mahdavi, M.: Polynomial reachability witnesses via stellensätze. In: PLDI, pp. 772–787 (2021)
9. Barbosa, H., et al.: cvc5: A versatile and industrial-strength SMT solver. In: TACAS, pp. 415–442 (2022)

10. Basu, S., Pollack, R., Roy, M.-F.: Algorithms in Real Algebraic Geometry. Springer, Berlin, Heidelberg (2006). https://doi.org/10.1007/3-540-33099-2
11. Bjørner, N.S., Janota, M.: Playing with quantified satisfaction. In: LPAR (short papers), vol. 35, pp. 15–27 (2015)
12. Brown, C.W.: Improved projection for cylindrical algebraic decomposition. J. Symb. Comput. **32**(5), 447–465 (2001)
13. Brown, C.W.: QEPCAD B: a program for computing with semi-algebraic sets using cads. SIGSAM Bull. **37**(4), 97–108 (2003)
14. Cachera, D., Jensen, T.P., Jobin, A., Kirchner, F.: Inference of polynomial invariants for imperative programs: a farewell to Gröbner bases. Sci. Comput. Program. **93**, 89–109 (2014)
15. Cai, Z., Farokhnia, S., Goharshady, A.K., Hitarth, S.: Asparagus: automated synthesis of parametric gas upper-bounds for smart contracts. Proc. ACM Program. Lang. **7**(OOPSLA2), 882–911 (2023)
16. Caviness, B.F., Johnson, J.R.: Quantifier elimination and cylindrical algebraic decomposition. Texts and Monographs in Symbolic Computation (1998)
17. Chatterjee, K., Fu, H., Goharshady, A.K.: Termination analysis of probabilistic programs through Positivstellensatz's. In: Chaudhuri, S., Farzan, A. (eds.) CAV 2016. LNCS, vol. 9779, pp. 3–22. Springer, Cham (2016). https://doi.org/10.1007/978-3-319-41528-4_1
18. Chatterjee, K., Fu, H., Goharshady, A.K.: Non-polynomial worst-case analysis of recursive programs. In: CAV, vol. 10427, pp. 41–63 (2017)
19. Chatterjee, K., Fu, H., Goharshady, A.K.: Non-polynomial worst-case analysis of recursive programs. ACM Trans. Program. Lang. Syst. **41**(4), 20:1–20:52 (2019)
20. Chatterjee, K., Fu, H., Goharshady, A.K., Goharshady, E.K.: Polynomial invariant generation for non-deterministic recursive programs. In: PLDI, pp. 672–687 (2020)
21. Chatterjee, K., Fu, H., Goharshady, A.K., Okati, N.: Computational approaches for stochastic shortest path on succinct MDPs. In: IJCAI, pp. 4700–4707. ijcai.org (2018)
22. Chatterjee, K., Goharshady, A.K., Goharshady, E.K., Karrabi, M., Zikelic, D.: Sound and complete witnesses for template-based verification of LTL properties on polynomial programs. In: FM (2024)
23. Chatterjee, K., Goharshady, A.K., Meggendorfer, T., Zikelic, D.: Quantitative bounds on resource usage of probabilistic programs. In: OOPSLA (2024)
24. Chatterjee, K., Goharshady, A.K., Meggendorfer, T., Zikelic, D.: Sound and complete certificates for quantitative termination analysis of probabilistic programs. In: CAV, vol. 13371, pp. 55–78 (2022)
25. Chen, C., Maza, M.M.: Quantifier elimination by cylindrical algebraic decomposition based on regular chains. In: ISSAC, pp. 91–98. ACM (2014)
26. Chen, C., Maza, M.M.: Quantifier elimination by cylindrical algebraic decomposition based on regular chains. J. Symb. Comput. **75**, 74–93 (2016)
27. Cimatti, A., Griggio, A., Schaafsma, B., Sebastiani, R.: The MathSAT5 SMT solver. In: Proceedings of TACAS (2013)
28. Collins, G.E.: Quantifier elimination for real closed fields by cylindrical algebraic decompostion. In: Automata Theory and Formal Languages (1975)
29. Collins, G.E.: Quantifier elimination by cylindrical algebraic decomposition - twenty years of progress. In: Quantifier Elimination and Cylindrical Algebraic Decomposition, pp. 8–23 (1998)
30. Collins, G.E., Hong, H.: Partial cylindrical algebraic decomposition for quantifier elimination. J. Symb. Comput. **12**(3), 299–328 (1991)

31. Corzilius, F., Kremer, G., Junges, S., Schupp, S., Ábrahám, E.: SMT-RAT: an open source C++ toolbox for strategic and parallel SMT solving. In: SAT, pp. 360–368 (2015)
32. Dantzig, G.B., Eaves, B.C.: Fourier-Motzkin elimination and its dual. J. Comb. Theory, Ser. A **14**(3), 288–297 (1973)
33. Dehnert, C., et al.: PROPhESY: a probabilistic parameter synthesis tool. In: CAV, vol. 9206, pp. 214–231 (2015)
34. Dolzmann, A., Sturm, T.: REDLOG: computer algebra meets computer logic. SIGSAM Bull. **31**(2), 2–9 (1997)
35. Dorato, P., Yang, W., Abdallah, C.T.: Robust multi-objective feedback design by quantifier elimination. J. Symb. Comput. **24**(2), 153–159 (1997)
36. Dutertre, B.: Yices 2.2. In: Computer Aided Verification, pp. 737–744 (2014)
37. Gao, S., Avigad, J., Clarke, E.M.: Delta-decidability over the reals. In: LICS, pp. 305–314 (2012)
38. Garcia-Contreras, I., K., H.G.V., Shoham, S., Gurfinkel, A.: Fast approximations of quantifier elimination. In: CAV, pp. 64–86 (2023)
39. Goharshady, A.K., Hitarth, S., Mohammadi, F., Motwani, H.J.: Algebro-geometric algorithms for template-based synthesis of polynomial programs. Proc. ACM Program. Lang. **7**(OOPSLA1), 727–756 (2023)
40. Gurobi Optimization, LLC: Gurobi Optimizer Reference Manual (2023). https://www.gurobi.com
41. Handelman, D.: Representing polynomials by positive linear functions on compact convex polyhedra. Pac. J. Math. **132**(1), 35–62 (1988)
42. Hong, H., Liska, R., Steinberg, S.L.: Testing stability by quantifier elimination. J. Symb. Comput. **24**(2), 161–187 (1997)
43. Huang, M., Fu, H., Chatterjee, K., Goharshady, A.K.: Modular verification for almost-sure termination of probabilistic programs. Proc. ACM Program. Lang. **3**(OOPSLA), 129:1–129:29 (2019)
44. Inc., W.R.: Mathematica, Version 14.0. https://www.wolfram.com/mathematica, Champaign, IL (2024)
45. Iwane, H., Yanami, H., Anai, H.: SyNRAC: a toolbox for solving real algebraic constraints. In: Hong, H., Yap, C. (eds.) Mathematical Software – ICMS 2014, pp. 518–522. Springer, Berlin, Heidelberg (2014). https://doi.org/10.1007/978-3-662-44199-2_78
46. Jirstrand, M.: Nonlinear control system design by quantifier elimination. J. Symb. Comput. **24**(2), 137–152 (1997)
47. John, A.K., Chakraborty, S.: A quantifier elimination algorithm for linear modular equations and disequations. In: CAV, vol. 6806, pp. 486–503 (2011)
48. John, A.K., Chakraborty, S.: A layered algorithm for quantifier elimination from linear modular constraints. Formal Methods Syst. Des. **49**(3), 272–323 (2016)
49. Jovanovic, D., de Moura, L.M.: Solving non-linear arithmetic. In: IJCAR, pp. 339–354 (2012)
50. Kapur, D.: A quantifier-elimination based heuristic for automatically generating inductive assertions for programs. J. Syst. Sci. Complex. **19**(3), 307–330 (2006)
51. Komuravelli, A., Gurfinkel, A., Chaki, S.: SMT-based model checking for recursive programs. Formal Methods Syst. Des. **48**(3), 175–205 (2016). https://doi.org/10.1007/S10703-016-0249-4
52. Kremer, G., Ábrahám, E.: Fully incremental cylindrical algebraic decomposition. J. Symb. Comput. **100**, 11–37 (2020)
53. Lafferriere, G., Pappas, G.J., Yovine, S.: Symbolic reachability computation for families of linear vector fields. J. Symb. Comput. **32**(3), 231–253 (2001)

54. Loos, R., Weispfenning, V.: Applying linear quantifier elimination. Comput. J. **36**(5), 450–462 (1993)
55. Magron, V., Henrion, D., Lasserre, J.: Semidefinite approximations of projections and polynomial images of semialgebraic sets. SIAM J. Optim. **25**(4), 2143–2164 (2015)
56. McCallum, S.: Partial solution of a path finding problem using the cad method. Electron. Proc. IMACS ACA (1995)
57. McCallum, S.: On projection in cad-based quantifier elimination with equational constraint. In: ISSAC, pp. 145–149. ACM (1999)
58. McCallum, S.: On propagation of equational constraints in cad-based quantifier elimination. In: ISSAC, pp. 223–231. ACM (2001)
59. Monniaux, D.: A quantifier elimination algorithm for linear real arithmetic. In: LPAR, pp. 243–257 (2008)
60. Monniaux, D.: Automatic modular abstractions for linear constraints. In: POPL, pp. 140–151. ACM (2009)
61. de Moura, L.M., Bjørner, N.S.: Z3: an efficient SMT solver. In: TACAS, pp. 337–340 (2008)
62. Müller-Olm, M., Seidl, H.: Computing polynomial program invariants. Inf. Process. Lett. **91**(5), 233–244 (2004)
63. Pugh, W.W.: The omega test: a fast and practical integer programming algorithm for dependence analysis. In: SC, pp. 4–13. ACM (1991)
64. Rodríguez-Carbonell, E., Kapur, D.: Automatic generation of polynomial loop. In: ISSAC, pp. 266–273. ACM (2004)
65. Sadeghimanesh, A., England, M.: An SMT solver for non-linear real arithmetic inside maple. ACM Commun. Comput. Algebra **56**(2), 76–79 (2022)
66. Sankaranarayanan, S., Sipma, H., Manna, Z.: Non-linear loop invariant generation using Gröbner bases. In: POPL, pp. 318–329. ACM (2004)
67. Seidenberg, A.: A new decision method for elementary algebra. Ann. Math. **60**(2), 365–374 (1954)
68. Strzebonski, A.W.: Solving systems of strict polynomial inequalities. J. Symb. Comput. **29**(3), 471–480 (2000)
69. Strzebonski, A.W.: Cylindrical algebraic decomposition using validated numerics. J. Symb. Comput. **41**(9), 1021–1038 (2006)
70. Sun, Y., Fu, H., Chatterjee, K., Goharshady, A.K.: Automated tail bound analysis for probabilistic recurrence relations. In: CAV, vol. 13966, pp. 16–39 (2023)
71. Tarski, A.: A Decision Method for Elementary Algebra and Geometry: Prepared for Publication with the Assistance of J.C.C. McKinsey. RAND Corporation, Santa Monica, CA (1951)
72. The Sage Developers: SageMath, the Sage Mathematics Software System (Version 10.2) (2023). https://www.sagemath.org
73. Wang, J., Sun, Y., Fu, H., Chatterjee, K., Goharshady, A.K.: Quantitative analysis of assertion violations in probabilistic programs. In: PLDI, pp. 1171–1186. ACM (2021)
74. Wang, P., Fu, H., Goharshady, A.K., Chatterjee, K., Qin, X., Shi, W.: Cost analysis of nondeterministic probabilistic programs. In: PLDI, pp. 204–220 (2019)
75. Weispfenning, V.: Quantifier elimination for real algebra - the cubic case. In: ISSAC, pp. 258–263. ACM (1994)
76. Weispfenning, V.: Quantifier elimination for real algebra - the quadratic case and beyond. Appl. Algebra Eng. Commun. Comput. **8**(2), 85–101 (1997)
77. Weispfenning, V.: Semilinear motion planning in REDLOG. Appl. Algebra Eng. Commun. Comput. **12**(6), 455–475 (2001)

78. Winkler, T., Junges, S., Pérez, G.A., Katoen, J.: On the complexity of reachability in parametric Markov decision processes. In: CONCUR, pp. 14:1–14:17 (2019)
79. Xue, B., Fränzle, M., Zhan, N.: Under-approximating reach sets for polynomial continuous systems. In: HSCC, pp. 51–60. ACM (2018)

A Divide-and-Conquer Approach to Variable Elimination in Linear Real Arithmetic

Valentin Promies$^{(\boxtimes)}$ ⓘ and Erika Ábrahám ⓘ

RWTH Aachen University, Aachen, Germany
{promies,abraham}@cs.rwth-aachen.de

Abstract. We introduce a novel variable elimination method for *conjunctions* of *linear* real arithmetic constraints. In prior work, we derived a variant of the Fourier-Motzkin elimination, which uses case splitting to reduce the procedure's complexity from doubly to singly exponential. This variant, which we call FMplex, was originally developed for satisfiability checking, and it essentially performs a depth-first search in a tree of sub-problems. It can be adapted straightforwardly for the task of quantifier elimination, but it returns *disjunctions* of conjunctions, even though the solution space can always be defined by a single conjunction. Our main contribution is to show how to efficiently extract an equivalent *conjunction* from the search tree. Besides the theoretical foundations, we explain how the procedure relates to other methods for quantifier elimination and polyhedron projection. An experimental evaluation demonstrates that our implementation is competitive with established tools.

Keywords: Variable Elimination · Linear Arithmetic · Projection

1 Introduction

The first-order theory of *linear real arithmetic (LRA)* allows reasoning about numerical variables by means of formulas, built from potentially quantified Boolean combinations of linear constraints, which compare linear combinations of variables to constants. Even though multiplication between variables is not supported, LRA is expressive enough to be widely applicable, for example in static program analysis [12], scheduling [26] or neural network verification [13].

These applications sometimes require determining the truth or, when free variables are involved, the satisfiability of LRA formulas. Other times, a representation of all solutions for a set of free variables is needed. Both problems can be solved by quantifier elimination, or *variable elimination* in the case of quantifier-free or purely existentially quantified formulas.

We focus on variable elimination for *conjunctions* of LRA constraints. That is, given a finite set of linear constraints in the variables $x_1, \ldots, x_n$, we want to compute a set of linear constraints in the variables $x_{q+1}, \ldots, x_n$, whose solutions coincide with the solutions of the original set, when the $x_1, \ldots, x_q$-dimensions are

© The Author(s) 2025
A. Platzer et al. (Eds.): FM 2024, LNCS 14933, pp. 131–148, 2025.
https://doi.org/10.1007/978-3-031-71162-6_7

removed. From a geometrical perspective, LRA constraint sets define by their solution sets *convex polyhedra*. Variable elimination corresponds to projecting a convex polyhedron onto a subspace, resulting in another (lower-dimensional) convex polyhedron which can be represented by LRA constraints without the eliminated variables. Therefore, this problem is also called *polyhedron projection*.

Related Work. One of the first methods for variable elimination in LRA was discovered independently by Fourier [10] and Motzkin [24]. It is still often used in practice, but quickly suffers from a doubly exponential worst case behavior (w.r.t. the number of eliminated variables) when the inputs become more complex. Different optimizations have been suggested to reduce the computational effort, most notably by avoiding redundant constraints in intermediate steps, e.g. [6, 14] and, more recently, [16].

An alternative approach is the Double-Description (DD) method [23], which was further developed and implemented by Fukuda and Prodon [11] in the CDD library [5], but also by others [2, 15]. A more recent development uses a reduction to parametric linear programming [17, 31]. These approaches stem from research focusing on the geometric, polyhedra-based view.

On the other hand, the algebraic view considers the more general problem of quantifier elimination for formulas with quantifier alternation and an arbitrary Boolean structure. As these methods are not optimized for our particular problem, we only highlight the *virtual term substitution* method proposed by Loos and Weispfenning [21] and thoroughly studied by others [19, 20], as well as the work by Monniaux [22], in which the authors reduce quantifier elimination for the general case to repeated polyhedron projections and satisfiability checking.

Most relevant for this work is the FMplex method [27], which was derived from the method of Fourier and Motzkin and aimed at satisfiability checking, but which can also be used for variable elimination from conjunctions of linear constraints. While a tree-shaped search allows FMplex to reduce the worst-case complexity from doubly to singly exponential, it has the consequence that the variable elimination result is provided only as a *disjunction* of conjunctions and not as a single conjunction, like provided by Fourier-Motzkin. These disjunctions are harder to interpret for the users, and they are larger than necessary.

Contributions. We overcome this limitation with the following contributions:

- We propose a new variable elimination approach for sets of LRA constraints, derived from the FMplex method presented in [27], but returning the result as a *set* (or *conjunction*) of LRA constraints.
- We show the correctness of this approach, give complexity estimates, and explain which of the improvements from [27] can be transferred to the new variable elimination algorithm.
- We discuss interesting relations between our method and the virtual term substitution method [21].
- We provide an implementation in the SMT-solving toolbox SMT-RAT.

– We present an experimental evaluation, which shows that our implementation outperforms other established tools on three different benchmark sets.

Outline. The rest of the paper is organized as follows: After a formal problem description in Sect. 2, we present the FMplex method and derive our new variable elimination method in Sect. 3. We compare it to other methods and evaluate its performance in Sects. 4 and 5. Finally, in Sect. 6, we conclude the paper and give an outlook on future work.

2 Preliminaries

Let $\mathbb{R}$, $\mathbb{Q}$ and $\mathbb{N}$ denote the real, rational, and natural numbers, respectively.

We use upper case letters (e.g. A) to denote matrices, bold lower case letters for vectors (e.g. $\boldsymbol{b}, \boldsymbol{f}$), and b_i to denote the i-th entry in $\boldsymbol{b}$. The i-th row and the j-th column vectors of a matrix A are denoted by $\boldsymbol{a}_{i,-}$ and $\boldsymbol{a}_{-,j}$, respectively. We assume $\mathbb{R}^n = \mathbb{R}^{n \times 1}$, i.e. $\boldsymbol{f} \in \mathbb{R}^n$ is a column vector. The transpose of $\boldsymbol{f}$ is $\boldsymbol{f}^\mathsf{T}$, and by $\boldsymbol{f} \geq \boldsymbol{0}$ we denote the component-wise comparison to zero, i.e. $f_1 \geq 0 \wedge \ldots \wedge f_n \geq 0$. We write $\boldsymbol{e}_i$ for the i-th unit vector and $\boldsymbol{0}$ for zero-matrices or zero-vectors; their dimensions will be clear from the context.

Linear Real Arithmetic: Syntax. We fix $n \in \mathbb{N}$ and a vector $\boldsymbol{x} = (x_1, \ldots, x_n)^\mathsf{T}$ of $\mathbb{R}$-valued variables. When convenient, we view variable vectors as ordered sets, writing e.g. $x_i \in \boldsymbol{x}$, or $\boldsymbol{y} \subseteq \boldsymbol{x}$ to denote that $\boldsymbol{y} = (x_{i_1}, \ldots, x_{i_k})^\mathsf{T}$ for some $0 \leq k \leq n$ and $1 \leq i_1 < \ldots < i_k \leq n$, and we write $|\boldsymbol{y}| = k$ for the length of $\boldsymbol{y}$.

Our main objects of interest are *linear constraints* (from here on simply *constraints*), which are inequations of the form

$$a_1 x_1 + a_2 x_2 + \ldots + a_n x_n \leq b, \text{ or equivalently } \boldsymbol{a}^\mathsf{T} \boldsymbol{x} \leq b$$

for some rational constants $\boldsymbol{a} = (a_1, \ldots, a_n)^\mathsf{T} \in \mathbb{Q}^n$ and $b \in \mathbb{Q}$. Expressions of the form $\boldsymbol{a}^\mathsf{T} \boldsymbol{x} + b$ are called *(linear) terms*. We sometimes write $s \leq t$ with linear terms s, t and implicitly assume a conversion to the above normal form.

Note that we do not consider strict inequations $\boldsymbol{a}^\mathsf{T} \boldsymbol{x} < b$; we will discuss their integration in Sect. 3.3. Note furthermore that $\boldsymbol{a}^\mathsf{T} \boldsymbol{x} \geq b$ is equivalent to $-\boldsymbol{a}^\mathsf{T} \boldsymbol{x} \leq -b$, and $\boldsymbol{a}^\mathsf{T} \boldsymbol{x} = b$ is equivalent to $\boldsymbol{a}^\mathsf{T} \boldsymbol{x} \leq b \wedge \boldsymbol{a}^\mathsf{T} \boldsymbol{x} \geq b$.

A variable x_i *occurs* in $\boldsymbol{a}^\mathsf{T} \boldsymbol{x} \leq b$ if $a_i \neq 0$. Let $vars(c)$ be the set of all variables that occur in the constraint c, and $vars(C) := \cup_{c \in C} vars(c)$ for any constraint set C. For a given $\boldsymbol{y} \subseteq \boldsymbol{x}$, we sometimes write $C(\boldsymbol{y})$ to indicate $vars(C) \subseteq \boldsymbol{y}$. Note that in this paper, we always have $vars(C) \subseteq \boldsymbol{x}$.

LRA formulas are built from constraints using Boolean connectives ($\wedge, \vee, \neg$) and quantifiers ($\exists, \forall$), according to the syntax of first-order logic. For an LRA formula φ, a variable $x_i \in \boldsymbol{x}$, and a term t, we write $\varphi[t/x_i]$ to denote the substitution of t for each free occurrence of x_i in φ.

Throughout the paper, we sometimes interpret sets of constraints as conjunctions, and sometimes as systems $A\boldsymbol{x} \leq \boldsymbol{b}$, with $A \in \mathbb{Q}^{m \times n}$ and $\boldsymbol{b} \in \mathbb{Q}^m$, representing the set $\{a_{i,-}x \leq b_i \mid i \in \{1, \ldots m\}\}$. Note that every finite set of constraints can be represented this way for a suitable A and b. We use the representations as set, conjunction or system interchangeably.

Linear Real Arithmetic: Semantics. An *assignment for* $y \subseteq x$ with $|y| = i \in \mathbb{N}$ is a vector $\alpha \in \mathbb{R}^i$. We define $\varphi[\alpha/y] := \varphi[\alpha_1/y_1] \ldots [\alpha_i/y_i]$, and say that α is a *solution* for φ, written $\alpha \models \varphi$, if $\varphi[\alpha/y]$ evaluates to true under the standard semantics.

If every solution of φ is also a solution of the formula ψ, then we say that φ implies ψ and write $\varphi \models \psi$. If both $\varphi \models \psi$ and $\psi \models \varphi$ hold, then the solution sets are equal and the formulas are equivalent, denoted by $\varphi \equiv \psi$. Note that, when interpreting a set C of constraints as their conjunction, the statement $\alpha \models C$ is to be interpreted as $\alpha \models \bigwedge_{c \in C} c$.

A well-known result for such constraint systems is Farkas' Lemma, which we will use in the following formulation.

Theorem 1 (Farkas' Lemma [9]). *Let* $A \in \mathbb{Q}^{m \times n}$ *and* $b \in \mathbb{Q}^m$. *A constraint* c *is implied by* $Ax \leq b$ *if and only if there are* $f \in \mathbb{R}^m$ *and* $f_0 \in \mathbb{R}$ *with* $f \geq 0$, $f_0 \geq 0$ *and* $c = (f^\mathsf{T} Ax \leq f^\mathsf{T} b + f_0)$.

Variable Elimination. Consider a finite set C of linear constraints, and let $x^Q \subseteq x$. W.l.o.g. we assume $x^Q = (x_1, \ldots, x_q)^\mathsf{T}$ for some $1 \leq q \leq n$, and we set $x^P := (x_{q+1}, \ldots, x_n)^\mathsf{T}$ and $p := |x^P| = n - q$. Our goal is to find a - preferably small - constraint set $D(x^P)$ with $D \equiv \exists x_1 \ldots \exists x_q . C$. That is, $\alpha^P \in \mathbb{R}^p$ is a solution for D if and only if it can be extended to a solution $\alpha \in \mathbb{R}^n$ for C.

We refer to the variables in x^Q as *quantified* and to those in x^P as *parameters*, and formulate constraint sets also as $A^Q x^Q + A^P x^P \leq b$. We fix x^Q, x^P, q and p as given above for the rest of this paper.

Example 1. A possible solution to the variable elimination of x_1 and x_2 from

$$C := \{-x_1 + x_2 - x_3 \leq -3, \; -x_1 + x_2 + x_3 \leq 4, \; x_1 \leq 3, \; -x_2 \leq -1\}$$

is the set $\{-x_3 \leq -1, \; x_3 \leq 6\}$.

It is important to note that the ordering of the existential quantifiers does not change the task, as is illustrated in Fig. 1. Thus, it is possible and indeed helpful to change this order dynamically.

Polyhedron Projection. The above variable elimination problem is also known as *polyhedron projection*. This name comes from the fact that the solutions of a constraint set $Ax \leq b$ describe a convex polyhedron in the n-dimensional space and eliminating the variables x^Q corresponds to a projection onto the dimensions from x^P. That is, $(Dx^P \leq f) \equiv (\exists x^Q . A^Q x^Q + A^P x^P \leq b)$ if and only if

$$\{\alpha^P \in \mathbb{R}^p \mid D\alpha^P \leq f\} = \{\alpha^P \in \mathbb{R}^p \mid \exists \alpha^Q \in \mathbb{R}^q : A^Q \alpha^Q + A^P \alpha^P \leq b\}.$$

$$\begin{bmatrix} -1 & 1 \\ -1 & 1 \\ 1 & 0 \\ 0 & -1 \end{bmatrix} \begin{bmatrix} x_1 \\ x_2 \end{bmatrix} + \begin{bmatrix} -1 \\ 1 \\ 0 \\ 0 \end{bmatrix} x_3 \le \begin{bmatrix} -3 \\ 4 \\ 3 \\ -1 \end{bmatrix}$$

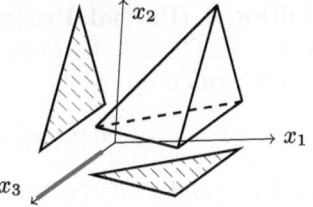

Fig. 1. The constraint set from Example 1 in matrix representation (left) and its solution set, as well as the projections of that set onto the x_1-x_3-plane (blue), the x_2-x_3-plane (red) and the x_3-axis (violet). (Color figure online)

3   A Divide-and-Conquer Approach

3.1   Divide: The FMplex Method

We now summarize the idea of the FMplex method introduced in [27] and then refine it to make it better suited for the task of polyhedron projection.

Originally, this method was developed as a branching version of the Fourier-Motzkin (FM) variable elimination method. However, [27] does not further study the general task of variable elimination, but focuses on using FMplex for checking the satisfiability of a constraint set.[1]

To eliminate a variable $x_i \in \boldsymbol{x}$ from a constraint set C, FMplex partitions the constraints into three sets as follows.

Definition 1. *For each constraint set C and variable $x_i \in \boldsymbol{x}$, we define*

- $C^-(x_i) := \{(\boldsymbol{a}^\mathsf{T}\boldsymbol{x} \le b) \in C \mid a_i < 0\}$, *called the* lower bounds *of C on x_i,*
- $C^+(x_i) := \{(\boldsymbol{a}^\mathsf{T}\boldsymbol{x} \le b) \in C \mid a_i > 0\}$, *called the* upper bounds *of C on x_i,*
- $C^0(x_i) := \{(\boldsymbol{a}^\mathsf{T}\boldsymbol{x} \le b) \in C \mid a_i = 0\}$, *called the* non-bounds *of C on x_i,*

Moreover, for each $c = (\boldsymbol{a}^\mathsf{T}\boldsymbol{x} \le b) \in C^-(x_i) \cup C^+(x_i)$, we define the term

$$bnd(x_i, c) := 1/a_i \cdot (b - (a_1 x_1 + \ldots + a_{i-1} x_{i-1} + a_{i+1} x_{i+1} + \ldots + a_n x_n)).$$

Each constraint $c \in C^-(x_i)$ is equivalent to $bnd(x_i, c) \le x_i$, and it bounds from below the x_i-value of solutions for C w.r.t. the other variables. Similarly, $c \in C^+(x_i)$ is equivalent to $x_i \le bnd(x_i, c)$. For $c \in C^0(x_i)$ we have $x_i \notin vars(c)$.

The method then uses the insight that at each point in the projection onto $vars(C) \backslash (x_i)$, one of the lower bounds is a *greatest* and one of the upper bounds is a *lowest*. Thus, the projection can be divided into a disjunction of sub-problems, each stating that a particular lower bound is a greatest and that no upper bound is below it. Symmetrically, one can express that a particular upper bound is a lowest and that no lower bound is above it. Theorem 2 formalizes the division into sub-problems by which FMplex eliminates the variable x_i.

---

[1] In that context, FMplex exhibits similarities to the simplex method, hence the name.

Definition 2 (Partial Projection). *Let C be a constraint set, $x_i \in \boldsymbol{x}$ and $c \in C^-(x_i) \cup C^+(x_i)$. Further, let $t := bnd(x_i, c)$, then the* partial projection *of x_i from C with c is*

$$C[c//x_i] := \{c'[t/x_i] \mid c' \in C \setminus \{c\}\}.$$

Using $L := \{bnd(x_i, c') \mid c' \in C^-(x_i)\}$ and $U := \{bnd(x_i, c') \mid c' \in C^+(x_i)\}$, this is equivalent to $\{l \le t \mid l \in L \setminus \{c\}\} \cup \{t \le u \mid u \in U \setminus \{c\}\} \cup C^0(x_i)$.

Theorem 2 ([27]). *If $C^+(x_i) = \emptyset$ or $C^-(x_i) = \emptyset$, then $\exists x_i.C \equiv C^0(x_i)$.*

Otherwise, $\exists x_i.C \quad \equiv \bigvee_{c \in C^-(x_i)} C[c//x_i] \quad \equiv \bigvee_{c \in C^+(x_i)} C[c//x_i]$.

To eliminate multiple variables, the disjuncts can be handled independently. That is, in each of the disjuncts, one can eliminate any of the remaining variables to again receive a disjunction. Essentially, the method constructs a tree of constraint sets where the root is the initial input C, and the children of any node are the disjuncts that result from eliminating a variable from that node using Theorem 2. At the leafs of the tree, all desired variables are eliminated, but different paths from the root to a leaf may eliminate the variables in different orders and may alternate between using lower or upper bounds for branching.

Example 2. We revisit Example 1 and start by eliminating x_1 using greatest lower bounds. With $C^-(x_1) = \{-x_1 + x_2 - x_3 \le -3, -x_1 + x_2 + x_3 \le 4\}$, $C^+(x_1) = \{x_1 \le 3\}$ and $C^0(x_1) = \{-x_2 \le -1\}$, we get

$$\begin{aligned}
\exists x_1.C \quad &\equiv \quad C[(-x_1 + x_2 - x_3 \le -3)//x_1] \quad \lor \quad C[(-x_1 + x_2 + x_3 \le 4)//x_1] \\
&\equiv \quad \{2x_3 \le 7, \quad x_2 - x_3 \le 0, \quad -x_2 \le -1\} \quad \lor \\
&\qquad \{-2x_3 \le -7, \quad x_2 + x_3 \le 7, \quad -x_2 \le -1\}
\end{aligned}$$

We eliminate x_2 from the two sets independently, using their only lower bound:

$$\exists x_1, x_2.C \equiv \quad \{2x_3 \le 7, \quad -x_3 \le -1\} \quad \lor \quad \{-2x_3 \le -7, \quad x_3 \le 6\}.$$

3.2   Conquer: Obtaining a Conjunctive Result

When using FMplex for satisfiability checking (like in [27]), one eliminates all variables of the given constraint set and if *any* leaf is satisfiable, then the input is satisfiable as well. But for quantifier elimination, we need to consider *all* leafs. The problem here is that the final result is going to be a potentially large disjunction of conjunctions or, geometrically, a union of convex polyhedra. We know from Fourier-Motzkin that this union is again a single convex polyhedron and thus can be represented as a single conjunction. However, naively computing the union of the polyhedra would be too much effort, and we will show a more efficient way to extract a conjunction from the computations.

Our first step is to observe that all constraints constructed by the above method can be understood as linear combinations of the original constraints.

Lemma 1. *Let $A \in \mathbb{Q}^{m \times n}$ and $\boldsymbol{b} \in \mathbb{Q}^m$. For every constraint $\boldsymbol{v}^\mathsf{T}\boldsymbol{x} \leq w$ constructed by FMplex (repeated application of Theorem 2) on the input $A\boldsymbol{x} \leq \boldsymbol{b}$, there is $\boldsymbol{f} \in \mathbb{Q}^m$ with $\boldsymbol{f}^\mathsf{T}A = \boldsymbol{v}^\mathsf{T}$ and $\boldsymbol{f}^\mathsf{T}\boldsymbol{b} = w \in \mathbb{Q}$.*

Proof. For any $\boldsymbol{a}_{k,-}\boldsymbol{x} \leq b_k$, we can simply choose $\boldsymbol{f} = \boldsymbol{e}_k$. Let $c = (\boldsymbol{a}^\mathsf{T}\boldsymbol{x} \leq d)$ with $a_i \neq 0$, $t := bnd(x_i, c)$, and $c' = (\boldsymbol{a'}^\mathsf{T}\boldsymbol{x} \leq d')$. Assume that we already have $\boldsymbol{f}, \boldsymbol{f'} \in \mathbb{Q}^m$ with $c = (\boldsymbol{f}^\mathsf{T}A\boldsymbol{x} \leq \boldsymbol{f}^\mathsf{T}\boldsymbol{b})$ and $c' = (\boldsymbol{f'}^\mathsf{T}A\boldsymbol{x} \leq \boldsymbol{f'}^\mathsf{T}\boldsymbol{b})$. Then

$$c'[t/x_i] \equiv \left(\left(\boldsymbol{a'} - \frac{a_i'}{a_i}\boldsymbol{a}\right)^\mathsf{T}\boldsymbol{x} \leq d' - \frac{a_i'}{a_i}d\right) = \left(\left(\boldsymbol{f'} - \frac{a_i'}{a_i}\boldsymbol{f}\right)^\mathsf{T}A\boldsymbol{x} \leq \left(\boldsymbol{f'} - \frac{a_i'}{a_i}\boldsymbol{f}\right)^\mathsf{T}\boldsymbol{b}\right).$$

Note that new constraints are only constructed by this kind of substitution. □

It can happen that the same constraint is derived in multiple ways, and from now on, we want to distinguish constraints also by the way they are generated.

Definition 3 (Annotated Constraints). *An* annotated constraint *has the form $c{:}\boldsymbol{f}$ with some constraint c and an $\boldsymbol{f} \in \mathbb{Q}^m$, also called the* construction vector. *Constraints with different annotations are considered as different.*

Instead of constraint sets, we now consider sets of annotated constraints. Most notions can be adapted straightforwardly, in particular the definitions for $C^-(x_i), C^+(x_i), C^0(x_i)$ and $vars(C)$. For the restricted projection $C[c{:}\boldsymbol{f}/\!/x_i]$, the construction vector of a new constraint can easily be computed from the construction vectors of its parents, according to the proof of Lemma 1.

Our main result, which we will show in Theorem 3, is that the final disjunction computed by FMplex is equivalent to the conjunction of those constraints whose construction vectors have no negative entries. This is fairly easy to see for the elimination of a single variable, since the non-negative combinations are exactly the constraints the Fourier-Motzkin method would compute. The constraints whose construction vectors do have negative entries stem from the assumptions that some lower (upper) bound is larger or equal to another lower (upper) bound. This means that these constraints do not define the boundary of the solution space, but they only cut it into multiple parts, causing the disjunction. This intuition can be generalized for the elimination of multiple variables.

Example 3. When going through Example 2 with annotations, we get the result

$$\exists x_1, x_2.C \equiv \{2x_3 \leq 7{:}(-1, 1, 0, 0)^\mathsf{T}, \; -x_3 \leq -1{:}(1, 0, 1, 1)^\mathsf{T}\} \vee$$
$$\{-2x_3 \leq -7{:}(1, -1, 0, 0)^\mathsf{T}, \; x_3 \leq 6{:}(0, 1, 1, 1)^\mathsf{T}\}.$$

Collecting the constraints with non-negative construction vectors gives the equivalent set $\{-x_3 \leq -1, \; x_3 \leq 6\}$, as in Example 1. Note how the other two constraints partition the solution space, but they do not change it.

Theorem 3. *Let C be a constraint set and $\exists \boldsymbol{x}^Q.C \equiv D_1 \vee \ldots \vee D_k$, such that the disjunction on the right-hand side was constructed using the FMplex method, i.e. by repeated application of Theorem 2 with constraint annotation. Let further $D_{pos} := \{c \mid c{:}\boldsymbol{f} \in \bigcup_{i=1}^k D_i, \; \boldsymbol{f} \geq 0\}$. Then $\exists \boldsymbol{x}^Q.C \equiv D_{pos}$.*

Proof. We show that for every $\boldsymbol{\alpha}^P \in \mathbb{R}^p$ holds $(\boldsymbol{\alpha}^P \models \exists \boldsymbol{x}^Q.C) \Leftrightarrow (\boldsymbol{\alpha}^P \models D_{pos})$. Farkas' Lemma (Theorem 1) immediately yields $(\boldsymbol{\alpha}^P \models \exists \boldsymbol{x}^Q.C) \Rightarrow (\boldsymbol{\alpha}^P \models D_{pos})$. So, it remains to show $\boldsymbol{\alpha}^P \not\models \exists \boldsymbol{x}^Q.C \Rightarrow \boldsymbol{\alpha}^P \not\models D_{pos}$. Assume that C has the form $A^Q \boldsymbol{x}^Q + A^P \boldsymbol{x}^P \leq \boldsymbol{b}$ and consider the following system, with $\boldsymbol{b}' := \boldsymbol{b} - A^P \boldsymbol{\alpha}^P \in \mathbb{R}^m$:

$$C' \quad := \quad C[\boldsymbol{\alpha}^P / \boldsymbol{x}^P] \quad = \quad (A^Q \boldsymbol{x}^Q + A^P \boldsymbol{\alpha}^P \leq \boldsymbol{b}) \quad \equiv \quad A^Q \boldsymbol{x}^Q \leq \boldsymbol{b}'.$$

Since $\boldsymbol{\alpha}^P \not\models \exists \boldsymbol{x}^Q.C$, this system is unsatisfiable and there is a minimal unsatisfiable subset $K' \subseteq C'$. We know that there is $K \subseteq C$ with $K[\boldsymbol{\alpha}^P / \boldsymbol{x}^P] = K'$. We will show that there is $c \in D_{pos}$, constructed only from K and so that $\alpha \not\models c$.

For this purpose, we will construct a sequence $(C_1, C_2, \ldots, C_{q+1})$, starting with $C_1 := C$, corresponding to a path in the elimination tree of FMplex from the initial system to a leaf (where all variables in $\boldsymbol{x}^Q$ have been eliminated). Starting with $K_1 := K$, we will construct a second sequence $(K_1, K_2, \ldots, K_{q+1})$ so that for all $1 \leq i \leq q+1$ holds $K_i \subseteq C_i$, the set $K_i[\boldsymbol{\alpha}^P / \boldsymbol{x}^P]$ is unsatisfiable and K_i is minimal in the sense that for all $L \subsetneq K_i$, the set $L[\boldsymbol{\alpha}^P / \boldsymbol{x}^P]$ is satisfiable.

W.l.o.g. let x_i be the variable eliminated next from C_i. It holds $K_i^-(x_i) \neq \emptyset$ if and only if $K_i^+(x_i) \neq \emptyset$, because otherwise $K_i^0(x_i)$ would be a strict subset of K_i and $K_i^0(x_i)[\boldsymbol{\alpha}^P / \boldsymbol{x}^P]$ would be unsatisfiable, contradicting the minimality of K_i. Therefore, either $x_i \notin vars(K_i)$ or $K_i^-(x_i) \neq \emptyset \neq K_i^+(x_i)$ holds.

- If $x_i \notin vars(K_i)$, then $K_i \subseteq C_i^0(x_i)$, therefore K_i is included in all children of C_i. We choose one of them as C_{i+1} and use $K_{i+1} := K_i$.
- In the other case, there is a constraint $c : \boldsymbol{f} \in K_i$ so that one of the constructed children is $C_{i+1} := C_i[c : \boldsymbol{f} // x_i]$.
  Note that $K_i[c : \boldsymbol{f} // x_i] \subseteq C_i[c : \boldsymbol{f} // x_i]$ holds and $K_i[c : \boldsymbol{f} // x_i][\boldsymbol{\alpha}^P / \boldsymbol{x}^P]$ is unsatisfiable (since otherwise K' would be satisfiable). Thus, there is a minimal subset $K_{i+1} \subseteq K_i[c : \boldsymbol{f} // x_i]$ so that $K_{i+1}[\boldsymbol{\alpha}^P / \boldsymbol{x}^P]$ is unsatisfiable.

In the end, $K_{q+1} \neq \emptyset$, $vars(K_{q+1}) \cap \boldsymbol{x}^Q = \emptyset$ and $K_{q+1}[\boldsymbol{\alpha}^P / \boldsymbol{x}^P]$ is unsatisfiable. Thus, there is $c : \boldsymbol{f} \in K_{q+1}$ with $\boldsymbol{\alpha}^P \not\models c$. We now show $\boldsymbol{f} \geq 0$ and thus $c \in D_{pos}$.

For $i \in \{1, \ldots, m\}$, let $c_i := ((\boldsymbol{a}^Q)_{i,-} \boldsymbol{x}^Q + (\boldsymbol{a}^P)_{i,-} \boldsymbol{x}^P \leq b_i)$. For all i with $c_i \in C \setminus K$ holds $f_i = 0$, by construction. Towards a contradiction, assume there was $1 \leq j \leq m$ with $c_j \in K$ and $f_j < 0$. By Farkas' Lemma and the minimality of K, there exists $\boldsymbol{f}' \in \mathbb{R}^m$ so that $f_i' > 0$ for all $c_i \in K$, $f_i' = 0$ for all $c_i \in C \setminus K$, and $(\boldsymbol{f}'^\mathsf{T} A^Q \boldsymbol{x}^Q + \boldsymbol{f}'^\mathsf{T} A^P \boldsymbol{x}^P \leq \boldsymbol{f}'^\mathsf{T} \boldsymbol{b}) = c$.

Using $\lambda := \max\{\frac{-f_j}{f_j'} \mid 1 \leq j \leq m, \ f_j < 0\}$ and $\boldsymbol{g} := \boldsymbol{f} + \lambda \boldsymbol{f}'$, we observe $\boldsymbol{g}^\mathsf{T} A^Q = 0$ and $\boldsymbol{\alpha}^P \not\models (\boldsymbol{g}^\mathsf{T} A^P \boldsymbol{x}^P \leq \boldsymbol{g}^\mathsf{T} \boldsymbol{b})$, but $\{c_i \mid 1 \leq i \leq m, \ g_i \neq 0\} \subsetneq K$, contradicting the minimality of K. Therefore, $c \in D_{pos}$ and $\alpha \not\models D_{pos}$. $\qquad \square$

Our method is formulated in Algorithm 1. It maintains a stack `node_stack` of annotated constraint sets, which correspond to the nodes of the elimination tree traversed by FMplex. The function `push` inserts the given set at the top of the stack, and `pop` removes its top element and returns that set.

Since a node's children are smaller than that node, i.e. $|N[c : \boldsymbol{f} // x_i]| < |N|$, and the tree branching is bounded by m, i.e. $|N^-(x_i)| \leq |N|, |N^+(x_i)| \leq |N|$, the algorithm has an exponential complexity ($\mathcal{O}(m^{q+1})$) in space and time, with respect to $|\boldsymbol{x}^Q|$. In fact, the stack never contains more than $m^2 \cdot (q+1)$ total constraints at the same time and only the output needs exponentially large space. Interestingly, we only insert new constraints into the output set and never read or remove something from it during the procedure.

Algorithm 1: $\texttt{project}(C, \boldsymbol{x}^Q)$

Input : A constraint set $C = \{c_1, \ldots c_m\}$ and $\boldsymbol{x}^Q = \{x_1, \ldots x_q\} \subseteq \boldsymbol{x}$.
Output: A constraint set D with $vars(D) \cap \boldsymbol{x}^Q = \emptyset$ and $D \equiv \exists x_1 \ldots x_q.C$

---

1 Initialize $\texttt{result} = \{\}$, $\texttt{node\_stack} = [\,]$
2 $\texttt{node\_stack.push}(\{c_i{:}e_i \mid c_i \in C\})$
3 **while** not $\texttt{node\_stack.empty}()$ **do**
4 $\quad$ $N = \texttt{node\_stack.pop}()$
5 $\quad$ $\texttt{result} = \texttt{result} \cup \{c \mid c{:}\boldsymbol{f} \in N \wedge \boldsymbol{f} \geq 0 \wedge \boldsymbol{x}^Q \cap vars(c) = \emptyset\}$
6 $\quad$ **if** $vars(N) \cap \boldsymbol{x}^Q \neq \emptyset$ **then**
7 $\quad\quad$ Choose $x_i \in vars(N) \cap \boldsymbol{x}^Q$
8 $\quad\quad$ **if** $N^-(x_i) = \emptyset$ or $N^+(x_i) = \emptyset$ **then**
9 $\quad\quad\quad$ $\texttt{node\_stack.push}(N^0(x_i))$
10 $\quad\quad$ **else**
11 $\quad\quad\quad$ Choose $* \in \{-, +\}$
12 $\quad\quad\quad$ **foreach** $c{:}\boldsymbol{f} \in N^*(x_i)$ **do** $\texttt{node\_stack.push}(N[c{:}\boldsymbol{f}/\!/x_i])$
13 **return** $\texttt{result}$

3.3 Further Improvements

Thanks to its disjunctive structure, our approach admits many optimizations. The original paper for FMplex [27] describes several improvements for the version developed for satisfiability checking. We will now show, which of these improvements can be transferred to the new setting of variable elimination.

Variable and Branch Choice. In each of the processed nodes, we can choose the eliminated variable and whether to branch on lower or upper bounds. This choice is independent of the other nodes and can have a massive impact on the runtime of the algorithm. To minimize the number of children for each node N, we choose an x_i for which $\min(|N^-(x_i)|, |N^+(x_i)|)$ is minimal and, if necessary, choose the branching $* \in \{-, +\}$ accordingly.

Equations and Strict Constraints. In the presence of equations $\boldsymbol{a}^\mathsf{T}\boldsymbol{x} = b$, we employ Gauss-elimination before the actual call to our procedure, in order to eliminate some of the desired variables using the equations.

To handle strict constraints $\boldsymbol{a}^\mathsf{T}\boldsymbol{x} < b$, we introduce a new variable δ as a placeholder for some infinitesimal value and instead consider $\boldsymbol{a}^\mathsf{T}\boldsymbol{x} + \delta \leq b$. We eliminate δ from the final result using the additional constraint $\delta > 0$. That is, for a resulting constraint $\boldsymbol{a}^\mathsf{T}\boldsymbol{x}^P + d\delta \leq b$, if $d \neq 0$, then $d > 0$ and we can deduce $\boldsymbol{a}^\mathsf{T}\boldsymbol{x}^P < b$. This is a fairly standard way of dealing with strict constraints.

Pruning Equivalent Nodes. An interesting result in [27] is that for each node N in the elimination tree, one can partition the original input C into two sets $\mathcal{N}, \mathcal{B}$, so that each constraint $c \in N$ was constructed from the constraints in $\mathcal{N}$ and exactly one of the constraints in $\mathcal{B}$. The intuition is that we start with $\mathcal{N} := \emptyset$ and $\mathcal{B} := C$ and when constructing $N[c//x_i]$, the constraint corresponding to c moves from $\mathcal{B}$ to $\mathcal{N}$. In that sense, $\mathcal{N}$ contains the assumed strictest bounds.

Multiple nodes can have the same corresponding sets $\mathcal{N}, \mathcal{B}$, with the intuition that the same bounds are chosen in a different order. Then, the nodes are equivalent, and [27] avoids visiting more than one of them using some bookkeeping.

This optimization can be transferred straightforwardly, as the relevant results are about equivalence and not just satisfiability.

Pruning Unsatisfiable Nodes. In the case of satisfiability checking, the goal is to find *any* satisfiable node in the elimination tree. Therefore, it is helpful to identify and prune unsatisfiable parts of the tree. A node is easily recognized as unsatisfiable if it contains a trivially false constraint, e.g. $0 \leq -1$. Then, the children of that node can be ignored, since they will also contain that constraint.

This can also be used in our version for variable elimination, though we omit the proof here for brevity. Essentially, one can show that the construction in the proof for Theorem 3 still works when leaving out the pruned nodes.

This idea is taken even further in [27], by analyzing how the trivially false constraints are constructed. If an unsatisfiable node is encountered, one may find an ancestor of that node in the elimination tree which already implies the trivially false constraint. Therefore, the remaining children of that ancestor can also be pruned. However, this can *not* be used for variable elimination, as illustrated by the following example, which was already considered in [27]:

Example 4. We eliminate all variables with the static order x_3, x_2, x_1 from

$$\{-x_3 \leq 0, \quad x_1 - x_2 - x_3 \leq 0, \quad x_1 \leq -1, \quad -x_1 + x_2 \leq -1, \quad -x_2 + x_3 \leq 0\},$$

always branching on lower bounds and first considering greatest lower bounds whose construction vectors have negative entries. When pruning nodes according to which ancestor implied the unsatisfiability, our algorithm would incorrectly return the (satisfiable) empty constraint set, while the input is unsatisfiable.

There is one exception, though. If a trivially false constraint is annotated with an $\boldsymbol{f} \geq 0$, then it is implied by the input system. Thus, it is added to the result, which is then unsatisfiable and we can stop immediately. However, in usual applications of polyhedron projection, the input is rarely unsatisfiable.

Splitting Into Unrelated Systems. It can happen that the input system consists of several parts that are unrelated with regard to the eliminated variables. That is, we can find a decomposition $C = C_1 \cup \ldots \cup C_k$ so that for all $i \neq j$ holds $vars(C_i) \cap vars(C_j) \cap x^Q = \emptyset$. In that case, x^Q can be eliminated from each single C_i independently. To avoid eliminating the variables in $vars(C_1) \cap x^Q$ and then performing the elimination for C_2 in every resulting subtree, we can split the node C into nodes $C_1, C_2, \ldots$ and put them on the stack. Such a partition can easily be found by computing the connected components in a graph that has the constraints of C as vertices and has an edge between c and c' if $vars(c) \cap vars(c') \cap x^Q \neq \emptyset$. Note that this can be applied to the initial input to help any projection method. However, our method can apply it to all the intermediate nodes, potentially leading to more savings. This improvement is not relevant for satisfiability checking, and it is a novel contribution.

4   Relation to Virtual Term Substitution

Although the original approach was derived from the Fourier-Motzkin method, it exhibits striking similarities to *virtual term substitution (VTS)* introduced by Loos and Weispfenning [21]. The VTS method also eliminates variables from LRA formulas in a tree-like manner. In each step, it collects terms from the individual constraints and substitutes them for the eliminated variable, obtaining a disjunction similar to the result of Theorem 2. In fact, these terms can be chosen to be exactly like in our approach, i.e. so that they correspond to the lower bounds or the upper bounds. However, the special case that there are no lower bounds or no upper bounds is handled by an additional disjunct $C[-\infty//x_i]$ or $C[\infty//x_i]$, performing a *virtual* substitution of an infinite value for the variable.

It was observed in [19] that the constraints derived by the VTS are linear combinations of the original input, in the same sense as described in Sect. 3.2. Thus, we are certain that our main result, Theorem 3, can be transferred to the VTS method. To our knowledge, this has not been shown before. In particular, [19] is only about satisfiability checking and does not construct an equivalent conjunction. Interestingly though, it introduces a pruning mechanism which is similar to the ones described in the previous section.

All this only applies to the case where existential quantifiers are eliminated from a conjunction of weak linear constraints. In general, VTS can be applied to formulas with quantifier alternation and arbitrary Boolean structure, and non-linear constraints with quadratic polynomials.[2] Our results cannot be easily generalized to that setting (and, in that general case, the result of quantifier elimination is not necessarily defining a convex polyhedron).

5   Experimental Evaluation

We implemented our algorithm in the *Satisfiability Modulo Theories Real Arithmetic Toolbox* (SMT-RAT, [7]) and compared the following tools.

---

[2] In fact, it can be adapted to handle polynomials of a fixed higher degree.

SMT-RAT The implementation of the algorithm presented in this paper, including the optimizations described in Sect. 3.3. For source code see [29].

FM A basic implementation of the Fourier-Motzkin method in SMT-RAT, without any further optimizations. This is merely a baseline, and it should be noted that there exist substantial improvements.

CDD The projection method of the library CDDlib which uses the double description method. For source version, see [5].

Redlog An optimized VTS implementation provided by the Redlog package of the computer algebra system Reduce [8]. For source version, see [28].

Z3 The z3 prover [25], which offers quantifier elimination based on quantifier instantiation and model based projections [4]. For source version, see [32].

The methods provided by Redlog and Z3 are directed at much more general quantifier elimination tasks than polyhedron projection. As a consequence, they generally return disjunctions, which are harder to interpret and to use. The comparisons are still interesting, since firstly, VTS is closely related to our method and secondly, Z3 is state of the art for most SMT related tasks.

All tools use exact arithmetic. We tested the tools on three benchmark sets.

Random. We randomly generated a set of satisfiable conjunctions and varied certain parameters to ensure diversity. More precisely, for each combination of $n \in \{3, 6, \ldots, 30\}$, $m \in \{3, 6, \ldots, 60\}$ and $d \in \{0.1, 0.3, 0.5, 0.7, 0.9\}$, we generated 10 conjunctions of m constraints with n variables and so that the density of the coefficients is around d (i.e., the probability that an entry is non-zero is set to d). The coefficients are random integers between -100 and 100, though the right-hand sides are non-negative to ensure satisfiability. For each of the conjunctions, half of the variables are chosen at random as the quantified variables. This amounted to 10000 test cases.

SMT-LIB. The standard SMT-LIB [3] quantifier elimination benchmarks are not suitable as they contain universal quantifiers and more complex Boolean structures. Instead, we executed a DPLL(T)-style SMT-solver on the *quantifier free* linear real arithmetic benchmarks (QF_LRA) and collected all maximal conjunctions that were passed to the theory solver during the execution, leaving out disequalities ($\neq$) and replacing $<$ by $\leq$, as CDD does not natively handle strict constraints. For each conjunction, half of the variables are chosen randomly to be eliminated. This produced 4798 test cases.

NN-Verif. Neural network verification approaches like [1, 30] use convex polyhedra to over-approximate the set of all possible outputs of a neural network for a given input set. This approximation uses auxiliary variables, whose elimination might simplify the representation and speed up computations.

ACAS Xu is a standard data set with 45 neural networks belonging to an airborne collision avoidance system [18]. For each network, we over-approximated its output for two different input sets, using the method from [1]. The resulting constraint matrices have an almost triangular structure, with decreasing column density from left to right. Therefore, we derived three test cases from each polyhedron: one eliminating the first five variables, one eliminating the last five and one for five randomly chosen variables. This amounted to 270 instances.

We executed each tool on each test instance with a time limit of 5 min and a memory limit of 4 GB. The experiments were conducted on identical machines with two Intel Xeon Platinum 8160 CPUs (2.1 GHz, 24 cores). Consult the Data Availability Statement for more details on the collected data.

Table 1. Number of solved instances for each tool and benchmark set.

Set	#instances	SMT-RAT	CDD	Redlog	FM	Z3
Random	10000	**7482**	7347	6712	4632	3688
SMT-LIB	4798	**4740**	1306	4545	4731	4456
NN-Verif	270	**124**	116	105	75	76

Table 1 summarizes the results. In each of the benchmark suites, our implementation in SMT-RAT solves more instances than any of the other tools. As was to be expected, the simple implementation of FM does not perform well and quickly uses too much memory as the number of constructed constraints explodes. In fact, all failures of FM were due to exceeding the memory limit. The weakness of FM becomes apparent especially for the random benchmarks.

Surprisingly, Z3 did not perform better than FM, though it never exceeded the memory limit. As mentioned before, the method implemented by Z3 is not specialized for our task and, while it solves more general and complex problems efficiently, it cannot compete with the specialized methods.[3]

Redlog is not far behind our method: for each benchmark set, the difference in solved instances does not exceed 8% of the total number of instances. It is not surprising to see some similarities between the two, considering that they are closely related, as discussed in Sect. 4. However, note that the outputs of Redlog or Z3 are not always suitable for the respective application, as they can contain disjunctions. This is the case for 3352 (resp. 2069 for Z3) random instances, 1934 (2646) of the SMT-LIB set and 39 (76) of the NN-Verif set.

On the random and neural network verification benchmarks, CDD is the strongest contender after SMT-RAT. Compared to Redlog and FM, it is a more specialized implementation for the task at hand. However, its performance dramatically drops for the set derived from SMT-LIB, and we will see why this happens when we further inspect that benchmark set below.

Random Instances. With respect to the running time, our implementation clearly outperforms FM, Z3 and Redlog. FM solves 2648 instances faster than SMT-RAT, and Z3 does so on 430 instances. However, SMT-RAT solves most

---

[3] Z3 offers some flexibility and control over the solver's behavior and it is possible that specific settings improve the results; but this is out of scope for our evaluation.

of them within 0.5 s and all within 10 s. Only in 154 cases is Redlog faster than SMT-RAT, in contrast to 7329 cases where SMT-RAT is faster.

The comparison to CDD, however, is more ambiguous. CDD is faster in "only" 1657 cases, but SMT-RAT significantly struggles with these cases and times out on 148 of them. On the other hand, many of the instances where SMT-RAT is faster are solved by both tools within one second. In such small time, implementation details, e.g. how the input is processed, can have a big impact, making it harder to interpret the results. Nevertheless, there are 1060 instances for which SMT-RAT is faster and CDD takes more than a second.

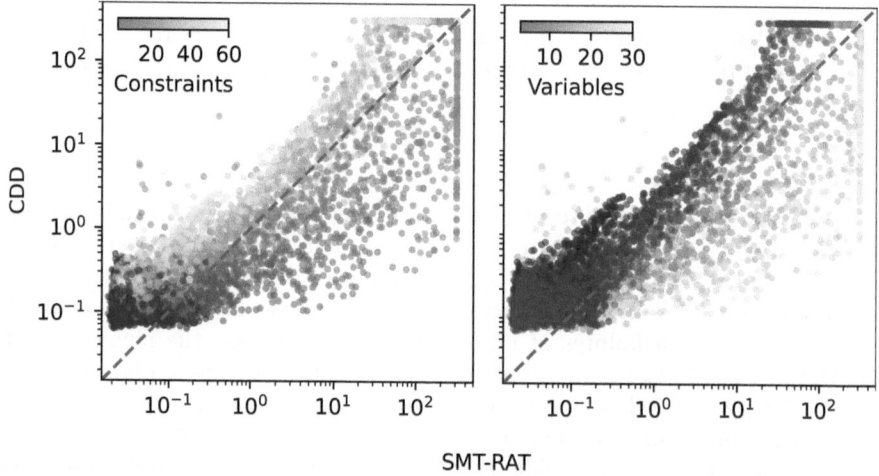

Fig. 2. Running times in seconds of CDD compared to SMT-RAT, colored by the number of input constraints (left) and the number of input variables (right). Each dot represents one instance of the random benchmark set. Timeouts are clamped to 5 min (lines on the very right/top).

To further investigate the strengths and weaknesses of the two tools, we consider Fig. 2, which shows the running times of SMT-RAT compared to CDD on each individual random instance. On the left, the instances are colored according to the number of input constraints; on the right, the same image is colored according to the number of input variables. We can see that SMT-RAT usually performs better if the number of constraints is high, but there are not more than 15 variables. On the other hand, CDD seems to have an advantage for problems with a medium number (20 to 40) of constraints and many variables.

A similar analysis with regard to the sparsity of the input showed no clear pattern. However, we will see next that extreme sparsity can make a difference.

SMT-LIB. The problems derived from the SMT-LIB satisfiability checking benchmarks are structurally quite different from the other two sets. They contain many variables and constraints, but are extremely sparse. In numbers: over 88% of the instances contain 50 or more variables and over 90% contain 100 or more constraints. On the other hand, over 87% of the instances have a density of 0.05 or lower, which is much lower than in any of the random benchmarks.

This sparsity makes it very likely that the flexibility and the structural savings of our approach have a big impact. It also favors FM, since memory and the combinatorial blow-up inherent to FM are less of an issue. CDD on the other hand cannot exploit the sparsity that well. It is based on the double description method which is generally more expensive for larger numbers of constraints.

Neural Network Verification. All instances in the NN-Verif set have a density between 0.25 and 0.4, which nicely complements the set derived from SMT-LIB. The instances are still sizable, containing 20–102 variables and 55–301 constraints.

As described before, the NN-Verif set has three categories of 90 instances each, depending on which variables are eliminated. SMT-RAT, Redlog and CDD were able to solve all 90 problems where the last five variables were eliminated. FM and Z3 only solved 75 (76) of those and none in the other categories. Of the instances where five randomly chosen variables were eliminated, SMT-RAT solved 31, CDD 25 and Redlog 15. When eliminating the first five variables, SMT-RAT solved 3 and CDD 1. The structure of these benchmarks has a big impact, and they are generally more challenging than the other sets we tried.

Output Size. When variable elimination is used by an external algorithm, a concise representation of the projection helps to reduce the effort of further computations by that algorithm. Thus, we are also interested in the output size, i.e. the number of constraints in the result.

On all three benchmark sets, FM and CDD never give a smaller output than SMT-RAT, and the same holds for Redlog and Z3 on most of the instances. In fact, their output can be bigger than SMT-RAT's by up to four orders of magnitude (FM, Redlog), three orders of magnitude (Z3) or two orders of magnitude (CDD), respectively. For roughly 3600 instances in the random and SMT-LIB-derived benchmarks, Redlog yields significantly fewer (by up to four orders of magnitude) constraints than SMT-RAT. These instances contain very few variables, and the difference is likely due to some redundancy removal used by Redlog, which could also be implemented in the other tools. Z3 yields fewer (by up to one order of magnitude) constraints than SMT-RAT for 53 random instances, and there are 64 instances of the SMT-LIB-derived set where Z3 recognizes that the input is unsatisfiable and returns a single unsatisfiable constraint, while SMT-RAT returns up to several hundred constraints. This difference could be elided by having SMT-RAT perform a satisfiability check first. Note that only 68 total instances are unsatisfiable, and all of them are derived from SMT-LIB.

6   Conclusion

We adapted the FMplex method from [27] to eliminate (existentially quantified) variables from conjunctions of linear inequations. While a straightforward adaption of the original method yields a disjunction as output, we showed that it is possible to find an equivalent conjunction with little additional effort.

Our new approach admits many improvements and structural savings, as the processing of the individual steps is quite flexible. We revealed strong similarities to the VTS method and are certain that our results can be easily transferred to it, in the case of a conjunctive linear input. First experiments show that our implementation outperforms other tools, though a comparison to more alternatives, like the ones in [2,15,16], would be interesting. Depending on the application, our method, just like other established tools, can hit its limitations even for few eliminated variables, as observed on our neural network verification benchmarks.

Accordingly, there is potential for further improvements. For example, one could try to find and remove redundant constraints during the computation, or prune more nodes of the elimination tree. The difficulty there is to ensure that the final result still contains all necessary constraints. Finally, our procedure is easily parallelizable, as the nodes in the search tree can be processed independently.

Acknowledgments. Valentin Promies was supported by the Deutsche Forschungsgemeinschaft (DFG) as part of AB 461/9-1 *SMT-ART*.

Data Availability Statement. The considered benchmark sets are available at https://doi.org/10.5281/zenodo.10605373. An artifact containing the compared tools and the collected results is available at https://zenodo.org/doi/10.5281/zenodo.12080344.

References

1. Antal, L., Masara, H., Ábrahám, E.: Extending neural network verification to a larger family of piece-wise linear activation functions. In: Proceedings of the 5th International Workshop on Formal Methods for Autonomous Systems (FMAS@iFM'23). EPTCS, vol. 395, pp. 30–68 (2023). https://doi.org/10.4204/EPTCS.395.4
2. Bagnara, R., Hill, P.M., Zaffanella, E.: The parma polyhedra library: toward a complete set of numerical abstractions for the analysis and verification of hardware and software systems. Sci. Comput. Program. **72**(1–2), 3–21 (2008). https://doi.org/10.1016/J.SCICO.2007.08.001
3. Barrett, C., Fontaine, P., Tinelli, C.: The Satisfiability Modulo Theories Library (SMT-LIB) (2016). www.SMT-LIB.org
4. Bjørner, N.S., Janota, M.: Playing with quantified satisfaction. In: Proceedings of the 20th International Conference on Logic for Programming, Artificial Intelligence and Reasoning, (LPAR 2015). EPiC Series in Computing, vol. 35, pp. 15–27. EasyChair (2015). https://doi.org/10.29007/VV21
5. CDDlib. Commit aff2477. https://github.com/cddlib/cddlib/tree/aff2477f8ab25e826da93c6650731dd1717d6b4a

6. Chernikov, S.N.: Contraction of systems of linear inequalities. Dokl. Akad. Nauk SSSR **152**(5), 1075–1078 (1963)
7. Corzilius, F., Kremer, G., Junges, S., Schupp, S., Ábrahám, E.: SMT-RAT: an open source C++ toolbox for strategic and parallel SMT solving. In: Heule, M., Weaver, S. (eds.) SAT 2015, pp. 360–368. Springer, Cham (2015). https://doi.org/10.1007/978-3-319-24318-4_26
8. Dolzmann, A., Sturm, T.: REDLOG: computer algebra meets computer logic. ACM SIGSAM Bull. **31**(2), 2–9 (1997). https://doi.org/10.1145/261320.261324
9. Farkas, J.: Theorie der einfachen Ungleichungen. J. für die reine und angewandte Mathematik (Crelles J.) **1902**(124), 1–27 (1902). https://doi.org/10.1515/crll.1902.124.1
10. Fourier, J.B.J.: Analyse des travaux de l'Académie Royale des Sciences pendant l'année 1824. Partie Mathématique (1827)
11. Fukuda, K., Prodon, A.: Double description method revisited. In: Deza, M., Euler, R., Manoussakis, I. (eds.) CCS 1995. LNCS, vol. 1120, pp. 91–111. Springer, Heidelberg (1996). https://doi.org/10.1007/3-540-61576-8_77
12. Giesl, J., et al.: Analyzing program termination and complexity automatically with approve. J. Autom. Reason. **58**(1), 3–31 (2017). https://doi.org/10.1007/S10817-016-9388-Y
13. Huang, X., Kwiatkowska, M., Wang, S., Wu, M.: Safety verification of deep neural networks. In: Majumdar, R., Kuncak, V. (eds.) CAV 2017. LNCS, vol. 10426, pp. 3–29. Springer, Heidelberg (2017). https://doi.org/10.1007/978-3-319-63387-9_1
14. Imbert, J.: Fourier's elimination: which to choose? In: Proceedings of the 2nd Workshop on Principles and Practice of Constraint Programming (PPCP 1993), pp. 117–129 (1993)
15. Jeannet, B., Miné, A.: APRON: a library of numerical abstract domains for static analysis. In: CAV 2009. LNCS, vol. 5643, pp. 661–667. Springer, Heidelberg (2009). https://doi.org/10.1007/978-3-642-02658-4_52
16. Jing, R., Maza, M.M., Talaashrafi, D.: Complexity estimates for Fourier-Motzkin elimination. In: CASC 2020. LNCS, vol. 12291, pp. 282–306. Springer, Heidelberg (2020). https://doi.org/10.1007/978-3-030-60026-6_16
17. Jones, C., Kerrigan, E., Maciejowski, J.M.: On polyhedral projection and parametric programming. J. Optimiz. Theory Appl. **138**, 207–220 (2008). https://doi.org/10.1007/s10957-008-9384-4
18. Julian, K.D., Kochenderfer, M.J., Owen, M.P.: Deep neural network compression for aircraft collision avoidance systems. J. Guid. Control. Dyn. **42**(3), 598–608 (2019). https://doi.org/10.2514/1.G003724
19. Korovin, K., Kosta, M., Sturm, T.: Towards conflict-driven learning for virtual substitution. In: CASC 2014. LNCS, vol. 8660, pp. 256–270. Springer, Heidelberg (2014). https://doi.org/10.1007/978-3-319-10515-4_19
20. Košta, M.: New Concepts for Real Quantifier Elimination by Virtual Substitution. Ph.D. thesis, Universität des Saarlandes, Germany (2016). http://dx.doi.org/10.22028/D291-26679
21. Loos, R., Weispfenning, V.: Applying linear quantifier elimination. Comput. J. **36**(5), 450–462 (1993). https://doi.org/10.1093/COMJNL/36.5.450
22. Monniaux, D.: A quantifier elimination algorithm for linear real arithmetic. In: Proceedings of the 15th International Conference on Logic for Programming, Artificial Intelligence, and Reasoning (LPAR 2008). LNCS, vol. 5330, pp. 243–257. Springer, Heidelberg (2008). https://doi.org/10.1007/978-3-540-89439-1_18

23. Motzkin, T.S., Raiffa, H., Thompson, G.L., Thrall, R.M.: The Double Description Method, pp. 51–74. Princeton University Press, Princeton (1953). https://doi.org/10.1515/9781400881970-004

24. Motzkin, T.S.: Beiträge zur Theorie der linearen Ungleichungen (Dissertation). Buchdrückeri Azriel, Jerusalem (1936)

25. de Moura, L., Bjørner, N.: Z3: an efficient SMT solver. In: Ramakrishnan, C.R., Rehof, J. (eds.) TACAS 2008. LNCS, vol. 4963, pp. 337–340. Springer, Heidelberg (2008). https://doi.org/10.1007/978-3-540-78800-3_24

26. de Moura, L.M., Bjørner, N.S.: Satisfiability modulo theories: introduction and applications. Commun. ACM **54**(9), 69–77 (2011). https://doi.org/10.1145/1995376.1995394

27. Nalbach, J., Promies, V., Ábrahám, E., Kobialka, P.: FMplex: a novel method for solving linear real arithmetic problems. In: Proceedings of the 14th International Symposium on Games, Automata, Logics, and Formal Verification (GandALF 2023). EPTCS, vol. 390, pp. 16–32 (2023). https://doi.org/10.4204/EPTCS.390.2

28. Reduce, Snapshot 2023-03-08. https://sourceforge.net/projects/reduce-algebra/files/snapshot_2023-03-08/linux64/reduce-complete_6547_amd64.deb

29. SMT-RAT, a toolbox for strategic and parallel Satisfiability Modulo Theories solving. https://github.com/ths-rwth/smtrat/tree/pub/fmplex-qe-3

30. Tran, H.-D., et al.: Star-based reachability analysis of deep neural networks. In: ter Beek, M.H., McIver, A., Oliveira, J.N. (eds.) FM 2019. LNCS, vol. 11800, pp. 670–686. Springer, Cham (2019). https://doi.org/10.1007/978-3-030-30942-8_39

31. Yu, H., Monniaux, D.: An efficient parametric linear programming solver and application to polyhedral projection. In: Chang, B.-Y.E. (ed.) SAS 2019. LNCS, vol. 11822, pp. 203–224. Springer, Cham (2019). https://doi.org/10.1007/978-3-030-32304-2_11

32. z3 theorem prover, commit 520e692. https://github.com/Z3Prover/z3/tree/520e692a43c41e8981eb091494bef0297ecbe3c6

Foundations

Free Facts: An Alternative to Inefficient Axioms in Dafny

Tabea Bordis[1]([✉])[iD] and K. Rustan M. Leino[2][iD]

[1] Karlsruhe Institute of Technology, Karlsruhe, Germany
tabea.bordis@kit.edu
[2] Amazon Web Services, Seattle, WA, USA
leino@amazon.com

Abstract. Formal software verification relies on properties of functions and built-in operators. Unless these properties are handled directly by decision procedures, an automated verifier includes them in verification conditions by supplying them as universally quantified axioms or theorems. The use of quantifiers sometimes leads to bad performance, especially if automation causes the quantifiers to be instantiated many times.

This paper proposes *free facts* as an alternative to some axioms. A free fact is a pre-instantiated axiom that is generated alongside the formulas in a verification condition that can benefit from the facts. Replacing an axiom with free facts thus reduces the number of quantifiers in verification conditions. Free facts are statically triggered by syntactic occurrences of certain patterns in the proof terms. This is less powerful than the dynamically triggered patterns used during proof construction. However, the paper shows that free facts perform well in practice.

Keywords: SMT-based reasoning · proof brittleness · Dafny · formal verification

1 Introduction

Complex software is used in almost every domain, including safety-critical or security-critical domains that require strong guarantees of correctness. Formal methods have successfully been applied to guarantee correctness of large-scale, complex software (e.g., [12, 13, 21, 22, 26, 31, 36, 37]). Especially successful are Satisfiability Modulo Theories (SMT) solvers [5, 9, 33] and SMT-based, automated program verifiers, such as Dafny [29], Frama-C [25], AutoProof [19], VeriFast [24], and F* [39]. In Dafny, for example, the developer writes specifications and code, which are then translated into proof obligations that are automatically checked by an SMT solver. The verification result is displayed in the IDE, including descriptive error messages in case of a negative result.

The underlying idea of automated verifiers is to transfer most of the verification effort from the developer to the SMT solver, i.e., to automate the verification task as much as possible. For instance, axioms for properties that are known to be

© The Author(s) 2025
A. Platzer et al. (Eds.): FM 2024, LNCS 14933, pp. 151–169, 2025.
https://doi.org/10.1007/978-3-031-71162-6_8

true are automatically generated such that the developer does not have to specify and prove said properties themselves. As a result, automation has increased user-friendliness, leading to more users and the application to larger and more complex systems, including their application in industry. However, with increasing complexity, a certain *proof brittleness*[1] has been observed among SMT-based verifiers [22,30]. Proof brittleness describes a problem where seemingly irrelevant changes, such as renaming a variable or using a newer version of the tool, can lead to a variation in the verification time and even result. The impact of this is severe, as it drastically increases debugging time and may even require refactoring of the code and specification. Additionally, confidence in the tool and the user experience decreases, as the focus shifts from developing correct software to refactoring the code to make the proof complexity manageable for the solver.

In Dafny, many axioms, for example, describing properties for collection types, are automatically defined in the background whenever a proof is triggered. The solver can then use this information provided by the axiom to prove the correctness of the program. There are some problems with axioms that affect proof brittleness, and which we found during our experiments to remove certain axioms from Dafny. (1) Axioms increase the complexity of the proof obligations. The more information there is for the solver, the more options there are to discharge a proof. (2) Universally quantified axioms provide properties and the solver decides where to instantiate the property. Therefore, the developer cannot control this. (3) Not every property is easily expressible in an axiom, because the solver can quickly run into matching loops, where the SMT solver keeps instantiating quantified axioms for new terms.

In this paper, we propose *free facts* as an alternative automatic mechanism for giving properties similar to those defined in axioms, but on concrete instances of the program code. For example, when we detect a set union of sets A and B, we generate a property describing how to retain the original sets from the union; the property specifically mentions the instances A and B, rather than using an axiom that quantifies over any two sets. The advantage is that the property is already instantiated without giving the solver the option to use it elsewhere. Furthermore, the developer does not have to change their behavior because the behavior is fully automated.

In this paper, we make the following contributions:

- We introduce *free facts* as an alternative to universally quantified axioms.
- We define *free facts* for properties of different collection types in Dafny.
- We provide an implementation of *free facts* in Dafny as a proof of concept.
- We evaluate the impact of *free facts* with regard to proof brittleness in Dafny and compare them to universally quantified axioms.

2 Dafny and Its Verifier

Our work is in the context of the Dafny programming language. Dafny supports formal reasoning about programs and for that purpose features an automated

---

[1] Also referred to as *proof instability*.

program verifier. The verifier operates in two phases: it first prescribes proof obligations (using the intermediate verification language Boogie) and then attempts to discharge these proof obligations using automatic decision procedures (which are provided in an SMT solver). In this section, we describe the general structure of how the proof obligations are prescribed. The full details of how (an early version of) Dafny is translated into the intermediate verification language Boogie are recorded in Marktoberdorf Summer School lecture notes [28].

2.1   Proof Obligations

To prescribe proof obligations, Dafny uses the Boogie intermediate verification language [6]. Boogie features first-order declarations of types, functions, and axioms, as well as imperative procedures. Procedure bodies consist of statements from a simple while language. The Boogie tool generates a verification condition for each procedure. More precisely, given axioms A, and with a procedure whose pre- and postconditions are Pre and $Post$, respectively, and whose body is a statement S, Boogie generates the logical verification condition

$$A \land Pre \implies \mathsf{wp}[S, Post]$$

where $\mathsf{wp}[S, Post]$ is first expanded to be the weakest precondition of S with respect to $Post$ [18].

For the purposes of this paper, it suffices to understand three kinds of statements in Boogie:

- Assignment statement $x := E$ evaluates expression E and then assigns its value to variable x.
- Assertion statement **assert** P adds condition P as a verification debit.
- Assumption statement **assume** Q adds condition Q as a verification credit.

Expressions in Boogie are *total*; that is, it is legal to apply operators and functions to any arguments. If the source language (Dafny, in our case) wants to prescribe a proof obligation for one of its expressions, then it must introduce an assertion in Boogie. For example, the translation of the Dafny statement $x := y/z$ into Boogie is

assert $z \neq 0$; x := Div(y, z)

This instructs the Boogie tool to check the condition $z \neq 0$, reporting an error if the condition cannot be proved, and then assign the variable x.

An assumption is used to state a condition that the verifier is allowed to use. Sound verification requires that every assumption be justified in some way, but such justification lies outside the use of Boogie; Boogie allows verification-tool authors to introduce such assumptions. Sometimes, an assumption is justified by some property of the programming language or by a limitation of the program verifier. For example, a program verifier for a C-like language may choose to verify only those runs of a program that do not exceed the available memory. For an allocation statement $x := \mathbf{malloc}(1024)$, such a verifier would introduce an assumption along the lines of

```
x := ...;   assume x ≠ 0 ∧ size(x) = 1024
```

Procedure pre- and postconditions (introduced, respectively, with **requires** and **ensures** clauses) provide a convenient way to introduce verification debits and credits at procedure boundaries. In particular, a precondition turns into an implicit **assert** statement at a call site and a matching implicit **assume** statement at the beginning of the procedure body. Conversely, a postcondition turns into an implicit **assert** statement at the end of the procedure body and a matching implicit **assume** statement on return from each call.

Here is a small Boogie example that illustrates these features:

```
axiom A
procedure M(x: X) returns (y: Y)
  requires Pre(x) ensures Post(x, y)
{
  assert P(x);
  assume Q(x);
  y := E(x)
}
```

Procedure M declares one in-parameter (x) and one out-parameter (y). For this example, Boogie generates the verification condition

$$A \wedge Pre(x) \implies P(x) \wedge (Q(x) \implies Post(x, E(x)))$$

and passes it to the decision procedures in Boogie's underlying SMT solver.

2.2   Axioms Versus Assumptions

In the example above, the proof goal $Post(x, E(x))$ has three antecedents: the axioms A, the precondition $Pre(x)$, and the assumption $Q(x)$. Further antecedents in other examples include guard conditions from control flow like **if** and the postconditions of any calls. Logically, there is no difference between these kinds of antecedents. Instead, they are all assumptions, but stated in different contexts and different scopes.

Stylistically, **assume** statements are used to introduce assumptions about local variables (like the result of a procedure call), whereas axioms are used to describe properties of global functions or operators of the language (like Div from a previous example above).

2.3   Expression Translation

As further background for our paper, let us describe the general translation of expressions from the source language (Dafny) into the intermediate verification language (Boogie). The expression translation is part of the translation of any statement, so we will use a Dafny assignment statement $x := E$ as a running example; other statements are similar (see [28]). There are three parts to the translation of expressions from Dafny to Boogie.

Translation Mapping. The translation of $x := E$ will map the Dafny variables into corresponding variables in Boogie. For our purposes, we will assume the Boogie variables have the same names. Thus, the left-hand side x in Dafny simply maps into a Boogie variable x.

The right-hand side of the assignment is more interesting. Its translation also needs to map Dafny operators and functions into Boogie counterparts. For example, we can imagine that Dafny's integer-division operator / is translated into a Boogie function Div, as we saw in an example above. For this purpose, we introduce a translation function Tr:

$$x := \mathsf{Tr}[E]$$

where, for example, $\mathsf{Tr}[E0/E1] = Div(\mathsf{Tr}[E0], \mathsf{Tr}[E1])$. (In many of our examples that follow, we will use the same operator symbol in Boogie as in Dafny.)

Checking Well-Formedness. As we mentioned above, expressions in Boogie are total. In contrast, operators and functions in Dafny can be *partial*. The translation from Dafny to Boogie therefore prescribes *well-formedness checks*, as we will indicate with the translation function Wf. With these in mind, the translation of an assignment statement $x := E$ becomes

assert $\mathsf{Wf}[E]$; $x := \mathsf{Tr}[E]$

For example, we have

$$\mathsf{Wf}[E0/E1] = \mathsf{Wf}[E0] \wedge \mathsf{Wf}[E1] \wedge \mathsf{Tr}[E0] \neq 0$$

Introducing Assumptions. Translation functions like Tr and Wf have been described before (e.g., [27,28]). What Dafny also uses, but which has not been described, is a template for introducing assumptions. Previously, this part of the translation has been limited in focus, mostly to try to speed up verifier performance of function calls. We will not describe the details of these previous assumptions, since they are not the subject of this paper. Relevant to this paper is just that the translation process includes not only the translation mapping Tr and the well-formedness checks Wf, but also an *assumption generator* Ag. The assumption generator is used as follows, as we can now show the complete translation of expressions from Dafny to Boogie:

assert $\mathsf{Wf}[E]$; **assume** $\mathsf{Ag}[E]$; $x := \mathsf{Tr}[E]$

As we mentioned, assumption generators have had limited use in Dafny. Indeed, for most expressions E, we have $\mathsf{Ag}[E] = true$. It is into these assumption generators that we will incorporate our *free facts*, as we will describe next.

3   Free Facts

In this section, we present and discuss our concept for free facts. First, as motivation, we show a common pattern that currently needs manual proof effort. Then, we define its automated mechanism and provide free facts for Dafny's collection types. Finally, we discuss free facts in terms of use cases and limitations.

3.1   Motivating Example

Axioms for Operations of Built-in Types. The general strategy for axiom-atizing the operators of built-in types in Dafny is to define them in terms of primitive operators. For example, set operations are defined in terms of set membership as follows:

$$\forall x, S, T \cdot \quad x \in S \cup T \iff x \in S \vee x \in T$$

This strategy gives rise to a kind of rewriting that moves toward smaller terms, and hence (by itself) terminates. However, this strategy alone does not give equality between terms, a property that logic gives the name *extensionality*. Extensionality becomes important when terms are used as arguments to other functions. Dafny thus also uses an extensionality axiom. For example, the one for sets looks like

$$\forall S, T \cdot \quad S =_{set} T \implies S = T$$

where $=_{set}$ is the set-equality operator in Dafny and $=$ is the verifier's equality.

How Axioms Get Used. Universal quantifiers in Dafny's verifier are used through instantiation. To control this process, each quantifier has a *matching pattern* [17]. The verifier instantiates an axiom if, during proof construction, some of the prover's ground terms look like the matching pattern.

For example, the matching pattern for each of the quantifiers in the examples above are the left-hand side of the main connective in the quantifier body. So, if the prover's ground terms happen to contain $y \in A \cup B$ for some expressions y, A, B, then the first quantifier above is instantiated with $x, S, T := y, A, B$. But note that the quantifier is not instantiated if the ground terms only contain $y \in A$ and $y \in B$. In the same way, the quantifier in the extensionality axiom is instantiated only if there already is a ground term that mentions $=_{set}$.

Derived Properties. Using the defining axioms and the axiom of extensionality, it is possible to prove additional properties as theorems, such as

$$\forall x, S \cdot \quad x \notin S \implies (S \cup \{x\}) \backslash \{x\} = S$$

This property is often used in proofs of Dafny programs. A sketch of a prototypical example thereof is a loop that wants to maintain $P(S)$ as a loop invariant, where P is some predicate on the set S, and the loop body contains an assignment $S := S \cup \{x\}$.

Since the theorem above is useful, it is tempting, as developers of the Dafny verifier, to include the theorem among the verifier's axioms. Unfortunately, it far too often instead has a negative effect on prover performance, because the quantifiers end up being instantiated too often. So, the theorem above is not included in Dafny. Instead, programs that need the property tend to include a user-defined assertion of the property, which the Dafny verifier proves and then uses. For example, it is typical to see Dafny code snippets like

```
S' := S ∪ {x};
assert S' \ {x} =_set S
```

Similar code snippets are frequently used for other types and operators as well. For instance, here is an example that uses sequences:

```
x := A[0];
A' := A[1..];
assert [x] · A' =seq A
```

3.2 Free Facts

Our aim is to obtain the desired automation in cases like our motivating example, but without risk of causing the verifier to instantiate the derived-property theorems too many times. We do this by instantiating such theorems *before* sending verification conditions to the verifier. We call the result of such an instantiation a *free fact*, and we include free facts among the generated assumptions (translation function Ag in Sect. 2.3). For example, as motivated by the example in the previous subsection, the free facts we generate

$$
\begin{aligned}
\mathsf{Ag}[S \cup T] \; = \\
\mathsf{Ag}[S] \, \wedge \, \mathsf{Ag}[T] \, \wedge \\
\mathsf{Tr}[S] = (\mathsf{Tr}[S] \setminus \mathsf{Tr}[T]) \cup (\mathsf{Tr}[S] \cap \mathsf{Tr}[T])
\end{aligned}
$$

Note that this generalized property works for any set T, not just a singleton set $\{x\}$ as we showed in our motivating example above.

To support free facts Dafny, we first decide on some candidate theorems (more about that in Sect. 3.3). The mechanism we then use to control instantiations is similar to what the verifier does with matching patterns, but with an important difference: While the verifier's set of ground terms grows as the verifier performs inferences, the terms available to free-fact generation are those that occur syntactically in the program. To understand this syntactic-terms limitation, suppose we tried to encode the associativity of set union as a free fact:

$$
\begin{aligned}
\mathsf{Ag}[S \cup (T \cup U)] \; = \\
\mathsf{Ag}[S] \, \wedge \, \mathsf{Ag}[T] \, \wedge \, \mathsf{Ag}[U] \, \wedge \\
\mathsf{Tr}[S] \cup (\mathsf{Tr}[T] \cup \mathsf{Tr}[U]) \; = \; (\mathsf{Tr}[S] \cup \mathsf{Tr}[T]) \cup \mathsf{Tr}[U]
\end{aligned}
$$

This would generate the free fact only if the Dafny program contained an expression of the form $S \cup (T \cup U)$. However, it would not generate the free fact if the syntax was slightly different. For example, the free fact would not be generated for a code snippet like

```
a := T ∪ U;
b := S ∪ a
```

since no single expression contains two union operators. Because of this syntactic limitation, free facts are most effective when the matching pattern has just one operator.

3.3   Free Facts for Collection Types

Collections are nontrivial data types, yet are widely used in software systems. In Sect. 2, we explained how axioms are used to describe properties of built-in types in Dafny. In Sect. 3.1, we gave an example of a property that performs poorly as an axiom and therefore has to be provided as a user-defined assertion. Hence, we looked for assertions on collection types in different systems that are implemented in Dafny and defined our free fact properties based on our findings. In Table 1, we show a complete list of all free facts that we defined for this paper. Only the last two properties are defined as axioms in the current version of Dafny. The other properties have to be defined by the developer in an assertion if needed and are therefore new properties in the automatic encoding.

Table 1. Free Fact Properties for Collection Types in Dafny.

Collection Type	Operation in Code	Free Fact Property
Set	$S \cup T,\ S \backslash T$	$S = (S \backslash T) \cup (S \cap T)$
		$T = (T \backslash S) \cup (S \cap T)$
Multiset (allows duplicates)	$S \cup T,\ S \backslash T$	$S = (S \backslash T) \cup (S \cap T)$
		$T = (T \backslash S) \cup (S \cap T)$
Map	$M + N$	$M.keys \cap N.keys = \emptyset \implies M = M + N - N.keys$
		$M.keys \cap N.keys = \emptyset \implies N = M + N - M.keys$
Sequence	$X \cdot Y$	$X = (X \cdot Y)[0..|X|]$
		$Y = (X \cdot Y)[|X|..|(X \cdot Y)|]$
	$X[i..|X|],\ X[0..i]$	$X = X[0..i] \cdot X[i..|X|]$
	$X[i..j]$	$X[0..j] = X[0..i] \cdot X[i..j]$
		$X[i..|X|] = X[i..j] \cdot X[j..|X|]$

Operations: Map merge: $+$, Map difference: $-$, Seq. concatenation: $\cdot$, Seq. length: $|X|$, Subsequence: $X[i..j]$
See Dafny reference manual for further explanations of the operations [3].

Sets and Multisets. In contrast to ordinary sets, multisets allow duplicate entries. Apart from that, we define the same free fact properties for sets and multisets. Whenever we detect a (multi-)set union or (multi-)set difference in the Dafny code, we generate the two free fact properties in the very right column that describe a relationship between the (multi-)set operations $\backslash$, $\cup$, and $\cap$.

Maps. We define similar free fact properties as the ones for sets for finite maps, as well. The merge of two maps is not commutative, because values are overriden if the key already exists in the left-hand side map; hence, the key sets of the two maps need to be disjoint.

Sequences. For sequences, we define free fact properties for the concatenation of two sequences and the subsequence operation $X[i..j]$ (from index i inclusive to index j exclusive). For the concatenation of two sequences $X \cdot Y$, we get the original set X by taking the subsequence of the concatenation from 0 to the length of X ($|X|$). Respectively, set Y is equal to the subsequence of the concatenation from $|X|$ to $|(X \cdot Y)|$. For the subsequence operation, we define a free fact for the special case where one of the indices is 0 or the length of the sequence, i.e., dropping the start or the end of the sequence, and a general one for arbitrary indices. The latter is generated only if the special case is not true.

3.4 Discussion

Applicability Limitations. Free facts rely on syntactically detectable operations in the Dafny code. Collections are particularly well suited, because (1) they often require additional properties in the form of assertions and (2) their operations are easy to detect since they are not scattered over multiple statements.

During our experiments, we encountered proof brittleness when using the non-linear arithmetic setting of the SMT solver. As an alternative, we tried to define free facts for non-linear arithmetic properties. Unfortunately, the distribution properties of $+$ and $*$ are not possible under our syntactic-terms limitation.

Free Facts as Replacement for Axioms. Our aim is not to replace axioms altogether. Axioms are an effective way of globally providing certain properties that do not require a proof. SMT solvers use the given information dynamically and quickly and decide about their instantiation. However, the instantiation of axioms must always be regulated by matching patterns. Otherwise, the solver will quickly run into matching loops. For some properties, it is difficult to define the matching pattern in a way that is not too restrictive, such that the axiom is never really instantiated or that it is instantiated too often, resulting in performance issues. For example, if we would define the first free fact property from Table 1 as a quantified axiom with $S \cup T$ as trigger, this leads to an endless instantiation of this property as the trigger matches part of the term. For these properties, we propose free facts as an alternative because they are defined on concrete instances of the code and the solver cannot instantiate them arbitrarily, i.e., even if a free fact that we generate is not used, it does not keep generating additional facts, like universally quantified axioms can. The overall goal is to replace only inefficient axioms and to add properties for further automation where it fits the conditions of free facts.

Increasing the Level of Automation. The high degree of automation in verification tools has led to complex queries for the SMT solver in the backend which increases proof brittleness. Therefore, it may seem unintuitive to propose another automatic mechanism to be added on top of Dafny to counter proof brittleness. With free facts, we propose a change in the automatic encoding of the proof obligations to *avoid* universally quantified axioms. Other parts of the automatic encoding could possibly also be improved. In other places, however, it may be better to reduce automation, giving control back to the developer. Overall, a composition of multiple solutions, not only for automatic encoding from Dafny to Boogie, but also for the way programs and proofs are defined and how the solver is used in the backend, will bring progress regarding the overall problem.

4 Evaluation

Proof brittleness is a problem that can occur when the proof obligations and information for the program verifier are too complex. In this section, we evaluate *free facts* in terms of their usefulness with regard to proof brittleness and compare them to axioms in Dafny.

4.1   Research Questions

In particular, we define the following research questions:

RQ1: Is it possible to define free facts in Dafny?
RQ2: To what extent can free facts reduce the proof brittleness in Dafny?
RQ3: Are free facts superior to axioms in terms of their verification time and resource count?

With **RQ1**, we want to assess the feasibility of free facts. By answering **RQ2**, we gain insights into how well suited *free facts* are to reduce the proof brittleness problem. With **RQ3**, we may estimate how *free facts* compare to axioms by comparing both approaches using the collection type properties (see Sect. 3.3).

4.2   Methodology

To answer our research questions, we created three different branches of Dafny that we used to compare the verification results. All branches can be used like the regular Dafny version.

Master: The master branch[2] is the original version of Dafny, and we use this branch as the baseline for our evaluation.
Free Facts: The free facts branch[3] implements all properties of Sect. 3.3 as free facts and none as axioms.
Axioms: The axioms branch[4] implements most properties from Sect. 3.3 as axioms and none as free facts. The differences between the axioms and the free facts in Table 1 are: The free facts for (multi-)set union and (multi-)set difference are implemented with only set difference as trigger. The free fact for sequence concatenation has a more restrictive trigger. Without adaptions, the SMT solver ran into matching loops.

To answer **RQ1**, we implement free facts for collection type properties as described in Sect. 3 in the free facts branch. Afterwards, we run the Dafny test suite to check whether the free fact branch of Dafny is working as intended. To reason about **RQ2** and **RQ3**, we perform a mutation-based analysis using an internal tool on three subject systems that are implemented in Dafny and compare the performance of our different Dafny branches. The idea of the mutation-based analysis is to syntactically mutate the subject systems to mimic the developer that observes proof brittleness when they make slight changes to their program. Furthermore, we collect metrics that indicate proof brittleness. For **RQ2**,

---

[2] https://github.com/dafny-lang/dafny, commit 2e7de95.
[3] https://github.com/dafny-lang/dafny/tree/tb-experiment-freefacts, 62b2a90.
[4] https://github.com/dafny-lang/dafny/tree/tb-experiment-freefactaxioms, e9a1bd2.

Table 2. Subject Systems and their Characteristics.

Subject Systems	# Procedures	LOC	# Specifications	# CTs
Cedar[a]	1,454	19,695	5,974	589
Dafny Libraries[b]	6,398	15,729	4,668	638
Internal System	14,504	17,858	4,003	371

Procedures include methods, functions, and lemmas.

LOC — Non-whitespace lines of Code. # CTs — Explicit mentions of collection types.

[a] https://github.com/cedar-policy/cedar
[b] https://github.com/dafny-lang/libraries

we compare the free facts branch with the master branch, and for **RQ3**, we compare the free facts branch with the axiom branch. We describe the tool, the metrics, and the subject systems in the following.

Mutation-Based Analysis of Two Dafny Versions. For the evaluation, we use an internal tool that syntactically mutates our subject systems and collects different metrics for two different branches of Dafny. It mutates every procedure of the subject systems five times, randomly changing the names of all identifiers and the order of declarations, and runs each mutant with a random seed that the SMT solver uses when making decisions that can be arbitrary. The tool collects the following metrics for each procedure on the two different branches: The number of failed runs, the verification time, and the resource count (a Z3-specific metric for the proof complexity).

The number of failed runs can be used as an indicator for proof brittleness if some runs fail and some do not. We sum up the number of failed runs of the single procedures in one subject system to a total number of failed runs for each branch. If the number for branch A is higher than the number for branch B, this gives the indication that branch A is more brittle than branch B. To obtain a holistic evaluation, we combine the number of failed runs with two further metrics that indicate proof brittleness, namely, the average verification time and the average resource count. It has been observed that both metrics correlate with the proof brittleness problem [41].

Subject Systems. We evaluate *free facts* on three large-scale subject systems that are implemented in Dafny. One of the subjects is an internal policy-checking system. The other two systems, Cedar[5] and the Dafny Libraries[6], are openly accessible on GitHub. We selected the internal subject system because it has a high usage of sequence collections and it lets us discuss the results with domain experts to verify our results and prevent potential errors. In Table 2, we give an overview on the subject systems and provide metrics that show their size and complexity. All subject systems contain assertions in the code that are similar to our free fact properties (cf. Sect. 3.1).

---

[5] https://github.com/cedar-policy/cedar.
[6] https://github.com/dafny-lang/libraries.

4.3   Results and Discussion

RQ1: Is it possible to define free facts in Dafny?
We implemented free facts as described in Sect. 3. In the Dafny integration test suite, we found seven test cases with assertions that can be removed because of free facts. In some cases, such removal led to a higher resource count, but at the other end of the spectrum, one case had a resource count that was 12 times lower than the failing verification without free facts. We can therefore answer RQ1 positively for collection type properties. In Sect. 3.4, we have already discussed the applicability of our concept in terms of its limitations due to the syntactical detection.

RQ2: To what extent can free facts reduce the proof brittleness in Dafny?
In Table 3, we show the results of the mutation-based analysis of the master and the free facts branch for our three subject systems. We give the average improvement for the runtime and resource count in percent, and the difference between the total number of failed runs between the master and the free facts branch. For runtime and resource count, a positive percentage ($+x\%$) means that the free facts branch performed on average x percent faster/with less resources than the master branch. For the difference in failed runs, a negative number ($-y$) means that the free facts branch failed y fewer times than the master.

The largest effect of free facts was seen in the Dafny Libraries, where we measure an average improvement in the runtime of 41%. In contrast, the resource count worsened by 4% on average. The difference in the number of failed runs is only minor with 25 additional failed runs. For the internal system, we observe an improvement in runtime by 9% and resource count by 8%. However, the difference in the number of failed runs increased by 367 failed runs. Compared to the total number of runs (72,520) this is still just a change of 0.5%. Besides the average of the whole system, we also looked at the maximum average improvement of the procedures in Cedar and the Dafny libraries, which was +748% runtime and +160% resource count for Cedar and +19597% runtime and +277% for the Dafny libraries. The procedure in the Dafny libraries that had the extreme improvement in runtime actually went from being brittle with only 2/5 succeeding runs on the master to being stable with 5/5 succeeding runs with free facts.

Overall, we can answer RQ2 neither positively nor negatively. The average resource count suggests a slight deterioration compared to the master branch for Cedar and the Dafny Libraries. With free facts, we generate certain properties automatically that previously had to be defined manually. As long as those assertions are not removed from the code, the assertions still provide a verification debit for the solver and therefore obfuscate the benefit of free facts. We discuss this in detail in Sect. 4.4. In contrast, the runtime improved for all subject systems. We conclude from this that, even though the proofs seem to be slightly more complex (potentially because the subject systems still contain

Table 3. Results: Master vs. Free Facts

Subject Systems	Runtime	Resource Count	# Failed Runs		
			total		Diff.
	Avg. Improvement	Avg. Improvement	master	free facts	
Cedar[a]	+1%	-6%	38	66	+28
Dafny Libraries[b]	+41%	-4%	392	417	+25
Internal System	+9%	+8%	51	418	+367

The total number of all runs (5 * #procedures): Cedar - 7,270. Libraries - 31,990. Internal - 72,520.

[a] https://github.com/cedar-policy/cedar
[b] https://github.com/dafny-lang/libraries

Table 4. Results: Axioms vs. Free Facts

Subject Systems	Runtime	Resource Count	# Failed Runs		
			total		Diff.
	Avg. Improvement	Avg. Improvement	axioms	free facts	
Cedar[a]	+7%	-1%	40	69	+29
Dafny Libraries[b]	+23%	+9%	557	511	-46
Internal System	+9%	+6%	386	391	+5

The total number of all runs (5 * #procedures): Cedar - 7,270. Libraries - 31,990. Internal - 72,520.

[a] https://github.com/cedar-policy/cedar
[b] https://github.com/dafny-lang/libraries

assertions that could be removed), but easier and therefore faster to close given the additional information. Additionally, we observed strong improvements for individual procedures, such as in the case of the maximum values, which shows the great potential of free facts as a concept. We expect an alignment of the resource count to the positive trend of the runtime once free facts are deployed, and developers adapt their behavior to the free fact generation of Dafny.

RQ3: Are free facts superior to axioms in terms of their verification time and resource count?

In Table 4, we summarize the results for the mutation-based analysis between the free facts and the axiom branch. While the difference in the number of failed runs between the two branches is rather small (+29 failed runs for Cedar, −46 failed runs for the Dafny libraries, and +5 failed runs for the internal system), there is an improvement in favor of the free facts branch in both the average runtime and resource count. The average improvement of free facts for the Dafny libraries and the internal system is higher (+23% runtime and +9% resources for the libraries and +9% runtime and +6% resources) than the one for Cedar (+7% runtime and −1% resources), which we explain again by the fact that Cedar uses fewer collections.

Overall, we can answer RQ3 positively, since the free facts branch took less time and resources on average than the axiom branch. Note that we were not able to implement all free fact properties as axioms, as some led to matching loops, which would quickly lead to a timeout for a majority of the procedures. In fact, this supports our argument that free facts are an alternative automatic mechanism that is superior in certain cases where axioms are inefficient.

4.4   Threats to Validity

Removal of Assertions in the subject systems. As explained in Sect. 3.1, we are automating the generation of certain properties in Dafny that previously had to be defined as assertions by the developer. Therefore, the full potential of free facts can only be observed if these assertions are removed from the code as they are translated into a proof debit for the SMT solver. Leaving the assertions in the code does not affect the correctness, but it does affect the runtime and resource count. In our evaluation, we did not remove these assertions from the subject systems, as the manual effort would be too high since we used large-scale systems. As a result, this benefit is not measurable in our experiments, and the values for newly built systems using free facts might be better as we expect developers to adapt their proofs accordingly. It is conceivable that such a change in behavior would make free facts better overall.

Reproducibility. Parts of our experiments are not reproducible for externals because we used (1) an internal tool to perform the variability analysis and (2) an internal subject system. However, the implementation of all branches is publicly available, as well as the other two subject systems. With that, a similar report can be generated, also including mutations. Detailed instructions can be found in the Dafny documentation in Section *Measuring proof brittleness* [3].

Since both the mutation-based analysis and the decision process of the SMT solver involve randomness, and the subject systems are productively used systems that are regularly modified, the exact results will still vary from run to run. However, the overall trend is reproducible.

Transferability. We have only performed our evaluation on Dafny with Z3 as SMT solver. We cannot claim that our results are fully representative for other automated verifiers or SMT solvers. Nevertheless, the concept is transferable to other verifiers as well. We believe that our results provide valuable insight into the proof brittleness problem and may influence future work.

5   Related Work

Resolving Proof Brittleness. Few approaches have addressed proof brittleness, mainly because: (1) it is a rather new challenge stemming from the recent verification of complex systems, and (2) the complexity of the SMT-solvers decision process using heuristics and randomness to a certain degree. We categorize the papers into the Dafny pipeline, writing program, specification, and proof

(proof engineering); automatic encoding of Dafny to SMT; the SMT solver itself. Five of the papers have been presented at this year's Dafny workshop [1].

Proof Engineering. McLaughlin et al. [32] introduce Dafny64, a mode of using Dafny that significantly reduces verification resources by stripping back automation for proofs. Cutler et al. [15] improved the stability of type safety proofs in Dafny by making functions opaque (i.e., making the body of the function unavailable) and specifying them manually such that the solver does not have to reason about multiple large definitions simultaneously. Ho and Pit-Claudel [23] improved the debugging of brittle lemmas by using Dafny's abstract modules to achieve an induction principle similar to that in the theorem prover Coq [7]. These papers highlight the necessity to reduce automation, such that the developer gains more control over the verification task. Although we agree with this suggestion, with *free facts* we aim to improve the automatic encoding in the next step of the pipeline. We reduce the options for the solver while maintaining the usability of Dafny as an automatic verifier. The proposed approaches and free facts can be applied in parallel to maximize results.

Automatic Encoding. Srinivasan et al. [38] identify the boundaries where information from other modules should be made opaque to leverage the automation of Dafny in the best possible way. In particular, they concentrate on quantifier instantiations. With *free facts*, we also propose a technique that improves the automatic encoding; however, we focus on code-based detection of the need and instantiate properties to avoid universally quantified axioms.

SMT Solver. Mugnier et al. [34] propose a portfolio of SMT solvers meaning that different SMT solvers and different versions of SMT solvers are used to get more performant proofs. This work is orthogonal to *free facts* and can be applied later to further increase the performance.

Detection of Proof Brittleness. The detection of proof brittleness is indirectly related to our work, because detecting proof brittleness does not directly reduce brittleness. However, detection can be used to evaluate approaches to resolve proof brittleness and may lead to a better understanding of the problem and more targeted solutions in the future.

As a first measure, for early detection, Dafny and F* provide a command-line flag to execute multiple randomized verification runs [2,3]. Mariposa [41] is a tool that performs a mutation-based analysis to detect and quantify SMT-based proof brittleness. In their paper, they performed an evaluation on six different verification projects, provide a benchmark, and describe their findings. The Axiom Profiler [10] is a tool that analyzes instantiation problems, e.g., matching loops caused by axioms, by logging information of SMT runs.

Quantifier Instantiation. Since the Simplify prover introduced E-matching [17], it has been adapted and improved in a number of SMT solvers [4,8,16], as well as the pattern selection in many SMT-based automated verifiers (including Dafny) [14,30,35]. However, there are also a few approaches that focus on avoiding quantifier instantiation altogether. The tool Leon [11] (a predecessor of Stainless [20]) is an SMT-based verifier for programs written in Scala. It avoids quantifiers by unfolding recursive definitions as needed. Liquid Haskell adds refinement types to Haskell and implements a recursive technique similar to Leon called refinement reflection [40]. The idea of both approaches is comparable to free facts, but they are applied to functions and the detection of the need to unfold is more dynamic than our syntactic detection.

6 Conclusion

Proof brittleness is a persistent issue in automated verification, particularly with complex and large-scale software. Research is still in its early stages of understanding and improving the sources of proof brittleness. The complexity stems from the high degree of automation. We believe that the entire process, from proof engineering to the automation of the verifier and the SMT solver itself, requires revision. We aim to improve the automatic encoding in Dafny by generating pre-instantiated *free facts*. This approach reduces the number of quantifiers in the verification conditions compared to quantified axioms without increasing manual effort for the developer. With collections, we found a good use case for free facts, and we plan to experiment with further use cases in the future.

References

1. Dafny 2024 - POPL 2024. https://popl24.sigplan.org/home/dafny-2024#event-overview. Accessed 15 Mar 2024
2. Understanding how F* uses Z3 - Proof-Oriented Programming in F* documentation. https://fstar-lang.org/tutorial/book/under_the_hood/uth_smt.html. Accessed 01 July 2024
3. Dafny Documentation (2024). https://dafny.org/dafny/DafnyRef/DafnyRef.html. Accessed 18 Mar 2024
4. Bansal, K., Reynolds, A., King, T., Barrett, C., Wies, T.: Deciding local theory extensions via e-matching. In: Kroening, D., Păsăreanu, C.S. (eds.) CAV 2015. LNCS, vol. 9207, pp. 87–105. Springer, Cham (2015). https://doi.org/10.1007/978-3-319-21668-3_6
5. Barbosa, H., et al.: cvc5: a versatile and industrial-strength SMT solver. In: TACAS 2022. LNCS, vol. 13243, pp. 415–442. Springer, Cham (2022). https://doi.org/10.1007/978-3-030-99524-9_24
6. Barnett, M., Chang, B.-Y.E., DeLine, R., Jacobs, B., Leino, K.R.M.: Boogie: a modular reusable verifier for object-oriented programs. In: de Boer, F.S., Bonsangue, M.M., Graf, S., de Roever, W.-P. (eds.) FMCO 2005. LNCS, vol. 4111, pp. 364–387. Springer, Heidelberg (2006). https://doi.org/10.1007/11804192_17

7. Barras, B., et al.: The Coq Proof Assistant Reference ManualâĂŕ: Version. vol. 6, p. 1 (2006)
8. Barrett, C., et al.: Cvc4. In: Computer Aided Verification: 23rd International Conference, CAV 2011, Snowbird, pp. 171–177. Springer, Heidelberg (2011)
9. Barrett, C., Tinelli, C.: Satisfiability modulo theories. In: Handbook of Model Checking, pp. 305–343. Springer, Cham (2018). https://doi.org/10.1007/978-3-319-10575-8_11
10. Becker, N., Müller, P., Summers, A.J.: The axiom profiler: interderstanding and debugging SMT quantifier instantiations. In: Vojnar, T., Zhang, L. (eds.) TACAS 2019. LNCS, vol. 11427, pp. 99–116. Springer, Cham (2019). https://doi.org/10.1007/978-3-030-17462-0_6
11. Blanc, R., Kuncak, V., Kneuss, E., Suter, P.: An overview of the Leon verification system: verification by translation to recursive functions. In: Proceedings of the 4th Workshop on Scala (SCALA 2013), pp. 1–10. Association for Computing Machinery (2013)
12. Bornholt, J., et al.: Using lightweight formal methods to validate a key-value storage node in Amazon S3. In: Proceedings of the ACM SIGOPS 28th Symposium on Operating Systems Principles (SOSP 2021), pp. 836–850. Association for Computing Machinery (2021)
13. Chudnov, A., et al.: Continuous formal verification of Amazon s2n. In: Chockler, H., Weissenbacher, G. (eds.) CAV 2018. LNCS, vol. 10982, pp. 430–446. Springer, Cham (2018). https://doi.org/10.1007/978-3-319-96142-2_26
14. Cohen, E., et al.: VCC: a practical system for verifying concurrent C. In: Theorem Proving in Higher Order Logics: 22nd International Conference, TPHOLs 2009, Munich, 17–20 August 2009, pp. 23–42. Springer, Heidelberg (2009)
15. Cutler, J.W., Hicks, M., Torlak, E.: Improving the Stability of Type Safety Proofs in Dafny (2024). https://popl24.sigplan.org/details/dafny-2024-papers/3/Improving-the-Stability-of-Type-Safety-Proofs-in-Dafny. in [1]
16. De Moura, L., Bjørner, N.: Efficient E-matching for SMT solvers. In: Automated Deduction–CADE-21: 21st International Conference on Automated Deduction Bremen, 17–20 July 2007, pp. 183–198. Springer, Heidelberg (2007)
17. Detlefs, D., Nelson, G., Saxe, J.B.: Simplify: a theorem prover for program checking. J. ACM **52**(3), 365–473 (2005)
18. Dijkstra, E.W.: A Discipline of Programming. Prentice Hall (1976)
19. Furia, C.A., Nordio, Martín and Polikarpova, N., Tschannen, J.: AutoProof: auto-active functional verification of object-oriented programs. Int. J. Softw. Tools Technol. Transf
20. Hamza, J., Voirol, N., Kunčak, V.: System FR: formalized foundations for the stainless verifier. Proc. ACM Program. Lang. **3**, 1–30 (2019)
21. Hance, T., Lattuada, A., Hawblitzel, C., Howell, J., Johnson, R., Parno, B.: Storage Systems are Distributed Systems (So Verify Them That Way!), pp. 99–115 (2020)
22. Hawblitzel, C., et al.: IronFleet: proving practical distributed systems correct. In: Proceedings of the 25th Symposium on Operating Systems Principles (SOSP 2015), pp. 1–17. Association for Computing Machinery (2015)
23. Ho, S., Pit-Claudel, C.: Incremental Proof Development in Dafny with Module-Based Induction (2024). in [1]
24. Jacobs, B., Smans, J., Philippaerts, P., Vogels, F., Penninckx, W., Piessens, F.: VeriFast: a powerful, sound, predictable, fast verifier for C and Java. NASA Formal Methods **6617**, 41–55 (2011)
25. Kirchner, F., Kosmatov, N., Prevosto, V., Signoles, J., Yakobowski, B.: Frama-C: a software analysis perspective. Formal Aspects Comput. **27**(3), 573–609 (2015)

26. Klein, G., et al.: seL4: formal verification of an operating-system kernel. Commun. ACM **53**(6), 107–115 (2010)
27. Leino, K.R.M.: Ecstatic: an object-oriented programming language with an axiomatic semantics. In: The Fourth International Workshop on Foundations of Object-Oriented Languages (1997)
28. Leino, K.R.M.: Specification and verification of object-oriented software. In: Broy, M., Sitou, W., Hoare, T. (eds.) Engineering Methods and Tools for Software Safety and Security, NATO Science for Peace and Security Series D: Information and Communication Security, vol. 22, pp. 231–266. IOS Press (2009)
29. Leino, K.R.M.: Dafny: an automatic program verifier for functional correctness. In: Clarke, E.M., Voronkov, A. (eds.) LPAR 2010. LNCS (LNAI), vol. 6355, pp. 348–370. Springer, Heidelberg (2010). https://doi.org/10.1007/978-3-642-17511-4_20
30. Leino, K.R.M., Pit-Claudel, C.: Trigger selection strategies to stabilize program verifiers. In: Chaudhuri, S., Farzan, A. (eds.) CAV 2016. LNCS, vol. 9779, pp. 361–381. Springer, Cham (2016). https://doi.org/10.1007/978-3-319-41528-4_20
31. Liu, J., et al.: P4v: practical verification for programmable data planes. In: Proceedings of the 2018 Conference of the ACM Special Interest Group on Data Communication (SIGCOMM 2018), pp. 490–503. Association for Computing Machinery (2018)
32. McLaughlin, S., Jaloyan, G.A., Xiang, T., Rabe, F.: Enhancing Proof Stability (2024). https://popl24.sigplan.org/details/dafny-2024-papers/14/Enhancing-Proof-Stability, in [1]
33. de Moura, L., Bjørner, N.: Z3: an efficient SMT solver. In: Ramakrishnan, C.R., Rehof, J. (eds.) TACAS 2008. LNCS, vol. 4963, pp. 337–340. Springer, Heidelberg (2008). https://doi.org/10.1007/978-3-540-78800-3_24
34. Mugnier, E., McLaughlin, S., Tomb, A.: Portfolio Solving for Dafny (2024). https://popl24.sigplan.org/details/dafny-2024-papers/8/Portfolio-Solving-for-Dafny, in [1]
35. Müller, P., Schwerhoff, M., Summers, A.J.: Viper: a verification infrastructure for permission-based reasoning. In: Jobstmann, B., Leino, K.R.M. (eds.) VMCAI 2016. LNCS, vol. 9583, pp. 41–62. Springer, Heidelberg (2016). https://doi.org/10.1007/978-3-662-49122-5_2
36. Nelson, L., Bornholt, J., Gu, R., Baumann, A., Torlak, E., Wang, X.: Scaling symbolic evaluation for automated verification of systems sode with serval. In: Proceedings of the 27th ACM Symposium on Operating Systems Principles (SOSP 2019), pp. 225–242. Association for Computing Machinery (2019)
37. Protzenko, J., et al.: EverCrypt: a fast, verified, cross-platform cryptographic provider. In: 2020 IEEE Symposium on Security and Privacy (SP), pp. 983–1002 (2020)
38. Srinivasan, P., Padon, O., Howell, J., Lattuada, A.: Domesticating Automation (2024). https://popl24.sigplan.org/details/dafny-2024-papers/2/Domesticating-Automation. in [1]
39. Swamy, N., et al.: Dependent types and multi-monadic effects in F*. In: Proceedings of the 43rd Annual ACM SIGPLAN-SIGACT Symposium on Principles of Programming Languages (POPL 2016), pp. 256–270. Association for Computing Machinery (2016)

40. Vazou, N., et al.: Refinement reflection: complete verification with SMT. Proc. ACM Program. Lang. **2**(POPL), 1–31 (2017)
41. Zhou, Y., Bosamiya, J., Takashima, Y., Li, J., Heule, M., Parno, B.: Mariposa: measuring SMT instability in automated program verification. In: Proceedings of the 23rd Conference on Formal Methods in Computer-Aided Design (FMCAD 2023), pp. 178–188 (2023)

Understanding Synthesized Reactive Systems Through Invariants

Rüdiger Ehlers[✉][iD]

Clausthal University of Technology, Clausthal-Zellerfeld, Germany
ruediger.ehlers@tu-clausthal.de

Abstract. In many applications for which reactive synthesis is attractive, computed implementations need to have understandable behavior. While some existing synthesis approaches compute finite-state machines with a structure that supports their understandability, such approaches do not scale to specifications that can only be realized with a large number of states. Furthermore, asking the engineer to understand the internal structure of the implementation is unnecessary when only the behavior of the implementation is to be understood.

In this paper, we present an approach to computing understandable safety invariants that every implementation satisfying a generalized reactivity(1) specification needs to fulfill. Together with the safety part of the specification, the invariants completely define which transitions between input and output proposition valuations any correct implementation can take. We apply the approach in two case studies and demonstrate that the computed invariants highlight the strategic decisions that implementations for the given specification need to make, which not only helps the system designer with understanding what the specification entails, but also supports specification debugging.

1 Introduction

In reactive synthesis, a reactive system implementation is automatically computed from its specification. Such systems continuously interact with their environment (as usual in *embedded systems*) and synthesis promises to drastically increase developer productivity by freeing her/him from having to write the implementation along with the specification. As a consequence, a developer can then focus on getting the specification correct and complete, which is needed in development processes for safety- or business-critical systems anyway.

There are however two major obstacles that currently prevent the widespread use of reactive synthesis in the field. The first one is *scalability*: for instance, reactive synthesis from linear temporal logic (LTL) specifications has a doubly-exponential time complexity [33]. This problem is partially mitigated by work on practical reactive synthesis, which spurred substantial performance increases over the last two decades [16]. Furthermore, by focusing on specification formalisms with a lower synthesis complexity that pair well with symbolic reasoning, such as *generalized reactivity(1) specifications* [8] in combination with *binary*

© The Author(s) 2025
A. Platzer et al. (Eds.): FM 2024, LNCS 14933, pp. 170–187, 2025.
https://doi.org/10.1007/978-3-031-71162-6_9

decision diagrams, the scalability of reactive synthesis can be further improved, which led to the successful execution of the first practical case studies [6,7,12,26]. The corresponding synthesis approach is also commonly called *GR(1) synthesis*, in which the specifications consist of safety properties (which restrict the transitions allowed by the environment and the system) and liveness properties.

The second obstacle to the widespread use of reactive synthesis in the field is, somewhat unintuitively, a lack of trust in the *correctness* of the synthesized implementations. While the computed implementations are guaranteed to be correct-by-construction, they are only correct with respect to the specification written by the system's engineer and not the implicit expectations that the engineer or the later user of the system have [23]. Indeed it has been noticed that the high degree of specification engineering needed for reactive synthesis is a substantial challenge [3,13,31]. Ensuring system correctness in reactive synthesis however goes beyond getting the specification right, as a synthesized system typically needs to also convey trust in its correct functioning. Synthesized systems often behave in unexpected ways, for instance by working against their environments [5,30], which causes several problems. Firstly, if the system is to interact with a human, the human may lose trust in the system if the system behaves in unexpected ways [24]. Similarly, to allow engineers to rely on the correct functioning of a synthesized component when using it in the context of a bigger system, they need to understand why a synthesized system behaves the way it does (also called *predictable* behavior [36]). Finally, when servicing bigger systems with synthesized components, unexpected system behavior can misinform the error diagnosis of a deployed system. In all three cases, we see that a system's behavior needs to be *understandable* for the system to be useful.

This understandability question could be addressed by accompanying the synthesized implementation with a human-readable *explanation* of how it operates. While the specification sets the boundaries of a synthesized system's behavior, the synthesis process concretizes them by the *strategic choices* that a system needs to make to avoid the eventual violation of its specification. These necessary strategic choices, in a sense, represent how the system needs to plan ahead to be able to satisfy the specification regardless of the future input. For instance, a robot controller operating in a shared workspace with humans needs to avoid situations in which it can be trapped by humans, and an explanation of what the robot needs to avoid as a consequence could be a side-output of a synthesis process to document that the system's behavior is reasonable. This explanation would also help with system integration activities in which the synthesized implementation is used as a component.

But how can an explanation look like? It has to be *readable* in order to be useful, but readability is a soft target. For systems with a low number of states, the implementation itself (or the set of changes made during the development process to accommodate all specification parts) could be used as an explanation, but especially when synthesizing from generalized reactivity(1) specifications, the generated implementations often need to be large, and the approach is unattractive in such cases. Furthermore, it normally suffices to explain the *behavior* of the synthesized system, rather than its internal structure. For generalized reactivit(1) specifications, we can however observe that since the safety part of a specification provides boundaries on the transitions that a system can make, the specification itself already provides a large part of the explanation of how a system behaves by defining which transitions are *allowed* by the system. As the safety specification part is manually written, it needs to be understandable, as otherwise the specifier cannot know if it is correct. What is still left to explain are however the strategic choices that a correct implementation needs to make in order to accommodate all possible future input. In other words, we could explain the system's behavior by identifying the *invariants* that a synthesized implementation needs to maintain in addition to satisfying the safety specification. If these are in human-readable form, then we obtain an explanation of the system behavior.

In this paper, we present an approach to identifying invariants that *all* synthesized implementations need to maintain. We target GR(1) synthesis, which can be reduced to finding a winning strategy in a *synthesis game* in which the states are exactly the valuations to the input and output variables. We show that in this context, both the strongest and weakest possible invariants are Boolean functions that characterize which input/output combinations must never occur during the execution of a correct system implementation, and these functions are called *local input/output invariants* in this paper. Since neither the strongest nor weakest local input/output invariants are necessarily easy to interpret, we present an approach to pick and decompose some invariant in between them so that we obtain a minimal number of *mixed monotone/antitone* invariants. In this class, every invariant consists of a single *worst-case variable valuation* and a couple of cases that are *"also bad"*. Every variable valuation that is some mixture of the worst case and a bad case is then also a state to avoid. Our invariant class is quite general and for instance contains all linear inequalities over state variables, including when variables together binary-encode a number.

Our algorithm is intended to be used in the scope of an iterative specification development process, where after each addition to the specification, the engineer checks which invariants the specification *entails*. These invariants can then be added to the specification as documentation and to restrict the set of reachable states in the game, which also ensures that the invariants are not found again after subsequent specification refinements. As the invariants are added step-by-step and are mixed monotone/antitone, they tend to be comparably simple and understandable, as we demonstrate in two case studies, which concern the synthesis of graphical user interface glue code and a generalized buffer controller [7]. We also demonstrate in the case studies that identifying invariants is a useful specification debugging step: by examining the invariants, an engineer can get some insight into whether the specification is correct and complete.

1.1 Related Work

While invariant identification is a classical task in many sub-fields of formal methods, such as software verification [32], in reactive synthesis, this problem is less explored. Work on inferring (safety) *assumptions* on the environment that make a specification *realizable* can however be seen as related [1,11,27]. Such assumptions represent a kind of invariant: if the environment fulfills the assumptions all of the time, the system under design also fulfills its specification. The focus in this context is however not on fostering the understandability of a synthesized implementation, but making a specification realizable.

In order to improve the understandability of synthesized systems, one can enforce a certain structure of the solutions. For instance, Lustig and Vardi [28] show how to compute an implementation consisting only of components from a library. Aminof et al. [2] on the other hand show how to generate an implementation consisting of a hierarchy of components, hence enforcing a certain structure. Finally, Khalimov and Jacobs [21] gave an approach to compute *parameterized* arbitrarily scalable systems. All these approaches however do not come with a guarantee that their results are indeed easy to understand. On a smaller scale, there are also works that aim at making a synthesized finite-state machine easier to understand. For instance, Finkbeiner and Klein [17] presented an approach for synthesizing controllers that are as small as possible while bounding the size of cycles, which allows engineers to understand a controller by looking at small implementation parts in isolation. Baumeister et al. [3] proposed to explain a controller by looking at its evolution when successively adding new specification parts. After each addition, a small *repair* is generated that explains how the controller had to be changed to accommodate the additional specification part. An implementation can also be made more understandable by making use of typical program structures rather than representing the implementation as a finite-state machine. For instance, a synthesis approach based on two-way automata [18,29] generates small programs in a simple programming language. However, the scalability of the approach is currently also limited to very small programs. Further related work on synthesizing understandable implementations is given in the survey paper on challenges in reactive synthesis by Torfah and Kress-Gazit [25]. In contrast to all aforementioned work on synthesizing understandable implementations, we focus on synthesizing understandable invariants that *augment* the specification parts that the system engineer already understands. As such, the approach scales to specifications that require large numbers of states in an implementation, which is commonly the case for generalized reactivity(1) specifications.

The survey paper by Torfah and Kress-Gazit [25] also discusses a wide variety of existing methods for helping with *specification debugging* in reactive synthesis. The difficulty of writing correct temporal specifications has been acknowledged in multiple application domains, including software [20], hardware design [15] and autonomous system verification [19]. In reactive synthesis, specification debugging is particular important [13], as all relevant properties of a system under design need to be specified in order to guarantee them. Our invariant generation approach augments existing specification debugging techniques because it allows to check for surprising invariants (which indicate problems with the specification) and the absence of expected implied invariants (which indicates that satisfying the new specification part in the intended way can be side-stepped by the implementation).

2   Preliminaries

Sets and Variables: For a finite *alphabet* Σ, we denote the set of finite sequences of Σ as Σ^* and the set of infinite such sequences as Σ^ω. We will typically use the Boolean valuations $2^{\mathcal{V}}$ to some variable set $\mathcal{V}$ as alphabet. For notational conciseness, we treat assignments $x : \mathcal{V} \to \mathbb{B}$ and subsets of $\mathcal{V}$ representing the variables with **true** values interchangeably. We use 0 and 1 as shorter representatives for the Boolean values **false** and **true**, respectively.

Boolean Formulas: A Boolean formula over some set of variables $\mathcal{V}$ is in *conjunctive normal form* if it is a conjunction of *clauses*, which are disjunctions of *literals*, which are in turn variables or their negation. Boolean formulas represent *Boolean functions*, which map variable valuations to **false** and **true**. In the latter case, we call the valuation *satisfying*. We will sometimes treat a Boolean function as a set of assignments satisfying it. *Satisfiability (SAT) solving* is the process of checking if a Boolean formula has a satisfying assignment (and computing such a valuation). We say that among a set of Boolean functions $f_1, \ldots, f_n$, a Boolean function f_i (for $1 \leq i \leq n$) is the *strongest* if every *model* (satisfying assignment) of f_i is a model of f_j for all $1 \leq j \leq n$. Boolean functions can also be represented as *reduced ordered binary decision diagrams (BDDs, [10])*. These are acyclic directed graphs with a root node and 0 and 1 as sink nodes. Each non-sink-node n is labeled with a variable $\text{var}(n)$ and has a *then-successor* $\text{then}(n)$ and an *else-successor* $\text{else}(n)$. The BDD maps those valuations to **true** that include a path from the root node along which the 1 node is eventually reached, where we take the then-successor of a node whenever the variable by which the node is labeled has a **true** value in the valuation, and we take the else-successor otherwise. We do not consider the extension of *complemented else-edges* [9], which some BDD libraries offer, in the presentation of this paper, and on a technical level translate these on-the-fly to BDDs without complemented else-edges for the implementation of the presented approach.

Generalized Reactivity(1) Synthesis: The GR(1) synthesis approach [8] targets a specific class of specifications. Given as input to the synthesis process are disjoint finite sets of input and output variables (also called *propositions*) AP^I and AP^O and a specification φ of the following form:

$$\varphi = \left(\varphi_I^A \wedge \varphi_S^A \wedge \varphi_L^A\right) \to_s \left(\varphi_I^G \wedge \varphi_S^G \wedge \varphi_L^G\right)$$

The left-hand side of this equation contains the *assumptions* that, intuitively, encode what environment behavior the implementation to synthesize can assume. The right-hand side of the equation contains the *guarantees*, which the implementation needs to satisfy. Both assumptions and guarantees are split into:

- *initialization properties*, which define the allowed initial values of the propositions AP^I and AP^O,

- *safety properties*, which restrict the possible changes between the valuations of $\mathcal{V} = \mathsf{AP}^I \cup \mathsf{AP}^O$ when the system makes a transition, and
- *liveness properties*, which define valuations of $\mathcal{V}$ that should occur infinitely often along a trace of the system.

Traces of synthesized systems are, as usual, finite or infinite sequences of valuations of $\mathcal{V}$. The $\rightarrow_s$ symbol in the above GR(1) specification shape denotes *strict implication* (explained in detail in [22] without naming it), which intuitively means that the implementation must not violate the guarantees *before* the environment violates its assumptions. More formally, the strict implication holds if along all possible traces $w = \rho_0\rho_1 \ldots \in (2^{\mathcal{V}})^\omega$ of the system, we have:

(a) if $\rho_0 \models \varphi_I^A$, then $\rho_0 \models \varphi_I^G$,
(b) if $\rho_0 \models \varphi_I^A \wedge \varphi_I^G$, then for the smallest index $i \in \mathbb{N} \cup \{\infty\}$ such that $(\rho_i, \rho_{i+1}) \not\models \varphi_S^G$ or $i = \infty$, we have that for some $i' \leq i$, we have $(\rho_{i'}, \rho_{i'+1}) \not\models \varphi_S^A$, or
(c) if the previous two cases not already define whether a trace satisfies φ, then the trace satisfies φ if and only if the trace satisfies $\varphi_L^A \rightarrow \varphi_L^G$.

We say that a specification is *realizable* if there exists an implementation such that along all of its traces the specification is satisfied. Such an implementation can be represented as a *Mealy machine*, which induces the system's executions as its set of traces, where we consider both finite and infinite traces (and their prefixes). For the simplicity of presentation, we assume that a synthesized Mealy machine for a specification φ does not induce traces along which the environment assumptions of φ are violated. As a consequence, there may exist finite traces for the Mealy machine that cannot be extended to an infinite trace of it.

Details on GR(1) synthesis and all further constraints on the specification shape can be found in the paper by Bloem et al. [7], who also presented a synthesis algorithm based on reducing the synthesis problem to solving a game between an input and an output player. The states in this game are the possible valuations to $\mathcal{V}$, and each state $v \subseteq \mathcal{V}$ is either *losing* or *winning* for the system player, where the latter means that the system player can enforce that a trace starting with v satisfies $\varphi_{\backslash I} = (\varphi_S^A \wedge \varphi_L^A) \rightarrow_s (\varphi_S^G \wedge \varphi_L^G)$. Determining the winning states W for the system player can be done using Boolean operations over BDDs, and checking realizability then amounts to checking if for all input proposition valuations $x \subseteq \mathsf{AP}^I$ with $x \models \varphi_I^A$, there exists some $y \subseteq \mathsf{AP}^O$ such that $(x, y) \models \varphi_I^G$ and $(x, y) \in W$.

We denote the set of traces that does not violate φ after a finite number of steps by the rules above as L_φ. We say that some subset of finite traces $L \subseteq (2^{\mathcal{V}})^*$ is a *safety property* if it is *prefix-closed*, i.e., for every word $\rho_0 \ldots \rho_n \in L$ for some $n \in \mathbb{N}$, we also have $\rho_0 \ldots \rho_{n-1} \in L$.

3   Computing Mixed Monotone/Antitone Invariants

In this paper, we present an approach to computing invariants that are satisfied by *any* implementation of a given realizable GR(1) specification. In this context, we only need to consider invariants that restrict the set of input/output combinations that can occur along a system's trace, as we show next.

Definition 1. *Let* $\mathcal{V} = \mathsf{AP}^I \cup \mathsf{AP}^O$ *be a set of atomic propositions and* $\mathcal{M}$ *be a Mealy machine. Let us furthermore for some Boolean formula* B *over* $\mathcal{V}$ *define the language* $L_B = \{\rho_0\rho_1\ldots\rho_{n-1} \in (2^{\mathcal{V}})^* \mid \forall 0 \leq i \leq n-1. \rho_i \models B\}$, *i.e., the language over finite words for which each letter in each word in the language satisfies* B. *We say that* B *is a* local input/output invariant *of* $\mathcal{M}$ *if every finite trace of* $\mathcal{M}$ *is in* L_B.

The following lemma proves that for GR(1) specifications, the restriction to local input/output invariants does not restrict the generality of our approach.

Lemma 1. *Let* $\mathcal{V} = \mathsf{AP}^I \cup \mathsf{AP}^O$ *and* $\varphi = (\varphi_I^A \wedge \varphi_S^A \wedge \varphi_L^A) \to_s (\varphi_I^G \wedge \varphi_S^G \wedge \varphi_L^G)$ *be a GR(1) specification. There exists a unique strongest Boolean formula* B *over* $\mathcal{V}$ *with the following property: Let* $L \subseteq (2^{\mathcal{V}})^*$ *be a safety property that is satisfied by every trace of* every *Mealy machine over* $(\mathsf{AP}^I, \mathsf{AP}^O)$ *that implements a GR(1) specification* φ. *Then, we have* $L \supseteq L_\varphi \cap L_B$, *i.e.,* L *is not a stronger invariant than* L_B *when considering* L_φ *as already set.*

Proof. Let $W \subseteq 2^{\mathcal{V}}$ be the set of positions that are winning in the GR(1) game for φ. We show that $B = \bigvee_{i \in \mathbb{N}} B_i$ for $B_0 = \{v \in W \mid v \models \varphi_I^A \wedge \varphi_I^G\}$ and $B_{i+1} = \{v' \in W \mid \exists v \in B_i. (v, v') \models \varphi_S^A \wedge \varphi_S^G\}$ for every $i \in \mathbb{N}$ has this property. Note that B characterizes the set of winning positions in the synthesis game reachable from some initial winning position while taking only transitions through winning positions. If for some $j \in \mathbb{N}$, we have $B_0 \vee \ldots \vee B_j = B_0 \vee \ldots \vee B_{j-1}$, then we know that $B = B_0 \vee \ldots \vee B_{j-1}$, hence B can be computed in a finite number of steps as there are only finitely many variables in $\mathcal{V}$.

Let us first show that B is a local input/output invariant. To see this, consider the converse, i.e., there exists a correct implementation having a finite trace $\rho = \rho_0 \ldots \rho_{n-1}$ such that $\rho_{n-1} \not\models B$. Let ρ be a shortest such trace, so for all $0 \leq i < n-1$, we have $\rho_i \models B$. If now ρ_{n-1} is not in B, then either (a) $n > 1$ and ρ_{n-1} is not reachable from ρ_{n-2} via a transition satisfying φ_S^A and φ_S^G, (b) ρ_{n-1} is not in W, or (c) $n = 1$ and $\rho_{n-1} \not\models \varphi_I^A \wedge \varphi_I^G$. In case (a), the transition from ρ_{n-2} to ρ_{n-1} is not an allowed part of a correct implementation, which is a contradiction. In case (b), we have that by the construction of the synthesis game, since $\rho_{n-1} \notin W$, there exists a strategy for the environment to make $\varphi_{\backslash I}$ violated when starting with ρ_{n-1}, so the implementation needs to have *some* trace violating $\varphi_{\backslash I}$ and which starts with an initial state (satisfying $\varphi_I^A \wedge \varphi_I^G$), which overall contradicts the satisfaction of φ by the implementation. In case (c), either the assumption from page 6 that along no trace of the Mealy machine, assumptions are violated, does not hold, or φ_I^G is violated, which means that the specification is violated along the trace.

Finally, let us now prove that $L \supseteq L_\varphi \cap L_B$ holds. Assume that the converse holds, i.e., we have some $\rho = \rho_0 \ldots \rho_{n-1} \in (2^{\mathcal{V}})^*$ such that $\rho \notin L$ but $\rho \in L_\varphi \cap L_B$. An implementation can have ρ as a (prefix) trace by for the first n steps of its execution choosing arbitrary output allowed by φ while staying in the set of winning positions and after n steps following some winning strategy, which exists from a winning state. As ρ is in L_φ and has $\rho_{n-1} \in W$, indeed ρ can be a prefix trace of a satisfying implementation. But then, L is not an invariant of *all* implementations, yielding a contradiction.   □

This lemma essentially states that for every safety property that every implementation of a specification satisfies along every trace in addition to the specification, we can provide a local input/output invariant achieving the same, and hence if our interest is in computing safety properties that every implementation satisfies in addition to the specification, we only need to compute a strongest possible local input/output invariant. The proof of the lemma above provides a procedure for doing so, which can also be executed with BDDs.

While the computed strongest local input/output invariant B can be represented as a conjunctive or disjunctive normal form Boolean formula or as a BDD to explain what the specification *entails*, this is often not useful. The set B contains only reachable and winning states, and hence specifications implying a set of reachable positions that is complex to represent often cause B to have a complex representation, too. For invariants that augment the specification, we however have some flexibility regarding which local input/output invariant we choose, which can be exploited.

Definition 2. *Let B be the unique strongest local input/output invariant for a given specification φ. We say that another Boolean function B' over $\mathcal{V}$ satisfies the B-boundary condition if for every $v, v' \in 2^{\mathcal{V}}$, if $v \models B$, then $v \models B'$, and if furthermore $v' \not\models B$ and $(v, v') \models \varphi_S^A \wedge \varphi_S^G$ hold, we have $v' \not\models B'$.*

Lemma 2. *Let B' be a Boolean function satisfying the B-boundary condition for the strongest local input/output invariant B for a specification φ. We have that B' is also a local input/output invariant satisfied by all implementations of φ.*

Proof. For a proof by contradiction, assume that there exists an implementation satisfying φ with a trace $\rho = \rho_0 \ldots \rho_{n-1}$ such that $\rho_{n-1} \not\models B$, but $\rho_{n-1} \models B'$. Without loss of generality, let ρ be a shortest such trace. If $n = 1$, then as $\rho_0 \models \varphi_I^A \wedge \varphi_I^G$, this means that ρ_0 is not a winning position, which contradicts that the implementation satisfies the specification. Otherwise, if $n > 1$, then $\rho_{n-2} \models B$, but $\rho_{n-1} \not\models B$. By the definition of B, there are two reasons for why ρ_{n-1} is not included in B then. If ρ_{n-1} is not reachable from ρ_{n-2} while satisfying $\varphi_S^A \wedge \varphi_S^G$, then this contradicts that the implementation satisfies φ. The other possible reason is that ρ_{n-1} is not a winning position in the game, which also contradicts that the implementation under concern satisfies φ.   □

Note that the Boolean functions B' satisfying the B-boundary condition are not unique in general, which we can exploit in order to choose one that is easier to represent and to explain. However, there is a *weakest* such invariant.

Lemma 3. *Let $\{B_1', \ldots, B_m'\}$ be all possible local input/output invariants satisfying the B-boundary condition for the strongest local input/output invariant B for some specification φ. Then we have that $\tilde{B} = \bigvee_{1 \le i \le m} B_i'$ is also a local input/output invariant for every implementation of φ, and the invariant satisfies the B-boundary condition.*

Proof. We prove that for a pair of Boolean local input/output invariants B_i' and B_{i+1}', we have that $B_i' \vee B_{i+1}'$ is also a local input/output invariant. The claim then follows by applying this argument $m - 1$ times.

Note that $B_i' \vee B_{i+1}'$ is indeed a local input/output invariant, as if along any trace of any system satisfying φ, we only have letters that are models of B_i' and we only have letters that are models of B_{i+1}', then this holds for $B_i' \vee B_{i+1}'$ by definition.

Now let both B_i' and B_{i+1}' satisfy the B-boundary condition. If $v \models B$, then we know $v \models B_i'$ and $v \models B_{i+1}'$, and hence $v \models B_i' \vee B_{i+1}'$ as well. If furthermore $v' \not\models B$ and $(v, v') \models \varphi_S^A \wedge \varphi_S^G$ hold, then since B_i' and B_{i+1}' satisfy the B-boundary condition, we know that $v' \not\models B_i'$ and $v' \not\models B_{i+1}'$, and hence $v' \not\models B_i' \vee B_{i+1}'$. $\qquad\square$

Note that $\tilde{B}$ can be obtained by computing the set of positions v' that $\tilde{B}$ must not map to **true** according to Definition 2 and choosing its complement as $\tilde{B}$.

In this paper, we propose a process that computes a local input/output invariant *between* B and $\tilde{B}$ (i.e., an invariant B' such that both $B \rightarrow B'$ and $B' \rightarrow \tilde{B}$ are Boolean functions that are equivalent to **true**) along with its decomposition into *mixed monotone/antitone* invariants, which are defined as follows.

Definition 3. *Let $\mathcal{V}$ be a set of variables. We say that a subset of valuations $I \subseteq 2^{\mathcal{V}}$ is a* mixed monotone/antitone *invariant if there exists a worst case valuation w and a set of bad cases $b_0^w, \ldots, b_{m-1}^w$, all in $2^{\mathcal{V}}$ such that the following holds: A valuation $v \subseteq \mathcal{V}$ has that $v \not\models I$ if and only if there exists some bad case b_i^w such that for some selection of variables $V \subseteq \mathcal{V}$, we have $v = (w \cap V) \cup (b_i^w \setminus V)$.*

The last condition in the definition essentially states that every variable valuation that does not satisfy a mixed monotone/antitone invariant is a mixture of the variable values in the worst case valuation and a corresponding bad case. Note that in the special case of an empty set of bad cases, the mixed monotone/antitone invariant accepts all variable valuations.

Many invariants are mixed monotone/antitone. For instance, the linear inequality $3 \cdot x_1 + 6 \cdot x_2 - 4 \cdot x_3 - 8 \cdot x_4 \geq 1$ over the variables $\{x_1, x_2, x_3, x_4\}$ is mixed monotone/antitone. The worst case is the valuation for which the sum on the left-hand side is as small as possible, i.e., $\{x_3, x_4\}$, and the possible bad cases are the other valuations violating the inequality. In this context, only the valuations $\emptyset, \{x_1, x_3\}, \{x_1, x_4\}, \{x_2, x_4\}, \{x_1, x_2, x_3, x_4\}$ are actually needed as bad cases, because all other valuations violating the equality can be obtained by mixing one of them with the worst case. In general, every inequality $f(x_1, \ldots, x_n) \leq c$ for some constant c is a mixed monotone/antitone invariant if the function f is either monotone or antitone in every argument. This includes all polynomial inequalities in which the monotone and antitone elements are never mixed.

Not all local input/output invariants B' are mixed monotone/antitone (such as the exclusive or function between two variables). However, every local input/output invariant B' can be represented as the conjunction of mixed monotone/antitone invariants. From an algorithmic point of view, we solve the following core problem in this paper:

Algorithm 1. Algorithm for computing n mixed monotone/antitone invariants

1: **function** COMPUTEINVARIANTS($\mathcal{V},\varphi,W,m$)
2:     $B \leftarrow \varphi_A^I \wedge \varphi_G^I \wedge W$
3:     **while** fixed point of B not reached **do**
4:         $B \leftarrow B \vee \{v' \in 2^{\mathcal{V}} \mid \exists v \in B.(v,v') \models \varphi_S^A \wedge \varphi_S^G, v' \models W\}$
5:     $\tilde{B} = \{v' \in 2^{\mathcal{V}} \mid \forall v \in 2^{\mathcal{V}}.v \in B \wedge (v,v') \models \varphi_S^A \wedge \varphi_S^G \rightarrow v' \in W\}$
6:     $\psi \leftarrow$ **true**, $BAD \mapsto \emptyset$
7:     **while** ψ is satisfiable **do**
8:         $a \leftarrow$ satisfying assignment of ψ
9:         $w_i = \{x_j \mapsto a(b_{i,j}) \mid 1 \le j \le |\mathcal{V}|\}$ for $1 \le i \le m$
10:        $I_i = 2^{\mathcal{V}} \setminus \{f \in \mathcal{V} \mapsto \mathbb{B} \mid \exists \theta \in BAD : a(c_{i,\theta}) =$ **true**$, \forall 1 \le j \le |\mathcal{V}|.f(x_j) =$
           $w_i(j) \vee f(x_j) = \theta(j)\}$ for all $1 \le i \le m$
11:        **if** $I_1 \wedge \ldots \wedge I_m \wedge \neg \tilde{B} \equiv$ **false then**
12:            **return** $w_1,\ldots,w_m, I_1,\ldots,I_m$ as solution
13:        Sample a random assignment θ from $I_1 \wedge \ldots \wedge I_m \wedge \neg \tilde{B}$ and add θ to BAD
14:        $\psi \leftarrow \psi \wedge \bigvee_{1 \le i \le m} c_{i,\theta}$
15:        $\psi \leftarrow \psi \wedge \bigwedge_{1 \le i \le m, 1 \le j \le |\mathcal{V}|}(c_{i,\theta} \rightarrow (b_{i,j} \leftrightarrow d_{i,\theta}))$
16:        **for** all BDD nodes ξ in the BDD for B **do**
17:            **if** $x_j \leftarrow var(y) \in \mathcal{V}$ **then**
18:                $\psi \leftarrow \psi \wedge \{(e_{\xi,\theta} \wedge (d_{j,\theta} \vee \neg \theta(x_j)) \rightarrow e_{\text{then}(\xi),\theta}\}$
19:                $\psi \leftarrow \psi \wedge \{(e_{\xi,\theta} \wedge (\neg d_{j,\theta} \vee \theta(x_j)) \rightarrow e_{\text{else}(\xi),\theta}\}$
20:        $\psi \leftarrow \psi \wedge e_{B,\theta} \wedge \neg e_{1,\theta}$
21:    **return** no solution found

Definition 4. *Let B and $\tilde{B}$ be Boolean functions over a set of variables $\mathcal{V}$ and $m \in \mathbb{N}$. We want to compute a set of mixed monotone/antitone invariants $I_1,\ldots,I_m$ (along with their worst and bad cases) such that $B' = I_1 \wedge \ldots \wedge I_m$ for some Boolean function B' such that $B \rightarrow B'$ and $B' \rightarrow \tilde{B}$ each are Boolean formulas that are equivalent to **true**.*

By computing B and $\tilde{B}$ according to Lemma 1 and Lemma 3, we can use a solution to the problem from Definition 4 to compute a set of m mixed monotone/antitone invariants that together induce a local input/output invariant in between B and $\tilde{B}$. By first trying to solve this problem for $m = 0$, and increasing m one by one until a solution is found, we can find a *smallest* possible set of mixed monotone/antitone invariants. Note that for every realizable specification, such a set of invariants can be found – in the worst case, we use a separate mixed monotone/antitone invariant for each valuation not in $\tilde{B}$.

3.1 Computing a Set of Mixed Monotone/antitone Invariants

Algorithm 1 describes an approach to computing a minimally sized set of mixed monotone/antitone invariants in pseudocode, where for notational simplicity, we assume that the variable set in the specification is $\mathcal{V} = \{x_1,\ldots,x_n\}$. Lines 1-5 are concerned with computing the state sets B and $\tilde{B}$ defined above. The remaining lines of the algorithm then solve the problem from Definition 4. For this purpose, we employ *counter-example guided inductive synthesis* [34] (CEGIS) using an incremental satisfiability (SAT) solver. An empty SAT instance is allocated in line 6 together with the initially empty set of bad cases. The rest of the algorithm consists of the main CEGIS loop. It starts by the SAT solver finding a list of worst cases and an assignment of the bad cases to the worst cases such that no induced mixed monotone/antitone invariant rules out a variable valuation that is a model of B. We employ the following set of SAT variables:

– The variables $\{b_{i,j}\}_{1\leq i\leq m, 1\leq j\leq|\mathcal{V}|}$ are used for the value of variable x_j in worst case number i.
– The variables $\{c_{i,\theta}\}_{1\leq i\leq m,\theta\in BAD}$ are used for encoding that bad case θ is assigned to the worst case number i.
– The variables $\{d_{j,\theta}\}_{1\leq j\leq|\mathcal{V}|,\theta\in BAD}$ are used for encoding the worst case valuation that will be used for the bad case θ.

For the simplicity of presentation, we assume in Algorithm 1 that variables are allocated in the SAT solver on-the-fly. Furthermore, for readability, we use some non-clausal constraints. Since every of them has a fixed number of elements, we can translate them easily without helper SAT variables to clauses in an implementation of Algorithm 1.

Initially, the solver's SAT instance is empty, so that an arbitrary list of worst cases is computed in line 9. In the following line, the corresponding invariants are computed based on the assignment of bad cases to invariants. If the invariants together cover all states not in $\tilde{B}$, this is detected in line 11 and the found invariants are returned along with their worst cases.

Whenever it is instead found that some state not in $\tilde{B}$ still needs to be covered by some invariant, in line 13, a random new bad case is computed. Randomness is used to get a diverse set of bad cases in order to heuristically improve the coverage of $2^{\mathcal{V}} \setminus \tilde{B}$ by the mixed monotone/antitone invariants regardless of which worst cases are chosen by the SAT solver.

For the new bad case θ, in lines 14 and 15, clauses are added that require the SAT solver to assign the bad case to one of the worst cases and to copy the values of the chosen worst case to the variables $\{d_{i,\theta}\}_{1\leq i\leq|\mathcal{V}|}$. Finally, in lines 16 to 19, we encode the check if in a BDD for B, any Boolean valuation between the worst case and the bad case leads to the 1 sink, which would indicate that safe reachable states are ruled out by the mixed monotone/antitone invariant (which is disallowed as we compute invariants that *every* implementation must fulfill). For this purpose, we use the following set of additional variables:

– The variables $\{e_{\xi,\theta}\}_{\xi \text{ is a node in the BDD of } B, \theta\in BAD}$ are used to encode that for some variable valuation between bad case θ and its assigned worst case, the BDD node ξ in the BDD for B is reachable from the root.

When iterating over the BDD nodes of B, the then/else successor of a reachable node is reachable if the respective variable value in the worst case valuation is **true/false**, respectively. In case the value of the bad case and the worst case differ, the respective other BDD successor node is also reachable.

If at some point, the SAT solver finds no satisfying assignment, we know that the bad cases cannot be allocated to any set of m worst cases, and then the algorithm terminates without a solution in line 21.

We can also employ a couple of optimizations in addition to the core components of our approach shown in Algorithm 1. First of all, symmetry breaking on the SAT instance can be applied to require the worst case variable valuations to be in lexicographical order. The respective clauses are added once before the main CEGIS loop. Furthermore, whenever for some value of m, no set of invariants is found, in the algorithm run for $m + 1$ invariants, the SAT instance can be bootstrapped by executing lines 14 to 19 for bad examples found previously. Also, input/output variables of the synthesis problem instance that do not appear in the BDD for B can be removed from consideration in the whole algorithm.

We also apply some BDD optimizations to the computed mixed monotone/ antitone invariants to reduce their representation as BDDs (which we give to the user) while keeping their values on all positions in $B \vee \neg \tilde{B}$, which are the relevant positions for the correctness of an invariant. This includes trying to existentially or universally quantify variables from the invariant as well as using a *BddRestrict* optimization on $B \vee \neg \tilde{B}$, which heuristically merges some BDD nodes.

4   Experiments and Case Studies

We implemented the approach from this paper as a plugin for the reactive synthesis tool `slugs` [14], available in a branch with experimental plugins at https://github.com/VerifiableRobotics/slugs/tree/unstable-linuxonly-extensions. The SAT solver `CaDiCaL` [4] is used for incremental SAT solving and compiled into the `slugs` executable. We also use the `CUDD` binary decision diagram library [35]. Computation times (single-threaded) were taken on a computer with an i9-12900H CPU and 32 Gigabyte of RAM.

We demonstrate our invariant computation approach on two case studies. The first case study concerns GUI glue code synthesis [12], while the second one concerns the classical *generalized buffer* GR(1) synthesis benchmark (from [7]).

4.1   GUI Glue Code Synthesis

When developing programs with a graphical user interface, its developer needs to write *event handlers* that define how the program reacts in response to events such as button clicks and background computation threads terminating. We consider here a GR(1) specification for the GUI↔backend interaction for a whiteboard photo postprocessing application, which we modeled after an existing such application that can be downloaded from https://github.com/progirep/ BBPhoto. The application has a *wizard*-like user interface with four views that can be switched between using *forward* and *backward* buttons. The overall invariant computation time for this case study is 7.5 s. For the final specification with the invariants, the `slugs` tool computes an implementation with 172 (explicit) states.

Step 1: We start by specifying GUI behavior on the first view of the wizard, where the user clicks four times to define the boundaries of the screen part showing the whiteboard. The GUI glue code also has to trigger redrawing the view after every click. We also declare the forward and backward buttons to switch between the views. The specification is realizable, and a single invariant BDD over four propositions (shown in Fig. 1a) is computed that states that at every time, only one proposition for the currently selected boundary may have a **true** value.

Step 2: In this step, the first parts of the specification for the second view of the wizard are added. The tool computes that no additional invariant is needed.

Step 3: Now, the remaining specification parts for a second wizard view with a preview of the processed whiteboard photo is added. A computation thread for updating the preview is defined, and there are sliders for changing some image processing setting. Whenever a slider moves, the preview update thread needs to eventually run.

Two invariants are generated, shown in Fig. 1b and Fig. 1c. The minimized first invariant is just a 4-literal clause stating that if the second view is shown while the computation thread is running and a state variable tracking if the thread still has to be started has a **false** value, the forward button of the wizard has to be enabled. The second invariant encodes that if the computation thread is running or is marked as that it still needs to run, the forward button must not be enabled. The invariants together show an error in the specification, which already has a constraint defining when exactly the forward button is to be enabled—this constraint however erroneously talks about the state before a transition rather than after a transition, and the found invariants identify this oversight.

Step 4: In this step, the third "please wait" view is added that is used when computing the full-resolution image after clicking "next" on the previous view. An additional computation thread is executed while this view is active. As upon completion of the thread, the view of the wizard changes to the next final one, propositions defining the existence of the final view are also added in this step.

A single invariant is computed, with 13 BDD nodes (not counting sinks). During some manual variable reordering, one can find that the BDD tends to get smaller when moving some variables of the one-hot encoding of the current view to the top. We move all of them to the top (as exactly one should have a **true** value at every point in time), and we obtain the BDD in Fig. 1d from which we can make observations. The BDD has paths corresponding to the first two views being visible at the same time as well as no view being visible, which indicates that there is no specification part enforcing that this cannot happen. Other than that, the BDD paths leading to the 0 node represent the condition that if the please wait view is shown, the forward button should not be enabled, and if the resolution selection page is shown, the computation thread of the previous view must not be running. Together, these constraints implement the invariant.

Step 5: Additional specification parts are added in this step that represent that on the final view, a thread for computing final images in different resolutions run in the background, and since the threads access the same data, they must not run concurrently. Some other specification parts encode when the new thread need to start. The specification becomes unrealizable, and an analysis reveals that by the user going quickly forward and backwards through the views, she can enforce to start multiple threads at the same time, which is disallowed.

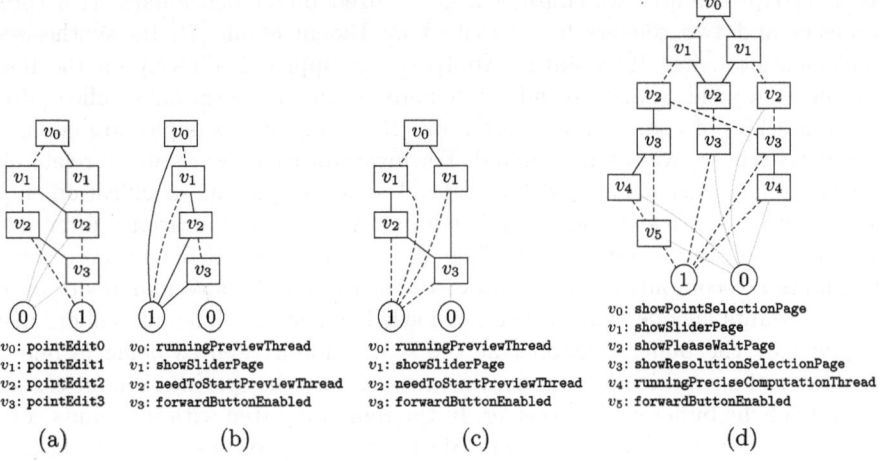

Fig. 1. Some mixed monotone/antitone invariants represented as BDDs. Then-Edges are drawn solid, Else-edges are dashed. Paths to the 0 sink are drawn with gray color (Color figure online).

Step 6: The possibility for the system to deactivate the "back" button is added to address unrealizability. A new invariant is computed whose BDD has 15 nodes. It can be decomposed manually step-by-step by looking at BDD paths to the 0 node, adding specification parts ruling out this path, and recomputing an invariant with a smaller BDD representation to read off the next specification part after each addition. The first constraint states that if the preview computation thread still needs to start after the forward button has been pressed, the backward button needs to be disabled (to avoid the user going back-and-forth). The second invariant part states that if any thread apart from the preview thread is running and the second view is shown, no variable indicating an outstanding thread starting may have a **true** value. The third invariant part is more complex and lists cases in which the backward button must not be enabled. All of them have in common that the third view is shown. We realize at this point that a specification part for ensuring that the button is always disabled on the third view is missing and add it as a *strengthened* invariant.

Finally, we can identify an invariant part that states that whenever the final view is shown, the computation thread of the "please wait" page runs, and the preview thread still needs to be run, then the backward button should not be enabled. This invariant shows that it is possible for an implementation to have background threads of other views running in the final view, which is undesired and indicates that the specification should be changed.

4.2 Generalized Buffer

As a second example, we consider a generalized buffer benchmark with three receivers and two senders, as described by Bloem et al. [7]. Its synthesized implementation has 1098 states. Applying our approach directly on the final specification yields that three mixed monotone/antitone invariants suffice (after 9 min and 20 s of computation time), and 1349 negative examples are enumerated before these invariants are found. The invariant BDDs are however relatively large and have between 58 and 195 nodes. We hence split the specification engineering process into steps again while adding the computed invariants after each step, with an overall computation time of 3.5 s. In three out of the seven steps, invariants are computed and in two of them, the BDDs have four nodes each. The invariants encode that no two acknowledgements to different senders may be given by the buffer controller at the same time as well as being in one of two states of a specification automaton encoded into the specification for certain requests of the buffer's data receiver. In the remaining step with invariants computed, however, two large invariants BDDs are found. We identified that this is caused by B containing few positions, so that it is possible for the algorithm to spuriously squeeze the reachable but non-winning positions into two invariants. When using W instead of B in line 16 of Algorithm 1 and removing the conjunction with W in line 2, three invariants become necessary (which are found after 1.8 s of computation time), which are at least partially readable (with 10, 38, and 106 nodes). After adding the invariants for the first two BDDs and rerunning the tool, the change in reachable states results in a BDD with 17 nodes for the final invariant, which is then easier to encode.

5 Conclusion

In this paper, we presented an approach to computing a minimal set of mixed monotone/antitone invariants implied by a specification in generalized reactivity(1) synthesis. We provided two case studies that show that the approach is indeed suitable for computing readable invariants in all cases except for the final invariants in the second case study, where we had to compute *stronger* invariants to improve their representation. The first case study also demonstrates the use of computing invariants for specification debugging. We leave exploiting such invariants to speed up synthesis and utilizing them in order to compute smaller implementations to future work. Furthermore, we note that computing invariants for synthesized *implementations* that can be used to structure their representation (e.g., as a circuit or as program code) is also still to be explored.

Most of the invariants in the case studies were already readable because our approach performs a decomposition into multiple Boolean functions, hence making each of them more readable. Also, it uses the fact that *any* invariant between two specific Boolean functions is suitable. Yet, we plan to replace BDDs as invariant representation in future work and to develop solver-based techniques for computing smaller Boolean formula representations for the decomposed invariants.

Acknowledgements. This work was supported by the DFG through Grant No. 322591867. The author thanks Ayrat Khalimov for feedback on the work.

References

1. Alur, R., Moarref, S., Topcu, U.: Pattern-based refinement of assume-guarantee specifications in reactive synthesis. In: 21st International Conference on Tools and Algorithms for the Construction and Analysis of Systems (TACAS), pp. 501–516 (2015)
2. Aminof, B., Mogavero, F., Murano, A.: Synthesis of hierarchical systems. In: Arbab, F., Ölveczky, P.C. (eds.) FACS 2011. LNCS, vol. 7253, pp. 42–60. Springer, Heidelberg (2012). https://doi.org/10.1007/978-3-642-35743-5_4
3. Baumeister, T., Finkbeiner, B., Torfah, H.: Explainable reactive synthesis. In: 18th International Symposium on Automated Technology for Verification and Analysis (ATVA), pp. 413–428 (2020)
4. Biere, A., Fazekas, K., Fleury, M., Heisinger, M.: CaDiCaL, Kissat, Paracooba, Plingeling and Treengeling entering the SAT Competition 2020. In: Balyo, T., Froleyks, N., Heule, M., Iser, M., Järvisalo, M., Suda, M. (eds.) SAT Competition 2020 – Solver and Benchmark Descriptions. Department of Computer Science Report Series B, vol. B-2020-1, pp. 51–53. University of Helsinki (2020)
5. Bloem, R., Ehlers, R., Könighofer, R.: Cooperative reactive synthesis. In: Finkbeiner, B., Pu, G., Zhang, L. (eds.) ATVA 2015. LNCS, vol. 9364, pp. 394–410. Springer, Cham (2015). https://doi.org/10.1007/978-3-319-24953-7_29
6. Bloem, R., Galler, S.J., Jobstmann, B., Piterman, N., Pnueli, A., Weiglhofer, M.: Interactive presentation: automatic hardware synthesis from specifications: a case study. In: 2007 Design, Automation and Test in Europe Conference and Exposition (DATE), pp. 1188–1193 (2007)
7. Bloem, R., Galler, S.J., Jobstmann, B., Piterman, N., Pnueli, A., Weiglhofer, M.: Specify, compile, run: hardware from PSL. In: Proceedings of the Workshop on Compiler Optimization meets Compiler Verification (COCV@ETAPS 2007), pp. 3–16 (2007)
8. Bloem, R., Jobstmann, B., Piterman, N., Pnueli, A., Sa'ar, Y.: Synthesis of reactive(1) designs. J. Comput. Syst. Sci. **78**(3), 911–938 (2012)
9. Brace, K.S., Rudell, R.L., Bryant, R.E.: Efficient implementation of a BDD package. In: 27th ACM/IEEE Design Automation Conference (DAC), pp. 40–45 (1990). https://doi.org/10.1145/123186.123222

10. Bryant, R.E.: Symbolic manipulation of Boolean functions using a graphical representation. In: 22nd ACM/IEEE Conference on Design automation (DAC), pp. 688–694 (1985)

11. Chatterjee, K., Henzinger, T.A., Jobstmann, B.: Environment assumptions for synthesis. In: van Breugel, F., Chechik, M. (eds.) CONCUR 2008. LNCS, vol. 5201, pp. 147–161. Springer, Heidelberg (2008). https://doi.org/10.1007/978-3-540-85361-9_14

12. Ehlers, R., Adabala, K.: Reactive synthesis of graphical user interface glue code. In: 17th International Symposium on Automated Technology for Verification and Analysis (ATVA), pp. 387–403 (2019)

13. Ehlers, R., Raman, V.: Low-effort specification debugging and analysis. In: Proceedings 3rd Workshop on Synthesis, SYNT 2014, Vienna, July 23–24, 2014, pp. 117–133 (2014)

14. Ehlers, R., Raman, V.: Slugs: extensible GR(1) synthesis. In: Chaudhuri, S., Farzan, A. (eds.) CAV 2016. LNCS, vol. 9780, pp. 333–339. Springer, Cham (2016). https://doi.org/10.1007/978-3-319-41540-6_18

15. Fey, G., Ghasempouri, T., Jacobs, S., Martino, G., Raik, J., Riener, H.: Design understanding: from logic to specification. In: IFIP/IEEE International Conference on Very Large Scale Integration (VLSI-SoC), pp. 172–175 (2018)

16. Finkbeiner, B.: Synthesis of reactive systems. In: Dependable Software Systems Engineering, NATO Science for Peace and Security Series - D: Information and Communication Security, vol. 45, pp. 72–98. IOS Press (2016)

17. Finkbeiner, B., Klein, F.: Bounded cycle synthesis. In: Chaudhuri, S., Farzan, A. (eds.) CAV 2016. LNCS, vol. 9779, pp. 118–135. Springer, Cham (2016). https://doi.org/10.1007/978-3-319-41528-4_7

18. Gerstacker, C., Klein, F., Finkbeiner, B.: Bounded synthesis of reactive programs. In: Lahiri, S.K., Wang, C. (eds.) ATVA 2018. LNCS, vol. 11138, pp. 441–457. Springer, Cham (2018). https://doi.org/10.1007/978-3-030-01090-4_26

19. Gladisch, C., Heinz, T., Heinzemann, C., Oehlerking, J., von Vietinghoff, A., Pfitzer, T.: Experience paper: search-based testing in automated driving control applications. In: 34th IEEE/ACM International Conference on Automated Software Engineering (ASE), pp. 26–37 (2019)

20. Holzmann, G.J.: The logic of bugs. ACM SIGSOFT Softw. Eng. Notes **27**(6), 81–87 (2002)

21. Khalimov, A., Jacobs, S., Bloem, R.: Towards efficient parameterized synthesis. In: Giacobazzi, R., Berdine, J., Mastroeni, I. (eds.) VMCAI 2013. LNCS, vol. 7737, pp. 108–127. Springer, Heidelberg (2013). https://doi.org/10.1007/978-3-642-35873-9_9

22. Klein, U., Pnueli, A.: Revisiting synthesis of GR(1) specifications. In: Barner, S., Harris, I., Kroening, D., Raz, O. (eds.) HVC 2010. LNCS, vol. 6504, pp. 161–181. Springer, Heidelberg (2011). https://doi.org/10.1007/978-3-642-19583-9_16

23. Könighofer, R., Hofferek, G., Bloem, R.: Debugging formal specifications: a practical approach using model-based diagnosis and counterstrategies. Int. J. Softw. Tools Technol. Transf. **15**(5–6), 563–583 (2013)

24. Kress-Gazit, H., et al.: Formalizing and guaranteeing human-robot interaction. Commun. ACM **64**(9), 78–84 (2021)

25. Kress-Gazit, H., Torfah, H.: The challenges in specifying and explaining synthesized implementations of reactive systems. In: 3rd Workshop on formal reasoning about Causation, Responsibility, and Explanations in Science and Technology (CREST@ETAPS), pp. 50–64 (2018)

26. Kress-Gazit, H., Wongpiromsarn, T., Topcu, U.: Correct, reactive, high-level robot control. IEEE Robot. Autom. Mag. **18**(3), 65–74 (2011)
27. Li, W., Dworkin, L., Seshia, S.A.: Mining assumptions for synthesis. In: 9th IEEE/ACM International Conference on Formal Methods and Models for Codesign, MEMOCODE 2011, Cambridge, 11–13 July 2011, pp. 43–50 (2011)
28. Lustig, Y., Vardi, M.Y.: Synthesis from component libraries. Int. J. Softw. Tools Technol. Transf. **15**(5–6), 603–618 (2013)
29. Madhusudan, P.: Synthesizing reactive programs. In: Bezem, M. (ed.) 20th Annual Conference of the EACSL (CSL). LIPIcs, vol. 12, pp. 428–442. Schloss Dagstuhl - Leibniz-Zentrum für Informatik (2011). http://drops.dagstuhl.de/opus/portals/extern/index.php?semnr=11007
30. Majumdar, R., Piterman, N., Schmuck, A.-K.: Environmentally-friendly GR(1) synthesis. In: Vojnar, T., Zhang, L. (eds.) TACAS 2019. LNCS, vol. 11428, pp. 229–246. Springer, Cham (2019). https://doi.org/10.1007/978-3-030-17465-1_13
31. Maoz, S., Ringert, J.O.: Spectra: a specification language for reactive systems. Softw. Syst. Model. **20**(5), 1553–1586 (2021)
32. Neider, D., Madhusudan, P., Saha, S., Garg, P., Park, D.: A learning-based approach to synthesizing invariants for incomplete verification engines. J. Autom. Reason. **64**(7), 1523–1552 (2020)
33. Pnueli, A., Rosner, R.: On the synthesis of an asynchronous reactive module. In: Automata, Languages and Programming, 16th International Colloquium, ICALP89, Stresa, 11–15 July 1989, pp. 652–671 (1989)
34. Solar-Lezama, A., Tancau, L., Bodík, R., Seshia, S.A., Saraswat, V.A.: Combinatorial sketching for finite programs. In: 12th International Conference on Architectural Support for Programming Languages and Operating Systems (ASPLOS), pp. 404–415. ACM (2006). https://doi.org/10.1145/1168857.1168907
35. Somenzi, F.: CUDD: CU decision diagram package, release 3.0.0 (2015)
36. Sztipanovits, J., et al.: Toward a science of cyber-physical system integration. Proc. IEEE **100**(1), 29–44 (2012)

Combining Classical and Probabilistic Independence Reasoning to Verify the Security of Oblivious Algorithms

Pengbo Yan[1]([✉])[iD], Toby Murray[1][iD], Olga Ohrimenko[1][iD],
Van-Thuan Pham[1][iD], and Robert Sison[2][iD]

FM
Artifact
Evaluation
★
Available

[1] The University of Melbourne, Melbourne, Australia
pengboy@student.unimelb.edu.au,
{toby.murray,oohrimenko,thuan.pham}@unimelb.edu.au
[2] UNSW Sydney, Sydney, Australia
r.sison@unsw.edu.au

Abstract. We consider the problem of how to verify the security of probabilistic oblivious algorithms formally and systematically. Unfortunately, prior program logics fail to support a number of complexities that feature in the semantics and invariants needed to verify the security of many practical probabilistic oblivious algorithms. We propose an approach based on reasoning over perfectly oblivious approximations, using a program logic that combines both classical Hoare logic reasoning and probabilistic independence reasoning to support all the needed features. We formalise and prove our new logic sound in Isabelle/HOL and apply our approach to formally verify the security of several challenging case studies beyond the reach of prior methods for proving obliviousness.

1 Introduction

Side-channel attacks allow attackers to infer sensitive information by eavesdropping on a program's execution, when the sensitive data are not directly observable (e.g. because they are encrypted). For example, sensitive documents or secret images can be reconstructed by only observing a program's memory access pattern [15,20,24]. Many algorithms are charged with the protection of secrets in application contexts where such attacks are realistic, for example, cloud computing [28,35], secure processors [8,21] and multiparty computation [19].

The goal of an <u>oblivious algorithm</u> (e.g. path ORAM [32], Melbourne shuffle [25]) is to hide its secrets from an attacker that can observe memory accesses. <u>Probabilistic</u> oblivious algorithms aim to do so while achieving better performance than <u>deterministic</u> oblivious algorithms. The various programming disciplines to defend against such attacks for deterministic algorithms [1,22] often lead to poor performance: e.g. to hide the fact that an array is accessed at a

---

This work has been supported in part by the joint CATCH MURI-AUSMURI and the Melbourne Graduate Research Scholarship.

A. Platzer et al. (Eds.): FM 2024, LNCS 14933, pp. 188–205, 2025.
https://doi.org/10.1007/978-3-031-71162-6_10

certain position, one may have to iterate over the entire array [5]. Probabilistic oblivious algorithms avoid this inefficiency by performing random choices at runtime to hide their secrets from attackers more efficiently. Unfortunately, probabilistic methods for achieving obliviousness are error prone and some have been shown insecure, as a result requiring non-trivial fixes [10,13].

In this paper we develop a program logic to verify the security of probabilistic oblivious algorithms formally and systematically. We adopt the standard threat model for such programs, in which the attacker is assumed to be able to infer the memory access pattern (e.g. either by explicitly observing memory requests in case of untrusted/compromised operating system or by measuring the time its own memory accesses take due to shared resources like caches) [4,9,11,32].

Although some previous works [3,7,31,34] exist, many oblivious algorithms have complex semantics and invariants that are beyond the reach of those prior methods to reason about. For example, path ORAM [32] maintains an invariant stating that virtual addresses are independent of each other and of the program's memory access patterns; whereas the oblivious sampling algorithm [28] contains secret- or random-variable-dependent random choices, conditional branches and loops, whose details we introduce in Sect. 2 and Sect. 5.

Also, to achieve efficiency, some oblivious algorithms [25,30,32] forgo perfection and have a very small probability of failure, which means that they do not perfectly hide their secrets. Fortunately, they are intentionally designed so that the failure probability is bounded by some negligible factor (e.g. of the size of the secret data), meaning that they are secure in practice. Following prior work [25,32], this means that we can prove them secure by reasoning over perfectly oblivious approximations, the theoretical and perfect version of the practical algorithms that are free of failure by construction (Appendix A.1 of the extended version of this paper [33] justifies this claim). Proving negligible error probability bounds on oblivious algorithms is an important goal, but is out of scope of this present work.

Reasoning over the perfectly oblivious approximations requires an approach that supports for all of the following:

- Assertions that describe probability distributions and independence;
- Reasoning about dynamic random choices over secrets and random variables
  - e.g. a random choice of integers from 1 to random secret variable s;
- Reasoning about branches that depend on secret random variables;
- Reasoning over loops that have a random number of iterations.

Our approach addresses these challenges simultaneously.

Following preliminaries (Sect. 3), in Sect. 4 we build a program logic that combines classical and probabilistic reasoning to address the aforementioned challenges, which we prove sound in Isabelle/HOL. Our logic is situated atop the Probabilistic Separation Logic (PSL) [3]; proving the soundness of our logic revealed several oversights in PSL [3], which we fixed (see Sect. 4.4).

To our knowledge, the reasoning our logic supports is beyond all prior methods for verifying obliviousness, including PSL [3], ObliCheck [31], λ_{OADT} [34], and λ_{obliv} [7]. The combination of classical and probabilistic reasoning also makes our logic more expressive than previous probabilistic Hoare logics (e.g., [12], VPHL [26] and pRHL [2]) which, because they lack assertions for describing distributions and independence, are ill-suited to direct proofs of obliviousness.

Finally, we demonstrate the power of our logic by applying it on pen-and-paper to verify, for the first time, the obliviousness of several non-trivial case studies (Sect. 5). Their verification is a significant achievement in that they constitute the fundamental building blocks for secure oblivious systems.

2   Overview

2.1   Challenges for Verification

Many probabilistic oblivious algorithms use probabilistic independence as a core intermediate condition to prove their obliviousness informally on pen and paper [25,28,30,32], which is intuitive and simple. However, such algorithms present a range of challenges for formally verifying their obliviousness systematically.

We have constructed the example algorithm in Fig. 1 to illustrate in a simplified form the kinds of complexities that will feature in the semantics and invariants needed to prove our case studies (Sect. 5). The teal-coloured parts show the verification and will be introduced in the next subsection. Our synthetic algorithm takes an input array S with size n containing secret elements: each either 0 or 1. The list O is empty initially but will be filled with some data later. We want to prove O will not leak any information about S. The synthetic algorithm first initialises array A with two random values sampled from the integers between 0 and 7. Its nested loop illustrates the following challenges:

1. The outer loop iterates n times where the ith iteration will append $A[S[i]]$ to O (line 4). It simulates a simplified version of path ORAM [32], which maintains an invariant that virtual addresses are independent of each other and of the program's memory access patterns. The secret S can be seen as a sequence of secret virtual addresses and the output O represents the memory access pattern. We need to prove an invariant that the elements in O are independent of each other and independent of each element $A[S[i]]$ appended to O by the outer loop. Note: the assignment on line 4 breaks the independence between O and $A[S[i]]$, so lines 4–11 update $A[S[i]]$ with a fresh random value to re-establish the independence for the next loop iteration. This ensures O is independent of S and will not leak secret information.
2. After initialising m with 8 on line 5, we have the inner loop containing a probabilistic and secret-dependent if-conditional. Its secret dependence makes the control flow different over different values of the secret. The iteration count for the inner loop is truly random, depending on $A[S[i]]$ (where each iteration doubles m and increases j by 1 or 2 depending on whether $j + S[i]\%3 = 0$). These kinds of loops and conditionals are common in real-world oblivious algorithms (Sect. 5), yet necessarily complicate reasoning.

Let $\text{eight}(i) = \{[x_0, x_1, \cdots, x_{i-1}] \mid \forall j.\ 0 \leq x_j \leq 7\}$
Let $\text{pre} = \{\forall i \in \{0, 1, \cdots, n-1\}.\ S[i] \in \{0, 1\}\}$
Let $\text{inv}(x) = \{\text{Ct}(\text{pre} \wedge i \leq n) \wedge \mathbf{U}_{\text{eight}(x)}[O]\}$
$\textbf{synthetic}(S, O, n):$
　　　$\{\text{Ct}(\text{pre} \wedge O = [])\}$

1　　$A[0] \leftarrow_\$ \mathbf{U}_{\{0,1,2,\cdots,7\}};$
　　　$\{\text{Ct}(\text{pre} \wedge O = []) \wedge \mathbf{U}_{\{0\cdots7\}}[A[0]]\}$

2　　$A[1] \leftarrow_\$ \mathbf{U}_{\{0,1,2,\cdots,7\}};\ i \leftarrow 0;$
　　　$\{\text{Ct}(\text{pre} \wedge O = [] \wedge i = 0) \wedge \mathbf{U}_{\{0\cdots7\}}[A[0]] * \mathbf{U}_{\{0\cdots7\}}[A[1]]\}$

3　　$\textbf{while } i < n \textbf{ do}$　　　　　　　　　　　$\text{because eight}(0) = \{[]\}$
　　　$\{\text{inv}(i) * \mathbf{U}_{\{0\cdots7\}}[A[S[i]]] * \mathbf{U}_{\{0\cdots7\}}[A[1 - S[i]]]\}$

4　　　　$O \leftarrow O + A[S[i]];$　　　　　　　　　　$\text{using proposition 1.8}$
　　　　　$\{\text{inv}(i+1) * \mathbf{U}_{\{0\cdots7\}}[A[1 - S[i]]]\}$

5　　　　$m \leftarrow 8;\ j \leftarrow 0;$
　　　　　$\{\text{inv}(i+1) * \mathbf{U}_{\{0\cdots7\}}[A[1 - S[i]]] \wedge \text{Ct}(m = 8 \wedge j = 0)\}$

6　　　　$\textbf{while } A[S[i]] > j \textbf{ do}$
　　　　　　$\{\text{Ct}(m > 7 \wedge m \,\%\, 8 = 0)\}$

7　　　　　　$m \leftarrow m * 2;\ j \leftarrow j + 1;$

8　　　　　　$\textbf{if } (j + S[i]) \,\%\, 3 == 0 \textbf{ then}$

9　　　　　　　$j \leftarrow j + 1;$
　　　　　$\{\text{Ct}(m > 7 \wedge m \,\%\, 8 = 0)\}\,\text{using Const rule around the loop}$
　　　　　$\{\text{inv}(i+1) * \mathbf{U}_{\{0\cdots7\}}[A[1 - S[i]]] \wedge \text{Ct}(m > 7 \wedge m \,\%\, 8 = 0)\}$

10　　　　$t \leftarrow_\$ \mathbf{U}_{\{1,2,3,\cdots,m\}};$　　　　　　　　using RSample
　　　　　$\{\text{inv}(i+1) * \mathbf{U}_{\{0\cdots7\}}[A[1 - S[i]]] \wedge \mathbf{U}_{\{0\cdots7\}}[t \,\%\, 8]\}$

11　　　　$A[S[i]] \leftarrow t \,\%\, 8;$　　　　　　$\text{using Rassign, Unif-Idp rule}$
　　　　　$\{\text{inv}(i+1) * \mathbf{U}_{\{0\cdots7\}}[A[1 - S[i]]] * \mathbf{U}_{\{0\cdots7\}}[A[S[i]]]\}$

12　　　　$i \leftarrow i + 1;$
　　　$\{\text{inv}(n)\}$

Fig. 1. Verification of the motivating algorithm.

3. On line 10, the algorithm makes what we call a <u>dynamic random choice</u>, which is one over a truly random set (here, from 1 to the random variable m), assigning the chosen value to t. Then, (line 11) $A[S[i]]$ is assigned $t \,\%\, 8$. This requires reasoning that $t \,\%\, 8$ satisfies the uniform distribution on $\{0 \cdots 7\}$, because m is certainly a multiple of 8. Dynamic random choices are also common in real-world oblivious algorithms, as Sect. 5 demonstrates.

Lines $5 - 11$ are derived from the oblivious sampling algorithm [28] (see Appendix C.2 of the extended version [33]) to demonstrate challenges 2 and 3.

2.2　Mixing Probabilistic and Classical Reasoning

We show how to construct a program logic that combines classical and probabilistic (and independence) reasoning over different parts of the program so that it can verify our running example, as shown in Fig. 1. Namely, certain parts of the algorithm (lines $1, 2, 4, 10$) require careful probabilistic reasoning, while others do not, but that each style of reasoning can benefit the other.

Our program logic is constructed by situating these ideas in the context of the Probabilistic Separation Logic (PSL) [3]. PSL is an existing program logic for reasoning about probabilistic programs. PSL employs the separating conjunction (here written $\star$) familiar from separation logic [23] to capture when two probability distributions are independent. In situating our work atop PSL we extend its assertion forms with the new $\mathsf{Ct}(\cdot)$ assertion, to capture classical information. More importantly, however, we significantly extend the resulting logic with a range of novel reasoning principles for mixing classical and probabilistic reasoning embodied in a suite of new rules (Fig. 3), which we will present more fully in Sect. 4. These new rules show how classical reasoning (captured by $\mathsf{Ct}(\cdot)$ assertions) can be effectively harnessed, and allow reasoning about dynamic random choices, secret-dependent if-statements, and random loops, making our logic significantly more applicable than PSL; while leveraging PSL's support for intuitive reasoning about probability distributions makes our logic also more expressive than prior probabilistic program logics [2, 12, 26]. We also harness the close interaction between classical and probabilistic reasoning to allow new ways to prove security (e.g., the UNIF-IDP rule and the final proposition of Proposition 1, which will be introduced in Fig. 3 and Sect. 4.1), and new ways to reason about random sampling (embodied in the RSAMPLE rule, Fig. 3). Each represents a non-trivial insight, and all are necessary for reasoning about real-world oblivious algorithms (Sect. 5). The increase in expressiveness, beyond prior probabilistic program logics [2, 3, 12, 26], within a principled and clean extension of PSL attests to the careful design of our logic.

The combination of classical and probabilistic reasoning means that our logic tracks two kinds of <u>atomic assertions</u>, as follows.

Certain Assertions. Classical reasoning is supported by certain assertions $\mathsf{Ct}(e_r)$ that state that some property e_r (which may mention random variables) is true with absolute certainty, i.e. is true in all memories supported by the current probabilistic state of the program. With certain assertions and classical reasoning, our logic can reason about **loops with random iteration numbers and randomly secret-dependent if statements**. Doing so requires distinguishing classical from distribution (independence) assertions, because the latter are ill-suited for reasoning about random loops and conditionals.

For example, from line 5 to 9, although the random loop and the probabilistic- and secret-dependent if statement complicate the algorithm, we only need classical reasoning to conclude that after the loop m is certainly a multiple of 8 (using the RLOOP and RCOND rules in Fig. 3, which have the classic form). This information is sufficient to verify the remainder of the algorithm.

Distribution Assertions. On the other hand, reasoning about probability distributions is supported by distribution assertions, which we adopt and extend from PSL: for a set expression e_d (which is allowed to mention non-random program variables), $\mathbf{U}_{e_d}[e_r]$ states that expression e_r is uniformly distributed over the set denoted by e_d in the sense that when e_r is evaluated in the current probabilistic state of the program it yields a uniform distribution over the evaluation of e_d. We define these concepts formally later in Sect. 4.1 (see Definition 2). With this reasoning style, we support **dynamic random choice** (e.g. line 10, the value is sampled from a truly probabilistic set), which is not supported by previous works [2,3,7,12,26,31,34]. Note that we require e_d to be deterministic here because if e_d can be probabilistic, then it means a probabilistic expression satisfies a <u>uniform distribution on a probabilistic set</u>—a clear contradiction.

For example, at line 10, even if we do not specify the detailed distribution of m, we can conclude $t \% 8$ satisfies the uniform distribution on the set $\{0 \cdots 7\}$, as m is certainly a multiple of 8, by an argument based on our concept of an <u>even partition</u> (Definition 4). This reasoning is supported by our novel RSAMPLE rule (Fig. 3). Here, it requires that all the possible sets (in this case, $\{1 \cdots 8\}$ or $\{1 \cdots 16\}$ or ...) over which t was sampled, can each be evenly mapped to (and thus partitioned by) the target set (here $\{0 \cdots 7\}$) by the applied function (here $\%8$). Thus $t \% 8$ must satisfy the uniform distribution on $\{0 \cdots 7\}$.

Unifying Classical and Probabilistic Independence Reasoning. Another important feature of our logic is that it allows independence to be <u>derived</u> by leveraging classical reasoning. For example, considering line 10, 11, if a variable ($A[S[i]]$) always satisfies the same distribution (uniform distribution on $\{0 \cdots 7\}$) over any possible values of some other variables (O and $A[1 - S[i]]$), then the former is independent of the latter (because O and $A[1 - S[i]]$ will not influence the values of $A[S[i]]$). The new rule UNIF-IDP (Fig. 3) embodies this reasoning (where $\star$ denotes independence and $\mathbf{D}()$ stands for an arbitrary distribution).[1]

Our logic also includes a set of useful propositions (Proposition 1) that aid deriving independence information from classical reasoning.

Returning to the example, with the conclusion that $A[S[i]]$ is independent of other variables, we can construct the loop invariant of the outer loop ($\mathsf{inv}(i)$) stating that the output array O always satisfies a uniform distribution following the ith iteration, which is captured by $\mathsf{eight}(i)$. We use the final proposition of Proposition 1 here. Intuitively, this proposition says given a reversible function (whose inputs can be decided by looking at its outputs, e.g. array appending), if its two inputs satisfy uniform distribution and are independent of each other, then the result of the function should satisfy the uniform distribution on the product (by the function) of the two inputs' distribution.

By the invariant, we can conclude finally the output array always satisfies the uniform distribution on $\mathsf{eight}(n)$, regardless of secret S, which means the output will not leak any secret information.

---

[1] In this case we cannot use PSL's frame rule because m is not independent of A.

3 Preliminaries

3.1 Programming Language and Semantics

In this paper we define a probability distribution over a countable set A is a function $\mu : A \to [0, 1]$ where $\Sigma_{a \in A}\mu(a) = 1$. We write $\mu(B)$ for $\Sigma_{b \in B}\mu(b)$ where B can be any subset of A and $\mathbf{D}(A)$ for the set of all distributions over A.

The support of a distribution μ, $\mathsf{supp}(\mu)$, is the set of all elements whose probability is greater than zero, $\{a \in A \mid \mu(a) > 0\}$.

A unit distribution over a single element, $\mathsf{unit}(a)$, is $(\lambda x.$ If $a = x$ then 1 else $0)$. A uniform distribution over a set, Unif_S, is $(\lambda x.$ If $x \in S$ then $1/|S|$ else $0)$.

Given a distribution μ over A and a function f from elements of A to a distribution, $f : A \to \mathbf{D}(B)$, we define $\mathsf{bind}(\mu, f) = \lambda b.\ \Sigma_{a \in A}\mu(a) \cdot f(a)(b)$, used to give semantics to random selections and assignments to random variables.

Given two distributions μ_A and μ_B over the sets A and B, we define $\mu_A \otimes \mu_B = \lambda a, b.\ \mu_A(a) \cdot \mu_B(b)$. Given a distribution μ over $A \times B$, we define $\pi_1(\mu) = \lambda a.\ \Sigma_{b \in B}\mu(a, b)$ and $\pi_2(\mu) = \lambda b.\ \Sigma_{a \in A}\mu(a, b)$. We say these two distributions are independent if and only if $\mu = \pi_1(\mu) \otimes \pi_2(\mu)$.

Given a distribution μ over some set A, and $S \subseteq A$ where $\mu(S) > 0$, let $E \subseteq A$, we define $(\mu|S) = \lambda E.\ \frac{\mu(E \cap S)}{\mu(S)}$, used to give semantics to conditional statements, as is the following. Given two distribution μ_1, μ_2, and a number $p \in [0, 1]$, we define $\mu_1 \oplus_p \mu_2 = \lambda x.\ p \cdot \mu_1(x) + (1 - p) \cdot \mu_2(x)$. When p is 1 or 0, we unconditionally define the result to be μ_1 or μ_2 respectively.

Same as PSL's memory model, we also distinguish deterministic from random variables: only the latter can be influenced by random selections (i.e. by probabilistic choices). We define $\mathbf{DV}$ as a countable set of deterministic variables and $\mathbf{RV}$ as a countable set of random variables, disjoint from $\mathbf{DV}$.

Let $\mathbf{Val}$ be the countable set of values, which we assume contains at least the values true and false. When applying our logic, we will freely assume it contains integers, lists, sets, and any other standard data types as required. Let op be a set of operations on values, including binary functions on values of type $(\mathbf{Val} \times \mathbf{Val}) \to \mathbf{Val}$. In practice, we will assume it includes the standard arithmetic, list and set operations, and others as required. Finally, let $\mathsf{vset}()$ be a function of type $\mathbf{Val} \to \mathcal{P}(\mathbf{Val})$, taking one value and returning a non-empty, finite set of values, for giving semantics to dynamic random choice.

Then let $\mathbf{DetM} = \mathbf{DV} \to \mathbf{Val}$ be the set of deterministic memories, and $\mathbf{RanM} = \mathbf{RV} \to \mathbf{Val}$ the set of random variable memories. A semantic configuration is a pair (σ, μ), where $\sigma \in \mathbf{DetM}$ and $\mu \in \mathbf{D}(\mathbf{RanM})$ (a probability distribution over $\mathbf{RanM}$). Configurations represent program states.

As with program variables, we define sets of deterministic and random expressions, denoted $\mathbf{DE}$ and $\mathbf{RE}$ respectively. $\mathbf{DE}$ cannot mention random variables.

Definition 1 (Expressions). *Expressions are either deterministic or random, defined as follows:*

$$Deterministic\ expressions:\ \mathbf{DE} \ni e_d ::= \mathbf{Val} \mid \mathbf{DV} \mid \mathsf{op}\ \mathbf{DE}\ \mathbf{DE}$$
$$Random\ expressions:\ \mathbf{RE} \ni e_r ::= \mathbf{Val} \mid \mathbf{DV} \mid \mathbf{RV} \mid \mathsf{op}\ \mathbf{RE}\ \mathbf{RE}$$

Note that **DE** is a subset of **RE**. Given a deterministic memory σ and a random variable memory m, we write $[[e_r]]\,(\sigma, m)$ as the evaluation of expression e_r. Expression evaluation is entirely standard and its definition is omitted for brevity. The evaluation of deterministic expressions e_d depends only on the deterministic memory σ and so we often abbreviate it $[[e_d]]\,\sigma$.

Following the distinction between deterministic and random variables, the programming language also distinguishes deterministic and random conditionals and loops. We define two sets of program commands for our language, where **C** is the complete set of commands and **RC** is a subset of **C** containing so-called "random" commands that cannot assign to deterministic variables. We write **if**$_D$ b **then** c to abbreviate **if**$_D$ b **then** c **else skip** and likewise for **if**$_R$ b **then** c. As with PSL, our logic is defined for programs that always terminate.

$$
\begin{aligned}
\mathbf{RC} \ni c ::=\ & \mathbf{skip} \mid \mathbf{RV} \leftarrow \mathbf{RE} \\
\mid\ & \mathbf{RV} \leftarrow_\$ \mathbf{U_{RE}} \mid \mathbf{RC};\mathbf{RC} \\
\mid\ & \mathbf{if}_D\ \mathbf{DE}\ \mathbf{then}\ \mathbf{RC}\ \mathbf{else}\ \mathbf{RC} \\
\mid\ & \mathbf{if}_R\ \mathbf{RE}\ \mathbf{then}\ \mathbf{RC}\ \mathbf{else}\ \mathbf{RC} \\
\mid\ & \mathbf{while}_D\ \mathbf{DE}\ \mathbf{do}\ \mathbf{RC} \\
\mid\ & \mathbf{while}_R\ \mathbf{RE}\ \mathbf{do}\ \mathbf{RC}
\end{aligned}
\qquad
\begin{aligned}
\mathbf{C} \ni c ::=\ & \mathbf{skip} \mid \mathbf{DV} \leftarrow \mathbf{DE} \\
\mid\ & \mathbf{RV} \leftarrow \mathbf{RE} \mid \mathbf{RV} \leftarrow_\$ \mathbf{U_{RE}} \mid \mathbf{C};\mathbf{C} \\
\mid\ & \mathbf{if}_D\ \mathbf{DE}\ \mathbf{then}\ \mathbf{C}\ \mathbf{else}\ \mathbf{C} \\
\mid\ & \mathbf{if}_R\ \mathbf{RE}\ \mathbf{then}\ \mathbf{RC}\ \mathbf{else}\ \mathbf{RC} \\
\mid\ & \mathbf{while}_D\ \mathbf{DE}\ \mathbf{do}\ \mathbf{C} \\
\mid\ & \mathbf{while}_R\ \mathbf{RE}\ \mathbf{do}\ \mathbf{RC}
\end{aligned}
$$

In practical verification, given an algorithm, we try to set all the variables as deterministic variables at the beginning. Then, all the variables sampled from the uniform distribution or assigned by an expression containing random variables must be random variables. All the loop and if-conditions containing random variables must be random loops/conditionals. All the variables assigned in a random loop/conditional must be random variables. We repeat the above process until no variable and loop/conditional will change their type.

The semantics (Fig. 2) of a command $c \in \mathbf{C}$ is denoted $[[c]]$, which is a configuration transformer of type $(\mathbf{DetM} \times \mathbf{D}(\mathbf{RanM})) \to (\mathbf{DetM} \times \mathbf{D}(\mathbf{RanM}))$. Our programming language extends that of PSL by allowing dynamic random choice, in which a value is chosen from a set denoted by an random expression $e_r \in \mathbf{RE}$ rather than a constant set. We also add random loops, whose condition can depend on random expressions (rather than only deterministic expressions as in PSL). These improvements increase the expressivity of the language, necessary to capture the kinds of practical oblivious algorithms that we target in Sect. 5. Unlike PSL, which defines its loop semantics somewhat informally, ours enables direct mechanisation (in Isabelle/HOL).

4 Logic

4.1 Assertions

The assertions of our logic include those of PSL, which we extend with the certainty assertion $\mathsf{Ct}(e_r)$ while extending the uniform distribution assertion $\mathbf{U}_{e_d}[e_r]$ by allowing the set to be specified by an expression e_d (rather than a constant as in PSL). The free variables of an expression e are denoted $\mathsf{FV}(e)$.

$$[[\textbf{skip}]](\sigma, \mu) = (\sigma, \mu)$$

$$[[x_d \leftarrow e_d]](\sigma, \mu) = (\sigma[x_d \mapsto [[e_d]]\sigma], \mu)$$

$$[[x_r \leftarrow e_r]](\sigma, \mu) = (\sigma, \text{bind}(\mu, m \mapsto \text{unit}(m[x_r \mapsto [[e_r]](\sigma, m)])))$$

$$[[x_r \leftarrow_{\$} \mathbf{U}_{e_r}]](\sigma, \mu) = (\sigma, \text{bind}(\mu, m \mapsto \text{bind}(\text{Unif}_{\text{vset}([[e_r]](\sigma, m))}, u \mapsto \text{unit}(m[x_r \mapsto u]))))$$

$$[[c;\ c']](\sigma, \mu) = [[c']]([[c]](\sigma, \mu))$$

$$[[\textbf{if}_D\ b\ \textbf{then}\ c\ \textbf{else}\ c']](\sigma, \mu) = \begin{cases} [[c]](\sigma, \mu) & : [[b]]\sigma \neq \textsf{false} \\ [[c']](\sigma, \mu) & : [[b]]\sigma = \textsf{false} \end{cases}$$

$$[[\textbf{if}_R\ b\ \textbf{then}\ c\ \textbf{else}\ c']](\sigma, \mu) = [[c]](\sigma, \mu|[[b]]\sigma \neq \textsf{false}) \oplus_{\mu([[b]]\sigma \neq \textsf{false})}$$
$$[[c']](\sigma, \mu|[[b]]\sigma = \textsf{false})$$

$$[[\textbf{while}_D\ b\ \textbf{do}\ c]](\sigma, \mu) = [[\textbf{if}_D\ b\ \textbf{then}\ (c;\ \textbf{while}_D\ b\ \textbf{do}\ c)]](\sigma, \mu)$$

$$[[\textbf{while}_R\ b\ \textbf{do}\ c]](\sigma, \mu) = [[\textbf{if}_R\ b\ \textbf{then}\ (c;\ \textbf{while}_R\ b\ \textbf{do}\ c)]](\sigma, \mu)$$

Fig. 2. Programming Language Semantics

The domain of distribution μ over memories, written $\text{dom}(\mu)$, is the set of random variables in the memories in the support of μ. **AP** denotes the set of atomic assertions.

For a random variable expression e_r, $\text{Ct}(e_r)$ asserts that e_r evaluates to true in every memory consistent with the current configuration, i.e. it holds with absolute certainty. Note that the set of random variable expressions e_r can accommodate all standard assertions from classical Hoare logic.

Definition 2 (Atomic Assertion Semantics).

$$[[\text{Ct}(e_r)]] = \{(\sigma, \mu) \mid \forall m \in \text{supp}(\mu).\ \ [[e_r]]\,(\sigma, m) = \textsf{true}\}$$
$$[[\mathbf{U}_{e_d}[e_r]]] = \{(\sigma, \mu) \mid \text{FV}(e_r) \cup \text{FV}(e_d) \subseteq \text{dom}(\sigma) \cup \text{dom}(\mu)$$
$$and\ \text{Unif}_{\text{vset}([[e_d]]\sigma)} = [[e_r]]\,(\sigma, \mu)\}$$

The assertion $\mathbf{U}_{e_d}[e_r]$ asserts that the evaluation of random variable expression e_r yields the uniform distribution over the set denoted by the deterministic expression e_d when evaluated in the current deterministic memory, where the vset() function is used to retrieve that denotation after evaluating e_d (Sect. 3.1). We require the expression e_d to be deterministic as otherwise this assertion can introduce contradictions (e.g. if the set expression instead denoted a truly random set including possible sets $\{1, 2\}$ and $\{0\}$, then e_r will not be uniformly distributed on any set).

From PSL our logic inherits its other assertions and Kripke resource monoid semantics. The assertions $\top$ (which holds always), $\bot$ (which never holds), and connectives $\wedge, \vee, \rightarrow$ have their standard meaning. The separation logic [23] connectives are $*$, which is separating conjunction and is used to assert probabilistic independence; and $-\!\!*$ is separating implication. See extended Appendix A.2 [33].

Note that $\text{Ct}(P) \wedge \text{Ct}(Q)$ is equivalent to $\text{Ct}(P \wedge Q)$, but $\text{Ct}(a = 1) \vee \text{Ct}(a = 2)$ is different to $\text{Ct}(a = 1 \vee a = 2)$: the former asserts that either a is always 1 or a is always 2 (stronger); the latter asserts that always a is either 1 or 2 (weaker).

We also write $\mathbf{D}(x)$ to abbreviate $\mathsf{Ct}(x = x)$, which asserts that the variable x is in the domain of the partial configuration. Any distribution of x satisfies this assertion.

Finally, we introduce several useful propositions about assertions implication. They are very useful in the verification and reflect the interplay between classical and probabilistic independence reasoning, especially the last one.

Proposition 1.

$$\models (\phi * \psi) \wedge \eta \rightarrow (\phi \wedge \eta) * \psi \text{ ,where } \models \phi \rightarrow \mathbf{D}(\mathsf{FV}(\eta) \cap \mathbf{RV}) \tag{1}$$

$$\models (\phi * \psi) \rightarrow (\phi \wedge \psi) \tag{2}$$

$$\models \mathbf{U}_S[e] \wedge \mathsf{Ct}(f \text{ is a bijection from } S \text{ to } S') \rightarrow \mathbf{U}_{S'}[f(e)] \tag{3}$$

$$\models (\mathsf{Ct}(\phi \wedge \psi)) \rightarrow (\mathsf{Ct}(\phi) \wedge \mathsf{Ct}(\psi)) \tag{4}$$

$$\models (\mathsf{Ct}(\phi) \wedge \mathsf{Ct}(\psi)) \rightarrow (\mathsf{Ct}(\phi \wedge \psi)) \tag{5}$$

$$\models \mathbf{U}_S[e] \rightarrow \mathsf{Ct}(e \in S) \tag{6}$$

$$\models \mathbf{U}_S[e] \wedge \mathsf{Ct}(e = e') \rightarrow \mathbf{U}_S[e'] \tag{7}$$

$$\models \mathsf{Ct}(x = e \wedge x \notin \mathsf{FV}(e')) \wedge \mathbf{D}(e) * \mathbf{D}(e') \implies \mathbf{D}(x) * \mathbf{D}(e') \tag{8}$$

$$\models \begin{aligned}&\mathsf{Ct}(\forall a, b \in S, c, d \in S'.f(a,c) = f(b,d) \rightarrow a = b \wedge c = d) \wedge \mathbf{U}_S[x] * \mathbf{U}_{S'}[e'] \\ &\rightarrow \mathbf{U}_{S \times_f S'}[f(x, e')], \text{ where } S \times_f S' = \{f(a,b) \mid a \in S \wedge b \in S'\}\end{aligned} \tag{9}$$

The first two are inherited from PSL. The third one generalises a similar proposition of PSL [3] over possibly different sets S and S'. The fourth and fifth show the equivalence of $\wedge$ whether inside or outside the certain assertions. The sixth shows the straightforward consequence that if e is uniformly distributed over set S, then the value of e must be in S. The seventh shows two expressions satisfy the same distribution if they are certainly equal. The eighth shows if we know that e is independent of e' and we know another variable $x = e$ additionally, we can conclude that x is also independent of e' if x is not a free variable in e'.

The last one also generalises a proposition of PSL [3] by leveraging $\mathsf{Ct}(\cdot)$ conditions: it restricts binary function f by requiring it to produce different outputs when given two different pairs of inputs. In practice, we will use this lemma letting f be the concatenation function on two arrays where S is a set of possible arrays with the same length. We conclude the concatenated array satisfies the uniform distribution on S times S' if those premises hold.

4.2   Judgements and Rules

The judgements $\vdash \{\phi\} c \{\psi\}$ of our program logic are simple Hoare logic correctness statements, in which c is a program command and ϕ and ψ are preconditions and postconditions respectively.

Definition 3 (Judgement Validity). *Given two assertions ϕ, ψ and a program command c, a judgement $\{\phi\}c\{\psi\}$ is valid if for all configuration (σ, μ) satisfying $(\sigma, \mu) \models \phi$, we have $[[c]](\sigma, \mu) \models \psi$, denoted $\vdash \{\phi\} c \{\psi\}$.*

RAssign
$$\frac{\phi \in \mathbf{AP}}{\vdash \{\phi[e_r/x_r]\}\ x_r \leftarrow e_r\ \{\phi\}}$$

RSample
$$\vdash \{\mathsf{Ct}(\mathsf{El}(f, S, S'))\}\ x_r \leftarrow_\$ \mathbf{U}_S\ \{\mathbf{U}_{S'}[f(x_r)]\}$$

$$\frac{\vdash \{\mathsf{Ct}(\phi \wedge b \neq \mathsf{false})\}\ c\ \{\mathsf{Ct}(\psi)\} \qquad \vdash \{\mathsf{Ct}(\phi \wedge b = \mathsf{false})\}\ c'\ \{\mathsf{Ct}(\psi)\}}{\vdash \{\mathsf{Ct}(\phi)\}\ \mathbf{if}_R\ b\ \mathbf{then}\ c\ \mathbf{else}\ c'\ \{\mathsf{Ct}(\psi)\}}\text{RCond}$$

$$\frac{\vdash \{\phi\}\ \mathbf{if}_R\ b\ \mathbf{then}\ c\ \{\phi\}}{\vdash \{\phi\}\ \mathbf{while}_R\ b\ \mathbf{do}\ c\ \{\phi \wedge \mathsf{Ct}(b = \mathsf{false})\}}\text{RLoop}$$

Unif-Idp
$$\frac{\mathsf{FV}(a) \cap \mathsf{MV}(c) = \emptyset \qquad b \notin \mathsf{FV}(a) \qquad \vdash \{\mathsf{Ct}(a \in A) * Q \wedge \mathsf{Ct}(P)\}\ c\ \{\mathbf{U}_S[b]\}}{\vdash \{\mathsf{Ct}(a \in A) * Q \wedge \mathsf{Ct}(P)\}\ c\ \{(\mathbf{D}(a) * \mathbf{U}_S[b])\}}$$

Fig. 3. Rules capturing the interplay of classical and probabilistic reasoning.

Our logic inherits all of PSL's original rules [3] (see extended Appendix A.3 [33] for details); many of them use the $\mathsf{Ct}(\cdot)$ assertion to encode equality tests, which were encoded instead in PSL primitively.

Figure 3 depicts the rules of our logic that embody its new reasoning principles, and support the requirements listed at Sect. 2.1. The random assignment rule RAssign has the classical Hoare logic form. It requires the postcondition ϕ is atomic to avoid unsound derivations, e.g. $\{0 = 0 * 0 = 0\}\ x = 0\ \{x = x * x = x\}$.

As mentioned in Sect. 2.2, the RSample rule is another embodiment of the general principle underlying the design of our logic, of classical and probabilistic reasoning enhancing each other. Specifically, it allows us to deduce when a randomly sampled quantity $f(x_r)$ (a function f applied to a random variable x_r) is uniformly distributed over set S' when the random variable x_r was uniformly sampled over set S. It is especially useful when S is itself random. It relies on the function f <u>evenly partitioning</u> the input set S into S', as defined below.

Definition 4 (Even Partition). *Given two sets S, S' and a function f, we say that f <u>evenly partitions</u> S into S' if and only if $S' = \{f(s) | s \in S\}$ and there exists an integer k such that $\forall s' \in S'. |\{s \in S | f(s) = s'\}| = k$. In this case we write $\mathsf{El}(f, S, S')$.*

RSample allows reasoning over random choices beyond original PSL [3], and in particular dynamic random sampling from truly random sets. For example, at line 10 of Fig. 1, we have $\mathsf{Ct}(\mathsf{El}(f, S, S'))$ where $f = \%\ 8$, $S = \{0 \cdots m\}$, $S' = \{0 \cdots 7\}$. Letting $k = m/8$ with the above definition, we can prove the precondition implies $\mathsf{Ct}(\mathsf{El}(f, S, S'))$. Note that if $m = 9$ then $\mathsf{Ct}(\mathsf{El}(f, S, S'))$ will not hold because we cannot find k. The existence of k makes sure that S can be evenly partitioned to S' by f. Also, from our new random sample rule RSample, one can obtain PSL's original rule by letting $S' = S$ and $f = (\lambda x.\ x)$.

Besides PSL's random conditional rule, we also include the RCond rule for random conditions that operate over certainty assertions $\mathsf{Ct}(\cdot)$. It is in many cases more applicable because it does not require the branching condition to be independent of the precondition and, while it reasons only over certainty assertions, other conditions can be added by applying the CONST rule [3]. The new random loop rule RLOOP is straightforward, requiring proof of the invariant ϕ over a random conditional.

The final new rule UNIF-IDP unifies two methods to prove the independence of an algorithm's output b from its input a: it says that if given any arbitrary distribution of a we can always prove that the result b is uniformly distributed, then a and b are independent because the distribution of a does not influence b, where $\mathsf{MV}(c)$ is the variables c may write to (same as PSL's definition). It is useful for programs that consume their secrets by random choice at runtime (e.g. Fig. 1 we verified in Sect. 2.2 and the Oblivious Sampling algorithm [28] we verify in extended Appendix C.2 [33]).

As an example, we used this rule between line 10 and line 11 in Fig. 1 by letting $a = (O,\ A[1 - S[i]])$ and P, Q be the other information in the assertion before line 10. The first premise of the rule is true because these two lines of code never modify O and $A[1 - S[i]]$. The second premise is also trivially true. The third premise is proved by the RSAMPLE and RASSIGN rules. This yields the conclusion that O and $A[1 - S[i]]$ are independent of $A[S[i]]$.

Note that the pre-condition $\mathsf{Ct}(a \in A) * Q \land \mathsf{Ct}(P)$ appears in both premise and conclusion of the rule. Considering the WEAK rule [3] (aka the classical consequence rule), when the precondition is in the premise, we want it be as strong as it can so that the premise is easier to be proved. When it is in conclusion, we want it be as weak as it can so that the conclusion is more useful. These two requirements guide us to design the rule with two free assertions connected by $\land$ and $*$ respectively so that it is very flexible. If we change the pre-condition to $\mathbf{D}(a)$ (deleting A, P, Q), this rule is still sound (which can be proved by letting A be the universe set and P, Q be true) but much less applicable.

4.3   Soundness

Theorem 1. *All the rules in Fig. 3, plus the other original PSL rules [3], are sound, i.e. are valid according to Definition 3.*

We formalised our logic and proved it sound in Isabelle/HOL (see the accompanying artifact). It constitute 7K lines of Isabelle and required approx. 8 person-months to complete. Some of our Isabelle proofs follow PSL's pen-and-paper proofs but we also found several problems in PSL's definitions and proofs. We briefly discuss those now, to highlight the value and importance of machine-checked proofs for establishing the soundness of program logics.

4.4   Oversights in Original PSL

Our machine-checked proofs identified various oversights in the pen-and-paper formalisation of original PSL [3]. We fixed them either by modifying specific definitions or by finding an alternative—often much more complicated, but sound—proof strategy.

PSL [3] defines the notion of when a formula ϕ is <u>supported</u> (**SP**), requiring that for any deterministic memory σ, there exists a distribution over random variable memories μ such that if $(\sigma, \mu') \models \phi$, then $\mu \sqsubseteq \mu'$ (meaning that μ is a marginal distribution of μ' where $\mathsf{dom}(\mu) \subseteq \mathsf{dom}(\mu')$) [3, Definition 6].

This definition aims to restrict the assertions used in PSL's original rule for random conditionals [3, rule RCOND of Fig. 3], but it is not strong enough. All the assertions satisfy it because μ can always be instantiated with the unit distribution over the empty memory $\mathsf{unit}(\emptyset \rightarrow \mathbf{Val})$, $\sqsubseteq$ all others. This means the second example in their paper [3, Example 2] is a counterexample to their rule for random conditionals because there is not any non-supported assertion.

We fixed this by altering their definition of **SP**. Note that simply excluding the empty memory case is not enough to fix this problem. Instead, we have Definition 5 and our Isabelle proofs ensure its soundness. It does not have a big impact on adjusting the proofs strategy of relevant rules.

Definition 5 (Supported). *An assertion ϕ is Supported (**SP**) if for any deterministic memory σ, there exists a randomised memory μ such that if $(\sigma, \mu') \models \phi$, then $\mu \sqsubseteq \mu'$ and $(\sigma, \mu) \models \phi$.*

Additionally, key lemmas that underpin PSL's soundness argument turned out to be true, but not for the reasons stated in their proofs [3, Lemmas 1 and 2, Appendix B]. PSL's Lemma 1 proof has mistakes in the implication case. The second sentence of the implication case said, "there exists a distribution μ" such that ...". However μ" may not exist because μ and μ' may disagree on some variables in $\mathsf{FV}(\phi_1, \phi_2)$. PSL's Lemma 2 proof also has mistakes. They said "we have $(\sigma_1, \mu_1) \models \eta$" on the third line of proof but this is not true because σ_1 may not equal σ (the domain of σ_1 could be smaller than σ). The actual proof of these needs a different strategy which we found and formalized in Isabelle.

Without mechanising the soundness of our program logic, it is unlikely we would have uncovered these issues. This shows the vital importance of mechanised soundness proofs.

5   Case Studies

We applied our program logic to verify the obliviousness of four non-trivial oblivious algorithms: the Melbourne Shuffle [25], Oblivious Sampling [28], Path ORAM [32] and Path Oblivious Heap [30]. The details are in Appendix C of the extended version of this paper [33].

While these proofs are manual, each took less than a person-day to complete, except for Path Oblivious Heap, which took approx. 2 days of proof effort.

To our knowledge, the Melbourne Shuffle, Oblivious Sampling, and Path Oblivious Heap have never been formally verified as each requires the combination of features that our approach uniquely supports. Path ORAM has received some formal verification [16,27] (see later in Sect. 6) and also comes with an informal but rigorous proof of security [32]. We verified it to show that our logic can indeed encode existing rigorous security arguments.

In practice we need to distinguish the public memory locations and private locations, where we assume any access to public memory locations is visible to attackers. We add ghost code to record all public accesses in an array "Trace" and finally we aim to prove that array is independent of secrets.

The Melbourne Shuffle [25] (see extended Appendix C.1 [33]) is an effective oblivious shuffling algorithm used in cloud storage and also a basic building block for other higher-level algorithms (e.g. oblivious sampling [28]). Its operation is non-trivial, including rearranging array elements with dummy values and other complexities. Its verification employs much classical reasoning because, while it is probabilistic, its memory access pattern is deterministic (absent failure).

Oblivious sampling [28] (see extended Appendix C.2 [33]) is another important building block having applications in differential privacy, oblivious data analysis and machine learning. The algorithm obliviously samples from a data set, by producing a uniformly-distributed memory access pattern, and includes random and secret-dependent looping and if-statements, plus dynamic random choices (shuffling on a truly probabilistic array). Thus our logic's interplay between classical and probabilistic reasoning is essential to verifying its security.

Path ORAM [32] (see extended Appendix C.3 [33]) is a seminal oblivious RAM algorithm with practical efficiency, providing general-purpose oblivious storage. Path oblivious heap (extended Appendix C.4 [33]) is inspired by Path ORAM and the two share the same idea: using a binary tree with a random and virtual location table to store secret data, where the mappings between each physical and virtual location are always independent of each other and of the memory access pattern. Thus probabilistic independence is crucial to express and prove these algorithms' key invariants.

6   Related Work

Our program logic naturally extends PSL [3] non-trivially, including support for classical reasoning, dynamic random choice, improved support for random conditionals, random loops, and random assignments. Our mechanisation of PSL identified and fixed a number of oversights (see Sect. 4.4).

Its unique synergy of classical and probabilistic independence reasoning means our program logic is more expressive not only than PSL but also prior probabilistic Hoare logics, such as [12], VPHL [26] and Easycrypt's pRHL [2].

Probabilistic coupling (supported by pRHL and Easycrypt [2]) is another popular way for proving the security of probabilistic algorithms. It does so by proving the output distribution is equal between any pair of different secret inputs, witnessed by a bijection probabilistic coupling for each probabilistic choice. However, for dynamic random choice, the bijection probabilistic coupling may not exist or may even be undefined (e.g. Fig. 1 and [28]). Sometimes, finding the correct coupling can be far more challenging than proving the conclusion directly via probabilistic independence. Indeed, the original informal security proofs of our case studies [25, 28, 30, 32] all use probabilistic independence to argue their obliviousness, instead of coupling.

Other program logics or type systems for verifying obliviousness also exist. For example, ObliCheck [31] and λ_{OADT} [34] can check or prove obliviousness but only for deterministic algorithms. λ_{obliv} [7] is a type system for a functional language for proving obliviousness of probabilistic algorithms but it forbids branching on secrets, which is prevalent in many oblivious algorithms including those in Sect. 5. It also forbids outputting a probabilistic value (and all other values influenced by it) more than once. Our approach suffers no such restriction.

Path ORAM has received some verification attention [16,27]. [27] reason about this algorithm but in a non-probabilistic model, instead representing it as a nondeterministic transition system, and apply model counting to prove a security property about it. Their property says that for any observable output, there is a sufficient number of inputs to hide which particular input would have produced that output. This specification seems about the best that can be achieved for a nondeterministic model of the algorithm, but would also hold for an implementation that used biased choices (which would necessarily reveal too much of the input). Ours instead says that for each input the output is identically distributed, and would not be satisfied for such a hypothetical implementation. Nonetheless, it would be interesting to compare the strengths and weaknesses of their complementary approach to ours. Hannah Leung et al. [16] recently proposed to verify this algorithm in Coq, but as far as we are aware ours is the first verification of Path ORAM via a probabilistic program logic.

Other recent work extends PSL in different ways. Ugo Dal Lago et al. [14] extended PSL to computational security, but it cannot deal with loops (neither deterministic nor probabilistic) so their target algorithms are very different to ours. Lilac [17] also uses separating conjunction to model probabilistic independence. Crucially, it supports reasoning about conditional probability and conditional independence; John M. Li et al. [18] validated the design decisions of Lilac. However, Lilac's programming language is functional whereas ours is imperative. Lilac does not support random loops or dynamic random choice, which are essential for our aim.

IVL [29] reasons about probabilistic programs with nondeterminism. In doing so it supports classical reasoning (e.g. for the nondeterministic parts) and probabilistic reasoning for the probabilistic parts. Our logic reasons only about probabilistic programs (with no nondeterminism) but allows using classical reasoning to reason about parts of the probabilistic program, and for the classical and probabilistic reasoning styles to interact and enhance each other.

Some oblivious algorithms and their security definition (e.g. Differentially Oblivious Algorithms [6]) are not based on independence and they are beyond the reach of our approach.

7   Conclusion and Future Work

We presented the first program logic that, to our knowledge, is able to verify the obliviousness of real-world foundational probabilistic oblivious algorithms whose implementations combine challenging features like dynamic random choice and secret- and random-variable-dependent control flow. Our logic harnesses the interplay between classical and probabilistic reasoning, is situated atop PSL [3], and proved sound in Isabelle/HOL. We applied it to several challenging case studies, beyond the reach of prior approaches.

Artifact Availability Statement

We published our Isabelle/HOL formalisation on
https://doi.org/10.5281/zenodo.12518321.

References

1. Almeida, J.B., Barbosa, M., Barthe, G., Dupressoir, F., Emmi, M.: Verifying constant-time implementations. In: USENIX Security Symposium, vol. 16, pp. 53–70 (2016)
2. Barthe, G., Dupressoir, F., Grégoire, B., Kunz, C., Schmidt, B., Strub, P.-Y.: EasyCrypt: a tutorial. In: Aldini, A., Lopez, J., Martinelli, F. (eds.) FOSAD 2012-2013. LNCS, vol. 8604, pp. 146–166. Springer, Cham (2014). https://doi.org/10.1007/978-3-319-10082-1_6
3. Barthe, G., Hsu, J., Liao, K.: A probabilistic separation logic. Proc. ACM Program. Lang. 4(POPL), 1–30 (2019). https://doi.org/10.1145/3371123
4. Bittau, A., et al.: Prochlo: strong privacy for analytics in the crowd. In: Proceedings of the 26th Symposium on Operating Systems Principles (SOSP 2017), pp. 441–459. Association for Computing Machinery, New York (2017). https://doi.org/10.1145/3132747.3132769
5. Cauligi, S., et al.: Fact: a DSL for timing-sensitive computation. In: Proceedings of the 40th ACM SIGPLAN Conference on Programming Language Design and Implementation, pp. 174–189 (2019)
6. Chan, T.H.H., Chung, K.M., Maggs, B., Shi, E.: Foundations of differentially oblivious algorithms. J. ACM 69(4), 1–49 (2022). https://doi.org/10.1145/3555984
7. Darais, D., Sweet, I., Liu, C., Hicks, M.: A language for probabilistically oblivious computation. Proc. ACM Program. Lang. 4(POPL), 1–31 (2019). https://doi.org/10.1145/3371118
8. Fletcher, C.W., Ren, L., Kwon, A., van Dijk, M., Stefanov, E., Devadas, S.: RAW path ORAM: a low-latency, low-area hardware ORAM controller with integrity verification. IACR Cryptol. ePrint Arch. 431 (2014). http://eprint.iacr.org/2014/431
9. Goldreich, O., Ostrovsky, R.: Software protection and simulation on oblivious rams. J. ACM 43(3), 431–473 (1996). https://doi.org/10.1145/233551.233553
10. Goodrich, M.T., Mitzenmacher, M.: Privacy-preserving access of outsourced data via oblivious RAM simulation. In: Aceto, L., Henzinger, M., Sgall, J. (eds.) ICALP 2011. LNCS, vol. 6756, pp. 576–587. Springer, Heidelberg (2011). https://doi.org/10.1007/978-3-642-22012-8_46
11. Gruss, D., Spreitzer, R., Mangard, S.: Cache template attacks: automating attacks on inclusive last-level caches. In: 24th USENIX Security Symposium (USENIX Security 15), pp. 897–912. USENIX Association, Washington, D.C. (2015). https://www.usenix.org/conference/usenixsecurity15/technical-sessions/presentation/gruss

12. Hartog, J.I.: Verifying probabilistic programs using a hoare like logic. In: Thiagarajan, P.S., Yap, R. (eds.) ASIAN 1999. LNCS, vol. 1742, pp. 113–125. Springer, Heidelberg (1999). https://doi.org/10.1007/3-540-46674-6_11

13. Kushilevitz, E., Lu, S., Ostrovsky, R.: On the (in)security of hash-based oblivious ram and a new balancing scheme. In: Proceedings of the Twenty-Third Annual ACM-SIAM Symposium on Discrete Algorithms (SODA 2012), pp. 143–156. Society for Industrial and Applied Mathematics (2012)

14. Lago, U.D., Davoli, D., Kapron, B.M.: On separation logic, computational independence, and pseudorandomness (extended version) (2024). https://arxiv.org/abs/2405.11987

15. Lee, S., Shih, M.W., Gera, P., Kim, T., Kim, H., Peinado, M.: Inferring finegrained control flow inside SGX enclaves with branch shadowing. In: 26th USENIX Security Symposium (USENIX Security 17), pp. 557–574. USENIX Association, Vancouver (2017). https://www.usenix.org/conference/usenixsecurity17/technical-sessions/presentation/lee-sangho

16. Leung, H., Ringer, T., Fletcher, C.W.: Towards formally verified path Oram in COQ (2023). https://dependenttyp.es/pdf/oramproposal.pdf

17. Li, J.M., Ahmed, A., Holtzen, S.: Lilac: a modal separation logic for conditional probability. Proc. ACM Program. Lang. 7(PLDI), 148–171 (2023). https://doi.org/10.1145/3591226

18. Li, J.M., Aytac, J., Johnson-Freyd, P., Ahmed, A., Holtzen, S.: A nominal approach to probabilistic separation logic. In: Proceedings of the 39th Annual ACM/IEEE Symposium on Logic in Computer Science (LICS 2024). Association for Computing Machinery, New York (2024). https://doi.org/10.1145/3661814.3662135

19. Liu, C., Wang, X.S., Nayak, K., Huang, Y., Shi, E.: Oblivm: a programming framework for secure computation. In: 2015 IEEE Symposium on Security and Privacy, pp. 359–376 (2015). https://doi.org/10.1109/SP.2015.29

20. Liu, F., Yarom, Y., Ge, Q., Heiser, G., Lee, R.B.: Last-level cache side-channel attacks are practical. In: 2015 IEEE Symposium on Security and Privacy, pp. 605–622 (2015). https://doi.org/10.1109/SP.2015.43

21. Maas, M., et al.: Phantom: practical oblivious computation in a secure processor. In: Proceedings of the 2013 ACM SIGSAC Conference on Computer and Communications Security (CCS 2013), pp. 311–324. Association for Computing Machinery, New York (2013). https://doi.org/10.1145/2508859.2516692

22. Molnar, D., Piotrowski, M., Schultz, D., Wagner, D.: The program counter security model: automatic detection and removal of control-flow side channel attacks. In: Won, D.H., Kim, S. (eds.) ICISC 2005. LNCS, vol. 3935, pp. 156–168. Springer, Heidelberg (2006). https://doi.org/10.1007/11734727_14

23. O'Hearn, P., Reynolds, J., Yang, H.: Local reasoning about programs that alter data structures. In: Fribourg, L. (ed.) CSL 2001. LNCS, vol. 2142, pp. 1–19. Springer, Heidelberg (2001). https://doi.org/10.1007/3-540-44802-0_1

24. Ohrimenko, O., Costa, M., Fournet, C., Gkantsidis, C., Kohlweiss, M., Sharma, D.: Observing and preventing leakage in mapreduce. In: Proceedings of the 22nd ACM SIGSAC Conference on Computer and Communications Security (CCS 2015), pp. 1570–1581. Association for Computing Machinery, New York (2015). https://doi.org/10.1145/2810103.2813695

25. Ohrimenko, O., Goodrich, M.T., Tamassia, R., Upfal, E.: The Melbourne shuffle: improving oblivious storage in the cloud. In: Esparza, J., Fraigniaud, P., Husfeldt, T., Koutsoupias, E. (eds.) ICALP 2014. LNCS, vol. 8573, pp. 556–567. Springer, Heidelberg (2014). https://doi.org/10.1007/978-3-662-43951-7_47

26. Rand, R., Zdancewic, S.: VPHL: a verified partial-correctness logic for probabilistic programs. Electron. Notes Theor. Comput. Sci. **319**, 351–367 (2015). https://doi.org/10.1016/j.entcs.2015.12.021

27. Sahai, S., Subramanyan, P., Sinha, R.: Verification of quantitative hyperproperties using trace enumeration relations. In: Lahiri, S.K., Wang, C. (eds.) CAV 2020. LNCS, vol. 12224, pp. 201–224. Springer, Cham (2020). https://doi.org/10.1007/978-3-030-53288-8_11

28. Sasy, S., Ohrimenko, O.: Oblivious sampling algorithms for private data analysis. In: Proceedings of the 33rd International Conference on Neural Information Processing Systems. Curran Associates Inc., Red Hook (2019)

29. Schröer, P., Batz, K., Kaminski, B.L., Katoen, J.P., Matheja, C.: A deductive verification infrastructure for probabilistic programs. Proc. ACM Program. Lang. **7**(OOPSLA2), 2052–2082 (2023). https://doi.org/10.1145/3622870

30. Shi, E.: Path oblivious heap: optimal and practical oblivious priority queue. Cryptology ePrint Archive, Paper 2019/274 (2019). https://eprint.iacr.org/2019/274

31. Son, J., Prechter, G., Poddar, R., Popa, R.A., Sen, K.: ObliCheck: efficient verification of oblivious algorithms with unobservable state. In: 30th USENIX Security Symposium (USENIX Security 21), pp. 2219–2236. USENIX Association (2021). https://www.usenix.org/conference/usenixsecurity21/presentation/son

32. Stefanov, E., et al.: Path Oram: an extremely simple oblivious ram protocol. J. ACM **65**(4), 1–26 (2018). https://doi.org/10.1145/3177872

33. Yan, P., Murray, T., Ohrimenko, O., Pham, V.T., Sison, R.: Combining classical and probabilistic independence reasoning to verify the security of oblivious algorithms (extended version). arXiv preprint arXiv:2407.00514 (2024)

34. Ye, Q., Delaware, B.: Oblivious algebraic data types. Proc. ACM Program. Lang. **6**(POPL), 1–29 (2022). https://doi.org/10.1145/3498713

35. Zheng, W., Dave, A., Beekman, J.G., Popa, R.A., Gonzalez, J.E., Stoica, I.: Opaque: an oblivious and encrypted distributed analytics platform. In: 14th USENIX Symposium on Networked Systems Design and Implementation (NSDI 17), pp. 283–298. USENIX Association, Boston (2017). https://www.usenix.org/conference/nsdi17/technical-sessions/presentation/zheng

Efficient Formally Verified Maximal End Component Decomposition for MDPs

Arnd Hartmanns, Bram Kohlen[✉], and Peter Lammich

University of Twente, Enschede, The Netherlands
b.kohlen@utwente.nl

Abstract. Identifying a Markov decision process's maximal end components is a prerequisite for applying sound probabilistic model checking algorithms. In this paper, we present the first mechanized correctness proof of a maximal end component decomposition algorithm, which is an important algorithm in model checking, using the Isabelle/HOL theorem prover. We iteratively refine the high-level algorithm and proof into an imperative LLVM bytecode implementation that we integrate into the MODEST TOOLSET's existing mcsta model checker. We bring the benefits of interactive theorem proving into practice by reducing the trusted code base of a popular probabilistic model checker and we experimentally show that our new verified maximal end component decomposition in mcsta performs on par with the tool's previous unverified implementation.

1 Introduction

Model checking [12] is a verification technique that determines the validity of properties specified as temporal logics formulae on formal models of systems ranging from hardware circuits [6,13] and concurrent programs [21] to cyber-physical systems [15,45]. The model's semantics is traditionally some form of transition system [3]. Extended model checking approaches deal with, for example, real-time systems using a timed automata semantics [1,7], or probabilistic systems [2] using Markov chains or Markov decision processes (MDP) [5,47]. Given the often safety- or mission-critical nature of the systems being model-checked, the correctness of the model checker is of utmost importance.

As of today, however, few model checkers themselves are formally verified, and none of those is widely used. The CAVA LTL model checker [8,18], for example, is fully verified, from algorithmic correctness all the way down to a correct implementation. Yet, for the same purpose, SPIN [31] remains the tool of choice for practitioners despite being unverified. This is because CAVA supports only a fragment of the PROMELA input language [44], and is much slower due

Authors are listed in alphabetical order. This work was supported by the European Union's Horizon 2020 research and innovation programme under Marie Skłodowska-Curie grant agreement 101008233 (MISSION), the Interreg North Sea project STORM_SAFE, NWO grant OCENW.KLEIN.311, NWO VIDI grant VI.Vidi.223.110 (TruSty) and NWO grant OCENW.M.21.291 (VESPA).

A. Platzer et al. (Eds.): FM 2024, LNCS 14933, pp. 206–225, 2025.
https://doi.org/10.1007/978-3-031-71162-6_11

to its purely functional-programming implementation, while SPIN's algorithms and code have been highly optimised. Similarly, the fully verified MUNTA model checker for timed automata [55] is significantly slower than the de-facto standard tool UPPAAL [4], despite MUNTA's refinement resulting in Standard ML code that uses imperative elements such as arrays to obtain better performance.

While initiatives like CAVA and MUNTA constitute major achievements in interactive theorem proving (ITP) research, they have not managed to bring the benefits of ITP into verification practice. Their approach towards the goal of a fully-verified model checker is top-down: Create a new tool from scratch, necessarily starting (and ultimately remaining) with a limited scope that prevents practical adoption. In addition, they are limited by the technology available in their time for refining abstract algorithms into executable code.

We instead propose a bottom-up approach: Starting from an existing model checker that is competitive and has an established user base, replace its unverified code by provably correct implementations component-by-component. In this way, the tool is not immediately fully verified, but the trusted code base is reduced step-by-step. Crucially, by exploiting recent advances in refinement technology [39,41] that deliver highly-efficient LLVM bytecode, our verified replacement components perform similarly to the unverified originals implemented in e.g. C or C#. The incremental approach is thus "invisible" to the users, leading to an immediate adoption of the benefits of ITP in verification practice.

Our contributions are to formalise an algorithm for *maximum end component* (MEC) decomposition in MDPs with Isabelle/HOL, prove its correctness, and iteratively refine the abstract algorithm to imperative code and data structures in LLVM bytecode. We integrate the resulting verified implementation into an existing probabilistic model checker and experimentally show that it performs on par with the previous unverified implementation.

A MEC is a subset of the states of an MDP for which a strategy exists that remains within the MEC with probability 1. In an MDP with nontrivial MECs, the Bellman operator used in sound numeric algorithms for probabilistic model checking (PMC) for indefinite-horizon properties [22,26,48] has multiple fixed points, leading to divergence [22] and/or breaking the algorithm's correctness proof [26]. Eliminating or later deflating [17] the MECs of an MDP is thus a necessary step in PMC. To the best of our knowledge, ours is **the first mechanical formalisation and correctness proof of MEC decomposition**. We use the Isabelle Refinement Framework [42] to refine our algorithm down to LLVM code which we integrate into an existing model checker. We target mcsta of the MODEST TOOLSET [25]. Its performance is competitive [9], and it has been used for various case studies by different teams of researchers [24,50,53]. Our verification and refinement of MEC decomposition constitutes a critical step on the long-term bottom-up path towards a fully-verified probabilistic model checker, laying the foundation for verifying the actual numeric algorithm as the next step. MEC decomposition is also used in probabilistic planning [57] as part of the FRET[1]

---

[1] Here, end components are called "traps"; FRET is "find, revise, eliminate traps" [33].

approach [33,51], and can be generalised from MDP to stochastic games where it is equally necessary for sound algorithms [17]. Our work can thus be transferred to tools in these areas.

Our MEC decomposition algorithm, or *MEC algorithm* for short, follows the standard approach [3, Algorithm 47]: (i) find all strongly connected components (SCCs) of the MDP's graph, (ii) identify all bottom SCCs as MECs and remove them, (iii) delete all transitions with nonzero probability to leave an SCC, and (iv) repeat until no more states remain. After defining MDPs and MECs in Sect. 2, we present the algorithm, our formalisation in Isabelle/HOL, and our correctness proof in Sect. 3. We introduce the efficient data structures for the implementation in Sect. 4. We had earlier verified Gabow's SCC-finding algorithm and refined it into efficient LLVM code for mcsta [28]. We were able to integrate the SCC algorithm's high-level correctness proof into our MEC algorithm formalisation with minor technical adaptations. However, the SCC algorithm could assume the graph to be static, whereas the MEC algorithm iteratively changes the MDP graph. We thus need a new data structure that allows deleting states and transitions, which we describe together with the corresponding refinement proofs in Sect. 4. In this part, we also extended proofs and refinement relations for the SCC-finding aspect due to an extended data structure. In Sect. 5, we describe the LLVM code generation and integration into mcsta. By adopting mcsta's existing MDP representation, we minimise costly glue code and transformations or copies of the data. This is important for the scalability and performance of our end result, which we experimentally show in Sect. 6.

Related Work. Certification is an alternative to verification: A formally verified certifier checks the results of an unverified tool. This requires a practical certification mechanism and the support of the unverified model checker. Formally verified certification tools that work on significant problem sizes exist for e.g. timed automata model checking [54,56] and SAT solving [29,40].

Probabilistic models have been the subject of ITP work before. Notably, there are some formalisations of MDPs and the value iteration algorithm in Isabelle/HOL [30] and Coq [52], but executable code does not appear to have been extracted from these proofs. Additionally, there is a formalisation of value iteration for discounted expected rewards [43] which extracts Standard ML code from the proof. We note that MEC decomposition is not necessary in the discounted case, thus [43] and the many current works in machine learning/artificial intelligence based on reinforcement learning typically avoid the problem.

The standard MEC decomposition approach computes SCCs. SCC-finding algorithms have been formalised with various tools, including Isabelle/HOL [38], Coq [46], and Why3 [11]. Of these, only [38] extracted executable code, which however performed poorly. Our earlier verification and high-performance refinement of Gabow's SCC-finding algorithm [28] built upon ideas from [38]. An asymptotically faster MEC algorithm has been proposed [10]. It combines SCC-finding with a lock-step depth-first search. The algorithm has not been adopted by PMC tools so far, likely due to its implementation complexity.

2   Background

We introduce MDPs and MECs in the context of probabilistic model checking, then explain the refinement-based approach to program verification that we use.

Probabilistic Model Checking. Let $[0,1] \subseteq \mathbb{R}$ be the interval of real numbers from 0 to 1 and 2^X the power set of X. A (discrete) *probability distribution* over X is a function $\mu: X \to [0,1]$ where $\sum_{x \in X} \mu(x) = 1$ that has countable support $Sp(\mu) = \{ v \mid \mu(v) > 0 \}$. $Dist(X)$ is the set of probability distributions over X.

Definition 1. *A Markov decision process (MDP) is a pair (S, K) where S is a finite set of states and K is the kernel of type $S \to 2^{Dist(S)}$.*

An MDP models the interaction of an agent with a random environment: In current state u, the agent makes a decision, i.e. non-deterministically chooses a distribution $\mu \in K(u)$. The environment then updates the current state by sampling μ. By repeating this process, we trace a *path* with a certain probability. A *strategy* represents an agent's decisions of which distribution to pick next based on the path traced so far. Combining an MDP and a strategy removes all non-determinism, resulting in a Markov chain on which a probability measure over paths can be defined in the standard way [3]. We characterise interesting sets of paths via *properties*; for this work, we are particularly interested in *reachability*:

Definition 2. *Given sets $A, T \subseteq S$, a reachability property is an LTL formula $\neg A \cup T$ (characterising the set of paths that do not visit avoid states (A) before a target state (T) which is visited eventually). Under a given strategy, the probability of satisfying a property is the probability mass of the (measurable) set of paths satisfying that property.*

There is a strategy that *minimises* and one that *maximises* the probability of satisfying $\neg A \cup T$ [3], which induce the minimum/maximum reachability probabilities.

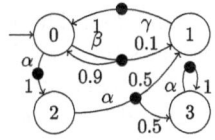

Fig. 1. MDP (S, K)

Example 1. Figure 1 shows an MDP with $S = \{0, 1, 2, 3\}$. The edges represent K where α, β and γ label the non-deterministic choices followed by the probability mass of each state. The minimum probability to satisfy $\neg\{1\} \cup \{3\}$ is 0 for the strategy that always chooses β and γ. The maximum probability is 0.5 by choosing α twice. After this, we are either in target state 3 or in avoid state 1.

The edges of an MDP kernel are $Edges(K) = \{ (u,v) \mid \exists \mu \in K(u): \mu(v) > 0 \}$. A *sub-MDP* of (S, K) is a pair (C, D) where $C \subseteq S$ and $D(u) \subseteq K(u)$.

Definition 3. *Given an MDP (S, K), an end component (EC) [14] is a sub-MDP (C, D) such that $C \times C \subseteq Edges(D)^*$ (it is strongly connected) and $(u, v) \in Edges(K) \wedge u \in C \Rightarrow v \in C$ (it is closed). A maximal end component (MEC) is an EC that is not a sub-MDP of another EC.*

SCCs are weaker than MECs: They are maximal strongly connected *subsets of states* rather than closed sub-MDPs. In other words, for every state, there exists a strategy such that the next state is in the SCC with probability > 0, while for a MEC the probability is 1. MECs play an essential role in sound algorithms for evaluating reachability probabilities: Collapsing the MECs (i.e. replacing every MEC by a single state that collects all edges out of the MEC) guarantees a single fixed point for these algorithms. We find MECs through a graph analysis that requires the computation of SCCs. *Graph analysis* means that we only need to know whether probabilities are non-zero, i.e. we work with the *MDP structure* that maps state u to its set of supports $\{ Sp(\mu) \mid \mu \in K(u) \} \subseteq 2^S$. We call elements of the outer set *transitions* and elements of the inner sets *branches*.

Example 2. In the MDP structure for Fig. 1, state 0 is mapped to $\{ \{ 0,1 \}, \{ 2 \} \}$. The MDP has two SCCs: $\{ 0,1,2 \}$ and $\{ 3 \}$. Set $\{ 0,1 \}$ is not an SCC as it is not maximal. There are three MECs: $\{ 0,1 \}$, $\{ 2 \}$, and $\{ 3 \}$. While state 2 has an edge to 1, it is not in the same MEC as it cannot go back with probability 1.

We also use models that are *Markov automata* (MA) [16] and *probabilistic timed automata* (PTA) [37]. Untimed reachability on a MA can be checked on its embedded MDP, while PTA can be converted to MDP using e.g. digital clocks [36].

Verification by Refinement. We aim for efficient verified executable code. This requires reasoning about the high-level behaviour of algorithms as well as about lower-level concepts like efficient data structures. To keep these independent concerns separate, we use an iterative *refinement* approach:

We represent the algorithm with the *nondeterministic result* (nres) monad of the Isabelle Refinement Framework (IRF) [42]. It has two possible states: *result* and *fail*. The former captures the set of outputs of all non-deterministic behaviours (e.g. picking an element of a set) of a program while the latter occurs if any behaviour of the program fails (e.g. non-termination). For abstract program A and concrete program C, the *refinement relation* $C \leq_{\Downarrow} R\,A$ holds iff each result of C relates to a result of A via relation R. If A fails, then C always refines it. We use predefined relations like R_{size} and R_{bool} to relate natural numbers and booleans to 64 and 1 bit words, respectively, or $br\ \alpha\ I = \{(c,a).\ a{=}\alpha\ c \wedge I\ c\}$ to build a relation from *abstraction function* α which converts concrete data to abstract data and *invariant* I that holds if the data is in valid form. We use notation $(C,A) \in [\lambda\ a_1...a_n.\ P\ a_1...a_n]\ R_1 \to ... \to R_n \to R$ for

$$P\ a_1...a_n \Longrightarrow (c_1,a_1) {\in} R_1 ... \Longrightarrow (c_n,a_n) {\in} R_n \Longrightarrow (C\ c_1...c_n) \leq \Downarrow R\ (A\,a_1...a_n)$$

where P is a precondition over the abstract program. To refine e.g. addition of natural numbers $(a+b)$ to addition of 64-bit words, we need the precondition $a+b \leq 2^{63} - 1$; the maximal value of 64-bit signed words.

As they are transitive, we can compose refinements. The final step is an automatic refinement to a model of LLVM using the sepref tool [39]. It uses *assertions* of separation logic [49] to map data structures to concrete memory contents; e.g. A'_{size} and A'_{bool} map 64 and 1 bit words to memory, respectively,

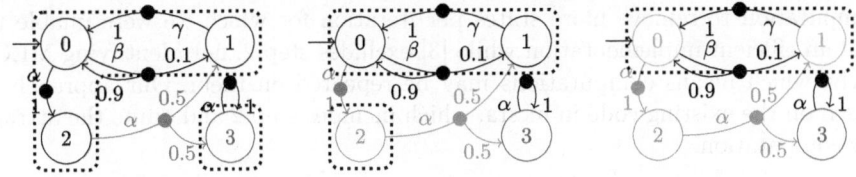

Fig. 2. An execution of the MEC algorithm using 3 iterations.

and A_{list} maps a list to memory using a heap. We combine relations and assertions through composition; e.g. $A_{size} = R_{size} \; O \; A'_{size}$ maps natural numbers to memory.

Example 3. We show an example of a bitset, abstractly represented as a *nat set*. We implement operation *sget*, which tests whether a value is in a bitset.

$(*1*)$ $sget \; bs \; i = i \in bs$ $bs\_get \; bs \; i \equiv (bi \; ! \; (i \; div \; 64) \; !! \; (i \; mod \; 64))$
$(*2*)$ $bs\_\alpha \; bs = Collect \; (\lambda \; i. \; bitset\_get \; i \; bs \land i < 64 * length \; bs)$
$bs\_inv \; n \; bs = (n \leq 64 * length \; bs)$ $R_{bs} = br \; bs\_\alpha \; bs\_inv$
$(*3*)$ $(bs\_get, sget) \in R_{bs} \; n \to (R_{nbn} \; n) \to R_{bool}$
$(*4*)$ $(bs\_geti, bs\_get) \in [\lambda(i,l). \; i{<}length \; l * 64] \; A_{size} \to A_{list} \to A_{bool}$
$(*5*)$ $A_{bs} = R_{bs} \; O \; A_{list}$ $(bs\_geti, sget) \in (A_{nbn} \; n) \to A_{bs} \to A_{bool}$

Here, we (1) define an abstract function *sget*, which is a membership test, and an implementation *bs_get* over *bs::64 word list* (i.e. a list of 64-bit binary words) and an index *i::nat* . This function obtains the i-th bit in the sequence: $bs \; ! \; j$ obtains the j-th word and $x \; !! \; k$ the k-th bit in word x. We then (2) relate *64 word list* to a *nat set* using R_{bs}; we provide bs_α as abstraction function to convert *64 word lists* to *nat sets*, and *bs_inv* as invariant that makes sure that n values fit in our bitset. Next, (3) we prove refinement of *sget* to *bs_get*. $R_{nbn} \; n$ maps all values up to n to themselves. (4) Function *bs_geti* is an LLVM program *automatically generated* by sepref and refines *bs_get*. The precondition guarantees that the index is in bounds. Finally (5) through composition we obtain A_{bs} that maps a *nat set* to a bitset on the heap. This allows sepref to generate LLVM code for every occurence of *sget*. Note that we simplified the notation e.g. to match the relation refinement and we omitted notation for (non-)destructive heap access.

3 Correctness of the MEC Algorithm

The standard MEC algorithm iteratively culls the MDP as follows: (1) Calculate the SCC decomposition of the current MDP, (2) find the SCCs that are MECs, and (3) remove the found MECs, and remove all transitions with branches to a different SCC. Figure 2 shows 3 iterations of this algorithm on the MDP of Fig. 1. SCCs are marked by dotted lines, states of SCCs that are MECs are coloured, and culled branches in the current/previous iteration are red/gray. This algorithm is loosely based on those of [3,10] where [10] uses an attractor computation to remove more states per iteration for which we were unable to find an efficient implementation while [3] excludes step 2, not identifying MECs early, which means computations may be repeated on them. Our approach is based on the existing code in mcsta, which includes step 2 and omits the attractor computation.

3.1   Abstract MDP Structure

We represent the MDP structure as mapping each state to a list of lists of states, i.e. it is of type $'a\ mdp\_K = 'a \Rightarrow 'a\ list\ list$. We chose a list-based representation over a set-based one for straightforward compatibility with our earlier SCC implementation [28] while still being abstract enough for our purposes. The MEC algorithm takes the states ($S_0 :: 'v\ set$) and the MDP kernel ($K_0 :: 'v\ mdp\_K$) as parameters. We use Isabelle/HOL's locale mechanism for general constructs. A locale creates a block in which user-specified assumptions hold. We define an MDP locale with some natural well-formedness assumptions:

definition $closed\_mdp\ S\ K \equiv \forall u \in S.\ \forall\ a \in set\ (K\ u).\ set\ a \subseteq S$
locale mdp = **fixes** $S :: 'v\ set$ **and** $K :: 'v\ mdp\_K$ +
   assumes $1: u \in S \Longrightarrow [] \notin set\ (K\ u)$ **and** $2: finite\ S$ **and** $3: closed\_mdp\ S\ K$

This locale states that transitions have at least one branch, the state space is finite, and the MDP is closed, i.e. all transitions starting in S end in S.

3.2   Specification

Let $sc\ S\ K$ denote that the MDP is strongly connected. Given $mdp\ S\ K$:

$sub\_mdp\ S_1\ K_1\ S_2\ K_2 \equiv S_1 \subseteq S_2 \wedge (\forall u \in S_1.\ set\ (K_1\ u) \subseteq set\ (K_2\ u))$
$is\_ec\ S'\ K' \equiv S' \neq \{\} \wedge sub\_mdp\ S'\ K'\ S\ K \wedge closed\_mdp\ S'\ K' \wedge sc\ S'\ K'$
$is\_mec\ S'\ K' \equiv is\_ec\ S'\ K' \wedge (\nexists S''\ K''.\ is\_ec\ S''\ K'' \wedge psub\_mdp\ S'\ K'\ S''\ K'')$

where $psub\_mdp$ is the proper sub_mdp. Here, $sub\_mdp\ S_1\ K_1\ S_2\ K_2$ holds if (S_1,K_1) is a sub-MDP of (S_2,K_2). We allow reorderings and (de)duplications of the transitions as they do not alter the MDP structure. An EC is a strongly connected, closed sub-MDP with at least one state. A MEC is an EC that is not a proper sub-MDP of another EC. With these definitions, we *specify* MEC algorithms as those that return a list with the MECs of the input MDP structure:

definition $compute\_MEC\_spec \equiv$ **spec** $(\lambda\ r.\ set\ r = \{S'\ |S'\ K'.\ is\_mec\ S'\ K'\ \})$

3.3   Abstract Algorithm

We now *define* the MEC algorithm, focusing on its abstract, high-level behaviour; we refine this to concrete data structures in Sect. 4. The definition in Isabelle is:

```
1    compute_MEC ≡ do {
2       let (M,S,K) = op_init_mdp (S₀,K₀);
3       (M,S,K) ← while (compute_MEC_invar S₀ K₀) op_states_non_empty
4           (λ(M,S,K). do {
5              C ← compute_sccs (M,S,K);
6              (C,V) ← identify_mecs C (M,S,K);
7              (M,S,K) ← cull_graph (C,V) (M,S,K);
8              return (M,S,K)
9           }) (M,S,K);
10      return (op_get_mecs (M,S,K))
```

We initialise the loop state in line 2 as an empty list M to store the MECs and $S = S_0$ and $K = K_0$. We bundle this data into one tuple so that we can refine them through a single assertion in Sect. 4.2. We iterate as long as there are states for which we have not found a MEC in line 3. We then perform the three-step process described earlier: We (1) compute C in line 5 such that $scc\_list\ C\ S\ K$ holds (i.e. C is a distinct list of all SCCs of the graph structure of S and K). We then (2) obtain list V which contains all SCCs of C that are also MECs in line 6. We finally (3) remove MECs and transitions between different SCCs in line 7. At the end of the program, we extract M which contains the MECs.

These operations are defined by high-level behaviour; e.g. for $cull\_graph$:

$$cull\_graph\ (C,V)\ (M,S,K) \equiv \textbf{spec}$$
$$(\lambda\ (M',S',K').\ M' = M@V \wedge S' = S{-}\textstyle\bigcup(set\ V) \wedge culled\_edges\ C\ V\ K\ K'))$$

We elided the definition of predicate $culled\_edges$ which holds if K' only contains the transitions in K whose branches all remain within the same SCC as their source. Also, $cull\_graph$ adds the identified MECs to M and removes them from S.

These definitions are still far from an efficient implementation. We first refine each operation to a control flow (definitions elided). The operations of that control flow are implemented in the respective data structures in Sect. 4. The SCC algorithm has been refined separately in [28].

Invariant. We define the following invariant for the main loop of the algorithm:

locale $compute\_MEC\_invar = mdp\ S_0\ K_0$ **for** $S_0\ K_0\ (M,S,K)\ +$
   assumes *1:* $S \cap \bigcup(set\ M) = \{\}$ **and** *2:* $S_0 = \bigcup(set\ M) \cup S$
   and *3: pairwise disjnt* $(set\ M)$ **and** *4: distinct* M **and** *5: sub_mdp_of* $S\ K\ S_0\ K_0$
   and *6: mdp* $S\ K$ **and** *7: is_mec* $S'\ K' \Longrightarrow S' \in set\ M \vee sub\_mdp\_of\ S'\ K'\ S\ K$
   and *8:* $S \neq \{\} \Longrightarrow mdp\_def.is\_mec\ S\ K\ S'\ K' \Longrightarrow is\_mec\ S'\ K'$
   and *9:* $S' \in set\ M \Longrightarrow \exists K'.\ is\_mec\ S'\ K'$ **and** *10: scc_list* $C\ S\ K \Longrightarrow a \in set\ (K_0\ u)$
      $\Longrightarrow S' \in set\ C \Longrightarrow u \in S' \Longrightarrow \forall v {\in} set\ a.\ v \in S' \Longrightarrow a \in set\ (K\ u)$

It states that (1) the states (S) and MECs (M) are disjoint and (2) cover the original statespace. Also, (3,4) M is pairwise disjoint and contains no duplicates. The current graph structure is (5) a sub-MDP of the input and (6) an MDP itself. Further, (7) all MECs are either in M or in the current graph structure, (8) a MEC of the current graph structure is a MEC of the original one, (9) each element of M is a MEC, and (10) transitions in the original graph structure within one SCC are preserved in the current one. We have proven that the invariant is preserved throughout the while-loop and if S is empty the specification holds.

Termination is guaranteed as every non-empty graph has at least one *bottom-SCC* (BSCC), i.e. an SCC with no outgoing edges. Our algorithms finds MECs by identifying BSCCs; we find at least one MEC per iteration and remove it from the state space. Since the state space is finite, we necessarily terminate.

4 Data Structures and Refinement

The next step is to define the data structures to efficiently implement the abstract operations specified in Sect. 3.3. For input and output, we formalize the data structures that mcsta uses, so that we can integrate our implementation without costly conversions. Using the IRF, the refinement is done modularly, and in multiple steps to structure the correctness proof and keep it manageable.

4.1 Supplementary Data Structures

We introduce auxiliary data structures that are part of mcsta's data structure:

Intervals. In mcsta, intervals of natural numbers $\{l..<h\}$ are represented as a single 64 bit word, where the 20 most significant bits encode the length, and the 44 remaining bits encode the starting point l. Like in [28], we express this refinement in two levels: the relation A_{sn} relates a 64 bit word to a pair (n,i) of type $sn = nat \times nat$, and the functions $sn\_intv\ (n,i) = \{i..<i+n\}$ and $ls\_intv\ (n,i) = [i..<i+n]$ represent these as set and list, respectively.

Disjoint Nat Set List. Our implementation requires a map from states to indices of MECs or SCCs. Low-valued indices are MECs while high-valued ones are SCCs. Abstractly, we represent this as two lists of sets of states such that each state occurs at most once. We highlight some operations here:

type_synonym $dslt = nat\ set\ list \times nat\ set\ list$
$d\_empty :: dslt$ **where** $d\_empty = ([],[])$
$d\_count1 :: dslt \Rightarrow nat$ **where** $d\_count1(xs,ys) = length\ xs$
$d\_move1 :: dslt \Rightarrow nat \Rightarrow nat \Rightarrow dslt$ **where** $d\_move1\ (xs,ys)\ v\ i =$
  $((map\ (\lambda\ x.\ x - \{v\})\ xs)[i:=(xs\ !\ i) \cup \{v\}], (map\ (\lambda\ y.\ y - \{v\})\ ys))$

Operation d_empty constructs a tuple of empty lists, d_count1 returns the length of the first list, and $d\_move1\ ds\ v\ i$ moves state v into index i of the first list (removing it from anywhere else if necessary). Every operation on the first list (with suffix 1) has a corresponding operation on the second one (with suffix 2). We omit some further operations for this data structure.

We implement the data structure as an array map that maps values to the index of the set that they are in. This means that we flatten the two lists into one map. We introduce a bound L which is the maximal size of the first list.

Indices $i < L$ represent indices to sets in the first list; indices $i \geq L$ represent index $i - L$ in the second list. Values that are not in any set get a -1 entry. We capture this mapping in assertion A_{dslt}.

Example 4. Let $L = 3$ and $N = 5$. Then A_{dslt} maps the abstract *nat dslt* $([\{1\}, \{\}, \{2\}], [\{0, 4\}])$ to array $a = [3, 0, 2, -1, 3]$: We have $a[1] < L$ so value 1 must be in the first list; since $a[1] = 0$, we find value 1 in the set at index 0. We also have $a[4] \geq L$ so value 4 is in the second list. Since $a[4] = 3$, we find it at index $3 - L = 0$. Lastly, we have $a[3] = -1$, which means that value 3 is not in any of the sets.

4.2   The mcsta Data Structure

The mcsta data structure is a tuple $SS = (St, Tr, Br, Av, Ta)$. St, Tr and Br represent the states, transitions, and branches of the MDP structure, respectively. Additionally, Av and Ta are sets representing the avoid and target states of the reachability property being verified (corresponding to sets A and T of Def. 2). We define a relation R_{Mdi} that relates our model of the mcsta data structure to an MDP structure:

$S_0\_\alpha \ N = \{0..{<}N\} \quad K_0\_\alpha \ N \ SS :: nat \ mdp\_K \ (* \ elided \ *)$
$MG_0\_\alpha \ N \ SS = (S_0\_\alpha \ N, \ K_0\_\alpha \ N \ SS)$

locale $Md\_input\_inv = mdp \ S_0::nat \ set \ K_0$ **fixes** $N \ (St,Tr,Br,Av,Ta) +$
assumes *1:* $N = length \ St$ **and** *2:* $Av \subseteq \{0..{<}N\}$ **and** *3:* $Ta \subseteq \{0..{<}N\}$
and *4:* $i < length \ St \Longrightarrow uid \ (St!i) \leq length \ Tr$ **and** *5:* $i < length \ Tr \Longrightarrow$
$uid \ (Tr!i) \leq length \ Br$ **and** *6:* $i < length \ Br \Longrightarrow Br!i < length \ St$
and *7:* $i < length \ St \Longrightarrow cnt \ (St!i){>}0$ **and** *8:* $i < length \ Tr \Longrightarrow cnt \ (Tr!i){>}0$
and *9:* $i < length \ Tr \Longrightarrow j < i \Longrightarrow sn\_intv \ (Tr \ ! \ i) \cap sn\_intv \ (Tr \ ! \ j) = \{\}$
and *10:* $S_0 = S_0\_\alpha \ N$ **and** *11:* $K_0 = K_0\_\alpha \ N \ (St,Tr,Br,Av,Ta)$

$R_{Mdi} \ S_0 \ K_0 \ N = br \ (MG_0\_\alpha \ N) \ (Md\_input\_inv \ S_0 \ K_0 \ N)$

The states of an MDP in mcsta are numbered from 0 to $N-1$. K_0_α derives the kernel from the data structure as follows: St and Tr are lists of intervals (represented as tuples, see Sect. 4.1) and Br is a list of state indices. If $St \ ! \ v = (n,i)$, the next n transitions starting at index i in Tr belong to state v. This means that a transition is an index $i \leq t < n + i$. Similarly, $Tr \ ! \ t$ is a tuple pointing to an interval of indices on Br. A branch is thus an index $i \leq b < n + i$ and $Br \ ! \ b$ is the target state of the branch. Furthermore, if $v \in Av \vee v \in Ta$, we ignore all outgoing edges. The invariant states the following: (1) it fixes the number of states to N for the bounds calculations in sepref. It states that (2,3) our target and avoid states are a subset of S_0. It also states that (4,5,6) St points to valid indices on Tr, Tr points to valid indices on Br and Br points to a valid indices on St, (7,8) St and Tr do not contain empty intervals, (9) transitions cannot overlap, and (10,11) the input MDP structure remains constant. The relation R_{Mdi} relates the input MDP structure to the concrete data structure. Using sepref and composition, we obtain the according assertion A_{Mdi} . We refine the concrete data structure to LLVM using the IRF standard library and the supplementary data structures from Sect. 4.1: We implement St and Tr as lists of bit-packed intervals, Br as a list of 64-bit values, and Av and Ta as bitsets.

Example 5. One possibility to represent Fig. 1 is $St = [(2,0),(1,2),(1,3),(1,3)]$, $Tr = [(1,0),(2,1),(1,3),(2,4),(1,6)]$, $Br = [2,0,1,0,3,1,3]$. For state 0 we have $St!0 = (2,0)$, i.e. it has 2 successors (α and β) starting at index 0. Similarly, for transition 1 (corresponding to β in this case) we have $Tr!1 = (2,1)$, which means that this transition has 2 branches starting at index 1 in Br (i.e. state $Br!1 = 0$ and $Br!2 = 1$). Note that we have not defined Av and Ta yet as these are dependent on the property. If we assume the property of Example 1 then $Av = \{1\}$ and $Ta = \{3\}$. These translate to the bitsets ...0010 and ...1000 respectively, which removes the outgoing transitions from those states (not visualized).

mcsta directly passes this data to our implementation. However, as we have seen in Sect. 3.3, our algorithm needs to be able to efficiently remove states and transitions. The data structure that we have presented so far cannot implement this functionality efficiently.

Cullable MDP Structure. The implementation of op_init_mdp from Sect. 3.3 supplements the input data structure with the $dslt$ data structure from Sect. 4.1, which is a tuple of lists of sets of states. States in the first list of the tuple are removed while states in the second one are not. Furthermore, a transition starting in some state v is "activated" if all branches of that transition are within the same set. If any branch connects different sets, the transition is deactivated. With this approach, we place states of the same SCC into the same set, disabling transitions between SCCs in the process. Additionally, we use the tuple structure to distinguish between MECs in the first list and SCCs in the second, which means that it eventually stores the MEC decomposition.

$is\_act\ u\ t\ =\ t{\in}sn\_intv\ (St!u)\ \wedge\ (\forall b{\in}sn\_intv\ (Tr!t)\ b\ \longrightarrow\ d\_eqset\ Mm\ u\ (Br!b))$
$S\_\alpha\ N\ Mm\ =\ \{v.\ v < N \wedge (\forall\ i < length\ (fst\ Mm).\ v \notin (fst\ Mm)\ !\ i)\}$
$K\_\alpha\ N\ (SS,Mm)\ ::\ nat\ mdp\_K\ (*\ elided\ *)$
$MSK\_\alpha\ N\ (SS,Mm)\ =\ (fst\ Mm, S\_\alpha\ N\ Mm, K\_\alpha\ N\ (SS,Mm))$

locale $Md\_mdp\_cullable\_inv = Md\_mdp\_input\_inv\ S_0\ K_0\ N\ (St,Tr,Br,Av,Ta)$ $+\ mdp\ S_0\ K_0$ **for** $S_0{::}nat$ **set and** $K_0\ N\ (St,Tr,Br,Av,Ta,Mm,Nr) + ...$

With is_act we test if a transition is activated by checking that all branches are in the same set (d_eqset which is a $dslt$ operation) as the source state. We use this to derive the culled kernel K_α which contains exactly the activated transitions of K_0_α. S_α omits the states that have been identified as a MEC. The MECs are stored in the first list of Mm directly. Variable Nr is the number of remaining states, i.e. for which no MEC has been identified. We use this for implementing the termination criterion. We omit the definition of the invariant which mainly concerns well-formedness of Mm. This data structure allows us to efficiently implement *cull_graph* from Sect. 3.3 by putting states from the same SCC into the same set. This update is straightforward to implement as it merely involves updating the value of unfinished states in the map to the corresponding index of the SCC, which is also stored in a map for the SCC algorithm.

Example 6. Assuming the middle situation in Fig. 2, consider the input data from Example 5 and additionally $Mm = ([\{3\}, \{2\}], [\{0, 1\}])$. For state 0, β is activated since its branches (to 0 and 1) are in the same set as the source (0). However, α branches to 2 which is in another set, so the transition was deleted.

4.3 Filter List

Given the number of states N and the number of MECs M, we have $M \leq N$. This is essential for our bounds calculation: Since the ID of a MEC is represented as a 64-bit value, we need to bound M. We require a "dense" indexing for the MECs, i.e. they must be numbered from 0 to $M - 1$ efficiently. This way, we can do our bounds calculation solely using N, which we know a priori. We do so by iterating over all states, and if we find any transitions leaving the SCC, the SCC is not a MEC and we filter it. We implemented a filter set and filter list to implement this memory- and time-efficiently.

The filter list is an extension of any data structure representing a list. On the abstract layer, it is of type $'a\ list \times 'a\ list$ where the first list of the pair is the original list that we want to filter and the second one is the filtered variant. Concretely, it is of type $'v\ list \times nat\ option\ list \times nat$. The first list ($xs$) is the original list, the second list (ids) is a map containing indices, and the natural number is a counter representing the length of the filtered list c. The list ids is the core of this data structure. It maps an index i of the unfiltered list to *None* if $xs\ !\ i$ is filtered or to *Some j* if $xs\ !\ i$ is at index j in the filtered list. The filter set is similar to the filter list but ids either maps to *None* (entry is filtered) or *Some 0* (entry is unfiltered). We then convert the filter set to a list by assigning a unique index to each unfiltered entry.

Example 7. Assume unfiltered list $[a, b, c, d]$ out of which we want to filter a and c. Abstractly, we have $([a, b, c, d], [b, d])$. Its concrete implementation is the triple $([a, b, c, d], [None, Some\ 0, None, Some\ 1], 2)$. Since a (index 0) and c (index 2) are filtered, we have $ids\ !\ 0 = ids\ !\ 2 = None$. Similarly, we find b (index 1) at index 0 in the filtered list. Therefore $ids\ !\ 1 = Some\ 0$.

5 Code Generation and Integration

Using the algorithm of Sect. 3 and the data structures of Sect. 4, we derive an LLVM program *Md_compute_MEC* using sepref. Through transitivity of the refinement relation, we can show that this program refines the specification from Sect. 3.2. The IRF provides the setup to extract a separation logic Hoare triple from our correctness proof. Let $\star$ be the separation conjunction. Then we obtain:

theorem *Md_compute_MEC_htriple: llvm_htriple (*
(∗*1*∗) A_{size} *N ni* $\star$ A_{Mdi} *N S_0 K_0 (S_0, K_0) mdpi*
(∗*2*∗) $\star$ *ll_pto mdpi p_mdpi* $\star$ *ll_pto anything resp*
(∗*3*∗) $\star$ *(mdp S_0 K_0 $\wedge$ N < 2^{62} $\wedge$ S_0={0..<N}))*
(∗*4*∗) *(Md_compute_MEC ni p_mdpi resp)*
(∗*5*∗) *(λ_. EXS M resi.*
(∗*6*∗) A_{size} *N ni* $\star$ A_{Mdi} *N S_0 K_0 (S_0, K_0) mdpi* $\star$ A_{Mdo} *N N M resi*
(∗*7*∗) $\star$ *ll_pto resi resp* $\star$ *ll_pto mdpi p_mdpi*
(∗*8*∗) $\star$ *(set M = {S' |S' K'. mdp.is_mec S_0 K_0 S' K' }))*

where A_{Mdo} is derived from A_{dslt} mapping only its first list to memory given
that the second list is empty. The precondition consists of several parts: (1) The
input consists of a value N representing the number of states with its 64 bit
representation ni and an input MDP structure (S_0, K_0) which is represented in
memory by $mdpi$. (2) We are provided a pointer to the MDP structure (p_mdpi)
and one to an address where we can store our output. (3) (S_0, K_0) is an MDP
structure that has fewer than 2^{62} states and a dense numbering S. Given these
preconditions we (4) run our program *Md_compute_MEC* with the specified input
parameters. We then get (5) a MEC decomposition M and its representation in
memory $resi$ such that (6) the input parameters are preserved and we additionally obtain the MEC decomposition, (7) the provided pointer ($resp$) points to
that decomposition and (8) M is the set of MECs.

The IRF has built-in functionality to translate *Md_compute_MEC* to LLVM
code with a header file, which can be called as an external function from mcsta.
Note that we use indirection through pointers to avoid problems with different
ABIs when passing structures as parameters or return values. It is invoked as:

export_llvm *Md_compute_MEC* **is**
  void compute_MEC(modest_size_t, modest_input_mdp_t ∗, *mec_output_t* ∗)

5.1   Compatibility with mcsta

We refer to the verified LLVM code as the *verified* implementation and to the pre-
existing C# implementation in mcsta as the *integrated* implementation. While
the data format of the verified implementation is compatible with mcsta, there
were some important differences that we fix using glue code for post-processing:

First, collapsing the MECs for interval iteration, which is currently not verified, requires the MECs to be sorted in exploration order. The algorithm we
formalised does not do that out of the box and we are not aware of an algorithm
that does preserve this order. That is why we decided to reorder the MEC indices
as a post-processing step.

Second, the integrated algorithm groups all target states into one collapsed
target state and does the same for avoid states. The verified algorithm puts each
target and avoid state in its own MEC. Both approaches are correct, but the
verified algorithm therefore calculates at least as many MECs as the integrated
one. We considered formalising this collapsing of states in our proofs, but we

decided against it as it would complicate them. Since we decided for the post-processing approach for reordering, we included the latter as well.

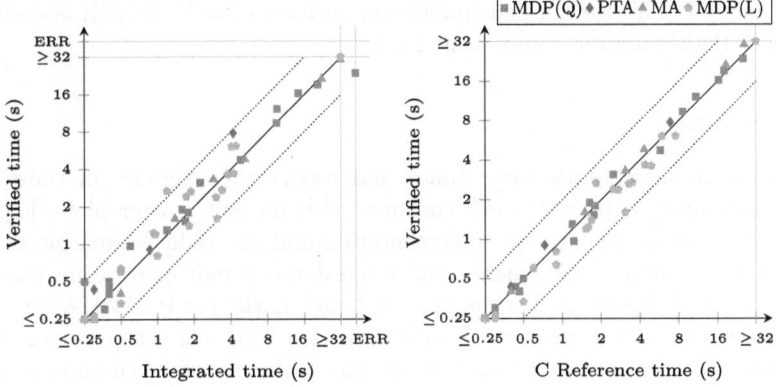

Fig. 3. Comparison of runtime to complete the MEC decomposition routine

6 Experimental Evaluation

We have embedded the verified implementation into the mcsta tool of the MOD-EST TOOLSET. Since it uses mcsta's regular input and output data structures, we do not need any expensive conversions and minimal glue code with negligible runtime. Furthermore, we implemented a *reference* implementation in C++ that we manually optimised. We now compare the performance of these two and the integrated implementation.

6.1 Experimental Setup

We use all applicable benchmarks (i.e. all MDP models, PTA models transformed into their digital clocks MDP, and MA transformed into the embedded MDP for untimed properties) from the Quantitative Verification Benchmark Set (QVBS) [27], which however rarely contain any nontrivial MECs. MEC decomposition is still necessary since we do not know a priori whether nontrivial MECs exist in a model and the algorithm may still require multiple iterations to obtain this result. To study the performance when nontrivial MECs exist, we adapt a benchmark set for long-run average rewards (LRA) from [20]. We test one reachability property per model to trigger the MEC algorithm and inflated the parameters to challenge the implementations. This benchmark set contains the *mer* Mars rover case study from [19], the *sensors* case study from [34], and other models from the PRISM benchmarks. We added parameters where sensible to allow scaling the model. We also created MDP adaptations of the stochastic games originally hand-crafted to contain interesting MEC structures for the evaluation of [35]. This gave us 61 benchmark instances to test our implementation on. We aimed to benchmark models between 500,000 and 100 million states. Smaller models terminate too quickly to benchmark while larger models run out of memory. We ran all benchmarks on an Intel Core i7-12700H system with 32 GB of RAM running Linux Mint 21.3.

6.2 Results

We ran each benchmark three times and report the averages of those runs. Figure 3 compares the wall clock runtime, with the left scatter plot comparing the verified to the integrated implementation and the right comparing the verified to the reference implementation. Each dot is a pair of runtime values for one benchmark instance. We distinguish benchmarks for PTA, MA and MDP from the QVBS (Q) or the LRA benchmarks (L). With our setup, we found that our verified implementation performs on par with the reference and integrated implementations, with a slight edge for the integrated implementation, but with little optimisation potential. We observe that this pattern also seems to hold independently of the type of model. One noteworthy outcome is the fact that the integrated implementation crashes for one instance whereas the reference and verified implementations do not. This is caused by the integrated implementation requiring more memory. We compared peak memory usage (working set) of the verified and integrated implementations. While this approach may be influenced by external factors like garbage collection, it can still provide a useful indication of relative memory consumption. Peak memory was higher for the integrated implementation in 42 out of the 61 instances. On average, the integrated implementation used about 8.2% more memory than the verified implementation. In isolated instances it reached up to 36.4% more. In comparison, the verified implementation used at most 28.4% more than the integrated implementation for isolated instances. The instance that crashed (*tireworld* with $n = 45$) lies on the verge of what a laptop with 32 GB of RAM can process: Peak memory reached almost 31 GB for this instance using the verified algorithm.

7 Conclusion

We have formally verified a MEC decomposition algorithm in Isabelle/HOL. As far as we know, this is the first such formalization. We have refined this algorithm down to LLVM and generated efficient executable code which we embedded into the mcsta probabilistic model checker of the MODEST TOOLSET. This is a step towards a fully verified model checking toolchain. We aim to replace algorithms in the toolchain piece by piece, monitoring the performance impact in each step. Where previous attempts at formally verified model checkers have not been competitive in terms of performance and functionality, our approach yields comparable performance to manual implementations. Additionally, if desired, cross-usage with other (unverified) functionality is possible. While the performance of our verified implementation is comparable to the integrated implementation, it is a clear improvement over the integrated implementation in terms of memory usage.

Future Work. Comparisons with the manual implementations suggest that the verified implementation does not have a lot of optimization potential. We consider it more useful to focus on other algorithms at this point. One candidate is the improved MEC algorithm by Chatterjee et al. [10], which has a better theoretical complexity than our implementation; deriving a competitive implementation from this would be highly relevant. Another candidate is the interval iteration algorithm [22] which uses the MEC algorithm as a pre-processing step. An efficient implementation of interval iteration requires a representation of real or rational numbers with low overhead. Unverified implementations rely on IEEE floating-point values (floats) which are suitable for high-performance computations but come with rounding errors [23]. This requires an extension of the IRF in order to refine real numbers to floats and reason about rounding.

Data availability. The proofs and benchmarks presented in this paper are archived and available at https://doi.org/10.4121/3f2a4539-e69b-4d16-b665-530c1abddfbc [32].

References

1. Alur, R., Dill, D.L.: A theory of timed automata. Theor. Comput. Sci. **126**(2), 183–235 (1994). https://doi.org/10.1016/0304-3975(94)90010-8
2. Baier, C., de Alfaro, L., Forejt, V., Kwiatkowska, M.: Model checking probabilistic systems. In: Handbook of Model Checking, pp. 963–999. Springer, Cham (2018). https://doi.org/10.1007/978-3-319-10575-8_28
3. Christel Baier and Joost-Pieter Katoen. Principles of Model Checking. MIT Press (2008)
4. Behrmann, G., David, A., Larsen, K.G.: A tutorial on UPPAAL. In: Bernardo, M., Corradini, F. (eds.) SFM-RT 2004. LNCS, vol. 3185, pp. 200–236. Springer, Heidelberg (2004). https://doi.org/10.1007/978-3-540-30080-9_7
5. Bellman, R.: A Markovian decision process. J. Math. Mech. **6**(5), 679–684 (1957)
6. Biere, A., Van Dijk, T., Heljanko, K.: Hardware model checking competition 2017. In: Stewart, D., Weissenbacher, G., (eds.) 2017 International Conference on Formal Methods in Computer Aided Design FMCAD, p. 9. IEEE (2017). https://doi.org/10.23919/FMCAD.2017.8102233
7. Bouyer, P., Fahrenberg, U., Larsen, K.G., Markey, N., Ouaknine, J., Worrell, J.: Model checking real-time systems. In: Handbook of Model Checking, pp. 1001–1046. Springer, Cham (2018). https://doi.org/10.1007/978-3-319-10575-8_29
8. Brunner, J., Lammich, P.: Formal verification of an executable LTL model checker with partial order reduction. J. Autom. Reasoning **60**(1), 3–21 (2018). https://doi.org/10.1007/s10817-017-9418-4
9. Budde, C.E., et al.: On correctness, precision, and performance in quantitative verification. In: Margaria, T., Steffen, B. (eds.) ISoLA 2020. LNCS, vol. 12479, pp. 216–241. Springer, Cham (2021). https://doi.org/10.1007/978-3-030-83723-5_15

10. Chatterjee, K., Henzinger, M.: Faster and dynamic algorithms for maximal end-component decomposition and related graph problems in probabilistic verification. In: Randall, D. (ed.) 22nd Annual ACM-SIAM Symposium on Discrete Algorithms (SODA), pp. 1318–1336. SIAM (2011). https://doi.org/10.1137/1.9781611973082.101

11. Chen, R., Lévy, J.-J.: A semi-automatic proof of strong connectivity. In: Paskevich, A., Wies, T. (eds.) VSTTE 2017. LNCS, vol. 10712, pp. 49–65. Springer, Cham (2017). https://doi.org/10.1007/978-3-319-72308-2_4

12. Clarke, E.M., Henzinger, T.A., Veith, H., Bloem, R. (eds.) Handbook of Model Checking. Springer (2018). https://doi.org/10.1007/978-3-319-10575-8

13. Clarke, E., Mishra, B.: Automatic verification of asynchronous circuits. In: Clarke, E., Kozen, D. (eds.) Logic of Programs 1983. LNCS, vol. 164, pp. 101–115. Springer, Heidelberg (1984). https://doi.org/10.1007/3-540-12896-4_358

14. Alfaro,L.: Formal verification of probabilistic systems. PhD thesis, Stanford University, USA (1997). https://searchworks.stanford.edu/view/3910936

15. Doyen, L., Frehse, G., Pappas, G.J., Platzer, A.: Verification of hybrid systems. In: Handbook of Model Checking, pp. 1047–1110. Springer, Cham (2018). https://doi.org/10.1007/978-3-319-10575-8_30

16. Eisentraut, C., Hermanns, H., Zhang, L.: On probabilistic automata in continuous time. In: Proceedings of the 25th Annual IEEE Symposium on Logic in Computer Science, LICS 2010, 11-14 July 2010, Edinburgh, United Kingdom, pp. 342–351. IEEE Computer Society (2010). https://doi.org/10.1109/LICS.2010.41

17. Eisentraut, J., Kelmendi, E., Křetínský, J., Weininger, M.: Value iteration for simple stochastic games: Stopping criterion and learning algorithm. Inf. Comput. 285(Part), 104886 (2022). https://doi.org/10.1016/J.IC.2022.104886

18. Esparza, J., Lammich, P., Neumann, R., Nipkow, T., Schimpf, A., Smaus, J.-G.: A fully verified executable LTL model checker. In: Sharygina, N., Veith, H. (eds.) CAV 2013. LNCS, vol. 8044, pp. 463–478. Springer, Heidelberg (2013). https://doi.org/10.1007/978-3-642-39799-8_31

19. Feng, L., Kwiatkowska, M., Parker, D.: Automated learning of probabilistic assumptions for compositional reasoning. In: Giannakopoulou, D., Orejas, F. (eds.) FASE 2011. LNCS, vol. 6603, pp. 2–17. Springer, Heidelberg (2011). https://doi.org/10.1007/978-3-642-19811-3_2

20. Grover, K., Weininger, M., Kretinsky, J.: QComp LRA results. Zenodo (2023). https://doi.org/10.5281/zenodo.8219191

21. Gupta, A., Kahlon, V., Qadeer, S., Touili, T.: Model checking concurrent programs. In: Handbook of Model Checking, pp. 573–611. Springer, Cham (2018). https://doi.org/10.1007/978-3-319-10575-8_18

22. Haddad, S., Monmege, B.: Interval iteration algorithm for MDPs and IMDPs. Theor. Comput. Sci. **735**, 111–131 (2018). https://doi.org/10.1016/J.TCS.2016.12.003

23. Hartmanns, A.: Correct probabilistic model checking with floating-point arithmetic. In: TACAS 2022. LNCS, vol. 13244, pp. 41–59. Springer, Cham (2022). https://doi.org/10.1007/978-3-030-99527-0_3

24. Hartmanns, A.: An overview of Modest models and tools for real stochastic timed systems. In: Dubslaff, C., Luttik, B. (eds.) 5th Workshop on Models for Formal Analysis of Real Systems (MARS), vol. 355 EPTCS, pp. 1–12 (2022). https://doi.org/10.4204/EPTCS.355.1

25. Hartmanns, A., Hermanns, H.: The Modest Toolset: an integrated environment for quantitative modelling and verification. In: Ábrahám, E., Havelund, K. (eds.) TACAS 2014. LNCS, vol. 8413, pp. 593–598. Springer, Heidelberg (2014). https://doi.org/10.1007/978-3-642-54862-8_51

26. Hartmanns, A., Kaminski, B.L.: Optimistic value iteration. In: Lahiri, S.K., Wang, C. (eds.) CAV 2020. LNCS, vol. 12225, pp. 488–511. Springer, Cham (2020). https://doi.org/10.1007/978-3-030-53291-8_26

27. Hartmanns, A., Klauck, M., Parker, D., Quatmann, T., Ruijters, E.: The quantitative verification benchmark set. In: Vojnar, T., Zhang, L. (eds.) TACAS 2019. LNCS, vol. 11427, pp. 344–350. Springer, Cham (2019). https://doi.org/10.1007/978-3-030-17462-0_20

28. Hartmanns, A., Kohlen, B., Lammich, P.: Fast verified SCCs for probabilistic model checking. In: André, É., Sun, J. (eds.) 21st International Symposium on Automated Technology for Verification and Analysis (ATVA). LNCS, vol. 14215, pp. 181–202. Springer, Cham (2023). https://doi.org/10.1007/978-3-031-45329-8_9

29. Heule, M., Hunt, W., Kaufmann, M., Wetzler, N.: Efficient, verified checking of propositional proofs. In: Ayala-Rincón, M., Muñoz, C.A. (eds.) ITP 2017. LNCS, vol. 10499, pp. 269–284. Springer, Cham (2017). https://doi.org/10.1007/978-3-319-66107-0_18

30. Hölzl, J.: Markov chains and Markov decision processes in Isabelle/HOL. J. Autom. Reason. **59**(3), 345–387 (2017). https://doi.org/10.1007/s10817-016-9401-5

31. Holzmann, G.J.: Software model checking with SPIN. Adv. Comput. **65**, 78–109 (2005). https://doi.org/10.1016/S0065-2458(05)65002-4

32. Kohlen, B., Hartmanns, A., Lammich, P.: Artifact for the paper "Efficient formally verified maximal end component decomposition for MDPs". 4TU.ResearchData (2024). https://doi.org/10.4121/3f2a4539-e69b-4d16-b665-530c1abddfbc

33. Kolobov, A., Mausam, M., Weld, D., Geffner, H.: Heuristic search for generalized stochastic shortest path MDPs. In: Bacchus, F., Domshlak, C., Edelkamp, S., Helmert, M. (eds.) 21st International Conference on Automated Planning and Scheduling (ICAPS). AAAI, (2011). http://aaai.org/ocs/index.php/ICAPS/ICAPS11/paper/view/2682

34. Komuravelli, A., Păsăreanu, C.S., Clarke, E.M.: Assume-guarantee abstraction refinement for probabilistic systems. In: Madhusudan, P., Seshia, S.A. (eds.) CAV 2012. LNCS, vol. 7358, pp. 310–326. Springer, Heidelberg (2012). https://doi.org/10.1007/978-3-642-31424-7_25

35. Křetínský, J., Ramneantu, E., Slivinskiy, A., Weininger, M.: Comparison of algorithms for simple stochastic games. Inf. Comput., 289(Part), 104885 (2022). https://doi.org/10.1016/J.IC.2022.104885

36. Kwiatkowska, M., Norman, G., Parker, D. et al.: Performance analysis of probabilistic timed automata using digital clocks. Formal Methods Syst. Des., 29(1), 33–78, (2006). https://doi.org/10.1007/s10703-006-0005-2

37. Kwiatkowska, M.Z., Norman, G., Segala, R., Sproston, J.: Automatic verification of real-time systems with discrete probability distributions. Theor. Comput. Sci. **282**(1), 101–150 (2002). https://doi.org/10.1016/S0304-3975(01)00046-9

38. Lammich, P.: Verified efficient implementation of Gabow's strongly connected component algorithm. In: Klein, G., Gamboa, R. (eds.) ITP 2014. LNCS, vol. 8558, pp. 325–340. Springer, Cham (2014). https://doi.org/10.1007/978-3-319-08970-6_21

39. Lammich, P.: Generating verified LLVM from Isabelle/HOL. In: Harrison,J., Leary, J., Tolmach, A. (eds.) 10th International Conference on Interactive Theorem Proving (ITP). LIPIcs, vol. 141, pp. 22:1–22:19. Schloss Dagstuhl – Leibniz-Zentrum für Informatik (2019). https://doi.org/10.4230/LIPIcs.ITP.2019.22

40. Lammich, P.: Efficient verified (UN)SAT certificate checking. J. Autom. Reason. **64**(3), 513–532 (2020). https://doi.org/10.1007/s10817-019-09525-z
41. Lammich, P.: Refinement of parallel algorithms down to LLVM. In: Andronick, J., Moura, L. (eds.) 13th International Conference on Interactive Theorem Proving (ITP). LIPIcs, vol. 237, pages 24:1–24:18. Schloss Dagstuhl – Leibniz-Zentrum für Informatik (2022). https://doi.org/10.4230/LIPIcs.ITP.2022.24
42. Lammich, P., Tuerk, T.: Applying data refinement for monadic programs to Hopcroft's algorithm. In: Beringer, L., Felty, A. (eds.) ITP 2012. LNCS, vol. 7406, pp. 166–182. Springer, Heidelberg (2012). https://doi.org/10.1007/978-3-642-32347-8_12
43. Schäffeler, M., Abdulaziz, M.: Formally verified solution methods for Markov decision processes. In: 37th AAAI Conference on Artificial Intelligence, pp. 15073–15081 (2022). https://doi.org/10.1609/aaai.v37i12.26759
44. Neumann, R.: Using Promela in a fully verified executable LTL model checker. In: Giannakopoulou, D., Kroening, D. (eds.) VSTTE 2014. LNCS, vol. 8471, pp. 105–114. Springer, Cham (2014). https://doi.org/10.1007/978-3-319-12154-3_7
45. Platzer, A.: Logical Foundations of Cyber-Physical Systems. (2018). https://doi.org/10.1007/978-3-319-63588-0
46. Pottier, F.: Depth-first search and strong connectivity in Coq. In: Vingt-sixièmes journées francophones des langages applicatifs (JFLA) (2015)
47. Puterman, M.L.: Markov Decision Processes: Discrete Stochastic Dynamic Programming. Wiley Series in Probability and Statistics. Wiley (1994). https://doi.org/10.1002/9780470316887
48. Quatmann, T., Katoen, J.-P.: Sound value iteration. In: Chockler, H., Weissenbacher, G. (eds.) CAV 2018. LNCS, vol. 10981, pp. 643–661. Springer, Cham (2018). https://doi.org/10.1007/978-3-319-96145-3_37
49. Reynolds, J.C.: Separation logic: a logic for shared mutable data structures. In: 17th IEEE Symposium on Logic in Computer Science (LICS 2002), 22-25 July 2002, Copenhagen, Denmark, Proceedings, pp. 55–74. IEEE Computer Society (2002). https://doi.org/10.1109/LICS.2002.1029817
50. Roberts, R., et al.: Probabilistic verification for reliability of a two-by-two network-on-chip system. In: Lluch Lafuente, A., Mavridou, A. (eds.) FMICS 2021. LNCS, vol. 12863, pp. 232–248. Springer, Cham (2021). https://doi.org/10.1007/978-3-030-85248-1_16
51. Steinmetz, M., Hoffmann, J., Buffet, O.: Goal probability analysis in probabilistic planning: exploring and enhancing the state of the art. J. Artif. Intell. Res. **57**, 229–271 (2016). https://doi.org/10.1613/JAIR.5153
52. Vajjha, K., Shinnar, A., Trager, B., Pestun, V., Fulton, N.: CertRL: formalizing convergence proofs for value and policy iteration in Coq. In: Hritcu, C., Popescu, A. (eds.) 10th ACM SIGPLAN International Conference on Certified Programs and Proofs (CPP), pp. 18–31. ACM, (2021). https://doi.org/10.1145/3437992.3439927
53. van den Berg, F., Remke, A., Haverkort, B.R.: iDSL: automated performance prediction and analysis of medical imaging systems. In: Beltrán, M., Knottenbelt, W., Bradley, J. (eds.) EPEW 2015. LNCS, vol. 9272, pp. 227–242. Springer, Cham (2015). https://doi.org/10.1007/978-3-319-23267-6_15
54. Wimmer, S., Herbreteau, F., van de Pol, J.: Certifying emptiness of timed Büchi automata. In: Bertrand, N., Jansen, N. (eds.) FORMATS 2020. LNCS, vol. 12288, pp. 58–75. Springer, Cham (2020). https://doi.org/10.1007/978-3-030-57628-8_4
55. Wimmer, S., Lammich, P.: Verified model checking of timed automata. In: Beyer, D., Huisman, M. (eds.) TACAS 2018. LNCS, vol. 10805, pp. 61–78. Springer, Cham (2018). https://doi.org/10.1007/978-3-319-89960-2_4

56. Wimmer, S., Mutius, J.: Verified certification of reachability checking for timed automata. In: TACAS 2020. LNCS, vol. 12078, pp. 425–443. Springer, Cham (2020). https://doi.org/10.1007/978-3-030-45190-5_24
57. Younes, H.L., Littman, M.L., Weissman, D., Asmuth, J.: The first probabilistic track of the international planning competition. J. Artif. Intell. Res. **24**, 851–887 (2005). https://doi.org/10.1613/JAIR.1880

Introducing SWIRL: An Intermediate Representation Language for Scientific Workflows

Iacopo Colonnelli[1] , Doriana Medić[1](✉) , Alberto Mulone[1] ,
Viviana Bono[1] , Luca Padovani[2] , and Marco Aldinucci[1]

[1] University of Turin, Turin, Italy
{iacopo.colonnelli,doriana.medic,alberto.mulone,
viviana.bono,marco.aldinucci}@unito.it
[2] University of Camerino, Camerino, Italy
luca.padovani@unicam.it

Abstract. In the ever-evolving landscape of scientific computing, properly supporting the modularity and complexity of modern scientific applications requires new approaches to workflow execution, like seamless interoperability between different workflow systems, distributed-by-design workflow models, and automatic optimisation of data movements. In order to address this need, this article introduces SWIRL, an intermediate representation language for scientific workflows. In contrast with other product-agnostic workflow languages, SWIRL is not designed for human interaction but to serve as a low-level compilation target for distributed workflow execution plans. The main advantages of SWIRL semantics are low-level primitives based on the send/receive programming model and a formal framework ensuring the consistency of the semantics and the specification of translating workflow models represented by Directed Acyclic Graphs (DAGs) into SWIRL workflow descriptions. Additionally, SWIRL offers rewriting rules designed to optimise execution traces, accompanied by corresponding equivalence. An open-source SWIRL compiler toolchain has been developed using the ANTLR Python3 bindings.

Keywords: Hybrid workflow · Interoperability · Formal methods

1 Introduction

Workflows have been widely used to model large-scale scientific workloads. The explicit definition of true dependencies between subsequent steps allows inferring concurrent execution strategies automatically, improving performances, and transferring input and output data wherever needed, fostering large-scale distributed executions. However, current Workflow Management Systems (WMSs) struggle to keep up with the ever-more demanding requirements of modern scientific applications, such as *interoperability* between different systems, *distributed-by-design* workflow models, and *automatic optimisation of data movements*.

A. Platzer et al. (Eds.): FM 2024, LNCS 14933, pp. 226–244, 2025.
https://doi.org/10.1007/978-3-031-71162-6_12

With the advent of BigData, adopting a proper *data management* strategy has become a crucial aspect of large-scale workflow orchestration. Avoiding unnecessary data movements and coalescing data transfers are two established techniques for performance optimisation in distributed executions. Moving computation near data to remove the need for data transfers is the underlying principle of several modern approaches to large-scale executions, like Resilient Distributed Datasets [42] and in-situ workflows [4].

WMSs' *interoperability* is an open problem in scientific workflows, which hinders reusability and composability. Despite several attempts to model product-agnostic workflow languages [11] and representations [28] present in the literature, these solutions capture only a subset of features, forcing WMSs to reduce their expressive power in the name of portability. The main issue in unifying workflow representations resides in the heterogeneity of different WMSs' APIs and programming models tailored to the needs of a domain experts. Conversely, moving the interoperability efforts to the lower level of the workflow execution plan representation is a promising but still relatively unexplored alternative.

The *heterogeneity* in contemporary hardware resources and their features, further exacerbated by the end-to-end co-design approach [30], requires WMSs to support a large ecosystem of execution environments (from HPC to cloud, to the Edge), optimisation policies (performance vs. energy efficiency) and computational models (from classical to quantum). However, maintaining optimised executors for such diverse execution targets is an overarching effort. In this setting, a just-in-time compilation of target-specific execution bundles, optimised for a single workflow running in a single execution environment, would be a game-changing approach. Indeed, this approach allows for the efficient use of resources, as the compilation is done at the time of execution, taking into account the specific characteristics of the execution environment. It also ensures the effectiveness of the execution, as the compiled bundle is optimised for the specific workflow, leading to improved performance.

This work presents SWIRL, a "Scientific Workflow Intermediate Representation Language". Unlike other product-agnostic workflow languages, SWIRL is not intended for human interaction but serves as a low-level compilation target for distributed workflow execution plans. It models the execution plan of a location-aware workflow graph as a distributed system with send/receive communication primitives. This work provides a formal method to encode a workflow instance into a distributed execution plan using these primitives, promoting interoperability and composability of different workflow models. It also includes a set of rewriting rules for automatic optimisation of data communications with correctness and consistency guarantees. The optimised SWIRL representation can then be compiled into one or more self-contained executable bundles, making it adaptable to specific execution environments and embracing heterogeneity.

The SWIRL implementation follows the same line as the theoretical approach, separating scientific workflows' design and runtime phases. A SWIRL-based compiler translates a workflow system W to a high-performance, self-contained workflow execution bundle based on send/receive communication protocols and runtime libraries, which can easily be included in a Research Object [5], significantly improving reproducibility.

In detail, Sect. 2 introduces a generic formalism for representing distributed scientific workflow models, while the related work and the comparison with the SWIRL language is given in Sect. 2.1. Section 3 introduces the SWIRL semantics, and Sect. 4 derives the rewriting rules used for optimisation. Section 5 describes the implementation of the SWIRL compiler toolchain while Sect. 6 shows how to model the 1000 Genomes workflow [35], a Bioinformatics pipeline aiming at fetching, parsing and analysing data from the 1000 Genomes Project [39] into SWIRL system. Finally, Sect. 7 concludes the article. Full proofs and additional material can be found in [10] while the experiment is in [9].

2   Background and Related Work

This section gathers the related work (Sect. 2.1) and introduces a formal representation of scientific workflows (Sect. 2.2) and their mapping onto distributed and heterogeneous execution environments (Sect. 2.3).

2.1   Related Work

Location-Aware WMSs. Grid-native WMSs typically support distributed workflows out of the box, providing automatic scheduling and data transfer management across multiple execution locations. However, all the orchestration aspects are delegated to external, grid-specific technologies, limiting the spectrum of supported execution environments. For instance, Triana [36], Askalon [14] and Pegasus [12] delegate tasks offloading and data transfers to the GAP interface [37], the GLARE library [34], and HTCondor [38], respectively.

Recently, a new class of location-aware WMSs is bringing advantages in performance and costs of workflow executions on top of heterogeneous distributed environments. StreamFlow [8] allows users to explicitly map each step onto one or more locations in charge of its execution. It relies on a set of connectors to support several execution environments, from HPC queue managers to microservices orchestrators. Jupyter Workflow [7] transforms a sequential computational notebook into a distributed workflow by mapping each cell into one or more execution locations, semi-automatically extracting inter-cell data dependencies from the code, and delegating the runtime orchestration to StreamFlow. Mashup [32] automatically maps each workflow step onto the best-suited location, choosing between traditional Cloud VMs and serverless platforms.

Each tool has its own strategy to derive an execution plan from a workflow graph without relying on an explicit and consolidated intermediate representation. Moreover, none of them formalise this derivation process, hiding its details inside the WMS's codebase. Instead, relying on a common intermediate language like SWIRL would allow interoperability between different tools and formal correctness guarantees on the adopted optimisation strategies.

Formal Models for Distributed Workflows. In the literature, the number of different WMSs is notable [3], however, up to our knowledge, there are only a few WMS for which formal models have been developed: Taverna [41], employing the lambda calculus [25] to define the workflow language in functional terms; Kepler [21] adopting Process Networks [18] and BPEL [26], where the workflow language is formalised with Petri Nets. YAWL [1] is another workflow language based on Petri Nets extended with constructs to address the multiple instances, advanced synchronisation, and cancellation patterns. It provides a detailed representation of workflow patterns [2] supported by an open-source environment.

Process algebra, in particular, different versions of π-calculus [33] are suited to model the workflow system due to the ability of processes to change their structure dynamically. A class of workflow patterns has been precisely defined using the execution semantics of π-calculus, in [29], while the basic control flow constructs modelled by π-calculus are given in [13]. A distributed extension of π-calculus [15] is examined as a formalisation for distributed workflow systems in [23], providing a discussion on the flexibility of the proposed representation. Aside from π-calculus, CCS (Calculus of Communication Systems) [24] models Web Service Choreography Interface descriptions.

2.2   Scientific Workflow Models

A generic workflow can be represented as a *directed bipartite graph*, where the nodes refer to either the computational *steps* of a modular application or the *ports* through which they communicate, and the edges encode *dependency relations* between steps.

Definition 1. *A workflow is a directed bipartite graph $W = (S, P, \mathcal{D})$ where S is the set of steps, P is the set of ports, and $\mathcal{D} \subseteq (S \times P) \cup (P \times S)$ is the set of dependency links.*

In the considered graph, one port can have multiple output edges meaning that more steps are dependent on it. The sets of input/output ports (steps) of a step (port) are defined with the following definition.

Definition 2. *Given a workflow $W = (S, P, \mathcal{D})$, a step $s \in S$ and a port $p \in P$, the sets of input and output ports of s are denoted with $In(s)$ and $Out(s)$, respectively, and defined as:*

$$In(s) = \{p' \mid (p', s) \in \mathcal{D}\} \qquad Out(s) = \{p' \mid (s, p') \in \mathcal{D}\}$$

while the sets of input and output steps of p are denoted with $In(p)$ and $Out(p)$, respectively, and defined as:

$$In(p) = \{s' \mid (s', p) \in \mathcal{D}\} \qquad Out(p) = \{s' \mid (p, s') \in \mathcal{D}\}$$

Traditionally, scientific workflows are modelled using a dataflow approach, i.e., following *token-pushing* semantics in which tokens carry *data values*. The step executions are enabled by the presence of tokens in their input ports and produce new tokens in their output ports. In general, a single workflow model can generate infinite *workflow instances*. Different instances preserve the same graph structure but differ in the values carried by each token.

Definition 3. *A workflow instance is a tuple $(W, D, \mathcal{I})$ where $W = (S, P, \mathcal{D})$ is a workflow, D is a set of data elements, and $\mathcal{I} \subseteq (D \times P)$ is a mapping relation connecting each data element $d \in D$ to the port $p \in P$ that contains it.*

Definition 4. *Given a workflow instance $(W, D, \mathcal{I})$, where $W = (S, P, \mathcal{D})$, and a step $s \in S$, the sets of input and output data elements of s are denoted with $In^D(s)$ and $Out^D(s)$, respectively, and defined as:*

$$In^D(s) = \{d \mid (d,p) \in \mathcal{I} \land p \in In(s)\} \qquad Out^D(s) = \{d \mid (d,p) \in \mathcal{I} \land p \in Out(s)\}$$

Introducing more precise evaluation semantics, triggering strategies, or limitations on the dependencies structure can specialise this general definition to an actual workflow model (e.g., a Petri Net [31] or Coloured Petri Nets [16], a Kahn Processing Network [17], or a Synchronous Dataflow Graph [20]).

2.3   Distributed Workflow Models

A *distributed workflow* is a workflow whose steps can target different *deployment locations* in charge of executing them. To compute the step, the corresponding location must have access to or store all the input data elements, additionally, it will store all the output data elements on its local scope. Locations can be *heterogeneous*, exposing different hardware devices, software libraries, and security levels. Consequently, the steps are explicitly mapped onto execution locations depending on their computing requests. Given that, a distributed workflow model must contain a specification of the workflow structure, the set of available locations, and a mapping relation between steps and locations.

Definition 5. *A distributed workflow is a tuple $(W, L, \mathcal{M})$, where $W = (S, P, \mathcal{D})$ is a workflow, L is the set of available locations, and $\mathcal{M} \subseteq (S \times L)$ is a mapping relation stating which locations are in charge of executing each workflow step.*

Each location can execute multiple steps on it, and a single step can be mapped onto multiple locations. Multiple steps related to a single location introduce a *temporal constraint*: all the involved steps compete to acquire the location's resources. They can be serialised if the location does not have enough resources to execute all of them concurrently. Conversely, multiple locations related to a single step express a *spatial constraint*: all involved locations must collaborate to execute the step. This work does not impose any particular strategy for scheduling different step executions on a single location when temporal constraints arise. However, it is helpful to know the *work queue* of a given location l, i.e., the set of steps mapped onto it.

Definition 6. *Given a distributed workflow $(W, L, \mathcal{M})$, where $W = (S, P, \mathcal{D})$, and a location $l \in L$, the set of steps mapped onto l is called the work queue of l, denoted as $Q(l)$ and defined as: $Q(l) = \{s \mid l \in \mathcal{M}(s)\}$.*

Similarly to what was discussed in Sect. 2.2, a single distributed workflow model can generate potentially infinite *distributed workflow instances* with different data elements and condition evaluations.

Definition 7. *A distributed workflow instance is a tuple* $I = (W, L, \mathcal{M}, D, \mathcal{I})$ *where* $(W, L, \mathcal{M})$ *is a distributed workflow,* D *is a set of data elements, and* $\mathcal{I} \subseteq (D \times P)$ *is a mapping relation connecting each data element* $d \in D$ *to the port* $p \in P$ *that contains it.*

Example 1. Fig. 1 shows an example of a distributed workflow model. A step s_1 produces two different output data elements d_1 and d_2, which are mapped to ports p_1 and p_2. The second and the third step, s_2 and s_3 depend on the data elements on the ports p_1 and p_2, respectively. None of them produces other outputs. This workflow is mapped onto four locations. Step s_1 is executed on location l_d, while s_2 is offloaded to l_1 and step s_3 is mapped to two locations l_2 and l_3. Using definitions above, Fig. 1 can be written as follows:

$$W = (\{s_1, s_2, s_3\}, \{p_1, p_2\}, \{(s_1, p_1), (s_1, p_2), (p_1, s_2), (p_2, s_3)\})$$

$$L = \{l_d, l_1, l_2, l_3\} \qquad \mathcal{M} = \{(s_1, l_d), (s_2, l_1), (s_3, l_2), (s_3, l_3)\}$$

$$D = \{d_1, d_2\} \qquad \mathcal{I} = \{(d_1, p_1), (d_2, p_2)\}$$

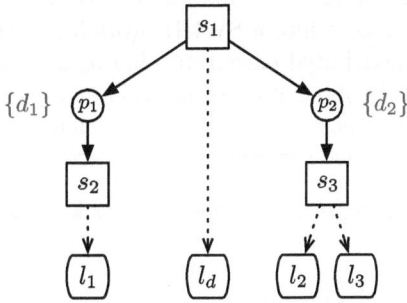

Fig. 1. Example of a distributed workflow model. Steps are represented as squares and ports as circles. Dependency links between steps and ports are depicted as arrows with black-filled heads. Locations are represented as squashed rectangles. Mapping relations are expressed as dotted arrows. A potential instance of this model can be derived by adding data elements, denoted as sets of values, near their related port.

3   The SWIRL Representation

This section introduces SWIRL, a "Scientific Workflow Intermediate Representation Language". Given a distributed workflow instance (Sect. 2.3), SWIRL can model a decentralised execution plan, called *workflow system*, by inferring and projecting execution traces on each involved location and specifying

$$(\text{ID}_{\,|}\,)\quad e\mid \mathbf{0} \equiv e \qquad (\text{ID.})\quad \mathbf{0}.e \equiv e \wedge e.\mathbf{0} \equiv e \qquad (\text{COMT}_u)\quad u\mid u' \equiv u'\mid u\,,\ u\in e, \mathtt{W}$$

Fig. 2. SWIRL structural congruence rules.

$$(\text{EXEC})\quad \frac{\forall l_i \in \mathcal{M}(s)\ \wedge\ In^D(s)\subseteq D_i}{\displaystyle\prod_{i,l_i\in\mathcal{M}(s)} \langle l_i, D_i, \mathbf{exec}(s,F(s),\mathcal{M}(s)).e_i\rangle \rightarrow \prod_{i,l_i\in\mathcal{M}(s)} \left\langle l_i, D_i \cup Out^D(s), e_i\right\rangle}$$

$$(\text{L-COMM})\quad \frac{d\in D}{\langle l, D, \mathbf{send}(d \rightarrowtail p,l,l).e\mid \mathbf{recv}(p,l,l).e'\rangle \rightarrow \langle l, D, e\mid e'\rangle}$$

$$(\text{COMM})\quad \frac{d\in D}{\langle l, D, \mathbf{send}(d \rightarrowtail p,l,l').e\rangle \mid \langle l', D', \mathbf{recv}(p,l,l').e'\rangle \rightarrow \langle l, D, e\rangle \mid \langle l', D'\cup\{d\}, e'\rangle}$$

$$(\text{L-PAR})\quad \frac{\langle l, D, e_1\rangle \rightarrow \langle l, D', e_1'\rangle}{\langle l, D, e_1\mid e_2\rangle \rightarrow \langle l, D', e_1'\mid e_2\rangle} \qquad (\text{SEC})\quad \frac{\langle l, D, e_1\rangle \rightarrow \langle l, D', e_1'\rangle}{\langle l, D, e_1.e_2\rangle \rightarrow \langle l, D', e_1'.e_2\rangle}$$

$$(\text{PAR})\quad \frac{\mathtt{W}_1 \rightarrow \mathtt{W}_1'}{\mathtt{W}_1\mid \mathtt{W}_2 \rightarrow \mathtt{W}_1'\mid \mathtt{W}_2} \qquad (\text{CONGR})\quad \frac{\mathtt{W}_1' \equiv \mathtt{W}_1 \rightarrow \mathtt{W}_2 \equiv \mathtt{W}_2'}{\mathtt{W}_1' \rightarrow \mathtt{W}_2'}$$

Fig. 3. SWIRL reduction semantics rules.

inter-location communications using send/receive primitives. The following sections introduce SWIRL syntax and semantics and derive a procedure to formally encode a workflow instance I into a SWIRL workflow system W.

SWIRL models a distributed execution plan as a workflow system W, which can be seen as a parallel composition of *location configurations*, tuples $\langle l, D, e\rangle$, containing the location name l, the set D of data elements laying on l at a given time, and the execution trace e representing the actions to be executed on l.

Definition 8. *The syntax of a workflow system W is defined by the following grammar:*

$$\mathtt{W} ::= \langle l, D, e\rangle \parallel (\mathtt{W}_1\mid \mathtt{W}_2)$$
$$e ::= \mu \parallel e_1.e_2 \parallel (e_1\mid e_2) \parallel \mathbf{0}$$
$$\mu ::= \mathbf{exec}(s, F(s), \mathcal{M}(s)) \parallel \mathbf{send}(d\rightarrowtail p,l,l') \parallel \mathbf{recv}(p,l,l')$$
$$F(s) ::= In^D(s) \mapsto Out^D(s)$$

Each execution trace e is constructed from the predicates μ, which can be composed using two operators: the *sequential execution* $e_1.e_2$ and the *parallel composition* $e_1\mid e_2$. The $\mathbf{0}$ symbol represents the empty trace.

A predicate μ represents an action to be performed during workflow execution. Predicates $\mathbf{send}(d\rightarrowtail p,l,l')$ and $\mathbf{recv}(p,l,l')$ allow transferring the data element d over port p from location l to location l'. Modelling ports and data separately seams redundant, but we prefer to keep them divided for the future extensions of the framework, as adding the loops. The $\mathbf{exec}(s, F(s), \mathcal{M}(s))$ action represents the execution of step s. Besides the name of the step, this predicate contains the set $\mathcal{M}(s)$ of locations onto which s is mapped and the *dataflow*

$F(s)$, i.e., the set $In^D(s)$ of input data needed by s and the set $Out^D(s)$ of output data produced on each $l \in \mathcal{M}(s)$ after the execution of s.

3.1 Semantics

The SWIRL semantics is defined in terms of a *reduction semantics*.

Definition 9. *The SWIRL semantics is defined by the reduction relation* $\longrightarrow$ *defined as a smallest relation closed under the rules of Figs. 2 and 3.*

The structural congruence properties are reported in Fig. 2. The commutativity of the parallel composition in location and the execution trace level is defined with rule ($\textsc{Comt}_u$). For both operators, parallel composition and sequential execution, the identity element is **0** (rules ($\textsc{Id}_|$) and ($\textsc{Id}_.$)).

The rules of a SWIRL semantics are depicted in Fig. 3. The step execution is performed by the ($\textsc{Exec}$) rule. It collects all the locations $\mathcal{M}(s)$ onto which step s is mapped and synchronises the execution action. The data $Out^D(s)$ produced by the step execution are added to the set D_i in all executing locations. Rule ($\textsc{L-Comm}$) describes local communication, while rule ($\textsc{Comm}$) represents a data transfer between two locations. In the latter case, the involved data element is *copied* to the targeted (receiving) location. Note that communications do not consume the data element on the sending location.

Assuming that configuration $\langle l, D, e_1 \rangle$ can be computed, rules ($\textsc{L-Par}$) and ($\textsc{Seq}$) allow for the execution of the parallel and the sequential composition inside the same location, respectively. The execution of the workflow sub-system as a part of a larger system is allowed by the rule ($\textsc{Par}$). The ($\textsc{Congr}$) rule allows the application of structural congruence.

When a step s is mapped onto multiple locations, each of them must contain an **exec** predicate with the set of involved locations. Such predicates introduce *synchronisation points* among different locations, as all involved execution traces must step forward in a single pass. Additionally, each location must have a copy of the input data $In^D(s)$, requiring multiple **send** operations for each element $d \in In^D(s)$, and will own a copy of $Out^D(s)$.

Example 2. The behaviour of the distributed workflow instance given in Fig. 1 can be modelled as a workflow system W with the following syntax:

$$\mathtt{W} = \langle l_d, \emptyset, e_d \rangle \mid \prod_{i=1}^{3} \langle l_i, \emptyset, e_i \rangle$$

$$
\begin{aligned}
e_d =\ & \mathbf{exec}(s_1, \emptyset \mapsto \{d_1, d_2\}, \{l_d\}).\big(\mathbf{send}(d_1 \rightarrowtail p_1, l_d, l_1) \mid \\
& \mathbf{send}(d_2 \rightarrowtail p_2, l_d, l_2) \mid \mathbf{send}(d_2 \rightarrowtail p_2, l_d, l_3)\big) \\
e_1 =\ & \mathbf{recv}(p_1, l_d, l_1).\mathbf{exec}(s_2, \{d_1\} \mapsto \emptyset, \{l_1\}) \\
e_2 =\ & \mathbf{recv}(p_2, l_d, l_2).\mathbf{exec}(s_3, \{d_2\} \mapsto \emptyset, \{l_2, l_3\}) \\
e_3 =\ & \mathbf{recv}(p_2, l_d, l_3).\mathbf{exec}(s_3, \{d_2\} \mapsto \emptyset, \{l_2, l_3\})
\end{aligned}
$$

In the execution trace e_d, step s_1 is sending output data d_2 to both locations $l_2, l_3 \in \mathcal{M}(s_3)$ through the same port p_2.

3.2   Workflow Model Encoding

Example 2 describes the encoding of a distributed workflow instance I into a workflow system W. This section introduces a formal methodology to perform this encoding automatically for any distributed workflow instance.

In SWIRL, the execution trace e_l of a location $l \in L$ models the actions required to execute all the steps in its work queue $Q(l)$. In this respect, e_l can be seen as the parallel composition of *building blocks* $B_l(s)$, one for each $s \in Q(l)$. Each building block $B_l(s)$ contains the same sequence of actions: (i) receives all the necessary data elements for the step execution in which case it is necessary to determine all input data elements $(In^D(s))$ and for each element to identify the step producing it $(In(\mathcal{I}(d_i)))$ and the locations on which the steps are mapped to $(\mathcal{M}(In(\mathcal{I}(d_i))))$ (ii) executes the step s; (iii) sends the produced data elements $(Out^D(s))$ to the locations onto which the receiving steps are mapped (one data element can be sent, over the same port, to the different steps/locations, therefore it is necessary to identify the steps data d_i is sent to with $Out(\mathcal{I}(d_i))$ and the locations l_j on which each step is deployed).

Definition 10. *Given a distributed workflow instance* $I = (W, L, \mathcal{M}, D, \mathcal{I})$, *a deployment location* $l \in L$ *and a step* $s \in S$ *s.t.* $l \in \mathcal{M}(s)$, *the building block representing* s *in* e_l *is denoted by* $B_l(s)$ *and defined as:*

$$B_l(s) = \left(\prod^{\forall d_i \in In^D(s)} \prod^{\forall l_j \in \mathcal{M}(In(\mathcal{I}(d_i)))} \mathtt{recv}(\mathcal{I}(d_i), l_j, l) \right).$$

$$\mathtt{exec}(s, In^D(s) \mapsto Out^D(s), \mathcal{M}(s)).$$

$$\left(\prod^{\forall d_i \in Out^D(s)} \prod^{\forall s_k \in Out(\mathcal{I}(d_i))} \prod^{\forall l_j \in \mathcal{M}(s_k)} \mathtt{send}(d_i \rightarrowtail \mathcal{I}(d_i), l, l_j) \right)$$

Definition 10 introduces the general form of $B_l(s)$, which holds for steps connected to both input and output ports. If a step does not consume input data, as in the case of step s_1 from Example 2, the receiving part of $B_l(s)$ is modelled with $\mathbf{0}$, resulting in $B_{l_d}(s_1) = \mathbf{0}.\mathtt{exec}(s, \emptyset \mapsto \{d_1\}, \{l_d\}).\mathtt{send}(d_1 \rightarrowtail p_1, l_d, l_1)$. The same applies to steps that do not produce output data.

The concept of building blocks $B_l(s)$ allows for the modular construction of execution traces by processing one pair (s, l) at a time. Intuitively, for each mapping pair step-location (s, l), corresponding building blocks $B_l(s)$ are made and added to the execution trace of the location l. Another important information is the *instance data distribution* on the locations, denoted by $G(l) = \{d | d \in D_l\}$.

Definition 11. *The encoding function* $[\![\cdot]\!] : \mathcal{W}_I \rightarrow \mathcal{W}_W$, *where* $\mathcal{W}_I$ *and* $\mathcal{W}_W$ *are the sets of distributed workflow instances and workflow systems represented in SWIRL, respectively, is inductively defined as follows:*

$$\llbracket \mathtt{I} \rrbracket = \llbracket \mathtt{I}, \mathcal{M}, G; \mathtt{W} \rrbracket \quad where \ \mathtt{W} = \prod_{\forall l_i \in L} \langle l_i, \emptyset, e_l \rangle$$

$$\llbracket \mathtt{I}, \mathcal{M} \cup (s, l), G; \mathtt{W} \mid \langle l, \emptyset, e_l \rangle \rrbracket = \llbracket \mathtt{I}, \mathcal{M}, G; \mathtt{W} \mid \langle l, \emptyset, e_l \mid B_l(s) \rangle \rrbracket$$

$$\llbracket \mathtt{I}, \mathcal{M}, G \cup G(l); \mathtt{W} \mid \langle l, \emptyset, e_l \rangle \rrbracket = \llbracket \mathtt{I}, \mathcal{M}, G; \mathtt{W} \mid \langle l, G(l), e_l \rangle \rrbracket$$

$$\llbracket \mathtt{I}, \emptyset, \emptyset; \mathtt{W} \rrbracket = \mathtt{W}$$

Formally, the encoding operator can be defined as a function with four input parameters: (i) a workflow instance $\mathtt{I}$ to be translated; (ii) the set of pairs (s, l) containing all mappings in $\mathcal{M}$; (iii) the set G representing the distribution of the data over locations; (iv) placeholder to build the workflow system $\mathtt{W}$. The translation starts by adding the auxiliary parameters into the encoding process and inside a SWIRL placeholder, creating a workflow containing locations configurations for each location in the workflow instance $\mathtt{I}$ (for all $l \in L$). The iteration process is divided in two phases, first at each iteration, the encoding function takes the pair (s, l), identify the location l and add the building block $B_l(s)$ into the execution trace to be executed on the location l. When all pairs are encoded, in the second phase, the iteration is on the distribution of the data over locations. Each set $G(l) \subseteq G$ is encoded to the corresponding locations. In that way, the trace e_l is the parallel composition of building blocks $B_l(s)$ for each $s \in Q(l)$. The encoding finishes when both sets $\mathcal{M}$ and G are empty.

3.3 Consistency of SWIRL Semantics

This section defines a concurrency relation on the derivations of a workflow system $\mathtt{W}$, which is then used to show the consistency of different execution diagrams through the semantics. As commonly done in the literature, this section only considers reachable workflow systems defined below.

Definition 12. *Given a distributed workflow instance* $\mathtt{I} = (W, L, \mathcal{M}, D, \mathcal{I})$ *and the function* $\llbracket \cdot \rrbracket : \mathcal{W}_{\mathtt{I}} \to \mathcal{W}_{\mathtt{w}}$, *the initial state of a distributed workflow system is*

$$\mathtt{W}_{Init} = \llbracket \mathtt{I}, L, * \rrbracket = \prod_{l_j \in L} \left\langle l_j, \emptyset, \prod_{s \in Q(l_j)} B(s) \right\rangle$$

Definition 13. *A state of a workflow system* $\mathtt{W}$ *is reachable if it can be derived from the initial state* $(\mathtt{W}_{Init})$ *by applying the rules in Figs. 2 and 3.*

Having a transition $t : \mathtt{W} \to \mathtt{W}'$, the workflow states $\mathtt{W}$ and $\mathtt{W}'$ are called *source* and *target* of the transition t, respectively. The *concurrency relation* is defined on the transitions having the same source. Formally:

Definition 14 (Concurrency relation). *Two different transitions* $t_1 : \mathtt{W} \to \mathtt{W}_1$ *and* $t_2 : \mathtt{W} \to \mathtt{W}_2$ *having the same source, are always concurrent, written* $t_1 \smile t_2$.

Following the standard notation, let t_2/t_1 represent a transition t_2 executed after the transition t_1. The concurrency relation is used to prove the *Church-Rosser property*, which states that when two concurrent transitions execute at the same time, the ordering of the executions does not impact the eventual result. This finding shows that the concurrent semantics is confluent. Formally:

Lemma 1 (Church-Rosser property). *Given two concurrent transitions t_1 : $W \rightarrow W_1$ and t_2 : $W \rightarrow W_2$, there exist two transitions t_2/t_1 : $W_1 \rightarrow W_3$ and t_1/t_2 : $W_2 \rightarrow W_3$ having the same target.*

4   Optimisation

This section introduces an *optimisation function* that scans the entire workflow system to remove redundant communications, improving performance. In particular, there are two cases in which execution traces can be optimised: (i) communications between steps deployed on the same location, which are always redundant; (ii) multiple communications of the same data element between a pair of locations, when different steps mapped onto the destination location require the same input data from the same ports.

The encoding function adds a communication to the workflow system W every time a data element is required for the execution of a step, no matter if it is already present at the destination location, creating unnecessary communications. For instance, consider a location $\langle l, D, e \rangle$ where $D = \emptyset$ and

$$e = \mathtt{recv}(p, l_1, l).\mathtt{exec}(s, \{d\} \mapsto \{d_1\}, \{l\}).\mathtt{send}(d_1 \rightarrowtail p_1, l, l) \mid$$
$$\mathtt{recv}(p_1, l, l).\mathtt{exec}(s_1, \{d_1\} \mapsto \emptyset, \{l\})$$

After the execution of the step s, the data element d_1 is saved on the location l ($D \cup \{d_1\}$), therefore the $\mathtt{send}/\mathtt{recv}$ pair does not affect the state of W. By removing the unnecessary communication, the trace e can be rewritten as:

$$e' = \mathtt{recv}(p, l_1, l).\mathtt{exec}(s, \{d\} \mapsto \{d_1\}, \{l\}) \mid \mathtt{exec}(s_1, \{d_1\} \mapsto \emptyset, \{l\})$$

The rule (EXEC) in Fig. 3, preserves dependency between steps s and s_1 by ensuring that step s_1 will not execute until the required data d_1 is produced.

The second optimisation step is to remove redundant communications between different pairs of locations when the same data element is sent multiple times through the same port. For instance, consider two locations $\langle l, D, e \rangle$ and $\langle l', D', e' \rangle$ where $D = D' = \emptyset$ and

$$e = \mathtt{recv}(p, l_1, l).\mathtt{exec}(s, \{d\} \mapsto \{d_1\}, \{l\}).(\prod_{i=1}^{3} \mathtt{send}(d_1 \rightarrowtail p_1, l, l'))$$

$$e' = \prod_{i=1}^{3} \mathtt{recv}(p_1, l, l').\mathtt{exec}(s_i, \{d_1\} \mapsto \emptyset, \{l'\})$$

The first location l sends the data element d_1 to three steps mapped onto location l'. Transferring the data element only once is enough, as the subsequent communications will not affect the state of W, hence, there is:

$$e = \mathtt{recv}(p, l_1, l).\mathtt{exec}(s, \{d\} \mapsto \{d_1\}, \{l\}).\mathtt{send}(d_1 \rightarrowtail p_1, l, l')$$

$$e' = \mathtt{recv}(p_1, l, l').\mathtt{exec}(s_k, \{d_1\} \mapsto \emptyset, \{l'\}) \mid \prod_{i=1, i \neq k}^{3} \mathtt{exec}(s_i, \{d_1\} \mapsto \emptyset, \{l'\})$$

The optimisation of a workflow system W is defined in terms of three functions: the first and the second[1] ones start the optimisation process and controls it till the end, by taking the additional parameter A (the set of all prefixes/actions) and calling the third function that actually rewrite the execution trace of a location. It goes through the execution traces of the workflow W and breaks them into single action (prefix) blocks. Analysing the blocks one by one, it performs the following actions: (i) if the predicate is a part of the communication on the same location, it is removed; (ii) if the predicate is already in the set A, it is removed as well (meaning the same data element was already sent to the same location through the same port, just to different step); (iii) otherwise, the predicate is added to the set A and the drilling function moves to the next element.

Definition 15. *Given the workflow system* W *and sets of workflow and optimised systems* $\mathcal{W}_\mathtt{W}$ *and* $\mathcal{W}_\mathtt{O}$, *respectively, the optimisation function* W, $[\![\cdot]\!] : \mathcal{W}_\mathtt{W} \to \mathcal{W}_\mathtt{O}$ *is defined in terms of the auxiliary functions,* $[\![\cdot]\!] : \mathcal{W}_\mathtt{W} \times A \to \mathcal{W}_\mathtt{O}$ *and* $\mathord{\wr}\cdot\mathord{\int} : \mathcal{W}_\mathtt{W} \to \mathcal{W}_\mathtt{O}$ *(where* $\mathtt{o} \in \{|, .\}$ *and* $A_{l,l} = \{\mathtt{send}(d \rightarrowtail p, l, l), \mathtt{recv}(p, l, l)\}$*) as follows:*

$$[\![\mathtt{W}]\!] = [\![\mathord{\wr}\mathtt{W}\mathord{\int}, \emptyset]\!]$$
$$[\![\mathord{\wr}\langle l, D, e\rangle\mathord{\int}, A]\!] = \langle l, D, [\![\mathord{\wr}e\mathord{\int}, A]\!]\rangle$$
$$[\![\mathord{\wr}\mathtt{W}_1 \mid \mathtt{W}_2\mathord{\int}, A]\!] = [\![\mathord{\wr}\mathtt{W}_1\mathord{\int}, A]\!] \mid [\![\mathord{\wr}\mathtt{W}_2\mathord{\int}, A]\!]$$
$$\mathord{\wr}e \mathbin{\mathtt{o}} e_1\mathord{\int} = \mathord{\wr}e\mathord{\int} \mathbin{\mathtt{o}} \mathord{\wr}e_1\mathord{\int}$$
$$[\![e \mathbin{\mathtt{o}} \mathord{\wr}\mu\mathord{\int} \mathbin{\mathtt{o}} \mathord{\wr}e_1\mathord{\int}, A]\!] = \begin{cases} [\![e \mathbin{\mathtt{o}} \mathbf{0} \mathbin{\mathtt{o}} \mathord{\wr}e_1\mathord{\int}, A]\!] & \text{if } \mu \in A \quad \vee \quad \mu \in A_{l,l} \\ [\![e \mathbin{\mathtt{o}} \mu \mathbin{\mathtt{o}} \mathord{\wr}e_1\mathord{\int}, A \cup \mu]\!] & \text{otherwise} \end{cases}$$
$$[\![e, A]\!] = e$$

The two workflow systems W and $\mathtt{O} = [\![\mathtt{W}]\!]$ are modelling the same behaviour of the distributed workflow system, i.e. the computations of the workflow steps are executed in the same order in both systems with the difference in the number of communications. Therefore, the weak barbed bisimulation [33] is used to define the relation between the distributed workflow system and its optimised version.

To highlight that the executing action is a communication, it is labelled by τ. Therefore, $\mathtt{W} \xrightarrow{\tau} \mathtt{W}'$ indicates that workflow system W can evolve into W′ by performing the communication (transfer) action. The reflexive and transitive closure of $\xrightarrow{\tau}$ is denoted with $\overset{\tau}{\Rightarrow}$ and the transition $\mathtt{W} \overset{\tau}{\Rightarrow} \mathtt{W}'$ express the ability of the system W to evolve into W′ by executing some number, possibly zero, of τ actions (communications). Given the transition $\mathtt{W} \to \mathtt{W}'$ (any type of action, including the communication), if the same action can be executed after a certain number of communication actions, it is denoted as $\mathtt{W} \overset{\tau}{\Rightarrow}\to \mathtt{W}'$.

The observable elements in this setting are the executions of the steps and it is denoted by $\mathtt{W} \downarrow_\nu$ (resp. $\mathtt{O} \downarrow_\nu$) where $\nu = \mathtt{exec}(s, F(s), \mathcal{M}(s))$ where the

---

[1] The two functions have the same notation to simplify the notation, they can be easily distinguished because of the different number of arguments.

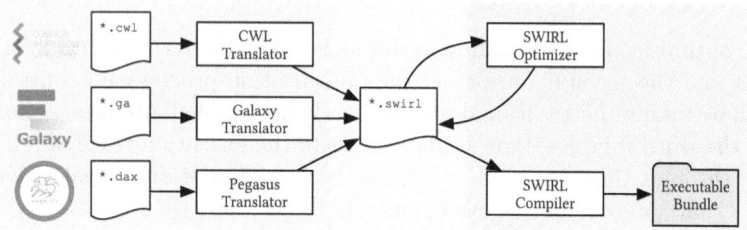

Fig. 4. The SWIRL compiler toolchain.

weak barb is denoted by $W \Downarrow_\nu$ (resp. $O \Downarrow_\nu$), and it is defined as $W \stackrel{\tau}{\Rightarrow} \downarrow_\nu$ (resp. $O \stackrel{\tau}{\Rightarrow} \downarrow_\nu$). Hence, the barbed bisimulation will check that all the step executions in a workflow system can be matched by the executions in the optimised one.

Definition 16. *A relation $\mathcal{R} \subseteq \mathcal{W} \times \mathcal{O}$ is a weak barbed simulation if* $W\mathcal{R}[\![W]\!]$:

- $W \downarrow_\nu$ *implies* $[\![W]\!] \Downarrow_\nu$
- $W \rightarrow W'$ *implies* $[\![W]\!] \Rightarrow [\![W']\!]$ *with* $W'\mathcal{R}[\![W']\!]$

A relation $\mathcal{R} \subseteq \mathcal{W} \times \mathcal{O}$ is a weak barbed bisimulation if $\mathcal{R}$ and $\mathcal{R}^{-1}$ are weak barbed simulations. Weak bisimilarity, $\approx$, is the largest weak barbed bisimulation.

The next theorem shows the operational correspondence between a distributed workflow system and its optimised term.

Theorem 1. *For any distributed workflow system W, $W \approx [\![W]\!]$.*

5   Implementation

The SWIRL compiler reference implementation[2], called `swirlc`, follows the same line as the theoretical approach, separating scientific workflows' design and runtime phases. On the one hand, it allows the translation of high-level, product-specific workflow languages designed for direct human interaction to chains of low-level primitives easily understood by distributed runtime systems. A common representation fosters composability and interoperability among different workflow models, which can be easily combined into a single workflow system. Moreover, the translation process is performed with the formal consistency guarantees discussed in Sect. 3.2.

Finally, a SWIRL-based compiler can translate a workflow system W to a high-performance, self-contained workflow execution bundle based on send/receive communication protocols and runtime libraries, which can easily be included in a Research Object [5], improving reproducibility. An advanced compiler can also generate multiple execution bundles from the same workflow system, each optimised for a different execution environment (e.g., Cloud, HPC, or Edge),

---

[2] https://github.com/alpha-unito/swirlc.

improving performance. As a bonus feature, the intrinsically distributed nature of SWIRL execution traces promotes decentralised runtime architectures, avoiding the single point of failure introduced by a centralised control plane.

Figure 4 sketches the SWIRL compiler toolchain. We implemented the SWIRL grammar using ANTLR [27], and we automatically generated Python3 parser classes to process the SWIRL syntax. All the components of the SWIRL toolchain rely on these parsers to process *.swirl files. An abstract SWIRLTranslator class implements the encoding function, producing a SWIRL file from a workflow instance I. A concrete implementation specialises the SWIRLTranslator logic to the semantics of a given workflow language, e.g., CWL

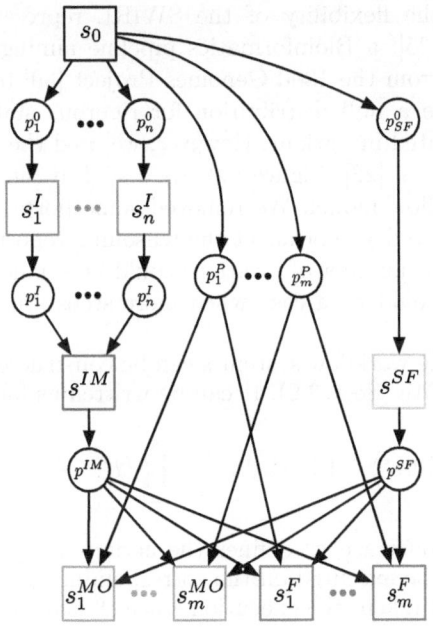

Fig. 5. Graphical representation of the 1000 Genomes workflow contains five classes of steps mapped to diverse locations: (i) **individuals** (blue), number of steps n, mapped to locations l^I_j, $j \in [1, a]$; (ii) **individuals_merge** (violet), a single step mapped to location l^{IM}; (iii) **sifting** (yellow), a single step mapped to location l^{IM}; (iv) **mutations_overlap** (red), number of steps m, mapped to locations l^{MO}_t, $t \in [1, b]$, and (v) **frequency** (green) number of steps m, mapped to locations l^F_k, $k \in [1, c]$. The initial step s_0, mapped to driver location l_d is a step that sends each input data element to the correct location for processing. The mapping between data elements and ports, where $i \in [1, n]$ and $h \in [1, m]$, is: $\mathcal{I} = \left\{ \begin{array}{l} (d^0_i, p^0_i), (d^P_h, p^P_h), (d^0_{SF}, p^0_{SF}), \\ (d^I_i, p^I_i), (d^{IM}, p^{IM}), (d^{SF}, p^{SF}) \end{array} \right\}$ (Color figure online)

[11], DAX (for Pegasus [12]), or the Galaxy Workflow Format (GWF) [40][3]. A `SWIRLOptimizer`[5] class implements the optimisation function $[\![\cdot]\!] : \mathcal{W}_W \to \mathcal{W}_0$, generating an optimised *.swirl file. Finally, an abstract `SWIRLCompiler` class produces an executable bundle from a *.swirl file and a declarative metadata file, which contains additional information not currently modelled in the SWIRL semantics, e.g., step commands, data types and location IP addresses. We have implemented a simple compiler class that generates a multithreaded Python program for each location, relying on TCP sockets for send/receive communications.

6   Evaluation

This section tests the flexibility of the SWIRL representation on the 1000 Genomes workflow [35], a Bioinformatics pipeline aiming at fetching, parsing and analysing data from the 1000 Genomes Project [39] to identify mutational overlaps and provide a null distribution for rigorous statistical evaluation of potential disease-related mutations. However, we used the 1000 Genomes applications written in C++ [22]. Figure 5 shows a slightly simplified version of the 1000 Genomes workflow model. We removed some ports to simplify the notation, but their absence does not affect the reasoning reported in the rest of this Section. Note that the number of locations could be smaller than the number of steps. Hence, there could be a case when more steps are mapped to the same location.

The corresponding workflow system W can be constructed using the encoding function $[\![\cdot]\!] : \mathcal{W}_I \to \mathcal{W}_W$ (Sect. 3.2). It can be written as follows:

$$\mathtt{W} = \prod_{i \in \{d, SF, IM\}} \left\langle l^i, \emptyset, e^i \right\rangle \mid \prod_{j=1}^{a} \left\langle l_j^I, \emptyset, e_j^I \right\rangle \mid \prod_{t=1}^{b} \left\langle l_t^{MO}, \emptyset, e_t^{MO} \right\rangle \mid \prod_{k=1}^{c} \left\langle l_k^F, \emptyset, e_k^F \right\rangle$$

where each execution trace e_*^* defines the actions (steps and data transfers) depicted in Fig. 5 to be executed on the corresponding location. For instance, if the driver location is taken, the execution trace e^d is defines as:

$$e^d = \prod_{i=1}^{n} \mathbf{send}(d_i^0 \rightarrowtail p_i^0, l^d, l_j^I) \mid \mathbf{send}(d_{SF}^0 \rightarrowtail p_{SF}^0, l^d, l^{SF}) \mid$$

$$\prod_{h=1}^{m} (\mathbf{send}(d_h^P \rightarrowtail p_h^P, l^d, l_t^{MO}) \mid \mathbf{send}(d_h^P \rightarrowtail p_h^P, l^d, l_k^F))$$

The full representation of W is discussed in [10]. The 1000 Genomes workflow modelled above can be reproduced using the SWIRL implementation (Sect. 5). To keep the experiment small and ease reproducibility, the ten homogeneous execution locations and a single chromosome, i.e., a single workflow instance, are considered. The necessary installing package and instructions on how to run the experiment can be find in [9].

---

[3] The implementation of the CWL and GWF translators and the `SWIRLOptimizer` are ongoing works.

7   Conclusion

This work introduced SWIRL, a "Scientific Workflow Intermediate Representation Language" based on send/receive communication primitives. An encoding function maps any workflow instance onto a distributed execution plan W, fostering interoperability and composability of different workflow models. A set of rewriting rules allows for automatic optimisation of data communications, improving performance with correctness and consistency guarantees. The optimised SWIRL representation can be compiled into one or more self-contained executable bundles addressing specific execution environments, ensuring reproducibility and embracing heterogeneity. SWIRL already proved itself to be flexible enough to model a real large-scale scientific workflow (even if still not supporting all features of modern WMSs).

The foundational contribution of SWIRL is to propose a novel direction to solve well-known problems in the field of scientific workflows. Indeed, SWIRL shifts the focus from high-level workflow languages, designed either for direct human interaction or to encode complex, product-specific features, to a low-level minimalistic representation of a workflow execution plan, which is far more manageable from both formalisation methods and compiler toolchains. In this context, we hope that SWIRL can pave the way to a novel, more formal approach to distributed workflow orchestration research.

The formal SWIRL representation gives the possibility to build the formally correct extensions, for instance, adding a type system where the multiparty sessions are enriched with security levels for messages (data in our case) [6] or deriving the causal-consistent reversible framework by applying the approach [19], that later can be used as a base to build fault-tolerance mechanism.

Acknowledgments. This work was supported by: the Spoke 1 "FutureHPC & Big-Data" of ICSC - Centro Nazionale di Ricerca in High-Performance Computing, Big Data and Quantum Computing, funded by European Union - NextGenerationEU; the EUPEX EU's Horizon 2020 JTI-EuroHPC research and innovation programme project under grant agreement No 101033975.

Data Availability Statement.. The artifact presented in this article is openly available at https://doi.org/10.5281/zenodo.12523000

References

1. van der Aalst, W.M.P., ter Hofstede, A.H.M.: YAWL: yet another workflow language. Inf. Syst. **30**(4), 245–275 (2005). https://doi.org/10.1016/j.is.2004.02.002
2. van der Aalst, W.M.P., ter Hofstede, A.H.M., Kiepuszewski, B., Barros, A.P.: Workflow patterns. Distributed Parallel Databases **14**(1), 5–51 (2003). https://doi.org/10.1023/A:1022883727209
3. Amstutz, P., Mikheev, M., Crusoe, M.R., Tijanic, N., Lampa, S., et al.: Existing workflow systems. common workflow language wiki (2022). https://s.apache.org/existing-workflow-systems. Accessed 05 Oct 2023

4. Ayachit, U., Bauer, A.C., Duque, E.P.N., Eisenhauer, G., Ferrier, N.J., et al.: Performance analysis, design considerations, and applications of extreme-scale in situ infrastructures. In: Proceedings of the International Conference for High Performance Computing, Networking, Storage and Analysis, SC 2016, Salt Lake City, UT, USA, November 13-18, 2016, pp. 921–932. IEEE Computer Society (2016). https://doi.org/10.1109/SC.2016.78

5. Bechhofer, S., Buchan, I.E., Roure, D.D., Missier, P., Ainsworth, J.D., et al.: Why linked data is not enough for scientists. Futur. Gener. Comput. Syst. 29(2), 599–611 (2013). https://doi.org/10.1016/j.future.2011.08.004

6. Capecchi, S., Castellani, I., Dezani-Ciancaglini, M.: Information flow safety in multiparty sessions. Math. Struct. Comput. Sci. 26(8), 1352–1394 (2016). https://doi.org/10.1017/S0960129514000619

7. Colonnelli, I., Aldinucci, M., Cantalupo, B., Padovani, L., Rabellino, S., et al.: Distributed workflows with Jupyter. Futur. Gener. Comput. Syst. 128, 282–298 (2022). https://doi.org/10.1016/j.future.2021.10.007

8. Colonnelli, I., Cantalupo, B., Merelli, I., Aldinucci, M.: StreamFlow: cross-breeding cloud with HPC. IEEE Trans. Emerg. Top. Comput. 9(4), 1723–1737 (2021). https://doi.org/10.1109/TETC.2020.3019202

9. Colonnelli, I., Medic, D., Mulone, A., Bono, V., Padovani, L., Aldinucci, M.: Artifact for paper "Introducing SWIRL: An Intermediate Representation Language for Scientific Workflows". https://doi.org/10.5281/zenodo.12523000 (2024). Accessed 26 June 2024

10. Colonnelli, I., Medić, D., Mulone, A., Bono, V., Padovani, L., Aldinucci, M.: Introducing swirl: an intermediate representation language for scientific workflows (2024). https://iris.unito.it/handle/2318/1989870

11. Crusoe, M.R., Abeln, S., Iosup, A., Amstutz, P., Chilton, J., et al.: Methods included: standardizing computational reuse and portability with the common workflow language. Commun. ACM (2022). https://doi.org/10.1145/3486897

12. Deelman, E., et al.: The evolution of the Pegasus workflow management software. Comput. Sci. Eng. 21(4), 22–36 (2019). https://doi.org/10.1109/MCSE.2019.2919690

13. Dong Yang, S.S.Z.: Approach for workflow modeling using π-calculus. J. Zhejiang Univ. Sci. 2003 4(6), 643–650 (2003). https://doi.org/10.1631/jzus.2003.0643

14. Fahringer, T., Prodan, R., Duan, R., Hofer, J., Nadeem, F., et al.: ASKALON: A development and grid computing environment for scientific workflows. In: Workflows for e-Science, Scientific Workflows for Grids, pp. 450–471. Springer (2007). https://doi.org/10.1007/978-1-84628-757-2_27

15. Hennessy, M.: A distributed Pi-calculus. Cambridge University Press (2007)

16. Jensen, K.: Coloured petri nets: A high level language for system design and analysis. In: Advances in Petri Nets 1990 [10th International Conference on Applications and Theory of Petri Nets, Bonn, Germany, June 1989, Proceedings], pp. 342–416 (1989). https://doi.org/10.1007/3-540-53863-1_31

17. Kahn, G.: The semantics of a simple language for parallel programming. In: Rosenfeld, J.L. (ed.) Information processing, pp. 471–475. North Holland, Amsterdam, Stockholm, Sweden (1974)

18. Kahn, G., MacQueen, D.B.: Coroutines and networks of parallel processes. In: Information Processing. In: Proceedings of the 7th IFIP Congress 1977, Toronto, Canada, August 8-12, 1977, pp. 993–998. North-Holland (1977)

19. Lanese, I., Medic, D.: A general approach to derive uncontrolled reversible semantics. In: 31st International Conference on Concurrency Theory, CONCUR 2020,

September 1-4, 2020, Vienna, Austria (Virtual Conference). LIPIcs, vol. 171, pp. 33:1–33:24. Schloss Dagstuhl - Leibniz-Zentrum für Informatik (2020). https://doi.org/10.4230/LIPICS.CONCUR.2020.33

20. Lee, E.A., Messerschmitt, D.G.: Synchronous data flow. Proc. IEEE **75**(9), 1235–1245 (1987). https://doi.org/10.1109/PROC.1987.13876

21. Ludäscher, B., et al.: Scientific workflow management and the Kepler system. Concurrency and Computation: Practice and Experience **18**(10), 1039–1065 (2006). https://doi.org/10.1002/cpe.994

22. Martinelli, A.R., Torquati, M., Aldinucci, M., Colonnelli, I., Cantalupo, B.: Capio: a middleware for transparent i/o streaming in data-intensive workflows. In: 2023 IEEE 30th International Conference on High Performance Computing, Data, and Analytics (HiPC). IEEE, Goa, India (2023). https://doi.org/10.1109/HiPC58850.2023.00031

23. Medic, D., Aldinucci, M.: Towards formal model for location aware workflows. In: 47th IEEE Annual Computers, Software, and Applications Conference, COMPSAC 2023, Torino, Italy, June 26-30, 2023, pp. 1864–1869. IEEE (2023). https://doi.org/10.1109/COMPSAC57700.2023.00289

24. Milner, R.: Communication and concurrency. PHI Series in computer science, Prentice Hall (1989)

25. Moggi, E.: Computational lambda-calculus and monads. In: Proceedings of the Fourth Annual Symposium on Logic in Computer Science (LICS 89), Pacific Grove, California, USA, 5–8 June, 1989, pp. 14–23. IEEE Computer Society (1989). https://doi.org/10.1109/LICS.1989.39155

26. Ouyang, C., Verbeek, E., van der Aalst, W.M.P., Breutel, S., Dumas, M., ter Hofstede, A.H.M.: Formal semantics and analysis of control flow in WS-BPEL. Sci. Comput. Program. **67**(2–3), 162–198 (2007). https://doi.org/10.1016/j.scico.2007.03.002

27. Parr, T.J., Quong, R.W.: ANTLR: a predicated- LL(k) parser generator. Softw. Pract. Exp. **25**(7), 789–810 (1995). https://doi.org/10.1002/spe.4380250705

28. Plankensteiner, K., Montagnat, J., Prodan, R.: IWIR: a language enabling portability across grid workflow systems. In: WORKS'11, Proceedings of the 6th Workshop on Workflows in Support of Large-Scale Science, pp. 97–106. ACM (2011). https://doi.org/10.1145/2110497.2110509

29. Puhlmann, F., Weske, M.: Using the *pi*-calculus for formalizing workflow patterns. In: Business Process Management, 3rd International Conference, BPM 2005, Nancy, France, September 5-8, 2005, Proceedings, vol. 3649, pp. 153–168 (2005). https://doi.org/10.1007/11538394_11

30. Reed, D.A., Gannon, D., Dongarra, J.J.: Reinventing high performance computing: Challenges and opportunities. CoRR abs/2203.02544 (2022). https://doi.org/10.48550/arXiv.2203.02544

31. Reisig, W., Rozenberg, G. (eds.): ACPN 1996. LNCS, vol. 1491. Springer, Heidelberg (1998). https://doi.org/10.1007/3-540-65306-6

32. Roy, R.B., Patel, T., Gadepally, V., Tiwari, D.: Mashup: making serverless computing useful for HPC workflows via hybrid execution. In: PPoPP '22: 27th ACM SIGPLAN Symposium on Principles and Practice of Parallel Programming, pp. 46–60. ACM (2022). https://doi.org/10.1145/3503221.3508407

33. Sangiorgi, D., Walker, D.: The Pi-Calculus - a theory of mobile processes. Cambridge University Press (2001)

34. Siddiqui, M., Villazón, A., Hofer, J., Fahringer, T.: GLARE: a grid activity registration, deployment and provisioning framework. In: Proceedings of the ACM/IEEE

SC2005 Conference on High Performance Networking and Computing, p. 52 (2005). https://doi.org/10.1109/SC.2005.30

35. da Silva, R.F., Filgueira, R., Deelman, E., Pairo-Castineira, E., Overton, I.M., Atkinson, M.P.: Using simple pid-inspired controllers for online resilient resource management of distributed scientific workflows. Futur. Gener. Comput. Syst. **95**, 615–628 (2019). https://doi.org/10.1016/j.future.2019.01.015

36. Taylor, I.J., Shields, M.S., Wang, I., Harrison, A.: The Triana workflow environment: architecture and applications. In: Workflows for e-Science, Scientific Workflows for Grids, pp. 320–339. Springer (2007). https://doi.org/10.1007/978-1-84628-757-2_20

37. Taylor, I.J., Shields, M.S., Wang, I., Rana, O.F.: Triana applications within grid computing and peer to peer environments. J. Grid Comput. **1**(2), 199–217 (2003). https://doi.org/10.1023/B:GRID.0000024074.63139.ce

38. Thain, D., Tannenbaum, T., Livny, M.: Distributed computing in practice: the Condor experience. Concurrency and Computation: Practice and Experience **17**(2–4), 323–356 (2005). https://doi.org/10.1002/cpe.938

39. The 1000 Genomes Project Consortium: A global reference for human genetic variation. Nature **526**(7571), 68–74 (2015). https://doi.org/10.1038/nature15393

40. The Galaxy Community: The Galaxy platform for accessible, reproducible and collaborative biomedical analyses: 2022 update. Nucleic Acids Res. **50**(W1), W345–W351 (2022). https://doi.org/10.1093/nar/gkac247

41. Turi, D., Missier, P., Goble, C.A., Roure, D.D., Oinn, T.: Taverna workflows: Syntax and semantics. In: Third International Conference on e-Science and Grid Computing, e-Science 2007, 10-13 December 2007, Bangalore, India, pp. 441–448. IEEE Computer Society (2007). https://doi.org/10.1109/E-SCIENCE.2007.71

42. Zaharia, M., Chowdhury, M., Das, T., Dave, A., Ma, J., et al.: Resilient distributed datasets: a fault-tolerant abstraction for in-memory cluster computing. In: Proceedings of the 9th USENIX Symposium on Networked Systems Design and Implementation, NSDI 2012, pp. 15–28. USENIX Association (2012)

Fast Attack Graph Defense Localization via Bisimulation

Nimrod Busany[1], Rafi Shalom[1,2], Dan Klein[1], and Shahar Maoz[2(✉)]

[1] Accenture Labs, Herzliya, Israel
{nimrod.busany,rafi.shalom,dan.klein}@accenture.com
[2] Tel Aviv University, Tel Aviv, Israel
maoz@cs.tau.ac.il

Abstract. System administrators, network engineers, and IT managers can learn much about the vulnerabilities of an organization's cyber system by constructing and analyzing analytical attack graphs (AAGs). An AAG consists of logical rule nodes, fact nodes, and derived fact nodes. It provides a graph-based representation that describes ways by which an attacker can achieve progress towards a desired goal, a.k.a. a crown jewel. Given an AAG, different types of analyses can be performed to identify attacks on a target goal, measure the vulnerability of the network, and gain insights on how to make it more secure. However, as the size of the AAGs representing real-world systems may be very large, existing analyses are slow or practically impossible. In this paper, we introduce and show how to compute an AAG's *defense core*: a locally minimal subset of the AAG's rules whose removal will prevent an attacker from reaching a crown jewel. Most importantly, in order to scale-up the performance of the detection of a defense core, we introduce a novel application of the well-known notion of bisimulation to AAGs. Our experiments show that the use of bisimulation results in significantly smaller graphs and in faster detection of defense cores, making them practical.

1 Introduction

System administrators, network engineers, and IT managers can learn much about the vulnerabilities of a cyber system by investigating and analysing analytical attack graphs (AAGs) [35]. An AAG provides a graph-based representation that describes ways by which an attacker can achieve progress towards a desired goal, a.k.a. a crown jewel, in a digital environment given an entry point, e.g., using social engineering. An AAG consists of logical rule nodes, fact nodes, and derived fact nodes. Given an AAG, different types of analyses can be performed to identify paths to reach a target goal, measure the vulnerability of the network, and gain insights on how to optimize the efforts to secure it. Several tools allow users to extract AAGs from their network, analyze the AAGs, and provide relevant reports for system administrators and IT managers, e.g., [11,22,30,34,44].

Yet, as the size of the AAGs representing real-world organizational networks may be very large, existing analyses are incomplete or very slow, to the extent

© The Author(s) 2025
A. Platzer et al. (Eds.): FM 2024, LNCS 14933, pp. 245–263, 2025.
https://doi.org/10.1007/978-3-031-71162-6_13

that make them impractical and hinder the wide-spread adoption of the technology. One such analysis is the detection of the AAG's rules that one should change in order to protect the crown jewels [11].

In this paper, we introduce and show how to compute an AAG's *defense core*: a locally minimal subset of the AAG's rules whose removal will prevent an attacker from reaching a crown jewel. Most importantly, in order to scale-up the performance of the detection of a defense core, we introduce a novel application of the well-known notion of bisimulation to AAGs.

Bisimulation is a binary relation between the nodes of two graphs that applies when the nodes have similar topological properties. Specifically, the result of computing a maximum bisimulation between a graph and itself, allows one to find a smaller representation of the graph that preserves important topological properties. Bisimulation is well-studied in theoretical computer science and has important applications in formal verification [3,7]. Multiple algorithms exist to compute a bisimulation relation [8,9,36]. To the best of our knowledge, we are the first to apply bisimulation to AAGs. The result of computing a maximum bisimulation of an AAG is a compact representation we call an AAG-fold.

Given an AAG, a defense core is a minimal subset of the AAG's rules whose removal will make the system safe, i.e., prevent an attacker from reaching a crown jewel. However, computing a defense core is computationally expensive and (as we show in our experiments) can become very slow or practically impossible on large AAGs. Thus, rather than computing it on the original AAG directly, we compute it on its AAG-fold. The correctness of our work relies on the fact that AAG-folds preserve attacks, which we formalize and prove in Sect. 5. The scalability of our work relies on (1) the ability to compute the AAG-fold efficiently and (2) that in practice, as we show in our experiments, the AAG-fold is typically much smaller than the original AAG.

Finally, note that defense minimality is important because system changes corresponding to logical rule change or removal may be expensive or technically difficult to apply. Typically, many different defense cores may exist and computing the minimal one is too expensive. As a pragmatic solution, we compute a locally minimal subset, one which may be larger than other possible cores but in itself, does not include any redundant rules. To compute it, we use a variant of the well-known minimization algorithm QuickXplain [18].

We implemented our ideas as an extension to AgiSC, developed by Accenture Labs and used by Accenture Security as part of its IT and consulting services to clients. The tool uses Datalog to represent facts and derivation rules about the system. Our experiments show that a direct approach to computing a defense core does not scale. They also show that the use of bisimulation results in significantly smaller graphs and in faster and scalable defense-core computations.

2   Illustrative Example

We use an example to semi-formally illustrate and motivate the use of AAGs and the problem of computing AAG defense cores. See Sect. 3.3 for a formal definition

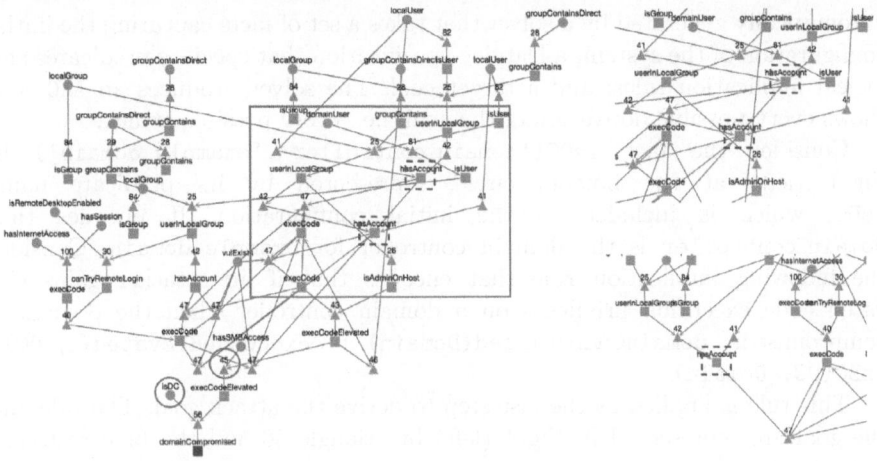

Fig. 1. An AAG (L), an excerpt of it (TR), and a folding of "hasAccount" (BR).

of an AAG based on Datalog specifications, and for an example of Datalog facts, rules, and a fact derivation. We consider a network with n domain users, each with a personal workstation and a server. All users belong to a special domain group with remote desktop protocol (RDP) access to all servers. All servers can use a network file sharing protocol (SMB) to share files and request services from the domain controller. One of the servers, namely *server1*, contains a local privilege escalation vulnerability, and the domain admin *admin@example.domain* is logged into the server.

Consider the following attack scenario. An attacker compromises a personal workstation using a social engineering technique that steals the user credentials. The attacker then connects to *server1* by logging into it via RDP with the stolen user credentials. The attacker escalates her privileges on *server1* using a local privilege escalation vulnerability. Then, the attacker uses a hacking tool to find the credentials of the logged domain admin. Finally, the attacker uses a Windows OS procedure with the stolen domain admin credentials to log on to domain controller via the SMB protocol with administrative privileges. From the domain controller the attacker effectively gains complete control over network, and so the domain is compromised.

Figure 1 shows an example of an AAG of a small network. Graph nodes shaped as circles, triangles, and rectangles represent facts, implication rules, and derived facts respectively. Rules are numbered and facts have only predicate names to avoid clutter. The blue dashed rectangles depict two nodes with the same label, namely hasAccount. The red rectangle highlights the excerpt that appears on the top right figure. The red circles highlight a fact and a rule that are relevant to the discussion below.

Figure 1 (left) shows a visualization of the AAG that captures the scenario described above when the network has one domain user, i.e., $n = 1$. This AAG is automatically generated by a solver that takes a set of facts capturing the initial configuration of the system; a Datalog specification that specifies predicates and logical implication rules; and a target goal. The solver produces an `AAG` that shows every possible derivation of the goal, i.e., every possible attack.

Consider the fact `isDC('domain_controller','example.domain')` in Fig. 1 (left) at the bottom circle, represented by its predicate name `isDC`, which is included in the initial configuration. It encodes that `domain_controller` is the domain controller for `example.domain`. Consider the following implication rule that encodes that if an attacker gains elevated code execution privileges on a domain controller, then the domain is compromised: `domainCompromised(Domain) :- execCodeElevated(_, DC)`, `isDC(DC, Domain)`

This rule is applied as the last step to derive the attack goal. The rule and the goal are represented in Fig. 1 (left) by triangle 56 and the blue rectangle respectively.

One common use of `AAG`s is to mitigate potential cyber threats. Different mitigation strategies exist, some focus on rectifying specific facts [1,10,15,41], while others on blocking potential lateral moves, represented by Datalog rules, by installing security controls [11,12]. In this work, we focus on the latter and search for a set of rules whose removal prevents all attacks towards the goal.

Consider the rule labeled 45 in our example. It encodes that if two hosts are connected via an SMB protocol and an attacker has elevated privileges on one, then the attacker can gain elevated privileges of the other. Removing this Datalog rule means that we prevent its applications, i.e., all rule nodes labeled 45 in the graph. As a result, the goal is no longer reachable, and thus the graph ceases to show possible attacks.

A major obstacle when searching for a defense core relates to the size of the `AAG`, which dramatically increases with the size of the network. Consider our example, scaling up the network by increasing the number of users $n = 1, 5, 50$ yields `AAG`s with 135, 2565, and $\approx 1.3M$ nodes and edges respectively. Thus, as the network grows, finding a defense becomes a computationally expensive and long if not an impractical task. We observe that while the number of possible attacks increases with the network size, many of the attacks share the same structure. Thus, we use bisimulation, and fold graph nodes with similar labels and graph topology. The motivation to use bisimulations relies on the fact that an `AAG` typically depicts many different attacks that differ only in agents and machines that share similar properties.

Figure 1 (bottom right) shows a visualization of a portion of the folded attack graph. Although the folded graph is smaller, the original graph and the folded one exhibit the same set of labeled paths. For example, the two nodes labelled `hasAccount` in the `AAG` that appear in Fig. 1 (top right), have same label and graph topology, e.g., the same outgoing edges to the equally labeled nodes. Both are folded into one node in the bottom right figure. The 135 nodes and edges of the `AAG`, are represented by 112 nodes and edges in the folded representation.

By folding the graphs of our example for $n = 1, 5, 50$, the original graphs of 135, 2565, and $\approx 1.3M$ nodes and edges are reduced to graphs with 112, 252, and 252 nodes and edges resp. Interestingly, the folded representation does not change when increasing n from 5 to 50, as in this case the newly added nodes are folded into existing folded nodes. The difference between a graph of size $1.3M$ and a graph of size 252 makes our work scalable. In this paper we leverage folding to achieve faster defense analysis time for large AAGs.

3 Preliminaries

3.1 Monotonic Criteria and Cores

Given a set T, and a monotonic criterion on subsets of T, a core is a local minimum that satisfies the criterion. Formally:

Definition 1 (Monotonic criterion). *A Boolean criterion over subsets of T is monotonic iff for any two sets A, B such that $A \subseteq B \subseteq T$, if A satisfies the criterion then B satisfies the criterion.*

Definition 2 (Core). *Given a set T and a monotonic criterion over its subsets, a set $C \subseteq T$ is a core of T iff C satisfies the criterion, and all its proper subsets $C' \subset C$ do not satisfy the criterion.*

Note that multiple cores may exist, not all of them minimal in size. There are several well-known domain-agnostic algorithms that compute a core, given a method that computes a monotonic criterion. We chose `QuickXplain` as our core computation algorithm. It has a worst-case complexity of $O(k + k log(\frac{|T|}{k}))$, where T is the minimized set, and k is the size of the largest core. See Sect. 7 for a discussion of core computation algorithms.

3.2 Bisimulation Relations

Bisimulation relations are equivalence relations on nodes that share topological properties. They can be extended by labels on nodes and edges that distinguish between different types of nodes and edges. Here we use strong bisimulation with labeled nodes [28]. This allows more succinct representations of graphs while keeping certain properties.

Two nodes v_1 and v_2 of a directed graph may be equivalent in terms of the paths starting from them. The equivalence of the paths means that for each path starting from v_1 there is a path starting from v_2 composed of equivalent nodes by the same relation, and vice versa. For example, every two leaves (i.e., nodes with no outgoing edges), may be considered equivalent.

Such an equivalence relation is called a bisimulation. The most fine grained bisimulation is the identity relation, and the most coarse is called a maximum bisimulation. We borrow the formal definitions and propositions from [8].

Definition 3 (Bisimulation relation). *Given graphs $G_1 = \langle V_1, E_1 \rangle$ and $G_2 = \langle V_2, E_2 \rangle$, a bisimulation between G_1 and G_2 is a relation $b \subseteq V_1 \times V_2$ such that*

1. $(u_1 \ b \ u_2 \land \langle u_1, v_1 \rangle \in E_1) \Rightarrow \exists v_2 \in V_2(v_1 \ b \ v_2 \land \langle u_2, v_2 \rangle \in E_2)$
2. $(u_1 \ b \ u_2 \land \langle u_2, v_2 \rangle \in E_2) \Rightarrow \exists v_1 \in V_1(v_1 \ b \ v_2 \land \langle u_1, v_1 \rangle \in E_1)$.

Definition 4 (Maximum bisimulation and minimum representation). *Given a graph $G = \langle V, E \rangle$, a maximum bisimulation $\equiv$ on G is the union of all bisimulation relations between G and itself. The minimum representation of G has nodes $V/\equiv$ and edges $\langle [u], [v] \rangle$, s.t. $\exists u_1 \in [u], v_1 \in [v](\langle u_1, v_1 \rangle \in E)$.*

Proposition 1 (Uniqueness and bisim. of minimum representations). *A maximum bisimulation $\equiv$ on G always exists. It is a unique equivalence relation over the nodes of G. A graph G and its minimum representation are bisimilar, i.e., there is a bisimulation relation between them.*

The definition of a bisimulation relation may be refined to consider labels on nodes. In this case, for example, nodes without outgoing edges are equivalent iff they have the same label.

Definition 5 (Labeled graph bisimulation). *Let L be a finite set of labels. Given a labeled graph $G = \langle V, E, l \rangle$ with $l : V \to L$, a labeled bisimulation on G is a bisimulation relation $b \subseteq V \times V$ on G such that $u \ b \ v$ implies $l(u) = l(v)$.*

Definition 4 and Proposition 1 apply as they are to maximum labeled bisimulations and to minimum representations of labeled graphs respectively.

Several algorithms for computing a maximum bisimulation exist. **PT** is an efficient algorithm suggested by Paige and Tarjan [36], with a complexity of $O(|E|log|V|)$ for a graph $G(V, E)$. We discuss other algorithms in Sect. 7. We used *BisPy* [2], an open-source project that includes an efficient implementation of PT for maximum bisimulation computation.

3.3   Analytical Attack Graphs

An analytical attack graph (**AAG**) provides a graph-based representation that describes ways by which an attacker can achieve progress towards a specified goal. An influential work by Ou et al. [34] presented MulVal, a framework for generating **AAG**s based on facts and vulnerabilities that are collected from the organizational network. Facts describe logical and physical entities of the network. They are formally modeled by Datalog predicates. Each predicate is an n-ary relation between such entities. The Datalog statement $P(arg_1, arg_2, \ldots)$. states that the literals $arg_1, arg_2, \ldots$ satisfy the predicate P. Literals are constant strings of characters.

For example, Listing 1 contains two facts. The predicate names of the facts are `entryPoint` and `hasSession`.

Derivation rules allow the deduction of new facts from given facts. Essentially, derivation rules derive a fact when a conjunction of facts is detected. The derivation may be a general one, as some of the arguments may be represented by variables. Thus, a single rule is usually applied to many different sets of facts.

The syntax of a Datalog rule is

$$P(a_1, a_2, \ldots) : -P_1(a_{11}, \ldots), P_2(a_{21}, \ldots), \ldots, P_n(a_{n1}, \ldots)$$

where P is the derived predicate name. If predicates $P_1, P_2, \ldots P_n$ hold, it is possible that several instances of P with some literals are derived, depending on the parameters of $P_1, P_2, \ldots P_n$. The parameters of predicates in rules are variables (that begin with a capital letter or underscore for variables not essential for the derivation) and literals.

Listing 1. Two Facts

```
1 entryPoint('SERVER_USER_1_PC.DOM1').
2 hasSession('SERVER_USER_1_PC.DOM1', 'SERVER_USER_1@DOM1').
```

Listing 2. A Derivation Rule

```
1 interaction_rule(
2     (execCode(User, Host) :-
3         hasSession(Host, User),
4         entryPoint(Host)
5     ),
6     rule_desc('Starting position of an attacker', 1.0)).
```

Listing 3. A Derived Fact

```
1 execCode('SERVER_USER_1@DOM1', 'SERVER_USER_1_PC.DOM1')
```

For example, Listing 2 shows a rule from one of our Datalog files stating that if the literal of **entryPoint** and the first literal of **hasSession** are the same, the predicate **execCode** with the same parameters as **hasSession** in reverse order is derivable. In our case, Listing 1 and Listing 2 together indicate the derived fact that appears in Listing 3. Note that Listing 1 and Listing 2 show real Datalog code while Listing 3 is a textual representation of the derived fact.

Given a Datalog representation of the network, one can use a reasoning engine, e.g., XSB [37], to check whether there exists an attack from the input facts to the target goal. Given primitive facts and rules, which describe the system, the reasoning engine deduces derived facts. Derived facts have the same syntax as primitive facts, i.e., predicates over literals. Given a goal, the reasoning provides two outputs, namely, deciding whether the goal is achievable, and if so, producing information about all possible attacks in the form of an AAG.

An AAG exists iff the goal is achievable. We borrow the definition of an AAG and its semantics from [10]

Definition 6 (Analytical attack graph (AAG)). *An analytical attack graph is a structure $A = \langle N_r, N_f, N_d, E, L, g \rangle$ where N_r, N_f, N_d are mutually exclusive sets of nodes denoting derivation rules, facts, and derived facts respectively. E is a set of edges that connects facts, either primitive or derived, to derivation rules, and derivation rules to derived facts. Formally, $E \subseteq ((N_f \cup N_d) \times N_r) \cup (N_r \times N_d)$. L is a mapping from a node to its label, i.e., fact nodes $N_f \cup N_d$, and rule nodes N_r are mapped to the facts and rules they represent respectively. Finally, $g \in N_d$ is the target node. We denote by $V = N_r \cup N_f \cup N_d$ the set of all the nodes.*

For example, an AAG that represents the facts and rules in Listings 1–3, has nodes v_1, v_2, v_3, v_4 and edges $(v_1, v_3), (v_2, v_3), (v_3, v_4)$. The two facts in Listing 1 are the labels $L(v_1), L(v_2)$ of two nodes, $v_1, v_2 \in N_f$. Listing 2 lines 2-4 is the label $L(v_3)$ of a rule node $v_3 \in N_r$. Listing 3 is the label $L(v_4)$ of a derived node $v_4 \in N_d$. The AAG will include three edges. $(v_1, v_3), (v_2, v_3) \in N_f \times N_r$ and $(v_3, v_4) \in N_r \times N_d$.

We defined an AAG to have a single goal. It is always possible to reduce an AAG that represents a set of goals, where either all or at least one of them must be achieved, to the AAG as defined in Definition 6, with additional rules.

An AAG is a special case of an And/Or graph [27], where each rule node instantiates only one (derived) fact. The semantics of an AAG is that derived facts are supported by a rule and facts that imply the derived fact in accordance with the rule. Formally:

Definition 7 (AAG semantics). *For every $v_r \in N_r$ and $v_d \in N_d$ s.t. $\langle v_r, v_d \rangle \in E$, it holds that $\wedge_{\langle v, v_r \rangle \in E} L(v) \to L(v_d)$ is an instance of the rule $L(v_r)$.*

An AAG indicates that the goal can be achieved. Since the reasoning engine deduces all possible derivable facts, an AAG represents all possible attacks, possibly including circular ones, which occur when two facts contribute to the deduction of each other. An attack or attack plan is intuitively a single attack scenario. Explicitly, it is a subgraphs of the AAG that contains the goal node, each derived fact node has an incoming degree 1, and each rule node is satisfied by its preconditions. For a formal definition of attack plans see [10].

4   The Defense Problem and a Naive Defense Algorithm

We now describe the defense problem, i.e., finding a subset of the rules whose removal prevents all possible attacks on the goal. We call the remaining set of rules safe, and define safe sets first. We then show a naive defense algorithm, i.e., one that uses an AAG directly.

Definition 8 (Safe sets of rules). *Given an AAG $A = \langle N_r, N_f, N_d, E, L, g \rangle$, we denote its set of rules by $R = \{r \in L(v_r) | v_r \in N_r\}$. A subset $R' \subseteq R$ is **safe** if any subgraph of A with a set of rules restricted to R' and the same goal g is not an AAG. A subset $R' \subseteq R$ is **maximally safe** if it is safe and every R'' such that $R' \subset R'' \subseteq R$ is not safe.*

Note that there may exist more than one maximally safe set of rules.
A defense-set is the complement of a safe set of rules. Formally,

Definition 9 (Defense-sets). *Given the notation of Definition 8, a subset $R' \subseteq R$ is a **defense-set** iff $R \setminus R'$ is safe.*

We define a defense problem: Given an AAG as input, output a defense-set.
The duality of locally maximal sets satisfying a property, and their complements being locally minimal sets the removal of which satisfies the property is trivial and well-known [21].

The direct way to compute a defense-set is to apply a domain-agnostic core computation algorithm to a set of rules of the AAG. This requires a method that computes the defense-set criterion, i.e., given a set of rules, decide if it a defense-set. We implemented a naive defense-set `check` algorithm. We call the application of `QuickXplain` to a set of rules with `check` as the monotonic criterion computation `AAG-Defense`. Since the criterion is evidently monotonic, the correctness of the algorithm follows. Moreover, since `QuickXplain` ensures a core the complement of the obtained defense-set is maximally safe.

5   Applying Bisimulation to Attack Graphs, and a Fast Defense Algorithm

An AAG may be folded using a bisimulation, which generates a succinct representation of it. The succinct representation may be helpful for various purposes, such as comprehension and computational efficiency of analyses.

We now present our contribution. In Sect. 5.1 we introduce the notion and the semantics of an AAG-fold which represents an AAG that has been folded using a bisimulation. We then prove that the AAG-fold semantics must hold. In Sect. 5.2 we introduce a faster defense algorithm, namely, AF-Defense.

5.1   Folding an AAG

To fold an AAG, we define a labeled bisimulation based on the predicate names, and ignore the arguments of primitive and derived facts. We first define an abstraction function for predicates and rules.

Definition 10 (Abstraction function). *The function abs ignores arguments in fact and rule labels. For a fact label* $l_1 :=$ *"$P(a_1, a_2, \ldots)$" let* $abs(l_1) =$ *"P". For rule label* $l_2 :=$ *"$P(a_1, a_2, \ldots) : -P_1(a_{11}, \ldots), P_2(a_{21}, \ldots)), \ldots, P_n(a_{n1}, \ldots))$" we define* $abs(l_2) =$ *"$P : -P_1, P_2, \ldots, P_n$".*

For example, the abstractions of the two facts in Listing 1 are the names of the predicates, namely `entryPoint` and `hasSession`. The abstraction of the rule in Listing 2 lines 2–4 is `execCode :- hasSession, entryPoint`.

Next, we define an AAG-fold to be the minimum representation of an AAG. We collapse the facts but not the rules according to a maximum labeled bisimulation. That is, apart from considering the topology of the graph, nodes can become equivalent only if they keep the exact rule for rule nodes, and can become equivalent if they have the same predicate name (regardless of the arguments) for fact nodes. Formally:

Definition 11 (AAG-fold). *Let* $A = \langle N_r, N_f, N_d, E, L, g \rangle$ *be an AAG. We define a label function* l *over nodes* $N_r \cup N_f \cup N_d$ *as follows.* $\forall v \in N_r\ l(v) = L(v)$, *and* $\forall v \in N_f \cup N_d\ l(v) = abs(L(v))$. *We apply the unique maximum labeled bisimulation relation* $\equiv$ *to obtain an AAG-fold* $AF = \langle N_r/ \equiv, N_f/ \equiv, N_d/ \equiv, E_\equiv, L_\equiv, [g] \rangle$ *where* $E_\equiv$ *is defined in accordance with the edges of the minimum representation in Definition 4, and* $L_\equiv$ *abstracts both rule nodes and fact nodes, namely,* $\forall v \in N_r \cup N_f \cup N_d\ L_\equiv([v]) = abs(L(v))$.

The maximum labeled bisimulation relation ≡ exists and is unique according to Proposition 1. Note that this equivalence relation ranges over the whole set of nodes V. It is possible that two nodes, one from N_f and one from N_d, are equivalent. The quotient set $N_d/ \equiv$ uses the restriction of the relation to the set N_d (and similarly for N_f). Note that the label function $L_\equiv$ is well defined. First, rule nodes use the syntax of the original rule as their label for the purpose of bisimulation. This means that only rules with the exact syntax may become equivalent. Thus, they must have the same abstraction. Second, fact nodes that become equivalent must have the same predicate name, which is also their abstraction. Thus the definition of $L_\equiv$ for equivalent fact nodes must agree.

The semantics of the **AAG-fold** is slightly different than that of an **AAG**:

Definition 12 (AAG-fold semantics). *Let $AF = \langle N_r, N_f, N_d, E, L, g \rangle$ be an* **AAG-fold.** *For every $v_r \in N_r$ and $v_d \in N_d$ s.t. $\langle v_r, v_d \rangle \in E$, then $\wedge_{\langle v, v_r \rangle \in E} L(v)$ implies $L(v_d)$ according to rule $L(v_r)$.*

Note that the implication involves only predicate names rather than predicates with literals, which is more relaxed. For example, $P_1 \wedge P_1 \wedge P_2$ and $P_1 \wedge P_2 \wedge P_2$ are equivalent, although they are not the same formula. The difference is that the number of instances of the same predicate name may vary in the **AAG-fold**, and we only require that one of each predicate name of the rule appears as a support. We discuss the effect of this in detail below.

We now prove our main claim, namely, that the **AAG-fold** of any **AAG** must adhere to **AAG-fold** semantics.

Theorem 1 (An AAG-fold adheres to AAG-fold semantics). *Given an* **AAG** *$A = \langle N_r, N_f, N_d, E, L, g \rangle$, AF as defined in Definition 11 has* **AAG-fold** *semantics as defined in Definition 12.*

Proof. Let $v_r' \in N_r/ \equiv$ and $v_d' \in N_d/ \equiv$ be nodes satisfying $\langle v_r', v_d' \rangle \in E_\equiv$. By Definition 4 there are $v_r \in v_r'$ and $v_d \in v_d'$ s.t. $\langle v_r, v_d \rangle \in E$. By Definition 5, all elements of v_r' have the same bisimulation label $r = l(v_r)$. Bisimulation labels of rule nodes are not abstracted (Definition 11), thus $r = L(v_r)$ is an **AAG** rule. According to **AAG** semantics, $\wedge_{\langle v, v_r \rangle \in E} L(v) \rightarrow L(v_d)$ is an instance of r (see Definition 7). By Proposition 1 A and AF are bisimilar, and according to Definition 3, for each v s.t. $\langle v, v_r \rangle \in E$ there is a (not necessarily unique) v' s.t. $\langle v', v_r' \rangle \in E_\equiv$, and s.t. v and v' satisfy the bisimilarity between A and AF. By Definition 11, the $L_\equiv(v')$ are abstractions of the facts of their corresponding $L(v)$, which, in turn, satisfy r. Thus, $\wedge_{\langle v', v_r' \rangle \in E_\equiv} L_\equiv(v')$ implies $L_\equiv(v_d')$ according to the abstracted rule $L_\equiv(v_r')$. This satisfies the semantics of $AAG_\equiv$ according to Definition 12.

The rationale of Theorem 1 implies that every attack plan of the **AAG** has a corresponding attack scenario in the **AAG-fold**, obtained by translating nodes and edges of the attack plan to their counterparts in the **AAG-fold**. Essentially this means that an **AAG-fold** maintains all possible attacks on the goal node.

The preconditions supporting a derived fact in the **AAG** match the list of predicates appearing in the rule, including multiple appearances of the same predicate. In the `AAG-fold`, however, we only need one node of each predicate name (in the rule's preconditions) to deduce the node. This may have the following consequences. First, a rule node may have more incoming edges than the preconditions in its declaration. This can occur if not all incoming predicate nodes that share a label were folded, due to topological differences. Second, if an `AAG` rule for deriving predicate P_1 requires two different instances of P_2 (i.e., $P_1(\ldots) : -P_2(\ldots), P_2(\ldots), \ldots$), two different instances of P_2 must appear in the `AAG`. However, as nodes may get folded in the `AAG-fold`, the two incoming instances may merge in the `AAG-fold`. This still complies with the semantics of the folded rule. The idempotency of the conjunction ensures that one instance of P_2 is enough for both instances of P_2 as they are indistinguishable without their arguments.

Note that the converse of Theorem 1 does not hold. For example, if we need predicates P_1 and P_2 in order to derive P, the `AAG-fold` may contain many instances of P_1 and P_2 nodes leading to the rule node. However, not all pairs of P_1 and P_2 represent `AAG` nodes that match the rule, so not any such pair necessarily supports the derived node. Thus, an `AAG-fold` which depicts an attack on the goal node does not necessarily indicate that the `AAG` it was produced from has a corresponding attack plan.

5.2   The `AF-Defense` Algorithm

Algorithm `AF-Defense` improves the naive approach of `AAG-Defense`. It first computes an `AAG-fold` of the `AAG` by applying the PT Algorithm (see Sect. 3.2 and Definition 11). Next, it applies `QuickXplain` on the `AAG-fold` to find a core, which it returns as a defense-set. The same `check` operation (described in the appendix available in the extended version of the paper), which is required for the `QuickXplain` algorithm, is applied to the `AAG-fold`, and uses the semantics of the `AAG-fold` instead of the semantics of `AAG`s.

From Theorem 1 follows the correctness of `AF-Defense`.

Theorem 2 (Correctness of `AAG-Defense`). *Algorithm `AF-Defense` computes a defense-set.*

Proof. Assume by contradiction that the computed set of rules R' is not a defense-set, thus the complementary set w.r.t. all the rules R is an unsafe set of rules $R \setminus R'$. According to Definition 8 there is a subgraph of the `AAG` which is an `AAG` with rules $R \setminus R'$ and the same goal node. According to Theorem 1 its induced `AAG-fold` maintains `AAG-fold` semantics, which implies that the goal of the `AAG-fold` is achievable with rules $R \setminus R'$ in the `AAG-fold`.

However, The criterion `check` directly checks that the goal of the `AAG-fold` is not achievable for a removed set of rules. The computed criterion is monotonic also for `AAG-fold`s similar to the check for `AAG`s. By correctness of `QuickXplain` the produced set R' is a core, which satisfies the checked criterion (Definition 2). Thus R' is a set of rules, the removal of which makes the goal of the `AAG-fold` unachievable, a contradiction. Thus, the computed set of rules R' is a defense-set.

In Sect. 5.1 we explained why the converse of Theorem 1 does not hold. Thus, in theory, `AAG-Defense` has the advantage of ensuring that the complement of the defense-set is a maximally safe set of rules, while `AF-Defense` does not ensure maximality. That said, in the appendix in the extended version of the paper we show that in practice, the actual difference in defense-set size is small, if any.

6   Evaluation

We provide an overview of our evaluation. Details appear in the appendix available in the extended version of the paper.

We implemented `AAG` folding and defense-set algorithms in Python. We used *BisPy* [2], an open-source project that includes an efficient implementation of PT for computing bisimulation over directed graphs. For minimization we implemented a variant of `QuickXplain` [18]. The end-to-end implementation allows the user to choose an `AAG`, a set of rules that can be removed (all the rules by default), and a flag to control whether the defense-set should be done directly or using the `AAG-fold`. The tool runs our algorithm and outputs a defense-set, i.e., a set of rules to be removed such that the remaining rules are safe (do not allow an attack).

In our experiments, we compared the performance of algorithms `AAG-Defense` and `AF-Defense`. Note that we were unable to compare to previous works directly as none of them computed defense-sets.

We considered the following research questions: RQA Can we compute an `AAG-fold` efficiently and how do the sizes of the original and folded graphs compare? RQB How do defense-set computation times compare between the original and the folded graphs? RQC How do sizes of defense-sets of `AAG-Defense` and `AF-Defense` compare?

We ran experiments over several datasets that include real-world examples of AAGs that were generated to detect potential vulnerabilities in different systems of two large manufacturing facilities in the automotive and retail industry, versions of an IT system created for the purpose of assessing segments of a managed organization network, examples taken from Hadar et al. [12], as well as synthetic examples that simulates a network with the vulnerability described in Sect. 2.

Tables and graphs summarizing the characteristics of these datasets and the experiment results appear in the extended version of the paper. We summarize the answers to the research questions as follows:

RQA: Computing the `AAG-fold` for graphs with thousands of nodes and edges requires a few milliseconds. For AAGs with millions of nodes and edges, computing the `AAG-fold` does not come for free. Yet, it is very effective in producing much smaller representations.

RQB: We can efficiently compute defense-sets for AAGs with thousands of nodes and edges. However, the running time increases considerably with the size of the AAG. For larger AAGs, `AAG-Defense` does not scale well, while `AF-Defense` never exceeds a few milliseconds.

RQC: `AF-Defense` is effective and produces similar or only slightly larger defense-sets compared to those produced by `AAG-Defense`. It achieved minimal cores in a large majority of experiments.

7 Related Work

Analytical Attack Graphs Analysis. Inference of analytical attack graphs (AAGs) [34,38] over real-world systems often produces large models that are hard to comprehend and analyze using existing techniques [13,16,20,23,26,33,47].

Yousefi et al. [47] present an algorithm that refines the attack graph and generates a simplified transition graph. The algorithm produced a smaller graph but provides no guarantees about soundness. Noel and Jajodia [31] describe a framework for managing attack graph complexity through interactive visualization, which includes hierarchical aggregation of graph elements. The aggregation collapses non-overlapping subgraphs to single vertices but is applied to a different model of attack graph and therefore cannot be directly compared to our work. Homer et al. [14] present two simplifying methods for AAGs. The first is a data filtering approach, which identifies portions of an attack graph that do not help users understand the security problems and trims them. The second is an abstraction approach, which groups similar attack steps as virtual nodes in a model of the network topology. These two methods can be viewed as complementary to our approach. Others [17,32] have suggested methods to simplify the attack graph by grouping similar hosts together and representing grouped hosts by single nodes, and by using hierarchical displays. These approaches still result in complex attack graphs that are difficult for system administrators to relate to the underlying analysed network [32]. Williams et al. [46] present an interactive tool with a cascade display that produces a compact representation, highlights critical attack steps that lead into new network areas, and displays both attack graph and reachability information over a multiple-prerequisite (MP) graph. They use treemaps to present hosts in subnets in close proximity. Hosts in each treemap are automatically grouped based on level of compromise, how the hosts are treated by firewalls, trust relationships the hosts participate in, and prerequisites required to compromise hosts. These groupings provide visual indications of the network security and greatly simplify the display. Recently, Sabur et al. [40] suggested a divide-and-conquer approach to divide a large attack graph into smaller segments based on similarity between services. A distributed firewall prevent the attacker from compromising separated segments. They optimize their approach by removing cycles from the graph, and computing the optimal number of segments, based on the implementation cost of the segmentation. Mjihil et al. [29] present the use of well-known efficient decomposition algorithms of graphs into strongly connected components, which in turn allows the use of parallel computation for faster analysis of the subgraphs. They acknowledge that their approach works better on sparse graphs.

In contrast to the aforementioned works, our work is unique in that it uses the well-known bisimulation relation, a topology preserving equivalence relation for graph abstraction. This allows us to create a sound abstraction of the attack graph that respects its topology and labeling; it eliminates redundancies while preserving all possible attacks. As opposed to works that attempt to decompose the attack graph, our approach is resilient to topological aspects that impede decomposition. To the best of our knowledge, no earlier work has made such guarantees. As we show, it can be computed efficiently and results in smaller graphs that allow faster analyses. Finally, several ways to speed up attack graph computation based on parallel and/or distributed computing have been proposed [5,19]. These methods do not reduce the size of the attack graph.

Symbolic Attack Detection. Several authors employed symbolic approaches such as model checking to detect attacks and compute attack graphs, e.g., [39]. More recently [43] modeled AWS IAM attacks using Boolean formulas. Solving those with SAT solvers allows proving no attacks are possible, and detecting attacks with the possibility of grouping similar attacks. Contrary to this approach, we exploit a representation of all possible attacks in a structure that tries to avoid repetitions of similar attacks. A recent work [6] presented a formal verification approach to handle attack graphs. The work models attack graphs as Kripke structures and proposes to use model-checking in order to verify whether an attacker can gain access to certain resources.

Bisimulation. Bisimulation is well-studied in theoretical computer science and has important applications in formal verification [3]. Multiple algorithms exist to compute a bisimulation relation [8,9,36]. To the best of our knowledge, we are the first to apply bisimulation to AAGs. For the bisimulation computation required to obtain an AAG-fold, we use the PT algorithm [36], which has an $O(|E|log|V|)$ complexity for a graph $G(V, E)$. Dovier et al. [8], propose algorithms for acyclic graphs, and labled graphs. They suggest some further improvements such as computing sets of ranks instead of ranks, which is finer. They also suggest symbolic computation using BDDs.

Cores. Core computations are applied in many domains, usually for fault-localization. For example, cores of unsatisfiable CNF formulas, a.k.a. MUS, minimal unsatisfiable subsets of clauses [21], are computed for Alloy [45] and for component and connector specifications [24]. Many different core computation algorithms exist, either single core domain-agnostic, e.g., DDMin [48] and QuickXplain [18], domain-specific [25] and all cores computations [4,21,25]. Cores have also been applied to the removal of redundant elements in valid specifications [42]. We chose QuickXplain for core computations thanks to its complexity and prioritization parameter (see below). We are the first to apply cores to attack graph defense.

Reducing Risk Based on Analytical Attack Graphs. Some works suggested means to select nodes whose removal from the AAG will reduce the risk of attack, based on different criteria such as centrality measures [1,10,15,41]. Hadar et al. [11,12] enumerate risk-reducing security requirements and suggest means to prioritize security controls to reduce risk. They do not aim to prevent attacks but focus on prioritizing between given security controls.

In contrast, given an `AAG`, we automatically compute a safe subset of the `AAG`'s rules for which no attack is possible. In the future, it may be interesting to consider prioritization in our work too. The `QuickXplain` algorithm allows prioritization as a parameter. See the last paragraph in Sect. 8.

8 Conclusion and Future Work

We presented fast means to compute an attack graph defense core, identifying a minimal set of changes to a cyber system that will prevent an attacker from reaching a crown jewel. To scale-up attack graph defense performance, we introduced a novel application of the well-known notion of bisimulation to attack graphs and showed how to compute a defense-set over the resulting graphs. Our experiments showed that the use of bisimulation results in significantly smaller graphs and in defense-set computations that are significantly faster than a direct solution, making them practical.

We consider the following future work. First, it is possible to improve the computation of the bisimulation with ideas from [8]. One example is the replacement of the notion of a rank of a node as a number, by the set of ranks the node points to. This may improve the running times of the computation. Another direction is the use of symbolic representations of sets of nodes, for example using BDDs. Symbolic computation of bisimulations were considered, e.g., in [9].

Second, we consider additional applications for `AAG-fold`, beyond defense-set computations. For example, faster detection of possible attacks, faster risk assessments of the vulnerability of the network, and possibly more user-friendly and scalable UIs for viewing and exploring `AAG`s.

Third, it may be possible to accelerate checks of the safety of subsets of rules. A simple case is when the goal node is disconnected from the primitive facts, which can be detected easily by finding connected components of an `AAG` limited to a set of rules. This is equivalently useful for an `AAG-fold`. Another possible approach is to find all locally minimal subsets of rules required for the validation of each derived node, using dynamic programming. By doing this once over an `AAG` or an `AAG-fold`, the validation detection for a given set of rules may become very efficient.

Finally, `QuickXplain` allows different ways to order the importance of rules. In our present work we ranked rules by their frequency in the graph. Other ways to rank rules exist, e.g., by employing centrality measures [11]. Moreover, not all rules are equally difficult or expensive to remove, and so users may be interested in using domain-knowledge for rule ranking. Different rule rankings will induce different notions of defense-set minimality, e.g., rather than computing a defense-set that includes a minimal number of rules, compute one whose set of rules is the least expensive to change. That is, investigating the *quality* of defense-sets while considering different notions of quality. We leave all these for future work.

Data Availability Statement. The experimental data and scripts, as well as a version of this paper that includes appendices, are available in Zenodo with the identifier: https://doi.org/10.5281/zenodo.12515137.

References

1. Albanese, M., Jajodia, S., Noel, S.: Time-efficient and cost-effective network hardening using attack graphs. In: Swarz, R.S., Koopman, P., Cukier, M. (eds.) IEEE/IFIP International Conference on Dependable Systems and Networks, DSN 2012, Boston, MA, USA, June 25–28, 2012, pp. 1–12. IEEE Computer Society (2012). https://doi.org/10.1109/DSN.2012.6263942
2. Andreuzzi, F.: BisPy: Bisimulation in Python (2021). https://doi.org/10.21105/joss.03519
3. Baier, C., Katoen, J.: Principles of model checking. MIT Press (2008)
4. Bendík, J., Černá, I.: MUST: minimal unsatisfiable subsets enumeration tool. In: TACAS 2020. LNCS, vol. 12078, pp. 135–152. Springer, Cham (2020). https://doi.org/10.1007/978-3-030-45190-5_8
5. Cao, N., Lv, K., Hu, C.: An attack graph generation method based on parallel computing. In: Liu, F., Xu, S., Yung, M. (eds.) SciSec 2018. LNCS, vol. 11287, pp. 34–48. Springer, Cham (2018). https://doi.org/10.1007/978-3-030-03026-1_3
6. Catta, D., Leneutre, J., Mijatovic, A., Ulin, J., Malvone, V.: A formal verification approach to handle attack graphs. In: Rocha, A.P., Steels, L., van den Herik, H.J. (eds.) Proceedings of the 16th International Conference on Agents and Artificial Intelligence, ICAART 2024, vol. 3, Rome, Italy, February 24-26, 2024, pp. 125–132. SCITEPRESS (2024). https://doi.org/10.5220/0012310000003636
7. Clarke, E.M., Grumberg, O., Peled, D.A.: Model checking. MIT Press (2001)
8. Dovier, A., Piazza, C., Policriti, A.: An efficient algorithm for computing bisimulation equivalence. Theor. Comput. Sci. **311**(1–3), 221–256 (2004). https://doi.org/10.1016/S0304-3975(03)00361-X
9. Fisler, K., Vardi, M.Y.: Bisimulation and model checking. In: Pierre, L., Kropf, T. (eds.) CHARME 1999. LNCS, vol. 1703, pp. 338–342. Springer, Heidelberg (1999). https://doi.org/10.1007/3-540-48153-2_29
10. Gonda, T., Pascal, T., Puzis, R., Shani, G., Shapira, B.: Analysis of attack graph representations for ranking vulnerability fixes. In: Lee, D.D., Steen, A., Walsh, T. (eds.) GCAI-2018, 4th Global Conference on Artificial Intelligence, Luxembourg, September 18-21, 2018. EPiC Series in Computing, vol. 55, pp. 215–228. EasyChair (2018). https://doi.org/10.29007/2c1q
11. Hadar, E., Hassanzadeh, A.: Big data analytics on cyber attack graphs for prioritizing agile security requirements. In: Damian, D.E., Perini, A., Lee, S. (eds.) 27th IEEE International Requirements Engineering Conference, RE 2019, Jeju Island, Korea (South), September 23-27, 2019, pp. 330–339. IEEE (2019). https://doi.org/10.1109/RE.2019.00042
12. Hadar, E., Kravchenko, D., Basovskiy, A.: Cyber digital twin simulator for automatic gathering and prioritization of security controls' requirements. In: Breaux, T.D., Zisman, A., Fricker, S., Glinz, M. (eds.) 28th IEEE International Requirements Engineering Conference, RE 2020, Zurich, Switzerland, August 31 - September 4, 2020, pp. 250–259. IEEE (2020). https://doi.org/10.1109/RE48521.2020.00035
13. Höfner, P., Möller, B.: Dijkstra, Floyd and Warshall meet Kleene. Formal Aspects Comput. **24**(4–6), 459–476 (2012). https://doi.org/10.1007/s00165-012-0245-4
14. Homer, J., Varikuti, A., Ou, X., McQueen, M.A.: Improving attack graph visualization through data reduction and attack grouping. In: Goodall, J.R., Conti, G., Ma, K.-L. (eds.) VizSec 2008. LNCS, vol. 5210, pp. 68–79. Springer, Heidelberg (2008). https://doi.org/10.1007/978-3-540-85933-8_7

15. Hong, J.B., Kim, D.S.: Scalable security analysis in hierarchical attack representation model using centrality measures. In: 43rd Annual IEEE/IFIP Conference on Dependable Systems and Networks Workshop, DSN Workshops 2013, Budapest, Hungary, June 24-27, 2013, pp. 1–8. IEEE Computer Society (2013). https://doi.org/10.1109/DSNW.2013.6615507

16. Idika, N.C., Bhargava, B.K.: Extending attack graph-based security metrics and aggregating their application. IEEE Trans. Dependable Secur. Comput. **9**(1), 75–85 (2012). https://doi.org/10.1109/TDSC.2010.61

17. Ingols, K., Lippmann, R., Piwowarski, K.: Practical attack graph generation for network defense. In: 22nd Annual Computer Security Applications Conference (ACSAC 2006), 11-15 December 2006, Miami Beach, Florida, USA, pp. 121–130. IEEE Computer Society (2006). https://doi.org/10.1109/ACSAC.2006.39

18. Junker, U.: QUICKXPLAIN: preferred explanations and relaxations for over-constrained problems. In: McGuinness, D.L., Ferguson, G. (eds.) Proceedings of the Nineteenth National Conference on Artificial Intelligence, Sixteenth Conference on Innovative Applications of Artificial Intelligence, July 25-29, 2004, San Jose, California, USA, pp. 167–172. AAAI Press/The MIT Press (2004). http://www.aaai.org/Library/AAAI/2004/aaai04-027.php

19. Kaynar, K., Sivrikaya, F.: Distributed attack graph generation. IEEE Trans. Dependable Secur. Comput. **13**(5), 519–532 (2016). https://doi.org/10.1109/TDSC.2015.2423682

20. Li, W., Vaughn, R.B.: Cluster security research involving the modeling of network exploitations using exploitation graphs. In: Sixth IEEE International Symposium on Cluster Computing and the Grid (CCGrid 2006), 16-19 May 2006, Singapore, p. 26. IEEE Computer Society (2006). https://doi.org/10.1109/CCGRID.2006.128

21. Liffiton, M.H., Sakallah, K.A.: Algorithms for computing minimal unsatisfiable subsets of constraints. J. Autom. Reason. **40**(1), 1–33 (2008). https://doi.org/10.1007/s10817-007-9084-z

22. Lippmann, R., et al.: Validating and restoring defense in depth using attack graphs. In: MILCOM 2006 - 2006 IEEE Military Communications Conference, pp. 1–10 (2006). https://doi.org/10.1109/MILCOM.2006.302434

23. Lu, L., Safavi-Naini, R., Hagenbuchner, M., Susilo, W., Horton, J., Yong, S.L., Tsoi, A.C.: Ranking attack graphs with graph neural networks. In: Bao, F., Li, H., Wang, G. (eds.) ISPEC 2009. LNCS, vol. 5451, pp. 345–359. Springer, Heidelberg (2009). https://doi.org/10.1007/978-3-642-00843-6_30

24. Maoz, S., Pomerantz, N., Ringert, J.O., Shalom, R.: Why is my component and connector views specification unsatisfiable? In: 20th ACM/IEEE International Conference on Model Driven Engineering Languages and Systems, MODELS 2017, Austin, TX, USA, September 17-22, 2017, pp. 134–144. IEEE Computer Society (2017). https://doi.org/10.1109/MODELS.2017.26

25. Maoz, S., Shalom, R.: Unrealizable cores for reactive systems specifications. In: 43rd IEEE/ACM International Conference on Software Engineering, ICSE 2021, Madrid, Spain, 22-30 May 2021, pp. 25–36. IEEE (2021). https://doi.org/10.1109/ICSE43902.2021.00016

26. Mehta, V., Bartzis, C., Zhu, H., Clarke, E., Wing, J.: Ranking attack graphs. In: Zamboni, D., Kruegel, C. (eds.) RAID 2006. LNCS, vol. 4219, pp. 127–144. Springer, Heidelberg (2006). https://doi.org/10.1007/11856214_7

27. de Mello, L.H., Sanderson, A.C.: AND/OR graph representation of assembly plans. IEEE Trans. Robotics Autom. **6**(2), 188–199 (1990). https://doi.org/10.1109/70.54734

28. Milner, R. (ed.): A Calculus of Communicating Systems. LNCS, vol. 92. Springer, Heidelberg (1980). https://doi.org/10.1007/3-540-10235-3
29. Mjihil, O., Huang, D., Haqiq, A.: Improving attack graph scalability for the cloud through SDN-based decomposition and parallel processing. In: Ubiquitous Networking - Third International Symposium. Lecture Notes in Computer Science, vol. 10542, pp. 193–205. Springer (2017). https://doi.org/10.1007/978-3-319-68179-5_17
30. Noel, S., Elder, M., Jajodia, S., Kalapa, P., O'Hare, S., Prole, K.: Advances in topological vulnerability analysis. In: 2009 Cybersecurity Applications and Technology Conference for Homeland Security, pp. 124–129 (2009). https://doi.org/10.1109/CATCH.2009.19
31. Noel, S., Jajodia, S.: Managing attack graph complexity through visual hierarchical aggregation. In: Brodley, C.E., Chan, P., Lippmann, R., Yurcik, W. (eds.) 1st ACM Workshop on Visualization and Data Mining for Computer Security, VizSEC/DMSEC 2004, Washington, DC, USA, October 29, 2004, pp. 109–118. ACM (2004). https://doi.org/10.1145/1029208.1029225
32. Noel, S., Jajodia, S.: Understanding complex network attack graphs through clustered adjacency matrices. In: 21st Annual Computer Security Applications Conference (ACSAC 2005), 5–9 December 2005, Tucson, AZ, USA, pp. 160–169. IEEE Computer Society (2005). https://doi.org/10.1109/CSAC.2005.58
33. Ortalo, R., Deswarte, Y., Kaâniche, M.: Experimenting with quantitative evaluation tools for monitoring operational security. IEEE Trans. Software Eng. **25**(5), 633–650 (1999). https://doi.org/10.1109/32.815323
34. Ou, X., Boyer, W.F., McQueen, M.A.: A scalable approach to attack graph generation. In: Juels, A., Wright, R.N., di Vimercati, S.D.C. (eds.) Proceedings of the 13th ACM Conference on Computer and Communications Security, CCS 2006, Alexandria, VA, USA, October 30 - November 3, 2006, pp. 336–345. ACM (2006). https://doi.org/10.1145/1180405.1180446
35. Ou, X., Govindavjhala, S., Appel, A.W.: Mulval: A logic-based network security analyzer. In: McDaniel, P.D. (ed.) Proceedings of the 14th USENIX Security Symposium, Baltimore, MD, USA, July 31 - August 5, 2005. USENIX Association (2005). https://www.usenix.org/conference/14th-usenix-security-symposium/mulval-logic-based-network-security-analyzer
36. Paige, R., Tarjan, R.E.: Three partition refinement algorithms. SIAM J. Comput. **16**(6), 973–989 (1987). https://doi.org/10.1137/0216062
37. Pemmasani, G., Guo, H.-F., Dong, Y., Ramakrishnan, C.R., Ramakrishnan, I.V.: Online justification for tabled logic programs. In: Kameyama, Y., Stuckey, P.J. (eds.) FLOPS 2004. LNCS, vol. 2998, pp. 24–38. Springer, Heidelberg (2004). https://doi.org/10.1007/978-3-540-24754-8_4
38. Phillips, C.A., Swiler, L.P.: A graph-based system for network-vulnerability analysis. In: Blakley, B., Kienzle, D.M., Zurko, M.E., Greenwald, S.J. (eds.) Proceedings of the 1998 Workshop on New Security Paradigms, Charlottsville, VA, USA, September 22-25, 1998, pp. 71–79. ACM (1998). https://doi.org/10.1145/310889.310919
39. Ritchey, R.W., Ammann, P.: Using model checking to analyze network vulnerabilities. In: 2000 IEEE Symposium on Security and Privacy, Berkeley, California, USA, May 14-17, 2000. pp. 156–165. IEEE Computer Society (2000). https://doi.org/10.1109/SECPRI.2000.848453
40. Sabur, A., Chowdhary, A., Huang, D., Alshamrani, A.: Toward scalable graph-based security analysis for cloud networks. Comput. Networks **206** (2022). https://doi.org/10.1016/j.comnet.2022.108795

41. Sawilla, R.E., Ou, X.: Identifying critical attack assets in dependency attack graphs. In: Jajodia, S., Lopez, J. (eds.) ESORICS 2008. LNCS, vol. 5283, pp. 18–34. Springer, Heidelberg (2008). https://doi.org/10.1007/978-3-540-88313-5_2

42. Shalom, R., Maoz, S.: Which of my assumptions are unnecessary for realizability and why should I care? In: 45th IEEE/ACM International Conference on Software Engineering, ICSE 2023, Melbourne, Australia, May 14-20, 2023, pp. 221–232. IEEE (2023). https://doi.org/10.1109/ICSE48619.2023.00030

43. Shevrin, I., Margalit, O.: Detecting multi-step IAM attacks in AWS environments via model checking. In: Calandrino, J.A., Troncoso, C. (eds.) 32nd USENIX Security Symposium, USENIX Security 2023, Anaheim, CA, USA, August 9–11, 2023, pp. 6025–6042. USENIX Association (2023). https://www.usenix.org/conference/usenixsecurity23/presentation/shevrin

44. Sheyner, O., Haines, J.W., Jha, S., Lippmann, R., Wing, J.M.: Automated generation and analysis of attack graphs. In: 2002 IEEE Symposium on Security and Privacy, Berkeley, California, USA, May 12-15, 2002, pp. 273–284. IEEE Computer Society (2002). https://doi.org/10.1109/SECPRI.2002.1004377

45. Torlak, E., Chang, F.S.-H., Jackson, D.: Finding minimal unsatisfiable cores of declarative specifications. In: Cuellar, J., Maibaum, T., Sere, K. (eds.) FM 2008. LNCS, vol. 5014, pp. 326–341. Springer, Heidelberg (2008). https://doi.org/10.1007/978-3-540-68237-0_23

46. Williams, L., Lippmann, R., Ingols, K.: An interactive attack graph cascade and reachability display. In: Goodall, J.R., Conti, G.J., Ma, K. (eds.) 4th International Workshop on Visualization for Computer Security, VizSEC 2007, Sacramento, CA, USA, October 29, 2007. pp. 221–236. Mathematics and Visualization. Springer (2007). https://doi.org/10.1007/978-3-540-78243-8_15

47. Yousefi, M., Mtetwa, N., Zhang, Y., Tianfield, H.: A novel approach for analysis of attack graph. In: 2017 IEEE International Conference on Intelligence and Security Informatics, ISI 2017, Beijing, China, July 22-24, 2017, pp. 7–12. IEEE (2017). https://doi.org/10.1109/ISI.2017.8004866

48. Zeller, A., Hildebrandt, R.: Simplifying and isolating failure-inducing input. IEEE Trans. Software Eng. 28(2), 183–200 (2002). https://doi.org/10.1109/32.988498

Learn and Repair

State Matching and Multiple References in Adaptive Active Automata Learning

Loes Kruger$^{(\boxtimes)}$ ⓘ, Sebastian Junges ⓘ, and Jurriaan Rot ⓘ

Radboud University, Nijmegen, The Netherlands
{loes.kruger,sebastian.junges,jurriaan.rot}@ru.nl

Abstract. Active automata learning (AAL) is a method to infer state machines by interacting with black-box systems. Adaptive AAL aims to reduce the sample complexity of AAL by incorporating domain specific knowledge in the form of (similar) reference models. Such reference models appear naturally when learning multiple versions or variants of a software system. In this paper, we present state matching, which allows flexible use of the structure of these reference models by the learner. State matching is the main ingredient of adaptive $L^\#$, a novel framework for adaptive learning, built on top of $L^\#$. Our empirical evaluation shows that adaptive $L^\#$ improves the state of the art by up to two orders of magnitude.

1 Introduction

Automata learning aims to extract state machines from observed input-output sequences of some system-under-learning (SUL). *Active* automata learning (AAL) assumes that one has black-box access to this SUL, allowing the learner to incrementally choose inputs and observe the outputs. The models learned by AAL can be used as a documentation effort, but are more typically used as basis for testing, verification, conformance checking, fingerprinting—see [9,23] for an overview of applications. The classical algorithm for AAL is L^*, introduced by Angluin [2]; state-of-the-art algorithms are, e.g., $L^\#$ [24] and TTT [11], which are available in toolboxes such as LearnLib [12] and AALpy [16].

The primary challenge in AAL is to reduce the number of inputs sent to the SUL, referred to as the *sample complexity*. To learn a 31-state machine with 22 inputs, state-of-the-art learners may send several million inputs to the SUL [24]. This is not necessarily unexpected: the underlying space of 31-state state machines is huge and it is nontrivial how to maximise information gain. The literature has investigated several approaches to accelerate learners, see the overview of [23]. Nevertheless, scalability remains a core challenge for AAL.

We study *adaptive* AAL [8], which aims to improve the sample efficiency by utilizing expert knowledge already given to the learner. In (regular) AAL, a learner commonly starts learning from scratch. In adaptive AAL, however,

This research is partially supported by the NWO grant No. VI.Vidi.223.096.

A. Platzer et al. (Eds.): FM 2024, LNCS 14933, pp. 267–284, 2025.
https://doi.org/10.1007/978-3-031-71162-6_14

the learner is given a *reference model*, which ought to be similar to the SUL. Reference models occur naturally in many applications of AAL. For instance: (1) Systems evolve over time due to, e.g., bug fixes or new functionalities—and we may have learned the previous system; (2) Standard protocols may be implemented by a variety of tools; (3) The SUL may be a variant of other systems, e.g., being the same system executing in another environment, or a system configured differently.

Several algorithms for adaptive AAL have been proposed [5–8,25]. Intuitively, the idea is that these methods try to *rebuild* the part of the SUL which is similar to the reference model. This is achieved by deriving suitable queries from the reference model, using so-called *access sequences* to reach states, and so-called *separating sequences* to distinguish these from other states. These algorithms rely on a rather strict notion of similarity that depends on the way we reach these states. In particular, existing rebuilding algorithms cannot effectively learn an SUL from a reference model that has a different initial state, see Sect. 2.

We propose an approach to adaptive AAL based on *state matching*, which allows flexibly identifying parts of the unknown SUL where the reference model may be an informative guide. More specifically, in this approach, we match states in the model that we have learned so far (captured as a tree-shaped automaton) with states in the reference model such that the outputs agree on all enabled input sequences. This matching allows for targeted re-use of separating sequences from the reference model and is independent of the access sequences. We refine the approach by using *approximate state matching*, where we match a current state with one from the reference model that agrees on most inputs.

Approximate state matching is the essential ingredient for the novel $AL^\#$ algorithm. This algorithm is a conservative extension of the recent $L^\#$ [24]. Along with approximate state matching, $AL^\#$ includes rebuilding steps, which are similar to existing methods, but tightly integrated in $L^\#$. Finally, $AL^\#$ is the first approach with *dedicated support* to use more than one reference model.

Contributions. We make the following contributions to the state-of-the-art in adaptive AAL. First, we present state matching and its generalization to approximate state matching which allows flexible re-use of separating sequences from the reference model. Second, we include state matching and rebuilding in an unifying approach, called $AL^\#$, which generalizes the $L^\#$ algorithm for non-adaptive automata learning. We analyse the resulting framework in terms of termination and complexity. This framework naturally supports using multiple reference models as well as removing and adding inputs to the alphabet. Our empirical results show the efficacy of $AL^\#$. In particular, $AL^\#$ may reduce the number of inputs to the SUL by two orders of magnitude.

Related work. Adaptive AAL goes back to [8]. That paper, and many of the follow-up approaches [4–7] re-use access sequences and separating sequences from the reference model (or from the data structures constructed when learning that model). The recent approach in [6] removes redundant access sequences during rebuilding and continues learning with informative separating sequences. In [25], an L^*-based adaptive AAL approach is proposed where the algorithm starts

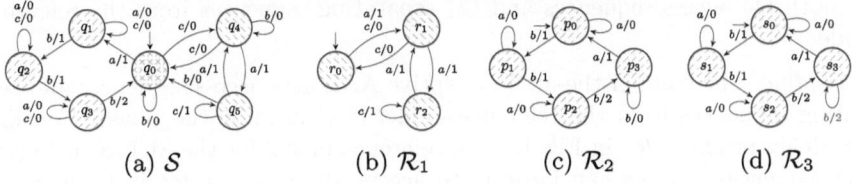

Fig. 1. An SUL $\mathcal{S}$ and three reference models $\mathcal{R}_1$, $\mathcal{R}_2$ and $\mathcal{R}_3$.

by including *all* separating sequences that arise when learning the reference model with L^*, ignoring access sequences. This algorithm is used in [10] for a general study of the usefulness of adaptive AAL: Among others, the authors suggest using more advanced data structures than the observation tables in L^*. Indeed, in [4] the internal data structure of the TTT algorithm is used [11] in the context of lifelong learning; the precise rebuilding approach is not described. The recent [7] proposes an adaptive AAL method based on discrimination trees as used in the Kearns-Vazirani algorithm [13]. We consider the algorithms proposed in [6, 7] the state-of-the-art and have experimentally compared $AL^{\#}$ in Sect. 8.

2   Overview

We illustrate (1) how adaptive AAL uses a reference model to help learn a system and (2) how this may reduce the sample complexity of the learner.

MAT Framework. We recall the standard setting for AAL: Angluin's MAT framework, cf. [9,23]. Here, the learner has no direct access to the SUL, but may ask *output queries (OQs)*: these return, for a given input sequence, the sequence of outputs from the SUL; and *equivalence queries (EQs)*: these take a Mealy machine $\mathcal{H}$ as input, and return whether or not $\mathcal{H}$ is equivalent to the SUL. In case it is not, a counterexample is provided in the form of a sequence of inputs for which $\mathcal{H}$ and the SUL return different outputs. EQs are expensive [3,19,22,26], therefore, we aim to learn the SUL using primarily OQs.

Apartness. Learning algorithms in the MAT framework typically assume that two states are equivalent as long as their *known* residual languages are equivalent. To *discover a new state*, we must therefore (1) access it by an input sequence and (2) prove this state distinct (*apart*) from the other states that we already know. Consider the SUL $\mathcal{S}$ in Fig. 1a. The access sequences c, ca access q_4 and q_5, respectively, from the initial state. These states are different because the response to executing c from q_4 and q_5 is distinct: We say c is a *separating sequence* for q_4 and q_5. This difference can be observed by posing OQs for cc and cac, consisting of the access sequences for q_4 and q_5 followed by their separating sequence c.

Aim. The aim of adaptive AAL is to learn SULs with fewer inputs, using knowledge in the form of a reference model, known to the learner and preferrably similar to the SUL. The discovery of states is accelerated by extracting candidates for both (1) access sequences and (2) separating sequences from the reference model.

Rebuilding. The state-of-the-art in adaptive AAL uses access sequences and separating sequences from the reference model [6,7] in an initial phase. Consider the Mealy machine $\mathcal{R}_1$ in Fig. 1b as a reference model for the SUL $\mathcal{S}$ in Fig. 1a. The sequences ε, c, ca can be used to access all orange states in both $\mathcal{S}$ and $\mathcal{R}_1$. The separating sequences c and ac for these states in $\mathcal{R}_1$ also separate the orange states in $\mathcal{S}$. By asking OQs combining the access sequences and separating sequences, we discover all orange states for $\mathcal{S}$.

Limits of Rebuilding. However, these rebuilding approaches have limitations. Consider $\mathcal{R}_2$ in Fig. 1c. The sequences ε, b, bb and bbb can be used to access all states in $\mathcal{R}_2$. Concatenating these with any separating sequences from $\mathcal{R}_2$ will not be helpful to learn SUL $\mathcal{S}$, because in $\mathcal{S}$ these sequences all access q_0. However, the separating sequences from $\mathcal{R}_2$ are useful if executed in the right state of $\mathcal{S}$. For instance, the sequence bb separates all states in $\mathcal{R}_2$, and the blue states in $\mathcal{S}$. Thus, rebuilding does not realise the potential of reusing the separating sequences from $\mathcal{R}_2$, since the access sequences for the relevant states are different.

State Matching. We extend adaptive AAL with *state matching*. State matching overcomes the strong dependency on the access sequences and allows the efficient usage of reference models where the residual languages of the individual states are similar. Suppose that while learning, we have not yet separated q_0 and q_1 in $\mathcal{S}$, but we do know the output of the b-transition from q_0. We may use that output to *match* q_0 with p_3 in $\mathcal{R}_2$: these two states agree on input sequences where both are defined. Subsequently, we can use the separating sequence bb between p_3 and p_0 to separate q_0 and q_1, through OQs bb and abb.

Approximate State Matching. It rarely happens that states in the SUL exactly match states in the reference model: Consider the scenario where we want to learn $\mathcal{S}$ with reference model $\mathcal{R}_3$ from Fig. 1d. States q_0 and s_3 do not match because they have different outputs for input b but are still similar. This motivates an approximate version of matching, where a state is matched to the reference state which maximises the number of inputs with the same output.

Outline. After the preliminaries (Sect. 3), we recall the $L^\#$ algorithm and extend it with rebuilding (Sect. 4). We then introduce adaptive AAL with state matching and its approximate variant (Sect. 5). Together with rebuilding, this results in the $AL^\#$ algorithm (Sect. 6). We proceed to define a variant that allows the use of multiple reference models (Sect. 7). This is helpful already in the example discussed in this section: given both $\mathcal{R}_1$ and $\mathcal{R}_2$, $AL^\#$ with multiple reference models allows to discover all states in $\mathcal{S}$ without any EQs, see App. F of [14].

3   Preliminaries

For a partial map $f\colon X \rightharpoonup Y$, we write $f(x){\downarrow}$ if $f(x)$ is defined and $f(x){\uparrow}$ otherwise.

Definition 3.1. *A* partial Mealy machine *is a tuple* $\mathcal{M} = (Q, I, O, q_0, \delta, \lambda)$, *where Q, I and O are finite sets of states, inputs and outputs respectively; $q_0 \in Q$ an initial state, $\delta \colon Q \times I \rightharpoonup Q$ a transition function, and $\lambda \colon Q \times I \rightharpoonup O$ an output function such that δ and λ have the same domain. A* (complete) Mealy machine *is a partial Mealy machine where δ and λ are total. If not specified otherwise, a Mealy machine is assumed to be complete.*

We write $\mathcal{M}|_I$ to denote $\mathcal{M}$ restricted to alphabet I. We use the superscript $\mathcal{M}$ to indicate to which Mealy machine we refer, e.g. $Q^{\mathcal{M}}$ and $\delta^{\mathcal{M}}$. The transition and output functions are naturally extended to input sequences of length $n \in \mathbb{N}$ as functions $\delta \colon Q \times I^n \rightharpoonup Q$ and $\lambda \colon Q \times I^n \rightharpoonup O^n$. We abbreviate $\delta(q_0, w)$ by $\delta(w)$.

Definition 3.2. *Let $\mathcal{M}_1$, $\mathcal{M}_2$ be partial Mealy machines. States $p \in Q^{\mathcal{M}_1}$ and $q \in Q^{\mathcal{M}_2}$* match, *written $p \stackrel{\leftrightarrow}{=} q$, if $\lambda(p, \sigma) = \lambda(q, \sigma)$ for all $\sigma \in (I^{\mathcal{M}_1} \cap I^{\mathcal{M}_2})^*$ with $\delta(p, \sigma)\!\downarrow$ and $\delta(q, \sigma)\!\downarrow$. If p and q do not match, they are* apart, *written $p \mathbin{\#} q$.*

If $p \mathbin{\#} q$, then there is a *separating sequence*, i.e., a sequence σ such that $\lambda(p, \sigma) \neq \lambda(q, \sigma)$; this situation is denoted by $\sigma \vdash p \mathbin{\#} q$. The definition of matching allows the input (and output) alphabets of the underlying Mealy machines to differ; it requires that they agree on all commonly defined input sequences. If $\mathcal{M}_1$ and $\mathcal{M}_2$ are complete and have the same alphabet, then the matching of states is referred to as *language equivalence*. Two complete Mealy machines are *equivalent* if their initial states are language equivalent.

Let $\mathcal{M}$ be a partial Mealy machine. A state $q \in Q^{\mathcal{M}}$ is *reachable* if there exists $\sigma \in I^*$ such that $\delta^{\mathcal{M}}(q_0, \sigma) = q$. The *reachable part* of $\mathcal{M}$ contains all reachable states in $Q^{\mathcal{M}}$. A sequence σ is an *access sequence* for $q \in Q^{\mathcal{M}}$ if $\delta^{\mathcal{M}}(\sigma) = q$. A set $P \subseteq I^*$ is a *state cover* for $\mathcal{M}$ if P contains an access sequence for every reachable state in $\mathcal{M}$. In this paper, a *tree* $\mathcal{T}$ is a partial Mealy machine where every state q has a *unique* access sequence, denoted by access(q).

Definition 3.3. *Let $\mathcal{M}$ be a complete Mealy machine. A set $W_q \subseteq (I^{\mathcal{M}})^*$ is a* state identifier *for $q \in Q^{\mathcal{M}}$ if for all $p \in Q^{\mathcal{M}}$ with $p \mathbin{\#} q$ there exists $\sigma \in W_q$ such that $\sigma \vdash p \mathbin{\#} q$. A* separating family *is a collection of state identifiers $\{W_p\}_{p \in Q^{\mathcal{M}}}$ such that for all $p, q \in Q^{\mathcal{M}}$ with $p \mathbin{\#} q$ there exists $\sigma \in W_p \cap W_q$ with $\sigma \vdash p \mathbin{\#} q$.*

We use $P^{\mathcal{M}}$ and $\{W_q\}^{\mathcal{M}}$ to refer to a minimal state cover and a separating family for $\mathcal{M}$ respectively. State covers and separating families can be constructed for every Mealy machine, but are not necessarily unique.

4 $L^{\#}$ with Rebuilding

We first recall the $L^{\#}$ algorithm for (standard) AAL [24]. Then, we consider adaptive learning by presenting an $L^{\#}$-compatible variant of rebuilding.

4.1   Observation Trees

$L^{\#}$ uses an observation tree as data structure to store the observed traces of $\mathcal{M}$.

Definition 4.1. *A tree $\mathcal{T}$ is an observation tree if there exists a mapping $f\colon Q^{\mathcal{T}} \to Q^{\mathcal{M}}$ such that $f(q_0^{\mathcal{T}}) = q_0^{\mathcal{M}}$ and $q \xrightarrow{i/o} q'$ implies $f(q) \xrightarrow{i/o} f(q')$.*

In an observation tree, a *basis* is a subtree that describes unique behaviour present in the SUL. Initially, a basis $B \subseteq Q^{\mathcal{T}}$ contains the root state. All states in the basis are pairwise apart, i.e., for all $q \neq q' \in B$ it holds that $q \# q'$. For a fixed basis, its *frontier* is the set of states $F \subseteq Q^{\mathcal{T}}$ which are immediate successors of basis states but which are not in the basis themselves.

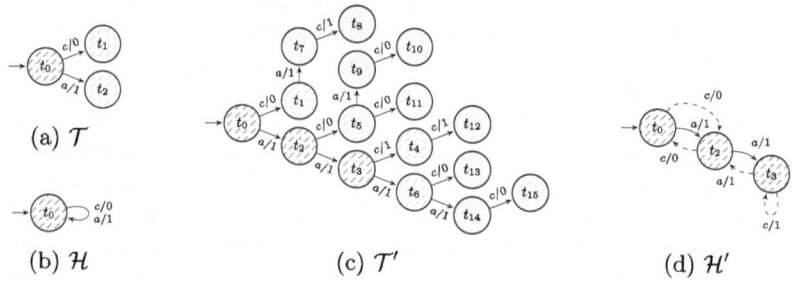

Fig. 2. Observation trees and hypotheses generated while learning $\mathcal{R}_1$ with $L^{\#}$. Basis states are displayed in pink and frontier states in yellow. (Color figure online)

Example 4.2. Figure 2c shows an observation tree $\mathcal{T}'$ for the Mealy machine $\mathcal{H}'$ from Fig. 2d. The separating sequences c and ac show that the states in basis $B = \{t_0, t_2, t_3\}$ are all pairwise apart. The frontier F is $\{t_1, t_4, t_5, t_6\}$.

We say that a frontier state is *isolated* if it is apart from all basis states. A frontier state is *identified* with a basis state q if it is apart from all basis states except q. We say the observation tree is *adequate* if all frontier states are identified, no frontier states are isolated and each basis state has a transition with every input. If every frontier state is identified and each basis state has a transition for every input, the observation tree can be *folded* to create a complete Mealy machine . The Mealy machine has the same states as the basis. The transitions between basis states are the same as in the observation tree. Transitions from basis states to frontier states are *folded back* to the basis state the frontier state is identified with. We call the resulting complete Mealy machine a *hypothesis* whenever this canonical transformation is used.

Example 4.3. In $\mathcal{T}'$ (Fig. 2c) the frontier states are identified as follows: $t_1 \mapsto t_2, t_4 \mapsto t_3, t_5 \mapsto t_0$ and $t_6 \mapsto t_2$. Hypothesis $\mathcal{H}'$ (Fig. 2d) can be folded back from $\mathcal{T}'$. The dashed transitions in Fig. 2d represent the folded transitions.

4.2 The $L^{\#}$ Algorithm

The $L^{\#}$ algorithm maintains an observation tree $\mathcal{T}$ and a basis B. Initially, $\mathcal{T}$ consists of just a root node q_0 and $B = \{q_0\}$. We denote the frontier of B by F. The $L^{\#}$ algorithm then repeatedly applies the following four rules.

- The *promotion* rule (**P**) extends B by $r \in F$ when r is isolated.
- The *extension* rule (**Ex**) poses OQ $\mathsf{access}(q)i$ for $q \in B, i \in I$ with $\delta(q,i)\uparrow$.
- The *separation* rule (**S**) takes a state $r \in F$ that is not apart from $q,q' \in B$ and poses OQ $\mathsf{access}(r)\sigma$ with $\sigma \vdash q \# q'$ that shows r is apart from q or q'.
- The *equivalence* rule (**Eq**) folds $\mathcal{T}$ into hypothesis $\mathcal{H}$, checks whether $\mathcal{H}$ and $\mathcal{T}$ agree on all sequences in $\mathcal{T}$ and poses an EQ. If $\mathcal{H}$ and the SUL are not equivalent, counterexample processing isolates a frontier state.

The pre- and postconditions of the rules are summarized in (the top rows of) Table 1. A detailed account is given in the paper introducing $L^{\#}$ [24].

Table 1. Extended $L^{\#}$ rules with parameters, preconditions and postconditions.

	Rule	Parameters	Precondition	Postcondition
Sec. 4.2	*promotion*	$r \in F$	$\forall q \in B, q \# r$	$r \in B$
	extension	$q \in B, i \in I$	$\delta^{\mathcal{T}}(q,i)\uparrow$	$\delta^{\mathcal{T}}(q,i)\downarrow$
	separation	$r \in F,$ $q,q' \in B$	$\neg(r \# q), \neg(r \# q'), q \neq q'$	$r \# q \vee r \# q'$
	equivalence	-	$\forall q \in B. \forall i \in I. \delta^{\mathcal{T}}(q,i)\downarrow,$ $\forall r \in F. \exists q \in B.$ $(\neg(r \# q) \wedge \forall q' \in B \setminus \{q\}. r \# q')$	$\exists r \in F$ s.t. $\forall q \in B. r \# q$
Sec. 4.3	*rebuilding*	$q,q' \in B,$ $i \in I$	$\delta^{\mathcal{T}}(q,i) \notin B, \neg(q' \# \delta^{\mathcal{T}}(q,i)),$ $\mathsf{access}^{\mathcal{T}}(q)i, \mathsf{access}^{\mathcal{T}}(q') \in P^{\mathcal{R}},$ $\sigma = \mathsf{sep}(\delta^{\mathcal{R}}(\mathsf{access}^{\mathcal{T}}(q)i), \delta^{\mathcal{R}}(\mathsf{access}^{\mathcal{T}}(q'))),$ $(\delta^{\mathcal{T}}(q,i\sigma)\uparrow \vee \delta^{\mathcal{T}}(q',\sigma)\uparrow)$	$\delta^{\mathcal{T}}(q,i\sigma)\downarrow,$ $\delta^{\mathcal{T}}(q',\sigma)\downarrow$
	prioritized promotion	$r \in F$	$\mathsf{access}^{\mathcal{T}}(r) \in P^{\mathcal{R}}, \forall q \in B. q \# r$	$r \in B$
Sec. 5.1, 5.2	*match separation*	$q,q' \in B,$ $p \in Q^{\mathcal{R}}, i \in I$	$\delta^{\mathcal{T}}(q,i) = r \in F, \neg(r \# q'), \delta^{\mathcal{R}}(p,i) = p'$ $\neg(\exists q'' \in B$ s.t. $p' \overset{\vee}{\preceq} q''), p \overset{\vee}{\preceq} q$	$r \# q' \vee$ $(p \overset{\vee}{\neq} q \wedge r \# p')$
	match refinement	$q \in B,$ $p,p' \in Q^{\mathcal{R}}$	$p \overset{\vee}{\preceq} q, p' \overset{\vee}{\preceq} q,$ $\sigma = \mathsf{sep}(p,p')$	$p \overset{\vee}{\neq} q \vee p' \overset{\vee}{\neq} q$
	prioritized separation	$r \in F,$ $q',q'' \in B$	$\neg(r \# q'), \neg(r \# q''), \exists i \in I$ s.t. $\delta^{\mathcal{T}}(q,i) = r,$ $\sigma \vdash q' \# q'', \sigma \in \bigcup_{p \overset{\vee}{\preceq} q} W_{\delta^{\mathcal{R}}(p,i)}$	$r \# q'' \vee$ $r \# q'$

Example 4.4. Suppose we learn $\mathcal{R}_1$ from Fig. 1. $L^{\#}$ applies the *extension* rule twice, resulting in $\mathcal{T}$ as in Fig. 2a. States t_1 and t_2 are identified with t_0 because

there is only one basis state. Next, $L^{\#}$ applies the *equivalence* rule using hypothesis $\mathcal{H}$ (Fig. 2b). Counterexample aac distinguishes $\mathcal{H}$ from $\mathcal{R}_1$. This sequence is added to $\mathcal{T}$ and processed further by posing OQ ac in the *equivalence* rule. Observations ac and aac show that the states accessed with ε, a and aa are pairwise apart. States t_2 and t_3 are added to the basis using the *promotion* rule. Next, $L^{\#}$ poses OQ aaa during the *extension* rule. To identify all frontier states, $L^{\#}$ may use $ac \vdash t_2 \# t_3$, $ac \vdash t_0 \# t_2$ and $c \vdash t_0 \# t_3$. Figure 2c shows one possible observation tree $\mathcal{T}'$ after applying the *separation* rule multiple times. Next, the *equivalence* rule constructs hypothesis $\mathcal{H}'$ (Fig. 2d) from $\mathcal{T}'$ and $L^{\#}$ terminates because $\mathcal{H}'$ and $\mathcal{R}_1$ are equivalent.

4.3   Rebuilding in $L^{\#}$

In this subsection, we combine rebuilding from [6,7] with $L^{\#}$ and implement this using two rules: *rebuilding* and *prioritized promotion*, see also Table 1. Both rules depend on a reference model $\mathcal{R}$, which is a complete Mealy machine, with a possibly different alphabet than the SUL $\mathcal{S}$. More precisely, these rules depend on a prefix-closed and minimal state cover $P^{\mathcal{R}}$ and a separating family $\{W_q\}^{\mathcal{R}}$ computed on $\mathcal{R}|_{IS}$ for maximal overlap with $\mathcal{S}$. The separating family can be computed with partition refinement [21]. We fix $\mathsf{sep}(p, p')$ with $p, p' \in Q^{\mathcal{R}}$ to be a unique sequence from $W_p \cap W_{p'}$ such that $\mathsf{sep}(p, p') \vdash p \# p'$. Below, we use q for states in B, r for states in F and p for states in $Q^{\mathcal{R}}$. In App. A of [14], we depict the scenarios in the observation tree and reference model required for the new rules to be applicable.

Rule (R): Rebuilding. Let $q \in B$, $i \in I$ and suppose $\delta^{\mathcal{T}}(q, i) \notin B$. The aim of the *rebuilding* rule is to show apartness between $\delta^{\mathcal{T}}(q, i)$ and a basis state q', using the state cover and separating family from $\mathcal{R}$. The rebuilding rule is applicable when $\mathsf{access}^{\mathcal{T}}(q)$ and $\mathsf{access}^{\mathcal{T}}(q)i$ are in $P^{\mathcal{R}}$. If $\mathsf{access}^{\mathcal{T}}(q') \in P^{\mathcal{R}}$ then there exists a sequence σ such that $\sigma = \mathsf{sep}(\delta^{\mathcal{R}}(\mathsf{access}^{\mathcal{T}}(q)i), \delta^{\mathcal{R}}(\mathsf{access}^{\mathcal{T}}(q')))$. We pose OQs $\mathsf{access}^{\mathcal{T}}(q)i\sigma$ and $\mathsf{access}^{\mathcal{T}}(q')\sigma$.

Lemma 4.5. *Suppose $\mathsf{access}^{\mathcal{T}}(q') \in P^{\mathcal{R}}$ for all $q' \in B$. Consider $q \in B$, $i \in I$ such that $\delta^{\mathcal{T}}(q, i) \notin B$ and $\mathsf{access}^{\mathcal{T}}(q)i \in P^{\mathcal{R}}$. If for all $q' \in B$ it holds that $\mathsf{sep}(\delta^{\mathcal{R}}(\mathsf{access}^{\mathcal{T}}(q)i), \delta^{\mathcal{R}}(\mathsf{access}^{\mathcal{T}}(q'))) \vdash \delta^{\mathcal{S}}(\mathsf{access}^{\mathcal{T}}(q)i) \# \delta^{\mathcal{S}}(\mathsf{access}^{\mathcal{T}}(q'))$, then after applying the rebuilding rule for q, i and all $q' \in B$ with $\neg(q' \# \delta^{\mathcal{T}}(q, i))$, state $\delta^{\mathcal{T}}(q, i)$ is isolated.*

If a state is isolated, it can be added to the basis using the *promotion* rule.

Rule (PP): Prioritized Promotion. Like (regular) promotion, *prioritized promotion* extends the basis. However, *prioritized promotion* only applies to states r with $\mathsf{access}^{\mathcal{T}}(r) \in P^{\mathcal{R}}$. This enforces that the access sequences for basis states are in $P^{\mathcal{R}}$ as often as possible, enabling the use of the *rebuilding* rule.

Example 4.6. Consider reference $\mathcal{R}_1$ and SUL $\mathcal{S}$ from Fig. 1. We learn the orange states similarly as described in Sect. 2: We apply the *rebuilding* rule with $\mathsf{access}^{\mathcal{T}}(q) = \varepsilon$, $\mathsf{access}^{\mathcal{T}}(q') = \varepsilon$, $i = c$ which results in OQs cac and ac. Next, we promote $\delta^{\mathcal{T}}(c)$ with the *prioritized promotion* rule. We apply the *rebuilding* rule with $\mathsf{access}^{\mathcal{T}}(q) = c$, $\mathsf{access}^{\mathcal{T}}(q') = c$ and $i = a$ which results in OQs cac (already present in $\mathcal{T}$) and cc. Lastly, we promote $\delta^{\mathcal{T}}(ca)$ with *prioritized promotion*.

The overlap between $\mathcal{S}$ and $P^{\mathcal{R}}$ and $\{W_q\}^{\mathcal{R}}$ determines how many states of $\mathcal{S}$ can be discovered via rebuilding. The statement follows from Lemma 4.5 above.

Theorem 4.7. *If $q_0^{\mathcal{R}}$ matches $q_0^{\mathcal{S}}$ and $\mathcal{T}$ only contains a root $q_0^{\mathcal{T}}$, then after applying only the* rebuilding *and* prioritized promotion *rules until they are no longer applicable, the basis consists of n states where n is the number of equivalence classes (w.r.t. language equivalence) in the reachable part of $\mathcal{S}|_{I^{\mathcal{R}}}$.*

Corollary 4.8. *Suppose we learn SUL $\mathcal{S}$ with reference $\mathcal{S}$. Using the* rebuilding *and* prioritized promotion *rules, we can add all reachable states in $\mathcal{S}$ to the basis.*

5 $L^{\#}$ Using State Matching

In this section, we describe another way to reuse information from references, called state matching, which is independent of the state cover. First, we present a version of state matching using the matching relation ($\overset{\vee}{=}$) from Def. 3.2 and then we weaken this notion to approximate state matching.

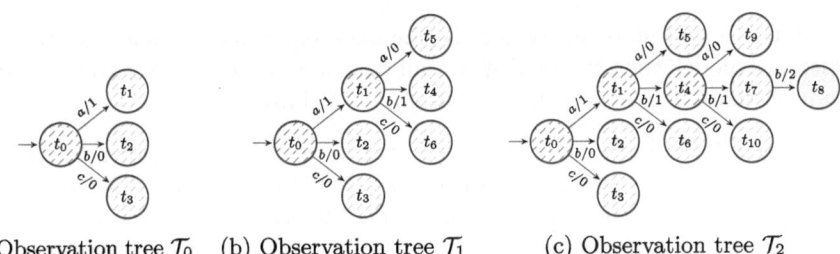

(a) Observation tree $\mathcal{T}_0$ (b) Observation tree $\mathcal{T}_1$ (c) Observation tree $\mathcal{T}_2$

Fig. 3. Observation trees generated while learning $\mathcal{S}$ with $\mathcal{R}_2$.

5.1 State Matching

With state matching, the learner maintains the matching relation $\overset{\vee}{=}$ between basis states and reference model states during learning. In the implementation, before applying a matching rule, the matching is updated based on the OQs asked since the previous match computation. We present two key rules here and an optimisation in the next subsection.

Rule (MS): Match separation. This rule aims to show apartness between the frontier and a basis state using separating sequences from the reference separating family. Let $q, q' \in B$, $r \in F$ with $\delta^{\mathcal{T}}(q, i) = r$ for some $i \in I$, and

$p, p' \in Q^{\mathcal{R}}$. Suppose that $\delta^{\mathcal{R}}(p, i) = p'$, $\neg(r \# q')$, $p \overset{\vee}{=} q$ and p' does not match any basis state. In particular, there exists some separating sequence σ for $p' \# q'$. The *match separation* rule poses OQ access$(q)i\sigma$ to either show $r \# q'$ or $q \overset{\vee}{\neq} p$ and $r \# p'$.

Example 5.1. Suppose we learn $\mathcal{S}$ using $\mathcal{R}_2$ from Fig. 1. After applying the *extension* rule three times, we get $\mathcal{T}_0$ (Fig. 3a). State t_0 matches p_3 as their outputs coincide on sequences from alphabet $I^{\mathcal{S}} \cap I^{\mathcal{R}_2} = \{a, b\}$. State p_3 transitions to the unmatched state p_0 with input a. The *match separation* rule conjectures t_1 may match p_0 which implies $t_1 \# t_0$. We use OQ access$(t_1)a$ to test this conjecture and indeed find that t_1 can be added to the basis using *promotion*.

Lemma 5.2. *We fix* $p \in Q^{\mathcal{R}}$, $q \in B$, $i \in I$ *and* $\delta^{\mathcal{T}}(q, i) = r \in F$. *Suppose* $\delta^{\mathcal{S}}(\text{access}^{\mathcal{T}}(q)) \overset{\vee}{=} p$. *If* $\delta^{\mathcal{R}}(p, i) \overset{\vee}{\neq} q'$ *for all* $q' \in B$, *then after applying the* match separation *rule with* q, p, i *for all* $q' \in B$ *with* $\neg(q' \# r)$, *state* r *is isolated.*

Rule (MR): Match Refinement. Let $q \in B$ and $p, p' \in Q^{\mathcal{R}}$. Suppose q matches both p and p' and let $\sigma = \text{sep}(p, p')$. The *match refinement* rule poses OQ access$(q)\sigma$ resulting in q no longer being matched to p or p'.

Example 5.3. Suppose we continue learning $\mathcal{S}$ using $\mathcal{R}_2$ from observation tree $\mathcal{T}_1$ (Fig. 3a). State t_1 matches both p_0 and p_1. After posing OQ access$(t_1)bb$ where $bb \vdash p_0 \# p_1$, t_1 no longer matches p_1.

If the initial state of SUL $\mathcal{S}$ is language equivalent to some state in the reference model, then we can discover all reachable states in $\mathcal{S}$ via state matching and $L^{\#}$ rules. The statement uses Lemma 5.2 above.

Theorem 5.4. *Suppose we have reference* $\mathcal{R}$ *and SUL* $\mathcal{S}$ *equivalent to* $\mathcal{R}$ *but with a possibly different initial state. Using only the* match refinement, match separation, promotion *and* extension *rules, we can add* n *states to the basis where* n *is the number of equivalence classes (w.r.t. language equivalence) in the reachable part of* $\mathcal{S}$.

5.2   Optimised Separation Using State Matching

In this subsection, we add an optimisation rule *prioritized separation* that uses the matching to guide the identification of frontier states. First, we highlight the differences between *prioritized separation* and the previous separation rules. Both *match separation* and *prioritized separation* require that $r \overset{\vee}{=} p$ for $r \in F$ and $p \in Q^{\mathcal{R}}$. The aim of *match separation* is to isolate r and requires that p does not match any basis state. Instead, the aim of *prioritized separation* is to guide the identification of r using the state identifier for a p matched with a basis state. The *prioritized separation* rule is also different from the *separation* rule (Sect. 4.2) which randomly selects $q, q' \in B$ to separate r from q or q'.

Rule (PS): Prioritized Separation. The *prioritized separation* rule uses the matching to find a separating sequence from the reference model that is expected to separate a frontier state from a basis state. Let $q', q'' \in B$ and $r \in F$. Suppose r is not apart from q' and q'' and $\sigma \vdash q' \# q''$. If σ is in $\{W_p\}^{\mathcal{R}}$ of a reference model state p that matches r, the *prioritized separation* rule poses OQ access$(r)\sigma$ resulting in r being apart from q' or q''[1].

Example 5.5. Suppose we learn $\mathcal{S}$ using $\mathcal{R}_1$ from Fig. 1. Assume we have discovered all states in $\mathcal{S}$ and want to identify $\delta^{\mathcal{T}}(ca, c) \in F$, which is currently not apart from any basis state. The *prioritized separation* rule can only be applied with basis states $q', q'' \in B$ such that $c \vdash q' \# q''$, as c is the only sequence in the state identifier of r_2 which is the state that matches $\delta^{\mathcal{T}}(ca, c)$. From the sequences $\{bb, ac, c\}$ possibly used by $L^{\#}$, only c immediately identifies $\delta^{\mathcal{T}}(ca, c)$.

5.3 Approximate State Matching

In this subsection, we introduce an approximate version of matching, by quantifying matching via a *matching degree*. Let $\mathcal{T}$ be a tree and $\mathcal{R}$ be a (partial) Mealy machine. Let $I = I^{\mathcal{T}} \cap I^{\mathcal{R}}$. We define $\mathsf{WI}(q) = \{(w, i) \in I^* \times I \mid \delta^{\mathcal{T}}(q, wi)\downarrow\}$ as prefix-suffix pairs that are defined from $q \in Q^{\mathcal{T}}$ onwards. Then, we define the matching degree $\mathsf{mdeg} : Q^{\mathcal{T}} \times Q^{\mathcal{R}} \to \mathbb{R}$ as

$$\mathsf{mdeg}(q, p) = \frac{\left| \{(w, i) \in \mathsf{WI}(q) \mid \lambda^{\mathcal{T}}\left(\delta^{\mathcal{T}}(q, w), i\right) = \lambda^{\mathcal{R}}\left(\delta^{\mathcal{R}}(p, w), i\right)\} \right|}{|\mathsf{WI}(q)|}.$$

Example 5.6. Consider t_1 from $\mathcal{T}_2$ (Fig. 3c) and p_0, p_1 from $\mathcal{R}_2$ (Fig. 1). We derive $\mathsf{WI}(t_1) = \{(\varepsilon, a), (\varepsilon, b), (b, a), (b, b), (bb, b)\}$ from $\mathcal{T}_2$ where $I = I^{\mathcal{T}_2} \cap I^{\mathcal{R}_2} = \{a, b\}$. On these pairs, all the suffix outputs for p_0 and t_1 are equivalent, $\mathsf{mdeg}(t_1, p_0) = 5/5 = 1$. The matching degree between t_1 and p_1 is only $3/5$ because $\lambda^{\mathcal{R}_2}(p_1, bbb) = 120 \neq 112 = \lambda^{\mathcal{T}}(t_1, bbb)$ which impacts pairs (b, b) and (bb, b).

A state q in an observation tree $\mathcal{T}$ *approximately matches* a state $p \in Q^{\mathcal{R}}$, written $q \overset{\vee}{=} p$, if there does not exist a $p' \in Q^{\mathcal{R}}$ such that $\mathsf{mdeg}(q, p') > \mathsf{mdeg}(q, p)$.

Lemma 5.7. *For any* $q \in Q^{\mathcal{T}}, p \in Q^{\mathcal{R}}$: $\mathsf{mdeg}(q, p) = 1$ *implies* $q \overset{\vee}{=} p$.

We define rules *approximate match separation* (**AMS**), *approximate match refinement* (**AMR**) and *approximate prioritized separation* (**APS**) that represent the approximate matching variations of *match separation*, *match refinement* and *prioritized separation* respectively. These rules have weaker preconditions and postconditions, see Table 3 in App A of [14].

---

[1] The precise specification is more involved, as the learner only keeps track of the match relation on $B \times Q^{\mathcal{R}}$.

6 Adaptive $L^{\#}$

The rebuilding, state matching and $L^{\#}$ rules described in Table 1 are ordered and combined into one adaptive learning algorithm called *adaptive $L^{\#}$* (written $AL^{\#}$). A non-ordered listing of the rules can be found in Algorithm 1 in App. A of [14]. We use the abbreviations for the rules defined in previous sections.

Definition 6.1. *The $AL^{\#}$ algorithm repeatedly applies the rules from Table 1 (see Algorithm 1), with the following ordering: Ex, APS, (S if APS was not applicable), P, if the observation tree is adequate we try AMR, AMS, Eq. The algorithm starts by applying R and PP until they are no longer applicable; these rules are not applied anymore afterwards.*

Similar to $L^{\#}$, the correctness of $AL^{\#}$ amounts to showing termination because the algorithm can only terminate when the teacher indicates that the SUL and hypothesis are equivalent. We prove termination of $AL^{\#}$ by proving that each rule application lowers a ranking function. The necessary ingredients for the ranking function are derived from the post-conditions of Table 1.

Theorem 6.2. *$AL^{\#}$ learns the correct Mealy machine within $\mathcal{O}(kn^2 + kno + no^2 + n \log m)$ output queries and at most $n-1$ equivalence queries where n is the number of equivalence classes for $\mathcal{S}$, o is the number of equivalence classes for $\mathcal{R}$, k is the number of input symbols and m the length of the longest counterexample.*

7 Adaptive Learning with Multiple References

Let $\mathcal{X}$ be a finite set of complete reference models with possibly different alphabets. Assume each reference model $\mathcal{R} \in \mathcal{X}$ has a state cover $P^{\mathcal{R}}$ and separating family $\{W_q\}^{\mathcal{R}}$. We adapt the arguments for the $AL^{\#}$ algorithm to represent the state cover and separating family for the set of reference models.

State Cover. We initialize the $AL^{\#}$ algorithm with the union of the state cover of each reference model, i.e., $\cup_{\mathcal{R} \in \mathcal{X}} P^{\mathcal{R}}$. To reduce the size of $P^{\mathcal{X}}$, the state cover for each reference model is computed using a fixed ordering on inputs.

Separating Family. We combine the separating families for multiple reference models using a stronger notion of apartness, called *total apartness*, which also separates states based on whether inputs are defined. When changing the alphabet of a reference model to the alphabet of the SUL, as is done when computing the separating family, the reference model may become partial. If states from different reference models behave the same on their common alphabet but their alphabets contain different inputs from the SUL, we still want to distinguish the reference models based on which inputs they enable.

Definition 7.1. *Let $\mathcal{M}_1, \mathcal{M}_2$ be partial Mealy machines and $p \in Q^{\mathcal{M}_1}, q \in Q^{\mathcal{M}_2}$. We say p and q are total apart, written $p \mathrel{\#_{\uparrow}} q$, if $p \# q$ or there exists $\sigma \in (I^{\mathcal{M}_1} \cap I^{\mathcal{M}_2})^*$ such that either $\delta^{\mathcal{M}_1}(p,w)\uparrow$ or $\delta^{\mathcal{M}_2}(q,w)\uparrow$ but not both.*

We use *total apartness* to define a *total state identifier* and a *total separating family*. This definition is similar to Definition 3.3 but $\#$ is be replaced by $\#_\uparrow$. We combine the multiple reference models into a single one with an arbitrary initial state, compute the *total separating family* and use this to initialize $AL^\#$.

Example 7.2. A total separating family for $\mathcal{X} = \{\mathcal{R}_1, \mathcal{R}_2\}$ and alphabet I^S is $W_{p_0} = W_{p_1} = \{c, b, bb\}, W_{p_2} = W_{p_3} = \{c, b\}, W_{r_0} = W_{r_1} = \{c, ac\}, W_{r_2} = \{c\}$.

We add an optimisation to $AL^\#$ that only chooses p and p' from the same reference model during rebuilding. Theorem 6.2 can be generalized to this setting where o represents the number of equivalence classes across the reference models.

8   Experimental Evaluation

In this section, we empirically investigate the performance of our implementation of $AL^\#$. The source code and all benchmarks are available online[2] [15]. We present four experiments to answer the following research questions:

R1 What is the performance of adaptive AAL algorithms, when ...
    Exp 1 ... learning models from a similar reference model?
    Exp 2 ... applied to benchmarks from the literature?
R2 Can multiple references help $AL^\#$, when learning ...
    Exp 3 ... a model from similar reference models?
    Exp 4 ... a protocol implementation from reference implementations?

Setup. We implement $AL^\#$ on top of the $L^\#$ LearnLib implementation[3]. We invoke conformance testing for the EQs, using the `random Wp method` from LearnLib with `minimal size=3` and `random length`$= 3$[4]. We run all experiments with 30 seeds. We measure the performance of the algorithms based on the number of inputs sent to the SUL during both OQs and EQs: *Fewer is better.*

Table 2. Summed inputs in millions for learning the mutated models with the original models.

Algorithm	mut_1	mut_2	mut_3	mut_4	mut_5	mut_6	mut_7	mut_8	mut_9	mut_{10}	mut_{11}	mut_{12}	mut_{13}	mut_{14}
L^*	115.2	24.2	49.4	69.7	78.7	60.5	50.7	132.9	294.2	36.8	52.5	38.0	18.3	301.9
KV	123.5	17.8	49.6	60.1	68.9	58.7	44.9	103.7	244.3	25.5	28.7	28.0	7.5	253.6
$L^\#$	101.7	14.3	50.0	49.2	73.0	58.7	39.9	100.1	313.9	25.4	38.9	28.0	8.0	234.9
∂L^*_M [6]	132.7	19.8	22.5	25.0	32.7	26.0	-	178.0	375.0	24.7	25.4	44.1	8.9	256.3
IKV [7]	114.8	18.6	1.6	2.4	0.9	0.8	-	56.6	373.9	11.0	2.1	1.1	5.8	7.0
$AL^\#$ (new!)	1.2	0.5	1.5	0.8	0.8	0.8	0.6	68.1	141.1	1.4	1.3	0.8	1.9	7.2
$L^\#_R$ (new!)	101.7	12.3	1.7	9.4	1.1	7.9	0.7	68.2	306.1	12.6	2.8	1.7	6.4	7.9
$L^\#_\ell$ (new!)	1.2	0.5	3.5	5.2	9.1	7.2	0.7	63.0	36.8	8.7	9.8	10.8	5.7	7.1
$L^\#_\ell$ (new!)	1.2	0.5	1.7	2.7	2.0	2.1	0.7	70.6	186.5	6.0	6.1	1.7	4.8	7.4
$L^\#_{R,\ell}$ (new!)	1.2	0.5	1.5	0.8	1.0	0.8	0.6	69.3	38.7	3.1	2.0	1.0	4.5	7.3

---

[2] https://gitlab.science.ru.nl/lkruger/adaptive-lsharp-learnlib/.
[3] Obtained from https://github.com/UCL-PPLV/learnlib.git [7].
[4] These hyperparameters are discussed in the LearnLib documentation, `learnlib.de`.

Experiment 1. We evaluate the performance of $AL^\#$ against non-adaptive and adaptive algorithms from the literature, in particular L^* [2], KV [13], and $L^\#$ [24] as well as ∂L_M^*[6] and (a Mealy machine adaptation of) IKV [7]. As part of an ablation study, we compare $AL^\#$ with simpler variations which we refer to as $L_R^\#$, $L_{\check{\vee}}^\#$, $L_{\check{\vee}}^\#$, $L_{R,\check{\vee}}^\#$. The subscripts indicate which rules are added:

R: $\mathbf{R} + \mathbf{PP}$, $\check{\vee}$: $\mathbf{MS} + \mathbf{MR} + \mathbf{PS}$, $\check{\vee}$: $\mathbf{AMS} + \mathbf{AMR} + \mathbf{APS}$.

We learn six models from the AutomataWiki benchmarks [17] also used in [24]. We limit ourselves to six models because we mutate every model in 14 different ways (and for 30 seeds). The chosen models represent different types of protocols with varying number of states. We learn the mutated models using the original models, referred to as $\mathcal{S}$, as a reference. The mutations may add states, divert transitions, remove inputs, perform multiple mutations, or compose the model with a mutated version of the model. We provide details on the used models and mutations in App. E of [14].

Results. Table 2 shows for an algorithm (rows) and a mutation (columns) the total number of inputs ($\cdot10^6$) necessary to learn all models, summed over all seeds[5]. The highlighted values indicate the best performing algorithm. We provide detailed pairwise comparisons between algorithms in App. E of [14].

Discussion. First, we observe that $AL^\#$ always outperforms non-adaptive learning algorithms, as is expected. By combining state matching and rebuilding, $AL^\#$ mostly outperforms algorithms from the literature, with IKV being competitive on some types of mutations. In $mut_9(\mathcal{S})$ we append $\mathcal{S}$ to $mut_{13}(\mathcal{S})$, $L_{\check{\vee}}^\#$ outperforms $L_{\check{\vee}}^\#$ because $L_{\check{\vee}}^\#$ incorrectly matches $mut_{13}(\mathcal{S})$ states with states in $\mathcal{S}$, making it harder to learn the $\mathcal{S}$ fragment.

Experiment 2. We evaluate $L^\#$, ∂L_M^*, IKV and $AL^\#$ on benchmarks that contain reference models. *Adaptive-OpenSSL* [18], used in [6], contains models learned from different git development branches for the OpenSSL server side. *Adaptive-Philips* [20] contains models representing some legacy code which evolved over time due to bug fixes and allowing more inputs.

Results. Figure 4a shows the mean total number of inputs required for learning a model from the associated reference model, depicting the $5^{th} - 95^{th}$ percentile (line) and average (mark) over the seeds.

Discussion. We observe that $L^\#$ and ∂L_M^* perform worse than $AL^\#$. $AL^\#$ often outperforms IKV by a factor 2–4, despite that these models are relatively small and thus easy to learn.

Experiment 3. We evaluate $AL^\#$ with one or multiple references on the models used in Experiment 1. We either (1) learn $\mathcal{S}$ using several mutations of $\mathcal{S}$ or (2) learn a mutation that represents a combination of the $\mathcal{S}$ and $mut_{13}(\mathcal{S})$.

---

[5] ∂L_M^* and IKV do not support removing input inputs, relevant for mutation M7.

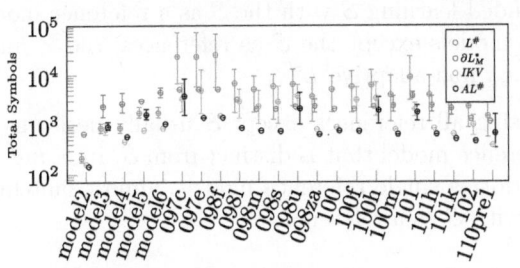

SUL	$\{mut_{10}(S)\}$	$\{mut_{12}(S)\}$	$\{mut_{10}(S),$ $mut_{12}(S)\}$	$\{mut_{12}(S),$ $mut_{10}(S),$ $mut_{13}(S)\}$
S	33.1	52.7	17.4	22.9

(b) Summed inputs in millions for learning some S.

SUL	$\{S\}$	$\{mut_{13}(S)\}$	$\{S, mut_{13}(S)\}$
$mut_8(S)$	68.1	96.3	25.7
$mut_9(S)$	141.1	263.0	35.3
$mut_{14}(S)$	7.2	212.1	3.2

(a) Averaged inputs for learning *Adaptive-Philips* (starting with m) and *Adaptive-OpenSSL*.

(c) Summed inputs in millions for learning some mutated S.

Fig. 4. Results Experiments 2 and 3.

Results. Figure 4b, 4c show for every type of SUL (rows) and every set of references (columns) the total number of inputs ($\cdot 10^6$) necessary to learn all models, summed over all seeds. Highlighted values indicate the best performing set of references. Column $\{S\}$ in Fig. 4c corresponds to values in row $AL^\#$ of Table 2; they are added in Fig. 4c for clarity.

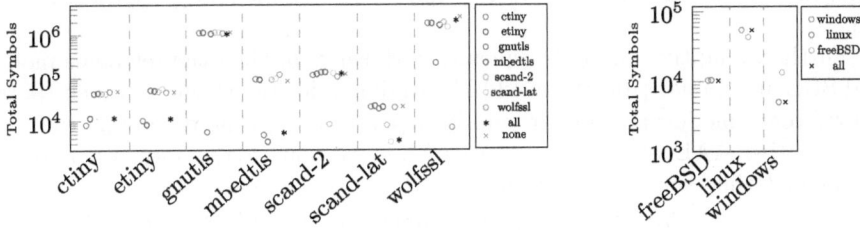

Fig. 5. Averaged inputs for learning S with multiple references.

Discussion. We observe that using multiple references outperforms using one reference, as is expected. We hypothesize that learning with reference $mut_{13}(S)$ instead of S often leads to an increase in total inputs because $mut_{13}(S)$ is less complex due to the random transitions. Therefore, discovering states belonging to the S fragment in $mut_8(S)$, $mut_9(S)$ and $mut_{14}(S)$ becomes more difficult.

Experiment 4. We evaluate the performance of $AL^\#$ with one or multiple references on learning *DTLS* and *TCP* models from AutomataWiki[6]. We consider seven *DTLS* implementations selected to have the same key exchange algorithm and certification requirement. We consider three *TCP* client implementations.

Results. Figure 5 shows the required inputs for learning S (x-axis) with only the reference model indicated by the colored data point, averaged over the seeds.

---

[6] References represent related models instead of previous models as in Experiment 2.

For each $DTLS$ model, we included learning S with the S as a reference model. The $*$ mark indicates using all models except the S as references, the $\times$ mark indicates using no references, e.g., non-adaptive $L^{\#}$.

Discussion. We observe that using all references except S usually performs as well as the best performing reference model that is distinct from S. In *scand-lat*, using a set of references outperforms single reference models, almost matching the performance of learning S with S as a reference.

9   Conclusion

We introduced the *adaptive $L^{\#}$* algorithm $(AL^{\#})$, a new algorithm for adaptive active automata learning that allows to flexibly use domain knowledge in the form of (preferably similar) reference models and thereby aims to reduce the sample complexity for learning new models. Experiments show that the algorithm can lead to significant improvements over the state-of-the-art (Sect. 8).

Future Work. Approximate state matching is sometimes too eager and may mislead the learner, as happens for mut_9 in Experiment 1 (Sect. 8). This may be addressed by only applying matching rules when the matching degree is above some threshold. It is currently unclear how to determine an appropriate threshold.

Further, adaptive methods typically perform well when the reference model and SUL are similar [10]. We would like to dynamically determine which (parts of) reference models are similar, and incorporate this in the rebuilding rule.

Adaptive AAL allows the re-use of information in the form of a Mealy machine. Other sources of information that can be re-used in AAL are, for instance, system logs, realised by combining active and passive learning [1,26]. An interesting direction of research is the development of a more general methodology that allows the re-use of various forms of previous knowledge.

Data Availability Statement. The datasets generated and analysed in this study and code to regenerate them are available in the accompanying artifact [15].

References

1. Aichernig, B.K., Muskardin, E., Pferscher, A.: Active vs. passive: a comparison of automata learning paradigms for network protocols. In: FMAS/ASYDE@SEFM. EPTCS, vol. 371, pp. 1–19 (2022)
2. Angluin, D.: Learning regular sets from queries and counterexamples. Inf. Comput. **75**(2), 87–106 (1987)
3. Aslam, K., Cleophas, L., Schiffelers, R.R.H., van den Brand, M.: Interface protocol inference to aid understanding legacy software components. Softw. Syst. Model. **19**(6), 1519–1540 (2020)

4. Bainczyk, A., Steffen, B., Howar, F.: Lifelong learning of reactive systems in practice. In: Ahrendt, W., Beckert, B., Bubel, R., Johnsen, E.B. (eds.) The Logic of Software. A Tasting Menu of Formal Methods. LNCS, vol. 13360, pp. 38–53. Springer, Cham (2022). https://doi.org/10.1007/978-3-031-08166-8_3
5. Chaki, S., Clarke, E.M., Sharygina, N., Sinha, N.: Verification of evolving software via component substitutability analysis. Formal Methods Syst. Des. **32**(3), 235–266 (2008)
6. Damasceno, C.D.N., Mousavi, M.R., da Silva Simao, A.: Learning to reuse: adaptive model learning for evolving systems. In: Ahrendt, W., Tapia Tarifa, S.L. (eds.) IFM 2019. LNCS, vol. 11918, pp. 138–156. Springer, Cham (2019). https://doi.org/10.1007/978-3-030-34968-4_8
7. Ferreira, T., van Heerdt, G., Silva, A.: Tree-based adaptive model learning. In: Jansen, N., Stoelinga, M., van den Bos, P. (eds.) A Journey from Process Algebra via Timed Automata to Model Learning. LNCS, vol. 13560, pp. 164–179. Springer, Cham (2022). https://doi.org/10.1007/978-3-031-15629-8_10
8. Groce, A., Peled, D.A., Yannakakis, M.: Adaptive model checking. Log. J. IGPL **14**(5), 729–744 (2006)
9. Howar, F., Steffen, B.: Active automata learning in practice. In: Bennaceur, A., Hähnle, R., Meinke, K. (eds.) Machine Learning for Dynamic Software Analysis: Potentials and Limits. LNCS, vol. 11026, pp. 123–148. Springer, Cham (2018). https://doi.org/10.1007/978-3-319-96562-8_5
10. Huistra, D., Meijer, J., van de Pol, J.: Adaptive learning for learn-based regression testing. In: Howar, F., Barnat, J. (eds.) FMICS 2018. LNCS, vol. 11119, pp. 162–177. Springer, Cham (2018). https://doi.org/10.1007/978-3-030-00244-2_11
11. Isberner, M., Howar, F., Steffen, B.: The TTT algorithm: a redundancy-free approach to active automata learning. In: Bonakdarpour, B., Smolka, S.A. (eds.) RV 2014. LNCS, vol. 8734, pp. 307–322. Springer, Cham (2014). https://doi.org/10.1007/978-3-319-11164-3_26
12. Isberner, M., Howar, F., Steffen, B.: The open-source LearnLib – a framework for active automata learning. In: Kroening, D., Păsăreanu, C.S. (eds.) CAV 2015. LNCS, vol. 9206, pp. 487–495. Springer, Cham (2015). https://doi.org/10.1007/978-3-319-21690-4_32
13. Kearns, M.J., Vazirani, U.V.: An Introduction to Computational Learning Theory. MIT Press (1994). https://mitpress.mit.edu/books/introduction-computational-learning-theory
14. Kruger, L., Junges, S., Rot, J.: State matching and multiple references in adaptive active automata learning (2024). https://arxiv.org/abs/2406.19714
15. Kruger, L., Junges, S., Rot, J.: State matching and multiple references in adaptive active automata learning: supplementary material (2024). https://doi.org/10.5281/zenodo.12517574
16. Muškardin, E., Aichernig, B.K., Pill, I., Pferscher, A., Tappler, M.: AALpy: an active automata learning library. In: Hou, Z., Ganesh, V. (eds.) ATVA 2021. LNCS, vol. 12971, pp. 67–73. Springer, Cham (2021). https://doi.org/10.1007/978-3-030-88885-5_5
17. Neider, D., Smetsers, R., Vaandrager, F., Kuppens, H.: Benchmarks for automata learning and conformance testing. In: Margaria, T., Graf, S., Larsen, K.G. (eds.) Models, Mindsets, Meta: The What, the How, and the Why Not? LNCS, vol. 11200, pp. 390–416. Springer, Cham (2019). https://doi.org/10.1007/978-3-030-22348-9_23

18. Ruiter, J.: A tale of the OpenSSL state machine: a large-scale black-box analysis. In: Brumley, B.B., Röning, J. (eds.) NordSec 2016. LNCS, vol. 10014, pp. 169–184. Springer, Cham (2016). https://doi.org/10.1007/978-3-319-47560-8_11

19. de Ruiter, J., Poll, E.: Protocol state fuzzing of TLS implementations. In: USENIX Security Symposium, pp. 193–206. USENIX Association (2015)

20. Schuts, M., Hooman, J., Vaandrager, F.: Refactoring of legacy software using model learning and equivalence checking: an industrial experience report. In: Ábrahám, E., Huisman, M. (eds.) IFM 2016. LNCS, vol. 9681, pp. 311–325. Springer, Cham (2016). https://doi.org/10.1007/978-3-319-33693-0_20

21. Smetsers, R., Moerman, J., Jansen, D.N.: Minimal separating sequences for all pairs of states. In: Dediu, A.-H., Janoušek, J., Martín-Vide, C., Truthe, B. (eds.) LATA 2016. LNCS, vol. 9618, pp. 181–193. Springer, Cham (2016). https://doi.org/10.1007/978-3-319-30000-9_14

22. Tappler, M., Aichernig, B.K., Bloem, R.: Model-based testing IoT communication via active automata learning. CoRR abs/1904.07075 (2019)

23. Vaandrager, F.W.: Model learning. Commun. ACM **60**(2), 86–95 (2017)

24. Vaandrager, F., Garhewal, B., Rot, J., Wißmann, T.: A new approach for active automata learning based on apartness. In: TACAS 2022. LNCS, vol. 13243, pp. 223–243. Springer, Cham (2022). https://doi.org/10.1007/978-3-030-99524-9_12

25. Windmüller, S., Neubauer, J., Steffen, B., Howar, F., Bauer, O.: Active continuous quality control. In: CBSE, pp. 111–120. ACM (2013)

26. Yang, N., et al.: Improving model inference in industry by combining active and passive learning. In: SANER, pp. 253–263. IEEE (2019)

Automated Repair of Information Flow Security in Android Implicit Inter-App Communication

Abhishek Tiwari[1]([⊠]), Jyoti Prakash[2], Zhen Dong[3], and Carlo A. Furia[1]

[1] Software Institute, USI Università della Svizzera italiana, Lugano, Switzerland

abhishek.tiwari@usi.ch

[2] University of Passau, Passau, Germany

jyotiprakash1@acm.org

[3] Fudan University, Shanghai, China

zhendong@fudan.edu.cn

https://bugcounting.net/

Abstract. Android's intents provide a form of inter-app communication with implicit, capability-based matching of senders and receivers. Such kind of implicit addressing provides some much-needed flexibility but also increases the risk of introducing information flow security bugs and vulnerabilities—as there is no standard way to specify what permissions are required to access the data sent through intents, so that it is handled properly.

To mitigate such risks of intent-based communication, this paper introduces INTENTREPAIR, an automated technique to detect such information flow security leaks and to automatically repair them. INTENTREPAIR first finds sender and receiver modules that may communicate via intents, and such that the sender sends sensitive information that the receiver forwards to a public channel. To prevent this flow, INTENTREPAIR patches the sender so that it also includes information about the permissions needed to access the data; and the receiver so that it will only disclose the sensitive information if it possesses the required permissions.

We evaluated a prototype implementation of INTENTREPAIR on 869 Android open-source apps, showing that it is effective in automatically detecting and repairing information flow security bugs that originate in implicit intent-based communication, introducing only a modest overhead in terms of patch size.

1 Introduction

Mobile applications ("apps") are often designed as a collection of specialized components that rely on each other to implement functionality for the end user. Thus, inter-app communication features prominently in their implementations, and mobile operating systems offer a variety of communication primitives that are sufficiently flexible to work in an open ecosystem of apps. Unfortunately, ease of communication also brings risks of introducing information flow security bugs and vulnerabilities that are hard to prevent, detect, and fix.

First and last author's work partially supported by SNF grant 200021-207919 (LastMile).

A. Platzer et al. (Eds.): FM 2024, LNCS 14933, pp. 285–303, 2025.

https://doi.org/10.1007/978-3-031-71162-6_15

A concrete instance of this problem occurs in the popular Android mobile operating system, which provides *intents* for flexible, asynchronous inter-app coordination. An app that wants to delegate an operation (for example, opening a web page) to another app instantiates an intent object specifying the operation and the data needed to execute it (for example, the web page's URL), and registers the object with the Android operating system. Any other app that is capable of executing the operation (for example, a web browser) can *receive* that intent object from the system and handle its request. This kind of *implicit* communication between apps is suitable for programming in an open ecosystem, where the app that makes a request (instantiating the intent object) does not need to know which apps can handle it (receiving the intent object). However, it may also introduce unintended leaks of sensitive information [14,17,18,22,24,26]: the sender has no way of specifying the sensitivity of the data packed within an intent, nor can it know in advance which apps will receive and how they will handle the intent. Conversely, the receivers do not know whether they are handling sensitive data, nor which privacy policies the sender app would like to enforce.

In this paper, we propose INTENTREPAIR: an automated technique to detect information leaks that originate in inter-app intent-based communication, and to automatically *repair* them by enforcing a preferred security policy. As we better discuss in Sect. 5, INTENTREPAIR's focus is quite novel: plenty of existing work [5,6,12,17,18,24,26] deals with detecting information-flow security violations in intent communication, but most of it focuses on intra-app communication. Furthermore, to our knowledge, no other work features the automated repair of such security flaws.

To *detect* leaks, INTENTREPAIR creates a summary of any app's usage of intents— whether the app sends or receives intent objects, for which operations, and the information flow of the intents' data. Then, it matches senders and receivers for the same operation to identify possible information leaks—when a sender's sensitive data is sent to a sink in the receiver. Unlike most existing approaches, INTENTREPAIR does not just detect information leaks but can also *automatically repair* them. The key idea is to repair both the senders—adding a sensitivity declaration to any data they add to intent objects—and the receivers—checking that the received data is handled according to the sender's preferred policy. To achieve high precision, INTENTREPAIR combines static analysis of Android bytecode with dynamic taint analysis, which validates whether certain information flow are actually possible at runtime.

We implemented the INTENTREPAIR technique in a tool with the same name. We evaluated it on 14 Android open-source apps from the DroidBench [1] and Repo-Droid [21] curated collections, as well as on 855 larger open-source apps from the FDroid repository. The experimental evaluation demonstrates that INTENTREPAIR can analyze apps of realistic size, successfully detect scenarios of insecure intent-based inter-app communication, and automatically generates patches that avoid the information-flow security bugs.

In summary, this paper makes the following contributions:

- INTENTREPAIR: an automated technique to detect and repair information flow privacy leaks in Android apps.
- A prototype implementation of INTENTREPAIR [25].
- An experimental evaluation of INTENTREPAIR on 869 Android apps.

2 Preliminaries

This section provides an overview of inter-app communication and its challenges in Android apps. First, Sects. 2.1 and 2.2 introduce the basics of Android apps and intent communication; then, Sect. 2.3 details the challenges in detecting and repairing the information flows via intents.

2.1 Android Basics

Android applications are usually written in Java or Kotlin, and consist of a collection of *components* of four kinds: activities, broadcast receivers, services, and content providers [4]. Activities usually implement user interfaces, such as a login screen. System and application events, such as boot-up notifications, are broadcasted to components registered as broadcast receivers. Services are active in the background and designed for lengthy or computationally intensive tasks, such as downloading a file in the background. Content providers shuffle data from one app to another by various means.

Each app contains a manifest file AndroidManifest.xml, which includes essential information, such as the app's name, its components, and any libraries it depends on. The manifest also specifies an app's *permissions*, that is the features of the Android operating system (and of the device that runs it) that the app may access.

2.2 How Intent Communication Works

Android provides *intents* as a flexible communication means between components. In a nutshell, intents implement a form of message-passing communication based on the component's capabilities (called "actions" in Android parlance).

Precisely, Android intents support two ways of *addressing*, that is of identifying the recipients of a message. With *explicit* intents, the sender explicitly specifies the component(s) that may receive the message; no other components are allowed to receive it. With *implicit* intents, the sender does not specify any explicit recipients, but rather an *action* (for example, opening a web page);[1] the Android system will dispatch the message to any components that support the action specified by the sender. In other words, implicit intents support a kind of implicit, capability-based addressing.

Explicit and implicit intents provide different trade offs between ease of communication and control over the recipients. Sending sensitive data via explicit intents is generally safe, in that the sender generally knows exactly who will receive that data (and how they will use it). In contrast, sending sensitive[2] data via implicit intents may be risky, since the sender of an implicit intent generally does not know exactly who will receive the data until when the app actually runs. Thus, enforcing privacy rules during

---

[1] Android offers a number of predefined actions, but apps may also define new custom actions.

[2] As defined more rigorously in Sect. 3.2.6, one can associate a permission level to any piece of data; sending high-permission data to a low-permission channel violates information flow security—whereas one is always allowed to send low-permission data to a high-permission channel.

app development is a challenge when using implicit intents; tackling this challenge is the main focus of the present work.

```
1  TelephonyManager tel = (TelephonyManager)
       getSystemService(TELEPHONY_SERVICE);
2  // sensitive data
3  String imei = tel.getDeviceId();
4  // create intent object
5  Intent i = new Intent("action_test");
6  // add sensitive data to intent
7  i.putExtra("data", imei);
8  // send intent object
9  startActivity(i);
```

(a) Sender app *S*: intent with sensitive data.

```
10  // non-sensitive data
11  String ping = "Ping";
12  // create intent object
13  Intent i = new Intent("action_test");
14  // add non-sensitive data to intent
15  i.putExtra("data", ping);
16  // send intent object
17  startActivity(i);
```

(b) Sender app *N*: intent with normal (non-sensitive) data.

```
18  // (This app's manifest specifies it handles "action_test")
19  // receive intent object for "action_test"
20  Intent i = getIntent();
21  // take data from intent
22  String data = i.getStringExtra("data");
23  // send data to public sink
24  smsManager.sendTextMessage("1234567890", null, data, null, null);
```

(c) Receiver app *R*, which handles intents "action_test".

Fig. 1. Android code of sender and receiver apps communicating through implicit intents.

2.3   An Example of the Challenges of Implicit Intent Communication

Figure 1 illustrates the risks of implicit intent communication through a simple example. Two sender apps each create an intent object for custom action "action_test": app *S* in Fig. 1a includes some sensitive data in the object—the host mobile device's unique identifier (also known as IMEI number). App *N* in Fig. 1b, instead, only includes information that is not sensitive.

Figure 1c shows the code of another app *R*, which is capable of *handling* action "action_test".[3] In a system where all three apps *S*, *N*, and *R* operate, Android would dispatch the intent messages sent by *S* and *N* to *R*, which would then retrieve the data and re-send it through a public channel (i.e., in a text message—Line 24 in Fig. 1c).

Such a scenario has two potential problems in terms of information-flow security. First, *S* is not aware that *R* sends its sensitive data to a public channel. Second, *R* may not even have the necessary permissions to receive that sensitive data. Both problems originate in the flexible nature of implicit intent-based communication: the sender of an implicit intent cannot specify the sensitive nature of the data it sends; and the receivers of an implicit intent may access its data even if it contains information that is beyond their permissions.

Addressing these problems when implementing apps *S*, *N*, and *R* would be infeasible or too expensive, and fundamentally at odds with the flexibility introduced by implicit intents. The receiver app *R* cannot know, in general, the sensitivity of the data

---

[3] An app's manifest file specifies the actions it can handle.

received through intents. Considering a priori all potential sender apps is also practically impossible in an open ecosystem of apps like Android. To address these issues, we propose a novel automated repair approach that works at *app deployment time*, which we describe in Sect. 3.2.

3 Methodology

This section presents our approach to automatically detect and repair information flow security leaks that originate with implicit intent communication. First, Sect. 3.1 introduces an abstract model of implicit intent-based communication; then, Sect. 3.2 gives an overview of our intent repair framework, followed by a detailed presentation of how its components work.

3.1 An Abstract Model of Implicit Intents

Before delving into the details of our framework, we present an abstract model of implicit intents. As is, Android offers a rich API for intent communication [3]. For example, there are 25 operations to initialize an intent object, 30 operations to add data to it, and 42 operations to extract data from it.

$$
\begin{array}{ll}
Statement ::= & i \in Intent := \texttt{createIntent}(a \in Action) & \text{Create intent object and assign it to } i \\
| & \texttt{send}(i \in Intent) & \text{Launch intent } i \\
| & i \in Intent := \texttt{receive}(a \in Action) & \text{Receive intent and assign it to } i \\
| & \texttt{put}(i \in Intent, k \in Key, d \in Data) & \text{Add data } d \text{ under key } k \text{ in intent } i \\
| & d \in Data := \texttt{get}(i \in Intent, k \in Key) & \text{Assign to } d \text{ data under key } k \text{ in intent } i \\
| & \texttt{sink}(d \in Data, p \in Perm) & \text{Send data } d \text{ to sink with security level } p
\end{array}
$$

Fig. 2. Tentative: An abstract model of intent programming.

```
i := createIntent("action_test")
put(i, "data", imei)
send(i)
```

```
i := receive("action_test")
data := get(i, "data")
sink(data, ⊤)
```

(a) Intent sender S fragment, corresponding to lines 5–9 in Figure 1a.

(b) Intent receiver R fragment, corresponding to lines 20–24 in Figure 1c.

Fig. 3. An example of intent communication in Tentative.

In this paper, we only consider *implicit* intents, where the sender does not know precisely which components will receive an intent message, but only what *actions* the receivers can handle. Figure 2 shows the syntax of Tentative: an abstract, minimal model of implicit intent communication, which we'll use in the paper to simplify the presentation of the core technical concepts. Tentative provides statements to create an intent object for a certain action a ($\texttt{createIntent}(a)$), to add a key-value pair k, d to an intent object i ($\texttt{put}(i, k, d)$), to retrieve the data stored under k from an intent object

$i\,(\texttt{get}(i,k))$, to send $\texttt{send}(i)$ and receive $\texttt{receive}(a)$ an intent object associated with action a, and to "sink" some information into a channel $(\texttt{sink}(d,p))$—public, or with some other security level p. In an Android app, the action associated with a receiver is declared in the receiver app's manifest; in Tentative, it is explicit in the call to $\texttt{receive}$. Figure 3 shows two snippets of Tentative code modeling a basic sender and receiver: the sender in Fig. 3a captures the same behavior as Fig. 1a's Android code; the receiver in Fig. 3b captures the same behavior as Fig. 1c's Android code, where $\texttt{sink}(\texttt{data},\,\top)$ denotes that the $\texttt{data}$ is sent to a public sink.

3.2   How Intent Repair Works

Figure 4 pictures the overall workflow of our intent repair framework; Algorithm 1 presents its corresponding high-level algorithm. The input to the intent repair process is a set of Android apps—given as APK files—whose intent-based information flow communication will be analyzed. The first step is the *receiver analysis* (described in Sect. 3.2.1): for each app that receives implicit intent objects, we determine which actions it supports, and what it does with the data extracted from the intent objects—in particular, whether it leaks any of it to a sink. Assuming that at least one "potentially insecure" receiver exists, the next step is the *sender analysis* (described in Sect. 3.2.2), which summarizes the behavior of apps that send implicit intent objects—in particular, whether they include any sensitive data in the intents. The next step (described in Sect. 3.2.3) *matches* senders and receivers, identifying pairs (s,r) such that s sends sensitive information through implicit intents, r may receive such information and send it to a non-secure sink. For each such pair, the last step performs the actual *repair*: it patches the sender s so that it includes information about the permissions required to use the data it sends via implicit intents (as described in Sect. 3.2.4); and it patches the receiver r so that it retrieves this information and uses it to check that it has the necessary permissions to use the intent data (as described in Sect. 3.2.5).[4]

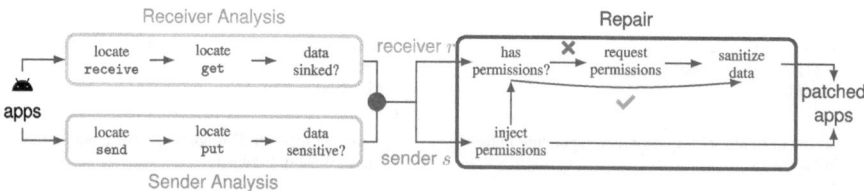

Fig. 4. An overview of how INTENTREPAIR works.

---

[4] In general, both the sender and receiver need repairing, as whether information flow security is enforced depends on how the receiver uses the data send by the sender. For example, a photo gallery app (sender) sends a private picture to a photo editing app (receiver); as long as the receiver does not make the private picture public, there is no privacy violation.

Algorithm 1: INTENTREPAIR's overall algorithm.

Input: a set of apps A
Output: a set of patches P

1 $R \leftarrow \varnothing$ // Receivers' summaries
2 $S \leftarrow \varnothing$ // Senders' summaries
3 **foreach** $a \in A$ **do**
4 | $R \leftarrow R \cup$ ReceiverAnalysis(a)
5 **if** $R \neq \varnothing$ **then**
6 | **foreach** $a \in A$ **do**
7 | | $S \leftarrow S \cup$ SenderAnalysis(a)
8 $P \leftarrow \varnothing$ // Patched apps
9 **foreach** $(s, r) \in Match(S, R)$ **do**
10 | $s' \leftarrow$ InjectPermissions(s)
11 | $r' \leftarrow$ CheckPermissions(r)
12 | $P \leftarrow P \cup \{s', r'\}$
13 **return** P

Algorithm 2: Analysis of receivers: ReceiverAnalysis.

Input: an app A
Output: a set of receivers' summaries R

1 $R \leftarrow \varnothing$ // Receivers' summaries
2 **foreach** $intent := $ receive$(action) \in A$ **do**
3 | **foreach** $value := $ get$(intent, key) \in$ Taint$(intent)$ **do**
4 | | **if** sink$(value) \in$ Taint$(value)$ **then**
5 | | | $R \leftarrow R \cup \{\langle A, action, key \rangle\}$
6 **return** R

3.2.1 Receiver Analysis

Algorithm 2 outlines INTENTREPAIR's receiver analysis. A receiver component is one that includes calls to the `receive` primitive (line 2).[5] INTENTREPAIR *taints* the intent object for each such call to `receive`, in order to find program locations that extract data from the object (primitive `get`, line 3). Then, it also taints the data objects to determine if they flow into an insecure *sink* (line 4). If this is the case, all the collected information about the receiver is stored as the receiver summary (line 5).

3.2.2 Sender Analysis

Algorithm 3 outlines INTENTREPAIR's sender analysis. A sender component is one that includes calls to the `send` primitive (line 2), which represents all variants of Android's `sendIntent` methods. For each such call to `send`, INTENTREPAIR computes the inter-procedural backward slice using the sent intent object as slicing criterion; thus, the slice will include all calls to the `createIntent` and `put` primitives that involve the

---

[5] As explained in Sect. 3.1, `receive` corresponds to any of the numerous Android API primitives to receive an implicit intent object, such as `getIntent()` in Fig. 1c.

Algorithm 3: Analysis of senders: SenderAnalysis.

Input: an app A
Output: a set of senders' summaries S

1 $S \leftarrow \emptyset$ // Senders' summaries
2 **foreach** send($intent$) $\in$ $class$ **do**
3   **foreach** $intent$:= createIntent($action$) $\in$ Slice($intent$) **do**
4   **foreach** put($intent, key, value$) $\in$ Slice($intent$) **do**
5   **if** Permission($value$) $\neq$ $\top$ **then**
6                  $S \leftarrow S \cup \{\langle A, action, key, \text{Permission}(value)\rangle\}$
7 **return** S

---

sent intent object. INTENTREPAIR considers all pairs of createIntent (line 3) and put (line 4) in the slice that target the same *action*. By analyzing the data that is stored by each put, INTENTREPAIR determines whether handling that data requires any non-trivial permission (line 5). If this is the case, all the collected information about the sender is stored as the sender summary (line 6).

3.2.3 Sender-Receiver Matching

Given a sender S's summary $\langle s, a_s, k_s, p\rangle$ and a receiver R's summary $\langle r, a_r, k_r\rangle$, *matching* them is straightforward: it amounts to determining if they send and receive intent objects associated with the same *action* ($a_s = a_r$), and exchange data using some shared *key* ($k_s = k_r$).

```
i := createIntent("action_test")
put(i, "data", imei)
// accessing imei requires
// permission "read phone state"
+put(i, "perm:data", "READ_PHONE_STATE")
send(i)
```

(a) Repairing Figure 1a's sender by injecting its intent object with information about the permissions that is required to access the intent data.

```
i := receive("action_test")                  1
data := get(i, "data")                        2
// retrieve required permission               3
+perm := get(i, "perm:data")                  4
// try to acquire permission                  5
+if (!request(perm)) exit()                   6
// sanitize data before sinking it            7
+data := sanitize(data, ⊤)                    8
sink(data, ⊤)                                 9
```

(b) Repairing Figure 3b's receiver by ensuring that it has the necessary permissions to access the intent data, and sanitizing the sensitive data before sending it to a non-secure sink.

Fig. 5. Abstract Repairs for the Senders and Receivers

3.2.4 Sender Repair

If at least one matching pair of sender and receiver exists, it means there is sensitive information that may flow to a sink; in this case, the repair process begins. The first step is "repairing" the sender, which means providing means of communicating its security policies to the receiver site Android provides no built-in mechanism to allow this kind of identification with intent objects—not even at runtime. To address this, we explicitly inject the intent object in the sender with additional data. The main idea is storing in the intent object pairs (k, p), where k is the *key* of a piece of data stored in the same object and p is the *permission* required to access that data.

Figure 5a illustrates this idea on the running example. Figure 1a's sender includes in intent object i sensitive data (an IMEI number) under key "data". Android permission READ_PHONE_STATE is required to access this sensitive data; thus, INTENTREPAIR injects the pair ("data", READ_PHONE_STATE) in the sender's intent object, using a fresh, unique key "perm:data".

3.2.5   Receiver Repair

As described in the previous section, INTENTREPAIR injects intent objects on the sender's side, so that the receivers know the required permissions. Correspondingly, INTENTREPAIR modifies all receiver apps so that they retrieve this information about permissions and use it appropriately.

First, the receiver should have the required permissions to handle the intent object. If this is not the case, INTENTREPAIR patches the receiver so that it asks the app user to upgrade its permissions. If the user denies the request, the app is not allowed to continue and can only abort its operations.

Once the receiver has acquired the necessary permissions—either statically or dynamically—INTENTREPAIR still has to sanitize the sensitive data it received through the intent object before dumping it into a public sink, so as not to violate any information flow security rules. To this end, INTENTREPAIR provides a simple anonymization of the data (which could also be used, in a pinch, in the scenario where the client lacks the necessary permissions). Within the same general repair scheme, one could implement custom declassification policies for the nature of the sensitive data; for instance, if the sensitive data is location information, the receiver could replace the precise location with an approximation. INTENTREPAIR supports customizing how receiver apps are repaired, so as to enforce the app developers' preferred policies and practices.

Figure 5b illustrates this idea on the running example. INTENTREPAIR modifies Fig. 1b's receiver so that it checks what permission perm is required to handle the data stored under key "data" in intent object i. If the receiver does not have nor cannot acquire permission perm, it simply terminates, so as to avoid any mishandling of sensitive information. Conversely, once it has acquired permission perm, it sanitizes the intent data before sending it to a public sink.

3.2.6   Repair Correctness

To make the presentation of INTENTREPAIR's repairs rigorous, let's extend Tentative with the set of *fix ingredients* shown in Fig. 6: INTENTREPAIR can avoid an information-flow security flaw in a receiver by terminating its execution (exit), sanitizing sensitive data (sanitize), or requesting a permission (request). As for the rest of Tentative, these operations generalize different Android library calls that can be used to change the permissions and a program's information-flow security—as demonstrated in Fig. 5b's example.

Figure 7 shows the main rules that formalize what it means for a Tentative program to be information-flow secure. To this end, a *permission state* P keeps track of

$$\textit{Repair} ::= \texttt{exit}() \qquad\qquad\qquad\qquad \text{Terminate the current activity}$$
$$| \quad w := \texttt{sanitize}(v \in \textit{Data}, p \in \textit{Perms}) \quad \text{Sanitize data } v \text{ to comply with permission } p$$
$$| \quad \texttt{request}(p \in \textit{Perms}) \qquad\qquad\quad \text{Try to acquire permission } p$$

Fig. 6. Repair operations for Tentative intent programs.

GET
$$\frac{P = (A, R) \qquad p = [\![\texttt{get(i, "perm:k")}]\!]}{\langle v := \texttt{get(i, "k")}, P \rangle \rightarrow (A, R \cup [v \mapsto p])}$$

USE
$$\frac{P = (A, R) \qquad R(v) \in A}{\langle \textit{stmt}[v], P \rangle \rightarrow P}$$

EXIT
$$\overline{\langle \texttt{exit}(), P \rangle \rightarrow \checkmark}$$

SANITIZE
$$\frac{P = (A, R) \qquad R(v) \in A}{\langle w := \texttt{sanitize}(v, p), (A, R) \rangle \rightarrow (A, R \cup [w \mapsto p])}$$

SINK
$$\frac{P = (A, R) \qquad R(w) \geq q}{\langle \texttt{sink}(w, q), P \rangle \rightarrow P}$$

UPGRADE
$$\frac{P = (A, R) \qquad [\![\texttt{request}(p)]\!]}{\langle \texttt{request}(p), P \rangle \rightarrow (A \cup \{p\}, R)}$$

NO-UPGRADE
$$\frac{P = (A, R) \qquad \neg [\![\texttt{request}(p)]\!]}{\langle \texttt{request}(p), P \rangle \rightarrow P}$$

Fig. 7. Rules to check whether a Tentative program is information-flow secure.

the permission as a program executes; P is a pair (A, R), where A is the set of permissions the running app currently has, whereas R maps each variable v to the permission $R(v)$ required to access that variable's content.[6] Each rule in Fig. 7 has the form $\langle s, P \rangle \rightarrow P'$, which denotes that executing statement s when the permission state is P is successful and leads to permission state P' (or to termination if $P' = \checkmark$). A program is information-flow safe if we can successfully apply these rules to all its statements.

Rule GET models how the information about which permissions are needed to access which variables is retrieved by INTENTREPAIR, which, in turn, relies on the sender repair algorithm described above. Rule USE indicates that, whenever a statement $\textit{stmt}[v]$ accessing some variable v executes, the app must possess the necessary permission $R(v)$. Rule SINK deals with primitive $\texttt{sink}$, which is secure only if the output channel's security level q is not more restrictive than the permission $R(w)$ required to access the sinked data w. The program can always safely terminate, without requiring any special permission (rule EXIT). Sanitizing a variable's content may change (usually, reduce) the permission required to access it (rule SANITIZE). Conversely, successfully acquiring a permission extends the set of current permissions (rules NO-/UPGRADE).

With this formalization, we can support our claim that INTENTREPAIR patches such as Fig. 5b's are information-flow safe by construction: Line 4 retrieves the required permission; Line 6 tries to acquire it, and terminates if this is not possible; Line 8 sanitizes the data, so that Line 9 is allowed to sink it.

3.2.7 Sanitize Operations

INTENTREPAIR can be customized and extended by providing different kinds of implementation of the $\texttt{sanitize}$ primitive that achieve a desired trade off between security preservation and app functionality. We distinguish between *declassify* operations, which reduce the precision of the data, and pure *sanitize* operations, which completely replace

---

[6] Without loss of generality, we assume that all permissions form a complete lattice, with $\top$ being the least restrictive permission (i.e., public data).

sensitive data with dummy values. The latter are straightforward to implement using default values or encryption. In contrast, declassify operations depend on the nature of the data that should be declassified. For example, location data can be declassified by replacing a precise location with an approximate one. Table 1 lists several declassify and sanitize operations implemented in INTENTREPAIR.

Table 1. INTENTREPAIR's declassification (top) and sanitization (bottom) operations on several kinds and types of sensitive data d.

DATA d	TRANSFORMATION	DESCRIPTION
location	$\mathtt{coarse}(d)$	approximate location d
device id	$\mathtt{substring}(d, n)$	keep only first n characters of device id d
event	$d.\mathtt{location} = \mathtt{coarse}(d.\mathtt{location})$	approximate event d's location
step count	$d + \mathtt{random}(-10000, 10000)$	add random noise to number d of walked steps
person height	$d * \mathtt{random}(0.5, 1.5)$	scale person height d by random factor
contacts	$\mathtt{filter}(d, \mathrm{name} = \mathrm{person})$	keep single person's contact data (instead of all contacts d)
String	" "	sanitize string data
int/Integer	0	sanitize integer data
T[]	$\{t, t, \ldots, t\}$	sanitize array of Ts, where t is T's sanitized default value

3.3 Implementation

We implemented our intent repair technique in a prototype tool also called INTENT-REPAIR. INTENTREPAIR takes APK files or Java source code as input, which it analyzes as described above, and directly injects patches into the input files. INTENT-REPAIR is implemented in Java and comprises around three thousand lines of code. INTENTREPAIR's static analysis uses the Wala framework [13] and APKTool [2] and works on the .dex and *Smali* intermediate representations. INTENTREPAIR also uses Axplorer [7,8] to detect sensitive sources based on an app's permissions. INTENT-REPAIR's implementation includes a few workarounds to handle unsupported operations of the Android framework. For example, whether the user grants the extra permissions needed by a repair is stored dynamically as a Boolean flag. If the patch were to be deployed officially, the extra permissions could be added to an app's manifest file.

4   Evaluation

We empirically evaluated the capabilities of INTENTREPAIR in repairing information flow security bugs in Android apps. Our experiments answer the research questions:

RQ1 How *effective* is INTENTREPAIR? ("Effectiveness" refers to how many information flow security bugs INTENTREPAIR can detect and repair.)

RQ2 Is INTENTREPAIR scalable? ("Scalability" refers to whether INTENTREPAIR can be applied to realistic-size apps.)

All experiments described in this section ran on a MacBook with a 2.6 GHz 6-Core Intel Core i7 processor and 16 GB of RAM. For lack of space, we only present the main results and refer to the artifact package for details.

4.1   RQ1: Effectiveness of INTENTREPAIR

4.1.1   Subjects

To assess INTENTREPAIR's effectiveness, we selected apps from two widely used curated collections of open-source Android apps: DroidBench [1] and RepoDroid [21]. Droid-Bench was originally introduced to specifically benchmark taint analyses, whereas RepoDroid encompasses a broader selection of apps; both include a ground truth about which apps incur information-flow security leaks.

Starting from 45 apps (21 in DroidBench and 24 in RepoDroid), we selected all those that *i)* send sensitive information via implicit intents; or *ii)* receive information via implicit intents (regardless of whether they sink it or not). According to DroidBench's and RepoDroid's ground truths, only 14 apps (3 in DroidBench and 11 in RepoDroid) satisfy one or both these criteria; the selected apps are generally small, as each of them consists of only 50–100 lines of code over 2–3 classes. This is arguably due to the focus of DroidBench and RepoDroid, which were curated to mainly include apps that use (inter-app) communication mechanisms other than implicit intents. (RQ2 will demonstrate INTENTREPAIR on a larger number of apps of realistic size.) Nevertheless, the 14 apps that we selected as experimental subjects do exhibit—in the small—significant patterns of information-flow exchanges. Figure 8 shows examples of code from some of these apps: Fig. 8a is a sender that sends out the IMEI device identifier to receivers that support action `testaction`; Figs. 8b and 8c are receivers supporting such action; Fig. 8b sinks this sensitive data, whereas Fig. 8c does not.

4.1.2   Sender/Receiver Analysis

Table 2 summarizes the outcome of INTENTREPAIR's sender and receiver analysis on RQ1's 14 experimental subjects.

INTENTREPAIR found 23 activities that can receive intent objects with 5 different actions; and 11 activities that can send intent objects with 4 different actions. This determines 36 potential instances of sender-receiver communication between activities. For example, app `icc_implicit_src_sink`'s `MainActivity` sends an intent object that stores Android device ids under key `"data"`; this data can be received by the `FooActivity` of the same app, as well as of the homonymous activity of apps `icc_implicit_nosrc_sink`, `icc_implicit_nosrc_nosink`, `icc_implicit_action`, and `icc_implicit_src_nosink`. We also confirmed that INTENTREPAIR detected all information-flow security leaks in DroidBench's and RepoDroid's ground truth.

4.1.3   Repair

Out of the 36 sender-receiver communication pairs, INTENTREPAIR reported 17 instances where the receiver may inappropriately send the intent information to a public sink. In the previous example, this happens when the receiver is app `icc_implicit_nosrc_sink`'s `FooActivity`. In all these cases, INTENTREPAIR patched the sender-receiver pairs so as to avoid any information-flow security leaks. We manually validated these patches by running the communicating apps while monitoring the information sent to the sink, confirming that the leak occurs in the original app version (before applying the patch) and no longer occurs with INTENTREPAIR's patch.

Table 2. INTENTREPAIR's sender and receiver summaries of the 14 apps analyzed for RQ1. For each APP and ACTIVITY, the table reports the actions it RECEIVES and/or SENDS; the KEY used to store the data in the intent object; the VALUE stored, and any PERMISSION needed to access the data. (Action main is android.intent.action.MAIN; action test is amandroid.impliciticctest_action.testaction; action send is android.intent.action.SEND; permission phone is READ_PHONE_STATE; location is ACCESS_FINE_LOCATION, SMS is SEND_SMS.)

APP	ACTIVITY	RECEIVES	SENDS	KEY	VALUE	PERMISSION
Echoer	MainActivity	send				
icc_implicit_action	MainActivity	main	test	"data"	*device id*	phone
	FooActivity	test				
icc_implicit_category	MainActivity	main	test	"data"	*device id*	phone
	FooActivity	test				
icc_implicit_data1	MainActivity	main		"data"	*device id*	phone
	FooActivity	test				
icc_implicit_data2	MainActivity	main	test/type	"data"	*device id*	phone
	FooActivity	test				
icc_implicit_mix1	MainActivity	main	test_action	"data"	*device id*	phone
	HookActivity	test_action2				
icc_implicit_mix2	MainActivity	main	test_action	"data"	*device id*	phone
	FooActivity	test_action				
icc_implicit_nosrc_nosink	MainActivity	main	test	"data"	"noSrc"	
	FooActivity	test				
icc_implicit_nosrc_sink	MainActivity	main	test	"data"	"noSrc"	
	FooActivity	test				
icc_implicit_src_sink	MainActivity	main	test	"data"	*device id*	phone
	FooActivity	test				
SendSms	MainActivity	main				phone, SMS
	Button1Listener		send	"secret"	*device id*	phone, SMS
WriteFile	MainActivity	main				location
	Button1Listener		send	"secret"	*location*	location
org.arguslab.icc_implicit_src_nosink	MainActivity	main	test	"data"	*device id*	phone
	FooActivity	test				

4.2 RQ2: Scalability of *INTENTREPAIR*

4.2.1 Subjects

To assess INTENTREPAIR's scalability, we selected apps from the well-known app hosting platform FDroid [19]. To only consider realistic-size apps, we first selected all apps greater than 5 MB in size (1301 apps); out of them, we further selected all those that use implicit intents (855 apps) as our experimental subjects. Table 3's left-hand half lists the five largest apps in this dataset, ranked by their size.

Although the intent communication API is very rich, Fig. 9a shows that a small fraction of them dominate usage in our subjects. Two out of 25 methods to broadcast an intent object (abstracted by primitive send in Tentative) are used 80% of

```
// More code
TelephonyManager tel=(TelephonyManager) getSystemService(TELEPHONY_SERVICE);
String imei = tel.getDeviceId(); // source
Intent i = new Intent("amandroid.impliciticctest_action.testaction");
i.putExtra("data", imei);
startActivity(i); // sink
```

(a) Sender module `MainActivity` in app `icc_implicit_src_sink` app.

```
// More Code
Intent i = getIntent();
String imei = "" + i.getStringExtra("data");
Log.d("deviceid", imei); //sink
```

```
// More Code
Intent i = getIntent();
String v = i.getStringExtra("data");
v.trim(); //No Leak
```

(b) Receiver module `FooActivity` in app `icc_implicit_src_sink`.

(c) Receiver module `FooActivity` in app `icc_implicit_nosrc_nosink`.

Fig. 8. Snippets of code from Android apps that send sensitive information via implicit intents.

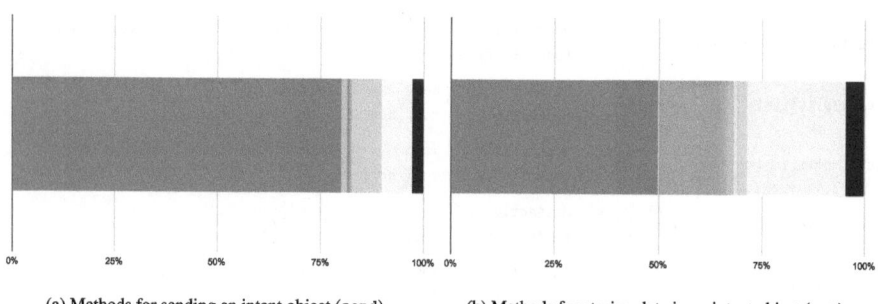

(a) Methods for sending an intent object (`send`).

(b) Methods for storing data in an intent object (`put`).

Fig. 9. Statistics about which intent API methods are used more frequently in RQ2's subjects.

the time; `startActivity(Intent)` alone covers 65% of usages. Similarly, method `putExtra(String, String)` (out of all 30 methods to store data in an intent object) covers 40% of usages; integer values are stored in another 26% of usages.

4.2.2 Analysis and Repair

INTENTREPAIR found 98 app modules (in 83 apps) that send sensitive data (location, file system, . . .) through implicit intents; for 70 of them (in 59 apps), INTENTREPAIR could also determine the 10 different intents' *actions*:[7]

```
android.intent.action.SEND                  ch.blinkenlights.android.vanilla.action.LAUNCH_PLUGIN
android.intent.action.SENDTO                 android.speech.action.RECOGNIZE_SPEECH
android.intent.action.RINGTONE_PICKER        android.intent.action.VIEW-URI
android.media.action.IMAGE_CAPTURE           de.azapps.mirakel.SHOW_TASK_FROM_WIDGET
android.app.action.ADD_DEVICE_ADMIN          android.intent.action.CREATE_DOCUMENT
```

Table 3's right-hand half lists the five largest apps among these 59 apps, ranked by their size. INTENTREPAIR also found 98 app modules that match some of these 70 senders; and 23 sender-receiver pairs where information-flow security leaks may happen. It successfully produced patches for all of these (validated as in RQ1).

---

[7] In the other 28 instances, the action was set dynamically and/or through complex string operations, which could not be resolved statically by INTENTREPAIR.

Table 3. The five largest apps among all RQ2's 855 experimental subjects (left) and among the 59 of them that send sensitive data through implicit intents (right).

AMONG 855 IMPLICIT INTENT APPS		RANK	AMONG 59 SENDER APPS	
APP	SIZE (MB)		APP	SIZE (MB)
org.openttd.fdroid	227	1	com.github.linwoodcloud.dev_doctor	78
org.olpc_france.sugarizer	186	2	org.dslul.openboard.inputmethod.latin	53
com.fr.laboussole.track	174	3	com.celzero.bravedns	47
network.mysterium.vpn	153	4	io.pslab	40
com.zhenxiang.superimage	152	5	org.kiwix.kiwixmobile	40

4.2.3 Scalability

In our experiments, INTENTREPAIR ran for 10.5 s per app on average: this includes sender and receiver analysis (3.5 s), followed by sender-receiver matching and repair (7 s). This performance is reasonable for a prototype implementation, and shows that INTENTREPAIR is also applicable to large apps.

4.3 Discussion

INTENTREPAIR repairs information-flow leaks by simultaneously patching senders and receivers that may communicate; thus, applying the patches only to the receiving apps does not suffice in general. In an ideal scenario, one may equip a receiver with the information obtained by sender analysis, and use that information at runtime to identify the sender's sensitive information (thus avoiding the need for patching the senders). Clearly, this would incur in all sorts of practical hurdles, as it is generally impossible to identify the sender apps with implicit intent communication.

Section 4's empirical evaluation of INTENTREPAIR demonstrated that it is applicable to realistic apps, and that it generates repairs that are effective at removing the source of information-flow leaks. While we informally inspected the patched apps, and tried them out by running them, to gain some confidence that they remain usable and their overall behavior consistent, we did not perform a rigorous analysis of usability. INTENTREPAIR repairs *senders* by simply injecting permission information in their intent objects; since the size of this information is negligible, we are fairly confident that these changes do not have any meaningful impact on the sender app's usability.

INTENTREPAIR's repairs of *receivers* are potentially more invasive, as they may: *i)* request new permissions to the app user, and *ii)* terminate an activity to avoid an security leak. These actions are necessary, in general, to enforce information-flow security, but they may worsen the user experience. As we discussed elsewhere, INTENTREPAIR's repair policies are customizable; thus, one may change it to achieve a different trade-off between usability and security (for example, by declassifying data instead of forcing app termination) depending on the practical application scenario.

5 Related Work

Previous work on automated repair of Android apps focused on bugs such as crashes, leaks, and configuration and compatibility issues. Tan et al. [23] describe how to repair null-pointer dereference crashes. Huang et al.'s technique [16] repairs inconsistent XML configuration files across Android versions. Zhao et al. [28] show how to generate fix templates for system- and device-compatibility issues. Guo et al. [15] detect and repair data losses that may occur when the user navigates from one UI component to another. Banerjee et al. [10] present a combined static and dynamic analysis technique to detect, validate, and repair energy bugs in Android apps. Xu et al. [27] tackle the problem of UI testing scripts becoming obsolete when an app's design changes; to this end, they propose a technique that can identify and remove obsolete testing scripts. Bhatt and Furia [11] present a static analysis tool that can detect and repair Android resource leaks. Unlike all these works, the present paper targets *information-flow* leaks in apps in accordance with the Android permission model; it combines static and dynamic analyses to automatically detect and repair such leaks.

To our knowledge, this paper is the first that can automatically *repair* information-flow security issues that occur in intent communication. In contrast, many approaches [5,6,9,12,17,18,24,26] have been proposed to *detect* information-flow violations; however, most of them focus on intra-app intent communication [5,17,18], whereas our INTENTREPAIR fully supports inter-app detection (as we demonstrated in Sect. 4's evaluation). The few previous approaches that can deal with inter-app communication have limitations—such as they only work on older Android versions [12,26], or rely on third-party slicers [24]—that restrict their effectiveness on realistic apps. Following a general-purpose approach, Mesecan [20] is a repair tool for information-flow bugs that is language- and system-agnostic, as it is based on genetic algorithms. In contrast to their work, our INTENTREPAIR is more specialized (on the Android permission model, and its intent-communication capabilities) and customizable, and is also capable of *detecting* information-flow bugs without requiring tests as input.

6   Conclusions and Future Work

In this paper, we presented INTENTREPAIR: the first automated framework to detect and repair information flow leaks that may occur in Android when apps communicate using implicit intents. To address the key issue that senders and receivers communicating via implicit intents do not have a standard way of identifying the sensitivity of the data they are sharing, INTENTREPAIR performs repair by *injecting* this information in the senders and processing it in the receivers, ensuring that their handling abides by the necessary permissions. We implemented INTENTREPAIR in a prototype tool with the same name. In a preliminary evaluation involving 14 apps from the popular DroidBench and RepoDroid benchmarks, and 855 larger apps from the FDroid repository, INTENT-REPAIR showed promise, as it was able to precisely identify all known information flow security flaws in these apps, and to automatically fix them.

INTENTREPAIR is flexible, in that users can decide how to balance enforcing security and preserving app functionality when they deploy automatically generated repairs. INTENTREPAIR's analysis is also fine-grained, as it can identify different permissions for different pieces of data sent through intents. As future work, we'll systematically evaluate how to implement common declassification patterns that are found in mature apps. Note that Android does offer an API to send intent objects only to receivers with certain permissions; however, this mechanism is coarse-grained and thus inapplicable to many scenarios of implicit intent communication—as we have seen in our experiments, where we found several apps that send data associated with different actions and permissions. In the future, our approach to enable privacy-compliant intent communication could be the basis for an official Android API, or perhaps be provided as an extension of the Android framework—for example, providing the capability of annotating any piece of data with the required permissions. Finally, a rigorous evaluation of INTENTREPAIR's practical usability would also benefit from a user study.

Data Availability. Our prototype implementation of INTENTREPAIR, as well as the detailed experimental results, are available at https://doi.org/10.5281/zenodo.11957919

References

1. Droidbench: A micro-benchmark suite to assess the stability of taint-analysis tools for android. Github. https://github.com/secure-software-engineering/DroidBench/tree/develop
2. Apktool: A tool for reverse engineering android apk files (2024). https://apktool.org
3. Intent communication in android (2024). https://developer.android.com/reference/android/content/Intent
4. Android platform architecture. https://developer.android.com/guide/platform/. Accessed 15 Jan 2024
5. Arzt, S., et al.: Flowdroid: precise context, flow, field, object-sensitive and lifecycle-aware taint analysis for android apps. In: Proceedings of the 35th ACM SIGPLAN Conference on Programming Language Design and Implementation. PLDI '14, pp. 259–269. Association for Computing Machinery, New York, NY, USA (2014). https://doi.org/10.1145/2594291.2594299
6. Arzt, S., et al.: Flowdroid: precise context, flow, field, object-sensitive and lifecycle-aware taint analysis for android apps. SIGPLAN Not. **49**(6), 259–269 (2014). https://doi.org/10.1145/2666356.2594299
7. Backes, M., Bugiel, S., Derr, E., McDaniel, P., Octeau, D., Weisgerber, S.: On demystifying the android application framework: re-visiting android permission specification analysis. In: Proceedings of the 25th USENIX Conference on Security Symposium. SEC'16, pp. 1101–1118. USENIX Association, USA (2016)
8. Backes, M., Bugiel, S., Derr, E., McDaniel, P., Octeau, D., Weisgerber, S.: Github: Axplorer–android permission mappings. GitHub (2024). https://github.com/reddr/axplorer/tree/master
9. Bai, G., et al.: Towards model checking android applications. IEEE Trans. Softw. Eng. **44**(6), 595–612 (2018). https://doi.org/10.1109/TSE.2017.2697848
10. Banerjee, A., Chong, L.K., Ballabriga, C., Roychoudhury, A.: Energypatch: repairing resource leaks to improve energy-efficiency of android apps. IEEE Trans. Softw. Eng. **44**(5), 470–490 (2018). https://doi.org/10.1109/TSE.2017.2689012
11. Bhatt, B.N., Furia, C.A.: Automated repair of resource leaks in android applications. J. Syst. Softw. **192**, 111417 (2022). https://doi.org/10.1016/j.jss.2022.111417, https://www.sciencedirect.com/science/article/pii/S0164121222001273
12. Bosu, A., Liu, F., Yao, D.D., Wang, G.: Collusive data leak and more: large-scale threat analysis of inter-app communications. In: Proceedings of the 2017 ACM on Asia Conference on Computer and Communications Security. ASIA CCS '17, pp. 71–85. Association for Computing Machinery, New York, NY, USA (2017). https://doi.org/10.1145/3052973.3053004
13. Center, I.T.W.R.: Wala T. J. Watson libraries for analysis (2024). https://github.com/wala/WALA

14. Groß, S., Tiwari, A., Hammer, C.: PIAnalyzer: a precise approach for pendingintent vulnerability analysis. In: Lopez, J., Zhou, J., Soriano, M. (eds.) ESORICS 2018. LNCS, vol. 11099, pp. 41–59. Springer, Cham (2018). https://doi.org/10.1007/978-3-319-98989-1_3

15. Guo, W., Dong, Z., Shen, L., Tian, W., Su, T., Peng, X.: Detecting and fixing data loss issues in android apps. In: Proceedings of the 31st ACM SIGSOFT International Symposium on Software Testing and Analysis. ISSTA 2022, pp. 605–616. Association for Computing Machinery, New York, NY, USA (2022). https://doi.org/10.1145/3533767.3534402

16. Huang, H., Xu, C., Wen, M., Liu, Y., Cheung, S.: Conffix: repairing configuration compatibility issues in android apps. ACM (2023). https://doi.org/10.1145/3597926

17. Klieber, W., Flynn, L., Bhosale, A., Jia, L., Bauer, L.: Android taint flow analysis for app sets. In: Proceedings of the 3rd ACM SIGPLAN International Workshop on the State of the Art in Java Program Analysis. SOAP '14, pp. 1–6. Association for Computing Machinery, New York, NY, USA (2014). https://doi.org/10.1145/2614628.2614633

18. Li, L., et al.: ICCTA: detecting inter-component privacy leaks in android apps. In: Proceedings of the 37th International Conference on Software Engineering - Volume 1. ICSE '15, pp. 280–291. IEEE Press (2015)

19. Limited, F.D., Contributors: F-droid (2023). https://f-droid.org

20. Mesecan, I., Blackwell, D., Clark, D., Cohen, M.B., Petke, J.: Hypergi: automated detection and repair of information flow leakage. In: 2021 36th IEEE/ACM International Conference on Automated Software Engineering (ASE), pp. 1358–1362 (2021). https://doi.org/10.1109/ASE51524.2021.9678758

21. Pauck, F.: Repodroid: android benchmark reproduction framework. Github (2024). https://foellix.github.io/ReproDroid/

22. Romdhana, A., Merlo, A., Ceccato, M., Tonella, P.: Assessing the security of inter-app communications in android through reinforcement learning. Comput. Secur. **131**, 103311 (2023)

23. Tan, S.H., Dong, Z., Gao, X., Roychoudhury, A.: Repairing crashes in android apps. In: 2018 IEEE/ACM 40th International Conference on Software Engineering (ICSE), pp. 187–198. ACM (2018). https://doi.org/10.1145/3180155

24. Tiwari, A., Groß, S., Hammer, C.: IIFA: modular inter-app intent information flow analysis of android applications. In: Chen, S., Choo, K.-K.R., Fu, X., Lou, W., Mohaisen, A. (eds.) SecureComm 2019. LNICST, vol. 305, pp. 335–349. Springer, Cham (2019). https://doi.org/10.1007/978-3-030-37231-6_19

25. Tiwari, A., Prakash, J., Dong, Z., Furia, C.A.: Artifacts for automated repair of information flow security in android implicit inter-app communication. Zenodo (2024). https://doi.org/10.5281/zenodo.11957919

26. Wei, F., Roy, S., Ou, X., Robby: amandroid: a precise and general inter-component data flow analysis framework for security vetting of android apps. ACM Trans. Priv. Secur. **21**(3) (2018). https://doi.org/10.1145/3183575

27. Xu, T., et al.: Guider: GUI structure and vision co-guided test script repair for android apps. In: Proceedings of the 30th ACM SIGSOFT International Symposium on Software Testing and Analysis. ISSTA 2021, pp. 191–203. Association for Computing Machinery, New York, NY, USA (2021). https://doi.org/10.1145/3460319.3464830

28. Zhao, Y., Li, L., Liu, K., Grundy, J.: Towards automatically repairing compatibility issues in published android apps. In: Proceedings of the 44th International Conference on Software Engineering. ICSE '22, pp. 2142–2153. Association for Computing Machinery, New York, NY, USA (2022). https://doi.org/10.1145/3510003.3510128

Learning Branching-Time Properties in CTL and ATL via Constraint Solving

Benjamin Bordais[1,2]($\boxtimes$), Daniel Neider[1,2], and Rajarshi Roy[3]

[1] TU Dortmund University, Dortmund, Germany
benjamin.bordais@tu-dortmund.de
[2] Center for Trustworthy Data Science and Security,
University Alliance Ruhr, Dortmund, Germany
[3] Max Planck Institute for Software Systems, Kaiserslautern, Germany

Abstract. We address the problem of learning temporal properties from the branching-time behavior of systems. Existing research in this field has mostly focused on learning linear temporal properties specified using popular logics, such as Linear Temporal Logic (LTL) and Signal Temporal Logic (STL). Branching-time logics such as Computation Tree Logic (CTL) and Alternating-time Temporal Logic (ATL), despite being extensively used in specifying and verifying distributed and multi-agent systems, have not received adequate attention. Thus, in this paper, we investigate the problem of learning CTL and ATL formulas from examples of system behavior. As input to the learning problems, we rely on the typical representations of branching behavior as Kripke structures and concurrent game structures, respectively. Given a sample of structures, we learn concise formulas by encoding the learning problem into a satisfiability problem, most notably by symbolically encoding both the search for prospective formulas and their fixed-point based model checking algorithms. We also study the decision problem of checking the existence of prospective ATL formulas for a given sample. We implement our algorithms in a Python prototype and have evaluated them to extract several common CTL and ATL formulas used in practical applications.

1 Introduction

Formal verification relies on the fact that formal specifications, which are precise descriptions of the design requirements, are either readily available or can be constructed easily. This assumption, however, often proves to be unrealistic as constructing specifications manually is not only tedious but also prone to errors. As a result, for years, the availability of precise, functional, and usable specifications has been one of the biggest bottlenecks of formal methods [3,14,50].

To tackle this serious limitation, recent research has concentrated on automatically generating specifications, especially in temporal logics. There is a large body of works targeted towards learning specifications in linear-time logics such as Linear Temporal Logic (LTL) [19,41], Metric Temporal Logic (MTL) [45], Signal Temporal Logic (STL) [15,39], etc. These approaches not only generate

A. Platzer et al. (Eds.): FM 2024, LNCS 14933, pp. 304–323, 2025.
https://doi.org/10.1007/978-3-031-71162-6_16

reliable specifications but can also be used to infer interpretable descriptions for complex temporal behaviors.

Along with linear-time logics, branching-time logics have had a significant impact on formal verification. Computation Tree Logic (CTL) [24], which combines temporal operators such as $\mathbf{X}$ (next), $\mathbf{F}$ (finally), $\mathbf{G}$ (globally) with the branching quantifiers $\mathbf{E}$ (exists) and $\mathbf{A}$ (all), is a specification language of choice for numerous verification tools [11,22,30]. Alternating-time Temporal Logic (ATL) [1], which augments CTL with a "cooperation" quantifier $\langle\langle \cdot \rangle\rangle$ to reason about interaction of multiple agents, is popular in specifying properties for distributed and multi-agent systems [2,36] and has several applications in AI domains [29,38].

Despite the significance of branching-time logics, learning such specifications has received considerably less attention. The few existing works handle the problem of completing user-defined queries [20], i.e., specifications with missing parts, or searching for specifications based on few restricted templates [54] such as $\mathbf{AF}?$, $\mathbf{AG}(?_1 \rightarrow \mathbf{F}?_2)$, etc. These works are limited in their generality and require one to handcraft queries/templates suitable for learning.

Towards learning arbitrary branching-time properties, we consider the *passive learning* problem for both CTL and ATL. This problem requires, given a sample $\mathcal{S}$ of positive (or desirable) and negative (or undesirable) structures, to infer a minimal CTL/ATL formula that is consistent with $\mathcal{S}$. Passive learning is widely studied in the literature [13,27,41] and forms a significant part of many learning frameworks [19,48] (see Sect. 3 for elaboration). In our learning problem, we consider, as input, structures typical for describing branching behavior: Kripke structures (KSs) and concurrent game structures (CGSs), which model single and multi-agent systems, respectively.

To address the passive learning problem, we design algorithms for CTL and ATL that employ constraint-solving techniques to learn prospective formulas. Following Neider and Gavran [41], our algorithms search for prospective formulas of size n for a given sample $\mathcal{S}$, by encoding the problem into the satisfiability of a propositional formula $\Omega_n^{\mathcal{S}}$. This formula is then solved using an off-the-shelf SAT solver to obtain a CTL/ATL formula of size n if one exists. The crux of the SAT encoding lies in symbolically encoding both the structure of the formula and the standard fixed-point based model-checking for the symbolic formula.

To present the technical details of the encoding, we focus on passive learning of ATL formulas from CGSs, as ATL and CGSs generalize CTL and KSs for multi-agent settings, respectively. In particular, restricting the number of agents to one simply reduces ATL to CTL and CGSs to KSs. Nonetheless, we highlight aspects of the learning algorithm that improve in the case of CTL passive learning.

We also initiate the theoretical study of the ATL passive learning problem . We study the decision problem of whether there is an ATL formula consistent with $\mathcal{S}$. We extend already existing results for CTL to the case of ATL: we show that the decision problem for full ATL can be solved in polynomial time (Theorem 1, extending [17, Thm. 3.2, 3.9]). We also show that, for any fragment of ATL, the same decision problem can be decided in exponential time (Theorem 2, extending [34, Thm. 3]). In the same theorem, we exhibit an exponential bound on the size of the formulae that need to be considered to find a consistent one, regardless of the fragment considered (parallelizing [43, Coro. 1]).

We have implemented our learning algorithms in an open-source prototype that can access an array of SAT solvers. We evaluate the prototype on synthetic benchmarks consisting of samples of KSs and CGSs that reflect typical branching-time properties. We observed that our algorithms display the ability to learn formulas from samples of varying sizes. Further, we demonstrated improvements to the SAT encoding for enhanced runtime performance.

We include all missing proofs and experiments in an extended version [16].

Related Works. As alluded to above, most of the works in inferring temporal logics focus on linear-time logics. For LTL, many works consider learning based on handcrafted templates or queries, which are incomplete formulas [31,35,51]. Few others learn formulas of arbitrary syntactic structure in LTL (or its important fragments) either by exploiting constraint solving [19,41,46] or efficient enumerative search [44,52]. Some recent works rely on neuro-symbolic approaches to learn LTL formulas from noisy data [37,53]. For STL, most works focus on learning formulas of particular syntactic structure [15,15] or searching time intervals for STL formulas of known structure [6,32,33]. A handful of works consider learning STL formulas of arbitrary structure [39,42]. There are also works on learning several other logics such as Metric Temporal Logic [45], Past LTL [5], Property Specification Language [47], etc. In contrast, research on learning branching-time properties remains relatively sparse. Chan [20] considers the problem of completing CTL queries—incomplete CTL formulas with missing (Boolean combinations of) atomic propositions. A related work by Wasylkowski and Zeller [54] considers inferring operational preconditions for Java methods in CTL. Both of these works are limited in their ability to search through large number of CTL formulas of arbitrary syntactic structure. As a result, they resort to user-defined queries or handcrafted templates to reduce the search space of specifications.

A recent paper by Pommellet et al. [43] addresses the problem of learning CTL formulas from a sample of Kripke structures (KSs). Their learning algorithm follows a SAT-based paradigm and uses an encoding similar to ours. Our encoding for CTL was developed independently [49]. In this paper, we study the more general problem of learning ATL formulas from CGSs, which conceptually subsumes the problem of learning CTL formulas from KSs.

Another work that devises a similar encoding is the one by Bertrand et al. [12]. Their SMT encoding, albeit similar, is tailored towards solving a different problem of synthesizing small models for probabilistic CTL (PCTL) formulas.

2 Preliminaries

We refer to the set of positive integers by $\mathbb{N}_1$. For $n \in \mathbb{N}_1$, we let $[1, n] \subseteq \mathbb{N}_1$ denote the set $\{1, \ldots, n\}$. For a non-empty set Q, we let Q^*, Q^+, Q^ω denote the set of finite, non-empty finite, and infinite sequences of elements in Q, respectively. For all $\bullet \in \{*, +, \omega\}$, $\rho \in Q^\bullet$, and $i \in \mathbb{N}$, if ρ has at least $i + 1$ elements, we let $\rho[i] \in Q$ denote the $(i+1)$-th element in ρ, $\rho[:i] \in Q^+$ denote the finite sequence $\rho_0 \cdots \rho_i \in Q^+$, and $\rho[i:] \in Q^\bullet$ denote the sequence $\rho_i \cdots \in Q^\bullet$.

2.1   Concurrent Game Structure (CGS) and Kripke Structure

We model multi-agent systems with concurrent game structures defined below.

Definition 1. *A concurrent game structure (CGS for short) is a tuple $C = \langle Q, I, k, \mathcal{P}, \pi, d, \delta \rangle$ where Q is the finite set of states, $I \subseteq Q$ is the set of initial states, $k \in \mathbb{N}_1$ is the number of agents, we denote by $\mathsf{Ag} := [\![1,k]\!]$ the set of k agents. Furthermore, $\mathcal{P}$ is the finite set of propositions (or observations) , $\pi : Q \mapsto 2^{\mathcal{P}}$ maps each state $q \in Q$ to the set of propositions $\pi(q) \subseteq \mathcal{P}$ that hold in q. Finally, $d : Q \times \mathsf{Ag} \to \mathbb{N}_1$ maps each state and agent to the number of actions available to that agent at that state, and $\delta : Q_{\mathsf{Act}} \to Q$ is the function mapping every state and tuple of one action per agent to the next state, where $Q_{\mathsf{Act}} := \cup_{q \in Q} Q_{\mathsf{Act}}(q)$ with $Q_{\mathsf{Act}}(q) := \{(q, \alpha_1, \ldots, \alpha_k) \mid \forall a \in \mathsf{Ag}, \alpha_a \in [\![1, d(q,a)]\!]\}$ representing the set of tuples of actions available to the players at state q.*

For all $q \in Q$ and $A \subseteq \mathsf{Ag}$, we let $\mathsf{Act}_A(q) := \{\alpha = (\alpha_a)_{a \in A} \in \prod_{a \in A} \{a\} \times [\![1, d(q,a)]\!]\}$. Then, for all tuple $\alpha \in \mathsf{Act}_A(q)$ of one action per agent in A, we let:

$$\mathsf{Succ}(q, \alpha) := \{q' \in Q \mid \exists \alpha' \in \mathsf{Act}_{\mathsf{Ag}\setminus A}(q),\ \delta(q, (\alpha, \alpha')) = q'\}$$

When $k = 1$, the CGS C is called a Kripke structure. In that case, for all states $q \in Q$, we have the set $\mathsf{Succ}(q) \subseteq Q$ of the successor states of Q.

Finally, we define the size $|C|$ of the structure C by $|C| = |Q_{\mathsf{Act}}| + |\mathcal{P}| + |\mathsf{Ag}|$.

Unless otherwise stated, a CGS C refers to the tuple $C = \langle Q, I, k, \mathcal{P}, \pi, d, \delta \rangle$.

In a CGS, a strategy for an agent is a function that prescribes to the agent what to do as a function of the history of the game, i.e., the finite sequence of states seen so far. Moreover, given a coalition of agents and a tuple of one strategy per agent in the coalition, we define the set of infinite sequences of states that can occur with this tuple of strategies. Formally, we define this as follows.

Definition 2. *Consider a CGS C and an agent $a \in \mathsf{Ag}$. A strategy for Agent a is a function $s_a : Q^+ \to \mathbb{N}_1$ such that, for all $\rho = \rho_0 \ldots \rho_n \in Q^+$, we have $s_a(\rho) \le d(\rho_n, a)$. We let S_a denote the set of strategies available to Agent a.*

Given a coalition (or subset) of agents $A \subseteq \mathsf{Ag}$, a strategy profile for the coalition A is a tuple $s = (s_a)_{a \in A}$ of one strategy per agent in A. We denote by S_A the set of strategy profiles for the coalition A. For all $s \in \mathsf{S}_A$ and $q \in Q$, we let $\mathsf{Out}^Q(q, s) \subseteq Q^\omega$ denote the set of infinite paths ρ compatible with s from q:

$$\mathsf{Out}^Q(q, s) := \{\rho \in Q^\omega \mid \rho[0] = q,\ \forall i \in \mathbb{N}, \rho[i+1] \in \mathsf{Succ}(\rho[i], (s_a(\rho[:i]))_{a \in A})\}$$

2.2   Alternating-Time Temporal Logic

Alternating-time Temporal Logic (ATL) is a temporal logic that takes into accounts strategic behavior of the agents. It can be seen as a generalization

of Computation Tree Logic (CTL) with more than one agent. There are two
different kinds of ATL formulas: state formulas—where propositions and strategic operators occur—and path formulas – where temporal operators occur. To
avoid confusion, we denote state formulas and path formulas with Greek capital
letters and Greek lowercase letters, respectively. ATL state formulas over a set
of propositions $\mathcal{P}$ and a set of agents Ag are given by the grammar:

$$\Phi ::= p \mid \neg\Phi \mid \Phi \wedge \Phi \mid \langle\!\langle A \rangle\!\rangle \varphi,$$

where $p \in \mathcal{P}$ is a proposition, $A \subseteq \mathsf{Ag}$ is a coalition of agents and φ is a path
formula. We include the Boolean constants *true* and *false* and other operators
such as $\Phi \vee \Phi_2$ and $\Phi_1 \Rightarrow \Phi_2$. Next, ATL path formulas are given by the grammar:

$$\varphi ::= \mathbf{X}\,\Phi \mid \Phi\,\mathbf{U}\,\Phi \mid \mathbf{G}\,\Phi$$

where $\mathbf{X}$ is the neXt operator, $\mathbf{U}$ is the Until operator, and $\mathbf{G}$ is the Globally operator. As syntactic sugar, we allow standard temporal operators $\mathbf{F}$, the
Finally operator, which is defined in the usual manner: for any coalition of agents
$A \subseteq \mathsf{Ag}$: $\langle\!\langle A \rangle\!\rangle \mathbf{F}\,\Phi := \langle\!\langle A \rangle\!\rangle (\mathit{true}\,\mathbf{U}\,\Phi)$.

A CTL formula is an ATL formula on a single agent $\mathsf{Ag} = \{1\}$. In particular,
the path quantifiers of CTL can be obtained as follows: $\mathbf{E} \equiv \langle\!\langle 1 \rangle\!\rangle$ and $\mathbf{A} \equiv \langle\!\langle\rangle\!\rangle$.

The size $|\Phi|$ of an ATL formula Φ is then defined as size of the set of sub-
formulas: $|\Phi| := |\mathsf{SubF}(\Phi)|$, which is defined inductively as follows:

- $\mathsf{SubF}(p) := \{p\}$ for all $p \in \mathcal{P}$;
- $\mathsf{SubF}(\neg\Phi) := \{\neg\Phi\} \cup \mathsf{SubF}(\Phi)$;
- $\mathsf{SubF}(\Phi_1 \wedge \Phi_2) := \{\Phi_1 \wedge \Phi_2\} \cup \mathsf{SubF}(\Phi_1) \cup \mathsf{SubF}(\Phi_2)$;
- $\mathsf{SubF}(\langle\!\langle A \rangle\!\rangle \bullet \Phi) := \{\langle\!\langle A \rangle\!\rangle \bullet \Phi\} \cup \mathsf{SubF}(\Phi)$ for $\bullet \in \{\mathbf{X}, \mathbf{G}\}$ and $A \subseteq \mathsf{Ag}$;
- $\mathsf{SubF}(\langle\!\langle A \rangle\!\rangle(\Phi_1 \mathbf{U} \Phi_2)) := \{\langle\!\langle A \rangle\!\rangle(\Phi_1 \mathbf{U} \Phi_2)\} \cup \mathsf{SubF}(\Phi_1) \cup \mathsf{SubF}(\Phi_2)$ for $A \subseteq \mathsf{Ag}$.

We interpret ATL formulas over CGSs C using the standard definitions [1].
Given a state $q \in Q$, we define when a state formula Φ holds in state q—denoted
by $q \models \Phi$—inductively as follows:

$$q \models p \ \text{iif} \ p \in \pi(q),$$
$$q \models \neg\Phi \ \text{iif} \ q \not\models \Phi,$$
$$q \models \Phi_1 \wedge \Phi_2 \ \text{iif} \ q \models \Phi_1 \ \text{and} \ q \models \Phi_2,$$
$$q \models \langle\!\langle A \rangle\!\rangle \varphi \ \text{iif} \ \exists s \in S_A, \ \forall \rho \in \mathsf{Out}^Q(q, s), \ \rho \models \varphi$$

Similarly, given a path $\rho \in Q^\omega$ and a path formula φ, we define when φ holds
on path ρ, denoted $\rho \models \varphi$ as above, inductively as follows:

$$\rho \models \mathbf{X}\,\Phi \ \text{iif} \ \rho[1:] \models \Phi$$
$$\rho \models \Phi_1 \mathbf{U} \Phi_2 \ \text{iif} \ \exists j \in \mathbb{N}, \ \rho[j] \models \Phi_2, \ \text{and} \ \forall k < j, \rho[k:] \models \Phi_1$$
$$\rho \models \mathbf{G}\,\Phi \ \text{iif} \ \forall j \in \mathbb{N}, \ \rho[j:] \models \Phi$$

We say that an ATL formula Φ accepts (resp. rejects) a state q if $q \models \Phi$ (resp. $q \not\models \Phi$). We say that it distinguishes two states q, q' if it accepts one and rejects the other. Finally, we then say that the ATL formula Φ accepts a CGS C, denoted by $C \models \Phi$, if Φ accepts all initial states of C.

Remark 1. When evaluated on turn-based game structures (i.e., where, at each state, at most one player has more than one action available), the formulas $\langle\!\langle A \rangle\!\rangle\varphi$ and $\neg\langle\!\langle \mathsf{Ag} \setminus A \rangle\!\rangle\neg\varphi$ are equivalent (However, it is not the case when they are evaluated on arbitrary CGSs.)

3 Passive Learning for ATL

In this problem, we are given a sample $\mathcal{S} = (P, N)$ consisting of a set P of positive structures and a set N of negative structures. The goal is to find a minimal formula Φ that is *consistent* with $\mathcal{S}$, i.e., Φ must hold on all positive structures and must not hold on any negative structure. We are specifically searching for a minimal formula and the reason for this is two-fold: (1) the prospective formula will be more interpretable, and (2) it will not overfit the sample [41,47]. Formally:

Problem 1 (Passive learning of ATL). Given a sample $\mathcal{S} = (P, N)$ consisting of two finite sets P and N of concurrent game structures (CGSs) with the same set Ag of agents, find a minimal size ATL formula Φ on Ag that is consistent with $\mathcal{S}$.

The passive learning problem of CTL can be obtained by simplifying Problem 1 by use of a single agent $\mathsf{Ag} = \{1\}$, which reduces CGSs to KSs and ATL to CTL.

Before describing our solution to Problem 1, we briefly discuss the source of the positive and negative structures. Passive learning, among several applications, constitutes a critical subroutine of certain learning frameworks. Active learning [4], which involves learning black-box systems by interacting with a teacher, often involves repeated passive learning on the counter-example models, i.e., the feedback, received from the teacher [19]. Furthermore, one-class classification, or learning from positive examples, leverages passive learning to derive candidate formulas [8,48]. These formulas facilitate the generation of negative examples, which help refine the search for more concise and descriptive formulas.

A concrete application of Problem 1 would be to provide contrastive explanations [31] in a multi-agent setting. Consider a multi-agent system that is deemed to have some "good" positions and some "bad" positions. This system would yield positive and negative CGSs corresponding to the good and bad positions. To explain the dichotomy between these good and bad positions, one can learn an ATL formula that accepts the positive CGSs and rejects the negative ones.

3.1 SAT-Based Learning Algorithm

Our approach to solving Problem 1 is by reducing it to satisfiability problems in propositional logic. We thus provide a brief introduction to propositional logic.

Propositional Logic. Let Var be a set of propositional variables that can be set to Boolean values from $\mathbb{B} = \{0, 1\}$ (0 representing *false* and 1 representing *true*). Formulas in Propositional Logic are inductively constructed as follows:

$$\Omega ::= true \mid false \mid x \in \mathsf{Var} \mid \neg\Omega \mid \Omega \vee \Omega \mid \Omega \wedge \Omega \mid \Omega \Rightarrow \Omega \mid \Omega \Leftrightarrow \Omega$$

To avoid confusion with ATL formulas, we will be exclusively using the letter Ω (along with its variants) to denote propositional formulas.

To assign values to propositional variables, we rely on a valuation function $v : \mathsf{Var} \to \mathbb{B}$. We exploit the valuation function v to define the satisfaction $v \models \Omega$ of a propositional formula Ω; we use standard definitions for this. When $v \models \Omega$, we say that v satisfies Ω and call it a *satisfying valuation* of Ω. A formula Ω is *satisfiable* if there exists a satisfying valuation v of Φ. The satisfiability (SAT) problem for propositional logic is a well-known NP-complete problem, which asks if a propositional formula given as input is satisfiable. To handle SAT, numerous optimized decision procedures have been designed in recent years [7,10,40].

We now describe a reduction of Problem 1 to SAT , inspired by [19,41]. Following their work, we design a propositional formula $\Omega_n^{\mathcal{S}}$ that enables the search for an ATL formula of size at most n that is consistent with a sample $\mathcal{S}$. The formula $\Omega_n^{\mathcal{S}}$ has the following properties:

1. $\Omega_n^{\mathcal{S}}$ is satisfiable if and only if there exists an ATL formula of size at most n that is consistent with $\mathcal{S}$; and
2. from a satisfying valuation of $\Omega_n^{\mathcal{S}}$, one can easily extract a suitable ATL formula of size at most n.

One can then iteratively search for a minimal, consistent formula: increment n by 1, check satisfiability of $\Omega_n^{\mathcal{S}}$ and extract a formula if satisfiable; else repeat.

The formula $\Omega_n^{\mathcal{S}}$ is defined as a conjunction of subformulas with distinct roles: $\Omega_n^{\mathcal{S}} := \Omega_n^{\mathsf{str}} \wedge \Omega_n^{\mathsf{sem}} \wedge \Omega_n^{\mathsf{con}}$. The subformula Ω^{str} encodes the structure of the prospective ATL formula Φ. The subformula Ω^{sem} encodes that the correct semantics of ATL is used to interpret the prospective ATL formula on the given CGSs. Finally, the subformula Ω^{con} ensures that the prospective ATL formula holds on the models in P and not in the models in N. The formula used for CTL learning has an identical high-level structure, with similar subformulas.

We now describe the subformulas of $\Omega_n^{\mathcal{S}}$ in detail.

Encoding the Structure of ATL Formulas. The structure of an ATL formula is symbolically encoded as a *syntax DAG*. A syntax DAG of an ATL formula is simply a syntax tree in which the common nodes are merged. Figure 1 depicts an example of a syntax tree and DAG of an ATL formula.

To conveniently encode the syntax DAG of an ATL formula, we first fix a naming convention for its nodes. For a formula of size at most n, we assign to each of its nodes an identifier in $[\![1, n]\!]$ such that the identifier of each node is larger than those of its children, if applicable. Note that such a naming convention may not be unique. We then denote the sub-formula of Φ rooted at Node i as $\Phi[i]$. Thus, $\Phi[n]$ denotes the entire formula Φ.

Fig. 1. Syntax DAG with identifiers (indicated above nodes) of $\langle\langle 2 \rangle\rangle \mathbf{X}\, p \vee \langle\langle 1 \rangle\rangle (p \,\mathbf{U}\, \langle\langle 1,3 \rangle\rangle \mathbf{G}\, q)$.

Next, to encode a syntax DAG symbolically, we introduce the following propositional variables: (i) $x_{i,\lambda}$ for $i \in [\![1,n]\!]$ and $\lambda \in \mathcal{P} \cup \Lambda$ with $\Lambda :=$ $\{\neg, \wedge, \langle\langle \cdot \rangle\rangle\mathbf{X}, \langle\langle \cdot \rangle\rangle\mathbf{G}, \langle\langle \cdot \rangle\rangle\mathbf{U}\}$; (ii) $A_{i,a}$ for $i \in [\![1,n]\!]$ and $a \in \mathsf{Ag}$; and (iii) $l_{i,j}$ and $r_{i,j}$ for $i \in [\![1,n]\!]$ and $j \in [\![1, i-1]\!]$. The variable $x_{i,\lambda}$ tracks the operator labeled in Node i, meaning, $x_{i,\lambda}$ is set to true if and only if Node i is labeled with λ. The variable $A_{i,a}$ is relevant only if $x_{i,\langle\langle\cdot\rangle\rangle\bullet}$ is set to true for some temporal operator $\bullet \in \{\mathbf{X}, \mathbf{G}, \mathbf{U}\}$. In such a case, the variables $(A_{i,a})_{a\in\mathsf{Ag}}$ track which agents are in the coalition $\langle\langle\cdot\rangle\rangle$ at Node i. The variable $l_{i,j}$ (resp., $r_{i,j}$) tracks the left (resp., right) child of Node i, meaning, $l_{i,j}$ (resp., $r_{i,j}$) is set to true if and only if the left (resp., right) child of Node i is Node j.

To ensure that these variables encode a valid syntax DAG, we impose structural constraints similar to the ones proposed by Neider and Gavran [41]. For instance, the constraint below ensures that each node is labeled with a unique operator:

$$\Big[\bigwedge_{i\in[\![1,n]\!]} \bigvee_{\lambda\in\Lambda} x_{i,\lambda} \Big] \wedge \Big[\bigwedge_{i\in[\![1,n]\!]} \bigwedge_{\lambda\neq\lambda'\in\Lambda} \neg x_{i,\lambda} \vee \neg x_{i,\lambda'} \Big]$$

We impose similar constraints to ensure that each node has a unique left and right child. The formula Ω_n^{str} is simply the conjunction of all such structural constraints.

Based on a satisfying valuation v of Ω_n^{str}, one can construct a unique ATL formula: label each Node i with the operator λ for which $v(x_{i,\lambda}) = 1$, include players in a coalition for which $v(A_{i,a}) = 1$, and mark the left (resp., right) child with Nodes j (resp., j') for which $v(l_{i,j}) = 1$ (resp., $v(r_{i,j'}) = 1$).

For encoding the structure of CTL, the only difference from that of ATL is that we rely on CTL operators, e.g., $\Lambda := \{\neg, \wedge, \mathbf{EX}, \mathbf{EG}, \mathbf{EU}\}$.

Encoding the Semantics of ATL Formulas. To symbolically encode the semantics of the prospective ATL formula Φ for a given CGS C, we rely on encoding the ATL model-checking procedure developed in [1, Section 4]. The procedure involves calculating, for each sub-formula Φ' of Φ, the set $\mathsf{SAT}_C(\Phi') = \{q \in Q \mid q \models \Phi'\}$ of the states of C where Φ' holds. Since we consider ATL formulas, we need to handle the strategic operators $\langle\langle A \rangle\rangle$ for $A \subseteq \mathsf{Ag}$. To do so, given a coalition of agents $A \subseteq \mathsf{Ag}$ and some subset of states $S \subseteq Q$, we let $\mathsf{Pre}_A(S) \subseteq Q$ denote the set of states from which the coalition A has a strategy to enforce reaching the set S in one step. That is: $\mathsf{Pre}_A(S) := \{q \in Q \mid \exists \alpha \in \mathsf{Act}_A(q),\ \mathsf{Succ}(q, \alpha) \subseteq S\}$.

We can now describe how to compute the set $\mathrm{SAT}_C(\Phi)$. It is done inductively on the structure of the ATL formula Φ as follows:

$$\mathrm{SAT}_C(p) = \{q \in Q \mid p \in \pi(q)\}, \text{ for any } p \in \mathcal{P}, \tag{1}$$

$$\mathrm{SAT}_C(\Phi \wedge \Psi) = \mathrm{SAT}_C(\Phi) \cap \mathrm{SAT}_C(\Psi), \tag{2}$$

$$\mathrm{SAT}_C(\neg\Phi) = Q \setminus \mathrm{SAT}_C(\Phi), \tag{3}$$

$$\mathrm{SAT}_C(\langle\!\langle A \rangle\!\rangle \mathbf{X}\, \Phi) = \mathsf{Pre}_A(\mathrm{SAT}_C(\Phi)), \tag{4}$$

$\mathrm{SAT}_C(\langle\!\langle A \rangle\!\rangle(\Phi_1\, \mathbf{U}\, \Phi_2))$ is the smallest $T \subseteq Q$, such that

$$(1)\ \mathrm{SAT}_C(\Phi_2) \subseteq T \text{ and } (2)\ \mathrm{SAT}_C(\Phi_1) \cap \mathsf{Pre}_A(T) \subseteq T, \tag{5}$$

$\mathrm{SAT}_C(\langle\!\langle A \rangle\!\rangle \mathbf{G}\, \Phi)$ is the largest $T \subseteq Q$, such that

$$(1)\ T \subseteq \mathrm{SAT}_C(\Phi) \text{ and } (2)\ T \subseteq \mathsf{Pre}_A(T) \tag{6}$$

Our goal is to symbolically encode the above-described computation. To do so, we introduce the propositional variables $y_{i,q}^C$ for each $i \in [\![1, n]\!]$, $q \in Q$ that track whether a state $q \in Q$ belongs to $\mathrm{SAT}_C(\Phi[i])$ for a sub-formula $\Phi[i]$ of Φ . That is, $y_{i,q}^C$ is set to true if and only if $\Phi[i]$ holds in state q, i.e. $q \in \mathrm{SAT}_C(\Phi[i])$.

Before defining the propositional formulas that ensure the desired meaning of the variables $y_{i,q}^C$, we introduce formulas to keep track of whether a state belongs to the set $\mathsf{Pre}_A(S)$. Formally, for all $q \in Q$ and $i \in [\![1, n]\!]$, given any predicate $y_S : Q \Rightarrow \mathbb{B}$ (encoding a set $S = (y_S)^{-1}[true] \subseteq Q$), we define the formula $\Omega_{q,i}^{\mathsf{Pre}}(y_S)$ that encodes the fact that $q \in \mathsf{Pre}_{A_i}(S)$, where A_i is the coalition of agents defined by the variables $(A_{i,a})_{a \in \mathsf{Ag}}$. This formula is defined as follows:

$$\Omega_{q,i}^{\mathsf{Pre},C}(y_S) := \bigvee_{\alpha \in \mathsf{Act}_{\mathsf{Ag}}(q)} \bigwedge_{\alpha' \in \mathsf{Act}_{\mathsf{Ag}}(q)} \left[\left(\bigwedge_{a \in \mathsf{Ag}} A_{i,a} \Rightarrow (\alpha_a = \alpha'_a) \right) \Rightarrow y_S(\delta(q, \alpha')) \right]$$

This formula can be informally read as follows: there exists an action tuple for the coalition A (the disjunction), such that for all action tuples for the opposing coalition (the conjunction), the corresponding state is in the set S (indicated by $y_S(\delta(q, \alpha'))$). Since we do not know, a priori, what the coalition A_i is, we quantify over action tuples for all the agents both in the disjunction and the conjunction. However, the rightmost implication of the formula ensures that the only relevant tuples of actions $\alpha' \in \mathsf{Act}_{\mathsf{Ag}}(q)$ are those for which the action for the agents in the coalition A_i are given by the tuple of actions $\alpha \in \mathsf{Act}_{\mathsf{Ag}}(q)$.

We define the formulas ensuring the intended meaning of the variables $y_{i,q}$.

$$\Omega^{\text{sem}}_{\mathcal{P},C} := \bigwedge_{p\in\mathcal{P}} \bigwedge_{i\in[\![1,n]\!]} \left[x_{i,p} \Rightarrow \bigwedge_{q\in Q,\, p\in\pi(q)} y^C_{i,q} \wedge \bigwedge_{q\in Q,\, p\notin\pi(q)} \neg y^C_{i,q} \right]$$

$$\Omega^{\text{sem}}_{\wedge,C} := \bigwedge_{\substack{i\in[\![1,n]\!]\\ j,j'\in[\![1,i-1]\!]}} \left[[x_{i,\wedge} \wedge l_{i,j} \wedge r_{i,j'}] \Rightarrow \bigwedge_{q\in Q} [y^C_{i,q} \Leftrightarrow [y^C_{j,q} \wedge y^C_{j',q}]] \right]$$

$$\Omega^{\text{sem}}_{\neg,C} := \bigwedge_{\substack{i\in[\![1,n]\!]\\ j\in[\![1,i-1]\!]}} \left[[x_{i,\neg} \wedge l_{i,j}] \Rightarrow \bigwedge_{q\in Q} [y^C_{i,q} \Leftrightarrow \neg y^C_{j,q}] \right]$$

$$\Omega^{\text{sem}}_{\mathbf{X},C} := \bigwedge_{\substack{i\in[\![1,n]\!]\\ j\in[\![1,i-1]\!]}} \left[[x_{i,\langle\!\langle\cdot\rangle\!\rangle\mathbf{X}} \wedge l_{i,j}] \Rightarrow \bigwedge_{q\in Q} [y^C_{i,q} \Leftrightarrow \Omega^{\text{Pre},C}_{q,i}(y^C_{j,\cdot})] \right]$$

The above formulas encode, via a straightforward translation, the SAT_C computation for the propositions, Boolean operators and the $\langle\!\langle\cdot\rangle\!\rangle\mathbf{X}$ operator.

The case of the $\langle\!\langle\cdot\rangle\!\rangle\mathbf{U}$ and $\langle\!\langle\cdot\rangle\!\rangle\mathbf{G}$ operators require some innovation. Indeed, as can be seen in Eqs. (5) and (6), the SAT_C involves a least and greatest fixed-point, respectively . To circumvent this difficulty, we mimic the steps of the fixed-point computation algorithm [1, Fig. 3] in propositional logic. Let us recall how they are computed. Given an ATL formula $\Phi = \langle\!\langle A\rangle\!\rangle\Phi_1\, \mathbf{U}\,\Phi_2$, the way $\text{SAT}_C(\Phi)$ is computed from $\text{SAT}_C(\Phi_1)$ and $\text{SAT}_C(\Phi_2)$ is described in Algorithm 1. Similarly, given an ATL formula $\Phi = \langle\!\langle A\rangle\!\rangle\mathbf{G}\,\Phi'$, the way $\text{SAT}_C(\Phi)$ is computed from $\text{SAT}_C(\Phi')$ is described in Algorithm 2. Note that, instead of using *while* loops, as in [1, Fig. 3], that are necessarily exited after at most $|Q|$ steps, we use *for* loops.

Algorithm 1. Compute $\text{SAT}_C(\Phi)$ for $\Phi = \langle\!\langle A\rangle\!\rangle\Phi_1\,\mathbf{U}\,\Phi_2$

Input: CGS C, coalition A, $\text{SAT}_C(\Phi_1)$ and $\text{SAT}_C(\Phi_2)$
1: $S := \text{SAT}_C(\Phi_2)$
2: **for** $1 \le k \le |Q|$ **do**
3:    $S \leftarrow S \cup \{q \in \text{SAT}_C(\Phi_1) \cap \text{Pre}_A(S)\}$
4: **return** S

Algorithm 2. Compute $\text{SAT}_C(\Phi)$ for $\Phi = \langle\!\langle A\rangle\!\rangle\, \mathbf{G}\,\Phi'$

Input: CGS C, coalition A and $\text{SAT}_C(\Phi')$
1: $S := \text{SAT}_C(\Phi')$
2: **for** $1 \le k \le |Q|$ **do**
3:    $S \leftarrow S \cap \text{Pre}_A(S)$
4: **return** S

As can be seen in both algorithms, the fixed-point computation algorithm internally maintains an estimate of the SAT_C set and updates it iteratively. Thus, to encode the fixed-point computation, we introduce propositional variables that encode whether a state q of a CGS C belongs to a particular estimate of SAT_C. Formally, we introduce propositional variables $y^C_{i,q,k}$ for each $i \in [\![1, n]\!]$, $q \in A$, and $k \in [\![0, |Q|]\!]$, where the parameter $k \in [\![0, |Q|]\!]$ tracks which iterative step of the fixed-point computation the variable $y^C_{i,q,k}$ encodes. We define the formulas below to ensure the intended meaning of these introduced variables:

$$\Omega^{\mathsf{sem}}_{\mathsf{U},C} := \bigwedge_{\substack{i \in [\![1,n]\!] \\ j,j' \in [\![1,n]\!]}} [x_{i,\langle\!\langle \cdot \rangle\!\rangle \mathsf{U}} \wedge l_{i,j} \wedge r_{i,j'}] \Rightarrow \bigwedge_{q \in Q} \Big[[y^C_{i,q,0} \Leftrightarrow y^C_{j',q}] \wedge$$

$$\bigwedge_{0 \leq k \leq |Q|-1} [y^C_{i,q,k+1} \Leftrightarrow [y^C_{i,q,k} \vee [y^C_{j,q} \wedge \Omega^{\mathsf{Pre}}_{q,i}(y^C_{i,\cdot,k})]]] \wedge [y^C_{i,q} \Leftrightarrow y^C_{i,q,|Q|}] \Big]$$

$$\Omega^{\mathsf{sem}}_{\mathsf{G},C} := \bigwedge_{\substack{i \in [\![1,n]\!] \\ j \in [\![1,i-1]\!]}} [x_{i,\langle\!\langle \cdot \rangle\!\rangle \mathsf{G}} \wedge l_{i,j}] \Rightarrow \bigwedge_{q \in Q} \Big[[y^C_{i,q,0} \Leftrightarrow y^C_{j,q}] \wedge$$

$$\bigwedge_{0 \leq k \leq |Q|-1} [y^C_{i,q,k+1} \Leftrightarrow [y^C_{i,q,k} \wedge \Omega^{\mathsf{Pre}}_{q,i}(y^C_{i,\cdot,k})]] \wedge [y^C_{i,q} \Leftrightarrow y^C_{i,q,|Q|}] \Big]$$

The formula Ω^{sem}_n is simply defined as the conjunction of all the formulas above.

For the semantics of CTL, the main difference is that the formula $\Omega^{\mathsf{Pre}}_{q,i}(y_S)$ encoding the fact that $q \in \mathsf{Pre}(S)$ can be greatly simplified (for the quantifier **E**):

$$\hat{\Omega}^{\mathsf{Pre}}_{q,i}(y_S) := \bigvee_{q' \in \mathsf{Succ}(q)} y_S(q')$$

Encoding the Consistency with the Models. Finally, to encode that the prospective formula is consistent with S, we have the following formula:

$$\Omega^{\mathsf{con}}_n := \Big[\bigwedge_{C \in P} \bigwedge_{s \in I} y^C_{n,s} \Big] \wedge \Big[\bigwedge_{C \in N} \bigvee_{s \in I} \neg y^C_{n,s} \Big]$$

The size of the formula Ω^S_n, and the number of variables involved in it, is polynomial in n and the size of S, $|S| := \sum_{C \in P \cup N} |C|$. Furthermore, we have the lemma below establishing the correctness of the encoding.

Proposition 1. *Let $S = (P, N)$ be a sample and $n \in \mathbb{N} \setminus \{0\}$. Then:*

1. *If an ATL formula of size at most n consistent with S exists, then the propositional formula Ω^S_n is satisfiable.*
2. *If a valuation v is such that $v \models \Omega^S_n$, then there is an ATL formula Φ^v of size at most n that is consistent with S.*

3.2 Deciding the Separability

Given a sample $\mathcal{S}$, by iteratively checking if $\Omega_0^{\mathcal{S}}$ is satisfiable, if $\Omega_1^{\mathcal{S}}$ is satisfiable, etc., we can find a minimal size formula consistent with $\mathcal{S}$ if one exists. However, if there is no such formula, the above iteration would not terminate. To circumvent that issue, there are two possibilities. We may first decide the separability of the sample, i.e., if there exists an ATL formula consistent with it; or we may exhibit a bound B, expressed as a function of $\mathcal{S}$, such that if there is a separating formula, there is one of size at most B. In this subsection, we tackle both of these issues.

It was shown in [17, Section 3, Thm. 3.2, 3.9] that the separability can be decided in polynomial time for full CTL (i.e., all operators can be used) with Kripke structures. Furthermore, in [43, Coro. 1], the results of [17] are used to exhibit an exponential bound on the size of the CTL formulas to be considered.

For fragments of CTL (i.e. CTL formulas that can use only some operators), it was shown in [34, Thm. 3], as a corollary of a "meta theorem" with applications to various logic, that the separability can be decided in exponential time.

Here, we extend these results to ATL formulas. We consider two settings: full ATL and any fragment of ATL. In the first setting, we show that separability can also be decided in polynomial time. In the second setting, we show that separability can be decided in exponential time. We deduce an exponential bound on the size of the formulas that need to be considered, which hold regardless of the fragment considered (including full ATL).

Separability for full ATL. For full ATL, our goal is to show the theorem below.

Theorem 1. *Given a sample $\mathcal{S} = (P, N)$ of CGS, we can decide in time polynomial in $|\mathcal{S}|$ if the sample $\mathcal{S}$ is separable with (arbitrary) ATL formulas.*

Due to space constraint, we only provide an informal explanation here. The first step is to prove that it is sufficient to consider only ATL-**X** formulas, i.e., ATL formulas whose only used temporal operator is **X**. This may seem counter-intuitive since given an ATL formula Φ using the operator **G** (or the operator **U**), there does not exist ATL-**X** formula equivalent to Φ because the number of states of the CGS on which Φ may be evaluated is arbitrarily large. However, given a sample $\mathcal{S}$ of finitely many CGS, there is a bound on the number of states used in all the CGS of $\mathcal{S}$. Hence, there is an ATL-**X** formula equivalent to Φ on all the CGS of $\mathcal{S}$.

Lemma 1. *Consider a sample $\mathcal{S} = (P, N)$ of CGS. If there exists an ATL formula consistent with $\mathcal{S}$, then there is one that is an ATL-**X** formula.*

Let us now consider the set $\mathsf{Distinguish}(\mathcal{S}) \subseteq Q^2$ of pairs of states that we can distinguish with an ATL-**X** formula.

Definition 3. *Consider a sample $\mathcal{S}$ of CGS. We let Q denote the set of all the states occurring in all CGS of $\mathcal{S}$. We let:*

$\mathsf{Distinguish}(\mathcal{S}) \coloneqq \{(q, q') \in Q^2 \mid \text{there is ATL-}\mathbf{X} \text{ formula } \Phi \text{ s.t. } q \models \Phi \Leftrightarrow q' \not\models \Phi\}$

Given a sample $\mathcal{S}$, we claim the following: 1) it is possible to compute in time polynomial in $|\mathcal{S}|$ the set $\mathsf{Distinguish}(\mathcal{S})$, and 2) given $\mathsf{Distinguish}(\mathcal{S}) \subseteq Q^2$, we can decide in polynomial time if there is an ATL-$\mathbf{X}$ formula consistent with $\mathcal{S}$.

We start with the second claim. The reason why it holds is the following: there is an ATL-$\mathbf{X}$ formula consistent with $\mathcal{S}$ iff, for all negative structures C_N of $\mathcal{S}$, there is a starting state $q_N \in I_{C_N}$ such that, for all starting states q_P of all positive structures of $\mathcal{S}$, we have $(q_P, q_N) \in \mathsf{Distinguish}(\mathcal{S})$, which can be checked in polynomial time. The "only if" implication comes directly from the definition of a formula consistent with a sample. The "if" implication is a consequence of the fact that ATL-$\mathbf{X}$ formulas can use conjunctions, disjunctions, and negations.

Let us now consider the first claim. We say that two sets of states $T, T' \subseteq Q$ are ATL-$\mathbf{X}$ distinguishable if there is an ATL-$\mathbf{X}$ formula $\varPhi$ and a state $t' \in T'$ such that for all $t \in T$, $t \models \varPhi$ and $t' \not\models \varPhi$. Now, given a set R of pairs of states , let us define the set $\mathsf{Dist_X}(R) \subseteq Q^2$ of pairs of states that we know can be distinguished by ATL-$\mathbf{X}$ formulas whose first operator used is $\mathbf{X}$, assuming all pairs of states in R can be distinguished by ATL-$\mathbf{X}$ formulas.

Definition 4. *Given a sample $\mathcal{S}$ of CGS and some $R \subseteq Q^2$, we let:*

$$\mathsf{Dist_X}(R) := \{(q, q'), (q', q) \in Q^2 \mid \exists A \subseteq \mathsf{Ag}, \exists \alpha \in \mathsf{Act}_A(q), \forall \alpha' \in \mathsf{Act}_A(q'),$$
$$\mathsf{Succ}(q, \alpha) \text{ and } \mathsf{Succ}(q', \alpha') \text{ are ATL-}\mathbf{X} \text{ distinguishable} \}$$

Given a set R, we can compute in polynomial time the set $\mathsf{Dist_X}(R)$. This may be counterintuitive since checking all coalitions of agents $A \subseteq \mathsf{Ag}$ would take time exponential in $|\mathcal{S}|$. However, to compute the set $\mathsf{Dist_X}(R)$, it is sufficient to consider coalitions of agents $A \subseteq \mathsf{RelAg}(q, q')$, where $\mathsf{RelAg}(q, q') := \{a \in \mathsf{Ag} \mid d(q, a) \cdot d(q', a) \geq 2\}$. Indeed, the agents not in $\mathsf{RelAg}(q, q')$ have only one action available at both states q and q'. They are, therefore, irrelevant in those states to determine the set of states reachable by a coalition. Looking over all such coalitions now takes time polynomial in $|\mathcal{S}|$ because $|2^{\mathsf{RelAg}(q,q')}| \leq |Q_{\mathsf{Act}}(q)| \times |Q_{\mathsf{Act}}(q')|$.

Interestingly, we have the following characterization of the set $\mathsf{Distinguish}(\mathcal{S})$.

Lemma 2. *Consider a sample $\mathcal{S}$ of CGS. The set $\mathsf{Distinguish}(\mathcal{S})$ is the smallest set of Q^2 such that: $\{(q, q') \in Q^2 \mid \pi(q) \neq \pi(q')\} \subseteq \mathsf{Distinguish}(\mathcal{S})$, and $\mathsf{Dist_X}(\mathsf{Distinguish}(\mathcal{S})) \subseteq \mathsf{Distinguish}(\mathcal{S})$.*

With the help of this lemma, given a sample $\mathcal{S}$ of CGS, it follows that we can compute in polynomial time the set $\mathsf{Distinguish}(\mathcal{S})$. Indeed, this can be done with a computation similar to that of the set $\mathsf{SAT}_C(\langle\!\langle A \rangle\!\rangle \varPhi_1 \mathbf{U} \varPhi_2)$ in Algorithm 1, where $\mathsf{SAT}_C(\langle\!\langle A \rangle\!\rangle \varPhi_1 \mathbf{U} \varPhi_2)$ is defined as a smallest set satisfying a specific property in Eq. (5). Overall, from both our claims 1) and 2), we do obtain that the separability of a sample of CGS can be decided in polynomial time.

Separability for any Fragment of ATL. Let us now consider the case of an arbitrary fragment of ATL. Now, the above-described algorithm a priori does not work. Among other things, one of the issues is that, possibly, we may not be able to use the operator $\mathbf{X}$. Therefore, given a sample $\mathcal{S}$, instead of iteratively constructing a subset of $\mathsf{Distinguish}(\mathcal{S}) \subseteq Q^2$ of distinguishable pairs of states, we iteratively compute a subset $\mathsf{Acc}(\mathcal{S}) \subseteq 2^Q$ of sets of states that can be accepted with a formula in the fragment considered, while the complement set is rejected. We can then prove a lemma similar to Lemma 2 except that we additionally have to be able to handle the operators $\mathbf{G}$ and $\mathbf{U}$, which is done by using Algorithms 1, 2.

Since we manipulate subsets of 2^Q, we obtain an exponential time algorithm. Interestingly, the correctness proof of this algorithm gives information on the size of consistent ATL formulas. Indeed, we can show that when there is a consistent formula, there is one for which each of its sub-formulas corresponds to a different set in $\mathsf{Acc}(\mathcal{S}) \subseteq 2^Q$. Therefore, the size of this formula is at most $|2^Q| = 2^{|Q|}$.

Theorem 2. *Consider a sample $\mathcal{S}$ and a fragment ATL' of ATL. We can decide in time exponential in $|\mathcal{S}|$ if the sample $\mathcal{S}$ is separable with ATL' formulas. If it is, then there exists an ATL' formula consistent with $\mathcal{S}$ of size at most $2^{|Q|}$.*

4   Experimental Evaluation

To test the ability of our learning algorithms (from Sect. 3.1), we implement them in an open-source prototype[1]. The prototype is developed in Python3 and utilizes the PySMT library [26], providing us access to an array of SAT solvers. Moreover, it offers configurable parameters for learning, including options to specify the model type (KS or CGS) and the formula type (CTL or ATL).

To test various aspects of our algorithms, we rely on synthetic benchmarks generated from a set of chosen formulas as is common in the literature [19,41]. We first identified some common CTL and ATL formulas from standard sources: the book on model-checking by Baier and Katoen [9, Example 6.3] for CTL and the seminal work by Alur et al. [1, Examples 3.1,3.2] for ATL. Figure 2 displays a selection of formulas (with the rest in the extended version [16]); we used abstract propositions and players in the formulas to maintain uniformity. The CTL formulas reflect properties occurring in distributed systems, such as mutual exclusion, request-response progress, etc. The ATL formulas describe various properties of a train-controller (multi-agent) system.

We generated samples following a random generation technique. To construct a structure C for a sample, we iteratively added states to C ensuring its connectedness; assigned random propositions to each state of C; and added random edges, labeled with action tuples if generating a CGS. For CGSs, we focussed on generating turn-based games, i.e., games where only one player has actions in each state, due to their prevalence in verification and synthesis. We split the randomly generated structures into P and N based on the selected formula.

Overall, from six CTL formulas and six ATL formulas, we generated two benchmark suites, the first one consisting of 144 samples of KSs and the second

---

[1] https://github.com/rajarshi008/learning-branching-time.

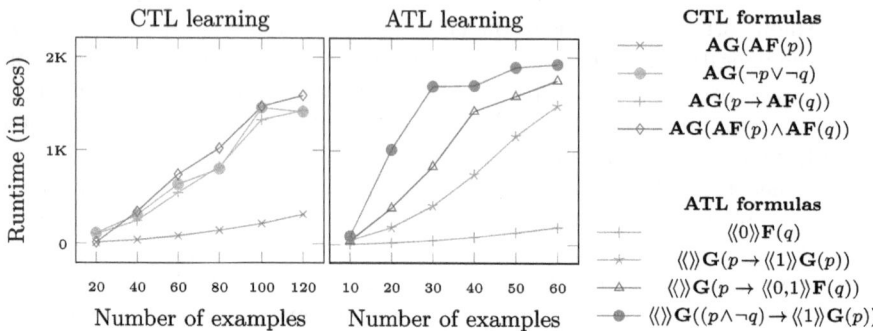

Fig. 2. Runtime of CTL and ATL learning algorithms on samples with varying number of examples (considering structures of size ≤ 20).

one consisting of 144 samples of CGSs, respectively. The number of examples in the suites ranges from 20 to 120 and 10 to 60, respectively. Moreover, the sizes of the KSs range from 1 to 40, while the size of the CGSs range from 1 to 20.

All tests were run on Intel Xeon Gold 6142 CPU (at 2.6 GHz) using up to 10 GB of RAM using MathSAT solver [23][2], with a timeout of 2400 s.

How effective are the algorithms in learning CTL/ATL formulas? To answer this, we ran the CTL and ATL learning algorithms on the first and second benchmark suites, respectively. Figure 2 depicts runtimes of both algorithms for samples generated from a selection of formulas. Both algorithms exhibit reasonable runtime performance for small samples. As the samples size increases, the runtime also increases, more prominently for the larger formulas in our selection. For the smaller formulas, however, the runtime of the algorithms remains reasonable even when the samples size increases.

Which parts of the SAT encoding contribute significantly towards the runtime? To understand this, we profiled both algorithms to identify the constraints responsible for significant runtime increases. Notably, generating constraints for the **U** operators (i.e., **EU**, **AU** for CTL and $\langle\!\langle \cdot \rangle\!\rangle$**U** for ATL) turned out to be the most time-consuming among all operators. Consequently, we compared runtime performance with and without these operators. (Note that we included **F** and **G** operators in both cases.) Learning without the **U** operator is often justified, since several properties do not require the **U** operator [44]. Figure 3a depicts this comparison for CTL learning; the average runtime improvement is 46%.

Moreover, computing the constraints for $\Omega_{q,i}^{\mathsf{Pre}}(y)$ happens to be expensive due to the nesting of conjunction and disjunction of propositional formulas. As a result, we noticed an improvement when we used the following optimized encoding designed specifically for turn-based games:

$$\bar{\Omega}_{q,i}^{\mathsf{Pre}}(y_S) := [A_{i,\sigma(q)} \Rightarrow \bigvee_{\alpha \in \mathsf{Act}_{\mathsf{Ag}}(q)} y_S(\delta(q,\alpha)] \wedge [\neg A_{i,\sigma(q)} \Rightarrow \bigwedge_{\alpha \in \mathsf{Act}_{\mathsf{Ag}}(q)} y_S(\delta(q,\alpha)],$$

---

[2] MathSAT [23] performed better than Z3 [40] and Boolector [18] in our experiments.

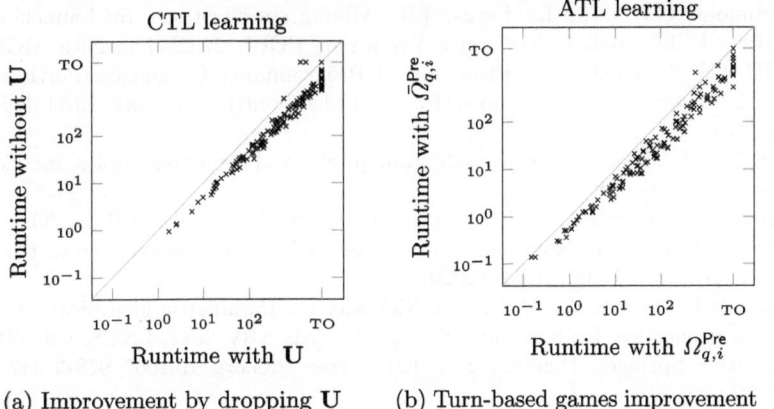

(a) Improvement by dropping **U**   (b) Turn-based games improvement

Fig. 3. Runtime improvement with optimized encodings for CTL and ATL learning on first and second benchmark suites, respectively. The runtimes are in seconds and 'TO' represents timeout.

where $\sigma(q)$ denotes the Agent owning the state q. Figure 3b illustrates this improvement; the average runtime improvement is 52%.

Overall, we demonstrated that our learning algorithms can successfully infer several CTL and ATL formulas from samples of varying sizes.

5   Conclusion

In this work, we address the passive learning problem for CTL and ATL, proposing a constraint-solving technique that encodes search and model-checking of formulas in propositional logic. We additionally investigate the separability of ATL formulas and develop decision procedures for it. Our experimental evaluations validate the efficacy of our algorithms in inferring useful CTL/ATL formulas.

As future work, we like to explore the computational hardness of the passive learning problems for CTL/ATL, similar to [25]. We also plan to improve our prototype by adding heuristics, such as the ones discussed in [43]. Finally, we like to lift our techniques to probabilistic logics such as PCTL [28] and PATL [21].

References

1. Alur, R., Henzinger, T.A., Kupferman, O.: Alternating-time temporal logic. J. ACM **49**(5), 672–713 (2002). https://doi.org/10.1145/585265.585270
2. Alur, R., Henzinger, T.A., Mang, F.Y.C., Qadeer, S., Rajamani, S.K., Tasiran, S.: MOCHA: modularity in model checking. In: CAV. Lecture Notes in Computer Science, vol. 1427, pp. 521–525. Springer (1998)

3. Ammons, G., Bodík, R., Larus, J.R.: Mining specifications. In: Launchbury, J., Mitchell, J.C. (eds.) Conference Record of POPL 2002: The 29th SIGPLAN-SIGACT Symposium on Principles of Programming Languages, Portland, OR, USA, January 16-18, 2002, pp. 4–16. ACM (2002). https://doi.org/10.1145/503272. 503275

4. Angluin, D.: Learning regular sets from queries and counterexamples. Inf. Comput. **75**(2), 87–106 (1987)

5. Arif, M.F., Larraz, D., Echeverria, M., Reynolds, A., Chowdhury, O., Tinelli, C.: SYSLITE: syntax-guided synthesis of PLTL formulas from finite traces. In: FMCAD, pp. 93–103. IEEE (2020)

6. Asarin, E., Donzé, A., Maler, O., Nickovic, D.: Parametric identification of temporal properties. In: Khurshid, S., Sen, K. (eds.) RV 2011. LNCS, vol. 7186, pp. 147–160. Springer, Heidelberg (2012). https://doi.org/10.1007/978-3-642-29860-8_12

7. Audemard, G., Simon, L.: On the glucose SAT solver. Int. J. Artif. Intell. Tools **27**(1), 1840001:1–1840001:25 (2018)

8. Avellaneda, F., Petrenko, A.: Inferring DFA without negative examples. In: Unold, O., Dyrka, W., Wieczorek, W. (eds.) Proceedings of the 14th International Conference on Grammatical Inference, ICGI 2018, Wrocław, Poland, September 5-7, 2018. Proceedings of Machine Learning Research, vol. 93, pp. 17–29. PMLR (2018). http://proceedings.mlr.press/v93/avellaneda19a.html

9. Baier, C., Katoen, J.: Principles of model checking. MIT Press (2008)

10. Barbosa, H., Barrett, C., Brain, M., Kremer, G., Lachnitt, H., Mann, M., Mohamed, A., Mohamed, M., Niemetz, A., Nötzli, A., Ozdemir, A., Preiner, M., Reynolds, A., Sheng, Y., Tinelli, C., Zohar, Y.: cvc5: a versatile and industrial-strength SMT solver. In: TACAS 2022. LNCS, vol. 13243, pp. 415–442. Springer, Cham (2022). https://doi.org/10.1007/978-3-030-99524-9_24

11. Bengtsson, J., Larsen, K., Larsson, F., Pettersson, P., Yi, W.: UPPAAL — a tool suite for automatic verification of real-time systems. In: Alur, R., Henzinger, T.A., Sontag, E.D. (eds.) HS 1995. LNCS, vol. 1066, pp. 232–243. Springer, Heidelberg (1996). https://doi.org/10.1007/BFb0020949

12. Bertrand, N., Fearnley, J., Schewe, S.: Bounded satisfiability for PCTL. In: Cégielski, P., Durand, A. (eds.) Computer Science Logic (CSL'12) - 26th International Workshop/21st Annual Conference of the EACSL, CSL 2012, September 3-6, 2012, Fontainebleau, France. LIPIcs, vol. 16, pp. 92–106. Schloss Dagstuhl - Leibniz-Zentrum für Informatik (2012). https://doi.org/10.4230/LIPIcs.CSL.2012.92

13. Biermann, A.W., Feldman, J.A.: On the synthesis of finite-state machines from samples of their behavior. IEEE Trans. Comput. **21**(6), 592–597 (1972)

14. Bjørner, D., Havelund, K.: 40 years of formal methods. In: Jones, C., Pihlajasaari, P., Sun, J. (eds.) FM 2014. LNCS, vol. 8442, pp. 42–61. Springer, Cham (2014). https://doi.org/10.1007/978-3-319-06410-9_4

15. Bombara, G., Vasile, C.I., Penedo, F., Yasuoka, H., Belta, C.: A decision tree approach to data classification using signal temporal logic. In: Proceedings of the 19th International Conference on Hybrid Systems: Computation and Control, HSCC 2016, pp. 1–10. Association for Computing Machinery, New York (2016). https://doi.org/10.1145/2883817.2883843

16. Bordais, B., Neider, D., Roy, R.: Learning branching-time properties in ctl and atl via constraint solving. CoRR abs/2406.19890 (2024). https://arxiv.org/abs/2406.19890

17. Browne, M.C., Clarke, E.M., Grumberg, O.: Characterizing finite kripke structures in propositional temporal logic. Theor. Comput. Sci. **59**, 115–131 (1988). https://doi.org/10.1016/0304-3975(88)90098-9
18. Brummayer, R., Biere, A.: Boolector: an efficient SMT solver for bit-vectors and arrays. In: Kowalewski, S., Philippou, A. (eds.) TACAS 2009. LNCS, vol. 5505, pp. 174–177. Springer, Heidelberg (2009). https://doi.org/10.1007/978-3-642-00768-2_16
19. Camacho, A., McIlraith, S.A.: Learning interpretable models expressed in linear temporal logic. In: ICAPS, pp. 621–630. AAAI Press (2019)
20. Chan, W.: Temporal-logic queries. In: Emerson, E.A., Sistla, A.P. (eds.) CAV 2000. LNCS, vol. 1855, pp. 450–463. Springer, Heidelberg (2000). https://doi.org/10.1007/10722167_34
21. Chen, T., Lu, J.: Probabilistic alternating-time temporal logic and model checking algorithm. In: FSKD (2), pp. 35–39. IEEE Computer Society (2007)
22. Cimatti, A., Clarke, E., Giunchiglia, F., Roveri, M.: NuSMV: a new symbolic model verifier. In: Halbwachs, N., Peled, D. (eds.) CAV 1999. LNCS, vol. 1633, pp. 495–499. Springer, Heidelberg (1999). https://doi.org/10.1007/3-540-48683-6_44
23. Cimatti, A., Griggio, A., Schaafsma, B.J., Sebastiani, R.: The MathSAT5 SMT solver. In: Piterman, N., Smolka, S.A. (eds.) TACAS 2013. LNCS, vol. 7795, pp. 93–107. Springer, Heidelberg (2013). https://doi.org/10.1007/978-3-642-36742-7_7
24. Clarke, E.M., Emerson, E.A.: Design and synthesis of synchronization skeletons using branching-time temporal logic. In: Logic of Programs. Lecture Notes in Computer Science, vol. 131, pp. 52–71. Springer (1981)
25. Fijalkow, N., Lagarde, G.: The complexity of learning linear temporal formulas from examples. In: ICGI. Proceedings of Machine Learning Research, vol. 153, pp. 237–250. PMLR (2021)
26. Gario, M., Micheli, A.: Pysmt: a solver-agnostic library for fast prototyping of smt-based algorithms. In: SMT Workshop 2015 (2015)
27. Gold, E.M.: Complexity of automaton identification from given data. Inf. Control **37**(3), 302–320 (1978)
28. Hansson, H., Jonsson, B.: A logic for reasoning about time and reliability. Formal Aspects Comput. **6**(5), 512–535 (1994)
29. van der Hoek, W., Wooldridge, M.J.: Cooperation, knowledge, and time: alternating-time temporal epistemic logic and its applications. Stud. Logica. **75**(1), 125–157 (2003)
30. Holzmann, G.J.: The model checker SPIN. IEEE Trans. Software Eng. **23**(5), 279–295 (1997)
31. Kim, J., Muise, C., Shah, A., Agarwal, S., Shah, J.: Bayesian inference of linear temporal logic specifications for contrastive explanations. In: IJCAI, pp. 5591–5598. ijcai.org (2019)
32. Kong, Z., Jones, A., Belta, C.: Temporal logics for learning and detection of anomalous behavior. IEEE Trans. Autom. Control **62**(3), 1210–1222 (2017). https://doi.org/10.1109/TAC.2016.2585083
33. Kong, Z., Jones, A., Medina Ayala, A., Aydin Gol, E., Belta, C.: Temporal logic inference for classification and prediction from data. In: Proceedings of the 17th International Conference on Hybrid Systems: Computation and Control, HSCC 2014, pp. 273–282. Association for Computing Machinery, New York (2014). https://doi.org/10.1145/2562059.2562146
34. Krogmeier, P., Madhusudan, P.: Languages with decidable learning: a meta-theorem. Proc. ACM Program. Lang. **7**(OOPSLA1), 143–171 (2023). https://doi.org/10.1145/3586032

35. Li, W., Dworkin, L., Seshia, S.A.: Mining assumptions for synthesis. In: MEM-OCODE, pp. 43–50. IEEE (2011)
36. Lomuscio, A., Raimondi, F.: MCMAS: a model checker for multi-agent systems. In: Hermanns, H., Palsberg, J. (eds.) TACAS 2006. LNCS, vol. 3920, pp. 450–454. Springer, Heidelberg (2006). https://doi.org/10.1007/11691372_31
37. Luo, W., Liang, P., Du, J., Wan, H., Peng, B., Zhang, D.: Bridging ltlf inference to GNN inference for learning ltlf formulae. In: AAAI, pp. 9849–9857. AAAI Press (2022)
38. Mogavero, F., Murano, A., Perelli, G., Vardi, M.Y.: Reasoning about strategies: on the model-checking problem. ACM Trans. Comput. Log. **15**(4), 34:1–34:47 (2014). https://doi.org/10.1145/2631917
39. Mohammadinejad, S., Deshmukh, J.V., Puranic, A.G., Vazquez-Chanlatte, M., Donzé, A.: Interpretable classification of time-series data using efficient enumerative techniques. In: HSCC '20: 23rd ACM International Conference on Hybrid Systems: Computation and Control, Sydney, New South Wales, Australia, April 21-24, 2020, pp. 9:1–9:10. ACM (2020). https://doi.org/10.1145/3365365.3382218
40. de Moura, L., Bjørner, N.: Z3: an efficient SMT solver. In: Ramakrishnan, C.R., Rehof, J. (eds.) TACAS 2008. LNCS, vol. 4963, pp. 337–340. Springer, Heidelberg (2008). https://doi.org/10.1007/978-3-540-78800-3_24
41. Neider, D., Gavran, I.: Learning linear temporal properties. In: Bjørner, N.S., Gurfinkel, A. (eds.) 2018 Formal Methods in Computer Aided Design, FMCAD 2018, Austin, TX, USA, October 30 - November 2, 2018, pp. 1–10. IEEE (2018). https://doi.org/10.23919/FMCAD.2018.8603016
42. Nenzi, L., Silvetti, S., Bartocci, E., Bortolussi, L.: A robust genetic algorithm for learning temporal specifications from data. In: McIver, A., Horvath, A. (eds.) QEST 2018. LNCS, vol. 11024, pp. 323–338. Springer, Cham (2018). https://doi.org/10.1007/978-3-319-99154-2_20
43. Pommellet, A., Stan, D., Scatton, S.: Sat-based learning of computation tree logic. CoRR abs/2402.06366 (2024). https://doi.org/10.48550/ARXIV.2402.06366
44. Raha, R., Roy, R., Fijalkow, N., Neider, D.: Scalable anytime algorithms for learning fragments of linear temporal logic. In: TACAS 2022. LNCS, vol. 13243, pp. 263–280. Springer, Cham (2022). https://doi.org/10.1007/978-3-030-99524-9_14
45. Raha, R., Roy, R., Fijalkow, N., Neider, D., Pérez, G.A.: Synthesizing efficiently monitorable formulas in metric temporal logic. In: VMCAI (2). Lecture Notes in Computer Science, vol. 14500, pp. 264–288. Springer (2024)
46. Riener, H.: Exact synthesis of LTL properties from traces. In: FDL, pp. 1–6. IEEE (2019)
47. Roy, R., Fisman, D., Neider, D.: Learning interpretable models in the property specification language. In: IJCAI, pp. 2213–2219. ijcai.org (2020)
48. Roy, R., Gaglione, J., Baharisangari, N., Neider, D., Xu, Z., Topcu, U.: Learning interpretable temporal properties from positive examples only. CoRR abs/2209.02650 (2022)
49. Roy, R., Neider, D.: Inferring properties in computation tree logic. CoRR abs/2310.13778 (2023)
50. Rozier, K.Y.: Specification: the biggest bottleneck in formal methods and autonomy. In: Blazy, S., Chechik, M. (eds.) VSTTE 2016. LNCS, vol. 9971, pp. 8–26. Springer, Cham (2016). https://doi.org/10.1007/978-3-319-48869-1_2
51. Shah, A., Kamath, P., Shah, J.A., Li, S.: Bayesian inference of temporal task specifications from demonstrations. In: NeurIPS, pp. 3808–3817 (2018)
52. Valizadeh, M., Fijalkow, N., Berger, M.: LTL learning on gpus. CoRR abs/2402.12373 (2024). https://doi.org/10.48550/ARXIV.2402.12373

53. Wan, H., Liang, P., Du, J., Luo, W., Ye, R., Peng, B.: End-to-end learning of ltlf formulae by faithful ltlf encoding. In: AAAI, pp. 9071–9079. AAAI Press (2024)
54. Wasylkowski, A., Zeller, A.: Mining temporal specifications from object usage. Autom. Softw. Eng. **18**(3–4), 263–292 (2011)

A Zonotopic Dempster-Shafer Approach to the Quantitative Verification of Neural Networks

Eric Goubault [ID] and Sylvie Putot[(✉)] [ID]

LIX, CNRS, Ecole Polytechnique, Institut Polytechnique de Paris,
91120 Palaiseau, France
{goubault,putot}@lix.polytechnique.fr

Abstract. The reliability and usefulness of verification depend on the ability to represent appropriately the uncertainty. Most existing work on neural network verification relies on the hypothesis of either set-based or probabilistic information on the inputs. In this work, we rely on the framework of imprecise probabilities, specifically p-boxes, to propose a quantitative verification of ReLU neural networks, which can account for both probabilistic information and epistemic uncertainty on inputs. On classical benchmarks, including the ACAS Xu examples, we demonstrate that our approach improves the tradeoff between tightness and efficiency compared to related work on probabilistic network verification, while handling much more general classes of uncertainties on the inputs and providing fully guaranteed results.

Keywords: neural networks · probability bounds · p-boxes · Dempster-Shafer structures · zonotopes

1 Introduction

Verifying that neural networks satisfy desirable properties has become crucial for ensuring the safety of learning-enabled autonomous systems. However, most existing approaches that provide guarantees on the satisfaction of a specification are designed for adversarial input uncertainties, and offer only qualitative assessments. Complete methods return whether or not the property is satisfied but are often not scalable, while sound methods return either that a property is satisfied or that the answer is unknown, due to over-approximation errors. For instance, the analyzers DeepZ [27], DeepPoly [28] and Verinet [13] propagate respectively zonotopes, polyhedra, and symbolic intervals through the layers of a neural network, to ensure that certain specifications are met. In addition, many analyzers have considered producing also robustness bounds of networks, as specifically done by CROWN [35], FCROWN [16] and CNN-Cert [5].

In contrast, quantitative verification has been little explored for neural networks, despite providing a better understanding of the system by refining information about property satisfaction. This is especially true for probabilistic verification. Some authors have considered estimating the statistics of the output of

A. Platzer et al. (Eds.): FM 2024, LNCS 14933, pp. 324–342, 2025.
https://doi.org/10.1007/978-3-031-71162-6_17

neural networks, given a multivariate probabilistic law for its inputs. This app-roach has been used in particular for assessing the robustness of neural networks [31,36] and for probabilistically certifying their correctness under adversarial attacks [2,3,14,20,34]. But these estimates, using improved sampling methods, do not give guaranteed bounds. Even fewer articles have considered guaranteed probabilistic bounds. In [32], the authors describe the analyzer PROVEN, which provides probability certificates of neural network robustness when the input perturbation is given by a probabilistic distribution, based on abstractions. For networks with ReLU activation function, methods have been developed in [21,22] to find the probability of the output or of the input-output relationships. In [8], the authors consider an ellipsoid input space with Gaussian random variables and compute confidence ellipsoids for the outputs of ReLU networks, using semi-definite programming. In [29], the authors consider truncated multivariate Gaus-sian distribution inputs and abstract them by probabilistic stars (ProbStars), a variation of the star set abstraction [1] recently introduced in the context of reachability analysis. They propagate them in a guaranteed manner in a net-work, and estimate the probability of violating a safety property on the output by computing each probstar's probability. In a way, ProbStar is a hybrid method, relying on guaranteed set-based computations, but estimating the probabilities in a non guaranteed manner.

The works mentioned above rely on the hypothesis of either set-based or probabilistic information on the inputs. However, in real-world systems, precise models representative of the data are not always available. For instance, several probabilistic models may be plausible for describing of a problem, or a prob-abilistic model may be known but with uncertain parameters. Therefore, we need to consider both aleatory information and epistemic uncertainty. Imprecise probabilities [4,30] offer a framework that unifies probabilistic and set-based information. This framework includes a wide variety of mathematical models, among which probability boxes (p-boxes in short) [9], which characterize an uncertain random variable by all probability distributions consistent with lower and upper bounds on its cumulative distribution function (CDF in short). A p-box can be seen as interval bounds on a probability distribution. An Interval-based discrete over-approximation of p-boxes, Interval Dempster-Shafer struc-ture [25] (DSI in short) has been proposed. Algorithms for arithmetic operations on DSI can be derived [9,33], which can be seen as a unification of standard interval analysis with traditional probability theory, allowing probability bound analysis on arithmetic expressions. It gives the same answer as interval analy-sis does when only range information is available. And it gives sound bounds on the distribution function, as a sound counterpart of a Monte Carlo simu-lation, when information is precise enough to fully specify input distributions and their dependencies. However, DSI arithmetic is expensive and suffers from the conservativeness of interval arithmetic, on which it relies. Probabilistic affine forms have been proposed as an alternative [6,7], improving both precision and efficiency by combining affine forms or zonotopes and DSI structures.

In this work, we first extend for the analysis of ReLU neural networks, the Interval Dempster Shafer arithmetic in Sect. 3 and probabilistic affine arithmetic in Sect. 4. We then introduce in Sect. 5 a new abstraction, Zonotopic Dempster Shafer structures, which exhibits much better computational properties (complexity and tightness of the approximations). This new abstraction is directly related to the general notion of random sets [24] which generalize one-dimensional Dempster-Shafer structures such as the DSI. Finally, in Sect. 6 we demonstrate on benchmarks from the state of the art that our approach improves in terms of tradeoff between tightness and efficiency compared to the most closely related work [29], while being able to handle much more general classes of uncertainties on the inputs and providing fully guaranteed results.

2   Problem Statement

We consider an L-layer feedforward ReLU network with input $x^0 \in \mathbb{R}^{h_0}$ and output $y = f(x^0) = x^L \in \mathbb{R}^{h_L}$, with f being the composition of L layers, $f = f^{L-1} \circ \ldots \circ f^0$. The k-th layer of the ReLU network is defined by $f^k : \mathbb{R}^{h_k} \to \mathbb{R}^{h_{k+1}}$ of the form $x^{k+1} = f^k(x^k) = \sigma(A^k x^k + b^k)$, where $A^k \in \mathbb{R}^{h_{k+1} \times h_k}$ is the weight matrix, $b^k \in \mathbb{R}^{h_{k+1}}$ is the bias, and $\sigma(x_j^k) := \max(0, x_j^k)$ is the component-wise ReLU function, where x_j^k is the jth component of $x^k \in \mathbb{R}^{h_k}$.

For a multi-dimensional distribution $X \in \mathbb{R}^n$, we note $P(X \leq x) := \mathbb{P}(X_1 \leq x_1 \wedge X_2 \leq x_2 \ldots \wedge X_n \leq x_n)$, and in what follows, we systematically use $\leq$ as the componentwise order. We are interested in the following two problems, extending, in particular to a larger class of inputs, the quantitative verification properties of [29]:

Problem 1 (Probability Bounds Analysis). Given a ReLU network f and a constrained probabilistic input set $\mathcal{X} = \{X \in \mathbb{R}^{h_0} \mid CX \leq d \wedge \underline{F}(x) \leq \mathbb{P}(X \leq x) \leq \overline{F}(x), \forall x\}$ where $\underline{F}$ and $\overline{F}$ are two cumulative distribution functions, compute a constrained probabilistic output set $\mathcal{Y}$ guaranteed to contain $\{f(X), X \in \mathcal{X}\}$.

Problem 2 (Quantitative Property Verification). Given a ReLU network f, a constrained probabilistic input set $\mathcal{X}$ and a linear safety property $Hy \leq w$, bound the probability of the network output vector y satisfying this property.

We illustrate throughout the paper the approach on the toy example below. The details on the analyzes of this example, which results are stated in further sections, are provided in the Appendix of preprint [10].

Example 1. We consider the ReLU network defined by the matrices of weights and biases: $A_1 = \begin{bmatrix} 1 & -1 \\ 1 & 1. \end{bmatrix}, b_1 = \begin{bmatrix} 0.0 \\ 0.0 \end{bmatrix}, A_2 = \begin{bmatrix} 1 & -1 \\ 1 & 1 \end{bmatrix}, b_2 = \begin{bmatrix} 0.0 \\ 0.0 \end{bmatrix}$. We take only one ReLU layer and an affine output layer. After the ReLU layer, we note $x^1 = \sigma(A_1 x^0 + b_1) = \sigma(x_1^0 - x_2^0, x_1^0 + x_2^0)$, and after the output layer $x^2 = A_2 x^1 + b_2$.

The problem is to verify the network against the unsafe output set $x_1^2 \leq -2 \wedge x_2^2 \geq 2$ for an input $x^0 = (x_1^0, x_2^0) \in [-2, 2] \times [-1, 1]$. This writes $Hx^2 \leq w$ with $H = \begin{bmatrix} 1 & 0 \\ 0 & -1 \end{bmatrix}, w = [-2 \ -2]$.

3 Analysis with Interval Dempster-Shafer Structures

Probability-Boxes and Interval Dempster-Shafer Arithmetic. We characterize a real-valued random variable X by its cumulative probability distribution function (CDF in short) $F : \mathbb{R} \to [0,1]$ defined by $F(x) = \mathbb{P}(X \leq x)$. A p-box [9] is defined by a pair of CDF:

Definition 1 (P-box). *Given two CDF $\overline{F}, \underline{F}$, the p-box $[\underline{F}, \overline{F}]$ represents the set of distribution functions F such that $\underline{F}(x) \leq F(x) \leq \overline{F}(x)$ for all $x \in \mathbb{R}$.*

P-boxes can be combined in mathematical calculations, but analytical solutions are usually not available. Interval Dempster-Shafer structures [25] provide a simple way to soundly over-approximate the set of cdfs using a discrete representation, for which the arithmetic operations can be converted into a series of elementary interval calculations.

Definition 2
(Interval Dempster-Shafer Structure). *An interval Dempster-Shafer structure (DSI in short) is a finite set of intervals, named focal elements, associated with a probability, written $d = \{\langle \boldsymbol{x_1}, w_1 \rangle, \langle \boldsymbol{x_2}, w_2 \rangle, \ldots, \langle \boldsymbol{x_n}, w_n \rangle\}$, where $\boldsymbol{x_i}$ is an interval and $w_i \in (0,1]$ is its probability, with $\sum_{k=1}^{n} w_k = 1$.*

Proposition 1 (CDF of an Interval Dempster-Shafer Structure). *A DSI $d = \{\langle \boldsymbol{x_1}, w_1 \rangle, \langle \boldsymbol{x_2}, w_2 \rangle, \ldots, \langle \boldsymbol{x_n}, w_n \rangle\}$ defines the discrete p-box $[\underline{F_d}, \overline{F_d}]$ representing the sets of distributions such that $\underline{F_d}(u) \leq \mathbb{P}(X \leq u) \leq \overline{F_d}(u)$ with $\underline{F_d}(u) = \sum_{\overline{x_i} < u} w_i$ and $\overline{F_d}(u) = \sum_{\underline{x_i} \leq u} w_i$, noting $\underline{x_i}$ (resp. $\overline{x_i}$) the greatest lower bound (resp. least upper bound) of set $\boldsymbol{x_i}$.*

Conversely, discrete upper and lower approximations of distribution functions can be constructed, for instance using the inverse CDF as in [33]. Given a discretization size N, they define a DSI with N focal elements where all weights are equal to $1/N$. The focal elements $\boldsymbol{x_i}$ are defined evaluating the quantiles or inverse cdfs for uniformly spaced probability levels $p_i = \frac{i-1}{N}$ for $i = 1, \ldots, N+1$, by $\boldsymbol{x_i} = [\overline{F_d}^{-1}(p_i), \underline{F_d}^{-1}(p_{i+1})]$ where $F_d^{-1}(p) = \inf\{x \mid F_d(x) \geq p\}$.

The arithmetic operators on DSI structures [9,33] compute guaranteed enclosures of all possible distributions of an output variable if the input p-boxes enclose the input distributions. Let two random variables X and Y represented by DSI structures $d_X = \{\langle \boldsymbol{x_i}, w_i \rangle, i \in [1,n]\}$ and $d_Y = \{\langle \boldsymbol{y_j}, w'_j \rangle, j \in [1,m]\}$, and Z be the random variable such that $Z = X + Y$ (the algorithms for other arithmetic operations are similar). In particular, they define algorithms for the extreme cases of unknown dependence and independence between X and Y.

Definition 3 (Probabilistic Dependence and Dependence Graph). *Two random variables X_1 and X_2 are independent if and only if their CDF can be decomposed as $F(x_1, x_2) = F_1(x_1)F_2(x_2)$. Otherwise, the random variables are called correlated. The probabilistic dependence graph G over a set of n variables $X_1, \ldots, X_n$ is an undirected graph where the X_i are the vertices and there exists an edge (X_i, X_j) in the graph iff variables X_i and X_j are correlated.*

The addition of DSI independent variables is obtained as a discrete convolution of the two input distributions [9,33]:

Definition 4 (Addition of Independent DSIs). *If X and Y are independent random variables, then the DSI for $Z = X \oplus Y$ is $d_Z = \{\langle z_{i,j}, r_{i,j} \rangle,\ i \in [1,n],\ j \in [1,m]\}$ such that: $\forall i \in [1,n],\ j \in [1,m],\ z_{i,j} = x_i + y_j$ and $r_{i,j} = w_i \times w'_j$.*

The number of focal elements grows exponentially with the number of such operations. In order to keep the computation tractable, the number of focal elements is usually bounded, at the cost of some over-approximations.

Different algorithms have been proposed for the addition of DSIs with unknown dependence, relying on the Fréchet-Hoeffding copula bounds or on linear programming, most of them produce the same result [9,23,33].

DSI Analysis of Neural Networks. We now define a sound probability bounds analysis of ReLU neural networks.

Modelling the Network Inputs. Consider an h_0-dimensional uncertain input vector $x^0 = (x_1^0, \ldots, x_{h_0}^0)$, which can be represented as a vector $d^0 = (d_1^0, \ldots, d_{h_0}^0)$ of h_0 DSI, each with the same number n of focal elements for simplicity of presentation: $d_i^0 = \{\langle x_{i,1}^0, w_{i,1}^0 \rangle, \langle x_{i,2}^0, w_{i,2}^0 \rangle, \ldots, \langle x_{i,n}^0, w_{i,n}^0 \rangle\}$ for $i \in 1, \ldots, h_0$, where $x_{i,j}^0 \in \mathbb{IR}$ is an interval and $w_{i,j}^0 \in [0,1]$ is the associated probability, with $\sum_{j=1}^n w_{i,j}^0 = 1$, for all $i \in 1, \ldots, h_0$. A dependence graph is assumed to be known between the components of the input vector.

Affine Transform of a Vector of DSI Structures. Given a vector of random variables $X = (X_1, \ldots, X_k)$ represented as a vector $d = (d_1, \ldots, d_k)$ of DSI structures, and a dependence graph G, we define a DSI $d^y = \sum_{j=1}^k a_j d_j + b$ which includes the result of $Y = \sum_{j=1}^k a_j X_j + b$ on the DSI d by:

- we note $a_j d_j$ where $a_j \in \mathbb{R}$ and d_j is a DSI $\{\langle x_{j,i}, w_{j,i} \rangle \mid i = 1, \ldots, n\}$, the result of the multiplication of a constant by a DSI: $\{\langle a_j x_{j,i}, w_{j,i} \rangle \mid i = 1, \ldots, n\}$,
- we arbitrarily choose to compute the sum $\sum_{j=1}^k a_j d_j$ as $((a_1 d_1 + a_2 d_2) + a_3 d_3) + \ldots a_k d_k)$, applying for the j-th sum the right operators depending of the dependence between X_{j+1} and X_1 to X_j,
- we note $d + b$ where d is a DSI $\{\langle x_i, w_i \rangle \mid i = 1, \ldots, n\}$ and $b \in \mathbb{R}$ the result of the addition of a constant to a DSI: $\{\langle b + x_i, w_i \rangle \mid i = 1, \ldots, n\}$,
- the dependence graph is updated by adding an edge between Y and all X_j such that a_j is non zero

Interpreting the action of the ReLU function $Y = \max(0, X)$ means enforcing the constraints $Y \geq X$ and $Y \geq 0$. This means that Y is obtained by intersecting the focal elements of the representation of X with $[0, \infty)$:

Lemma 1 (ReLU of a DSI). *Given a random variable X represented by the DSI $d = \{\langle x_i, w_i \rangle, i \in [1, n]\}$, then the CDF of $Y = \sigma(X) = \max(0, X)$ is included in the DSI $\{\langle y_i, w_i \rangle, i \in [1, n]\}$ with $y_i = [\max(0, \underline{x_i}), \max(0, \overline{x_i})]$.*

This leads to Algorithm 1 for the analysis of an L-layer ReLU network with the notations of Sect. 2.

Algorithm 1. ReLU feedforward neural network analysis by DSI arithmetic

---

Input: d^0 a h_0-dimensional vector of DSI
1: **for** $k = 0$ to $L - 1$ **do**
2:     **for** $l = 1$ to h_{k+1} **do**
3:         $d_l^{k+1} \leftarrow \sigma(\sum_{j=1}^{h_k} a_{lj}^k d_j^k + b_l^k)$ ▷ Affine transform and Lemma 1
4:     **end for**
5: **end for**
6: **return** $(d^L, \text{cdf}(Hd^L, w))$

Output The output after propagation in the network consists in:

- the vector of DSI d^L characterizing the network output (solving Problem 1)
- interval bounds noted $cdf(Hd^L, w)$ on the probability $\mathbb{P}(Hx^L \leq w)$ (solving Problem 2). Let $[\underline{P_m}, \overline{P_m}]$, with m ranging over the rows of H and w, be the interval for the probability $\mathbb{P}(\sum_{i=1}^{h_L} h_{mi} x_i^L \leq w_m)$. It is obtained applying Proposition 1 to compute the CDF at w on each component of the vector Hd^L. We define $cdf(Hd^L, w) = [\min_m \underline{P_m}, \min_m \overline{P_m}]$.

The DSI computation encodes the marginal distribution of each component of a vector x^i as a DSI. The probability of a conjunction Hx^L is thus computed considering each inequality independently and expressing that the probability of the conjunction is lower or equal than the probability of each term.

Analysis of the Toy Example. Consider Example 1. A classical interval analysis of the network from the input set $x^0 = (x_1^0, x_2^0) \in [-2, 2] \times [-1, 1]$ yields the output ranges $x_1^2 \in [-3, 3]$ and $x_2^2 \in [0, 6]$. As these have non empty intersection with the property $x_1^2 \leq -2 \wedge x_2^2 \geq 2$, this analysis does not allow to conclude.

Uniform Distribution on Inputs Abstracted by DSI with 2 Focal Elements. Let us now suppose that we additionally know that the 2 components of the input follow a uniform distribution. We first choose a discretization of the inputs by DSI with 2 focal elements, $d_1^0 = \{\langle [-2, 0], 0.5 \rangle, \langle [0, 2], 0.5 \rangle\}$ and $d_2^0 = \{\langle [-1, 0], 0.5 \rangle, \langle [0, 1], 0.5 \rangle\}$. Let us suppose the inputs independent, the first output after the first affine layer, $d_{y_1} = d_1^0 - d_2^0$, computed following Definition 4, is $\{\langle [-2, 1], 0.25 \rangle, \langle [-3, 0], 0.25 \rangle, \langle [0, 3], 0.25 \rangle, \langle [-1, 2], 0.25 \rangle\}$. In order to limit the complexity of computation, the result of each operation on DSI can be reduced by a sound overapproximation with a fixed number of focal elements. This can be done by joining some focal elements and adding the corresponding weights. For instance here, when reducing to 2 focal elements by joining the first 2 and the last 2 focal elements, this results in $d_{y_1} = \{\langle[-3,1],0.5\rangle;\langle[-1,3],0.5\rangle\}$. Then, applying to d_{y_1} the ReLU function by Lemma 1 produces $d_1^1 = \{\langle[0,1],0.5\rangle,\langle[0,3],0.5\rangle\}$. The other output x_2^1 of the first layer has the same DSI representation. After the output layer, the first output is $d_1^2 = d_1^1 - d_2^1 = \{\langle[-3,1],0.5\rangle,\langle[-1,3],0.5\rangle\}$. Here x_1^1 and x_2^1 can no longer be considered as independent as they both are correlated to x_1^0 and x_2^0, the subtraction of their DSI representation is computed accordingly. The second output is $d_2^2 = d_1^1 + d_2^1 = \{\langle[0,4],0.5\rangle,\langle[0,6],0.5\rangle\}$.

Take now the property $x_1^2 \leq -2 \land x_2^2 \geq 2$. Using Proposition 1, we deduce from d_1^2 and d_2^2 that $\mathbb{P}(x_1^2 \leq -2) \in [0,0.5]$ and $\mathbb{P}(x_2^2 \geq 2) \in [0.0,1.0]$, from which $\mathbb{P}(x_1^2 \leq -2 \land x_2^2 \geq 2) \in [0,0.5]$. Consider $\mathbb{P}(x_1^2 \leq -2)$ evaluated using $d_1^2 = \{\langle[-3,1],0.5\rangle,\langle[-1,3],0.5\rangle\}$. Its lower bound is obtained using Proposition 1 by $\underline{P}(-2) = \sum_{\overline{x_i} < -2} w_i = 0$, as the upper bounds of the 2 focal elements $[-3,1]$ and $[-1,3]$ are both greater than -2. The upper bound is $\overline{P}(-2) = \sum_{\underline{x_i} \leq u} w_i = 0.5$, as the lower bound of $[-3,1]$ is lower than -2, which is not the case for $[-1,3]$.

Increasing the Number of Focal Elements. refines the over-approximation of the input distributions and the sets of CDF obtained for the outputs. For instance for 100 focal elements, in the case inputs can be considered as independent, we obtain $\mathbb{P}(x_1^2 \leq -2) \in [0,0.07]$ and $\mathbb{P}(x_2^2 \geq 2) \in [0.05,0.52]$. In the case of inputs with unknown correlation, $\mathbb{P}(x_1^2 \leq -2) \in [0,0.26]$ and $\mathbb{P}(x_2^2 \geq 2) \in [0,1]$. However, the supports of the sets of distribution remain unchanged and are equal to the ranges obtained through interval analysis. Indeed, the affine layers introduce some conservatism due to the wrapping effect of the intervals used as focal elements. Additionally, joint distribution are not naturally represented in the DSI framework, making it difficult to accuractely verify general properties.

4   Analysis with Probabilistic Zonotopes

Probabilistic affine forms [6,7] are affine forms where the symbolic variables or noise symbols are constrained by DSI structures instead of being simply bounded in $[-1,1]$. This can be seen as a simple way to encode affine correlations between uncertain variables abstracted by p-boxes, or a quantitative version of affine forms. We first introduce the probabilistic affine forms, presented as probabilistic zonotopes, which represent vectors of probabilistic affine forms. Then we propose an analysis of neural networks relying on these probabilistic zonotopes.

Affine Forms, Zonotopes and Probabilistic Zonotopes. An affine form is a linear expression $\alpha_0 + \sum_{j=1}^p \alpha_j \varepsilon_j$ with real coefficients α_j and symbolic variables ε_j called noise symbols which values range in $[-1,1]$. A zonotope is the geometric concretization of a vector of affine forms:

Definition 5 (Zonotope). *An n-dimensional zonotope $\mathcal{Z}$ with center $c \in R^n$ and a vector $\Gamma = \begin{bmatrix} g_1 \ldots g_p \end{bmatrix} \in \mathbb{R}^{n,p}$ of p generators $g_j \in \mathbb{R}^n$ for $j = 1,\ldots,p$ is defined as $\mathcal{Z} = \langle c, \Gamma \rangle = \{c + \Gamma\varepsilon \mid \|\varepsilon\|_\infty \leq 1\}$.*
We note $\gamma_i(\mathcal{Z}) = c_i + \sum_{j=1}^{p} g_{ij}[-1,1]$ the range of its i-th component.

Zonotopes are closed under affine transformations:

Proposition 2 (Affine Transforms of a Zonotope). *For $A \in \mathbb{R}^{m,n}$ and $b \in \mathbb{R}^m$ we define $A\mathcal{Z}+b = \langle Ac+b, A\Gamma \rangle$ as the m-dimensional resulting zonotope.*

Definition 6 (Probabilistic Zonotope). *For ε a vector of random variables of $\mathbb{R}^p$, a zonotope $\mathcal{Z} = \langle c, \Gamma \rangle$ with $c \in \mathbb{R}^n$ and $\Gamma \in \mathbb{R}^{n,p}$ can be interpreted as a probabilistic zonotope noted $p\mathcal{Z}(\varepsilon) = \langle c, \Gamma, \varepsilon \rangle$ representing the $n-$dimensional random variable $Z = c + \Gamma\varepsilon$. Let d_ε be a $p-$dimensional vector of DSI structures with support in $[-1,1]^p$ and G a dependence graph on the components $\varepsilon_1, \ldots, .\varepsilon_p$. The marginal of each component of $p\mathcal{Z}(d_\varepsilon)$ is the affine transform on DSI structures: $c^i + \sum_{j=1}^{p} g_{ij}d_{\varepsilon_j}$, $i = 1, \ldots, n$ computed as in Sect. 3.*

Zonotopes represent affine relations that hold between uncertain quantities. In the case of probabilistic zonotopes, *imprecise* affine relations hold:

Example 2. Let $x_1 = 1 + \varepsilon_1 - \varepsilon_2$, $x_2 = -\frac{1}{2}\varepsilon_1 + \frac{1}{4}\varepsilon_2$, $d_{\varepsilon_1} = \{\langle [-1,0], \frac{1}{2}\rangle, \langle [0,1], \frac{1}{2}\rangle\}$, $d_{\varepsilon_2} = \{\langle [-\frac{1}{10}, 0], \frac{1}{2}\rangle, \langle [0, \frac{1}{10}], \frac{1}{2}\rangle\}$, Then $x_1 + 2x_2 = 1 - \frac{1}{2}\varepsilon_2$, represented by the DSI $d = 1 - \frac{1}{2}d_{\varepsilon_2} = \{\langle [\frac{19}{20}, 1], \frac{1}{2}\rangle, \langle [1, \frac{21}{20}], \frac{1}{2}\rangle\}$, by (a simple version of) the Affine Transform of a Vector of DSI Structures. Thus the lower probability that $x_1 + 2x_2 \leq \frac{21}{20}$ is 1; and the upper probability that $x_1 + 2x_2 < \frac{19}{20}$ is 0. But $x_1 + 2x_2 \leq 1$ has upper probability $\frac{1}{2}$ and lower probability 0 and is thus an imprecise relation.

Probabilistic Zonotopes for the Analysis of Neural Networks. We detail hereafter Algorithm 2 using probabilistic zonotopes.

Algorithm 2. Neural network analysis by Probabilistic Zonotopes

---

Input: d^0 a h_0-dimensional vector of DSI
1: $p\mathcal{Z}^0(\varepsilon) = \langle c^0, \Gamma^0, d_\varepsilon \rangle \leftarrow$ dsi-to-pzono(d^0)
2: **for** $k = 0$ to $L - 1$ **do**
3:     $\mathcal{Z}^{k+1} \leftarrow \sigma(A^k \mathcal{Z}^k + b^k)$ ▷ Proposition 2 and Proposition 3
4: **end for**
5: $d^L \leftarrow$ pzono-to-dsi($\mathcal{Z}^L, d_\varepsilon$)   ▷ Definition 6
6: **return** $(d^L, \text{cdf}(\text{pzono-to-dsi}(H\mathcal{Z}^L, d_\varepsilon), w))$

Input and Initialization. The input of the algorithm is the same as in Sect. 3, the uncertain input is modelled as a vector $d^0 = (d_1^0, \ldots, d_{h_0}^0)$ of h_0 DSI. We can then define $\boldsymbol{x}^0 \in \mathbb{IR}^{h_0}$ the h_0-dimensional box obtained as the support of d^0, computed for each DSI as the union of its focal elements with non-zero weight. Finally, we define $p\mathcal{Z}^0(\varepsilon) = \langle c^0, \Gamma^0, d_\varepsilon \rangle$ in Line 1 of Algorithm 2 by:

- $\mathcal{Z}^0 = \langle c^0, \Gamma^0 \rangle$, is built from the box $\boldsymbol{x}^0$,
- d_ε is the vector of DSI obtained by rescaling d^0 between -1 and 1.

Propagation in the Layers. The propagation in the affine layers can be expressed directly as affine transform on the zonotope by Proposition 2, and later interpreted as a probabilistic zonotope. Proposition 3 introduces the ReLU transformer proposed in [26], encoded in zonotope matrix form. The ReLU transform is applied componentwise (on each row) and a new noise symbol (and thus a new column in the generator matrix) is added whenever an over-approximation is needed, that is when the input is not either always positive or negative.

Proposition 3 (ReLU Transform of a Zonotope). *Let $\mathcal{Z} = \langle c, \Gamma \rangle$ with $\Gamma = (g_{ij})_{i,j} \in \mathbb{R}^{n,p}$ be a zonotope, we note $[l_i, u_i] = \gamma_i(\mathcal{Z})$ the range of its i-th component. The result of applying componentwise the ReLU activation function is a zonotope $\mathcal{Z}' = \langle c', \Gamma' \rangle$ where $c' \in \mathbb{R}^n$ and $\Gamma' \in \mathbb{R}^{n,p+n}$, with $c'_i = \lambda_i c_i + \mu_i$ and*

$$
\Gamma' = \begin{bmatrix} \lambda_1 g_{11} & \ldots & \lambda_1 g_{1p} & \mu_1 & 0 & \ldots & 0 \\ \lambda_2 g_{21} & \ldots & \lambda_2 g_{2p} & 0 & \mu_2 & \ldots & 0 \\ & \ldots & & & & \\ \lambda_n g_{n1} & \ldots & \lambda_n g_{np} & 0 & 0 & \ldots & \mu_n \end{bmatrix}, (\lambda_i, \mu_i) = \begin{cases} (1,0) & \text{if } l_i \geq 0, \\ (0,0) & \text{if } u_i \leq 0, \\ \left(\frac{u_i}{u_i - l_i}, -\frac{u_i l_i}{2(u_i - l_i)}\right) & \text{otherwise.} \end{cases}
$$

Output. The output zonotope after the L layers is $\mathcal{Z}^L = \langle c^L, \Gamma^L \rangle$ with $c^L \in \mathbb{R}^{h_L}$ and $\Gamma^L \in \mathbb{R}^{h_L, \sum_{k=0}^L h_k}$. At line 5 of Algorithm 2, the probabilistic zonotope $p\mathcal{Z}^L(d_\varepsilon)$ is converted into a vector of DSI, following Definition 6. In this interpretation as a probabilistic zonotope, we must define the DSI structures corresponding to the $\sum_{k=1}^L h_k$ new noise symbols introduced by the ReLU transformers. A sound although conservative interpretation is to take the interval $[-1, 1]$ as DSI for them. This corresponds to considering that there is no available information about the distribution of the variable represented by these new noise symbols.

At line 6, the transform $H\mathcal{Z}^L$, interpreted as a probabilistic zonotope, is converted in a vector of DSI and used to bound the probability $\mathbb{P}(Hy \leq w)$.

Analysis of the Toy Example. We consider again Example 1.

Deterministic Zonotopes Analysis. From the input sets $x^0 \in [-2,2] \times [-1,1]$, the zonotopic interpretation is initialized with the affine forms $x_1^0 = 2\varepsilon_1$, $x_2^0 = \varepsilon_2$ with $\varepsilon_1, \varepsilon_2 \in [-1,1]$, encoded: $\mathcal{Z}^0 = \langle c^0, \Gamma^0 \rangle$ with $c^0 = \begin{bmatrix} 0 \\ 0 \end{bmatrix}$, $\Gamma^0 = \begin{bmatrix} 2 & 0 \\ 0 & 1 \end{bmatrix}$. Using the affine transforms on zonotopes and Proposition 3 for the ReLU layer with $(\lambda, \mu) = (0.5, 0.75)$ for both neurons, we obtain after the second affine layer:

$$\mathcal{Z}^2 = A_2 \mathcal{Z}^1 + b_2 = \langle \begin{bmatrix} 0 \\ 1.5 \end{bmatrix}, \begin{bmatrix} 0 & -1 & 0.75 & -0.75 \\ 2 & 0 & 0.75 & 0.75 \end{bmatrix} \rangle \subseteq \begin{bmatrix} [-2.5, 2.5] \\ [-2, 5] \end{bmatrix}$$

The first output x_1^2 is bounded in a tighter interval than with interval propagation ([-3,3]), the second ouput x_2^2 is incomparable to the interval computation ([0,6]).

Probabilistic Zonotopes Analysis. Let us now suppose that the inputs x_1^0 and x_2^0 follow a uniform law, which can be abstracted as in Sect. 3 with DSI structures d_1^0 and d_2^0. Algorithm 2 produces the same input zonotope and propagation through the network as above. Let us discretize the inputs with 2 focal elements. The rescaling of the DSI d_1^0 and d_2^0 between -1 and 1 yields $d_{\varepsilon_1} = \{\langle [-1,0], 0.5 \rangle, \langle [0,1], 0.5 \rangle\}$ and $d_{\varepsilon_2} = \{\langle [-1,0], 0.5 \rangle, \langle [0,1], 0.5 \rangle\}$.

The concretization of the final probabilistic zonotope $p\mathcal{Z}^2(d_\varepsilon)$ to a vector of DSI writes: $d_1^2 = -d_{\varepsilon_2} + 0.75 d_{\varepsilon_3} - 0.75 d_{\varepsilon_4}$ and $d_2^2 = 1.5 + 2d_{\varepsilon_1} + 0.75 d_{\varepsilon_3} + 0.75 d_{\varepsilon_4}$, where d_{ε_3} and d_{ε_4} are the DSI corresponding to the noise symbols introduced in the analysis by the ReLU function, with unknown distribution in $[-1,1]$. We get $d_1^2 = \{\langle [-2.5, 1.5], 0.5 \rangle, \langle [-1.5, 2.5], 0.5 \rangle\}$ and $d_2^2 = \{\langle [-2., 3.], 0.5 \rangle, \langle [0., 5.], 0.5 \rangle\}$ and deduce $\mathbb{P}(x_1^2 \leq -2) \in [0, 0.5]$ and $\mathbb{P}(x_2^2 \geq 2) \in [0,1]$.

The supports of the DSI are equal to the range obtained by the classical zonotopic analysis, thus incomparable to the support of the DSI obtained by Algorithm 1. The results are more generally not strictly comparable to those of DSI computation. For instance here with 100 focal elements, we have $\mathbb{P}(x_1^2 \leq -2) \in [0, 0.26]$ and $\mathbb{P}(x_2^2 \geq 2) \in [0, 0.76]$ both in the case of independent inputs x_1^0 and x_2^0 and unknown correlation, which is better than DSI in the case of unknown correlation, while DSI are better for independent inputs. The reason why the results do not depend here on the correlation between inputs is that d_{ε_1} does not appear in the expression of d_1^2 and d_{ε_2} in the expression of d_2^2, so that the information of correlation between inputs is not used.

5   Analysis with Zonotopic Dempster-Shafer Structures

In Sect. 4, a unique initial zonotope is built and propagated in the network. This propagation is exact through affine layers, but can be highly conservative for nonlinear operations such as the activation functions. In Algorithm 3, we suppose that the inputs are independent and perform the zonotopic propagation at a finer grain, on each tuple of focal elements of the inputs. This can be seen as using zonotopic focal elements to represent the input vector of a layer, instead of interval focal elements to represent each component of the input vector.

Algorithm 3. Neural network analysis by Dempster-Shafer zonotopic layers

---

Input: d^0 a h_0-dimensional vector of DSI

1: $d_{\mathcal{Z}}^0 = \{\langle \mathcal{Z}_{i_1\dots i_{h_0}}^0, w_{1,i_1}^0 \dots w_{h_0,i_{h_0}}^0\rangle, (i_1,\dots,i_{h_0}) \in [1,n]^{h_0}\} \leftarrow$ dsi-to-dsz(d^0)

2: **for** $k = 0$ to $L - 1$ **do**

3:     **for** $(i_1, i_2, \dots, i_{h_0}) \in [1,n]^{h_0}$ **do**

4:         $\mathcal{Z}_{i_1\dots i_{h_0}}^{k+1} \leftarrow \sigma(A^k \mathcal{Z}_{i_1\dots i_{h_0}}^k + b^k)$ ▷ Proposition 2 and Proposition 3

5:     **end for**

6: **end for**

7: $d_{\mathcal{Z}}^L = \{\langle \mathcal{Z}_{i_1\dots i_{h_0}}^L, w_{1,i_1}^0 \dots w_{h_0,i_{h_0}}^0\rangle, (i_1,\dots,i_{h_0}) \in [1,n]^{h_0}\}$

8: $d^L \leftarrow$ dsz-to-dsi($d_{\mathcal{Z}}^L$)

9: **return** (d^L, cdf(($H d_{\mathcal{Z}}^L, w$))

Input and Initialization. The input is the same as in Sects. 3 and 4: the uncertain input is modelled as a vector $d^0 = (d_1^0, \dots, d_{h_0}^0)$ of h_0 DSI. Assuming the input components as independent, we perform the convolution of the distributions of the input components to build a DSZ abstraction of the input vector: we construct one zonotope per possible h_0-tuple of focal elements representing the input vector of DSI d^0, with weight the product of the weights of each interval focal elements: we define for each $(i_1, i_2, \dots, i_{h_0}) \in [1,n]^{h_0}$ the zonotope $\mathcal{Z}_{i_1\dots i_{h_0}}^0 = \langle c_{i_1\dots i_{h_0}}^0, \Gamma_{i_1\dots i_{h_0}}^0\rangle$, built from the box $\boldsymbol{x}_{1i_1}^0 \times \boldsymbol{x}_{2i_2}^0 \times \dots \times \boldsymbol{x}_{h_0 i_{h_0}}^0$ and define the input $d_{\mathcal{Z}}^0$ as a Dempster Shafer structure with zonotopic focal elements (DSZ in short): $d_{\mathcal{Z}}^0 = \{\langle \mathcal{Z}_{i_1\dots i_{h_0}}^0, w_{1,i_1}^0 w_{2,i_2}^0 \dots w_{h_0,i_{h_0}}^0\rangle, (i_1, i_2, \dots, i_{h_0}) \in [1,n]^{h_0}\}$.

The number of focal elements does not have to be identical for each component of the input vector d^0, this choice was made here for simplicity of notation.

The propagation in the layers then consists in propagating each zonotope focal elements. Note that the number of focal elements remains constant through the propagation in the layers because all convolutions were computed at initialization, only the zonotopes size evolves with the layer dimensions.

Output. The DSZ $d_{\mathcal{Z}}^L$ is projected on the output vector, defined for each $i \in [1, h_L]$ by the DSI $d_i^L = \{\langle \gamma_i(\mathcal{Z}_{i_1\dots i_{h_0}}^0), w_{1,i_1}^0 w_{2,i_2}^0 \dots w_{h_0,i_{h_0}}^0\rangle, (i_1, i_2, \dots, i_{h_0}) \in [1,n]^{h_0}\rangle\}$.

The property can be assessed by evaluating the set of joint cumulative distributions represented by the DSZ $H d_{\mathcal{Z}}^L$, by generalizing the definition of Proposition 1 from interval to zonotopic focal elements:

Proposition 4 (CDF of a Zonotopic Dempster-Shafer Structure). *Let* X *be a random variable in* $\mathbb{R}^n$ *and* $d_{\mathcal{Z}} = \{\langle \mathcal{Z}_1, w_1\rangle, \langle \mathcal{Z}_2, w_2\rangle, \ldots, \langle \mathcal{Z}_u, w_u\rangle\}$ *be a DSZ with* $\mathcal{Z}_k = \langle c_k, \Gamma_k\rangle$ *with* $c_k \in \mathbb{R}^n$ *and* $\Gamma_k \in R^{n,p}$ *and* $w_k \in]0,1]$ *and* $\sum_{k=1}^u w_u = 1$. *The DSZ* $d_{\mathcal{Z}}$ *defines a discrete p-box representing the sets of joint cumulative distribution functions such that for* $v \in \mathbb{R}^n$,

$$\sum_{k\in[1,u],\,\mathcal{Z}_k \subset \downarrow v} w_k = \underline{P}_v \leq \mathbb{P}(X \leq v) \leq \overline{P}_v = \sum_{k\in[1,u],\,\mathcal{Z}_k \cap \downarrow v \neq \emptyset} w_k$$

where $\downarrow v$ *is the set of points in* $\mathbb{R}^n$ *less or equal than* v *in the componentwise ordering. Practically, we can use the ranges or projections of each component of* $\mathcal{Z}_k$ *to get a conservative over-approximation of the p-box:*

$$\underline{P}_v \geq \sum_{k\in[1,u],\,\bigwedge_{i\in[1,n]} \overline{\gamma_i(\mathcal{Z}_k)} < v_i} w_k \wedge \overline{P}_v \leq \sum_{k\in[1,u],\,\bigwedge_{i\in[1,n]} \underline{\gamma_i(\mathcal{Z}_k)} \leq v_i} w_k$$

This proposition can be derived from the notion of cdf of a random set of [24]. The bounds obtained by Proposition 4 are always at least as good than by first converting the DSZ as a vector and then applying Proposition 1.

DSZ Analysis of the Toy Example. We consider again Example 1. with 2 focal elements for each input, we have $d_1^0 = \{\langle[-2,0],0.5\rangle, \langle[0,2],0.5\rangle\}$ and $d_2^0 = \{\langle[-1,0],0.5\rangle, \langle[0,1],0.5\rangle\}$. At Line 1 of Algorithm 3, $d_{\mathcal{Z}}^0$ is a DSZ structure with 4 zonotopic focal elements, each with weight 0.25: $\mathcal{Z}_{11}^0 = \langle \begin{bmatrix} -1 \\ -0.5 \end{bmatrix}, \begin{bmatrix} 1 & 0 \\ 0 & 0.5 \end{bmatrix}\rangle$, $\mathcal{Z}_{12}^0 = \langle \begin{bmatrix} -1 \\ 0.5 \end{bmatrix}, \begin{bmatrix} 1 & 0 \\ 0 & 0.5 \end{bmatrix}\rangle$, $\mathcal{Z}_{21}^0 = \langle \begin{bmatrix} 1 \\ -0.5 \end{bmatrix}, \begin{bmatrix} 1 & 0 \\ 0 & 0.5 \end{bmatrix}\rangle$, $\mathcal{Z}_{22}^0 = \langle \begin{bmatrix} 1 \\ 0.5 \end{bmatrix}, \begin{bmatrix} 1 & 0 \\ 0 & 0.5 \end{bmatrix}\rangle$. After the output layer, the 4 zonotopic elements, each with weight 0.25, are: $\mathcal{Z}_{11}^2 = \langle \begin{bmatrix} \frac{1}{6} \\ \frac{1}{6} \end{bmatrix}, \begin{bmatrix} \frac{1}{3} & -\frac{1}{6} & \frac{1}{3} \\ \frac{1}{3} & -\frac{1}{6} & \frac{1}{3} \end{bmatrix}\rangle$, $\mathcal{Z}_{12}^2 = \langle \begin{bmatrix} -\frac{1}{6} \\ \frac{1}{6} \end{bmatrix}, \begin{bmatrix} -\frac{1}{3} & -\frac{1}{6} & -\frac{1}{3} \\ \frac{1}{3} & \frac{1}{6} & \frac{1}{3} \end{bmatrix}\rangle$, $\mathcal{Z}_{21}^2 = \langle \begin{bmatrix} \frac{5}{6} \\ \frac{13}{6} \end{bmatrix}, \begin{bmatrix} \frac{1}{3} & -\frac{5}{6} & -\frac{1}{3} \\ \frac{10}{6} & \frac{1}{6} & \frac{1}{3} \end{bmatrix}\rangle$, $\mathcal{Z}_{22}^2 = \langle \begin{bmatrix} -\frac{5}{6} \\ \frac{13}{6} \end{bmatrix}, \begin{bmatrix} -\frac{1}{3} & -\frac{5}{6} & \frac{1}{3} \\ \frac{10}{6} & \frac{1}{6} & \frac{1}{3} \end{bmatrix}\rangle$. From these and their projected ranges for x_1^2 and x_2^2, we deduce (see Appendix of preprint [10]) using Proposition 4 that $\mathbb{P}(x_1^2 \leq -2) \in [0,0.25]$ and $\mathbb{P}(x_2^2 \geq 2) \in [0,0.5]$ and the conjunction $\mathbb{P}(Hy \leq w) \in [0.0,0.25]$.

6 Evaluation

Implementation. We implemented our approach[1] using the Julia library ProbabilityBoundsAnalysis.jl [11] for Interval Dempster Shafer abstraction and arithmetic. In this library, the focal elements of a DSI structure all have same weight. The result is reduced after each arithmetic operation to keep a constant number of focal elements. We rely on this DSI implementation, but our DSZ implementation does not present the same restrictions. The focal elements are bounded, but

---

[1] available from https://doi.org/10.5281/zenodo.12519084.

a flag allows the user to specify that a distribution may have unbounded support, and this knowledge is used to produce a sound CDF estimation for unbounded distributions. In our current implementation, we do not use this possibility, but we believe that the work presented here can be extended to unbounded support. Timings for our analysis are on a MacBook Pro 2.3 GHz Intel Core i9 with 8 cores (the implementation is not parallel, although obviously parallelizable).

Comparing DSI, Probabilistic Zonotopes and DSZ on the Toy Example. We compare in Table 1 our 3 abstractions in the case of independent inputs, varying the number of focal elements and the input distributions: $U(n)$ denotes a uniform distribution represented with n focal elements, and $N(n)$ a truncated normal law in the same range with n focal elements.

On this example, the DSZ analysis is by far more precise, followed by the DSI and finally the probabilistic zonotopes. Refining the input discretization with more focal elements tightens the output of all analyzes, but only the DSZ converges to actually tight bounds. In particular, for DSI and probabilistic zonotopes, the support of the output distribution is unchanged when the input is refined. The computation times are, on this example, of the same order of magnitude for all three analyzes, slightly higher for DSZ, and lower for probabilistic zonotopes. The reason for the probabilistic zonotopes to have lower cost is that affine transforms are computed on the zonotopes, and the costly operations between DSI are delayed until the final representation as a DSI. It is not surprising that the DSZ have slightly higher cost, because of the exponential number of zonotopic focal elements. However, the computation is obviously parallelizable.

Table 1. Probability bounds for the toy example, independent inputs.

Law (#FE)	DSI			Prob. Zono.			DSZ		
	$\mathbb{P}(x_1^2 \leq -2)$	$\mathbb{P}(x_2^2 \geq 2)$	time	$\mathbb{P}(x_1^2 \leq -2)$	$\mathbb{P}(x_2^2 \geq 2)$	time	$\mathbb{P}(x_1^2 \leq -2)$	$\mathbb{P}(x_2^2 \geq 2)$	time
$U(2)$	$[0, 0.5]$	$[0, 1]$	$< e^{-3}$	$[0, 0.5]$	$[0, 1]$	$< e^{-3}$	$[0, 0.25]$	$[0, 0.5]$	$< e^{-3}$
$U(10)$	$[0, 0.2]$	$[0, 0.7]$	e^{-3}	$[0, 0.3]$	$[0, 0.8]$	e^{-3}	$[0, 0.03]$	$[0.2, 0.3]$	$< e^{-3}$
$U(10^2)$	$[0, 0.07]$	$[0.05, 0.52]$	0.022	$[0, 0.26]$	$[0, 0.76]$	0.013	$[0, 0.0014]$	$[0.25, 0.26]$	0.026
$U(10^3)$	$[0, 0.063]$	$[0.062, 0.502]$	2.4	$[0, 0.251]$	$[0, 0.751]$	1.2	$[0, 3.e^{-6}]$	$[0.25, 0.251]$	3
$N(10)$	$[0, 0.017]$	$[0, 0.277]$	e^{-3}	$[0, 0.1]$	$[0, 1]$	e^{-3}	$[0, 0.01]$	$[0, 0.1]$	$< e^{-3}$
$N(10^2)$	$[0, 0.004]$	$[0, 0.186]$	0.022	$[0, 0.07]$	$[0, 0.94]$	0.013	$[0, 4.e^{-4}]$	$[0.06, 0.07]$	0.026
$N(10^3)$	$[0, 0.004]$	$[0.003, 0.182]$	2.4	$[0, 0.067]$	$[0, 0.934]$	1.2	$[6e^{-5}, 1.1e^{-4}]$	$[0.066, 0.067]$	3

We can also note the strong impact of the input hypotheses on the results, advocating the need of such an approach which can account in a same framework and computation for large classes of inputs. For instance, changing the input distribution from a uniform to a Gaussian truncated to same support produces very different probability bounds. In Table 1, we supposed the inputs independent. For instance, the DSI analysis for 100 focal elements and a uniform law, produces for independent inputs $\mathbb{P}(x_1^2 \leq -2) \in [0, 0.07]$ and $\mathbb{P}(x_2^2 \geq 2) \in [0.05, 0.52]$, while for inputs with unknown dependence, $\mathbb{P}(x_1^2 \leq -2) \in [0, 0.26]$ and $\mathbb{P}(x_2^2 \geq 2) \in [0, 1]$.

For independent inputs, the DSZ is the best choice among our approaches. In the case of correlated inputs, it is hard to conclude from such a simple example between DSI and probabilistic zonotopes. In the context of discrete dynamical systems where probabilistic zonotopes were proposed [6,7], they were much better than DSI both in terms of efficiency and accuracy. The context of neural networks is less favorable, but it is probable that probabilistic zonotopes can be more interesting than DSI for larger networks. However, our focus is to explore in the future the encoding of multivariate probabilistic distributions as input distributions, and lift this current restriction on the DSZ analysis.

Comparing DSZ to Probstar [29]. We now compare our approach to the results of the closely related approach [29] on their two benchmark examples. Similarly to [29], we consider the inputs as independent.

ACAS Xu We consider the ACAS Xu networks benchmark, where the networks have 5 inputs and 5 outputs, with the same input configurations and properties $(P_2 : y_1 > y_2 \land y_1 > y_3 \land y_1 > y_4 \land y_1 > y_5, P_3/P_4 : y_1 < y_2 \land y_1 < y_3 \land y_1 < y_4 \land y_1 < y_5)$ as in [29]. The lower and upper bounds on the inputs, lb and ub, depend on the property, and are used in [29] to define probabilistic input sets by Gaussian distributions with mean $m = (ub + lb)/2$ and standard deviation $(ub - m)/a$, where $a = 3$, truncated between lb and ub. In our work, after creation of the input DSI from the above Gaussian distribution, we truncate all focal elements so that the support of the DSI is restricted to the input range $[lb, ub]$. In [29], an argument is used to deduce bounds for the probability for non truncated distributions. We could use a similar argument here but we focus on the results for the truncated distributions, and compare our results to the interval $[US - Prob - LB, US - Prob - UB]$ with the notations of [29].

We choose for our approach an over-approximation of the input distributions using a different number of focal elements for each component of the vector input, based on the relative widths of the input intervals. We represent these as vectors of number of focal elements, taking [5, 80, 50, 6, 5] for Property 2, [5, 20, 1, 6, 5] for Properties 3 and 4. In Table 2, we compare our results with the Probstar approach with two parametrizations: $p_f = 0$ corresponds to an exact set-based propagation, while $p_f = e^{-5}$ corresponds to the level of over-approximation in propagation most widely used in [29].

The running times for Probstar in Table 2 are those of [29], hence not computed on the same computer. We reproduced Property 2 on Net 1–6 with Probstars on our MacBook: for $p = 0$, it takes 3614 s on 8 cores, 5045 s on 4 cores, 12542 on 1 core, to be compared to the 1424 s in Table 2; for $p = e^{-5}$, it takes 425 s on 8 cores, 489 on 4 cores, 1489 on 1 core, to be compared to the 206 s in Table 2) and to the 46 s with DSZ.

The tightness of the enclosures of the DSZ is comparable to Probstars with $p = e^{-5}$, for an analysis being generally an order of magnitude faster. The results look consistent between the 2 analyzes for Property 2. Properties 3 and 4 (originally from [15]) are true on the whole input range, which can be proven by classical set-based analysis, and our approach accordingly produces a probability

Table 2. Probability bounds for the ACAS Xu example.

Prop	Net	DSZ $\mathbb{P}$	time	Probstar $p_f = e^{-5}$ $\mathbb{P}$	time	Probstar $p_f = 0$ $\mathbb{P}$	time
2	1–6	[0, 0.01999]	46.4	[2.8e-06,0.05283]	206.7	1.87224e-05	1424
2	2–2	[0.00423 0.0809]	47.9	[0.0195,0.094]	299.0	0.0353886	2102.5
2	2–9	[0, 0.0774684]	51.0	[0.000255,0.107]	504.5	0.000997678	4561.2
2	3–1	[0.0165, 0.08787]	43.8	[0.0305, 0.07263]	202.7	0.044535	1086.4
2	3–6	[0.0167, 0.1111]	52.4	[0.02078,0.1069]	452.0	0.0335763	5224.4
2	3–7	[6e-05, 0.1361]	43.7	[0.002319,0.075]	331.1	0.00404731	2598
2	4–1	[1e-05, 0.05353]	40.9	[0.00104,0.07162]	305.3	0.00231247	1870.7
2	4–7	[0.0129, 0.1056]	44.4	[0.02078,0.1081]	418.9	0.04095	3407.8
2	5–3	[0, 0.03939]	40.0	[1.59e-09,0.0326]	139.7	1.81747e-09	418.8
3	1–7	[1, 1]	0.25	[0.9801,0.9804]	4.7	0.976871	3.6
4	1–9	[1, 1]	0.2	[0.9796,0.98]	3.6	0.989244	3.6

equal to 1. The approach of [29] produces more precise, 'exact' results, when $p = 0$, than our approach. However, only the set-based propagation is exact, there is also a part of probabilistic estimation. For instance, when reproducing Property 2 on Net 1–6 with Probstars, we obtained for $p = 0$, the probabilities 1.56119e-05 with 8 cores, 6.76052e-06 with 4 cores, 7.22045e-06 with 1 core, to be compared to the 'exact' 1.87224e-05 in the table. In contrast, our approach produces fully guaranteed bounds while allowing a much richer classes of inputs.

In Table 2, we manually chose the number of focal element per input component. Although we refrained from optimizing too much, choosing for instance the same discretization for different networks, this impairs the practicality of the approach. As a first answer, we implemented a simple loop to automatically refine the discretization starting from a very rough one, by some basic sensitivity analysis. For instance, for Property 2 and net-1-6, the total refinement process with as stopping criterion the width of the probability interval lower than 0.05 takes 112 s and leads to the number of focal elements [5, 81, 38, 5, 5] and a probability in [0, 0.0276], with bounds twice tighter than Probstars with $p = e^{-5}$.

Rocket Lander. Let us now consider the rocket lander example of [29], with the same inputs and properties. The networks have here 9 inputs. Taking the vector of focal elements [7, 12, 10, 17, 9, 7, 1, 1, 2, 1, 1] produces the results of Table 3

Again, the timings for Probstars are those of [29]; we executed for instance on our MacBook the analysis of Property 1 on network 0 with 4 cores, the running times were 1351.2 s for $p_f = 1e-5$ and 12127 s for $p_f = 0$.

Table 3. Comparing probability bounds for the rocket lander example.

Prop	Net	DSZ		Probstar $p_f = 1e-5$		Probstar $p_f = 0$	
		$\mathbb{P}$	time	$\mathbb{P}$	time	$\mathbb{P}$	time
1	0	[0, 0.03387]	77.8	[4.15e-09, 0.06748]	1158.6	7.978e-08	5903.7
2	0	[0, 0.01352]	83.7	[0,0.1053]	2216	0	13132.7
1	1	[0, 0.01985]	80.5	[0,0.0536]	1229.7	8.68e-08	5163.9
2	1	[0, 0.00055]	69.1	[0, 0.0161751]	448.5	0	1495.6

7   Conclusion

A central notion for dealing with multivariate probabilistic distributions is that of a copula [18], and in particular Sklar's theorem which links multivariate cdf with the cdf of its marginals. Multiple authors have considered generalizing Sklar's theorem to imprecise probabilities, [17,19], with e.g. applications in [12] to the analysis of non-linear dynamical systems. In this work, we developed the case of multidimensional imprecise probabilites described by the independence copula. Future work includes the tractable treatment of other copulas in our framework. Finally, we focused here on ReLU-based networks, but the approach is by no means restricted to this activation function.

Acknowledgement. This work was partially supported by the SAIF project, funded by the France 2030 government investment plan managed by the French National Research Agency, under the reference ANR-23-PEIA-0006, and by the 2021 project FARO, funded by Agence de l'Innovation de Défense AID through the Centre Interdisciplinaire d'Etudes pour la Défense et la Sécurité CIEDS.

Data Availability Statement. The Julia implementation of our approach and the examples to reproduce results of this paper are available from https://doi.org/10.5281/zenodo.12519084.

References

1. Bak, S., Duggirala, P.S.: Simulation-equivalent reachability of large linear systems with inputs. In: Majumdar, R., Kunčak, V. (eds.) CAV 2017. LNCS, vol. 10426, pp. 401–420. Springer, Cham (2017). https://doi.org/10.1007/978-3-319-63387-9_20
2. Baluta, T., Chua, Z.L., Meel, K.S., Saxena, P.: Scalable quantitative verification for deep neural networks (2021)
3. Baluta, T., Shen, S., S., S., Meel, K.S., Saxena, P.: Quantitative verification of neural networks and its security applications. In: Computer and Communications Security (2019)
4. Beer, M., S.F., Kreinovich, V.: Imprecise probabilities in engineering analyses. Mech. Syst. Signal Process. **37**(1), 4–29 (2013)
5. Boopathy, A., Weng, T.W., Chen, P.Y., Liu, S., Daniel, L.: CNN-cert: an efficient framework for certifying robustness of convolutional neural networks. In: AAAI (2019)

6. Bouissou, O., Goubault, E., Goubault-Larrecq, J., Putot, S.: A generalization of p-boxes to affine arithmetic. Computing **94**(2–4), 189–201 (2012)

7. Bouissou, O., Goubault, E., Putot, S., Chakarov, A., Sankaranarayanan, S.: Uncertainty propagation using probabilistic affine forms and concentration of measure inequalities. In: Chechik, M., Raskin, J.-F. (eds.) TACAS 2016. LNCS, vol. 9636, pp. 225–243. Springer, Heidelberg (2016). https://doi.org/10.1007/978-3-662-49674-9_13

8. Fazlyab, M., Morari, M., Pappas, G.J.: Probabilistic verification and reachability analysis of neural networks via semidefinite programming. In: 2019 IEEE 58th Conference on Decision and Control (CDC), pp. 2726–2731 (2019). https://doi.org/10.1109/CDC40024.2019.9029310

9. Ferson, S., Kreinovich, V., Ginzburg, L., Myers, D.: Constructing probability boxes and dempster-shafer structures. Tech. rep., Sandia National Laboratories, SAND2002-4015, Albuquerque, New Mexico (2003)

10. Goubault, E., Putot, S.: A Zonotopic Dempster-Shafer Approach to the Quantitative Verification of Neural Networks (2024). https://hal.science/hal-04546350. Working paper or preprint

11. Gray, A., Ferson, S., Patelli, E.: `ProbabilityBoundsAnalysis.jl`: arithmetic with sets of distributions. In: Proceedings of JuliaCon (2021)

12. Gray, A., Forets, M., Schilling, C., Ferson, S., Benet, L.: Verified propagation of imprecise probabilities in non-linear ODEs. Int. J. Approx. Reason. **164**, 109044 (2024). https://doi.org/10.1016/j.ijar.2023.109044

13. Henriksen, P., Lomuscio, A.R.: Efficient neural network verification via adaptive refinement and adversarial search. In: Giacomo, G.D., et al. (eds.) ECAI 2020 - 24th European Conference on Artificial Intelligence, 2020 - Including 10th Conference on Prestigious Applications of Artificial Intelligence (PAIS 2020). Frontiers in Artificial Intelligence and Applications, vol. 325, pp. 2513–2520. IOS Press (2020)

14. Huang, C., Hu, Z., Huang, X., Pei, K.: Statistical certification of acceptable robustness for neural networks. In: Farkaš, I., Masulli, P., Otte, S., Wermter, S. (eds.) ICANN 2021. LNCS, vol. 12891, pp. 79–90. Springer, Cham (2021). https://doi.org/10.1007/978-3-030-86362-3_7

15. Katz, G., Barrett, C., Dill, D.L., Julian, K., Kochenderfer, M.J.: Reluplex: an efficient SMT solver for verifying deep neural networks. In: Majumdar, R., Kunčak, V. (eds.) CAV 2017. LNCS, vol. 10426, pp. 97–117. Springer, Cham (2017). https://doi.org/10.1007/978-3-319-63387-9_5

16. Lyu, Z., Ko, C.Y., Kong, Z., Wong, N., Lin, D., Daniel, L.: Fastened crown: tightened neural network robustness certificates. Proc. AAAI Conf. Artif. Intell. **34**(04), 5037–5044 (2020)

17. Montes, I., Miranda, E., Pelessoni, R., Vicig, P.: Sklar's theorem in an imprecise setting. Fuzzy Sets and Systems **278**, 48–66 (2015). https://doi.org/10.1016/j.fss.2014.10.007, https://www.sciencedirect.com/science/article/pii/S0165011414004539, special Issue on uncertainty and imprecision modelling in decision making (EUROFUSE 2013)

18. Nelsen, R.B.: An Introduction to Copulas, 2nd edn. Springer, New York (2006)

19. Omladič, M., Stopar, N.: A full scale sklar's theorem in the imprecise setting. Fuzzy Sets and Systems **393**, 113–125 (2020). https://doi.org/10.1016/j.fss.2020.02.001, https://www.sciencedirect.com/science/article/pii/S0165011420300348, copulas and Related Topics

20. Pautov, M., Tursynbek, N., Munkhoeva, M., Muravev, N., Petiushko, A., Oseledets, I.: Cc-cert: A probabilistic approach to certify general robustness of neural net-

works. Proceedings of the AAAI Conference on Artificial Intelligence **36**, 7975–7983 (06 2022). https://doi.org/10.1609/aaai.v36i7.20768

21. Pilipovsky, J., Sivaramakrishnan, V., Oishi, M., Tsiotras, P.: Probabilistic verification of Relu neural networks via characteristic functions. In: Matni, N., Morari, M., Pappas, G.J. (eds.) Proceedings of The 5th Annual Learning for Dynamics and Control Conference. Proceedings of Machine Learning Research, vol. 211, pp. 966–979. PMLR (2023)

22. Păsăreanu, C., Converse, H., Filieri, A., Gopinath, D.: On the probabilistic analysis of neural networks. In: 2020 IEEE/ACM 15th International Symposium on Software Engineering for Adaptive and Self-Managing Systems (SEAMS), pp. 5–8 (2020). https://doi.org/10.1145/3387939.3391594

23. Regan, H., Ferson, S., Berleant, D.: Equivalence of methods for uncertainty propagation of real-valued random variables. Int. J. Approx. Reason. **36**, 1–30 (2004). https://doi.org/10.1016/j.ijar.2003.07.013

24. Schmelzer, B.: Random sets, copulas and related sets of probability measures. Int. J. Approx. Reason. **160**, 108952 (2023). https://doi.org/10.1016/j.ijar.2023.108952

25. Shafer, G.: A Mathematical Theory of Evidence. Princeton University Press (1976)

26. Singh, G., Gehr, T., Mirman, M., Püschel, M., Vechev, M.: Fast and effective robustness certification. In: Bengio, S., Wallach, H., Larochelle, H., Grauman, K., Cesa-Bianchi, N., Garnett, R. (eds.) Advances in Neural Information Processing Systems. vol. 31. Curran Associates, Inc. (2018). https://proceedings.neurips.cc/paper_files/paper/2018/file/f2f446980d8e971ef3da97af089481c3-Paper.pdf

27. Singh, G., Gehr, T., Mirman, M., Püschel, M., Vechev, M.T.: Fast and effective robustness certification. In: Advances in Neural Information Processing Systems, NeurIPS, pp. 10825–10836 (2018)

28. Singh, G., Gehr, T., Püschel, M., Vechev, M.: An abstract domain for certifying neural networks. Proc. ACM Program. Lang. (POPL) (2019)

29. Tran, H.D., Choi, S., Okamoto, H., Hoxha, B., Fainekos, G., Prokhorov, D.: Quantitative verification for neural networks using probstars. In: Proceedings of the 26th ACM International Conference on Hybrid Systems: Computation and Control (HSCC 2023). Association for Computing Machinery, New York (2023). https://doi.org/10.1145/3575870.3587112

30. Walley, P.: Statistical Reasoning with Imprecise Probabilities. Chapman & Hall (1991)

31. Webb, S., Rainforth, T., Teh, Y.W., Kumar, M.P.: A statistical approach to assessing neural network robustness. ICLR. arXiv preprint arXiv:1811.07209 (2019)

32. Weng, L., et al.: PROVEN: Verifying robustness of neural networks with a probabilistic approach. In: Chaudhuri, K., Salakhutdinov, R. (eds.) Proceedings of the 36th International Conference on Machine Learning. Proceedings of Machine Learning Research, vol. 97, pp. 6727–6736. PMLR (2019). https://proceedings.mlr.press/v97/weng19a.html

33. Williamson, R.C., Downs, T.: Probabilistic arithmetic: numerical methods for calculating convolutions and dependency bounds. Journ. Approx. Reas. (1990)

34. Zhang, D., Ye, M., Gong, C., Zhu, Z., Liu, Q.: Black-box certification with randomized smoothing: a functional optimization based framework. In: Proceedings of the 34th International Conference on Neural Information Processing Systems (NIPS 2020). Curran Associates Inc., Red Hook (2020)

35. Zhang, H., Weng, T.W., Chen, P.Y., Hsieh, C.J., Daniel, L.: Efficient neural network robustness certification with general activation functions. In: Bengio, S., Wallach, H., Larochelle, H., Grauman, K., Cesa-Bianchi, N., Garnett, R. (eds.)

Advances in Neural Information Processing Systems, vol. 31, pp. 4939–4948. Curran Associates, Inc. (2018). https://proceedings.neurips.cc/paper/2018/file/d04863f100d59b3eb688a11f95b0ae60-Paper.pdf

36. Zhang, T., Ruan, W., Fieldsend, J.E.: Proa: a probabilistic robustness assessment against functional perturbations. In: ECML PKDD 2022, Part III. LNCS, pp. 154–170. Springer, Heidelberg (2023). https://doi.org/10.1007/978-3-031-26409-2_10

Certified Quantization Strategy Synthesis
for Neural Networks

Yedi Zhang[1], Guangke Chen[2], Fu Song[3,4], Jun Sun[5(✉)], and Jin Song Dong[1]

[1] National University of Singapore, Singapore 117417, Singapore
[2] ShanghaiTech University, Shanghai 201210, China
[3] Key Laboratory of System Software (Chinese Academy of Sciences) and State Key Laboratory of Computer Science, Institute of Software, Chinese Academy of Sciences, Beijing 100190, China
[4] Nanjing Institute of Software Technology, Nanjing 211135, China
[5] Singapore Management University, Singapore 178902, Singapore
junsun@smu.edu.sg

Abstract. Quantization plays an important role in deploying neural networks on embedded, real-time systems with limited computing and storage resources (e.g., edge devices). It significantly reduces the model storage cost and improves inference efficiency by using fewer bits to represent the parameters. However, it was recently shown that critical properties may be broken after quantization, such as robustness and backdoor-freeness. In this work, we introduce the first method for synthesizing quantization strategies that verifiably maintain desired properties after quantization, leveraging a key insight that quantization leads to a data distribution shift in each layer. We propose to compute the preimage for each layer based on which the preceding layer is quantized, ensuring that the quantized reachable region of the preceding layer remains within the preimage. To tackle the challenge of computing the exact preimage, we propose an MILP-based method to compute its under-approximation. We implement our method into a tool **Quadapter** and demonstrate its effectiveness and efficiency by providing certified quantization that successfully preserves model robustness and backdoor-freeness.

1 Introduction

While deep neural networks (DNNs) have achieved notable success in various application domains [5,31], their deployment on resource-constrained,

This study was funded by the National Natural Science Foundation of China (62072309), CAS Project for Young Scientists in Basic Research (YSBR-040), ISCAS New Cultivation Project (ISCAS-PYFX-202201), ISCAS Fundamental Research Project (ISCAS-JCZD-202302), the Ministry of Education, Singapore under its Academic Research Fund Tier 3 (Award ID: MOET32020-0004), and the Ministry of Education, Singapore under its Academic Research Fund Tier 3 (Award ID: MOE-MOET32020-0003). Any opinions, findings, conclusions, or recommendations expressed in this material are those of the author(s) and do not reflect the views of the Ministry of Education, Singapore.

A. Platzer et al. (Eds.): FM 2024, LNCS 14933, pp. 343–362, 2025.
https://doi.org/10.1007/978-3-031-71162-6_18

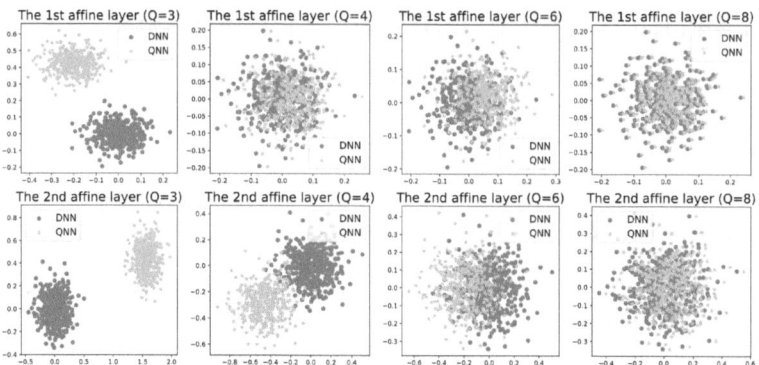

Fig. 1. Visualized data distribution shift using 400 random samples centered around an input image. These inputs are processed through both a DNN (trained on MNIST [20]) and its counterparts quantized with bit-width $Q \in \{4, 6, 8, 10\}$. The resulting high-dimensional convex shapes are visualized in 2D. The blue and brown scatters demonstrate the distribution of output values of each affine layer of the DNN and QNNs. (Color figure online)

embedded, real-time systems is currently impeded by their substantial demand for computing and storage resources [27]. Quantization is one of the most popular and promising techniques to address this issue [8,39]. By storing the full-precision values in a DNN (such as parameters and/or activation values) into low bit-width fixed-point numbers, quantization facilitates the compression of a DNN and leads to a quantized neural network (QNN), making the network more efficient.

While a lot of techniques have been proposed to minimize the loss of accuracy induced by quantization [8,15,21,22,32,33,42,44,48], an important side-effect of quantization is overlooked, that is the risk of breaking desired critical properties, e.g., robustness [24,41] and backdoor-freeness [13,26,34,55], thereby raising great concerns, especially when they are deployed in safety-critical applications. While quantization-aware training techniques have been proposed to improve the robustness for a given fixed quantization strategy [23,24,41,43], they fail to provide robustness guarantees. Therefore, it becomes imperative to devise a quantization strategy synthesis technique, ensuring that the resulting QNNs retain specific desired properties. Noting that although various verification methods for QNNs have been proposed [3,9,12,52–54], they exclusively focus on post-hoc analyses rather than synthesis, namely, these methods merely verify or falsify the properties but offer no solutions for those that are falsified.

Contributions. In this work, we propose the first quantization strategy synthesis method, named Quadapter, such that the desired properties are verifiably maintained by the quantization. Given a DNN $\mathcal{N}$ and a property $\langle \mathcal{I}, \mathcal{O} \rangle$ where $\mathcal{I}$ and $\mathcal{O}$ are the pre- and post-condition for the input and output, our general idea is first to compute the preimage of each layer w.r.t. the output region formed by $\mathcal{O}$. Then, considering the typical data distribution shift caused by quantization in each layer (cf. Fig. 1), we identify the minimal bit-width for each layer such that the shifted quantized reachable region w.r.t. $\mathcal{I}$ always remains within the corresponding preimage. This method allows us to derive a quantization strategy for the entire network, preserving the desired property $\langle \mathcal{I}, \mathcal{O} \rangle$ after quantization.

A key technical question is how to represent and compute the preimage for each layer effectively and efficiently. In this work, we propose to compute an under-approximation of the preimage for each layer and represent it by adapting the abstract domain of DeepPoly [40]. Specifically, we devise a novel Mixed Integer Linear Programming (MILP) based method to propagate the (approximate) preimage layer-by-layer in a backward fashion, where we encode the affine transformation and activation function precisely as linear constraints and compute under-approximate preimage via MILP solving.

We implement our methods as an end-to-end tool Quadapter and extensively evaluate our tool on a large set of synthesis tasks for DNNs trained using two widely used datasets MNIST [20] and Fashion-MNIST [46], where the number of hidden layers varies from 2 to 6 and the number of neurons in each hidden layer varies from 100 to 512. The experimental results demonstrate the effectiveness and efficiency of Quadapter in synthesizing certified quantization strategies to preserve robustness and backdoor-freeness. The quantization strategy synthesized by Quadapter generally preserves the accuracy of the original DNNs (with only minor degradation). We also show that by slightly relaxing the under-approximate preimages of the hidden layers (without sacrificing the overall soundness), Quadapter can synthesize quantization strategies with much smaller bit-widths while preserving the desired properties and accuracy.

The remainder of this paper is organized as follows. Section 2 gives the preliminaries and formulates the problem. Section 3 presents the details of our approach and Sect. 4 demonstrates its applications. Section 5 reports our experimental results. We discuss related work in Sect. 6 and finally, Sect. 7 concludes. The source code for our tool, along with the benchmarks, is available in [50], which also includes a long version of the paper containing all missing proofs, design choices, implementation details, and additional experimental results.

2   Preliminaries

We denote by $\mathbb{R}$ the set of real numbers. Given an integer n, let $[n] := \{1, \ldots, n\}$ and $\mathbb{R}^n$ be the set of the n-tuples of real numbers. We use **bold lowercase letters** (e.g., $\mathbf{x}$) and **BOLD UPPERCASE** (e.g., $\mathbf{W}$) to denote vectors and matrices. We denote by $\mathbf{W}_{i,:}$ (resp. $\mathbf{W}_{:,i}$) the i-th row (resp. column) vector of the matrix $\mathbf{W}$, and by $\mathbf{x}_j$ (resp. $\mathbf{W}_{i,j}$) the j-th entry of the vector $\mathbf{x}$ (resp. $\mathbf{W}_{i,:}$). $\mathbf{M}$ denotes an extremely large number.

A *Deep Neural Network* (DNN) with $2d$ layers is a function $\mathcal{N} : \mathbb{R}^{n_0} \to \mathbb{R}^{n_{2d}}$ such that $\mathcal{N} = f_{2d} \circ \cdots \circ f_1$, where $f_1 : \mathbb{R}^{n_0} \to \mathbb{R}^{n_1}$ is the input layer, $f_{2d} : \mathbb{R}^{n_{2d-1}} \to \mathbb{R}^{n_{2d}}$ is the output layer, and the others are hidden layers. The hidden layers alternate between affine layers $f_{2i} : \mathbb{R}^{n_{2i-1}} \to \mathbb{R}^{n_{2i}}$ and activation layers $f_{2i+1} : \mathbb{R}^{n_{2i}} \to \mathbb{R}^{n_{2i+1}}$ for $i \in [d-1]$. The semantics of each layer is defined as follows: $\mathbf{x}^1 = f_1(\mathbf{x}) = \mathbf{x}$, $\mathbf{x}^{2i} = f_{2i}(\mathbf{x}^{2i-1}) = \mathbf{W}^{2i}\mathbf{x}^{2i-1} + \mathbf{b}^{2i}$ for $i \in [d]$ and $\mathbf{x}^{2i+1} = f_{2i+1}(\mathbf{x}^{2i}) = \mathrm{ReLU}(\mathbf{x}^{2i})$ for $i \in [d-1]$, where $\mathbf{W}^{2i}$ and $\mathbf{b}^{2i}$ are the weight matrix and the bias vector of the $2i$-th layer, $n_0 = n_1$ and $n_{2i} = n_{2i+1}$ for $i \in [d-1]$. Note that for the sake of presentation, we regard affine and activation layers separately as hidden layers, some prior work regards the composition of an affine layer and an activation layer as one hidden layer, e.g., [4,25,38]. Given a DNN $\mathcal{N}$ with $2d$ layers, we use $\mathcal{N}_{[i:j]} : \mathbb{R}^{n_{i-1}} \to \mathbb{R}^{n_j}$ to denote the composed function $f_j \circ \cdots \circ f_i$. By $\mathcal{N}(\mathcal{I})$ (resp. $\mathcal{N}(\mathcal{I})_g$), we refer to the output region of the network $\mathcal{N}$ (resp. neuron $\mathbf{x}_g^{2d}$) w.r.t. the input region $\mathcal{I}$.

A *Quantized Neural Network* (QNN) is structurally identical to a DNN but uses fixed-point values for its parameters and/or layer outputs. In this work, we focus on QNNs where only parameters are quantized using the most hardware-efficient quantization scheme, i.e., *signed power-of-two quantization* [33].

A *quantization configuration* ξ is a pair $\langle Q, F \rangle$, where Q denotes the total bit-width and F denotes the bit-width for the fractional part of the value. Given a quantization configuration ξ and a real-valued number u, its fixed-point counterpart $\hat{u}$ is defined as $\hat{u} = \min(\max(\frac{\lfloor u \cdot 2^F \rceil}{2^F}, -2^{Q-1}), 2^{Q-1} - 1)$, where $\lfloor \cdot \rceil$ is the round-to-nearest operator. Given a DNN $\mathcal{N} : \mathbb{R}^{n_0} \to \mathbb{R}^{n_{2d}}$ with $2d$ layers and a set of quantization configurations for affine and output layers $\Xi = \{\xi_1, \ldots, \xi_d\}$, its quantized version $\widehat{\mathcal{N}} : \mathbb{R}^{n_0} \to \mathbb{R}^{n_{2d}}$ is a composed function as $\widehat{\mathcal{N}} = \hat{f}_{2d} \circ \cdots \circ \hat{f}_1$, where each layer is defined the same as that in the DNN $\mathcal{N}$ except that the parameters $\mathbf{W}^{2i}$ and $\mathbf{b}^{2i}$ for $i \in [d]$ from the DNN $\mathcal{N}$ are quantized into fixed-point values $\widehat{\mathbf{W}}^{2i}$ and $\widehat{\mathbf{b}}^{2i}$ in the QNN $\widehat{\mathcal{N}}$ according to the quantization configuration ξ_i. In this work, we call the set Ξ a *quantization strategy* of the DNN $\mathcal{N}$.

Definition 1. *Given a DNN $\mathcal{N} : \mathbb{R}^{n_0} \to \mathbb{R}^{n_{2d}}$, a property of $\mathcal{N}$ is a pair $\langle \phi, \psi \rangle$ where ϕ is a pre-condition over the input $\mathbf{x} \in \mathbb{R}^{n_0}$ and ψ is a post-condition over the output $\mathbf{y} = \mathcal{N}(\mathbf{x}) \in \mathbb{R}^{n_{2d}}$. $\mathcal{N}$ satisfies the property $\langle \phi, \psi \rangle$, denoted by $\mathcal{N} \models \langle \phi, \psi \rangle$, if $\phi(\mathbf{x}) \Rightarrow \psi(\mathcal{N}(\mathbf{x}))$ holds for any input $\mathbf{x} \in \mathbb{R}^{n_0}$.*

Following prior work [49], we assume that the pre-condition ϕ and post-condition ψ are expressible by polyhedra, namely, $\mathcal{I}$ and $\mathcal{O}$, respectively. It is reasonable since, for typical properties such as robustness, both conditions can be effectively represented by a set of linear constraints. For simplicity, we will use $\langle \mathcal{I}, \mathcal{O} \rangle$ to denote the property directly. We are now ready to define our problem.

Definition 2. *Given a DNN $\mathcal{N}$ and a property $\langle \mathcal{I}, \mathcal{O} \rangle$ such that $\mathcal{N} \models \langle \mathcal{I}, \mathcal{O} \rangle$, the problem of certified quantization strategy synthesis is to find a quantization strategy Ξ such that $\widehat{\mathcal{N}} \models \langle \mathcal{I}, \mathcal{O} \rangle$, where $\widehat{\mathcal{N}}$ is the QNN obtained from $\mathcal{N}$ under the quantization strategy Ξ.*

Review of DeepPoly. The core idea of DeepPoly is to (approximately) represent the transformation of each layer using an abstract transformer, and compute lower/upper bounds for the output of each neuron. Fix a neuron $\mathbf{x}_j^i$, its abstract element $\mathcal{A}_j^{i,\sharp}$ is given by a tuple $\langle \mathbf{a}_j^{i,\leq}, \mathbf{a}_j^{i,\geq}, l_j^i, u_j^i \rangle$, where $\mathbf{a}_j^{i,\leq}$ (resp. $\mathbf{a}_j^{i,\geq}$) is a symbolic lower (resp. upper) bound in the form of a linear combination of variables from its preceding layers, l_j^i (resp. u_j^i) is the concrete lower (resp. upper) bound of $\mathbf{x}_j^i$. We denote by $\mathbf{a}^{i,\leq}$ (resp. $\mathbf{a}^{i,\geq}$) the vector of symbolic bounds $\mathbf{a}_j^{i,\leq}$

(resp. $\mathbf{a}_j^{i,\geq}$) of the neurons $\mathbf{x}_j^i$'s in the i-th layer. The concretization of $\mathcal{A}_j^{i,\sharp}$ is defined as $\gamma(\mathcal{A}_j^{i,\sharp}) = \{\mathbf{x}_j^i \in \mathbb{R} \mid \mathbf{a}_j^{i,\leq} \leq \mathbf{x}_j^i \leq \mathbf{a}_j^{i,\geq}\}$. By repeatedly substituting each variable $x_{j'}^{i'}$ in $\mathbf{a}_j^{i,\leq}$ (resp. $\mathbf{a}_j^{i,\geq}$) using $\mathbf{a}_{j'}^{i',\leq}$ or $\mathbf{a}_{j'}^{i',\geq}$ according to the coefficient of $x_{j'}^{i'}$, until no further substitution is possible, $\mathbf{a}_j^{i,\leq}$ (resp. $\mathbf{a}_j^{i,\geq}$) will be a linear combination over the input variables of the DNN. We denote by $f_j^{i,\leq}$ and $f_j^{i,\geq}$ the resulting linear combinations of $\mathbf{a}_j^{i,\leq}$ and $\mathbf{a}_j^{i,\geq}$. Then, the concrete lower bound l_j^i (resp. concrete upper bound u_j^i) of the neuron $\mathbf{x}_j^i$ can be derived using the input region $\mathcal{I}$ and $f_j^{i,\leq}$ (resp. $f_j^{i,\geq}$). All the abstract elements $\mathcal{A}_j^{i,\sharp}$ are required to satisfy the domain invariant: $\gamma(\mathcal{A}_j^{i,\sharp}) \subseteq [l_j^i, u_j^i]$. We denote by $\mathcal{A}_j^i$ the abstract element $\langle f_j^{i,\leq}, f_j^{i,\geq}, l_j^i, u_j^i \rangle$. For an affine function $\mathbf{x}^i = \mathbf{W}^i\mathbf{x}^{i-1} + \mathbf{b}^i$, the abstract affine transformer sets $\mathbf{a}^{i,\leq} = \mathbf{a}^{i,\geq} = \mathbf{W}^i\mathbf{x}^{i-1} + \mathbf{b}^i$. Given the abstract element $\mathcal{A}_j^{i,\sharp} = \langle \mathbf{a}_j^{i,\leq}, \mathbf{a}_j^{i,\geq}, l_j^i, u_j^i \rangle$ of the neuron $\mathbf{x}_j^i$, $\mathcal{A}_j^{i+1,\sharp}$ of the neuron $\mathbf{x}_j^{i+1} = \text{ReLU}(\mathbf{x}_j^i)$ have three cases as follows, where $\lambda_j^i = \frac{u_j^i}{u_j^i - l_j^i}$: i) if $l_j^i \geq 0$, then $\mathbf{a}_j^{i+1,\leq} = \mathbf{a}_j^{i+1,\geq} = \mathbf{x}_j^i$, $l_j^{i+1} = l_j^i$, $u_j^{i+1} = u_j^i$; ii) if $u_j^i \leq 0$, then $\mathbf{a}_j^{i+1,\leq} = \mathbf{a}_j^{i+1,\geq} = l_j^{i+1} = u_j^{i+1} = 0$; iii) if $l_j^i u_j^i < 0$, then $\mathbf{a}_j^{i+1,\geq} = \lambda_j^i(\mathbf{x}_j^i - l_j^i)$, $\mathbf{a}_j^{i+1,\leq} = \kappa \cdot \mathbf{x}_j^i$ where $\kappa \in \{0, 1\}$ such that the area of resulting shape by $\mathbf{a}_j^{i+1,\leq}$ and $\mathbf{a}_j^{i+1,\geq}$ is minimal, $l_j^{i+1} = \kappa \cdot l_j^i$ and $u_j^{i+1} = u_j^i$.

3   Our Approach

In the following, we fix a DNN $\mathcal{N}$ with $2d$ layers and a property $\langle \mathcal{I}, \mathcal{O} \rangle$.

3.1   Foundation of Quadapter

Consider a function f and an output set Y, the *preimage* $f^{-1}(Y)$ of the output set Y for f is the set $\{x \mid f(x) \in Y\}$. An *under-approximation* of $f^{-1}(Y)$ is a set $\mathcal{P}$ such that $\mathcal{P} \subseteq f^{-1}(Y)$.

Definition 3. *A set $\mathfrak{P} = \{\mathcal{P}^{2i} \mid i \in [d-1]\}$ is an under-approximate preimage of the output region $\mathcal{O}$ for the DNN $\mathcal{N}$ if for every $i \in [d-1]$, $\mathcal{P}^{2i} \subseteq \mathcal{N}_{[2i+1:2d]}^{-1}(\mathcal{O})$.*

Intuitively, $\mathcal{P}^{2i}$ (resp. $\mathcal{P}_j^{2i}$) is the preimage of the activation layer f_{2i+1} (resp. neuron $\mathbf{x}_j^{2i+1}$) w.r.t. the output region $\mathcal{O}$. Since it suffices to consider preimages of the activation layers in the set $\mathfrak{P}$ for computing bit-widths of affine layers, the preimages of the affine layers are excluded.

Proposition 1. *Let $\widehat{\mathcal{N}}^{2i}$ be a network obtained from $\mathcal{N}$ by quantizing the first $2i$ layers. If $\mathfrak{P} = \{\mathcal{P}^{2i} \mid i \in [d-1]\}$ is an under-approximate preimage of the output region $\mathcal{O}$ for the DNN $\mathcal{N}$, then $\widehat{\mathcal{N}}_{[1:2i]}^{2i}(\mathcal{I}) \subseteq \mathcal{P}^{2i} \Rightarrow \widehat{\mathcal{N}}^{2i} \models \langle \mathcal{I}, \mathcal{O} \rangle$.* $\qquad\square$

Intuitively, Proposition 1 states that regardless of the quantization configurations of the first $2i$ layers, the property $\langle \mathcal{I}, \mathcal{O} \rangle$ is always preserved in the resulting QNN, as long as the reachable region of the quantized layer $\hat{f}_{2i}$ w.r.t. the input

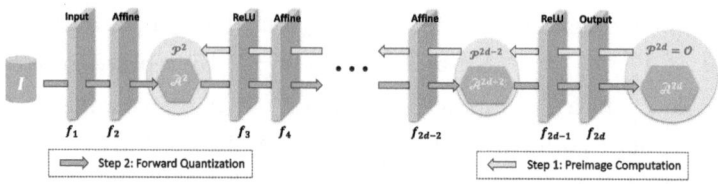

Fig. 2. An overview of our method.

region $\mathcal{I}$ remains within the preimage $\mathcal{P}^{2i}$. This proposition allows us to repeatedly compute a quantization configuration ξ_i for each layer f_{2i} ($i \in [d]$), from the first affine layer to the output layer, that guarantees the reachable region of each quantized layer $\hat{f}_{2i}$ remains within its respective preimage $\mathcal{P}^{2i}$. Putting all the quantization configurations of the affine layers and the output layer together yields a quantization strategy Ξ that preserves the desired property $\langle \mathcal{I}, \mathcal{O} \rangle$.

However, it is non-trivial to compute the preimages $\mathcal{N}_{[2i+1:2d]}^{-1}(\mathcal{O})$ from the functions $\mathcal{N}_{[2i+1:2d]}^{-1}$ for $i \in [d-1]$. To resolve this issue, we propose to repeatedly compute a preimage $\mathcal{P}^{2i}$ of each activation layer f_{2i+1} starting from the output layer to the first activation layer by analyzing the function $\mathcal{N}_{[2i+1:2i+2]}^{-1}$ instead of the function $\mathcal{N}_{[2i+1:2d]}^{-1}$, according to the following proposition.

Proposition 2. *Let $\mathfrak{P} = \{\mathcal{P}^{2i} \mid i \in [d-1]\}$ be a set such that for every $i \in [d-1]$, i) if $i = d-1$, $\mathcal{P}^{2i} \subseteq \mathcal{N}_{[2i+1:2i+2]}^{-1}(\mathcal{O})$; ii) if $i \leq d-2$, $\mathcal{P}^{2i} \subseteq \mathcal{N}_{[2i+1:2i+2]}^{-1}(\mathcal{P}^{2i+2})$. $\mathfrak{P}$ is an under-approximate preimage of the output region $\mathcal{O}$ for the DNN $\mathcal{N}$.* $\square$

3.2 Overview of Quadapter

Let $\mathcal{P}^{2d} = \mathcal{O}$. The overall workflow of Quadapter is depicted in Fig. 2 which consists of the following two steps:

- **Step 1: Preimage Computation.** We first compute an under-approximate preimage $\mathcal{P}^{2d-2}$ for the output layer s.t. $\mathcal{P}^{2d-2} \subseteq \mathcal{N}_{[2d-1:2d]}^{-1}(\mathcal{O})$, and then propagate it through the network until reaching the first affine layer. Finally, we obtain the under-approximate preimage $\mathfrak{P} = \{\mathcal{P}^{2i} \mid i \in [d-1]\}$ for the DNN $\mathcal{N}$ (the yellow part);
- **Step 2: Forward Quantization.** We then conduct a forward quantization procedure layer-by-layer to find a quantization configuration $\xi_i = \langle Q_i, F_i \rangle$ with minimal bit-width Q_i for each layer f_{2i}, ensuring that the reachable region characterized by the quantized abstract element $\hat{\mathcal{A}}^{2i}$ (the blue part) is included in the preimage $\mathcal{P}^{2i}$, i.e., $\gamma(\hat{\mathcal{A}}^{2i}) \subseteq \mathcal{P}^{2i}$ for $1 \leq i \leq d$.

The overall algorithm is given in Algorithm 1. Given a DNN $\mathcal{N}$, a property $\langle \mathcal{I}, \mathcal{O} \rangle$, and the minimum (resp. maximum) fractional bit-width $\mathfrak{B}_l$ (resp. $\mathfrak{B}_u$) for each layer, we first apply DeepPoly on the DNN $\mathcal{N}$ w.r.t. input region $\mathcal{I}$ to obtain the abstract elements $\mathcal{A}^{2i}$ for $i \in [d]$. Then, the first for-loop computes the preimage by invoking the function UnderPreImage($\mathcal{N}, \mathcal{A}^{2i}, \mathcal{P}^{2i+2}$) which propagates

---

Algorithm 1: $Certified\_Quantization(\mathcal{N}, \mathcal{I}, \mathcal{O}, \mathfrak{B}_l, \mathfrak{B}_u)$

1   Apply DeepPoly on the DNN $\mathcal{N}$ w.r.t. $\mathcal{I}$ to obtain abstract elements $\{\mathcal{A}^{2i} \mid 1 \leq i \leq d\}$;

2   Let $\mathcal{P}^{2d} = \mathcal{O}$ and $\widehat{\mathcal{N}} = \mathcal{N}$;

3   **for** $i = d - 1$ to 1 **do**

4     $\lfloor$ $\mathcal{P}^{2i} = \texttt{UnderPreImage}(\mathcal{N}, \mathcal{A}^{2i}, \mathcal{P}^{2i+2})$; $//get~\mathcal{P}^{2i}~s.t.~\mathcal{P}^{2i} \subseteq \mathcal{N}^{-1}_{[2i+1:2i+2]}(\mathcal{P}^{2i+2})$

5   **for** $i = 1$ to d **do**

6     $\xi_i = \bot$;

7     $\mathfrak{I}$ = the minimal bit-width to encode integer parts of $\mathbf{W}^{2i}$ and $\mathbf{b}^{2i}$ without overflow;

8   **for** $F = \mathfrak{B}_l$ to $\mathfrak{B}_u$ **do**

9   Quantize $\mathbf{W}^{2i}, \mathbf{b}^{2i}$ w.r.t. $\check{\xi}_i = \langle F + \mathfrak{I}, F \rangle$ on $\widehat{\mathcal{N}}$ to obtain $\widehat{\mathcal{N}}^{2i}$;

10   Apply DeepPoly on $\widehat{\mathcal{N}}^{2i}_{[1:2i]}$ w.r.t. $\mathcal{I}$ to obtain $\widehat{\mathcal{A}}^{2i}$;

11   **if** $\gamma(\widehat{\mathcal{A}}^{2i}) \subseteq \mathcal{P}^{2i}$ **then**

12         $\lfloor$ $\xi_i = \check{\xi}_i$; $\widehat{\mathcal{N}} = \widehat{\mathcal{N}}^{2i}$; $//accept~\check{\xi}_i~and~update~quantized~parameters$

13   **break**

14     $\lfloor$ **if** $\xi_i == \bot$ **then return** UNKNOWN

15   **return** $\Xi = \{\xi_1, \ldots, \xi_d\}$;

$\mathcal{P}^{2i+2}$ to the preceding activation layer and returns the approximate preimage $\mathcal{P}^{2i}$ with $\mathcal{P}^{2i} \subseteq \mathcal{N}^{-1}_{[2i+1:2i+2]}(\mathcal{P}^{2i+2})$. The second for-loop performs a forward quantization procedure, where the i-th iteration is used to compute the quantization configuration ξ_i for layer f_{2i}. First, we obtain the minimal bit-width $\mathfrak{I}$ for the integer part of weights and biases to prevent overflow. Then, we iterate through all the possible configurations $\check{\xi}_i = \langle F + \mathfrak{I}, F \rangle$ by varying the fractional bit-width F from the smallest one $\mathfrak{B}_l$ to the largest one $\mathfrak{B}_u$. For each $F \in [\mathfrak{B}_l, \mathfrak{B}_u]$, we compute a partially quantized DNN $\widehat{\mathcal{N}}^{2i}$, where only the first i affine layers (and the output layer) are quantized using $\xi_1, \cdots, \xi_{i-1}, \check{\xi}_i$. Next, we apply DeepPoly on $\widehat{\mathcal{N}}^{2i}_{[1:2i]}$ w.r.t. the input region $\mathcal{I}$ to obtain the abstract element $\widehat{\mathcal{A}}^{2i}$ of the quantized layer f_{2i}, resulting in reachable region as the blue part in Fig. 2. We then check whether this reachable region is strictly contained in the preimage $\mathcal{P}^{2i}$, i.e., $\gamma(\widehat{\mathcal{A}}^{2i}) \subseteq \mathcal{P}^{2i}$. If this is the case, we update ξ_i as $\check{\xi}_i$, stop the iteration, and proceed to find the quantization configuration ξ_{i+1} for the next layer f_{2i+2}. If there is no such quantization configuration, we return UNKNOWN.

Below, we present the details of function $\texttt{UnderPreImage}(\mathcal{N}, \mathcal{A}^{2i}, \mathcal{P}^{2i+2})$ and the method of checking the condition $\gamma(\widehat{\mathcal{A}}^{2i}) \subseteq \mathcal{P}^{2i}$. We first introduce the template of preimage $\mathcal{P}^{2i}$ utilized in this work.

3.3   Template $\mathcal{T}^{2i}$ of Preimage $\mathcal{P}^{2i}$

Given the abstract elements $\mathcal{A}^{2i} = \{\mathcal{A}^{2i}_j \mid j \in [n_{2i}]\}$ of the neurons in the layer f_{2i}, where $\mathcal{A}^{2i}_j = \langle f^{2i,\leq}_j, f^{2i,\geq}_j, l^{2i}_j, u^{2i}_j \rangle$, we define the template $\mathcal{T}^{2i}$ of the preimage $\mathcal{P}^{2i}$ as $\bigwedge_{j \in [n_{2i}]} \mathcal{T}^{2i}_j$, where $\mathcal{T}^{2i}_j = \{\mathbf{x}^{2i}_j \in \mathbb{R} \mid f^{2i,\leq}_j - \alpha^{2i}_j \leq \mathbf{x}^{2i}_j \leq f^{2i,\geq}_j + \beta^{2i}_j\}$, $\alpha^{2i}_j = \beta^{2i}_j = (\frac{u^{2i}_j - l^{2i}_j}{2})\chi^{2i}$, and χ^{2i} is an additional variable over the domain $\mathbb{R}$. Intuitively, $\mathcal{T}^{2i}_j$ is a scaling of $\mathcal{A}^{2i}_j$ using the scaling variable χ^{2i} and step $\frac{u^{2i}_j - l^{2i}_j}{2}$. Thus, $\mathcal{T}^{2i}_j$ is $\mathcal{A}^{2i}_j$ when $\chi^{2i} = 0$, and is super-region (resp. sub-region) of $\mathcal{A}^{2i}_j$ when $\chi^{2i} > 0$ (resp. $\chi^{2i} < 0$).

3.4 Details of Function `UnderPreImage`

We present an MILP-based method to implement `UnderPreImage`($\mathcal{N}, \mathcal{A}^{2i}$, $\mathcal{P}^{2i+2}$). Given the abstract element $\mathcal{A}^{2i}$ and preimage $\mathcal{P}^{2i+2}$, we construct a maximization problem with objective function χ^{2i} subject to the constraints $\mathcal{T}^{2i} \subseteq \mathcal{N}_{[2i+1:2i+2]}^{-1}(\mathcal{P}^{2i+2})$, where $\mathcal{T}^{2i}$ is the template of $\mathcal{P}^{2i}$ with the scaling variable χ^{2i}. The solution, i.e., the value of χ^{2i}, yields the tightest under-approximate preimage $\mathcal{P}^{2i}$ such that $\mathcal{P}^{2i} \subseteq \mathcal{N}_{[2i+1:2i+2]}^{-1}(\mathcal{P}^{2i+2})$. Hence, the key is addressing $\mathcal{T}^{2i} \subseteq \mathcal{N}_{[2i+1:2i+2]}^{-1}(\mathcal{P}^{2i+2})$, for which we present an MILP-based method. We first express $\mathcal{T}^{2i} \subseteq \mathcal{N}_{[2i+1:2i+2]}^{-1}(\mathcal{P}^{2i+2})$ as the following maximization problem:

$$\text{maximize } \chi^{2i} \text{ s.t. } \mathcal{N}_{[2i+1:2i+2]}(\mathcal{T}^{2i}) \subseteq \mathcal{P}^{2i+2}. \tag{1}$$

However, Problem (1) is not an MILP, due to the "forall"-type of constraints. To address this issue, we construct the following minimization problem:

$$\text{minimize } \chi^{2i} \text{ s.t. } \mathbf{x}^{2i+2} \in \mathcal{N}_{[2i+1:2i+2]}(\mathcal{T}^{2i}) \wedge \mathbf{x}^{2i+2} \notin \mathcal{P}^{2i+2}. \tag{2}$$

Intuitively, given the solution to Problem (2), e.g., $\chi_{\min}^{2i,*}$, we can always get a value for χ^{2i} by subtracting an extremely small value from $\chi_{\min}^{2i,*}$. The resulting value of χ^{2i} is close to the optimal solution of Problem (1), within a negligible margin of error. Such a transformation to an "existential" constraint provides an alternative way for handling $\mathcal{T}^{2i} \subseteq \mathcal{N}_{[2i+1:2i+2]}^{-1}(\mathcal{P}^{2i+2})$, allowing the problem to be effectively tackled within the MILP framework.

Suppose $\mathcal{T}_j^{2i} = \{\mathbf{x}_j^{2i} \in \mathbb{R} \mid f_j^{2i,\leq} - \alpha_j^{2i} \leq \mathbf{x}_j^{2i} \leq f_j^{2i,\geq} + \beta_j^{2i}\}$ for $j \in [n_{2i}]$ and $\mathcal{P}_k^{2i+2} = \{\mathbf{x}_k^{2i+2} \in \mathbb{R} \mid f_k^{2i+2,\leq} - a_k^{2i+2} \leq \mathbf{x}_k^{2i+2} \leq f_k^{2i+2,\geq} + b_k^{2i+2}\}$ for $k \in [n_{2i+2}]$ and $i \leq d-2$. We reformulate Problem (2) as the following MILP problem:

$$\text{minimize } \chi^{2i} \text{ s.t. } \Psi_{\in\mathcal{I}} \cup \Psi_{\mathcal{T}^{2i}} \cup \Psi_{\mathcal{T}^{2i+1}} \cup \Psi_{\mathcal{T}^{2i+2}} \cup \Psi_{\notin\mathcal{P}^{2i+2}}, \tag{3}$$

where $\Psi_{\in\mathcal{I}}$ and $\Psi_{\notin\mathcal{P}^{2d}}$ will be given in Sect. 4 which entail $\mathbf{x} \in \mathcal{I}$ and $\mathbf{x}^{2d} \notin \mathcal{P}^{2d}$ respectively, as they depend on the property $\langle \mathcal{I}, \mathcal{O} \rangle$. $\Psi_{\mathcal{T}^{2i}}$, $\Psi_{\mathcal{T}^{2i+1}}$, $\Psi_{\mathcal{T}^{2i+2}}$, and $\Psi_{\notin\mathcal{P}^{2i+2}}$ are defined as follows ($\{\eta_j^{2i+1}, \eta_j^{2i+2}, \zeta_j^{2i+2}\}$ are Boolean variables):

- $\Psi_{\mathcal{T}^{2i}} = \{f_j^{2i,\leq} - \alpha_j^{2i} \leq \mathbf{x}_j^{2i} \leq f_j^{2i,\geq} + \beta_j^{2i} \mid j \in [n_{2i}]\}$ expressing template $\mathcal{T}^{2i}$;
- $\Psi_{\mathcal{T}^{2i+1}} = \{\mathbf{x}^{2i+1} \geq 0, \mathbf{x}^{2i+1} \geq \mathbf{x}^{2i}, \mathbf{x}^{2i+1} \leq \mathbf{M} \cdot \eta_j^{2i+1}, \mathbf{x}^{2i+1} \leq \mathbf{x}^{2i} + \mathbf{M} \cdot (1 - \eta_j^{2i+1}) \mid j \in [n_{2i+1}]\}$ encoding the activation layer f_{2i+1} (cf. [54]);
- $\Psi_{\mathcal{T}^{2i+2}} = \{\mathbf{x}_j^{2i+2} = \mathbf{W}_{j,:}^{2i+2}\mathbf{x}^{2i+1} + \mathbf{b}_j^{2i+2} \mid j \in [n_{2i+2}]\}$ encoding the affine layer f_{2i+2} (cf. [54]). Note that $\Psi_{\mathcal{T}^{2i}}$, $\Psi_{\mathcal{T}^{2i+1}}$ and $\Psi_{\mathcal{T}^{2i+2}}$ together express the condition $\mathbf{x}^{2i+2} \in \mathcal{N}_{[2i+1:2i+2]}(\mathcal{T}^{2i})$.

- $\Psi_{\notin\mathcal{P}^{2i+2}} = \left\{ \begin{array}{l} \mathbf{x}_j^{2i+2} > f_j^{2i+2,\geq} + b_j^{2i+2} + \mathbf{M} \cdot (\eta_j^{2i+2} - 1), \\ \mathbf{x}_j^{2i+2} \leq f_j^{2i+2,\geq} + b_j^{2i+2} + \mathbf{M} \cdot \eta_j^{2i+2}, \\ \mathbf{x}_j^{2i+2} \geq f_j^{2i+2,\leq} - a_j^{2i+2} - \mathbf{M} \cdot \zeta_j^{2i+2}, \\ \mathbf{x}_j^{2i+2} < f_j^{2i+2,\leq} - a_j^{2i+2} - \mathbf{M} \cdot (\zeta_j^{2i+2} - 1), \\ j \in [n_{2i+2}] \wedge \sum_{k=1}^{n_{2i+2}} (\eta_k^{2i+2} + \zeta_k^{2i+2}) \geq 1 \end{array} \right\}$ expressing the condition $\mathbf{x}^{2i+2} \notin \mathcal{P}^{2i+2}$.

Theorem 1. *Problems (2) and (3) are equivalent.*   □

3.5 Checking $\gamma(\widehat{\mathcal{A}}^{2i}) \subseteq \mathcal{P}^{2i}$

Fix the abstract elements $\widehat{\mathcal{A}}^{2i} = \{\widehat{\mathcal{A}}_j^{2i} \mid j \in [n_{2i}]\}$ for the quantized layer $\hat{f}_{2i}$ with $\widehat{\mathcal{A}}_j^{2i} = \langle \hat{f}_j^{2i,\leq}, \hat{f}_j^{2i,\geq}, \hat{l}_j^{2i}, \hat{u}_j^{2i} \rangle$, we have $\gamma(\widehat{\mathcal{A}}_j^{2i}) = \{\mathbf{x}_j^{2i} \in \mathbb{R} \mid \hat{f}_j^{2i,\leq} \leq \mathbf{x}_j^{2i} \leq \hat{f}_j^{2i,\geq}\}$. Let $\mathcal{P}_j^{2i} = \{\mathbf{x}_j^{2i} \in \mathbb{R} \mid \hat{f}_j^{2i,\leq} - a_j^{2i} \leq \mathbf{x}_j^{2i} \leq \hat{f}_j^{2i,\geq} + b_j^{2i}\}$ for $j \in [n_{2i}]$ be the preimage obtained by the function `UnderPreImage` for $i \leq d-1$, where a_j^{2i} and b_j^{2i} are real-valued numbers.

Since reformulating the problem of checking $\gamma(\widehat{\mathcal{A}}^{2i}) \subseteq \mathcal{P}^{2i}$ into an MILP problem directly is infeasible due to its inherent nature of "forall"-type constraint, we instead check the negation of this statement.

Let $\Phi_{\not\subseteq \mathcal{P}^{2i}}$ be the following set of the linear constraints:

$$\Phi_{\not\subseteq \mathcal{P}^{2i}} = \Psi_{\in \mathcal{I}} \cup \left\{ \begin{array}{c} f_j^{2i,\geq} + b_j^{2i} + \mathbf{M} \cdot (\eta_j^{2i} - 1) < \hat{f}_j^{2i,\geq} \leq f^{2i,\geq} + b_j^{2i} + \mathbf{M} \cdot \eta_j^{2i}, \\ f^{2i,\leq} - a_j^{2i} - \mathbf{M} \cdot \zeta_j^{2i} \leq \hat{f}_j^{2i,\leq} < f^{2i,\leq} - a_j^{2i} - \mathbf{M} \cdot (\zeta_j^{2i} - 1), \\ j \in [n_{2i}], \qquad \sum_{k=1}^{n_{2i}} \left(\eta_k^{2i} + \zeta_k^{2i} \right) \geq 1 \end{array} \right\}$$

where η_j^{2i} and ζ_j^{2i} are two additional Boolean variables, and $\Psi_{\in \mathcal{I}}$ and $\Phi_{\not\subseteq \mathcal{P}^{2d}}$ will be given in Sect. 4 such that $\Psi_{\in \mathcal{I}}$ entails $\mathbf{x} \in \mathcal{I}$ and $\neg \Phi_{\not\subseteq \mathcal{P}^{2d}}$ entails $\gamma(\widehat{\mathcal{A}}^{2d}) \subseteq \mathcal{P}^{2d}$ respectively, as they depend on the property $\langle \mathcal{I}, \mathcal{O} \rangle$.

Theorem 2. *If $\Phi_{\not\subseteq \mathcal{P}^{2i}}$ does not hold, then $\gamma(\widehat{\mathcal{A}}^{2i}) \subseteq \mathcal{P}^{2i}$.* □

4 Applications: Robustness and Backdoor-Freeness

4.1 Certified Quantization for Robustness

We use Algorithm 1 to synthesize quantization strategies for preserving robustness.

Definition 4. *Let $\mathcal{N} : \mathbb{R}^{n_0} \to \mathbb{R}^{n_{2d}}$ be a DNN, $\mathcal{I}_{\mathbf{u}}^r = \{\mathbf{x} \in \mathbb{R}^{n_0} \mid ||\mathbf{x} - \mathbf{u}||_\infty \leq r\}$ be a perturbation region around an input $\mathbf{u} \in \mathbb{R}^{n_0}$, and $\mathcal{O}_g = \{\mathbf{x}^{2d} \in \mathbb{R}^{n_{2d}} \mid argmax(\mathbf{x}^{2d}) = g\}$ be the output region corresponding to a specific class g. Then, $\langle \mathcal{I}_{\mathbf{u}}^r, \mathcal{O}_g \rangle$ is a (local) robustness property of the DNN $\mathcal{N}$.*

We now give the encoding details that are not covered in Sect. 3, i.e., $\Psi_{\in \mathcal{I}}$ and $\Psi_{\not\subseteq \mathcal{P}^{2d}}$ in Problem (3), and $\Phi_{\not\subseteq \mathcal{P}^{2d}}$ in Sect. 3.5 for the property $\langle \mathcal{I}_{\mathbf{u}}^r, \mathcal{O}_g \rangle$[1]:

- $\Psi_{\in \mathcal{I}} = \{\max(\mathbf{u}_j - r, 0) \leq \mathbf{x}_j \leq \min(\mathbf{u}_j + r, 1) \mid j \in [n_0]\}$ specifying the feasible input range $\mathcal{I}_{\mathbf{u}}^r$;
- $\Psi_{\not\subseteq \mathcal{P}^{2d}} = \left\{ \begin{array}{c} \mathbf{x}_g^{2d} + \mathbf{M} \cdot (\eta_j^{2d} - 1) \leq \mathbf{x}_j^{2d} \leq \mathbf{x}_g^{2d} + \mathbf{M} \cdot \eta_j^{2d}, \\ j \in [n_{2d}] \setminus g, \qquad \sum_{k \in [n_{2d}] \setminus g} \eta_k^{2d} \geq 1 \end{array} \right\}$ stating $\mathbf{x}^{2d} \notin \mathcal{O}_g$, i.e., $argmax(\mathbf{x}^{2d}) \neq g$, where η_j^{2d} is a Boolean variable;

---

[1] For simplicity, we assume that the output layer of $\mathcal{N}$ has a unique maximum value for any given input. This assumption can be avoided by adapting $\Psi_{\not\subseteq \mathcal{P}^{2d}}$ and $\Phi_{\not\subseteq \mathcal{P}^{2d}}$.

$$- \varPhi_{\notin \mathcal{P}^{2d}} = \left\{ \begin{array}{c} \hat{f}_g^{2d,\leq} + \mathbf{M} \cdot (\eta_j^{2d} - 1) \leq \hat{f}_j^{2d,\geq} \leq \hat{f}_g^{2d,\leq} + \mathbf{M} \cdot \eta_j^{2d}, \\ j \in [n_{2d}] \backslash g, \qquad \sum_{k \in [n_{2d}] \backslash g} \eta_k^{2d} \geq 1 \end{array} \right\} \text{ whose unsat-}$$

isfiability ensuring $\gamma(\widehat{\mathcal{A}}^{2d}) \subseteq \mathcal{O}_g$, where η_j^{2d} is a Boolean variable.

The soundness of the algorithm is captured by the theorem below.

Theorem 3. $\varPsi_{\in \mathcal{I}} \Leftrightarrow \mathbf{x} \in \mathcal{I}_{\mathbf{u}}^r$, $\varPsi_{\notin \mathcal{P}^{2d}} \Leftrightarrow \mathbf{x}^{2d} \notin \mathcal{O}_g$, $\neg \varPhi_{\notin \mathcal{P}^{2d}} \Rightarrow \gamma(\widehat{\mathcal{A}}^{2d}) \subseteq \mathcal{O}_g$. $\qquad \square$

4.2   Certified Quantization for Backdoor-Freeness

Given a DNN $\mathcal{N} : \mathbb{R}^{n_0} \to \mathbb{R}^{n_{2d}}$ and an input $\mathbf{u} \in \mathbb{R}^{n_0}$, assume that the 2D-shape of $\mathbf{u}$ is a rectangle (h_u, w_u) (i.e., $n_0 = h_u \times w_u$). A backdoor trigger is any 2D input $\mathbf{s} \in \mathbb{R}^{h_s \times w_s}$ with a shape of rectangle (h_s, w_s) such that $h_s \leq h_u$ and $w_s \leq w_u$. We use $\mathbf{u}[x, y]$ to denote the element located in the x-th row and y-th column within the 2D-input $\mathbf{u}$. Let (h_p, w_p) denote the position of (i.e., the top-left corner of) the trigger $\mathbf{s}$ such that $h_p + h_s \leq h_u$ and $w_p + w_s \leq w_u$. Then, $\mathbf{u^s}$ is the stamped input where $\mathbf{u^s}[x, y] = \mathbf{s}[x - h_p, y - w_p]$ if $h_p \leq x \leq h_p + h_s \wedge w_p \leq y \leq w_p + w_s$, and $\mathbf{u^s}[x, y] = \mathbf{u}[x, y]$ otherwise.

Definition 5. *Let $\mathcal{N} : \mathbb{R}^{n_0} \to \mathbb{R}^{n_{2d}}$ be a DNN, (h_s, w_s), (h_p, w_p), t, and θ be the shape, position, target class, and attack success rate of potential triggers. Then, the DNN $\mathcal{N}$ satisfies the backdoor-freeness property if there does not exist a backdoor trigger $\mathbf{s}$ which has an attack success rate of at least θ, i.e., the probability of $\mathcal{N}(\mathbf{u^s}) = t$ for any $\mathbf{u} \in \mathbb{R}^{n_0}$ is at least θ [37].*

Given an input $\mathbf{u} \in \mathbb{R}^{n_0}$, let $\langle \mathcal{I}_{\mathbf{u}}^B, \mathcal{O}_t^B \rangle$ be a property such that $\mathcal{I}_{\mathbf{u}}^B = \{ \mathbf{u^s} \in \mathbb{R}^{n_0} \mid \mathbf{s} \in \mathbb{R}^{h_s \times w_s} \text{ is any trigger at position } (h_p, w_p) \}$ and $\mathcal{O}_t^B = \{ \mathbf{x}^{2d} \in \mathbb{R}^{n_{2d}} \mid \text{argmax}(\mathbf{x}^{2d}) \neq t \}$. Intuitively, $\langle \mathcal{I}_{\mathbf{u}}^B, \mathcal{O}_t^B \rangle$ entails that no trigger exists whereby the input $\mathbf{u}$, once stamped, would be classified as class t.

The overall algorithm is given in Algorithm 2 by applying a hypothesis testing (a type I/II error σ/ϱ and a half-width of the indifference region δ), i.e., the SPRT algorithm [1]. The while loop first keeps randomly selecting a set of K properties and collects the preimage with the highest value of the scaling variable of the first affine layer, along with the property, until one of the hypotheses is accepted. When the null hypothesis H_0 is accepted (line 9), we try to find a shared quantization strategy for all the properties collected before, following Algorithm 1, with the innermost for-loop to traverse all properties. Due to space limitations, details of the hypothesis testing and input parameters are explained in [50].

Table 1. Benchmarks of DNNs on MNIST and Fashion-MNIST.

Accuracy	P1: 2×100	P2: 4×100	P3: 6×100	P4: 4×512
MNIST	97.79%	97.63%	97.39%	98.17%
Fashion-MNIST	87.86%	88.45%	87.22%	88.7%

Algorithm 2: $CQ\_Backdoor(\mathcal{N}, \mathfrak{B}_l, \mathfrak{B}_u, (h_s, w_s), (h_p, w_p), t, \theta, K, \epsilon, \sigma, \varrho, \delta)$

---

1 Let $\mathcal{P}^{2d} = \mathcal{O}_t^B$, $\widehat{\mathcal{N}} = \mathcal{N}$, $All_{\mathcal{I}} = \emptyset$, $All_{\mathfrak{P}} = \emptyset$, $n = z = 0$;
2 Let $p_0 = 1 - \theta^K + \delta$, $p_1 = 1 - \theta^K - \delta$;
3 **while** *true* **do**
4 $\quad$ $n = n + 1$;
5 $\quad$ Randomly select a set of K properties $X = \{\langle \mathcal{N}_{\mathbf{u}_1}^B, \mathcal{O}_t^B \rangle, \ldots, \langle \mathcal{N}_{\mathbf{u_K}}^B, \mathcal{O}_t^B \rangle\}$;
6 $\quad$ Compute under-approximate preimage for each property in X (cf. Alg. 1), and let
   $\quad$ $\langle \mathcal{I}_{\mathbf{u}^*}^B, \mathcal{O}_t^B \rangle$ be the property with the highest value of the scaling variable χ^{2*} for layer f_2
   $\quad$ and $\mathfrak{P}^*$ be the corresponding under-approximate preimage;
7 $\quad$ **if** $\chi^{2*} \geq \epsilon$ **then**
8 $\quad$ $\quad$ $z = z + 1$; $All_{\mathcal{I}}$.append($\mathcal{I}_{\mathbf{u}^*}^B$); $All_{\mathfrak{P}}$.append($\mathfrak{P}^*$);
9 $\quad$ **if** $\frac{p_1^z}{p_0^z} \times \frac{(1-p_1)^{n-z}}{(1-p_0)^{n-z}} \leq \frac{\varrho}{1-\sigma}$ **then**
10 $\quad$ $\quad$ **for** $i = 1$ to d **do**
11 $\quad$ $\quad$ $\quad$ $\xi_i = \perp$;
12 $\quad$ $\quad$ $\quad$ Let $\mathfrak{I}$ be the minimal bit-width to encode integer parts of $\mathbf{W}^{2i}$ and $\mathbf{b}^{2i}$
    $\quad$ $\quad$ $\quad$ without overflow;
13 $\quad$ $\quad$ $\quad$ **for** $F = \mathfrak{B}_l$ to $\mathfrak{B}_u$ **do**
14 $\quad$ $\quad$ $\quad$ $\quad$ Quantize $\mathbf{W}^{2i}$, $\mathbf{b}^{2i}$ w.r.t. $\check{\xi}_i = (F + \mathfrak{I}, F)$ on $\widehat{\mathcal{N}}$ and obtain $\widehat{\mathcal{N}}^{2i}$;
15 $\quad$ $\quad$ $\quad$ $\quad$ **for** $k = 1$ to z **do**
16 $\quad$ $\quad$ $\quad$ $\quad$ $\quad$ Apply DeepPoly on $\widehat{\mathcal{N}}_{[1:2i]}^{2i}$ w.r.t. $All_{\mathcal{I}}[k]$ and obtain $\widehat{\mathcal{A}}^{2i,k}$;
17 $\quad$ $\quad$ $\quad$ $\quad$ $\quad$ **if** $\gamma(\widehat{\mathcal{A}}^{2i,k}) \subseteq All_{\mathfrak{P}}[k][i]$ is UNSAT **then**
18 $\quad$ $\quad$ $\quad$ $\quad$ $\quad$ $\quad$ **break**   *//jump to line 13 for next iteration of F*
19 $\quad$ $\quad$ $\quad$ $\quad$ $\xi_i = \check{\xi}_i$; $\widehat{\mathcal{N}} = \widehat{\mathcal{N}}^{2i}$;   *//accept $\check{\xi}_i$ and update quantized parameters*
20 $\quad$ $\quad$ $\quad$ $\quad$ **break**   *//jump to line 10 to quantize next layer f_{2i+2}*
21 $\quad$ $\quad$ $\quad$ **if** $\xi_i == \perp$ **then return** UNKNOWN
22 $\quad$ $\quad$ **return** $\Xi = \{\xi_1, \ldots, \xi_d\}$
23 $\quad$ **else if** $\frac{p_1^z}{p_0^z} \times \frac{(1-p_1)^{n-z}}{(1-p_0)^{n-z}} \leq \frac{1-\varrho}{\sigma}$ **then**
24 $\quad$ $\quad$ **return** UNKNOWN;

We now give the encoding details that are not covered in Sect. 3, i.e., $\Psi_{\in\mathcal{I}}$ and $\Psi_{\notin\mathcal{P}^{2d}}$ in Problem (3), and $\Phi_{\notin\mathcal{P}^{2d}}$ in Sect. 3.5 for the property $\langle \mathcal{I}_{\mathbf{u}}^B, \mathcal{O}_t^B \rangle$:

$$- \ \Psi_{\in\mathcal{I}} = \left\{ \begin{array}{l} 0 \leq \mathbf{x}[a, b] \leq 1 \text{ if } h_p \leq a \leq h_p + h_s \wedge w_p \leq b \leq w_p + w_s, \\ \qquad\qquad \mathbf{x}[a, b] = \mathbf{u}[a, b] \text{ otherwise} \end{array} \right\};$$

$$- \ \Psi_{\notin\mathcal{P}^{2d}} = \{\mathbf{x}_t^{2d} \geq \mathbf{x}_j^{2d} \mid j \in [n_{2d}]\};$$

$$- \ \Phi_{\notin\mathcal{P}^{2d}} = \{\hat{f}_j^{2d,\leq} \leq \hat{f}_t^{2d,\geq} \mid j \in [n_{2d}] \setminus t\}.$$

Theorem 4. *(1)* $\Psi_{\in\mathcal{I}} \Leftrightarrow \mathbf{x} \in \mathcal{I}_{\mathbf{u}}^B$, $\Psi_{\notin\mathcal{P}^{2d}} \Leftrightarrow \mathbf{x}^{2d} \notin \mathcal{O}_t^B$, $\neg\Phi_{\notin\mathcal{P}^{2d}} \Rightarrow \gamma(\widehat{\mathcal{A}}^{2d}) \subseteq \mathcal{O}_t^B$, *and (2) there is sufficient evidence (subject to type 1 error σ and type 2 error ϱ) that there are no backdoor attacks with the featured triggers within the QNN obtained by Algorithm 2.* $\square$

5 Evaluation

We have implemented our methods as a tool **Quadapter** with Gurobi [11] as the back-end MILP solver. To address the numerical stability problem using big-M, we use alternative formulations for the ReLU activation function and tighter bounds for other big-M. Details refer to [50]. All experiments are run on a machine with Intel(R) Xeon(R) Platinum 8375C CPU@2.90GHz, using 30 threads in total. The time limit for each task is 2 h.

Benchmarks. We train 8 DNNs using the MNIST [20] and Fashion-MNIST [46] datasets based on their popularity in previous verification studies with comparable size [9,12,19,36,37]. To evaluate the performance of Quadapter, these DNNs vary in architectures, whose details are given in Table 1, where $x \times y$ means that the network has x hidden layers and y neurons per each hidden layer. Hereafter, we use MPx (resp. FPx) with $x \in \{1, 2, 3, 4\}$ to denote the network of architecture Px trained using MNIST (resp. Fashion-MNIST).

5.1   Performance of UnderPreImage Function

We evaluate the effectiveness and efficiency of the MILP-based method introduced in Sect. 3.4 for computing the under-approximate preimage of DNNs MPx with $x \in \{1, 2, 3, 4\}$ for robustness properties. Specifically, we randomly select 50 inputs from the test set of MNIST and set the perturbation radius as $r \in \{2, 4\}$, resulting in a total of 400 robustness properties, each of which can be certified using DeepPoly. The time limit for each computation task is 2 h. We also implement an abstraction-based method (ABS) to compute the preimages for comparative analysis. Details refer to [50].

The results are depicted in Fig. 3. The boxplot shows the distribution of the values of the scaling variables obtained by the two methods for each layer, where Ax and Mx denote the results of layer f_x obtained by the ABS and MILP methods, respectively. (Note that some Ax and Mx may be missing because the DNN has no f_x layer.) The table reports the average computation time in seconds, where (i) indicates the number of tasks that run out of time in 2 h. We find that compared to the MILP method,

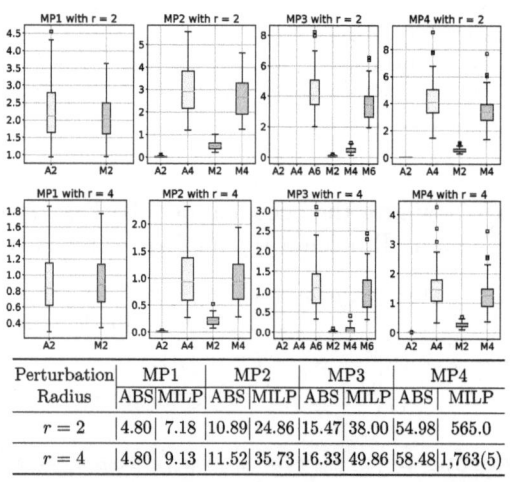

Perturbation	MP1		MP2		MP3		MP4	
Radius	ABS	MILP	ABS	MILP	ABS	MILP	ABS	MILP
$r = 2$	4.80	7.18	10.89	24.86	15.47	38.00	54.98	565.0
$r = 4$	4.80	9.13	11.52	35.73	16.33	49.86	58.48	1,763(5)

Fig. 3. Results of preimage computation.

the ABS method tends to obtain significantly smaller values for scaling variables in earlier layers, albeit requiring less time. It is mainly attributed to the inherent over-approximation in the abstract transformers. Note that the scaling variable for the last affine layer returned by the ABS method is typically larger than that obtained via the MILP method. However, we argue that the scaling variables of preceding layers are more significant, with larger values being preferable for a successful forward quantization process subsequently. Therefore, we opt for the MILP method to implement UnderPreImage, despite its longer execution time. Integrating both methods is an interesting direction for future work.

Table 2. Certified quantization strategy synthesis results for robustness.

Network	Quadapter with $(\mathfrak{B}_l, \mathfrak{B}_l) = (1, 16)$						Quadapter* with $(\mathfrak{B}_l, \mathfrak{B}_l) = (2, 16)$					
	#S	#F	Bit-width	Acc.	PTime(s)	QTime(s)	#S	#F	Bit-width	Acc.	PTime(s)	QTime(s)
MP1	250	0	(6,3)	95.57%	8.17	10.80	250	0	(4,4)	96.59%	8.75	3.96
MP2	248	2	(8,6,3)	94.11%	30.49	29.18	249	1	(5,4,4)	96.35%	31.60	13.38
MP3	175	75	(11,9,6,3)	95.47%	39.55	58.63	208	32	(8,5,4,4)	96.08%	42.37	78.22
MP4	228	0	(8,6,3)	94.48%	1,066	160.2	227	0	(4,4,4)	96.97%	1,066	32.99
FP1	250	0	(6,4)	78.54%	6.93	10.48	250	0	(4,4)	83.89%	7.80	3.63
FP2	249	1	(8,6,3)	79.43%	29.82	28.86	248	2	(5,4,4)	84.56%	33.13	11.39
FP3	180	70	(11,9,6,3)	74.23%	36.90	59.45	222	26	(7,5,4,4)	85.74%	39.71	39.44
FP4	221	2	(8,7,3)	75.98%	564.0	160.7	220	2	(4,4,4)	83.07%	565.3	64.23

Unsurprisingly, we also observe the decrease of scaling variables as r increases or the layer index decreases. The former is attributed to the enlargement of the reachable region of each neuron with an increasing r, leading to a diminution in the theoretical range of the amplification. The latter is because we propagate the preimage towards the input layer and the preimage returned by UnderPreImage increasingly under-approximates the ground truth. Additionally, we find a more pronounced impact of the number of layers in a DNN on the scaling, as opposed to the impact of the number of neurons per each layer. For example, when $r = 4$, while the scaling of the last affine layer is similar across MP2, MP3, and MP4, a notable divergence is observed as the preimage computation progresses to the preceding layer, i.e., the scaling of f_4 in MP3 largely diminishes compared to that of f_2 in MP2 and MP4, and even approaches zero in some tasks. We conjecture that as the DNN gets deeper and r gets larger, DeepPoly shows enhanced efficacy in its symbolic propagation such that the region delineated by $\mathcal{A}^{2i+2}$ becomes significantly tighter compared to the region confined by $\mathcal{N}_{[2i+1:2i+2]}(\mathcal{A}^{2i})$. Finally, we find that the preimage computation time is predominantly impacted by the number of neurons per each layer (e.g., MP2 vs MP4).

5.2   Certified Quantization for Robustness

We evaluate Quadapter in terms of robustness properties on all the networks listed in Table 1 with the fractional bit-width range $[\mathfrak{B}_l, \mathfrak{B}_u] = [1, 16]$. For each network, we randomly select 50 inputs from the test set of the respective dataset and set the perturbation radius as $r \in \{1, 2, 3, 4, 5\}$. It results in a total of 250 synthesis tasks for each network, each of which can be certified by DeepPoly.

The results are reported in Columns 2 to 7 in Table 2. Columns (#S) and (#F) list the number of quantization successes and quantization failures due to small values of scaling variables. Column (Bit-width) lists the average bit-width for each layer within the quantization strategies synthesized by Quadapter and Column (Acc.) lists the average accuracy of the resulting QNNs. Columns (PTime) and (QTime) show the average execution time in seconds for the preimage computation and forward quantization procedures, respectively. Overall, Quadapter solves almost all the tasks of MPx and FPx for $x \in \{1, 2\}$, and most tasks of MP4 and FP4, where all timeout cases occur in the preimage computation process. For MP3 and FP3, all quantization failures are due to the excessively small preimage returned by `UnderPreImage`, posing a great challenge in finding a feasible quantization strategy, which requires that the quantized region must be strictly included within the preimage. Given the distribution shift phenomenon shown in Fig. 1, we hypothesize that it may be alleviated by relaxing such "strict-inclusion" requirement on the early layer quantization while not compromising soundness. Thus, we next relax the restriction by permitting the quantized regions of some portion of neurons, e.g., 25%, in each affine layer (except the output layer to guarantee the soundness of the approach) to deviate from the preimage returned by `UnderPreImage`. Note that, when using the relaxed version of our tool, named Quadapter*, we set $\mathfrak{B}_l = 2$ to circumvent situations where the use of the smallest bit-width (specifically, 1-bit), while theoretically yielding a viable solution for the current layer, may lead to a lack of feasible quantization for subsequent layers. Experimental results are shown in Columns 8 to 13 in Table 2. We observe that Quadapter* usually synthesizes quantization strategies with smaller bit-widths for earlier layers, larger bit-widths for the last later, better accuracy, and solves more tasks on average. While the accuracy drops slightly, it also slightly drops using the same but non-certified quantization scheme and our certified quantization achieved comparable accuracy [50].

Network	$(h_s, w_s) = (3,3)$					$(h_s, w_s) = (5,5)$				
	#S	#F	Bit-width	Acc.	Time(s)	#S	#F	Bit-width	Acc.	Time(s)
MP1	49	0	(12,4)	96.87%	474.9	44	6	(10,4)	96.94%	595.4
MP2	43	7	(15,8,4)	97.06%	1,100	26	24	(12,8,4)	97.09%	1,293
FP1	50	0	(12,4)	85.29%	466.7	46	4	(9,4)	85.38%	511.4
FP2	40	10	(13,7,4)	86.61%	1,114	32	18	(11,8,4)	86.71%	1,063

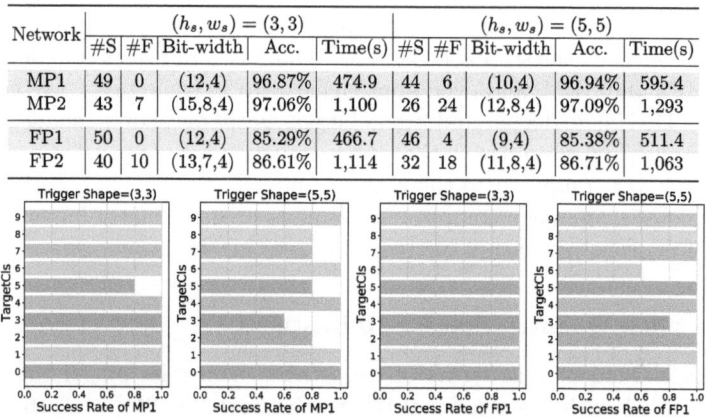

Fig. 4. Certified quantization strategies synthesis results for backdoor-freeness.

5.3   Certified Quantization for Backdoor-Freeness

We evaluate Quadapter in terms of backdoor-freeness on MP1, MP2, FP1 and FP2. For each network, we randomly select 5 trigger positions and consider all the 10 output classes as target labels of the backdoor attacks with two shapes of triggers, i.e., $h_s = w_s = 3$ and $h_s = w_s = 5$, resulting in $5 \times 10 \times 2 =$

100 backdoor-freeness properties. Following [37], we set the input parameters of Algorithm 2 as $(\mathfrak{B}_l, \mathfrak{B}_u) = (2, 16)$, $\theta = 0.9$, $K = 5$, $\epsilon = 0.01$, and $\sigma = \varrho = \delta = 0.05$. Note that these parameters do not affect the soundness of Algorithm 2.

The results are given in Fig. 4. We observe that for $(h_s, w_s) = (3, 3)$, Quadapter solves almost all the tasks of MP1 and FP1, and most tasks on MP2 and FP2. For $(h_s, w_s) = (5, 5)$, over half of the tasks are solved by Quadapter. All the quantization failures (due to small values of scaling variables) may be solvable with the relaxed version of Quadapter which is left as future work. The histogram shows the distribution of target classes in the solved tasks on MP1 and FP1, where the x-axis gives the synthesis success rate. We also observe that Quadapter is more likely to successfully find certified quantization strategies w.r.t. target classes $\{0, 1, 4, 6, 9\}$ on MP1 and target classes $\{1, 2, 4, 5, 7, 8, 9\}$ on FP1, compared to its efficacy w.r.t. other classes. Due to the black-box nature, we currently cannot explain the discrepancy in performance between target classes.

6 Related Work

Numerous methods have been proposed to verify (local) robustness of DNNs (e.g., [7, 10, 17, 40, 45, 47]) and QNNs (e.g., [9, 12, 14, 19, 52–54]). Recently, backdoor-freeness verification for DNNs has been explored leveraging a similar hypothesis testing method [37]. Methods for verifying quantization error bound [30, 35, 36, 51] and Top-1 equivalence [16] between DNNs and QNNs have also been proposed. Except for [16], these works only verify properties without adjusting quantization strategies for falsified properties. The concurrent work [16] iteratively searches for a quantization strategy and verifies Top-1 equivalence after quantization, refining strategies if equivalence is violated. However, it does not support general properties (e.g., backdoor freeness or robustness of multi-label classification [6]). Additionally, [16] requires frequent equivalence verification, which is computationally expensive and inefficient (e.g., networks with 100 neurons in 20 min). Comparison experiments are given in [50].

The primary contribution of this work is the first certified quantization strategy synthesis approach utilizing preimage computation as a crucial step. Hence, any (under-approximate) preimage computation methods can be integrated. [28] introduced an exact preimage computation method that, while precise, is impractical due to its exponential time complexity. The inverse abstraction approach [4] circumvents the intractability of exact preimage computation by using symbolic interpolants [2] for compact symbolic abstractions of preimages. However, it still faces scalability issues due to the complexity of the interpolation process. [18, 49] considered over-approximate preimages, which are unsuitable for our purpose.

Quantization-aware training has been studied to improve robustness for a given fixed quantization strategy [19, 23, 24, 41, 43], but only [19] provides robustness guarantees by lifting abstract interpretation-based training [29] from DNNs to QNNs. In contrast, our work aims to obtain a better quantification strategy for preserving given properties. Thus, our work is orthogonal to and could be combined with them. We leave this as interesting future work.

7   Conclusion

In this work, we have presented a pioneering method Quadapter to synthesize a fine-grained quantization strategy such that the desired properties are preserved within the resulting quantized network. We have implemented our methods as an end-to-end tool and conducted extensive experiments to demonstrate the effectiveness and efficiency of Quadapter in preserving robustness and backdoor-freeness properties. For future work, it would be interesting to explore the adaptation of Quadapter to other activation functions and network architectures, towards which this work makes a significant step.

Disclosure of Interests. The authors have no competing interests to declare that are relevant to the content of this article.

References

1. Agha, G., Palmskog, K.: A survey of statistical model checking. ACM Trans. Model. Comput. Simul. **28**(1), 1–39 (2018)
2. Albarghouthi, A., McMillan, K.L.: Beautiful interpolants. In: Sharygina, N., Veith, H. (eds.) CAV 2013. LNCS, vol. 8044, pp. 313–329. Springer, Heidelberg (2013). https://doi.org/10.1007/978-3-642-39799-8_22
3. Amir, G., Wu, H., Barrett, C.W., Katz, G.: An SMT-based approach for verifying binarized neural networks. In: Proceedings of the 27th International Conference on Tools and Algorithms for the Construction and Analysis of Systems (TACAS), vol. 12652, pp. 203–222 (2021). https://doi.org/10.1007/978-3-030-72013-1_11
4. Dathathri, S., Gao, S., Murray, R.M.: Inverse abstraction of neural networks using symbolic interpolation. In: Proceedings of the 33rd AAAI Conference on Artificial Intelligence (AAAI), pp. 3437–3444 (2019). https://doi.org/10.1609/AAAI.V33I01.33013437
5. Dong, S., Wang, P., Abbas, K.: A survey on deep learning and its applications. Comput. Sci. Rev. **40**, 100379 (2021). https://doi.org/10.1016/J.COSREV.2021.100379
6. Eleftheriadis, C., Kekatos, N., Katsaros, P., Tripakis, S.: On neural network equivalence checking using SMT solvers. In: Proceedings of the 20th International Conference on Formal Modeling and Analysis of Timed Systems, vol. 13465, pp. 237–257 (2022). https://doi.org/10.1007/978-3-031-15839-1_14
7. Gehr, T., Mirman, M., Drachsler-Cohen, D., Tsankov, P., Chaudhuri, S., Vechev, M.T.: AI²: safety and robustness certification of neural networks with abstract interpretation. In: Proceedings of the 2018 IEEE Symposium on Security and Privacy, pp. 3–18 (2018)
8. Gholami, A., Kim, S., Dong, Z., Yao, Z., Mahoney, M.W., Keutzer, K.: A survey of quantization methods for efficient neural network inference. In: Low-Power Computer Vision, pp. 291–326. Chapman and Hall/CRC (2022)
9. Giacobbe, M., Henzinger, T.A., Lechner, M.: How many bits does it take to quantize your neural network? In: TACAS 2020. LNCS, vol. 12079, pp. 79–97. Springer, Cham (2020). https://doi.org/10.1007/978-3-030-45237-7_5
10. Guo, X., Wan, W., Zhang, Z., Zhang, M., Song, F., Wen, X.: Eager falsification for accelerating robustness verification of deep neural networks. In: Proceedings of the 32nd IEEE International Symposium on Software Reliability Engineering, pp. 345–356 (2021)

11. Gurobi. A most powerful mathematical optimization solver (2018). https://www.gurobi.com/
12. Henzinger, T.A., Lechner, M., Zikelic, D.: Scalable verification of quantized neural networks. In: Proceedings of the 35th AAAI Conference on Artificial Intelligence (AAAI), pp. 3787–3795 (2021). https://doi.org/10.1609/AAAI.V35I5.16496
13. Hong, S., Panaitescu-Liess, M., Kaya, Y., Dumitras, T.: Qu-anti-zation: exploiting quantization artifacts for achieving adversarial outcomes. In: Proceedings of the Annual Conference on Neural Information Processing Systems (NeurIPS), pp. 9303–9316 (2021)
14. Huang, P., et al.: Towards efficient verification of quantized neural networks. In: Proceedings of the 38th AAAI Conference on Artificial Intelligence, pp. 21152–21160 (2024). https://doi.org/10.1609/AAAI.V38I19.30108
15. Jacob, B., et al.: Quantization and training of neural networks for efficient integer-arithmetic-only inference. In: Proceedings of the IEEE Conference on Computer Vision and Pattern Recognition (CVPR), pp. 2704–2713 (2018)
16. Jr., J.B.P.M., de Lima Filho, E.B., Bessa, I., Manino, E., Song, X., Cordeiro, L.C.: Counterexample guided neural network quantization refinement. IEEE Trans. Comput. Aided Des. Integr. Circuits Syst. **43**(4), 1121–1134 (2024). https://doi.org/10.1109/TCAD.2023.3335313
17. Katz, G., Barrett, C.W., Dill, D.L., Julian, K., Kochenderfer, M.J.: Reluplex: an efficient SMT solver for verifying deep neural networks. In: Proceedings of the 29th International Conference on Computer Aided Verification, pp. 97–117 (2017)
18. Kotha, S., Brix, C., Kolter, J.Z., Dvijotham, K., Zhang, H.: Provably bounding neural network preimages. Adv. Neural Inf. Process. Syst. **36** (2024)
19. Lechner, M., Žikelić, Đ., Chatterjee, K., Henzinger, T.A., Rus, D.: Quantization-aware interval bound propagation for training certifiably robust quantized neural networks. In: Proceedings of the AAAI Conference on Artificial Intelligence (AAAI), pp. 14964–14973 (2023). https://doi.org/10.1609/AAAI.V37I12.26747
20. LeCun, Y., Cortes, C.: Mnist handwritten digit database (2010)
21. Li, Z., Ni, B., Zhang, W., Yang, X., Gao, W.: Performance guaranteed network acceleration via high-order residual quantization. In: IEEE International Conference on Computer Vision (ICCV), pp. 2603–2611 (2017). https://doi.org/10.1109/ICCV.2017.282
22. Lin, D.D., Talathi, S.S., Annapureddy, V.S.: Fixed point quantization of deep convolutional networks. In: Proceedings of the 33nd International Conference on Machine Learning (ICML). pp. 2849–2858 (2016)
23. Lin, H., Lou, J., Xiong, L., Shahabi, C.: Integer-arithmetic-only certified robustness for quantized neural networks. In: Proceedings of the IEEE/CVF International Conference on Computer Vision (CVPR), pp. 7808–7817. IEEE (2021). https://doi.org/10.1109/ICCV48922.2021.00773
24. Lin, J., Gan, C., Han, S.: Defensive quantization: when efficiency meets robustness. In: International Conference on Learning Representations (2018)
25. Liu, J., Xing, Y., Shi, X., Song, F., Xu, Z., Ming, Z.: Abstraction and refinement: towards scalable and exact verification of neural networks. arXiv preprint arXiv:2207.00759 (2022)
26. Ma, H., et al.: Quantization backdoors to deep learning commercial frameworks. IEEE Trans. Depend Secure Comput. (2023). https://doi.org/10.1109/TDSC.2023.3271956
27. Marco, V.S., Taylor, B., Wang, Z., Elkhatib, Y.: Optimizing deep learning inference on embedded systems through adaptive model selection. ACM Trans. Embed. Comput. Syst. **19**(1), 2:1–2:28 (2020). https://doi.org/10.1145/3371154

28. Matoba, K., Fleuret, F.: Exact preimages of neural network aircraft collision avoidance systems. In: Proceedings of the Workshop on Machine Learning for Engineering Modeling, Simulation, and Design, pp. 1–9 (2020)
29. Mirman, M., Gehr, T., Vechev, M.T.: Differentiable abstract interpretation for provably robust neural networks. In: Proceedings of the 35th International Conference on Machine Learning, vol. 80, pp. 3575–3583 (2018)
30. Mohammadinejad, S., Paulsen, B., Deshmukh, J.V., Wang, C.: DiffRNN: differential verification of recurrent neural networks. In: Dima, C., Shirmohammadi, M. (eds.) FORMATS 2021. LNCS, vol. 12860, pp. 117–134. Springer, Cham (2021). https://doi.org/10.1007/978-3-030-85037-1_8
31. Musa, A.A., Hussaini, A., Liao, W., Liang, F., Yu, W.: Deep neural networks for spatial-temporal cyber-physical systems: a survey. Future Internet **15**(6), 199 (2023). https://doi.org/10.3390/FI15060199
32. Nagel, M., Amjad, R.A., Van Baalen, M., Louizos, C., Blankevoort, T.: Up or down? Adaptive rounding for post-training quantization. In: Proceedings of the 37th International Conference on Machine Learning (ICML), vol. 119, pp. 7197–7206 (2020)
33. Nagel, M., Fournarakis, M., Amjad, R.A., Bondarenko, Y., van Baalen, M., Blankevoort, T.: A white paper on neural network quantization. arXiv preprint arXiv:2106.08295 (2021)
34. Pan, X., Zhang, M., Yan, Y., Yang, M.: Understanding the threats of trojaned quantized neural network in model supply chains. In: Proceedings of the Annual Computer Security Applications Conference (ACSAC), pp. 634–645 (2021). https://doi.org/10.1145/3485832.3485881
35. Paulsen, B., Wang, J., Wang, C.: Reludiff: differential verification of deep neural networks. In: 2020 IEEE/ACM 42nd International Conference on Software Engineering (ICSE), pp. 714–726. IEEE (2020)
36. Paulsen, B., Wang, J., Wang, J., Wang, C.: NeuroDiff: scalable differential verification of neural networks using fine-grained approximation. In: Proceedings of the 35th IEEE/ACM International Conference on Automated Software Engineering, pp. 784–796 (2020)
37. Pham, L.H., Sun, J.: Verifying neural networks against backdoor attacks. In: Proceedings of the 34th International Conference on Computer Aided Verification (CAV), pp. 171–192 (2022). https://doi.org/10.1007/978-3-031-13185-1_9
38. Prabhakar, P., Afzal, Z.R.: Abstraction based output range analysis for neural networks. In: Proceedings of the Annual Conference on Neural Information Processing Systems, pp. 15762–15772 (2019)
39. Rokh, B., Azarpeyvand, A., Khanteymoori, A.: A comprehensive survey on model quantization for deep neural networks in image classification. ACM Trans. Intell. Syst. Technol. **14**(6), 97:1–97:50 (2023). https://doi.org/10.1145/3623402
40. Singh, G., Gehr, T., Püschel, M., Vechev, M.T.: An abstract domain for certifying neural networks. Proc. ACM Program. Lang. (POPL) **3**, 41:1–41:30 (2019). https://doi.org/10.1145/3290354
41. Song, C., Fallon, E., Li, H.: Improving adversarial robustness in weight-quantized neural networks. arXiv preprint arXiv:2012.14965 (2020)
42. Song, X., Sun, Y., Mustafa, M.A., Cordeiro, L.C.: QNNRepair: qneural network repair. In: Proceedings of the 21st International Conference on Software Engineering and Formal Methods, vol. 14323, pp. 320–339 (2023)
43. Tang, Z., Dong, Y., Su, H.: Error-silenced quantization: bridging robustness and compactness. In: Proceedings of the Workshop on Artificial Intelligence Safety (AISafety@IJCAI) (2020)

44. Wang, P., Hu, Q., Zhang, Y., Zhang, C., Liu, Y., Cheng, J.: Two-step quantization for low-bit neural networks. In: Proceedings of the IEEE/CVF Conference on Computer Vision and Pattern Recognition (CVPR), pp. 4376–4384 (2018). https://doi.org/10.1109/CVPR.2018.00460

45. Wang, S., et al.: Beta-crown: efficient bound propagation with per-neuron split constraints for neural network robustness verification. In: Proceedings of the Annual Conference on Neural Information Processing Systems, pp. 29909–29921 (2021)

46. Xiao, H., Rasul, K., Vollgraf, R.: Fashion-MNIST: a novel image dataset for benchmarking machine learning algorithms. arXiv preprint arXiv:1708.07747 (2017)

47. Yang, P., et al.: Improving neural network verification through spurious region guided refinement. In: TACAS 2021. LNCS, vol. 12651, pp. 389–408. Springer, Cham (2021). https://doi.org/10.1007/978-3-030-72016-2_21

48. Zhang, D., Yang, J., Ye, D., Hua, G.: LQ-Nets: learned quantization for highly accurate and compact deep neural networks. In: Ferrari, V., Hebert, M., Sminchisescu, C., Weiss, Y. (eds.) ECCV 2018. LNCS, vol. 11212, pp. 373–390. Springer, Cham (2018). https://doi.org/10.1007/978-3-030-01237-3_23

49. Zhang, X., Wang, B., Kwiatkowska, M.: On preimage approximation for neural networks. arXiv preprint arXiv:2305.03686 (2023)

50. Zhang, Y., Chen, G., Song, F., Sun, J., Dong, J.S.: Certified quantization strategy synthesis for neural networks. https://github.com/zhangyedi/Quadapter (2024)

51. Zhang, Y., Song, F., Sun, J.: Qebverif: quantization error bound verification of neural networks. In: Proceedings of the 35th International Conference on Computer Aided Verification, vol. 13965, pp. 413–437 (2023). https://doi.org/10.1007/978-3-031-37703-7_20

52. Zhang, Y., Zhao, Z., Chen, G., Song, F., Chen, T.: BDD4BNN: a BDD-based quantitative analysis framework for binarized neural networks. In: Silva, A., Leino, K.R.M. (eds.) CAV 2021. LNCS, vol. 12759, pp. 175–200. Springer, Cham (2021). https://doi.org/10.1007/978-3-030-81685-8_8

53. Zhang, Y., Zhao, Z., Chen, G., Song, F., Chen, T.: Precise quantitative analysis of binarized neural networks: a BDD-based approach. ACM Trans. Softw. Eng. Methodol. **32**(3), 62:1–62:51 (2023). https://doi.org/10.1145/3563212

54. Zhang, Y., Zhao, Z., Chen, G., Song, F., Zhang, M., Chen, T., Sun, J.: Qvip: an ilp-based formal verification approach for quantized neural networks. In: Proceedings of the 37th IEEE/ACM International Conference on Automated Software Engineering (ASE), pp. 82:1–82:13 (2022). https://doi.org/10.1145/3551349.3556916

55. Zhu, Y., et al.: Towards robustness evaluation of backdoor defense on quantized deep learning model. SSRN: https://ssrn.com/abstract=4578346

Partially Observable Stochastic Games with Neural Perception Mechanisms

Rui Yan[1]([✉])[iD], Gabriel Santos[1][iD], Gethin Norman[1,2][iD], David Parker[1][iD], and Marta Kwiatkowska[1][iD]

[1] University of Oxford, Oxford OX1 2JD, UK
{rui.yan,gabriel.santos,david.parker,marta.kwiatkowska}@cs.ox.ac.uk,
gethin.norman@glasgow.ac.uk
[2] University of Glasgow, Glasgow G12 8QQ, UK

Abstract. Stochastic games are a well established model for multi-agent sequential decision making under uncertainty. In practical applications, though, agents often have only partial observability of their environment. Furthermore, agents increasingly perceive their environment using data-driven approaches such as neural networks trained on continuous data. We propose the model of neuro-symbolic partially-observable stochastic games (NS-POSGs), a variant of continuous-space concurrent stochastic games that explicitly incorporates neural perception mechanisms. We focus on a one-sided setting with a partially-informed agent using discrete, data-driven observations and another, fully-informed agent. We present a new method, called one-sided NS-HSVI, for approximate solution of one-sided NS-POSGs, which exploits the piecewise constant structure of the model. Using neural network pre-image analysis to construct finite polyhedral representations and particle-based representations for beliefs, we implement our approach and illustrate its practical applicability to the analysis of pedestrian-vehicle and pursuit-evasion scenarios.

1 Introduction

Strategic reasoning is essential to ensure stable multi-agent coordination in complex environments, e.g., autonomous driving or multi-robot planning. *Partially-observable stochastic games* (POSGs) are a natural model for settings involving multiple agents, uncertainty and partial information. They allow the synthesis of optimal (or near-optimal) strategies and equilibria that guarantee expected outcomes, even in adversarial scenarios. But POSGs also present significant challenges: key problems are undecidable, already for the single-agent case of partially observable Markov decision processes (POMDPs) [24], and practical algorithms for finding optimal values and strategies are lacking.

Computational tractability can be improved using *one-sided POSGs*, a subclass of two-agent, zero-sum POSGs where only one agent has partial information while the other agent is assumed to have full knowledge of the state [40,41]. This can be useful when making worst-case assumptions about one agent, such as in

A. Platzer et al. (Eds.): FM 2024, LNCS 14933, pp. 363–380, 2025.
https://doi.org/10.1007/978-3-031-71162-6_19

an adversarial setting (e.g., an attacker-defender scenario) or a safety-critical domain (e.g., a pedestrian in an autonomous driving application).

From a computational perspective, one-sided POSGs avoid the need for nested beliefs [39], i.e., reasoning about beliefs not only over states but also over opponents' beliefs. This is because the fully-informed agent can reconstruct beliefs from observation histories. Recent advances [19] have led to the first practical variant of heuristic search value iteration (HSVI) [31] for computing approximately optimal values and strategies in (finite) one-sided POSGs.

However, in many realistic autonomous coordination scenarios, agents perceive *continuous* environments using *data-driven* observation functions, typically implemented as neural networks (NNs). Examples include autonomous vehicles using NNs to perform object recognition or to estimate pedestrian intention, and NN-enabled vision in an airborne pursuit-evasion scenario.

In this paper, we introduce *one-sided neuro-symbolic POSGs (NS-POSGs)*, a variant of continuous-space POSGs that explicitly incorporates neural perception mechanisms. We assume one partially-informed agent with a (finite-valued) observation function synthesised in a data-driven fashion, and a second agent with full observation of the (continuous) state. Continuous-space models with neural perception mechanisms have already been developed, but are limited to the simpler cases of POMDPs [36] and (fully-observable) stochastic games [33]. Our model provides the ability to reason about an agent with a realistic perception mechanism *and* operating in an adversarial or worst-case setting.

Solving continuous-space models, even approximately, is computationally challenging. One approach is to discretise and then use techniques for finite-state models (e.g., [19] in our case). But this can yield exponential growth of the state space, depending on the granularity and time-horizon used. Furthermore, decision boundaries for data-driven perception are typically irregular and can be misaligned with gridding schemes for discretisation, limiting precision.

An alternative is to exploit structure in the underlying model and work directly with the continuous-state model. For example, classic dynamic programming approaches to solving MDPs can be lifted to continuous-state variants [12]: a piecewise constant representation of the value function is computed, based on a partition of the state space created dynamically during solution. It is demonstrated that this approach can outperform discretisation and that it can also be generalised to solving POMDPs. We can adapt this approach to models with neural perception mechanisms [36], exploiting the fact that ReLU NN classifiers induce a finite decomposition of the continuous environment into polyhedra.

Contributions. The contributions of this paper are as follows. We first define the model of one-sided NS-POSGs and motivate it via an autonomous driving scenario based on a ReLU NN classifier for pedestrian intention learnt from public datasets [28]. We then prove that the (discounted reward) value function for NS-POSGs is continuous and convex, and is a fixed point of a minimax operator. Based on mild assumptions about the model, we give a piecewise linear and convex representation of the value function, which admits a finite polyhedral representation and which is closed with respect to the minimax operator.

In order to provide a feasible approach to approximating values of NS-POSGs, we present a variant of HSVI, which is a popular anytime algorithm for POMDPs that iteratively computes lower and upper bounds on values. We build on ideas from HSVI for finite one-sided POSGs [19] (but there are multiple challenges when moving to a continuous state space and NNs) and for POMDPs with neural perception mechanisms [36] (but, for us, the move to games brings a number of complications); see Sect. 6 for a detailed discussion.

We implement our one-sided NS-HSVI algorithm using the popular particle-based representation for beliefs and employing NN pre-image computation [25] to construct an initial finite polyhedral representation of perception functions. We apply this to the pedestrian-vehicle interaction scenario and a pursuit-evasion game inspired by mobile robotics applications, demonstrating the ability to synthesise agent strategies for models with complex perception functions, and to explore trade-offs when using perception mechanisms of varying precision.

Related Work. Solving POSGs is largely intractable. Methods based on exact dynamic programming [17] and approximations [11,23] exist but have high computational cost. Further approaches exist for *zero-sum* POSGs, including conversion to extensive-form games [3], counterfactual regret minimisation [21,22,42] and methods based on reinforcement learning and search [5,26]. In [9], an HSVI-like finite-horizon solver that provably converges to an ε-optimal solution is proposed; [32] provides convexity and concavity results but no algorithmic solution.

Methods exist for *one-sided* POSGs: a space partition approach when actions are public [40], a point-based approximate algorithm when observations are continuous [41] and projection to POMDPs based on factored representations [7]. But these are all restricted to *finite-state* games. Closer to our work, but still for finite models, is [19], which proposes an HSVI method for POSGs.

For the *continuous-state* but *single-agent* (POMDP) setting, point-based value iteration [6,27,38] and discrete space approximation [4] can be used; the former also uses α-functions but works with (approximate) Gaussian mixtures or beta-densities, whereas we exploit structure, similarly to [12]. As discussed above, in earlier work, we proposed models and techniques for extending several simpler probabilistic models with neural perception mechanisms [33,34,36]. Recent work [37] builds on the one-sided NS-POSG model proposed in this paper, but focuses instead on *online* methods for strategy synthesis.

2   Background

POSGs. The semantics of our models are continuous-state *partially observable concurrent stochastic games* (POSGs) [5,18,21]. Letting $\mathbb{P}(X)$ denote the space of probability measures on a Borel space X, POSGs are defined as follows.

A two-player POSG is a tuple $\mathsf{G} = (N, S, A, \delta, \mathcal{O}, Z)$, where: $N = \{1, 2\}$ is a set of two agents; S a Borel measurable set of states; $A \triangleq A_1 \times A_2$ a finite set of joint actions where A_i are actions of agent i; $\delta : (S \times A) \to \mathbb{P}(S)$ a probabilistic transition function; $\mathcal{O} \triangleq \mathcal{O}_1 \times \mathcal{O}_2$ a finite set of joint observations where $\mathcal{O}_i$ are observations of agent i; and $Z : (S \times A \times S) \to \mathcal{O}$ an observation function.

In a state s of a POSG G, each agent i selects an action a_i from A_i. The probability to move to a state s' is $\delta(s, (a_1, a_2))(s')$, and the subsequent observation is $Z(s, (a_1, a_2), s') = (o_1, o_2)$, where agent i can only observe o_i. A *history* of G is a sequence of states and joint actions $\pi = (s^0, a^0, s^1, \ldots, a^{t-1}, s^t)$ such that $\delta(s^k, a^k)(s^{k+1}) > 0$ for each k. For a history π, we denote by $\pi(k)$ the $(k+1)$th state, and $\pi[k]$ the $(k+1)$th action. A (local) *action-observation history (AOH)* is the view of a history π from agent i's perspective: $\pi_i = (o_i^0, a_i^0, o_i^1, \ldots, a_i^{t-1}, o_i^t)$. If an agent has full information about the state, then we assume the agent is also informed of the history of joint actions. Let $FPaths_G$ and $FPaths_{G,i}$ denote the sets of finite histories of G and AOHs of agent i, respectively.

A (behaviour) *strategy* of agent i is a mapping $\sigma_i : FPaths_{G,i} \to \mathbb{P}(A_i)$. We denote by Σ_i the set of strategies of agent i. A *profile* $\sigma = (\sigma_1, \sigma_2)$ is a pair of strategies for each agent and we denote by $\Sigma = \Sigma_1 \times \Sigma_2$ the set of profiles.

Objectives. Agents 1 and 2 maximise and minimise, respectively, the expected value of the *discounted reward* $Y(\pi) = \sum_{k=0}^{\infty} \beta^k r(\pi(k), \pi[k])$, where π is an infinite history, $r : (S \times A) \to \mathbb{R}$ a reward structure and $\beta \in (0, 1)$. The expected value of Y starting from state distribution b under profile σ is denoted $\mathbb{E}_b^\sigma[Y]$.

Values and Minimax Strategies. If $V^\star(b) \triangleq \sup_{\sigma_1 \in \Sigma_1} \inf_{\sigma_2 \in \Sigma_2} \mathbb{E}_b^{\sigma_1, \sigma_2}[Y] = \inf_{\sigma_2 \in \Sigma_2} \sup_{\sigma_1 \in \Sigma_1} \mathbb{E}_b^{\sigma_1, \sigma_2}[Y]$ for all $b \in \mathbb{P}(S)$, then $V^\star$ is called the *value* of G. A profile $\sigma^\star = (\sigma_1^\star, \sigma_2^\star)$ is a *minimax strategy profile* if, for any $b \in \mathbb{P}(S)$, $\mathbb{E}_b^{\sigma_1^\star, \sigma_2}[Y] \geq \mathbb{E}_b^{\sigma_1^\star, \sigma_2^\star}[Y] \geq \mathbb{E}_b^{\sigma_1, \sigma_2^\star}[Y]$ for all $\sigma_1 \in \Sigma_1$ and $\sigma_2 \in \Sigma_2$.

3   One-Sided Neuro-Symbolic POSGs

We now introduce our model, aimed at commonly deployed multi-agent scenarios with data-driven perception, necessitating the use of continuous environments.

One-Sided NS-POSGs. A *one-sided neuro-symbolic POSG (NS-POSG)* comprises a *partially informed, neuro-symbolic* agent and a *fully informed* agent in a continuous-state environment. The first agent has a finite set of local states, and is endowed with a data-driven perception mechanism, through which (and only through which) it makes finite-valued observations of the environment's state, stored locally as *percepts*. The second agent can directly observe both the local state and percept of the first agent, and the state of the environment.

Definition 1 (NS-POSG). *A one-sided NS-POSG C comprises agents* $\mathsf{Ag}_1 = (S_1, A_1, obs_1, \delta_1)$ *and* $\mathsf{Ag}_2 = (A_2)$, *and environment* $E = (S_E, \delta_E)$, *where:*

- $S_1 = Loc_1 \times Per_1$ *is a set of states for* Ag_1, *where* Loc_1 *and* Per_1 *are finite sets of local states and percepts, respectively;*
- $S_E \subseteq \mathbb{R}^e$ *is a closed set of continuous environment states;*
- A_i *is a finite set of actions for* Ag_i *and* $A \triangleq A_1 \times A_2$ *is a set of joint actions;*
- $obs_1 : (Loc_1 \times S_E) \to Per_1$ *is* Ag_1*'s perception function;*
- $\delta_1 : (S_1 \times A) \to \mathbb{P}(Loc_1)$ *is* Ag_1*'s local probabilistic transition function;*
- $\delta_E : (Loc_1 \times S_E \times A) \to \mathbb{P}(S_E)$ *is a finitely-branching probabilistic transition function for the environment.*

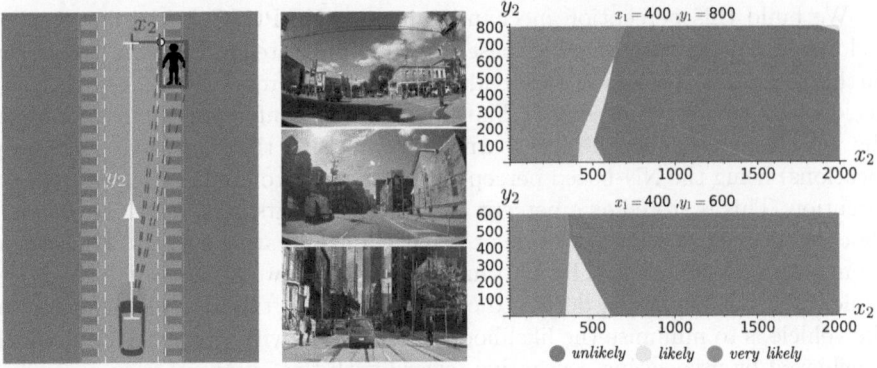

Fig. 1. Pedestrian-vehicle example. Left: Positions of two agents. Middle: Sample images from the PIE dataset [28]. Right: Slices of learnt perception function, where $(x_1, y_1), (x_2, y_2)$ are two successive (relative) positions of the pedestrian.

One-sided NS-POSGs are a subclass of two-agent, hybrid-state POSGs with discrete observations (S_1) and actions for Ag_1, and continuous observations $(S_1 \times S_E)$ and discrete actions for Ag_2. Additionally, Ag_1 is informed of its own actions and Ag_2 of joint actions. Thus, Ag_1 is partially informed, without access to environment states and actions of Ag_2, and Ag_2 is fully informed. Since Ag_2 needs no percepts, its local state and transition function are omitted.

The game executes as follows. A global state of C comprises a state $s_1 = (loc_1, per_1)$ for Ag_1 and an environment state s_E. In state $s = (s_1, s_E)$, the two agents concurrently choose one of their actions, resulting in a joint action $a = (a_1, a_2) \in A$. Next, the local state of Ag_1 is updated to some $loc_1' \in Loc_1$, according to $\delta_1(s_1, a)$. At the same time, the environment state is updated to some $s_E' \in S_E$ according to $\delta_E(loc_1, s_E, a)$. Finally, the first agent Ag_1, based on loc_1', generates a percept $per_1' = obs_1(loc_1', s_E')$ by observing the environment state s_E' and C reaches the global state $s' = ((loc_1', per_1'), s_E')$.

We focus on neural perception functions, i.e., for each local state loc_1, we associate an NN classifier $f_{loc_1} : S_E \to \mathbb{P}(Per_1)$ that returns a distribution over percepts for each environment state $s_E \in S_E$. Then $obs_1(loc_1, s_E) = f_{loc_1}^{\max}(s_E)$, where $f_{loc_1}^{\max}(s_E)$ is the percept with the largest probability in $f_{loc_1}(s_E)$ (a tie-breaking rule is applied if multiple percepts have the largest probability).

Motivating Example: Pedestrian-Vehicle Interaction. A key challenge for autonomous driving in urban environments is predicting pedestrians' intentions or actions. One solution is NN classifiers, e.g., trained on video datasets [28, 29]. To illustrate our NS-POSG model, we consider decision making for an autonomous vehicle using an NN-based intention estimation model for a pedestrian at a crossing [28]. We use their simpler "vanilla" model, which takes two successive (relative) locations of the pedestrian (the top-left coordinates (x_1, y_1) and (x_2, y_2) of two fixed size bounding boxes around the pedestrian) and classifies its intention as: *unlikely*, *likely* or *very likely* to cross. We train a feed-forward NN classifier with ReLU activation functions over the PIE dataset [28].

We build this perception mechanism into an NS-POSG model of a vehicle yielding at a pedestrian crossing, based on [13], illustrated in Fig. 1. A pedestrian further ahead at the side of the road may decide to cross and the vehicle must decide how to adapt its speed. The first, partially-informed agent represents the vehicle. It observes the environment (comprising the successive pedestrian locations) using the NN-based perception mechanism to predict the pedestrian's intention. This is stored as a percept and its speed as its local state. The vehicle chooses between selected (positive or negative) acceleration actions. The second agent, the pedestrian, is fully informed, providing a worst-case analysis of the vehicle decisions, and can decide to cross or return to the roadside. The goal of the vehicle is to minimise the likelihood of a collision with the pedestrian, which is achieved by associating a negative reward with this event.

Figure 1 also shows selected slices of the state space decomposition obtained by computing the pre-image [25] of the learnt NN classifier, for each of the three predicted intentions. The decision boundaries are non-trivial, justifying our goal of performing a formal analysis, but some intuitive characteristics can be seen. When $x_2 \geq x_1$, meaning that the pedestrian is stationary or moving away from the road, it will generally be classified as *unlikely* to cross. We also see the prediction model is *cautious* when trying to make an estimation if its first observation is made from greater distance. More details are in [35].

One-Sided NS-POSG Semantics. A one-sided NS-POSG C induces a POSG $[\![C]\!]$, where we restrict to states that are *percept compatible*, i.e., where $per_1 = obs_1(loc_1, s_E)$ for $s = ((loc_1, per_1), s_E)$. The semantics of a one-sided NS-POSG is closed with respect to percept compatible states.

Definition 2 (Semantics). *Given a one-sided NS-POSG C, as in Definition 1, its semantics is the POSG $[\![C]\!] = (N, S, A, \delta, \mathcal{O}, Z)$ where:*

- $N = \{1, 2\}$ *is a set of two agents and* $A = A_1 \times A_2$;
- $S \subseteq S_1 \times S_E$ *is the set of percept compatible states;*
- *for* $s = (s_1, s_E), s' = (s'_1, s'_E) \in S$ *and* $a \in A$ *where* $s_1 = (loc_1, per_1)$ *and* $s'_1 = (loc'_1, per'_1)$, *we have* $\delta(s, a)(s') = \delta_1(s_1, a)(loc'_1)\delta_E(loc_1, s_E, a)(s'_E)$;
- $\mathcal{O} = \mathcal{O}_1 \times \mathcal{O}_2$, *where* $\mathcal{O}_1 = S_1$ *and* $\mathcal{O}_2 = S$;
- $Z(s, a, s') = (s'_1, s')$ *for* $s \in S$, $a \in A$ *and* $s' = (s'_1, s'_E) \in S$.

Strategies. As $[\![C]\!]$ is a POSG, we consider (behaviour) *strategies* for the two agents. Since Ag_2 is fully informed, it can recover the beliefs of Ag_1, thus removing nested beliefs. Hence, the AOHs of Ag_2 are equal to the histories of $[\![C]\!]$, i.e., $FPaths_{[\![C]\!],2} = FPaths_{[\![C]\!]}$. We also consider the *stage strategies* at a history of $[\![C]\!]$, which will later be required for solving the induced zero-sum normal-form games in the minimax operator. For a history π of $[\![C]\!]$, a stage strategy for Ag_1 is a distribution $u_1 \in \mathbb{P}(A_1)$ and a stage strategy for Ag_2 is a function $u_2 : S \to \mathbb{P}(A_2)$, i.e., $u_2 \in \mathbb{P}(A_2 \mid S)$.

Beliefs. Since Ag_1 is partially informed, it may need to infer the current state from its AOH. For an Ag_1 state $s_1 = (loc_1, per_1)$, we let $S_E^{s_1}$ be the set of environment states compatible with s_1, i.e., $S_E^{s_1} = \{s_E \in S_E \mid obs_1(loc_1, s_E) = $

per_1}. Since the states of Ag_1 are also the observations of Ag_1 and states of $[\![C]\!]$ are percept compatible, a *belief* for Ag_1, which can also be reconstructed by Ag_2, can be represented as a pair $b = (s_1, b_1)$, where $s_1 \in S_1$, $b_1 \in \mathbb{P}(S_E)$ and $b_1(s_E) = 0$ for all $s_E \in S_E \setminus S_E^{s_1}$. We denote by S_B the set of beliefs of Ag_1.

Given a belief (s_1, b_1), if action a_1 is selected by Ag_1, Ag_2 is *assumed* to take stage strategy $u_2 \in \mathbb{P}(A_2 \mid S)$ and s_1' is observed, then the updated belief of Ag_1 via Bayesian inference is denoted $(s_1', b_1^{s_1, a_1, u_2, s_1'})$; see [35] for details.

4   Values of One-Sided NS-POSGs

We establish the *value function* of a one-sided NS-POSG C with semantics $[\![C]\!]$, which gives the minimax expected reward from an initial belief, and show its convexity and continuity. Next, to compute it, we introduce minimax and max-sup operators specialised for one-sided NS-POSGs, and prove their equivalence. Finally, we provide a fixed-point characterisation of the value function.

Value Function. We assume a fixed reward structure r and discount factor β. The *value function* of C represents the minimax expected reward in each possible initial belief of the game, given by $V^* : S_B \to \mathbb{R}$, where $V^*(s_1, b_1) = \mathbb{E}_{(s_1, b_1)}^{\sigma^*}[Y]$ for all $(s_1, b_1) \in S_B$ and σ^* is a minimax strategy profile of $[\![C]\!]$.

The value function for zero-sum POSGs may not exist when the state space is uncountable [2,14,30] as in our case. In this paper, we only consider one-sided NS-POSGs that are determined, i.e., for which the value function exists.

Convexity and Continuity. Since r is bounded, the value function V^* has lower and upper bounds $L = \min_{s \in S, a \in A} r(s, a)/(1 - \beta)$ and $U = \max_{s \in S, a \in A} r(s, a)/(1 - \beta)$. The proof of the following and all other results can be found in [35].

Theorem 1 (Convexity and continuity). *For $s_1 \in S_1$, $V^*(s_1, \cdot) : \mathbb{P}(S_E) \to \mathbb{R}$ is convex and continuous, and for $b_1, b_1' \in \mathbb{P}(S_E) : |V^*(s_1, b_1) - V^*(s_1, b_1')| \le K(b_1, b_1')$ where $K(b_1, b_1') = \frac{1}{2}(U - L) \int_{s_E \in S_E^{s_1}} |b_1(s_E) - b_1'(s_E)| ds_E$.*

Minimax and maxsup operators. We give a fixed-point characterisation of the value function V^*, first introducing a minimax operator and then simplifying to an equivalent maxsup variant. The latter will be used in Sect. 5 to prove closure of our representation for value functions and in Sect. 6 to formulate HSVI. For $f : S \to \mathbb{R}$ and belief (s_1, b_1), let $\langle f, (s_1, b_1) \rangle = \int_{s_E \in S_E} f(s_1, s_E) b_1(s_E) ds_E$ and $\mathbb{F}(S_B)$ denote the space of functions mapping the beliefs S_B to reals $\mathbb{R}$.

Definition 3 (Minimax). *The minimax operator $T : \mathbb{F}(S_B) \to \mathbb{F}(S_B)$ is given by:*

$$[TV](s_1, b_1) = \max_{u_1 \in \mathbb{P}(A_1)} \min_{u_2 \in \mathbb{P}(A_2|S)} \mathbb{E}_{(s_1, b_1), u_1, u_2}[r(s, a)]$$

$$+ \beta \sum_{(a_1, s_1') \in A_1 \times S_1} P(a_1, s_1' \mid (s_1, b_1), u_1, u_2) V(s_1', b_1^{s_1, a_1, u_2, s_1'}) \quad (1)$$

for $V \in \mathbb{F}(S_B)$ and $(s_1, b_1) \in S_B$, where $\mathbb{E}_{(s_1, b_1), u_1, u_2}[r(s, a)] = \int_{s_E \in S_E} b_1(s_E) \sum_{(a_1, a_2) \in A} u_1(a_1) u_2(a_2 \mid s_1, s_E) r((s_1, s_E), (a_1, a_2)) ds_E$.

Motivated by [19], which proposed an equivalent operator for the discrete case, we instead prove that the minimax operator has an equivalent simplified form over convex continuous functions of $\mathbb{F}(S_B)$.

For $\Gamma \subseteq \mathbb{F}(S)$, we let $\Gamma^{A_1 \times S_1}$ denote the set of vectors of elements of the convex hull of Γ indexed by $A_1 \times S_1$. Furthermore, for $u_1 \in \mathbb{P}(A_1)$, $\overline{\alpha} = (\alpha^{a_1, s_1'})_{(a_1, s_1') \in A_1 \times S_1} \in \Gamma^{A_1 \times S_1}$ and $a_2 \in A_2$, we define $f_{u_1, \overline{\alpha}, a_2} : S \to \mathbb{R}$ to be the function such that, for $s \in S$:

$$
f_{u_1, \overline{\alpha}, a_2}(s) = \sum_{a_1 \in A_1} u_1(a_1) r(s, (a_1, a_2))
$$

$$
+ \beta \sum_{(a_1, s_1') \in A_1 \times S_1} u_1(a_1) \sum_{s_E' \in S_E} \delta(s, (a_1, a_2))(s_1', s_E') \alpha^{a_1, s_1'}(s_1', s_E') \quad (2)
$$

where the sum over s_E' is due to the finite branching of $\delta(s, (a_1, a_2))$.

Definition 4 (Maxsup). For $\varnothing \neq \Gamma \subseteq \mathbb{F}(S)$, if $V(s_1, b_1) = \sup_{\alpha \in \Gamma} \langle \alpha, (s_1, b_1) \rangle$ for $(s_1, b_1) \in S_B$, then the maxsup operator $T_\Gamma : \mathbb{F}(S_B) \to \mathbb{F}(S_B)$ is defined as $[T_\Gamma V](s_1, b_1) = \max_{u_1 \in \mathbb{P}(A_1)} \sup_{\overline{\alpha} \in \Gamma^{A_1 \times S_1}} \langle f_{u_1, \overline{\alpha}}, (s_1, b_1) \rangle$ for $(s_1, b_1) \in S_B$ where $f_{u_1, \overline{\alpha}}(s) = \min_{a_2 \in A_2} f_{u_1, \overline{\alpha}, a_2}(s)$ for $s \in S$.

In the maxsup operator, u_1 and $\overline{\alpha}$ are aligned with Ag_1's goal of maximising the objective, where u_1 is over action distributions and $\overline{\alpha}$ is over convex combinations of elements of Γ. The minimisation by Ag_2 is simplified to an optimisation over its finite action set in the function $f_{u_1, \overline{\alpha}}$. Note that each state may require a different minimiser a_2, as Ag_2 knows the current state before taking an action.

The maxsup operator avoids the minimisation over Markov kernels with continuous states in the original minimax operator. Given u_1 and $\overline{\alpha}$, the minimisation can induce a pure best-response stage strategy $u_2 \in \mathbb{P}(A_2 \mid S)$ such that, for any $s \in S$, $u_2(a_2' \mid s) = 1$ for some $a_2' \in \arg\min_{a_2 \in A_2} f_{u_1, \overline{\alpha}, a_2}(s)$. Using Theorem 1, the operator equivalence and fixed-point result are as follows.

Theorem 2 (Operator equivalence and fixed point). For $\varnothing \neq \Gamma \subseteq \mathbb{F}(S)$, if $V(s_1, b_1) = \sup_{\alpha \in \Gamma} \langle \alpha, (s_1, b_1) \rangle$ for $(s_1, b_1) \in S_B$, then the minimax operator T and maxsup operator T_Γ are equivalent and their unique fixed point is $V^\star$.

5   P-PWLC Value Iteration

We next discuss a representation for value functions using *piecewise constant* (PWC) α-functions, called P-PWLC (*piecewise linear and convex under PWC*), originally introduced in [36]. This representation extends the α-functions of [6,27,38] for continuous-state POMDPs, but a key difference is that we work with polyhedral representations (induced precisely from NNs) rather than approximations based on Gaussian mixtures [27] or beta densities [15].

We show that, given PWC representations for an NS-POSG's perception, reward and transition functions, and under mild assumptions on model structure, P-PWLC value functions are closed with respect to the minimax operator. This yields a (non-scalable) *value iteration* algorithm and, subsequently, the basis for a more practical point-based HSVI algorithm in Sect. 6.

PWC Representations. A *finite connected partition* (FCP) of S, denoted Φ, is a finite collection of disjoint connected *regions* (subsets) of S that cover it.

Definition 5 (PWC function). *A function $f : S \to \mathbb{R}$ is piecewise constant (PWC) if there exists an FCP Φ of S such that $f : \phi \to \mathbb{R}$ is constant for $\phi \in \Phi$. Let $\mathbb{F}_C(S)$ be the set of PWC functions in $\mathbb{F}(S)$.*

Since we focus on NNs for Ag_1's perception function obs_1, it is PWC (as for the one-agent case [36]) and the state space S of a one-sided NS-POSG can be decomposed into a finite set of *regions*, each with the same observation. Formally, there exists a *perception FCP* Φ_P, the smallest FCP of S such that all states in any $\phi \in \Phi_P$ are observationally equivalent, i.e., if $(s_1, s_E), (s'_1, s'_E) \in \phi$, then $s_1 = s'_1$. We can use Φ_P to find the set $S_E^{s_1}$ for any agent state $s_1 \in S_1$. Given an NN representation of obs_1, the corresponding FCP Φ_P can be extracted (or approximated) offline by analysing its pre-image [25].

We also need to make some assumptions about the transitions and rewards of one-sided NS-POSGs (in a similar style to [36]). Informally, we require that, for any decomposition Φ' of the state-space into regions (i.e., an FCP), there is a second decomposition Φ, the *pre-image FCP*, such that states in regions of Φ have the same rewards and transition probabilities into regions of Φ'. The transitions of the (continuous) environment must also be decomposable into regions.

Assumption 1 (Transitions and rewards). *Given any FCP Φ' of S, there exists an FCP Φ of S, called the* pre-image *FCP of Φ', where for $\phi \in \Phi$, $a \in A$ and $\phi' \in \Phi'$ there exists $\delta_\Phi : (\Phi \times A) \to \mathbb{P}(\Phi')$ and $r_\Phi : (\Phi \times A) \to \mathbb{R}$ such that $\delta(s,a)(s') = \delta_\Phi(\phi, a)(\phi')$ and $r(s,a) = r_\Phi(\phi, a)$ for $s \in \phi$ and $s' \in \phi'$. In addition, δ_E can be expressed in the form $\sum_{i=1}^{n} \mu_i \delta_E^i$, where $n \in \mathbb{N}$, $\mu_i \in [0,1]$, $\sum_{i=1}^{n} \mu_i = 1$ and $\delta_E^i : (Loc_1 \times S_E \times A) \to S_E$ are piecewise continuous functions.*

The need for this assumption also becomes clear in our later algorithms, which compute a representation for an NS-POSG's value function over a (polyhedral) partition of the state space. This partition is created dynamically over the iterations of the solution, using a pre-image based splitting operation.

We now show, using results for continuous-state POMDPs [27,36], that V^* is the limit of a sequence of α-functions, called *piecewise linear and convex under PWC α-functions*, first introduced in [36] for neuro-symbolic POMDPs.

Definition 6 (P-PWLC Function). *A function $V : S_B \to \mathbb{R}$ is piecewise linear and convex under PWC α-functions (P-PWLC) if there exists a finite set $\Gamma \subseteq \mathbb{F}_C(S)$ such that $V(s_1, b_1) = \max_{\alpha \in \Gamma} \langle \alpha, (s_1, b_1) \rangle$ for $(s_1, b_1) \in S_B$, where the functions in Γ are called PWC α-functions.*

If $V \in \mathbb{F}(S_B)$ is P-PWLC, then it can be represented by a set of PWC functions over S, i.e., as a finite set of FCP regions and a value vector. Recall that $\langle \alpha, (s_1, b_1) \rangle = \int_{s_E \in S_E} \alpha(s_1, s_E) b_1(s_E) ds_E$, and therefore computing the value for a belief involves integration. For one-sided NS-POSGs, we demonstrate, under Assumption 1, closure of the P-PWLC representation for value functions under the minimax operator and the convergence of value iteration.

LP, Closure Property and Convergence. By showing that $f_{u_1,\overline{\alpha},a_2}$ in (2) is PWC in S (see [35]), we use Theorem 2 to demonstrate that, if V is P-PWLC, the minimax operation can be computed by solving an LP.

Lemma 1 (LP for Minimax and P-PWLC). *If $V \in \mathbb{F}(S_B)$ is P-PWLC, then $[TV](s_1, b_1)$ is given by an LP for $(s_1, b_1) \in S_B$.*

Using Lemma 1, we show that the P-PWLC representation is closed under the minimax operator. This closure property enables iterative computation of a sequence of such functions to approximate $V^\star$ to within a convergence guarantee.

Theorem 3 (P-PWLC closure and convergence). *If $V \in \mathbb{F}(S_B)$ is P-PWLC, then so is $[TV]$. If $V^0 \in \mathbb{F}(S_B)$ is P-PWLC, then the sequence $(V^t)_{t=0}^{\infty}$, such that $V^{t+1} = [TV^t]$, is P-PWLC and converges to $V^\star$.*

An implementation of value iteration for one-sided NS-POSGs is therefore feasible, since each α-function involved is PWC and thus allows for a finite representation. However, as the number of α-functions grows exponentially in the number of iterations, it is not scalable in practice.

6   Heuristic Search Value Iteration for NS-POSGs

To provide a more practical approach to solving one-sided NS-POSGs, we now present a variant of HSVI (heuristic search value iteration) [31], an anytime algorithm that approximates the value function $V^\star$ via lower and upper bound functions, updated through heuristically generated beliefs.

Our approach broadly follows the structure of HSVI for *finite* POSGs [19], but every step presents challenges when extending to continuous states and NN-based observations. In particular, we must work with integrals over beliefs and deal with uncountability, using P-PWLC (rather than PWLC) functions for lower bounds, and therefore different ingredients to prove convergence. Value computations are also much more complex because NN perception function induce FCPs, which are used to compute images, pre-images and intersections.

We also build on ideas from HVSI for (single-agent) neuro-symbolic POMDPs in [36]. The presence of two opposing agents brings three main challenges. First, value backups at belief points require solving normal-form games instead of maximising over one agent's actions. Second, since the first agent is not informed of the joint action, in the value backups and belief updates of the maxsup operator uncountably many stage strategies of the second agent have to be considered, whereas, in the single-agent variant, the agent can decide the transition probabilistically on its own. Third, the forward exploration heuristic is more complex as it depends on the stage strategies of the agents in two-stage games.

6.1   Lower and Upper Bound Representations

We first discuss representing and updating the lower and upper bound functions.

Lower Bound Function. Selecting an appropriate representation for α-functions requires closure properties with respect to the maxsup operator. Motivated by [36], we represent the lower bound $V_{lb}^{\Gamma} \in \mathbb{F}(S_B)$ as the P-PWLC function for a finite set $\Gamma \subseteq \mathbb{F}_C(S)$ of PWC α-functions (see Definition 6), for which the closure is guaranteed by Theorem 3. The lower bound V_{lb}^{Γ} has a finite representation as each α-function is PWC, and is initialised as in [19].

Upper Bound Function. The upper bound $V_{ub}^{\Upsilon} \in \mathbb{F}(S_B)$ is represented by a finite set of belief-value points $\Upsilon = \{((s_1^i, b_1^i), y_i) \in S_B \times \mathbb{R} \mid i \in I\}$, where y_i is an upper bound of $V^{\star}(s_1^i, b_1^i)$. Similarly to [36], for any $(s_1, b_1) \in S_B$, the upper bound $V_{ub}^{\Upsilon}(s_1, b_1)$ is the lower envelope of the lower convex hull of the points in Υ satisfying the following LP problem: minimise

$$\sum_{i \in I_{s_1}} \lambda_i y_i + K_{ub}(b_1, \sum_{i \in I_{s_1}} \lambda_i b_1^i) \text{ subject to } \lambda_i \geq 0 \text{ and } \sum_{i \in I_{s_1}} \lambda_i = 1 \quad (3)$$

for $i \in I_{s_1}$ where $I_{s_1} = \{i \in I \mid s_1^i = s_1\}$ and $K_{ub} : \mathbb{P}(S_E) \times \mathbb{P}(S_E) \to \mathbb{R}$ measures the difference between two beliefs such that, if K is the function from Theorem 1, then for any $b_1, b_1', b_1'' \in \mathbb{P}(S_E)$: $K_{ub}(b_1, b_1) = 0$,

$$K_{ub}(b_1, b_1') \geq K(b_1, b_1') \quad \text{and} \quad |K_{ub}(b_1, b_1') - K_{ub}(b_1, b_1'')| \leq K_{ub}(b_1', b_1''). \quad (4)$$

Note that (3) is close to the upper bound in regular HSVI for finite-state spaces, except for the function K_{ub} that measures the difference between two beliefs (two continuous-state functions). With respect to the upper bound used in [36], K_{ub} here needs to satisfy an additional triangle property in (4) to ensure the continuity of V_{ub}^{Υ}, for the convergence of the point-based algorithm below. The properties of K_{ub} imply that (3) is an upper bound after a value backup, as stated in Lemma 3 below. The upper bound V_{ub}^{Υ} is initialised as in [19].

Lower Bound Updates. For the lower bound V_{lb}^{Γ}, in each iteration we add a new PWC α-function $\alpha^{\star}$ to Γ at a belief $(s_1, b_1) \in S_B$ such that:

$$\langle \alpha^{\star}, (s_1, b_1) \rangle = [TV_{lb}^{\Gamma}](s_1, b_1) = \langle f_{\overline{p}_1^{\star}, \overline{\alpha}^{\star}}, (s_1, b_1) \rangle \quad (5)$$

where the second equality follows from Lemma 1 and $(\overline{p}_1^{\star}, \overline{\alpha}^{\star})$ is computed via the optimal solution to the LP in Lemma 1 at (s_1, b_1).

Using $\overline{p}_1^{\star}$, $\overline{\alpha}^{\star}$ and the perception FCP Φ_P, Algorithm 1 computes a new α-function $\alpha^{\star}$ at belief (s_1, b_1). To guarantee (5) and improve efficiency, we only compute the backup values for regions $\phi \in \Phi_P$ over which (s_1, b_1) has positive probabilities, i.e., $s_1^{\phi} = s_1$ (where s_1^{ϕ} is the unique agent state appearing in ϕ) and $\int_{(s_1, s_E) \in \phi} b_1(s_E) ds_E > 0$, and assign the trivial lower bound L otherwise.

For each region ϕ either $\alpha^{\star}(\hat{s}_1, \hat{s}_E) = f_{\overline{p}_1^{\star}, \overline{\alpha}^{\star}}(\hat{s}_1, \hat{s}_E)$ or $\alpha^{\star}(\hat{s}_1, \hat{s}_E) = L$ for all $(\hat{s}_1, \hat{s}_E) \in \phi$. Computing the backup values in line 4 of Algorithm 1 state by state is computationally intractable, as ϕ contains an infinite number of states.

ALGORITHM 1. Point-based $Update(s_1, b_1)$ of $(V_{lb}^\Gamma, V_{ub}^\Upsilon)$

1: $(\overline{p}_1^\star, \overline{\alpha}^\star) \leftarrow [TV_{lb}^\Gamma](s_1, b_1)$ via an LP in Lemma 1
2: **for** $\phi \in \Phi_P$ **do**
3:     **if** $s_1^\phi = s_1$ and $\int_{(s_1, s_E) \in \phi} b_1(s_E) \mathrm{d}s_E > 0$ **then**
4:         $\alpha^\star(\hat{s}_1, \hat{s}_E) \leftarrow f_{\overline{p}_1^\star, \overline{\alpha}^\star}(\hat{s}_1, \hat{s}_E)$ for $(\hat{s}_1, \hat{s}_E) \in \phi$ ▷ ISPP backup
5:     **else** $\alpha^\star(\hat{s}_1, \hat{s}_E) \leftarrow L$ for $(\hat{s}_1, \hat{s}_E) \in \phi$
6: $\Gamma \leftarrow \Gamma \cup \{\alpha^\star\}$
7: $y^\star \leftarrow [TV_{ub}^\Upsilon](s_1, b_1)$ via (1) and (3)
8: $\Upsilon \leftarrow \Upsilon \cup \{((s_1, b_1), y^\star)\}$

However, the following lemma shows that $\alpha^\star$ is PWC, allowing a tractable region-by-region backup, called Image-Split-Preimage-Product (ISPP) backup, which is adapted from the single-agent variant in [36]. The details of the ISPP backup for one-sided NS-POSGs are in [35]. The lemma also shows that the lower bound function increases and is valid after each update.

Lemma 2 (Lower bound). *The function $\alpha^\star$ generated by Algorithm 1 is a PWC α-function satisfying (5), and if $\Gamma' = \Gamma \cup \{\alpha^\star\}$, then $V_{lb}^\Gamma \leq V_{lb}^{\Gamma'} \leq V^\star$.*

Upper Bound Updates. For the upper bound V_{ub}^Υ, due to representation (3), at a belief $(s_1, b_1) \in S_B$ in each iteration, we add a new belief-value point $((s_1, b_1), y^\star)$ to Υ such that $y^\star = [TV_{ub}^\Upsilon](s_1, b_1)$. Computing $[TV_{ub}^\Upsilon](s_1, b_1)$ via (1) and (3) requires the concrete formula for K_{ub} and the belief representations. Thus, we will show how to compute $[TV_{ub}^\Upsilon](s_1, b_1)$ when introducing belief representations below. The following lemma shows that $y^\star \geq V^\star(s_1, b_1)$ required by (3), and the upper bound function is decreasing and is valid after each update.

Lemma 3 (Upper bound). *Given a belief $(s_1, b_1) \in S_B$, if $y^\star = [TV_{ub}^\Upsilon](s_1, b_1)$, then $y^\star$ is an upper bound of $V^\star$ at (s_1, b_1), i.e., $y^\star \geq V^\star(s_1, b_1)$, and if $\Upsilon' = \Upsilon \cup \{((s_1, b_1), y^\star)\}$, then $V_{ub}^\Upsilon \geq V_{ub}^{\Upsilon'} \geq V^\star$.*

6.2   One-Sided NS-HSVI

Algorithm 2 presents our NS-HSVI algorithm for one-sided NS-POSGs.

Forward Exploration Heuristic. The algorithm uses a heuristic approach to select which belief will be considered next. Similarly to finite-state one-sided POSGs [19], we focus on a belief that has the highest *weighted excess gap*. The excess gap at a belief (s_1, b_1) with depth t from the initial belief is defined by $excess_t(s_1, b_1) = V_{ub}^\Upsilon(s_1, b_1) - V_{lb}^\Gamma(s_1, b_1) - \rho(t)$, where $\rho(0) = \varepsilon$ and $\rho(t+1) = (\rho(t) - 2(U - L)\bar{\varepsilon})/\beta$, and $\bar{\varepsilon} \in (0, (1 - \beta)\varepsilon/(2U - 2L))$. Using this excess gap, the next action-observation pair $(\hat{a}_1, \hat{s}_1)$ for exploration is selected from:

$$\mathrm{argmax}_{(a_1, s_1') \in A_1 \times S_1} P(a_1, s_1' \mid (s_1, b_1), u_1^{ub}, u_2^{lb}) excess_{t+1}(s_1', b_1^{s_1, a_1, u_2^{lb}, s_1'}). \quad (6)$$

ALGORITHM 2. One-sided NS-HSVI for one-sided NS-POSGs

1: **while** $V_{ub}^{\Upsilon}(s_1^{init}, b_1^{init}) - V_{lb}^{\Gamma}(s_1^{init}, b_1^{init}) > \varepsilon$ **do** $Explore((s_1^{init}, b_1^{init}), 0)$
2: **return** V_{lb}^{Γ} and V_{ub}^{Υ} via sets Γ and Υ
3: **function** $Explore((s_1, b_1), t)$
4:    $(u_1^{lb}, u_2^{lb}) \leftarrow$ minimax strategy profile in $[TV_{lb}^{\Gamma}](s_1, b_1)$
5:    $(u_1^{ub}, u_2^{ub}) \leftarrow$ minimax strategy profile in $[TV_{ub}^{\Upsilon}](s_1, b_1)$
6:    $Update(s_1, b_1)$ ▷ Algorithm 1
7:    $(\hat{a}_1, \hat{s}_1) \leftarrow$ select according to forward exploration heuristic
8:    **if** $P(\hat{a}_1, \hat{s}_1 \mid (s_1, b_1), u_1^{ub}, u_2^{lb}) excess_{t+1}(\hat{s}_1, b_1^{s_1, \hat{a}_1, u_2^{lb}, \hat{s}_1}) > 0$ **then**
9:        $Explore((\hat{s}_1, b_1^{s_1, \hat{a}_1, u_2^{lb}, \hat{s}_1}), t+1)$
10:       $Update(s_1, b_1)$ ▷ Algorithm 1

To compute the next belief via lines 8 and 9 of Algorithm 2, the minimax strategy profiles in stage games $[TV_{lb}^{\Gamma}](s_1, b_1)$ and $[TV_{ub}^{\Upsilon}](s_1, b_1)$, i.e., (u_1^{ub}, u_2^{lb}), are required. Since V_{lb}^{Γ} is P-PWLC, using Lemma 1, the strategy u_2^{lb} is obtained by solving an LP. However, the computation of the strategy u_1^{ub} depends on the representation of (s_1, b_1) and the measure function K_{ub}, and thus will be discussed later. One-sided NS-HSVI has the following convergence guarantees.

Theorem 4 (One-sided NS-HSVI). *For any* $(s_1^{init}, b_1^{init}) \in S_B$ *and* $\varepsilon > 0$, *Algorithm 2 will terminate and upon termination:* $V_{ub}^{\Upsilon}(s_1^{init}, b_1^{init}) - V_{lb}^{\Gamma}(s_1^{init}, b_1^{init}) \le \varepsilon$ *and* $V_{lb}^{\Gamma}(s_1^{init}, b_1^{init}) \le V^{\star}(s_1^{init}, b_1^{init}) \le V_{ub}^{\Upsilon}(s_1^{init}, b_1^{init})$.

6.3 Belief Representation and Computations

Implementing one-sided NS-HSVI depends on belief representations, as closed forms are needed. We use the popular *particle-based representation* [10,27], which can approximate arbitrary beliefs and handle non-Gaussian systems. However, compared to region-based representations [36], it is more vulnerable to disturbances and can require many particles for a good approximation.

Particle-Based Beliefs. A *particle-based belief* $(s_1, b_1) \in S_B$ is represented by a weighted particle set $\{(s_E^i, \kappa_i)\}_{i=1}^{n_s}$ with a normalised weight κ_i for each particle $s_E^i \in S_E$, where $b_1(s_E) = \sum_{i=1}^{n_b} \kappa_i D(s_E - s_E^i)$ for $s_E \in S_E$ and $D(s_E - s_E^i)$ is a Dirac delta function centred at 0.

To implement one-sided NS-HSVI using particle-based beliefs, we prove that V_{lb}^{Γ} and V_{ub}^{Υ} are eligible representations, as the belief update $b_1^{s_1, a_1, u_2, s_1'}$, expected values $\langle \alpha, (s_1, b_1) \rangle$, $\langle r, (s_1, b_1) \rangle$ and probability $P(a_1, s_1' \mid (s_1, b_1), u_1, u_2)$ are computed as simple summations for a particle-based belief (s_1, b_1) ([35]).

Lower Bound. Since V_{lb}^{Γ} is P-PWLC with PWC α-functions Γ, for a particle-based belief (s_1, b_1) represented by $\{(s_E^i, \kappa_i)\}_{i=1}^{n_b}$, using Definition 6, $V_{lb}^{\Gamma}(s_1, b_1) = \max_{\alpha \in \Gamma} \sum_{i=1}^{n_b} \kappa_i \alpha(s_1, s_E^i)$. The stage game $[TV_{lb}^{\Gamma}](s_1, b_1)$ and minimax strategy profile (u_1^{lb}, u_2^{lb}) follow from solving the LP in Lemma 1.

Upper Bound. To compute V_{ub}^{Υ} in (3), we need a function K_{ub} to measure belief differences that satisfies (4). We take $K_{ub} = K$, which does so by definition. Given $\Upsilon = \{((s_1^i, b_1^i), y_i) \mid i \in I\}$, the upper bound and stage game can be computed by solving an LP, respectively, as demonstrated by the following theorem, and then the minimax strategy profile (u_1^{ub}, u_2^{ub}) is synthesised (see [35]).

Theorem 5 (LPs for upper bound). *For a particle-based belief* $(s_1, b_1) \in S_B$, $V_{ub}^{\Upsilon}(s_1, b_1)$ *and* $[TV_{ub}^{\Upsilon}](s_1, b_1)$ *are the optimal value of an LP, respectively.*

7   Experimental Evaluation

We have built a prototype implementation in Python, using Gurobi [16] to solve the LPs needed for computing lower and upper bound values, and the minimax values and strategies of one-shot games. We use the Parma Polyhedra Library [1] to operate over polyhedral pre-images of NNs, α-functions and reward structures.

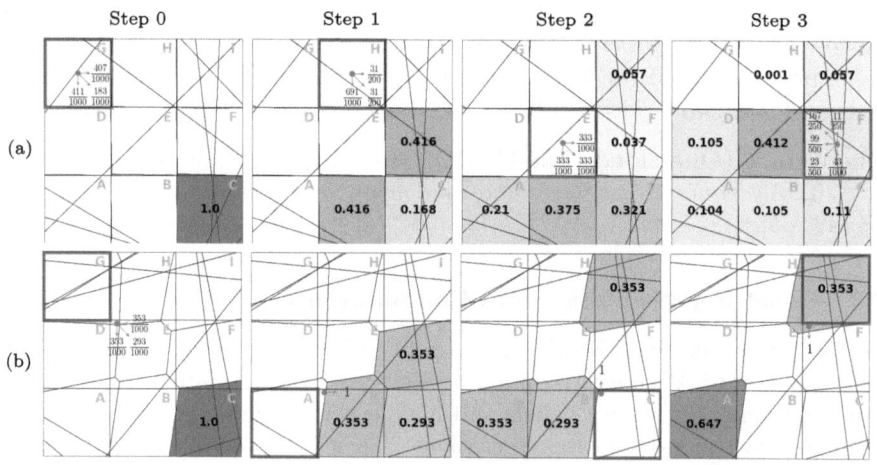

Fig. 2. Simulations of strategies for the pursuer, showing actual location (red), perceived location (blue), belief of evader location (green) and strategy (pink) for two different NN perception functions: (a) more precise; (b) coarser. (Color figure online)

Our evaluation uses two one-sided NS-POSG examples: a *pursuit-evasion* game and the *pedestrian-vehicle* scenario from Sect. 3. Below, we discuss the applicability and usefulness of our techniques on these examples. Due to limited space, we refer to [35] for more details of the models, including the training of the ReLU NN classifiers, and empirical results on performance.

Pursuit-Evasion. A pursuit-evasion game models a *pursuer* trying to catch an *evader* aiming to avoid capture. We build a continuous-space variant of the model from [19] inspired by mobile robotics applications [8,20]. The environment includes the exact position of both agents. The (partially informed) pursuer uses an NN classifier to perceive its own location, which maps to one of 3×3 grid cells.

To showcase the ability of our methodology to assess the performance of realistic NN perception functions, we train two NNs, the second with a coarser accuracy.

Figure 2 shows simulations of strategies synthesised for the pursuer, using the two different NNs. Its actual location is a red dot, and the pink arrows denote the strategy. Blue squares show the cell that is output by the pursuer's perception function, and black lines mark the underlying polyhedral decomposition. The pursuer's belief over the evader's location is shown by the green shading and annotated probabilities; it initially (correctly) believes that the evader is in cell C and the belief evolves based on the optimal counter-strategy of the evader.

The plots show we can synthesise non-trivial strategies for agents using NN-based perception in a partially observable setting. We can also study the impact of a poorly trained perception function. Figure 2(b), for the coarser NN, shows the pursuer repeatedly mis-detecting its location because the grid cells shapes are poorly approximated, and subsequently taking incorrect actions. This is exploited by the evader, leading to considerably worse performance for the pursuer.

Pedestrian-Vehicle Interaction. Figure 3 shows several simulations from strategies synthesised for the pedestrian-vehicle example described in Sect. 3 (Fig. 1), plotting the position (x_2, y_2) of the pedestrian, relative to the vehicle. We fix the pedestrian's strategy, to simulate a crossing scenario: it moves from right to left, i.e., decreasing x_2. The (partially informed) vehicle's perception function predicts the intention of the pedestrian (green/yellow/red = *unlikely/likely/very likely* to cross), shown as coloured dots. Above and below each circle, we indicate the acceleration actions taken (black) and current speeds (orange), respectively, which determine the distance y_2 to the pedestrian crossing.

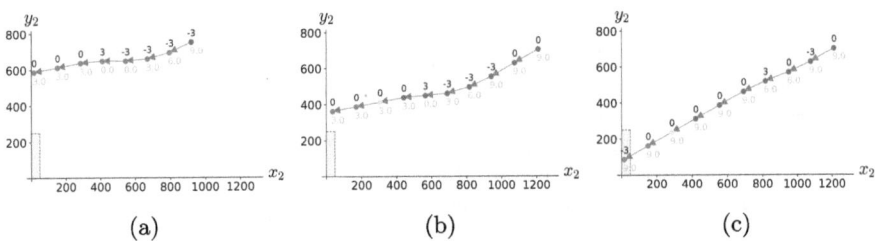

(a)   (b)   (c)

Fig. 3. Simulations of strategies for the vehicle, plotted as the pedestrian's current position (x_2, y_2) relative to it. Also shown: perceived pedestrian intention (green/yellow/red = *unlikely/likely/very likely* to cross), current speed (orange), acceleration (black) and crash region (shaded purple region). (Color figure online)

Again, we investigate the feasibility of generating strategies for agents with realistic NN-based perception. Here, the goal is to avoid a crash scenario, denoted by the shaded region at the bottom left of the plots. We find that, in many cases, safe strategies can be synthesised. Figure 3(a) shows an example; notice that the pedestrian intention is detected early. This is not true in (b) and (c), which show two simulations from a strategy and starting point where the perception function results in much later detection; (c) shows we were then unable to synthesise a strategy for the vehicle that is always safe.

8 Conclusions

We have proposed one-sided neuro-symbolic POSGs, designed to reason formally about partially observable agents equipped with neural perception mechanisms. We characterised the value function for discounted infinite-horizon rewards, and designed, implemented and evaluated a HSVI algorithm for approximate solution. Computational complexity is high due to expensive polyhedral operations. Nevertheless, our method provides an important baseline that can reason about true decision boundaries for game models with NN-based perception, against which efficiency improvements can later be benchmarked. We plan to investigate ways to improve performance, e.g., merging of adjacent polyhedra or Monte-Carlo planning methods, and to study restricted cases of two-sided NS-POSGs, e.g., those with public observations [18].

Acknowledgements. This project was funded by the ERC under the European Union's Horizon 2020 research and innovation programme (FUN2MODEL, grant agreement No.834115).

References

1. Bagnara, R., Hill, P.M., Zaffanella, E.: The Parma Polyhedra Library: toward a complete set of numerical abstractions for the analysis and verification of hardware and software systems. Sci. Comput. Programm. **72**(1), 3–21 (2008). https://www.bugseng.com/ppl

2. Bhabak, A., Saha, S.: Partially observable discrete-time discounted Markov games with general utility. arXiv:2211.07888 (2022)

3. Bosansky, B., Kiekintveld, C., Lisy, V., Pechoucek, M.: An exact double-oracle algorithm for zero-sum extensive-form games with imperfect information. J. Artif. Intell. Res. **51**, 829–866 (2014)

4. Brechtel, S., Gindele, T., Dillmann, R.: Solving Continuous POMDPs: value iteration with incremental learning of an efficient space representation. In: Proceedings of ICML'13, pp. 370–378. PMLR (2013)

5. Brown, N., Bakhtin, A., Lerer, A., Gong, Q.: Combining deep reinforcement learning and search for imperfect-information games. In: Proceedings of NeurIPS'20, pp. 17057–17069. Curran Associates, Inc. (2020)

6. Burks, L., Loefgren, I., Ahmed, N.R.: Optimal continuous state POMDP planning with semantic observations: a variational approach. IEEE Trans. Rob. **35**(6), 1488–1507 (2019)

7. Carr, S., Jansen, N., Bharadwaj, S., Spaan, M.T., Topcu, U.: Safe policies for factored partially observable stochastic games. In: Robotics: Science and System XVII (2021)

8. Chung, T.H., Hollinger, G.A., Isler, V.: Search and pursuit-evasion in mobile robotics. Auton. Robot. **31**(4), 299–316 (2011)

9. Delage, A., Buffet, O., Dibangoye, J.S., Saffidine, A.: HSVI can solve zero-sum partially observable stochastic games. Dyn. Games Appl., 1–55 (2023)
10. Doucet, A., Freitas, N., Gordon, N. (eds.): Sequential Monte Carlo Methods in Practice. Springer, New York, NY (2001). https://doi.org/10.1007/978-1-4757-3437-9
11. Emery-Montemerlo, R., Gordon, G., Schneider, J., Thrun, S.: Approximate solutions for partially observable stochastic games with common payoffs. In: Proceedings of AAMAS'04, pp. 136–143. IEEE (2004)
12. Feng, Z., Dearden, R., Meuleau, N., Washington, R.: Dynamic programming for structured continuous Markov decision problems. In: Proceedings of UAI'04, pp. 154–161 (2004)
13. Fu, T., Miranda-Moreno, L., Saunier, N.: A novel framework to evaluate pedestrian safety at non-signalized locations. Accid. Anal. Prev. **111**, 23–33 (2018)
14. Ghosh, M.K., McDonald, D., Sinha, S.: Zero-sum stochastic games with partial information. J. Optim. Theory Appl. **121**, 99–118 (2004)
15. Guestrin, C., Hauskrecht, M., Kveton, B.: Solving factored MDPs with continuous and discrete variables. In: Proceedings of UAI'04, pp. 235–242 (2004)
16. Gurobi Optimization, LLC: Gurobi Optimizer Reference Manual (2021). https://www.gurobi.com
17. Hansen, E.A., Bernstein, D.S., Zilberstein, S.: Dynamic programming for partially observable stochastic games. In: Proceedings of AAAI'04, vol. 4, pp. 709–715 (2004)
18. Horák, K., Bošanský, B.: Solving partially observable stochastic games with public observations. In: Proceedings of AAAI'19, vol. 33, pp. 2029–2036 (2019)
19. Horák, K., Bošanský, B., Kovařík, V., Kiekintveld, C.: Solving zero-sum one-sided partially observable stochastic games. Artif. Intell. **316**, 103838 (2023)
20. Isler, V., Nikhil, K.: The role of information in the cop-robber game. Theoret. Comput. Sci. **399**(3), 179–190 (2008)
21. Kovařík, V., Schmid, M., Burch, N., Bowling, M., Lisý, V.: Rethinking formal models of partially observable multiagent decision making. Artif. Intell. **303**, 103645 (2022)
22. Kovařík, V., Seitz, D., Lisý, V., Rudolf, J., Sun, S., Ha, K.: Value functions for depth-limited solving in zero-sum imperfect-information games. Artif. Intell. **314**, 103805 (2023)
23. Kumar, A., Zilberstein, S.: Dynamic programming approximations for partially observable stochastic games. In: Proceedings of FLAIRS'09, pp. 547–552 (2009)
24. Madani, O., Hanks, S., Condon, A.: On the undecidability of probabilistic planning and related stochastic optimization problems. Artif. Intell. **147**(1–2), 5–34 (2003)
25. Matoba, K., Fleuret, F.: Computing preimages of deep neural networks with applications to safety (2020). https://openreview.net/forum?id=FN7_BUOG78e
26. Moravčík, M., et al.: DeepStack: expert-level artificial intelligence in heads-up no-limit poker. Science **356**(6337), 508–513 (2017)
27. Porta, J.M., Vlassis, N., Spaan, M.T., Poupart, P.: Point-based value iteration for continuous POMDPs. J. Mach. Learn. Res. **7**, 2329–2367 (2006)
28. Rasouli, A., Kotseruba, I., Kunic, T., Tsotsos, J.K.: PIE: a large-scale dataset and models for pedestrian intention estimation and trajectory prediction. In: Proceedings of ICCV'19, pp. 6262–6271 (2019)
29. Rasouli, A., Kotseruba, I., Tsotsos, J.K.: Are they going to cross? A benchmark dataset and baseline for pedestrian crosswalk behavior. In: Proceedings of ICCV'17, pp. 206–213 (2017)
30. Saha, S.: Zero-sum stochastic games with partial information and average payoff. J. Optim. Theory Appl. **160**(1), 344–354 (2014)

31. Smith, T., Simmons, R.: Heuristic search value iteration for POMDPs. In: Proceedings of UAI'04, pp. 520–527. AUAI (2004)
32. Wiggers, A.J., Oliehoek, F.A., Roijers, D.M.: Structure in the value function of two-player zero-sum games of incomplete information. Front. Artif. Intell. Appl. **285**, 1628–1629 (2016)
33. Yan, R., Santos, G., Norman, G., Parker, D., Kwiatkowska, M.: Strategy synthesis for zero-sum neuro-symbolic concurrent stochastic games. arXiv 2202.06255 (2022)
34. Yan, R., Santos, G., Duan, X., Parker, D., Kwiatkowska, M.: Finite-horizon equilibria for neuro-symbolic concurrent stochastic games. In: Proceedings of UAI'22, pp. 2170–2180. AUAI Press (2022)
35. Yan, R., Santos, G., Norman, G., Parker, D., Kwiatkowska, M.: Partially observable stochastic games with neural perception mechanisms. arXiv:2310.11566 (2023)
36. Yan, R., Santos, G., Norman, G., Parker, D., Kwiatkowska, M.: Point-based value iteration for POMDPs with neural perception mechanisms. arXiv 2306.17639 (2023)
37. Yan, R., Santos, G., Norman, G., Parker, D., Kwiatkowska, M.: HSVI-based online minimax strategies for partially observable stochastic games with neural perception mechanisms. In: Proceedings of L4DC'24 (2024)
38. Zamani, Z., Sanner, S., Poupart, P., Kersting, K.: Symbolic dynamic programming for continuous state and observation POMDPs. In: Advances in Neural Information Processing Systems, vol. 25 (2012)
39. Zettlemoyer, L., Milch, B., Kaelbling, L.: Multi-agent filtering with infinitely nested beliefs. In: Advances in Neural Information Processing Systems, vol. 21 (2008)
40. Zheng, W., Jung, T., Lin, H.: The Stackelberg equilibrium for one-sided zero-sum partially observable stochastic games. Automatica **140**, 110231 (2022)
41. Zheng, W., Jung, T., Lin, H.: Continuous-observation one-sided two-player zero-sum partially observable stochastic game with public actions. IEEE Trans. Autom. Control, 1–15 (2023)
42. Zinkevich, M., Johanson, M., Bowling, M., Piccione, C.: Regret minimization in games with incomplete information. In: Advances in Neural Information Processing Systems, vol. 20 (2007)

Bridging Dimensions: Confident Reachability for High-Dimensional Controllers

Yuang Geng[1]([✉]) [iD], Jake Brandon Baldauf[1] [iD], Souradeep Dutta[2] [iD],
Chao Huang[3] [iD], and Ivan Ruchkin[1] [iD]

[1] University of Florida, Gainesville, FL, USA
{yuang.geng,jakebaldauf}@ufl.edu, iruchkin@ece.ufl.edu
[2] University of Pennsylvania, Philadelphia, PA, USA
duttaso@seas.upenn.edu
[3] University of Southampton, Southampton, UK
chao.huang@soton.ac.uk

Abstract. Autonomous systems are increasingly implemented using end-to-end learning-based controllers. Such controllers make decisions that are executed on the real system, with images as one of the primary sensing modalities. Deep neural networks form a fundamental building block of such controllers. Unfortunately, the existing neural-network verification tools do not scale to inputs with thousands of dimensions—especially when the individual inputs (such as pixels) are devoid of clear physical meaning. This paper takes a step towards connecting exhaustive closed-loop verification with high-dimensional controllers. Our key insight is that the behavior of a high-dimensional vision-based controller can be approximated with several low-dimensional controllers. To balance the approximation accuracy and verifiability of our low-dimensional controllers, we leverage the latest verification-aware knowledge distillation. Then, we inflate low-dimensional reachability results with statistical approximation errors, yielding a high-confidence reachability guarantee for the high-dimensional controller. We investigate two inflation techniques—based on trajectories and control actions—both of which show convincing performance in three OpenAI gym benchmarks.

Keywords: reachability · neural-network control · conformal prediction

1 Introduction

End-to-end deep neural network controllers have been extensively used in executing complex and safety-critical autonomous systems in recent years [13,40, 51,52]. In particular, *high-dimensional controllers* (HDCs) based on images and other high-dimensional inputs have been applied in areas such as autonomous car navigation [49,61] and aircraft landing guidance [47]. For example, recent work

© The Author(s) 2025
A. Platzer et al. (Eds.): FM 2024, LNCS 14933, pp. 381–402, 2025.
https://doi.org/10.1007/978-3-031-71162-6_20

has shown the high performance of controlling aircraft to land on the runway with a vision-based controller [65]. For such critical applications, it is important to develop techniques with strong safety guarantees for HDC-controlled systems.

However, due to the high-dimensional nature of the input space, modern verification cannot be applied directly to systems controlled by HDCs [2,43]. Current closed-loop verification tools, such as NNV [54], Verisig [30], Sherlock [18], and ReachNN* [28], are capable of combining a dynamical system and a *low-dimensional controller* (LDC) to verify a safety property starting from an initial region of the low-dimensional input space, such as position-velocity states of a car. DeepReach [5] has pushed the boundary of applying Hamilton-Jacobi (HJ) reachability to systems with tens of state dimensions. However, such verification tools fail to scale for an input with thousands of dimensions (e.g., an image). One issue is that the dynamics of these dimensions are impractical to describe. Furthermore, the structure of an HDC is usually more complicated than that of an LDC, with convolution and pooling layers. For example, an image-based HDC may have hundreds of layers with thousands of neurons, whereas an LDC usually contains several layers with dozens of neurons, making HDC verification difficult.

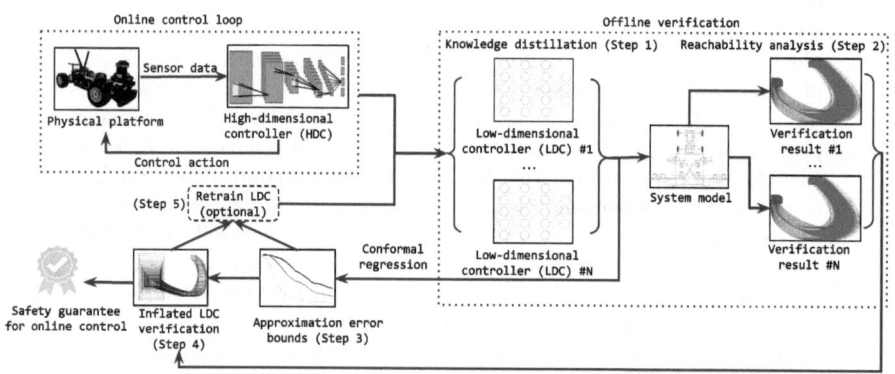

Fig. 1. Our verification approach for systems with high-dimensional controllers.

To deal with these challenges, researchers have built perception abstractions into the verification process. One work [31] verified a generative adversarial network (GAN) that creates images from states. Such methods cannot guarantee the GAN's accuracy or relation to reality, which becomes a major falsifiable assumption of their verification outcomes. Another work [47] built a precise mathematical model capturing the exact relationship between states and image pixels to verify the image-based controller, which is effortful and needs to be redone for each system. Inspired by previous work on decreasing the dimensions, we skillfully create verifiable low-dimensional controllers from high-dimensional ones.

This paper proposes an **end-to-end methodology** to verify systems with HDCs by employing the steps displayed in Fig. 1. Instead of verifying an HDC's safety directly over a complicated input space, our key idea is to approximate it with several LDCs so that we can reduce the HDC reachability problem to several LDC reachability problems. A crucial step is to upper-bound the difference between LDC and HDC, which we do statistically. Finally, we extend the reachable sets with the statistical bounds to obtain a safety guarantee for the HDC.

Since the input space and structure of the HDC are too complex to verify, we leverage *knowledge distillation* [25]—a model compression method—to train simplified "student models" (LDC) based on the information from the sophisticated "teacher model" (HDC). This training produces an LDC that is lightweight and amenable to closed-loop verification because it operates on dynamical states, not images. Moreover, due to the importance of the Lipschitz to minimizing the overapproximation error [28,29], our methodology adopts *two-objective gradient descent* [21], decreasing both the approximation error and Lipschitz constant.

After training the LDCs, we calculate the statistical upper bound of the discrepancy between the two controllers, since obtaining the true discrepancy is impractical. To this end, we rely on *conformal prediction* [22,45,48], one of the cutting-edge statistical methods to provide a lower bound of the confidence interval for prediction residuals without distributional assumptions or explicit dependency on the sample count. We propose *two conformal techniques* to quantify the difference between HDC- and LDC-controlled systems, by bounding: (i) the distance between their trajectories, and (ii) the difference between the actions produced by the HDC and LDC. We inflate reachable sets of the LDC system based on both bounds to obtain safety guarantees on the HDC system.

We evaluate our approach on three popular case studies in OpenAI Gym [7]: inverted pendulum, mountain car, and cartpole. Our contributions are three-fold:

1. Two verification approaches for high-dimensional controllers that combine reachability analysis and statistical inference to provide a safety guarantee for systems controlled by neural networks with thousands of inputs.
2. A novel neural-network approximation technique for training multiple LDCs that collectively mimic an HDC and reduce overapproximation error.
3. An implementation and evaluation of our verification approaches on three case studies: inverted pendulum, mountain car, and cartpole.

Section 2 provides the background and our problem. Section 3 describes our verification approach, which is evaluated in Sect. 4. Finally, we review the related work in Sect. 5 and conclude in Sect. 6. More details are in the extended online version [67].

2 Background and Problem Setting

High- and Low-Dimensional Systems. The original *high-dimensional closed-loop system* is a tuple $M_{hd} = (S, Z, U, s_0, f, c_{hd}, g)$. Here, the S is the state space,

Z is the high-dimensional sensor space of so-called "images" (e.g., camera images or LIDAR scans), and the U is the control action space, s_0 is the initial state, $f : S \times U \to S$ is the dynamics, and $c_{hd} : Z \times S \to U$ is the HDC. Note that c_{hd} only uses a *subset* of state dimensions as input (e.g., a convolutional neural network with image and velocity inputs, but not position), getting the rest of the information from the image.

For mathematical convenience, we also define an (unknown) deterministic state-to-image generator as $g : S \to Z$ and the role and assumptions of generator g are stated below. As a verifiable approximation of M_{hd}, our *low-dimensional closed-loop system* is defined as $M_{ld} = (S, U, s_0, f, c_{ld})$. Both M_{hd} and M_{ld} have the same state space and action space. The only difference is that the M_{ld} has a low-dimensional controller $c_{ld} : S \to U$, which operates on the exact states.

System Execution. The execution of M_{hd} starts from the initial state s_0. Next, an image z can be generated by image generator g from that state. Then it is fed into c_{hd} to obtain a corresponding control action $u = c_{hd}(z)$, which is used to update the state via dynamics f. For M_{ld}, the execution proceeds similarly, except that the current state s directly results in a control action $u = c_{ld}(s)$. Thus, we denote the *state at time* t starting from s_0 executed by M_{hd} or M_{ld} as $\varphi_{hd}(s_0, t)$ and $\varphi_{ld}(s_0, t)$ respectively. The *trajectory* of M_{hd} is defined as a state sequence: $\tau_{hd}(s_0, T) = [s_0, \varphi_{hd}(s_0, 1), \dots, \varphi_{hd}(s_0, T)]$, and similarly for τ_{hd}.

Based on previous background, we define reachable sets and tubes:

Definition 1 (Reachable set). *Given an initial set S_0 and an integer time t, a reachable set $\mathsf{rs}_M(S_0, t)$ for (either) system M contains all the states that can be reached from S_0 in t steps: $\mathsf{rs}_M(S_0, t) = \{\varphi_M(s_0, t) \mid \forall s_0 \in S_0\}$.*

Definition 2 (Reachable tube). *Given an initial set S_0 and time horizon T, a reachable tube $\mathsf{rt}_M(S_0, T)$ for (either) system M is a sequence of all the reachable sets from S_0 until time T: $\mathsf{rt}_M(S_0, T) = [S_0, \mathsf{rs}_M(S_0, 1), ..., \mathsf{rs}_M(S_0, T)]$.*

Assumptions on Image-State Mapping g. Our key challenge is establishing a mapping between the high-dimensional image space Z and the low-dimensional state space S. Our verification methodology is based on the existence of a deterministic image generator g that is part of M_{hd}. This generator is the true and *unknown* mechanism that creates images from states (e.g., a camera system). We do *not* assume or use an analyzable closed-form description of g. We also do not assume or verify any perception model (which obtains states from images).

We only use g in the training process for a limited state-image dataset, analogously to a "lab study" of an instrumented system M_{hd} (e.g., with positioning sensors or human annotators) to label each image z with a corresponding low-dimensional state s. Further, to check our robustness to this assumption, we will perform a sensitivity analysis by adding zero-mean Gaussian noise to the state-image mapping. The results of this evaluation will be discussed in Sect. 4.

Verification Problem. Our problem is to guarantee that the high-dimensional system M_{hd} reaches the goal set G from an initial set S_0 within time T. To this end, we aim to compute reachable sets of the high-dimensional system M_{hd} and intersect them with the goal set to obtain the verification verdict. Set G

is specified in low dimensions (i.e., using physical variables); however, the M_{hd} behavior is determined by the images from generator g and the HDC's response to them.

Thus, given an initial set S_0, goal set G, system M_{hd}, and time horizon T, our goal is to verify this assertion:

$$\forall s_0 \in S_0 \cdot \mathsf{rs}_{M_{hd}}(S_0, T) \subseteq G \tag{1}$$

This problem can be divided into two parts: (a) approximating M_{hd} with low-dimensional systems $M_{ld}^1, \ldots, M_{ld}^n$ and verifying them; (b) combining these reachability results based on the approximation error bounds into a reachability verdict to solve the above M_{hd} problem with statistical confidence.

3   Verification of High-Dimensional Systems

Considering the challenges of complex structure and dynamics of high-dimensional systems, and the difficulties of defining safety in high dimensions, our end-to-end approach is structured in five steps: (1) train low-dimensional controller(s), (2) perform reachability analysis on them, (3) compute statistical discrepancy bounds between high- and low-dimensional controllers, (4) inflate the reachable tubes from low-dimensional verification with these bounds, and (5) combine the verification results and repeat the process as if needed on different states/LDCs.

Step 1: Training Low-Dimensional Controllers

Given the aforementioned challenges of directly verifying M_{hd}, we plan to first verify the behavior in the low dimensions according to M_{ld}. Hence, we train a c_{ld} to imitate the performance of c_{hd} starting from a given state region, which serves as an input to Step 1 (our first iteration uses the full initial state region S_0 to train one c_{ld}). As a start, we collect the training data for c_{ld}: given the c_{hd}, access to image generator g, and the initial state space region S_0, we construct a supervised training dataset $\mathcal{D}_{tr} = \left\{ \left(\tau_{hd}(s_i, T), (u_1, \ldots, u_T)_i \right) \right\}_{i=1}^m$ by sampling the initial states $s_i \sim D_0$ from some given distribution D_0 (in practice, $D_0 = \mathrm{Uniform}(S_0)$).

Training a verifiable LDC has two conflicting objectives. On the one hand, we want to approximate the given c_{hd} with minimal Mean Squared Error (MSE) on $\mathcal{D}_{tr}$. On the other hand, neural networks with smaller Lipschitz constants are more predictable and verifiable [15,23,50].

We balance the ability of the c_{ld} to mimic the c_{hd} and the verifiability of c_{ld} by using a recent *verification-aware knowledge distillation technique* [21]. Originally, this method was developed to compress low-dimensional neural networks for better verifiability—and we extend it to approximate an HDC with LDCs using the supervised dataset $\mathcal{D}_{tr}$. Specifically, we implement knowledge distillation with *two-objective gradient descent*, which aims to optimize the MSE loss function L_{mse} and Lipschitz constant loss function L_{lip}. First, it computes the directions of two gradients with respect to the c_{ld} parameters θ:

$$d_{L_{mse}} = \frac{\partial L_{mse}}{\partial \theta}, \quad d_{L_{lip}} = \frac{\partial L_{lip}}{\partial \theta} \tag{2}$$

The two-objective descent operates case-by-case to optimize at least one objective as long as possible. If $d_{L_{mse}} \cdot d_{L_{lip}} > 0$, the objectives can be optimized simultaneously by following the direction of the angular bisector of the two gradients. If $d_{L_{mse}} \cdot d_{L_{lip}} < 0$, then it is impossible to improve both objectives. Then, weights are updated along the vector of $d_{L_{mse}}$ (the higher priority) projected onto the hyperplane perpendicular to $d_{L_{lip}}$. The thresholds for MSE and Lipschitz constants in our system M_{ld} are denoted as ϵ and λ respectively. The stopping condition is met when both loss functions are below their thresholds or the training time exceeds the limit. Later on, Step 1 will be referred to with function TRAINLDC, and our way of tuning ϵ and λ will be described later in Step 5.

Step 2: Reachability Analysis In Low Dimensions

After training LDCs $\{c_{ld}^1, ..., c_{ld}^m\}$, we construct overapproximate reachable tubes for each. We perform reachability analysis for systems $M_{ld}^1, ..., M_{ld}^m$ with the respective controllers and the initial set S_0 specified in the original verification problem. This will result in a set of reachable tubes $\mathrm{rt}_{M_{ld}^1}(S_0, T), ..., \mathrm{rt}_{M_{ld}^m}(S_0, T)$.

To implement reachability analysis, we use the *POLAR toolbox* (https://github.com/ChaoHuang2018/POLAR_Tool), version of December 2022 [27,62], which computes univariate Bernstein polynomials to overapproximate activation functions in c_{ld}, and then tightly and selectively overapproximates c_{ld} with Taylor/Bernstein polynomials. For dynamics reachability, alternating with neural-network overapproximation, POLAR relies on the mature Flow* tool with Taylor model approximations [9]. The latest experimental results [62] show that POLAR outperforms other neural-network verification tools in both computational efficiency and tightness. The verification details are formalized in Algorithm 2 in Step 5.

Step 3a: Defining Discrepancy Bounds

The LDC reachable tubes from Step 2 cannot be used directly to obtain HDC guarantees because of the discrepancy between LDC and HDC behaviors, which inevitably arises when compressing a higher-parameter neural network [24]. Therefore, we will quantify the difference between LDCs and HDCs using *discrepancy functions*, inspired by the prior work on testing hybrid systems [19,20,44]. We introduce and investigate two types of discrepancy functions in our setting:

1. Trajectory-based discrepancy β considers the difference between the HDC and LDC *trajectories* starting from a *matched* state-image pair (s, z), i.e., $z =$

$g(s)$. It is defined as the least upper bound on the maximum L1 distance between two trajectories, i.e., $\|\tau_{hd}(s_0, T) - \tau_{ld}(s_0, T)\|_1$, over time T for all initial states s_0 within the initial set S_0. Therefore, each initial set S_0 gives rise to its trajectory-based discrepancy $\beta(S_0)$.

2. Action-based discrepancy γ considers the difference between LDC and HDC *actions* on a *matched* state-image pair (s, z), i.e., $z = g(s)$. Similarly to the above, it is defined as the least upper bound on the difference between control actions over time horizon T starting from any initial state s_0 within the initial set S_0. Note that the control difference, $\|c_{hd}(g(s_{hd}^t)) - c_{ld}(s_{ld}^t)\|_1$, is considered at each time step, where the s is each state in the two trajectories.

Step 3b: Computing Statistical Discrepancy Bounds

Unfortunately, obtaining the true discrepancies is impractical: it would require solving optimization/feasibility problems in high-dimensional image spaces. Instead, we calculate the statistical upper bounds for these discrepancies via *conformal prediction*, which is a distribution-free statistical technique to provide probabilistically valid uncertainty regions for complex prediction models—without strong assumptions about these models or their error distributions [55].

Below we briefly summarize basic conformal prediction. Consider $k + 1$ independent and identically distributed random variables $\Delta, \Delta^1, ..., \Delta^k$, also known as *non-conformity scores*. Conformal prediction computes an uncertainty region for Δ via a function $\bar{\Delta} : \mathbb{R}^k \to \mathbb{R}$ from the other k values. Given a failure probability $\alpha \in (0, 1)$, conformal prediction provides an uncertainty bound on $\bar{\Delta}$ such that $\Pr(\Delta \leq \bar{\Delta}) \geq 1 - \alpha$. This is performed with a surprisingly simple quantile argument, where the uncertainty bound $\bar{\Delta}$ is calculated as the $(1 - \alpha)$-th quantile of the empirical distribution over the values of $\Delta^1, \Delta^2, ..., \Delta^k$, and ∞. The guarantee is formalized in the lemma below, and for details see a popular tutorial [48].

Lemma 1. *(Lemma 1 in [22]) Let $\Delta, \Delta^1, \Delta^2, ..., \Delta^k$ be $k+1$ independent identically distributed real-valued random variables. Without loss of generality, let $\Delta, \Delta^1, \Delta^2, ..., \Delta^k$ be stored in non-decreasing order and define $\Delta^{k+1} := \infty$. For $\alpha \in (0, 1)$, it holds that $\Pr(\Delta \leq \bar{\Delta}) \geq 1 - \alpha$ where $\bar{\Delta} := \Delta^{(r)}$, which is the r-ranked variable with $r = \lceil (k + 1)(1 - \alpha) \rceil$, and $\lceil . \rceil$ is the ceiling function.*

Leveraging conformal prediction, we define the statistical versions of our discrepancy functions. For the trajectory-based one, we define the non-conformity as the maximum L1 distance between states at the same time in two matched trajectories $\tau_{ld}(s_0, T)$ and $\tau_{hd}(s_0, T)$ starting from a random state $s_0 \sim D_0$ sampled independently and identically distributed (i.i.d.) from a given distribution D_0 over the initial region S_0, similar to recent works [11,44]. This leads to a trajectory dataset $\mathcal{D}_{tb}$, from which k non-conformity scores are calculated.

Definition 3 (Statistical trajectory-based discrepancy). *Given distribution D_0 over S_0, confidence $\alpha \in (0, 1)$, and state functions $\varphi_{hd}(s, t)$ and $\varphi_{ld}(s, t)$*

for systems M_{hd} and M_{ld}, a statistical trajectory-based discrepancy $\bar{\beta}(D_0)$ is an α-confident upper bound on the max trajectory distance starting from $s_0 \sim D_0$:

$$\Pr{}_{s_0 \sim D_0} \left[\max_{t=0..T} \|\varphi_{hd}(s_0, t) - \varphi_{ld}(s_0, t)\|_1 \leq \bar{\beta}(D_0) \right] \geq 1 - \alpha$$

To obtain this bound $\bar{\beta}(D_0)$, we leverage conformal prediction as follows. Dataset $\mathcal{D}_{tb}$ contains i.i.d. samples $s_1, s_2, ..., s_k$ from our chosen distribution D_0. In practice, we choose the uniform distribution, namely $s \sim \text{Uniform}(S)$, because we value the safety of each state equally. We compute the corresponding non-conformity scores $\delta^1, \delta^2, ..., \delta^k, \delta^{k+1}$ as the maximum L1 distances between the same-time states in the two trajectories over all times $t \in [0..T]$:

$$\delta^i = \max_{t=0..T} \|\varphi_{hd}(s_i, t) - \varphi_{ld}(s_i, t)\|_1 \text{ for } i = 1 \ldots k; \text{ and } \delta^{k+1} = \infty$$

We sort the scores in the increasing order and set $\bar{\beta}(S_0)$ to the r-th quantile:

$$\bar{\beta}(D_0) := \delta^{(r)} \text{ with } r = \lceil (k+1)(1-\alpha) \rceil \tag{3}$$

We follow a similar procedure for the statistical action-based discrepancy, except that now the non-conformity scores are defined as the maximum differences between actions at the same time in two paired trajectories.

Definition 4 (Statistical action-based discrepancy). *Given confidence $\alpha \in (0, 1)$, distribution D_0 over S_0, and systems M_{ld} and M_{hd}, a statistical action-based discrepancy $\bar{\gamma}(D_0)$ is an α-confident upper bound on maximum action discrepancy in two trajectories starting from $s_0 \sim D_0$:*

$$\Pr{}_{D(S_0)} \left[\max_{t=0..T} \|c_{hd}\big(g(\varphi_{hd}(s_0, t))\big) - c_{ld}\big(\varphi_{ld}(s_0, t)\big)\|_1 \leq \bar{\gamma}(D_0) \right] \geq 1 - \alpha$$

To implement this statistical action-based discrepancy function, we sample initial states $s_1, s_2, ..., s_k$ from a given set S_0 following the distribution D_0 (in practice, uniform) and obtain the corresponding low-dimensional trajectories. Then we generate with g the corresponding images matched to each state in each trajectory—and these pairs form our action-based dataset $\mathcal{D}_{ab}$. The corresponding nonconformity scores $\delta^1, \delta^2, ..., \delta^k, \delta^{k+1}$ are maximum action differences:

$$\delta^i = \max_{t=0..T} \|c_{hd}(g(\varphi_{hd}(s_0, t))) - c_{ld}(\varphi_{ld}(s_0, t))\|_1 \text{ for } i = 1 \ldots k; \delta^{k+1} = \infty.$$

Then we sort these non-conformity scores in the non-decreasing order and determine the statistical bound for the action-based discrepancy as:

$$\bar{\gamma}(D_0) := \delta^{(r)} \text{ with } r = \lceil (k+1)(1-\alpha) \rceil \tag{4}$$

Step 4: Inflating Reachability With Discrepancies

This step combines low-dimensional reachable tubes (Step 2) with statistical discrepancies (Step 3b) to provide a safety guarantee on the high-dimensional system. Thus, we inflate the original LDC reach tubes with either trajectory or action discrepancy to contain the (unknown) true HDC tube with chance $1 - \alpha$.

Trajectory-Based Inflation. The trajectory-based approach inflates the LDC reachable set starting in region S_0 with the statistical trajectory-based discrepancy $\bar{\beta}(D_0)$. Since the final reachable tube for a given initial set of c_{ld} is represented as a sequence of discrete state polytopes calculated by concretizing the Taylor model with interval arithmetic on the initial set [27], we inflate these polygons by adding $\bar{\beta}(D_0)$ to their boundaries.

Definition 5 (Trajectory-inflated reachable set). *Given a distribution D_0 over initial set S_0 that is controlled by LDC c_{ld}, reachable set $\mathsf{rs}(S_0, t)$, and its trajectory discrepancy $\bar{\beta}(D_0)$, a trajectory-inflated reachable set is defined as:*

$$\mathsf{irs}(S_0, t, \bar{\beta}(D_0)) = \left\{ s \in S \mid \exists s' \in \mathsf{rs}(S_0, t) \cdot \|s - s'\|_1 \leq \bar{\beta}(D_0) \right\}$$

Definition 6 (Trajectory-inflated reachable tube). *Given a distribution D_0 over initial set S_0 that is controlled by LDC c_{ld}, a reachable tube $\mathsf{rt}(S_0, t) = \left[S_0, \mathsf{rs}(S_0, 1), \ldots, \mathsf{rs}(S_0, T) \right]$ over time horizon T, and its trajectory discrepancy $\bar{\beta}(D_0)$ over the initial set S_0, a trajectory-inflated reachable tube $\mathsf{irt}(S_0, \bar{\beta}(D_0))$ is defined as:*

$$\mathsf{irt}(S_0, \bar{\beta}(D_0)) = \left[\mathsf{irs}(S_0, 0, \bar{\beta}(D_0)), \mathsf{irs}(S_0, 1, \bar{\beta}(D_0)), \ldots, \mathsf{irs}(S_0, T, \bar{\beta}(D_0)) \right].$$

Based on Definitions 5 and 6, we establish Theorem 1 that the trajectory-inflated LDC reachable tube contains the HDC reachable tube with at least $1 - \alpha$ probability.

Theorem 1 (Confident trajectory-based overapproximation). *Consider distribution D_0 over initial set S_0, confidence α, a high-dimensional system M_{hd}, approximated with a low-dimensional system controlled by c_{ld} with an α-confident statistical trajectory-based discrepancy function $\bar{\beta}(S_0)$. Then the trajectory-inflated low-dimensional tube $\mathsf{irt}_{M_{ld}}(S_0, \bar{\beta}(D_0))$ contains the high-dimensional reachable tube $\mathsf{rt}_{M_{hd}}(S_0)$ with probability $1 - \alpha$:*

$$\mathrm{Pr}_{D_0} \left[\mathsf{rt}_{M_{hd}}(S_0) \subseteq \mathsf{irt}_{M_{ld}}(S_0, \bar{\beta}(S_0)) \right] \geq 1 - \alpha$$

Proof. All the proofs are found in the extended online version [67].

Definitions 5 and 6 and Theorem 1 describe inflation and guarantees with a *single LDC*. However, one LDC usually cannot mimic the behavior of the HDC accurately. Therefore, we train several LDCs $\{c_{ld}^1, c_{ld}^2, \ldots, c_{ld}^m\}$, one for each subregion of initial set $\{S_1, S_2, \ldots, S_m\}$ with respective distributions $D_0 = \{D_1, D_2, \ldots, D_m\}$. Subsequently, the trajectory-inflated tube with multiple LDCs can be represented as a union of all the single trajectory-inflated tube $\mathsf{irt}(S_0, \bar{\beta}(D_0)) := \bigcup_{i=1}^{m} \mathsf{irt}(S_i, \bar{\beta}(D_i))$.

Action-Based Inflation. Action-based inflation is less direct than with trajectories: we inflate the neural network's *output set* that is represented by a *Taylor* *model* $\mathrm{TM}(p(S_0), I)$ [27], where $p(S_0)$ is a polynomial representing order-k Taylor series expansion of the c_{ld} activation functions in region S_0, and the remainder interval I ensures that Taylor model overapproximates the neural network's output. In this context, we widen the bounds of the remainder interval I in the last layer of the c_{ld} by our statistical action-based discrepancy $\bar{\gamma}(D_0)$, ensuring that the potential outputs of c_{hd} are contained in the resulting Taylor model.

Definition 7 (Action-inflated reachable set). *Given distribution D_0 over set S_0 that is controlled by LDC c_{ld}, statistical action-based discrepancy $\bar{\gamma}(D_0)$, and low-dimensional control bounds $[u_{min}(t), u_{max}(t)] \supseteq c_{ld}(S_0)$, the action-inflated reachable set contains states reachable by inflating the action bounds:*

$$\mathrm{irs}(S_0, \bar{\gamma}(D_0)) = \left\{ f(s, u) \mid s \in S_0, u \in [u_{min}(t) - \bar{\gamma}(D_0), u_{max}(t) + \bar{\gamma}(D_0)] \right\}$$

Definition 8 (Action-inflated reachable tube). *Given an distribution D_0 over initial set S_0 that is controlled by LDC c_{ld}, dynamics f, time horizon T, and action-based discrepancy functions $\bar{\gamma}(D_0)$, the action-inflated reachable tube is a recursive sequence of inflated action-based reachable sets:*

$$\mathrm{irt}(S_0, \bar{\gamma}(D_0)) = \left[S_0, \mathrm{irs}_1(S_0, \bar{\gamma}(D_0)), \mathrm{irs}_2(\mathrm{irs}_1, \bar{\gamma}(D_0)), \dots, \mathrm{irs}_T(\mathrm{irs}_{T-1}, \bar{\gamma}(D_0)) \right].$$

Based on Definitions 7 and 8, we put forward Theorem 2 below for the lower probability bound of the action-inflated LDC tube containing the true HDC tube.

Theorem 2 (Confident action-based overapproximation). *Consider distribution D_0 over initial set S_0, high-dimensional system M_{hd} with controller c_{hd}, approximated by low-dimensional system M_{ld} controlled by c_{ld} with α-confident statistical action-based discrepancies $\bar{\gamma}(S_0)$. Then the action-inflated low-dimensional tube $\mathrm{irt}_{M_{ld}}(S_0, \bar{\gamma}(S_0))$ contains the high-dimensional tube $\mathrm{rt}_{M_{hd}}(S_0)$ with probability $1 - \alpha$:*

$$\Pr_{D_0} \left[\mathrm{rt}_{M_{hd}}(S_0) \subseteq \mathrm{irt}_{M_{ld}}(S_0, \bar{\gamma}(S_0)) \right] \geq 1 - \alpha$$

Definitions 7 and 8 describe inflation with a *single LDC*, which we extend to multiple LDCs by taking the union of all the LDCs' inflated tubes. Given a partitioned initial set $S_0 = \{S_1, ..., S_m\}$ with respective controllers $\{c_{ld}^1, ..., c_{ld}^m\}$ and distributions $D_0 = \{D_1, ..., D_m\}$, the multiple LDCs action-inflated reachable tube is $\mathrm{irt}(S_0, \bar{\gamma}(D_0)) := \bigcup_{i=1}^m \mathrm{irt}(S_i, \bar{\gamma}(D_i))$. As it turns out, this reachable tube also contains the HDC tube with at least $1 - \alpha$ chance.

Step 5: Iterative Retraining and Re-gridding

Once the inflated reachable tubes are obtained in Step 4, we focus on the regions of the initial set where HDC simulations succeed—yet safety verification fails. This can happen for two reasons: (i) overly high overapproximation error in the LDC reachability, or (ii) overly high conformal discrepancy bounds from $\bar{\beta}$ or $\bar{\gamma}$.

Algorithm 1. Iterative LDC training for the action-based approach

---

function IterativeTrainingAB(HDC c_{hd}, image generator g, sample count N,
initial state space S_0, confidence α, discrepancy thresh. ξ, time steps T, goal set G)

   $\lambda, \epsilon \leftarrow$ initial values
   $S \leftarrow$ initial gridding of $S_0 : S_1, S_2, \ldots$
   while Computing resources last **do**
      for $i = 1$ to $|S|$ **do**
         $c_{ld}^i \leftarrow$ TrainLDC(c_{hd}, g, S_i, λ, ϵ)
         $\delta^i \leftarrow$ ComputeActionDiscr(c_{ld}^i, c_{hd}, g, S_i, α, N)
         if $\delta^i > \xi$ **then**
            $\epsilon \leftarrow \epsilon/2$ ▷ Reduce MSE threshold
         end if
      end for
      if $\hat{\delta} > \xi$ in some sub-region $\hat{S} \subseteq S$ **then**   ▷ Too much discrepancy
         $S' \leftarrow S$ with refined re-gridding of $\hat{S}$
      end if
      if $\hat{\delta} \leq \xi \wedge \mathsf{rs}_{M_{ld}}(\hat{S}, T) \not\subseteq G$ in some sub-region $\hat{S} \subseteq S$ **then**
         $\lambda \leftarrow \lambda/2$ and keep the same ϵ in $\hat{S}$ ▷ Reduce Lipschitz threshold
      end if
      $S \leftarrow S'$ ▷ Use the updated grid
   end while
   $\bar{\gamma} \leftarrow \delta^1, \delta^2, \ldots$
   return $c_{ld}^1, c_{ld}^2, \ldots, \bar{\gamma}$
end function

Reducing Reachability Overapproximation Error. We lower the threshold for the Lipschitz constant λ to retrain the respective LDCs in Step 1. In our experience, this almost always reduces the overapproximation in the LDC analysis and makes low-dimensional reachable tubes tighter—but may result in higher statistical discrepancy bounds, which we address below.

Reducing Conformal Discrepancy Bounds. When these bounds are loose, our LDC imitates the HDC poorly in some state-space region. Here, we take inspiration from refinement techniques in testing [45,66]. When a desired discrepancy bound ξ is exceeded in a state-space region, we split it into subregions by taking its midpoints in each dimension, leading to an updated state-space grid S'. Then in each sub-region, we retrain an LDC as per Step 1 with a reduced MSE threshold ϵ and re-compute its bounds as per Step 3b. leading to tighter statistical overapproximations of HDC reachable tubes.

To summarize, Algorithm 1 shows our iterative training procedure for the action-based approach (its trajectory-based counterpart proceeds analogously, except for computing the discrepancies over trajectories).

Combining all the five steps together, we present Algorithm 2 that displays our end-to-end verification of a given HDC with either trajectory-based or action-based discrepancies. The LDCs and their discrepancies are input into the reachability analysis, implemented with the function Reach, to calculate the inflated

---

Algorithm 2. End-to-end reachability verification of an HDC

---

function ENDTOENDVERIFICATION(HDC c_{hd}, generator g, sample count N, state space S, initial set S_0, confidence α, discrepancy threshold ξ, time horizon T, goal set G, approach selection $J \in \{$ trajectory-based, action-based $\})$

    if $J =$ trajectory-based **then**

        $c_{ld}^1 \ldots c_{ld}^n, \bar{\beta} \leftarrow$ ITERATIVETRAININGTB$(c_{hd}, g, N, S_0, \alpha, \xi, T)$

        $X \leftarrow \bar{\beta}$ ▷ Store the trajectory discrepancies

    else

        $c_{ld}^1 \ldots c_{ld}^n, \bar{\gamma} \leftarrow$ ITERATIVETRAININGAB$(c_{hd}, g, N, S, \alpha, \xi, T, G)$

        $X \leftarrow \bar{\gamma}$ ▷ Store the action discrepancies

    end if

    $\mathbf{S_{ver}} \leftarrow$ split S_0 into regions: $S_0^1, S_0^2, \ldots$ ▷ Gridding for parallel verification

    $S_{safe}, S_{unsafe} \leftarrow \emptyset$ ▷ Initialize safe and unsafe regions

    for $j = 1$ to $|\mathbf{S_{ver}}|$ **do**

        irs$(S_0^j, X, T) \leftarrow$ REACH$(c_{ld}^1, \ldots, c_{ld}^n, S_0^j, X, T)$

        if irs$(S_0^j, X, T) \subseteq G$ **then**

            $S_{safe} \leftarrow S_{safe} \cup S_0^j$

        else

            $S_{unsafe} \leftarrow S_{unsafe} \cup S_0^j$

        end if

    end for

    return S_{safe}, S_{unsafe}

end function

---

reachable tubes (using the POLAR toolbox in practice). Note that the verification regions of $\mathbf{S_{ver}}$ in Algorithm 2 are much smaller partitions of larger gridding regions $\mathbf{S}$ defined in Algorithm 1 for training. Each gridding region, which for instance is a 0.5×0.5 square, corresponds to one LDC. Inside each gridding region, the verification region $\mathbf{S_{ver}}$ is a 0.01×0.01 square. Our end-to-end algorithm guarantees that an affirmative answer to our verification problem is correct with at least $1 - \alpha$ probability, as per Theorem 3.

Theorem 3 (Confident guarantee of HDC safety). *Consider a partitioned initial set grid $S_0 = \{S_1, \ldots, S_m\}$, a set of corresponding distributions $\{D_1, \ldots D_m\}$, a high-dimensional system M_{hd} with controller c_{hd}, and a set of low-dimensional systems $M_{ld}^1, \ldots, M_{ld}^m$ with respective controllers $c_{ld}^1, \ldots, c_{ld}^n$ that approximate c_{hd} with either an α-confident trajectory discrepancy or action discrepancy, the probability that HDC safe set S_{safe} calculated by Algorithm 2 with either discrepancy belongs to ground truth safe set S_{safe}^* is at least $(1 - \alpha)$:*

$$\Pr_{D_1 \ldots D_m} \left[S_{safe} \subseteq S_{safe}^* \right] \geq (1 - \alpha)$$

4 Experimental Evaluation

Benchmark Systems and Controllers. We evaluate our approach on three benchmarks from OpenAI Gym [7]: two two-dimensional case studies—an *inverted pendulum* (IP) with angle θ and angular velocity $\dot{\theta}$; a *mountain car* (MC) with position x and velocity v, and a four-dimensional case study—a *cart pole* (CP) with cart position x, cart velocity v, angle θ, and angular velocity $\dot{\theta}$. Our selection of case studies is limited because of the engineering challenge of setting up *both* vision-based control and low-dimensional verification for the same system. Our continuous-action, convolutional HDCs c_{hd} for these systems were trained with deep deterministic policy gradient (DDPG) [36]. To imitate the performance of c_{hd}, we train simpler feedforward neural networks c_{ld} with only low-dimensional state inputs. See the Appendix for their architecture and dynamics, and our code can be accessed from GitHub[1]

Experimental Procedure. Our verification's goal is to check whether the system will stay inside the specified goal set G after T time steps (e.g., the mountain car's position must stay within the target set $[0.45, \infty]$ after 60 steps). The verification returns "safe" if the inflated reachable set for $t = T$ lies entirely in G—and "unsafe" otherwise. The details are found in the Appendix.

For both approaches, we calculate the discrepancies in 0.25-sized state squares within the initial set in IP, hence creating $8 \times 8 = 64$ regions (MC has $8 \times 9 = 72$ regions; CP has $5 \times 5 \times 5 \times 5 = 625$). In each, we sample 60 trajectories to compute both trajectory-based discrepancies $\bar{\beta}$ and action-based discrepancies $\bar{\gamma}$ because it is a relatively small sample count that avoids the highest non-conformity score or the infinity as the conformal bound. We also implement a *pure conformal prediction baseline* and, for a fair comparison, give it the same data/regions. This results in 3840 sampled trajectories in IP, 4320 in MC, and 76800 for CP.

We use closed-loop simulation to obtain the (approximate) ground truth (GT) of safety. For IP and CP, we grid the initial set into squares with an interval of 0.01. For MC, we grid the initial set with the position step 0.01 and velocity step 0.001. Within each grid cell, we uniformly sample 10 initial states and simulate a trajectory from each. If all 10 trajectories end in the goal set G, we mark this cell as "truly safe", otherwise "truly unsafe". In IP, the truly safe-to-unsafe cell ratio is 0.56, 0.78 in MC, and 0.58 in CP. The verification process uses the same grid cells as its initial state regions, leading to 40k low-dimensional verification runs for IP, 14k for MC, and 50k for CP. The trajectory-based verification time for IP, MC, and CP are 6.2, 5.8, and 6.4 h respectively; the action-based verification takes 6.3, 6.1, and 6.6 h respectively.

Success Metrics. We evaluate verification as a binary classifier of the GT safety, with "safe" being the positive class and "unsafe" being the negative. Our evaluation metrics are the (i) *true positive rate* (TPR, a.k.a. sensitivity and recall), indicating the fraction of truly safe regions that were successfully verified; (ii) *true negative rate* (TNR, a.k.a. specificity), indicating the fraction of truly unsafe regions that failed verification; (iii) *precision*, indicating the fraction of safe verification verdicts that are truly safe (which is essential for safety-critical systems and controlled by rate α as per Theorem 3); and (iv) *F1 score*, which is

---

[1] https://github.com/Trustworthy-Engineered-Autonomy-Lab/Bridging-dimensions.

a harmonic mean of precision and recall to provide a class-balanced assessment of predictions.

Table 1. Verification performance ($M = 4$ for IP and CP, $M = 10$ for MC).

Benchmark	Metrics	Pure conformal prediction	Trajectory-based approach		Action-based approach	
		HDC	1 LDC	M LDCs	1 LDC	M LDCs
Inverted Pendulum (IP)	True positive rate	0.6564	0.4662	**0.7938**	0.0603	0.4050
	True negative rate	**0.9999**	0.9976	**0.9995**	**1.0000**	0.9999
	Precision	**0.9998**	0.9880	**0.9985**	**1.0000**	0.9997
	F1-score	0.7925	0.6335	**0.8844**	0.1137	0.5765
Mountain Car (MC)	True positive rate	0.4686	**0.7220**	0.7207	0.1050	0.2659
	True negative rate	**0.9967**	0.9693	0.9872	0.9964	1.0000
	Precision	**0.9916**	0.9621	0.9793	0.9999	1.0000
	F1-score	0.6364	0.8249	**0.8303**	0.1900	0.4201
Cartpole (CP)	True positive rate	0.6697	0.7225	**0.7450**	0.6554	0.7238
	True negative rate	**1.0000**	0.9998	**1.0000**	**1.0000**	**1.0000**
	Precision	**1.0000**	0.9999	**1.0000**	**1.0000**	**1.0000**
	F1-score	0.8022	0.8389	**0.8539**	0.7918	0.8398

Table 2. Verification performance for multiple LDCs with zero-mean Gaussian noise added to true state before image generator g.

Benchmark	Metrics	Trajectory-based method		Action-based method	
Inverted Pendulum (IP)	STD of θ, $\dot{\theta}$ noise	0.01	0.1	0.01	0.1
	True positive rate	**0.6732**	0.5272	0.3675	0.1924
	True negative rate	**1.0000**	**1.0000**	0.9999	**1.0000**
	Precision	**1.0000**	**1.0000**	0.9997	0.9997
	F1-score	**0.8046**	0.6904	0.5374	0.3228
Mountain Car (MC)	STD of x noise	0.01	0.1	0.01	0.1
	STD of v noise	0.0001	0.003	0.0001	0.003
	True positive rate	**0.6797**	0.4189	0.1558	0.0658
	True negative rate	0.9878	0.9889	1.0000	1.0000
	Precision	0.9790	0.9753	1.0000	1.0000
	F1-score	**0.8023**	0.5861	0.2696	0.1235
Cartpole (CP)	STD of $x,v,\theta,\dot{\theta}$ noise	0.03	0.1	0.03	0.1
	True positive rate	**0.7108**	0.6253	0.6724	0.6040
	True negative rate	**0.9998**	**0.9998**	0.9996	0.9996
	Precision	**0.9995**	**0.9995**	0.9990	0.9989
	F1-score	**0.8308**	0.7692	0.8038	0.7528

Verification Results. The quantitative results of the three case studies are summarized in Table 1. Confidence α is set to 0.05 for all methods, which sets the minimum precision to 0.95, satisfied by all the approaches. The pure conformal prediction baseline shows high precision and TNR, but loses in TPR to our approaches—thus being able to correctly verify a significantly smaller region of the state space. When it comes to well-balanced safety prediction in practice, F1 score shows that our trajectory-based approach outperforms the other two.

Across all case studies, the baseline is significantly more conservative than the requested 95% precision. While this can be an advantage in safety-critical settings, excessive conservatism can also hamper adoption, so the approach should be sensitive to the desired confidence—which our trajectory-based approach demonstrates in the mountain car case study (see Precision in Table 1).

Across all case studies, the multi-LDC approaches always match or outperform the one-LDC approaches. This result demonstrates the utility of modularizing the HDC approximation problem. Also, our single-LDC action-based approach successfully verifies relatively few regions, leading to its low TPR. That is because unlike in the case of trajectory discrepancies, only one LDC cannot provide tight statistical upper bounds for control actions, causing large overapproximation in the inflated reachable sets, resulting in false negatives.

Sensitivity to Noisy Images. Despite adding Gaussian noise to generator g, our approaches perform similarly to noise-free g when under low noise variance as per Table 2, thus showing some robustness. However, we saw a significant decline in the verification coverage (TPR, but not the TNR and α-guaranteed precision) under substantial noise variance (up to 0.5, not shown in Table 2).

Limitations. Our approach relies on statistical inference based on i.i.d. sampling from a fixed distribution, which downgrades the exhaustive guarantees of formal verification. However, it may be possible to exhaustively bridge this gap with neural-network conformance analysis based on satisfiability solving [41]. We also envision relaxing the i.i.d. assumption with time-series conformal prediction [3, 58], as well as uncertainty-guided gridding [37] to reduce our discrepancy bounds.

5   Related Work

Low-Dimensional Verification of Closed-Loop Systems. Neural-network controlled systems have been used widely [42,46,52], which has highlighted the challenges of verifying their correctness within closed-loop systems. Since it's impossible to calculate all the exact states, especially in non-linear systems, current approaches primarily focus on how to make tight overapproximate reachable sets [2,9,10]. For sigmoid-based NNCS, Verisig [30] toolbox can transform the neural-network controlled system into a hybrid system, which can be verified by other tools like flow*. NNV [54] performs overapproximation analysis by combining star sets [38,53] for feed-forward neural networks with zonotopes for non-linear plant dynamics in CORA [2]. POLAR [27] overcame the challenges of non-differentiable activation functions by combining the Bernstein-Bézier Form [28] and the symbolic remainder. This method achieves state-of-the-art performance in both the tightness of reachable tubes and computation times. Another type of verification called *Hamilton-Jacobi* (HJ) reachability [4], is inspired by optimal control. The DeepReach [5] technique can solve the verification problem with tens of dimensions by leveraging a deep neural network to represent the value function in the HJ reachability analysis. Nonetheless, such methods remain ill-suited for handling inputs with hundreds or thousands of dimensions.

These verification tools cannot deal with complicated neural network controllers. Therefore, an alternative approach is to simplify complex controllers into smaller, verifiable controllers by model reduction techniques [16,33], such as parameter pruning, compact convolution filters, and knowledge distillation [25].

Abstractions of Perception Models. Given the challenge of verifying the image-based closed-loop systems directly, many methods construct abstractions of the perception model to map the relationship between the image and the states for verification [43]. One abstraction approach [31] employs the generative model, especially Generative Adversarial Network (GAN), mapping states to images. The generated images will be put into the controller in the verification phase. Hence, the accuracy of the verification results depends on the quality of the image produced by the generative model. Other researchers [26] construct the exact mathematical formula mapping the real state into the simplified image [47], which can be verified in another neural network checker [32]. One limitation of exact modeling is the effort to generalize for other systems or scenarios. For instance, their implementation may be specific to a proportional controller in the aircraft landing or lane-keeping scenarios, which may not be suitable for the more complicated image-based systems in other cases.

Statistical Verification. Statistical verification draws samples to determine the property satisfaction from a finite number of trajectories [1,11,34,35]. One advantage of such algorithms is that they provide assurance for arbitrarily complex black-box systems, merely requiring the ability to simulate them [59,60]. Conformal prediction [55], which has been a popular choice for distribution-free uncertainty quantification, has recently been used to provide probabilistic guarantees on the satisfaction of a given STL property [37,45]. Purely statistical methods come at the price of drawing sufficient samples—and only obtaining the guarantees at some level of statistical confidence, which can be difficult to interpret in the context of a dynamical system. Our work restricts the use of sampling only to the most challenging aspects and leverages exhaustive verification for the rest of the system, thus reducing our reliance on statistical assurance.

6 Conclusion

This paper takes a significant step towards addressing the major challenge of verifying end-to-end controllers implemented with high-dimensional neural networks. Our insight is that the behavior of such neural networks can be effectively approximated by several low-dimensional neural networks operating over physically meaningful space. To balance approximation error and verifiability in our low-dimensional controllers, we harness the state-of-the-art knowledge distillation. To close the gap between low- and high-dimensional controllers, we apply conformal prediction and provide a statistical upper bound on their difference either in trajectories or actions. Finally, by inflating the reachable tubes with two discrepancy types, we establish a high-confidence reachability guarantee for high-dimensional controllers. Future work may further reduce the role of sampling.

Acknowledgments. The authors thank Kang Gao, Zhenjiang Mao, Priyanshu Mathur, and Sukanth Sundaran for helping implement the verification and case studies as well as providing valuable feedback on this manuscript.

This work was supported in part by the NSF Grant CCF-2403616, ARO MURI W911NF-20-1-0080, and grant EP/Y002644/1 under the EPSRC ECR International Collaboration Grants program, funded by the International Science Partnerships Fund (ISPF) and the UK Research and Innovation. Any opinions, findings, conclusions, or recommendations expressed in this material are those of the authors and do not necessarily reflect the views of the National Science Foundation (NSF), Army Research Office (ARO), the Department of Defense, or the United States Government.

References

1. Agha, G., Palmskog, K.: A survey of statistical model checking. ACM Trans. Modeling Comput. Simul. **28** (2018,1), Publisher Copyright: 2018 ACM

2. Althoff, M.: An introduction to CORA 2015. In: Proc. of the Workshop on Applied Verification for Continuous And Hybrid Systems, pp. 120-151 (2015)

3. Auer, A., Gauch, M., Klotz, D., Hochreiter, S.: Conformal prediction for time series with modern hopfield networks. In: Proceedings Of The 37th International Conference On Neural Information Processing Systems (2024)

4. Bansal, S., Chen, M., Herbert, S.L., Tomlin, C.J.: Hamilton-jacobi reachability: a brief overview and recent advances. 2017 IEEE 56th Annual Conference on Decision and Control (CDC), pp. 2242–2253 (2017). https://api.semanticscholar.org/CorpusID:35768454

5. Bansal, S., Tomlin, C.J.: Deepreach: a deep learning approach to high-dimensional reachability. In: 2021 IEEE International Conference on Robotics and Automation (ICRA), pp. 1817–1824. IEEE (2021)

6. Bassan, S., Katz, G.: Towards formal xai: formally approximate minimal explanations of neural networks. In: International Conference on Tools and Algorithms for the Construction and Analysis of Systems, pp. 187–207. Springer (2023)

7. Brockman, G., Cheung, V., Pettersson, L., Schneider, J., Schulman, J., Tang, J., Zaremba, W.: OpenAI Gym (Jun 2016). http://arxiv.org/abs/1606.01540, arXiv:1606.01540 [cs]

8. Chakraborty, K., Bansal, S.: Discovering closed-loop failures of vision-based controllers via reachability analysis. IEEE Robot. Automation Lett. **8**(5), 2692–2699 (2023)

9. Chen, X., Ábrahám, E., Sankaranarayanan, S.: Flow*: An analyzer for non-linear hybrid systems. In: International Conference on Computer Aided Verification (2013)

10. Chen, X., Sankaranarayanan, S.: Reachability analysis for cyber-physical systems: Are we there yet? In: NASA Formal Methods Symposium, pp. 109-130 (2022)
11. Cleaveland, M., Lee, I., Pappas, G., Lindemann, L.: Conformal prediction regions for time series using linear complementarity programming. In: Proceedings of the AAAI Conference on Artificial Intelligence, vol. 38, pp. 20984–20992 (2024)
12. Cleaveland, M., Sokolsky, O., Lee, I., Ruchkin, I.: Conservative safety monitors of stochastic dynamical systems. In: Proc. of the NASA Formal Methods Conference, May 2023
13. Codevilla, F., Müller, M., López, A., Koltun, V., Dosovitskiy, A.: End-to-end driving via conditional imitation learning. In: 2018 IEEE International Conference On Robotics And Automation (ICRA), pp. 4693-4700 (2018)
14. Cofer, D., et al.: Run-time assurance for learning-based aircraft taxiing. In: 2020 AIAA/IEEE 39th Digital Avionics Systems Conference (DASC), pp. 1–9 (2020)
15. Combettes, P.L., Pesquet, J.C.: Lipschitz Certificates for Layered Network Structures Driven by Averaged Activation Operators. SIAM Journal on Mathematics of Data Science 2(2), 529–557 (Jan 2020). https://doi.org/10.1137/19M1272780, publisher: Society for Industrial and Applied Mathematics
16. Deng, L., Li, G., Han, S., Shi, L., Xie, Y.: Model compression and hardware acceleration for neural networks: a comprehensive survey. Proc. IEEE 108(4), 485–532 (2020)
17. Dutta, S., et al.: Distributionally robust statistical verification with imprecise neural networks (Aug 2023). https://doi.org/10.48550/arXiv.2308.14815, arXiv:2308.14815 [cs]
18. Dutta, S., Chen, X., Jha, S., Sankaranarayanan, S., Tiwari, A.: Sherlock-a tool for verification of neural network feedback systems: demo abstract. In: Proceedings of the 22nd ACM International Conference On Hybrid Systems: Computation And Control, pp. 262–263 (2019)
19. Fan, C., Mitra, S.: Bounded verification with on-the-fly discrepancy computation. In: Finkbeiner, B., Pu, G., Zhang, L. (eds.) ATVA 2015. LNCS, vol. 9364, pp. 446–463. Springer, Cham (2015). https://doi.org/10.1007/978-3-319-24953-7_32
20. Fan, C., Qi, B., Mitra, S., Viswanathan, M.: DRYVR: data-driven verification and compositional reasoning for automotive systems. In: Majumdar, R., Kunčak, V. (eds.) CAV 2017. LNCS, vol. 10426, pp. 441–461. Springer, Cham (2017). https://doi.org/10.1007/978-3-319-63387-9_22
21. Fan, J., Huang, C., Li, W., Chen, X., Zhu, Q.: Towards verification-aware knowledge distillation for neural-network controlled systems: Invited paper. In: 2019 IEEE/ACM International Conference on Computer-Aided Design (ICCAD), pp. 1–8 (2019). https://api.semanticscholar.org/CorpusID:209497572
22. Fannjiang, C., Bates, S., Angelopoulos, A., Listgarten, J., Jordan, M.: Conformal prediction under feedback covariate shift for biomolecular design. Proc. Natl. Acad. Sci. 119, e2204569119 (2022)
23. Fazlyab, M., Robey, A., Hassani, H., Morari, M., Pappas, G.: Efficient and accurate estimation of lipschitz constants for deep neural networks. In: Advances in Neural Information Processing Systems, vol. 32. Curran Associates, Inc. (2019). https://proceedings.neurips.cc/paper_files/paper/2019/hash/95e1533eb1b20a97777749fb94fdb944-Abstract.html
24. Gou, J., Yu, B., Maybank, S.J., Tao, D.: Knowledge distillation: a survey. Int. J. Comput. Vision 129, 1789–1819 (2021)
25. Hinton, G., Vinyals, O., Dean, J.: Distilling the knowledge in a neural network. arXiv preprint arXiv:1503.02531 (2015)

26. Hsieh, C., Li, Y., Sun, D., Joshi, K., Misailovic, S., Mitra, S.: Verifying controllers with vision-based perception using safe approximate abstractions. IEEE Trans. Comput. Aided Des. Integr. Circuits Syst. **41**(11), 4205–4216 (2022). https://doi. org/10.1109/TCAD.2022.3197508

27. Huang, C., Fan, J., Chen, X., Li, W., Zhu, Q.: Polar: A polynomial arithmetic framework for verifying neural-network controlled systems. In: International Symposium on Automated Technology for Verification and Analysis, pp. 414–430. Springer (2022)

28. Huang, C., Fan, J., Li, W., Chen, X., Zhu, Q.: Reachnn: reachability analysis of neural-network controlled systems. ACM Trans. Embedded Comput. Syst. (TECS) **18**(5s), 1–22 (2019)

29. Fazlyab, M., Robey, A., Hassani, H., Morari, M., Pappas, G.: Efficient and accurate estimation of lipschitz constants for deep neural networks. In: Advances In Neural Information Processing Systems. **32** (2019)

30. Ivanov, R., Weimer, J., Alur, R., Pappas, G., Lee, I.: Verisig: verifying safety properties of hybrid systems with neural network controllers. In: Proceedings of the 22nd ACM International Conference on Hybrid Systems: Computation And Control, pp. 169-178 (2019)

31. Katz, S.M., Corso, A.L., Strong, C.A., Kochenderfer, M.J.: Verification of image-based neural network controllers using generative models. J. Aerospace Inf. Syst. **19**(9), 574–584 (2022)

32. Khedr, H., Ferlez, J., Shoukry, Y.: Peregrinn: Penalized-relaxation greedy neural network verifier. In: Computer Aided Verification: 33rd International Conference, CAV 2021, Virtual Event, July 20-23, 2021, Proceedings, Part I, pp. 287-300 (2021). https://doi.org/10.1007/978-3-030-81685-8_13

33. Ladner, T., Althoff, M.: Specification-driven neural network reduction for scalable formal verification. arXiv preprint arXiv:2305.01932 (2023)

34. Larsen, K.G., Legay, A.: Statistical model checking: past, present, and future. In: Margaria, T., Steffen, B. (eds.) ISoLA 2016. LNCS, vol. 9952, pp. 3–15. Springer, Cham (2016). https://doi.org/10.1007/978-3-319-47166-2_1

35. Lew, T., Janson, L., Bonalli, R., Pavone, M.: A Simple and Efficient Sampling-based Algorithm for General Reachability Analysis. In: Proceedings of the 4th Annual Learning for Dynamics and Control Conference. 168, pp. 1086–1099 (2022,6,23). https://proceedings.mlr.press/v168/lew22a.html

36. Lillicrap, T., Hunt, J., Pritzel, A., Heess, N., Erez, T., Tassa, Y., Silver, D., Wierstra, D.: Continuous control with deep reinforcement learning. CoRR. abs/1509.02971 (2015). https://api.semanticscholar.org/CorpusID:16326763

37. Lindemann, L., Qin, X., Deshmukh, J.V., Pappas, G.J.: Conformal prediction for stl runtime verification. In: Proceedings of the ACM/IEEE 14th International Conference on Cyber-Physical Systems (with CPS-IoT Week 2023), pp. 142–153. ICCPS '23, Association for Computing Machinery, New York (2023). https://doi. org/10.1145/3576841.3585927

38. Lopez, D.M., Musau, P., Tran, H.D., Johnson, T.T.: Verification of closed-loop systems with neural network controllers. EPiC Series in Computing **61**, 201–210 (2019)

39. Luo, R., Zhao, S., Kuck, J., Ivanovic, B., Savarese, S., Schmerling, E., Pavone, M.: Sample-efficient safety assurances using conformal prediction. In: International Workshop on the Algorithmic Foundations of Robotics, pp. 149–169. Springer (2022)

40. Matsumoto, E., Saito, M., Kume, A., Tan, J.: End-to-end learning of object grasp poses in the amazon robotics challenge. In: Causo, A., Durham, J., Hauser, K., Okada, K., Rodriguez, A. (eds.) Advances on Robotic Item Picking, pp. 63–72. Springer, Cham (2020). https://doi.org/10.1007/978-3-030-35679-8_6

41. Mohammadinejad, S., Paulsen, B., Deshmukh, J.V., Wang, C.: DiffRNN: differential verification of recurrent neural networks. In: Dima, C., Shirmohammadi, M. (eds.) FORMATS 2021. LNCS, vol. 12860, pp. 117–134. Springer, Cham (2021). https://doi.org/10.1007/978-3-030-85037-1_8

42. Pan, Y., Cheng, C., Saigol, K., Lee, K., Yan, X., Theodorou, E., Boots, B.: Agile Autonomous Driving using End-to-End Deep Imitation Learning. Robotics: Science And Systems XIV (2017). https://api.semanticscholar.org/CorpusID: 53873353

43. Păsăreanu, C.S., Mangal, R., Gopinath, D., Getir Yaman, S., Imrie, C., Calinescu, R., Yu, H.: Closed-loop analysis of vision-based autonomous systems: A case study. In: International Conference on Computer Aided Verification, pp. 289–303. Springer (2023)

44. Qin, X., Hashemi, N., Lindemann, L., Deshmukh, J.V.: Conformance testing for stochastic cyber-physical systems. In: Conference on Formal Methods in Computer-Aided Design–FMCAD 2023, p. 294 (2023)

45. Qin, X., Xia, Y., Zutshi, A., Fan, C., Deshmukh, J.V.: Statistical verification of cyber-physical systems using surrogate models and conformal inference. In: 2022 ACM/IEEE 13th International Conference on Cyber-Physical Systems (ICCPS), pp. 116–126 (2022). https://doi.org/10.1109/ICCPS54341.2022.00017

46. Ruchkin, I., Cleaveland, M., Ivanov, R., Lu, P., Carpenter, T., Sokolsky, O., Lee, I.: Confidence composition for monitors of verification assumptions. In: ACM/IEEE 13th Intl. Conf. on Cyber-Physical Systems (ICCPS), pp. 1–12, May 2022. https://doi.org/10.1109/ICCPS54341.2022.00007

47. Santa Cruz, U., Shoukry, Y.: Nnlander-verif: a neural network formal verification framework for vision-based autonomous aircraft landing. Springer, Heidelberg (2022). https://doi.org/10.1007/978-3-031-06773-0_11

48. Shafer, G., Vovk, V.: A Tutorial on Conformal Prediction. J. Mach. Learn. Res. **9**, 371–421 (2008). http://dl.acm.org/citation.cfm?id=1390681.1390693

49. Stocco, A., Nunes, P.J., D'Amorim, M., Tonella, P.: Thirdeye: Attention maps for safe autonomous driving systems. In: Proceedings of the 37th IEEE/ACM International Conference on Automated Software Engineering, ASE 2022. Association for Computing Machinery, New York (2023). https://doi.org/10.1145/3551349.3556968

50. Szegedy, C., Zaremba, W., Sutskever, I., Bruna, J., Erhan, D., Goodfellow, I., Fergus, R.: Intriguing properties of neural networks. In: International Conference on Learning Representations (2014)

51. Teeti, I., Khan, S., Shahbaz, A., Bradley, A., Cuzzolin, F.: Vision-based Intention and Trajectory Prediction in Autonomous Vehicles: A Survey, vol. 6, pp. 5630–5637 (Jul 2022). https://www.ijcai.org/proceedings/2022/785, iSSN: 1045-0823

52. Topcu, U., Bliss, N., Cooke, N., Cummings, M., Llorens, A., Shrobe, H., Zuck, L.: Assured Autonomy: Path Toward Living With Autonomous Systems We Can Trust, October 2020. http://arxiv.org/abs/2010.14443, arXiv:2010.14443 [cs]

53. Tran, H.D., Manzanas Lopez, D., Musau, P., Yang, X., Nguyen, L.V., Xiang, W., Johnson, T.T.: Star-based reachability analysis of deep neural networks. In: Formal Methods–The Next 30 Years: Third World Congress, FM 2019, Porto, Portugal, October 7–11, 2019, Proceedings 3, pp. 670–686. Springer (2019)

54. Tran, H., et al.: NNV: the neural network verification tool for deep neural networks and learning-enabled cyber-physical systems. In: International Conference on Computer Aided Verification, pp. 3-17 (2020)
55. Vovk, V., Gammerman, A., Shafer, G.: Algorithmic Learning in a Random World. Springer, New York, 2005 edition edn. (2005)
56. Xiang, W., Shao, Z.: Approximate bisimulation relations for neural networks and application to assured neural network compression. In: 2022 American Control Conference (ACC), pp. 3248–3253. IEEE (2022)
57. Xiang, W., Shao, Z.: Safety verification of neural network control systems using guaranteed neural network model reduction. In: 2022 IEEE 61st Conference on Decision and Control (CDC), pp. 1521–1526. IEEE (2022)
58. Xu, C., Xie, Y.: Conformal prediction interval for dynamic time-series. In: Proceedings of the 38th International Conference on Machine Learning, pp. 11559–11569. PMLR, July 2021. https://proceedings.mlr.press/v139/xu21h.html, iSSN: 2640-3498
59. Xue, B., Zhang, M., Easwaran, A., Li, Q.: Pac model checking of black-box continuous-time dynamical systems. IEEE Trans. Comput.-Aided Des. Integrated Circuits Syst. **39** (07 2020). https://doi.org/10.1109/TCAD.2020.3012251
60. Zarei, M., Wang, Y., Pajic, M.: Statistical verification of learning-based cyber-physical systems. In: Proceedings of the 23rd International Conference on Hybrid Systems: Computation and Control, HSCC 2020. Association for Computing Machinery, New York (2020). https://doi.org/10.1145/3365365.3382209
61. Zhang, M., Zhang, Y., Zhang, L., Liu, C., Khurshid, S.: Deeproad: Gan-based metamorphic testing and input validation framework for autonomous driving systems. In: Proceedings of the 33rd ACM/IEEE International Conference on Automated Software Engineering, pp. 132-142. ASE 2018. Association for Computing Machinery, New York, NY, USA (2018). https://doi.org/10.1145/3238147.3238187
62. Wang, Y., Zhou, W., Fan, J., Wang, Z., Li, J., Chen, X., Huang, C., Li, W. and Zhu, Q.: Polar-express: Efficient and precise formal reachability analysis of neural-network controlled systems. In: IEEE Transactions on Computer-Aided Design of Integrated Circuits and Systems. (2023)
63. Xin, L., Tang, Z., Gai, W., Liu, H.: Vision-based autonomous landing for the UAV: A review. Aerospace **9**, 634 (2022)
64. Tang, C., Lai, Y.: Deep reinforcement learning automatic landing control of fixed-wing aircraft using deep deterministic policy gradient. In: 2020 International Conference On Unmanned Aircraft Systems (ICUAS), pp. 1-9 (2020)
65. Oszust, M., et al.: A vision-based method for supporting autonomous aircraft landing. Aircraft Eng. Aerospace Technol. **90**, 973–982 (2018)
66. Menghi, C., Nejati, S., Briand, L., Parache, Y.: Approximation-refinement testing of compute-intensive cyber-physical models: an approach based on system identification. In: 2020 IEEE/ACM 42nd International Conference On Software Engineering (ICSE), pp. 372–384 (2020)
67. Geng, Y., Baldauf, J. B., Dutta, S., Huang, C., Ruchkin, I.: Bridging Dimensions: Confident Reachability for High-Dimensional Controllers. 2024. arXiv preprint arXiv:2311.04843. https://arxiv.org/abs/2311.04843

VeriQR: A Robustness Verification Tool for Quantum Machine Learning Models

Yanling Lin[1,2]⬤, Ji Guan[2](✉)⬤, Wang Fang[2]⬤, Mingsheng Ying[3]⬤, and Zhaofeng Su[1](✉)⬤

[1] University of Science and Technology of China,
Hefei 230026, China
zfsu@ustc.edu.cn

[2] Key Laboratory of System Software (Chinese Academy
of Sciences) and State Key Laboratory of Computer Science,
Institute of Software, Chinese Academy of Sciences, Beijing 100190, China
guanj@ios.ac.cn

[3] Centre for Quantum Software and Information, University of Technology Sydney,
NSW 2007, Australia

Abstract. Adversarial noise attacks present a significant threat to quantum machine learning (QML) models, similar to their classical counterparts. This is especially true in the current Noisy Intermediate-Scale Quantum era, where noise is unavoidable. Therefore, it is essential to ensure the robustness of QML models before their deployment. To address this challenge, we introduce *VeriQR*, the first tool designed specifically for formally verifying and improving the robustness of QML models, to the best of our knowledge. This tool mimics real-world quantum hardware's noisy impacts by incorporating random noise to formally validate a QML model's robustness. *VeriQR* supports exact (sound and complete) algorithms for both local and global robustness verification. For enhanced efficiency, it implements an under-approximate (complete) algorithm and a tensor network-based algorithm to verify local and global robustness, respectively. As a formal verification tool, *VeriQR* can detect adversarial examples and utilize them for further analysis and to enhance the local robustness through adversarial training, as demonstrated by experiments on real-world quantum machine learning models. Moreover, it permits users to incorporate customized noise. Based on this feature, we assess *VeriQR* using various real-world examples, and experimental outcomes confirm that the addition of specific quantum noise can enhance the global robustness of QML models. These processes are made accessible through a user-friendly graphical interface provided by *VeriQR*, catering to general users without requiring a deep understanding of the counter-intuitive probabilistic nature of quantum computing.

Keywords: Robustness Verification · Quantum Machine Learning · Formal Verification · Quantum Classifiers · Quantum Noise

© The Author(s) 2025
A. Platzer et al. (Eds.): FM 2024, LNCS 14933, pp. 403–421, 2025.
https://doi.org/10.1007/978-3-031-71162-6_21

1   Introduction

Over the last decade, machine learning (ML) has driven technological advancements in various fields. The combination of machine learning with quantum computing has given rise to a new field of research known as *quantum machine learning (QML)*. In classical ML, classification models are vulnerable in adversarial scenarios [5,8]. Specifically, the addition of intentionally crafted noises to the original data can cause classifiers to make incorrect predictions with high confidence. An illustrative example is the misclassification of a panda image as a gibbon with a confidence level exceeding 99% after adding imperceptible noise [37]. Although studies have shown the potential superiority of quantum computers over classical counterparts in certain well-known ML tasks [4], the presence of noise in quantum computation is inevitable due to the limitations of quantum hardware devices in the current Noisy Intermediate-Scale Quantum (NISQ) era [34], which may cause quantum learning systems to suffer from adversarial perturbations from environmental noises. Research on the vulnerability of QML models has garnered widespread attention [15,19,20,23,30,31,41]. In particular, formal methods have been employed to verify the robustness of QML models against noises. Various algorithms have been developed to verify both local and global robustness, which have established a formal framework for verifying the robustness of QML models, allowing for detecting non-robust quantum states (also known as quantum adversarial examples) during the verification process.

Numerous tools have been developed to verify the robustness of classical ML models and improve robustness through adversarial training. Notable examples include NNV [39], Reluplex [27], DeepG [2], PRODeep [28], VerifAI [14] and AI² [18]. These tools have simplified the process for users to verify the robustness of their ML models. However, understanding the counter-intuitive principles of quantum mechanics, which serve as the inherent probabilistic foundation of quantum systems, poses a distinctive challenge for the average user. Therefore, there is a requirement for automated tools in the analysis of quantum systems.

In recent years, formal methods-based tools have emerged to verify the correctness of quantum systems. For instance, the development of a specification language and an automated tool called AUTOQ enables symbolic verification of quantum circuits [10]. Similarly, CoqQ, integrated into the Coq proof assistant, provides a means to reason about quantum programs [45]. A measurement-based linear-time temporal logic (MLTL) has been proposed to formally check the quantitative properties of quantum algorithms [21]. Furthermore, model checkers like QMC [33] and QPMC [16] have been proposed for verifying quantum programs and communication protocols. However, to the best of our knowledge, there are currently no dedicated tools available for verifying the robustness of QML models and then improving robustness.

Contributions. To fill the gap mentioned above, we introduce a tool named *VeriQR*. *VeriQR* is built upon the aforementioned theoretical formal verification techniques [19,20] for automatically quick robustness verification of QML models and the improvement strategies for enhancing robustness. The architecture of *VeriQR* is shown in Fig. 1 and its main advantages are listed in the following.

1. For *universality*, *VeriQR* supports the verification of two distinct robustness properties. These are referred to as *local robustness* for QML classification models and *global robustness* for all existing QML models.
2. For *usability*, *VeriQR* offers support for QML models that are represented in the OpenQASM 2.0 format of IBM [11]. This format is widely utilized as a programming language for describing quantum circuits and algorithms.
3. For *reality*, *VeriQR* formally verifies the robustness of a QML model by adding random noise to the model. This functionality enables simulations of the noisy effects of real-world quantum hardware on the robustness verification of various QML models.
4. For *efficiency*, in addition to basic verification methods, *VeriQR* incorporates various optimization techniques. These include approximation techniques for *local robustness* and tensor network contractions for *global robustness*, which enhance the performance of the verification process.
5. For *local robustness enhancement*, *VeriQR* can utilize the identified adversarial examples from the verification process for adversarial training, akin to traditional methods. Additionally, users have the option to introduce customized noise for *improving global robustness*, as discussed in [15, 20, 25]. This customized noise extends beyond standard quantum noise to include user-defined quantum noise models.

In Sect. 4, we present experimental results demonstrating the versatility and practicality of *VeriQR* in verifying and improving the robustness of different QML models in real-world scenarios. The experiments cover a range of noise types and levels, showcasing the efficacy and reliability of *VeriQR*.

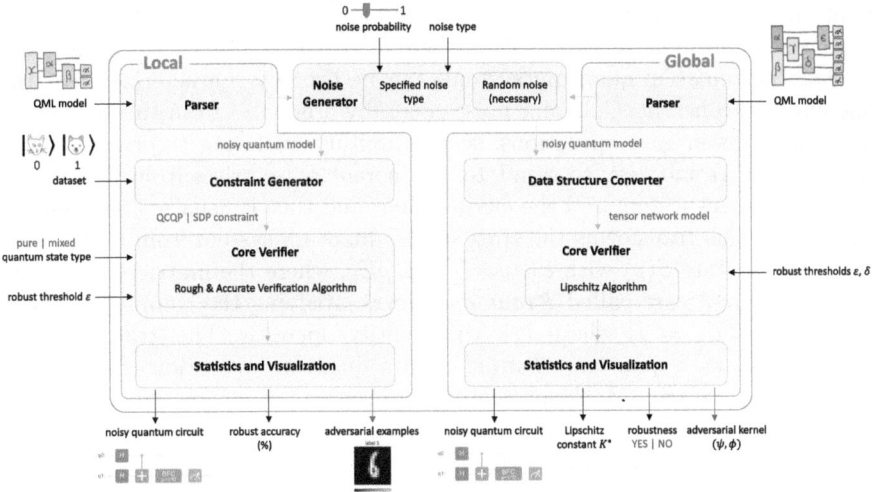

Fig. 1. An overview of the architecture of *VeriQR*.

2   Robustness for Quantum Machine Learning Models

For the convenience of the reader, we briefly introduce the concepts of quantum computing used in this paper and QML models (algorithms). We then review the local and global robustness verification problems for QML models in their most basic form, which can be handled by our tool *VeriQR*. For more details, please refer to [19,20,32].

2.1   Quantum Machine Learning Model

A QML model $\mathcal{A}$ is composed of input quantum states, a quantum circuit, and a quantum measurement.

Quantum state. The input quantum state ρ refers to the data that is processed by the quantum model. Mathematically, ρ is a positive semi-definite matrix with a size of 2^n-by-2^n, where n represents the number of quantum bits (qubits). It is important to note that the quantum state ρ can not only represent quantum information, such as the state of a physical Hamiltonian system, for physical computational tasks but also encode classical information, such as image data or financial data, for classical computational tasks.

Quantum circuit. The noisy quantum circuit $\mathcal{E}$ is used to describe the computational aspect of the QML model. A quantum circuit consists of a sequence of *quantum logic gates* and *quantum noises* (represented by yellow and brown boxes in Fig. 2, respectively).

Quantum logic gates are the building blocks of quantum circuits and can transform a quantum state into a new quantum state, like classical logic gates are for conventional digital circuits. They are described as unitary matrices relative to some orthogonal basis. Mathematically, a gate that acts on an n-qubit quantum state ρ is represented by a $2^n \times 2^n$ unitary matrix U, and its output is a evolved quantum state $\rho' = U\rho U^\dagger$, where $U^\dagger$ is the conjugate transpose of U.

Quantum noise in quantum systems can be broadly characterized as either coherent or incoherent. Coherent noise generally originates from the noisiness of the parameters in gate operations, so it is unitary evolution (represented by a unitary matrix) and easy to simulate; incoherent noise arises from the interaction between the system and the environment and thus is usually a non-unitary evolution, which transforms the state of the quantum system from a pure state ρ to a mixed state $\mathcal{E}(\rho)$ with $\mathcal{E}(\rho) = \sum_k E_k \rho E_k^\dagger$, where the matrices $\{E_k\}$ with a size of 2^n-by-2^n are called *Kraus operators*, satisfying the completeness conditions $\sum_k E_k^\dagger E_k = I$, where I is the identity operator. This transformation is also known as a *quantum channel*, it is a quantum operation characterized by a 2^n-by-2^n matrix. Mathematical representations of common 1-qubit quantum channels, including *bit flip channel (BFC)*, *phase flip channel (PFC)*, and *depolarizing channel (DC)*, are described as follows:

$$\mathcal{E}_{\text{BFC}}(\rho) = (1-p)I\rho I + pX\rho X$$
$$\mathcal{E}_{\text{PFC}}(\rho) = (1-p)I\rho I + pZ\rho Z$$
$$\mathcal{E}_{\text{DC}}(\rho) = (1-p)I\rho I + \frac{p}{3}(X\rho X + Y\rho Y + Z\rho Z)$$

and

$$X = \begin{bmatrix} 0 & 1 \\ 1 & 0 \end{bmatrix}, Y = \begin{bmatrix} 0 & -i \\ i & 0 \end{bmatrix}, Z = \begin{bmatrix} 1 & 0 \\ 0 & -1 \end{bmatrix}.$$

Here p represents the likelihood of the state ρ undergoing further manipulation by a quantum gate. For instance, in a bit flip channel, p signifies the chance of a bit flip operation affecting the quantum state. These three categories of quantum channels are frequently encountered noise in real-world quantum hardware. In this context, p serves as a measure of the noise level. A higher value of p corresponds to a more pronounced alteration in the initial state ρ. Therefore, the state of the quantum system after a noisy quantum circuit $\mathcal{E}$ represented by a set of matrices $\{E_k\}$ is $\mathcal{E}(\rho) = \sum_k E_k \rho E_k^\dagger$.

Quantum Measurement. At the end of each quantum circuit, a quantum measurement (represented by red boxes in Fig. 2) is performed to extract the computational outcome, which contains classical information, from $\mathcal{E}(\rho)$. This information is a probability distribution over the possible outcomes of the measurement. Mathematically, a quantum measurement is modeled by a set $\{M_c\}_{c\in\mathcal{C}}$ of positive semi-definite matrices with a size of 2^n-by-2^n. Here, $\mathcal{C}$ represents a finite set of measurement outcomes or class labels. The observation process is probabilistic: for the current state $\mathcal{E}(\rho)$, the measurement outcome $c \in \mathcal{C}$ is obtained with probability $p_c = \text{tr}(M_c\mathcal{E}(\rho))$, which is the summation of diagonal entries of $M_c\mathcal{E}(\rho)$.

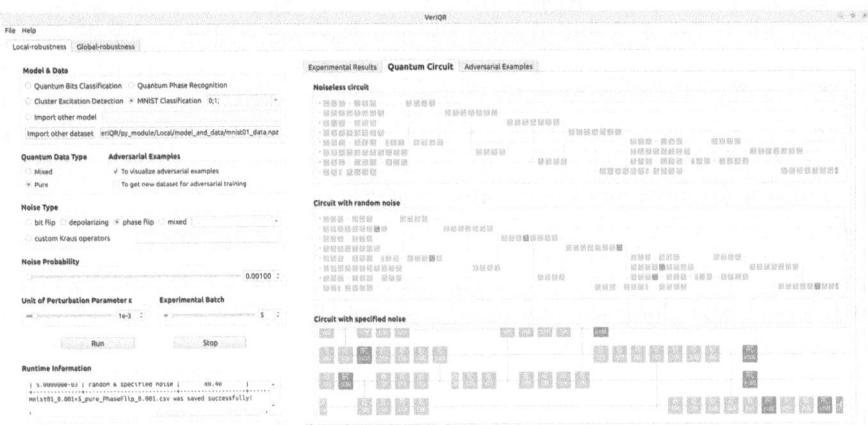

Fig. 2. GUI: the main tabs for verification task and (8-qubit) quantum circuit diagrams corresponding to the QML model to be verified. In this diagram representation, yellow boxes represent 1-qubit gates, blue ones represent controlled gates (not shown in this example), brown ones represent quantum noises, and red ones represent measurements.

In summary, a QML model, denoted as $\mathcal{A} = (\mathcal{E}, \{M_c\}_{c \in \mathcal{C}})$, can be viewed as a randomized mapping. For any input quantum state ρ, the model outputs a probability distribution $\mathcal{A}(\rho) = \{\text{tr}(M_c \mathcal{E}(\rho))\}_{c \in \mathcal{C}}$.

Pure Versus Mixed Quantum States. It is essential to note that quantum states fall into two main categories: pure and mixed states. A quantum system with a known exact state $|\psi\rangle$ containing n qubits is considered to be in a pure state, which can be represented by a column vector of size 2^n in a complex vector space. In this scenario, the density matrix (operator) representing the system is $\rho = |\psi\rangle\langle\psi|$, characterized by positive semidefinite matrices with a trace of 1. On the other hand, if the state of the quantum system is not precisely known, it is classified as a mixed state, which comprises an ensemble of pure states $(p_1, |\psi_1\rangle)$, $(p_2, |\psi_2\rangle)$, ..., $(p_n, |\psi_n\rangle)$, denoted as $\rho = \sum_i p_i |\psi_i\rangle\langle\psi_i|$. This indicates that the system is in state $|\psi_j\rangle$ with a probability of p_j. A pure state $|\psi\rangle$ can be considered a special instance of the mixed state $\rho = |\psi\rangle\langle\psi|$, implying that the collection of pure quantum states is a subset of mixed quantum states. Pure states are mainly employed to safeguard against deliberate classical attacks (by humans) embedded in input quantum states, while mixed states are utilized in a broader array of situations, including defense against quantum noise. To accommodate different application contexts, our tool *VeriQR* empowers users to choose the specific type of quantum states they wish to work with.

2.2   Robustness Verification of QML Models

Similar to their classical counterparts, QML models can be delineated into two primary categories: *regression models* and *classification models*. Consequently, two distinct forms of robustness verification are requisite.

Global Robustness for Regression Models. A *regression model* $\mathcal{A}$ uses the output distribution $\mathcal{A}(\rho)$ directly to determine the predicted value for the regression variable ρ. Naturally, a regression model that is robust to adversarial noise attacks should have the ability to maintain stable predictions with a certain degree of tolerance for small changes, which could induce incorrect predictions, in the initial data. In other words, it is necessary to treat all similar input states with minor differences similarly to ensure robustness for regression models, which is called *global robustness*.

Problem 1 (Global Robustness Formal Verification). Let $\mathcal{A} = (\mathcal{E}, \{M_c\}_{c \in \mathcal{C}})$ be a QML model, and check whether $\mathcal{A}$ is (ε, δ)-globally robust, i.e., for any pair of quantum state ρ and σ with $D(\rho, \sigma) \leq \varepsilon$, we have $d(\mathcal{A}(\rho), \mathcal{A}(\sigma)) \leq \delta$. If not, provide such a pair of quantum states violating the robustness.

Here $D(\cdot, \cdot)$ and $d(\cdot, \cdot)$ represent the trace distance of two density matrices and the total variance distance of the measurement outcome probability distributions on quantum states, respectively. These distances are used to quantify the similarities in input and output states, respectively. To solve the formal verification problem (Problem 1), the Lipschitz constant K^* of $\mathcal{A}$ is introduced with the fact that $\mathcal{A}$

is (ε, δ)-globally robust, if and only if $\delta \geq \varepsilon$ [20]. Here the Lipschitz constant K^* is the smallest K such that $d(\mathcal{A}(\rho), \mathcal{A}(\sigma)) \leq KD(\rho, \sigma)$ for all quantum states ρ and σ. So the key is to compute K^* which is done by our tool *VeriQR*.

Local Robustness for Classification Models. A *classification model (classifier)* $\mathcal{A}$ utilizes the probability distribution $\mathcal{A}(\rho)$ to assign a class label $c \in \mathcal{C}$ to the input state ρ. The most commonly used approach is to assign the label with the highest corresponding probability in the output distribution $\{tr(M_c \mathcal{E}(\rho))\}_{c \in \mathcal{C}}$. Naturally, a robust classifier should be able to classify all similar input states in the same class to ensure robustness, which is referred to as *local robustness*.

Problem 2 (Local Robustness Formal Verification). Let $\mathcal{A} = (\mathcal{E}, \{M_c\}_{c \in \mathcal{C}})$ be a QML model. Given an input state ρ with label $c \in \mathcal{C}$, check whether $\mathcal{A}$ is ε-locally robust, i.e., $\mathcal{A}(\sigma) = c$ for all $\sigma \in \mathcal{N}_\varepsilon(\rho)$, the ε-neighbourhood of ρ. If not, provide an adversarial example (counter-example) $\sigma \in \mathcal{N}_\varepsilon(\rho)$ with label $l \neq c$.

Here, the ε-neighbourhood of ρ is defined as $\mathcal{N}_\varepsilon(\rho) = \{\sigma : \bar{F}(\rho, \sigma) \leq \varepsilon\}$, and $\bar{F}(\rho, \sigma)$ quantifies the similarity between states ρ and σ using fidelity [32]. To evaluate the ε-robustness of a given finite set of labeled quantum states, we assess each input example individually. Subsequently, we generate a collection of concrete adversarial examples and determine the proportion of ε-robust states in the dataset. This measure, referred to as the ε-robust accuracy of the quantum classifier $\mathcal{A}$, provides insight into its *local robustness* on the dataset.

2.3   Challenges of Implementation

When it comes to implementing a verification tool for QML models, we encounter distinct challenges compared to dealing with classical ML models.

Continuous State Space. Quantum systems that operate within a linear space of finite dimensions possess a continuous state space. This implies that QML models must account for an infinite number of quantum states when conducting global robustness verification. In contrast, classical models mainly work with discrete input datasets that have a finite number of data. This distinction renders classical robustness verification techniques [1] unsuitable for quantum systems, such as the reachability method [38] and abstract interpretation [18]. Consequently, we develop *VeriQR* as an independent tool that does not rely on any existing classical robustness tools. Instead, we implement the algorithms proposed in [19,20] to verify the robustness of QML models.

State Explosion. The size of QML models, which is given by the dimension 2^n, grows exponentially as the number of qubits n increases. This poses challenges in terms of memory usage and runtime when performing robustness verification on large-scale systems. To address this, we employ tensor networks as an efficient data structure for storing quantum circuits, effectively optimizing memory usage. Furthermore, we utilize Google's tensor network calculator [36] with heuristic methods as a subroutine to enhance the efficiency of verifying global robustness (Problem 1). Furthermore, we have implemented the approximate verification algorithm [19] for local robustness verification (Problem 2). These optimization techniques allow *VeriQR* to handle robustness verification of noisy QML models with up to 20 qubits on a small service for general users (refer to Sect. 4 for experimental results). Without these optimizations, *VeriQR* is only able to handle models with up to 8 qubits.

QML Benchmarks. Currently, there are only a few benchmarks available for quantum circuits (e.g., [9]), and there is a lack of benchmarks specifically designed for QML models. To broaden the range of applicable scenarios, we have incorporated the use of OpenQASM 2.0 files as inputs. Moreover, to further enhance this capability, we have developed built-in scripts for translating QML models on several platforms (such as Huawei's MindSpore Quantum [43] and Google's Cirq [13]) into the OpenQASM 2.0 format. This enables the establishment of a unified verification benchmark framework for QML models deployed on various popular quantum platforms, including IBM's Qiskit [26], Google's TensorFlow Quantum [7], and others. In addition, we have visualized the framework by providing a graphical user interface (GUI) that converts inputted OpenQASM 2.0 code, used for describing quantum circuits, into visual representations (see the right side of Fig. 2).

3   Overview and Features of *VeriQR*

VeriQR is a graphical user interface (GUI) tool developed using C++. The decision to use C++ was influenced by the widespread use of Qt [6] in GUI programming. As shown in Fig. 1, *VeriQR* consists of two main parts: *Local robustness verification* and *Global robustness verification*.

Inputs. To utilize *VeriQR*, the user is required to import a relevant example, specifically a QML model and a dataset that contains quantum states and their corresponding ground truth labels and can be sourced from either a training or testing dataset. *VeriQR* accepts a model in the following formats, each of which represents a quantum circuit with a measurement at the end of the circuit.

1. *A NumPy data file (.npz format)* is utilized to package a quantum circuit, quantum measurement, and training dataset. This format is particularly beneficial for individuals who are not experts in quantum computing but have proficiency in classical formal methods and machine learning. By incorporating NumPy, *VeriQR* becomes more accessible to average users without requiring extensive learning. Moreover, *VeriQR* provides four popular testing examples (see the upper left corner of Fig. 2) of quantum classifiers in .npz, catering to beginners.
2. *An OpenQASM 2.0 file (.qasm format)* expresses the quantum circuit corresponding to the QML model to be checked. OpenQASM 2.0 is an IBM-introduced format widely adopted in the quantum computing community for constructing quantum circuits [11]. *QML models trained on different quantum platforms can be converted into this format. This allows for unified and reliable verification of robustness, addressing the challenge of "QML Benchmarks" discussed in Sect. 2.3.*

It is important to mention that the verification of *global robustness* does not require the use of the original dataset as input. Therefore, users only need to import a QML model in a .qasm file for the circuit and the measurement, without the need for additional training data. Once this step is completed, users can proceed to configure parameters for the specific case of interest. These parameters consist of the following: (i) the types and levels (probabilities ranging from 0 to 1) of noise: *VeriQR* inherently provides users with the option to select three standard types of noise, namely *depolarizing, phase flip, bit flip* [32]. Furthermore, users can also customize a new noise themselves, or even choose a combination of all types of noise; (ii) the type of quantum state, which can be either mixed or pure in the local component and is set as mixed by default in the global component. The choice for the global component is predetermined as global robustness verification for mixed states can be reduced to that for pure states; and (iii) perturbation parameters, specifically two thresholds for robustness (ε, δ in Problem 1) for the verification of *global robustness* and a threshold for robustness (ε in Problem 2) for the verification of *local robustness*.

3.1 Verifying Robustness

Verification of Local Robustness. This part is comprised of five modules:

1) **Parser**: This module handles a quantum classifiers file to obtain the corresponding quantum circuit object.
2) **Noise Generator**: The input for this module is a quantum circuit object. *First*, it generates a noisy quantum circuit by adding a random noise to each qubit at random points in the circuit with a randomly determined noise probability. The purpose of this is to simulate the effect of noise to verify the robustness of the QML model on real-world quantum hardware. *In addition*, users can also use *VeriQR* to actively add noises of specific types, including commonly used standard quantum noise models and user-defined quantum noise models (using Kraus representation) with specific noise probabilities, to the noisy model. Here, user-specified noises are added at the end of the circuit, which is a common assumption. This functionality enables robustness improvements, illustrated by our experimental results in Sect. 4.
3) **Constraint Generator**: This module generates constraints based on the (noisy) quantum model and the input dataset, which are then submitted to the core verifier.
4) **Core Verifier**: This module receives the constraints, a perturbation parameter ε, and the quantum state type as inputs. Based on the state type, it chooses the appropriate constraint solver: a Semidefinite Programming solver for mixed states, and a Quadratically Constrained Quadratic Program solver for pure states [19]. It then utilizes both the under-approximation and exact algorithms to initiate the verification analysis procedure for ε-robustness. *These algorithms and solvers are specifically designed to tackle the challenge of "Continuous State Space" discussed in Sect. 2.3 when verifying the robustness of QML models. In particular, the under-approximation algorithm is implemented to address the "State Explosion" issue.*

5) **Statistics and Visualization**: This module is responsible for visualizing and displaying the results in the GUI of *VeriQR*. The computed robust accuracy of the quantum classifier, which indicates the validity of the robustness property, is outputted by *VeriQR*. Additionally, the detected adversarial examples (quantum states) are stored in a NumPy data file for further analysis and to improve robustness through adversarial training. The GUI also presents the original and noisy quantum circuit diagrams for the classifier (see Fig. 2), providing users with an intuitive way to analyze the model construction. Moreover, for the MNIST handwritten digit classification task, *VeriQR* displays pictures of the detected adversarial examples based on the digits specified by the user in the GUI. These adversarial examples are obtained by adding noisy perturbations to a set of legitimate input examples, as illustrated in Fig. 3.

Verification of Global Robustness. This part also includes five modules similar to validating *local robustness*. However, instead of being verified directly by the verifier, *the noisy model generated by the noise generator is first passed to the data structure converter and is transformed into the corresponding* tensor networks *model to improve efficiency and overcome the challenge of "State Explosion" discussed in Sect. 2.3*. The core verifier then takes the tensor network model as input and calculates the required constant K^* for model validation, following the procedure outlined in Algorithm 1 of [20]. In addition to this, the core verifier receives perturbation parameters ε and δ in Problem 1 for validation and finally determines whether the global robustness property holds by checking if $\delta \geq K^*\varepsilon$. If not, it will provide an adversarial kernel (ψ, ϕ), which is capable of generating infinitely many pairs of quantum states that violate the global robustness of the QML model.

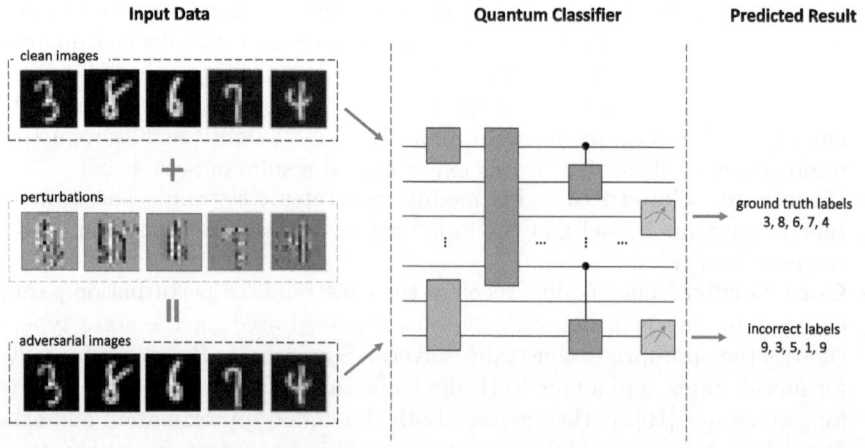

Fig. 3. The adversarial examples and the corresponding adversarial perturbations found by *VeriQR* in MINIST handwritten digit classification.

3.2 Improving Robustness

VeriQR offers adversarial training and adding specific noise to enhance the local and global robustness of QML models, respectively. The effectiveness of these strategies is validated through experiments on various QML models in Sect. 4.

Adversarial training. *VeriQR* empowers users with adversarial training capabilities, an extension of traditional machine learning. When the ε-local robustness of ρ with label l is compromised, our robustness verification algorithms embedded in *VeriQR* automatically generate an adversarial example σ. By incorporating (σ, l) into the training dataset, users can then retrain the QML model to enhance its local robustness against the adversarial examples.

Specific noise. Previous research [15, 20, 25] suggests that introducing specific quantum noise at strategic points in the circuits of QML models can improve global robustness. The *VeriQR* tool empowers users to apply standard or personalized noise at various locations in quantum circuits for robustness enhancement.

4 Evaluation

In this section, we evaluate the effectiveness of *VeriQR* in verifying and enhancing both the local and global robustness of various QML models. These models utilize popular parameterized quantum circuits like Quantum Neural Networks (QNN), Quantum Convolutional Neural Networks (QCNN), Quantum Approximate Optimization Algorithms (QAOA), Variational Quantum Eigensolver Algorithms (VQE) and Quantum Supremacy Algorithms. All these networks have previously demonstrated successful implementation on practical quantum hardware [44]. All the experiments are performed on a workstation with a Intel(R) Xeon(R) Gold 6254 CPU @ 3.10GHz × 72 Cores Processor and 314 GB RAM.

4.1 Local Robustness

We conducted several experiments to test the *local robustness* of various quantum classifiers with different numbers of qubits. These classifiers were trained on labeled datasets that were encoded using different quantum encoders in platforms such as Mindspore Quantum [43] and Tensorflow Quantum [7]. The classifiers examined in our study include the *qubit* classifier, which determines the qubit's position in the X-Z plane of a Bloch sphere [7]; the *iris* classifier, which categorizes irises from various subgenera [17]; the *mnist* classifier, which identifies handwritten digits, specifically 1 & 3 [12]; the *fashion* classifier, which classifies images of T-shirts and ankle boots [42]; and the *tfi* classifier, which recognizes wavefunctions at different phases in a quantum many-body system [7].

Table 1. Experimental results of the *local robustness* verification of different QML models.

Model	#Qubits	ε	Circuit	Noise Setting (noise_p)	Rough Verif		Accurate Verif	
					RA (%)	VT (s)	RA (%)	VT (s)
qubit	1	0.001	c_0	noiseless	88.12	0.0038	90	2.4226
			c_1	random	88.12	0.0039	90	2.4623
			c_2	depolarizing_0.001	88.00	0.0038	90	2.4873
			c_2	depolarizing_0.005	87.62	0.0053	90	2.7140
iris	4	0.005	c_0	noiseless	98.75	0.0013	100	0.4924
			c_1	random	97.50	0.0009	100	0.8876
			c_2	mixed_0.01	97.50	0.0019	100	0.8808
			c_2	mixed_0.05	96.25	0.0021	100	3.1675
tfi	4	0.005	c_0	noiseless	86.41	0.0039	100	6.5220
			c_1	random	85.94	0.0038	100	6.6438
			c_2	mixed_0.01	85.78	0.0061	100	6.7117
			c_2	mixed_0.05	85.16	0.0063	100	7.0374
tfi	8	0.005	c_0	noiseless	98.44	0.0372	100	2.3004
			c_1	random	96.56	0.1061	100	3.9492
			c_2	bit-flip_0.01	96.56	37.0965	100	42.1246
			c_2	bit-flip_0.05	95.94	32.7195	100	38.8139
fashion	8	0.001	c_0	noiseless	90.60	0.0420	97.40	25.3777
			c_1	random	90.30	0.0934	97.30	27.4964
			c_2	bit-flip_0.01	89.90	15.6579	97.20	42.1063
			c_2	bit-flip_0.05	87.60	14.0342	96.70	48.5805
mnist (1&3)	8	0.003	c_0	noiseless	93.80	0.0543	96.00	18.5063
			c_1	random	92.60	0.0785	95.70	23.2905
			c_2	phase-flip_0.001	92.60	12.9728	95.70	36.2348
			c_2	phase-flip_0.01	92.60	11.6704	95.70	33.7894

Experiment Setting for Verification: To investigate the impact of random and specific noise on local robustness verification, we conducted experiments on four different circuits for each model as outlined in Table 1: the noiseless ideal QML model with quantum circuit c_0; circuit c_1 created by introducing random noise at various random points in circuit c_0 to simulate noise effects on NISQ devices; and circuit c_2 modified by adding specific noise with a noise level p (referred to as "noisename_p" below c_2) of four types: *depolarizing, phase flip, bit flip,* and *mixed* (a combination of the three) noise, introduced in Sect. 2.1, applied to each qubit after the random noise manipulation on circuit c_1.

Experiment Setting for Approximate Versus Exact Verification: In each robustness verification scenario, we employed two verification techniques:

a coarse method labeled "Rough Verif" and a precise method labeled "Accurate Verif". We must emphasize here the difference between accurate and rough verification methods for local robustness verification. The *rough verification* method detects non-robust states only by applying the robust bound condition from the work in [19]. However, quantum states that do not satisfy this condition may also be robust, leading to an underestimation of the robust accuracy. Therefore, the *accurate verification* method first filters out possible non-robust states using the condition, and then uses a Semidefinite Programming solver to obtain the optimal robust bound for these states, thus verifying the local robustness of each state precisely.

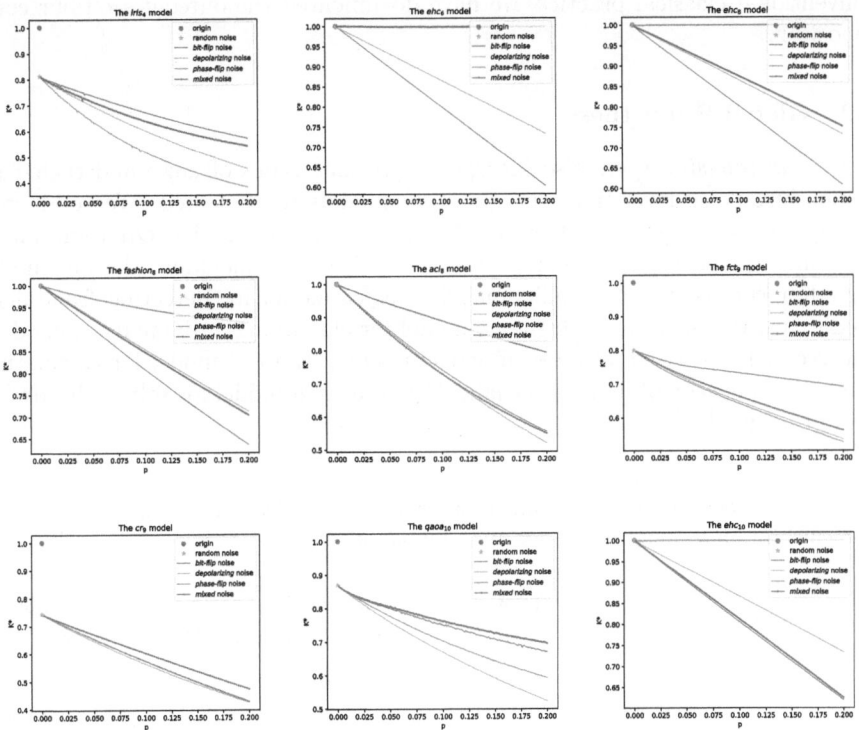

Fig. 4. Experimental results of the trade-off between the Lipschitz constant K^* (measuring *global robustness*) and noise level p in different QML models.

Table 1 presents a summary of the outcomes obtained from our experiments on *local robustness* verification. In this table, the robust accuracy of the classifiers is represented as "RA", while the verification time (in seconds) is indicated as "VT". The experimental results reveal two key aspects:

1. By examining the RA values in rows c_0, c_1, and c_2 for each QML experiment in Table 1, it becomes evident that both random noise and specific noise cannot enhance robustness, particularly in the *fashion* and *mnist* experiments.

2. When comparing the RA (VT) values between the "Rough Verif" and "Accurate Verif" columns, it is observed that the under-approximation of robust accuracy scales well in almost all cases with faster verification time, supporting the conclusions drawn in [19].

Remark 1. Our tool, *VeriQR*, serves as a formal instrument capable of identifying all non-robust quantum states (adversarial examples) during the verification process of all quantum classifiers. Analogous to classical methodologies, adversarial training can be utilized to fortify non-robust states within the retrained models. In our study, we have incorporated the adversarial training technique as outlined in Sect. 2.2 for all QML models listed in Table 1. Despite being a conventional classical practice, we have documented the outcomes on our code repository.

4.2   Global Robustness

For *global robustness*, we also incorporate various types of noise and their corresponding noise levels into the quantum models to be tested. We conducted multiple experiments on different QML models using the *VeriQR* tool. These experiments encompass a wide range of applications, including the *aci* model for adult census income prediction [3], the *fct* model for detecting fraudulent credit card transactions [40], the *cr* model for classifying individuals as good or bad credit risks based on a set of attributes [24], the *ehc* model for calculating the binding energy of hydrogen chains [35], the *qaoa* model for solving hardware grid problems [22].

Table 2. Experimental comparison of tensor network-based verification with a baseline implementation lacking tensors for assessing *global robustness*.

Model	#Qubits	Noise	p	(ε, δ)	Baseline		TN		Robust
					K^*	time (s)	K^*	time (s)	
ehc	8	bit flip	0.0001	(0.0003, 0.0075)	0.99980	0.26	0.99976	26.17	YES
		depolarizing	0.05	(0.001, 0.0075)	0.93333	0.26	0.93304	27.87	YES
		phase flip	0.025	(0.075, 0.0003)	1	0.26	0.99968	28.46	NO
		mixed	0.0005	(0.005, 0.005)	0.99938	0.24	0.99905	25.75	YES
aci	8	bit flip	0.0001	(0.003, 0.0001)	0.99985	0.18	0.99985	6.44	NO
		depolarizing	0.025	(0.03, 0.0005)	0.92640	0.25	0.92440	7.70	NO
		phase flip	0.05	(0.05, 0.001)	0.88450	0.19	0.85990	8.58	NO
		mixed	0.005	(0.005, 0.005)	0.98384	0.22	0.98326	6.06	YES
fct	9	bit flip	0.05	(0.075, 0.003)	0.99024	0.98	0.97683	13.89	NO
		depolarizing	0.05	(0.0003, 0.0001)	0.92638	0.76	0.92486	40.73	NO
		phase flip	0.01	(0.01, 0.0075)	0.98730	0.87	0.98290	10.45	NO
		mixed	0.05	(0.075, 0.0075)	0.94531	0.89	0.92949	9.06	NO

continued

Table 2. continued

Model	#Qubits	Noise	p	(ε, δ)	Baseline		TN		Robust
					K^*	time (s)	K^*	time (s)	
cr	9	bit flip	0.025	(0.01, 0.0005)	0.93964	0.65	0.93819	14.44	NO
		depolarizing	0.005	(0.075, 0.005)	0.98637	1.21	0.98515	6.49	NO
		phase flip	0.025	(0.0003, 0.0001)	0.94753	0.97	0.93772	9.63	NO
		mixed	0.025	(0.0001, 0.0001)	0.95579	0.93	0.94980	12.15	YES
qaoa	10	bit flip	0.005	(0.05, 0.0005)	0.99843	5.23	0.98507	16.98	NO
		depolarizing	0.0001	(0.01, 0.003)	0.99983	6.15	0.99965	16.10	NO
		phase flip	0.005	(0.075, 0.0075)	0.99224	5.14	0.98516	17.95	NO
		mixed	0.001	(0.03, 0.0075)	0.99923	4.98	0.99657	16.16	NO
ehc	10	bit flip	0.075	(0.05, 0.0003)	0.85409	3.37	0.85262	82.25	NO
		depolarizing	0.0005	(0.03, 0.001)	0.99933	5.69	0.99924	40.33	NO
		phase flip	0.01	(0.0003, 0.0075)	1	4.36	0.99857	66.67	YES
		mixed	0.0001	(0.005, 0.001)	0.99981	5.26	0.99977	38.13	NO
ehc	12	bit flip	0.005	(0.0005, 0.0003)	0.99001	169.42	0.98965	76.77	NO
		depolarizing	0.0005	(0.0001, 0.005)	0.99933	253.11	0.99926	189.35	YES
		phase flip	0.075	(0.001, 0.0075)	1	163.61	0.99880	675.50	YES
		mixed	0.001	(0.01, 0.0001)	0.99997	195.48	0.99984	64.50	NO
inst	16	bit flip	0.005	(0.0005, 0.0003)	-	TO	0.98009	1052.73	NO
		depolarizing	0.0005	(0.0003, 0.005)	-	TO	0.99833	33.99	YES
		phase flip	0.05	(0.001, 0.0075)	-	TO	0.95131	381.15	YES
		mixed	0.001	(0.005, 0.0003)	-	TO	0.99899	123.25	NO
qaoa	20	bit flip	0.05	(0.005, 0.001)	-	TO	0.91194	2402.32	NO
		depolarizing	0.075	(0.005, 0.003)	-	TO	0.83488	433.05	NO
		phase flip	0.0005	(0.0001, 0.0001)	-	TO	0.99868	70.00	YES
		mixed	0.05	(0.075, 0.0003)	-	TO	0.89682	4635.55	NO

Noise improving global robustness. Fig. 4 depicts the scaling of the Lipschitz constant K^* (which quantifies global robustness as discussed in Sect. 2.2) across various models at different noise levels p for four distinct noise types. The figure also showcases the experimental outcomes of the original model alongside a model derived from the original version with random noise. These results indicate that *the global robustness of all models improves due to quantum noise*, as evidenced by the reduced K^* value in the models. This outcome validates earlier theoretical findings suggesting that specific quantum noise can boost global robustness [15, 20, 25]. The presence of "_n" in each model name in the figure signifies the model's utilization of n qubits.

High efficiency of tensor network. Importantly, *VeriQR* transformed quantum models into tensor network models and applied a tensor network-driven algorithm (referred to as "TN" in Table 2) for global robustness assessment. Table 2 provides an experimental comparison with a baseline implementation (labeled as "Baseline") that does not incorporate tensors in global robustness evaluation. In this evaluation, a timeout threshold ("TO" entries) of 7,200 s was imposed. The results demonstrate that *the tensor network approach significantly enhances verification speed for a large number of qubits (more than 12)*, thereby improving the scalability compared to the precise *local robustness* verification outlined in Table 1.

Remark 2. To further verify the robustness of *VeriQR* both locally and globally, we have conducted additional experiments. These experiments involved testing the QML models presented in Tables 1 and 2 but with varying numbers of qubits and different types and levels of noise. Furthermore, the experimental QML models encompass 45 MNIST classifiers that have been designed to classify all possible combinations of handwritten digits $\{0, 1, 2, \ldots, 9\}$. All of these experiment results, along with the corresponding artifact for this paper, can be accessed in our code repository.

5   Conclusion

This paper presented *VeriQR*, a graphical user interface (GUI) tool developed to verify the robustness of QML models in the current NISQ era, where noise is unavoidable. *VeriQR* offers exact, under-approximate, and tensor network-based algorithms for local and global robustness verification of real-world QML models in the presence of quantum noise. Throughout the verification process, *VeriQR* can identify quantum adversarial examples (states) and utilize them for adversarial training to improve the local robustness as the same as classical machine learning. Additionally, *VeriQR* applies specific quantum noise to enhance the global robustness. Furthermore, *VeriQR* is capable of accommodating any quantum model in the OpenQASM 2.0 format and can convert QML models into this format to establish a unified benchmark framework for robustness verification.

Acknowledgments. We would like to thank Runhong He for his valuable discussion. This work was partly supported by the Youth Innovation Promotion Association, Chinese Academy of Sciences (Grant No. 2023116), the Australian Research Council (Grant No. DP220102059), National Natural Science Foundation of China (Grants No. 62002333) and Innovation Program for Quantum Science and Technology (Grants No. 2021ZD0302901). This work was done when Yanling Lin was a remote research intern supervised by A/Prof. Ji Guan at the Institute of Software, Chinese Academy of Sciences.

Data Availability Statement. The raw (classical) data underlying this article are available in the article, and the corresponding quantum version data can be found in the online supplement material - the github code repository https://github.com/Veri-Q/VeriQR or the artifacts at [29].

References

1. Albarghouthi, A., et al.: Introduction to neural network verification. Found. Trends® Programm. Lang. **7**(1–2), 1–157 (2021)
2. Balunovic, M., Baader, M., Singh, G., Gehr, T., Vechev, M.: Certifying geometric robustness of neural networks. In: Advances in Neural Information Processing Systems, vol. 32 (2019)
3. Becker, B., Kohavi, R.: Adult. UCI Machine Learning Repository (1996)
4. Biamonte, J., Wittek, P., Pancotti, N., Rebentrost, P., Wiebe, N., Lloyd, S.: Quantum machine learning. Nature **549**(7671), 195–202 (2017)
5. Biggio, B., Roli, F.: Wild Patterns: ten years after the rise of adversarial machine learning. In: Proceedings of the 2018 ACM SIGSAC Conference on Computer and Communications Security, pp. 2154–2156 (2018)
6. Blanchette, J., Summerfield, M.: C++ GUI programming with Qt 4. Prentice Hall Professional (2006)
7. Broughton, M., et al.: TensorFlow Quantum: a software framework for quantum machine learning. arXiv preprint arXiv:2003.02989 (2020)
8. Chakraborty, A., Alam, M., Dey, V., Chattopadhyay, A., Mukhopadhyay, D.: A survey on adversarial attacks and defences. CAAI Trans. Intell. Technol. **6**(1), 25–45 (2021)
9. Chen, K., et al.: VeriQBench: a benchmark for multiple types of quantum circuits. arXiv preprint arXiv:2206.10880 (2022)
10. Chen, Y.-F., Chung, K.-M., Lengál, O., Lin, J.-A., Tsai, W.-L.: AutoQ: An Automata-Based Quantum Circuit Verifier. In: Enea, C., Lal, A. (eds.) Computer Aided Verification: 35th International Conference, CAV 2023, Paris, France, July 17–22, 2023, Proceedings, Part III, pp. 139–153. Springer Nature Switzerland, Cham (2023). https://doi.org/10.1007/978-3-031-37709-9_7
11. Cross, A.W., Bishop, L.S., Smolin, J.A., Gambetta, J.M.: Open quantum assembly language. arXiv preprint arXiv:1707.03429 (2017)
12. Deng, L.: The mnist database of handwritten digit images for machine learning research. IEEE Signal Process. Mag. **29**(6), 141–142 (2012)
13. Developers, C.: Cirq. https://quantumai.google/cirq
14. Dreossi, T., et al.: VERIFAI: a toolkit for the formal design and analysis of artificial intelligence-based systems. In: International Conference on Computer Aided Verification, pp. 432–442. Springer (2019). https://doi.org/10.1007/978-3-030-25540-4_25
15. Du, Y., Hsieh, M.H., Liu, T., Tao, D., Liu, N.: Quantum noise protects quantum classifiers against adversaries. Phys. Rev. Res. **3**(2), 023153 (2021)
16. Feng, Y., Hahn, E.M., Turrini, A., Zhang, L.: QPMC: a model checker for quantum programs and protocols. In: Bjørner, N., de Boer, F. (eds.) FM 2015. LNCS, vol. 9109, pp. 265–272. Springer, Cham (2015). https://doi.org/10.1007/978-3-319-19249-9_17
17. Fisher, R.A.: Iris. UCI Machine Learning Repository (1988)
18. Gehr, T., Mirman, M., Drachsler-Cohen, D., Tsankov, P., Chaudhuri, S., Vechev, M.: AI2: safety and robustness certification of neural networks with abstract interpretation. In: 2018 IEEE Symposium on Security and Privacy (SP), pp. 3–18. IEEE (2018)
19. Guan, J., Fang, W., Ying, M.: Robustness verification of quantum classifiers. In: Silva, A., Leino, K.R.M. (eds.) Computer Aided Verification: 33rd International Conference, CAV 2021, Virtual Event, July 20–23, 2021, Proceedings, Part I,

pp. 151–174. Springer International Publishing, Cham (2021). https://doi.org/10.1007/978-3-030-81685-8_7

20. Guan, J., Fang, W., Ying, M.: Verifying fairness in quantum machine learning. In: Shoham, S., Vizel, Y. (eds.) Computer Aided Verification: 34th International Conference, CAV 2022, Haifa, Israel, August 7–10, 2022, Proceedings, Part II, pp. 408–429. Springer International Publishing, Cham (2022). https://doi.org/10.1007/978-3-031-13188-2_20

21. Guan, J., Feng, Y., Turrini, A., Ying, M.: Measurement-based verification of quantum Markov chains. In: Gurfinkel, A., Ganesh, V. (eds.) Computer Aided Verification: 36th International Conference, CAV 2024, Montreal, QC, Canada, July 24–27, 2024, Proceedings, Part III, pp. 533–554. Springer Nature Switzerland, Cham (2024). https://doi.org/10.1007/978-3-031-65633-0_24

22. Harrigan, M.P., et al.: Quantum approximate optimization of non-planar graph problems on a planar superconducting processor. Nat. Phys. **17**(3), 332–336 (2021). https://doi.org/10.1038/s41567-020-01105-y

23. Helstrom, C.W.: Detection theory and quantum mechanics. Inf. Control **10**(3), 254–291 (1967)

24. Hofmann, H.: Statlog (German Credit Data). UCI Machine Learning Repository (1994)

25. Huang, J.C., et al.: Certified robustness of quantum classifiers against adversarial examples through quantum noise. In: ICASSP 2023-2023 IEEE International Conference on Acoustics, Speech and Signal Processing (ICASSP), pp. 1–5. IEEE (2023)

26. IBM: Learn quantum computation using Qiskit. https://qiskit.org/textbook/preface.html (Accessed 2021)

27. Katz, G., Barrett, C., Dill, D.L., Julian, K., Kochenderfer, M.J.: Reluplex: an efficient SMT solver for verifying deep neural networks. In: Majumdar, R., Kunčak, V. (eds.) CAV 2017. LNCS, vol. 10426, pp. 97–117. Springer, Cham (2017). https://doi.org/10.1007/978-3-319-63387-9_5

28. Li, R., et al.: PRODeep: a platform for robustness verification of deep neural networks. In: Proceedings of the 28th ACM Joint Meeting on European Software Engineering Conference and Symposium on the Foundations of Software Engineering, pp. 1630–1634 (2020)

29. Lin, Y., Guan, J., Fang, W., Ying, M., Su, Z.: Artifact for veriQR (2024). https://doi.org/10.5281/zenodo.12526235

30. Liu, N., Wittek, P.: Vulnerability of quantum classification to adversarial perturbations. Phys. Rev. A **101**(6), 062331 (2020)

31. Lu, S., Duan, L.M., Deng, D.L.: Quantum adversarial machine learning. Phys. Rev. Res. **2**(3), 033212 (2020)

32. Nielsen, M.A., Chuang, I.L.: Quantum computation and quantum information. Phys. Today **54**(2), 60 (2001)

33. Gay, S.J., Nagarajan, R., Papanikolaou, N.: QMC: a model checker for quantum systems. In: Gupta, A., Malik, S. (eds.) CAV 2008. LNCS, vol. 5123, pp. 543–547. Springer, Heidelberg (2008). https://doi.org/10.1007/978-3-540-70545-1_51

34. Preskill, J.: Quantum computing in the NISQ era and beyond. Quantum **2**, 79 (2018)

35. Quantum, G.A., et al.: Hartree-Fock on a superconducting qubit quantum computer. Science **369**(6507), 1084–1089 (2020)

36. Roberts, C., et al.: TensorNetwork: a library for physics and machine learning (2019). https://tensornetwork.readthedocs.io/en/latest/index.html

37. Goodfellow, I.J., Shlens, J., Szegedy, C.: Explaining and harnessing adversarial examples. arXiv preprint arXiv:1412.6572 (2014)
38. Tran, H.-D., et al.: Robustness verification of semantic segmentation neural networks using relaxed reachability. In: Silva, A., Leino, K.R.M. (eds.) Computer Aided Verification: 33rd International Conference, CAV 2021, Virtual Event, July 20–23, 2021, Proceedings, Part I, pp. 263–286. Springer International Publishing, Cham (2021). https://doi.org/10.1007/978-3-030-81685-8_12
39. Tran, H.-D., et al.: NNV: the neural network verification tool for deep neural networks and learning-enabled cyber-physical systems. In: Lahiri, S.K., Wang, C. (eds.) Computer Aided Verification: 32nd International Conference, CAV 2020, Los Angeles, CA, USA, July 21–24, 2020, Proceedings, Part I, pp. 3–17. Springer International Publishing, Cham (2020). https://doi.org/10.1007/978-3-030-53288-8_1
40. ULB, M.L.G.: Credit card fraud detection. https://www.kaggle.com/datasets/mlg-ulb/creditcardfraud
41. Weber, M., Liu, N., Li, B., Zhang, C., Zhao, Z.: Optimal provable robustness of quantum classification via quantum hypothesis testing. NPJ Quant. Inf. **7**(1), 76 (2021)
42. Xiao, H., Rasul, K., Vollgraf, R.: Fashion-MNIST: a novel image dataset for benchmarking machine learning algorithms. arXiv preprint arXiv:1708.07747 (2017)
43. Xu, X., et al.: MindSpore Quantum: a user-friendly, high-performance, and AI-compatible quantum computing framework. arXiv preprint arXiv:2406.17248 (2024)
44. Zeguendry, A., Jarir, Z., Quafafou, M.: Quantum machine learning: a review and case studies. Entropy **25**(2), 287 (2023)
45. Zhou, L., Barthe, G., Strub, P.Y., Liu, J., Ying, M.: CoqQ: foundational verification of quantum programs. In: Proceedings of the ACM on Programming Languages, vol. 7(POPL), pp. 833–865 (2023)

Programming Languages

Formal Semantics and Analysis
of Multitask PLC ST Programs
with Preemption

Jaeseo Lee and Kyungmin Bae

Pohang University of Science and Technology,
Pohang, South Korea
{sean96,kmbae}@postech.ac.kr

Abstract. Programmable logic controllers (PLCs) are widely used in industrial applications. Ensuring the correctness of PLC programs is important due to their safety-critical nature. Structured text (ST) is an imperative programming language for PLC. Despite recent advances in executable semantics of PLC ST, existing methods neglect complex multitasking and preemption features. This paper presents an executable semantics of PLC ST with preemptive multitasking. Formal analysis of multitasking programs experiences the state explosion problem. To mitigate this problem, this paper also proposes state space reduction techniques for model checking multitask PLC ST programs.

Keywords: Programmable logic controller · Structured Text · Formal semantics · Preemptive multitasking · Partial order reduction

1 Introduction

Programmable logic controllers (PLCs) are industrial computer systems designed to manage tasks in diverse applications, from assembly lines to robotic devices. The IEC 61131-3 international standard [9] defines the programming languages tailored for developing PLC programs, such as Structured Text (ST), a high-level imperative language. The critical role of PLCs lies in their ability to improve the flexibility, efficiency, and reliability of complex industrial control systems.

Ensuring the correctness of PLC programs is of paramount importance due to their safety-critical nature in industrial applications. Over the years, formal analysis of PLC programs has received significant attention from both academia and industry. In response to this demand, many techniques and tools have been developed for formally analyzing PLC programs, including [2,4,10,13,19,25,34], written in various PLC programming languages. In particular, ST is the most expressive of all PLC languages and is widely used for formal analysis [11].

Recent advances introduce a complete executable semantics of PLC ST [18,38]. Traditional "translation-based" methods (e.g., [4,10,13]) convert PLC ST programs into the input language of another analysis tool. They are inherently limited to a particular syntactic subset of the language, determined by the capabilities of the target input language. In contrast, the complete semantics [18,38] can directly deal with the full syntactic subset of the language.

© The Author(s) 2025
A. Platzer et al. (Eds.): FM 2024, LNCS 14933, pp. 425–442, 2025.
https://doi.org/10.1007/978-3-031-71162-6_22

While the existing complete semantics [18, 24, 38] detail the language constructs of PLC ST, they overlook complex multitasking aspects. PLC programs run in iterative rounds, called *scan cycles*, interacting with their controlled entities at each iteration. They manage multiple tasks with different periods, deadlines, and priorities, allowing high-priority tasks to preempt low-priority tasks. Capturing this complex nondeterministic behavior remains an unresolved problem.

Our goal is to extend the PLC ST semantics [24, 38] for preemptive multitask programs. There are two central challenges to achieve this goal:

- Although PLC ST programs operate within fixed time intervals, they can be executed or preempted at any moment within a dense time domain. It is essential to completely capture all possible behaviors.
- Task execution and preemption, despite their arbitrariness, often lead to indistinguishable outcomes. It is crucial to identify and focus on the minimal interactions without compromising completeness.

To address these issues, we first define a "time-complete" semantics that naturally captures all possible behaviors over time points. We then introduce an abstraction to identify equivalent behaviors over time intervals.

Our time-complete semantics of PLC ST, based on the K framework [35], explicitly considers each time point within a dense time domain, and faithfully models task execution and preemption at arbitrary times. In particular, a state in our semantics contains a global time, and the `tick` rule can advance the global time by any amount before the deadline caused by intervals of tasks. Since this semantics involves an infinite number of behaviors within a finite time period, it is *not executable* and is unsuitable for automated analysis.

To deal with the non-executability problem, we define an abstraction of the time-complete semantics, resulting in a time-abstract semantics of PLC ST. In contrast to the time-complete semantics, it restricts the focus to a finite number of interleaving scenarios within a finite time period. Each global time in a state is abstracted into the time interval spanning from the earliest start time to the earliest deadline of the tasks involved. Importantly, our semantics is equivalent to the time-complete semantics in terms of bisimulation.

The nondeterministic nature of preemptive multitasking can still lead to the state explosion problem. To illustrate, consider two tasks T_1 and T_2, where T_2 has a higher priority. If T_1 runs a sequence of code $s_1; s_2; \cdots ; s_n$, then T_2 can preempt T_1 after executing any of s_i, resulting in n potential preemption scenarios. However, only statements that interact with global variables can produce different results. To avoid such redundant behavior, we propose state space reduction methods for our semantics, based on partial order reduction [33].

This paper is organized as follows. Section 2 gives some background on the basic K semantics of PLC ST and partial order reduction. Section 3 explains details of multitask PLC with preemption and introduces a running example. Section 4 presents the time-complete semantics of PLC ST, and Sect. 5 presents the time-abstract semantics. Section 6 presents the state space reduction methods for our semantics, and Sect. 7 shows the experimental results. Section 8 discusses related work. Finally, Sect. 9 presents some concluding remarks.

2   Preliminaries

K Framework. K [35] is a semantic framework for programming languages, based on rewriting logic [27]. It has been widely used to formalize a variety of languages, including C [12], Java [3], JavaScript [31], PLC ST [38], AADL [21,22], and so on. There are several tools that can be used to execute and analyze programming languages using K, including the K tool [20] and Maude [8,37].

In K, program states are represented as multisets of nested cells, called *configurations*. Each cell represents a component of a program state, such as computations and stores. Transitions between configurations are specified as (labeled) K rules, written in a notation that specifies only the relevant parts.

A computation in K is defined as a $\curvearrowright$-separated sequence of computational tasks. For example, $t_1 \curvearrowright t_2 \curvearrowright \ldots \curvearrowright t_n$ represents the computation consisting of t_1 followed by t_2 followed by t_3, and so on. A task can be decomposed into simpler tasks, and the result of a task is forwarded to the subsequent tasks. E.g., $(5+x)*2$ is decomposed into $x \curvearrowright 5 + \square \curvearrowright \square * 2$, where $\square$ is a placeholder for the result of a previous task. If x evaluates to some value, say 4, then $4 \curvearrowright 5 + \square \curvearrowright \square * 2$ becomes $5 + 4 \curvearrowright \square * 2$, which eventually becomes 18.

The following shows a typical example of K rules for variable lookup, where `lookup` is a label, the k cell contains a computation, *env* contains a map from variables to locations, and *store* contains a map from locations to values:

$$\text{lookup:} \quad \frac{\langle x \curvearrowright \ldots \rangle_k}{v} \ \langle \ldots x \mapsto l \ldots \rangle_{env} \ \langle \ldots l \mapsto v \ldots \rangle_{store}$$

A horizontal line represents a state change, and "..." indicates irrelevant parts. A cell without horizontal lines is not changed by the rule. By the `lookup` rule, if the first item in k is x, then x is replaced by the value v of x in its location l.

PLC ST and its K Semantics. Structured text (ST) is a textual programming language defined in the IEC 61131-3 standard [9]. ST supports common features of imperative programming language, such as (local and global) variable assignments, conditionals, loops, and functions. ST also has unique constructs, such as function blocks, which are callable "objects" with state variables. Functions, function blocks, and programs are called *program organization units* (POUs).

We briefly summarize the syntax of PLC ST. A program is declared with the syntax **PROGRAM** *Name* ... **END_PROGRAM**. A program consists of variable declarations and code. A variable declaration section is declared with the syntax **VAR** *SectionType* ... **END_VAR**, where *SectionType* is one of **GLOBAL**, **INPUT**, and **OUTPUT**, or omitted (local in this case). A global variable section can be written outside of a program. A body of code begins after variable sections.

We give an overview of the K semantics of PLC ST [18,24,38]. Figure 1 shows part of the structure of K configurations. The k, *env*, and *store* cells are explained above. The *stack* cell contains a call stack, which stores the caller's environment and computation when a function block is called. The *pouDef* cell is a map from POU identifiers to POU declarations, each of which contains variable declarations and code. The *pList* cell contains a list of programs to run.

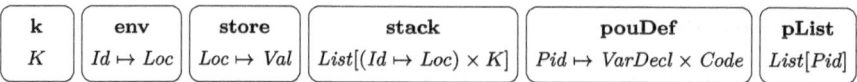

Fig. 1. Examples of K cells for PLC ST.

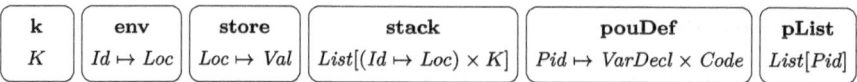

Fig. 2. Examples of K rules for PLC ST.

Figure 2 shows some of the K rules in the PLC ST semantics. Thanks to the modularity of the K technique [35,36], the K rules for common imperative language constructs, such as `assign` for variable assignment, and `if-true` and `if-false` for conditional statements, are (almost) identical to those for other imperative languages, except for slight syntactic differences.

When a function block is called (`fbCall`), the POU instance $[fb, \eta]$ is obtained, where η is a local environment, and tasks of binding the arguments and executing the code S are loaded in k. When the code S is executed (`fbExec`), the current environment ρ and the remaining computation κ are pushed to *stack*, and η becomes a new environment in *env*. When there are no more tasks in k (`fbQuit`), the previous environment ρ and the computation κ are restored from *stack*.

Transition Systems. A *transition system* $\mathcal{S}$ is a tuple (S, s_0, T, AP, L) [1,33], where S is a set of states, $s_0 \in S$ is an initial state, T is a set of transitions such that $\alpha \in T$ is a partial function $\alpha : S \to S$, AP is a set of atomic propositions, and $L : S \to 2^{AP}$ is a state labeling function. A transition $\alpha \in T$ is *enabled* in a state $s \in S$ if $\alpha(s)$ is defined. We denote by *enabled(s)* the set of transitions enabled in s. We often write $s \xrightarrow{\alpha} s'$ to denote $\alpha(s) = s'$ for $s, s' \in S$.

For two transition systems $\mathcal{S}_i = (S_i, s_0^i, T_i, AP, L_i)$, $i = 1, 2$, a binary relation $R \in S_1 \times S_2$ is a *simulation* [7] from $\mathcal{S}_1$ to $\mathcal{S}_2$ iff: (i) $(s_0^1, s_0^2) \in R$; and (ii) for any $(s_1, s_2) \in R$, $L(s_1) = L(s_2)$ holds, and if $s_1 \xrightarrow{\alpha} s_1'$, there exists $s_2' \in S$ such that $s_2 \xrightarrow{\alpha} s_2'$ and $(s_1', s_2') \in R$. A simulation R from $\mathcal{S}_1$ to $\mathcal{S}_2$ is called a *bisimulation* iff R^{-1} is also a simulation from $\mathcal{S}_2$ to $\mathcal{S}_1$.

The K semantics of PLC ST naturally defines a transition system, provided that AP and L are given. States are given by K configurations. Each transition α_l is identified by a rule label l such that $s \xrightarrow{\alpha_l} s'$ iff s is reduced to s' by a K rule with label l. For the "single-task" case, α_l is well defined as a partial function because single-task PLC programs are deterministic. For the "multitask" case, we also need task identifiers as well as rule labels (see Sect. 4.2).

Partial Order Reduction. Consider a transition system $S = (S, s_0, T, AP, L)$. A transition $\alpha \in T$ is *invisible* iff $s \xrightarrow{\alpha} s'$ implies $L(s) = L(s')$. An *independence relation* $I \subseteq T \times T$ is a symmetric and anti-reflexive relation such that for any pair of transitions $(\alpha, \beta) \in I$ and state $s \in S$, where $\alpha, \beta \in enabled(s)$, (i) $\alpha \in enabled(\beta(s))$ and $\beta \in enabled(\alpha(s))$, and (ii) $\alpha(\beta(s)) = \beta(\alpha(s))$. Its complement $D = (T \times T) \setminus I$ is called a dependency relation.

We consider partial order reduction using ample sets [33]. An *ample set* of a state $s \in S$ is a subset of the enabled transitions $ample(s) \subseteq enabled(s)$. A state $s \in S$ is called *fully expanded* when $ample(s) = enabled(s)$. When exploring the state space, only the transitions in $ample(s)$ are explored instead of all the transitions in $enabled(s)$. This results in a reduced transition system $\hat{S}$ that is behaviorally equivalent when ample sets are chosen appropriately.

The following conditions guarantee that a transition system S and its reduced version $\hat{S}$ are behaviorally equivalent [33]: (i) $ample(s) \neq \emptyset$ iff $enabled(s) \neq \emptyset$; (ii) a transition that is dependent on a transition in $ample(s)$ cannot occur before a transition in $ample(s)$ occurs first.[1]; (iii) if s is not fully expanded, all transitions in $ample(s)$ are invisible; and (iv) any cycle in the reduced state space $\hat{S}$ contains at least one fully expanded state.

3 Multitask PLC and a Running Example

In multitask PLC, each program is assigned an *interval* and a *priority*. A program is scheduled to run periodically, where the interval determines the duration of each period. Priorities are given as natural numbers, where a lower number indicates a higher priority. A program with a higher priority can preempt the execution of a program with a lower priority. The execution of each program must be completed before the beginning of its next round.

Multitask PLC programs are difficult to analyze because of their complex interleaving possibilities. Due to the nondeterministic nature of preemption, the number of different interleavings can grow exponentially with the number of programs. E.g., if a program with k statements is preempted, preemption can occur after the i-th statement for any $1 \leq i \leq k$, Therefore, for n programs with different priorities, there are $O(k^{n-1})$ interleaving possibilities by preemption.

Our running example is inspired by the two-wheeled self-balancing robot [6]. The robot moves on flat ground while maintaining its balance. It is equipped with a sonar sensor that detects nearby obstacles. The current state information is displayed on the attached panel. It takes control input from a remote controller to move forward, backward, and turn.

The system consists of three programs: `balanceControl`, `sonar`, and `display`, with intervals of 3 ms, 4 ms, and 12 ms, and priorities of 1, 2, and 3, respectively. Figure 3 shows a code snippet of `balanceControl` and `sonar`, where the intervals and priorities are declared in `CONFIGURATION`. The global variables `mode` and `obstacle_flag` are used for communication between different programs.

---

[1] For $s \xrightarrow{\beta_1} \cdots \xrightarrow{\beta_n} s_n \xrightarrow{\alpha} t$, if α depends on $ample(s)$, $\beta_i \in ample(s)$ for some $i \leq n$.

```
CONFIGURATION Config                          PROGRAM balanceControl
  RESOURCE Res ON PLC                           VAR_INOUT
    TASK T1(INTERVAL:= T#3ms, PRIORITY := 1);     cmd_forward : DINT; cmd_turn: DINT ;
    TASK T2(INTERVAL:= T#4ms, PRIORITY := 2);     gyro_sensor : REAL;
    TASK T3(INTERVAL:= T#12ms, PRIORITY := 3);    ...
    PROGRAM bCtrl WITH T1 : balanceControl;     END_VAR
    PROGRAM sonar WITH T2 : sonar;
    PROGRAM dsply WITH T3 : display;            VAR
  END_RESOURCE                                    avg_cnt : REAL := 0 ;

  VAR_GLOBAL                                    END_VAR
    mode : MODE := CAL;
    obstacle_flag : BOOL := FALSE;              CASE mode OF
  END_VAR                                         CAL:
END_CONFIGURATION                                   offset := offset + gyro_sensor;
                                                    avg_cnt := avg_cnt + 1;
PROGRAM sonar                                       IF avg_cnt >= 1 THEN
  VAR_INPUT                                           offset := offset / avg_cnt;
    sonar : REAL;                                     mode := CONTROL;
    ...                                               ...
  END_VAR                                            END_IF;
                                                  CONTROL:
  IF mode = CONTROL AND sonar <= 100 THEN           IF obstacle_flag THEN
    obstacle_flag := 1;                               cmd_forward := -100;
    ...                                               ...
  END_IF;                                           END_IF;
  ...                                             END_CASE;
END_PROGRAM                                     END_PROGRAM
```

Fig. 3. Two-wheeled self-balancing robot code.

The balanceControl program takes control inputs (such as cmd_forward and cmd_turn) and balancing inputs (such as gyro_sensor). The robot has two modes CAL and CONTROL, where the global variable mode indicates the current mode. When balanceControl is executed for the first time, it calibrates and sets the appropriate initial settings for the robot and sets mode to CONTROL. The program starts controlling the robot from the second round.

The sonar program takes sonar sensor inputs (such as sonar). When mode is CONTROL, the program measures the distances to nearby objects to detect an imminent collision hazard. If so, it sets the global variable obstacle_flag to TRUE. At this point, balanceControl ignores its control input and attempts to stop the robot by setting cmd_forward to −100.

Figure 4 shows two interleaving scenarios that reach different outcomes. Each rectangle denotes the range from the *earliest possible start time* to the *deadline* for a task. The heads and tails of horizontal arrows denote the start and end of program execution. The curved vertical arrows denote preemption and its return. In Scenario 1, there is no preemption.

4   Formal Semantics of Multitask PLC

This section presents an executable semantics of PLC ST with preemptive multitasking, which extends the existing K semantics of PLC ST [18,24,38]. Our semantics specifies all possible interleavings by nondeterministic preemption over a dense time domain. We take into account a global time that can be advanced by any amount up to the deadline, determined by the intervals of tasks.

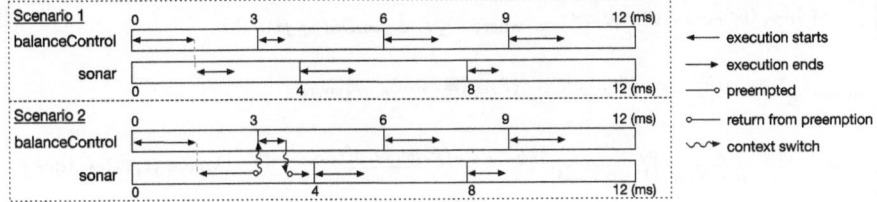

Fig. 4. Two interleaving scenarios of the robot example.

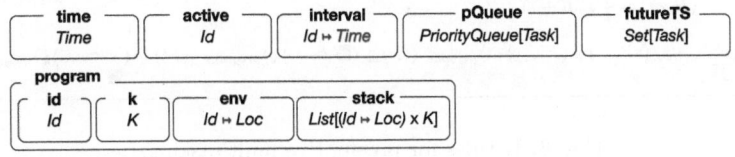

Fig. 5. K configurations for multitask PLC.

4.1 K Configuration for Multitask PLC

Figure 5 depicts the K cells for specifying preemptive multitasking behaviors, in addition to the existing cells in the original semantics [18, 24, 38]: (1) *time* denotes the current time; (2) *active* denotes the identifier of the currently running program; (3) *interval* has a map from program identifiers to their intervals; (4) *pQueue* contains a priority queue of tasks that are ready to run according to *time* and *interval*; and (5) *futureTS* contains tasks that are not ready.

Tasks are represented as a tuple (id, pr, es, dl), where id is the identifier of the program, pr is the program's priority, es is the earliest start time, and dl is the deadline. Each program can start after its earliest start time and must end before its deadline. When the current time is 0, es is 0 and dl is the interval.

The *Program* cell encompasses the program's identifier, a computation, and an environment and a call stack. Unlike the single-task semantics in Sect. 2, in our multi-task semantics, each program maintains its own computation, environment, and stack. That is, a full K configuration has the nested structure of the form (where other K cells not used in this paper are omitted):

$$\langle \cdots \rangle_{time}\ \langle \cdots \rangle_{active}\ \langle \cdots \rangle_{interval}\ \langle \cdots \rangle_{pQueue}\ \langle \cdots \rangle_{futureTS}\ \langle \cdots \rangle_{store}\ \langle \cdots \rangle_{pouDef}\ \cdots$$
$$\langle\langle \cdots \rangle_{id}\ \langle \cdots \rangle_{k}\ \langle \cdots \rangle_{env}\ \langle \cdots \rangle_{stack}\ \cdots \rangle_{program}\ \cdots\ \langle\langle \cdots \rangle_{id}\ \langle \cdots \rangle_{k}\ \langle \cdots \rangle_{env}\ \langle \cdots \rangle_{stack}\ \cdots \rangle_{program}$$

4.2 K Rules for Multitask PLC

Figure 6 shows the K rules to specify preemptive multitasking behaviors. The `tick` rule (nondeterministically) increments the current time up to the minimum deadline of the tasks, where $minDL(pq, ft) = \min(deadlines(pq) \cup deadlines(ft))$, with $deadlines(A)$ denoting the set of deadlines in A. The side condition of `tick` maintains the following validity constraint: the value of the *time* cell should not exceed any of the deadlines of the tasks in *pQueue* and *futureTS*.

$$\text{tick: } \frac{\langle t \rangle_{time} \langle pq \rangle_{pQueue} \langle ft \rangle_{futureTS}}{t'} \qquad \text{where } t \leq t' < minDL(pq, ft)$$

$$\text{execute: } \frac{\langle \cdot \rangle_{active} \langle\!\langle (P, \_, es, dl) \dots \rangle_{pQueue} \langle\!\langle P \rangle_{id} \langle \blacksquare \curvearrowright \dots \rangle_k \dots \rangle_{program}}{P}$$

$$\text{placeT: } \langle t \rangle_{time} \langle \frac{pq}{insert(pq, (P, pr, t, dl))} \rangle_{pQueue} \langle \dots \frac{(P, pr, es, dl)}{\cdot} \dots \rangle_{futureTS} \qquad \text{where } \{t\} \cap [es, dl] \neq \emptyset$$

$$\text{endProgram: } \langle t \rangle_{time} \langle \dots P \mapsto \iota \dots \rangle_{interval} \langle\!\langle P \rangle_{id} \langle \frac{\cdot}{\blacksquare \curvearrowright code} \rangle_k \rangle_{program} \langle \dots \frac{(P, pr, es, dl)}{\cdot} \dots \rangle_{pQueue}$$

$$\langle \dots \frac{\cdot}{(P, pr, es + \iota, dl + \iota)} \dots \rangle_{futureTS} \frac{\langle P \rangle_{active}}{\cdot} \langle \dots P \mapsto (\_, code) \dots \rangle_{pouDef} \qquad \text{where } es < t$$

$$\text{preempt: } \frac{\langle P' \rangle_{active} \langle\!\langle (P, \_) \dots (P', \_) \dots \rangle_{pQueue} \langle\!\langle P \rangle_{id} \langle \blacksquare \curvearrowright \dots \rangle_k \rangle_{program} \langle\!\langle P' \rangle_{id} \langle \frac{\cdot}{\blacksquare} \curvearrowright \dots \rangle_k \rangle_{program}}{P}$$

Fig. 6. K rules for preemptive multitasking.

Lemma 1. *For a K configuration that satisfies the validity constraint, any next configuration obtained by applying a rule also satisfies the constraint.*

The `execute` rule executes the top task in *pQueue* if no task is currently running. Before the rule is applied, the *active* cell is empty, and the execution of each program is "blocked" by ■ at the top of its *k* cell. Suppose P is the program for the top task in *pQueue*. When `execute` is applied, the *active* cell is updated with the program's identifier P, and ■ is removed from the top of P's *k* cell.

The `placeT` rule moves a task in *futureTS* into *pQueue*, when the task is ready to run according to *time* and *interval*. The function $insert(pq, T)$ inserts task T into the priority queue *pq*. The side condition states that the current time is between its earliest start time and the deadline. It also sets the third item of the task to the current time t to record when this happens.

The `endProgram` rule is applied when the execution of the active program is finished. Suppose P is the active program and the *k* cell of P is empty. When `endProgram` is applied, the *active* cell becomes empty and the corresponding task is removed from *pQueue*. The subsequent task for P is added to *futureTS*, where the earliest start time and deadline are increased by P's interval ι. Finally, the code of P, where the execution is blocked by ■, is loaded into the *k* cell of P. The side condition asserts that the execution of P takes non-zero time.

The `preempt` rule preempts a lower-priority task, and executes a higher-priority task in *pQueue*. In the rule, P has a higher priority than P' because it is the top element in *pQueue*. The *active* becomes P, and ■ moves to P' from P.

It is worth noting that the rules in Fig. 6 are all nondeterministic. The time can be increased by any value up to the deadline, and different tasks can have the same priority and interval. For this reason, transitions with `tick` are identified by time differences (e.g., `tick(1)` increases the time by 1), and transitions with the other four rules are identified by rule labels and program identifiers (e.g., `placeT(P)` moves a task $(P, \dots)$ from *futureTS* to *pQueue*).

$$s_1 \quad \frac{\langle 0 \rangle_{time} \ \langle \cdot \rangle_{active} \ \langle (P_b, 1, 0, 3), (P_s, 2, 0, 4) \rangle_{pQueue}}{\langle \cdot \rangle_{futureTS} \ \langle\langle P_b \rangle_{id} \ \langle \blacksquare \curvearrowright ... \rangle_k ... \rangle_{program} \ \langle\langle P_s \rangle_{id} \ \langle \blacksquare \curvearrowright ... \rangle_k ... \rangle_{program} ...}$$

$$s_2 \quad \frac{\langle 0 \rangle_{time} \ \langle P_b \rangle_{active} \ \langle (P_b, 1, 0, 3), (P_s, 2, 0, 4) \rangle_{pQueue}}{\langle \cdot \rangle_{futureTS} \ \langle\langle P_b \rangle_{id} \ \langle ... \rangle_k ... \rangle_{program} \ \langle\langle P_s \rangle_{id} \ \langle \blacksquare \curvearrowright ... \rangle_k ... \rangle_{program} ...}$$

$$s_3 \quad \frac{\langle 1 \rangle_{time} \ \langle \cdot \rangle_{active} \ \langle (P_s, 2, 0, 4) \rangle_{pQueue}}{\langle (P_b, 1, 3, 6) \rangle_{futureTS} \ \langle\langle P_b \rangle_{id} \ \langle \cdot \rangle_k ... \rangle_{program} \ \langle\langle P_s \rangle_{id} \ \langle \blacksquare \curvearrowright ... \rangle_k ... \rangle_{program} ...}$$

$$s_4 \quad \frac{\langle 3 \rangle_{time} \ \langle P_s \rangle_{active} \ \langle (P_b, 1, 3, 6), (P_s, 2, 0, 4) \rangle_{pQueue}}{\langle \cdot \rangle_{futureTS} \ \langle\langle P_b \rangle_{id} \ \langle \blacksquare \curvearrowright ... \rangle_k ... \rangle_{program} \ \langle\langle P_s \rangle_{id} \ \langle ... \rangle_k ... \rangle_{program} ...}$$

$$s_5 \quad \frac{\langle 3 \rangle_{time} \ \langle P_b \rangle_{active} \ \langle (P_b, 1, 3, 6), (P_s, 2, 0, 4) \rangle_{pQueue}}{\langle \cdot \rangle_{futureTS} \ \langle\langle P_b \rangle_{id} \ ... \rangle_k ... \rangle_{program} \ \langle\langle P_s \rangle_{id} \ \langle \blacksquare \curvearrowright ... \rangle_k ... \rangle_{program} ...}$$

Fig. 7. An example of execution sequences, where $P_b = balanceControl$ and $P_s = sonar$.

4.3 Example of K Rule Applications

Figure 7 shows a sequence of states simulating an execution path for Scenario 2 in Fig. 4. Applying `execute` to state s_1 to execute `balanceControl` gives s_2. After 1 s, `balanceControl` executes its code (using other K rules) and then `endProgram` is applied, resulting in s_3. The following shows the transitions:

$$s_1 \xrightarrow{\text{execute}(P_b)} s_2 \xrightarrow{\text{tick}(1)} \cdots \xrightarrow{\text{endProgram}(P_b)} s_3$$
$$\xrightarrow{\text{execute}(P_s)} \cdots \xrightarrow{\text{tick}(2)} \cdots \xrightarrow{\text{placeT}(P_b)} s_4 \xrightarrow{\text{preempt}(P_b)} s_5 \longrightarrow \cdots$$

Likewise, Scenario 1 can be simulated by the following sequence of transitions. It is the same as the above up to s_3, and has different states after that.

$$s_1 \xrightarrow{\text{execute}(P_b)} s_2 \xrightarrow{\text{tick}(1)} \cdots \xrightarrow{\text{endProgram}(P_b)} s_3$$
$$\xrightarrow{\text{execute}(P_s)} \cdots \xrightarrow{\text{tick}(2)} \cdots \xrightarrow{\text{endProgram}(P_s)} s_4' \xrightarrow{\text{placeT}(P_b)} s_5' \xrightarrow{\text{execute}(P_b)} \cdots$$

5 Time Abstraction

A single program execution can produce an infinite number of cases, due to *nondeterministic time advances*. In Scenario 2 of Fig. 4, the first execution of `balanceControl` can end in 1 *ms*, 0.5 *ms*, 0.25 *ms*, and so on. However, there are only a finite number of critical times that may change the possible behaviors.

This section presents a time abstraction for our multitask PLC ST semantics. The main idea is to express time abstractly with a time interval that represents an infinite number of time points. We define an abstract function that maps a concrete K configuration to its abstract version and apply it globally to the K rules defined in Sect. 4.2. We show that the resulting abstract semantics is equivalent to the concrete PLC semantics in terms of bisimulation.

$$\texttt{placeT'}: \frac{\langle|\ \underline{\quad t_{min}\quad}, t_{max}\ |\rangle_{time}\ \langle\ \underline{\qquad pq\qquad}\ \rangle_{pQueue}\ \langle ... \underline{(P, pr, es, dl)} ...\rangle_{futureTS}}{max(t_{min}, es) \qquad\qquad insert(pq, (P, pr, es, dl)) \qquad\qquad\qquad \cdot}$$

$$\text{where } [t_{min}, t_{max}] \cap [es, dl] \neq \emptyset$$

$$\texttt{endProgram'}: \frac{\langle|\ \underline{\qquad t_{min}\qquad}, \underline{\qquad t_{max}\qquad}\ |\rangle_{time}\ \langle ... P \mapsto \iota ...\rangle_{interval}\ \langle\underline{P}\rangle_{active}\ \langle\underline{pq}\rangle_{pQueue}}{max(maxES(pq'), es)\ \ minDL(pq', ft') \qquad\qquad \cdot \qquad\qquad\quad pq'}$$

$$\frac{\langle\underline{ft}\rangle_{futureTS}\ \langle\langle\underline{P}\rangle_{id}\ \langle\ \underline{\qquad\cdot\qquad}\ \rangle_k\rangle_{program}\ \langle ... P \mapsto (\_, code) ...\rangle_{pouDef}}{ft' \qquad\qquad\qquad \blacksquare \curvearrowright code}$$

$$\text{where } (P, pr, es, dl) \in pq, \text{ and } pq' = pq \setminus \{(P, pr, es, dl)\}, \text{ and } ft' = ft \cup \{(P, pr, es + \iota, dl + \iota)\}$$

Fig. 8. K rules for multitask interleaving with abstract time

5.1 Abstraction Function

The abstraction function takes a K configuration with a time value and returns the K configuration with a time interval that (i) contains the original time, and (ii) encompasses all other times that have equivalent behaviors. Now the *time* cell contains a pair of times $|\ t_1, t_2\ |$, and represents the set of all the times that are contained in the left-closed right-open interval $[t_1, t_2)$.

Definition 1. *Given a K configuration* $s = \langle t\rangle_{time}\ \langle pq\rangle_{pQueue}\ \langle ft\rangle_{futureTS}\ \cdots$, *its time abstraction is defined as follows, where* $maxES(pq) = \min(startTimes(pq))$, *with* $startTimes(pq)$ *denoting the set of earliest start times in pq:*

$$\lambda(s) = \langle|\ max(maxES(pq), t), minDL(pq,\ ft)\ |\rangle_{time}\ \langle pq\rangle_{pQueue}\ \langle ft\rangle_{futureTS}\ \cdots$$

Figure 8 shows the interleaving rules with the abstract time. Except `tick`, `endProgram`, and `placeT`, all other K rules, including `execute` and `preempt`, are the same before and after the abstraction. The `tick` rule is now identity. The `endProgram` and `placeT` rules move the possible time range of the system. It moves the minimum time value (left) to *maximum earliest start times* of the tasks in *pQueue* or remains unchanged if the priority queue is empty. The maximum time value (right) is moved to the *minimum deadlines* of the tasks in *pQueue* and *futureTS* altogether.

5.2 Equivalence Before and After Abstraction

The concrete semantics and the abstract semantics are equivalent in terms of bisimulation. Let R be a binary relation between concrete configurations and abstract configurations such that $(s, \lambda(s)) \in R$ for each configuration s. Then, R is a bisimulation with respect to atomic propositions not depending on *time*.

By construction, for a concrete transition $s \xrightarrow{\alpha} s'$, there exists an abstract transition $\lambda(s) \xrightarrow{\alpha} \lambda(s')$. For an abstract transition $\hat{s} \xrightarrow{\alpha} \hat{s}'$, there also exists a corresponding concrete transition $s \xrightarrow{\alpha} s'$, where the *time* values t and t' of s and s', respectively, can be any values in the corresponding intervals such that: (i) $t \leq t'$ if $\alpha = \texttt{tick}$, and (ii) $t = t'$ if $\alpha \neq \texttt{tick}$. The complete proof of the following theorem can be found in [23].

Theorem 1. *Given an initial K configuration s_0 satisfying the validity constraint, R is a bisimulation between the concrete transition system S from s_0 and the abstract transition system $\hat{S}$ from $\lambda(s_0)$.*

6 State Space Reduction

In this section, we introduce two state space reduction methods that reduce the state space. Since the K rules we introduced involve many nondeterministic choices, it results in a large state space that makes it hard to analyze.

The first technique is the application of the ample set approach. Based on the observation that interleaving of placeT with other rules spawns many different but essentially the same execution paths, we include placeT in the ample set, if not fully expanded. It is not simple because not all enabled placeT can be prioritized without consequences. The second technique is to put rules that do not change the local memory first. This is possible because the atomic properties of interest in this paper only depend on the local memory.

6.1 Our Ample Set Approach

Consider state $\langle \cdot \rangle_{active}$ $\langle (P_1, 1, 0, 20) \rangle_{pQueue}$ $\langle (P_2, 2, 5, 25) \rangle_{futureTS}$ .... From this state, both execute and placeT are applicable. In either order, it converges to $\langle P \rangle_{active}$ $\langle (P_1, 1, 0, 20)$ $\langle (P_2, 2, 5, 25) \rangle_{pQueue}$ $\langle \cdot \rangle_{futureTS}$ ..., and all states in this procedure including the intermediate states share the same set of atomic properties held. Thus, we only need to explore one of these paths. This phenomenon stems from the independence of these two rules. Just like this case, when placeT does not change the top element of $pQueue$, it is only dependent on tick.

Definition 2. *For a state s, if* placeT$(P) \in enabled(s)$ *and* placeT(P) *does not change the top element of pQueue, ample$(s) = \{$placeT(P), tick$(\tau)\}$; otherwise, ample$(s) = enabled(s)$.*

To prove that Definition 2 satisfies the ample set conditions, we first show the following lemma for Condition (ii). Lemma 2 shows that placeT is independent of any other rule except tick if it does not change the top element of $pQueue$, since only the top element of $pQueue$ decides what to execute or preempt. Lemma 2 also shows that tick is independent of any other rule except placeT, since the other rules do not restrain the side condition of tick.

Lemma 2. *(1)* placeT(P) *is independent of all other transitions except* tick(τ), *if it does not change the top element of the pQueue cell. (2)* tick(τ) *is independent of all other transitions except* placeT$(\cdot)$.

The following theorem states that *ample* in Definition 2 satisfies the ample set conditions regarding atomic propositions that do not modify *time, pQueue*, and *futureTS*. (See [23] for the full proof.)

Theorem 2. *For any execution path without continuous infinite application of* `tick`, *ample satisfies the four conditions for partial order reduction.*

Proof (Sketch). (i) It immediately follows from Definition 2. (ii) It holds since transitions in $ample(s)$ are only dependent on other transitions in *ample* and no other enabled transitions. When `placeT`(P) does not change the top element of *pQueue*, Lemma 2 shows the independence of `placeT`(P) and of `tick` with all other rules. (iii) When it is not fully expanded, $ample(s)$ contains `tick` and `placeT`. These two rules are invisible since they only look and modify *time, pQueue,* and *futureTS* cells, which are irrelevant to any atomic propositions of interest. (iv) By Definition 2, when $ample(s) \neq enabled(s)$, $ample(s) =$ {`placeT`(P), `tick`(τ)}. The number `placeT` is bounded by the number of tasks in *futureTS*. With the assumption that there is no cycle only consisting of `tick`, if there is a cycle in the reduced system, it must contain at least one fully expanded state.   □

6.2   Internal Transitions Without Memory Update

Certain scenarios may be equivalent even if they are not addressed by our ample set approach. Consider the following state: $s = \langle P \rangle_{active} \langle\langle x \curvearrowright ...\rangle_k \langle P \rangle_{id} \rangle_{program} \langle\langle (P', 1, 0, 30) \ (P, 2, 0, 20)\rangle_{pQueue} ....$ Both `lookup` and `preempt` are enabled in s. Applying `preempt` results in $\langle P' \rangle_{active} \langle\langle \blacksquare \curvearrowright x \curvearrowright ...\rangle_k \langle P \rangle_{id} \rangle_{program} \langle\langle (P', 1, 0, 30) \ (P, 2, 0, 20)\rangle_{pQueue} ...,$ where `lookup` is not enabled anymore. This makes `lookup` dependent on `preempt` and cannot satisfy Condition (ii) of ample set. All rules such as `if-T`, `if-F`, and `fbCall`, which operate internally in a k cell of a program without modifying the memory state show the same phenomena. We call these rules *internal rules*.

Figure 9 shows a state space diagram when an internal transition τ and `preempt` is possible. Each circle represents a state and the active task is shown below each circle. We start from the bottom-left state. Whether we choose τ or `preempt`, it converges to the same state in the top-right state. States within the same dashed oval are indistinguishable from outside because τ does not modify any part of the memory in the system. Therefore, we only need to explore the top path by prioritizing internal rules over `preempt`.

Suppose a state labeling function satisfies the following condition: for any two states s and s' with the same *store* cell, $L(s) = L(s')$. Based on the above observation, we have the following theorem (the proof is in [23]).

Theorem 3. *Consider a state s such that* `preempt`(Q), $\tau \in enabled(s)$, *where τ is internal. For any $s \xrightarrow{\text{preempt}(Q)} s_1 \xrightarrow{\alpha_1} \cdots \xrightarrow{\alpha_{n-1}} s_n \xrightarrow{\tau} t$, there exists $s \xrightarrow{\tau} s' \xrightarrow{\text{preempt}(Q)} s'_1 \xrightarrow{\alpha_1} \cdots \xrightarrow{\alpha_{n-1}} t$, such that $L(s_i) = L(s'_i)$ for $1 \leq i \leq n$.*

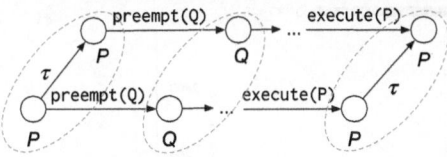

Fig. 9. State diagram when an internal transition and `preempt` are available

7   Experimental Evaluation

To evaluate the effectiveness of our methods, we have implemented our semantics and state space reduction methods in Maude [8].[2] We have conducted experiments to measure the performance of state space exploration up to a given model time bound. We first compare time and the number of states before and after the abstraction. To emphasize the strength of the abstracted semantics, we also compare it with the sampling-based approach, which is very fast but skips a significant part of the full state space. Then, we compare the time and state space with and without each of the reduction methods in the abstract setting. We refer to the longer report [23] for more details.

We consider seven models, each with 2 priority settings and 3 model time bounds. The first model is the self-balancing robot in Sect. 3. We manually adapted and translated the original source's C program into PLC ST programs. The second model is the traffic light example from [24] adapted to a multitask setting. There are four light controllers, two for cars and two for pedestrians. There is one task for a timer, thus there are up to 5 programs in total. The LOC of the robot model is 75 and the LOC of the traffic light model is 259. The third to the sixth model is a variant of the second model with different numbers of traffic lights. The seventh model is from the PLCOpen library [4]; it is a single-task model but adapted to a multitask model (the LOC is 2154).

In the case of concrete semantics, since the nondeterministic `tick` rule is not executable per se, we symbolically execute this semantics using the approach in [24]. In the sampling-based semantics, we increase the time by the greatest common divisor of the intervals of the programs. The sampling method samples the time of the greatest common divisor of the intervals of all the programs. All experiments were conducted on Intel Xeon 2.8 GHz with 256 GB memory. Timeout is set to 1 h in all settings.

Figure 10 shows the analysis time comparison in scale between concrete and abstract (left) and sampling and abstract (right). The timed-out data is marked at the edge of the graph. In all cases, state space exploration with time abstraction takes less state space and time than the concrete semantics. In cases where the execution with concrete semantics is not timed out, the abstract semantics takes at most a hundredth of time. Except for only one case, abstract semantics outperforms the sampling-based semantics.

---

[2] As mentioned in Sect. 2, the K tool and Maude can be used to run K semantics. We use Maude since it is easier to perform model checking with state space reduction.

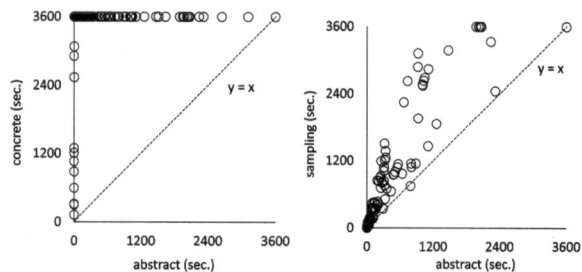

Fig. 10. Analysis time comparison between concrete, sampling, and abstract semantics

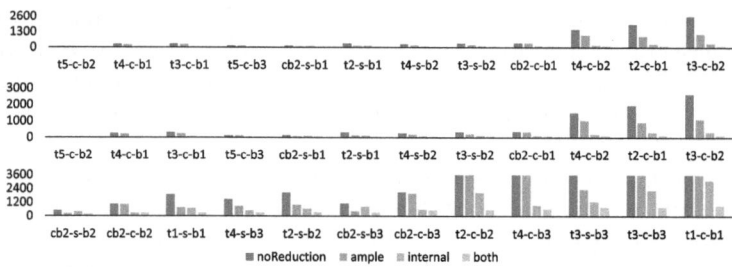

Fig. 11. Analysis time comparison with and without reduction techniques

Figure 11 shows the state space exploration time comparison of abstract semantics with and without each reduction technique. 'noReduction' is the result without any reduction methods, 'ample' with our ample set approach, 'internal' with the reduction using internal memory, and 'both' with both reduction methods. The x-axis shows the benchmark models with their settings. 'r' means our robot models and 't1'–'t5' are the traffic light models with varying numbers of traffic lights. 'cb2' is the one from PLCOpen safety library. 's' and 'c' respectively note the priority setting with fewer possible preemptions (simple) and with greater preemption points (complex). 'b1'–'b3' shows the model's time bound. 'bn' maps to the bound of the greatest common divisor of intervals $\times n$. The y-axis shows the analysis time in seconds. Both methods proved their effectiveness. The internal rule reduction is effective throughout all the settings. The ample set approach is more effective in settings with more equal-priority programs. Applying both reductions proved to be the most efficient.

8 Related Work

Numerous methods exist for formally analyzing PLC programs written in various languages, including Function Block Diagram [25,32], Sequential Function Chart [2,15,19], Ladder Diagram [26,34], Instruction List [5], and Structured Text [4,10,13]. Most of these approaches utilize a model checking methodology.

As mentioned in Sect. 1, they typically involve translating PLC programs into models that are compatible with existing model checking tools.

The K framework, along with its methodology for semantic definition [35], has been successfully applied to a variety of programming languages, including C [12,16], Java [3], JavaScript [31], Ethereum Virtual Machine [17], etc. In particular, several studies [18,24,38] propose a K semantics for PLC ST. However, preemptive multitasking features and their state-space reduction methods are not considered in these previous K semantics for PLC ST.

A relatively small number of studies deal with multitask PLC. In [14], a technique for symbolic execution of multitask PLC with preemption is presented. However, it is aimed at generating test inputs rather than formal analysis. Another paper [28] focuses on the verification of multitask PLCs with preemption. It is used to verify a specific class of timed multitask PLC program with input delay using the Uppaal tool. However, [28] focuses on Sequential Function Chart (SFC) and Ladder Diagram (LD), whereas our work focuses on ST.

Real-Time Maude [30] provides several formal analysis methods for real-time systems, along with time-complete abstraction [29]. It is based on the *maximal time elapse* strategy, where time elapses until the earliest time at which any event is enabled. However, the maximal time elapse strategy is not complete for multitask PLC ST, because events may happen in arbitrary time. In contrast, our time-optimal semantics is equivalent to the time-complete semantics.

9   Concluding Remarks

We have presented an executable semantics of multitask PLC ST with preemption, based on the K framework. Our semantics efficiently and faithfully covers all possible interleaving scenarios by nondeterministic preemption. We have defined a time-complete semantics that explicitly considers a dense time domain. We have then defined a time abstraction to identify equivalent behaviors across time intervals, resulting in behaviorally equivalent time-abstract semantics.

To cope with the state explosion problem by nondeterministic preemptive multitasking, we have proposed state space reduction techniques based on partial order reduction. We have evaluated the effectiveness of our techniques using several multitask PLC ST benchmarks. The experimental results have shown a significant improvement in the performance of state space exploration using our time-abstract semantics and state space reduction techniques.

There are several limitations to be addressed in the future work. We should develop more case studies on model checking multitask PLC ST programs, including industrial case studies. Our current implementation lacks tool support and we plan to integrate our framework with existing analysis tools, such as STBMC [24]. Since our framework does not yet support multi-PLC configurations, we should expand our semantics to support multi-PLC.

Acknowledgement. This work was supported in part by the National Research Foundation of Korea (NRF) grants funded by the Korea government (MSIT) (No. 2021R1A5A1021944 and No. RS-2023-00251577), and by the NATO Science for Peace and Security Programme project SymSafe (grant number G6133).

Data Availability Statement. The artifact for reproducing the experiments is available at https://doi.org/10.5281/zenodo.12530343.

References

1. Baier, C., Katoen, J.P.: Principles of Model Checking. MIT Press (2008)
2. Bauer, N., et al.: Verification of PLC programs given as sequential function charts. In: Ehrig, H., et al. (eds.) Integration of Software Specification Techniques for Applications in Engineering. LNCS, vol. 3147, pp. 517–540. Springer, Heidelberg (2004). https://doi.org/10.1007/978-3-540-27863-4_28
3. Bogdanas, D., Roşu, G.: K-Java: a complete semantics of Java. In: Proceedings of the 42nd ACM SIGPLAN-SIGACT Symposium on Principles of Programming Languages, pp. 445–456. ACM (2015). https://doi.org/10.1145/2676726.2676982
4. Bohlender, D., Hamm, D., Kowalewski, S.: Cycle-bounded model checking of PLC software via dynamic large-block encoding. In: Proceedings of the 33rd ACM Symposium on Applied Computing, pp. 1891–1898. ACM (2018). https://doi.org/10.1145/3167132.3167334
5. Canet, G., Couffin, S., Lesage, J.J., Petit, A., Schnoebelen, P.: Towards the automatic verification of PLC programs written in instruction list. In: Proceedings of the IEEE International Conference on Systems, Man and Cybernetics, vol. 4, pp. 2449–2454. IEEE (2000). https://doi.org/10.1109/ICSMC.2000.884359
6. Chikamasa, T.: NXTway-GS C API for a two wheeled self-balancing robot. https://lejos-osek.sourceforge.net/nxtway_gs.htm. Accessed 19 Apr 2024
7. Clarke, Jr., E.M., Grumberg, O., Kroening, D., Peled, D., Veith, H.: Model Checking. MIT Press (2018)
8. Clavel, M., et al.: Maude manual (version 3.4). Tech. rep., SRI International, Menlo Park (2024)
9. Commission, I.E.: Programmable controllers-part 3: programming languages. IEC 61131-3 (1993)
10. Darvas, D., Blanco Vinuela, E., Fernández Adiego, B.: PLCverif: a tool to verify PLC programs based on model checking techniques. In: Proceedings of the 15th International Conference on Accelerator and Large Experimental Physics Control Systems (2015)
11. Darvas, D., Majzik, I., Viñuela, E.B.: PLC program translation for verification purposes. Periodica Polytech. Electric. Eng. Comput. Sci. **61**(2), 151–165 (2017). https://doi.org/10.3311/PPee.9743
12. Ellison, C., Rosu, G.: An executable formal semantics of C with applications. In: Proceedings of the 39th ACM SIGPLAN-SIGACT Symposium on Principles of Programming Languages, vol. 47, pp. 533–544. ACM (2012). https://doi.org/10.1145/2103656.2103719
13. Gourcuff, V., De Smet, O., Faure, J.M.: Efficient representation for formal verification of PLC programs. In: International Workshop on Discrete Event Systems, pp. 182–187. IEEE (2006). https://doi.org/10.1109/WODES.2006.1678428

14. Guo, S., Wu, M., Wang, C.: Symbolic execution of programmable logic controller code. In: Proceedings of the Joint Meeting on Foundations of Software Engineering, pp. 326–336. ACM (2017). https://doi.org/10.1145/3106237.3106245
15. Hassapis, G., Kotini, I., Doulgeri, Z.: Validation of a SFC software specification by using hybrid automata. IFAC Proceedings Volumes 31(15), 107–112 (1998). https://doi.org/10.1016/S1474-6670(17)40537-4
16. Hathhorn, C., Ellison, C., Roşu, G.: Defining the undefinedness of C. In: Proceedings of the ACM SIGPLAN Conference on Programming Language Design and Implementation, vol. 50, pp. 336–345. ACM (2015). https://doi.org/10.1145/2737924.2737979
17. Hildenbrandt, E., et al: KEVM: a complete formal semantics of the ethereum virtual machine. In: Proceedings of IEEE Computer Security Foundations Symposium, pp. 204–217. IEEE (2018). https://doi.org/10.1109/CSF.2018.00022
18. Huang, Y., Bu, X., Zhu, G., Ye, X., Zhu, X., Shi, J.: KST: executable formal semantics of IEC 61131-3 Structured Text for verification. IEEE Access 7, 14593–14602 (2019). https://doi.org/10.1109/ACCESS.2019.2894026
19. Lampérière-Couffin, S., Lesage, J.J.: Formal Verification of the Sequential Part of PLC Programs, pp. 247–254. Springer (2000). https://doi.org/10.1007/978-1-4615-4493-7_25
20. Lazar, D., et al.: Executing formal semantics with the K tool. In: Proceedings of the International Symposium on Formal Methods. LNCS, vol. 7436, pp. 267–271. Springer, Heidelberg (2012). https://doi.org/10.1007/978-3-642-32759-9_23
21. Lee, J., Bae, K., Ölveczky, P.C., Kim, S., Kang, M.: Modeling and formal analysis of virtually synchronous cyber-physical systems in AADL. Int. J. Softw. Tools Technol. Transf. 24(6), 911–948 (2022). https://doi.org/10.1007/s10009-022-00665-z
22. Lee, J., Kim, S., Bae, K., Ölveczky, P.C.: HybridSynchAADL: modeling and formal analysis of virtually synchronous CPSs in AADL. In: International Conference on Computer Aided Verification, pp. 491–504. Springer, Cham (2021). https://doi.org/10.1007/978-3-030-81685-8_23
23. Lee, J., Bae, K.: Supplementary materials and technical report (2024). https://github.com/postechsv/plc-release/releases/tag/v1.1
24. Lee, J., Kim, S., Bae, K.: Bounded model checking of PLC ST programs using rewriting modulo SMT. In: Proceedings of the ACM SIGPLAN International Workshop on Formal Techniques for Safety-Critical Systems, pp. 56–67. ACM (2022). https://doi.org/10.1145/3563822.3568016
25. Li, J., Qeriqi, A., Steffen, M., Yu, I.C.: Automatic translation from FBD-PLC-programs to NuSMV for model checking safety-critical control systems. In: Proceedings of the Norsk Informatikkonferanse. Bibsys Open Journal Systems, Norway (2016). https://dblp.org/rec/conf/nik/LiQSY16.html
26. Lobov, A., Lastra, J.L.M., Tuokko, R., Vyatkin, V.: Modelling and verification of PLC-based systems programmed with ladder diagrams. IFAC Proceedings Volumes 37(4), 183–188 (2004). https://doi.org/10.1016/S1474-6670(17)36116-5
27. Meseguer, J.: Conditional rewriting logic as a unified model of concurrency. Theoret. Comput. Sci. 96(1), 73–155 (1992). https://doi.org/10.1016/0304-3975(92)90182-F
28. Mokadem, H.B., Berard, B., Gourcuff, V., De Smet, O., Roussel, J.M.: Verification of a timed multitask system with Uppaal. IEEE Trans. Autom. Sci. Eng. 7(4), 921–932 (2010). https://doi.org/10.1109/TASE.2010.2050199
29. Ölveczky, P.C., Meseguer, J.: Abstraction and completeness for Real-Time Maude. Electron. Notes Theor. Comput. Sci. 176(4), 5–27 (2007). https://doi.org/10.1016/j.entcs.2007.06.005

30. Ölveczky, P.C., Meseguer, J.: Semantics and pragmatics of Real-Time Maude. High. Order Symbol. Comput. **20**, 161–196 (2007)
31. Park, D., Ştefănescu, A., Roşu, G.: KJS: a complete formal semantics of JavaScript. In: Proceedings of the ACM SIGPLAN Conference on Programming Language Design and Implementation, pp. 346–356. ACM (2015). https://doi.org/10.1145/2737924.2737991
32. Pavlovic, O., Ehrich, H.D.: Model checking PLC software written in function block diagram. In: Proceedings of the International Conference on Software Testing, Verification and Validation, pp. 439–448. IEEE (2010). https://doi.org/10.1109/ICST.2010.10
33. Peled, D.: Handbook of Model Checking, pp. 173–190. Springer, Cham (2018). https://doi.org/10.1007/978-3-319-10575-8
34. Rausch, M., Krogh, B.H.: Formal verification of PLC programs. In: Proceedings of the American Control Conference, vol. 1, pp. 234–238. IEEE (1998). https://doi.org/10.1109/ACC.1998.694666
35. Rosu, G., Serbănută, T.F.: An overview of the K semantic framework. J. Logic Algeb. Program. **79**(6), 397–434 (2010). https://doi.org/10.1016/j.jlap.2010.03.012
36. Roşu, G., Şerbănuţă, T.F.: K overview and SIMPLE case study. Electron. Notes Theor. Comput. Sci. **304**, 3–56 (2014). https://doi.org/10.1016/j.entcs.2014.05.002
37. Şerbănuţă, T.F., Roşu, G.: K-Maude: a rewriting based tool for semantics of programming languages. In: International Workshop on Rewriting Logic and its Applications, pp. 104–122. Springer, Heidelberg (2010). https://doi.org/10.1007/978-3-642-16310-4_8
38. Wang, K., Wang, J., Poskitt, C.M., Chen, X., Sun, J., Cheng, P.: K-ST: a formal executable semantics of the Structured Text language for PLCs. IEEE Trans. Softw. Eng. **49**(10), 4796–4813 (2023). https://doi.org/10.1109/TSE.2023.3315292

Accurate Static Data Race Detection
for C

Emerson Sales[(✉)] ⓘ, Omar Inverso ⓘ, and Emilio Tuosto ⓘ

Gran Sasso Science Institute, L'Aquila, Italy
{emerson.sales,omar.inverso,emilio.tuosto}@gssi.it

Abstract. Data races are a particular kind of subtle, unintended program behaviour arising from thread interference in shared-memory concurrency. In this paper, we propose an automated technique for static detection of data races in multi-threaded C programs with POSIX threads. The key element of our technique is a reduction to reachability. Our prototype implementation combines such reduction with context-bounded analysis. The approach proves competitive against state-of-the-art tools, finding new issues in the implementation of well-known lock-free data structures, and shows a considerably superior accuracy of analysis in the presence of complex shared-memory access patterns.

1 Introduction

Multi-threaded programming is notoriously prone to subtle software glitches that are difficult to identify and reproduce [29]. In addition, for the C language, the specifications represent another factor of complexity [2,43,68]. Indeed, to leave room for improving compiler efficiency and hardware support, so-called *undefined behaviour* [22,40] is deliberately introduced in many points of the specifications. Such loose ends place further burden on the programmer, who is assumed to have a very good knowledge of the specific compiler and target architecture.

A *data race* is a rather insidious case of undefined behaviour in C. Such undesirable situation, triggered by conflicting access from multiple threads to overlapping memory locations, can be seen as a specific class of *safety* violations.

```
f() {
  x = x*2;
}
g() {
  x = x+1;
}
```

Let us consider two parallel threads respectively executing functions f and g on the left. Assuming that shared variable x is initially 0, one might be tempted to conclude that the value of x will eventually be either 1 or 2, depending on which thread is executed first. However, this reasoning incorrectly implies that the two threads are executed in sequence. In fact, f and g may interleave and interfere with each other: if f is pre-empted right after its read access to x, then g increases x to 1, and finally f multiplies the previously stored value of x by two, the final value of x will be 0.

Many techniques for static checking of generic safety properties are available, e.g. traditional symbolic execution and testing [10,44], well-known

---

Work partially funded by projects MUR-PRIN DREAM (20228*FT*78*M*), MUR-PRO3 Software Quality, MUR-PNRR VITALITY (*ECS*00000041), and PRIN PNRR DeLICE (*F*53*D*23009130001).

A. Platzer et al. (Eds.): FM 2024, LNCS 14933, pp. 443–462, 2025.
https://doi.org/10.1007/978-3-031-71162-6_23

under- and over-approximated analyses [5,12], and more recent inductive methods [9]. Mature off-the-shelf static analysers typically accommodate such techniques within modular workflows, in form of mechanised encodings for efficient general-purpose decision procedures. Concurrency, as well as specific aspects thereof, can similarly be handled separately, as e.g. in context-bounded analysis [47,59] and in the emulation of weak memory models under sequential consistency [1].

Driven by the same modularity principle, in this paper we focus on *static detection of data races* in multi-threaded C programs [39]. Much like dynamic detection, we wish to (*i*) monitor shared-memory access to keep track of the operating thread along with the relevant locations, and at the same time (*ii*) check for interfering operations from other threads. Remarkably, unlike dynamic detection, we cannot rely on low-level facilities offered by the operating system to inspect memory access. Conducive to static detection is thus the embedding of the whole detection mechanism within the program of interest. Intuitively, we instrument each relevant statement with a few operations on auxiliary variables and assertions; by construction, a feasible violation of any such assertion will indicate a feasible data race at the corresponding point of the program.

The above encoding yields a reduction to *reachability*. The in-program detection system hinges on a diligent bookkeeping of the relevant memory locations. Our instrumentation introduces no spurious or missed data races w.r.t. the feasible behaviour of the program, while avoiding any explicit representation or direct manipulation of memory locations. This transparently delegates all complexities (e.g. pointer aliasing, complex data structures, etc.) to the technology chosen for reachability analysis, while retaining maximum *accuracy* of detection.

We implemented a prototype data race detector, CSEQ-DR, by integrating our encoding within an existing sequentialisation-based workflow [37] for context-bounded analysis. We compared CSEQ-DR against four state-of-the-art data race detectors, including the best-performing tools at SV-COMP 2022 and 2023 [3,4]. CSEQ-DR proves competitive on the SV-COMP23 benchmarks; most notably, it discovers new issues in the implementation of well-known lock-free data structures [25,34]. Guided by a detailed static analysis of the SV-COMP23 benchmarks, we designed a second set of benchmarks, EDR, to improve the coverage of specific features that are particularly relevant to data race detection, e.g. complex synchronisation, shared composite data types, and pointers. CSEQ-DR shows a superior precision in the analysis on this second set of benchmarks.

Structure of the Paper. Section 2 introduces the syntax, semantics, and execution model of C programs with POSIX threads. Section 3 illustrates our main technical contribution, i.e. our reduction from data race detection to reachability. Section 4 sketches our prototype implementation and presents the experimental results. Sections 5 and 6 discuss related work and report final considerations, respectively.

2   Multi-threaded C Programs

A multi-threaded C program with POSIX threads [39] consists of multiple threads that can perform local computations, interact through the shared memory, and invoke pthread routines for thread creation, synchronisation, etc. At any point during the execution of the program, only the *active* thread can perform computations. Initially the *main thread* is active, and it is the only existing thread. New threads are spawned from the active thread, and added to the pool of *inactive* threads. On a *context switch* the active thread is *pre-empted* and becomes inactive, and one from the pool of inactive threads is activated. When a thread becomes active for the first time, its execution starts from the beginning; otherwise the thread continues from where it was last pre-empted.

```
#include <pthread.h>

int x = 0;

g() { x = x+1; }
f() { x = x*2; }

main() {
  int tid1, tid2;
  pthread_create(&tid1,f);
  pthread_create(&tid2,g);
  pthread_join(tid1);
  pthread_join(tid2);
  assert(x != 0);
}
```

Fig. 1. Running example

Let us now refer to the example program of Fig. 1 to informally introduce the syntax of multi-threaded C programs. A program consists of a sequence of declarations of *global* variables (in this case, only x) shared by all threads, followed by a sequence of function definitions (in this case g, f, and main, without input and output parameters for simplicity). The body of a function is composed of the declaration of *local* variables (like tid1 and tid2 in the main function) and the statements to be executed upon invocation. A *compound statement* or *block* is a sequence of statements enclosed in curly brackets. A statement (or an expression) involving only operations on the local memory without calls to a pthread routine is *non-visible*, otherwise *visible* (as all the statements in the example). The pthread routines include **pthread_create** to spawn a thread from a function (in the example with a simplified call) and **pthread_join** to wait for a specific thread to terminate. Other routines, e.g. for synchronisation via locks, conditional waiting, barriers, etc. are supported but not relevant here; it is also possible to explicitly declare **atomic** compound statements, whose execution cannot be pre-empted (as in compare-and-swap operations [32], GCC built-in atomics, and so on). We finally add the usual primitives for program verification, namely **assume** to discard all executions not satisfying a given condition, **assert** to express safety properties of interest, and **nondet** to non-deterministically assign to a variable any value allowed by its data type.

In the example program of Fig. 1 there are three threads. The main thread of the program, corresponding to its **main** function, is spawned at the beginning. The main thread in turn spawns two threads (from functions f and g respectively) and waits for them to terminate; it then checks whether the value of x is unchanged. The two threads update the value of x concurrently as shown.

The *state* of a multi-threaded program consists of the identifier of the active thread, a snapshot of the shared memory (i.e. an evaluation of the variables stored therein), and the *local state* of each thread (i.e. active or not); the local state of a thread consists of a local memory snapshot, the thread's *program counter* pointing to the statement being executed, and a stack to handle procedure calls. In the *initial state*, the identifier of the active thread corresponds to the main thread, the program counter of the only thread points to the first statement of the **main** function, the call stack is empty, and each variable is assigned its init expression, if any, or either 0 or `nondet`, respectively for global and local variables. A *transition* is a change of state in the program resulting from the execution of a statement. An *execution* is a sequence of consecutive transitions from the initial state. An *execution context* is a sequence of transitions performed by a thread between it activation and the following pre-emption (or termination). A *round-robin execution* is an execution where the threads are activated in a round-robin fashion (or *rounds*) according to their static order of creation in the program. A *context-bounded execution* is an execution with a given number of context switches. Considering the example program, an execution invoking `main`, `f`, `g`, `main`, `g`, and `f` takes 3 rounds, or 5 context switches.

Throughout the paper we assume *sequential consistency* [48]; it is worth noticing that this does not inherently limit the applicability of our technique, since so-called *weak memory models* for modern hardware can be soundly simulated under sequential consistency with extra computations and nondeterminism [1]. Without loss of generality, we also assume that each non-compound statement involves at most either one global variable or a pointer, without side effects. We call such statements *simple*, observing that any *complex* (i.e. non-simple) statement can be transformed into an equivalent sequence of simple statements with temporary variables [13,53]. Similarly, we assume that branch and loop conditions only refer to a single local scalar variable, and that function calls input parameters and return values are passed through local variables.

3   Encoding Data Race Checking as Reachability

In this section, we define a program transformation that encodes data race checking as reachability. We say that a multi-threaded program contains a *data race* if it can execute two *conflicting* actions (i.e. one thread writes to a memory location and another one reads from or writes to the same location), at least one of which is *not atomic*, and neither *happens before* the other [40]. In the rest of the paper we refer to a program as *unsafe* or *safe* depending on whether or not that program contains a data race.

We initially sketch our program transformation for simple cases and then progressively generalise it, elaborating a correctness argument as we go along. The key idea of our technique is to decorate each visible statement of the program under analysis with guarded assertions and operations on auxiliary variables. Such variables are synchronously updated to keep track of the threads and memory locations potentially involved in conflicting actions, while the guarded assertions combine extracted fragments of the visible statement in question to predicate on them. By construction, a violation of any of the assertions will indicate a feasible data race at the corresponding point of the initial program.

Auxiliary Variables. We initially add to the program under analysis the auxiliary global variables `waddr` and `wtid` to store the *target address* of the current shared-memory write operation and the *identifier* of the writing thread, respectively. Both variables are initialised to 0, indicating that no shared memory location is being written and no thread is writing to the shared memory.

Basic Operations. We transform a simple read operation from a shared variable as shown in Fig. 2. The program fragment being transformed is 1 = g, where the value of a global variable g is assigned to a local variable 1 (line 5). Right before such operation, we check that the thread wtid (if any) currently about to write to the shared

```
1   atomic {
2     if (wtid != pthread_self()) {
3       assert(waddr != &g);
4     }
5     1 = g;
6   }
```

Fig. 2. Basic encoding for a read operation on a shared variable.

memory and the current thread pthread_self are not the same. If so, we further check whether the read address &g of g and the write address waddr match: if they do, the assertion fails; otherwise, the access is completed. Observe that the above check and the statement being encoded are wrapped into a single atomic statement to prevent in-between context switching.

Let us dissect the transformation for a simple write operation g = 3, where a shared variable is assigned a constant value (Fig. 3). It consists of two atomic blocks. The first one is similar to the encoding of a read operation, except that right before the actual assignment (line 7) we set the writing thread wtid to the current thread and waddr to the address &g of g (lines 5–6). As in the case of a read operation, the guarded assertion checks upfront that no other thread is currently trying to write to the same address (lines 2–3).

```
1    atomic {
2      if (wtid != pthread_self()) {
3        assert(waddr != &g);
4      }
5      wtid = pthread_self();
6      waddr = &g;
7      g = 3;
8    }
9    atomic {
10     waddr = 0; wtid = 0;
11   }
```

Fig. 3. Basic encoding for a write operation on a shared variable.

If so, we update g as originally intended (line 7). In the second block we simply re-set waddr and wtid.

Proof Sketch (Reduction to Reachability). Intuitively, the race detection mechanism exploits the possible pre-emption of an encoded write operation right before the auxiliary variables waddr and wtid are re-set (line 9 in Fig. 3): at that point, another thread competing for a read or write operation can become active and reach an assertion violation. More concretely, suppose that the program under analysis is composed of a *reader* thread and a *writer* thread respectively executing 1 = g and g = 3 without synchronisation. Clearly, this program is unsafe according to the definition at the beginning of the section. The transformed program with the two threads encoded as in Figs. 2 and 3 must therefore contain a reachable assertion failure. Indeed, the writer thread can become active first, and then it can be pre-empted right before the second atomic block (line 9 in Fig. 3), so that the reader will become active, failing the assertion (line 3 in Fig. 2). Conversely, suppose the two threads are properly synchronised, e.g. via a shared lock. If the reader becomes active first, the assertion in there cannot fail as wtid and waddr are initialised to zero; since the reader does not modify such variables, the assertion checked by the writer thread activated subsequently will not fail either. If the writer becomes active first, wtid and waddr are both set and re-set within the same execution context, therefore the reader will not be able to fail the assertion check later. Observe that the argument for two writer threads would be similar as above. Finally two readers cannot trigger any assertion failure, because both `wtid` and `waddr` will be always 0.

Multiple Access. The encoding seen so far covers the basic case of a single access to a shared variable. In practice, multiple accesses to possibly different shared variables may occur within a statement. Since non-compound complex statements are assumed to be transformed into simple statements upfront (Sect. 2), this circumstance is limited to compound statements. For a regular block, we just encode the statements therein one by one. For an atomic block, however, this would not work because the pre-emption of encoded writes (Fig. 3) necessary for race detection would be disallowed. We thus encode atomic blocks in one go, as follows.

Let us consider the statement `atomic {stmt_1; stmt_2; ...}`, where every $stmt_i$ is simple. The encoding template for such statement (Fig. 4) generalises the previous simple cases (Figs. 2, 4 and 3). The different x_i and w_j are placeholders to be replaced with syntactic fragments of the statement in question that involve access to the shared memory. We refer to every such fragment as a *target expression*. Let us denote with $X = \{x_1, \ldots, x_n\}$ the set of target expressions for either a read or a write operation, and $W = \{w_1, \ldots, w_m\}$ the set of target expressions for write operations. For example, we would have $X = \{\&g\}$ and $W = \{\}$

```
1   atomic {
2     if (wtid != pthread_self()) {
3       assert(waddr != x_1);
4       ...
5       assert(waddr != x_n);
6     }
7     wtid = pthread_self();
8     waddr = w_1;
9     waddr = nondet() ? waddr : w_2;
10    ...
11    waddr = nondet() ? waddr : w_m;
12    stmt_1; stmt_2; ...
13  }
14  atomic {
15    waddr = 0; wtid = 0;
16  }
```

Fig. 4. Encoding multiple shared-memory access

for the read operation `l = g` considered in Fig. 2, while $X = W = \{\&g\}$ for the write operation `g = 3` of Fig. 3. The guarded assertion for race detection is now expanded into multiple assertions (one per target in X, lines 3–5 in Fig. 4), whereas `waddr` is non-deterministically assigned to any of the write targets in W (lines 8–11). The non-deterministic assignment to `waddr` keeps the encoding compact; in particular, it avoids having to store the different target addresses for write operations separately (for instance by representing `waddr` as an array of m elements), which would in turn result in $m \cdot n$ assertions at lines 3–5. We finally omit the second atomic block (lines 14–16) when $W = \{\}$.

Proof sketch (Over-Approximation of Target ESxpressions). In order to build the sets X and W for a given statement, it is crucial to categorise its visible expressions as read-or-write or write-only target expressions. While this is relatively straightforward, deciding whether an expression entails shared-memory access is generally undecidable in the presence of pointers. In that respect, a convenient feature of our encoding is in that non-visible expressions can be added to X and W without detriment to soundness. To see why, let us suppose that some non-visible expressions x_i and w_j are added to X and W, causing a violation of one of the assertions (lines 3–5 of Fig. 4). Observe that both elements will result in additional checks at those lines; in the case of w_j indirectly, through a preceding non-deterministic assignment to `waddr` (lines 9–11) from another thread `wtid`. If only one of the expressions (i.e. only x_i or w_j) in the failing assertion is non-visible, a match with the other (visible) expression would not be possible, since the local storage of a thread and the shared memory cannot overlap. If instead the failing assertion compares w_j to x_i, these would necessarily refer to the local storage space of two distinct threads (respectively `wtid` and `pthread_self`, as enforced by the guard at line 2), and therefore no match would be possible either. Given this argument, one could dispense with the detection of visible expressions and just populate X and W as if every expression was visible, without having to worry about false positives; this can be particularly useful for an actual implementation.

Composite Data Types and Pointers. Conflicting access to composite data types, possibly via pointers, requires some further ingenuity to achieve a precise representation of memory interference, and avoid unsoundess.

Fig. 5. Byte-precise tracking of memory locations

In the diagram of Fig. 5 (left), an array `A` of `short` integers (two bytes each element) is concurrently accessed at different positions. No data race is actually taking place as the memory locations being accessed are disjunct. However, an imprecise analysis based on a simple match of the base address of the shared data structure being accessed can raise false alarms. A similar situation can arise in the case of concurrent access to different fields of a shared `struct` (but not for a `union`, since all fields of a union have the same base address). Handling such cases requires to take into account the memory offsets for the different indexes of the array. Since our technique does not represent the target memory locations explicitly, but only through extracted program fragments that are pasted verbatim where appropriate, this entails no extra effort.

In the diagram of Fig. 5 (right), a producer and a consumer thread operate a shared buffer by respectively writing blocks of 8 bytes using `long` integers, and reading from the buffer byte by byte (e.g. to compute some low-level operation like byte-wise CRC [56]) into a `char` as soon as new data becomes available. The two threads access the buffer via local pointers of different types, while a shared index signposts available data not yet consumed. Due to a programming glitch in the handling of the shared index, the two operations may end up targeting different base addresses within the buffer, yet overlapping memory locations. Without taking into account the byte-width of the data being accessed, such conflicting access would be unsoundly marked as safe. We accommodate this in our encoding with an additional auxiliary variable `wlen` to be updated along with the others right before each write operation, and amend the guarded assertions accordingly.

We can finally define a general template for our encoding for data race detection. The memory locations currently about to be written span from `waddr` to `waddr+wlen`, and from x_i and x_i+xlen_i, respectively for the competing thread `wtid` and for the i-th access operation in the statement being encoded. The encoding is shown in Fig. 6. The amended checks (assertions at lines 3–7) detect overlaps in the above intervals. The non-deterministic assignment of `waddr` to any w_i in the set W of write target expressions (lines 10–13) is unchanged, and the subsequent assignment of `wlen` accounts for the size of the appropriate write target expression (line 14).

```
1   atomic {
2     if (wtid != pthread_self()) {
3       assert(waddr+wlen <= x₁
4             || x₁+xlen₁ <= waddr);
5       ...
6       assert(waddr+wlen <= xₙ
7             || xₙ+xlenₙ <= waddr);
8     }
9     wtid = pthread_self();
10    waddr = w₁;
11    waddr = nondet() ? waddr : w₂;
12    ...
13    waddr = nondet() ? waddr : wₘ;
14    wlen = sizeof(*waddr);
15    stmt₁; stmt₂; ...
16  }
17  atomic {
18    waddr = 0; wtid = 0;
19  }
```

Fig. 6. Encoding for data race checking, general case

4   Experimental Evaluation

Prototype. We have developed a prototype tool, CSEQ-DR, that can detect data races in multi-threaded programs with POSIX threads in (a representative fragment of) C99 extended with atomic compound statements (Sect. 2).

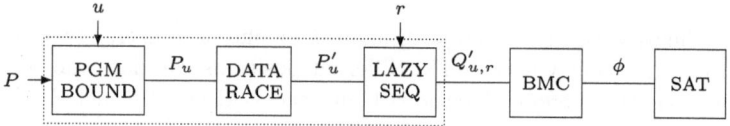

Fig. 7. Prototype verification flow for data race detection

The overall verification flow is shown in Fig. 7. The three leftmost boxes integrate our encoding for data race detection (Sect. 3) within CSEQ-LAZY [36], a sequentialisation-based tool for context-bounded analysis. Program P is unfolded into a bounded program P_u, equivalent to P up to the given unwinding bound u. Program P_u is then instrumented for data-race checking, obtaining program P'_u. Observe that P_u is instrumented, not P: the simpler structure of P_u makes it easier to build the sets X and W of targets (Sect. 3). To identify potentially-visible statements we distinguish between local and global variables, pointers and non-pointers, and structures and non-structures, possibly following structure fields recursively, and conservatively considering pointers as global variables.[1] Finally, P'_u is turned into a sequential program $Q'_{u,r}$ that simulates all executions of P up to u loop iterations and r rounds, and fails an assertion if and only if an execution of P can lead to a data race within the given bounds. At this point, different tools can be plugged in to analyse $Q'_{u,r}$ [37]. We use the CBMC [12],

---

[1] Over-approximating visible statements does not affect detection accuracy (Sect. 3).

which reduces reachability in $Q'_{u,r}$ to propositional satisfiability of ϕ, and in turn invokes MINISAT [19] to find a satisfiable assignment for ϕ, if any.

Benchmarks. We adopted as a first benchmark set the programs from the *ConcurrencySafety* track of the software verification competition (SV-COMP23) [4]. This widely used set yields a good coverage of the core features of the C programming language as well as of the basic concurrency mechanisms. All the tools we compare against have been fine-tuned on this set for the competition, which include different elements of complexity related to program analysis, such as complex control flow, deep loops, use of pointers, non-determinism, large amounts of threads, and so on. However, the set it not specific for data race checking.

In addition, we prepared an extended data race (EDR) benchmark set to specifically improve the coverage of a variety of cases that are particularly relevant to data race analysis. The benchmarks are organised into different subcategories: *arrays-ptrs* for operations on shared arrays and pointers, referencing and dereferencing, and type casting; *structs-unions* for other shared composite data structures (and combinations thereof); *mixed-structs* for different combinations of the first two subcategories; *nested-locks* for synchronisation with nested locks and atomic sections; *multiple-rw* for multiple read-write access to the shared memory; *prod-cons* for variants of the traditional producer-consumer example with shared-memory access via pointers of mixed types.

The complementarity of the SV-COMP23 and EDR benchmarks can be observed in Table 1, which compares them in terms of different complexity metrics and feature coverage. The two groups of rows refer to SV-COMP23 (top) and EDR (bottom). The two groups of columns refer to common sources of complexity for program analysis in general (left) and features that are of particular interest for data-race detection (right). The reported measures are the average number of lines of code (LOC), cyclomatic complexity (CC), number of threads (T), with starred values computed excluding instances with an infinite number of threads. The vertical bars represent the percentage of instances with

Table. 1. Summary of benchmarks features

Subcategory	LOC	CC	T	Nondet	Ptr	Arr	Struct	Sync	Multi	Ptr-+
goblint-regression	867	3.8	3301							
ldv-linux	10425	1.9	4.8							
ldv-races	1724	1.6	2.7							
pthread	936	1.8	3.6							
pthread-atomic	745	2.3	3.6							
pthread-C-DAC	1263	3.0	*2.3							
pthread-complex	1675	2.7	5.0							
pthread-deagle	836	2.4	3.0							
pthread-divine	824	1.4	2.3							
pthread-drv-races	7036	1.9	3.0							
pthread-ext	733	1.8	*2.0							
pthread-lit	750	1.5	2.0							
pthread-wmm	845	13.6	4.3							
weaver	98	8.9	4.0							
arrays-ptrs	24	1.0	2.9							
structs-unions	30	1.0	3.0							
mixed-structs	30	1.0	3.0							
nested-locks	31	1.0	3.0							
multiple-rw	25	1.0	3.0							
prod-cons	62	1.7	3.0							

specific characteristics, namely non-determinism (*Nondet*), pointers (*Ptr*), arrays (*Arr*), other composite data types such as struct or unions (*Struct*), non-trivial synchronisation (*Sync*), multiple shared-memory write operations (*Multi*), and pointer arithmetics (*Ptr+*).

As shown in the table, the SV-COMP23 benchmarks are not very representative of the sources of complexity specifically related to data race checking (top-right part of the table), and these always occur, when at all, together with generic elements of complexity (top-left part). The EDR set effectively counterbalances that by limiting generic sources of complexity (bottom-left) to focus on instances that are more interesting for race detection (bottom-right).

Setup. We evaluated CSEQ-DR against a selection of four state-of-the-art data race checkers. DARTAGNAN [26,50] is an SMT-based bounded model checker that leverages common LLVM [49] compiler optimisations to simplify the input program. DEAGLE [33,65] is a SAT-based bounded model checker built on top of CBMC [12] with an efficient handling of concurrency and a tailored SAT decision procedure; it was the winner in the *ConcurrencySafety* category at SV-COMP 2023 [4], which subsumes the *NoDataRace* demo category of the previous edition of the competition. ULTIMATE GEMCUTTER [45] is based on counterexample-guided abstraction refinement; it ranked first at SV-COMP 2022 [3] for the *NoDataRace* demo category. GOBLINT [61,66] is a static analyser for data race checking based on thread-modular abstract interpretation. We used the following versions of the selected verifiers: DARTAGNAN 3.1.1 [15], DEAGLE 2.1 [16], GEMCUTTER 0.2.2 [27], GOBLINT 1.8.2 [28].

We run the experiments on an otherwise idle workstation equipped with a dual Xeon E5-2687W 8-core 3.10 Hz processor and 128 GB of memory, running 64-bit GNU/Linux 5.10.27, with a memory limit of 16 GB and a timeout of 15 min for each instance (as in SV-COMP). In terms of parameters, bounded model checking requires a default unwinding bound to be used whenever a precise number of iterations for a loop cannot be computed upfront. We set an unwinding bound of 3 for DARTAGNAN and CSEQ-DR, observing that our tool fully unwinds a loop whenever a bound can be statically computed; DEAGLE does not allow setting the unwinding bound but hardcodes a specific unwinding strategy which is fine-tuned for the SV-COMP benchmarks. Our prototype also requires another bound for context-bounded analysis, which we set to 3 rounds. GEMCUTTER and GOBLINT implement over-approximate analyses which require no bounds; for these two tools we adopted their default configurations.

Experimental Results (SV-COMP23). The experimental results on the SV-COMP23 benchmarks are summarised in Table 2. Here, the columns left to right report the subcategory, the total number of instances (*Count*), correct results (races found or confirmed race freedom) (*Correct*), incorrect results (races missed or false alarms) (*Wrong*), internal errors (i.e. the tool crashed, threw an error, was unable to answer) (*Error*), and resources limits hits (*Unknown*). The maximum values for each subcategory are boxed. Our prototype CSEQ-DR

Table. 2. Verification verdicts (SV-COMP23)

Subcategory	Count	CSEQ-DR				DARTAGNAN				DEAGLE				GEMCUTTER				GOBLINT			
		Correct	Wrong	Error	Unknown	Correct	Wrong	Error	Unknown	Correct	Wrong	Error	Unknown	Correct	Wrong	Error	Unknown	Correct	Wrong	Error	Unknown
goblint-regression	197	130	·	10	57	116	3	72	6	123	·	72	2	132	·	38	27	194	2	·	1
ldv-linux	6	·	·	6	·	·	·	2	4	·	·	1	5	·	·	2	4	1	5	·	·
ldv-races	18	18	·	·	·	18	·	·	·	17	·	1	·	11	·	·	7	10	8	·	·
pthread	28	19	·	·	9	15	·	2	11	22	·	6	·	16	·	1	11	28	·	·	·
pthread-atomic	13	13	·	·	·	12	·	·	1	9	·	4	·	13	·	·	·	7	6	·	·
pthread-C-DAC	5	4	·	·	1	2	·	2	1	4	·	·	1	3	·	2	·	4	1	·	·
pthread-complex	4	2	·	·	2	·	·	·	4	·	·	1	3	·	·	1	3	2	2	·	·
pthread-deagle	4	4	·	·	·	3	·	·	1	2	·	2	·	4	·	·	·	4	·	·	·
pthread-divine	3	2	·	1	·	·	·	·	3	·	·	·	3	·	·	2	1	2	1	·	·
pthread-drv-races	18	·	·	18	·	·	·	·	18	14	·	4	·	5	·	·	13	14	4	·	·
pthread-ext	31	30	·	·	1	17	1	·	13	5	·	26	·	9	·	1	21	20	11	·	·
pthread-lit	2	2	·	·	·	2	·	·	·	2	·	·	·	2	·	·	·	2	·	·	·
pthread-wmm	283	283	·	·	·	283	·	·	·	283	·	·	·	114	·	1	168	283	·	·	·
weaver	171	158	·	·	13	62	·	98	11	170	·	1	·	121	·	6	44	170	1	·	·
Total	**783**	665	0	35	83	530	4	201	48	651	0	121	11	430	0	54	299	741	41	0	1

provides 665 correct verification verdicts, 0 incorrect verdicts, fails to produce an answer in 35 instances, and hits the resource limits on 83 instances.[2]

In the *goblint-regression* subset, CSEQ-DR fails to analyse 10 programs due to unsupported pthread library functions, parsing issues, and other internal errors. The analysis turns out to be too expensive on 57 instances; 50 of these are specifically crafted examples with ten thousands threads on which all verifiers struggle, except GOBLINT itself (also see relevant entry in Table 1). CSEQ-DR is unable to handle any of the 6 *ldv-linux* instances due to embedded assembly code, 1 instance of *pthread-divine* causing an internal error, and all the 18 instances of *pthread-drv-races* due to function pointers causing the function inlining module to crash. In *pthread* and *pthread-C-DAC*, our tool hits the resource limits on a total of 10 programs with large loops (up to one thousand iterations); the loop unfolding module is able to statically determine the loops bound and fully unwind these loops, but the unfolded encoding ends up being too large to be analysed within the given resource limits. The *pthread-complex* subcategory is a small collection of programs with complex implementations of *lock-free* data structures whose analysis is notoriously difficult [38], and our tool does indeed struggle in 2 out of 4 instances. Interestingly, CSEQ-DR is able to discover new issues in the remaining two instances, `elimination_backoff_stack` and `workstealqueue_mutex-2`, respectively containing well-known implemen-

---

[2] We amended the SV-COMP23 categorisation from safe to unsafe for 10 instances, which affects the count; further details are discussed later on in this section.

tations of a stack [34] and a queue [25].[3] Finally, CSEQ-DR hits the resource limits in 1 instance of *pthread-ext*[4], and on 13 *weaver* instances containing loops with non-deterministic exit conditions, and dynamic allocation of blocks of non-deterministic size.

DARTAGNAN categorises 530 programs correctly, rejects 201 programs due to unsupported features and internal errors, times out on 48 instances, and incorrectly classifies 4 instances. DEAGLE produces 651 correct results, fails to provide a verdict in 121 cases due to unsupported syntax and internal errors, and times out on 11 instances. GEMCUTTER correctly categorises 430 instances, with internal errors on 54 instances, and 299 timeouts. GOBLINT achieves 741 correct verification verdicts. However, it reports the incorrect verification verdict for 41 instances due to over-approximation.[5] The tool times out on a single instance.

Experimental Results (EDR). Table 3 reports the verification verdicts on the EDR benchmarks, divided by sub-category. For each sub-category, the results are split in two separate rows for unsafe (top) and safe instances (bottom). CSEQ-DR correctly verifies all benchmarks.

DARTAGNAN misses 1 data race in *arrays-ptrs* due to type casting. It also misses races on struct-to-struct assignments, generating 4 incorrect results on *structs-unions*. Pointers cause 3 missed races on *mixed-structs*, and non-synchronised read-write access causes 7 incorrect results on *nested-locks* and 5 on *multiple-rw*. The tool hits the resources limits on 10 instances of *prod-cons*.

DEAGLE misses 12 races on *arrays-ptrs* due to pointer operations, type casting, aliasing, and arrays. It misses 9 races on *structs-unions*. On *mixed-structs*, it generates 3 false and misses 8 races, totalising 11 errors. On *nested-locks*, it misses 2 races due to multiple shared-memory access, and rejects 4 programs due to use of locks occurring within atomic blocks. On *multiple-rw*, it misses 1 data race involving multiple writes to composite structures. Lastly, DEAGLE misses 6 races in *prod-cons* where the shared memory is accessed via pointers.

GEMCUTTER generates 2 false races on *arrays-ptrs* caused by dereferenced null pointers. Although this is in fact undefined behaviour, it does not strictly cause data races as null pointers are guaranteed to compare unequal to a pointer

---

[3] The counterexamples provided by our tool turn out to be feasible upon manual inspection. Among all the competitors, only GOBLINT categorises the files as unsafe, but (due to over-approximation) without providing counterexamples. DEAGLE times out but does confirm the race on a manually simplified version of one of the programs. We amended the SV-COMP23 categorisation from safe to unsafe for both instances.

[4] During preliminary runs we found 8 safe instances where the atomic sections were defined in a syntax apparently allowed in previous editions of the competition, but no longer supported in SV-COMP 2023 (and by none of the tools considered in our comparison). We fixed those instances to use the correct syntax, but our prototype reported all of them to be unsafe; we could confirm all counterexamples upon manual inspection. Therefore, we amended the categorisation of these instances accordingly.

[5] The reported incorrect verification verdicts are not consistent with the official SV-COMP results because for the competition GOBLINT outputs UNKNOWN on potentially unsafe programs to avoid losing points on false positives.

Table. 3. Verification verdicts (EDR)

Subcategory	Count	CSEQ-DR Correct	Wrong	Error	Unknown	DARTAGNAN Correct	Wrong	Error	Unknown	DEAGLE Correct	Wrong	Error	Unknown	GEMCUTTER Correct	Wrong	Error	Unknown	GOBLINT Correct	Wrong	Error	Unknown
arrays-ptrs	12	12	·	·	·	11	1	·	·	·	12	·	·	12	·	·	·	9	3	·	·
	12	12	·	·	·	12	·	·	·	12	·	·	·	10	2	·	·	5	7	·	·
structs-unions	9	9	·	·	·	5	4	·	·	·	9	·	·	6	3	·	·	2	7	·	·
	5	5	·	·	·	5	·	·	·	5	·	·	·	5	·	·	·	5	·	·	·
mixed-structs	10	10	·	·	·	7	3	·	·	2	8	·	·	3	7	·	·	2	8	·	·
	10	10	·	·	·	10	·	·	·	7	3	·	·	10	·	·	·	7	3	·	·
nested-locks	16	16	·	·	·	9	7	·	·	13	2	1	·	16	·	·	·	16	·	·	·
	26	26	·	·	·	26	·	·	·	23	·	3	·	26	·	·	·	25	1	·	·
multiple-rw	10	10	·	·	·	5	5	·	·	9	1	·	·	10	·	·	·	9	1	·	·
	7	7	·	·	·	7	·	·	·	7	·	·	·	7	·	·	·	6	1	·	·
prod-cons	6	6	·	·	·	2	·	·	4	·	6	·	·	4	·	·	2	6	·	·	·
	6	6	·	·	·	·	·	·	6	6	·	·	·	·	·	·	6	·	6	·	·
Total	129	129	0	0	0	99	20	0	10	84	41	4	0	109	12	0	8	92	37	0	0

to any object or function [40]. The tool also misses 3 races on *structs-unions* and 7 on *mixed-structs*, and times out on 8 instances on *prod-cons*.

GOBLINT incorrectly classifies 10 programs in *arrays-ptrs*, missing 3 races involving pointer arithmetic, aliasing, and type casting, and generating 7 false alarms on array operations. On *structs-unions*, GOBLINT misses 7 races. On *mixed-structs*, it generates 8 false alarms and misses 3 races. On *nested-locks*, it generates 1 false alarm. On *multiple-rw*, it misses 1 race and generates 1 false alarm. At last, it generates 6 false alarms on *prod-cons*.

Summary. The experiments demonstrate the superiority of our prototype in terms of data-race detection accuracy. In particular, CSEQ-DR is the only tool that produces no false positives or negatives (Tables 2 and 3). The accuracy is particularly evident in the presence of sources of complexity that stress the memory representation, where all competitors struggle in many cases (Table 3).

On the SV-COMP23 benchmarks (Table 2), our approach proves to be competitive against the considered state-of-the-art tools. On programs with a large number of threads and complex control flow (e.g. some instances of *goblint-regression*), CSEQ-DR hits the resource limits; however, it does spot two previously undetected data races in complex lock-free data structures. Additionally, CSEQ-DR rejects or crashes on considerably fewer instances than the other tools, outperforming DEAGLE (winner in the *ConcurrencySafety* category of SV-COMP 2023), GEMCUTTER (which ranked first in the *NoDataRace* demo category of SV-COMP 2022), and DARTAGNAN in terms of correct results.

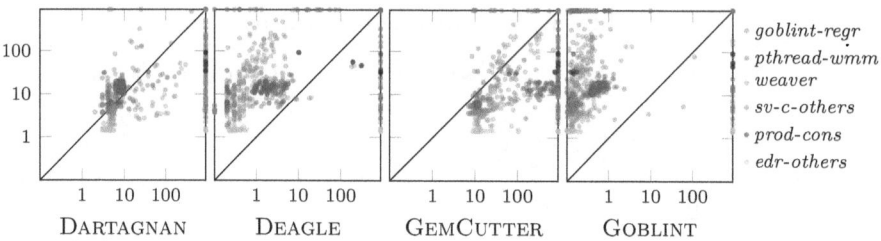

Fig. 8. Analysis runtime comparison (SV-COMP23, EDR)

As for speed (Fig. 8), CSEQ-DR outperforms GEMCUTTER and DARTAGNAN. GOBLINT proves comparatively quite fast, but its overly conservative approximation yields numerous false alarms on both benchmarks, resulting in the overall highest number of incorrect verification verdicts (Tables 2 and 3). DEAGLE proves capable of fast analysis too, also thanks to the unwinding strategy fine-tuned for SV-COMP23, but looses precision considerably on EDR (Table 3).

5   Related Work

As a recent trend in the development of programming languages and memory models, considerable effort has been devoted to balance the conflicting desiderata of programmers, compiler developers, and hardware vendors by moving towards stricter semantics to limit the possibility of data races upfront. For instance, in data race freedom semantics, all data-race-free parts of a program are guaranteed to have sequential semantics [18]; other approaches let the compiler synchronise shared-memory access in the likelihood of races [42], certify that some compiler optimisations will not introduce incorrectness [42,57], or even disallow some of them [18]. Nevertheless, such efforts are hardly effective e.g. with legacy code, low-level device drivers, and existing codebase in currently still widespread programming languages and platforms.

Program transformation to handle concurrency (or specific aspects thereof) is relied upon, among the others, by preprocessors in the style of REK [11] and early versions of CSEQ [24], both implementing so-called *eager* sequentialisation to reduce to sequential reachability [47], and in the mentioned semantic-preserving encodings from weak memory models to sequential consistency [1]. An early proof-of-concept implementation [14] of CSEQ-DR could only handle basic memory access, achieving modest results (5th place with 6 false positives) at SV-COMP 2022 [3]. GEMCUTTER also relies on program transformation for detecting races [17], but needs one auxiliary variable per global variable in the program, while we only introduce three variables for the whole program; similarly to [14], its analysis beyond basic memory access can be inaccurate. An extension of lazy sequentialisation for deadlock checking is proposed in [35].

Besides the ones considered in this paper (Sect. 4), static techniques for race detection usually rely on locksets to determine safe synchronisation of memory access [20,21,41,58,62,63,67,69]. Known tools include LOCKSMITH [58] and RELAY [67], which introduce relative locksets for scalability; these tools may return incorrect verdicts in presence of pointers. Lockset-based analysis is usually over-approximated, thus it can prove the absence of races or report *potential* races. Possible ways to reduce spurious warnings are considered in [41]. Static tools for other languages include LLOV [8] for OpenMP programs in C, C++, and FORTRAN [55], and RACERD [6] and CHORD [54] for Java.

Dynamic data race detection looks for conflicting memory access at runtime. Known tools include PACER [7], which uses sampling strategies for performance improvement, THREADSANITIZER [63] for C++ and Go, ROMP [31] for parallel OpenMP applications, NONDETERMINATOR [23] for the Cilk language, and TSVD [51], a thread-safety violation detector that injects delays on the program to expose races. Dynamic analysis can spot potential races in real software projects, but due to thread interleaving without a measurable coverage of the feasible behaviours of the system under analysis; on particularly critical software components, static analyses such as the one proposed in this paper can complement that with a systematic coverage and greater accuracy, when feasible.

6   Conclusion

C programs are particularly vulnerable to subtle data races. We have addressed this problem with a technique that automatically annotates a program and, combined with lazy sequentialisation and bounded model checking, yields effective under-approximate data race detection.

Our prototype implementation has proved competitive with state-of-the-art technology, showing an unmatched precision of analysis in the presence of complex synchronisation patterns and particularly relevant language features such as shared composite data types, and pointers. The approach can, in general, yield great detection accuracy at additional computational effort, which may be beneficial in the analysis of particularly critical software components. At the same time, our specific implementation has shown that context-bounded analysis can effectively mitigate the overhead introduced with our encoding.

Our program instrumentation allows to build the set of target expressions via relatively inexpensive yet conservative static analysis, at the cost of additional overhead but with no detriment to detection accuracy. Our prototype refines the sets of visible expressions by recursively inspecting composite data structures, but stops short of performing any pointer analysis. But of course one can plug in more sophisticated static analyses to calculate the target expressions. We leave for future work the investigation of different trade-offs between a more precise static analysis for working out the target expressions and overall performance of race detection. We also plan to explore the combination of our encoding with dynamic partial order reduction [46] for potential efficiency gains.

As commonplace for under-approximated analyses, our approach can miss bugs if bounds are insufficiently large. Nonetheless, out of 665 correct verification verdicts of the SV-COMP23 benchmarks, our prototype was able to compute static loop bounds and fully unfold 431 safe instances, basically failing to do so only on unbounded or non-deterministic loops. Also, it is empirically known that concurrency errors on real software typically occur within a few context switches [60] or a few memory operations [52]. In the future, we plan to experiment with alternative techniques to handle loops, such as k-induction [64], sequentialisation without unfolding [24,47], and context-unbounded sequentialisation on top of modern back ends for unbounded analysis such as Kratos2 [30].

Data Availability Statement. CSEQ-DR and EDR Benchmarks are publicly available and can be accessed at https://doi.org/10.5281/zenodo.11582694. All relevant data analyzed during this study are included in this published tool. Further inquiries regarding the data can be directed to the corresponding author.

References

1. Alglave, J., Kroening, D., Nimal, V., Tautschnig, M.: Software verification for weak memory via program transformation. In: Felleisen, M., Gardner, P. (eds.) ESOP 2013. LNCS, vol. 7792, pp. 512–532. Springer, Heidelberg (2013). https://doi.org/10.1007/978-3-642-37036-6_28

2. Batty, M., Memarian, K., Nienhuis, K., Pichon-Pharabod, J., Sewell, P.: The problem of programming language concurrency semantics. In: Vitek, J. (ed.) ESOP 2015. LNCS, vol. 9032, pp. 283–307. Springer, Heidelberg (2015). https://doi.org/10.1007/978-3-662-46669-8_12

3. Beyer, D.: Progress on software verification: SV-COMP 2022. In: TACAS 2022. LNCS, vol. 13244, pp. 375–402. Springer, Cham (2022). https://doi.org/10.1007/978-3-030-99527-0_20

4. Beyer, D.: Competition on software verification and witness validation: SV-COMP 2023. In: Sankaranarayanan, S., Sharygina, N. (eds) TACAS (2). LNCS, vol. 13994, pp. 495–522. Springer, Cham (2023). https://doi.org/10.1007/978-3-031-30820-8_29

5. Beyer, D., Henzinger, T.A., Jhala, R., Majumdar, R.: The software model checker BLAST. Int. J. Softw. Tools Technol. Transf. **9**(5–6), 505–525 (2007)

6. Blackshear, S., Gorogiannis, N., O'Hearn, P.W., Sergey, I.: RacerD: compositional static race detection. Proc. ACM Program. Lang. **2**(OOPSLA), 144:1–144:28 (2018)

7. Bond, M.D., Coons, K.E., McKinley, K.S.: PACER: proportional detection of data races. In: PLDI, pp. 255–268. ACM (2010)

8. Bora, U., Das, S., Kukreja, P., Joshi, S., Upadrasta, R., Rajopadhye, S.: LLOV: a fast static data-race checker for openMP programs. ACM Trans. Archit. Code Optim. **17**(4), 35:1–35:26 (2020)

9. Bradley, A.R.: SAT-based model checking without unrolling. In: Jhala, R., Schmidt, D. (eds.) VMCAI 2011. LNCS, vol. 6538, pp. 70–87. Springer, Heidelberg (2011). https://doi.org/10.1007/978-3-642-18275-4_7

10. Cadar, C., Dunbar, D., Engler, D.R.: KLEE: unassisted and automatic generation of high-coverage tests for complex systems programs. In: OSDI, pp. 209–224. USENIX Association (2008)

11. Chaki, S., Gurfinkel, A., Strichman, O.: Time-bounded analysis of real-time systems. In: FMCAD, pp. 72–80. FMCAD Inc. (2011)

12. Clarke, E., Kroening, D., Lerda, F.: A tool for checking ANSI-C programs. In: Jensen, K., Podelski, A. (eds.) TACAS 2004. LNCS, vol. 2988, pp. 168–176. Springer, Heidelberg (2004). https://doi.org/10.1007/978-3-540-24730-2_15

13. Clarke, E.M., Kroening, D., Yorav, K.: Behavioral consistency of C and Verilog programs using bounded model checking (2000)

14. Coto, A., Inverso, O., Sales, E., Tuosto, E.: A prototype for data race detection in CSeq 3. In: TACAS 2022. LNCS, vol. 13244, pp. 413–417. Springer, Cham (2022). https://doi.org/10.1007/978-3-030-99527-0_23

15. Dartagnan 3.1.1. https://github.com/hernanponcedeleon/Dat3M

16. Deagle 2.1. https://gitlab.com/sosy-lab/sv-comp/archives-2023

17. Dietsch, D., Heizmann, M., Klumpp, D., Schüssele, F., Podelski, A.: Ultimate Taipan and race detection in Ultimate - (competition contribution). In: Sankaranarayanan, S., Sharygina, N. (eds.) TACAS (2). LNCS, vol. 13994, pp. 582–587. Springer, Cham (2023). https://doi.org/10.1007/978-3-031-30820-8_40

18. Dolan, S., Sivaramakrishnan, K.C., Madhavapeddy, A.: Bounding data races in space and time. In: PLDI, pp. 242–255. ACM (2018)

19. Eén, N., Sörensson, N.: An extensible SAT-solver. In: SAT, pp. 502–518 (2003)

20. Elmas, T., Qadeer, S., Tasiran, S.: Goldilocks: efficiently computing the happens-before relation using locksets. In: Havelund, K., Núñez, M., Roşu, G., Wolff, B. (eds.) FATES/RV -2006. LNCS, vol. 4262, pp. 193–208. Springer, Heidelberg (2006). https://doi.org/10.1007/11940197_13

21. Engler, D.R., Ashcraft, K.: RacerX: effective, static detection of race conditions and deadlocks. In: SOSP, pp. 237–252. ACM (2003)

22. Ertl, M.A.: The intended meaning of undefined behaviour in c programs. In: KPS, pp. 20–28 (2017)

23. Feng, M., Leiserson, C.E.: Efficient detection of determinacy races in Cilk programs. Theory Comput. Syst. **32**(3), 301–326 (1999)

24. Fischer, B., Inverso, O., Parlato, G.: CSeq: a concurrency pre-processor for sequential C verification tools. In: ASE, pp. 710–713. IEEE (2013). https://doi.org/10.1109/ASE.2013.6693139

25. Frigo, M., Leiserson, C.E., Randall, K.H.: The implementation of the Cilk-5 multithreaded language. In: PLDI, pp. 212–223. ACM (1998)

26. Gavrilenko, N., Ponce-de-León, H., Furbach, F., Heljanko, K., Meyer, R.: BMC for weak memory models: relation analysis for compact SMT encodings. In: Dillig, I., Tasiran, S. (eds.) CAV 2019. LNCS, vol. 11561, pp. 355–365. Springer, Cham (2019). https://doi.org/10.1007/978-3-030-25540-4_19

27. Gemcutter 0.2.2. https://github.com/ultimate-pa/ultimate/releases

28. Goblint 1.8.2. https://github.com/goblint/analyzer

29. Gray, J.: Why do computer stop and what can be about it? In: Büroautomation. Berichte des German Chapter of the ACM, vol. 25, pp. 128–145. Teubner (1985)

30. Griggio, A., Jonás, M.: Kratos2: An SMT-based model checker for imperative programs. In: Enea, C., Lal, A. (eds.) CAV (3). LNCS, vol. 13966, pp. 423–436. Springer, Cham (2023). https://doi.org/10.1007/978-3-031-37709-9_20

31. Gu, Y., Mellor-Crummey, J.M.: Dynamic data race detection for openMP programs. In: SC, pp. 61:1–61:12. IEEE/ACM (2018)

32. Harris, T.L., Fraser, K., Pratt, I.A.: A practical multi-word compare-and-swap operation. In: Malkhi, D. (ed.) DISC 2002. LNCS, vol. 2508, pp. 265–279. Springer, Heidelberg (2002). https://doi.org/10.1007/3-540-36108-1_18

33. He, F., Sun, Z., Fan, H.: Deagle: An SMT-based verifier for multi-threaded programs (competition contribution). In: TACAS 2022. LNCS, vol. 13244, pp. 424–428. Springer, Cham (2022). https://doi.org/10.1007/978-3-030-99527-0_25

34. Hendler, D., Shavit, N., Yerushalmi, L.: A scalable lock-free stack algorithm. J. Parallel Distrib. Comput. **70**(1), 1–12 (2010)
35. Inverso, O., Nguyen, T.L., Fischer, B., Torre, S.L., Parlato, G.: Lazy-CSeq: a context-bounded model checking tool for multi-threaded c-programs. In: ASE, pp. 807–812. IEEE Computer Society (2015). https://doi.org/10.1109/ASE.2015.108
36. Inverso, O., Tomasco, E., Fischer, B., La Torre, S., Parlato, G.: Bounded model checking of multi-threaded C programs via lazy sequentialization. In: Biere, A., Bloem, R. (eds.) CAV 2014. LNCS, vol. 8559, pp. 585–602. Springer, Cham (2014). https://doi.org/10.1007/978-3-319-08867-9_39
37. Inverso, O., Tomasco, E., Fischer, B., Torre, S.L., Parlato, G.: Bounded verification of multi-threaded programs via lazy sequentialization. ACM Trans. Program. Lang. Syst. **44**(1), 1:1–1:50 (2022)
38. Inverso, O., Trubiani, C.: Parallel and distributed bounded model checking of multi-threaded programs. In: PPoPP, pp. 202–216. ACM (2020)
39. ISO/IEC: Information technology—Portable Operating System Interface (POSIX) Base Specifications, Issue 7, ISO/IEC/IEEE 9945:2009 (2009)
40. ISO/IEC: ISO/IEC 9899:2018: Information technology – Programming languages – C (2018)
41. Kahlon, V., Yang, Yu., Sankaranarayanan, S., Gupta, A.: Fast and accurate static data-race detection for concurrent programs. In: Damm, W., Hermanns, H. (eds.) CAV 2007. LNCS, vol. 4590, pp. 226–239. Springer, Heidelberg (2007). https://doi.org/10.1007/978-3-540-73368-3_26
42. Kang, J., Hur, C., Lahav, O., Vafeiadis, V., Dreyer, D.: A promising semantics for relaxed-memory concurrency. In: POPL, pp. 175–189. ACM (2017)
43. Kelly, T., Pan, Y.: Catch-23: the new C standard sets the world on fire. ACM Queue **21**(1), 12–30 (2023)
44. King, J.C.: Symbolic execution and program testing. Commun. ACM **19**(7), 385–394 (1976)
45. Klumpp, D., et al.: ULTIMATE GEMCUTTER and the axes of generalization. In: TACAS 2022. LNCS, vol. 13244, pp. 479–483. Springer, Cham (2022). https://doi.org/10.1007/978-3-030-99527-0_35
46. Kokologiannakis, M., Marmanis, I., Gladstein, V., Vafeiadis, V.: Truly stateless, optimal dynamic partial order reduction. Proc. ACM Program. Lang. **6**(POPL), 1–28 (2022). https://doi.org/10.1145/3498711
47. Lal, A., Reps, T.W.: Reducing concurrent analysis under a context bound to sequential analysis. Formal Methods Syst. Des. **35**(1), 73–97 (2009)
48. Lamport, L.: How to make a correct multiprocess program execute correctly on a multiprocessor. IEEE Trans. Comput. **46**(7), 779–782 (1997)
49. Lattner, C., Adve, V.S.: LLVM: a compilation framework for lifelong program analysis & transformation. In: CGO, pp. 75–88. IEEE Computer Society (2004)
50. Ponce-de-León, H., Haas, T., Meyer, R.: DARTAGNAN: leveraging compiler optimizations and the price of precision (competition contribution). In: TACAS 2021. LNCS, vol. 12652, pp. 428–432. Springer, Cham (2021). https://doi.org/10.1007/978-3-030-72013-1_26
51. Li, G., Lu, S., Musuvathi, M., Nath, S., Padhye, R.: Efficient scalable thread-safety-violation detection: finding thousands of concurrency bugs during testing. In: SOSP, pp. 162–180. ACM (2019)
52. Lu, S., Park, S., Seo, E., Zhou, Y.: Learning from mistakes: a comprehensive study on real world concurrency bug characteristics. In: ASPLOS, pp. 329–339. ACM (2008)

53. Müller-Olm, M.: Variations on Constants. LNCS, vol. 3800. Springer, Heidelberg (2006). https://doi.org/10.1007/11871743
54. Naik, M., Aiken, A., Whaley, J.: Effective static race detection for Java. In: PLDI, pp. 308–319. ACM (2006)
55. Organization, O.: The OpenMP API specification for parallel programming (2019). https://www.openmp.org/
56. Perez, A.: Byte-wise CRC calculations. IEEE Micro **3**(3), 40–50 (1983)
57. Podkopaev, A., Lahav, O., Vafeiadis, V.: Bridging the gap between programming languages and hardware weak memory models. Proc. ACM Program. Lang. **3**(POPL), 69:1–69:31 (2019)
58. Pratikakis, P., Foster, J.S., Hicks, M.: LOCKSMITH: practical static race detection for C. ACM Trans. Program. Lang. Syst. **33**(1), 3:1–3:55 (2011)
59. Qadeer, S., Rehof, J.: Context-bounded model checking of concurrent software. In: Halbwachs, N., Zuck, L.D. (eds.) TACAS 2005. LNCS, vol. 3440, pp. 93–107. Springer, Heidelberg (2005). https://doi.org/10.1007/978-3-540-31980-1_7
60. Qadeer, S., Wu, D.: KISS: keep it simple and sequential. In: PLDI, pp. 14–24. ACM (2004)
61. Saan, S., et al.: GOBLINT: Thread-modular abstract interpretation using side-effecting constraints. In: TACAS 2021. LNCS, vol. 12652, pp. 438–442. Springer, Cham (2021). https://doi.org/10.1007/978-3-030-72013-1_28
62. Savage, S., Burrows, M., Nelson, G., Sobalvarro, P., Anderson, T.E.: Eraser: A dynamic data race detector for multithreaded programs. ACM Trans. Comput. Syst. **15**(4), 391–411 (1997)
63. Serebryany, K., Iskhodzhanov, T.: ThreadSanitizer: data race detection in practice. In: WBIA, 9p. 62–71. Association for Computing Machinery (2009)
64. Sheeran, M., Singh, S., Stålmarck, G.: Checking safety properties using induction and a SAT-solver. In: Hunt, W.A., Johnson, S.D. (eds.) FMCAD 2000. LNCS, vol. 1954, pp. 127–144. Springer, Heidelberg (2000). https://doi.org/10.1007/3-540-40922-X_8
65. Sun, Z., Fan, H., He, F.: Consistency-preserving propagation for SMT solving of concurrent program verification. Proc. ACM Program. Lang. **6**(OOPSLA2), 929–956 (2022)
66. Vojdani, V., Apinis, K., Rõtov, V., Seidl, H., Vene, V., Vogler, R.: Static race detection for device drivers: the Goblint approach. In: ASE, pp. 391–402. ACM (2016)
67. Voung, J.W., Jhala, R., Lerner, S.: RELAY: static race detection on millions of lines of code. In: ESEC/FSE, pp. 205–214. ACM (2007)
68. Yodaiken, V.: How ISO C became unusable for operating systems development. In: PLOS, pp. 84—90. ACM (2021)
69. Yu, Y., Rodeheffer, T., Chen, W.: RaceTrack: efficient detection of data race conditions via adaptive tracking. In: SOSP, pp. 221–234. ACM (2005)

CFAULTS: Model-Based Diagnosis for Fault Localization in C with Multiple Test Cases

Pedro Orvalho[1](✉) ⓘ, Mikoláš Janota[2] ⓘ, and Vasco Manquinho[1] ⓘ

[1] INESC-ID, IST, Universidade de Lisboa, Lisboa, Portugal
{pmorvalho,vasco.manquinho}@tecnico.ulisboa.pt
[2] Czech Technical University in Prague, Prague, Czechia
mikolas.janota@cvut.cz

Abstract. Debugging is one of the most time-consuming and expensive tasks in software development. Several formula-based fault localization (FBFL) methods have been proposed, but they fail to guarantee a set of diagnoses across all failing tests or may produce redundant diagnoses that are not subset-minimal, particularly for programs with multiple faults.

This paper introduces a novel fault localization approach for C programs with multiple faults. CFAULTS leverages Model-Based Diagnosis (MBD) with multiple observations and aggregates all failing test cases into a unified MaxSAT formula. Consequently, our method guarantees consistency across observations and simplifies the fault localization procedure. Experimental results on two benchmark sets of C programs, TCAS and C-PACK-IPAs, show that CFAULTS is faster than other FBFL approaches like BUGASSIST and SNIPER. Moreover, CFAULTS only generates subset-minimal diagnoses of faulty statements, whereas the other approaches tend to enumerate redundant diagnoses.

Keywords: Fault Localization · Model-Based Diagnosis · Formula-based Fault Localization · Debugging · Maximum Satisfiability

1 Introduction

Localizing system faults has always been one of the most time-consuming and expensive tasks. Given a buggy program, *fault localization (FL)* involves identifying locations in the program that could cause a faulty behaviour (bug).

Given a faulty program and a test suite with failing test cases, current *formula-based fault localization (FBFL)* methods encode the localization problem into several optimization problems to identify a minimal set of faulty statements (diagnoses) within a program. Typically, these methods find a minimal diagnosis considering each failing test case individually rather than simultaneously with all failing test cases. Moreover, these FBFL methods enumerate all *Minimal Correction Subsets (MCSes)* [22] to cover all diagnoses.

For instance, BUGASSIST [17,18], a prominent FBFL tool, implements a ranking mechanism for bug locations. For each failing test, BUGASSIST enumerates all

A. Platzer et al. (Eds.): FM 2024, LNCS 14933, pp. 463–481, 2025.
https://doi.org/10.1007/978-3-031-71162-6_24

Listing 1.1: Faulty program example. Faulty lines: $\{5,8,11\}$.

```
1    int main(){
2        // finds maximum of 3 numbers
3        int f,s,t;
4        scanf("%d%d%d",&f,&s,&t);
5        if (f < s && f >= t)
6            // fix: f >= s
7            printf("%d",f);
8        if (f > s && s <= t)
9            // fix: f < s and s >= t
10           printf("%d",s);
11       if (f > t && s > t)
12           // fix: f < t and s < t
13           printf("%d",t);
14
15       return 0;
16   }
```

Table 1. Test-suite.

	Input			Output
t_0	1	2	3	3
t_1	6	2	1	6
t_2	-1	3	1	3

Table 2. Number of diagnoses (faulty statements) generated by BugAssist [17] and SNIPER [21] per test.

	BugAssist	SNIPER
#Diagnoses t_0	8	8
#Diagnoses t_1	21	21
#Diagnoses t_2	9	9
#Total Unique Diagnoses	32	1297
Final Diagnosis	$\{4,13\}$	$\{5,8,11\}$

diagnoses of a Maximum Satisfiability (MaxSAT) formula corresponding to bug locations. Subsequently, BugAssist ranks diagnoses based on their frequency of appearance in each failing test. Other FBFL tools, like SNIPER [21], also enumerate all diagnoses for each failing test. However, the set of SNIPER's diagnoses is obtained by taking the Cartesian product of the diagnoses gathered using each failing test. As a result, while FBFL methods can determine minimal diagnoses per failing test, BugAssist cannot guarantee a minimal diagnosis considering all failing tests, and SNIPER may enumerate a significant number of redundant diagnoses that are not minimal [16]. These limitations may pose challenges for programs with multiple faulty statements, as shown in Example 1.

Example 1 (Motivation). Consider the program presented in Listing 1.1, which aims to determine the maximum among three given numbers. However, based on the test suite shown in Table 1, the program is faulty, as its output differs from the expected. The set of minimally faulty lines in this program is $\{5, 8, 11\}$, as all three if-conditions are incorrect according to the test suite. Fixing any subset of these lines would be insufficient to repair the program. One possible fix is to replace all these conditions with the suggested fixes in lines $\{6, 9, 12\}$.

In a typical FBFL approach, the minimal set of statements identified as faulty might include, for example, lines 4 and 5. Removing the scanf statement and an if-statement would allow an FBFL tool to assign any value to the input variables in order to always produce the expected output. However, considering an approach that prioritizes identifying faulty statements within the program's logic before evaluating issues in the input/output statements (such as scanf and printf), one might identify lines $\{5, 8, 11\}$ as the faulty statements. When applying BugAssist's and SNIPER's approach on the program in Listing 1.1 with the described optimization criterion and utilizing the inputs/outputs detailed in Table 1 as specification, distinct sets of faults are identified for each failing test. Table 2 presents the diagnosis (set of faulty lines) produced by each tool, along with the number of diagnoses enumerated for each failing test case and the total number of unique diagnoses after aggregating the diagnoses from all tests, using each tool's respective method.

In the case of BugAssist, diagnoses are prioritized based on their occurrence frequency. Consequently, BugAssist yields 32 unique diagnoses and selects {4, 13} since this diagnosis is identified in every failing test. In contrast, SNIPER computes the Cartesian product of all diagnoses, resulting in 1297 unique diagnoses. Note that BugAssist's diagnoses may not adequately identify all faulty program statements. Conversely, SNIPER's diagnosis {5, 8, 11} is minimal, even though it enumerates an additional 1296 diagnoses. Hence, existing FBFL methods do not ensure a minimal diagnosis across all failing tests (e.g., BugAssist) or may produce an overwhelming number of redundant sets of diagnoses (e.g., SNIPER), especially for programs with multiple faults.

This paper tackles this challenge by formulating the FL problem as a single optimization problem in Sect. 3. We leverage MaxSAT and the theory of *Model-Based Diagnosis (MBD)*, integrating all failing test cases simultaneously. This approach allows us to generate only minimal diagnoses to identify all faulty program components within a C program. Furthermore, we have implemented the MBD problem with multiple test cases in CFaults, a fault localization tool for ANSI-C programs, presented in Sect. 4. CFaults begins by unrolling and instrumentalizing C programs at the code-level, ensuring independence from the bounded model checker. Next, CFaults utilizes CBMC [5], a well-known bounded model checker for C, to generate a trace formula of the program. Finally, CFaults encodes the problem into MaxSAT to identify the minimal set of diagnoses corresponding to the buggy statements.

Experimental results presented in Sect. 5 on two benchmarks of C programs, TCAS [10] (industrial), and C-Pack-IPAs [29] (programming exercises), show that CFaults effectively detects minimal sets of diagnoses. In contrast, SNIPER and BugAssist either generate an overwhelming number of redundant diagnoses or fail to produce a minimal set required to fix each program.

To summarize, the contributions of this work are: (1) we tackle the fault localization problem in C programs using a Model-Based Diagnosis (MBD) approach considering multiple failing test cases, and formulating it as a unified optimization problem; (2) we implement this MBD approach in a publicly available tool called CFaults [30][1] that unrolls and instrumentalizes C programs at the code level, making it independent of the bounded model checker used; (3) CFaults allows refinement of localized faults to pinpoint the bug's location more precisely; (4) we evaluate CFaults on two sets of C programs (TCAS and C-Pack-IPAs), showing that CFaults is fast and only produces subset-minimal diagnoses, unlike other state-of-the-art formula-based fault localization tools.

2   Preliminaries

This section provides definitions and notations that are used throughout the paper. We start by presenting basic definitions of propositional logic and programs and then address standard *model-based diagnosis (MBD)* definitions.

---

[1] https://github.com/pmorvalho/CFaults.

The *Boolean Satisfiability (SAT)* problem is the decision problem for propositional logic [3]. A propositional formula in Conjunctive Normal Form (CNF) is a conjunction of clauses where each clause is a disjunction of literals. A literal is a propositional variable x_i or its negation $\neg x_i$. Given a CNF formula ϕ, the SAT problem corresponds to deciding if there is an assignment to the variables in ϕ such that ϕ is satisfied or prove that no such assignment exists. When applicable, set notation will be used for formulas and clauses. A formula can be represented as a set of clauses (meaning its conjunction) and a clause as a set of literals (meaning its disjunction).

The *Maximum Satisfiability (MaxSAT)* problem is an optimization version of the SAT problem. Given a CNF formula ϕ, the goal is to find an assignment that maximizes the number of satisfied clauses in ϕ. In partial MaxSAT, ϕ is split into hard clauses (ϕ_h) and soft clauses (ϕ_s). Given a formula $\phi = (\phi_h, \phi_s)$, the goal is to find an assignment that satisfies all hard clauses in ϕ_h while minimizing the number of unsatisfied soft clauses in ϕ_s. Moreover, in the weighted version of the partial MaxSAT problem, each soft clause is assigned a weight, and the goal is to find an assignment that satisfies all hard clauses and minimizes the sum of the weights of the unsatisfied soft clauses. Let $\phi = (\phi_h, \phi_s)$ be a partial MaxSAT formula. A Minimal Correction Subset (MCS) μ of ϕ is a subset $\mu \subseteq \phi_s$ where $\phi_h \cup (\phi_s \setminus \mu)$ is satisfiable and, for all $c \in \mu$, $\phi_h \cup (\phi_s \setminus \mu) \cup \{c\}$ is unsatisfiable. A dual concept of MCSes are *Minimal Unsatisfiable Subsets (MUSes)* [16,22].

Programs. A program is considered sequential, comprising standard statements such as assignments, conditionals, loops, and function calls, each adhering to their conventional semantics in C. A program is deemed to contain a bug when an assertion violation occurs during its execution with input I. Conversely, if no assertion violation occurs, the program is considered correct for input I. In cases where a bug is detected for input I, it is possible to define an error trace, representing the sequence of statements executed by program P on input I.

A Trace Formula (TF) is a propositional formula that is SAT iff there exists an execution of the program that terminates with a violation of an assert statement while satisfying all assume statements. For further information on TFs, interested readers are referred to [5,8].

Model-Based Diagnosis (MBD). The following definitions are commonly used in the *MBD* theory [16,24,34]. A system description $\mathcal{P}$ is composed of a set of components $\mathcal{C} = \{c_1, \ldots, c_n\}$. Each component in $\mathcal{C}$ can be declared healthy or unhealthy. For each component $c \in \mathcal{C}$, $h(c) = 0$ if c is unhealthy, otherwise, $h(c) = 1$. As in prior works [16,25], $\mathcal{P}$ is described by a CNF formula, where $\mathcal{F}_c$ denotes the encoding of component c:

$$\mathcal{P} \triangleq \bigwedge_{c \in \mathcal{C}} (\neg h(c) \vee \mathcal{F}_c) \tag{1}$$

Observations represent deviations from the expected system behaviour. An observation, denoted as o, is a finite set of first-order sentences [16,34], which is assumed to be encodable in CNF as a set of unit clauses. In this work, the failing test cases represent the set of observations.

A system $\mathcal{P}$ is considered faulty if there exists an inconsistency with a given observation o when all components are declared healthy. The problem of model-based diagnosis (MBD) aims to identify a set of components which, if declared unhealthy, restore consistency. This problem is represented by the 3-tuple $\langle \mathcal{P}, \mathcal{C}, o \rangle$, and can be encoded as a CNF formula:

$$\mathcal{P} \wedge o \wedge \bigwedge_{c \in \mathcal{C}} h(c) \models \bot \tag{2}$$

For a given MBD problem $\langle \mathcal{P}, \mathcal{C}, o \rangle$, a set of system components $\Delta \subseteq \mathcal{C}$ is a diagnosis iff:

$$\mathcal{P} \wedge o \wedge \bigwedge_{c \in \mathcal{C} \setminus \Delta} h(c) \wedge \bigwedge_{c \in \Delta} \neg h(c) \nvDash \bot \tag{3}$$

A diagnosis Δ is minimal iff no subset of Δ, $\Delta' \subsetneq \Delta$, is a diagnosis, and Δ is of minimal cardinality if there is no other diagnosis $\Delta'' \subseteq \mathcal{C}$ with $|\Delta''| < |\Delta|$.

A diagnosis is redundant if it is not subset-minimal [16].

To encode the Model-Based Diagnosis problem with one observation with partial MaxSAT, the set of clauses that encode $\mathcal{P}$ (1) represents the set of hard clauses. The soft clauses consists of unit clauses that aim to maximize the set of healthy components, i.e., $\bigwedge_{c \in \mathcal{C}} h(c)$ [24,36]. This MaxSAT encoding of MBD enables enumerating minimum cardinality diagnoses and subset minimal diagnoses, considering a single observation. Furthermore, a minimal diagnosis is a minimal correction subset (MCS) of the MaxSAT formula. Given an inconsistent formula that encodes the MDB problem (2), a minimal diagnosis Δ satisfies (3), thereby making Δ an MCS of the MaxSAT formula. BUGASSIST [18], SNIPER [21], and other model-based diagnosis (MBD) tools for fault localization in circuits [16,24,36] encode the localization problem with partial MaxSAT.

More recently, the MaxSAT encoding for MBD [16] has been generalized to multiple inconsistent observations. Let $\mathcal{O} = \{o_1, \dots o_m\}$ be a set of observations. Each observation is associated with a replica $\mathcal{P}_i$ of the system $\mathcal{P}$. The system remains unchanged given different observations, where the components are replicated for each observation, but the healthy variables are shared. For a given observation o_i, a diagnosis is given by the following:

$$\mathcal{P}_i \wedge o_i \wedge \bigwedge_{c \in \mathcal{C} \setminus \Delta} h(c) \wedge \bigwedge_{c \in \Delta} \neg h(c) \nvDash \bot \tag{4}$$

The goal is to find a minimal diagnosis $\Delta \subseteq \mathcal{C}$, such that Δ is a minimal set of components when deactivated the system becomes consistent with all observations $\mathcal{O} = \{o_1, \dots o_m\}$. Moreover, when considering multiple observations, an aggregated diagnosis is a subset of components that includes one possible diagnosis for each given observation.

3   Model-Based Diagnosis with Multiple Test Cases

This paper encodes the fault localization problem as a Model-Based Diagnosis with multiple observations using a single optimization problem. We simultaneously integrate all failing test cases (observations) in a single MaxSAT formula. This approach allows us to generate only minimal diagnoses capable of identifying all faulty components within the system, in our case, a C program.

Given m observations, $\mathcal{O} = \{o_1, \ldots, o_m\}$, a distinct replica of the system, denoted as $\mathcal{P}_i$, is required for each observation o_i. The hard clauses, ϕ_h, in our MaxSAT formulation correspond to each observation's encoding (o_i) and m system replicas, one for each observation, $\mathcal{P}_i$. Hence, $\phi_h = \bigwedge_{o_i \in \mathcal{O}} (\mathcal{P}_i \wedge o_i)$. Additionally, we aim to maximize the set of healthy components. Therefore, the soft clauses are formulated as: $\phi_s = \bigwedge_{c \in \mathcal{C}} h(c)$. Thus, given the MaxSAT solution of (ϕ_h, ϕ_s), its complement, i.e., the set of unhealthy components $(h(c) = 0)$, corresponds to a subset-minimal aggregated diagnosis. This diagnosis is a subset-minimal of components that, when declared unhealthy (deactivated), make the system consistent with all observations, as follows:

$$\bigwedge_{o_i \in \mathcal{O}} (\mathcal{P}_i \wedge o_i) \wedge \bigwedge_{c \in \mathcal{C} \setminus \Delta} h(c) \wedge \bigwedge_{c \in \Delta} \neg h(c) \nvDash \bot \tag{5}$$

We assume that the system remains unchanged given different observations, where the components are replicated for each observation, but the healthy variables are shared. This is necessary because we analyze all observations jointly, which can affect the component's behaviour. In our work, the observations consist of a test suite containing failing test cases.

The HSD [16] algorithm was proposed to localize single faults in circuits given multiple observations. The HSD algorithm is based on hitting set dualization (HSD). For each observation o_i, this algorithm computes minimal unsatisfiable subsets (MUSes) of the MaxSAT formula encoded by (4). Next, the HSD algorithm computes a minimum hitting set $\mathcal{H}$ on the MUSes, and checks if $\mathcal{H}$ makes the system consistent with each observation individually. Hence, to compute all subset-minimal aggregated diagnoses of a faulty system $\mathcal{P}$, the algorithm performs at least m oracle calls for each minimum hitting set computed, where m is the number of observations. Each oracle call uses a different system replica (4).

Our approach encodes the problem into a single MaxSAT formula, while HSD [16] divides the problem into m MaxSAT formulas, one for each observation. Additionally, for each minimal hitting set computed in HSD, m oracle calls are needed to check if a diagnosis is consistent with all observations. However, in our case, we just need to perform a single MaxSAT call that returns a minimal diagnosis, which is, by definition, consistent with all observations since all observations are encoded into the formula. Furthermore, the HSD algorithm was solely evaluated using single faults in circuits given multiple observations, and it was not implemented to work with programs. A potential drawback is that our MaxSAT formula grows with the number of observations. This could result in a large formula and affect the performance of the MaxSAT solver. However, this scenario was not observed in our experimental results (see Sect. 5).

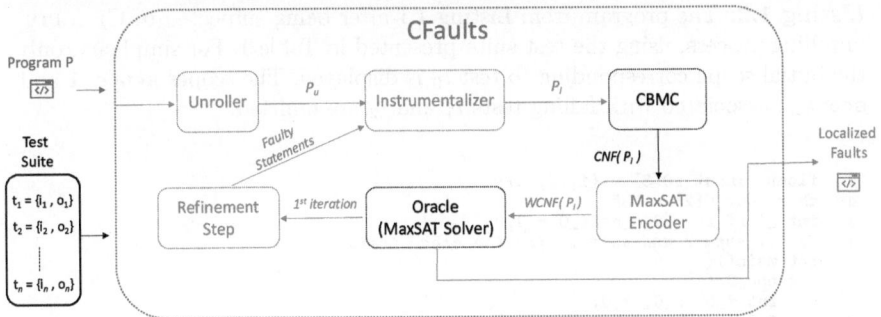

Fig. 1. Overview of CFAULTS.

4 *CFAULTS*: MBD with Multiple Observations for C

CFAULTS is a new model-based diagnosis (MBD) tool for fault localization in C programs with multiple test cases. Unlike previous works, CFAULTS uses the approach proposed in Sect. 3, and C programs are relaxed at the code level, enabling users to leverage other bounded model checkers effectively. Figure 1 provides an overview of CFAULTS consisting of six main steps: program unrolling, program instrumentalization, bounded model checking (CBMC), encoding to MaxSAT, an Oracle (MaxSAT solver), and a refinement step. Hence, CFAULTS formulates the MBD problem with multiple test cases as the 3-tuple $\langle \mathcal{P}, \mathcal{C}, \mathcal{O} \rangle$, where the observations $\mathcal{O}$ consist of failing test cases (inputs and assertions), the components $\mathcal{C}$ represent the set of program statements, and the system description $\mathcal{P}$ is a trace formula of the unrolled and instrumentalized program. The program is instrumented at the code level with relaxation variables corresponding to our *healthy variables*.

Program Unrolling. CFAULTS starts the unrolling process by expanding the faulty program using the set of failed tests from the test suite. In this context, an unrolled program signifies the original program expanded m times (m program scopes), where m denotes the number of failed test cases. An unrolled program encodes the execution of all failing tests within the program, along with their corresponding inputs and specifications (assertions).

The unrolling process encompasses three primary steps. Initially, CFAULTS generates fresh variables and functions for each of the m program scopes, ensuring each scope possesses unique variables and functions. Subsequently, CFAULTS establishes variables representing the inputs and outputs for each program scope corresponding to the failing tests. Input operations, such as `scanf`, undergo translation into read accesses to arrays corresponding to the inputs, while output operations, such as `printf`, are replaced by write operations into arrays representing the program's output. Every exit point of the program (e.g., a `return` statement in the `main` function) is replaced with a `goto` statement directing the

Listing 1.2: The program from Listing 1.1 after being subjected to CFAULTS'
unrolling process, using the test suite presented in Table 1. For simplicity, only
the initial scope corresponding to test t_0 is displayed. The scopes `scope_1` and
`scope_2` associated with failing tests t_1 and t_2 are omitted.

```
1   float _input_f0[3] = {1, 2, 3};
2   char _out_0[2] = "3";
3   int _ioff_f0 = 0, _ooff_0 = 0;
4   // ... inputs and outputs for the other tests
5   int main(){
6     scope_0:{
7       int f_0, s_0, t_0;
8       f_0 = _input_f0[_ioff_f0++];
9       s_0 = _input_f0[_ioff_f0++];
10      t_0 = _input_f0[_ioff_f0++];
11      if ((f_0 < s_0) && (f_0 >= t_0))
12          _ooff_0 = printInt(_out_0, _ooff_0, f_0);
13      if ((f_0 > s_0) && (s_0 <= t_0))
14          _ooff_0 = printInt(_out_0, _ooff_0, s_0);
15      if ((f_0 > t_0) && (s_0 > t_0))
16          _ooff_0 = printInt(_out_0, _ooff_0, t_0);
17      goto scope_1;
18    }
19    // ... scope_1 and scope_2
20    final_step:
21    assert(strcmp(_out_0, "3") != 0 || // other assertions);
22  }
```

program flow to the next failing test's scope. Lastly, at the end of the unrolled
program, CFAULTS embeds an assertion capturing all the specifications of the
failing tests. Consequently, the unrolled program encapsulates the execution of
all failing tests within a single program.

Listing 1.2 exhibits a program segment generated through the unrolling process applied to Listing 1.1. CFAULTS establishes global variables to represent the
inputs and outputs of each failing test (lines 1–3, Listing 1.2). For the sake of
simplicity, the depicted listing illustrates solely the initial scope corresponding to
test 0 from the test suite outlined in Table 1. Distinct variables are introduced
for each failing test. Furthermore, the `scanf` function call is substituted with
input array operations (lines 8–10), while the `printf` calls are replaced with
CFAULTS' print functions, akin to `sprintf` functions, which direct output to a
buffer. Lastly, the unrolled program concludes with an assertion representing the
disjunction of the negation of all failing test assertions. For instance, suppose
there are m failing tests, where A_i denotes the assertion of test t_i. In this scenario,
CFAULTS injects the following assertion into the program: $\neg A_1 \vee \cdots \vee \neg A_m$.

Program Intrumentalization. After integrating all possible executions and
assertions from failing tests during the unrolling step, CFAULTS proceeds to
instrumentalize the unrolled C program by introducing relaxation variables for
each program component (statement/instruction). Each relaxation variable activates (or deactivates) the program component being relaxed when assigned to
true (or false) respectively. CFAULTS ensures that there are no conflicts between
the names of the relaxation variables and the names of the program's original
variables. For this step, CFAULTS needs to receive a maximum number of iterations that the program should be unwound.

Listing 1.3: Program statements. **Listing 1.4:** Program statements relaxed.

```
1    int i;
2    int n;
3    int s;
4
5    s = 0;
6    n = _input_f0[_ioff_f0++];
7
8    if (n == 0)
9        return 0;
10
11   for (i=1; i < n; i++){
12       s = s + i;
13   }
```

```
1    //main scope
2    bool _rv1, _rv2, _rv3, _rv5;
3    bool _rv6[UNWIND],..., _rv8[UNWIND];
4    int _los; // loop1 offset
5
6    //test scope
7    bool _ev4;
8    int i,n,s;
9    _los=1;
10
11   if (_rv1) s = 0;
12   if (_rv2) n = _input_f0[_ioff_f0++];
13
14   if ( _rv3 ? (n == 0) : _ev4)
15       return 0;
16
17   for (_rv5 ? (i = 1) : 1;
18       !_rv6[_los] || (i<n);
19       _rv8[_los] ? i++ : 1, _los++){
20       if (_rv7[_los]) s = s + i;
21   }
```

The relaxation process introduces relaxation variables that deactivate or activate program components. This process involves four distinct relaxation rules for: (1) conditions of if-statements, (2) expression lists (e.g., an expression list executed at the beginning of a for-loop), (3) loop conditions, and (4) other program statements.

Example 2. Listings 1.3 shows a code snippet that sums all the numbers between 1 and n. Listings 1.4 depicts the same program statements after undergoing relaxation by CFAULTS. For the sake of simplicity, all relaxation variables' and offsets' names were simplified.

In more detail, the rule for relaxing a general program statement is to envelop the statement with an if-statement, whose condition is a relaxation variable. For example, consider lines 5 and 6 in the program on Listings 1.3. These lines are relaxed by CFAULTS using relaxation variables _rv1 and _rv2 respectively, appearing as lines 11 and 12 on Listings 1.4.

Furthermore, when relaxing if-statements, the statements inside the then and else blocks adhere to the previously explained relaxation rule. However, the conditions of if-statements are relaxed using a ternary operator, as shown in line 14 of Listings 1.4. Note that if the relaxation variable is assigned true, then the original if condition is executed. Otherwise, a different relaxation variable (e.g., _ev4 in Listings 1.4) determines whether the program execution enters the then-block or the else-block (if one exists). These relaxation variables (else's *relaxation variables*) are local to each failing test scope and enable different tests to determine whether to enter the then or else-block.

When handling expression lists, CFAULTS adopts a comparable strategy to that of generic program statements, enclosing each expression within a ternary operator instead of an if-statement. If the program component is deactivated, the expression is replaced by 1. For example, the initialization of variable i in line 11 of Listings 1.3 is relaxed into the ternary operation in line 17 of Listings 1.4.

Lastly, all relaxation variables inside a loop are Boolean vectors to relax statements within a loop. Each entry of these vectors relaxes the loop's statements for a given iteration. The maximum number of iterations of the loops is defined by the CFAULTS user. CFAULTS follows a similar approach for inner loops, creating arrays of arrays. Thus, for simple program statements within a loop, CFAULTS encapsulates them with if-statements, with the relaxation variables indexed to the iteration number. Line 20 of Listings 1.4 illustrates a relaxed statement inside a loop. The loop's condition is relaxed by implication of the relaxation variable, as demonstrated in line 18 of Listings 1.4. Furthermore, each loop has its own offsets to index relaxation variables. These offsets are initialized just before the loop and incremented at the end of each iteration (e.g., line 19 in Listing 1.4).

When handling auxiliary functions, CFAULTS declares the relaxation variables needed in the main scope of the program and passes these variables as parameters. Hence, CFAULTS ensures that the same variables are used throughout the auxiliary functions' calls.

Listing 1.5 depicts the program resulting from the instrumentalization process of Listing 1.2 performed by CFAULTS. The same program components (statements/instructions) across different failing test scopes are assigned the same relaxation variable declared in the main scope. Consequently, if a relaxation variable is set to 0, the corresponding program component is deactivated across all test executions. Additionally, the relaxation variables are left uninitialized, allowing CFAULTS to determine the minimal number of faulty components requiring deactivation. Note that relaxation variables are not declared as global variables but as local variables within the main scope. This is to prevent the C compiler from automatically initializing all these variables to 0.

CBMC. After unrolling and instrumentalizing the C program, CFAULTS invokes CBMC, a bounded model checker for C [5]. CBMC initially transforms the unrolled and relaxed program into *Static Single Assignment (SSA)* form, an intermediate representation ensuring that variables are assigned values only once and are defined before use [9]. SSA achieves this by converting existing variables into multiple versions, each uniquely representing an assignment. Next, CBMC translates the SSA representation into a CNF formula, which represents the trace formula of the program. During the CNF formula generation, CBMC negates the program's assertion $(\neg(\neg A_1 \vee \cdots \vee \neg A_m))$ to compute a counter-example. Moreover, the CNF formula, ϕ, encodes each failing test's input (I_i), assertion (A_i), and all execution paths of the unrolled and relaxed incorrect program encoded by the trace formula (P), i.e., $\phi = (I_1 \wedge \ldots \wedge I_m) \wedge P \wedge (A_1 \wedge \cdots \wedge A_m)$. Thus, if ϕ is *SAT*, an assignment exists that activates or deactivates each relaxation variable and makes all failing test assertions true. Hence, each satisfiable assignment is a diagnosis of the C program, considering all failing tests.

Listing 1.5: Instrumentalized program.

```
1   //global vars
2   int main(){
3     bool _rv1, _rv2, ..., _rv12;
4     scope_0:{
5       bool _ev5, _ev8, _ev11;
6       int f_0, s_0, t_0;
7       if (_rv1) f_0 = _input_f0[_ioff_f0++];
8       if (_rv2) s_0 = _input_f0[_ioff_f0++];
9       if (_rv3) t_0 = _input_f0[_ioff_f0++];
10      if (_rv4 ? ((f_0 < s_0) && (f_0 >= t_0)) : _ev5 ){
11          if (_rv6) _ooff_0 = printInt(_out_0, _ooff_0, f_0);
12      }
13      if (_rv7 ? ((f_0 > s_0) && (s_0 <= t_0)) : _ev8 ){
14          if (_rv9) _ooff_0 = printInt(_out_0, _ooff_0, s_0);
15      }
16      if (_rv10? ((f_0 > t_0) && (s_0 > t_0)) : _ev11 ){
17          if (_rv12) _ooff_0 = printInt(_out_0, _ooff_0, t_0);
18      }
19      goto scope_1;
20    }
21    // scope_1 and scope_2
22    final_step:
23    assert(strcmp(_out_0, "3") != 0 || ... // other assertions);
24  }
```

MaxSAT Encoder. Let ϕ denote the CNF formula generated by CBMC in the previous step. Next, CFAULTS generates a weighted partial MaxSAT formula $(\mathcal{H}, \mathcal{S})$ to maximize the satisfaction of relaxation variables in the program, aiming to minimize the necessary code alterations. The set of hard clauses is defined by CBMC's CNF formula (i.e., $\mathcal{H} = \phi$), while the soft clauses consist of unit clauses representing relaxation variables used to instrument the C program, expressed as $\mathcal{S} = \bigwedge_{c \in \mathcal{C}} (rv_c)$. Additionally, we assign a hierarchical weight to each relaxation variable based on the height of its sub-AST (Abstract Syntax Tree). For instance, in the case of an if-statement without an else-block, the relaxation variable for its condition will be assigned a weight equal to the sum of the weights of the relaxation variables within the then-block. Furthermore, to prioritize the identification of faulty statements within the program's logic over evaluating issues in the input/output, these statements (such as scanf and printf) are assigned a significantly higher cost compared to other program statements. Moreover, due to the use of hierarchical weights in the relaxation variables, CFAULTS enumerates all MaxSAT solutions to identify all subset-minimal diagnoses since there can be more than one MaxSAT solution (with the same cost) that differ in the number of relaxed program statements.

Oracle. CFAULTS invokes a MaxSAT solver to determine the program's minimal set of faulty statements, aligning with the principles of Model-Based Diagnosis (MBD) theory. By consolidating all failing tests into a unified, unrolled, and instrumentalized program, the MaxSAT solution identifies the minimum subset of statements requiring removal to fulfil the assertions of all failing tests.

Refinement. The standard Model-Based Diagnosis (MBD) theory focuses on faulty components (program statements) whose removal can rectify the system (program's assertions). However, addressing program faults in software may necessitate introducing, relocating, or replacing statements. Hence, CFAULTS incorporates a refinement step that introduces nondeterminism into the program, enabling the Oracle to simulate actions such as introducing, reallocating or replacing existing program statements. During the first iteration of CFAULTS, the refinement step is invoked to introduce non-determinism, with the aim of minimizing the number of faulty statements. This step can improve fault localization by conducting a more detailed analysis of previously identified faulty statements. For example, in the scenario outlined in Example 1, refining line ·5 into

```
if ((_rv1? (f < s) : nondet_bool()) && (_rv2? (f >= t) : nondet_bool()))
```

enables CFAULTS to determine that only the left part of the binary operation (f < s) is faulty, while the right part remains unaffected. This fine-grained approach allows for more precise detection of program faults. When the refinement step is triggered, CFAULTS instrumentalizes the program again, introducing nondeterminism exclusively to the statements previously identified as faulty during the initial Oracle call. Through this process, CFAULTS aims to reduce the set of faulty program components by executing them or assigning them to nondeterministic functions. All remaining program components are executed, meaning their relaxation variables are activated during this step.

5   Experimental Results

All of the experiments were conducted on an Intel(R) Xeon(R) Silver computer with 4210R CPUs @ 2.40 GHz running Linux Debian 10.2, using a memory limit of 32 GB and a timeout of 3600 s, for each program. CFAULTS has been evaluated using two distinct benchmarks of C programs: TCAS [10] and C-PACK-IPAs [27]. TCAS stands out as a well-known program benchmark extensively utilized in the fault localization literature [18,21]. This benchmark comprises a C program from Siemens and 41 versions with intentionally introduced faults, with known positions and types of these faults. Conversely, C-PACK-IPAs is a set of student programs collected during an introductory programming course. For this evaluation, we used the first lab class of C-PACK-IPAs, which consists of ten programming assignments, comprising 486 faulty programs and 799 correct implementations. C-PACK-IPAs has proven successful in evaluating various works across program analysis [32], program transformation [28], and clustering [31].

CFAULTS uses `pycparser` [33] for unrolling and instrumentalizing C programs. Additionally, CBMC version 5.11 is used to encode C programs into CNF formulas. Furthermore, since the source code of BUGASSIST and SNIPER is either unavailable or no longer maintained (resulting in compilation and linking issues), prototypes of their algorithms were implemented. It is worth noting that the original version of SNIPER could only analyze programs that utilized

Table 3. BUGASSIST, SNIPER and CFAULTS fault localization results.

Benchmark: **TCAS**				Benchmark: **C-Pack-IPAs**			
	Valid Diagnosis	Memouts	Timeouts		Valid Diagnosis	Memouts	Timeouts
BugAssist	41 (100.0%)	0 (0.0%)	0 (0.0%)	BugAssist	454 (93.42%)	0 (0.0%)	32 (6.58%)
SNIPER	7 (17.07%)	34 (82.93%)	0 (0.0%)	SNIPER	446 (91.77%)	4 (0.82%)	36 (7.41%)
CFaults	41 (100.0%)	0 (0.0%)	0 (0.0%)	CFaults	483 (99.38%)	1 (0.21%)	2 (0.41%)
CFaults-Refined	41 (100.0%)	0 (0.0%)	0 (0.0%)	CFaults-Refined	482 (99.18%)	1 (0.21%)	3 (0.62%)

a subset of ANSI-C, lacked support for loops and recursion, and could only partially handle global variables, arrays, and pointers. In this work, both SNIPER and BUGASSIST handle ANSI-C programs, as their algorithms are built on top of CFAULTS's unroller and instrumentalizer modules. For the MaxSAT oracle, RC2Stratified [15] from the PySAT toolkit [14] (v. 0.1.7.dev19) was used.

Furthermore, all three FBFL algorithms evaluated (CFAULTS, BUGASSIST, and SNIPER) consistently generate diagnoses that are consistent with (5), indicating that all proposed diagnoses undergo validation by CBMC once the algorithm provides a diagnosis. However, this validation primarily serves to verify diagnoses generated by BUGASSIST, as it has the capability to produce diagnoses that may not align with all failing test cases. In contrast, CFAULTS' MaxSAT solution, by definition, aligns with all observations, and SNIPER's aggregation method (Cartesian product) produces only valid diagnoses, although they may not always be subset-minimal. When considering BUGASSIST, we iterate through all computed diagnoses based on BUGASSIST's voting score, until we identify one diagnosis that is consistent with all observations, i.e., conforms to (5).

Table 3 provides an overview of the results obtained using SNIPER, BUGASSIST, and CFAULTS on the two benchmarks of C programs. The TCAS program comprises approximately 180 lines of code and has a maximum of 131 failing tests for each program. This leads SNIPER to reach the memory limit of 32 GB for almost 83% of the programs when aggregating the sets of MCSes computed for each failing test. Additionally, a higher rate of timeouts is observed for SNIPER and BUGASSIST than for CFAULTS. Figure 2a and 2b depict cactus plots that present the CPU time spent on fault localization in each program (y-axis) versus the number of programs with all faults successfully localized (x-axis) using BUGASSIST, SNIPER, and CFAULTS (with and without refinement) on TCAS and C-PACK-IPAs, respectively. Notably, CFAULTS generally exhibits faster performance compared to BUGASSIST and SNIPER across both benchmarks. In Fig. 2a, SNIPER's performance is due to its memout rate on TCAS.

In TCAS, CFAULTS, whether invoking the refinement step or not, identifies faults in the entire dataset. However, in C-PACK-IPAs, CFAULTS localizes faults in one additional program when the refinement step is not called. Even if the refinement step reaches the time limit, CFAULTS still possesses a subset-minimal diagnosis from the preceding step that has not undergone refinement. The refinement step slightly slows down CFAULTS, as shown in Fig. 2a and 2b. Nonetheless, Fig. 2c illustrates a scatter plot comparing the optimum costs (MaxSAT solu-

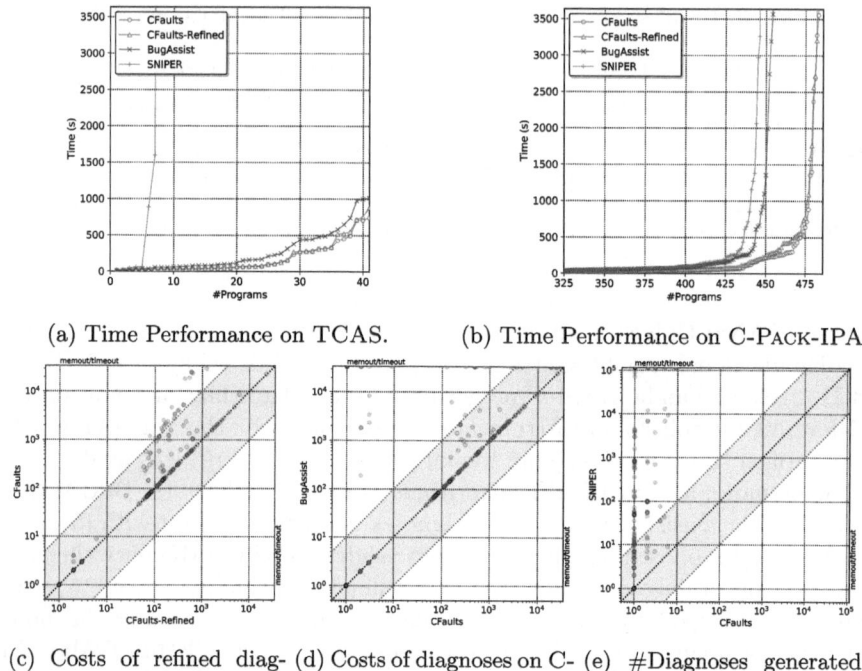

(a) Time Performance on TCAS.   (b) Time Performance on C-Pack-IPAs.

(c) Costs of refined diag- (d) Costs of diagnoses on C- (e) #Diagnoses generated
noses on C-Pack-IPAs.   Pack-IPAs.   on C-Pack-IPAs.

Fig. 2. Comparison between BugAssist's, SNIPER's and CFaults' diagnoses.

tion's cost) achieved by CFaults with and without calling the refinement step on C-Pack-IPAs. Each point on this plot represents a faulty program, where the x-value (resp. y-value) represents the optimum cost of CFaults' with refinement (resp. without refinement) diagnosis. If a point lies above the diagonal, it indicates that a non-refined diagnosis has a higher cost than a refined diagnosis for the same program. Therefore, while the refinement step may marginally slow down CFaults, it enables CFaults to identify smaller diagnoses at a reduced cost in approximately 16% of C-Pack-IPAs's programs. Moreover, this observation was not noted in the TCAS dataset, as each program contains a maximum of two faults, and the refinement step did not yield improved outcomes in this particular dataset.

Additionally, Fig. 2d illustrates a scatter plot comparing the diagnoses' costs achieved by CFaults (x-axis) against BugAssist (y-axis) on C-Pack-IPAs. BugAssist fails to provide an optimal diagnosis in almost 6% of cases. In the TCAS benchmark, although BugAssist manages to localize faults in all programs, it yields a non-optimal diagnosis in 10% of the programs. Furthermore, Fig. 2e depicts a scatter plot comparing the number of diagnoses generated by CFaults (x-axis) against SNIPER (y-axis). While CFaults needs to enumerate all MaxSAT solutions due to the weighted MaxSAT formula, it is evident that SNIPER generates significantly more diagnoses than CFaults. This discrepancy suggests that SNIPER overlooks the possibility of redundant diagnoses being computed. The number of such redundant diagnoses is much larger than the subset-minimal diagnoses generated by CFAULTS. Figure 2e illustrates that in some instances, SNIPER may enumerate up to 100K diagnoses, whereas CFAULTS generates less than 10.

As a validation step for our implementation, we analyzed all three fault localization methods on the collection of 799 correct programs in C-PACK-IPAS. This was done to ensure that all methods yielded zero faults for all correct implementations of each programming exercise. Moreover, we conducted a comparison between CFAULTS and the HSD algorithm [16] (see Sect. 3) on the ISCAS85 dataset [13], which is a widely studied collection of single-fault circuits. It is worth noting that HSD's implementation currently only supports fault localization in circuits. We encountered no performance issues during this comparison, and both approaches successfully localized all faults within each circuit.

6 Related Work

Fault localization (FL) techniques typically fall into two main families: *spectrum-based (SBFL)* and *formula-based (FBFL)*. SBFL methods [1,2,26,38–40] estimate the likelihood of a statement being faulty based on test coverage information from both passing and failing test executions. While SBFL techniques are generally fast, they may lack precision, as not all identified statements are likely to be the cause of failures [23,35]. In contrast, FBFL approaches [11,12,17–21,41,42] are considered exact. FBFL methods encode the fault localization problem into several optimization problems aimed at identifying the minimum number of faulty statements within a program. Typically, these methods perform a MaxSAT call for each failing test, allowing them to individually identify a minimal set of faults for each failing test case rather than simultaneously addressing all failing test cases. *Program slicing* [35,37,43] has also emerged as a technique for localizing faults within programs. A more syntactic FBFL approach [35] is to use program slicing to enumerate all minimal sets of repairs for a given faulty program. Another method for identifying the causes of faulty program behaviour involves analyzing the variances between various versions of the software [43]. *Refinement* has a long-standing tradition in verification; particularly for refining abstractions of reachable states [4,6,7]. In that sense, our form of refinement is different because it enables us to more precisely pinpoint faults of the user, at the sub-expression level.

7 Conclusion

This paper introduces a novel formula-based fault localization technique for C programs capable of addressing any number of faults. Leveraging Model-Based Diagnosis (MBD) with multiple observations, CFAULTS consolidates all failing test cases into a unified MaxSAT formula, ensuring consistency in the fault localization process. Experimental evaluations on TCAS and C-PACK-IPAS, show that CFAULTS is faster than other FBFL approaches like BUGASSIST and SNIPER. Furthermore, CFAULTS only generates minimal diagnoses of faulty statements, while other methods tend to produce redundant diagnoses.

Acknowledgements. This work was partially supported by Portuguese national funds through FCT, under projects UIDB/50021/2020 (DOI: 10.54499/UIDB/50021/-2020), PTDC/CCI-COM/2156/2021 (DOI: 10.54499/PTDC/CCI-COM/2156/2021) and 2022.03537.PTDC (DOI: 10.54499/2022.03537.PTDC) and grant SFRH/BD/-07724/2020 (DOI: 10.54499/2020.07724.BD). PO acknowledges travel support from the European Union's Horizon 2020 research and innovation programme under ELISE Grant Agreement No 951847. This work was also supported by the MEYS within the program ERC CZ under the project POSTMAN no. LL1902 and co-funded by the European Union under the project *ROBOPROX* (reg. no. CZ.02.01.01/00/-22_008/0004590). This article is part of the RICAIP project that has received funding from the EU's Horizon 2020 research and innovation program under grant agreement No 857306.

Data Availability Statement. CFAULTS' implementation, our prototypes for BUGASSIST and SNIPER, and the evaluation benchmarks, TCAS [10] and C-PACK-IPAs [29], used for the evaluation in this paper, are publicly available on Zenodo [30].

References

1. Abreu, R., Zoeteweij, P., van Gemund, A.J.C.: Spectrum-based multiple fault localization. In: ASE 2009, 24th IEEE/ACM International Conference on Automated Software Engineering, Auckland, New Zealand, November 16-20 2009, pp. 88–99. IEEE Computer Society (2009). https://doi.org/10.1109/ASE.2009.25
2. Abreu, R., Zoeteweij, P., Golsteijn, R., van Gemund, A.J.C.: A practical evaluation of spectrum-based fault localization. J. Syst. Softw. **82**(11), 1780–1792 (2009). https://doi.org/10.1016/J.JSS.2009.06.035
3. Biere, A., Heule, M., van Maaren, H., Walsh, T. (eds.): Handbook of Satisfiability, Frontiers in Artificial Intelligence and Applications, vol. 185. IOS Press (2009)
4. Clarke, E.M., Grumberg, O., Kroening, D., Peled, D.A., Veith, H.: Model checking, 2nd Edition. MIT Press (2018). https://mitpress.mit.edu/books/model-checking-second-edition
5. Clarke, E., Kroening, D., Lerda, F.: A tool for checking ANSI-C programs. In: Jensen, K., Podelski, A. (eds.) TACAS 2004. LNCS, vol. 2988, pp. 168–176. Springer, Heidelberg (2004). https://doi.org/10.1007/978-3-540-24730-2_15
6. Clarke, E.M., Kroening, D., Sharygina, N., Yorav, K.: Predicate abstraction of ANSI-C programs using SAT. Formal Methods Syst. Des. **25**(2–3), 105–127 (2004). https://doi.org/10.1023/B:FORM.0000040025.89719.F3
7. Clarke, E., Kroening, D., Sharygina, N., Yorav, K.: SATABS: SAT-based predicate abstraction for ANSI-C. In: Halbwachs, N., Zuck, L.D. (eds.) TACAS 2005. LNCS, vol. 3440, pp. 570–574. Springer, Heidelberg (2005). https://doi.org/10.1007/978-3-540-31980-1_40
8. Clarke, E.M., Kroening, D., Yorav, K.: Behavioral consistency of C and verilog programs using bounded model checking. In: Proceedings of the 40th Design Automation Conference, DAC 2003, Anaheim, CA, USA, 2-6 June 2003, pp. 368–371. ACM (2003). https://doi.org/10.1145/775832.775928

9. Cytron, R., Ferrante, J., Rosen, B.K., Wegman, M.N., Zadeck, F.K.: Efficiently computing static single assignment form and the control dependence graph. ACM Trans. Program. Lang. Syst. **13**(4), 451–490 (1991). https://doi.org/10.1145/115372.115320

10. Do, H., Elbaum, S.G., Rothermel, G.: Supporting controlled experimentation with testing techniques: an infrastructure and its potential impact. Empir. Softw. Eng. **10**(4), 405–435 (2005). https://doi.org/10.1007/S10664-005-3861-2

11. Feser, J.K., Chaudhuri, S., Dillig, I.: Synthesizing data structure transformations from input-output examples. In: Proceedings of the 36th ACM SIGPLAN Conference on Programming Language Design and Implementation, Portland, OR, USA, 15-17 June 2015, pp. 229–239 (2015)

12. Griesmayer, A., Staber, S., Bloem, R.: Automated fault localization for C programs. In: Bloem, R., Roveri, M., Somenzi, F. (eds.) Proceedings of the Workshop on Verification and Debugging, V&D@FLoC 2006, Seattle, WA, USA, 21 August 2006. Electronic Notes in Theoretical Computer Science, vol. 174, pp. 95–111. Elsevier (2006). https://doi.org/10.1016/J.ENTCS.2006.12.032

13. Hansen, M.C., Yalcin, H., Hayes, J.P.: Unveiling the ISCAS-85 benchmarks: a case study in reverse engineering. IEEE Des. Test Comput. **16**(3), 72–80 (1999). https://doi.org/10.1109/54.785838

14. Ignatiev, A., Morgado, A., Marques-Silva, J.: PySAT: a Python toolkit for prototyping with SAT oracles. In: Beyersdorff, O., Wintersteiger, C.M. (eds.) SAT 2018. LNCS, vol. 10929, pp. 428–437. Springer, Cham (2018). https://doi.org/10.1007/978-3-319-94144-8_26

15. Ignatiev, A., Morgado, A., Marques-Silva, J.: RC2: an efficient MaxSAT solver. J. Satisf. Boolean Model. Comput. **11**(1), 53–64 (2019)

16. Ignatiev, A., Morgado, A., Weissenbacher, G., Marques-Silva, J.: Model-based diagnosis with multiple observations. In: Kraus, S. (ed.) Proceedings of the Twenty-Eighth International Joint Conference on Artificial Intelligence, IJCAI 2019, Macao, China, 10-16 August 2019, pp. 1108–1115. (2019). https://doi.org/10.24963/IJCAI.2019/155, https://www.ijcai.org/

17. Jose, M., Majumdar, R.: Bug-Assist: assisting fault localization in ANSI-C programs. In: Gopalakrishnan, G., Qadeer, S. (eds.) CAV 2011. LNCS, vol. 6806, pp. 504–509. Springer, Heidelberg (2011). https://doi.org/10.1007/978-3-642-22110-1_40

18. Jose, M., Majumdar, R.: Cause clue clauses: error localization using maximum satisfiability. In: Proceedings of the 32nd ACM SIGPLAN Conference on Programming Language Design and Implementation, PLDI 2011, pp. 437–446. ACM (2011)

19. Könighofer, R., Bloem, R.: Automated error localization and correction for imperative programs. In: Bjesse, P., Slobodová, A. (eds.) International Conference on Formal Methods in Computer-Aided Design, FMCAD 2011, Austin, TX, USA, October 30 - November 02, 2011, pp. 91–100. FMCAD Inc. (2011). http://dl.acm.org/citation.cfm?id=2157671

20. Lamraoui, S.-M., Nakajima, S.: A formula-based approach for automatic fault localization of imperative programs. In: Merz, S., Pang, J. (eds.) ICFEM 2014. LNCS, vol. 8829, pp. 251–266. Springer, Cham (2014). https://doi.org/10.1007/978-3-319-11737-9_17

21. Lamraoui, S., Nakajima, S.: A formula-based approach for automatic fault localization of multi-fault programs. J. Inf. Process. **24**(1), 88–98 (2016). https://doi.org/10.2197/IPSJJIP.24.88

22. Liffiton, M.H., Sakallah, K.A.: Algorithms for computing minimal unsatisfiable subsets of constraints. J. Autom. Reason. **40**(1), 1–33 (2008). https://doi.org/10.1007/S10817-007-9084-Z

23. Liu, K., Koyuncu, A., Bissyandé, T.F., Kim, D., Klein, J., Le Traon, Y.: You cannot fix what you cannot find! an investigation of fault localization bias in benchmarking automated program repair systems. In: 2019 12th IEEE Conference on Software Testing, Validation and Verification (ICST), pp. 102–113. IEEE (2019)

24. Marques-Silva, J., Janota, M., Ignatiev, A., Morgado, A.: Efficient model based diagnosis with maximum satisfiability. In: Yang, Q., Wooldridge, M.J. (eds.) Proceedings of the Twenty-Fourth International Joint Conference on Artificial Intelligence, IJCAI 2015, Buenos Aires, Argentina, 25-31 July 2015, pp. 1966–1972. AAAI Press (2015). http://ijcai.org/Abstract/15/279

25. Metodi, A., Stern, R., Kalech, M., Codish, M.: A novel sat-based approach to model based diagnosis. J. Artif. Intell. Res. **51**, 377–411 (2014). https://doi.org/10.1613/JAIR.4503

26. Naish, L., Lee, H.J., Ramamohanarao, K.: A model for spectra-based software diagnosis. ACM Trans. Softw. Eng. Methodol. **20**(3), 11:1–11:32 (2011). https://doi.org/10.1145/2000791.2000795

27. Orvalho, P., Janota, M., Manquinho, V.: C-Pack of IPAs: a C90 program benchmark of introductory programming assignments. CoRR **abs/2206.08768** (2022). https://doi.org/10.48550/arXiv.2206.08768

28. Orvalho, P., Janota, M., Manquinho, V.: MultIPAs: applying program transformations to introductory programming assignments for data augmentation. In: Proceedings of the 30th ACM Joint European Software Engineering Conference and Symposium on the Foundations of Software Engineering, ESEC/FSE 2022, pp. 1657–1661. ACM, Singapore (2022). https://doi.org/10.1145/3540250.3558931

29. Orvalho, P., Janota, M., Manquinho, V.: C-Pack of IPAs: a C90 program benchmark of introductory programming assignments. In: International Workshop on Automated Program Repair, APR@ICSE 2024, Lisbon, Portugal, April 20, 2024, pp. – (2024). https://doi.org/10.1145/3643788.3648010

30. Orvalho, P., Janota, M., Manquinho, V.: CFaults: model-based diagnosis for fault localization in C with multiple test cases (2024). https://doi.org/10.5281/zenodo.12510220, https://github.com/pmorvalho/CFaults

31. Orvalho, P., Janota, M., Manquinho, V.: InvAASTCluster: on applying invariant-based program clustering to introductory programming assignments (2022). https://doi.org/10.48550/ARXIV.2206.14175, https://arxiv.org/abs/2206.14175

32. Orvalho, P., Piepenbrock, J., Janota, M., Manquinho, V.M.: Graph neural networks for mapping variables between programs. In: ECAI 2023 - 26th European Conference on Artificial Intelligence. Frontiers in Artificial Intelligence and Applications, vol. 372, pp. 1811–1818. IOS Press, Poland (2023). https://doi.org/10.3233/FAIA230468

33. pycparser (2024). https://github.com/eliben/pycparser. Accessed 18 April 2024

34. Reiter, R.: A theory of diagnosis from first principles. Artif. Intell. **32**(1), 57–95 (1987). https://doi.org/10.1016/0004-3702(87)90062-2

35. Rothenberg, B.-C., Grumberg, O.: Must fault localization for program repair. In: Lahiri, S.K., Wang, C. (eds.) CAV 2020. LNCS, vol. 12225, pp. 658–680. Springer, Cham (2020). https://doi.org/10.1007/978-3-030-53291-8_33

36. Safarpour, S., Mangassarian, H., Veneris, A.G., Liffiton, M.H., Sakallah, K.A.: Improved design debugging using maximum satisfiability. In: Formal Methods in Computer-Aided Design, 7th International Conference, FMCAD 2007, Austin,

Texas, USA, 11-14 November 2007, Proceedings, pp. 13–19. IEEE Computer Society (2007). https://doi.org/10.1109/FAMCAD.2007.26
37. Soremekun, E.O., Kirschner, L., Böhme, M., Zeller, A.: Locating faults with program slicing: an empirical analysis. Empir. Softw. Eng. **26**(3), 51 (2021). https://doi.org/10.1007/S10664-020-09931-7
38. Wong, W.E., Debroy, V., Choi, B.: A family of code coverage-based heuristics for effective fault localization. J. Syst. Softw. **83**(2), 188–208 (2010). https://doi.org/10.1016/J.JSS.2009.09.037
39. Wong, W.E., Debroy, V., Gao, R., Li, Y.: The Dstar method for effective software fault localization. IEEE Trans. Reliab. **63**(1), 290–308 (2014). https://doi.org/10.1109/TR.2013.2285319
40. Wong, W.E., Gao, R., Li, Y., Abreu, R., Wotawa, F.: A survey on software fault localization. IEEE Trans. Software Eng. **42**(8), 707–740 (2016). https://doi.org/10.1109/TSE.2016.2521368
41. Wotawa, F., Nica, M., Moraru, I.: Automated debugging based on a constraint model of the program and a test case. J. Log. Algebraic Methods Program **81**(4), 390–407 (2012). https://doi.org/10.1016/J.JLAP.2012.03.002
42. Xie, Y., Aiken, A.: Scalable error detection using Boolean satisfiability. In: Palsberg, J., Abadi, M. (eds.) Proceedings of the 32nd ACM SIGPLAN-SIGACT Symposium on Principles of Programming Languages, POPL 2005, Long Beach, California, USA, 12-14 January 2005, pp. 351–363. ACM (2005). https://doi.org/10.1145/1040305.1040334
43. Zeller, A.: Yesterday, my program worked. today, it does not. why? In: Nierstrasz, O., Lemoine, M. (eds.) ESEC/SIGSOFT FSE -1999. LNCS, vol. 1687, pp. 253–267. Springer, Heidelberg (1999). https://doi.org/10.1007/3-540-48166-4_16

Detecting Speculative Execution Vulnerabilities on Weak Memory Models

Nicholas Coughlin, Kait Lam, Graeme Smith[(✉)], and Kirsten Winter

Defence Science and Technology Group, Australia
School of Electrical Engineering and Computer Science,
The University of Queensland, Brisbane, Australia
g.smith1@uq.edu.au

Abstract. Speculative execution attacks affect all modern processors and much work has been done to develop techniques for detection of associated vulnerabilities. Modern processors also operate on weak memory models which allow out-of-order execution of code. Despite this, there is little work on looking at the interplay between speculative execution and weak memory models. In this paper, we provide an information flow logic for detecting speculative execution vulnerabilities on weak memory models. The logic is general enough to be used with any modern processor, and designed to be extensible to allow detection of vulnerabilities to specific attacks. The logic has been proven sound with respect to an abstract model of speculative execution in Isabelle/HOL.

1 Introduction

Speculative execution is a hardware optimisation in which the processor uses latent processing cycles to continue executing instructions based on a predicted value of an unevaluated expression, such as a branch condition. If the subsequent evaluation of the expression agrees with the prediction, the results of the executed instructions are committed to main memory, otherwise they are rolled back. This optimisation came to the forefront of computer security in 2018 with the disclosure of two related security attacks, Spectre [24] and Meltdown [25]. These were followed by the publication of a number of other speculative execution attacks [4,5,9,22,34,35,42], each taking advantage of traces of the speculatively executed code remaining in caches, and other micro-architectural features, after roll-back.

While much has been done to detect speculative vulnerabilities in code [8], most of this work has not considered additional hardware optimisations related to a processor's *weak memory model* [39]. All commercial processors (x86 processors of Intel and AMD, ARM processors, IBM Power, etc.) operate under a weak memory model which, again to make use of latent processing cycles, allows out-of-order execution of instructions. This out-of-order execution is constrained on individual threads so that only syntactically independent instructions may execute out-of-order, thereby guaranteeing behaviour equivalent to the original program order.

A. Platzer et al. (Eds.): FM 2024, LNCS 14933, pp. 482–500, 2025.
https://doi.org/10.1007/978-3-031-71162-6_25

While many programmers can therefore ignore weak memory effects, those utilising data races for efficiency (e.g., programmers of low-level code of operating system routines or library components) cannot. In the presence of data races, weak memory effects can result in behaviour not apparent in the code itself. As we show in this paper, this can lead to additional speculative execution vulnerabilities. To the best of our knowledge, we are the first to show that such vulnerabilities are possible.

Early work on weak memory models and security includes that by Vaughan and Milstein [41] (for the x86 weak memory model TSO) and Mantel et al. [27] (for TSO, PSO and IBM-370). These papers highlight security violations that are not detectable using standard approaches to information flow security. In [37,38], Smith et al. provide an information flow logic for the significantly weaker memory models of ARMv8 and IBM Power processors. This approach builds on the work of Mantel et al. [28] which uses a restricted form of rely/guarantee reasoning [23,44] to allow reasoning to be done over one thread of a concurrent program at a time. The approach is adapted to more general rely/guarantee reasoning on the ARMv8 weak memory model by Coughlin and Smith [13]. While this approach has been automated using symbolic execution, its inherent complexity limits the size of the programs that can be effectively handled. In further work by Coughlin et al. [14,15], this complexity is significantly reduced via a general approach that allows standard reasoning (assuming instructions execute in program order) to be augmented with additional *reordering interference freedom* (*rif*) checks to account for the effects of a given weak memory model. As well as being simpler to apply, the approach is parameterised by the weak memory model and hence can be applied to any currently available processor.

In this paper, we adopt the *rif* approach and use it with an information flow logic developed specifically for detecting speculative execution vulnerabilities. In Sect. 2, we provide a brief overview of Spectre-like attacks and show via an example how weak memory effects can introduce additional speculative execution vulnerabilities. In Sect. 3, we provide an overview of the work on which we build: an existing information flow logic for concurrent programs [43] and the aforementioned work on *rif* to capture weak memory effects [14]. Our logic for detecting speculative execution vulnerabilities is presented and applied to our example from Sect. 2 in Sect. 4. We compare our approach to the current literature in Sect. 5 before concluding in Sect. 6.

2 Speculative Execution Attacks

Speculative execution has been liberally applied in processor design as chipmakers seek to maximise performance. As a result, there are many sources of speculation and hence many associated attacks. Canella et al. [6] taxonomise speculative execution attacks and, in doing so, reveal additional avenues for mistraining applicable to all such attacks.

Spectre attacks [24] exploit deficiencies in the process of reverting incorrect speculations. Although their primary effects are reversed, their microarchitectural side-effects are reverted incompletely or not at all. Through timing side channels, an attacker can trace these side-effects and infer information accessed during the speculation—potentially exposing sensitive information and breaking traditional software isolation. Variants of Spectre differ in the root of the speculation they exploit and also in the side channel they use to extract the information. In this paper, we focus on Spectre-PHT, variant 1 reported in the initial discovery of Spectre vulnerabilities by Kocher et al. [24].

2.1   Spectre-PHT

In Spectre-PHT, the source of speculation is a conditional branch. By mistraining the pattern history table (PHT), an attacker forces the victim code to bypass a bounds check, indexing an array out of bounds and potentially accessing sensitive information. If that information is used to index another array, the array's value at that index is loaded into the cache. Since the cache line is not reverted when speculation is cancelled, the sensitive information can be revealed by a timing difference when accessing values of the array.

The typical Spectre-PHT gadget (from [24]) is shown below. If the second line is speculatively executed when the guard in the first line is false, the value of array1[x] multiplied by the cache line size (4096) is used to load a value of array2. After roll-back, a cache timing attack will reveal the cache line which was used from which the value of array1[x] can be derived.

```
if (x < array1_size)
    y := array2[array1[x] * 4096]
```

2.2   Spectre-PHT and Weak Memory

As well as speculative execution, multicore processors employ pipelining and superscalar design to improve the efficiency of executed code. Several instructions are evaluated simultaneously and may take effect in an order different to their order in the program. These additional *weak memory* effects can largely be ignored when code is either not concurrent, or is concurrent but data-race free. However, these effects do need to be considered when writing efficient low-level code for device drivers and concurrent data structures. Low-level programming constructs, in particular *fences*, can be used to control instruction ordering where required.

Consider a program in which a variable c may hold sensitive information whenever both of the lock variables, a and b, are non-zero indicating they are held by a writing thread. Furthermore, neither a nor b change value once set to 0. In the example, we use a, b and c for global variables shared between threads, and r0 to r3 for thread-local registers. We use the notation [r] for dereferencing the address held in register r.

The reading thread below checks whether a is 0 before entering the branch. The instructions before the if statement may take time leading to speculation on the branch condition. In the branch, b and c are read and if b is 0, c's value is used as an offset from a non-sensitive base address in a subsequent read.

The check of b is done using a conditional expression which is not subject to speculation. Hence, when ignoring weak memory effects, the code does not enable a Spectre-PHT attack based on the final read: when speculatively executing the branch when a is non-zero, the conditional expression evaluates to 0 when b is also non-zero.

```
r0 := a;
r1 := r1 ^ r1;      // exclusive-or sets r1 to 0
if (r0 = r1)
    r0 := b;        // this line could reorder with the next
    r1 := c;
    r2 := (r0=0) ? base + r1 : 0;
    r3 := [r2];     // Spectre attack enabled if r2 is sensitive
```

On all current microprocessors, however, the syntactically independent reads of b and c could reordered leading to the following scenario. During speculative execution of the branch, a sensitive value held in c is read due to both a and b being non-zero. A thread in the environment then sets c to a non-sensitive value and a and b to 0. Finally, b is read and, since it is now 0, the earlier sensitive value of c is used in the final read.

It is precisely such vulnerabilities that this paper aims to detect. Weak memory reasoning or speculative execution analysis alone would not reveal the issue.

3   Background

Our information flow logic for detecting Spectre-style vulnerabilities builds on the existing information flow logic of Winter et al. [43]. That logic introduces *proof obligations* during weakest precondition (*wp*) reasoning [16,17] to detect insecure information flow: the failure of such a proof obligation implies it is possible for sensitive information to leak to a variable accessible by an attacker.

The logic is sound with respect to the standard notion of *non-interference* [19] where the values of variables with a particular security classification are not influenced by the values of those with higher classifications. Hence, an attacker who can observe the former cannot deduce anything about the latter. This has been demonstrated in Isabelle/HOL over a programming language introduced in [43] with an extension to support simple array operations.

The logic also supports *value-dependent security policies* which enable a variable's security classification to change as the program executes [26,30,32], and thread-local analysis of concurrent code using rely/guarantee reasoning [23,44]. It does not, however, support reasoning on weak memory models. Hence, in this paper we also employ the notion of *reordering interference freedom* (*rif*) checks [14] to detect additional vulnerabilities due to weak memory. As detailed in [14,15], *rif* is readily customised to different processor architectures. It has also been automated and shown to be sound both on a simple while language and an abstraction of ARMv8 assembly code using Isabelle/HOL.

3.1   Weakest Precondition Based Information Flow Reasoning

As is standard in information flow logics, Winter et al. [43] define the security levels relevant to a program as the elements of a lattice $(L, \sqsubseteq)$ where each pair of elements $a, b \in L$ has a *join*, i.e., least upper bound, denoted by $a \sqcup b$, and a *meet*, i.e., greatest lower bound, denoted by $a \sqcap b$. The top of the lattice $\top$ represents the highest security classification, and the bottom $\bot$ the lowest.

A weakest precondition logic traditionally captures, at each point in a program, the weakest predicate needed to maintain correctness from that point in the code. To additionally capture information flow, the wp_{if} logic defined in [43] includes for each variable v an additional variable Γ_v (of type L) denoting the security level of the information currently held by the variable.

Variables are partitioned into *global* variables, which can be accessed by more than one thread, and *local* variables which cannot. In a secure program, for all global variables the security level of the information it holds is less than the variable's security classification. The latter, denoted $\mathcal{L}(v)$, is a conditional expression that evaluates to a value of type L depending on the current program state, i.e., its classification may depend on other variables referred to in this context as *control variables*. Formally, a global variable in a secure program always satisfies $\Gamma_v \sqsubseteq \mathcal{L}(v)$. That is, variables never hold information at a higher security level than their classification, ensuring non-interference. Local variables are not accessible by an attacker, and thus may hold information at any security level. Hence, their security classification is by default the top of the lattice.

When checking whether a particular line of code can leak information, it is assumed that the program is secure up to that point. Hence, for global variables $\Gamma_x \sqcap \mathcal{L}(x)$ is used to denote the security level of the information in variable x. When it is not possible to deduce Γ_x from a program's code, e.g., when x has been assigned to an input, the meet in this expression ensures that its value will not exceed $\mathcal{L}(x)$.

The security level of an expression e in terms of local variables and literals, denoted $\Gamma_E(e)$, is defined as the join of the security levels of the variables to which e refers. That is, $\Gamma_E(e) = \bigsqcup_{r \in vars(e)} \Gamma_r$ where $vars(e)$ denotes the variables occurring in e.

As an example, the wp_{if} rule for an assignment to a global variable $x := e$ replaces each occurrence of variable x with expression e in the post-state Q, and each occurrence of Γ_x with $\Gamma_E(e)$ (denoted $Q[x, \Gamma_x \backslash e, \Gamma_E(e)]$). Additionally, a proof obligation is added to Q to ensure that this change does not violate non-interference. This amounts to checking that

(i) the security level of e is not higher than the security classification of x, and
(ii) since x's value may affect the security classification of other global variables, for each such variable y, y's current security level Γ_y does not exceed its updated security classification with e in place of x.

$$wp_{if}(x := e, Q) = Q[x, \Gamma_x \backslash e, \Gamma_E(e)] \wedge \Gamma_E(e) \sqsubseteq \mathcal{L}(x) \wedge$$
$$(\forall y \cdot \Gamma_y \sqcap \mathcal{L}(y) \sqsubseteq \mathcal{L}(y)[x \backslash e])$$

Note that if y is not dependent on x, then $\mathcal{L}(y)[x \backslash e]$ simplifies to $\mathcal{L}(y)$ making the final proof obligation trivially true.

To analyse a thread within this framework, we would start with the predicate *true* holding after the program and step backwards through the code, transforming the predicate (from Q to Q') with $Q' = wp_{if}(\alpha, Q)$ for each instruction α. A *true* postcondition is used since we are focussed on information flow security (whose proof obligations are introduced by the logic) and not functional correctness (which would require a postcondition). The proof obligations added by the wp_{if} transformer at each step have been proven to ensure non-interference, i.e., that sensitive information is not leaked [43].

3.2   Extending with Rely/Guarantee Reasoning

To support reasoning about threads in a concurrent program, the wp_{if} logic is extended with rely/guarantee reasoning [23,44]. Each thread has a rely condition $\mathcal{R}$ and guarantee condition $\mathcal{G}$. The rely condition is a reflexive and transitive relation on states that abstractly captures changes that the environment may make to global variables. The guarantee condition is a reflexive relation on states that abstractly captures changes to global variables that the thread itself is allowed to make. Both conditions are expressed in terms of global variables x and x', the latter representing the variable in the post-state of the relation.

For each instruction α which updates global variables, the corresponding wp_{if} rule is updated to include a proof obligation $guar(\mathcal{G}, \alpha)$ which captures the conditions under which executing α will ensure $\mathcal{G}$. Additionally, all rules are updated with a proof obligation that their other proof obligations are stable, i.e., cannot be falsified, under $\mathcal{R}$. Given P comprises $wp_{if}(\alpha, Q)$ and $guar(\mathcal{G}, \alpha)$ if applicable, stability of P is defined as $stable_{\mathcal{R}}(P) = P \wedge (\forall glb' \cdot \mathcal{R} \Rightarrow P')$ where glb' is the list of post-state global variables, and P' is the predicate P with all global variables x replaced by x'. The resulting logic is referred to as wp_{if}^{RG}.

3.3   Reordering Interference Freedom

To take into account instruction reordering due to executing on a weak memory model it is sufficient to check that such reordering cannot invalidate the logic's outcome for a particular program. To do this, we employ the *reordering interference freedom (rif)* approach of Coughlin et al. [14]. This approach covers most modern processor architectures (such as x86 and ARMv8) and can be extended to cover all others as shown in [15]. Essentially the approach checks, for every pair of reorderable instructions, α and β, that executing the instructions in the reverse order does not introduce new behaviour. Reorderable instructions are defined in terms of the specific hardware memory model, e.g., TSO, ARMv8, based on the approach of Colvin and Smith [10].

For instructions α and β, let $\beta' \prec \alpha \prec \beta$ be the predicate that β may reorder before α where it is executed as β' (changes to β are due to the possibility of forwarding values from a later write instruction to an earlier read [10]). Given the rely and guarantee conditions under which α and β execute, we define

$$rif_{\mathsf{a}}(\alpha, \beta) \,\,\widehat{=}\,\, \forall\, Q \cdot wp_{if}^{RG}(\alpha; \beta, Q) \Rightarrow wp_{if}^{RG}(\beta'; \alpha, Q)$$

which expresses that the order of execution of α and β does not affect the security of their execution. This extends to programs p such that

$$rif(p) \,\,\widehat{=}\,\, \forall\, \alpha, \beta \in p \cdot (\beta' \prec \alpha \prec \beta) \Rightarrow rif_{\mathsf{a}}(\alpha, \beta).$$

The *rif* approach is sound because it is defined over all possible post-states Q. Hence, all traces (arising from different sequences of reorderings) under which a reordering could occur are taken into account.

The approach separates the inter-thread interference (using rely/guarantee) from the intra-thread (reordering) interference (using *rif*). That is, *rif* is thread-local. For a thread with n instructions, the worst case is that every instruction can reorder giving us $n(n-1)/2$ reorderable pairs (significantly less than the $n!$ traces that such reordering would introduce). Note also that this worst case is extremely unlikely. Instructions which refer to the same variable are not generally reorderable.

Pairs of potentially reorderable instructions can be identified via a dataflow analysis, similar to dependence analysis commonly used in compiler optimisation. We have previously provided such an automation for both a simple while language and an abstraction of ARMv8 assembly code using Isabelle/HOL [14].

4   Information Flow Logic

Our approach to extend the logic of Winter et al. [43] with speculation is to develop a weakest precondition transformer, wp_s, which operates over *pairs* of predicates $\langle Q_s, Q \rangle$. The predicate Q_s (resp. Q) represents the weakest precondition at that point in the program, assuming the processor is speculating (resp. is not speculating).

Furthermore, proof obligations within Q_s must distinguish between two versions of each global variable: *base* variables (those in the global state visible to all threads), and *frame* variables (those in the local speculation frame of this thread only). While speculating, writes and subsequent reads of global variables will only access the frame variables. Reads of global variables without a previous write during speculation will access the base variables. Other threads will concurrently read and write to the base variables. Within Q_s, we denote base variables with a b superscript so that predicates in terms of them will not be transformed by wp_s over speculative instructions.

Conceptually, wp_s can be understood as two wp transformers, one for the speculative case and one for the non-speculative case, running in parallel over each instruction. For a program to be secure, its precondition must imply the non-speculative weakest precondition. The speculative weakest precondition is merged into the speculative one at each branching point. This framework enables reasoning about speculation, even nested speculation, in a manner very similar to ordinary wp reasoning and with minimal added complexity.

4.1 Weakest Precondition with Speculation

For ease of presentation, we define wp_s over the instructions of a high-level programming language representing assembly programs (as in [10]). The syntax of an instruction, α, and a program, p, is defined as follows.

$$\alpha ::= \mathsf{skip} \mid r := e \mid r := x \mid x := e \mid \mathsf{fence} \mid \mathsf{leak}\ e$$
$$p ::= \alpha \mid p\,;\,p \mid \mathsf{if}\ b\ \mathsf{then}\ p\ \mathsf{else}\ p \mid \mathsf{while}\ b\ \mathsf{do}\ p$$

where r is a local variable, x is a global variable, b a Boolean condition and e an expression. Both b and e are in terms of local variables and literals only, reflecting the use of registers for these values in assembly code. The language includes a fence instruction which prevents reordering of instructions and also terminates current speculative execution. A special *ghost* instruction[1] leak e is inserted into a program to indicate that the following instructions are a gadget that leaks information through a micro-architectural side channel when executed (speculatively, or otherwise).

Before analysing a program with our logic, we insert leak instructions before each gadget of interest during a pre-pass over the code. Since typical gadgets can be detected syntactically, this is a straightforward task to mechanise. The expression e of the inserted leak instruction is based on what information leaks when the gadget is used in an attack. For the example of Sect. 2.2 where the memory access [r2] would leak r2, e would be $r2$. After this pre-pass the code is analysed using our logic to determine whether the information leaked is possibly sensitive and hence the gadget causes a security vulnerability. Note that not all code conforming to the syntactic form of a gadget will enable a successful attack on sensitive information.

Since the pre-pass can be customised for different gadgets, the overall approach can be adapted to a variety of attacks, including new attacks as they are discovered. We discuss adapting the approach for a number of existing speculative execution attacks in Sect. 4.5.

The rules for our speculative execution logic wp_s build on those of wp_{if} [43]. We extend them with rely/guarantee reasoning in Sect. 4.2. A formal proof in Isabelle/HOL of the soundness of the resulting rules with respect to an abstract semantics of speculative execution [11] is available online [12].

Skip: A skip instruction does not change the $\langle Q_s, Q \rangle$ tuple.

$$wp_s(\mathsf{skip}, \langle Q_s, Q \rangle) = \langle Q_s, Q \rangle$$

Local assignment: Local variables may hold information at any security level and cannot be used as control variables. Hence, we do not need the proof obligations

---

[1] A ghost instruction is not part of the actual code and is used for analysis purposes only.

of global assignments detailed in Sect. 3.1. For assigning an expression e to a
local variable, we have

$$wp_s(r := e, \langle Q_s, Q \rangle) = \langle Q_s[r, \Gamma_r \backslash e, \Gamma_E(e)], Q[r, \Gamma_r \backslash e, \Gamma_E(e)] \rangle .$$

For assigning the value of a global variable x to a local variable, $r := x$,
we need to modify the weakest precondition in the speculative state. Since we
do not know whether a load of x during speculation is of a frame variable or a
base variable (which is subject to interference from other threads) we need to
consider both cases. Let glb be the list of $globals$, i.e., all global variables x and
their associated Γ_x variables. For the case where the load is of the base variable,
we replace each $y \in glb$ with y^b. This ensures the predicate is not transformed
by speculative assignments as we reason backwards through the code. It is only
transformed by the assignments of other threads via the rely condition (as will
be described in Sect. 4.2), and so remains consistent with the actual values and
classifications of globals in terms of the base variables (which are shared with
other threads).

To ensure in the reasoning that the correct case is used, we distinguish the
cases by qualifying them with whether x has been written to during the speculation and hence is defined in the frame, or not. To do this, we introduce a
ghost variable x_{def} which is true when x is defined within the frame, and false
otherwise. When x is defined by an earlier write during speculation (and hence
the later load was from the frame) then x_{def} will be set to true (see the global
assignment rule below). This will cause the base case to be ignored, leaving just
the frame case.

If, on the other hand, there is no such earlier write to x, both cases reach
the start of speculation where x_{def} will be set to false (see the if and while rules
below). This will cause the frame case to be ignored, leaving just the base case.

Formally, we have

$$wp_s(r := x, \langle Q_s, Q \rangle) = \langle (x_{def} \Rightarrow Q_s[r, \Gamma_r \backslash x, \Gamma_x]) \wedge$$
$$(\neg x_{def} \Rightarrow Q_s[r, \Gamma_r \backslash x^b, \Gamma_x^b \sqcap \mathcal{L}(x)[glb \backslash glb^b]]),$$
$$Q[r, \Gamma_r \backslash x, \Gamma_x \sqcap \mathcal{L}(x)] \rangle .$$

where glb^b is the list glb with each element y replaced by y^b. Note that in the
base case of the speculative precondition all globals y are replaced by y^b. This
ensures that they refer to the values of the base variables. In the frame case, on
the other hand, x and Γ_x refer to the frame variables and will be transformed
by wp_s over earlier speculative assignments.

Global assignment: An assignment to a global variable $x := e$ sets x_{def} to true
and replaces each occurrence of variable x and Γ_x with expression e and security
level $\Gamma_E(e)$, respectively, in both Q_s and Q. Additionally, in the non-speculative
case we have the proof obligations of wp_{if} described in Sect. 3.1. The speculative case does not have these proof obligations. Since a speculatively executed
assignment does not write to memory, it has no effect on the classification of
other variables.

$$wp_s(x := e, \langle Q_s, Q \rangle) = \langle Q_s[x, \Gamma_x, x_{def} \backslash e, \Gamma_E(e), true],$$
$$Q[x, \Gamma_x \backslash e, \Gamma_E(e)] \wedge \Gamma_E(e) \sqsubseteq \mathcal{L}(x) \wedge$$
$$(\forall y \cdot \Gamma_y \sqcap \mathcal{L}(y) \sqsubseteq \mathcal{L}(y)[x \backslash e]) \rangle$$

Fence: The fence instruction terminates any current speculative execution. Hence, any proof obligations in the speculative state beyond the fence do not need to be considered at the point in the program where a fence occurs. Q_s is therefore replaced by *true* and Q is unchanged.

$$wp_s(\text{fence}, \langle Q_s, Q \rangle) = \langle true, Q \rangle$$

Leak: The instruction leak e leaks the value of expression e via a microarchitectural side channel, introducing a proof obligation into both Q_s and Q.

$$wp_s(\text{leak } e, \langle Q_s, Q \rangle) = \langle Q_s \wedge \Gamma_E(e) = \bot, Q \wedge \Gamma_E(e) = \bot \rangle$$

where $\bot$ denotes the lowest value of the security lattice. Requiring that the leaked information is at this level ensures that the attacker cannot deduce anything new from the information, regardless of the level of information they can observe.

Sequential composition: As in standard *wp* reasoning, sequentially composed instructions transform the tuple one at a time.

$$wp_s(p_1 ; p_2, \langle Q_s, Q \rangle) = wp_s(p_1, wp_s(p_2, \langle Q_s, Q \rangle))$$

If-then-else: In general, an if statement might occur within a speculative context (when nested in or following an earlier if, for example). The branch that is followed speculatively is, in general, independent of that actually executed later. Hence, the speculative proof obligations from both branches are conjoined to form the speculative precondition.

Additionally, given that the if statement might initiate speculation, the speculative proof obligations need to be merged into the non-speculative precondition. We do this by (i) setting x_{def} for all global variables x to false in the speculative precondition, leaving just the base case, and then (ii) renaming each global $y^\flat$ to y so that the resulting speculative precondition Q_s can be conjoined with the non-speculative precondition Q.

Finally, a proof obligation $\Gamma_E(b) = \bot$ is added to the non-speculative precondition. Such a proof obligation is common in information flow logics for concurrent programs since the value of b can readily be deduced using timing attacks on such programs [31,37]. It is not necessary to also check this proof obligation in the speculative case whose purpose is to detect vulnerabilities that are *not* detectable in the non-speculative case.

With $\langle Q_{s1}, Q_1 \rangle = wp_s(p_1, \langle Q_s, Q \rangle)$ and $\langle Q_{s2}, Q_2 \rangle = wp_s(p_2, \langle Q_s, Q \rangle)$, we have

$$
\begin{aligned}
wp_s(\text{if } b \text{ then } p_1 \text{ else } p_2, \langle Q_s, Q \rangle) = \\
\langle\, Q_{s1} \wedge Q_{s2}, \Gamma_E(b) = \bot \wedge (b \Rightarrow Q_1) \wedge (\neg\, b \Rightarrow Q_2) \wedge \\
(Q_{s1} \wedge Q_{s2})[glb^\flat, d_1, ..., d_n \backslash glb, false, ..., false]\,\rangle.
\end{aligned}
$$

where $glb^\flat$ is the list glb with all elements y replaced by $y^\flat$, and $d_1, .., , d_n$ is the list of introduced ghost variables of the form x_{def}.

While-do: Similar to standard wp reasoning, we can soundly approximate the weakest precondition of a loop by finding invariants which imply our speculative and non-speculative postconditions, Q_s and (when the loop guard is false) Q, and which are maintained by the loop body (when the loop guard is true in the non-speculative case). As with the if rule, a proof obligation $\Gamma_E(b) = \bot$ must hold in the non-speculative case.

$$
wp_s(\text{while } b \text{ do } p, \langle Q_s, Q \rangle) = \langle Inv_s, Inv \rangle
$$

where $Inv_s \Rightarrow Q_s$ and $Inv \Rightarrow \Gamma_E(b) = \bot \wedge Inv_s[glb^\flat, d_1, ..., d_n \backslash glb, false, ...,$ $false]$ and $Inv \wedge \neg\, b \Rightarrow Q$, and given $wp_s(p, \langle Inv_s, Inv \rangle) = \langle P_s, P \rangle$, then $Inv_s \Rightarrow P_s$ and $Inv \wedge b \Rightarrow P$. Like the if rule, the while rule copies the proof obligations in the speculative precondition to the non-speculative precondition, and maintains those in the speculative precondition in case the loop is reached within an existing speculative context.

4.2 Rely/Guarantee and Reordering

Given $\langle P_s, P \rangle = wp_s(\alpha, \langle Q_s, Q \rangle)$, we account for a thread's rely and guarantee conditions, $\mathcal{R}$ and $\mathcal{G}$, by ensuring that P_s and P are *stable*, i.e., cannot be made false under changes allowed by $\mathcal{R}$, and that α's effects on global variables satisfy $\mathcal{G}$.

For P_s, frame variables y will be unaffected by the environment whereas base variables $y^\flat$ represent the actual globals and will be subject to environmental change. P_s, therefore, needs to be stable under $id_{glb} \wedge \mathcal{R}[glb \backslash glb^\flat]$ where id_{glb} equates each $y \in glb$ with y', and $glb^\flat$ is the list glb with all elements y renamed to $y^\flat$.

The guarantee $\mathcal{G}$ need only be considered for global assignments $x := e$ as these are the only instructions that affect the shared environment. For such assignments, we require that $\mathcal{G}$ holds in P when e is used in place of x', and y is used in place of y' for all other variables, i.e., these variables are unchanged by the assignment. This is not needed for P_s, as globals are unchanged when executing speculatively.

Given glb' (resp. $glb^{b'}$) is the list glb with each element y replaced by y' (resp. $y^{b'}$), and $\langle P_s, P \rangle = wp_s(\alpha, \langle Q_s, Q \rangle)$, we define wp_s^{RG} for instructions as

$$wp_s^{RG}(\alpha, \langle Q_s, Q \rangle) = \langle\, P_s \wedge (\forall\, glb', glb^{b'} \cdot id_{glb} \wedge \mathcal{R}[glb \backslash glb^b] \Rightarrow P'_s),$$
$$P \wedge \mathcal{G}^\alpha \wedge (\forall\, glb' \cdot \mathcal{R} \Rightarrow (P \wedge \mathcal{G}^\alpha)[glb \backslash glb']) \,\rangle$$

where $\mathcal{G}^\alpha$ is defined as $\mathcal{G}[x' \backslash e][glb' \backslash glb]$ when α is $x := e$ and as $true$ for all other instructions.

For program structures, e.g., sequential composition, wp_s^{RG} is defined equivalently to wp_s, with all recursive invocations replaced with wp_s^{RG} and all loop invariants stable under $\mathcal{R}$.

4.3 Reordering Interference Freedom

Once a thread of our program has been proven secure with the logic wp_s^{RG}, we separately check reordering interference freedom (rif). This will uncover any problems due to reordering interference such as that in the example of Sect. 2.2. For reasoning over state tuples of the logic wp_s^{RG}, we define rif_a as

$$rif_a(\alpha, \beta) = \forall\, Q_s, Q \cdot wp_s^{RG}(\alpha; \beta, \langle Q_s, Q \rangle) \Rightarrow wp_s^{RG}(\beta'; \alpha, \langle Q_s, Q \rangle)$$

where $\langle Q_{s1}, Q_1 \rangle \Rightarrow \langle Q_{s2}, Q_2 \rangle$ is defined to be $(Q_{s1} \Rightarrow Q_{s2}) \wedge (Q_1 \Rightarrow Q_2)$.

4.4 Example Revisited

Applying wp_s^{RG} to the example of Sect. 2.2 results in a weakest precondition of true, revealing no security vulnerability as expected when weak memory is not taken into account. A rif check, however, reveals that the reordering of the syntactically independent instructions r0 := b and r1 := c can lead to different behaviour, indicating that the program may be insecure.

We investigate this possibility by applying wp_s^{RG} to the example with the instructions reordered in Fig. 1. We customise Γ_E so that $\Gamma_E(r^\hat{}\, r) = \bot$ given that the result of this expression will always be 0, and $\Gamma_E(e\ ?\ t : f) = \Gamma_E(e) \sqcup$ (if e then $\Gamma_E(t)$ else $\Gamma_E(f)$) to reflect that the security level of the expression will depend on just one of t or f. To improve precision, such customisations would be built into the logic for expressions in the given programming language to which it is applied.

We let $\mathcal{R} = (a = 0 \Rightarrow a' = 0) \wedge (b = 0 \Rightarrow b' = 0)$ to capture that once either a or b is zero it never changes. $\mathcal{L}(a)$ and $\mathcal{L}(b)$ are $\bot$ (the lowest security level) in any state, and $\mathcal{L}(c)$ is $\bot$ whenever $a = 0 \vee b = 0$. Where two predicate pairs appear between lines of code, the upper one is a simplification of the lower. Since there are no writes to global variables in the branch, for presentation purposes we have only included those predicates in the speculative states corresponding to all global variables being identified with the base variables (other predicates are replaced with ...).

None of the instructions change global variables, and hence there are no guarantee checks. Stability checks are required, however, for those predicates in terms of globals. The conjunct $\Gamma_{r1} = \bot$ above the line r0 := b is introduced as there are no states in which the predicate $b \neq 0$ is stable, i.e., $b = 0 \Rightarrow \Gamma_{r1} = \bot$ is stable only when $\Gamma_{r1} = \bot$.

Since a and b do not change when they are 0, and c does not hold sensitive information when a or b are 0, the predicate $\Gamma_c = \bot \vee a = 0 \vee b = 0$ (above the line r1 := c) is stable when $a = 0 \vee b = 0$. Similarly, for the speculative predicate $\Gamma_c^b = \bot \vee a^b = 0 \vee b^b = 0$. Also, the predicate $r0 = r1 \Rightarrow a = 0 \vee b = 0$ (above the line if (r0=r1)) is stable when $a = 0 \vee b = 0$.

The calculated weakest precondition at the beginning of the example code is $a = 0 \vee b = 0$, indicating that the code is only secure when both locks are not held. Therefore, the checks of a and b do not have the effect that the programmer intended. The check on b fails due to the reordered loads on c and b, whereas the check on a fails due to the incorrect speculation of the branch if (r0 = r1). The latter is evident in its precondition constraining $a = 0 \vee b = 0$ regardless of the branch condition. Since not taking into account either instruction reordering

```
⟨..., a = 0 ∨ b = 0⟩
r0 := a;
⟨..., Γr0 = ⊥ ∧ (a = 0 ∨ b = 0)⟩
r1:= r1^r1;
⟨..., Γr0 ⊔ Γr1 = ⊥ ∧ (a = 0 ∨ b = 0)⟩
⟨..., ΓE(r0 = r1) = ⊥ ∧ (r0 = r1 ⇒ a = 0 ∨ b = 0) ∧ (a = 0 ∨ b = 0)⟩
if (r0 = r1)
    ⟨... ∧ (¬bdef ∧ ¬cdef ⇒ a^b = 0 ∨ b^b = 0), a = 0 ∨ b = 0⟩
    ⟨... ∧ (¬bdef ∧ ¬cdef ⇒ P[glb\glb^b]), P⟩
      where P ≙ (Γc = ⊥ ∨ a = 0 ∨ b = 0) ∧ (a = 0 ∨ b = 0)
    r1 := c;
    ⟨... ∧ (¬bdef ⇒ Γr1 = ⊥), Γr1 = ⊥⟩
    ⟨... ∧ (¬bdef ⇒ P[glb\glb^b]), P⟩
      where P ≙ Γb ⊓ ℒ(b) = ⊥ ∧ (b = 0 ⇒ Γr1 = ⊥) ∧ Γr1 = ⊥
    r0 := b;
    ⟨Γr0 = ⊥ ∧ (r0 = 0 ⇒ Γr1 = ⊥), Γr0 = ⊥ ∧ (r0 = 0 ⇒ Γr1 = ⊥)⟩
    ⟨ΓE((r0 = 0) ? base + r1 : 0)) = ⊥, ΓE((r0 = 0) ? base + r1 : 0) = ⊥⟩
    r2 := (r0 = 0) ? base + r1 : 0;
    ⟨Γr2 = ⊥, Γr2 = ⊥⟩
    leak(r2);
    ⟨true, true⟩
    r3 := [r2]
    ⟨true, true⟩
else
    ⟨true, true⟩
    skip
    ⟨true, true⟩         where glb^b is the list glb with all elements y replaced by y^b.
```

Fig. 1. Applying wp_s^{RG} to a reordering of the example from Sect. 2.2.

or speculation would be sufficient to establish $a = 0 \lor b = 0$ (resulting in the weakest precondition being true), this vulnerability can only be identified by considering both.

4.5   Discussion

The use of leak instructions in our logic means we can readily customise it to detect various speculative execution vulnerabilities. For example, to detect Spectre variant 1 vulnerabilities, we would extend the logic with arrays (as was done for the Isabelle/HOL encoding of wp_{if} [43]). The expression e of the leak instruction would be the value used for the final read in the standard gadget (see Sect. 2.1). This simple extension of the logic would also allow us to detect (i) BranchSpec vulnerabilities [9] where a sensitive value from a speculative array-out-of-bounds access is used as a branching condition, and (ii) vulnerabilities to the data variant of the PACMAN attack [34]. During speculation, this attack obtains a sensitive value related to a Pointer Authentication Code (PAC), a recent security feature of ARM processors. It then performs a load using this sensitive value as the address to make the value accessible to the attacker (via a cache timing attack) after the speculation.

On the other hand, the instruction variant of PACMAN relies on a speculatively executed indirect branch to a sensitive address. Indirect branches could also be incorporated as in the weakest precondition calculus in [2]. A proof obligation that such a branch is only taken on values with security level $\perp$ could then be added to the speculative precondition of the branch.

Ren et al. [35] describe two gadgets relying on a sensitive value accessed during speculation being leaked by the micro-op cache of Intel and AMD processors. These gadgets are based on function calls, and fetches of indirect branches. The latter allows bypassing of a fence intended to stall speculative execution. To detect related vulnerabilities, we would need to further extend our programming language with function calls, and change the fence rule to allow later instructions to be "fetched" but not executed.

As well as Spectre-PHT, the initial paper by Kocher et al. [24] describe Spectre-BTB (or variant 2), which targets the branch target buffer used by the processor to predict destinations of indirect branch instructions. Compared to Spectre-PHT, this is more powerful. Any indirect branch is potentially vulnerable, and an attacker's mistraining can direct speculation towards a convenient gadget anywhere in the program or library code. Detecting such gadgets may still be possible in our approach if used in conjunction with recent compiler-based mitigations, Serbeus [29] or Switchpoline [3], which vastly reduce the potential target addresses of indirect branch instructions. This also applies to other approaches based on a speculative indirect branch (call, jump or return) to a gadget, such as SMoTherSpectre [4] and RETBLEED [42].

5   Related Work

Cauligi et al. [8] provide a comprehensive overview of existing semantics and tools aimed at providing formal reasoning about speculative execution. Only 7 of the 24 papers they examine consider out-of-order execution. These either model the mechanism for instruction reordering directly (in terms of a multi-stage *fetch-execute-retire* pipeline) [7,20,21,40], or capture the effects of instruction reordering via higher level abstractions: reordering relations [11], pomsets [18] and event graphs [33].

The former provide more precise characterisations of the hardware and hence the potential to detect a wider variety of vulnerabilities than more abstract approaches. However, such detailed models also add complexity to the verification task. For this reason, all of these models support analysis on only a single thread, and hence are unable to detect the kinds of leakage illustrated by our running example from Sect. 2.2.

The abstraction-based approaches of Disselkoen et al. (based on pomsets) [18] and Ponce de León and Kinder (based on event graphs) [33], use intra- and inter-thread relations between instructions to capture instruction ordering in concurrent programs (unrelated instructions can be reordered). The inter-thread relations are necessary for these approaches, but preclude thread-local reasoning. Instead, reasoning is over individual executions of a full program.

Our approach builds directly on the abstract semantics of Colvin and Winter [11]. That paper introduces the idea of a speculative context that operates on a fresh copy of the program state, which is key to our approach. It models out-of-order execution via a relation capturing which pairs of instructions in a given thread can reorder. Since the relation only imposes intra-thread constraints, the semantics can be used in a thread-local analysis, avoiding analysis over the exponential explosion of behaviours possible due to interleaving in a full concurrent program. The *rif* approach we adopt from [14] also uses such a reordering relation enabling our thread-local approach.

We extend the semantics of [11] with an information flow logic which defines the capabilities of an attacker in terms of which parts of memory they can observe, and their ability to observe control flow (via timing). The latter, in particular, is listed as an open problem by Cauligi et al. [8] for semantics based on abstractions of out-of-order execution.

6   Conclusion

In this paper, we have shown how information leakage can occur due to a combination of speculative execution and out-of-order execution, both of which are features of modern processors. To the best of our knowledge, this is the first paper to demonstrate that such a leak is possible. To enable detection of such leaks, we have developed a novel information flow logic using weakest precondition reasoning over a tuple of states comprising the actual and speculative states of the program. For scalability, the logic supports thread-local reasoning, and a notion of reordering interference freedom (*rif*), both of which significantly reduce the number of behaviours that must be analysed: the former allows us to abstract from concurrent interleaving of threads in a program, and the latter allows us to replace reasoning over behaviours resulting from instruction reordering by pair-wise checks over reorderable instructions. Our logic has been proven sound with respect to an abstract semantics of speculative execution [11] using Isabelle/HOL [12].

Our future goals include mechanising the information flow logic in the auto-active program verifier Boogie [1]. This will build on an existing encoding of information flow and rely/guarantee reasoning in Dafny [36], and require a way to support our novel representation of program state as a tuple of speculative and actual state spaces.

Acknowledgments. We would like to thank the anonymous referees for their insightful comments and suggestions.

Data Availability Statement. The formalisation of the logic and the proof of soundness and non-interference with respect to a semantics of speculative execution are available as Isabelle/HOL theories at https://doi.org/10.5281/zenodo.11910360.

Disclosure of Interests. The authors have no competing interests to declare that are relevant to the content of this article.

References

1. Barnett, M., Chang, B.-Y.E., DeLine, R., Jacobs, B., Leino, K.R.M.: Boogie: a modular reusable verifier for object-oriented programs. In: de Boer, F.S., Bonsangue, M.M., Graf, S., de Roever, W.-P. (eds.) FMCO 2005. LNCS, vol. 4111, pp. 364–387. Springer, Heidelberg (2006). https://doi.org/10.1007/11804192_17

2. Barnett, M., Leino, K.R.M.: Weakest-precondition of unstructured programs. In: Ernst, M.D., Jensen, T.P. (eds.) Proceedings of the 2005 ACM SIGPLAN-SIGSOFT Workshop on Program Analysis For Software Tools and Engineering, PASTE'05, pp. 82–87. ACM (2005). https://doi.org/10.1145/1108792.1108813

3. Bauer, M., Hetterich, L., Rossow, C., Schwarz, M.: Switchpoline: a software mitigation for Spectre-BTB and Spectre-BHB on ARMv8. In: 2024 ACM ASIA Conference on Computer and Communications Security, AsiaCCS 2024. ACM (2024). https://doi.org/10.60882/cispa.25304857.v1

4. Bhattacharyya, A., et al.: SMoTherSpectre: exploiting speculative execution through port contention. In: Cavallaro, L., Kinder, J., Wang, X., Katz, J. (eds.) CCS 2019, pp. 785–800. ACM (2019). https://doi.org/10.1145/3319535.3363194

5. Bulck, J.V., et al.: Foreshadow: extracting the keys to the intel SGX kingdom with transient out-of-order execution. In: Enck, W., Felt, A.P. (eds.) 27th USENIX Security Symposium, USENIX Security 2018, pp. 991–1008. USENIX Association (2018)

6. Canella, C., et al.: A systematic evaluation of transient execution attacks and defenses. In: Heninger, N., Traynor, P. (eds.) 28th USENIX Security Symposium, USENIX Security 2019, Santa Clara, CA, USA, August 14–16, 2019. pp. 249–266. USENIX Association (2019)

7. Cauligi, S., et al.: Constant-time foundations for the new Spectre era. In: Donaldson, A.F., Torlak, E. (eds.) Proceedings of the 41st ACM SIGPLAN International Conference on Programming Language Design and Implementation, PLDI 2020, pp. 913–926. ACM (2020). https://doi.org/10.1145/3385412.3385970

8. Cauligi, S., Disselkoen, C., Moghimi, D., Barthe, G., Stefan, D.: SoK: practical foundations for software Spectre defenses. In: 43rd IEEE Symposium on Security and Privacy, SP 2022, pp. 666–680. IEEE (2022). https://doi.org/10.1109/SP46214.2022.9833707

9. Chowdhuryy, M.H.I., Liu, H., Yao, F.: Branchspec: information leakage attacks exploiting speculative branch instruction executions. In: 38th IEEE International Conference on Computer Design, ICCD 2020, pp. 529–536. IEEE (2020). https://doi.org/10.1109/ICCD50377.2020.00095

10. Colvin, R.J., Smith, G.: A wide-spectrum language for verification of programs on weak memory models. In: Havelund, K., Peleska, J., Roscoe, B., de Vink, E. (eds.) FM 2018. LNCS, vol. 10951, pp. 240–257. Springer, Cham (2018). https://doi.org/10.1007/978-3-319-95582-7_14

11. Colvin, R.J., Winter, K.: An abstract semantics of speculative execution for reasoning about security vulnerabilities. In: Sekerinski, E., et al. (eds.) FM 2019, Part II. LNCS, vol. 12233, pp. 323–341. Springer, Cham (2020). https://doi.org/10.1007/978-3-030-54997-8_21

12. Coughlin, N., Lam, K., Winter, K.: Weak memory rely/guarantee logic with speculative execution (2024). https://github.com/UQ-PAC/wmm-rg/tree/paperwork-st

13. Coughlin, N., Smith, G.: Compositional noninterference on hardware weak memory models. Sci. Comput. Program. **217**, 102779 (2022). https://doi.org/10.1016/j.scico.2022.102779

14. Coughlin, N., Winter, K., Smith, G.: Rely/guarantee reasoning for multicopy atomic weak memory models. In: Huisman, M., Păsăreanu, C., Zhan, N. (eds.) FM 2021. LNCS, vol. 13047, pp. 292–310. Springer, Cham (2021). https://doi.org/10.1007/978-3-030-90870-6_16

15. Coughlin, N., Winter, K., Smith, G.: Compositional reasoning for non-multicopy atomic architectures. Formal Aspects Comput. **35**(2), 8:1–8:30 (2023). https://doi.org/10.1145/3574137

16. Dijkstra, E.W.: A Discipline of Programming. Prentice-Hall (1976). https://www.worldcat.org/oclc/01958445

17. Dijkstra, E.W., Scholten, C.S.: Predicate Calculus and Program Semantics. Springer, Heidelberg (1990). https://doi.org/10.1007/978-1-4612-3228-5

18. Disselkoen, C., Jagadeesan, R., Jeffrey, A., Riely, J.: The code that never ran: modeling attacks on speculative evaluation. In: 2019 IEEE Symposium on Security and Privacy, SP 2019, pp. 1238–1255. IEEE (2019). https://doi.org/10.1109/SP.2019.00047

19. Goguen, J.A., Meseguer, J.: Security policies and security models. In: 1982 IEEE Symposium on Security and Privacy, 1982, pp. 11–20. IEEE Computer Society (1982). https://doi.org/10.1109/SP.1982.10014

20. Guanciale, R., Balliu, M., Dam, M.: InSpectre: breaking and fixing microarchitectural vulnerabilities by formal analysis. In: Ligatti, J., Ou, X., Katz, J., Vigna, G. (eds.) CCS '20: 2020 ACM SIGSAC Conference on Computer and Communications Security, pp. 1853–1869. ACM (2020). https://doi.org/10.1145/3372297.3417246

21. Guarnieri, M., Köpf, B., Reineke, J., Vila, P.: Hardware-software contracts for secure speculation. In: 42nd IEEE Symposium on Security and Privacy, SP 2021, pp. 1868–1883. IEEE (2021). https://doi.org/10.1109/SP40001.2021.00036

22. Islam, S., et al.: SPOILER: speculative load hazards boost Rowhammer and cache attacks. In: Heninger, N., Traynor, P. (eds.) 28th USENIX Security Symposium, USENIX Security 2019, pp. 621–637. USENIX Association (2019)

23. Jones, C.B.: Specification and design of (parallel) programs. In: IFIP Congress, pp. 321–332 (1983)

24. Kocher, P., et al.: Spectre attacks: Exploiting speculative execution. In: 2019 IEEE Symposium on Security and Privacy, SP 2019, pp. 1–19. IEEE (2019). https://doi.org/10.1109/SP.2019.00002

25. Lipp, M., et al.: Meltdown: reading kernel memory from user space. In: Enck, W., Felt, A.P. (eds.) 27th USENIX Security Symposium, USENIX Security 2018, pp. 973–990. USENIX Association (2018)

26. Lourenço, L., Caires, L.: Dependent information flow types. In: Rajamani, S.K., Walker, D. (eds.) Proceedings of the 42nd Annual ACM SIGPLAN-SIGACT Symposium on Principles of Programming Languages, POPL 2015, pp. 317–328. ACM (2015). https://doi.org/10.1145/2676726.2676994

27. Mantel, H., Perner, M., Sauer, J.: Noninterference under weak memory models. In: IEEE 27th Computer Security Foundations Symposium, CSF 2014. pp. 80–94. IEEE Computer Society (2014). https://doi.org/10.1109/CSF.2014.14

28. Mantel, H., Sands, D., Sudbrock, H.: Assumptions and guarantees for compositional noninterference. In: Proceedings of the 24th IEEE Computer Security Foundations Symposium, CSF 2011, pp. 218–232. IEEE Computer Society (2011). https://doi.org/10.1109/CSF.2011.22

29. Mosier, N., Nemati, H., Mitchell, J.C., Trippel, C.: Serberus: protecting cryptographic code from spectres at compile-time. In: 2024 IEEE Symposium on Security and Privacy, SP 2024. IEEE (2024). https://doi.org/10.1109/SP54263.2024.00048

30. Murray, T.C.: Short paper: On high-assurance information-flow-secure programming languages. In: Clarkson, M., Jia, L. (eds.) Proceedings of the 10th ACM Workshop on Programming Languages and Analysis for Security, PLAS@ECOOP 2015, pp. 43–48. ACM (2015). https://doi.org/10.1145/2786558.2786561

31. Murray, T.C., Sison, R., Engelhardt, K.: COVERN: a logic for compositional verification of information flow control. In: 2018 IEEE European Symposium on Security and Privacy, EuroS&P 2018, pp. 16–30. IEEE (2018). https://doi.org/10.1109/EuroSP.2018.00010

32. Murray, T.C., Sison, R., Pierzchalski, E., Rizkallah, C.: Compositional verification and refinement of concurrent value-dependent noninterference. In: IEEE 29th Computer Security Foundations Symposium, CSF 2016, pp. 417–431. IEEE Computer Society (2016). https://doi.org/10.1109/CSF.2016.36

33. Ponce de León, H., Kinder, J.: Cats vs. Spectre: an axiomatic approach to modeling speculative execution attacks. In: 43rd IEEE Symposium on Security and Privacy, SP 2022, pp. 235–248. IEEE (2022). https://doi.org/10.1109/SP46214.2022.9833774

34. Ravichandran, J., Na, W.T., Lang, J., Yan, M.: PACMAN: attacking ARM pointer authentication with speculative execution. IEEE Micro 43(4), 11–18 (2023). https://doi.org/10.1109/MM.2023.3273189

35. Ren, X., Moody, L., Taram, M., Jordan, M., Tullsen, D.M., Venkat, A.: I see dead μops: leaking secrets via Intel/AMD micro-op caches. In: 48th ACM/IEEE Annual International Symposium on Computer Architecture, ISCA 2021, pp. 361–374. IEEE (2021). https://doi.org/10.1109/ISCA52012.2021.00036

36. Smith, G.: A Dafny-based approach to thread-local information flow analysis. In: 11th IEEE/ACM International Conference on Formal Methods in Software

Engineering, FormaliSE 2023, pp. 86–96. IEEE (2023). https://doi.org/10.1109/FormaliSE58978.2023.00017

37. Smith, G., Coughlin, N., Murray, T.: Value-dependent information-flow security on weak memory models. In: ter Beek, M.H., McIver, A., Oliveira, J.N. (eds.) FM 2019. LNCS, vol. 11800, pp. 539–555. Springer, Cham (2019). https://doi.org/10.1007/978-3-030-30942-8_32

38. Smith, G., Coughlin, N., Murray, T.: Information-flow control on ARM and POWER multicore processors. Formal Methods Syst. Des. **58**(1–2), 251–293 (2021). https://doi.org/10.1007/S10703-021-00376-2

39. Sorin, D.J., Hill, M.D., Wood, D.A.: A Primer on Memory Consistency and Cache Coherence. Synthesis Lectures on Computer Architecture, Morgan & Claypool Publishers (2011). https://doi.org/10.2200/S00346ED1V01Y201104CAC016

40. Vassena, M., Disselkoen, C., von Gleissenthall, K., Cauligi, S., Kici, R.G., Jhala, R., Tullsen, D.M., Stefan, D.: Automatically eliminating speculative leaks from cryptographic code with Blade. Proc. ACM Program. Lang. **5**(POPL), 1–30 (2021). https://doi.org/10.1145/3434330

41. Vaughan, J.A., Millstein, T.D.: Secure information flow for concurrent programs under Total Store Order. In: Chong, S. (ed.) 25th IEEE Computer Security Foundations Symposium, CSF 2012, pp. 19–29. IEEE Computer Society (2012). https://doi.org/10.1109/CSF.2012.20

42. Wikner, J., Razavi, K.: RETBLEED: arbitrary speculative code execution with return instructions. In: Butler, K.R.B., Thomas, K. (eds.) 31st USENIX Security Symposium, USENIX Security 2022, pp. 3825–3842. USENIX Association (2022)

43. Winter, K., Coughlin, N., Smith, G.: Backwards-directed information flow analysis for concurrent programs. In: 34th IEEE Computer Security Foundations Symposium, CSF 2021, pp. 1–16. IEEE (2021). https://doi.org/10.1109/CSF51468.2021.00017

44. Xu, Q., de Roever, W.P., He, J.: The rely-guarantee method for verifying shared variable concurrent programs. Formal Aspects Comput. **9**(2), 149–174 (1997). https://doi.org/10.1007/BF01211617

Staged Specification Logic for Verifying Higher-Order Imperative Programs

Darius Foo[⊠][iD], Yahui Song[iD], and Wei-Ngan Chin[iD]

School of Computing, National University of Singapore, Singapore, Singapore
{dariusf,yahuis,chinwn}@comp.nus.edu.sg

Abstract. Higher-order functions and imperative states are language features supported by many mainstream languages. Their combination is expressive and useful, but complicates specification and reasoning, due to the use of yet-to-be-instantiated function parameters. One inherent limitation of existing specification mechanisms is its reliance on *only two stages* : an initial stage to denote the precondition at the start of the method and a final stage to capture the postcondition. Such two-stage specifications force *abstract properties* to be imposed on unknown function parameters, leading to less precise specifications for higher-order methods. To overcome this limitation, we introduce a novel extension to Hoare logic that supports *multiple stages* for a call-by-value higher-order language with ML-like local references. Multiple stages allow the behavior of unknown function-type parameters to be captured abstractly as uninterpreted relations; and can also model the repetitive behavior of each recursion as a separate stage. In this paper, we define our staged logic with its semantics, prove its soundness and develop a new automated higher-order verifier, called Heifer, for a core ML-like language.

1 Introduction

Programs written in modern languages today are rife with higher-order functions [3,35], but specifying and verifying them remains challenging, especially if they contain imperative effects. Consider the *foldr* function from OCaml. Here is a good specification for it in Iris [19], a state-of-the-art framework for higher-order concurrent separation logic that is built using Coq proof assistant.

$$\forall P, Inv, f, xs, l. \left\{ \begin{array}{c} (\forall x, a', ys. \{P\ x * Inv\ ys\ a'\}\ f(x, a')\ \{r.\ Inv\ (x::ys)\ r\}) \\ * isList\ l\ xs * all\ P\ xs * Inv\ []\ a \end{array} \right\}$$

$$foldr\ f\ a\ l$$

$$\{r.\ isList\ l\ xs * Inv\ xs\ r\}$$

While this specification is conventional in weakest-precondition calculi like Iris, one might argue that that this specification is not the best possible specification for *foldr*, since it requires two *abstract properties* Inv and P to summarize the

© The Author(s) 2025
A. Platzer et al. (Eds.): FM 2024, LNCS 14933, pp. 501–518, 2025.
https://doi.org/10.1007/978-3-031-71162-6_26

behaviour of f. Moreover, the input list l is also immutable, through the same *isList* predicate in both its pre- and postcondition. (If mutation of list is allowed, a more complex *Inv* with an extra mutated list parameter is required.)

These abstract properties must be correspondingly instantiated for each instance of f, but unfortunately some usage scenarios (to be highlighted later in Sect. 2.2) of *foldr* cannot be captured by this particular pre/post specification of Iris, despite how well-designed it was. Thus, the conventional pre/post approach to specifying higher-order functions currently suffers from possible *loss in precision* in its specifications since the presence of these abstract properties implicitly *strengthens* the preconditions for higher-order imperative methods.

This paper proposes a new logic, *Higher-Order Staged Specification Logic* (*HSSL*), for specifying and verifying higher-order imperative methods. It is designed for automated verification via SMT and uses separation logic as its core stateful logic, aiming at more precise specifications of heap-based changes. While we have adopted separation logic to support heap-based mutations, *HSSL* may also be used with other base logics, such as those using dynamic frames [25]. We next provide an overview of our methodology by examples before providing formal details and an experimental evaluation of our proposal.

2   Illustrative Examples

We provide three examples to highlight the key features of our methodology.

2.1   A Simple Example

We introduce the specification logic using a simple example (Fig. 1), to highlight a key challenge we hope to solve, namely how should we specify the behavior of *hello* without pre-committing to some abstract property on f? To do that, we can model f using an *uninterpreted relation*. We use uninterpreted relation rather than a function here

```
1   let hello f x y =
2       x := !x + 1;
3       let r = f y in
4       let r2 = !x + r in
5       y := r2;
6       r2
```

Fig. 1. A Simple Example

in order to model both over-approximation and possible side-effect. Since f is effectful and may modify arbitrary state, including the references x and y, a modular specification of *hello* must express the ordering of the call to f with respect to the other statements in it so that the caller of *hello* may reason precisely about its effects. Therefore, a first approximation is the following specification. We adopt standard separation logic pre/post assertions and extend them with *sequential composition* and *uninterpreted relations*. A final parameter (named as *res* here) is added to denote the result of each staged specification's relation (*hello* here), a convention we follow henceforth.

$hello(f, x, y, res) =$

$\exists a . \mathbf{req}\, x \mapsto a;$	// Stage 1: requiring x be pre-allocated
$\mathbf{ens}[\_]\, x \mapsto a{+}1;$	// Stage 2: ensuring x is updated
$\exists r . f(y, r);$	// Stage 3: unknown higher-order f call
$\exists b . \mathbf{req}\, x \mapsto b * y \mapsto \_;$	// Stage 4: requiring x, y be pre-allocated
$\mathbf{ens}[res]\, x \mapsto b * y \mapsto res \wedge res{=}b{+}r$	// Stage 5: y is updated, and x is unchanged

We can summarize the imperative behavior of *hello* before the call to f with a read from x, followed by a write to x, as captured by Stages 1–2. The same applies to the portion after the call to f (lines 4–6), but here we only consider the scenario when x and y are disjoint[1]. Stages 4 and 5 state that memory location x is being read while y will be correspondingly updated.

The ordering of the unknown f call with respect to the parts before and after does matter, so the call can be seen as *stratifying* the temporal behavior of the function into *stages*. Should a specification for f become known, usually at a call site, its *instantiation* may lead to a staged formula with only **req**/**ens** stages; which can always be *compacted* into a single **req**/**ens** pair. We detail a *normalization* procedure to do this in Sect. 3.2.

As mentioned before, f can modify x despite not having direct access to it via an argument, as it could capture x from the environment of the caller of *hello*. To model this, we make worst-case assumptions on the footprints of unknown functions, resulting in the precondition $x \mapsto b$ in stage 4.

2.2 Pre/Post Vs Staged Specifications via *foldr*

We now specify *foldr* and compare it with the Iris specification from Sect. 1.

```
1  let rec foldr f a l =
2    match l with
3    | [] => a
4    | h :: t =>
5      f h (foldr f a t)
```

$foldr(f, a, l, rr) =$
$\quad \mathbf{ens}[rr]\, l{=}[] \wedge rr{=}a$
$\quad \vee\; \exists x, r, l_1 .\; \mathbf{ens}[\_]\, l{=}x{::}l_1;$
$\qquad foldr(f, a, l_1, r); f(x, r, rr)$

We model *foldr* as a recursive predicate whose body is a staged formula. The top-level disjunction represents the two possible paths that result from pattern matching. In the base case, when l is the empty list, and the result of *foldr* is a. In the recursive case, when l is nonempty, the specification expresses that the behavior of *foldr* is given by a recursive call to *foldr* on the tail of l to produce a result r, followed by a call to f with r to produce a value for rr. Crucially, we are able to represent the call to the unknown function f directly in the specification, without being forced to impose a stronger precondition on f.

foldr's specification's is actually very precise, to the point of mirroring the *foldr* program. Nevertheless, abstraction may readily be recovered by proving that this predicate entails a weaker formula, and a convenient point for this

---

[1] For simplicity, the intersection of specifications $\wedge_{sp}$ that arises from disjoint preconditions is omitted (with some loss in precision) in the main paper, but its core mechanism is briefly described in Appendix D [15].

would be when the unknown function-typed parameter is instantiated at each of *foldr*'s call sites; we discuss an example of this shortly. The point of specifying *foldr* this way is that the precision of stages enables us not to have to commit to an abstraction prematurely. We should, of course, summarize as early as is appropriate to keep our proving process tractable.

Recursive staged formulae are needed mainly to specify higher-order functions with unknown function-typed parameters. Otherwise, our preference is to apply summarization to obtain non-recursive staged formulae whenever unknown function-type parameters have been suitably instantiated. Under this scenario, we may still use recursive pure predicates or recursive shape predicates in order to obtain best possible modular specifications for our program code.

Now, we show how the staged specification for *foldr* can be used by proving that we can sum a list by folding it. *sum* can be specified in a similar way to *foldr*, but since this is a pure function that can be additionally checked for termination, we can automatically convert it into a *pure predicate* (without any stages or imperative side effects) to be used in (the pure fragment of) our specification logic. Termination of pure predicates is required for them to be safely used in specifications. (Techniques to check for purity and termination are well-known and thus omitted.) Also, each pure predicate may be used as either a staged predicate or a pure predicate. In case a pure predicate $p(v^*, res)$ is used as a staged predicate; its staged definition is:

$$p(v^*, res) = \mathbf{req}\ emp \wedge pre(v^*); \mathbf{ens}[\_]\ emp \wedge p(v^*, res)$$

where $pre(v^*)$ denotes the precondition to guarantee termination and avoids exceptions. Note that $p(v^*, res)$ is overloaded to be used as either a staged predicate or a pure predicate. This is unambiguous from the context of its use.

```
6   let rec sum li =
7       match li with
8       | [] -> 0
9       | x :: xs -> x + sum xs
```

$$sum(li, res) =$$
$$l=[] \wedge res=0$$
$$\vee\ \exists r, l_1 . l=x::l_1 \wedge sum(l_1, r) \wedge res=x+r$$

We can now re-summarize an imperative use of *foldr* with the help of *sum*.

```
10   let foldr_sum_state x xs init
```
$$foldr\_sum\_state(x, xs, init, res) =$$
$$\exists i, r . \mathbf{req}\ x \mapsto i; \mathbf{ens}[res]\ x \mapsto i+r \wedge res=r+init \wedge sum(xs, r)$$
```
12   = let g c t = x := !x + c; c + t in foldr g xs init
```

This summarization gives rise to the following entailment:

$$\forall m, xs, init, res . foldr(g, xs, init, res)$$
$$\sqsubseteq\ \exists i, r . \mathbf{req}\ x \mapsto i; \mathbf{ens}[res]\ x \mapsto i+r \wedge res=r+init \wedge sum(xs, r)$$

We have implemented a proof system for subsumption (denoted by $\sqsubseteq$) between staged formulae in our verifier, called Heifer [13]. This particular entailment can be proved automatically by induction on xs. While Iris's earlier pre-/post specification for *foldr* can handle this example through a suitable instantiation of $(Inv\ \_\ \_)$, it is <u>unable</u> to handle the following three other call instances.

```
13   let foldr_ex1 l = foldr (fun x r -> let v = !x
14                                        in x := v+1; v+r) l 0
15   let foldr_ex2 l = foldr (fun x r -> assert(x+r>=0);x+r) l 0
16   let foldr_ex3 l = foldr (fun x r -> if x>=0 then x+r
17                                       else raise Exc()) l 0
```

The first example cannot be handled since Iris's current specification for *foldr* expects its input list l to be immutable. The second example fails since the precondition required cannot be expressed using just the abstract property $(P\ x)$. The last example fails because the abstract property $(Inv\ (x::ys)\ r)$ used in the postcondition of f expects its method calls to return normally. In contrast, using our approach via staged specification , we can re-summarize the above three call instances to use the following subsumed specifications.

$$foldr\_ex1\,(l, res) \sqsubseteq \exists xs\,.\,\textbf{req}\,List(l, xs)\,;\,\exists ys\,.$$
$$\textbf{ens}[res]\,List(l, ys)\wedge mapinc(xs, ys)\wedge sum(xs, res)$$
$$foldr\_ex2\,(l, res) \sqsubseteq \textbf{req}\,allSPos(l)\,;\,\textbf{ens}[res]\,sum(l, res)$$
$$foldr\_ex3\,(l, res) \sqsubseteq \textbf{ens}[res]\,allPos(l)\wedge sum(l, res)\,\vee\,(\textbf{ens}[\_]\,\neg allPos(l);Exc())$$

Note that the first example utilizes a recursive spatial $List(l, xs)$ predicate, while the last example used $Exc()$ as a relation to model exception as a stage in our specification. The three pure predicates and one spatial predicate used in the above can be formally defined, as shown below.

$$mapinc(xs, ys) = (xs=[]\wedge ys=[]) \vee (\exists x, xs_1, ys_1\,.\,xs=x::xs_1\wedge ys=(x+1)::ys_1$$
$$\wedge\ mapinc(xs_1, ys_1))$$
$$allPos(l) = (l=[]) \vee (\exists x, l_1\,.\,l=x::l_1\wedge allPos(l_1)\wedge x\geq 0)$$
$$allSPos(l) = (l=[]) \vee (\exists x, r, l_1\,.\,l=x::l_1\wedge allSPos(l_1)\wedge sum(l, r)\wedge r\geq 0)$$
$$List(l, rs) = (emp\wedge l=[]) \vee (\exists x, rs_1, l_1\,.\,x\mapsto r * List(l_1, rs_1)\wedge l=x::l_1\wedge rs=r::rs_1)$$

We emphasize that our proposal for staged logics is strictly more *expressive* than traditional two-stage pre/post specifications, since the latter can be viewed as an instance of staged logics. As an example, the earlier two-stage specification for *foldr* can be modelled non-recursively in our staged logics as:

$$foldr(f, a, l, res) =$$
$$\exists P, Inv, xs\,.\,\textbf{req}\,List(l, xs) * Inv([], a)\wedge all(P, xs)$$
$$\wedge f(x, a', r)\sqsubseteq(\exists ys\,.\,\textbf{req}\,Inv(ys, a')\wedge P(x);\textbf{ens}[r]\,Inv(x::ys, r))\,;$$
$$\textbf{ens}[res]\,List(l, xs) * Inv(xs, res)$$

2.3   Inferrable Vs User-Provided Specifications via *map*

Our methodology for higher-order functions is further explicated by the *map* method, shown in Fig. 2. Specifications typeset in lavender must be user-supplied, whereas those shown in °red (with the small circle) may be automated or inferred (using the rules of Sect. 4). Like *sum* before, *length* and *incrg* may be viewed as *ghost* functions, written only for their specifications to be used to describe behavior. These specifications are also routine and can be mechanically derived; we elide them here and provide them in Appendix A [15]. The method *map_incr*

```
1   let rec length xs =
2     °length(xs, res) = ...
3     match xs with
4     | [] -> 0
5     | x :: xs1 ->
6         1 + length xs1
7
8   let rec incrg init li =
9     °incrg(init, li, res) = ...
10    match li with
11    | [] -> []
12    | x :: xs -> init ::
13        incrg (init + 1) xs

14  let rec map f xs =
15    °map(f, xs, res) = ...
16    match xs with
17    | [] -> []
18    | x :: xs1 ->
19        f x :: map f xs1
20
21  let map_incr xs x =
22  map_incr(xs, x, r) =
          ∃i. req x ↦ i; ∃m. ens[r] x ↦ i+m
          ∧ length(xs, m)∧incrg(i+1, xs, r)
23  = let f a = x := !x+1; !x
24    in map f xs
```

Fig. 2. Implementation of *map_incr* with a Summarized Specification from *map*

describes the scenario we are interested in, where *the state of the closure affects the result of map*. Its specification states that the pointer x must have its value incremented by the length of xs. Moreover, the *contents* of the resulting list is captured by another pure function *incrg*, which builds a list of as many increasing values as there are elements in its input list.

These examples illustrate the methodology involved with staged specifications. They inherit the modular verification and biabduction-based [4] specification inference of separation logic, adding the ability to describe imperative behavior using function stages to the mix; biabduction then doubles as a means to normalize and compact stages. There is emphasis on the inference of specifications and proof automation, and proofs are built out of simple lemmas, which help summarize behavior and the shapes of data, and either remove recursion or move it into a pure ghost function where it is easier to comprehend.

In summary, staged logic for specifying imperative higher-order functions represents a fundamentally new approach that is *more general* and yet can be *more precise* than what is currently possible via state-of-the-art pre/post specification logics for imperative higher-order methods. Our main technical contributions to support this new approach include:

1. **Higher-Order Staged Specification Logic (*HSSL*):** we design a novel program logic to specify the behaviors of imperative higher-order methods and give its formal semantics.
2. **Biabduction-based Normalization:** we propose a normalization procedure for *HSSL* that serves two purposes: (i) it allows us to produce succinct staged formulae for programs automatically, and (ii) it helps structure entailment proof obligations, allowing them to be discharged via SMT.
3. **Entailment:** we develop a proof system to solve subsumption entailments between normalized *HSSL* formulae, prove its soundness, and implement an automated prover based on it.
4. **Evaluation:** we report on initial experimental results, and present various case studies highlighting *HSSL*'s capabilities.

3 Language and Specification Logic

We target a minimal OCaml-like imperative language with higher-order functions and state. The syntax is given in Fig. 3. Expressions are in ANF (A-normal form); sequencing and control over evaluation order may be achieved using let-bindings, which define immutable variables. Mutation may occur through heap-allocated *refs*. Functions are defined by naming lambda expressions, which may be annotated with a specification Φ (covered below). For simplicity, they are always in tupled form and their calls are always fully applied. Pattern matching is encoded using recognizer functions (e.g., *is_cons*) and *if* statements. *assert* allows proofs of program properties to be carried out at arbitrary points.

(Expressions)	$e ::= v \mid x \mid let\ x{=}e_1\ in\ e_2 \mid f(x^*) \mid ref\ x \mid x_1 := x_2 \mid !x \mid$	
	$\quad assert\ D \mid if\ x\ then\ e_1\ else\ e_2$	
(Values)	$v ::= c \mid nil \mid x_1{::}x_2 \mid fun\ (x^*)\ \Phi[r] {\mapsto} e$	
(Staged)	$\Phi ::= E \mid \Phi_1 \vee \Phi_2 \mid \Phi_1 ; \Phi_2 \mid \exists x^* . \Phi$	
(Stage)	$E ::= \mathbf{req}\,D \mid \mathbf{ens}[r]\,D \mid f(x^*, r)$	*(State)* $\quad D ::= \sigma \wedge \pi$
(Heap)	$\sigma ::= emp \mid x_1 \mapsto x_2 \mid \sigma_1 * \sigma_2$	
(Pure)	$\pi ::= true \mid \pi_1 \vee \pi_2 \mid \neg\pi \mid \exists x.\ \pi \mid t_1{=}t_2 \mid a_1{<}a_2 \mid \Phi_1 \sqsubseteq \Phi_2$	
(A-Terms)	$a ::= i \mid x \mid a_1 + a_2 \mid -a$	
(Terms)	$t ::= nil \mid t_1{::}t_2 \mid c \mid a \mid f \mid \lambda\,(x^*, r) {\mapsto} \Phi$	

$c \in \mathbb{B} \cup \mathbb{Z} \cup \mathbf{unit}$	$i \in \mathbb{Z}$	$x, f, r \in var$

Fig. 3. Syntax of the Core Language and Staged Logics

Program behavior is specified using *staged formulae* Φ, which are disjunctions and/or sequences of *stages* E. A stage is an assertion about program state *at a specific point*. Each stage takes one of three forms: a precondition $\mathbf{req}\,D$, a postcondition $\mathbf{ens}[r]\,D$ with a named result r, or a *function stage* $f(v^*, r)$, representing the specification of a (possibly-unknown) function call. For brevity, we use a context notation $\Phi[r]$ where r explictly identifies the final result of specification Φ. Program states D are described using separation logic formulae from the *symbolic heap* fragment [4], without recursive spatial predicates (for simplicity of presentation). Most values of the core language are as usual also terms of the (pure) logic; a notable exception is the lambda expression $fun\ (x^*)\ \Phi[r] \to e$, which occurs in the logic as $\lambda\,(x^*, r) \to \Phi[r]$, without its body. Subsumption assertions between two staged formulae (Sect. 5) are denoted by $\Phi_1 \sqsubseteq \Phi_2$.

3.1 Semantics of Staged Formulae

From Triples to Stages. Staged formulae generalize standard Hoare triples. The standard partial-correctness interpretation of the separation logic Hoare triple $\{\ P(v^*, x^*)\ \}\ e\ \{\ \exists y^* . Q(v^*, x^*, y^*, res)\ \}$ where v^* denote valid program variables and x^* denote specification variables (e.g., ghost variables) is that for all states st satisfying $P(v^*, x^*)$, given a reduction $e, st \rightsquigarrow^* v, st'$, if $e, st \not\rightsquigarrow^* fault$, then st' satisfies $\exists y^* . Q(v^*, x^*, y^*, res)$. The staged equivalent is $\{ \Phi \} e \{ \Phi; \exists x^* . \mathbf{req}\, P(v^*, x^*); \exists y^* . \mathbf{ens}[\_]\, Q(v^*, x^*, y^*, res) \}$. Apart from mentioning the *history* Φ, which remains unchanged, its meaning is identical. Consider, then, $\{ \Phi \} e \{ \Phi; \mathbf{req}\, P_1; \mathbf{ens}[\_]\, Q_1; \mathbf{req}\, P_2; \mathbf{ens}[\_]\, Q_2 \}$ – an intuitive extension of the semantics of triples is that given $e, st \rightsquigarrow^* e_1, st_1$, where st_1 satisfies Q_1, the extended judgment holds if st_1 *further* satisfies P_2, and reduction from there, $e_1, st_1 \rightsquigarrow^* e_2, st_2$, results in a state st_2 that satisfies Q_2.

While heap formulae are satisfied by program states, staged formulae (like triples), are satisfied by traces which begin and end at particular states. Uninterpreted function stages further allow stages to describe the *intermediate states* of programs in specifications – a useful ability in the presence of unknown higher-order imperative functions, as we illustrate in Sect. 2 and Appendix C [15]. To formalize all this, we give a semantics for staged formulae next.

Formal Semantics. We first recall the standard semantics for separation logic formulae in Fig. 4, which provides a useful starting point.

$$
\begin{array}{lll}
S, h \models \sigma \wedge \pi & \text{iff} & [\![\pi]\!]s \text{ and } S, h \models \sigma \\
S, h \models emp & \text{iff} & dom(h) = \{\} \\
S, h \models x \mapsto y & \text{iff} & dom(h) = \{S(x)\} \text{ and } h(S(x)) = [\![y]\!]s \\
S, h \models \sigma_1 * \sigma_2 & \text{iff} & \exists h_1 h_2.\ h_1 \circ h_2 = h \text{ such that } S, h_1 \models \sigma_1 \text{ and } S, h_2 \models \sigma_2
\end{array}
$$

Fig. 4. Semantics of Separation Logic Formulae

Let var be the set of program variables, val the set of primitive values, and $loc \subset val$ the set of heap locations; ℓ is a metavariable ranging over locations. The models are program states, comprising a *store* of variables S, a partial mapping from a finite set of variables to values $var \rightharpoonup val$, and the heap h, a partial mapping from locations to values $loc \rightharpoonup val$. $[\![\pi]\!]_S$ denotes the valuation of pure formula π under store S. $dom(h)$ denotes the domain of heap h. $h_1 \circ h_2 = h$ denotes disjoint union of heaps; if $dom(h_1) \cap dom(h_2) = \{\}$, $h_1 \cup h_2 = h$. We write $h_1 \subseteq h_2$ to denote that h_1 is a subheap of h_2, i.e., $\exists h_3 . h_1 \circ h_3 = h_2$. $s[x := v]$ and $s[x :\neq]$ stand for store/heap updates and removal of keys.

We define the semantics of *HSSL* formulae in Fig. 5. Let $S, h \rightsquigarrow S_1, h_1, R \models \Phi$ denote the *models* relation, i.e., starting from the program state with store S and heap h, the formula Φ transforms the state into S_1, h_1, with an intermediate result R. R is either $Norm(r)$ for partial correctness, Err for precondition failure, or $\top$ for *possible* precondition failure in one of its execution paths.

When Φ is of the form $\mathbf{req}\, \sigma \wedge \pi$, the heap h is split into a heaplet h_1 satisfying $\sigma \wedge \pi$, which is consumed, and a frame h_2, which is left as the new heap. *Read-only heap assertions* $(\sigma \wedge \pi)@R$ under $\mathbf{req}$ check but do not change the heap.

$$S, h \rightsquigarrow S, h_1, Norm(\_) \models \textbf{req}\,\sigma \wedge \pi \qquad \textit{iff } h_1 {\subseteq} h \textit{ and } S, h_1 \models \sigma \wedge \pi$$

$$S, h \rightsquigarrow S, h, Err \models \textbf{req}\,\sigma \wedge \pi \qquad \textit{iff } \forall h_1 \,.\, h_1 {\subseteq} h \Rightarrow S, h_1 \not\models \sigma \wedge \pi$$

$$S, h \rightsquigarrow S, h, R \models \textbf{req}\,(\sigma \wedge \pi)@R \qquad \textit{iff } S, h \rightsquigarrow S, h_1, R \models \textbf{req}\,(\sigma \wedge \pi)$$

$$S, h \rightsquigarrow S, h \circ h_1, Norm(r) \models \textbf{ens}[r]\,\sigma \wedge \pi \textit{ iff } S, h_1 \models \sigma \wedge \pi \textit{ and } dom(h_1) \cap dom(h) {=} \{\}$$

$$S, h \rightsquigarrow S_1, h_1, R \models f(x^*, r) \qquad \qquad \textit{iff } S(f) = \textit{fun}\,(y^*)\,\Phi[r'] \rightarrow e,$$
$$S, h \rightsquigarrow S_1, h_1, R \models [r' {:=} r][y^* {:=} x^*]\Phi$$

$$S, h \rightsquigarrow S_1, h_1, R \models \exists x \,.\, \Phi \qquad \textit{iff } \exists v \,.\, S[x {:=} v], h \rightsquigarrow S_1, h_1, R \models \Phi$$

$$S, h \rightsquigarrow S_2, h_2, R \models \Phi_1 ; \Phi_2 \qquad \textit{iff } S, h \rightsquigarrow S_1, h_1, Norm(r) \models \Phi_1,$$
$$S_1, h_1 \rightsquigarrow S_2, h_2, R \models \Phi_2$$

$$S, h \rightsquigarrow S_1, h_1, \top \models \Phi_1 ; \Phi_2 \qquad \textit{iff } S, h \rightsquigarrow S_1, h_1, \top \models \Phi_1$$

$$S, h \rightsquigarrow S_3, h_3, Norm(r_3) \models \Phi_1 \vee \Phi_2 \quad \textit{iff } \exists h_1, h_2, r_1, r_2 \,.\, S, h \rightsquigarrow S_1, h_1, Norm(r_1) \models \Phi_1$$
$$\text{and } S, h \rightsquigarrow S_2, h_2, Norm(r_2) \models \Phi_2, \text{ and}$$
$$(S_3, h_3, r_3) {\in} \{(S_1, h_1, r_1), (S_2, h_2, r_2)\}$$

$$S, h \rightsquigarrow S_1, h_1, \top \models \Phi_1 \vee \Phi_2 \qquad \textit{iff } S, h \rightsquigarrow S_1, h_1, \top \models \Phi_1 \textit{ or } S, h \rightsquigarrow S_1, h_1, \top \models \Phi_2$$

Fig. 5. Semantics of Staged Formulae

When Φ is of the form $\textbf{ens}[\_]\,\sigma \wedge \pi$, σ describes locations which are to be added to the current heap. The semantics allows some concrete heaplet h_1 that satisfies $\sigma \wedge \pi$ (containing new or updated locations) be (re-)added to heap h.

When Φ is a function stage $f(x^*, r)$, its semantics depends on the specification of f. A staged existential causes the store to be extended with a binding from x to an existential value v. Sequential composition $\Phi_1 ; \Phi_2$ results in a failure $\top$ if Φ_1 does, while disjunction $\Phi_1 \vee \Phi_2$ requires both branches not to fail.

3.2 Compaction

Staged formulae subsume separation logic triples, but triples suffice for many verification tasks, particularly those without calls to unknown functions, and we would like to recover their succinctness in cases where intermediate states are not required. This motivates a *compaction* or *normalization* procedure for staged formulae, written $\Phi \Longrightarrow \Phi$ (Fig. 6). Compaction is also useful for aligning staged formulae, allowing entailment proofs to be carried out stage by stage; we elaborate on this use in Sect. 5.

$$\textbf{req}\,D_1 ; \textbf{req}\,D_2 \Longrightarrow \textbf{req}\,(D_1 * D_2)$$

$$\textbf{ens}[\_]\,\textit{false} ; \Phi \Longrightarrow \textbf{ens}[\_]\,\textit{false} \qquad \textbf{ens}[\_]\,D_1 ; \textbf{ens}[r]\,D_2 \Longrightarrow \textbf{ens}[r]\,(D_1 * D_2)$$

$$\textit{emp}; \Phi \Longrightarrow \Phi$$

$$\Phi; \textit{emp} \Longrightarrow \Phi \qquad \qquad \frac{D_A * D_1 \vdash D_2 * D_F}{\textbf{ens}[r]\,D_1 ; \textbf{req}\,D_2 \Longrightarrow \textbf{req}\,D_A ; \textbf{ens}[r]\,D_F}$$

Fig. 6. Select compaction rules

The three rules on the left simplify flows. A false postcondition (**ens** $\sigma \wedge false$) models an unreachable or nonterminating program state, so the rest of a flow may be safely ignored. *emp* in the next two rules is *either* (**req** $emp \wedge true$) or (**ens** $emp \wedge true$); either may serve as an identity for flows. The first two rules on the right merge consecutive pre- and postconditions. Intuitively, they are sound because symbolic heaps separated by sequential composition must be disjoint to be meaningful – this follows from the use of disjoint union in Fig. 5. The last rule allows a precondition **req** D_2 to be transposed with a preceding postcondition **ens** D_1. This is done using biabduction [4], which computes a pair of antiframe D_A and frame D_F such that the antiframe is the new precondition required, and frame is what remains after proving the known precondition. The given rule assumes that D_1 and D_2 are disjoint[2]. A read-only @R heap assertion under **req** would be handled by matching but not removing from D_F (see [7]).

Thus staged formulae can always be compacted into the following form, consisting of a disjunction of *flows* θ (a disjunction-free staged formula)[3], each consisting of a prefix of function stages (preceded by a description of the intermediate state at that point), followed by a final pre- and postcondition, capturing any behavior remaining after calling unknown functions.

$$\Phi ::= \theta \mid \Phi \vee \Phi$$
$$\theta ::= (\exists x^* . \, \textbf{req}\, D; \exists x^* . \, \textbf{ens}[\_]\, D; f(v^*, r)\; ;)^* \; \exists x^* . \, \textbf{req}\, D; \exists x^* . \, \textbf{ens}[\_]\, D$$

An example of compaction is given below (Fig. 7, left). We start at the first two stages of the flow and solve a biabduction problem (shown on the right, with solution immediately below) to infer a precondition for the whole flow, or, more operationally, to "push" the **req** to the left. We will later be able to rely on the new precondition to know that $a = 1$ when proving properties of the rest of the flow. Finally, we may combine the two **ens** stages because sequential composition guarantees disjointness. Normalization is *sound* in the sense that it transforms staged formulae without changing their meaning.

$$\textbf{ens}\; x \mapsto 1 * y \mapsto 2; \textbf{req}\; x \mapsto a; \textbf{ens}\; x \mapsto a{+}1$$
$$\Longleftrightarrow \textbf{req}\, a{=}1; \textbf{ens}\; y \mapsto 2; \textbf{ens}\; x \mapsto a{+}1 \qquad\qquad D_A * x \mapsto 1 * y \mapsto 2 \vdash x \mapsto a * D_F$$
$$\Longleftrightarrow \textbf{req}\, a{=}1; \textbf{ens}\; y \mapsto 2 * x \mapsto a{+}1 \qquad\qquad\qquad D_A{=}(a{=}1),\; D_F{=}(y \mapsto 2)$$

Fig. 7. An example of compaction

Theorem 1. (Soundness of Normalization). *Given* $\Phi_1 \Longrightarrow \Phi_2$, *if* $S, H \rightsquigarrow S_1, H_1, R_1 \models \Phi_1$, *then* $S, H \rightsquigarrow S_1, H_1, R_1 \models \Phi_2$.

Proof. By case analysis on the derivation of $\Phi_1 \Longrightarrow \Phi_2$. See Appendix I.2 [15]. ∎

---

[2] More exhaustive aliasing scenarios are considered in Appendix D [15].
[3] Using further normalization rules such as $(\Phi_1 \vee \Phi_2); \Phi_3 \Longrightarrow (\Phi_1; \Phi_3) \vee (\Phi_2; \Phi_3)$.

4   Forward Rules for Staged Logics

To verify that a program satisfies a given specification Φ_s, we utilize a set of rules (presented in Fig. 8) to compute an abstraction or summary of the program Φ_p, then discharge the proof obligation $\Phi_p \sqsubseteq \Phi_s$ (covered in Sect. 5), in a manner similar to strongest postcondition calculations.

We make use of the following notations. _ denotes an anonymous existentially quantified variable. $[x{:=}v]\Phi$ denotes the substitution of x with v in Φ, giving priority to recently bound variables. We lift sequencing from flows to disjunctive staged formulae in the natural way: $\Phi_1 ; \Phi_2 \triangleq \bigvee \{\theta_1 ; \theta_2 \mid \theta_1 \in \Phi_2, \theta_2 \in \Phi_2 \}$.

The first two rules in Fig. 8 are structural. The Conseq rule uses *specification subsumption* (detailed in Sect. 5) in place of implication – a form of behavioral subtyping. The Frame rule has both a *temporal* interpretation, which is that the reasoning rules are compositional with respect to the *history* of the current flow, and a *spatial* interpretation, consistent with the usual one from separation logic, if one uses the normalization rules (Sect. 3.2) to move untouched p from the final states of Φ_1 and Φ_2 into the frame Φ.

$$\frac{\Phi_1 \sqsubseteq \Phi_3 \quad \{\Phi_3\}\, e\, \{\Phi_4\} \quad \Phi_4 \sqsubseteq \Phi_2}{\{\Phi_1\}\, e\, \{\Phi_2\}} \; \text{Conseq} \qquad \frac{\{\Phi_1\}\, e\, \{\Phi_2\}}{\{\Phi; \Phi_1\}\, e\, \{\Phi; \Phi_2\}} \; \text{Frame}$$

$$\frac{}{\{\Phi\}\, x\, \{\Phi; \mathbf{ens}[x]\, emp\}} \; \text{Var} \qquad \frac{fresh\; r \quad v ::= c \mid nil \mid x_1{::}x_2}{\{\Phi\}\, v\, \{\Phi; \exists r.\, \mathbf{ens}[r]\, r{=}v\}} \; \text{Val}$$

$$\frac{fresh\; r}{\{\Phi\}\, ref\; x\, \{\Phi; \exists r.\, \mathbf{ens}[r]\, r \mapsto x\}} \; \text{Ref}$$

$$\frac{fresh\; a, res}{\{\Phi\}\, !x\, \{\Phi; \exists a, res.\, \mathbf{req}\, x \mapsto a;\mathbf{ens}[res]\, x \mapsto a \wedge res{=}a\}} \; \text{Deref}$$

$$\frac{}{\{\Phi\}\, x_1{:=}x_2\, \{\Phi; \mathbf{req}\, x_1 \mapsto \_;\mathbf{ens}[\_]\, x_1 \mapsto x_2\}} \; \text{Assign}$$

$$\frac{\{\Phi; \mathbf{ens}[\_]\, x\}\, e_1\, \{\Phi_1\} \quad \{\Phi; \mathbf{ens}[\_]\, \neg x\}\, e_2\, \{\Phi_2\}}{\{\Phi\}\, if\; x\; then\; e_1\; else\; e_2\, \{\Phi_1 \vee \Phi_2\}} \; \text{If}$$

$$\frac{fresh\; x \quad \{\Phi\}\, e_1\, \{\exists r.\, \Phi_1[r]\} \quad \{[r{:=}x]\Phi_1\}\, e_2\, \{\Phi_2\}}{\{\Phi\}\, let\; x{=}e_1\; in\; e_2\, \{\exists x.\, \Phi_2\}} \; \text{Let}$$

$$\frac{fresh\; res \quad \{\mathbf{ens}[\_]\, Pure(\Phi)\}\, e\, \{\exists r'.\, \Phi_p[r']\} \quad ([r'{:=}r]\Phi_p) \sqsubseteq \Phi_s}{\{\Phi\}\, fun\, (x^*)\exists r.\, \Phi_s[r] \to e\, \{\Phi; \exists res.\, \mathbf{ens}[res]\, res{=}\lambda\, (x^*, r) \to \Phi_s\}} \; \text{Lambda}$$

$$\frac{fresh\; r}{\{\Phi\}\, f(x^*)\, \{\Phi; \exists r.\, f(x^*, r)\}} \; \text{Call} \qquad \frac{}{\{\Phi\}\, assert\; D\, \{\Phi; \mathbf{req}\, D@R\}} \; \text{Assert}$$

Fig. 8. Forward Reasoning Hoare Rules with Staged Logics

The **Var** and **Val** rules illustrate how the results of pure expressions are tracked via named **ens** results. The **Ref** rule results in a new, existentially-quantified location being added to the current state. The **Deref** and **Assign** rules are similar, both requiring proof that a named location exists with a value, then respectively either returning the value of the location and leaving it unchanged, or changing the location and returning the unit value. **Assert** checks the current heap state without modifying it using the @R read-only annotation. **If** introduces disjunction. **Let** sequences expressions, renaming the intermediate result of e_1 accordingly; the scope of x in e_2 is represented by the scope of the introduced existential in the conclusion of the rule.

The **Lambda** rule handles function definition annotated with a given specification Φ_s. The body of the lambda is summarized into Φ_p starting from pure information $Pure(\Phi)$ from its program context. Its behavior must be subsumed by the given specification. The result is then the lambda expression itself.

The **Call** rule is completely trivial, yet perhaps the most illuminating as to the design of *HSSL*. A standard modular verifier would utilize this rule to look up the specification associated with f, prove its precondition, then assume its postcondition. In our setting, however, there is the possibility that f is higher-order, unknown, and/or unspecified. Moreover, there is no need to prove the precondition of f immediately, due to the use of flows for describing program behaviors. Both of these point to the simple use of a function stage, which stands for a *possibly-unknown* function call. Utilizing the specification of f, if it is provided, is deferred to the unfolding done in the entailment procedure.

We prove soundness of these rules, which is to say that derived specifications faithfully overapproximate the programs they are derived from. In the following theorem, $e, h, S \leadsto h_1, S_1$ is a standard big-step reduction relation whose definition we leave to Appendix I.1 [15]. Termination is also considered in Appendix I.5 [15]. However, completeness is yet to be established.

Theorem 2. (Soundness of Forward Rules). *Given* { *emp* } e { Φ }, *then* $\forall S, h, S_2, h_1 . (S, h \leadsto S_2, h_1, Norm(r) \models \Phi) \Rightarrow \exists S_1 . e, h, S \leadsto Norm(v), h_1, S_1$ *and* $S_1 \subseteq S_2$ *and* $S_1(r) = v$.

Proof. By induction on the derivation of $e, h, S_1 \leadsto R_1, h_1, S_1$. See Appendix I.3 [15].

5   Staged Entailment Checking and Its Soundness

In this section, we outline how entailments of the form $F \vdash \Phi_p \sqsubseteq \Phi_s$ may be automatically checked. F denotes heap and pure frames that are propagated by our staged logics entailment rules. Our entailment is always conducted over the compacted form where non-recursive staged predicate definitions are unfolded, while unknown predicates are matched exactly. Lemmas are also used to try re-summarize each instantiation of recursive staged predicates to simpler forms, where feasible. As staged entailment ensures that all execution traces that satisfy Φ_p must also satisfy Φ_s, we rely on theory of *behavioral subtyping* [20] to relate them. Specifically, we check that *contravariance holds* for pre-condition entailment, while *covariance holds* for post-condition entailment, as follows:

$$\frac{fresh\ y^* \qquad F_0 * D_2 \vdash (\exists x^*.D_1) * F \qquad F \vdash \theta_a \sqsubseteq \theta_c}{F_0 \vdash (\exists x^*.\mathbf{req}\ D_1; \theta_a) \sqsubseteq (\exists y^*.\mathbf{req}\ D_2; \theta_c)} \text{ EntReq}$$

$$\frac{fresh\ x^* \qquad F_0 * D_1 \vdash (\exists y^*.D_2) * F \qquad F \vdash \theta_a \sqsubseteq \theta_c}{F_0 \vdash (\exists x^*.\mathbf{ens}[r]\ D_1; \theta_a) \sqsubseteq (\exists y^*.\mathbf{ens}[r]\ D_2; \theta_c)} \text{ EntEns}$$

More details of staged entailment rules are given in Appendix G [15]. Note that we use another entailment over separation logic $D_1 \vdash D_2 * F_r$ that can propagate residual frame, F_r. Lastly, we outline the soundness of staged entailemt against the semantics of staged formulae, ensuring that all derivations are valid.

Theorem 3. (Soundness of Entailment). *Given* $\Phi_1 \sqsubseteq \Phi_2$ *and* S, $h \rightsquigarrow Norm(r_1), S_1, h_1 \models \Phi_1$, *then there exists* h_2 *such that* $S, h \rightsquigarrow Norm(r_1), S_2$, $h_2 \models \Phi_2$ *where* $h_2 \subseteq h_1$. *(Here,* $h_1 \subseteq h_2$ *denotes that* $\exists h_3.h_1 \circ h_3 = h_2$.*)*

Proof. By induction on the derivation of $\Phi_1 \sqsubseteq \Phi_2$. See Appendix I.4 [15].

6   Implementation and Initial Results

We prototyped our verification methodology in a tool named Heifer [13]. Our tool takes input programs written in a subset of OCaml annotated with user-provided specifications. It analyzes input programs to produce normalized staged formulae

Table 1. A Comparison with Cameleer and Prusti. (Programs that are natively inexpressible are marked with "✗". Programs that cannot be reproduced from Prusti's artifact [1] are marked with "-" denoting incomparable. We use T to denote the total verification time (in seconds) and T_P to record the time spent on the external provers.)

Benchmark	Heifer				Cameleer [23]			Prusti [32]		
	LoC	LoS	T	T_P	LoC	LoS	T	LoC	LoS	T
map	13	11	0.66	0.58	10	45	1.25	-		
map_closure	18	7	1.06	0.77	✗			-		
fold	23	12	1.06	0.87	21	48	8.08	-		
fold_closure	23	12	1.25	0.89	✗			-		
iter	11	4	0.40	0.32	✗			-		
compose	3	1	0.11	0.09	2	6	0.05	-		
compose_closure	23	4	0.44	0.32	✗			✗		
closure [28]	27	5	0.37	0.27	✗			13	11	6.75
closure_list	7	1	0.15	0.09	✗			-		
applyN	6	1	0.19	0.17	12	13	0.37	-		
blameassgn [12]	14	6	0.31	0.28	✗			13	9	6.24
counter	16	4	0.24	0.18	✗			11	7	6.37
lambda	13	5	0.25	0.22	✗			-		
	197	73			45	112		37	27	

(Sect. 3.2, Sect. 4), which it then translates to first-order verification conditions (Sect. 5) suitable for an off-the-shelf SMT solver. Here, our prototype targets SMT encodings via Why3 [11]. As an optimization, it uses Z3 [8] directly for queries which do not require Why3's added features.

We have verified a suite of programs [14] involving higher-order functions and closures (Table 1). As the focus of our work is to explore a new program logic and subsumption-based verification methodology (rather than to verify existing programs), the benchmarks are small in size, and are meant to illustrate the style of specification and give a flavor of the potential for automation.

Table 1 provides an overview of the benchmark suite. The first two sub-columns show the size of each program (LoC) and the number of lines of user-provided specifications (LoS) required. The next two give the total wall-clock time taken (in seconds) to verify all functions in each program against the provided specifications, and the amount of time spent in external provers.

The next column shows the same programs verified using Cameleer [23,26], a state-of-the-art deductive verifier. Cameleer serves as a good baseline for several reasons: it is representative of the dominant paradigm of pre/post specifications and, like Heifer, targets (a subset of) OCaml. It supports higher-order functions in both programs and specifications [27]. The most significant differences between Cameleer and Heifer are that Cameleer does not support *effectful* higher-order functions and is intended to be used via the Why3 IDE in a semi-interactive way (allowing tactic-like *proof transformations*, used in the above programs).

The last column shows results for Prusti [32]. Despite Rust's ownership type system, we compare it against Prusti because of its state-of-the-art support for mutable closures, highlighting differences below. While we were able to reproduce the claims made in Prusti's OOPSLA 2021 artifact [1], we were not able to verify many of our own benchmark programs due to two technical reasons, namely lacking support for Rust's impl Trait (to return closures) and ML-like cons lists (which caused timeouts and crashes). Support for closures is also not yet in mainline Prusti [2]. Nevertheless, we verified the programs we could use for the artifact, the results of which are shown in Table 1. All experiments were performed on macOS using a 2.3 GHz Quad-Core Intel Core i7 CPU with 16 GB of RAM. Why3 1.7.0 was used, with SMT solvers Z3 4.12.2, CVC4 1.8, and Alt-Ergo 2.5.2. The Prusti artifact, a Docker image, was run using Moby 25.0.1.

User annotations required. Significantly less specification than code is required in Heifer, with an average LoS/LoC ratio of 0.37. This is helped by two things: the use of function stages in specifications, and the use of biabduction-based normalization, which allows the specifications of functions to be mostly automated, requiring only properties and auxiliary lemmas to be provided. In contrast, Cameleer's ratio is 2.49, due to the need to adequately summarize the behaviors of the function arguments and accompany these summaries with invariants and auxiliary lemmas. Two examples illustrating this are detailed in Appendix F [15]. Prusti's ratio is 0.73, but a caveat is that in the programs for it, only closure reasoning was used, without lemmas or summarization.

Expressiveness. Heifer is able to express many programs that Cameleer cannot, particularly closure-manipulating ones. This accounts for the ✗ rows in Table 1. While some of these can be verified with Prusti, unlike stages, Prusti's call descriptions do not capture ordering [1,10]; an explicit limitation as shown by the ✗ rows in Prusti's column. Prusti is able to use history invariants and the ownership of the Rust type system, but this difference is more than mitigated in Heifer with the adoption of an expressive staged logic with spatial heap state; more appropriate for the weaker (but more general) type system of OCaml.

7   Related Work

The use of sequential composition in specifications goes back to classic theories of program refinement, such as Morgan's refinement calculus [21] and Hoare and He's Unifying Theories [17], as well session types [9] and logics [6]. It has also been used to structure verification conditions and give users control over the order in which they are given to provers [16], allowing more reliable proof automation. We extend both lines of work, developing the use of sequential composition as a precise specification mechanism for higher-order imperative functions, and using it to guide entailment proofs of staged formulae.

Higher-order imperative functions were classically specified in program logics using *evaluation formulae* [18] and *reference-reachability predicates* [34]. The advent of separation logic has allowed for simpler specifications using *invariants* and *nested triples* (Sect. 1). These techniques are common in higher-order separation logics, such as HTT [22], CFML [5], Iris [19] and Steel/Pulse [30], which are encoded in proof assistants (e.g. Coq, F⋆ [29]) which do not natively support closures or heap reasoning. While the resulting object logics are highly expressive, they are much more complex (owing to highly nontrivial encodings) and consequently less automated than systems that discharge obligations via SMT. We push the boundaries in this area by proposing stages as a new, precise specification mechanism which is compatible with automated verification.

The guarantees of an expressive type system can significantly simplify how higher-order state is specified and managed. Prusti [32] exploits this with *call descriptions* (an alternative to function stages, as pure assertions saying that a call has taken place with a given pre/post) and *history invariants*, which rely on the ownership of mutable locations that closures have in Rust. Creusot [10] uses a *prophetic mutable value semantics* to achieve a similar goal with pre/post specifications of closures. Our solution is not dependent on an ownership type system, applying more generally to languages with unrestricted mutation.

Defunctionalization [24] is another promising means of reasoning about higher-order effectful programs [27], pioneered by the Why3-based Cameleer [23]. This approach currently does not support closures.

Our approach to automated verification is currently based on strict evaluation. It would be interesting to see how staged specifications can be extended to support verification of lazy programs, as had been explored in [31,33].

8   Conclusion

We have explored how best to *modularly specify and verify higher-order imperative programs*. Our contributions are manifold: we propose a new staged specification logic, rules for deriving staged formulae from programs and normalizing them using biabduction, and an entailment proof system. This forms the basis of a new verification methodology, which we validate with our prototype Heifer.

To the best of the authors' knowledge, this work is the first to introduce a *fundamental* staged specification mechanism for verifying higher-order imperative programs *without* any presumptions; being *more concise* (without the need for specifying abstract properties) and *more precise* (without imposing preconditions on function-typed parameters) when compared to existing solutions.

Acknowledgments. This research is supported by the Ministry of Education, Singapore, under the Academic Research Fund Tier 1 (FY2023) (Project Title: Automated Verification for Imperative Higher-Order Programs).

References

1. Modular specification and verification of closures in Rust (artefact). https://zenodo.org/records/5482557 (2021)
2. Documentation of closures. https://github.com/viperproject/prusti-dev/issues/1431 (2024)
3. Alves, F., Oliveira, D., Madeiral, F., Castor, F.: On the bug-proneness of structures inspired by functional programming in JavaScript projects. CoRR, abs/2206.08849 (2022)
4. Calcagno, C., Distefano, D., O'Hearn, P., Yang, H.: Compositional shape analysis by means of bi-abduction. In: Shao, Z., Pierce, B.C., eds, Proceedings of the 36th ACM SIGPLAN-SIGACT Symposium on Principles of Programming Languages, POPL 2009, Savannah, GA, USA, January 21-23, 2009, pp. 289–300. ACM (2009)
5. Charguéraud, A.: Characteristic formulae for the verification of imperative programs. In: Chakravarty, M.M.T., Hu, Z., Danvy, O., eds, Proceeding of the 16th ACM SIGPLAN international conference on Functional Programming, ICFP 2011, Tokyo, Japan, September 19-21, 2011 pp. 418–430. ACM (2011)
6. Costea, A., Chin, W.-N., Qin, S., Craciun, F.: Automated modular verification for relaxed communication protocols. In: Ryu, S. (ed.) APLAS 2018. LNCS, vol. 11275, pp. 284–305. Springer, Cham (2018). https://doi.org/10.1007/978-3-030-02768-1_16
7. David, C., Chin, WN.: Immutable specifications for more concise and precise verification. In: Lopes, C.V., Fisher, K., eds, Proceedings of the 26th Annual ACM SIGPLAN Conference on Object-Oriented Programming, Systems, Languages, and Applications, OOPSLA 2011, part of SPLASH 2011, Portland, OR, USA, October 22 - 27, 2011, pp. 359–374. ACM (2011)
8. de Moura, L., Bjørner, N.S.: Z3: an efficient SMT solver. In: Ramakrishnan, C.R., Rehof, J., eds, Tools and Algorithms for the Construction and Analysis of Systems, 14th International Conference, TACAS 2008, Held as Part of the Joint European Conferences on Theory and Practice of Software, ETAPS 2008, Budapest, Hungary,

March 29-April 6, 2008. Proceedings, vol. 4963 of Lecture Notes in Computer Science, pp. 337–340. Springer (2008). https://doi.org/10.1007/978-3-540-78800-3_24

9. Deniélou, P.M., Yoshida, N., Bejleri, A., Hu, R.: Parameterised multiparty session types. Log. Methods Comput. Sci. **8**(4) (2012)

10. Denis, X., Jourdan, J.H.: Specifying and verifying higher-order Rust iterators. In: Sankaranarayanan, S., Sharygina, N., eds, Tools and Algorithms for the Construction and Analysis of Systems - 29th International Conference, TACAS 2023, Held as Part of the European Joint Conferences on Theory and Practice of Software, ETAPS 2022, Paris, France, April 22-27, 2023, Proceedings, Part II, vol. 13994 of Lecture Notes in Computer Science, pp. 93–110. Springer (2023). https://doi.org/10.1007/978-3-031-30820-8_9

11. Filliâtre, J.C., Paskevich, A.: Why3 - where programs meet provers. In: European Symposium on Programming (2013)

12. Findler, R.B., Felleisen, M.: Contracts for higher-order functions. In: Wand, M., Jones, S.L.P., eds, Proceedings of the Seventh ACM SIGPLAN International Conference on Functional Programming (ICFP '02), Pittsburgh, Pennsylvania, USA, October 4-6, 2002, pp. 48–59. ACM (2002)

13. Foo, D., Song, Y., Chin, W.N.: Heifer. https://github.com/hipsleek/Heifer (2024)

14. Foo, D., Song, Y., Chin, W.N.: Staged specification logic for verifying higher-order imperative programs. https://doi.org/10.5281/zenodo.12513074 (2024)

15. Foo, D., Song, Y., Chin, W.N.: Staged specification logic for verifying higher-order imperative programs (technical report). https://github.com/hipsleek/Heifer/blob/StagedSL/docs/FM2024_TR.pdf (2024)

16. Gherghina, C., David, C., Qin, S., Chin, W.N.: Structured specifications for better verification of heap-manipulating programs. In Michael J. Butler, M.J., Schulte, W., eds, FM 2011: Formal Methods - 17th International Symposium on Formal Methods, Limerick, Ireland, June 20-24, 2011. Proceedings, vol. 6664 of Lecture Notes in Computer Science, pp. 386–401. Springer (2011)

17. He, J., and Hoare, C.A.R.: Unifying theories of programming. In: RelMiCS (1998)

18. Honda, K., Yoshida, N., Berger, M.: An observationally complete program logic for imperative higher-order frame rules. In: 20th IEEE Symposium on Logic in Computer Science (LICS 2005), 26-29 June 2005, Chicago, IL, USA, Proceedings, pp. 270–279. IEEE Computer Society (2005)

19. Jung, R., Krebbers, R., Jourdan, J.-H., Bizjak, A., Birkedal, L., Dreyer, D.: Iris from the ground up: a modular foundation for higher-order concurrent separation logic. J. Funct. Program. **28**, e20 (2018)

20. Leavens, G.T., Naumann, D.A.: Behavioral subtyping, specification inheritance, and modular reasoning. ACM Trans. Program. Lang. Syst. **37**(4), 1–88 (2015)

21. Morgan, C.: The refinement calculus. In: NATO ASI PDC (1994)

22. Nanevski, A., Morrisett, J.G., Birkedal, L.: Hoare type theory, polymorphism and separation. J. Funct. Program. **18**(5-6), 865–911 (2008)

23. Pereira, M., Ravara, A.: Cameleer: a deductive verification tool for OCaml. In: Silva, A., Rustan, K., Leino, M., eds, Computer Aided Verification - 33rd International Conference, CAV 2021, Virtual Event, July 20-23, 2021, Proceedings, Part II, vol. 12760 of Lecture Notes in Computer Science, pp. 677–689. Springer (2021). https://doi.org/10.1007/978-3-030-81688-9_31

24. Reynolds, J.C., Definitional interpreters for higher-order programming languages. In: Donovan, J.J., Shields, R., editors, Proceedings of the ACM annual conference, ACM 1972, 1972, Volume 2, pp. 717–740. ACM (1972)

25. Smans, J., Jacobs, B., Piessens, F.: Implicit dynamic frames. ACM Trans. Program. Lang. Syst. **34**(1), 1–58 (2012)
26. Soares, T., Pereira, M.: A framework for the automated verification of algebraic effects and handlers (extended version). ArXiv, abs/2302.01265, 2023
27. Soares, T.L.: A deductive verification framework for higher order programs. CoRR, abs/2011.14044 (2020)
28. Svendsen, K.: Modular specification and verification for higher-order languages with state. IT-Universitetet i København (2013)
29. Swamy, N., et al.: Dependent types and multi-monadic effects in F. In: Bodík, R., Majumdar, R., eds, Proceedings of the 43rd Annual ACM SIGPLAN-SIGACT Symposium on Principles of Programming Languages, POPL 2016, St. Petersburg, FL, USA, January 20 - 22, 2016, pp. 256–270. ACM (2016)
30. Swamy, N., Rastogi, A., Fromherz, A., Merigoux, D., Ahman, D., Martínez, G.: Steelcore: an extensible concurrent separation logic for effectful dependently typed programs. Proc. ACM Program. Lang. **4**(ICFP), 1–30 (2020)
31. Vazou, N., Seidel, E.L., Jhala, R.: LiquidHaskell: experience with refinement types in the real world. In: Swierstra, W., edr, Proceedings of the 2014 ACM SIGPLAN symposium on Haskell, Gothenburg, Sweden, September 4-5, 2014, pp. 39–51. ACM (2014)
32. Wolff, F., Bílý, A., Matheja, C., Müller, P., Summers, A.J.: Modular specification and verification of closures in Rust. Proc. ACM Program. Lang. **5**(OOPSLA), 1–29 (2021)
33. Xu, D.N., Peyton Jones, S.L., Claessen, K.: Static contract checking for Haskell. In: Shao, Z., Pierce, B.C., eds, Proceedings of the 36th ACM SIGPLAN-SIGACT Symposium on Principles of Programming Languages, POPL 2009, Savannah, GA, USA, January 21-23, 2009, pp. 41–52. ACM (2009)
34. Yoshida, N., Honda, K., Berger, M.: Logical reasoning for higher-order functions with local state. In: Seidl, H., edr, Foundations of Software Science and Computational Structures, 10th International Conference, FOSSACS 2007, Held as Part of the Joint European Conferences on Theory and Practice of Software, ETAPS 2007, Braga, Portugal, March 24-April 1, 2007, Proceedings, vol. 4423 of Lecture Notes in Computer Science, pp. 361–377. Springer (2007)
35. Zampetti, F., Belias, F., Zid, C., Antonioland, G., Di Penta, M.: An empirical study on the fault-inducing effect of functional constructs in Python. In: 2022 IEEE International Conference on Software Maintenance and Evolution (ICSME), pp. 47–58 (2022)

Unifying Weak Memory Verification Using Potentials

Lara Bargmann[1]([⊠]) [iD], Brijesh Dongol[2] [iD], and Heike Wehrheim[1] [iD]

[1] Carl von Ossietzky Universität Oldenburg, Oldenburg, Germany
{lara.bargmann,heike.wehrheim}@uol.de
[2] University of Surrey, Guildford, UK
b.dongol@surrey.ac.uk

Abstract. Concurrency verification for weak memory models is inherently complex. Several deductive techniques based on proof calculi have recently been developed, but these are typically tailored towards a single memory model through specialised assertions and associated proof rules. In this paper, we propose an extension to the logic Piccolo to generalise reasoning across different memory models. Piccolo is interpreted on the semantic domain of thread *potentials*. By deriving potentials from weak memory model states, we can define the validity of Piccolo formulae for multiple memory models. We moreover propose unified proof rules for verification on top of Piccolo. Once (a set of) such rules has been shown to be sound with respect to a memory model MM, all correctness proofs employing this rule set are valid for MM. We exemplify our approach on the memory models SC, TSO and SRA using the standard litmus tests Message-Passing and IRIW.

1 Introduction

Weak memory models [1,4] are now a standard feature of concurrent systems and programmers may choose to exploit them at both the level of hardware (e.g., Intel TSO, Arm) and the level of programming languages (e.g., C11, Java). However, these models differ significantly from each other and are generally incomparable (i.e., allowed behaviours in one memory model are not necessarily a subset of the behaviours allowed by another [21,38]). This means that reasoning about a particular memory model can be challenging since one needs bespoke logics and assertions for verification. A variety of separation logics (e.g., [13,19, 37]) and (timestamp-based) Owicki-Gries logics (e.g., [7,11,12,27,39]) have been developed for specific weak memory models, but are not a generic technique.

In this paper, we aim to simplify weak memory reasoning by developing a unifying framework that captures the behaviours of different weak memory models. Our motivation is similar to prior works [3,14,16,22], which also aim

Bargmann and Wehrheim are supported by DFG grant WE 2290/14-1. Dongol is supported by VeTSS and EPSRC grants EP/Y036425/1, EP/X037142/1, EP/X015149/1, EP/V038915/1, EP/R025134/2.

A. Platzer et al. (Eds.): FM 2024, LNCS 14933, pp. 519–537, 2025.
https://doi.org/10.1007/978-3-031-71162-6_27

to uniformly reason about programs under different memory models within a single verification framework. Our point of departure is a new interval-based framework, Piccolo [25], that uses a notion of *potentials* to describe a program's behaviour, which is both intuitive to use and simple to describe. Thus far, Piccolo has been applied to a memory model known as *strong release-acquire* (SRA [23]), which strengthens the release-acquire memory model used by C11 [24].

We extend Piccolo and show that potential-based reasoning can also be used in other memory models, namely *sequential consistency* (SC) [28] and *total store order* (TSO) [31,35]. While the extension to SC is straightforward, the TSO memory model presents a new set of challenges. Namely, unlike SRA, TSO is a weak memory model that guarantees *multi-copy atomicity* (MCA), which means that all threads see the writes to each location in the same order. As we shall see, our logic provides a novel insight into reasoning about memory models that satisfy MCA. In particular, we develop a proof rule, which shows that for particular memory configurations, one can make a deduction on a thread based on the observations made by *another thread*.

Related Work. A number of works have proposed program logics for reasoning about concurrent programs on weak memory models [7,11,19,25,27,36], all specific to one memory model. Bargmann and Wehrheim [6] build proof rules on top of the generic approach of [14], using the program logic proposed in [11]. This logic is, however, not able to express sequences of values seen by threads, as possible in Piccolo (and needed for IRIW). Rely-guarantee reasoning on weak memory models (without defining specific logics) is furthermore studied in [9,10].

Alglave et al. [3] enhance Owicki-Gries reasoning [32] with so-called Pythia variables and communication-based proof obligations between different read and write events. This however introduces additional complexity since validity of the communication assertions must be proved in addition to the local correctness and non-interference proof obligations of the Owicki-Gries method. Doherty et al. [14] work with a timestamp-based operational semantics using a large set of axioms to characterise the properties of each memory model. By introducing assertions that directly describe the communication state, this method avoids an extra set of checks, allowing correctness to be proved by establishing local correctness and interference freedom of the assertions (as in the standard setting [32]). However, the timestamp model tends to induce a large set of bespoke assertions that describe a range of different phenomena and state configurations [7,11,12,14,39]. Besides these deductive approaches, Gavrilenko et al. [16] and Kokologiannakis et al. [22] propose model checking techniques for weak memory models, both parametric in the memory model, but only provide a bounded proof (i.e., a proof of correctness for paths of bounded length).

Our work encompasses a logic for TSO. While many prior works have studied verification under TSO, only a handful [9,14,34] consider program logics.

Contributions. The main contribution of this article is the use of potentials and its associated logical framework as a unifying model for reasoning across SC, TSO and SRA. While SRA is already defined in terms of potentials [25], we provide a novel technique for potential-based reasoning for SC and TSO by mapping their existing operational semantics into a potential domain. This unification requires two extensions to the existing logic for potentials: **(a)** assertions for reasoning about *views* of threads (e.g., view-maximality), and **(b)** a new proof rule for reasoning about the behaviour of reads in the presence of multi-copy atomicity (as guaranteed by memory models SC and TSO). Finally, we show how our proof rules can be applied to reason about key examples from the literature.

2 Motivation

As a first illustration of our reasoning framework, consider the concurrent program called the *message-passing* litmus test (see Fig. 1), typically used for demonstrating the causal consistency of a memory model. Thread T_1 updates x (representing some data) to 1, then updates y (representing a flag) to 1. Thread T_2 reads from y, then from x and guarantees that seeing the flag to be set (i.e., a = 1), it must also read the data written by T_1. Causal consistency holds for all three memory models that we consider, but does not hold for weaker models such as C11 (when using relaxed atomics) or Arm [15]. That is, for these weaker memory models, even if T_2 reads 1 for y, it may subsequently read a stale (in this case initial) value for x, missing the updated to x at line 1.

We seek to develop a correctness proof that demonstrates causal consistency (i.e., a proof showing that the postcondition $a = 1 \Rightarrow b = 1$ holds) which uniformly applies to several memory models. The proof outline in Fig. 1 is slightly adapted from the proof outline by Lahav et al. [25] for the SRA memory model. It shows correctness of message passing using a notion of *potentials* and an extension of the logic Piccolo to reason over potentials. The logic aims to exploit an operational semantics comprising a state domain over mappings

$$\{T_1 \uparrow x \wedge T_2 \ltimes [y \neq 1]\}$$

Thread T_1	**Thread T_2**
$\{T_1 \uparrow x\}$	$\{T_2 \ltimes [y \neq 1] ; [x = 1]\}$
1 : STORE(x, 1);	3 : a := LOAD(y);
$\{T_1 \ltimes [x = 1]\}$	$\{a = 1 \Rightarrow T_2 \ltimes [x = 1]\}$
2 : STORE(y, 1)	4 : b := LOAD(x)
$\{true\}$	$\{a = 1 \Rightarrow b = 1\}$

$$\{a = 1 \Rightarrow b = 1\}$$

Fig. 1. Message-passing proof using potentials that is valid for SC, TSO and SRA, adapted from [25]. The highlighted assertions are new for our unified proof.

from threads to potentials. Potentials are *lists* (sequences) of stores (which themselves are mappings from shared locations to values). Thereby, the semantic domain accounts for the fact that in weak memory models (a) threads do not all see the same value of a shared location at the same time, and (b) threads see written values in a certain order. Assertions formalise such states using an interval-based logic. The assertion $T_2 \ltimes [y \neq 1]$ states the list of stores corresponding to T_2 are such that, for all stores in the list, $y \neq 1$ holds. The values of other shared locations (including x) are unconstrained. Similarly, $T_2 \ltimes [y \neq 1] ; [x = 1]$ states that the list of stores corresponding to T_2 may be split into an initial (possibly empty) list, say L_1, such that $y \neq 1$ for all stores in L_1, and a remaining (possibly empty) list, say L_2, such that $x = 1$ for all stores in L_2. Shared locations different from y (resp., x) are unconstrained in L_1 (resp., L_2). Finally, the assertion $T_1 \uparrow x$ states that thread T_1 is currently viewing the last update to shared location x.

The prior work on Piccolo [25] employs a Hoare logic for atomic steps (stores and loads) and potential-based assertions, allowing one to discharge the standard (Owicki-Gries [32]) proof obligations[1] generated by the proof outline in Fig. 1. Namely, the framework requires that we establish local correctness of the assertions within a thread, as well as interference freedom from other thread(s). As an example, consider again Fig. 1. Local correctness of the assertions in T_1 for instance is straightforward. The only non-trivial assertion is the precondition to line 2, which we refer to as $T_1.2$ (second assertion in T_1). Local correctness of $T_1.2$ is straightforward since execution of STORE$(x, 1)$ directly establishes $T_1.2$, while interference freedom holds because T_2 only contains loads, which cannot affect the potentials of T_1. In thread T_2, local correctness of $T_2.1$ is established by the precondition of the program (since the second interval of $T_2.1$ is allowed to be empty). Interference freedom against line 1 holds because line 1 executes in a state in which T_1 is view maximal on x, and hence can only introduce a store with $x = 1$ at the *end* of T_2's potential. These and similar correctness arguments are captured as proof rules in the reasoning framework (see Sect. 4 and Sect. 5).

Our main motivation for this paper is to generalise and unify this approach. Namely, is it possible for the *same proof outline to be valid for several memory models?* Showing this would mean that a verifier only needs to understand a single proof system, and for the resulting proof to apply to *multiple memory models*. We seek to answer this question in the context of potentials and the logic Piccolo, avoiding the shortcomings of previous approaches as discussed in the introduction.

To this end, we provide a mapping from the operational semantics of both SC and TSO to a potential-based semantics, allowing one to interpret (extended) Piccolo assertions and proof rules for these memory models. Using this technique we show that the proof outline in Fig. 1 also holds for SC and TSO, allowing us to validate that both models satisfy causal consistency. Later, from Sect. refsec:IRIW onwards, we shall see proof outlines that only hold in *some* of our memory models (i.e., for SC and TSO, but not for SRA). A distinguishing feature between these memory models is then that some proof rules used to construct proof outlines are sometimes sound in one, but *unsound* in another model.

3   Background

In this section, we define the program syntax, and present the potential-based domain to unify weak memory models. Later, in Sect. 4, we present a logic over this domain.

---

[1] In [25], Owicki-Gries proof obligations are systematised within a rely-guarantee framework. While the generic framework in [25] applies to any causally consistent memory model, the specific instance of the program logic only applies to SRA.

Notation. Lists over an alphabet A are written as $L = \langle a_1 \cdot \ldots \cdot a_n \rangle$ where $a_1, \ldots, a_n \in A$. We use $\cdot$ to concatenate lists, write $\langle \rangle$ for the empty list, $L[i]$ for the i'th element of L and $\#L$ for the length of L. We assume the first element to be $L[1]$ and write $a \in L$ to say that element a occurs in the list L. We furthermore use $\mathbb{Q}^+$ to denote the positive rational numbers including 0. Given a function f, we let $f[y \mapsto v] = \lambda x.\ \textbf{if}\ x = y\ \textbf{then}\ v\ \textbf{else}\ f(x)$ denote functional override.

$$
\begin{array}{ll}
\textit{values} \quad v \in \mathsf{Val} = \{0, 1, \ldots\} & \textit{shared variables} \quad x, y \in \mathsf{Loc} = \{\mathsf{x}, \mathsf{y}, \ldots\} \\
\textit{local registers} \quad a \in \mathsf{Reg} = \{\mathsf{a}, \mathsf{b}, \ldots\} & \textit{thread identifiers} \quad \tau, \pi \in \mathsf{Tid} = \{\mathsf{T_0}, \mathsf{T_1}, \ldots\}
\end{array}
$$

$$
\begin{array}{ll}
e ::= a \mid v \mid e + e \mid e = e \mid e > e \mid \neg e \mid e \wedge e \mid e \vee e \mid \ldots & \\
c ::= a := e \mid \mathsf{STORE}(x, e) \mid a := \mathsf{LOAD}(x) \mid \ldots & \tilde{c} ::= c \mid \langle c, a := e \rangle \\
C ::= \tilde{c} \mid \mathsf{SKIP} \mid C\,;C \mid \ldots &
\end{array}
$$

Fig. 2. Program syntax

$$
\frac{\gamma' = \gamma[a \mapsto \gamma(e)]}{a := e \gg \atop \gamma \xrightarrow{\varepsilon} \gamma'} \qquad
\frac{l = \mathsf{W}(x, \gamma(e))}{\mathsf{STORE}(x, e) \gg \atop \gamma \xrightarrow{l} \gamma} \qquad
\frac{\begin{array}{c} l = \mathsf{R}(x, v_\mathsf{R}) \\ \gamma' = \gamma[a \mapsto v_\mathsf{R}] \end{array}}{a := \mathsf{LOAD}(x) \gg \atop \gamma \xrightarrow{l} \gamma'} \qquad
\frac{c \gg \gamma \xrightarrow{l_\varepsilon} \gamma' \quad a := e \gg \gamma' \xrightarrow{\varepsilon} \gamma''}{\langle c, a := e \rangle \gg \gamma \xrightarrow{l_\varepsilon} \gamma_n}
$$

$$
\frac{}{\langle \mathsf{SKIP};C, \gamma \rangle \xrightarrow{\tau, \varepsilon} \langle C, \gamma' \rangle} \qquad
\frac{\tilde{c} \gg \gamma \xrightarrow{\tau, l_\varepsilon} \gamma'}{\langle \tilde{c};C, \gamma \rangle \xrightarrow{\tau, l_\varepsilon} \langle C, \gamma' \rangle} \qquad
\frac{\langle \mathcal{C}(\tau), \gamma \rangle \xrightarrow{\tau, l_\varepsilon} \langle C', \gamma' \rangle}{\langle \mathcal{C}, \gamma \rangle \xrightarrow{\tau, l_\varepsilon} \langle \mathcal{C}[\tau \mapsto C'], \gamma' \rangle}
$$

Fig. 3. Local semantics of commands ($l \in \mathsf{Lab}, l_\varepsilon \in \mathsf{Lab} \cup \{\varepsilon\}$)

Program Syntax. The syntax of programs, given in Fig. 2, is mostly standard, comprising primitive (atomic) commands c and compound commands C. The non-standard components are instrumented commands $\tilde{c}$ (typically used to support auxiliary variables), which atomically execute a primitive command c and a local assignment $a := e$. Atomic commands (such as CAS), are elided since they induce a different set of proof rules. Rules for compound statements such as if-then-else and loops are straightforward to derive [25].

We assume top-level parallelism[2], i.e., that programs are of the form $\mathcal{C} \triangleq (\lambda \tau \in \mathsf{Tid}.\ C)$, mapping threads (of type Tid) to sequential commands. Often, we write $C_1 \| C_2 \| \ldots \| C_n$ (ignoring thread ids) for a program $\mathcal{C}$.

Semantics. As in prior works (e.g., [7,14,25,26]), we present the semantics of the language in three steps.

---

[2] An extension with join and fork statements could be done along the lines of [25].

Local Semantics. Here, the label (of type $\mathsf{Lab} = \{\mathtt{R}(x, v_\mathtt{R}), \mathtt{W}(x, v_\mathtt{W})\}$) for each action (read/write) associated with each command is extracted. This semantics (see Fig. 3) also tracks and updates a local register store, $\gamma \in \mathsf{Reg} \to \mathsf{Val}$. In this semantics, in the read rule, the value read is parametric and determined by the transition label. Later, in the combined program semantics, this value will be fixed so that the read value is consistent with the memory semantics.

Memory semantics. The semantics of memory models given by a labelled transition system (LTS), $\mathcal{M}$, with set of states denoted by $\mathcal{M}.\mathsf{Q}$, initial states $\mathcal{M}.\mathsf{Q}_0$, and transitions denoted by $\xrightarrow{k}_\mathcal{M}$. Transition labels, k, of $\mathcal{M}$ consist of program transition labels (elements of $\mathsf{Tid} \times (\mathsf{Lab} \cup \{\varepsilon\})$) and a (disjoint) set $\mathcal{M}.\Theta$ of internal memory steps. As an example, we present the SC memory model below. The SRA model is presented in Example 2 and the TSO model in Sect. 6.

Example 1 (SCmemory model). The memory model SC simply tracks the most recent value written to each variable (plus the id of the writing thread). SC has no internal memory transitions (i.e., $\mathsf{SC}.\Theta \triangleq \emptyset$), and the initial state is defined by $\mathsf{SC}.\mathsf{Q}_0 \triangleq \lambda x. \langle 0, \mathtt{T}_0 \rangle$ (where $\mathtt{T}_0$ is a special initialising thread), and transitions are given by:

$$\text{WRITE} \quad \frac{l = \mathtt{W}(x, v_\mathtt{W}) \qquad m' = m[x \mapsto \langle v_\mathtt{W}, \tau \rangle]}{m \xrightarrow{\tau, l}_{\mathsf{SC}} m'} \qquad\qquad \text{READ} \quad \frac{l = \mathtt{R}(x, v_\mathtt{R}) \qquad m(x) = \langle v_\mathtt{R}, \cdot \rangle}{m \xrightarrow{\tau, l}_{\mathsf{SC}} m}$$

Combined Program Semantics. This semantics combines the local with the memory semantics using the three generic rules below for steps corresponding to the external memory (left), non-memory (middle) and internal memory (right):

$$\frac{\langle \mathcal{C}, \gamma \rangle \xrightarrow{\tau, l} \langle \mathcal{C}', \gamma' \rangle \quad l \in \mathsf{Lab} \quad m \xrightarrow{\tau, l}_\mathcal{M} m'}{\langle \mathcal{C}, \gamma, m \rangle \xrightarrow{\tau, l}_{\overline{\mathcal{M}}} \langle \mathcal{C}', \gamma', m' \rangle} \qquad \frac{\langle \mathcal{C}, \gamma \rangle \xrightarrow{\tau, \varepsilon} \langle \mathcal{C}', \gamma' \rangle}{\langle \mathcal{C}, \gamma, m \rangle \xrightarrow{\tau, \varepsilon}_{\overline{\mathcal{M}}} \langle \mathcal{C}', \gamma', m \rangle} \qquad \frac{\theta \in \mathcal{M}.\Theta \quad m \xrightarrow{\theta}_\mathcal{M} m'}{\langle \mathcal{C}, \gamma, m \rangle \xrightarrow{\theta}_{\overline{\mathcal{M}}} \langle \mathcal{C}, \gamma, m' \rangle}$$

Potential Domain. Under weak memory models, a thread may read from several possible writes to a location when determining the location's value, and different semantics have been developed to capture this phenomenon. In this paper, our unifying model is based on the notion of *potentials* [24,25]. Each potential store is a mapping from shared locations to values as well as the thread that performed the write plus some auxiliary information required by specific memory models. This auxiliary information differs between memory models: SC requires no additional auxiliary information, TSO keeps track of *timestamps*, while SRA keeps track of *update flags*. As we shall see, the SRA memory model is defined directly over potentials, whereas for SC and TSO, we develop a mapping from the memory model to the potential domain.

Definition 1. *A potential store is a function $\delta : \mathsf{Loc} \to \mathsf{Val} \times \mathsf{Tid} \times \mathsf{Aux}$, where* Aux *captures the auxiliary information required by the memory model at hand.*

We use $\delta(x).\mathtt{val}$ and $\delta(x).\mathtt{tid}$ to retrieve the value and thread id of $\delta(x)$, respectively. Additionally, in TSO, we use $\delta(x).\mathtt{ts}$ to retrieve the (auxiliary) timestamp and in SRA, we use $\delta(x).\mathtt{flag}$ to retrieve the (auxiliary) update flag.

Definition 2. *A potential is a non-empty set of store lists. We let $\mathcal{L}$ be the set of all potentials. A potential mapping (of the set of all potential mappings $\mathcal{P}$) is a partial function $\mathcal{D} : \mathsf{Tid} \to 2^{\mathcal{L}} \setminus \{\emptyset\}$ that maps thread identifiers to potentials such that all lists agree on the last store.*

$$\text{WRITE} \frac{\begin{array}{c} \forall L' \in \mathcal{D}'(\tau). \exists L \in \mathcal{D}(\tau). L' = L[x \mapsto \langle v_{\mathtt{W}}, \tau, \mathtt{RMW}\rangle] \\ \forall \pi \in dom(\mathcal{D}) \setminus \{\tau\}, L' \in \mathcal{D}'(\pi). \exists L_0, L_1. \\ L_0 \cdot L_1 \in \mathcal{D}(\pi) \wedge L_1 \in \mathcal{D}(\tau) \wedge \\ L' = L_0[x \mapsto \mathtt{R}] \cdot L_1[x \mapsto \langle v_{\mathtt{W}}, \tau, \mathtt{RMW}\rangle] \end{array}}{\mathcal{D} \xrightarrow{\tau,\mathtt{W}(x,v_{\mathtt{W}})}_{\text{SRA}} \mathcal{D}'}$$

$$\text{READ} \frac{\begin{array}{c} \exists \pi. \forall L \in \mathcal{D}(\tau). \\ L[1](x).\mathtt{val} = v_{\mathtt{R}} \wedge \\ L[1](x).\mathtt{tid} = \pi \end{array}}{\mathcal{D} \xrightarrow{\tau,\mathtt{R}(x,v_{\mathtt{R}})}_{\text{SRA}} \mathcal{D}}$$

$$\text{LOSE} \frac{\mathcal{D}' \sqsubseteq \mathcal{D}}{\mathcal{D} \xrightarrow{\text{lose}}_{\text{SRA}} \mathcal{D}'} \qquad \text{DUP} \frac{\mathcal{D} \preceq \mathcal{D}'}{\mathcal{D} \xrightarrow{\text{dup}}_{\text{SRA}} \mathcal{D}'}$$

Fig. 4. SRA semantics of [25] ($L[x \mapsto \mathtt{R}]$ changes the update flag of x to $\mathtt{R}$ in L)

Example 2 (SRA memory model). The operational semantics of the memory model SRA is directly defined on the potential domain using *update flags* as auxiliary information, i.e., $\mathsf{SRA.Aux} \triangleq \{\mathtt{R}, \mathtt{RMW}\}$. With this, $\mathsf{SRA.Q} \triangleq \mathcal{P}$, $\mathsf{SRA.Q_0} \triangleq \lambda\tau.\{\langle \lambda x.\langle 0, T_0, \mathtt{RMW}\rangle\rangle\}$, $\mathsf{SRA.\Theta} \triangleq \{\mathsf{lose}, \mathsf{dup}\}$ and the transitions are defined in Fig. 4. Reading requires all lists in a thread's potential to agree on the first value of a location. Writing changes the value of a location in all stores in the writer thread τ, and on a suffix of the store lists in other threads. Potential stores can furthermore be arbitrarily dropped from store lists in potentials (and can thus enable reading) as well as duplicated. This is modelled by two internal transitions, LOSE and DUP. For this, we employ two relations on store lists, $L' \sqsubseteq L$ for losing (e.g., $\delta_1 \cdot \delta_2 \cdot \delta_3 \sqsubseteq \delta_2 \cdot \delta_3$) and $L \preceq L'$ for duplication (e.g., $\delta_1 \cdot \delta_2 \preceq \delta_1 \cdot \delta_2 \cdot \delta_2$). The relations are lifted to potential mappings as expected.

We refer the interested reader to [25] for full details of the SRA semantics.

Example 3 Consider the MP litmus test from Fig. 1. After executing instructions 1 and 2 of T_1, thread T_2 could have the potential:

$$\begin{bmatrix} \mathtt{x} \mapsto \langle 0, T_0, \mathtt{R}\rangle \\ \mathtt{y} \mapsto \langle 0, T_0, \mathtt{R}\rangle \end{bmatrix} \cdot \begin{bmatrix} \mathtt{x} \mapsto \langle 1, T_1, \mathtt{RMW}\rangle \\ \mathtt{y} \mapsto \langle 0, T_0, \mathtt{R}\rangle \end{bmatrix} \cdot \begin{bmatrix} \mathtt{x} \mapsto \langle 1, T_1, \mathtt{RMW}\rangle \\ \mathtt{y} \mapsto \langle 1, T_1, \mathtt{RMW}\rangle \end{bmatrix}$$

in which it currently sees both $\mathtt{x}$ and $\mathtt{y}$ to have the value 0. In the future (i.e., after some lose steps) T_2 will first observe $\mathtt{x}$ to become 1, then $\mathtt{y}$ to become 1. Note that once T_2 reads 1 for $\mathtt{y}$, it can only read 1 for the value of $\mathtt{x}$.

4   A Logic for Potentials

In this section, we present an extension of Piccolo [25], an interval-based logic for weak memory models formalised using a notion of potentials. Piccolo (originally developed for SRA [25]) comprises a set of assertions over potential-based states and a set of proof rules that allow one to formalise the values that a thread may see now, and in the future. The extended version of Piccolo that we develop enables reasoning about SC and TSO in addition to SRA.

Figure 5 gives the syntax of our extension to Piccolo. The extension concerns two concepts: First, we add assertions for specifying *view maximality*. Informally, a thread τ is view maximal on a location x, $\tau \uparrow x$, if it can only see the "last" write to x. Second, we incorporate the possibility for specifying a writer thread's id within the logic (by stating the writer to a location x to be τ, $x.\text{tid} = \tau$). We require this to later be able to formulate the proof rule stating MCA. Besides these new concepts, the other operators inherited from Piccolo are *intervals*: a list fulfills an interval assertion $[E]$ when all elements in the list satisfy E, and a list L satisfies $[I_1] ; [I_2]$ (where ; is the *chop* operator [8,29]) iff L can be split into lists L_1 and L_2 such that L_1 satisfies $[I_1]$ and L_2 satisfies $[I_2]$.

value expressions	$E_{\text{val}} ::= e \mid x.\text{val} \mid E_{\text{val}} + E_{\text{val}} \mid E_{\text{val}} - E_{\text{val}} \mid \ldots$
thread id expressions	$E_{\text{tid}} ::= \tau \mid x.\text{tid}$
extended expression	$E \quad ::= E_{\text{val}} = E_{\text{val}} \mid E_{\text{tid}} = E_{\text{tid}} \mid \neg E \mid E \wedge E \mid \ldots$
interval assertions	$I \quad ::= [E] \mid I ; I \mid I \wedge I \mid I \vee I$
assertions	$\varphi, \psi ::= \tau \ltimes I \mid \tau \uparrow x \mid e \mid \varphi \wedge \varphi \mid \varphi \vee \varphi$

Fig. 5. Assertions of Piccolo (extended)

Notation. For an assertion φ, we let $fv(\varphi) \subseteq \text{Reg} \cup \text{Loc} \cup \text{Tid}$ be the set of registers, locations and thread identifiers occurring in φ. Instead of writing $x.\text{val} = e$, we often simply write $x = e$.

Next, we formally define the interpretation of Piccolo on the domain of potentials.

Definition 3. *Let γ be a register store, δ a potential store, L a store list, and $\mathcal{D}$ a potential mapping. We let $[\![e]\!]_{\langle \gamma, \delta \rangle} \triangleq \gamma(e)$, $[\![x.\text{val}]\!]_{\langle \gamma, \delta \rangle} \triangleq \delta(x).\text{val}$ and $[\![x.\text{tid}]\!]_{\langle \gamma, \delta \rangle} \triangleq \delta(x).\text{tid}$. The extension of this notation to any extended expression E is standard. The validity of assertions in $\langle \gamma, \mathcal{D} \rangle$, denoted by $\langle \gamma, \mathcal{D} \rangle \models \varphi$, is defined as follows:*

1. *$\langle \gamma, L \rangle \models [E]$ if $[\![E]\!]_{\langle \gamma, \delta \rangle} = true$ for every $\delta \in L$.*
2. *$\langle \gamma, L \rangle \models I_1 ; I_2$ if $\langle \gamma, L_1 \rangle \models I_1$ and $\langle \gamma, L_2 \rangle \models I_2$ for some (possibly empty) L_1 and L_2 such that $L = L_1 \cdot L_2$.*
3. *$\langle \gamma, L \rangle \models I_1 \wedge I_2$ if $\langle \gamma, L \rangle \models I_1$ and $\langle \gamma, L \rangle \models I_2$ (similarly for $\vee$).*
4. *$\langle \gamma, \mathcal{D} \rangle \models \tau \ltimes I$ if $\langle \gamma, L \rangle \models I$ for every $L \in \mathcal{D}(\tau)$.*
5. *$\langle \gamma, \mathcal{D} \rangle \models \tau \uparrow x$ if $L[i](x) = L[1](x)$ for every $L \in \mathcal{D}(\tau), 1 \leq i \leq \#L$.*

6. $\langle \gamma, \mathcal{D} \rangle \models e$ *if* $\gamma(e) = true$.

7. $\langle \gamma, \mathcal{D} \rangle \models \varphi_1 \wedge \varphi_2$ *if* $\langle \gamma, \mathcal{D} \rangle \models \varphi_1$ *and* $\langle \gamma, \mathcal{D} \rangle \models \varphi_2$ *(similarly for* $\vee$*).*

View maximality of a thread is determined by inspecting its entries for a location x: if they are all the same (including thread id and auxiliary information), the thread can only see the value of the last update to x.

Before discussing the concrete rules, we note an important property of program logics for weak memory, namely the *stability* of assertions under internal memory transitions [14,25]. That is, for every assertion φ, register store γ and memory state m the following must be satisfied:

$$\langle \gamma, m \rangle \models \varphi \wedge m \xrightarrow{\theta}_{\mathcal{M}} m' \Rightarrow \langle \gamma, m' \rangle \models \varphi .$$

This property holds for all assertions described by Fig. 5 with respect to the lose and dup steps of SRA (see [25]), and trivially for SC. This property also holds for TSO and its internal memory transition (flush), see Sect. 6.

Assumption	Pre	Command	Post	Reference	Mem. Model
$x \notin fv(\varphi)$	$\{\varphi\}$	$\tau \mapsto \mathsf{STORE}(x, e)$	$\{\varphi\}$	STABLE-ST	SC,TSO,SRA
$a \notin fv(\varphi)$	$\{\varphi\}$	$\tau \mapsto a := \mathsf{LOAD}(x)$	$\{\varphi\}$	STABLE-LD	SC,TSO,SRA
	$\{\varphi(a := e)\}$	$\tau \mapsto a := e$	$\{\varphi\}$	SUBST	SC,TSO,SRA
	$\{\tau\!\uparrow\!x\}$	$\tau \mapsto \mathsf{STORE}(x, e)$	$\left\{ \begin{array}{l} \tau\!\uparrow\!x \wedge \\ \tau \ltimes [x = e \wedge \\ x.tid = \tau] \end{array} \right\}$	ST-OWN	SC,TSO,SRA
$\pi \neq \tau$	$\left\{ \begin{array}{l} \tau\!\uparrow\!x \wedge \\ \pi \ltimes I \end{array} \right\}$	$\tau \mapsto \mathsf{STORE}(x, e)$	$\left\{ \begin{array}{l} \pi \ltimes I ; [x = e \wedge \\ x.tid = \tau] \end{array} \right\}$	ST-OTHER1	SC,TSO,SRA
$\pi \neq \tau$, $x \notin fv(I_\tau)$	$\left\{ \begin{array}{l} \tau \ltimes I_\tau \wedge \\ \pi \ltimes I ; I_\tau \end{array} \right\}$	$\tau \mapsto \mathsf{STORE}(x, e)$	$\{\pi \ltimes I ; I_\tau\}$	ST-OTHER2	SC,TSO,SRA
P	$\{\tau \ltimes [e(a := x)]\}$	$\tau \mapsto a := \mathsf{LOAD}(x)$	$\{e\}$	LD-SINGLE	SC,TSO,SRA
	$\{\tau \ltimes [e(a := x)]; I\}$	$\tau \mapsto a := \mathsf{LOAD}(x)$	$\{e \vee \psi\}$	LD-SHIFT	SC,TSO,SRA
$\tau \neq \pi_i$, $i \in \{1, 2\}$	$\left\{ \begin{array}{l} \pi_i \ltimes [x \neq e]; \\ [x = e \wedge \\ x.tid = \tau] \end{array} \right\}$	$\pi_1 \mapsto a := \mathsf{LOAD}(x)$	$\left\{ \begin{array}{l} a = e \Rightarrow \\ \pi_2 \ltimes [x = e] \end{array} \right\}$	MCA	SC,TSO

Fig. 6. Piccolo proof rules ($\varphi(a := e)$ means replacement of a by e in φ), where $P \triangleq \{\tau \ltimes I\}\tau \mapsto a := \mathsf{LOAD}(x)\{\psi\}$

Proof Rules. The proof rules we introduce here solely concern *primitive* instructions. These can be used either within an Owicki-Gries-like proof framework [32] constructing proof outlines and showing these to be interference-free, or within a rely-guarantee approach [18,40].

Figure 6 gives the proof rules[3]. Note that we do not explicitly state a proof rule for instrumented primitive commands; for these, we can employ combinations of rules for primitive commands with rule SUBST. First, we have rules for

---

[3] Note that this set of rules is not complete, i.e., is not sufficient for proving all valid postconditions of programs for memory models SC, SRA and TSO.

stability, STABLE-LD and STABLE-ST, stating that Piccolo formulae not referring to registers or locations, respectively, are not affected by load and store
instructions. Rule Subst next states the standard axiom of assignment of Hoare
logic [17], which is here only defined with respect to registers and local expressions.

The next three rules concern store instructions. Rule ST-OWN describes the
changes a store has on the potential of the writing thread, namely if a thread is
view-maximal, the only value it can see for location x after the store is its own
value (and the id of the writer is its own id). Rule ST-OTHER1 states a similar
effect for the non-writing threads, which however can also still see "old" values for
x after the store instruction. Rule ST-OTHER2 states that properties of suffixes
of lists are preserved when the writing thread τ satisfies the same property. This
rule is essential for proving message-passing-like properties (e.g., in Fig. 1).

Rules LD-SINGLE and LD-SHIFT describe the loading of values of shared
locations   into   registers   when
the thread sees a list satisfying an interval assertion (consisting of one interval or several intervals, respectively). These rules are for instance required for
$\{T_2 \ltimes [y \neq 1]\,;\,[x = 1]\}\, \mathsf{a} := \mathsf{LOAD}(y)\, \{\mathsf{a} = 1 \Rightarrow T_2 \ltimes [x = 1]\}$ in the proof outline
of T_2 in Fig. 1.

Finally, the novel rule MCA describes the property of multi-copy atomicity.
It has not occurred in [25] as the memory model SRA studied there is not multi-
copy atomic. It details the fact that in multi-copy atomic memory models threads
(other than the writer) will all get to see a written value at the same time. Here,
we formulate it via intervals: if thread π_1 loads the value e to a, then thread π_2 is
also able to see this value. This rule is essential for building a proof outline for the
litmus test IRIW (see Sect. 5). This is the only rule requiring the specification
of thread identifiers: we need to be able to state that threads π_1 and π_2 are
different from the writing thread τ, and that π_1 loads the value written by τ.

5   Example Proofs

As examples we employ two standard litmus tests for weak memory models, the
message-passing example MP already seen in Fig. 1 and a concurrent program
called Independent-Reads-of-Independent-Writes (IRIW). For both litmus tests,
we give *proof outlines* (programs interspersed with assertions) which can be
derived using our proof rules. As underlying base reasoning technique, we employ
Owicki-Gries reasoning [5,32], replacing the normal rule of assignment by our
proof rules. Owicki-Gries reasoning requires performing two correctness checks:

Local Correctness. For every command $\tilde{c}$ of thread τ with pre-assertion φ and
post-assertion ψ, we need to prove $\{\varphi\}\, \tau \mapsto \tilde{c}\, \{\psi\}$.

Global Correctness. For every assertion φ in the proof outline of a thread τ
and every command $\tilde{c}$ in a thread π ($\tau \neq \pi$) with pre-assertion ψ, we need to
show $\{\varphi \wedge \psi\}\, \pi \mapsto \tilde{c}\, \{\varphi\}$ (non-interference).

Each proof rule employed in these checks must furthermore be shown to be sound w.r.t. the memory model of interest; if this is not the case, the proof outline is not valid for the particular memory model. In §7, we study soundness of our proof rules for SC, TSO and SRA.

Message-Passing. Figure 1 already gives the proof outline of MP. Note that we can also employ the standard rules of conjunction, disjunction and consequence of Hoare logic [17] for checking local and global correctness. The interesting cases in MP concern the non-interference checks of the first assertion in T_2 with respect to the store instructions of thread T_1. For this, we need to prove

$$\{T_2 \ltimes [y \neq 1]\,;[x = 1] \wedge T_1 \uparrow x\}\; T_1 \mapsto \mathsf{STORE}(x, 1)\; \{T_2 \ltimes [y \neq 1]\,;[x = 1]\}$$

(an instance of St-Other1) as well as the following (by St-Other2):

$$\left\{\begin{matrix} T_2 \ltimes [y \neq 1]\,;[x = 1] \\ \wedge T_1 \uparrow x \wedge T_1 \ltimes [x = 1] \end{matrix}\right\}\; T_1 \mapsto \mathsf{STORE}(y, 1)\; \{T_2 \ltimes [y \neq 1]\,;[x = 1]\}$$

Independent-Reads-of-Independent-Writes. Our next litmus test IRIW (see Fig. 7) gives an example of a proof outline which is only valid for SC and TSO (as the employed proof rules are all sound in SC and TSO, but one rule is not sound for SRA, see Sect. 7). IRIW is typically employed to show differences in the behaviour of multi-copy atomic and non multi-copy atomic memory models. In IRIW, we have two writer and two reader threads, the two readers reading values of x and y in opposite order. When IRIW runs on a memory model guaranteeing multi-copy atomicity, the threads T_2 and T_3 either both see

$$\{[x = 0] \wedge [y = 0] \wedge f = 0 \wedge g = 0\}$$

Thread T_1

$$\left\{\begin{matrix} T_2 \ltimes [x = 0] \\ \wedge T_3 \ltimes [x = 0] \\ \wedge T_1 \uparrow x \end{matrix}\right\}$$
$\mathsf{STORE}(x, 1);$
$\{true\}$

$\|$

Thread T_4

$$\left\{\begin{matrix} T_2 \ltimes [y = 0] \\ \wedge T_3 \ltimes [y = 0] \\ \wedge T_4 \uparrow y \end{matrix}\right\}$$
$\mathsf{STORE}(y, 1);$
$\{true\}$

$\|$

Thread T_2

$$\left\{\begin{matrix} (g = 3 \wedge c = 1 \Rightarrow T_2 \ltimes [y = 1]) \\ \wedge \neg(g = 0 \wedge f = 3) \\ \wedge g \in \{0, 3\} \wedge f \in \{0, 3\} \\ \wedge T_2 \ltimes [x = 0]; [x = 1 \wedge x.tid = T_1] \\ \wedge T_3 \ltimes [x = 0]; [x = 1 \wedge x.tid = T_1] \end{matrix}\right\}$$
$\langle a := \mathsf{LOAD}(x); f := 10 * f + 2\rangle$
$$\left\{\begin{matrix} (a = 1 \Rightarrow T_3 \ltimes [x = 1]) \\ \wedge (g = 3 \wedge c = 1 \Rightarrow T_2 \ltimes [y = 1]) \\ \wedge \neg(g = 0 \wedge f = 32) \\ \wedge g \in \{0, 3\} \wedge f \in \{2, 23, 32\} \end{matrix}\right\}$$
$\langle b := \mathsf{LOAD}(y); g := 10 * g + 2\rangle$
$$\left\{\begin{matrix} (a = 1 \Rightarrow T_3 \ltimes [x = 1]) \\ \wedge (g = 32 \wedge c = 1 \Rightarrow b = 1) \\ \wedge \neg(g = 2 \wedge f = 32) \\ \wedge \neg(g = 23 \wedge f = 32) \\ \wedge g \in \{2, 23, 32\} \\ \wedge f \in \{2, 23, 32\} \end{matrix}\right\}$$

$\|$

Thread T_3

$$\left\{\begin{matrix} (f = 2 \wedge a = 1 \Rightarrow T_3 \ltimes [x = 1]) \\ \wedge \neg(f = 0 \wedge g = 2) \\ \wedge g \in \{0, 2\} \wedge f \in \{0, 2\} \\ \wedge T_2 \ltimes [y = 0]; [y = 1 \wedge y.tid = T_4] \\ \wedge T_3 \ltimes [y = 0]; [y = 1 \wedge y.tid = T_4] \end{matrix}\right\}$$
$\langle c := \mathsf{LOAD}(y); g := 10 * g + 3\rangle$
$$\left\{\begin{matrix} (c = 1 \Rightarrow T_2 \ltimes [y = 1]) \\ \wedge (f = 2 \wedge a = 1 \Rightarrow T_3 \ltimes [x = 1]) \\ \wedge \neg(f = 0 \wedge g = 23) \\ \wedge g \in \{3, 23, 32\} \wedge f \in \{0, 2\} \end{matrix}\right\}$$
$\langle d := \mathsf{LOAD}(x); f := 10 * f + 3\rangle$
$$\left\{\begin{matrix} (c = 1 \Rightarrow y = 1) \\ \wedge (f = 23 \wedge a = 1 \Rightarrow d = 1) \\ \wedge \neg(f = 3 \wedge g = 23) \\ \wedge \neg(f = 32 \wedge g = 23) \\ \wedge g \in \{3, 23, 32\} \\ \wedge f \in \{3, 23, 32\} \end{matrix}\right\}$$

$$\{(a = 1 \wedge c = 1) \Rightarrow b = 1 \vee d = 1\}$$

Fig. 7. Piccolo proof of IRIW using $[x = 0]$ as shorthand for $\tau \ltimes [x = 0]$ for all τ

the write to x before the one to y or the other way around. In the first case, since the two reads in each thread are in program order, if $a = 1$ and $c = 1$ then T_3 has to see the write to x when reading from it. Hence, then $d = 1$. Equally, in the second case $b = 1$ when $a = 1$ and $c = 1$. Both cases together are described in the postcondition of Fig. 7 ($\{(a = 1 \wedge c = 1) \Rightarrow b = 1 \vee d = 1\}$).

Again, we use the notation $T_k.i$ to describe the i'th assertion in thread T_k. For reasoning about IRIW (and thus construct a proof outline) we need to describe the possible orders in which the two reads can happen. To this end, we employ two auxiliary variables [32] here, f (for orderings on reads of x) and g (for y). These are set atomically together with their respective load instructions. If at the end of the program, auxiliary

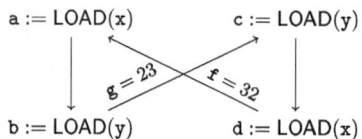

Fig. 8. Impossible reading order and values of auxiliary variables

variable f is 23, this means that thread T_2 has read from x before T_3 did. Therefore, $f = 23$ and $a = 1$ implies $d = 1$ (see line 2 of $T_3.3$). In the case where $f = 32$ at the end of the program, T_3 has read from x first. Analogously, auxiliary variable g describes the ordering of reads from y.

The proof outline contains several assertions detailing possible values of the two auxiliary variables and the registers. They basically state that certain orders of reads and thus certain combinations of values of registers a, b, c and d are excluded. In particular, we cannot have the ordering (cycle) depicted by the graph in Fig. 8, and hence we cannot have $g = 23 \wedge f = 32$ at the end of the program. We use this fact in our proof outline as for example seen in $T_2.3$.

Next, we exemplarily show one correctness check required for showing validity of the proof outline, namely the non-interference of $T_2.1$ with respect to the store in T_1, i.e. proving $\{T_1.1 \wedge T_2.1\}T_1 \mapsto \mathrm{STORE}(x, 1)\{T_2.1\}$. Its pre-assertion can be weakened to

$$\left\{ \begin{array}{l} T_2 \ltimes [x = 0] \wedge T_3 \ltimes [x = 0] \wedge T_1 \uparrow x \\ \wedge (g = 3 \wedge c = 1 \Rightarrow T_2 \ltimes [y = 1]) \wedge \neg(g = 0 \wedge f = 3) \wedge g \in \{0, 3\} \wedge f \in \{0, 3\} \end{array} \right\}$$

For the upper part of the assertion we apply the ST-OTHER1-rule twice and get

$$\left\{ \begin{array}{l} T_2 \ltimes [x = 0] \wedge T_3 \ltimes [x = 0] \\ \wedge T_1 \uparrow x \end{array} \right\} T_1 \mapsto \mathrm{STORE}(x, 1) \left\{ \begin{array}{l} T_2 \ltimes [x = 0]; [x = 1 \wedge x.\mathrm{tid} = T_1] \\ \wedge T_3 \ltimes [x = 0]; [x = 1 \wedge x.\mathrm{tid} = T_1] \end{array} \right\}$$

Since neither c, f, g nor y are changed by the store instruction, the STABLE-ST-rule tells us that the lower part of the assertion remains unchanged.

The key rule making this proof outline sound for TSO (and SC[4]) but not for SRA is MCA. We need MCA to show the local correctness of $\langle a := \mathrm{LOAD}(x); f := 10 * f + 2\rangle$ (analogous for $\langle c := \mathrm{LOAD}(y); g := 10 * g + 3\rangle$). For this, we prove

---

[4] A pure SC version of the proof outline has been checked with the proof assistant Isabelle using the encoding of the Owicki-Gries framework [30].

$\{T_2.1\}T_2 \mapsto \langle a := \mathsf{LOAD}(x); f := 10 * f + 2\rangle\{T_2.2\}$ by dividing the pre-assertion in two parts. For the first part

$$\{T_2 \ltimes [x = 0]; [x = 1 \wedge x.\mathtt{tid} = T_1] \wedge T_3 \ltimes [x = 0]; [x = 1 \wedge x.\mathtt{tid} = T_1]\}$$

we apply the MCA-rule and receive (eliding the id of the executing thread)

$$\left\{\begin{matrix} T_2 \ltimes [x = 0]; [x = 1 \wedge x.\mathtt{tid} = T_1] \wedge \\ T_3 \ltimes [x = 0]; [x = 1 \wedge x.\mathtt{tid} = T_1] \end{matrix}\right\} \langle a := \mathsf{LOAD}(x); f := 10 * f + 2\rangle \left\{\begin{matrix} a = 1 \Rightarrow \\ T_3 \ltimes [x = 1] \end{matrix}\right\}$$

For the second part, by applying the rules STABLE-ST and SUBST, we get

$$\left\{\begin{matrix} (g = 3 \wedge c = 1 \Rightarrow T_2 \ltimes [y = 1]) \\ \wedge \neg (g = 0 \wedge f = 3) \\ \wedge g \in \{0, 3\} \wedge f \in \{0, 3\} \end{matrix}\right\} \left\langle\begin{matrix} a := \mathsf{LOAD}(x); \\ f := 10 * f + 2 \end{matrix}\right\rangle \left\{\begin{matrix} (g = 3 \wedge c = 1 \Rightarrow T_2 \ltimes [y = 1]) \\ \wedge \neg (g = 0 \wedge f = 32) \\ \wedge g \in \{0, 3\} \wedge f \in \{2, 32\} \end{matrix}\right\}$$

By combining the two Hoare-triples and weaken $f \in \{2, 32\}$ to $f \in \{2, 23, 32\}$ we show local correctness.

6 Lifting SC and TSO to Potentials

The previous section has introduced a proof calculus for Piccolo which allows to construct proof outlines and thus enables reasoning over concurrent programs on weak memory models. The validity of proof outlines for a specific memory model depends on the soundness of the employed rules within the memory model. To this end, we first of all need to *lift* states of memory models to the level of potentials (and thus to Piccolo), which we will next do for SC and TSO.

$$\frac{l = R(x, v_R) \qquad v_R = val_\sigma(\tau, x)}{\sigma \xrightarrow{\tau, l}_{\mathsf{TSO}} \sigma} \qquad \frac{l = W(x, v_W) \qquad fresh_\sigma(\tau, q)}{\sigma \xrightarrow{\tau, l}_{\mathsf{TSO}} \langle \sigma.s, \sigma.wb[\tau \mapsto \sigma.wb(\tau) \cdot \langle\langle x, v_W, q\rangle\rangle]\rangle}$$

$$\frac{l = \mathsf{flush} \qquad wb(\tau) = \langle\langle x, v, q\rangle\rangle \cdot w \qquad nextFlush_\sigma(\tau)}{\sigma \xrightarrow{l}_{\mathsf{TSO}} \langle \sigma.s[x \mapsto \langle v, \tau, q\rangle], \sigma.wb[\tau \mapsto w]\rangle}$$

Fig. 9. Operational semantics of prophetic TSO using colours to highlight the updated shared memory and write buffer components

SC Memory Model. To interpret Piccolo formulae on SC states, we provide a mapping $map_{\mathsf{SC}} : \mathsf{SC.Q} \to \mathcal{P}$. For SC, Aux is empty and every thread sees the same one value only. Thus, we define:

$$map_{\mathsf{SC}}(m) \triangleq \lambda\tau.\{\langle\lambda x.\langle m(x).\mathtt{val}, m(x).\mathtt{tid}\rangle\rangle\}$$

Let γ be a register store and φ a Piccolo formula. Then $\langle\gamma, m\rangle \models \varphi$ is defined as $\langle\gamma, map_{\mathsf{SC}}(m)\rangle \models \varphi$. In the memory model SC, all proof rules of Fig. 6 are sound (see §7) and assertions of Piccolo are stable under internal memory transitions (since there are none).

TSO Memory Model. Next, we consider TSO [31,35], for this define an operational semantics for TSO and derive potentials out of TSO states. We base our semantics on the prophetic, timestamp-based version given in [14].

Operational Semantics. TSO has one memory-model internal action which is a flush, i.e. $\mathsf{TSO}.\Theta \triangleq \{\mathsf{flush}\}$. A state $\sigma = \langle s, wb \rangle$ in prophetic TSO consists of the shared memory $s : \mathsf{Loc} \to (\mathsf{Val} \times \mathsf{Tid} \times \mathbb{Q}^+)$ (recording value, writing thread and timestamp) and write buffers wb for all threads. The entries in write buffers record the location, written value and timestamp (to determine the order in which writes are flushed to shared memory). Together, $\mathsf{TSO}.\mathsf{Q} \triangleq (\mathsf{Loc} \to (\mathsf{Val} \times \mathsf{Tid} \times \mathbb{Q}^+)) \times (\mathsf{Tid} \to (\mathsf{Loc} \times \mathsf{Val} \times \mathbb{Q}^+)^*)$. Initially, we have $\mathsf{TSO}.\mathsf{Q}_0 \triangleq (\lambda x. \langle 0, \mathsf{T}_0, 0 \rangle, \lambda \tau. \langle \rangle)$ where T_0 is the thread initializing shared locations.

The transition relation $\to_{\mathsf{TSO}}$ is given in Fig. 9. The read transition needs to determine the value which thread τ can read in state σ for location x (either from its own write buffer or from shared memory):

$$val_\sigma(\tau, x) \triangleq \text{if } x \in \sigma.wb(\tau) \text{ then } wbVal_\sigma(\tau, x) \text{ else } \sigma.s(x)$$

with $wbVal_\sigma(\tau, x)$ a partial function extracting values out of write buffers. It is defined iff $\langle x, \_, \_ \rangle \in wb(\tau)$. If defined, we have $wbVal_\sigma(\tau, x) \triangleq \mathsf{last}((\sigma.wb(\tau))_{|x}).\mathsf{val}$, where $\mathsf{last}((\sigma.wb(\tau))_{|x})$ extracts the last entry for x in the write buffer of τ.

The write transition is writing the value to the writer's write buffer and to this end has to choose a new timestamp (which determines the time of flushing). The timestamp has to be larger than any other timestamp of writes of this thread, larger than all timestamps of entries in shared memory and different from any other timestamp:

$$fresh_\sigma(\tau, q) \triangleq (\forall x \in \mathsf{Loc}.\ \sigma.s(x).\mathsf{ts} < q) \wedge$$
$$(\forall \pi \in \mathsf{Tid}.\ \langle \_, \_, q \rangle \notin \sigma.wb(\pi)) \wedge (\forall \langle \_, \_, q' \rangle \in \sigma.wb(\tau).\ q > q')$$

Finally, flushing needs to determine which write buffer entry to flush next.

$$nextFlush_\sigma(\tau) \triangleq \exists q.\ \langle \_, \_, q \rangle = \sigma.wb(\tau)[1] \wedge$$
$$\forall \pi \in \mathsf{Tid}\backslash\{\tau\}.\forall \langle \_, \_, q' \rangle \in \sigma.wb(\pi).\ q' > q$$

Potentials of TSO States. For TSO, the auxiliary information Aux in the potentials concerns timestamps, i.e. $\mathsf{Aux} = \mathbb{Q}^+$. A state in prophetic TSO determines one potential per thread. In this, the ordering in which a thread sees values of shared locations depends on the timestamps. The first potential store thread τ sees in a state σ is fixed by shared memory and its own write buffer.

$$\Delta_\tau(\sigma) : \mathsf{Loc} \rightarrow (\mathsf{Val} \times \mathsf{Tid} \times \mathbb{Q}^+)$$
$$x \mapsto \langle val_\sigma(\tau, x), tid_\sigma(\tau, x), ts_\sigma(\tau, x) \rangle$$

where we let $tid_\sigma(\tau, x) \triangleq$ **if** $x \in \sigma.wb(\tau)$ **then** τ **else** $\sigma.s(x).\mathtt{tid}$ and $ts_\sigma(\tau, x) \triangleq$ **if** $x \in \sigma.wb(\tau)$ **then** $\mathsf{last}((\sigma.wb(\tau))_{|x}).\mathtt{ts}$ **else** $\sigma.s(x).\mathtt{ts}$.

With this at hand, we can define a mapping which relates prophetic TSO states to entire potentials: $map_{\mathsf{TSO}} : \mathsf{TSO}.\mathbb{Q} \rightarrow \mathcal{P}$ is defined as

$$map_{\mathsf{TSO}}(\sigma)(\tau) \triangleq \{mkLst(\sigma)(\tau)\}$$

where $mkLst(\sigma)(\tau) \triangleq$ **if** $\sigma \xrightarrow{\text{flush}}_{\mathsf{TSO}} \sigma'$ **then** $\langle \Delta_\tau(\sigma) \rangle \cdot mkLst(\sigma')(\tau)$ **else** $\langle \Delta_\tau(\sigma) \rangle$. This definition recursively builds a potential by flushing the next entry in a state σ and then constructing the next element of a list. The else case applies when all write buffers are empty.

Alike SC, we can now fix $\langle \gamma, \sigma \rangle \models \varphi$ to be $\langle \gamma, map_{\mathsf{TSO}}(\sigma) \rangle \models \varphi$. All assertions of Piccolo are stable under internal memory transition flush.

7 Soundness of Rules in Memory Models

With the lifting for SC and TSO at hand, we can formally study the soundness of Piccolo proof rules for our three memory models, SC, TSO and SRA. A proof rule $\{\varphi\}\tau \mapsto c\{\psi\}$ is sound for a memory model MM if for all states $\langle \gamma, m \rangle$ satisfying φ and all states $\langle \gamma', m' \rangle$ reached by executing c in MM, the formula ψ is true in $\langle \gamma', m' \rangle$.

Sequential Consistency. As already stated, we get:

Theorem 1. *Rules* STABLE-LD, STABLE-ST, SUBST, ST-OWN, ST-OTHER1, ST-OTHER2, LD-SINGLE, LD-SHIFT *and* MCA *are sound for* SC.

The proof is straightforward and therefore elided. Moreover, we have a stronger proof rule for store instructions, reflecting the essential property of sequential consistency: all threads directly see written values.

$$\text{ST-SC} \; \frac{}{\{true\}\tau \mapsto \mathsf{STORE}(x, e)\{\pi \ltimes [x = e]\}}$$

Total Store Ordering. For TSO, we get:

Theorem 2. *Rules* STABLE-LD, STABLE-ST, SUBST, ST-OWN, ST-OTHER1, ST-OTHER2, LD-SINGLE, LD-SHIFT *and* MCA *are sound for* SC. *Rule* ST-SC *is not sound for* TSO.

Proof. Due to space restrictions, we only provide a proof sketch for one rule here, the rule MCA. Let $\langle \gamma, \sigma \rangle \models \pi_i \ltimes [x \neq e]; [x = e \wedge x.\mathtt{tid} = \tau]$, i.e., there are lists L^i s.t. $mkLst(\sigma)(\pi_i) = L^i$ and exists L_1^i, L_2^i with $L^i = L_1^i \cdot L_2^i$ and $\langle \gamma, L_1^i \rangle \models [x \neq e]$ and $\langle \gamma, L_2^i \rangle \models [x = e \wedge x.\mathtt{tid} = \tau]$. If $a = e$ after loading x by π_1, then at least L_2^1 has to be non-empty. Moreover, L_1^1 has to be empty because load instructions read the value $val_\sigma(\pi_1, x)$ and by definition of $mkLst$ this is the entry for x in the first potential store. The question is thus why L_1^2 has to be empty as well.

If $\pi_1 \ltimes [x = e \wedge x.\mathtt{tid} = \tau]$ holds and $\tau \neq \pi_1$, then $\sigma.s(x).\mathtt{val} = e$ and $\sigma.s(x).\mathtt{tid} = \tau$. Moreover, for all σ' such that $\sigma \xrightarrow{\mathsf{flush}}_{\mathsf{TSO}} {}^* \sigma'$ this holds as well. Hence, $\pi_2 \ltimes [x = e \wedge x.\mathtt{tid} = \tau]$ by definition of $mkLst$ and L_1^2 is empty. $\square$

Strong Release-Acquire. As SRA already has an operational semantics with potentials as semantic domain, no lifting is required here and we get:

Theorem 3. *Rules* STABLE-LD, STABLE-ST, SUBST, ST-OWN, ST-OTHER1, ST-OTHER2, LD-SINGLE *and* LD-SHIFT *are sound for* SRA. *Rules* MCA *and* ST-SC *are not sound for* SRA.

Proof. The soundness follows from [25]. Rule MCA is not sound for SRA, because SRA is not multi-copy atomic. As an example, consider a state $\mathcal{D}$ in which both π_1 and π_2 can see $[x = 0]; [x = 1]$ (and for both intervals the lists are non-empty). Now assume step LOSE makes $\mathcal{D}(\pi_1)$ lose the entire list with $[x = 0]$. Then it can load x and read 1, whereas π_2 is still able to see the old value 0. $\square$

Knowing the soundness of rules, we get:

Theorem 4. *The proof outline in Fig. 1 is valid for* SC, TSO *and* SRA. *The proof outline in Fig. 7 is valid for* SC *and* TSO, *but not for* SRA.

8   Conclusion

This paper proposes the use of the domain of potentials and the logic Piccolo to build unified proof calculi for concurrent programs on weak memory models. As future work, we see the study of other memory models and semantics (like C11 [26], PSO [2]) and the treatment of read-modify-write operations. We do not expect our technique to be applicable to promise-based semantics [20, 36], though. We furthermore aim at developing tool support for reasoning, e.g. as in [12] or [33].

References

1. dve, S.V., Boehm, H.J.: Memory Models. In: Padua, D. (eds.) Encyclopedia of Parallel Computing, pp. 1107–1110. Springer (2011). https://doi.org/10.1007/978-0-387-09766-4_419
2. Adve, S.V., Gharachorloo, K.: Shared memory consistency models: a tutorial. Computer **29**(12), 66–76 (1996). https://doi.org/10.1109/2.546611

3. Alglave, J., Cousot, P.: Ogre and Pythia: an invariance proof method for weak consistency models. In: Castagna, G., Gordon, A.D. (eds.) POPL, pp. 3–18. ACM (2017). https://doi.org/10.1145/3009837.3009883

4. Alglave, J., Maranget, L., Tautschnig, M.: Herding cats: modelling, simulation, testing, and data mining for weak memory. ACM Trans. Program. Lang. Syst. **36**(2), 7:1-7:74 (2014). https://doi.org/10.1145/2627752

5. Apt, K.R., de Boer, F.S., Olderog, E.-R.: Verification of Sequential and Concurrent Programs. Texts in Computer Science. Springer (2009)

6. Bargmann, L., Wehrheim, H.: Lifting the reasoning level in generic weak memory verification. In: Herber, P., Wijs, A. (eds.) Integrated Formal Methods. iFM 2023. Lecture Notes in Computer Science, vol 14300. Springer, Cham (2023). https://doi.org/10.1007/978-3-031-47705-8_10

7. Bila, E.V., Dongol, B., Lahav, O., Raad, A., Wickerson, J.: View-based owicki–gries reasoning for persistent x86-TSO. In: ESOP 2022. LNCS, vol. 13240, pp. 234–261. Springer, Cham (2022). https://doi.org/10.1007/978-3-030-99336-8_9

8. Chaochen, Z., Hoare, C.A.R., Ravn, A.P.: A calculus of durations. Inf. Process. Lett. **40**(5), 269–276 (1991). https://doi.org/10.1016/0020-0190(91)90122-X

9. Coughlin, N., Winter, K., Smith, G.: Rely/guarantee reasoning for multicopy atomic weak memory models. In: Huisman, M., Păsăreanu, C., Zhan, N. (eds.) FM 2021. LNCS, vol. 13047, pp. 292–310. Springer, Cham (2021). https://doi.org/10.1007/978-3-030-90870-6_16

10. Coughlin, N., Winter, K., Smith, G.: Compositional reasoning for non-multicopy atomic architectures. Formal Aspects Comput. **35**(2), 8:1-8:0 (2023). https://doi.org/10.1145/3574137

11. Dalvandi, S., Doherty, S., Dongol, B., Wehrheim, H.: Owicki-Gries Reasoning for C11 RAR. In: Hirschfeld, R., Pape, T (eds.) ECOOP, LIPIcs, pp. 11:1–11:26. Schloss Dagstuhl - Leibniz-Zentrum für Informatik (2020). https://doi.org/10.4230/LIPIcs.ECOOP.2020.11

12. Dalvandi, S., Dongol, B., Doherty, S., Wehrheim, H.: Integrating Owicki-Gries for C11-style memory models into Isabelle/HOL. J. Autom. Reason. **66**(1), 141–171 (2022). https://doi.org/10.1007/S10817-021-09610-2

13. Dang, H.-H., Jourdan, J.-H., Kaiser, J.-O., Dreyer, D.: Rustbelt meets relaxed memory. Proc. ACM Program. Lang. **4**(POPL), 34:1–34:29 (2020). https://doi.org/10.1145/3371102

14. Doherty, S., Dalvandi, S., Dongol, B., Wehrheim, H.: Unifying operational weak memory verification: an axiomatic approach. ACM Trans. Comput. Log. **23**(4), 27:1-27:39 (2022). https://doi.org/10.1145/3545117

15. Flur, S., et al.: Modelling the ARMv8 architecture, operationally: Concurrency and ISA. In: Bodík, R., Majumdar, R. (eds.) POPL, pp. 608–621. ACM (2016). https://doi.org/10.1145/2837614.2837615

16. Gavrilenko, N., Ponce-de-León, H., Furbach, F., Heljanko, K., Meyer, R.: BMC for weak memory models: relation analysis for Compact SMT encodings. In: Dillig, I., Tasiran, S. (eds.) CAV 2019. LNCS, vol. 11561, pp. 355–365. Springer, Cham (2019). https://doi.org/10.1007/978-3-030-25540-4_19

17. Hoare, C.A.R.: An axiomatic basis for computer programming. Commun. ACM **12**(10), 576–580 (1969). https://doi.org/10.1145/363235.363259

18. Jones, C.B.: Tentative steps toward a development method for interfering programs. ACM Trans. Program. Lang. Syst. **5**(4), 596–619 (1983). https://doi.org/10.1145/69575.69577

19. Kaiser, J.-O., Dang, H.-H., Dreyer, D., Lahav, O., Vafeiadis, V.: Strong Logic for Weak Memory: Reasoning About Release-Acquire Consistency in Iris. In: Müller, P. (eds.) ECOOP, vol. 74. LIPIcs, pp. 17:1–17:29. Schloss Dagstuhl - Leibniz-Zentrum für Informatik (2017). https://doi.org/10.4230/LIPICS.ECOOP.2017.17

20. Kang, J., Hur, C.-K., Lahav, O., Vafeiadis, V., Dreyer, D.: A promising semantics for relaxed-memory concurrency. In: Castagna, G., Gordon, A.D. (eds.) POPL, pp. 175–189. ACM (2017). https://doi.org/10.1145/3009837.3009850

21. Kokologiannakis, M., Lahav, O., Vafeiadis, V.: Kater: Automating weak memory model metatheory and consistency checking. Proc. ACM Program. Lang. 7(POPL), 544–572 (2023). https://doi.org/10.1145/3571212

22. Kokologiannakis, M., Vafeiadis, V.: GENMC: a model checker for weak memory models. In: Silva, A., Leino, K.R.M. (eds.) CAV 2021. LNCS, vol. 12759, pp. 427–440. Springer, Cham (2021). https://doi.org/10.1007/978-3-030-81685-8_20

23. Lahav, O., Boker, U.: Decidable verification under a causally consistent shared memory. In: Donaldson, A.F., Torlak, E. (eds.) PLDI, pp. 211–226. ACM (2020). https://doi.org/10.1145/3385412.3385966

24. Lahav, O., Boker, U.: What's decidable about causally consistent shared memory? ACM Trans. Program. Lang. Syst. 44(2), 8:1–8:55 (2022). https://doi.org/10.1145/3505273

25. Lahav, O., Dongol, B., Wehrheim, H.: Rely-guarantee reasoning for causally consistent shared memory. In: Enea, C., Lal, A. (eds.) CAV, vol. 13964. LNCS, pp. 206–229. Springer (2023). https://doi.org/10.1007/978-3-031-37706-8_11

26. Lahav, O., Giannarakis, N., Vafeiadis, V.: Taming release-acquire consistency. In: Bodík, R., Majumdar, R. (eds.)POPL, pp. 649–662. ACM (2016). https://doi.org/10.1145/2837614.2837643

27. Lahav, O., Vafeiadis, V.: Owicki-Gries reasoning for weak memory models. In: Halldórsson, M.M., Iwama, K., Kobayashi, N., Speckmann, B. (eds.) ICALP 2015. LNCS, vol. 9135, pp. 311–323. Springer, Heidelberg (2015). https://doi.org/10.1007/978-3-662-47666-6_25

28. Lamport, L.: How to make a multiprocessor computer that correctly executes multiprocess programs. IEEE Trans. Computers 28(9), 690–691 (1979). https://doi.org/10.1109/TC.1979.1675439

29. Moszkowski, B.C.: A complete axiom system for propositional interval temporal logic with infinite time. Log. Methods Comput. Sci. 8(3) (2012). https://doi.org/10.2168/LMCS-8(3:10)2012

30. Nipkow, T., Nieto, L.P.: Owicki/Gries in Isabelle/HOL. In: Finance, J.-P. (ed.) FASE 1999. LNCS, vol. 1577, pp. 188–203. Springer, Heidelberg (1999). https://doi.org/10.1007/978-3-540-49020-3_13

31. Owens, S., Sarkar, S., Sewell, P.: A better x86 memory model: x86-TSO. In: Berghofer, S., Nipkow, T., Urban, C., Wenzel, M. (eds.) TPHOLs 2009. LNCS, vol. 5674, pp. 391–407. Springer, Heidelberg (2009). https://doi.org/10.1007/978-3-642-03359-9_27

32. Owicki, S.S., Gries, D.: An axiomatic proof technique for parallel programs I. Acta Inf. 6, 319–340 (1976). https://doi.org/10.1007/BF00268134

33. Raad, A., Lahav, O., Wickerson, J., Balcer, P., Dongol, B.: Intel PMDK transactions: specification, validation and concurrency. In: Weirich, S. (eds.) ESOP, vol. 14577 LNCS, pp.150–179. Springer (2024). https://doi.org/10.1007/978-3-031-57267-8_6

34. Ridge, T.: A rely-guarantee proof system for x86-TSO. In: Leavens, G.T., O'Hearn, P., Rajamani, S.K. (eds.) VSTTE 2010. LNCS, vol. 6217, pp. 55–70. Springer, Heidelberg (2010). https://doi.org/10.1007/978-3-642-15057-9_4

35. Sewell, P., Sarkar, S., Owens, S., Nardelli, F.Z., Myreen, M.O.: x86-TSO: a rigorous and usable programmer's model for x86 multiprocessors. Commun. ACM **53**(7), 89–97 (2010). https://doi.org/10.1145/1785414.1785443
36. Svendsen, K., Pichon-Pharabod, J., Doko, M., Lahav, O., Vafeiadis, V.: A separation logic for a promising semantics. In: Ahmed, A. (ed.) ESOP 2018. LNCS, vol. 10801, pp. 357–384. Springer, Cham (2018). https://doi.org/10.1007/978-3-319-89884-1_13
37. Simon Friis Vindum and Lars Birkedal: Spirea: a mechanized concurrent separation logic for weak persistent memory. Proc. ACM Program. Lang. **7**(OOPSLA2), 632–657 (2023). https://doi.org/10.1145/3622820
38. Wickerson, J., Batty, M., Sorensen, T., Constantinides, G.A.: Automatically comparing memory consistency models. In: Castagna, G., Gordon, A.D (eds.) POPL, pp. 190–204. ACM (2017). https://doi.org/10.1145/3009837.3009838
39. Wright, D., Dalvandi, S., Batty, M., Dongol, B.: Mechanised operational reasoning for C11 programs with relaxed dependencies. Formal Aspects Comput. **35**(2), 10:1–10:27 (2023). https://doi.org/10.1145/3580285
40. Xu, Q., de Roever, W.P., He, J.: The Rely-Guarantee Method for Verifying Shared Variable Concurrent Programs. Formal Aspects Comput. **9**(2), 149–174 (1997). https://doi.org/10.1007/BF01211617

Proving Functional Program Equivalence via Directed Lemma Synthesis

Yican Sun[1], Ruyi Ji[1], Jian Fang[1], Xuanlin Jiang[1], Mingshuai Chen[3],
and Yingfei Xiong[1,2(✉)]

[1] Key Laboratory of High Confidence Software Technologies (Peking University),
Ministry of Education; School of Computer Science, Peking University, Beijing, China
{sycpku,jiruyi910387714}@pku.edu.cn, {fangjian,xljiang}@stu.pku.edu.cn
[2] Zhongguancun Laboratory, Beijing, China
xiongyf@pku.edu.cn
[3] Zhejiang University, Hangzhou, China
m.chen@zju.edu.cn

Abstract. Proving equivalence between functional programs is a fundamental problem in program verification, which often amounts to reasoning about *algebraic data types* (ADTs) and compositions of *structural recursions*. Modern theorem provers provide *structural induction* for such reasoning, but a structural induction on the original theorem is often insufficient for many equivalence theorems. In such cases, one has to invent a set of lemmas, prove these lemmas by additional induction, and use these lemmas to prove the original theorem. There is, however, a lack of systematic understanding of what lemmas are needed for inductive proofs and how these lemmas can be synthesized automatically. This paper presents *directed lemma synthesis*, an effective approach to automating equivalence proofs by discovering critical lemmas using program synthesis techniques. We first identify two *induction-friendly* forms of propositions that give formal guarantees to the progress of the proof. We then propose two tactics that synthesize and apply lemmas, thereby transforming the proof goal into induction-friendly forms. Both tactics reduce lemma synthesis to a set of independent and typically small program synthesis problems that can be efficiently solved. Experimental results demonstrate the effectiveness of our approach: Compared to state-of-the-art equivalence checkers employing heuristic-based lemma enumeration, directed lemma synthesis saves 95.47% runtime on average and solves 38 more tasks over an extended version of the standard benchmark set.

Keywords: Program equivalence checking · Functional programs · Lemma synthesis

1 Introduction

Automatically proving the equivalence between functional programs is a fundamental problem in program verification. On the one hand, it is the basic way

© The Author(s) 2025
A. Platzer et al. (Eds.): FM 2024, LNCS 14933, pp. 538–557, 2025.
https://doi.org/10.1007/978-3-031-71162-6_28

to certify the correctness of optimizing functional programs. On the other hand, since modern theorem provers such as Isabelle [27], Coq [1], and Lean [22] are based on functional programming languages, many other verification problems reduce to reasoning about equivalence between functional programs.

The core of functional programming languages is built upon *algebraic data types* (ADTs). An ADT describes composite data structures by combining simpler types; it can be recursive when referring to itself in its own definition. ADTs are often processed by *structural recursions*, where recursive calls are invoked over the recursive substructures of the input value. As a result, the crux of verifying functional program equivalence is to reason about the *equivalence between composed structural recursions*, as demonstrated by the following example.

```
Inductive List = nil | cons Int List;

Let rev (l:List) =                    Let snoc (x:Int) (l:List) =
match l with                          match l with
| nil → nil                           | nil → cons x nil
| cons h t → snoc h (rev t)           | cons h t → cons h (snoc x t)
end;                                  end;

Let sort (l:List) =                   Let ins (x:Int) (l:List) =
match l with                          match l with
| nil → nil                           | nil → cons x nil
| cons h t → ins h (sort t)           | cons h t →
end;                                      if x ≤ h then cons x l
                                          else cons h (ins x t)
Let sum (l:List) =                    end;
match y with
| nil → 0
| cons h t → h + (sum t)
end;
```

Fig. 1. An algebraic data type and structurally recursive functions.

Example 1. Fig. 1 depicts a common ADT List with two constructors, nil and cons, and standard structurally recursive functions, rev that reverses a list, sort that applies insertion sort, and sum that calculates the sum of a list. Functions snoc and ins are for implementing these functions. We are interested in proving that summing a list after reverse is the equivalent of summing a list after sorting:

$$\forall\, xs : \mathtt{List}.\quad \mathtt{sum\ (rev\ xs)} \ = \ \mathtt{sum\ (sort\ xs)}\ . \tag{$\dagger$}$$

To prove the equivalence, it is natural to apply *structural induction*, which has been integrated into modern theorem provers. A structural induction certifies that proposition $P(x)$ holds for every instance x of some ADT by showing that $P(x)$ holds for each possible constructor of x, assuming the *induction hypothesis* that $P(x')$ holds for the substructure x' of x. For example, a structural induction for ($\dagger$) requires to prove two subgoals, each corresponds to a constructor of

List. The first subgoal is to show (†) holds when `xs = nil`. The second subgoal induces the following inductive hypothesis.

$$\text{sum (rev t)} = \text{sum (sort t)} . \tag{IH}$$

Proposition (†) holds for the `cons` case if: (†) is true, assuming `xs = cons h t` and (IH).   ◁

Challenge: Lemma Finding. Nonetheless, *many theorems cannot be proved by only induction over the original theorem* [12]. Example 1 is such a case: Its proof requires induction, but induction over (†) is insufficient since we cannot apply the inductive hypothesis (IH); see the full version [34] for a formal proof. To apply (IH), we have to transform (†) until there is a subterm matching either the left-hand-side (LHS) or right-hand-side (RHS) of (IH), such that we can apply (IH) to rewrite the transformed formula. However, such a subterm can never be derived through a deductive transformation (Details in Sect. 2)

In such cases, it is necessary to invent a set of lemmas, prove these lemmas by additional induction, and use these lemmas to prove the original proposition. Accordingly, the proof process boils down to (i) *lemma finding*, and (ii) *deductive reasoning with the aid of lemmas*. Whereas decision procedures for deductive reasoning have been extensively studied [3,21,25], *there is still a lack of systematic understanding of what lemmas are needed for inductive proofs and how these lemmas can be synthesized automatically*.

Due to the lack of theoretical understanding, many existing automatic proof approaches resort to *heuristic-based lemma enumeration* [4,7,11,20,26,29–32]. These approaches typically work as follows: (i) use heuristics to rank all possible lemma candidates in a syntactic space (the heuristics are commonly based on certain machine-learning models or the textual similarity to the original proposition), (ii) enumerate the candidates by rank and (iii) try to prove each lemma candidate and certify the original proposition using the lemma. Since there is no guarantee that the lemma candidates are helpful in advancing the proof, such solvers may waste time trying useless candidates, thus leading to inefficiency. For Example 1, the enumeration-based solver HIPSPEC [4] produces lemma ∀xs. `rev (rev xs) = xs`, which provides little help to the proof.

Approach. We present *directed lemma synthesis* to avoid enumerating useless lemmas. From Example 1, we can see that the key to the inductive proof lies in the *effective application* of the inductive hypothesis. Based on this observation, we identify two syntactic forms of propositions that guarantee the effective application of the inductive hypothesis, termed *induction-friendly forms*. Next, we propose two tactics that synthesize and apply lemmas. The lemmas synthesized by our tactics take the form of an equation, with one of its sides matching a term in the original proposition, and can be used to transform the original proposition by rewriting the matched term into the other side of the lemma. Consequently, the current proof goal splits into two subgoals – one for proving the transformed proposition and the other for proving the synthesized lemma itself. Our tactics have the following properties:

- *Progress*: The new proof goals after applying our tactics eventually fall into one of the induction-friendly forms. That is, compared with existing directionless lemma enumeration, our synthesis procedure is *directed*: it eventually produces subgoals that admit effective applications of the inductive hypothesis.
- *Efficiency*: The lemma synthesis problem in our tactics can be reduced to a set of independent and typically small *program synthesis* problems, thereby allowing an off-the-shelf program synthesizer to efficiently solve the problems.

Based on the two tactics, we propose AUTOPROOF, an automated approach to proving the equivalence between functional programs by *combining any existing decision procedure with our two tactics for directed lemma synthesis*.

For Example 1, AUTOPROOF synthesizes the lemma

$$\forall \, \mathtt{xs} : \mathtt{List.} \quad \mathtt{sum \ (rev \ xs)} \ = \ \mathtt{sum \ xs} \, ,$$

where the LHS matches the LHS of the original proposition (†). Therefore, we can use this lemma to rewrite (†) into

$$\forall \, \mathtt{xs} : \mathtt{List.} \quad \mathtt{sum \ xs} \ = \ \mathtt{sum \ (sort \ xs)} \, .$$

As will be shown later, both equations above fall into the first induction-friendly form, thus ensuring the application of the inductive hypothesis.

Evaluation. We have implemented AUTOPROOF on top of CVC4IND [30] – the available state-of-the-art equivalence checker with heuristic-based lemma enumeration. We conduct experiments on the program equivalence subset of an extended version of the standard benchmark in automated inductive reasoning. The results show that, compared with the original CVC4IND, our directed lemma synthesis saves 95.47% runtime on average and help solve 38 more tasks.

Contributions. The main contributions of this paper include the follows.

- The idea of *directed lemma synthesis*, i.e., synthesizing lemmas to transform the proof goal into desired forms.
- Two *induction-friendly forms* that guarantee the effective application of the inductive hypothesis, as well as two *tactics* that synthesize and apply lemmas to transform the proof goal into these forms. The lemma synthesis in our tactics can be reduced to a set of independent and typically small synthesis problems, ensuring the efficiency of the lemma synthesis.
- The implementation and evaluation of our approach, demonstrating the effectiveness of our approach in synthesizing lemmas to improve the state-of-the-art decision procedures.

Due to space limitations, we relegate the details to the full version [34].

2   Motivation and Approach Overview

In this section, we illustrate AUTOPROOF over examples. For simplicity, we consider only structurally recursive functions with one parameter in this section.

A Warm-up Example. To begin with, let us first consider an equation where the direct structural induction yields an effective application of the inductive hypothesis.

$$\forall \texttt{xs} : \texttt{List}. \quad \texttt{sum (rev xs)} \ = \ \texttt{sum xs} \qquad\qquad (\dagger_W)$$

To prove this equation, we conduct a structural induction on xs, the ADT argument that the structural recursion traverses, resulting in two cases xs = nil and xs = cons h t. The first case is trivial, and in the second case, we have an inductive hypothesis over the tail list t.

$$\texttt{sum (rev t)} \ = \ \texttt{sum t} \qquad\qquad (\text{IH}_W)$$

We first use the equation xs = cons h t to rewrite the original proposition $(\dagger_W)$, and obtain the following equation.

$$\texttt{sum (rev (cons h t))} \ = \ \texttt{sum (cons h t)}$$

Here sum and rev are both structural recursions, which use pattern matching to choose different branches based on the constructor of xs. With xs replaced as cons h t, we can now proceed with the pattern matching and obtain the following equation.

$$\texttt{sum (snoc h (rev t))} \ = \ \texttt{h + (sum t)} \qquad\qquad (1)$$

Now the equation contains a subterm sum t that matches the RHS of the inductive hypothesis (IH_W), which allows us to rewrite this equation with (IH_W), resulting in the following equation.

$$\texttt{sum (snoc h (rev t))} \ = \ \texttt{h + (sum (rev t))} \qquad\qquad (2)$$

There is a common "rev t" term on both sides of the equation above, and we can apply the standard generalization technique to replace it with a new fresh variable r, obtaining the following equation.

$$\texttt{sum (snoc h r)} \ = \ \texttt{h + (sum r)} \qquad\qquad (3)$$

This equation is simpler than the original one as snoc does not involve calls to other structurally recursive functions. By further applying induction on r, we can prove this equation.

We can see that the above proof contains two key steps: (i) using the inductive hypothesis to rewrite the equation, and (ii) using generalization to eliminate a common non-leaf subprogram. We call such two steps an *effective application* of the inductive hypothesis. Note that an effective application is guaranteed because the RHS of the original equation is a single structural recursion call, sum xs. Since a structural recursion applies itself to the substructure of the input, sum t is guaranteed to appear after reduction. Then, we can use the inductive hypothesis to rewrite, and the rewritten RHS contains rev t. Similarly, the inner-most function call, rev xs, is guaranteed to reduce to rev t. Therefore, a generalization is guaranteed.

Induction-Friendly Forms. In general, we identify *induction-friendly* forms, where for every equation in this form, there exists a variable such that performing induction on it yields an effective application of the inductive hypothesis for the cases involving a recursive substructure. From the discussion above, we have the simplified version of the first induction-friendly form.

(F0) *(Simplified (F1))*. One side of the equation is a single call to a structurally recursive function.

A Harder Example. Now let us consider the example equation (†) we have seen in Sect. 1. Recall this equation as follows.

$$\forall \, \mathtt{xs} : \mathtt{List.} \quad \mathtt{sum \; (rev \; xs)} \; = \; \mathtt{sum \; (sort \; xs)}$$

Since neither side of (†) is a single call to a structurally recursive function, this equation does not fall into (F0), and indeed, the induction over it will get stuck. To see this point, let us still consider the x = cons h t case, where the inductive hypothesis (IH) is as follows, which we have seen in Sect. 1.

$$\mathtt{sum \; (rev \; t)} \; = \; \mathtt{sum \; (sort \; t)}$$

By rewriting and reducing the original proposition with x = cons h t, we get the following equation.

$$\mathtt{sum \; (snoc \; h \; (rev \; t))} \; = \; \mathtt{sum \; (ins \; h \; (sort \; t))}$$

Unfortunately, neither side of (IH) appears, disabling the application of the inductive hypothesis. In fact, we can formally prove that this proposition cannot be proved by only induction over the original proposition [34].

If we can transform the original proposition (†) into (F0), we can ensure to effectively apply the inductive hypothesis. One way to perform this transformation is to find an equation where one side of the equation is the same as one side of the original proposition, and the other side is a single call to a structurally recursive function. This leads to the lemma (L1), which we have seen in the introduction.

$$\forall \, \mathtt{xs} : \mathtt{List.} \quad \mathtt{sum \; (rev \; xs)} \; = \; \mathtt{sum \; xs} \tag{L1}$$

Rewriting (†) with (L1), we obtain (L2) we have seen.

$$\forall \, \mathtt{xs} : \mathtt{List.} \quad \mathtt{sum \; xs} \; = \; \mathtt{sum \; (sort \; xs)} \tag{L2}$$

Now the original proof goal (†) splits into (L1) and (L2), both conforming to (F0). Now we have the guarantee that the inductive hypothesis can be applied in the inductive proofs of both (L1) and (L2).

Automation. Most steps of the above transformation process can be easily automated, and the only difficult step is to find a suitable lemma. Based on the form of the lemma, the key is finding the structurally recursive function sum to be used on the RHS, equivalent to a known term sum ∘ rev on the LHS. In general, synthesizing a function from scratch may be difficult. However, synthesizing a structural recursion is significantly easier for the following two reasons. First, the template fixes a large fraction of codes in a structural recursion. In this example, the structural recursion over xs with the following template.

```
Let f xs =
    match xs with
    | nil → base
    | cons h t → Let r = f t in comb h r
    end;
```

where the only unknown parts are *base* and *comb*. Second, we can separate the expression for each constructor as an independent synthesis task. In this example, we have the following two independent synthesis tasks for the constructors nil and cons, respectively.

$$\text{sum (rev nil)} = base$$
$$\forall \text{ h t.   sum (rev (cons h t))} = comb \text{ h (sum (rev t))}$$

Existing program synthesizers (e.g., AUTOLIFTER [13] in our implementation) can easily solve both tasks. We get *base* = 0 and *comb* h r = h + r. Thus, f coincides with sum. An additional benefit is that a typical synthesizer requires a verifier to verify the synthesis result. Here, we can omit the verifier and rely on tests to validate the result. This does not affect the soundness of our approach since the synthesized lemma is proved recursively.

Tactic. Summarizing the above process, we obtain the first tactic. Given a proof goal that does not conform to (F0), this tactic splits it into two proof goals, both conforming to (F0). This tactic has two variants, which rewrite the LHS and the RHS, respectively. We give only the RHS version here. In more detail, given an equation $\forall \bar{x}.p_1(\bar{x}) = p_2(\bar{x})$ that does not satisfy (F0), our first tactic proceeds as follows.

Step 1. Derive a lemma template in the form of $\forall \bar{x}, p_2(\bar{x}) = f(\bar{x})$, where f is a structurally recursive function to be synthesized.
Step 2. Generate a set of synthesis problems and solve them to obtain f.
Step 3. Generate two proof goals, $\forall \bar{x}.p_1(\bar{x}) = f(\bar{x})$ and $\forall \bar{x}.f(\bar{x}) = p_2(\bar{x})$.

Overall Process. Our approach AUTOPROOF combines any deductive solver with the two tactics to prove equivalence between functional programs. Given an equation, our approach first invokes the deductive solver to prove the equation. If the deductive solver fails to prove, we check if the equation is in an induction-friendly form and apply induction to generate new proof goals. Otherwise, we check if any tactic can be applied, and apply the tactic to generate new proof goals. Finally, we recursively invoke our approach to the new proof goals. The workflow of solving our harder example (†) is illustrated in Fig. 2.

Towards the Full Approach. The tactic we present here attempts to transform a complex term into a single structural recursion, but it may not be possible

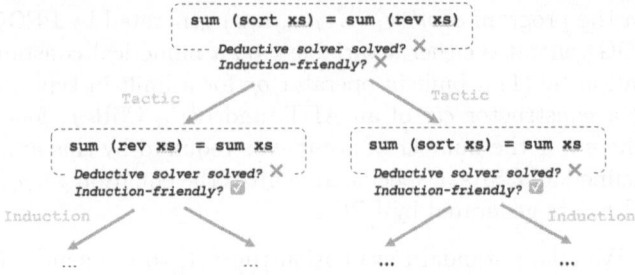

Fig. 2. Workflow of AUTOPROOF

in general. Thus, the full tactic transforms only a composition of two structural recursions into a single one each time, to significantly increase the chance of synthesis success.

Through out the section we consider only structurally recursive functions taking only one parameter, but there may be multiple ADT variables in general (e.g., proving the commutativity of natural number multiplications). Our second tactic deals with an issue caused by *inconsistent recursions*, that is, different recursions that traverse different ADT variables. Examples and details on this tactic can be found in Sect. 4.5.

3   Preliminary

This section presents the background of program equivalence checking. We first articulate the range of equivalence checking tasks. Throughout this paper, we use $p(v_1, \ldots, v_k)$ to denote a functional program p whose free variables range from $\{v_1, \ldots, v_k\}$.

Types. The family of types in AUTOPROOF consists of two disjoint parts: (1) the algebraic data types, and (ADTs) [28], and (2) the built-in types such as `Int` or `Bool`. For ease of presentation, we assume that there is only one built-in type `Int` for integers, and only one ADT for lists with integer elements. `List` has two constructors, `nil: List` for the empty list, and `cons: Int → List →` `List` that appends an integer at the head of a list. AUTOPROOF can be easily extended to handle all ADTs and more built-in types.

Syntax. As illustrated in Fig. 3, the specification for an equivalence checking task is generated by **SPEC**, where each task consists of two parts.

First, a specification defines a sequence of *canonical* structural recursions (CSRs), each generated by **CSRDef**. A CSR f is a function whose last argument is of an ADT. It applies pattern matching to the last argument v_k, which we call the *recursive argument*, and considers all top-level constructors of v_k. If $v_k = $ `nil`, i.e., an empty list, it invokes $base(v_1, \ldots, v_{k-1})$ generated by **PROG**. Otherwise, $v_k = $ `cons h t`. It recursively invokes itself over `t` with all other arguments unchanged, stores the result of the recursive call in `r`, and then combines the result via the program $comb(v_1 \ldots v_{k-1}, \mathbf{h}, \mathbf{r})$ generated by PROG. The non-terminal PROG generates either a variable *var*, a numerical constant *constant*, or an application by (1) a built-in operator *op* for a built-in type (e.g., $+, -, \times$ for Int), (2) a constructor *ctr* of an ADT, and (3) a CSR f, followed with k programs, where k is the number of arguments required by this application.

Having defined all CSRs, a specification gives the equation $\forall \bar{x}.p_1(\bar{x}) = p_2(\bar{x})$, where p_1 and p_2 are generated by PROG.

Semantics. We adapt standard evaluation rules [1] to the syntax (Fig. 3). We defer these details to the full version [34]. We use *term reduction* to refer to a single-step evaluation.

Abstraction. An *abstraction* is a syntactic transformation from a program p to another program p' performed in steps. In each step, given a program p, it introduces a fresh variable and replaces a subprogram of p with the fresh variable. For example, we can abstract the program p of sum (snoc (h + h) (rev t)) to p' of sum (snoc a b), which replaces (h + h) to a, and (rev t) to b.

Note that if p' is an abstraction of p, any transformation on p' yields another transformation on p by simply replacing each introduced fresh variable back with the corresponding subprogram. For example, the transformation from p' to a + (sum b) yields the transformation from p to (h + h) + sum (rev t).

$$
\begin{array}{rcl}
\text{SPEC} & ::= & \text{CSRDef}^* \; \forall \bar{x}.p_1 = p_2 \\
& & \text{where } p_1, p_2 \in \text{PROG} \\
\text{CSRDef} & ::= & \textbf{Let } f \; v_1 \; v_2 \ldots v_k = \\
& & \textbf{match } v_k \textbf{ with} \\
& & | \; \texttt{nil} \rightarrow base \\
& & | \; \texttt{cons h t} \rightarrow \textbf{Let } \mathbf{r} = f \; v_1 \ldots v_{k-1} \; \texttt{t in } comb \\
& & \textbf{end}; \\
& & \text{where } base, comb \in \text{PROG} \\
\text{PROG} & ::= & f \; \text{PROG}^* \mid ctr \; \text{PROG}^* \mid op \; \text{PROG}^* \mid var \mid const \\
& & \text{where } f \text{ is a CSR, } ctr \text{ is a constructor of ADT,} \\
& & const \text{ is a constant with the built-in type,} \\
& & op \text{ is a primitive operator, and } var \text{ is a free variable.}
\end{array}
$$

Fig. 3. Syntax of the surface language of AUTOPROOF.

Expressivity. Compared with widely-considered structural recursions [1], CSR has two additional restrictions. First, it applies pattern-matching to only one argument. Second, it keeps other parameters unchanged in recursive calls. However, we can transform any structural recursion into a composition of CSRs by refining *defunctionalization* [8]. Thus, restricting SRs to CSRs does not affect the expressivity of functional programs, see the full version [34] for details.

```
 1   class lemma_tactic:              11   # tactics: set of built-in
 2     # to be instantiated          12                tactics
 3     def precond(eq): pass         13   def Prove(pr,eq):
 4     def extract(eq): pass         14     if try_deductive(pr,eq) succeeds:
 5                                    15       return
 6     def t_apply(eq):              16     else:
 7       p's,v = extract(eq)         17       if induction-friendly(eq) then:
 8       lem = syn_lem(p's,v)        18         subgoals = split(pr,eq)
 9       eq' = apply_lem(eq, lem)    19         for sg in subgoals: Prove(sg)
10       return eq', lem             20         return
                                     21       for t in tactics:
                                     22         if t.precond(eq) then:
                                     23           eq',lem = t.t_apply(eq)
                                     24           Prove(pr,lem)
                                     25           Prove(pr.append(lem),eq')
                                     26           return
```

Fig. 4. Pseudocode of AUTOPROOF

4   AUTOPROOF in Detail

4.1   The Overall Approach

The pseudo-code of AUTOPROOF is shown in Fig. 4. The main procedure is Prove (Lines 11–24). The input of this procedure is a pair (pr, eq), termed as a *goal*, where pr is short for premises, which is a set of equations including all lemmas and inductive hypotheses, and eq is an equation denoting the current proposition to be proved. The target of a goal is to prove pr ⊢ eq.

Prove wraps an underlying deductive solver responsible for performing standard deductive reasoning, such as reduction or applying a premise. Prove first invokes the deductive solver to prove the input goal (Line 12). If the deductive solver succeeds, the proof procedure finishes (Lines 13–14). AUTOPROOF is compatible with any deductive solver. We choose the deductive reasoning module of the state-of-the-art solver CVC4IND [30] in our implementation.

Otherwise, the goal is too complex for the deductive solver to handle, which often requires finding a lemma. In this case, AUTOPROOF first invokes induction-friendly(e) to check if the input equation eq satisfies one of the two identified forms (F1) and (F2) (defined in Sect. 4.2). If so, then by the properties of induction-friendly forms, the original goal can be split into a set of subgoals (Line 18) by induction with effective applications of the inductive hypotheses.

If not, AUTOPROOF applies a built-in set of tactics to transform an input equation into an induction-friendly form gradually. We will discuss tactics in detail in Sect. 4.3. A tactic generally has a precondition, i.e., precond(·) indicating the set of applicable equations. If the tactic is applicable (Line 21), AUTO-PROOF invokes another procedure t_apply that synthesizes a lemma lem and applies this lemma to transform the input equation eq into another equation eq'. (Line 22). Then, Prove is recursively called to prove the lemma lem and the equation eq' with the aid of lem (Lines 24–25).

In this algorithm, induction is applied only when the proof goal is in the induction-friendly form, hence we need a *progress* property that, starting from any goal, if all lemmas are successfully synthesized, the initial goal can be eventually transformed into an induction-friendly form. This property is formally proved in Theorem 3.

4.2   Induction-Friendly Forms in AUTOPROOF

AUTOPROOF identifies two induction-friendly forms (defined at Sect. 2). Both forms guarantee the effective application of the inductive hypothesis.

(F1) The first induction-friendly form is $f\, v_1 \ldots\, v_k = p(v_1, \ldots, v_k)$, where

  (F1.1) One side of the equation is in the form $f v_1 \ldots v_k$, where f is a CSR and $v_1 \ldots v_k$ are different. From the definition of CSR, f applies pattern-matching on v_k.

  (F1.2) The other side of the equation is a program $p(v_1 \ldots v_k)$ satisfies the condition as follows. If v_k appears in p, then there exists an occurrence of v_k, such that (1) v_k appears as the recursive argument of the CSR it is passed to, and (2) all other arguments in this CSR invocation do not contain v_k.

```
Let app x y =                    Let sapp x y z =
match y with                     match z with
| nil → nil                      | nil → (sum x) + (sum y)
| cons h t →                     | cons h t → h + (sapp x y z)
    cons h (app x t)             end;
end;
```

Fig. 5. More CSRs for This Section

Intuitively, (F1.1) guarantees the applicability of the inductive hypothesis, and (F1.2) guarantees that there is a common term for generalization. To be more concrete, consider proving $\forall x, y, z.$ sapp x y z = sum (app (app y z) x), where app and sapp are defined in Fig. 5, app is the list concatenation function, and sapp caluclates the sum of three concatenated lists. Note that this equation fulfills (F1). Induction over z and consider the cons case where z = cons h t, the LHS can be reduced to:

$$h + (\text{sapp x y t}) = \text{sum (app (cons h (app y t)) x)}$$

Due to (F1.1), the LHS contains a single call, and due to the definition of the CSR, the recursive call must take t as the recursive argument and keep the other argument unchanged. Therefore, the LHS must contain sapp x y t as a subprogram, making the induction hypothesis applicable. Applying the induction hypothesis, we get

$$h + (\text{sum (app (app y t) x)}) = (\text{app (cons h (app y t)) x})$$

Due to (F1.2), either z do not appear in RHS, leading to exactly the same RHS as the inductive hypothesis, or we can find an occurrence of z in the RHS (app y z in this example), such that z is the recursive argument and all other arguments do not contain z. In this case, the reduction produces the recursive call app y t, a common subprogram on both sides. In both cases, we can generalize this subprogram to a fresh variable, yielding an effective application.

The second form is dedicated to our tactics. We propose this form to capture the lemmas proposed by our second tactic (Sect. 4.5).

The second form is $f\ v_1\ \ldots\ v_k\ =\ f'\ v_1'\ldots\ v_k'$, where $v_i \neq v_j \wedge v_i' \neq v_j'$ for all $1 \leq i < j \leq k$, i.e., each side is a single CSR call whose arguments are distinct variables.

When the equation fulfills (F2), we can guarantee an effective application of the induction hypothesis by a nested induction over v_k and v_k'. For example, consider proving $\forall x, y, z.$ sapp x y z = sapp x z y. We first perform induction over z and consider the cons case where z = cons $h_1 t_1$, the goal reduces to the following equation with the hypothesis sapp x y t_1 = sapp x t_1 y.

$$h_1 + \text{sapp x y } t_1 = \text{sapp x (cons } h_1\ t_1)\ y$$

Applying the hypothesis on LHS, we obtain the following subgoal:

$$h_1 + \text{sapp x } t_1\ y = \text{sapp x (cons } h_1\ t_1)\ y$$

Note that this subgoal falls into (F1), where the RHS is a single call and y is only used as a recursive argument, and thus an effective application of inductive hypothesis is guaranteed when we perform induction over y. We can see that this conformance to (F1) is guaranteed because the single call on the LHS guarantees the application of the inductive hypothesis, which will make the recursive arguments on both sides the same.

The following theorem establishes that both (F1) and (F2) are induction-friendly.

Theorem 1. *Both (F1) and (F2) are induction-friendly.*

4.3   General Routine of Tactics

In this part, we demonstrate the general routine of how tactics are applied to transform the input goal, i.e., the t.t_apply($\cdot$) function in Line 6 of Fig. 4. Let us start with the notation of *abstraction*.

Tactics. Informally, our tactics focus on lemmas that transform a fragment of the input equation into a single CSR invocation. Thus, it requires a subroutine extract($\cdot$), which needs to be instantiated per tactic, to extract the specification of a lemma synthesis problem from the equation to be proved. The output of extract($\cdot$) is a tuple (p_s', v), where p_s' is an abstraction of the subprogram to be transformed, and v is a free variable in p_s' (Line 7 in Fig. 4). The output (p_s', v) indicates the following lemma synthesis problem.

$$\forall \tilde{v}.\forall v.f^*\ \tilde{v}\ v\ =\ p_s'(\tilde{v}, v) \tag{eq_1}$$

where $\tilde{v}$ is the set of all free variables other than v.

The approach to finding f^* has been fully presented in Sect. 2 and thus is omitted here. As long as the program synthesis succeeds in finding f^*, we propose the lemma (eq_1) above. Since p'_s is an abstraction of some subprogram in the input equation, we can easily apply the lemma (eq_1) to transform the input equation and obtain a new equation eq_2 to be proved (Lines 8–9 in Fig. 4).

4.4   Tactic 1: Removing Compositions

Our first tactic is used to guarantee (F1.1). Thus, the precondition t.precond(eq) returns true if eq does not satisfy (F1.1). Below, we demonstrate the extract function in detail.

The extract function picks a non-leaf subprogram $c\ p_1\ p_2\ \ldots\ p_k$ of some side of the input equation eq, where c is a primitive operator, a constructor, or a CSR, $p_1 \ldots p_k$ are the arguments of c, and at least one of p_i is not a variable. Then, we abstract all arguments passed to each p_i with a fresh variable, obtaining the abstracted subprogram p'_s. We define the cost of this extraction as the number of fresh variables introduced. The extraction returns the extraction with the minimum cost. If there are several choices with the same minimum cost, we pick an arbitrary one.

For example, consider proving the equation app (rev a) (rev (rev b)) = rev (rev (app (rev a) b)), where app is the list concatenation function presented in Fig. 5. Then, we may choose the subprogram rev (rev (app (rev a) b)) and abstract the argument app (rev a) b of the inner rev with a fresh variable x, obtaining p'_s = rev (rev x). Since this extraction only introduces one variable, the cost is one, which is the minimum cost.

Having fixed p'_s, we then select a variable v in p'_s to be the recursive argument of the synthesized CSR f^*. We choose the variable whose corresponding lemma fulfills the maximum number of forms in (F1.1), (F1.2), and (F2). If there is a tie, we choose an arbitrary variable that reaches the maximum. Note that the lemma generated by this tactic satisfies at least (F1.1), which guarantees the applicability of the inductive hypothesis.

4.5   Tactic 2: Switching Recursive Arguments

Our second tactic is used to guarantee (F1.2), and synthesizes a lemma such as f x y = f' y x to switch the recursive argument of a function (recall that the recursive argument is always the last one). This tactic is only invoked when the first tactic (Sect. 4.4) cannot apply. Thus, the precondition precond(eq) returns true if eq satisfies (F1.1) but not (F1.2). Without loss of generality, we assume the LHS is a single CSR invocation with the recursive argument x.

The extraction algorithm picks the occurrence of x with the maximum depth in the AST, where x is passed to a CSR f. Then, each p_i is either the variable x or a program that does not contain x (otherwise, we find an occurrence of x with a larger depth). We introduce fresh variables $v_1 \ldots v_k$ to abstract $p_1 \ldots p_k$.

For some $1 \leq i < k$ such that $p_i = x$ (such i always exists since the equation violates (F1.2)), the extract outputs $p'_s = f\ v_1\ \dots\ v_k$ and $x = v_i$. Since all arguments of f are abstracted, the lemma proposed by this tactic must satisfy (F2). As a result, the lemma is induction-friendly.

For example, consider proving ∀x, y, z. plus3 y z x = plus (plus x y) z. Note that this equation satisfies (F1.1) but not (F1.2). We choose the subprogram plus x y and abstract it into p'_s = plus a b. Note that x appears as the first argument, thus the algorithm outputs (p'_s, a), which requires to synthesize a lemma ∀a, b. plus a b = plus' b a. As long as the lemma is synthesized, we can replace plus x y to plus' y x, making the equation satisfying (F1.2).

4.6 Properties

First, we show the soundness of AUTOPROOF, which is straightforward.

Theorem 2 (Soundness). *If* AUTOPROOF *proves an input goal, then the goal is true.*

Proof The proof of the input equation searched by AUTOPROOF is a sequence of induction, reduction, and application of lemmas. Thus, the soundness of AUTOPROOF follows from the soundness of these standard tactics.

Progress. As mentioned in Sect. 4.1, the effectiveness of AUTOPROOF comes from the following progress theorem.

Theorem 3 (Progress). *Starting from any goal, if all lemmas are successfully synthesized, the initial goal can be eventually transformed into an induction-friendly form.*

5   Evaluation

We implement AUTOPROOF on top of CVC4IND [30], an extension of CVC4 with induction and the available[1] state-of-the-art prover for proving equivalence between functional programs. We choose AUTOLIFTER [13] as the underlying synthesizer, which can solve the synthesis tasks in Sect. 4.3 over randomly generated tests. CVC4IND comes with a lemma enumeration module, our implementation invokes only the deductive reasoning module of CVC4IND. To compare the lemma enumeration with directed lemma synthesis, we evaluate AUTOPROOF against CVC4IND.

Dataset. We collect 248 *standard benchmarks* from the equivalence checking subset of CLAM [12], Isaplaaner [14], and "Tons of Inductive problems"

---

[1] PIRATE [37] is reported to have better performance than CVC4IND on *standard benchmarks* in our evaluation, but its code and its experimental data are not publicly accessible. Thus, we do not compare our approach against PIRATE. Note that AUTOPROOF can be combined with any deductive solver, including PIRATE.

Table 1. Experimental results on the number of the solved benchmarks.

	#Solved (Standard)	#Solved (Extension)	#Solved (Total)	#Fails (Timeout)
AutoProof	**140** (↑ **16.67%**)	**21** (↑ **600%**)	**161** (↑ **30.89%**)	**109**
Cvc4Ind	120	3	123	147

Table 2. Experimental results on the average runtime.

	AvgTime(s) (Standard)	AvgTime(s) (Extension)	AvgTime(s) (Total)
AutoProof	**1.31** (↑ **97.16%**)	**3.99** (↑ **98.71%**)	**3.64** (↑ **95.47%**)
Cvc4Ind	46.13	308.58	80.36

(TIP) [5], which have been widely employed in previous works [7,12,14,30,38]. We observe that these benchmarks do not consider the mix of ADTs and other theories (e.g., LIA for integer manipulation), which is also an important fragment in practice [6,10,17–19]. Thus, we created 22 *additional benchmarks* combining the theory of ADTs and LIA by converting ADTs to primitive types in existing benchmarks, such as converting `Nat` to `Int`. Our test suite thus consists of 270 benchmarks in total.

Procedure. We use our implementation and the baseline to prove the problems in the benchmarks. We set the time limit as 360 s for solving an individual benchmark, the default timeout of Cvc4Ind and is aligned with previous work [7, 29,30,38]. We obtain all results on the server with the Intel(R) Xeon(R) Platinum 8369HC CPU, 8GB RAM, and the Ubuntu 22.04.2 system.

Results. The comparison results are summarized in Tables 1–2. Overall, AutoProof solves 161 benchmarks, while the baseline Cvc4Ind solves 123, showing that directed lemma synthesis can make an enhancement with a ratio of 30.89%. On the solved benchmarks, AutoProof takes 3.64 s on average, while Cvc4Ind takes 80.36 s, indicating that directed lemma synthesis can save 95.47% runtime. The results justify our motivation: compared with the directionless lemma enumeration, directed lemma synthesis can avoid wasting time on useless lemmas. Note that AutoProof shows significant strength on additional benchmarks with a mixed theory. This is because the tactics and induction-friendly forms in our approach are *purely syntactic*, making AutoProof *theory-agnostic*. In contrast, Cvc4Ind is *theory-dependent*. Thus, it is hard for Cvc4Ind to tackle benchmarks with mixed theories.

Discussion. We observe that in the failed cases, the failure to synthesize a lemma is a common cause, and this in turn is due to two reasons. The first one is that the program synthesizer fails to produce a solution for a solvable synthesis problem. For example, one equation involves an exponential function, whose implementation is extremely slow on ADT types, and the synthesizer timed out on executing the randomly generated tests. The second one is that the potential lemma requires a structural recursion that is not canonical. Though in theory such a structural recursion can be converted into compositions of CSRs, our current algorithm only supports the synthesis of CSRs, and thus cannot synthesize such lemmas. This observation shows that, if we can further improve program synthesis in future, our approach may prove more theorems.

6   Related Work

Lemma Finding in Inductive Reasoning. Due to the necessity, the lemma finding algorithm has been integrated into various architectures of inductive reasoning, including theory exploration [4,31], superposition-based provers [7, 11,26,29], SMT solvers [23,30,36,38], and other customized approaches [20,32]. These approaches can be divided into two categories.

First, most of these approaches [4,7,11,20,26,29–32,38] apply lemma enumeration based on heuristics or user-provided templates, which often produce lemmas with little help to the proof, leading to inefficiency, as we have discussed in Sect. 1. Compared with these approaches, AUTOPROOF considers the *directed* lemma synthesis and application, eventually producing subgoals in induction-friendly forms.

Second, there are approaches [23,36] considering the lemma synthesis over a decision procedure based on bounded quantification and pre-fixed point computation. These approaches are restricted to structural recursions without nested function invocations or constructors, which cover only 19/248 (7%) benchmarks in our test suite (Sect. 5).

Other Approaches in Functional Program Verification. There are other approaches [2,16,24,35] verifying the properties of functional programs *without* induction. These tools require the user to manually provide an induction hypothesis. Thus, these approaches cannot prove any benchmark in our test suite (Sect. 5).

Invariant Synthesis. Lemma synthesis has also been applied to verifying the properties of imperative programs [9,15], where the lemma synthesis is often recognized as *invariant synthesis*. Since the core of imperative programs is the mutable atomic variables and arrays instead of ADTs, previous approaches for invariant synthesis [9,15] cannot be applied to our problem. It is future work to understand whether we can extend AUTOPROOF for verifying imperative programs.

7   Conclusion

We have presented AUTOPROOF, a prover for verifying the equivalence between functional programs, with a novel directed lemma synthesis engine. The conceptual novelty of our approach is the induction-friendly forms, which are propositions that give formal guarantees to the progress of the proof. We identified two forms and proposed two tactics that synthesize and apply lemmas, transforming the proof goal into induction-friendly forms. Both tactics reduce lemma synthesis to a specialized class of program synthesis problems with efficient algorithms. We conducted experiments, showing the strength of our approach. In detail, compared to state-of-the-art equivalence checkers employing heuristic-based lemma enumeration, directed lemma synthesis saves 95.47% runtime on average and solves 38 more tasks over a standard benchmark set.

Acknowledgement. We sincerely thank the anonymous reviewers for their valuable feedback on this paper. This work is sponsored by the National Key Research and Development Program of China under Grant No. 2022YFB4501902, the National Natural Science Foundation of China under Grant Nos. 62161146003, the ZJNSF Major Program under grant No. LD24F020013, and the ZJU Education Foundation's Qizhen Talent program.

Data Availability Statement. The artifact in this paper is publicly available on Zenodo [33].

References

1. Bertot, Y., Casteran, P.: Interactive Theorem Proving and Program Development. Springer, Heidelberg (2004). https://doi.org/10.1007/978-3-662-07964-5
2. Blanc, R., Kuncak, V., Kneuss, E., Suter, P.: An overview of the Leon verification system: Verification by translation to recursive functions. In: Proceedings of the 4th Workshop on Scala, pp. 1–10 (2013)
3. Bradley, A.R., Manna, Z.: The Calculus of Computation - Decision Procedures with Applications to Verification. Springer, Heidelberg (2007). https://doi.org/10.1007/978-3-540-74113-8
4. Claessen, K., Johansson, M., Rosén, D., Smallbone, N.: Automating inductive proofs using theory exploration. In: Bonacina, M.P. (ed.) CADE 2013. LNCS (LNAI), vol. 7898, pp. 392–406. Springer, Heidelberg (2013). https://doi.org/10.1007/978-3-642-38574-2_27
5. Claessen, K., Johansson, M., Rosén, D., Smallbone, N.: TIP: tons of inductive problems. In: Kerber, M., Carette, J., Kaliszyk, C., Rabe, F., Sorge, V. (eds.) CICM 2015. LNCS (LNAI), vol. 9150, pp. 333–337. Springer, Cham (2015). https://doi.org/10.1007/978-3-319-20615-8_23
6. Codish, M., Fekete, Y., Fuhs, C., Giesl, J., Waldmann, J.: Exotic semi-ring constraints. SMT@ IJCAR **20**, 88–97 (2012)
7. Cruanes, S.: Superposition with structural induction. In: Dixon, C., Finger, M. (eds.) FroCoS 2017. LNCS (LNAI), vol. 10483, pp. 172–188. Springer, Cham (2017). https://doi.org/10.1007/978-3-319-66167-4_10
8. Danvy, O., Nielsen, L.R.: Defunctionalization at work. In: Proceedings of the 3rd ACM SIGPLAN International Conference on Principles and Practice of Declarative Programming, pp. 162–174. PPDP 2001, Association for Computing Machinery, New York, NY, USA (2001). https://doi.org/10.1145/773184.773202
9. Garg, P., Löding, C., Madhusudan, P., Neider, D.: ICE: A robust framework for learning invariants. In: Biere, A., Bloem, R. (eds.) CAV 2014. LNCS, vol. 8559, pp. 69–87. Springer, Cham (2014). https://doi.org/10.1007/978-3-319-08867-9_5

10. Gavrilenko, N., Ponce-de-León, H., Furbach, F., Heljanko, K., Meyer, R.: BMC for weak memory models: relation analysis for compact SMT encodings. In: Dillig, I., Tasiran, S. (eds.) CAV 2019. LNCS, vol. 11561, pp. 355–365. Springer, Cham (2019). https://doi.org/10.1007/978-3-030-25540-4_19

11. Hajdú, M., Hozzová, P., Kovács, L., Schoisswohl, J., Voronkov, A.: Induction with generalization in superposition reasoning. In: Benzmüller, C., Miller, B. (eds.) CICM 2020. LNCS (LNAI), vol. 12236, pp. 123–137. Springer, Cham (2020). https://doi.org/10.1007/978-3-030-53518-6_8

12. Ireland, A., Bundy, A.: Productive Use of Failure in Inductive Proof, pp. 79–111. Springer Netherlands, Dordrecht (1996). https://doi.org/10.1007/978-94-009-1675-3_3

13. Ji, R., Zhao, Y., Xiong, Y., Wang, D., Zhang, L., Hu, Z.: Decomposition-based synthesis for applying divide-and-conquer-like algorithmic paradigms. ACM Trans. Program. Lang. Syst. (2024). https://doi.org/10.1145/3648440, just Accepted

14. Johansson, M., Dixon, L., Bundy, A.: Case-analysis for rippling and inductive proof. In: Kaufmann, M., Paulson, L.C. (eds.) ITP 2010. LNCS, vol. 6172, pp. 291–306. Springer, Heidelberg (2010). https://doi.org/10.1007/978-3-642-14052-5_21

15. Kincaid, Z., Cyphert, J., Breck, J., Reps, T.: Non-linear reasoning for invariant synthesis. Proc. ACM Prog. Lang. 2(POPL), 1–33 (2017)

16. Leino, K.R.M.: Dafny: an automatic program verifier for functional correctness. In: Clarke, E.M., Voronkov, A. (eds.) LPAR 2010. LNCS (LNAI), vol. 6355, pp. 348–370. Springer, Heidelberg (2010). https://doi.org/10.1007/978-3-642-17511-4_20

17. Lopes, N.P., Monteiro, J.: Automatic equivalence checking of programs with uninterpreted functions and integer arithmetic. Int. J. Softw. Tools Technol. Transfer 18, 359–374 (2016)

18. Luick, D., et al.: ZKSMT: A VM for proving SMT theorems in zero knowledge. Cryptology ePrint Archive (2023)

19. McCarthy, J.: Towards a mathematical science of computation. In: Colburn, T.R., Fetzer, J.H., Rankin, T.L. (eds.) Program Verification: Fundamental Issues in Computer Science, vol. 14, pp. 35–56. Springer, Dordrecht (1993). https://doi.org/10.1007/978-94-011-1793-7_2

20. Milovančević, D., Kunčak, V.: Proving and disproving equivalence of functional programming assignments. Proc. ACM Program. Lang. 7(PLDI) (2023). https://doi.org/10.1145/3591258

21. de Moura, L., Bjørner, N.: Z3: An efficient SMT solver. In: Ramakrishnan, C.R., Rehof, J. (eds.) TACAS 2008. LNCS, vol. 4963, pp. 337–340. Springer, Heidelberg (2008). https://doi.org/10.1007/978-3-540-78800-3_24

22. de Moura, L., Kong, S., Avigad, J., van Doorn, F., von Raumer, J.: The lean theorem prover (system description). In: Felty, A.P., Middeldorp, A. (eds.) CADE 2015. LNCS (LNAI), vol. 9195, pp. 378–388. Springer, Cham (2015). https://doi.org/10.1007/978-3-319-21401-6_26

23. Murali, A., Peña, L., Blanchard, E., Löding, C., Madhusudan, P.: Model-guided synthesis of inductive lemmas for FOL with least fixpoints. Proc. ACM Program. Lang. 6(OOPSLA2) (2022). https://doi.org/10.1145/3563354

24. Murali, A., Peña, L., Jhala, R., Madhusudan, P.: Complete first-order reasoning for properties of functional programs. Proc. ACM Program. Lang. 7(OOPSLA2) (2023). https://doi.org/10.1145/3622835

25. Nelson, G., Oppen, D.C.: Simplification by cooperating decision procedures. ACM Trans. Program. Lang. Syst. **1**(2), 245–257 (1979). https://doi.org/10.1145/357073.357079
26. Passmore, G., Cruanes, S., Ignatovich, D., Aitken, D., Bray, M., Kagan, E., Kanishev, K., Maclean, E., Mometto, N.: The Imandra automated reasoning system (system description). In: Peltier, N., Sofronie-Stokkermans, V. (eds.) IJCAR 2020. LNCS (LNAI), vol. 12167, pp. 464–471. Springer, Cham (2020). https://doi.org/10.1007/978-3-030-51054-1_30
27. Paulson, L.C.: Isabelle: the next 700 theorem provers (2000)
28. Pierce, B.C., Casinghino, C., Gaboardi, M., Greenberg, M., Hriţcu, C., Sjöberg, V., Yorgey, B.: Software foundations, p. 16 (2010). http://www.cis.upenn.edu/bcpierce/sf/current/index.html
29. Reger, G., Voronkov, A.: Induction in saturation-based proof search. In: Fontaine, P. (ed.) CADE 2019. LNCS (LNAI), vol. 11716, pp. 477–494. Springer, Cham (2019). https://doi.org/10.1007/978-3-030-29436-6_28
30. Reynolds, A., Kuncak, V.: Induction for SMT solvers. In: D'Souza, D., Lal, A., Larsen, K.G. (eds.) VMCAI 2015. LNCS, vol. 8931, pp. 80–98. Springer, Heidelberg (2015). https://doi.org/10.1007/978-3-662-46081-8_5
31. Singher, E., Itzhaky, S.: Theory exploration powered by deductive synthesis. In: Silva, A., Leino, K.R.M. (eds.) CAV 2021. LNCS, vol. 12760, pp. 125–148. Springer, Cham (2021). https://doi.org/10.1007/978-3-030-81688-9_6
32. Sonnex, W., Drossopoulou, S., Eisenbach, S.: Zeno: an automated prover for properties of recursive data structures. In: Flanagan, C., König, B. (eds.) TACAS 2012. LNCS, vol. 7214, pp. 407–421. Springer, Heidelberg (2012). https://doi.org/10.1007/978-3-642-28756-5_28
33. Sun, Y., Ji, R., Fang, J., Jiang, X., Chen, M., Xiong, Y.: Artifact for FM paper: proving Functional program equivalence via directed lemma. Synthesis (2024). https://doi.org/10.5281/zenodo.12532389
34. Sun, Y., Ji, R., Fang, J., Jiang, X., Chen, M., Xiong, Y.: Proving functional program equivalence via directed lemma synthesis (2024). https://arxiv.org/abs/2405.11535
35. Vazou, N.: Liquid Haskell: Haskell as a theorem prover. University of California, San Diego (2016)
36. VK, H.G., Shoham, S., Gurfinkel, A.: Solving constrained horn clauses modulo algebraic data types and recursive functions. Proc. ACM Program. Lang. **6**(POPL), 1–29 (2022)
37. Wand, D.: Superposition: types and induction. Ph.D. thesis, Saarland University (2017)
38. Yang, W., Fedyukovich, G., Gupta, A.: Lemma synthesis for automating induction over algebraic data types. In: Schiex, T., de Givry, S. (eds.) CP 2019. LNCS, vol. 11802, pp. 600–617. Springer, Cham (2019). https://doi.org/10.1007/978-3-030-30048-7_35

Reachability Analysis for Multiloop Programs Using Transition Power Abstraction

Konstantin Britikov[1]([⊠])⬤, Martin Blicha[1,2]⬤, Natasha Sharygina[1]⬤, and Grigory Fedyukovich[3]⬤

[1] University of Lugano, Lugano, Switzerland
britik@usi.ch
[2] Charles University, Prague, Czech Republic
[3] Florida State University, Tallahassee, FL, USA

Abstract. A wide variety of algorithms is employed for the reachability analysis of programs with loops but most of them are restricted to single loop programs. Recently a new technique called Transition Power Abstraction (TPA) showed promising results for safety checks of software. In contrast to many other techniques TPA efficiently handles loops with a large number of iterations. This paper introduces an algorithm that enables the effective use of TPA for analysis of multiloop programs. The TPA-enabled loop analysis reduces the dependency on the number of possible iterations. Our approach analyses loops in a modular manner and both computes and uses transition invariants incrementally, making program analysis efficient. The new algorithm is implemented in the Golem solver. Conducted experiments demonstrate that this approach outperforms the previous implementation of TPA and other competing tools on a wide range of multiloop benchmarks.

1 Introduction

Model checking is one of the most active research fields within Formal Verification. Recent advancements both in Satisfiability Modulo Theory (SMT) [2] and Constrained Horn Clauses (CHC) [26] significantly increased model checking capabilities [4,5]. Nonetheless, there is still a wide range of problems that require attention, such as model checking for nonlinear arithmetic, search for deep counterexamples, or analysis of multiple-loop systems.

A significant amount of research in model checking is centered around the loop analysis. There exist a large number of different approaches, most of which target [10,19,30,37] specifically single-loop programs. Multi-loop approaches are less common, primarily because such systems are harder to analyze than single-loop software due to their complex inner structures with interconnected loops and branching. Nonetheless, developing such approaches is crucial, as multi-loop software is widespread.

This work was partially funded by the Swiss National Science Foundation project 200021_185031 and by the Czech Science Foundation project 23-06506S.

A. Platzer et al. (Eds.): FM 2024, LNCS 14933, pp. 558–576, 2025.
https://doi.org/10.1007/978-3-031-71162-6_29

One of the critical problems for multi-loop analysis is the presence of deep loops with a large number of iterations. The presence of such loops might significantly slow down the model checking of the whole program. Recently published papers on Transition Power Abstraction (TPA) [9,10] tried to improve the analysis of deep loops. TPA is driven by SMT, similar to other algorithms like Interpolation-based Model Checking (IMC) [30], Spacer [26] or Lazy Abstraction With Interpolants (LAWI) [31]; however, TPA abstracts over transitions rather than states, overapproximating them and summarizing a sequence of transitions into a single *abstract transition*. This idea is beneficial for the detection of deep counterexamples because, unlike classic symbolic approaches, the algorithm unfolds loop iterations exponentially faster. TPA also leverages interpolants to abstract the system properties and this allows it to prove safety of possibly unbounded loops by producing a loop invariant.

TPA was developed for reasoning about single-loop systems. It is still possible to apply it to the multi-loop programs using a straightforward transformation to merge multiple loops into a single loop [13]. However, this method would lose structural information about the initial program leading to a potential slowdown of the verification. In this paper, we introduce a novel algorithm that enables effective reasoning over multi-loop programs by applying TPA *modularly* and *incrementally* for each loop. It explores every possible execution path of the program, discovering safe *transition invariants* for each loop along a path and utilizing them during the exploration of other paths. Learned information about the safe states is propagated back and forth through the path being explored thus contributing to substantial runtime savings. Additionally, our approach efficiently conducts reachability analysis for loops with large numbers of iterations as a result of the usage of TPA. Our algorithm handles programs with branching and multiple loops efficiently as confirmed by experiments.

Our approach was implemented inside the Golem CHC solver [8]. We experimentally compared the new approach to classical TPA (multi-loop programs were transformed into single-loop in advance) and state-of-the-art tools, such as Z3 (Spacer) [32] and Eldarica [23]. Results demonstrate that our modular analysis is able to solve a significant amount of multi-loop benchmarks previously unmanageable both by Golem competitors and TPA.

The rest of the paper is ordered as follows: Sect. 2 provides a brief overview of the terminology and concepts used in this paper. The main contribution of the paper, the TPA-based reachability algorithm for multi-loop programs, is presented in detail in Sect. 3. In Sect. 4, the effectiveness of the approach is evaluated through a series of experiments. Section 5 discusses related work, and Sect. 6 concludes the paper.

2   Preliminaries

Our approach relies on a symbolic program representation by mapping its control flow to formulas in first-order logic. A set of logic formulas Fla are restricted to Linear Integer Arithmetic (LIA).

```
1 int x1 = nondet(), x2 = nondet(), x3 = 0;
2 assume(0 <= x1 <= 100 && 0 <= x2 <= 50);
3 while (x1 < 300) { ++x1; ++x2; --x3;}
4 while (x3 < x2) { ++x3; --x1; }
5 assert(x1 <= 0);
```

Fig. 1. Multi-loop example.

While *Language.* We restrict our attention to programs in the conventional **While** language [33]. This language has the following meta-variables and categories: n (over integers), x (over variables), a (over arithmetic expressions), b (over boolean expressions), and S (over statements):

$$a ::= n \mid \mathsf{nondet}() \mid x \mid a_1 + a_2 \mid a_1 * a_2 \mid a_1 - a_2$$
$$b ::= \mathit{true} \mid \mathit{false} \mid a_1 = a_2 \mid a_1 \leq a_2 \mid \neg b \mid b_1 \wedge b_2$$
$$S ::= \mathsf{assert}(b) \mid \mathsf{assume}(b) \mid x := a \mid \mathsf{skip} \mid$$
$$S; S \mid \mathsf{if}\ b\ \mathsf{then}\ S\ \mathsf{else}\ S \mid \mathsf{while}\ b\ \mathsf{do}\ S$$

Figure 1 gives an example of a program with two consecutive loops. We present it in a more familiar **C** syntax, but it could easily be translated to **While**. We also use this example to illustrate the solving process of our algorithm in Sect. 3.3. The first loop increments both x_1 and x_2 until $x_1 \geq 300$, aldo decrementing x_3. The second loop increments x_3 and decrements x_1 until $x_2 \leq x_3$. The safety property of the program is given in the assertion $x_1 \leq 0$. This program is safe as for any value of x_1 and x_2 the assertion will be satisfied. By changing the assumption $x_1 \leq 100$ to $x_1 \leq 300$, this program can be made unsafe.

Program Encoding and Cutpoint Graphs. Our representation of the program assumes a global set of variables denoted V. Conventional primed notation is used to represent "next-state" variables. We model multiloop programs using Cutpoint Graphs (CPG) [6] which offer more compact program representations than classic Control Flow Graphs (CFG). Every node in a CPG (except *entry* and *error*) represents a loophead in the corresponding program. For every single loop-free segment between the loopheads, there exists a single corresponding edge in CPG, even when there are multiple possible paths through it.

Definition 1. *Given a program $\mathcal{P}$, its* cutpoint graph *representation $G_\mathcal{P} = \langle N, E, L, entry, error \rangle$ is such where N is a finite set of cutpoints (graph nodes), representing loopheads in the program. E is a set of actions between the cutpoints (edges between the nodes) of a form (u, v), where $u, v \in N \cup \{entry, error\}$. L is a mapping $L : E \rightarrow Fla$ from edges to logic formulas over V and V', representing symbolic encodings of loop-free statements, and entry and error are such that $\forall u \in N : (error, u) \notin E \wedge (u, entry) \notin E.$*

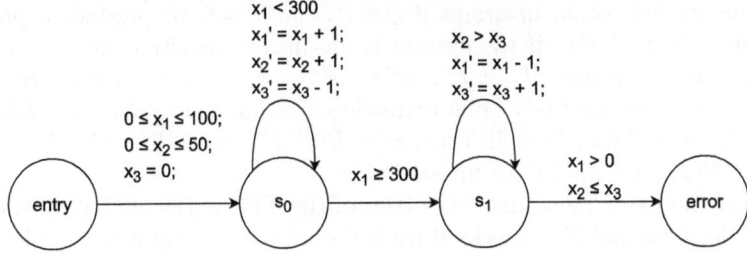

Fig. 2. Cutpoint Graph for program in Fig. 1. Transitions are labeled with constraints from *Fla*.

Based on Definition 1, it is possible to represent any program specified in **While** as a CPG. For example, the CPG for the program in Fig. 1 is given in Fig. 2.

We focus on programs without nested loops. Such programs can be represented with cutpoint graphs that do not have any cycles except for the self-loops. This is because our algorithm uses TPA to analyze reachability in individual loops and TPA is designed to handle loops that can be represented as a transition system. The example from Fig. 2 satisfies this condition as it does not have nested loops.

Transition System Reachability Analysis. Transition system can be defined as $\langle Init, Tr, V \rangle$, where $Init$ is an initial state of the system represented by a first-order logic formula, Tr is a transition formula, which represents the transition in the system, and V is a set of system's variables. Safety problem now can be defined as $\langle Init, Tr, Bad, V \rangle$ where Bad is a formula that represents a state violating the safety property. Reachability analysis in this context is the search for a path through the transition system to reach a Bad state.

Craig Interpolation. Given two logical formulas (A, B) such that $A \wedge B$ is unsatisfiable, a Craig interpolant [14] I is a formula that satisfies the following conditions: $A \rightarrow I$, $I \wedge B$ is unsatisfiable, and I contains only common variables of A and B. Interpolation can be used to prove the safety of a transition system by over-approximating the set of reachable states [30] or to extract information from unfeasible error path through the program [22].

Transition Power Abstraction. One of the interpolation-based model checking approaches, Transition Power Abstraction [9,10], is used in our algorithm. TPA is a model-checking algorithm that works based on the abstraction of the transition relation. It takes a safety problem $\langle Init, Tr, Bad, V \rangle$ as input and decides if any bad state is reachable from some initial state. Moreover, it can return a safe inductive transition invariant if the system is safe or produce a provably reachable subset of *Bad* if the system is unsafe. A transition formula $R(x, x')$ is a *transition invariant*, if $\forall x, x' : Tr^*(x, x') \implies R(x, x')$, where Tr^* is the reflexive transitive closure of Tr. A transition invariant R is *inductive* if $R(x, x') \wedge Tr(x', x'') \implies R(x, x'')$ or if $Tr(x, x') \wedge R(x', x'') \implies R(x, x'')$. It is *safe* if $Init(x) \wedge R(x, x') \wedge Bad(x')$ is unsatisfiable.

One of the most important properties of the TPA is the ability to efficiently execute deep reachability checks during the search for counterexamples. TPA runs iteratively, using transition abstractions $ATr^{\leq n}$, instead of exact transitions. $ATr^{\leq n}$ over-approximates the sequence of 2^n transitions for n-th iteration of the TPA, allowing it to double the amount of the considered transitions every iteration of the algorithm. For more details on TPA, we refer the reader to [9,10].

Example Continued. The example program in Fig. 1 has two interesting properties. First, the depth of the loops, which can overall result in up to 950 iterations. If it was an unsafe example, TPA would be more efficient than its competitors due to its ability to manage deep loops. Second, in the presence of multiple loops, TPA would verify this program only if loops in the program are merged into a single loop. The merged loop will be bigger in size and lose structural information about the program, which could cause a slowdown in verification.

On the other hand, TPA could be applied to the loops separately. However, that would require some intermediate assertion to define safety property for the first loop and initial conditions for the second loop. For example, the condition $x_1 \leq x_2 - x_3$ could serve as such intermediate assertion introduced between lines 3 and 4. Interestingly, the algorithm we present in the next section *automatically* infers similar helper information and applies TPA modularly.

3   Multi-loop Analysis with TPA

Our algorithm performs forward reachability analysis over the program's cut-point graph. It searches for a feasible path from *entry* to *error*, building the path gradually and backtracking when the current path cannot be extended further. Before backtracking from a blocked state, it generalizes the reason for the conflict and learns blocking lemmas (similar to IC3/PDR-style algorithms). These define states that are guaranteed to be safe (i.e., there is no feasible path to *error* from these states), so the algorithm will know to avoid them the next time it reaches the same CPG node.

3.1   Overview

To utilize the strengths of TPA, the algorithm alternates between two phases: i) reasoning about traversing from one loop to another loop, and ii) reasoning about traversing a single loop.

The first phase checks the feasibility of a single (large-block [6]) step in the traditional sense, and it can be reduced to a single SMT check. However, the second phase attempts to extend the current path by getting to the exit of the current loop in an arbitrary number of its iterations. This effectively means solving a reachability problem for a transition system where initial states are the currently reached states, transition relation encodes one iteration of the loop, and error states are the states at the loop exit not yet blocked by the algorithm. While any algorithm for answering reachability queries over transition systems could be applied here, TPA [9] has two advantages over traditional, state-focused model-checking algorithms. Its deep exploration makes it less likely to get stuck in a single loop that requires many iterations to traverse and, secondly, TPA is able to re-use bounded and unbounded *transition* invariants learned in previous queries to speed up current query to the same node. Note that when the algorithm reaches the same node but with a new state, the initial states (and possibly the error states too) of the reachability problem change, but the transition relation always stays the same. Thus, the transition invariants from previous queries are still valid, while state invariants would very likely be invalidated.

3.2 Core Algorithm

Algorithm 1 takes as input a CPG of a program with a safety property and decides if the error node is reachable (UNSAFE) or not (SAFE). For each node v in the graph, the algorithm keeps track of two versions of the node, v^{pre} and v^{post}, called the *pre-state* and the *post-state*, resp. The pre-state captures when the reachability analysis has reached v from another node. In programs, this represents execution reaching the loop header for the first time. The post-state captures when the reachability analysis is about to exit node v and continue to another node. In programs, this represents the execution exiting the loop. Each node version keeps track of a set of states already shown to be safe, denoted as $v^{pre}.safe$ and $v^{post}.safe$. These sets of states are represented as symbolic formulas initialized as $\perp$ (no states are proved safe at the start).

The algorithm also maintains the current feasible path prefix in the variable *path* as a stack of entries of the form $[v, \varphi]$ representing that the set of states φ has been reached at node v. At the beginning, *path* is initialized as leaving the entry node with no restriction on the states (Line 1). When *error* is added to *path*, the algorithm has discovered a feasible path from *entry* to *error* and the program is unsafe (Line 15). If the algorithm ever backtracks beyond the initial entry (*path* becomes empty), there is no feasible path from entry to error, and the program is safe (Line 25). Assuming *path* is not empty, the algorithm attempts to extend the current feasible path prefix. There are two distinct cases. If the last entry on the path is a post-state of some node v (Line 4), the algorithm attempts to use v's outgoing edges (ignoring the self-loop edge) to traverse to the pre-state of a *different* node w. Otherwise, the last entry is a pre-state of some node v (Line 18) and the algorithm attempts to get to the post-state of v by traversing v's self-looping edge some arbitrary number of times. Next, we describe these two cases in detail.

Algorithm 1: Multiloop-TPA

    Input : Cutpoint Graph $G = \langle N, E, L, entry, error \rangle$;
    Output: SAFE/UNSAFE

1 $path \leftarrow \{\lfloor entry^{post}, \top \rfloor\}$
2 **while** $path$ *is not empty* **do**
3 | **switch** $path.peek()$ **do**
4 | | **case** $[v^{post}, curr]$ **do**
5 | | | **if** $\forall w \in N,\ s.t.\ (v,w) \in E : (v,w).blocked \neq \bot$ **then**
6 | | | | $v^{post}.safe \leftarrow v^{post}.safe \vee \bigwedge\limits_{e \in v.outgoing} e.blocked$
7 | | | | $path.pop()$
8 | | | | **for** $e \in v.outgoing$ **do** $e.blocked \leftarrow \bot$
9 | | | **else**
10 | | | | pick $w \in N$ s.t. $(v,w) \in E$ and $(v,w).blocked = \bot$
11 | | | | let $t(x, x') = L((v,w))(x, x') \wedge \neg(w^{pre}.safe)(x')$
12 | | | | **if** $SAT?[curr(x) \wedge t(x,x')]$ **then**   // TraverseBridge
13 | | | | | let $M \models curr(x) \wedge t(x,x')$
14 | | | | | $path.push([w^{pre}, MBP(\exists x : curr(x) \wedge t(x,x'), M)])$
15 | | | | | **if** $w = error$ **then return** UNSAFE
16 | | | | **else**
17 | | | | | $(v,w).blocked \leftarrow Itp(curr(x), t(x,x'))$
18 | | **case** $[v^{pre}, curr]$ **do**   // TraverseLoop
19 | | | $(res, reached, TInv) = \text{TPA}(curr(x), L((v,v))(x,x'), \neg(v^{post}.safe)(x'))$
20 | | | **if** $res = reachable$ **then**
21 | | | | $path.push([v^{post}, reached])$
22 | | | **else**
23 | | | | $v^{pre}.safe \leftarrow v^{pre}.safe \vee Itp(curr(x), TInv(x,x') \wedge \neg(v^{post}.safe)(x'))$
24 | | | | $path.pop()$
25 **return** SAFE

Post: When the algorithm is leaving some node v with reached states $curr$ (Line 4), it searches for an unblocked outgoing edge as a candidate for extending the current path prefix (Line 5). An edge e is marked as blocked if the current path prefix cannot be extended with this edge, and the algorithm remembers the set of blocked source states (states for which it is not feasible to traverse the edge) in $e.blocked$. Algorithm 1 ensures the blocked states are superset of $curr$.

If all outgoing edges are blocked, it means that all outgoing edges have been considered as possible extensions, but all have failed eventually. The current path thus cannot be extended, and the algorithm backtracks to the pre-state of v (Line 7) to try a different continuation from that point. Before backtracking, the algorithm learns a new set of safe states as the intersection of states that are safe for individual outgoing edges (these are guaranteed to include all currently reached states) and unblocks all edges (Lines 6–8).

If, on the other hand, there is an unblocked edge (Line 10), the algorithm attempts to reach some potentially unsafe state of the edge's target node. The feasibility of this traversal, given the constraint of the edge, is checked in Lines 12-17 which, for simplicity, we call `TraverseBridge` throughout the rest of the paper. It decides if some potentially unsafe states are reachable and computes a set of definitely reached target states (in case of reachability) or a set of definitely blocked source states (in case of unreachability). If the traversal is feasible, the path is extended (Line 14), and the analysis will continue from the new reached point unless *error* has been reached, in which case the algorithm immediately terminates (Line 15). If the traversal is infeasible, the picked edge is blocked (Line 17), marked with superset of *curr* for which the traversal is infeasible (see more details on `TraverseBridge` below). In the next iteration, the algorithm tries to pick a different, unblocked edge.

Pre: When the algorithm is entering some node v with reached states *curr* (Line 18), it attempts to find a feasible traversal of the loop, i.e., to reach some potentially unsafe post-state of v (taking an arbitrary number of loop iterations). The feasibility of this traversal is checked in Lines 19-24, which for simplicity we call `TraverseLoop`. Similarly to `TraverseBridge`, `TraverseLoop` not only decides the feasibility of the traversal but also computes a set of definitely reached target states to extend the current path (Line 21) or a set of definitely blocked source states, which forces backtracking (Line 24). We provide further details on `TraverseBridge` and `TraverseLoop` in the next two paragraphs.

TraverseBridge. Given reached states *curr*, target states $\neg(w^{pre}.safe)$, and a transition constraint $L((v,w))$, the goal is to check if any target states are reachable from source states with *one* step of the transition constraint. The reachability check then amounts to the satisfiability check for the conjunction of the three formulas (denoted φ to simplify writing). Provably reached state can be defined exactly as $\exists x : \varphi$. To avoid quantifiers, we under-approximate the set of reached states with *model-based projection* (MBP) [26]. Provably blocked states can be characterized as $\neg \exists x' : L((v,w))(x,x') \wedge \neg(w^{pre}.safe)(x')$. It is again possible to avoid quantifiers but still obtain a generalization of the source states, using Craig interpolation [14].

TraverseLoop. Given reached states *curr*, target states $\neg(v^{post}.safe)$, and a transition constraint $L((v,v))$, the goal is to check if any target states are reachable from source states with *any number of steps* of $L((v,v))$. This is equivalent to deciding a safety problem for a transition system $\mathcal{S} = \langle Init, Tr, Bad \rangle$ with $Init = curr$, $Tr = L((v,v))$ and $Bad = \neg(v^{post}.safe)$. TPA can easily satisfy the additional requirements on `TraverseLoop`. It already internally computes provably reached states as part of the witness for reachability. Provably blocked states can be computed using a safe transition invariant that TPA computes as a witness for unreachability. Similarly to `TraverseBridge`, we leverage Craig interpolation to eliminate quantifiers. Note that computing a logically weak (more general) interpolant for $A = curr$ and $B = TInv \wedge \neg(v^{post}.safe)$ yields a potentially much larger set of blocked states than the source states themselves.

Using TPA for implementing `TraverseLoop` has the additional advantage that TPA learns bounded and unbounded *transition* invariants during a single reachability check, which can be leveraged to bootstrap the transition abstractions in future reachability queries for the same loop. Not starting from scratch has the potential to significantly speed up consequent queries.

3.3   Running Example

To demonstrate the execution of Algorithm 1, we utilize the motivating example from Fig. 2 as an input. The execution is depicted in Fig. 3.

Initially, the algorithm attempts to leave *entry* and picks the single (unblocked) outgoing edge leading to s_0. Potentially unsafe states at s_0^{pre} are $\top$ at this point, so TraverseBridge computes reached states at s_0^{pre} to be $0 \leq x_1 \leq 100 \wedge 0 \leq x_2 \leq 50 \wedge x_3 = 0$.

As the next step, the algorithm attempts to traverse loop s_0 with $\top$ as the potentially unsafe states at s_0^{post}. TraverseLoop determines that with one loop iteration state $1 \leq x_1 \leq 101 \wedge 1 \leq x_2 \leq 51 \wedge x_3 = -1$ is reached at s_0^{post}.

Attempting to continue from this state will now fail, because the only outgoing edge to s_1 is not feasible, as determined by TraverseBridge with $x_1 < 300$ being the blocked states.

The algorithm now backtracks to s_0^{pre} and attempts to traverse loop s_0 again, but this time with $x_1 \geq 300$ as the potentially unsafe states. Here TPA quickly determines that unsafe states are reachable, e.g. after 255 iterations of the loop the state $x_1 = 300 \wedge 255 \leq x_2 \leq 305 \wedge x_3 = -255$ is reached.

From this state at s_0^{post} it is possible to traverse to s_1^{pre}, reaching states defined by the same formula. Next, the algorithm attempts to traverse loop s_1.

Similarly to how it behaved for the first loop, TPA suggests exiting the second loop after one iteration, in state $x_1 = 299 \wedge 255 \leq x_2 \leq 305 \wedge x_3 = -254$. However, when checking the single outgoing edge to *error*, TraverseBridge determines the infeasibility of this attempt and computes $x_2 > x_3$ as safe states at s_1^{post}.

Thus, the algorithm backtracks again and attempts to traverse loop s_1 in a different way so that it ends up in a potentially unsafe state $x_2 \leq x_3$. Here TPA quickly determines that such a state can be reached after 511 iterations, with variable values $x_1 = -211 \wedge x_2 = 256 \wedge x_3 = 256$. However, this path cannot reach *error*, as determined by TraverseBridge with $x_1 \leq 0$ determined to be safe states at s_1^{post}.

In the final attempt to traverse s_1 TPAdetermines that no unsafe state is reachable anymore and computes $x_1 \leq 384 \wedge 384 \leq x_2 - x_3$ as new safe states at s_1^{pre}. Thus, the algorithm backtracks again and tries to find a different way to reach unsafe states of s_1^{pre} from s_0^{post}. TraverseBridge determines this to be impossible with $x_1 \leq 384 \wedge 384 \leq x_2 - x_3$ being safe at s_0^{post} as well. Note that this condition can be viewed as an intermediate assertions between the two loops (as we briefly mentioned in Sect. 2). It is sufficient to prove *error* cannot be reached by traversing the second loop, and, as we will see in a moment, it cannot be violated by traversing the first loop.

Finally, after backtracking to s_0^{pre}, an attempt to traverse loop s_0 to avoid the safe states at s_0^{post} fails, as TPA in TraverseLoop determines that $x_1 \leq$

$108 \wedge x_3 - x_2 \leq 0$ are safe states at $s_0{}^{pre}$. Finally, the algorithm backtracks to $entry^{post}$, and, with no new feasible way to extend the path, it concludes safety.

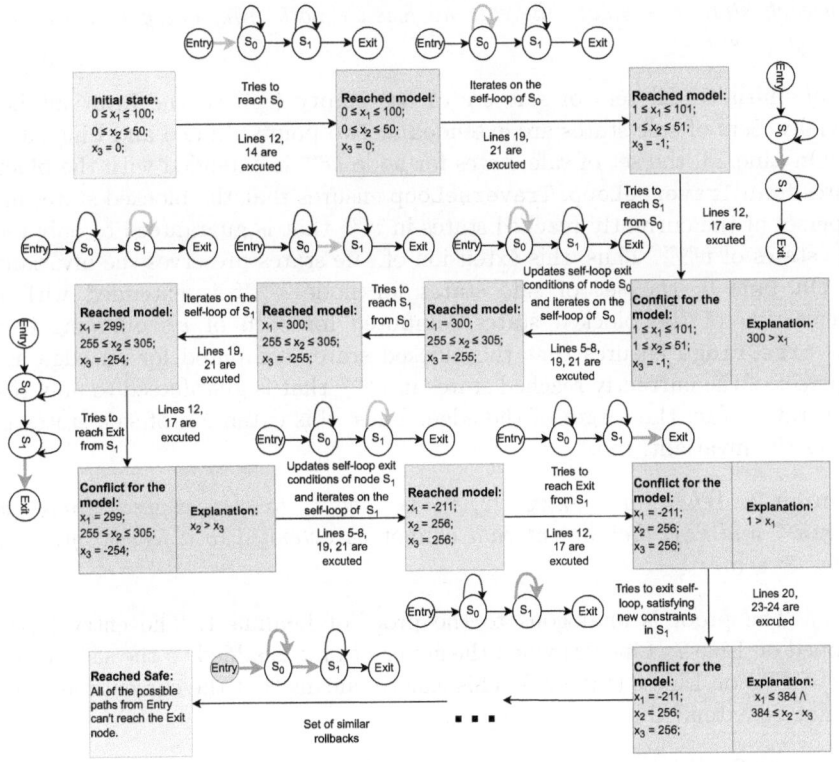

Fig. 3. Algorithm execution flow for Fig. 2.

3.4   Correctness

We first prove correctness when Algorithm 1 answers UNSAFE.

Theorem 1. *When Algorithm 1 returns UNSAFE, there exists a feasible path from entry to error.*

Proof. We show by induction that for every entry $[v, \varphi]$ that is added to *path*, states φ at node v are reachable from *entry*. This claim trivially holds for the initial entry $[entry^{post}, \top]$ added on Line 1. New entries are added to *path* at Lines 14 and 21. If follows from the properties of `TraverseBridge` and `TraverseLoop` that the new reached states added to *path* are indeed reachable from the previous entry in *path*.

Next, we prove the correctness of the SAFE answer using some auxiliary lemmas.

Lemma 1. *The following is an invariant of the algorithm: For each node $v \in N$ and each state $s \in v.safe$ there is no feasible path from entry to error going through $[v, s]$.*

Proof. Initially, all sets of safe states are empty ($\bot$), so the invariant holds trivially. Sets of safe states are extended at two points: Line 6 and Line 23.

On Line 23, the set of safe states for node v^{pre} is extended with the blocked states from TraverseLoop. TraverseLoop ensures that the blocked states are a superset of the currently reached states in v^{pre} that is guaranteed to only reach safe states of v^{post}. Thus, this extension of safe states preserves the invariant.

On Line 6, the set of safe states for node v^{post} is extended with the intersection of the blocked states computed for each of v's outgoing edges. TraverseBridge ensures that the blocked states computed for an edge are a superset of the currently reached states in v^{post} that is guaranteed to only reach safe states of w, the target of the edge. Thus, this extension of safe states preserves the invariant, too.

Lemma 2. *When an entry $[v, \varphi]$ is about to be popped from path (Lines 7 and 24), the current path cannot be extended to a feasible path from entry to error.*

Proof. The proof is analogous to the proof of Lemma 1. The entry $[v, \varphi]$ is popped on Line 7 (Line 24) when the superset of φ is added to the safe states of v^{post} (v^{pre}) on Line 6 (Line 23). This exactly means that the current path prefix cannot be extended to a feasible path.

Theorem 2. *When Algorithm 1 returns SAFE, there is no feasible path entry to error.*

Proof. Follows directly from Lemma 2 because Algorithm 1 returns SAFE when the initial entry $[entry, \top]$ is popped from *path*.

3.5   Witness Production

Here we show that Algorithm 1 can be extended to produce witnesses for both safe and unsafe programs (if it terminates).

Violation Witnesses. We show how a witness can be computed from *path* constructed by Algorithm 1. We use the standard notion of a violation witness as a counterexample path defined by a sequence of program states.

Definition 2 (Violation Witness). *Given a CPG $G_S = \langle N, E, L, entry, error \rangle$, a violation witness is an execution trace $[s_1, ..., s_n]$ such that*

– *for each $i \in [1, n]$, tuple $s_i = \langle v_i, st_i \rangle$ where $v_i \in N$ and st_i a program state, i.e., an assignment of all program variables,*

- $s_1 = \langle entry, \top \rangle$ and $s_n = \langle error, q \rangle$ for some $q \neq \bot$,
- for each consecutive pair $\langle v_i, st_i \rangle$ and $\langle v_{i+1}, st_{i+1} \rangle$, $(v_i, v_{i+1}) \in E$ and $L((v_i, v_{i+1}))(st_i, st_{i+1})$ is satisfiable.

When Algorithm 1 decides the input CPG to be unsafe (Line 15), the entries in *path* form a *blueprint* for the violation witness. It defines exactly which loops the counterexample traverses and in what order. However, the information that is missing is how many iterations are taken in each loop and what are the intermediate states of the program for those iterations. Fortunately, when TPA determines that target states are reachable it also computes how many steps are required. This number of loop iterations can be stored and used at the end to reconstruct the full execution trace. The *blueprint* from *path* combined with the precise number of unrollings of each loop defines the full step-by-step execution trace. To obtain concrete states at each execution step, an SMT query can be formed from the transitions defined by the trace, and concrete program states can be obtained directly from a model for such a query.

Safety Witnesses. We use inductive invariants as safety witnesses.

Definition 3 (Safety Witness). *Given a CPG $G_S = \langle N, E, L, entry, error \rangle$, a safety witness is a mapping $Inv : N \mapsto Fla$ from loops to state formulas such that $Inv(entry) = \top$, $Inv(error) = \bot$, and $\forall (v, u) = e \in E : Inv(v) \wedge L(e) \implies Inv(u)$.*

Note that this definition includes the requirement that $Inv(v)$ is an inductive invariant because the condition must hold also for self-loop edges (v, v).

We show how to compute inductive invariants from the information computed by Algorithm 1. Recall that the algorithm computes for each loop v the set of safe states $v^{pre}.safe$ and $v^{post}.safe$. We can compute a safety witness by computing, separately for each loop v, a safe inductive invariant for a reachability problem $\langle v^{pre}.safe, L((v, v)), \neg v^{post}.safe \rangle$ (which we know is safe).[1]

Lemma 3. *Suppose $Inv(v)$ is a safe inductive invariant for a reachability problem $\langle v^{pre}.safe, L((v, v)), \neg v^{post}.safe \rangle$ for all $v \in N$. Then Inv is a safety witness according to Definition 3, i.e., $\forall (u, v) = e \in E : Inv(u) \wedge L(e) \implies Inv(v)$.*

Proof. Each $Inv(v)$ is, by construction, an inductive invariant for its corresponding loop v. We show that these invariants are inductive also with respect to transitions between loops.

Consider an edge $e = (u, v)$ with $u \neq v$. Since $Inv(u)$ is a safe inductive invariant for the reachability problem $\langle u^{pre}.safe, L((u, u)), \neg u^{post}.safe \rangle$, it follows that $Inv(u) \implies u^{post}.safe$. Moreover, we know that $u^{post}.safe \wedge L(e) \implies v^{pre}.safe$ is valid based on how the set of safe states is constructed in Algorithm 1: only those states at u that cannot reach states outside of $v^{pre}.safe$ are ever added to $u^{post}.safe$. Finally, $v^{pre}.safe \implies Inv(v)$ is valid by construction of $Inv(v)$ as the inductive invariant for $\langle v^{pre}.safe, L((v, v)), \neg v^{post}.safe \rangle$. All three implications together yield the desired property $Inv(u) \wedge L(e) \implies Inv(v)$.

---

[1] Any model checking algorithm can be used here, including TPA.

4   Evaluation

We have implemented Algorithm 1 in our GOLEM CHC solver [8] and we refer to this implementation as GOLEM-MULTILOOP. In the experiments, GOLEM-MULTILOOP is compared with state-of-the-art tools Z3-SPACER (v4.13.0) [26, 32] and ELDARICA (v2.1.0) [23], as well as the existing TPA and SPACER engines of GOLEM (denoted as GOLEM-TPA and GOLEM-SPACER). Benchmarks are centered specifically around the multi-loop instances. All experiments were conducted on a machine with an AMD EPYC 7452 32-core processor and 8×32 GiB of memory.

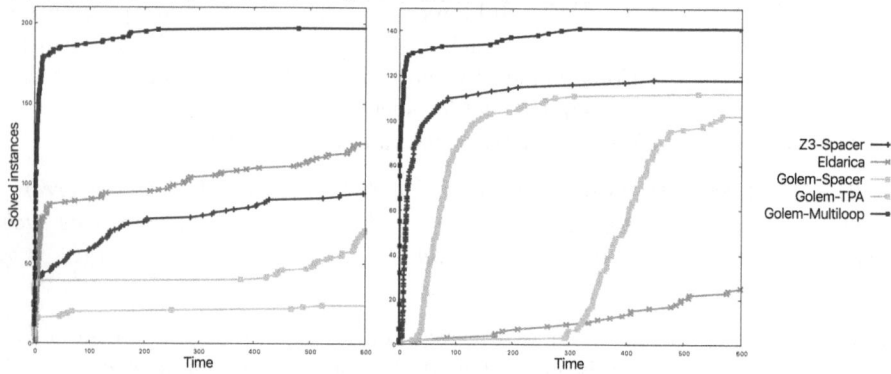

Fig. 4. Comparison of performance of GOLEM-MULTILOOP with other tools: Z3-SPACER, ELDARICA, GOLEM-SPACER and GOLEM-TPA. Plot on the left demonstrates amount of solved SAFE instances over time, plot on the the right shows UNSAFE instances.

The evaluation aims to answer the following two research questions:

- **RQ1:** How does the new *modular* algorithm compare to GOLEM-TPA running on a transformed single-loop program?
- **RQ2:** How does the performance of GOLEM-MULTILOOP fare against state-of-the-art tools?

The set of benchmarks[2] used in our experiments is partially composed of SV-COMP-23 instances[3] (specifically from the 'loops-crafted-1' set) and partially of crafted multi-loop examples. The benchmarks have a common structure, with multiple loops interconnected between each other without nested loops. Our motivating example from Fig. 1 illustrates the structure of these benchmarks. The benchmark set consists of 263 safe and 179 unsafe problems.

---

[2] https://github.com/BritikovKI/fv-benchmarks-2024.
[3] https://gitlab.com/sosy-lab/benchmarking/sv-benchmarks.

Quantile plots, shown in Fig. 4, compare the performance of individual tools on our benchmark set. A data point (x, y) in the plot represents the fact that the corresponding algorithm solved y problems given time x (in seconds). The results show that GOLEM-MULTILOOP outperforms GOLEM-TPA both for safe and unsafe instances. We attribute the large performance improvement for safe instances to GOLEM-MULTILOOP's modularity. While GOLEM-TPA has to find a single safe transition invariant for the whole (transformed) program, GOLEM-MULTILOOP builds separate transition invariants for individual loops *incrementally*.

For unsafe problems, the difference between the two approaches is smaller but still significant. We speculate that the modular nature of GOLEM-MULTILOOP also helps it to build better, more focused transition abstractions which, in turn, allow it to discover the real counter-example faster than GOLEM-TPA, which needs to spend more time refining the abstraction of the monolithic transition relation. To answer RQ1, we conclude that the incremental and modular nature of GOLEM-MULTILOOP delivers significant improvements over applying TPA in a monolithic way to a transformed single-loop program.

GOLEM-MULTILOOP also significantly outperforms state-of-the-art tools. From the safe problems, GOLEM-MULTILOOP solves 198 benchmarks, while the second best, ELDARICA, was able to solve 125 benchmarks. However, ELDARICA solved 10 safe instances uniquely, demonstrating some orthogonality to our approach. Similar results can be observed for the unsafe benchmarks. GOLEM-MULTILOOP solves 23 instances more than Z3-SPACER, the second-best tool, even though Z3-SPACER was able to solve 12 instances uniquely. To answer RQ2, our evaluation shows that GOLEM-MULTILOOP significantly improves upon the state-of-the-art solving more instances than the next-best competitor. Moreover, it is on average 4.1 times and 2.8 times faster than the next best competitor on unsafe and safe instances, respectively.

Overall, the evaluation demonstrates that our new algorithm is capable of successfully handling both safe and unsafe challenging multi-loop programs. It significantly improves not only over TPAapplied to transformed single-loop programs but also over existing state-of-the-art tools.

5 Related Work

A well-established research area around loop analysis embraces a multitude of approaches, many of which are overviewed below.

Loop Summarization. Several techniques aim to produce an abstraction that captures a relationship between the input and output of the loop as a set of symbolic constraints. Produced this way, a *loop summary* is then used to replace the loop in a subsequent analysis of the program. The approaches differ mainly due to the application of symbolic abstraction [11,27,35] or symbolic execution [21,36,37]. All those approaches are property-agnostic and thus could be more expensive or less effective than needed when potentially employed by our approach. By contrast, our technique abstracts loops following the guidance of the safety property.

Loop Acceleration. A group of related techniques produce quantifier-free first-order formulas that under-approximate loop behaviours [3,12,19,20]. They are motivated by and applied to verification approaches to improve scalability. We are however not aware if any such technique is applicable to complicated loops with control flow divergence or to loops over datatypes more complicated than just integers.

Invariant Generation. An older but more popular and more widely used technique in program analysis consists in the automated generation of inductive invariants. Intuitively, it aims at generating an over-approximation of all possible states that can be reached after a loop iteration, assuming it started from another over-approximation, and hoping to reach a fixpoint. There are multiple approaches to generate invariants, e.g. based on CEGAR and predicate abstraction [23,29], IC3/PDR [26], program transformation based [24], syntax-guided synthesis [18], or Machine Learning/Neural networks [25,34]. One of the most popular approaches for invariant generation is interpolant production, which is used in a wide variety of algorithms [9,23,26,28–31].

Other Techniques. Some algorithms try to analyze loops differently, for example, to simplify loops themselves, transforming them into a simpler version of the same loop [15,16]. These approaches are not comparable with our technique, as they simplify loops but not abstract them.

Multi-loop to Single-Loop Transformation. One of the important techniques for the analysis of multi-loop systems is the transformation of such systems into a single loop [1,13,17]. This set of approaches allows to apply algorithms like IMC, TPA, or other single-loop specific engines [7] to effectively analyze the multi-loop program as a whole.

6   Conclusion

Our paper introduces a novel approach for model checking of programs with multiple loops. Its main idea is a modular analysis of the program loops while propagating information about reachable and blocked states between consecutive loops. Utilization of Transition Power Abstraction for analysis of individual loops enables incremental computation and use of transition invariants for the program verification, which significantly improves the overall performance of the approach. We also proved the correctness of this algorithm and demonstrated how witnesses, both for SAFE and UNSAFE instances, can be generated. Experimental evaluation demonstrates that our algorithm significantly outperforms a straightforward application of TPA as well as other competitors in the analysis of multi-loop systems.

As a future work, we plan to modify this algorithm to manage multi-loop systems with nested loops. This would significantly expand the possible applications of our approach for the analysis of real-world programs.[4]

References

1. Aho, A.V., Sethi, R., Ullman, J.D.: Compilers: Principles, Techniques, and Tools. Addison-Wesley Series in Computer Science/World Student Series Edition. Addison-Wesley (1986). https://www.worldcat.org/oclc/12285707

2. Barbosa, H., et al.: cvc5: a versatile and industrial-strength SMT solver. In: Fisman, D., Rosu, G. (eds.) TACAS 2022. LNCS, vol. 13243, pp. 415–442. Springer, Cham (2022). https://doi.org/10.1007/978-3-030-99524-9_24

3. Bardin, S., Finkel, A., Leroux, J., Petrucci, L.: FAST: acceleration from theory to practice. Int. J. Softw. Tools Technol. Transf. **10**(5), 401–424 (2008). https://doi.org/10.1007/s10009-008-0064-3

4. Beyer, D.: Competition on software verification and witness validation: SV-COMP 2023. In: Sankaranarayanan, S., Sharygina, N. (eds.) TACAS 2023. LNCS, vol. 13994, pp. 495–522. Springer, Cham (2023). https://doi.org/10.1007/978-3-031-30820-8_29

5. Beyer, D.: Second competition on software verification - (summary of SV-COMP 2013). In: Piterman, N., Smolka, S.A. (eds.) TACAS 2013. LNCS, vol. 7795, pp. 594–609. Springer, Heidelberg (2013). https://doi.org/10.1007/978-3-642-36742-7_43

6. Beyer, D., Cimatti, A., Griggio, A., Keremoglu, M.E., Sebastiani, R.: Software model checking via large-block encoding. In: Proceedings of 9th International Conference on Formal Methods in Computer-Aided Design, FMCAD 2009, Austin, pp. 25–32. IEEE (2009). https://doi.org/10.1109/FMCAD.2009.5351147

7. Beyer, D., Lee, N., Wendler, P.: Interpolation and sat-based model checking revisited: adoption to software verification. arXiv preprint arXiv:2208.05046 (2022)

8. Blicha, M., Britikov, K., Sharygina, N.: The golem horn solver. In: Enea, C., Lal, A. (eds.) CAV 2023. LNCS, vol. 13965, pp. 209–223. Springer, Cham (2023). https://doi.org/10.1007/978-3-031-37703-7_10

9. Blicha, M., Fedyukovich, G., Hyvärinen, A.E.J., Sharygina, N.: Split transition power abstraction for unbounded safety. In: Griggio, A., Rungta, N. (eds.) 22nd Formal Methods in Computer-Aided Design, FMCAD 2022, Trento, pp. 349–358. IEEE (2022). https://doi.org/10.34727/2022/isbn.978-3-85448-053-2_42

10. Blicha, M., Fedyukovich, G., Hyvärinen, A.E.J., Sharygina, N.: Transition power abstractions for deep counterexample detection. In: Fisman, D., Rosu, G. (eds.) TACAS 2022. LNCS, vol. 13243, pp. 524–542. Springer, Cham (2022). https://doi.org/10.1007/978-3-030-99524-9_29

---

[4] Full set of benchmarks and an executable version of the algorithm described in the paper are available at https://zenodo.org/doi/10.5281/zenodo.12522510.

11. Blicha, M., Kofron, J., Tatarko, W.: Summarization of branching loops. In: Hong, J., Bures, M., Park, J.W., Cerný, T. (eds.) The 37th ACM/SIGAPP Symposium on Applied Computing, Virtual Event (SAC 2022), 25–29 April 2022, pp. 1808–1816. ACM (2022). https://doi.org/10.1145/3477314.3507042

12. Bozga, M., Iosif, R., Konecný, F.: Fast acceleration of ultimately periodic relations. In: Touili, T., Cook, B., Jackson, P.B. (eds.) CAV 2010. LNCS, vol. 6174, pp. 227–242. Springer, Heidelberg (2010). https://doi.org/10.1007/978-3-642-14295-6_23

13. Bueno, D.: Horn2vmt: Translating horn reachability into transition systems. Tech. rep., Sandia National Lab.(SNL-NM), Albuquerque, NM (United States) (2020)

14. Craig, W.: Three uses of the Herbrand-Gentzen theorem in relating model theory and proof theory. J. Symbol. Logic **22**(3), 269–285 (1957)

15. Darke, P., Chimdyalwar, B., Venkatesh, R., Shrotri, U., Metta, R.: Over-approximating loops to prove properties using bounded model checking. In: Nebel, W., Atienza, D. (eds.) Proceedings of the Design, Automation and Test in Europe Conference and Exhibition, DATE 2015, Grenoble, pp. 1407–1412. ACM (2015). http://dl.acm.org/citation.cfm?id=2757139

16. Darke, P., Khanzode, M., Nair, A., Shrotri, U., Venkatesh, R.: Precise analysis of large industry code. In: Leung, K.R.P.H., Muenchaisri, P. (eds.) 19th Asia-Pacific Software Engineering Conference, APSEC 2012, Hong Kong, 4–7 December 2012, pp. 306–309. IEEE (2012). https://doi.org/10.1109/APSEC.2012.97

17. Donaldson, A.F., Kroening, D., Rümmer, P.: Automatic analysis of DMA races using model checking and k-induction. Formal Methods Syst. Des. **39**(1), 83–113 (2011). https://doi.org/10.1007/s10703-011-0124-2

18. Fedyukovich, G., Kaufman, S.J., Bodík, R.: Learning inductive invariants by sampling from frequency distributions. Formal Methods Syst. Des. **56**(1), 154–177 (2020). https://doi.org/10.1007/s10703-020-00349-x

19. Frohn, F.: A calculus for modular loop acceleration. In: Biere, A., Parker, D. (eds.) TACAS 2020. LNCS, vol. 12078, pp. 58–76. Springer, Cham (2020). https://doi.org/10.1007/978-3-030-45190-5_4

20. Frohn, F., Giesl, J.: Proving non-termination via loop acceleration. arXiv preprint arXiv:1905.11187 (2019)

21. Godefroid, P., Luchaup, D.: Automatic partial loop summarization in dynamic test generation. In: Dwyer, M.B., Tip, F. (eds.) Proceedings of the 20th International Symposium on Software Testing and Analysis, ISSTA 2011, Toronto, pp. 23–33. ACM (2011). https://doi.org/10.1145/2001420.2001424

22. Henzinger, T.A., Jhala, R., Majumdar, R., McMillan, K.L.: Abstractions from proofs. In: Jones, N.D., Leroy, X. (eds.) Proceedings of the 31st ACM SIGPLAN-SIGACT Symposium on Principles of Programming Languages, POPL 2004, Venice, pp. 232–244. ACM (2004). https://doi.org/10.1145/964001.964021

23. Hojjat, H., Rümmer, P.: The ELDARICA horn solver. In: Bjørner, N.S., Gurfinkel, A. (eds.) Formal Methods in Computer Aided Design, FMCAD 2018, Austin, pp. 1–7. IEEE (2018). https://doi.org/10.23919/FMCAD.2018.8603013

24. Kafle, B., Gallagher, J.P., Morales, J.F.: Rahft: a tool for verifying horn clauses using abstract interpretation and finite tree automata. In: Chaudhuri, S., Farzan, A. (eds.) CAV 2016. LNCS, vol. 9779, pp. 261–268. Springer, Cham (2016). https://doi.org/10.1007/978-3-319-41528-4_14

25. Kamath, A., et al.: Finding inductive loop invariants using large language models. arXiv preprint arXiv:2311.07948 (2023)

26. Komuravelli, A., Gurfinkel, A., Chaki, S.: Smt-based model checking for recursive programs. Formal Methods Syst. Des. **48**(3), 175–205 (2016)

27. Kroening, D., Sharygina, N., Tonetta, S., Tsitovich, A., Wintersteiger, C.M.: Loop summarization using abstract transformers. In: Cha, S.D., Choi, J., Kim, M., Lee, I., Viswanathan, M. (eds.) ATVA 2008. LNCS, vol. 5311, pp. 111–125. Springer, Heidelberg (2008). https://doi.org/10.1007/978-3-540-88387-6_10

28. Lin, S., Sun, J., Xiao, H., Liu, Y., Sanán, D., Hansen, H.: Fib: squeezing loop invariants by interpolation between forward/backward predicate transformers. In: Rosu, G., Penta, M.D., Nguyen, T.N. (eds.) Proceedings of the 32nd IEEE/ACM International Conference on Automated Software Engineering, ASE 2017, Urbana, pp. 793–803. IEEE Computer Society (2017). https://doi.org/10.1109/ASE.2017.8115690

29. McMillan, K., Rybalchenko, A.: Computing relational fixed points using interpolation. Technical report. MSR-TR-2013-6 (2013)

30. McMillan, K.L.: Interpolation and sat-based model checking. In: Jr., W.A.H., Somenzi, F. (eds.) CAV 2003. LNCS, vol. 2725, pp. 1–13. Springer, Cham (2003). https://doi.org/10.1007/978-3-540-45069-6_1

31. McMillan, K.L.: Lazy abstraction with interpolants. In: Ball, T., Jones, R.B. (eds.) CAV 2006. LNCS, vol. 4144, pp. 123–136. Springer, Heidelberg (2006). https://doi.org/10.1007/11817963_14

32. de Moura, L.M., Bjørner, N.S.: Z3: an efficient SMT solver. In: Ramakrishnan, C.R., Rehof, J. (eds.) TACAS 2008. LNCS, vol. 4963, pp. 337–340. Springer, Heidelberg (2008). https://doi.org/10.1007/978-3-540-78800-3_24

33. Nielson, H.R., Nielson, F.: Semantics with applications - a formal introduction. In: Wiley Professional Computing. Wiley (1992)

34. Ryan, G., Wong, J., Yao, J., Gu, R., Jana, S.: CLN2INV: learning loop invariants with continuous logic networks. In: 8th International Conference on Learning Representations, ICLR 2020, Addis Ababa, Ethiopia. OpenReview.net (2020). https://openreview.net/forum?id=HJlfuTEtvB

35. Silverman, J., Kincaid, Z.: Loop summarization with rational vector addition systems. In: Dillig, I., Tasiran, S. (eds.) CAV 2019. LNCS, vol. 11562, pp. 97–115. Springer, Cham (2019). https://doi.org/10.1007/978-3-030-25543-5_7

36. Strejcek, J., Trtík, M.: Abstracting path conditions. In: Heimdahl, M.P.E., Su, Z. (eds.) International Symposium on Software Testing and Analysis, ISSTA 2012, Minneapolis, pp. 155–165. ACM (2012). https://doi.org/10.1145/2338965.2336772

37. Xie, X., Chen, B., Zou, L., Liu, Y., Le, W., Li, X.: Automatic loop summarization via path dependency analysis. IEEE Trans. Software Eng. 45(6), 537–557 (2019). https://doi.org/10.1109/TSE.2017.2788018

Logic and Automata

Misconceptions in Finite-Trace and Infinite-Trace Linear Temporal Logic

Ben Greenman[1,2]($\boxtimes$) , Siddhartha Prasad[2] , Antonio Di Stasio[3] ,
Shufang Zhu[3] , Giuseppe De Giacomo[3] , Shriram Krishnamurthi[2] ,
Marco Montali[4] , Tim Nelson[2] , and Milda Zizyte[2]

[1] University of Utah, Salt Lake City, USA
benjaminlgreenman@gmail.com
[2] Brown University, Providence, USA
[3] University of Oxford, Oxford, UK
[4] Free University of Bozen–Bolzano, Bolzano, Italy

Abstract. With the growing use of temporal logics in areas ranging from robot planning to runtime verification, it is critical that users have a clear understanding of what a specification means. Toward this end, we have been developing a catalog of semantic errors and a suite of test instruments targeting various user-groups. The catalog is of interest to educators, to logic designers, to formula authors, and to tool builders, e.g., to identify mistakes. The test instruments are suitable for classroom teaching or self-study.

This paper reports on five sets of survey data collected over a three-year span. We study misconceptions about finite-trace LTL_f in three LTL-aware audiences, and misconceptions about standard LTL in novices. We find several mistakes, even among experts. In addition, the data supports several categories of errors in both LTL_f and LTL that have not been identified in prior work. These findings, based on data from actual users, offer insights into what *specific ways* temporal logics are tricky and provide a groundwork for future interventions.

Keywords: LTL · LTLf · misconceptions · user studies

1 Introduction

Temporal logics are indispensable for specifying and verifying the behavior of complex systems. Linear temporal logic (LTL) and its restriction to finite traces (LTL_f) are two especially useful members of the family. LTL, for example, has been widely adopted by the robotics community [4,5,10,29,37,42,45,48,60,70]. LTL_f has applications to runtime verification [64], web-page testing [54], business process modeling [20,22], process mining [16], planning [13,24,25], reinforcement learning [21], and image processing [65]. Furthermore, both logics support good decision procedures [67] and enable program synthesis [2,3,7,11,49,56,62,71].

These successes all depend, however, on a crucial assumption: that users of the logics can actually write correct specifications. Given a well-formed but

A. Platzer et al. (Eds.): FM 2024, LNCS 14933, pp. 579–599, 2025.
https://doi.org/10.1007/978-3-031-71162-6_30

Globally / Always

$$\sigma \models G(x) \iff \forall j, \qquad\qquad \sigma(j) \models x$$
$$\sigma_N \models G(x) \iff \forall j : \mathrm{j} \leq \mathrm{N}, \sigma_N(j) \models x$$

Finally / Eventually

$$\sigma \models F(x) \iff \exists j, \qquad\qquad \sigma(j) \models x$$
$$\sigma_N \models F(x) \iff \exists j : \mathrm{j} \leq \mathrm{N}, \sigma_N(j) \models x$$

Next

$$\sigma \models X(x) \iff \qquad\qquad \sigma(1) \models x$$
$$\sigma_N \models X(x) \iff 1 \leq \mathrm{N} \ \wedge \ \sigma_N(1) \models x$$

Until

$$\sigma \models x\,U\,y \iff \exists j, \qquad\qquad \sigma(j) \models y$$
$$\wedge \ \forall i : i < j, \sigma(i) \models x$$
$$\sigma_N \models x\,U\,y \iff \exists j : \mathrm{j} \leq \mathrm{N}, \sigma_N(j) \models y$$
$$\wedge \ \forall i : i < j, \sigma_N(i) \models x$$

Fig. 1. Semantics of four LTL and LTL$_f$ operators: G, F, X, U

incorrect formula, synthesis will output a system that behaves as specified—whether or not that is the desired behavior. It is therefore critical to know the *specific* misunderstandings that lead to incorrect formulas in order to correct them via tools, logic design, and teaching. That is the focus of this paper.

Contributions and Outline. After a brief introduction to LTL, LTL$_f$, and our pedagogy (Sect. 2), we proceed with the following contributions:

- We introduce two test instruments (Sect. 3):
  - a *finite trace* instrument that tests respondents' understanding of the delta between LTL and LTL$_f$, and
  - an *introductory* instrument that promotes active learning of LTL.
- We present a dataset of over 3,000 responses collected from dozens of respondents over the past three years (Sect. 4). The data contains mistakes from beginning, knowledgeable, and expert respondents (Sect. 6).
- We present a catalog of LTL and LTL$_f$ misconceptions (Sect. 5) that is thoroughly grounded in the data (Sect. 7).

The main results are in Sects. 6 and 7. The paper concludes with threats to validity (Sect. 8), related work (Sect. 9), and a brief discussion (Sect. 10).

2   Background

LTL formulas are interpreted over infinite traces, $\sigma = s_0 s_1 s_2 \cdots$, where each s_i is a state that provides valuations for a set of atomic propositions [55]. LTL$_f$ formulas are interpreted over finite traces, $\sigma_N = s_0 s_1 \cdots s_N$ [69]. While LTL and LTL$_f$ share the same syntax, their semantics differ as shown by the highlighted constraints in Fig. 1. This figure uses the notation $\sigma(j)$ to select a suffix of σ starting from position j. For example, $\sigma(2)$ is equal to $s_2 \cdots$. An *always* (G) operator quantifies over all remaining states in the trace, an *eventually* (F) must find a satisfying suffix before the trace ends, a *next* (X, aka *strong next*) constrains the suffix after the current state, and an *until* (U) must find a satisfying suffix for its right operand and ensure that its left operand holds beforehand. Not pictured is the LTL$_f$ weak next (X_W, omitted to save space), which does not require that a next state exists.

2.1   LTL$_f$ Example: Concision via Finiteness

Finite prefixes can be expressed within an infinite LTL trace, but doing so may require intricate formulas. To illustrate, consider a busy philosopher sitting in front of a bowl of ice cream. She has a lot of thinking to do, but if she decides to eat ice cream, she needs to do so before the ice cream melts. In LTL$_f$, traces are finite. The end of a trace might correspond, e.g., to the termination of a program or the end of a data stream. Ending the trace at the point where the ice cream melts allows for a simple framing of this property:

$G(w \implies F(e))$ # where w means "wants to eat" and e means "is eating"

By contrast, LTL requires a larger formula with a new variable (m: ice cream has melted) and a gadget to encode a prefix of an infinite trace.

$!m \land F(m) \land$ # ice cream eventually melts
$G(m \implies G(m)) \land$ # once melted, ice cream stays melted
$G(m \lor$ # either ice cream is melted, or
     $(w \implies F(e \land !m)))$ # philosopher who wants to eat eventually does

2.2   Toward a Concept Inventory

This paper is part of a larger effort to create a set of *concept inventory* test instruments for LTL, LTL$_f$, and related logics. Our guiding example is the Force Concept Inventory for teaching physics [39, 40], a multiple choice test in which every incorrect choice is carefully designed to match *one* specific misconception. Unless test-takers select the wrong choice by mistake, their results strongly suggest which concepts they need to review. We are developing test instruments that use a variety of question types to identify the misconceptions that a temporal logic concept inventory should cover.

In a perfect world, every course subject would come with a concept inventory. However, developing an inventory takes several rounds of careful study (e.g., via think-aloud interviews) to identify misconceptions and reliably pinpoint them among test-takers [1, 63]. One impediment to development is the expert blind spot [51, 52]; namely, that test designers overlook concepts that learners struggle with. Our Spreading X misconception (Sect. 7.6), for example, is an issue that we were blind to.

This paper builds on prior LTL instruments [35, 58] that employed a learner-driven tool called Quizius [59] to reduce the up-front cost of discovering misconceptions. Prior work [35] refined the instruments through three post-Quizius surveys, finding support for some potential misconceptions and discarding others. This paper represents a significant step forward in the iterative development of concept inventories with four additional studies that find misconceptions in LTL and in the unexplored domain of LTL$_f$.

3   Instrument Design

This section describes the design of our study instruments. Complete instruments are in the artifact for this paper [34]. We contribute two instruments: a *finite-trace* instrument that contrasts LTL$_f$ with LTL and an *introductory* instrument

Q. Describe the formula $G(X(\text{red}))$ for LTL and LTL$_f$.

LTL:

LTL$_f$:

(a) Describe Formulas

Q. Write a formula for Red is on exactly once in LTL and LTL$_f$.

LTL:

LTL$_f$:

(b) Write Formulas

Q. Is the formula red $\wedge$ $G(X_W(\text{blue}))$ satisfied by this trace?

Answer: Yes / No

Rationale:

(c) Trace Matching

Q. Why does the formula $F(\text{red})$ reject this trace?

Answer:

(d) Explain Mismatches

Q. Is $G(!a) = {!}F(a)$ valid for any term a in LTL$_f$?
     This equation is valid in LTL.
Answer: Yes / No
Rationale:

(e) Check Equations

Fig. 2. Example questions

that assumes only minimal knowledge of LTL. The instruments are based on prior LTL work [35], reusing questions and question types that have proven effective in the past. The questions use simple state spaces with three on/off features such as the 3-color panel in Fig. 2.

The central question types ask about informal-to-formal translations:

Describe Formulas (Fig. 2a): Given an LTL or LTL$_f$ formula, translate it to an English-language description. This task is similar to what a person does when reading a specification and deciding whether it is correct.

Write Formulas (Fig. 2b): Given an English statement, translate it to LTL and/or LTL$_f$ or say that it is inexpressible. This is *the key skill* for doing formal verification. ("there must be a [informal-to-formal] transition" [26]).

Three other question types address specific goals. One type, Trace Matching, is from prior work [35]. The other two expose differences between LTL and LTL$_f$.

Trace Matching (Fig. 2c): Given a formula and a trace, mark the trace as either satisfying or violating. These questions test for specific, semantic misunderstandings. All traces were either finite or repeated the final state.

Explain Mismatches (Fig. 2d): Given an LTL$_f$ formula and a finite trace that violates the formula, explain the reason for the mismatch. The instructions suggest four potential explanations: (1) only an infinite trace can satisfy the formula; (2) the trace is too long, i.e., the formula accepts no traces of this length; (3) the trace is too short; or (4) trace content mismatch, i.e., the wrong lights are on/off in some states. These questions serve as a tutorial on the mismatches that can arise in a finite-trace setting.

Check Equations (Fig. 2e): Given an equation and a statement of its validity in LTL, determine whether it is valid in LTL$_f$ for non-empty traces. These questions test general ways in which LTL and LTL$_f$ formulas differ.

3.1   LTL$_f$ Instrument

The finite trace instrument is designed for an LTL-aware audience. This instrument has five parts, corresponding to the five question types above but arranged in order of difficulty rather than importance:

1. Explain Mismatches   2. Trace Matching   3. Describe Formulas
4. Write Formulas   5. Check Equations

Part 1 functions as an LTL$_f$ primer. It presents five mismatched formulas and traces and asks respondents to think critically about why the two disagree. For example, the trace in Fig. 2d is rejected by the formula $F(red)$ because it has no red states. Respondents who expect F to accept an empty trace (similar to weak next) may be able to use this example to correct their misconception.

Parts 2, 3, and 4 appear in order of increasing difficulty so that respondents can build confidence as they approach the harder questions. There are six Trace Matching questions, four Describe Formulas questions, and five Write Formulas questions. The translation questions each ask about LTL and LTL$_f$: respondents must provide two formulas (or two descriptions), or write "same" if the second would be identical. One question presents a formula that is insensitive to infiniteness [23], for which "same" is the correct response.

Part 5 presents three equations that are valid in LTL, such as $!X(a) = X(!a)$, and one that is invalid in LTL: $G(F(a)) = F(G(a))$. Respondents must decide whether the equations are valid in LTL$_f$.

3.2   LTL Instruments

We used two instruments with students: a new *introductory* instrument, and the LTL instrument from prior work [35]. Both instruments have three parts:

1. Trace Matching   2. Describe Formulas   3. Write Formulas

Part 1 uses lasso traces where the last shown state repeats indefinitely. The state space is a locomotive with three features: engine smoke, a door, and a headlight. Parts 2 and 3 ask for translations to and from LTL.

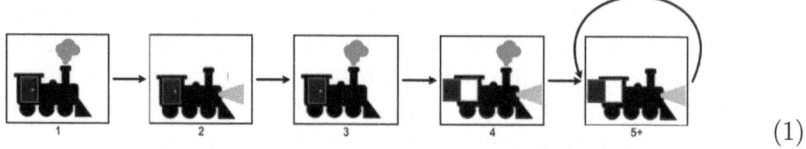

$$(1)$$

The first instrument is intended for students who have no knowledge of temporal logic. It presents nine of the easy-to-answer Trace Matching questions, and only two Describe questions and two Write questions. Some of the trace questions match the same formula with different traces to hone in on misconceptions. The translation questions intentionally do not ask about the until operator.

The second instrument is from prior work [35] with minor enhancements. It asks nine Match questions, five Describe questions, and five Write questions.

Table 1. Study contexts, number of respondents, and number of responses

Context	Instrument	Respondents	Total Responses
α'23	finite-trace	22	1132
α'24	finite-trace	18	693
FTAI	finite-trace	24	455
β_1	introductory	31	403
β_2	LTL [35]	24	456

4   Data

We deployed our instruments to four populations over three years. The finite-trace instrument went out to two semesters of students at a public UK university (α'23, α'24) and to the attendees of a symposium on LTL_f in artificial intelligence (FTAI—anonymized acronym). The introductory instrument was used in an embedded systems course at a private US university (β_1, β_2). Between 18 and 24 respondents completed each instrument, and each participant contributed dozens of individual responses to the overall dataset. Table 1 provides the details. We hosted each instrument on Qualtrics.

4.1   Student α: 2023 and 2024

Populations α'23 and α'24 consisted of students enrolled in an elective course on self-programming agents, which is dedicated to various forms of LTL_f reactive synthesis and planning in the context of autonomous agents. Students can take this course in the final year of a BSc in computer science or during an MSc on Advanced CS. Both α populations are similar and received comparable instruction, though we remark that the instructor joined the university in 2023. Early in the term, students received a lecture on LTL and completed the LTL instrument from prior work as a homework exercise. Shortly afterward, students received a lecture on LTL$_f$ and completed the finite-trace instrument as homework. The LTL responses were of very high quality (92% correct in α'23), so we analyze only the LTL$_f$ responses in this paper.

The α'23 instrument differs from the final, α'24 instrument in two ways: the Explain Mismatches questions are multiple choice and there are three additional Check Equations questions (which did not lead to interesting incorrect responses). Free response is better for Explain Mismatches because it is less constraining. Respondents struggled when two choices might reasonably apply, and forcing them to choose was not helpful in our search for misconceptions.

4.2   FTAI: 2023

FTAI is our anonymized name for a symposium on finite-trace temporal logics for AI that was held in 2023. The event brought together world-class researchers with deep expertise in temporal logics including LTL$_f$. Seventeen attendees (74%) self-reported AI as among their primary research areas, nine (39%) selected formal methods, and five (21%) selected machine learning. Eleven claimed to be knowledgeable in LTL$_f$ specifically. All but a few attendees were in-person.

On the first day of the symposium, we presented (via Zoom) a brief introduction to our work on logic misconceptions and gave respondents 15 min to fill out the instrument. This introduction did not explain LTL$_f$ semantics and it did not explain our question types; all instructions were in the instrument itself. Ten respondents completed the instrument in the allotted time. Eight respondents finished by the end of the conference. Six others finished later in Spring 2023; these may have been colleagues of symposium attendees, as we encouraged attendees to share the instrument link with their research groups.

Respondents in this study received only a subset of the α'23 instrument to maximize the completion rate, which explains the relatively low number of responses in Table 1. They completed 3 out of 5 Explain Mismatches questions, 3 of 6 Trace Matching questions, 2 of 4 Describe Formulas questions, 2 of 5 Write Formulas questions, and 5 of 7 Check Equations questions—all selected uniformly at random by Qualtrics.

4.3   Student β: 2022

Population β completed two instruments, β_1 and β_2, in the context of an elective undergraduate course on embedded systems taught at a private US university. The course has limited time to cover LTL-based model checking, making it critical to teach LTL quickly to students unfamiliar with temporal logic. In 2022, near the end of the semester, we assigned the introductory instrument as homework (β_1) without teaching LTL in lecture. Students had several days to read the course textbook [47] and submit. The next lecture featured LTL and assigned the full LTL instrument [35] as homework due the following week (β_2).

All homework in embedded systems was graded by participation. Furthermore, students were allowed to drop three homeworks during the term. We know from survey comments that at least two students were planning to drop an LTL homework, but since responses are anonymous and these comments appeared only in complete surveys, there is no reliable way to determine which of these students, if any, actually dropped an LTL homework.

5   Catalog Design

The catalog, or "code book" (in the qualitative analysis sense), is our rubric for temporal logic misconceptions. Figure 3 presents a short overview of the core semantic errors. Its aim is to provide just enough background for readers to understand our results in Sects. 6 and 7. The full catalog in our artifact comes with instructions showing how to apply the labels to new responses [34].

Length : too many/few states (LTL$_f$ only)
Last : attempt $X_W(\mathit{false})$ in LTL
Bad Prop : wrong $\wedge/\vee/\Rightarrow$/atom
Bad State Index : too many/few X
Bad State Quantification : wrong $F/G/U$
Cycle G : underspecified G term
Implicit F : missing/assumed F

Implicit G : missing/assumed G
Implicit Prefix : F missing context
Other Implicit : other underconstraint
Weak U : mistake U for W
Exclusive U : expect disjoint U terms
Trace-Split U : overspecified U
Spreading X : mistake XX for $X \wedge XX$

Fig. 3. Brief summary of misconceptions

In addition to the labels in Fig. 3, there are three meta labels: Precedence, RV, and Unlabeled. Precedence applies to responses that are ambiguous due to missing parentheses. RV stands for "Reasonable Variant," and applies to written formulas that support an unintended reading of an English prompt. Unlabeled is for responses that contain several mistakes or otherwise defy categorization.

The highlighted labels are new to this work. **Length** and **Last** apply only to LTL$_f$. **Cycle G**, **Implicit Prefix**, **Trace-Split U**, and **Spreading X** apply to both LTL$_f$ and LTL. The other labels originate in prior work [35]. We developed the new labels by starting from the prior catalog and applying techniques from grounded theory [33] to discover categories of mistakes. Two authors worked as labelers. First, the labelers independently assessed sample responses using the baseline catalog. Coding happened in small sessions to minimize labeler fatigue. Second, the labelers met to identify patterns among responses that did not fit the current rubric. Third, the labelers used the standard Cohen's κ score [17] to check agreement. This measure typically ranges from 0 to 1, where a score above 0.8 is considered excellent [61]. The coders quickly reached a high score, perhaps due to the well-tested baseline catalog. Further details on instrument development follow:

Finite Trace: $\kappa = 0.79$ after labeling 26 responses: 14 Write Formulas, 8 Describe Formulas, and 6 Check Equations.

Introductory: $\kappa = 0.83$ after labeling 13 responses: 9 Write Formulas and 4 Describe Formulas.

6   Results: Incorrect Responses, Specific Errors

Our instruments collected a variety of errors across the four populations. Table 2 presents the totals at a high-level. Table rows correspond to question types (with abbreviated names, such as Explain for Explain Mismatches), and table columns name the instrument deployments. Each cell counts the number of incorrect responses (*not* the number of respondents who contributed these responses) and reports it as a percentage of the total responses for that particular instrument and question type. Be advised that percentages are not comparable across columns because the number of questions in each part may have changed; for example, Check Equations has 7 questions in α'23 and 4 in α'24.

Table 2. Total incorrect responses

	α'23	α'24	FTAI	β_1	β_2
Explain	18 (20.00%)	4 (4.44%)	16 (22.22%)	N/A	N/A
Match	2 (1.85%)	3 (2.78%)	6 (8.33%)	76 (27.24%)	43 (19.91%)
Describe	23 (15.97%)	23 (15.97%)	19 (19.79%)	30 (48.39%)	47 (39.17%)
Write	38 (21.11%)	45 (25.00%)	32 (33.68%)	41 (66.13%)	76 (63.33%)
Check	9 (7.14%)	5 (6.94%)	25 (20.83%)	N/A	N/A

The main takeaway from Table 2 is that every question type attracted some incorrect responses, and some attracted quite a few (over 20%). Trace Matching was the easiest question across the board and Write Formulas was the hardest; even the FTAI respondents submitted a fair number of incorrect formulas. Students in β_1 submitted many incorrect responses. At a glance, it would seem that the β_2 responses are only marginally better percentage-wise, but there were nearly twice as many translation questions in the β_2 instrument and they were more difficult; the small percentage improvement is encouraging.

Each incorrect response may correspond to zero or more misconceptions in our catalog, depending on why it is incorrect. Table 3 presents the catalog classification of the incorrect responses. The columns are grouped by three question types: Trace Matching, Describe Formulas, and Write Formulas. We discuss the other question types in prose below. Within each question type, columns correspond to deployments. The rows are labels from the catalog. Each cell counts the number of incorrect responses; we use a dash (-) rather than a zero to make the nonzero numbers easier to see.

Table 3. Errors in incorrect responses (one response may match several labels)

(a) Finite trace instrument

Code	Match α'23	α'24	FTAI	Describe α'23	α'24	FTAI	Write α'23	α'24	FTAI	Total
Length	-	2	3	7	2	2	10	3	3	31
Last	-	-	-	-	-	-	1	5	-	6
Bad Prop	-	-	-	-	2	4	-	6	2	14
Bad State Index	-	-	-	-	-	-	2	9	5	17
Bad State Quantification	-	-	-	-	-	-	-	1	2	3
Cycle G	-	-	-	-	-	-	-	2	2	4
Implicit F	-	-	-	7	6	5	3	7	2	30
Implicit G	-	-	-	1	-	-	4	8	2	15
Implicit Prefix	-	-	-	-	-	-	8	4	8	20
Other Implicit	-	-	-	-	-	3	1	-	-	4
Weak U	2	1	2	-	1	1	-	-	-	7
Exclusive U	-	-	1	-	3	2	-	-	-	6
Trace-Split U	-	-	-	-	-	-	-	-	3	3
Spreading X	-	-	-	-	-	-	-	-	-	-
Precedence	-	-	-	-	-	-	-	1	1	2
RV	-	-	-	-	-	-	2	-	-	2
Unlabeled	-	-	-	8	10	4	13	2	9	46

(b) Introductory and LTL [35] instruments

Code	Match β_1	β_2	Describe β_1	β_2	Write β_1	β_2	Total
Bad Prop	9	7	3	8	16	14	57
Bad State Index	1	8	15	7	3	10	44
Bad State Quantification	7	3	5	9	4	4	32
Cycle G	-	-	-	-	-	-	-
Implicit F	11	11	1	1	-	4	28
Implicit G	13	1	1	7	23	23	68
Implicit Prefix	-	-	-	-	-	8	8
Other Implicit	-	-	-	-	-	5	5
Weak U	15	9	-	2	-	-	26
Exclusive U	8	5	-	4	-	-	17
Trace-Split U	-	-	-	-	-	2	2
Spreading X	6	-	1	3	10	3	23
Precedence	2	-	-	4	-	3	9
RV	-	-	-	-	-	-	-
Unlabeled	6	-	2	16	7	19	50

Every core label has at least some support from the responses, with **Bad State Index**, **Implicit F**, and **Implicit G** being among the most popular. The **Weak U** label has low numbers, but these came primarily from a Trace Matching question that specifically tests this issue; the fact that even one FTAI participant made this mistake is noteworthy. Issues with trace length constraints (**Length**) are common in LTL_f; see Sect. 7 for examples. Lastly, the low numbers for generic labels (**Bad State Quantification** and **Other Implicit**) and for reasonable variants (**RV**) suggest that the revised catalog is better at pinpointing issues and that the revised instruments are clearer to respondents.

We report some negative findings as well. Two labels, **Cycle G** and **Trace-Split U**, have little support overall and warrant targeted testing in the future. **Unlabeled** is unfortunately common, which suggests a need for interviews to learn the reasoning behind any deeply-incorrect responses. Some unlabeled responses in Table 3b do, however, have explanations. These are from respondents who were confused about LTL syntax, or who did not attempt the question.

Remaining Question Formats. The finite trace instruments include two question types that are not in Table 3a: Explain Mismatches and Check Equations. The incorrect Explain Mismatches responses are all **Unlabeled**; most of these are due to the multiple-choice ambiguity noted in Sect. 3.1. The incorrect Check Equations responses cannot be labeled definitively because these questions did not ask respondents to explain their reasoning (Fig. 2e). We merely note that the data suggests issues with **Length**, **OtherImplicit**, and a weak notion of F. The weak-F responses incorrectly marked $F(a) = a \vee X(F(a))$ as invalid in LTL_f.

7   Results: Categories of Errors

We turn now to the actual survey responses that support the new categories of errors; namely, the two LTL_f labels and four additional LTL labels. To ground the discussion, the subsections below present actual instrument questions ("Q") and representative sample responses ("WA" for "wrong answer"). We also discuss how tools might use our findings to provide feedback.

Certain questions appeared only in the finite-trace instruments and vice-versa. These are noted below. Also, to streamline the presentation, we have translated the introductory-instrument responses to use colors instead of locomotive characteristics (compare Fig. 2 and Eq. (1)).

7.1   Length (LTL_f only)

The **Length** label applies to responses that require too many or too few states. When writing an LTL_f formula, this issue can arise from the use of strong next instead of weak next. Tools might help by reporting the trace length(s) that a formula accepts.

- **Q.** Describe the LTL_f formula $red \wedge !X(blue)$.

– **WA.** "The first state must be red and the second state must not be blue."
This answer implies that a second state must exist, but the formula does not.
There are four responses of this sort in the dataset: two in α'23, one in α'24,
and one in FTAI.

– **Q.** Describe the LTL$_f$ formula $G(red \Rightarrow X(!red \wedge X(red)))$.
– **WA.** "For every state, if there is a red light on, the next state is with the
red light off, and the state afterward is with the red light on. The trace must
have at least have 3 states."
No finite trace with a red light can satisfy this formula, as every red light
demands another two states later. There are seven responses of this sort: five
in α'23 and one each in α'24 and FTAI.

– **Q.** Write an LTL$_f$ formula for: *Blue is on in the first state, off in the second
state, and alternates on/off for the remaining states.*
– **WA.** *blue* $\wedge$ $G(blue \Rightarrow X_W(!blue \wedge X_W(blue)))$
The prompt requires at least two states, but the formula accepts traces with
only one blue state. Interestingly, this formula is correct in LTL using X
instead of X_W, which underscores the subtlety of LTL$_f$. Eight α'23, one α'24,
and zero FTAI responses made this error.

7.2   Last (LTL$_f$ only)

The Last label applies to responses that attempt to encode a final state in infinite-
trace LTL instead of saying that the prompt is inexpressible. All such responses
stem from one formula-writing question.

– **Q.** Write (if possible) an LTL formula for: *Green is on in the final state.*
– **WA.** $F(G(green))$
While this response is correct for LTL$_f$ and is syntactically-valid LTL, it is
trying to answer an impossible question. There are six responses of this sort:
one from α'23, five from α'24, and zero from FTAI.

7.3   Cycle G

In LTL and LTL$_f$, the G operator imposes a constraint on every state. Yet, some
responses expect G to constrain one state, skip a few states, and reapply later.
The skipped states are precisely those captured by occurrences of X within the
G operand. A tool might help by highlighting atom constraints at each time
index (in the following example, index 2 would show a contradiction).

– **Q.** Write an LTL formula for: *Blue is on in the first state, off in the second
state, and alternates on/off for the remaining states.*
– **WA.** $G(blue \wedge X(!blue))$
This formula is unsatisfiable because it requires blue to be both on and off
in the second state. There are four responses of this sort, two from α'24 and
two from FTAI. However, we must caution that these responses came from
only two people who made the mistake consistently in LTL and LTL$_f$.

7.4   Implicit Prefix

The baseline catalog contains a generic label Other Implicit for responses that accept too many traces but do not fall under a more precise category. One such response from FTAI describes $G(red \Rightarrow X(!red \wedge X(red)))$ as "whenever red holds, it also holds two steps later," leaving the middle state underconstrained.

The Implicit Prefix label narrows the scope of Other Implicit. It applies to responses that correctly describe the suffix of valid traces but leave the prefix underconstrained. It does not apply to the example in the previous paragraph. Tools might help by showing example traces; for instance, traces with early states that satisfy some but not all constraints under an F may be informative.

- **Q.** Write an LTL formula for: *Red is on exactly once.*
- **WA.** $F(red \wedge X(G(!red)))$
  This formula describes a suffix in which red is on at one state and turns off afterward, but it does not prevent red from turning on before this point. There are 24 responses of this sort: eight each from α'23 and FTAI, and four each from α'24 and β_2. The finite-trace respondents made this mistake consistently in LTL and LTL$_f$, so the total in terms of people is only 14.

- **Q.** Write an LTL formula for: *Green is on for zero or more states, then turns off and remains off in the future.*
- **WA.** $G(F(!green))$
  Whereas the specification asks for green to stay on until it turns off, the formula allows green to turn on and off before reaching a non-green suffix. There are four responses of this sort in β_2. This question is not in the finite-trace instruments because it does not contrast LTL and LTL$_f$.

7.5   Trace-Split U

Several responses use F and G in the left operand of an until, as in $G(red)\ U\ blue$. These responses are usually incorrect. Some of them would be correct, however, if the left and right operands were interpreted on different parts of the full trace: a prefix on the left and a suffix on the right. (Interpreting on a prefix makes no sense in LTL, but is sensible in LTL$_f$.) The Trace-Split U label captures these responses. Tools can help by reporting such nested operands as a U antipattern.

- **Q.** Write an LTL formula for: *Blue is on in at least two states.*
- **WA.** $F(blue)\ U\ F(blue)$
  Any trace with one blue state satisfies the formula. There are two responses of this sort from FTAI and zero elsewhere.

- **Q.** Write an LTL formula for: *Green is on for zero or more states, then turns off and remains off in the future.*
- **WA.** $G(green)\ U\ G(!green)$
  Although a natural-language reading of this formula sounds compelling

(*always green until always not green*), the left G would entail a green light in every state. There are two responses of this sort in β_2. This question is not in the finite-trace instruments because it does not contrast LTL and LTL$_f$.

7.6   Spreading X

The X operator targets one specific state whereas G, F, and U quantify over an unknown future. This difference is evidently confusing to beginners, as several of the β_1 and β_2 responses expect one X to constrain both the current state and the next state. With nesting, these responses expect a longer interval, e.g., three red states for $X(X(red))$. Prior work with novices observed this issue as well [58]. We did not find evidence for it in our earlier studies [35], so perhaps the misconception is easily corrected. Tools can help by reminding users that an n-fold composition of X constrains one state n steps ahead.

- **Q.** Describe the LTL formula *blue* $\Rightarrow X(X(X(blue)))$.
- **WA.** "When the blue light is on, it will stay on for the next 3 states."
  There are three such responses. This question is only in the β_2 instrument.

- **Q.** Write an LTL formula for: *Red cannot stay on for 3 states in a row.*
- **WA.** $G(!X(X(X(red))))$
  There are eight such responses in β_1, and three in β_2. The finite-trace instrument does not include this question.

8   Threats to Validity

Qualitative coding inherently comes with biases, and our high agreement scores do not prove that these have been excised. To mitigate this issue, our data is available for other researchers to audit. Another threat is that the sets over which we computed agreement are not large.

One author manually classified responses for correctness and may have mislabeled some, despite our auditing. Write Formulas responses in particular might have leveraged automation, but the survey did not enforce an LTL syntax in order to lower the burden on respondents. Thus, there are variations such as or versus | and engine versus E that we had to normalize manually. One response uses next (perhaps inspired by PSL weak next [28]) without specifying a strong or weak interpretation. This ambiguity is a threat; fortunately, the response in question is incorrect in the same way with X or X_W. Operator precedence is another avenue for miscommunication; we assume, e.g., weak precedence for implication, but respondents may have had a different meaning in mind.

Regarding external validity, the two α studies took place at the same institution with the same instructor. The β study used a different institution and student population, and although the results are comparable to α they may not carry over to other populations, such as learners in industry. FTAI respondents were under time pressure due to the conference, and may have rushed through the more difficult translation questions.

Two question types require fluency in English. Although we did not specifically check for fluency, our respondents seem to meet this bar. Both universities that we worked with conduct all classes in English and expect a high degree of fluency. The FTAI symposium used English as well for all papers and talks. There were no indications of severe language issues in the responses.

Our instruments are rather weak ecologically because they ask basic questions about a rudimentary state space. Practical uses of LTL would involve systems with interacting components, and users would have access to verification tools. Performing studies in a realistic setting is an important topic for future work.

9   Related Work

Design tools [15,57], alternative languages and logics [6,8,28,46,66], pattern languages [27,36,43,50,57], natural-language translators [12,18,30] and error checkers [9,14,41,44,54], all seek to improve the usability of temporal logics such as LTL. Yet, none of these works study the misunderstandings of humans; at best, they address mistakes that a person *might* make.

Prior work on the Declare modeling language used think-aloud interviews to discover and validate errors [38]. Our work can help separate general LTL issues from Declare-specific issues. Other related user studies include two comparisons of LTL to similar logics [15,19], and an interface design study [15]. While these studies target learners, the focus is not directly on logic misconceptions.

Our translation questions are similar to those from Iltis [31,32], a tool for teaching logic. Iltis might serve as a framework for future studies, though it is aimed toward pedagogy rather than studies of misconceptions.

With the introductory instruments, we considered providing a link to Wickström's LTL visualizer [54,68]. We did not, due to concerns that misconceptions about the tool, which has not been validated, would be a confounding factor.

10   Looking Forward

We conducted a first study of LTL_f misconceptions in three populations with well-informed respondents, and studied LTL in two rounds with novices. The data offers insights into mis-specifications with two categories of LTL_f-specific mistakes, four new categories of LTL mistakes, and refined support for categories from prior work [35]. Given the very simple scenarios and formulas that we used, we suspect that many more issues lurk in more complicated settings.

Our work has obvious implications for learners and educators. We have already begun to employ its insights to create a new interactive learning environment called the LTL Tutor: https://www.ltl-tutor.xyz/. We have also had positive experiences in an undergraduate course on logical modeling [53] and in a graduate course on software verification. The instruments work well as an in-class activity followed by group discussion.

This work can also impact the design of future logics. Narrowly, it suggests different operator designs; broadly, it provides a methodology to identify misconceptions in the first place.

Finally, this work also has implications for tools that consume LTL or LTL$_f$. Currently, tools assume that a logical utterance precisely captures the user's intent, and verify, synthesize, or otherwise manifest exactly what was written. Our work can (and should!) be used to check for the presence of predictable errors, e.g., by checking that users really meant what they wrote (especially if they fall within a misconception category).

Acknowledgments. This collaboration began with a few comments on Facebook. We thank Moshe Vardi for the post that brought us together and Facebook for providing a discussion platform. Thanks to Mark Santolucito and Raven Rothkopf for conversations that influenced the introductory instruments. Thanks to the many students and researchers who participated in our studies.

This work has been partially supported by: the UNIBZ project ADAPTERS, the PRIN MIUR project PINPOINT Prot. 2020FNEB27, the ERC-ADG WhiteMech (No. 834228), and US National Science Foundation grants SHF-2227863, and 2030859.

Data Availability Statement. The survey instruments, final catalog, and labeled responses are available in the artifact for this paper [34].

Disclosure of Interests. The authors have no competing interests to declare.

References

1. Almstrum, V.L., et al.: Concept inventories in computer science for the topic discrete mathematics. ACM SIGCSE Bull. **38**(4), 132–145 (2006). https://doi.org/10.1145/1189136.1189182
2. Alur, R., Bansal, S., Bastani, O., Jothimurugan, K.: A framework for transforming specifications in reinforcement learning. CoRR abs/2111.00272 (2021). https://arxiv.org/abs/2111.00272
3. Amram, G., Bansal, S., Fried, D., Tabajara, L.M., Vardi, M.Y., Weiss, G.: Adapting behaviors via reactive synthesis. In: Silva, A., Leino, K.R.M. (eds.) CAV 2021. LNCS, vol. 12759, pp. 870–893. Springer, Cham (2021). https://doi.org/10.1007/978-3-030-81685-8_41
4. Antoniotti, M., Mishra, B.: Discrete events models + temporal logic = supervisory controller: automatic synthesis of locomotion controllers. In: ICRA, pp. 1441–1446. IEEE (1995). https://doi.org/10.1109/ROBOT.1995.525480
5. Araki, B., Li, X., Vodrahalli, K., DeCastro, J.A., Fry, M.J., Rus, D.: The logical options framework. In: ICML, vol. 139, pp. 307–317. PMLR (2021). http://proceedings.mlr.press/v139/araki21a.html
6. Armoni, R., et al.: The ForSpec temporal logic: a new temporal property-specification language. In: Katoen, J.-P., Stevens, P. (eds.) TACAS 2002. LNCS, vol. 2280, pp. 296–311. Springer, Heidelberg (2002). https://doi.org/10.1007/3-540-46002-0_21
7. Bansal, S., Li, Y., Tabajara, L.M., Vardi, M.Y., Wells, A.: Model checking strategies from synthesis over finite traces. In: André, É., Sun, J. (eds.) ATVA 2023. LNCS,

vol. 14215, pp. 227–247. Springer, Cham (2023). https://doi.org/10.1007/978-3-031-45329-8_11

8. Beer, I., Ben-David, S., Eisner, C., Fisman, D., Gringauze, A., Rodeh, Y.: The temporal logic sugar. In: Berry, G., Comon, H., Finkel, A. (eds.) CAV 2001. LNCS, vol. 2102, pp. 363–367. Springer, Heidelberg (2001). https://doi.org/10.1007/3-540-44585-4_33

9. Beer, I., Ben-David, S., Eisner, C., Rodeh, Y.: Efficient detection of vacuity in ACTL formulas. In: Grumberg, O. (ed.) CAV 1997. LNCS, vol. 1254, pp. 279–290. Springer, Heidelberg (1997). https://doi.org/10.1007/3-540-63166-6_28

10. Bhatia, A., Kavraki, L.E., Vardi, M.Y.: Sampling-based motion planning with temporal goals. In: ICRA, pp. 2689–2696. IEEE (2010). https://doi.org/10.1109/ROBOT.2010.5509503

11. Bloem, R., Jobstmann, B., Piterman, N., Pnueli, A., Sa'ar, Y.: Synthesis of reactive(1) designs. J. Comput. Syst. Sci. **78**(3), 911–938 (2012). https://doi.org/10.1016/j.jcss.2011.08.007

12. Brunello, A., Montanari, A., Reynolds, M.: Synthesis of LTL formulas from natural language texts: state of the art and research directions. In: TIME, vol. 147, pp. 17:1–17:19. Schloss Dagstuhl (2019). https://doi.org/10.4230/LIPIcs.TIME.2019.17

13. Camacho, A., McIlraith, S.A.: Strong fully observable non-deterministic planning with LTL and LTLf goals. In: IJCAI, pp. 5523–5531. ijcai.org (2019). https://doi.org/10.24963/IJCAI.2019/767

14. Chockler, H., Strichman, O.: Easier and more informative vacuity checks. In: MEMOCODE, pp. 189–198. IEEE Computer Society (2007). https://doi.org/10.1109/MEMCOD.2007.371225

15. Choi, W., Vazirani, M., Santolucito, M.: Program synthesis for musicians: a usability testbed for temporal logic specifications. In: Oh, H. (ed.) APLAS 2021. LNCS, vol. 13008, pp. 47–61. Springer, Cham (2021). https://doi.org/10.1007/978-3-030-89051-3_4

16. Ciccio, C.D., Montali, M.: Declarative process specifications: reasoning, discovery, monitoring. In: van der Aalst, W.M.P., Carmona, J. (eds.) Process Mining Handbook. LNBIP, vol. 448, pp. 108–152. Springer, Cham (2022). https://doi.org/10.1007/978-3-031-08848-3_4

17. Cohen, J.: A coefficient of agreement for nominal scales. Educ. Psychol. Measur. **20**(1), 37–46 (1960). https://doi.org/10.1177/001316446002000104

18. Cosler, M., Hahn, C., Mendoza, D., Schmitt, F., Trippel, C.: nl2spec: Interactively translating unstructured natural language to temporal logics with large language models. In: Enea, C., Lal, A. (eds.) CAV 2023. LNCS, vol. 13965, pp. 383–396. Springer, Cham (2023). https://doi.org/10.1007/978-3-031-37703-7_18

19. Czepa, C., Zdun, U.: On the understandability of temporal properties formalized in linear temporal logic, property specification patterns and event processing language. IEEE Trans. Softw. Eng. **46**(1), 100–112 (2020). https://doi.org/10.1109/TSE.2018.2859926

20. De Giacomo, G., De Masellis, R., Grasso, M., Maggi, F.M., Montali, M.: Monitoring business metaconstraints based on LTL and LDL for finite traces. In: Sadiq, S., Soffer, P., Völzer, H. (eds.) BPM 2014. LNCS, vol. 8659, pp. 1–17. Springer, Cham (2014). https://doi.org/10.1007/978-3-319-10172-9_1

21. De Giacomo, G., Iocchi, L., Favorito, M., Patrizi, F.: Restraining bolts for reinforcement learning agents. In: AAAI, pp. 13659–13662. AAAI Press (2020).https://doi.org/10.1609/AAAI.V34I09.7114

22. De Giacomo, G., Maggi, F.M., Marrella, A., Patrizi, F.: On the disruptive effectiveness of automated planning for LTLf-based trace alignment. In: Artificial Intelligence, pp. 1–7. AAAI (2017). https://doi.org/10.1609/aaai.v31i1.11020

23. De Giacomo, G., Masellis, R.D., Montali, M.: Reasoning on LTL on finite traces: insensitivity to infiniteness. In: AAAI, pp. 1027–1033. AAAI Press (2014). https://doi.org/10.1609/AAAI.V28I1.8872

24. De Giacomo, G., Rubin, S.: Automata-theoretic foundations of FOND planning for LTLf and LDLf goals. In: IJCAI, pp. 4729–4735. ijcai.org (2018). https://doi.org/10.24963/IJCAI.2018/657

25. De Giacomo, G., Vardi, M.Y.: Linear temporal logic and linear dynamic logic on finite traces. In: IJCAI, pp. 854–860. AAAI Press (2013). https://doi.org/10.5555/2540128.2540252

26. DeMillo, R.A., Lipton, R.J., Perlis, A.J.: Social processes and proofs of theorems and programs. CACM **22**(5), 271–280 (1979). https://doi.org/10.1145/359104.359106

27. Dwyer, M.B., Avrunin, G.S., Corbett, J.C.: Patterns in property specifications for finite-state verification. In: ICSE, pp. 411–420. ACM (1999). https://doi.org/10.1145/302405.302672

28. Eisner, C., Fisman, D.: A Practical Introduction to PSL. Springer, New York (2006). https://doi.org/10.1007/978-0-387-36123-9

29. Fainekos, G.E., Kress-Gazit, H., Pappas, G.J.: Temporal logic motion planning for mobile robots. In: ICRA, pp. 2020–2025. IEEE (2005). https://doi.org/10.1109/ROBOT.2005.1570410

30. Fuggitti, F., Chakraborti, T.: NL2LTL – a Python package for converting natural language (NL) instructions to linear temporal logic (LTL) formulas. In: AAAI Conference on Artificial Intelligence, vol. 37, no. 13, pp. 16428–16430 (2023). https://doi.org/10.1609/aaai.v37i13.27068

31. Geck, G., Ljulin, A., Peter, S., Schmidt, J., Vehlken, F., Zeume, T.: Introduction to Iltis: an interactive, web-based system for teaching logic. In: ITiCSE, pp. 141–146. ACM (2018). https://doi.org/10.1145/3197091.3197095

32. Geck, G., et al.: Iltis: teaching logic in the Web. CoRR abs/2105.05763 (2021)

33. Glaser, B., Strauss, A.: The Discovery of Grounded Theory: Strategies for Qualitative Research. Sociology Press, Mill Valley (1967)

34. Greenman, B., et al.: Artifact for misconceptions in finite-trace and infinite-trace linear temporal logic (2024). https://doi.org/10.5281/zenodo.12770102

35. Greenman, B., Saarinen, S., Nelson, T., Krishnamurthi, S.: Little tricky logic: misconceptions in the understanding of LTL. Programming **7**(2), 7:1–7:37 (2023). https://doi.org/10.22152/programming-journal.org/2023/7/7

36. Grunske, L.: Specification patterns for probabilistic quality properties. In: ICSE. ACM (2008). https://doi.org/10.1145/1368088.1368094

37. Gundana, D., Kress-Gazit, H.: Event-based signal temporal logic synthesis for single and multi-robot tasks. IEEE Robot. Autom. Lett. **6**(2), 3687–3694 (2021). https://doi.org/10.1109/LRA.2021.3064220

38. Haisjackl, C., et al.: Understanding Declare models: strategies, pitfalls, empirical results. Softw. Syst. Model. **15**(2), 325–352 (2016). https://doi.org/10.1007/S10270-014-0435-Z

39. Hestenes, D.: Toward a modeling theory of physics instruction. Am. J. Phys. **55**(5), 440–454 (1987). https://doi.org/10.1119/1.15129

40. Hestenes, D., Wells, M., Swackhamer, G.: Force concept inventory. Phys. Teach. **30**(3), 141–158 (1992). https://doi.org/10.1119/1.2343497

41. Hoskote, Y.V., Kam, T., Ho, P., Zhao, X.: Coverage estimation for symbolic model checking. In: Design Automation Conference, pp. 300–305. ACM (1999). https://doi.org/10.1145/309847.309936

42. Kantaros, Y., Zavlanos, M.M.: STyLuS*: a temporal logic optimal control synthesis algorithm for large-scale multi-robot systems. Int. J. Robot. Res. **39**(7), 812–836 (2020). https://doi.org/10.1177/0278364920913922

43. Konrad, S., Cheng, B.H.C.: Real-time specification patterns. In: ICSE, p. 372–381. ACM (2005). https://doi.org/10.1145/1062455.1062526

44. Kupferman, O., Vardi, M.Y.: Vacuity detection in temporal model checking. Int. J. Softw. Tools Technol. Transf. **4**(2), 224–233 (2003). https://doi.org/10.1007/s100090100062

45. Lahijanian, M., Almagor, S., Fried, D., Kavraki, L., Vardi, M.: This time the robot settles for a cost: a quantitative approach to temporal logic planning with partial satisfaction. In: AAAI, pp. 3664–3671. AAAI Press (2015). https://shaull.github.io/pub/LAFKV15.pdf

46. Lamport, L.: Specifying Systems: The TLA+ Language and Tools for Hardware and Software Engineers. Addison-Wesley, Boston (2002)

47. Lee, E.A., Seshia, S.A.: Introduction to Embedded Systems—A Cyber–Physical Systems Approach, 2nd edn. MIT Press, Cambridge (2017)

48. Loizou, S.G., Kyriakopoulos, K.J.: Automatic synthesis of multi-agent motion tasks based on LTL specifications. In: CDC, pp. 153–158. IEEE (2004). https://doi.org/10.1109/CDC.2004.1428622

49. Manna, Z., Wolper, P.: Synthesis of communicating processes from temporal logic specifications. TOPLAS **6**(1), 68–93 (1984). https://doi.org/10.1145/357233.357237

50. Menghi, C., Tsigkanos, C., Pelliccione, P., Ghezzi, C., Berger, T.: Specification patterns for robotic missions. IEEE Trans. Softw. Eng. **47**(10), 2208–2224 (2021). https://doi.org/10.1109/TSE.2019.2945329

51. Nathan, M.J., Koedinger, K.R., Alibali, M.W.: Expert blind spot: when content knowledge eclipses pedagogical content knowledge. In: International Conference on Cognitive Sciences, pp. 644–648 (2001). http://pact.cs.cmu.edu/koedinger/pubs/2001_NathanEtAl_ICCS_EBS.pdf

52. Nathan, M.J., Petrosino, A.: Expert blind spot among preservice teachers. Am. Educ. Res. J. **40**(4), 905–928 (2003). https://www.jstor.org/stable/3699412

53. Nelson, T., et al.: Forge: a tool and language for teaching formal methods. PACMPL **8**(OOPSLA1), 1–31 (2024). https://doi.org/10.1145/3649833

54. O'Connor, L., Wickström, O.: Quickstrom: property-based acceptance testing with LTL specifications. In: PLDI, pp. 1025–1038. ACM (2022). https://doi.org/10.1145/3519939.3523728

55. Pnueli, A.: The temporal logic of programs. In: FOCS, pp. 46–57. IEEE (1977). https://doi.org/10.1109/SFCS.1977.32

56. Pnueli, A., Rosner, R.: On the synthesis of a reactive module. In: POPL, pp. 179–190. ACM (1989). https://doi.org/10.1145/75277.75293

57. Rajhans, A., Mavrommati, A., Mosterman, P.J., Valenti, R.G.: Specification and runtime verification of temporal assessments in simulink. In: Feng, L., Fisman, D. (eds.) RV 2021. LNCS, vol. 12974, pp. 288–296. Springer, Cham (2021). https://doi.org/10.1007/978-3-030-88494-9_17

58. Saarinen, S.: Query strategies for directed graphical models and their application to adaptive testing. Ph.D. thesis, Brown University (2021). https://repository.library.brown.edu/studio/item/bdr:kgyft3b4/

59. Saarinen, S., Krishnamurthi, S., Fisler, K., Tunnell Wilson, P.: Harnessing the wisdom of the classes: classsourcing and machine learning for assessment instrument generation. In: SIGCSE, pp. 606–612. ACM (2019). https://doi.org/10.1145/3287324.3287504

60. Shah, A., Kamath, P., Shah, J.A., Li, S.: Bayesian inference of temporal task specifications from demonstrations. In: NeurIPS, pp. 3808–3817 (2018). https://proceedings.neurips.cc/paper/2018/hash/13168e6a2e6c84b4b7de9390c0ef5ec5-Abstract.html

61. Sim, J., Wright, C.C.: The kappa statistic in reliability studies: use, interpretation, and sample size requirements. Phys. Ther. **85**(3), 257–268 (2005). https://doi.org/10.1093/ptj/85.3.257

62. Tabajara, L.M., Vardi, M.Y.: LTLf synthesis under partial observability: from theory to practice. In: GandALF, pp. 1–17. Open Publishing Association (2020). https://doi.org/10.4204/eptcs.326.1

63. Taylor, C.B., Zingaro, D., Porter, L., Webb, K.C., Lee, C.B., Clancy, M.J.: Computer science concept inventories: past and future. Comput. Sci. Educ. **24**(4), 253–276 (2014). https://doi.org/10.1080/08993408.2014.970779

64. Tracy II, T., Tabajara, L.M., Vardi, M., Skadron, K.: Runtime verification on FPGAs with LTLf specifications. In: FMCAD, pp. 36–46 (2020). https://doi.org/10.34727/2020/isbn.978-3-85448-042-6_10

65. Umili, E., Capobianco, R., De Giacomo, G.: Grounding LTLf specifications in images. In: KR, pp. 45–63. ACM (2023).https://doi.org/10.24963/kr.2023/65

66. Vardi, M.Y.: Branching vs. linear time: final showdown. In: Margaria, T., Yi, W. (eds.) TACAS 2001. LNCS, vol. 2031, pp. 1–22. Springer, Heidelberg (2001). https://doi.org/10.1007/3-540-45319-9_1

67. Vardi, M.Y., Wolper, P.: An automata-theoretic approach to automatic program verification (preliminary report). In: LICS, pp. 332–344. IEEE Computer Society (1986)

68. Wickström, O.: Linear temporal logic visualizer. https://quickstrom.github.io/ltl-visualizer

69. Wilke, T.: Classifying discrete temporal properties. In: Meinel, C., Tison, S. (eds.) STACS 1999. LNCS, vol. 1563, pp. 32–46. Springer, Heidelberg (1999). https://doi.org/10.1007/3-540-49116-3_3

70. Wongpiromsarn, T., Ulusoy, A., Belta, C., Frazzoli, E., Rus, D.: Incremental temporal logic synthesis of control policies for robots interacting with dynamic agents. In: IROS, pp. 229–236. IEEE (2012). https://doi.org/10.1109/IROS.2012.6385575

71. Zhu, S., Tabajara, L.M., Li, J., Pu, G., Vardi, M.Y.: Symbolic LTLf synthesis. In: IJCAI, pp. 1362–1369 (2017). https://doi.org/10.24963/ijcai.2017/189

Sound and Complete Witnesses for Template-Based Verification of LTL Properties on Polynomial Programs

Krishnendu Chatterjee[1], Amir Goharshady[2], Ehsan Goharshady[1], Mehrdad Karrabi[1(✉)], and Đorđe Žikelić[3]

[1] Institute of Science and Technology Austria (ISTA), Klosterneuburg, Austria
{krishnendu.chatterjee,ehsan.goharshady, mehrdad.karrabi}@ist.ac.at
[2] The Hong Kong University of Science and Technology (HKUST), Clear Water Bay, Hong Kong
goharshady@cse.ust.hk
[3] Singapore Management University, Singapore, Singapore
dzikelic@smu.edu.sg

Abstract. We study the classical problem of verifying programs with respect to formal specifications given in the linear temporal logic (LTL). We first present novel sound and complete witnesses for LTL verification over imperative programs. Our witnesses are applicable to both verification (proving) and refutation (finding bugs) settings. We then consider LTL formulas in which atomic propositions can be polynomial constraints and turn our focus to polynomial arithmetic programs, i.e. programs in which every assignment and guard consists only of polynomial expressions. For this setting, we provide an efficient algorithm to automatically synthesize such LTL witnesses. Our synthesis procedure is both sound and semi-complete. Finally, we present experimental results demonstrating the effectiveness of our approach and that it can handle programs which were beyond the reach of previous state-of-the-art tools.

1 Introduction

Linear-Time Temporal Logic. The Linear-time Temporal Logic (LTL) [53] is one of the most classical and well-studied frameworks for formal specification, model checking and program verification. In LTL, we consider a set AP of atomic propositions and an infinite trace which tells us which propositions in AP hold at any given time. LTL formulas are then able to not only express propositional logical operations, but also modalities referring to the future. For example, X p requires that p holds in the next timeslot, whereas F q means q should hold at

Đorđe Žikelić: Part of the work done while the author was at the Institute of Science and Technology Austria (ISTA).

A. Platzer et al. (Eds.): FM 2024, LNCS 14933, pp. 600–619, 2025.
https://doi.org/10.1007/978-3-031-71162-6_31

some time in the future. This allows LTL to express common verification tasks such as termination, liveness, fairness and safety.

Witnesses. Given a specification φ and a program P, a *witness* is a mathematical object whose existence proves that the specification φ is satisfied by P. We say that a witness family is *sound and complete* when for every program P and specification φ, we have $P \models \varphi$ if and only if there is a witness in the family that certifies it. Witnesses are especially useful in dealing with undecidable problems in verification, which includes all non-trivial semantic properties [56]. This is because although the general case of the problem is undecidable, having a sound and complete notion of a witness can lead to algorithms that check for the existence of witnesses of a special form. For example, while termination is undecidable [64], and hence so is the equivalent problem of deciding the existence of a ranking function, there are nevertheless sound and complete algorithms for synthesis of *linear* ranking functions [54]. Similarly, while reachability (safety violation) is undecidable, it has sound and complete witnesses that can be automatically synthesized in linear and polynomial forms [1]. Our work subsumes both [54] and [1] and provides sound and complete witnesses for general LTL formulas.

Polynomial Programs. In this work, we mainly focus on imperative programs with polynomial arithmetic. More specifically, our programs have real variables and the right-hand-side of every assignment is a polynomial expression with respect to program variables. Similarly, the guard of every loop or branch is also a boolean combination of polynomial inequalities over the program variables.

Our Contributions. In this work, our contributions are threefold:

- On the theoretical side, by exploiting the connections to Büchi automata, we propose a novel family of sound and complete witnesses for general LTL formulas. This extends and unifies the known concepts of ranking functions [36], inductive reachability witnesses [1] and inductive invariants [25], which are sound and complete witnesses for termination, reachability and safety, respectively. Our theoretical result is not limited to polynomial programs.
- On the algorithmic side, we consider polynomial programs and present a sound and semi-complete template-based algorithm to synthesize polynomial LTL witnesses. This algorithm is a generalization of the template-based approaches in [1,25,54] which considered termination, reachability and safety. To the best of our knowledge, this is the most general model checking problem over polynomial programs to be handled by template-based approaches to date.
- Finally, on the experimental side, we provide an implementation of our approach and comparisons with state-of-the-art LTL model checking tools. Our experiments show that our approach is applicable in practice and can handle many instances that were beyond the reach of previous methods. Thus, our completeness result pays off in practice and enables us to solve new instances.

Motivation for Polynomial Programs. There are several reasons why we consider polynomial programs:

- Many real-world families of programs, such as, programs for cyber-physical systems and smart contracts, can be modeled in this framework [10,38,42].
- They are one of the most general families for which finding polynomial witnesses for reachability and safety are known to be decidable [1,12,57]. Hence, they provide a desirable tradeoff between decidability and generality.
- Using abstract interpretation, non-polynomial behavior in a program can be removed or replaced by non-determinism. Moreover, one can approximate any continuous function up to any desired level of accuracy by a polynomial. This is due to the Stone–Weierstrass theorem [30]. Thus, analysis of polynomial programs can potentially be applied to many non-polynomial programs via abstract interpretation or numerical approximation of the program's behavior.
- Previous works have studied (a) linear/affine programs with termination, safety, and reachability specifications [25,54,58], and (b) polynomial programs with termination, safety and reachability properties [1,11,12,57]. Since LTL subsumes all these specifications, polynomial program analysis with LTL provides a unifying and general framework for all these previous works.

Related Works on Linear Programs. There are many approaches focusing on linear witness synthesis for important special cases of LTL formulas. For example, [43,54] consider the problem of synthesizing linear ranking functions (termination witnesses) over linear arithmetic programs. The works [25,58] synthesize linear inductive invariants (safety witnesses), while [39] considers probabilistic reachability witnesses. The work [41] handles a larger set of verification tasks and richer settings, such as context-sensitive interprocedural program analysis. All these works rely on the well-known Farkas lemma [32] and can handle programs with linear/affine arithmetic and synthesize linear/affine witnesses. In comparison, our approach is (i) applicable to general LTL formulas and not limited to a specific formula such as termination or safety, and (ii) able to synthesize *polynomial* witnesses for *polynomial* programs with soundness and completeness guarantees. Thus, our setting is more general in terms of (a) formulas, (b) witnesses, and (c) programs that can be supported.

Related Works on Polynomial Programs. Similar to the linear case, there is a rich literature on synthesis of polynomial witnesses over polynomial programs. However, these works again focus on specific special formulas only and are not applicable to general LTL. For example, [11,15,16,44,49,51,59,68] consider termination analysis, [12] extends the invariant generation (safety witness synthesis) algorithm of [25] to the polynomial case and [14,17,18,35,62,69] add support for probabilistic programs. The works [22,70,71] consider alternative types of witnesses for safety (barriers) and obtain similarly successful synthesis algorithms. Finally, [1,63] synthesize reachability witnesses. Since we can handle any arbitrary LTL formula, our approach can be seen as an extension and unification of all these works. Indeed, our synthesis algorithm directly builds upon and extends [1].

In both cases above, some of the previous works are incomparable to ours since they consider probabilistic programs, whereas our setting has only non-probabilistic polynomial programs. Note that we do allow non-determinism.

Related Works on LTL Model Checking. There are thousands of works on LTL model checking and there is no way we can do justice to all. We refer to [24,60] for an excellent treatment of the finite-state cases. Some works that provide LTL model checking over infinite-state systems/programs are as follows:

- A prominent technique in this area is predicate abstraction [29,40,55], which uses a finite set of abstract states defined by an equivalence relation based on a finite set of predicates to soundly, but not completely, reduce the problem to the finite-state case.
- [19] uses a compositional approach to falsify LTL formulas and find an indirect description of a path that violates the specification.
- There are several symbolic approaches, including [26] which is focused on fairness and [4] which is applicable to LLVM. Another work in this category is [31], whose approach is to repeatedly rule out infeasible finite prefixes in order to find a run of the program that satisfies/violates the desired LTL formula. The work [27] uses CTL-based approaches that might report false counter-examples when applied to LTL. It then identifies and removes such spurious counterexamples using symbolic determinization.
- The work [33] presents a framework for proving liveness properties in multithreaded programs by using well-founded proof spaces.
- The recent work [52] uses temporal prophecies, inspired by classical prophecy variables, to provide significantly more precise reductions from general temporal verification to the special case of safety.
- There are many tools for LTL-based program analysis. For example, T2 [8] is able to verify a large family of liveness and safety properties, nuXmv [20] is a symbolic model checker with support for LTL, F3 [19] proves fairness in infinite-state transition systems, and Ultimate LTLAutomizer [31] is a general-purpose tool for verification of LTL specifications over a wide family of programs with support for various types of variables.
- Finally, we compare against the most recent related work [65]. This work provides relative-completeness guarantees for general programs with LTL specifications. Since it considers integer programs with recursive functions, there is no complexity guarantee provided. The earlier work [66] provides several special cases where termination is guaranteed. However, no runtime bounds are established. In contrast, our approach has both termination guarantees and sub-exponential time complexity for fixed degree.

As shown by our experimental results in Sect. 5, our completeness results enable our tool to handle instances that other approaches could not. On the other hand, our method is limited to polynomial programs and witnesses. Thus, there are also cases in which our approach fails but some of the previous tools succeed, e.g. when the underlying program requires a non-polynomial witness. In particular, Ultimate LTLAutomizer [31] is able to handle non-polynomial programs and witnesses, too.

2   Transition Systems, LTL and Büchi Automata

For a vector $e \in \mathbb{R}^n$, we use e_i to denote the i-th component of e. Given a finite set $\mathcal{V}$ of real-valued variables, a variable valuation $e \in \mathbb{R}^{|\mathcal{V}|}$ and a boolean predicate φ over $\mathcal{V}$, we write $e \models \varphi$ when φ evaluates to true upon substituting variables by the values given in e.

We consider imperative numerical programs with real-valued variables, containing standard programming constructs such as assignments, branching and loops. In addition, our programs can have finite non-determinism. We denote non-deterministic branching in our syntax by **if** $*$ **then**. See Fig. 1 for an example. We use transition systems to formally model programs.

Transition Systems. An infinite-state *transition system* is a tuple $\mathcal{T} = (\mathcal{V}, L, l_{init}, \theta_{init}, \mapsto)$, where:

- $\mathcal{V} = \{x_0, \ldots, x_{n-1}\}$ is a finite set of real-valued *program variables*.
- L is a finite set of *locations* with $l_{init} \in L$ the *initial location*.
- $\theta_{init} \subseteq \mathbb{R}^n$ is a set of *initial variable valuations*.
- $\mapsto$ is a finite set of *transitions*. Each transition $\tau \in \mapsto$ is of the form $\tau = (l, l', G_\tau, U_\tau)$, where l is the source location, l' is the target location, G_τ is the guard of the transition, which is a boolean predicate over $\mathcal{V}$, and $U_\tau : \mathbb{R}^n \to \mathbb{R}^n$ is the update function of the transition.

Translating programs into transition systems is a standard process. In what follows, we assume we are given a transition system $\mathcal{T} = (\mathcal{V}, L, l_{init}, \theta_{init}, \mapsto)$ of the program that we wish to analyze. An example is shown in Fig. 1.

States and Runs. A *state* in $\mathcal{T}$ is a pair (l, e) with $l \in L$ and $e \in \mathbb{R}^n$. A state (l, e) is said to be *initial* if $l = l_{init}$ and $e \in \theta_{init}$. We use $\mathscr{S}$ and $\mathscr{S}_{init}$ to denote the sets of all states and initial states. We assume the existence of a special *terminal location* l_t with a single outgoing transition which is a self-loop $(l_t, l_t, \text{true}, Id)$ with $Id(e) = e$ for each $e \in \mathbb{R}^n$. A state (l', e') is a *successor* of (l, e), denoted as $(l, e) \mapsto (l', e')$, if there exists a transition $\tau = (l, l', G_\tau, U_\tau) \in \mapsto$ such that $e \models G_\tau$ and $e' = U_\tau(e)$. We assume each state has at least one successor so that all runs are infinite and LTL semantics are well defined. This is without loss of generality, since we can introduce transitions to the terminal location. A *run* in $\mathcal{T}$ is an infinite sequence of successor states starting in $\mathscr{S}_{init}$.

Linear-Time Temporal Logic (LTL). Let AP be a finite set of atomic propositions. LTL formulas are inductively defined as follows:

- If $p \in$ AP, then p is an LTL formula.
- If φ and ψ are LTL formulas, then $\neg\varphi$, $\varphi \vee \psi$, $\varphi \wedge \psi$, $\mathbf{X}\,\varphi$, $\mathbf{G}\,\varphi$, $\mathbf{F}\,\varphi$ and $\varphi\,\mathbf{U}\,\psi$ are all LTL formulas.

$\neg, \vee$ and $\wedge$ are the propositional negation, disjunction and conjunction while $\mathbf{X}, \mathbf{G}, \mathbf{F}$ and $\mathbf{U}$ are the *next, globally, finally* and *until* temporal operators.

Atomic Propositions. To use LTL over the transition system $\mathcal{T}$, we first need to specify a finite set of atomic propositions AP. In this work, we let the set AP

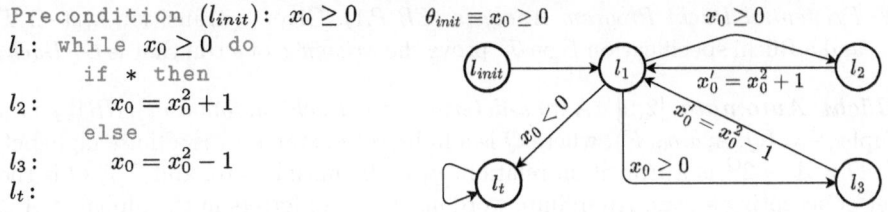

```
Precondition (l_init): x_0 ≥ 0
l_1:  while x_0 ≥ 0 do
         if * then
l_2:         x_0 = x_0^2 + 1
         else
l_3:         x_0 = x_0^2 - 1
l_t:
```

Fig. 1. An example program (left) and its transition system (right). Note that there is non-determinism at l_1.

consist of (i) finitely many constraints of the form $\exp(\mathbf{x}) \geq 0$ where $\exp: \mathcal{V} \to \mathbb{R}$ is an arithmetic expression over $\mathcal{V}$, and (ii) an atomic proposition $at(l)$ for each location l in $\mathcal{T}$. Note that unlike classical LTL settings, our atomic propositions are not necessarily independent. For example, if we have $p_1 := x \geq 0$ and $p_2 := x + 1 \geq 0$, it is impossible to have $p_1 \wedge \neg p_2$ at any point in time.

The semantics of LTL is standard, refer to the extended version of the paper [13] for details.

Program Analysis with LTL Specifications. We now define the LTL program analysis problems that we consider in this work. Given a transition system $\mathcal{T}$ and an LTL formula φ, we are interested in two problems:

1. *LTL Verification of Programs (LTL-VP).* Given a transition system $\mathcal{T}$ and an LTL formula φ in $\mathcal{T}$, prove that *all possible runs* of $\mathcal{T}$ satisfy φ.
2. *LTL Refutation of Programs (LTL-RP).* Given a transition system $\mathcal{T}$ and an LTL formula φ in $\mathcal{T}$, prove that there *exists a run* that violates φ, or equivalently, satisfies $\neg\varphi$.

Remark. *LTL Verification* asks about correctness of the program while *LTL Refutation* addresses the problem of finding bugs. Both problems have been widely studied in the literature [3,31,65]. Moreover, a witness for the refutation problem can be used in counterexample-guided techniques such as CEGAR [23].

Example. Consider the transition system in Fig. 1 and the LTL formula $\varphi = \neg[\mathtt{G}(at(l_3) \Rightarrow \mathtt{F}at(l_2))]$. The run that starts at $(l_{init}, 1)$ and chooses l_2 if $x_0 = 0$ and l_3 whenever $x_0 = 1$, does not satisfy φ. Therefore, in this case, the answer to the LTL-RP problem is positive. Additionally, deciding termination of a program with terminal location l_t is equivalent to the LTL-VP problem of $[\mathtt{F}\, at(l_t)]$ on the same program.

Program Analysis with Büchi Specifications. A Büchi specification is a subset $\mathcal{B} \subseteq \mathscr{S}$ of states. A run π is $\mathcal{B}-Büchi$ if it visits $\mathcal{B}$ infinitely many times, i.e. if $\{i \mid \pi(i) \in \mathcal{B}\}$ is infinite. Similar to LTL, Büchi specifications give rise to two main decision problems as follows:

1. *Universal Büchi Program Analysis (UB-PA).* Given a transition system $\mathcal{T}$ and a Büchi specification $\mathcal{B}$ on $\mathcal{T}$, prove that *all possible runs* of $\mathcal{T}$ are $\mathcal{B}-Büchi$.

2. *Existential Büchi Program Analysis (EB-PA)*. Given a transition system $\mathcal{T}$ and a Büchi specification $\mathcal{B}$ on $\mathcal{T}$, prove the *existence* of a run that is $\mathcal{B}-Büchi$.

Büchi Automata [2,9]. A *non-deterministic Büchi automaton (NBW)* is a tuple $N = (Q, A, \delta, q_0, F)$, where Q is a finite set of states, A is a finite alphabet, $\delta \colon Q \times A \to 2^Q$ is a transition relation, q_0 is the initial state, and $F \subseteq Q$ is the set of accepting states. An infinite word $a_0, a_1, \ldots$ of letters in the alphabet A is accepted by N if it gives rise to at least one accepting run in N, i.e. if there exists a run $q_0, q_1, \ldots$ such that $q_{i+1} \in \delta(q_i, a_i)$ for each i and F is visited infinitely many times. It is a classical result that for every LTL formula φ defined over atomic predicates AP there exists a non-deterministic Büchi automaton N with alphabet 2^{AP} which accepts exactly those traces that satisfy φ [24].

Let $\mathcal{T} = (\mathcal{V}, L, l_{init}, \theta_{init}, \mapsto)$ be a transition system and $N = (Q, 2^{AP}, \delta, q_0, F)$ be an NBW. In order to analyse $\mathcal{T}$ with respect to N, we utilize the Cartesian product $\mathcal{T} \times N$ and the Büchi specification $\mathcal{B}_N^{\mathcal{T}} = L \times F \times \mathbb{R}^n$. The state space of $\mathcal{T} \times N$ is exactly the Cartesian product of the state spaces of $\mathcal{T}$ and N. Moreover, for $l, l' \in L$ and $q, q' \in Q$, there is a transition from (l, q) to (l', q') if there is a transition in $\mathcal{T}$ from l to l' and a transition in N from q to q'. The formal definition of the product is available in [13]. See Fig. 2 for an example.

Lemma 1 (From LTL to Büchi Specifications, Proof in [13]). *Let $\mathcal{T}$ be a transition system, φ an LTL formula for $\mathcal{T}$ and N an NBW that accepts the same language as φ.*

- *The LTL-RP problem of $\mathcal{T}$ and $\neg\varphi$ is equivalent to the EB-PA problem of $\mathcal{T} \times N$ and $\mathcal{B}_N^{\mathcal{T}}$ [31].*
- *If N is deterministic, then the LTL-VP problem of $\mathcal{T}$ and φ is equivalent to the UB-PA problem of $\mathcal{T} \times N$ and $\mathcal{B}_N^{\mathcal{T}}$.*

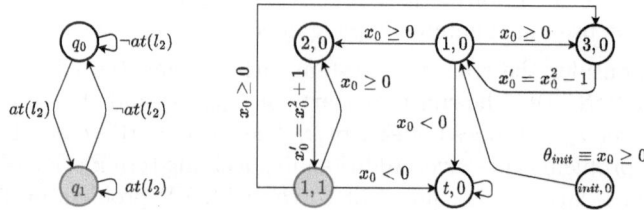

Fig. 2. An NBW accepting $\mathsf{G}\,\mathsf{F}\,at(l_2)$ with gray accepting nodes (left) and the product of the transition system in Fig. 1 and this NBW (right). A node labeled i, j represents location (l_i, q_j). Unreachable locations have been removed. (Color figure online)

Remark. Based on the lemma above, instead of designing witnesses for the LTL-RP problem, we only need to find sound and complete witnesses for EB-PA. Moreover, it is easy to see that LTL-VP is reducible to LTL-RP since all runs of $\mathcal{T}$ satisfy φ if and only if there is no run that satisfies $\neg\varphi$. So, finding sound and complete witnesses for EB-PA will theoretically solve both verification and refutation variants of LTL program analysis. Note that the second statement in Lemma 1 is more restrictive than the first one since it only applies to deterministic Büchi automata. Thus, if the LTL formula φ does not admit a deterministic Büchi automaton, the above sequence of reductions from LTL-VP to LTL-RP should be made and then the EB-PA witness should be used. However, if φ admits a DBW, then the reduction to UB-PA is preferable in practice. We will provide witness concepts for both EB-PA and UB-PA problems in the next section.

3   Sound and Complete B-PA Witnesses

Let $\mathcal{T} = (\mathcal{V}, L, l_{init}, \theta_{init}, \mapsto)$ be a transition system and $\mathcal{B} \subseteq \mathscr{S}$ a set of states in $\mathcal{T}$. In this section, we introduce our sound and complete witnesses for the EB-PA and UB-PA problems.

3.1   Sound and Complete Witnesses for Existential B-PA

Our witness concept for the EB-PA problem is a function that assigns a real value to each state in $\mathcal{T}$. The witness function is required to be non-negative in at least one initial state of $\mathcal{T}$, to preserve non-negativity in at least one successor state and to strictly decrease in value in at least one successor state whenever the current state is not contained in $\mathcal{B}$ and the value of the witness function in the current state is non-negative. Hence, starting in an initial state in which the witness function is non-negative, one can always select a successor state in which the witness function is non-negative and furthermore ensure that $\mathcal{B}$ is eventually reached due to the strict decrease condition, which will also be referred to as the *Büchi-ranking condition*. Intuitively, an EBRF is a function that overestimates the distance to $\mathcal{B}$ and guarantees that $\mathcal{B}$ is reached along at least one program run, at every program state in which the value of the EBRF is non-negative.

Definition 1 (EBRF). *Given two states $s_1, s_2 \in \mathscr{S}$, a function $f : \mathscr{S} \to \mathbb{R}$ is said to Büchi-rank (s_1, s_2) where $s_1 \mapsto s_2$, if it satisfies one of the following:*

- $s_1 \in \mathcal{B} \wedge \left[f(s_1) \geq 0 \Rightarrow f(s_2) \geq 0 \right]$; *or*
- $s_1 \notin \mathcal{B} \wedge \left[f(s_1) \geq 0 \Rightarrow 0 \leq f(s_2) \leq f(s_1) - 1 \right]$.

f is called a $\mathcal{B}$-Existential Büchi Ranking Function ($\mathcal{B}$-EBRF) if it satisfies the following conditions:

- $\exists s_{init} \in \mathscr{S}_{init}$ *where* $f(s_{init}) \geq 0$.
- *For every $s_1 \in \mathscr{S}$, there exists $s_2 \in \mathscr{S}$ such that $s_1 \mapsto s_2$ and (s_1, s_2) is Büchi-ranked by f.*

Example. The following is a $\{(l_1, q_1, *)\}$-EBRF for the transition system in Fig. 2: $f(l, x_0) = x_0 + 3$ if $l = (l_{init}, q_0)$, $f(l, x_0) = x_0 + 2$ if $l = (l_1, q_0)$, $f(l, x_0) = x_0 + 1$ if $l = (l_2, q_0)$, $f(l, x_0) = 0$ if $l = (l_1, q_1)$ and $f(l, x_0) = 0$ otherwise.

For example, the state $s_0 = ((l_1, q_0), 1)$ has two successors in the transition system: $s_1 = ((l_2, q_0), 1)$ and $s_2 = ((l_3, q_0), 1)$. It is easy to see that $0 \leq f(s_1) \leq f(s_0) - 1$ which shows that transition from s_0 to s_1 is Büchi-ranked by f.

The following theorem, proved in the extended version [13], establishes the soundness and completeness of EBRFs for the EB-PA problem, which is the main result of this section. Hence, since we showed in Lemma 1 that one can reduce the LTL-RP problem to EB-PA, as a corollary it also follows that EBRFs provide sound and complete certificates for LTL-RP.

Theorem 1 (Soundness and Completeness of EBRFs for EB-PA). *There exists a $\mathcal{B}$-EBRF f for $\mathcal{T}$ with Büchi specification $\mathcal{B}$ if and only if the answer to the EB-PA problem of $\mathcal{T}$ and $\mathcal{B}$ is positive.*

Corollary 1. *The answer to the LTL-RP problem of $\mathcal{T}$ and φ is positive if and only if there exists a $\mathcal{B}_N^{\mathcal{T}}$-EBRF for $\mathcal{T} \times N$, where N is the NBW accepting $\neg \varphi$.*

3.2   Sound and Complete Witnesses for Universal B-PA

Similarly to EBRFs, we can define a witness function for the UB-PA problem. The difference compared to EBRFs is that we now impose the Büchi ranking condition for *every* successor state of a state in which the witness function is non-negative. In contrast, in EBRFs we imposed the Büchi ranking condition only for *some* successor state.

Definition 2 (UBRF). *A function $f: \mathcal{S} \to \mathbb{R}^n$ is called a $\mathcal{B}$-Universal Büchi Ranking Function ($\mathcal{B}$-UBRF) if it satisfies the following conditions:*

- *$f(s) \geq 0$ for **every** $s \in \mathcal{S}_{init}$*
- *For **every** $s_1, s_2 \in \mathcal{S}$ such that $s_1 \mapsto s_2$, (s_1, s_2) is Büchi-ranked by f.*

We have the following theorem, which establishes that UBRFs provide a sound and complete certificate for the UB-PA problem. The proof is similar to the existential case and presented in the extended version [13]. The subsequent corollary then follows from Lemma 1 which shows that the LTL-VP problem can be reduced to the UB-PA problem if φ admits a deterministic Büchi automaton.

Theorem 2 (Soundness and Completeness of UBRFs for UB-PA). *There exists a $\mathcal{B}$-UBRF f for $\mathcal{T}$ with Büchi specification $\mathcal{B}$ if and only if the answer to the UB-PA problem of $\mathcal{T}$ and $\mathcal{B}$ positive.*

Corollary 2. *If φ is an LTL formula that admits a DBW D, the answer to the LTL-VP problem of $\mathcal{T}$ and φ is positive iff there exists a $\mathcal{B}_D^{\mathcal{T}}$-UBRF for $\mathcal{T} \times D$.*

Remark. Note that if the transition system $\mathcal{T}$ is deterministic, (i.e. it contains no non-determinism in initial states, assignments or branches) the LTL-VP of $\mathcal{T}$ and φ will be equivalent to the LTL-RP of $\mathcal{T}$ and $\neg\varphi$. Thus, in this case, the Büchi automaton determinism assumption can be relaxed as follows: if N is an NBW that accepts the same language as φ, the answer to the LTL-VP of $\mathcal{T}$ and φ is positive if and only if there exists a $\mathcal{B}_N^{\mathcal{T}}$-EBRF for $\mathcal{T} \times N$.

4 Template-Based Synthesis of Polynomial Witnesses

We now present our fully automated algorithms to synthesize polynomial EBRFs and UBRFs in polynomial transition systems. A transition system $\mathcal{T}$ is said to be *polynomial* if guards and updates of all transitions in $\mathcal{T}$ are polynomial expressions over program variables $\mathcal{V}$. Given a polynomial transition system $\mathcal{T}$ and a Büchi specification $\mathcal{B}$, which was obtained from an LTL formula as above, our approach synthesizes polynomial EBRFs and UBRFs of any desired degree, assuming that they exist. Our algorithms follow a template-based synthesis approach, similar to the methods used for reachability and termination analysis [1,12]. In particular, both EBRF and UBRF synthesis algorithms first fix a symbolic polynomial template function for the witness at each location in $\mathcal{T}$. The defining conditions of EBRFs/UBRFs are then expressed as entailment constraint of the form

$$\exists c \in \mathbb{R}^m \ \forall e \in \mathbb{R}^n \ (\phi \Rightarrow \psi), \tag{1}$$

where ϕ and ψ are conjunctions of polynomial inequalities. We show that this translation is sound and complete. However, such constraints are notoriously difficult to solve due to the existence of a quantifier alternation. Thus, we use the sound and semi-complete technique of [1] to eliminate the quantifier alternation and translate our constraints into a system of purely existentially quantified quadratic inequalities. Finally, this quadratic programming instance is solved by an SMT solver. We note that a central technical difficulty here is to come up with sound and complete witness notions whose synthesis can be reduced to solving entailment constraints of the form (1). While [1,12] achieved this for termination and reachability, our EBRF and UBRF notions significantly extend these results to arbitrary LTL formulas.

As is common in static analysis tasks, we assume that the transition system comes with an invariant θ_l at every location l in $\mathcal{T}$. Invariant generation is an orthogonal and well-studied problem. In polynomial programs, invariants can be automatically generated using the tools in [12,34,45]. Alternatively, one can encode an inductive invariant via constraints of the form (1). This has the extra benefit of ensuring that we always find an invariant that leads to a witness for our LTL formula, if such a witness exists, and thus do not sacrifice completeness due to potentially loose invariants. See [12] for details of the encoding. This is the route we took in our tool, i.e. our tool automatically generates the invariants it requires using the sound and complete method of [12]. For brevity, we removed the invariant generation part from the description of the algorithms below.

Synthesis of Polynomial EBRFs. We now present our algorithm for synthesis of a polynomial EBRF, given a polynomial transition system $\mathcal{T} = (\mathcal{V}, L, l_{init}, \theta_{init}, \mapsto)$ and Büchi specification $\mathcal{B}$ obtained from an LTL formula with polynomial inequalities in AP. We present a detailed example that illustrates the steps of the algorithm in the extended version of the paper [13]. The algorithm has five steps:

1. *Fixing Symbolic Templates.* Let $M_{\mathcal{V}}^D = \{m_1, m_2, \ldots, m_k\}$ be the set of all monomials of degree at most D over the set of variables $\mathcal{V}$. In the first step, the algorithm generates a symbolic polynomial template for the EBRF at each location $l \in L$ as follows: $f_l(x) = \Sigma_{i=1}^k c_{l,i} \cdot m_i$. Here, all the c-variables are fresh symbolic template variables that represent the coefficients of polynomial expressions in f. The goal of our synthesis procedure is to find a concrete valuation of c variables for which f becomes a valid $\mathcal{B}$-EBRF for $\mathcal{T}$.

2. *Generating Entailment Constraints.* For every location $l \in L$ and variable valuation $x \models \theta_l$, there must exist an outgoing transition τ such that $x \models G_\tau$ and τ is Büchi-ranked by f in x. The algorithm symbolically writes down this condition as an entailment constraint: $\forall x \in \mathbb{R}^n \quad x \models (\phi_l \Rightarrow \psi_l)$ with ϕ_l and ψ_l symbolically computed as follows: $\phi_l := \theta_l \wedge f_l(x) \geq 0$ and $\psi_l \equiv \bigvee_{\tau \in Out_l} G_\tau \wedge \mathcal{B}\text{-}Rank(\tau)$, where for each $\tau = (l, l', G_\tau, U_\tau)$ the predicate $\mathcal{B}\text{-}Rank$ is defined as

$$\mathcal{B}\text{-}Rank \equiv \begin{cases} f_{l'}(U_\tau(x)) \geq 0 \wedge f_{l'}(U_\tau(x)) \leq f_l(x) - 1 & l \notin \mathcal{B} \\ f_{l'}(U_\tau(x)) \geq 0 & l \in \mathcal{B} \end{cases}$$

The algorithm then writes ψ_l in disjunctive normal form as $\vee_{i=1}^k \psi_{l,i}$. Next, the algorithm rewrites $\phi_l \Rightarrow \psi_l$ equivalently as:

$$(\phi_l \wedge \bigwedge_{i=1}^{k-1} \neg \psi_{l,i}) \Rightarrow \psi_{l,k} \tag{2}$$

This rewriting makes sure that we can later manipulate the constraint in (2) to fit in the standard form of $(1)^1$. Intuitively, (2) ensures that whenever l was reached and each of the first $k-1$ outgoing transitions were either unavailable or not Büchi-ranked by f, then the last transition has to be available and Büchi-ranked by f. Our algorithm populates a list of all constraints and adds the constraint (2) to this list before moving to the next location and repeating the same procedure. Note that in all of the generated constraints of the form (2), both the LHS and the RHS of the entailment are boolean combinations of polynomial inequalities over program variables.

3. *Reduce Constraints to Quadratic Inequalities.* To solve the constraints generated in the previous step, we directly integrate the technique of [1] into our algorithm. This is a sound and semi-complete approach based on Putinar's Positivstellensatz. We will provide an example below, but refer to [1] for technical details and proofs of soundness/completeness of this step.
   In this step, for each constraint of the form $\Phi \Rightarrow \Psi$, the algorithm first rewrites

---

[1] We have to find values for c-variables that satisfy all these constraints conjunctively. This is why we have an extra existential quantifier in (1).

Φ in disjunctive normal form as $\phi_1 \vee \cdots \vee \phi_t$ and Ψ in conjunctive normal form as $\Psi \equiv \psi_1 \wedge \cdots \wedge \psi_r$. Then for each $1 \le i \le t$ and $1 \le j \le r$ the algorithm uses Putinar's Positivstellensatz in the exact same way as in [1] to generate a set of quadratic inequalities equivalent to $\phi_i \Rightarrow \psi_j$. The algorithm keeps track of a quadratic program Γ and adds these new inequalities to it conjunctively.

4. *Handling Initial Conditions.* Additionally, for every variable $x \in \mathcal{V}$, the algorithm introduces another symbolic template variable t_x, modeling the initial value of x in the program, and adds the constraint $[\theta_{init}(t) \wedge f_{l_{init}}(t) \ge 0]$ to Γ to impose that there exists an initial state in $\mathcal{T}$ at which the value of the EBRF f is non-negative.

5. *Solving the System.* Finally, the algorithm uses an external solver (usually an SMT solver) to compute values of t and c variables for which Γ is satisfied. If the solver succeeds in solving the system of constraints Γ, the computed values of c and t variables give rise to a concrete instance of an $\mathcal{B}$-EBRF for $\mathcal{T}$. This implies that the answer to the EB-PA problem is positive, and the algorithm return "Yes". Otherwise, the algorithm returns "Unknown", as there might exist a $\mathcal{B}$-EBRF for $\mathcal{T}$ of higher maximum polynomial degree D or a non-polynomial $\mathcal{B}$-EBRF.

Theorem 3 (Existential Soundness and Semi-completeness). *The algorithm above is a sound and semi-complete reduction to quadratic programming for synthesizing an EBRF in a polynomial transition system $\mathcal{T}$ given a Büchi specification $\mathcal{B}$ obtained from an LTL formula with polynomial inequalities in AP. Moreover, for any fixed D, the algorithm has sub-exponential complexity.*

In the above theorem, soundness means that every solution to the QP instance is a valid EBRF and semi-completeness means that if a polynomial EBRF exists and the chosen maximum degree D is large enough, then the QP instance will have a solution. In practice, we simply pass the QP instance to an SMT solver. Since it does not include a quantifier alternation, the SMT solvers have dedicated heuristics and are quite efficient on QP instances.

Synthesis of Polynomial UBRFs. Our algorithm for synthesis of UBRFs is almost the same as our EBRF algorithm, except that the constraints generated in Steps 2 and 4 are slightly different.

Changes to Step 2. Step 2 is the main difference between the two algorithms. In this step, for each location $l \in L$ and each transition $\tau \in Out_l$ the UBRF algorithm adds $(\phi_{l,\tau} \Rightarrow \psi_{l,\tau})$ to the set of constraints, where we have $\phi_{l,\tau} \equiv \theta_l \wedge G_\tau \wedge f_l(x) \ge 0$ and $\psi_{l,\tau} \equiv \mathcal{B}\text{-}Rank(\tau)$. The intuition behind this step is that whenever a transition is enabled, it has to be Büchi-ranked by f.

Changes to Step 4. In this step, instead of searching for a suitable initial valuation for program variables, the algorithm adds the quadratic inequalities equivalent to $(\theta_{init} \Rightarrow f_{l_{init}}(x) \ge 0)$ to Γ. The quadratic inequalities are obtained exactly as in Step 3. This is because the value of the UBRF must be non-negative on every initial state of the transition system.

In the universal case, we have a similar theorem of soundness and semi-completeness whose proof is exactly the same as Theorem 3.

Theorem 4 (Universal Soundness and Semi-completeness). *The algorithm above is a sound and semi-complete reduction to quadratic programming for synthesizing an UBRF in a polynomial transition system T given a Büchi specification B obtained from an LTL formula with polynomial inequalities in* AP. *Moreover, for any fixed maximum polynomial degree D, the algorithm has sub-exponential complexity.*

5   Experimental Results

General Setup of Experiments. We implemented a prototype[2] of our UBRF and EBRF synthesis algorithms in Java and used Z3 [50], Barcelogic [6] and MathSAT5 [21] to solve the generated systems of quadratic inequalities. More specifically, after obtaining the QP instance, our tool calls all three SMT solvers in parallel. We also used ASPIC [34] for invariant generation for benchmarks that are linear programs. Experiments were performed on a Debian 11 machine with a 2.60GHz Intel E5-2670 CPU and 6 GB of RAM with a timeout of 1800 s.

Baselines. We compare our tool with Ultimate LTLAutomizer [31], nuXmv [20], and MuVal [65] as well as with a modification of our method that instead of using Putinar's Positivstellensatz simply passes entailment constraints to the SMT-solver Z3 [50]:

– Ultimate LTLAutomizer makes use of "Büchi programs", which is a similar notion to our product of a transition system and a Büchi Automaton, to either prove that every lasso shaped path in the input program satisfies the given LTL formula, or find a path that violates it. However, in contrast to our tool, it neither supports non-linear programs nor provides completeness.
– nuXmv is a symbolic model checker with support for finite and infinite transition systems. It allows both existential and universal LTL program analysis and supports non-linear programs. It does not provide any completeness guarantees.
– MuVal [65] is a fixed-point logic validity checker based on pfwCSP solving [66]. It supports both linear and non-linear programs with integer variables and recursive functions.
– When directly applying Z3, instead of the dedicated quantifier elimination method (Step 3 of our algorithm), we directly pass the quantified formula (1) to the solver, which will in turn apply its own generic quantifier elimination. This is an ablation experiment to check whether Step 3 is needed in practice.

Benchmarks. We gathered benchmarks from two sources:

– 297 benchmarks from the "Termination of C-Integer Programs" category of TermComp'22 [37][3]. Among these, 287 programs only contained linear arith-

---

[2] Available at github.com/ekgma/LTL-VerP.

[3] There were originally 335 benchmarks, but we had to remove benchmarks with unbounded non-determinism and those without any variables, since they cannot be translated to transition systems and are not supported in our setting.

metic which is supported by all comparator tools, whereas 10 programs contained polynomial expressions not supported by Ultimate.

- 21 non-linear benchmarks from the "ReachSafety-Loops nl-digbench" category of SV-COMP'22 [5][4]. As these benchmarks are all non-linear, none of them are supported by Ultimate.

LTL Specifications. We used the four LTL specifications shown in Table 1. In all four considered specifications, x represents the alphabetically first variable in the input program. The motivation behind our specifications is as follows:

- *Reach-Avoid (RA) Specifications.* The first specification is an example of a reach-avoid specification, which specifies that a program run should terminate without ever making x negative. Reach-avoid specifications are standard in the analysis of dynamical and hybrid systems [48,61,67]. Another example is requiring a program to termination while satisfying all program assertions.
- *Overflow (OV) Specifications.* Intuitively, we want to evaluate whether our approach is capable of detecting variable overflows. The second specification specifies that each program run either terminates or the value of the variable x overflows. Specifically, suppose that an overflow is handled as a runtime error and ends the program. The negation (refutation) of this specification models the existence of a run that neither terminates nor overflows and so converges.
- *Recurrence (RC) Specifications.* The third specification is an instance of recurrence specifications which specify that a program run visits a set of states infinitely many times [47]. Our example requires that a program run contains infinitely many visits to states in which x has a non-negative value.
- *Progress (PR) Specifications.* The fourth specification is an example of progress specifications. In our experimental evaluation, progress specification specifies that a program run always makes progress from states in which the value of x is less than -5 to states in which the value of x is strictly positive.

Table 1. LTL specifications used in our experiments.

Name	Formula	Pre-condition θ_{init}
RA	$(F\ at(l_{term})) \wedge (G\ x \geq 0)$	$\forall x \in \mathcal{V}, 0 \leq x \leq 64$
OV	$F\ (at(l_{term}) \vee x < -64 \vee x > 63)$	$\forall x \in \mathcal{V}, -64 \leq x \leq 63$
RC	$G\ F\ (x \geq 0)$	$\forall x \in \mathcal{V}, -64 \leq x \leq 63$
PR	$G\ (x < -5 \Rightarrow F\ (x > 0))$	$\forall x \in \mathcal{V}, -64 \leq x \leq 63$

Results on Linear Programs. The top rows of Table 2 summarize our results over linear benchmarks to which all tools are applicable. First, we observe that in all cases our tool outperforms the method that uses Z3 for quantifier elimination, showing that our Step 3 is a crucial and helpful part of the algorithm. Compared

---

[4] The original benchmark set contains 28 programs, but 7 of them contain unsupported operators such as integer mod and are thus not expressible in our setting.

Table 2. Summary of our experimental results. For each class of benchmarks (linear/non-linear) and each formula, We report in how many cases the tool could successfully prove the formula (Yes) or refute it (No), total number of cases proved by the tool (Tot.), number of instances uniquely solved by each tool and no other tools (U.), and average runtime of each tool on programs that were successfully proved as correct with respect to each specification (Avg. T).

	Formula	Ours				Ultimate				nuXmv				MuVal				Z3			
		Yes	No	Tot.	U.	Yes	No	Tot.	U.	Yes	No	Tot.	U.	Yes	No	Tot.	U.	Yes	No	Tot.	U.
Linear	RA	141	114	255	5	142	121	263	7	76	91	137	0	118	76	194	0	56	36	92	0
	OV	199	47	246	4	212	55	267	5	110	50	160	0	205	47	252	3	48	27	75	0
	RC	87	187	274	0	86	194	280	0	83	183	266	0	86	191	277	0	44	71	115	0
	PR	43	222	265	1	45	237	282	0	44	227	271	0	42	235	277	0	29	77	106	0
	Avg. T	5.4	81.5	47.2	-	5.4	4.1	4.7	-	248.9	13.5	98.7	-	48.8	8.43	26.4	-	18.5	160.6	95.7	-
Non-linear	RA	24	3	27	8	-	-	-	-	1	0	1	0	18	1	19	2	0	0	0	0
	OV	26	0	26	2	-	-	-	-	7	0	7	0	25	0	25	1	0	0	0	0
	RC	20	6	26	0	-	-	-	-	17	9	26	2	17	7	24	2	0	0	0	0
	PR	11	16	27	1	-	-	-	-	9	16	25	0	5	16	21	1	0	0	0	0
	Avg. T	10.7	99.1	32.3	-	-	-	-	-	34.6	0.3	20.0	-	109.6	14.7	84.7	-	-	-	-	-

to nuXmv, our tool proves more instances in all but two LTL refutation and one LTL verification cases, i.e. the "No" column for the OV and PR specifications and the "Yes" column for the PR specification. On the other hand, our prototype tool is on par with Ultimate and MuVal, while proving 10 unique instances. Note that Ultimate is a state of the art and well-maintained competition tool that is highly optimized with heuristics that aim at the linear case. In contrast, it cannot handle polynomial instances. Our results shown in Table 2 demonstrate that our prototype tool is very competitive already on linear benchmarks, even though our main contribution is to provide practically-efficient semi-complete algorithms for the polynomial case.

Unique Instances. An important observation is that our tool successfully handles 10 unique *linear* instances that no other tool manages to prove or refute. Thus, our evaluation shows that our method handles not only polynomial, but even linear benchmarks that were beyond the reach of the existing methods. This shows that our algorithm, besides the desired theoretical guarantee of semi-completeness, provides an effective automated method. Future advances in invariant generation and SMT solving will likely further improve the performance.

Runtimes. Our tool and Ultimate are the fastest tools for proving LTL verification instances with an equal average runtime of 5.4 s. For LTL refutation, our tool is slower than other tools.

Results on Non-linear Programs. The bottom rows of Table 2 show the performance of our tool and the baselines on the non-linear benchmarks. Ultimate does not support non-linear arithmetic and Z3 timed out on every benchmark in this category. Here, compared to nuXmv, our tool succeeded in solving strictly more instances in all but one formula, i.e. *RC*, where both tools solve the same number of instances. In comparison with MuVal, our tool proves more instances for all four formulas. Moreover, the fact that Z3 timed out for every program in this table is further confirmation of the practical necessity of Step 3 (Quantifier

Elimination Procedure of [1]) in our algorithm. Note that our prototype could prove 11 instances that none of the other tools could handle.

Summary. Our experiments demonstrate that our automated algorithms are able to synthesize both LTL verification and refutation witnesses for a wide variety of programs. Our technique outperforms the previous methods when given non-linear polynomial programs (Bottom rows of Table 2). Moreover, even in the much more widely-studied case of linear programs, we are able to handle instances that were beyond the reach of previous methods and to solve the number of instances that is close to the state-of-the-art tools (Top Rows of Table 2).

6   Conclusion

We presented a novel family of sound and complete witnesses for template-based LTL verification. Our approach is applicable to both verification and refutation of LTL properties in programs. It unifies and significantly generalizes previous works targeting special cases of LTL, e.g. termination, safety and reachability. We also showed that our LTL witnesses can be synthesized in a sound and semi-complete manner by a reduction to quadratic programming. Our reduction works when the program and the witness are both polynomial. An interesting direction of future work would be to consider non-numerical programs that allow heap-manipulating operations. A common approach to handling heap-manipulating operations is to construct numerical abstractions of programs [7,46] and perform the analysis on numerical abstractions. Thus, coupling such approaches, e.g. [28], with our method is a compelling future direction.

Acknowledgements. This work was supported in part by the ERC-2020-CoG 863818 (FoRM-SMArt) and the Hong Kong Research Grants Council ECS Project Number 26208122.

Data Availability Statement. The implementations of the algorithms mentioned in the experiments section and the benchmarks are available at doi.org/10.5281/zenodo.12518217.

References

1. Asadi, A., Chatterjee, K., Fu, H., Goharshady, A.K., Mahdavi, M.: Polynomial reachability witnesses via stellensätze. In: PLDI, pp. 772–787 (2021)
2. Baier, C., Katoen, J.: Principles of Model Checking. MIT Press (2008)
3. Baresi, L., Kallehbasti, M.M.P., Rossi, M.: Efficient scalable verification of LTL specifications. In: ICSE (1), pp. 711–721. IEEE Computer Society (2015)
4. Bauch, P., Havel, V., Barnat, J.: LTL model checking of LLVM bitcode with symbolic data. In: MEMICS, pp. 47–59 (2014)
5. Beyer, D.: Progress on software verification: SV-COMP 2022. In: TACAS, pp. 375–402 (2022)

6. Bofill, M., Nieuwenhuis, R., Oliveras, A., Rodríguez-Carbonell, E., Rubio, A.: The barcelogic SMT solver. In: Gupta, A., Malik, S. (eds.) CAV 2008. LNCS, vol. 5123, pp. 294–298. Springer, Heidelberg (2008). https://doi.org/10.1007/978-3-540-70545-1_27

7. Bouajjani, A., Bozga, M., Habermehl, P., Iosif, R., Moro, P., Vojnar, T.: Programs with lists are counter automata. Formal Methods Syst. Des. **38**(2), 158–192 (2011)

8. Brockschmidt, M., Cook, B., Ishtiaq, S., Khlaaf, H., Piterman, N.: T2: temporal property verification. In: Chechik, M., Raskin, J.-F. (eds.) TACAS 2016. LNCS, vol. 9636, pp. 387–393. Springer, Heidelberg (2016). https://doi.org/10.1007/978-3-662-49674-9_22

9. Büchi, J.R.: Symposium on decision problems: on a decision method in restricted second order arithmetic. In: Studies in Logic and the Foundations of Mathematics, vol. 44, pp. 1–11 (1966)

10. Cai, Z., Farokhnia, S., Goharshady, A.K., Hitarth, S.: Asparagus: automated synthesis of parametric gas upper-bounds for smart contracts. In: OOPSLA (2023)

11. Chatterjee, K., Fu, H., Goharshady, A.K.: Termination analysis of probabilistic programs through positivstellensatz's. In: CAV, pp. 3–22 (2016)

12. Chatterjee, K., Fu, H., Goharshady, A.K., Goharshady, E.K.: Polynomial invariant generation for non-deterministic recursive programs. In: PLDI, pp. 672–687 (2020)

13. Chatterjee, K., Goharshady, A.K., Goharshady, E.K., Karrabi, M., Zikelic, D.: Sound and complete witnesses for template-based verification of LTL properties on polynomial programs. arXiv preprint arXiv:2403.05386 (2024)

14. Chatterjee, K., Goharshady, A.K., Meggendorfer, T., Zikelic, D.: Quantitative bounds on resource usage of probabilistic programs. In: OOPSLA (2024)

15. Chatterjee, K., Goharshady, A.K., Meggendorfer, T., Zikelic, D.: Sound and complete certificates for quantitative termination analysis of probabilistic programs. In: CAV, pp. 55–78 (2022)

16. Chatterjee, K., Goharshady, E.K., Novotný, P., Žikelić, D.: Proving non-termination by program reversal. In: PLDI, pp. 1033–1048 (2021)

17. Chatterjee, K., Goharshady, E.K., Novotný, P., Žikelić, U.: Equivalence and similarity refutation for probabilistic programs (PLDI) (2024). https://doi.org/10.1145/3656462

18. Chatterjee, K., Novotný, P., Žikelić, D.: Stochastic invariants for probabilistic termination. In: Proceedings of the 44th ACM SIGPLAN Symposium on Principles of Programming Languages, POPL 2017, Paris, 18–20 January 2017, pp. 145–160. ACM (2017). https://doi.org/10.1145/3009837.3009873

19. Cimatti, A., Griggio, A., Magnago, E.: LTL falsification in infinite-state systems. Inf. Comput. **289**, 104977 (2022)

20. Cimatti, A., Griggio, A., Magnago, E., Roveri, M., Tonetta, S.: Extending NUXMV with timed transition systems and timed temporal properties. In: Dillig, I., Tasiran, S. (eds.) CAV 2019. LNCS, vol. 11561, pp. 376–386. Springer, Cham (2019). https://doi.org/10.1007/978-3-030-25540-4_21

21. Cimatti, A., Griggio, A., Schaafsma, B.J., Sebastiani, R.: The mathsat5 SMT solver. In: TACAS, pp. 93–107 (2013)

22. Clark, A.: Verification and synthesis of control barrier functions. In: CDC, pp. 6105–6112 (2021)

23. Clarke, E.M., Grumberg, O., Jha, S., Lu, Y., Veith, H.: Counterexample-guided abstraction refinement. In: CAV (2000)

24. Clarke, E.M., Henzinger, T.A., Veith, H., Bloem, R.: Handbook of Model Checking. Springer (2018)

25. Colón, M.A., Sankaranarayanan, S., Sipma, H.B.: Linear invariant generation using non-linear constraint solving. In: CAV, pp. 420–432 (2003)

26. Cook, B., Khlaaf, H., Piterman, N.: Fairness for infinite-state systems. In: Baier, C., Tinelli, C. (eds.) TACAS 2015. LNCS, vol. 9035, pp. 384–398. Springer, Heidelberg (2015). https://doi.org/10.1007/978-3-662-46681-0_30

27. Cook, B., Koskinen, E.: Making prophecies with decision predicates. In: POPL, pp. 399–410 (2011)

28. Cook, B., Koskinen, E.: Reasoning about nondeterminism in programs. In: PLDI, pp. 219–230 (2013)

29. Daniel, J., Cimatti, A., Griggio, A., Tonetta, S., Mover, S.: Infinite-state liveness-to-safety via implicit abstraction and well-founded relations. In: Chaudhuri, S., Farzan, A. (eds.) CAV 2016. LNCS, vol. 9779, pp. 271–291. Springer, Cham (2016). https://doi.org/10.1007/978-3-319-41528-4_15

30. De Branges, L.: The Stone-Weierstrass theorem. Proc. AMS **10**(5), 822–824 (1959)

31. Dietsch, D., Heizmann, M., Langenfeld, V., Podelski, A.: Fairness modulo theory: a new approach to LTL software model checking. In: CAV, pp. 49–66 (2015)

32. Farkas, J.: Theorie der einfachen ungleichungen. Journal für die reine und angewandte Mathematik **1902**(124), 1–27 (1902)

33. Farzan, A., Kincaid, Z., Podelski, A.: Proving liveness of parameterized programs. In: LICS, pp. 185–196 (2016)

34. Feautrier, P., Gonnord, L.: Accelerated invariant generation for C programs with aspic and c2fsm. Electron. Notes Theor. Comput. Sci. 3–13 (2010)

35. Feng, Y., Zhang, L., Jansen, D.N., Zhan, N., Xia, B.: Finding polynomial loop invariants for probabilistic programs. In: ATVA, pp. 400–416 (2017)

36. Floyd, R.W.: Assigning meanings to programs. In: Program Verification: Fundamental Issues in Computer Science, pp. 65–81 (1993)

37. Frohn, F., Giesl, J., Moser, G., Rubio, A., Yamada, A., et al.: Termination competition 2022 (2021). https://termination-portal.org/wiki/Termination_Competition_2022

38. Fulton, N.: Verifiably safe autonomy for cyber-physical systems. Ph.D. thesis, Carnegie Mellon University (2018)

39. Funke, F., Jantsch, S., Baier, C.: Farkas certificates and minimal witnesses for probabilistic reachability constraints. In: TACAS, pp. 324–345 (2020)

40. Graf, S., Saïdi, H.: Construction of abstract state graphs with PVS. In: CAV, pp. 72–83 (1997)

41. Gulwani, S., Srivastava, S., Venkatesan, R.: Program analysis as constraint solving. In: PLDI, pp. 281–292 (2008)

42. Gurriet, T., Singletary, A., Reher, J., Ciarletta, L., Feron, E., Ames, A.D.: Towards a framework for realizable safety critical control through active set invariance. In: ICCPS, pp. 98–106 (2018)

43. Heizmann, M., Hoenicke, J., Leike, J., Podelski, A.: Linear ranking for linear Lasso programs. In: Van Hung, D., Ogawa, M. (eds.) ATVA 2013. LNCS, vol. 8172, pp. 365–380. Springer, Cham (2013). https://doi.org/10.1007/978-3-319-02444-8_26

44. Huang, M., Fu, H., Chatterjee, K., Goharshady, A.K.: Modular verification for almost-sure termination of probabilistic programs. Proc. ACM Program. Lang. **3**(OOPSLA), 129:1–129:29 (2019)

45. Kincaid, Z., Cyphert, J., Breck, J., Reps, T.W.: Non-linear reasoning for invariant synthesis. In: POPL, pp. 54:1–54:33 (2018)

46. Magill, S., Tsai, M., Lee, P., Tsay, Y.: Automatic numeric abstractions for heap-manipulating programs. In: POPL, pp. 211–222 (2010)

47. Manna, Z., Pnueli, A.: A hierarchy of temporal properties. In: PODC, pp. 377–410 (1990)
48. Meng, Y., Liu, J.: Lyapunov-barrier characterization of robust reach-avoid-stay specifications for hybrid systems (2022). https://doi.org/10.48550/ARXIV.2211. 00814
49. Moosbrugger, M., Bartocci, E., Katoen, J.-P., Kovács, L.: The probabilistic termination tool Amber. In: Huisman, M., Păsăreanu, C., Zhan, N. (eds.) FM 2021. LNCS, vol. 13047, pp. 667–675. Springer, Cham (2021). https://doi.org/10.1007/978-3-030-90870-6_36
50. de Moura, L., Bjørner, N.: Z3: an efficient SMT solver. In: Ramakrishnan, C.R., Rehof, J. (eds.) TACAS 2008. LNCS, vol. 4963, pp. 337–340. Springer, Heidelberg (2008). https://doi.org/10.1007/978-3-540-78800-3_24
51. Neumann, E., Ouaknine, J., Worrell, J.: On ranking function synthesis and termination for polynomial programs. In: CONCUR, pp. 15:1–15:15 (2020)
52. Padon, O., Hoenicke, J., McMillan, K.L., Podelski, A., Sagiv, M., Shoham, S.: Temporal prophecy for proving temporal properties of infinite-state systems. Formal Methods Syst. Des. **57**(2), 246–269 (2021)
53. Pnueli, A.: The temporal logic of programs. In: FOCS, pp. 46–57 (1977)
54. Podelski, A., Rybalchenko, A.: A complete method for the synthesis of linear ranking functions. In: Steffen, B., Levi, G. (eds.) VMCAI 2004. LNCS, vol. 2937, pp. 239–251. Springer, Heidelberg (2004). https://doi.org/10.1007/978-3-540-24622-0_20
55. Podelski, A., Rybalchenko, A.: Transition predicate abstraction and fair termination. In: POPL, pp. 132–144 (2005)
56. Rice, H.G.: Classes of recursively enumerable sets and their decision problems. Trans. AMS **74**(2), 358–366 (1953)
57. Sankaranarayanan, S., Sipma, H., Manna, Z.: Non-linear loop invariant generation using gröbner bases. In: POPL, pp. 318–329 (2004)
58. Sankaranarayanan, S., Sipma, H.B., Manna, Z.: Constraint-based linear-relations analysis. In: Giacobazzi, R. (ed.) SAS 2004. LNCS, vol. 3148, pp. 53–68. Springer, Heidelberg (2004). https://doi.org/10.1007/978-3-540-27864-1_7
59. Shen, L., Wu, M., Yang, Z., Zeng, Z.: Generating exact nonlinear ranking functions by symbolic-numeric hybrid method. J. Syst. Sci. Complex. **26**(2), 291–301 (2013)
60. Strejcek, J.: Linear temporal logic: expressiveness and model checking. Ph.D. thesis, Masaryk University (2004)
61. Summers, S., Lygeros, J.: Verification of discrete time stochastic hybrid systems: a stochastic reach-avoid decision problem. Autom. 1951–1961 (2010)
62. Sun, Y., Fu, H., Chatterjee, K., Goharshady, A.K.: Automated tail bound analysis for probabilistic recurrence relations. In: CAV, pp. 16–39 (2023)
63. Takisaka, T., Oyabu, Y., Urabe, N., Hasuo, I.: Ranking and repulsing supermartingales for reachability in randomized programs. TOPLAS **43**(2), 5:1–5:46 (2021)
64. Turing, A.M.: On computable numbers, with an application to the entscheidungsproblem. J. Math. **58**(345–363), 5 (1936)
65. Unno, H., Terauchi, T., Gu, Y., Koskinen, E.: Modular primal-dual fixpoint logic solving for temporal verification. In: POPL, pp. 2111–2140 (2023)
66. Unno, H., Terauchi, T., Koskinen, E.: Constraint-based relational verification. In: CAV, pp. 742–766 (2021)
67. Žikelić, D., Lechner, M., Henzinger, T.A., Chatterjee, K.: Learning control policies for stochastic systems with reach-avoid guarantees. In: AAAI, pp. 11926–11935 (2023)

68. Wang, J., Sun, Y., Fu, H., Chatterjee, K., Goharshady, A.K.: Quantitative analysis of assertion violations in probabilistic programs. In: PLDI, pp. 1171–1186 (2021)
69. Wang, P., Fu, H., Goharshady, A.K., Chatterjee, K., Qin, X., Shi, W.: Cost analysis of nondeterministic probabilistic programs. In: PLDI, pp. 204–220 (2019)
70. Wang, Q., Chen, M., Xue, B., Zhan, N., Katoen, J.: Synthesizing invariant barrier certificates via difference-of-convex programming. In: CAV, pp. 443–466 (2021)
71. Zhang, Y., Yang, Z., Lin, W., Zhu, H., Chen, X., Li, X.: Safety verification of nonlinear hybrid systems based on bilinear programming. IEEE Trans. Comput. Aided Des. Integr. Circuits Syst. **37**(11), 2768–2778 (2018)

The Opacity of Timed Automata

Jie An[1,3(✉)] ⓘ, Qiang Gao[1], Lingtai Wang[1], Naijun Zhan[1,2(✉)] ⓘ, and Ichiro Hasuo[3] ⓘ

[1] Institute of Software, Chinese Academy of Sciences, Beijing, China
{gaoqiang,wanglt,znj}@ios.ac.cn, anjie@iscas.ac.cn
[2] School of Computer Science, Peking University, Beijing, China
[3] National Institute of Informatics, Tokyo, Japan
i.hasuo@acm.org

Abstract. Opacity serves as a critical security and confidentiality property, which concerns whether an intruder can unveil a system's secret based on structural knowledge and observed behaviors. Opacity in timed systems presents greater complexity compared to untimed systems, and it has been established that opacity for timed automata is undecidable. However, the original proof cannot be applied to decide the opacity of one-clock timed automata directly. In this paper, we explore three types of opacity within timed automata: language-based timed opacity, initial-location timed opacity, and current-location timed opacity. We begin by formalizing these concepts and establishing transformation relations among them. Subsequently, we demonstrate the undecidability of the opacity problem for one-clock timed automata. Furthermore, we offer a constructive proof for the conjecture regarding the decidability of opacity for timed automata in discrete-time semantics. Additionally, we present a sufficient condition and a necessary condition for the decidability of opacity in specific subclasses of timed automata.

Keywords: Opacity · Timed opacity · Timed automata

1 Introduction

Opacity is a critical security and confidentiality property concerning information flow within systems, often utilized to describe security and privacy concerns across various scenarios. In general, it aims at safeguarding the secret information within a system from an intruder who has knowledge of the system structure but only partial observability of its behaviours.

Considering a Labelled Transition System (LTS), the secret information within it can be a set of system traces or states. An intruder observes the system behaviours, and based on the partial observations of system behaviours, the intruder estimates whether the actual behaviours contain secret information. The system is deemed opaque if for every secret run, there exists a non-secret

© The Author(s) 2025
A. Platzer et al. (Eds.): FM 2024, LNCS 14933, pp. 620–637, 2025.
https://doi.org/10.1007/978-3-031-71162-6_32

run exhibiting identical observations. Specifically, opacity is commonly categorized into two types based on the nature of the secret information: language-based opacity and state-based opacity. A system is called *language-opaque* if an intruder with partial observability can never determine whether a trace of the system is secret based on the observations. A system is termed *initial-state opaque* if an intruder is unable to determine whether a trace starts from a secret state, and it is termed *current-state opaque* if an intruder is unable to determine whether the current trace reaches a secret state. Extensive research has been conducted on untimed systems, such as Discrete Event Systems (DES) modeled by finite-state automata. The opacity problem of finite-state automata has been proved decidable in PSPACE [24,25]. We refer to [18] for a comprehensive survey.

However, timed systems introduce a level of complexity beyond untimed systems, as they encompass not only untimed event sequences but also the timestamps associated with actions or events. Moreover, it is recognized that time poses a potential security vulnerability for systems [10,14,19]. Therefore, considering that unobservable events also take a span of time, the opacity problem of timed systems becomes intriguing and considerably more intricate.

A simple example depicted in Fig. 1 illustrates an opacity problem inherent in timed systems. In this scenario, Alice, Bob, and Carlos can exchange messages, each with varying time durations between pairs. For instance, the transmission time between Alice and Bob, as well as vice versa, ranges from 1 to 4 time units, whereas between Alice and Carlos, it spans 1 to 2 time units. Let us consider Carlos as a secret participant within the system.

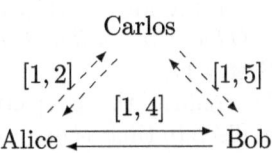

Fig. 1. A simple example for the opacity problem of timed systems

Meanwhile, an intruder named Eve, possessing only partial observability, can solely monitor the behaviors of Alice and Bob. For instance, consider a situation that the current real message passing is Alice $\xrightarrow{1.2}$ Carlos $\xrightarrow{2.1}$ Bob. With partial observability, what Eve observed is Alice $\xrightarrow{3.3}$ Bob. The opacity problem thus questions whether Eve can deduce Carlos's involvement in the message passing process, thereby exposing the secret behaviors. If Eve remains unaware of Carlos's participation, we conclude that the timed system is opaque to the intruder regarding the secret role of "Carlos" and the clandestine activities. This timed system is deemed non-opaque because Eve can ascertain the presence of a third participant when Eve observes that the time taken to pass messages between Alice and Bob exceeds 4 units. In essence, this scenario can be considered a special case of language-based opacity of timed systems if we view the dashed secret behaviors as a secret timed language.

Timed automata (TA) [2], which extend finite-state automata with clock variables, are widely used as a formal model for timed systems. In a seminal work by F. Cassez [11], it was proved that the opacity problem is undecidable for TA and even for deterministic timed automata (DTA). In the proof of the undecidability for L-opacity[1] of nondeterministic timed automata (NTA), Cassez reduced the universality problem of NTA to a specific instance of the L-opacity problem of NTA. Since the universality problem for NTA is known to be undecidable [2], it logically follows that the opacity problem for NTA is also undecidable. However, in the case of one-clock timed automata (OTA), where only a single clock is involved, the universality problem becomes decidable [1]. Consequently, the reduction does not yield a conclusion on the opacity of OTA. Additionally, at the end of [11], a conjecture is given that the opacity problem of TA is decidable in the discrete-time semantics. Therefore, all these factors serve as strong motivations for us to revisit the opacity problem of timed automata.

In this paper, we investigate three types of the opacity of timed automata, i.e., *language-based timed opacity* (LBTO), *initial-location timed opacity* (ILTO), and *current-location timed opacity* (CLTO). These concepts are adaptations of language-based opacity, initial-state opacity, and current-state opacity to the realm of timed automata, respectively. Our main contributions are as follows.

- We formalize and compare the three types of timed opacity, and present the transformations among them, i.e., ILTO and CLTO can be reduced to LBTO for TA while the inverse reductions are restricted to DTA. (Sect. 3)
- We provide proof of the undecidability of the opacity problem of OTA. Following the idea in [11], it is achieved by reducing the universality problem of *OTA with epsilon transitions* to an instance of CLTO problem of OTA. (Sect. 4.1)
- We confirm the conjecture regarding the decidability of opacity for TA in discrete-time semantics by transforming the opacity problem into the language inclusion problem of nondeterministic finite-state automata with epsilon transitions. (Sect. 4.2)
- We present both a sufficient condition and a necessary condition for the decidability of the opacity problem of specific subclasses of TA. Given a subclass of TA, a sufficient condition requires that the subclass is closed under product, complementation, and projection, and a necessary condition is that the universality problem of the subclass is decidable. (Sect. 4.3)

Related Work. Opacity problems have been extensively studied in Discrete Event Systems community [7,13,16,20,23,23,25,28,29]. We name just a few related works here. A comprehensive introduction to verification and enforcement of opacity can be found in [18]. Contrary to finite-state automata, which enjoy decidability in opacity, it has been proven that the opacity problem is undecidable for TA [11]. Therefore, various types of opacity for subclasses of TA with different restrictions have been investigated. The opacity problem of a subclass named Event-Recording Automata (ERA) [3] has also been proved undecidable in [11]. Later in [26,27], the language-based and state-based opacity problems have been proved decidable for RTA. A more comprehensive study on state-based opacity of RTA is given in [31], showing that the decision complexity is 2-EXPTIME. A kind of bounded-timed opacity is studied in [4]. Recently,

---

[1] It is equivalent to the current-location timed opacity (CLTO) defined in Sect. 3.

in [5,6], André et al. define a kind of timed opacity only considering the duration time of the executions but not the events, which is different from the classic concepts in [11]. There are also some works on the approximate opacity of Cyber-Physical Systems [21,30].

2   Preliminaries

In this section, we review the concepts of timed automata and recall several sub-classes. Let $\mathbb{N}$, $\mathbb{R}$ and $\mathbb{R}_{\geq 0}$ denote the set of natural, real and non-negative real numbers, respectively. The set of Boolean values is denoted as $\mathbb{B} = \{\top, \bot\}$, where $\top$ stands for *true* and $\bot$ for *false*. Let Σ, named alphabet, be a finite set of *events* or *actions*. Let ϵ be the special *empty action* and let $\Sigma_\epsilon = \Sigma \cup \{\epsilon\}$.

In what follows, suppose a symbol $\mathbb{A}$ represents a class of automata, we write ϵ-$\mathbb{A}$ for the *automata with epsilon transitions*. For instance, we write ϵ-TA for TA with epsilon transitions. Also, epsilon transitions are denoted as ϵ-transitions.

2.1   Timed Words, Timed Languages and Timed Automata

A *timed word* is a finite sequence of timed actions $\omega = (\sigma_1, t_1)(\sigma_2, t_2)\cdots$ $(\sigma_n, t_n) \in (\Sigma \times \mathbb{R}_{\geq 0})^*$, where $0 \leq t_1 \leq t_2 \leq \cdots \leq t_n$ are global timestamps, and *timed action* (σ_i, t_i) represents action σ_i occurs at time t_i for $1 \leq i \leq n$. The length of the timed word $|\omega| = n$ and the length of ϵ is 0. Particularly, a *timed word with empty action* ϵ is a sequence of timed actions and the empty action ϵ over $\Sigma_\epsilon \times \mathbb{R}_{\geq 0}$. A *timed language* $\mathcal{L}$ is a set of timed words, i.e., $\mathcal{L} \subseteq (\Sigma \times \mathbb{R}_{\geq 0})^*$.

Definition 1 (Projection). Given a subset $\Sigma_o \subseteq \Sigma$, a *projection* P_{Σ_o} on timed words w.r.t Σ_o is a function $(\Sigma \times \mathbb{R}_{\geq 0})^* \to (\Sigma_o \times \mathbb{R}_{\geq 0})^*$ s.t.

$$P_{\Sigma_o}(\epsilon) = \epsilon$$

$$P_{\Sigma_o}((\sigma, t) \cdot \omega) = \begin{cases} (\sigma, t) \cdot P_{\Sigma_o}(\omega) & \text{if } \sigma \in \Sigma_o \\ P_{\Sigma_o}(\omega) & \text{otherwise.} \end{cases}$$

Additionally, we extend P_{Σ_o} to timed languages, i.e., given a timed language $\mathcal{L}$, we have $P_{\Sigma_o}(\mathcal{L}) = \{P_{\Sigma_o}(\omega) \mid \omega \in \mathcal{L}\}$.

Example 1. Given a timed word $\omega = (\sigma_1, 2)(\sigma_2, 3.2)(\sigma_1, 5.7)(\sigma_3, 7)$, we have $P_{\{\sigma_1\}}(\omega) = (\sigma_1, 2)(\sigma_1, 5.7)$ and $P_{\{\sigma_2, \sigma_3\}}(\omega) = (\sigma_2, 3.2)(\sigma_3, 7)$. Note that, for timed words with empty action ϵ, say $\omega' = (\sigma_1, 2)(\epsilon, 3.2)(\sigma_1, 5.7)$, we also have $P_{\{\sigma_1\}}(\omega') = (\sigma_1, 2)(\sigma_1, 5.7)$.   ◁

Timed automata (TA) [2] extend finite-state automata with a finite set of clock variables. In each state, all clocks increase at the same rate, and a set of clocks can be reset to zero at each transition.

Let $\mathcal{C}$ be the set of clock variables and let $\Phi(\mathcal{C})$ denote the set of *clock constraints* of the form $\phi ::= \top \mid c \bowtie m \mid \phi \wedge \phi$, where $m \in \mathbb{N}$ and $\bowtie \in \{=, <, >, \leq, \geq\}$. A *clock valuation* $v : \mathcal{C} \to \mathbb{R}_{\geq 0}$ is a function assigning a non-negative real value to each clock $c \in C$. $v \in \phi$ represents that the clock valuation v *satisfies* the clock constraint ϕ, i.e. ϕ evaluates to true on v. For $d \in \mathbb{R}_{\geq 0}$, let $v + d$ be the clock valuation which maps every clock $c \in C$ to the value $v(c) + d$, and for a set $\mathcal{R} \subseteq \mathcal{C}$, let $[\mathcal{R} \to 0]v$ be the clock valuation which resets all clock variables in $\mathcal{R}$ to 0 and agrees with v for every clock in $\mathcal{C} \backslash \mathcal{R}$.

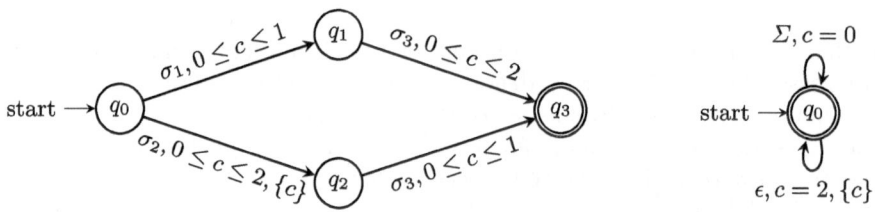

Fig. 2. An illustration for TA $\mathcal{A}$ (left side) and ϵ-TA $\mathcal{A}_\epsilon$ (right side).

Definition 2 (Timed automata). A (nondeterministic) *timed automaton* (NTA) is a 6-tuple $\mathcal{A} = (\Sigma, Q, Q_0, Q_f, \mathcal{C}, \Delta)$, where Σ is the alphabet; Q is a finite set of locations; Q_0 is a set of initial locations; Q_f is a set of accepting locations; $\mathcal{C}$ is a finite set of clocks; and $\Delta \subseteq Q \times \Sigma \times \Phi(\mathcal{C}) \times 2^{\mathcal{C}} \times Q$ is a transition relation.

A transition $(q, \sigma, \phi, \mathcal{R}, q') \in \Delta$ allows a jump from location q to q' if σ occurs and the constraint ϕ is satisfied by the current clock valuation. After that, the clocks in $\mathcal{R}$ are reset to zero, while other clocks remain unchanged.

A *state* of $\mathcal{A}$ is a pair (q, v), where $q \in Q$ is a location and v is a clock valuation. A *run* ρ of $\mathcal{A}$ over a timed word $\omega = (\sigma_1, t_1)(\sigma_2, t_2) \cdots (\sigma_n, t_n)$ is a sequence $\rho = (q_0, v_0) \xrightarrow{\tau_1, \sigma_1} (q_1, v_1) \xrightarrow{\tau_2, \sigma_2} \cdots \xrightarrow{\tau_n, \sigma_n} (q_n, v_n)$, satisfying (1) q_0 is an initial location and $v_0(c) = 0$ for each clock $c \in \mathcal{C}$; (2) for all $1 \leq i \leq n$, there is a transition $(q_{i-1}, \sigma_i, \phi_i, \mathcal{R}_i, q_i)$ such that $(v_{i-1} + \tau_i) \in \phi_i$ and $v_i = [\mathcal{R}_i \to 0](v_{i-1} + \tau_i)$; (3) $\tau_1 = t_1$ and $\tau_i = t_i - t_{i-1}$ for $2 \leq i \leq n$. Thus, each τ_i represents the delay time between the transitions. A run ρ is an *accepting* run if $q_n \in Q_f$.

The *trace* of a run ρ is the corresponding timed word $trace(\rho) = \omega$ or the empty timed word ϵ if $\rho = (q_0, v_0)$. Let $Tr_{\mathcal{A}}(q_0)$ be the set of all traces of runs from an initial location q_0 and let $Tr_{\mathcal{A}}(Q_0)$ be the set of traces of all traces of runs from any initial locations in Q_0. Additionally, given a location q and a subset $Q' \subseteq Q$, let $Tr_{\mathcal{A}}(Q_0, q)$ be the set of all traces of all runs starting from Q_0 and ending in location q, and $Tr_{\mathcal{A}}(Q_0, Q')$ be the set of all traces of all runs starting from Q_0 and ending in any locations in Q'. A timed automaton is a *deterministic timed automaton* (DTA) if $|Q_0| = 1$ and there is at most one run for each timed word.

Given a timed automaton $\mathcal{A}$, its *generated timed language* is the set of traces of runs of $\mathcal{A}$, i.e. $\mathcal{L}(\mathcal{A}) = Tr_{\mathcal{A}}(Q_0)$. The *recognized timed language* $\mathcal{L}_f(\mathcal{A})$ is the set of traces of accepting runs, i.e. $\mathcal{L}_f(\mathcal{A}) = Tr_{\mathcal{A}}(Q_0, Q_f)$.

An ϵ-NTA $\mathcal{A}_\epsilon = (\Sigma_\epsilon, Q, Q_0, Q_f, \mathcal{C}, \Delta)$ extends an NTA with ϵ-transitions in the form of $(q, \epsilon, \phi, \mathcal{R}, q')$. It can recognize timed words with ϵ over $\Sigma_\epsilon \times \mathbb{R}_{\geq 0}$.

The special empty action ϵ is viewed as invisible by default. Note that the timed language of an ϵ-NTA $\mathcal{A}_\epsilon$ is still a set of timed words defined on $(\Sigma \times \mathbb{R}_{\geq 0})^*$ [9].

Example 2. TA $\mathcal{A}$ on the left side of Fig. 2 has the unique clock c, where the alphabet $\Sigma = \{\sigma_1, \sigma_2, \sigma_3\}$. Timed word $\omega = (\sigma_2, 2)(\sigma_3, 3)$ is accepted by $\mathcal{A}$, since there is a run $\rho = q_0 \xrightarrow{2,\sigma_2} q_2 \xrightarrow{1,\sigma_3} q_3$ ending in the accepting location q_3. The recognized timed language $\mathcal{L}_f(\mathcal{A}) = \{(\sigma_1, t_1)(\sigma_3, t_2) | 0 \leq t_1 \leq 1 \wedge 0 \leq t_2 \leq 2\} \cup \{(\sigma_2, t_1)(\sigma_3, t_2) \mid 0 \leq t_1 \leq 2 \wedge 0 \leq t_2 - t_1 \leq 1\}$.

The ϵ-TA $\mathcal{A}_\epsilon$ with one clock c in Fig. 2 comes from [9]. Its generated timed language $\mathcal{L}(\mathcal{A}_\epsilon)$ is equivalent to its recognized timed language $\mathcal{L}_f(\mathcal{A}_\epsilon)$, i.e., $\mathcal{L}(\mathcal{A}_\epsilon) = \mathcal{L}_f(\mathcal{A}_\epsilon) = \{(\sigma_1, t_1) \cdots (\sigma_n, t_n) \in (\Sigma \times \mathbb{R}_{\geq 0})^* \mid \forall i \geq 0, t_i \in 2\mathbb{N} \wedge t_i \leq t_{i+1}\}$. It is clear that $P_\Sigma(\mathcal{L}(\mathcal{A}_\epsilon)) = \mathcal{L}(\mathcal{A}_\epsilon)$ and $P_\Sigma(\mathcal{L}_f(\mathcal{A}_\epsilon)) = \mathcal{L}_f(\mathcal{A}_\epsilon)$. ◁

2.2 Expressiveness and Decidability of Timed Automata

Unlike finite-state automata, TA are not closed under complementation. Moreover, the universality problem (i.e., whether $\mathcal{L}_f(\mathcal{A}) = (\Sigma \times \mathbb{R}_{\geq 0})^*$), inclusion problem (i.e., whether $\mathcal{L}_f(\mathcal{A}_1) \subseteq \mathcal{L}_f(\mathcal{A}_2)$), and equivalence problem (i.e., whether $\mathcal{L}_f(\mathcal{A}_1) = \mathcal{L}_f(\mathcal{A}_2)$) are proven undecidable for TA, nonetheless, decidable for DTA [2]. Consequently, various subclasses of TA with different restrictions have been introduced and extensively studied. In the following discussion, we will revisit some of these subclasses and provide a summary of their expressiveness.

We denote one-clock timed automata as OTA and refer to nondeterministic and deterministic OTA as NOTA and DOTA, respectively. The expressive power of NOTA strictly exceeds that of DOTA, i.e., DOTA $\subset$ NOTA. However, NOTA and DTA are *incomparable*. On one hand, there exist DTA languages that elude recognition by any NOTA. Conversely, NOTA lacks closure under complementation, while DTA retains closure. There exist NOTA languages that cannot be captured by any DTA. OTA with ϵ-transitions is denoted as ϵ-OTA.

Real-timed automata (RTA) [12] is a subclass of timed automata with a single clock resetting at every transition, resulting in RTA $\subset$ DOTA. Notably, any nondeterministic RTA can be determinized, thereby endowing deterministic RTA with the same expressive power as their nondeterministic counterparts. Additionally, RTA exhibits closure properties under product, complementation, and projection, as demonstrated in [12,27].

Event-recording automata (ERA) [3] is a kind of timed automata associating each action σ with a clock to record the time length from the last occurrence of σ to the current. As ERA is a class of *determinizable* timed automata, we have ERA $\subset$ DTA. However, ERA and RTA are *incomparable*. This distinction arises because RTA may accept languages consisting of two actions separated by an interval with integer length while ERA may not.

As shown in [2], NTA $\subset$ ϵ-NTA, since that ϵ-transitions will increase the expressive power if they reset clocks [9]. For example, in Fig. 2, the timed language of $\mathcal{A}_\epsilon$ can not be represented by any NTA.

In summary, the comparable expressive power among them is in the following order RTA $\subset$ DOTA $\subset$ DTA $\subset$ NTA $\subset$ ϵ-NTA. Note that we will ignore the character 'N' in general, such as NTA = TA and NOTA = OTA.

3   Opacity Problems of Timed Automata

In this section, we investigate three types of timed opacity, i.e., *language-based timed opacity* (LBTO), *initial-location timed opacity* (ILTO) and *current-location timed opacity* (CLTO), and demonstrate the transformations between them.

3.1   Language-Based and Location-Based Timed Opacity

Given a TA $\mathcal{A} = (\Sigma, Q, Q_0, Q_f, \mathcal{C}, \Delta)$, an observable alphabet $\Sigma_o \subseteq \Sigma$, and a *secret timed language* $\mathcal{L}_s$, we define LBTO as follows.

Definition 3 (Language-based timed opacity, LBTO). $\mathcal{A}$ is *language-based (strongly) timed opaque* w.r.t Σ_o and $\mathcal{L}_s$ iff

$$\forall \omega \in \mathcal{L}(\mathcal{A}) \cap \mathcal{L}_s, \exists \omega' \in \mathcal{L}(\mathcal{A}) \setminus \mathcal{L}_s \text{ s.t. } P_{\Sigma_o}(\omega) = P_{\Sigma_o}(\omega') \tag{1}$$

which is equivalent to $P_{\Sigma_o}(\mathcal{L}(\mathcal{A}) \cap \mathcal{L}_s) \subseteq P_{\Sigma_o}(\mathcal{L}(\mathcal{A}) \setminus \mathcal{L}_s)$.

LBTO requires that for each secret trace, there exists a non-secret trace such that their observations w.r.t the observable alphabet Σ_o are identical.

Let us consider a *secret set of locations* $Q_s \subseteq Q$ within $\mathcal{A}$, instead of a secret timed language $\mathcal{L}_s$. We define ILTO and CLTO as follows.

Definition 4 (Initial-location timed opacity, ILTO). $\mathcal{A}$ is *initial-location timed opaque* w.r.t Σ_o and $Q_s \subseteq Q_0$ iff

$$\forall \omega \in Tr_{\mathcal{A}}(Q_s), \exists \omega' \in Tr_{\mathcal{A}}(Q_0 \setminus Q_s) \text{ s.t. } P_{\Sigma_o}(\omega) = P_{\Sigma_o}(\omega') \tag{2}$$

which is equivalent to $P_{\Sigma_o}(Tr_{\mathcal{A}}(Q_s)) \subseteq P_{\Sigma_o}(Tr_{\mathcal{A}}(Q_0 \setminus Q_s))$.

ILTO requires that for each trace starting from a secret location, there exists a trace starting from a non-secret location such that their observations w.r.t Σ_o are identical.

Definition 5 (Current-location timed opacity, CLTO). $\mathcal{A}$ is *current-location timed opaque* w.r.t Σ_o and $Q_s \subseteq Q$ iff

$$\forall \omega \in Tr_{\mathcal{A}}(Q_0, Q_s), \exists \omega' \in Tr_{\mathcal{A}}(Q_0, Q \setminus Q_s) \text{ s.t. } P_{\Sigma_o}(\omega) = P_{\Sigma_o}(\omega') \tag{3}$$

which is equivalent to $P_{\Sigma_o}(Tr_{\mathcal{A}}(Q_0, Q_s)) \subseteq P_{\Sigma_o}(Tr_{\mathcal{A}}(Q_0, Q \setminus Q_s))$.

CLTO requires that for each trace reaching a secret location, there exists a trace reaching a non-secret location such that their observations w.r.t Σ_o are identical.

Example 3. In Fig. 2, suppose $\Sigma_o = \{\sigma_3\}$ and $\mathcal{L}_s = \{(\sigma_2, t_1)(\sigma_3, t_2) \mid 0 \le t_1 \le 2 \wedge 0 \le t_2 \le 3\}$, then $\mathcal{A}$ is not LBTO w.r.t $\mathcal{L}_s$ and Σ_o: If the intruder observes a 'σ_3' at time 3, they can infer that the previous action must have been 'σ_2' rather than 'σ_1', as there is no non-secret trace with an observation of 'σ_3' at time 3.

If we consider the opacity of the corresponding untimed system, the system language is $L = \{\sigma_1, \sigma_2, \sigma_1\sigma_3, \sigma_2\sigma_3\}$ and the secret language is $L_s = \{\sigma_2\sigma_3\}$. If the current observation is σ_3, the intruder cannot ascertain whether the actual behavior is $\sigma_1\sigma_3$ or $\sigma_2\sigma_3$. Therefore, the corresponding untimed system exhibits opacity. This illustrates that timed opacity presents a distinct and intriguingly more complex challenge compared to untimed systems. ◁

3.2 Transformation Between LBTO, ILTO and CLTO

We first present the transformations from ILTO to LBTO and from CLTO to LBTO with TA. Subsequently, we elucidate the reverse transformations from LBTO to ILTO and CLTO restricting to DTA.

Drawing from a common assumption in untimed systems' opacity, where a secret language is recognized by a finite-state automaton, we suppose that $\mathcal{L}_s$ can be recognized by a secret TA $\mathcal{A}_s$, i.e. $\mathcal{L}_s = \mathcal{L}_f(\mathcal{A}_s)$. The assumption is reasonable, given that every finite set of timed words can be modelled by a TA and every regular timed language can be recognized by a TA.

From ILTO to LBTO. Given a TA $\mathcal{A} = \{\Sigma, Q, Q_0, Q_f, \mathcal{C}, \Delta\}$, and a secret subset of locations $Q_s \subseteq Q_0$, the ILTO problem w.r.t Q_s and Σ_o formalized by (2) can be transformed to an LBTO problem as follows.

We first construct a TA $\mathcal{A}_s = \{\Sigma, Q, Q'_0, Q'_f, \mathcal{C}, \Delta\}$. Let $Q'_0 = Q_s$ and mark all locations as the accepting locations $Q'_f = Q$. Then we have $\mathcal{L}(\mathcal{A}_s) = \mathcal{L}_f(\mathcal{A}_s)$. Note that $Tr_{\mathcal{A}}(Q_s) = Tr_{\mathcal{A}_s}(Q_s)$. Let $\mathcal{L}_s = \mathcal{L}_f(\mathcal{A}_s)$ be the secret timed language. Then we have

$$\mathcal{L}(\mathcal{A}) \cap \mathcal{L}_s = \mathcal{L}(\mathcal{A}) \cap \mathcal{L}_f(\mathcal{A}_s) = \mathcal{L}(\mathcal{A}) \cap \mathcal{L}(\mathcal{A}_s) = \mathcal{L}(\mathcal{A}_s) = Tr_{\mathcal{A}_s}(Q_s) = Tr_{\mathcal{A}}(Q_s)$$

$$\mathcal{L}(\mathcal{A}) \setminus \mathcal{L}_s = \mathcal{L}(\mathcal{A}) \setminus \mathcal{L}_f(\mathcal{A}_s) = \mathcal{L}(\mathcal{A}) \setminus \mathcal{L}(\mathcal{A}_s) = Tr_{\mathcal{A}}(Q_0) \setminus Tr_{\mathcal{A}_s}(Q_s)$$
$$= Tr_{\mathcal{A}}(Q_0) \setminus Tr_{\mathcal{A}}(Q_s) = Tr_{\mathcal{A}}(Q_0 \setminus Q_s)$$

Hence, it is transformed to the following LBTO problem of $\mathcal{A}$ w.r.t $\mathcal{L}_s$ and Σ_o

$$\forall w \in \mathcal{L}(\mathcal{A}) \cap \mathcal{L}_s, \exists w' \in \mathcal{L}(\mathcal{A}) \setminus \mathcal{L}_s \text{ s.t. } P_{\Sigma_o}(w) = P_{\Sigma_o}(w')$$

□

From CLTO to LBTO. Given a TA $\mathcal{A} = \{\Sigma, Q, Q_0, Q_f, \mathcal{C}, \Delta\}$, and $Q_s \subseteq Q$, the CLTO problem w.r.t Q_s and Σ_o formalized by (3) can be transformed to an LBTO problem as follows.

We can construct a TA $\mathcal{A}' = \{\Sigma, Q, Q_0, Q'_f, \mathcal{C}, \Delta\}$ which is a copy of $\mathcal{A}$ except that the accepting locations are changed from Q_f to Q_s, i.e. $Q'_f = Q_s$.

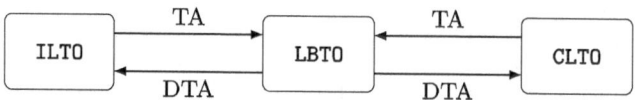

Fig. 3. The transformation between LBTO, ILTO, and CLTO.

Therefore, we have $\mathcal{L}(\mathcal{A}) = \mathcal{L}(\mathcal{A}')$, i.e., $Tr_A(Q_0) = Tr_{A'}(Q_0)$. Let $\mathcal{L}_s = \mathcal{L}_f(\mathcal{A}')$ be the secret language, then we have

$$\mathcal{L}(\mathcal{A}') \cap \mathcal{L}_s = \mathcal{L}_s = Tr_{A'}(Q_0, Q_f') = Tr_{A'}(Q_0, Q_s)$$
$$\mathcal{L}(\mathcal{A}') \setminus \mathcal{L}_s = Tr_{A'}(Q_0) \setminus Tr_{A'}(Q_0, Q_f') = Tr_{A'}(Q_0, Q \setminus Q_f') = Tr_{A'}(Q_0, Q \setminus Q_s)$$

Hence, it is transformed to the following LBTO problem of $\mathcal{A}'$ w.r.t $\mathcal{L}_s$ and Σ_o

$$\forall \omega \in \mathcal{L}(\mathcal{A}') \cap \mathcal{L}_s, \exists \omega' \in \mathcal{L}(\mathcal{A}') \setminus \mathcal{L}_s \text{ s.t. } P_{\Sigma_o}(\omega) = P_{\Sigma_o}(\omega')$$

□

From LBTO to CLTO. Given a DTA $\mathcal{A} = \{\Sigma, Q, Q_0, Q_f, \mathcal{C}, \Delta\}$, and a secret DTA $\mathcal{A}_s$ and let $\mathcal{L}_s = \mathcal{L}_f(\mathcal{A}_s)$, the LBTO problem w.r.t $\mathcal{L}_s$ and Σ_o formalized by (1) can be transformed to a CLTO problem as follows.

We construct a timed automaton $\mathcal{A}' = (\Sigma, Q', Q_0', Q_f', \mathcal{C}', \Delta')$ in the following steps. We first make a copy of $\mathcal{A}$ as $\mathcal{A}'' = (\Sigma, Q, Q_0, Q_f'', \mathcal{C}, \Delta)$ and let all locations be the accepting locations $Q_f'' = Q$. We have $\mathcal{L}_f(\mathcal{A}'') = \mathcal{L}(\mathcal{A})$. Since DTA are closed under product and complementation [2], we construct a product TA $\mathcal{A}_p = \mathcal{A}'' \times \mathcal{A}_s$ and then construct a product TA $\mathcal{A}_p' = \mathcal{A}'' \times \overline{\mathcal{A}_p}$. Therefore, we have

$$\mathcal{L}_f(\mathcal{A}_p) = \mathcal{L}_f(\mathcal{A}'') \cap \mathcal{L}_f(\mathcal{A}_s) = \mathcal{L}(\mathcal{A}) \cap \mathcal{L}_s$$
$$\mathcal{L}_f(\mathcal{A}_p') = \mathcal{L}_f(\mathcal{A}'') \cap (\overline{\mathcal{L}(\mathcal{A})} \cup \overline{\mathcal{L}_s}) = \mathcal{L}(\mathcal{A}) \cap \overline{\mathcal{L}_s} = \mathcal{L}(\mathcal{A}) \setminus \mathcal{L}_s.$$

Let $\mathcal{A}' = \mathcal{A}_p \cup \mathcal{A}_p'$ and let Q_s be the set of accepting locations of $\mathcal{A}_p$. We denote by $Q_f^{\mathcal{A}_p'}$ the set of accepting locations of $\mathcal{A}_p'$. It is clear that $Q_f^{\mathcal{A}_p'} \subset Q' \setminus Q_s$. Therefore, it is transformed to the following CLTO problem w.r.t Q_s and Σ_o

$$\forall \omega \in Tr_{A'}(Q_0', Q_s), \exists \omega' \in Tr_{A'}(Q_0', Q_f^{\mathcal{A}_p'}) \text{ s.t. } P_{\Sigma_o}(\omega) = P_{\Sigma_o}(\omega').$$

□

From LBTO to ILTO. The reduction is similar to the above reduction from LBTO to CLTO. Similar to [28], we suppose that $\mathcal{L}_s$ and $\mathcal{L}(\mathcal{A}) \setminus \mathcal{L}_s$ are both prefix-closed. Then we can build two DTA $\mathcal{A}_1$ and $\mathcal{A}_2$ such that $\mathcal{L}(\mathcal{A}_1) = \mathcal{L}_f(\mathcal{A}_p)$ and $\mathcal{L}(\mathcal{A}_2) = \mathcal{L}_f(\mathcal{A}_p')$. Let $\mathcal{A}' = \mathcal{A}_1 \cup \mathcal{A}_2$ and let the secret set Q_s be the initial location set of $\mathcal{A}_1$. Then, the LBTO problem is transformed to the following ILTO problem w.r.t Q_s and Σ_o

$$\forall \omega \in Tr_{A'}(Q_s), \exists \omega' \in Tr_{A'}(Q_0' \setminus Q_s) \text{ s.t. } P_{\Sigma_o}(\omega) = P_{\Sigma_o}(\omega').$$

□

Figure 3 summarizes the transformation between LBTO, ILTO, and CLTO. Since the complementation operation is involved in the transformations from LBTO to CLTO and to ILTO, we argue that the two transformations do not hold for general TA. Nevertheless, it is enough for supporting the results presented in Sect. 4.

4   Decidability and Undecidability of Timed Opacity Problems

This section serves to establish key results regarding the undecidability of opacity problems for OTA, the decidability of opacity problems for TA in discrete-time semantics, and a sufficient condition and a necessary condition for the decidability of opacity problems within various subclasses of TA. Consequently, our findings bridge a gap in the decidability of timed opacity problems and provide constructive proof of the conjecture proposed in [11]. These conditions delineate the system properties essential for designing opaque timed systems.

4.1   Undecidability of Opacity Problems of OTA

We first consider the CLTO problem of OTA and prove its undecidability. Moreover, our proof also holds for DOTA. Therefore, based on the transformations shown in Sect. 3.2, the three types of opacity problems of DOTA, OTA, and ϵ-OTA are all proven undecidable. The detailed proofs are presented as follows.

Lemma 1. *Given a OTA $\mathcal{A} = (\Sigma, Q, Q_0, Q_f, \{c\}, \Delta)$ and an observable alphabet $\Sigma_o \subset \Sigma$, there is an ϵ-OTA $\mathcal{A}'$ s.t. $\mathcal{A}$ is CLTO iff $\mathcal{A}'$ is CLTO.*

Proof. The ϵ-OTA $\mathcal{A}' = (\Sigma' \cup \{\epsilon\}, Q, Q_0, Q_f, \{c\}, \Delta')$ can be built as follows. Build a new alphabet Σ' s.t. $\Sigma_o \subset \Sigma' \subset \Sigma$. Suppose $\Sigma \setminus \Sigma' = \{\sigma'_1, \sigma'_2, \cdots, \sigma'_n\}$, the transition set Δ' is constructed from Δ by replacing σ'_i with ϵ for each transition $(q, \sigma'_i, \phi, \mathcal{R}, q') \in \Delta$.

Since each σ'_i is an unobservable action, i.e., $\sigma'_i \notin \Sigma_o$, it is equivalent to ϵ w.r.t the timed opacity problem with projection P_{Σ_o}. After replacing the corresponding transitions with ϵ-transitions, checking CLTO of OTA $\mathcal{A}$ is equivalent to checking CLTO of ϵ-OTA $\mathcal{A}'$.   □

The following lemma follows the proof idea in [11]. The difference is that we reduce the universality problem of ϵ-NTA, instead of NTA, to a CLTO problem.

Lemma 2. *Given an ϵ-NTA $\mathcal{A}_\epsilon = \{\Sigma \cup \{\epsilon\}, Q, Q_0, Q_f, \mathcal{C}, \Delta\}$, there is an NTA $\mathcal{A}'$ s.t. the universality problem of $\mathcal{A}_\epsilon$ is equivalent to the CLTO problem of $\mathcal{A}'$.*

Proof. Given ϵ-NTA $\mathcal{A}_\epsilon$, the universality problem asks if $\mathcal{L}_f(\mathcal{A}_\epsilon) = (\Sigma \times \mathbb{R}_{\geq 0})^*$. We first introduce a new non-accepting location $\tilde{q}$ and then build its complete ϵ-NTA $\tilde{\mathcal{A}}_\epsilon$, where the location set $\tilde{Q} = Q \cup \{\tilde{q}\}$ and the accepting locations are unchanged. We have $\mathcal{L}_f(\tilde{\mathcal{A}}_\epsilon) = \mathcal{L}_f(\mathcal{A}_\epsilon)$ and $\mathcal{L}(\tilde{\mathcal{A}}_\epsilon) = (\Sigma \times \mathbb{R}_{\geq 0})^*$. Based on $\tilde{\mathcal{A}}_\epsilon$, we build an NTA $\mathcal{A}' = (\Sigma', \tilde{Q}, Q_0, Q_f, \mathcal{C}, \Delta')$ by introducing an action $a \notin \Sigma$, i.e.,

$\Sigma' = \Sigma \cup \{a\}$ and replacing all ϵ-transitions in $\tilde{\mathcal{A}}_\epsilon$ with a-transitions. It is clear that $P_\Sigma(\mathcal{L}(\mathcal{A}')) = \mathcal{L}(\tilde{\mathcal{A}}_\epsilon) = (\Sigma \times \mathbb{R}_{\geq 0})^*$ and $P_\Sigma(\mathcal{L}_f(\mathcal{A}')) = P_\Sigma(\mathcal{L}_f(\tilde{\mathcal{A}}_\epsilon))$. Let the secret set $Q_s = \tilde{Q} \setminus Q_f$ and the observable alphabet $\Sigma_o = \Sigma$, the universality problem of $\mathcal{A}_\epsilon$ equals to the CLTO problem of $\mathcal{A}'$ w.r.t Q_s and Σ_o.   □

The proof of Lemma 2 is not related to the number of clocks, so the universality problem of ϵ-OTA can be reduced to the CLTO problem of OTA. According to [1], the former problem is undecidable.

Theorem 1. *The* CLTO *problems of OTA and ϵ-OTA are undecidable.*

Note that the reduction in Lemma 1 does not depend on the nondeterministic property. Therefore, it works for DOTA, i.e., given a DOTA $\mathcal{A}$, there is an ϵ-OTA $\mathcal{A}'$ s.t. $\mathcal{A}$ is CLTO iff $\mathcal{A}'$ is CLTO. Then by Theorem 1, the CLTO of DOTA is also undecidable. Depending on the transformation in Sect. 3.2, we have the conclusion.

Theorem 2. *The* LBTO, ILTO, *and* CLTO *problems of DOTA, OTA, and ϵ-OTA are all undecidable.*

4.2   Decidability in the Discrete-Time Semantics

The above discussions are under the continuous-time semantics. This section provides a constructive proof confirming the conjecture in [11] that language-based timed opacity of TA is decidable under discrete-time semantics, i.e., the time domain is $\mathbb{N}$.

At first, we introduce several concepts under the discrete-time semantics. In an *integral timed word* ω over $\Sigma \times \mathbb{N}$, all events have integral timestamps. An *integral timed language* L is a set of integral timed words, i.e., $L \subseteq (\Sigma \times \mathbb{N})^*$. Given a TA $\mathcal{A}$ under discrete-time semantics, the generated and recognized timed languages, denoted by $L(\mathcal{A})$ and $L_f(\mathcal{A})$, are integral timed languages. A function $Tick : (\Sigma \times \mathbb{N})^* \to (\Sigma \cup \{\checkmark\})^*$ maps an integral timed word to an untimed word over $\Sigma \cup \{\checkmark\}$.

The basic proof idea is as follows. Under the discrete-time semantics, by Definition 3, the LBTO problem is equivalent to the inclusion problem between the projections of two integral timed languages. According to [22], every integral timed language corresponds to an untimed *Tick* language, therefore we first build an integral automaton $\mathcal{A}^\checkmark$ accepting the integral timed language via the *Tick* language. Then, based on $\mathcal{A}^\checkmark$, we construct a nondeterministic finite-state automaton with ϵ-transitions (ϵ-NFA) accepting the projection of the integral timed language via the *Tick* language. *Therefore, we transform the* LBTO *problem to the language inclusion problem of ϵ-NFA, which is decidable.*

Definition 6 (Tick). Given an integral timed word $\omega = (\sigma_1, t_1)(\sigma_2, t_2)...$ (σ_n, t_n), $t_i \in \mathbb{N}$ for $1 \leq i \leq n$, $Tick(\omega) = \underbrace{\checkmark ... \checkmark}_{t_1} \sigma_1 \cdots \underbrace{\checkmark ... \checkmark}_{t_i - t_{i-1}} \sigma_i \cdots \sigma_n \in$

$(\Sigma \cup \{\checkmark\})^*$.

Hence, the number of $\checkmark$ between two events in the untimed word $Tick(\omega)$ is equal to the delay time length between two events in the timed word ω. For example, let $\omega = (\sigma_1, 2)(\sigma_2, 3)$, we have $Tick(\omega) = \checkmark\checkmark\sigma_1\checkmark\sigma_2$. We also extend $Tick$ to the integral timed languages, i.e., $Tick(L) = \{ Tick(\omega) \mid \omega \in L \}$. We call the untimed language $Tick(L)$ as $Tick$ language.

Therefore, we can transform the LBTO problem under discrete-time semantics into the inclusion problem of the corresponding $Tick$ languages.

Lemma 3. *Given the* LBTO *problem w.r.t* $L(\mathcal{A})$ *and* L_s, *we have* $P_{\Sigma_o}(L(\mathcal{A}) \cap L_s) \subseteq P_{\Sigma_o}(L(\mathcal{A}) \setminus L_s) \Leftrightarrow Tick(P_{\Sigma_o}(L(\mathcal{A}) \cap L_s)) \subseteq Tick(P_{\Sigma_o}(L(\mathcal{A}) \setminus L_s))$.

In the following, we present a procedure to construct an ϵ-NFA recognizing the $Tick$-language of the projection of the integral timed language of a given timed automaton $\mathcal{A}$.

According to [22], given a TA $\mathcal{A}$, we build an *integral automaton* (IA) recognizing the integral timed language of $\mathcal{A}$. The basic idea is to discretize the real-valued clock valuations based on the concept of *region equivalence* [2,8].

Let $\kappa : \mathcal{C} \to \mathbb{N}$ be the ceiling function, i.e., $\kappa(c)$ is the maximal integer constant appearing in the clock constraints of clock c on transitions. For $d \in \mathbb{R}$, let $\lfloor d \rfloor$ denote the integer part of d, and let $frac(d)$ denote the fractional part.

Definition 7 (Region equivalence [2,8]). Two clock valuations $v_1, v_2 : \mathcal{C} \to \mathbb{R}_{\geq 0}$ are region-equivalent, denoted by $v_1 \cong v_2$ iff

1. $\forall c \in \mathcal{C}$, either $\lfloor v_1(c) \rfloor = \lfloor v_2(c) \rfloor$, or $v_1(c) > \kappa(c) \wedge v_2(c) > \kappa(c)$.
2. $\forall c \in \mathcal{C}$, if $v_1(c) \leq \kappa(c)$, then $frac(v_1(c)) = 0$ iff $frac(v_2(c)) = 0$.
3. $\forall c_1, c_2 \in \mathcal{C}$, if $v_1(c_1) \leq \kappa(c_1) \wedge v_1(c_2) \leq \kappa(c_2)$, then $frac(v_1(c_1)) \leq frac(v_1(c_2))$ iff $frac(v_2(c_1)) \leq frac(v_2(c_2))$.

A *region* $[v] = \{\forall v' : \mathcal{C} \to \mathbb{R}_{\geq 0} \mid v' \cong v\}$ is an equivalence class induced by region equivalence $\cong$, which denotes the set of all clock valuations v' region-equivalent to v. Given a TA $\mathcal{A}$, we denote by $Reg(\mathcal{A})$ the set of regions. According to [2], $Reg(\mathcal{A})$ is finite and $|Reg(\mathcal{A})|$ is bounded by $|\mathcal{C}|! \cdot 2^{|\mathcal{C}|} \cdot \prod_{c \in \mathcal{C}}(2\kappa(c) + 2)$. Specifically, we denote by $IReg(\mathcal{A})$ the set of regions only contain the integer numbers, i.e. $IReg(\mathcal{A}) = \{[v] \mid \forall c \in \mathcal{C}, v(c) \in \{0, 1, ..., \kappa(c) + 1\}\}$. According to region equivalence, there is only one element v in a region $[v] \in IReg(\mathcal{A})$.

Definition 8 (Integral automata). Given a TA $\mathcal{A} = (\Sigma, Q, Q_0, Q_f, \mathcal{C}, \Delta)$, an integral automaton (IA) $\mathcal{A}^{\checkmark} = (\Sigma \cup \{\checkmark\}, Q^{\checkmark}, Q_0^{\checkmark}, Q_f^{\checkmark}, \Delta^{\checkmark})$ can be constructed as follows: the finite set of locations $Q^{\checkmark} = Q \times IReg(\mathcal{A})$; the set of initial locations $Q_0^{\checkmark} = Q_0 \times \{[0]\}$; the set of accepting locations $Q_f^{\checkmark} = Q_f \times IReg(\mathcal{A})$; and the transition relation $\Delta^{\checkmark} \subseteq Q^{\checkmark} \times \Sigma \cup \{\checkmark\} \times Q^{\checkmark}$ includes σ-translations and $\checkmark$-translations constructed based on transitions $(q, \sigma, \phi, \mathcal{R}, q') \in \Delta$:

- σ-translation: $(q, [v]) \xrightarrow{\sigma} (q', [v'])$, s.t. $\exists [v], [v'] \in IReg(\mathcal{A})$, $v \in \phi$ *and* $v' = [\mathcal{R} \to 0]v$.
- $\checkmark$-translation: $(q, [v]) \xrightarrow{\checkmark} (q, [v'])$, s.t. $\exists [v], [v'] \in IReg(\mathcal{A})$, $v' = v + 1$.

A σ-translation represents a discrete jump from a symbolic state (location) $(q, [v])$ to a symbolic state $(q', [v'])$. It simulates the transition $(q, \sigma, \phi, \mathcal{R}, q')$ in TA $\mathcal{A}$ but only triggered by the clock valuations containing integral assignments. A $\checkmark$-translation simulates the one time-unit passing in a location of $\mathcal{A}$. The generated and recognized languages, denoted by $L(\mathcal{A}^\checkmark)$ and $L_f(\mathcal{A}^\checkmark)$, are untimed languages over $\Sigma \cup \{\checkmark\}$.

The following lemma states that the corresponding IA $\mathcal{A}^\checkmark$ recognizes the integral timed language of TA $\mathcal{A}$ via the *Tick* language.

Lemma 4 (Proposition 10 in [22]). *Given a TA $\mathcal{A}$, there exists an IA $\mathcal{A}^\checkmark$ whose language $L_f(\mathcal{A}^\checkmark)$ is equivalent to $Tick(L_f(\mathcal{A}))$.*

ϵ-NFA Construction. Based on $\mathcal{A}^\checkmark$, we can construct an ϵ-NFA $\mathcal{A}_{\Sigma_o}^\checkmark$ that can accept the *Tick* language of the projection of the integral timed language of $\mathcal{A}$, i.e. $Tick(P_{\Sigma_o}(L_f(\mathcal{A})))$, by the following two steps.

1. Replace all $\sigma \notin \Sigma_o$ with ϵ.
2. For all traces that end up in $Q_f^\checkmark$ and contain only ϵ-translations and $\checkmark$-translations, construct a fresh set of ϵ-transitions Δ_ϵ by
   - Introducing a fresh location q_s as the unique accepting location.
   - For all $q \in Q^\checkmark$ s.t. $q \in Q_0^\checkmark$ or exist $(q', \sigma, q) \in \Delta^\checkmark$ with $\sigma \in \Sigma_o$, if (1) $q \in Q_f^\checkmark$ or (2) there exists a transition sequence from q to some location $q'' \in Q_f^\checkmark$ that only contains $\{\epsilon, \checkmark\}$-transitions, then adding an ϵ-transition (q, ϵ, q_s) into Δ_ϵ.

Therefore, we construct an ϵ-NFA $\mathcal{A}_{\Sigma_o}^\checkmark = (\Sigma^{\checkmark^{\Sigma_o}}, Q^{\checkmark^{\Sigma_o}}, Q_0^{\checkmark^{\Sigma_o}}, Q_f^{\checkmark^{\Sigma_o}}, \Delta^{\checkmark^{\Sigma_o}})$, where the alphabet $\Sigma^{\checkmark^{\Sigma_o}} = \Sigma_o \cup \{\epsilon, \checkmark\}$; the set of locations $Q^{\checkmark^{\Sigma_o}} = Q^\checkmark \cup \{q_s\}$; the set of initial locations $Q_0^{\checkmark^{\Sigma_o}} = Q_0^\checkmark$; the set of accepting locations $Q_f^{\checkmark^{\Sigma_o}} = \{q_s\}$; and the set of transitions $\Delta^{\checkmark^{\Sigma_o}} = \{(q, \sigma, q') \in \Delta^\checkmark \mid \sigma \in \Sigma_o \cup \{\checkmark\}\} \cup \{(q, \epsilon, q') \mid (q, \sigma, q) \in \Delta^\checkmark \wedge \sigma \notin \Sigma_o\} \cup \Delta_\epsilon$.

Lemma 5. *Given a TA $\mathcal{A}$, the language of the constructed ϵ-NFA $\mathcal{A}_{\Sigma_o}^\checkmark$ is equivalent to the Tick language of the projection of the integral timed language of $\mathcal{A}$, i.e., $L_f(\mathcal{A}_{\Sigma_o}^\checkmark) = Tick(P_{\Sigma_o}(L_f(\mathcal{A})))$.*

Given a TA $\mathcal{A}$ and a secret TA $\mathcal{A}_s$ under the discrete-time semantics, let $L_s = L_f(\mathcal{A}_s)$, by Lemma 4 and Lemma 5, we can always build two ϵ-NFA A_1 and A_2 such that $L_f(A_1) = Tick(P_{\Sigma_o}(L(\mathcal{A}) \cap L_s))$ and $L_f(A_2) = Tick(P_{\Sigma_o}(L(\mathcal{A}) \setminus L_s))$, since TA in the discrete-time semantics are closed under product and complementation [15]. Hence, by Lemma 3, the LBTO problem w.r.t the integral timed languages $L(\mathcal{A})$ and L_s can be transformed into the language inclusion problem between ϵ-NFA A_1 and A_2, and the latter is decidable in PSPACE-complete [17]. Therefore, we have the following conclusion.

Theorem 3. *The LBTO, ILTO, and CLTO of TA under the discrete-time semantics are decidable.*

4.3 Sufficient Condition and Necessary Condition

Given a subclass of TA, denoted by $\mathcal{X}$-automata, we present a sufficient condition and a necessary condition on the decidability of opacity problems of $\mathcal{X}$-automata. According to the transformation in Fig. 3, LBTO is the strongest property, i.e., ILTO and CLTO can be reduced to LBTO. Hence, we consider the sufficient condition of LBTO. For the necessary condition, we consider the CLTO problem.

Sufficient Condition of LBTO. Given an $\mathcal{X}$-automaton X, and a secret language $\mathcal{L}_s$ which can be recognized by a secret $\mathcal{X}$-automaton X_s, i.e., $\mathcal{L}_s = \mathcal{L}_f(X_s)$, by Definition 3, the LBTO problem asks if $\forall \omega \in \mathcal{L}(X) \cap \mathcal{L}_f(X_s), \exists \omega' \in \mathcal{L}(X) \backslash \mathcal{L}_f(X_s)$ s.t. $P_{\Sigma_o}(\omega) = P_{\Sigma_o}(\omega')$ which is equivalent to asking if $P_{\Sigma_o}(\mathcal{L}(X) \cap \mathcal{L}_f(X_s)) \subseteq P_{\Sigma_o}(\mathcal{L}(X) \setminus \mathcal{L}_f(X_s))$.

Theorem 4 (Sufficient condition). *If $\mathcal{X}$-automata are closed under product, complementation, and projection, then the LBTO of $\mathcal{X}$-automata is decidable.*

Proof. For the proof, we provide a decision procedure for the LBTO of $\mathcal{X}$-automata if $\mathcal{X}$-automata are closed under product, complementation, and projection.

First, we transform X to an $\mathcal{X}$-automaton X' by labeling all locations in X as accepting locations. Thus, we have $\mathcal{L}(X) = \mathcal{L}_f(X')$. Since $\mathcal{X}$-automata are closed under complementation, we can build the complemented $\mathcal{X}$-automaton of X_s, denoted by $\overline{X_s}$. By the product operation, we can build two product $\mathcal{X}$-automata $Y_s = X' \times X_s$ and $Y_{ns} = X' \times \overline{X_s}$. Therefore, Y_s represents the secret part, i.e., $\mathcal{L}_f(Y_s) = \mathcal{L}(X) \cap \mathcal{L}_f(X_s)$, and Y_{ns} represents the non-secret part $\mathcal{L}_f(Y_{ns}) = \mathcal{L}(X) \backslash \mathcal{L}_f(X_s)$. Since $\mathcal{X}$-automata are closed under projection P_{Σ_o}, we can build two projection $\mathcal{X}$-automata $Y_s^{\Sigma_o}$ and $Y_{ns}^{\Sigma_o}$. We have $\mathcal{L}_f(Y_s^{\Sigma_o}) = P_{\Sigma_o}(\mathcal{L}_f(Y_s)) = P_{\Sigma_o}(\mathcal{L}(X) \cap \mathcal{L}_f(X_s))$ and $\mathcal{L}_f(Y_{ns}^{\Sigma_o}) = P_{\Sigma_o}(\mathcal{L}_f(Y_{ns})) = P_{\Sigma_o}(\mathcal{L}(X) \setminus \mathcal{L}_f(X_s))$. For checking if $\mathcal{L}_f(Y_s^{\Sigma_o}) \subseteq \mathcal{L}_f(Y_{ns}^{\Sigma_o})$, we build a product $\mathcal{X}$-automaton $Z = Y_s^{\Sigma_o} \times \overline{Y_{ns}^{\Sigma_o}}$ and check the emptiness problem of Z. If $\mathcal{L}_f(Z) = \emptyset$, then X is LBTO w.r.t X_s and Σ_o. As shown in [2], the emptiness problem of timed automata is decidable in PSPACE. Since $\mathcal{X}$ is a sub-class of timed automata, the emptiness problem of $\mathcal{X}$-automata is also decidable.

Therefore, the LBTO of $\mathcal{X}$-automata is decidable if $\mathcal{X}$-automata are closed under product, complementation, and projection. □

For instance, we check our sufficient condition on the subclasses mentioned in Sect. 2.2. According to [12], RTA satisfy the sufficient condition, and we know that the opacity of RTA is decidable [27,31]. However, ϵ-NTA and NTA are not closed under complementation. Although DTA and ERA are closed under complementation, they are not closed under projection. [11] shows that the opacity problems of ϵ-NTA, NTA, DTA, and ERA are undecidable.

Necessary Condition of CLTO. Given an $\mathcal{X}$-automaton X, and a secret subset of locations $Q_s \subseteq Q$, by Definition 5, the CLTO problem asks if $\forall \omega \in Tr_X(Q_0, Q_s), \exists \omega' \in Tr_X(Q_0, Q \setminus Q_s)$ s.t. $P_{\Sigma_o}(\omega) = P_{\Sigma_o}(\omega')$.

The following lemma states that the universality problem of $\mathcal{X}$-automata can be reduced to an equivalent CLTO problem of $\mathcal{X}$-automata.

Lemma 6. *Given an $\mathcal{X}$-automaton X, there exists an $\mathcal{X}$-automaton X' s.t. the universality problem of X is equivalent to the CLTO problem of X'.*

Proof. Given an $\mathcal{X}$-automaton $X = (\Sigma, Q, Q_0, Q_f, \mathcal{C}, \Delta)$, the universality problem asks if $\mathcal{L}_f(X) = (\Sigma \times \mathbb{R}_{\geq 0})^*$.

Similar to the proof of Lemma 2, we first introduce a new non-accepting location $\tilde{q}$ and then build its complete $\mathcal{X}$-automaton $X' = (\Sigma, \tilde{Q}, Q_0, Q_f, C, \Delta')$ with $\tilde{Q} = Q \cup \tilde{q}$, which satisfies $\mathcal{L}_f(X) = \mathcal{L}_f(X')$ and $\mathcal{L}(X') = Tr_{X'}(Q_0) = (\Sigma \times \mathbb{R}_{\geq 0})^*$.

Let the observable subset $\Sigma_o = \Sigma$ and the secret location subsets $Q_s = \tilde{Q} \setminus Q_f$. By Definition 5, the CLTO problem of X' w.r.t Q_s and Σ_o asks if

$$\forall \omega \in Tr_{X'}(Q_0, Q_s), \exists \omega' \in Tr_{X'}(Q_0, \tilde{Q} \setminus Q_s) \text{ s.t. } P_\Sigma(\omega) = P_\Sigma(\omega')$$

which is equivalent to

$$\forall \omega \in Tr_{X'}(Q_0), \exists \omega' \in Tr_{X'}(Q_0, \tilde{Q} \setminus Q_s) \text{ s.t. } P_\Sigma(\omega) = P_\Sigma(\omega')$$
$$\Leftrightarrow \forall \omega \in \mathcal{L}(\mathcal{A}'), \exists \omega' \in \mathcal{L}_f(X') \text{ s.t. } P_\Sigma(\omega) = P_\Sigma(\omega')$$
$$\Leftrightarrow P_\Sigma(\mathcal{L}(X') \subseteq P_\Sigma(\mathcal{L}_f(X')).$$

By definition, for the same automaton, the recognized language is a subset of the generated language, then $P_\Sigma(\mathcal{L}_f(X')) \subseteq P_\Sigma(\mathcal{L}(X'))$. Therefore, it asks if $P_\Sigma(\mathcal{L}_f(X')) = P_\Sigma(\mathcal{L}(X'))$ which equals

$$P_\Sigma(\mathcal{L}_f(X')) = (\Sigma \times \mathbb{R}_{\geq 0})^*$$
$$\Leftrightarrow P_\Sigma(\mathcal{L}_f(X)) = (\Sigma \times \mathbb{R}_{\geq 0})^*$$
$$\Leftrightarrow \mathcal{L}_f(X) = (\Sigma \times \mathbb{R}_{\geq 0})^*$$

Therefore, it is equivalent to the universality problem of X. □

Theorem 5 (Necessary condition). *If the CLTO of $\mathcal{X}$-automata is decidable, then the universality problem of $\mathcal{X}$-automata is decidable.*

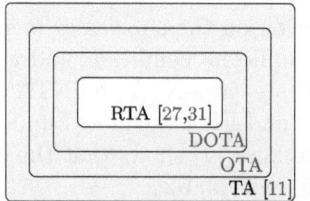
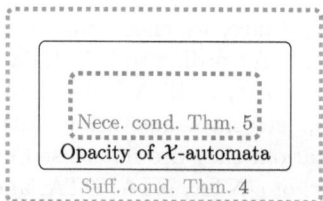

Fig. 4. Left: the decidability and undecidability results on the opacity of timed automata; **Right**: the sufficient condition and necessary condition for the decidability of the opacity of sub-class $\mathcal{X}$-automata.

5 Discussion and Conclusion

In this paper, we systematically examined three opacity problems (LBTO, ILTO, and CLTO) for TA with their transformations. We prove the undecidability of these opacity problems for one-clock timed automata, addressing a gap in prior work. Additionally, we provide a constructive proof confirming the decidability of opacity for TA under discrete-time semantics, offering a general verification algorithm. Finally, we propose a sufficient condition for LBTO and a necessary condition for CLTO, elucidating the system properties guiding the design of an opaque timed system.

In Fig. 4, the figure on the left side summarizes the decidability (for RTA) and undecidability (gray part in the figure) results on the opacity of different classes of timed automata; the figure on the right side illustrates the relation between the opacity problem, the necessary condition, and the sufficient condition. Hence, one question is if there exists a subclass $\mathcal{X}$-automata such that RTA $\subset$ $\mathcal{X}$-automata and the opacity of $\mathcal{X}$-automata is decidable. Another interesting question is whether we can find some tighter sufficient conditions and necessary conditions on the decidability of timed opacity or even a sufficient and necessary condition.

Acknowledgments. Thank the anonymous reviewers very much for their valuable suggestions. J. An, Q. Gao, and N. Zhan are partly supported by the NSFC under grants No. 62192732 and No. 62032024, and by the National Key R&D Program of China under grant No. 2022YFA1005101. J. An and I. Hasuo are supported by ERATO HASUO Metamathematics for Systems Design Project (No. JPMJER1603), JST.

Disclosure of Interests. The authors have no competing interests to declare that are relevant to the content of this article.

References

1. Abdulla, P.A., Deneux, J., Ouaknine, J., Quaas, K., Worrell, J.: Universality analysis for one-clock timed automata. Fundam. Informaticae **89**(4), 419–450 (2008). http://content.iospress.com/articles/fundamenta-informaticae/fi89-4-04
2. Alur, R., Dill, D.L.: A theory of timed automata. Theor. Comput. Sci. **126**(2), 183–235 (1994). https://doi.org/10.1016/0304-3975(94)90010-8
3. Alur, R., Fix, L., Henzinger, T.A.: Event-clock automata: a determinizable class of timed automata. Theor. Comput. Sci. **211**(1–2), 253–273 (1999). https://doi.org/10.1016/S0304-3975(97)00173-4
4. Ammar, I., Touati, Y.E., Yeddes, M., Mullins, J.: Bounded opacity for timed systems. J. Inf. Secur. Appl. **61**, 102926:1–102926:13 (2021). https://doi.org/10.1016/j.jisa.2021.102926
5. André, É., Lime, D., Marinho, D., Sun, J.: Guaranteeing timed opacity using parametric timed model checking. ACM Trans. Softw. Eng. Methodol. **31**(4), 64:1–64:36 (2022). https://doi.org/10.1145/3502851
6. André, É., Sun, J.: Parametric timed model checking for guaranteeing timed opacity. In: Chen, Y.-F., Cheng, C.-H., Esparza, J. (eds.) ATVA 2019. LNCS, vol. 11781, pp. 115–130. Springer, Cham (2019). https://doi.org/10.1007/978-3-030-31784-3_7

7. Badouel, É., Bednarczyk, M.A., Borzyszkowski, A.M., Caillaud, B., Darondeau, P.: Concurrent secrets. Discret. Event. Dyn. Syst. **17**(4), 425–446 (2007). https://doi.org/10.1007/s10626-007-0020-5

8. Bengtsson, J., Yi, W.: Timed automata: semantics, algorithms and tools. In: Desel, J., Reisig, W., Rozenberg, G. (eds.) ACPN 2003. LNCS, vol. 3098, pp. 87–124. Springer, Heidelberg (2004). https://doi.org/10.1007/978-3-540-27755-2_3

9. Bérard, B., Gastin, P., Petit, A.: On the power of non-observable actions in timed automata. In: Puech, C., Reischuk, R. (eds.) STACS 1996. LNCS, vol. 1046, pp. 255–268. Springer, Heidelberg (1996). https://doi.org/10.1007/3-540-60922-9_22

10. Bortz, A., Boneh, D.: Exposing private information by timing web applications. In: Williamson, C.L., Zurko, M.E., Patel-Schneider, P.F., Shenoy, P.J. (eds.) WWW 2007, pp. 621–628. ACM (2007). https://doi.org/10.1145/1242572.1242656

11. Cassez, F.: The dark side of timed opacity. In: Park, J.H., Chen, H.-H., Atiquzzaman, M., Lee, C., Kim, T., Yeo, S.-S. (eds.) ISA 2009. LNCS, vol. 5576, pp. 21–30. Springer, Heidelberg (2009). https://doi.org/10.1007/978-3-642-02617-1_3

12. Dima, C.: Real-time automata. J. Autom. Lang. Comb. **6**(1), 3–23 (2001). https://doi.org/10.25596/jalc-2001-003

13. Falcone, Y., Marchand, H.: Enforcement and validation (at runtime) of various notions of opacity. Discret. Event Dyn. Syst. **25**(4), 531–570 (2015). https://doi.org/10.1007/s10626-014-0196-4

14. Felten, E.W., Schneider, M.A.: Timing attacks on web privacy. In: Gritzalis, D., Jajodia, S., Samarati, P. (eds.) CCS 2000, pp. 25–32. ACM (2000). https://doi.org/10.1145/352600.352606

15. Gruber, H., Holzer, M., Kiehn, A., König, B.: On timed automata with discrete time – structural and language theoretical characterization. In: De Felice, C., Restivo, A. (eds.) DLT 2005. LNCS, vol. 3572, pp. 272–283. Springer, Heidelberg (2005). https://doi.org/10.1007/11505877_24

16. Han, X., Zhang, K., Li, Z.: Verification of strong k-step opacity for discrete-event systems. In: CDC 2022, pp. 4250–4255. IEEE (2022). https://doi.org/10.1109/CDC51059.2022.9993023

17. Hopcroft, J.E., Ullman, J.D.: Introduction to Automata Theory, Languages and Computation. Addison-Wesley (1979)

18. Jacob, R., Lesage, J., Faure, J.: Overview of discrete event systems opacity: models, validation, and quantification. Annu. Rev. Control. **41**, 135–146 (2016). https://doi.org/10.1016/j.arcontrol.2016.04.015

19. Jancar, J., et al.: "They're not that hard to mitigate": what cryptographic library developers think about timing attacks. In: S&P 2022, pp. 632–649. IEEE (2022). https://doi.org/10.1109/SP46214.2022.9833713

20. Lin, F.: Opacity of discrete event systems and its applications. Automatica **47**(3), 496–503 (2011). https://doi.org/10.1016/j.automatica.2011.01.002

21. Liu, S., Yin, X., Zamani, M.: On a notion of approximate opacity for discrete-time stochastic control systems. In: ACC 2020, pp. 5413–5418. IEEE (2020). https://doi.org/10.23919/ACC45564.2020.9147235

22. Ouaknine, J., Worrell, J.: Revisiting digitization, robustness, and decidability for timed automata. In: LICS 2003, pp. 198–207. IEEE Computer Society (2003). https://doi.org/10.1109/LICS.2003.1210059

23. Saboori, A., Hadjicostis, C.N.: Notions of security and opacity in discrete event systems. In: CDC 2007, pp. 5056–5061. IEEE (2007). https://doi.org/10.1109/CDC.2007.4434515

24. Saboori, A., Hadjicostis, C.N.: Verification of infinite-step opacity and complexity considerations. IEEE Trans. Autom. Control **57**(5), 1265–1269 (2012). https://doi.org/10.1109/TAC.2011.2173774

25. Saboori, A., Hadjicostis, C.N.: Verification of initial-state opacity in security applications of discrete event systems. Inf. Sci. **246**, 115–132 (2013). https://doi.org/10.1016/j.ins.2013.05.033

26. Wang, L., Zhan, N.: Decidability of the initial-state opacity of real-time automata. In: Jones, C., Wang, J., Zhan, N. (eds.) Symposium on Real-Time and Hybrid Systems. LNCS, vol. 11180, pp. 44–60. Springer, Cham (2018). https://doi.org/10.1007/978-3-030-01461-2_3

27. Wang, L., Zhan, N., An, J.: The opacity of real-time automata. IEEE Trans. Comput. Aided Des. Integr. Circuits Syst. **37**(11), 2845–2856 (2018). https://doi.org/10.1109/TCAD.2018.2857363

28. Wu, Y., Lafortune, S.: Comparative analysis of related notions of opacity in centralized and coordinated architectures. Discret. Event Dyn. Syst. **23**(3), 307–339 (2013). https://doi.org/10.1007/s10626-012-0145-z

29. Yin, X., Lafortune, S.: A new approach for the verification of infinite-step and k-step opacity using two-way observers. Automatica **80**, 162–171 (2017). https://doi.org/10.1016/j.automatica.2017.02.037

30. Yin, X., Zamani, M., Liu, S.: On approximate opacity of cyber-physical systems. IEEE Trans. Autom. Control **66**(4), 1630–1645 (2021). https://doi.org/10.1109/TAC.2020.2998733

31. Zhang, K.: State-based opacity of real-time automata. In: Castillo-Ramirez, A., Guillon, P., Perrot, K. (eds.) 27th IFIP WG 1.5 International Workshop on Cellular Automata and Discrete Complex Systems, AUTOMATA 2021. OASIcs, vol. 90, pp. 12:1–12:15. Schloss Dagstuhl - Leibniz-Zentrum für Informatik (2021). https://doi.org/10.4230/OASIcs.AUTOMATA.2021.12

Parameterized Verification
of Round-Based Distributed Algorithms
via Extended Threshold Automata

Tom Baumeister[1]([⊠])(iD), Paul Eichler[1](iD), Swen Jacobs[1](iD),
Mouhammad Sakr[2](iD), and Marcus Völp[2](iD)

[1] CISPA Helmholtz Center for Information Security,
Saarbrücken, Germany
tom.baumeister@cispa.de
[2] SnT, Luxembourg University, Esch-sur-Alzette,
Luxembourg

Abstract. Threshold automata are a computational model that has proven to be versatile in modeling threshold-based distributed algorithms and enabling their completely automatic parameterized verification. We present novel techniques for the verification of threshold automata, based on well-structured transition systems, that allow us to extend the expressiveness of both the computational model and the specifications that can be verified. In particular, we extend the model to allow decrements and resets of shared variables, possibly on cycles, and the specifications to general coverability. While these extensions of the model in general lead to undecidability, our algorithms provide a semi-decision procedure. We demonstrate the benefit of our extensions by showing that we can model complex round-based algorithms such as the phase king consensus algorithm and the Red Belly Blockchain protocol (published in 2019), and verify them fully automatically for the first time.

1 Introduction

Due to the increasing prevalence and importance of distributed systems in our society, ensuring reliability and correctness of these systems has become paramount. Computer-aided verification of distributed protocols and algorithms has been a very active research area in recent years [35,37,49,52,60]. To be practical, models of distributed algorithms need to take into account that communication or processes may be faulty, and correctness guarantees should be given based on a *resilience condition* that defines the quantity and quality of faults (e.g., how many processes may crash or even behave arbitrarily [13,45,48]).

Moreover, many distributed systems consist of an arbitrary number of communicating processes, thus requiring *parameterized verification* techniques that consider the number of processes as a parameter of the system, and that can provide correctness guarantees regardless of this parameter. However, the parameterized verification problem is in general undecidable, even in restricted settings

© The Author(s) 2025
A. Platzer et al. (Eds.): FM 2024, LNCS 14933, pp. 638–657, 2025.
https://doi.org/10.1007/978-3-031-71162-6_33

such as identical and anonymous finite-state processes that communicate by passing a binary-valued token in a ring [58].

Since undecidability arises so easily in this setting, the research into automatic parameterized verification can in principle be divided into two directions: (i) identifying *decidable* classes of systems and properties [1,3–7,15,24,26–30,32,33,36,38,41,54], which are often restricted to rather specialized use cases, and (ii) developing *semi-decision procedures* [2,16], which are usually much more versatile but come without a termination guarantee. In practice however, the line between these two approaches is not so clear. The line blurs when semi-decision procedures serve as decision procedures for a certain fragment of their possible inputs, and on the other hand, many decidable problems in parameterized verification have a huge complexity [24,54], and to an engineer it does not make a difference if the verification algorithm is guaranteed to terminate within a thousand years, or whether it comes without a termination guarantee.

In this paper, we aim for practical verification techniques that cover a large class of fault-tolerant distributed algorithms. Our focus is not decidability, but the development of techniques that can in practice verify a wide range of distributed algorithms, with full automation. We build on the formal model of threshold automata (TA) and existing techniques to verify them, which we combine with insights from the theory of well-structured transition systems (WSTS) [32] and with abstraction techniques. This combination allows us to lift some of the restrictions of the existing decidable fragments for TAs, and to verify distributed algorithms that are not supported by the existing techniques.

In particular, existing verification techniques for TAs are usually restricted to reason about shared variables that are monotonically increasing or decreasing over any run of the automaton. An extension of the model that allows both increasing and decreasing variables has been considered before [47], but only to show that the problem becomes undecidable, not to develop a verification technique for this case. In our setting, we can allow increments, decrements and resets of shared variables, while still obtaining a semi-decision procedure, and even a decision procedure in certain cases. In this paper, we demonstrate how this allows us to reason about round-based algorithms such as the phase king consensus algorithm [11] and the Red Belly Blockchain algorithm [23], which both use resets of shared variables at the beginning of a round, without a fixed bound on the number of rounds to be executed.

Contributions. In this paper,

1. we present an extension of threshold automata that allows increments, decrements and resets of shared variables (Sect. 2),
2. we develop a technique (based on well-structured transition systems) that is a decision procedure for general coverability properties of canonical threshold automata [47], and is a semi-decision procedure for our extension (Sect. 3–5),
3. we develop an additional abstraction that reduces the search space of this technique and additionally allows us to check another type of specification, called reachability properties, on extended threshold automata (Sect. 6),

4. we implement our techniques and demonstrate their performance on a number of examples from the literature, several of which—including the *phase king consensus* algorithm and the state-of-the-art Red Belly Blockchain algorithm—cannot be modeled in canonical threshold automata (Sect. 7).

2   System Model

In this section, we build on the existing notion of *threshold automata* (TAs) [45] and generalize their notion of shared variables. TAs are a model of distributed computation that encodes information exchange between processes into a fixed set of shared variables. Shared variables in TAs are usually required to be monotonically increasing along an execution to ensure decidability. We extend the definition such that it permits shared variables to be decreased or reset, which in general introduces undecidability [47]. We then define the semantics of an unbounded number of such TAs running in parallel. In Sect. 2.1, we introduce the notion of an abstract TA and provide the semantics for this abstraction.

Definition 1. *A threshold automaton is a tuple* $A = (L, \mathcal{I}, \Gamma, \Pi, \mathcal{R}, RC)$ *where:*

- L *is a finite set of* locations.
- $\mathcal{I} \subseteq L$ *is the set of* initial locations.
- $\Gamma = \{x_0, \ldots, x_m\}$ *is a finite set of* shared variables *over* $\mathbb{N}_0$.
- Π *is a finite set of* parameter variables *over* $\mathbb{N}_0$. *Usually,* $\Pi = \{n, t, f\}$, *where* n *is the total number of processes,* t *is a bound on the number of tolerated faulty processes , and* f *is the actual number of faulty processes.*
- RC, *the* resilience condition, *is a linear integer arithmetic formula over parameter variables. E.g.:* $RC = n > 3t \wedge t \geq f$.
  For a vector $\boldsymbol{p} \in \mathbb{N}_0^{|\Pi|}$, *we write* $\boldsymbol{p} \models RC$ *if* RC *holds after substituting parameter variables with values according to* $\boldsymbol{p}$. *Then the set of* admissible parameters *is* $\boldsymbol{P}_{RC} = \{\boldsymbol{p} \in \mathbb{N}_0^{|\Pi|} : \boldsymbol{p} \models RC\}$.
- $\mathcal{R}$ *is a set of rules where a rule is a tuple* $r = (\text{from}, \rightarrow, \varphi, \boldsymbol{uv}, \tau)$ *such that:*
  - *from,* $\rightarrow \in L$.
  - $\boldsymbol{uv} \in |\mathbb{Z}|^{|\Gamma|}$ *is an* update vector *for shared variables.*
  - φ *is a conjunction of lower guards and upper guards. A* lower guard *has the form:* $a_0 + \sum_{i=1}^{|\Pi|} a_i \cdot p_i \leq x$; *An* upper guard *has the form:* $a_0 + \sum_{i=1}^{|\Pi|} a_i \cdot p_i > x$, *with* $x \in \Gamma$, $a_0, \ldots, a_{|\Pi|} \in \mathbb{Q}$, $p_1, \ldots, p_{|\Pi|} \in \Pi$. *The left-hand side of a lower or upper guard is called a* threshold.
  - $\tau \subseteq \Gamma$ *is the set of shared variables to be reset to 0.*

Example 1. Figure 1 sketches a threshold automaton with $\mathcal{I} = \{v_0, v_1\}$, $L = \{v_0, v_1, Wait, d_0, d_1\}$, $\Gamma = \{x_0, x_1\}$, $\Pi = \{n, t, f\}$. A process in v_0 has a vote of 0 and a process in v_1 has a vote of 1. If at least $n-t$ processes vote with 0 (respectively, 1), the decision will be 0 (1), modeled by all processes moving to d_0 (d_1).

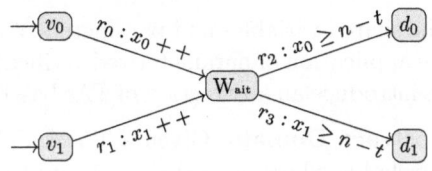

Fig. 1. A threshold automaton for simple voting.

Semantics of TA. Given a TA $A = (L, \mathcal{I}, \Gamma, \Pi, \mathcal{R}, RC)$, let the function $N : \boldsymbol{P}_{RC} \to \mathbb{N}_0$ determine the number of processes to be modelled (usually, $N(n, t, f) = n - f$). Then, the concrete semantics of a system composed of $N(\boldsymbol{p})$ threshold automata running in parallel are defined via a *counter system*.

Definition 2. *A* counter system *(CS) of a TA* $A = (L, \mathcal{I}, \Gamma, \Pi, \mathcal{R}, RC)$ *is a transition system* $\mathsf{CS}(\mathsf{A}) = (\Sigma, \Sigma_0, \mathcal{T})$ *where*

- Σ *is the set of configurations. A configuration is a tuple* $\sigma = (\boldsymbol{k}, \boldsymbol{g}, \boldsymbol{p})$ *where:*
  - $\boldsymbol{k} \in \mathbb{N}_0^{|L|}$ *is a vector of counter values, where* $\boldsymbol{k}[i]$ *represents the number of processes in location i. We refer to locations by their indices in L.*
  - $\boldsymbol{g} \in \mathbb{N}_0^{|\Gamma|}$ *is a vector of shared variables' values, where* $\boldsymbol{g}[i]$ *is the value of variable* $x_i \in \Gamma$.
  - $\boldsymbol{p} \in \boldsymbol{P}_{RC}$ *is an admissible vector of parameter values.*
- *The set* Σ_0 *contains all* initial *configurations, i.e., configurations that satisfy*

$$\forall x_i \in \Gamma : \; \sigma.\boldsymbol{g}[i] = 0 \; and \; \sum_{i \in \mathcal{I}} \sigma.\boldsymbol{k}[i] = N(\boldsymbol{p}) \; and \; \sum_{i \notin \mathcal{I}} \sigma.\boldsymbol{k}[i] = 0$$

- $\mathcal{T} \subseteq \Sigma \times \mathcal{R} \times \Sigma$ *is the set of* transitions, *where* $(\sigma, r, \sigma') \in \mathcal{T}$ *if and only if all of the following conditions hold:*
  - $\sigma'.\boldsymbol{p} = \sigma.\boldsymbol{p}$ *(parameter values never change).*
  - $\sigma'.\boldsymbol{k}[r. \to] = \sigma.\boldsymbol{k}[r. \to] + 1$ *(one process moves to $r. \to$).*
  - $\sigma'.\boldsymbol{k}[r.from] = \sigma.\boldsymbol{k}[r.from] - 1$ *(one process moves out of r.from)*
  - $\sigma.\boldsymbol{g} \models r.\varphi$ *(i.e., φ holds after replacing shared variables with values $\sigma.\boldsymbol{g}$)*
  - $\sigma'.\boldsymbol{g} = \sigma.\boldsymbol{g} + r.\boldsymbol{uv}$
  - $\forall x_i \in \tau \; \sigma'.\boldsymbol{g}[i] = 0$

Instead of $(\sigma, r, \sigma') \in \mathcal{T}$ *we also write* $\sigma \xrightarrow{r} \sigma'$. *If* $(\sigma, r, \sigma') \in \mathcal{T}$, *we say r is* enabled *in σ; otherwise it is* disabled.

Paths of CS. A sequence $\sigma_0, r_0, \sigma_1, \ldots, \sigma_{k-1}, r_{k-1}, \sigma_k$ of alternating configurations and rules is a *path* of a counter system $\mathsf{CS}(\mathsf{A}) = (\Sigma, \Sigma_0, \mathcal{T})$ if and only if $\sigma_0 \in \Sigma_0$ and $(\sigma_i, r_i, \sigma_{i+1}) \in \mathcal{T}$ for $0 \le i < k$. In this case we also write $\sigma_0 \to^* \sigma_k$. We denote by $Paths(\mathsf{CS}(\mathsf{A}))$ the set of all paths of $\mathsf{CS}(\mathsf{A})$.

Example 2. Let $N(n, t, f) = n - f$, $RC = n > 3t \wedge t \ge f$, then the following is a valid path of the counter system of the TA in Fig. 1:
$[(4, 0, 0, 0, 0)(0, 0)], r_0, [(3, 0, 1, 0, 0)(1, 0)], r_0, [(2, 0, 2, 0, 0)(2, 0)], r_0,$
$[(1, 0, 3, 0, 0)(3, 0)], r_0, [(0, 0, 4, 0, 0)(4, 0)], r_2, [(0, 0, 3, 1, 0)(4, 0)].$

2.1   Abstract Threshold Automata

The shared variables and parameters of a TA have infinite domains. To facilitate the application of parameterized verification techniques for finite-state processes, we introduce an abstraction of TAs based on parametric interval abstraction [40].

Abstract Domain. Given a TA A, define as $\mathcal{TH} = \{d_0, d_1, \ldots, d_k\}$ the set of thresholds where $d_0 = 0, d_1 = 1$ and $\forall i > 1$ d_i is a threshold in A. We assume that $\forall i, j$ $d_i < d_j$ if $i < j$. Note that this is always possible for a fixed $\boldsymbol{p} \in \boldsymbol{P}_{RC}$. If different $\boldsymbol{p} \in \boldsymbol{P}_{RC}$ result in different orders of the d_i, then we consider each of the finitely many such orders separately. Based on this, define the finite set of intervals $\mathcal{D} = \{I_0, I_1, \ldots, I_k\}$ where $I_i = [d_i, d_{i+1}[$ if $i < k$, and $I_k = [d_k, \infty[$.

Definition 3. Abstract Threshold Automata. *Given a threshold automaton* $A = (L, \mathcal{I}, \Gamma, \Pi, \mathcal{R}, RC)$, *we define the* abstract threshold automaton *(or* $\overline{TA}$*)* $\overline{A} = (L, \mathcal{I}, \overline{\Gamma}, \Pi, \overline{\mathcal{R}})$ *where:*

- *A and $\overline{A}$ share the components $L, \mathcal{I}, \Pi$.*
- *Let $\Gamma = \{x_0, \ldots, x_m\}$, then $\overline{\Gamma} = \{\overline{x}_0, \ldots, \overline{x}_m\}$, where each $\overline{x}_i$ is over the domain $\mathcal{D} = \{I_0, I_1, \ldots, I_k\}$.*
- *$\overline{\mathcal{R}}$ is the set of abstract rules. An abstract rule is a tuple $\overline{r} = (from, \rightarrow, \overline{\varphi}, \boldsymbol{uv}, \tau)$ where $from, \rightarrow, \boldsymbol{uv}, \tau$ are as before, and the abstract guard $\overline{\varphi}$ is a Boolean expression over equalities between shared variables and abstract values. Formally, let $\varphi = \varphi_0 \wedge \ldots \wedge \varphi_k$, then $\overline{\varphi} = \overline{\varphi}_0 \wedge \ldots \wedge \overline{\varphi}_k$ where for $\varphi_i = (d_j \leq x)$, we have $\overline{\varphi}_i = \bigvee_{c=j}^{k-1}(\overline{x} = [d_c, d_{c+1}[) \vee \overline{x} = [d_k, \infty[$, and for $\varphi_i = (d_j > x)$, we have $\overline{\varphi}_i = \bigvee_{c=0}^{j-1}(\overline{x} = [d_c, d_{c+1}[)$.*

Example 3. Consider again the TA in Fig. 1 with $N(n, t, f) = n - f$, $RC = n > 3t \wedge t \geq f > 1$. We have $\mathcal{TH} = \{0, 1, t, n - t\}$ and $\mathcal{D} = \{[0, 1[, [1, t[, [t, n - t[, [n - t, \infty[\}$ whose order is induced by RC. Moreover, we have $\overline{r}_0 = r_0, \overline{r}_1 = r_1$ (due to the absence of a guard), $\overline{r}_2.\overline{\varphi} = (\overline{x}_0 = [n - t, \infty[)$, $\overline{r}_3.\overline{\varphi} = (\overline{x}_1 = [n - t, \infty[)$.

To keep the presentation simple, in our definition all shared variables have the same abstract domain. The abstraction can be improved by considering different abstract domains for different variables: for a given shared variable x we can let $\mathcal{TH}_x = \{d_0, d_1, \ldots, d_l\}$ where $d_0 = 0, d_1 = 1$ and $\forall i > 1$ there is a guard $d_i * x$ with $* \in \{\geq, <\}$, to obtain a corresponding abstract domain $\mathcal{D}_x$ for x.

Semantics of $\overline{TA}$. We first over-approximate the semantics of a system composed of an arbitrary number of $\overline{TA}$s by an abstract counter system. We later show how to detect whether a behavior of the abstract counter system corresponds to a concrete behavior of a counter system.

Definition 4. *An* abstract counter system *(ACS) of* $\overline{A} = (L, \mathcal{I}, \overline{\Gamma}, \Pi, \overline{\mathcal{R}})$ *is a transition system* $\mathsf{ACS}(\overline{A}) = (\overline{\Sigma}, \overline{\Sigma}_0, \overline{\mathcal{T}})$ *where:*

- *$\overline{\Sigma}$ is the set of abstract configurations. A configuration of $\mathsf{ACS}(\overline{A})$ is a tuple $\overline{\sigma} = (\boldsymbol{k}, \overline{\boldsymbol{g}})$ where:*

- $\boldsymbol{k} \in \mathbb{N}_0^{|L|}$ is a vector of counter values where $\boldsymbol{k}[i]$ represents the number of processes in location i.
- $\overline{\boldsymbol{g}} \in \mathcal{D}^{|\Gamma|}$ is a vector of shared variables values, where $\overline{\boldsymbol{g}}[i]$ is the parametric interval currently assigned to $\overline{x}_i$.

- The set $\overline{\Sigma}_0$ contains all initial abstract configurations, i.e., those that satisfy

$$\forall \overline{x}_i \in \overline{\Gamma}: \ \overline{\sigma}.\overline{\boldsymbol{g}}[i] = I_0 \text{ and } \sum_{i \in \mathcal{I}} \overline{\sigma}.\boldsymbol{k}[i] \geq 0 \text{ and } \sum_{i \notin \mathcal{I}} \overline{\sigma}.\boldsymbol{k}[i] = 0$$

- $\overline{\mathcal{T}} \subseteq \overline{\Sigma} \times \overline{\mathcal{R}} \times \overline{\Sigma}$ is the set of transitions. A transition is a tuple $t = (\overline{\sigma}, \overline{r}, \overline{\sigma}')$ where:
  - $\overline{\sigma}'.\boldsymbol{k}[\overline{r}. \rightarrow] = \overline{\sigma}.\boldsymbol{k}[\overline{r}. \rightarrow] + 1$
  - $\overline{\sigma}'.\boldsymbol{k}[\overline{r}.from] = \overline{\sigma}.\boldsymbol{k}[\overline{r}.from] - 1$
  - $\overline{\sigma}.\overline{\boldsymbol{g}} \models \overline{r}.\overline{\varphi}$
  - $\overline{\sigma}'.\overline{\boldsymbol{g}} = \overline{\sigma}.\overline{\boldsymbol{g}} + \overline{r}.\boldsymbol{uv}$, defined as follows: $\forall i < |\Gamma|$:
    1. $\overline{\sigma}'.\overline{\boldsymbol{g}}[i] = \overline{\sigma}.\overline{\boldsymbol{g}}[i]$, if $\overline{r}.\boldsymbol{uv}[i] = 0$
    2. $(\overline{\sigma}'.\overline{\boldsymbol{g}}[i] = \overline{\sigma}.\overline{\boldsymbol{g}}[i]) \vee (\overline{\sigma}'.\overline{\boldsymbol{g}}[i] = \overline{\sigma}.\overline{\boldsymbol{g}}[i].next)$, if $\overline{r}.\boldsymbol{uv}[i] = 1$
    3. $(\overline{\sigma}'.\overline{\boldsymbol{g}}[i] = \overline{\sigma}.\overline{\boldsymbol{g}}[i]) \vee (\overline{\sigma}'.\overline{\boldsymbol{g}}[i] = \overline{\sigma}.\overline{\boldsymbol{g}}[i].previous)$, if $\overline{r}.\boldsymbol{uv}[i] = -1$
       the first disjunct in 2 and the second in 3 are omitted if $\overline{\sigma}.\overline{\boldsymbol{g}}[i] = I_0$.
    4. $\forall x_i \in \overline{r}.\tau: \ \overline{\sigma}'.\overline{\boldsymbol{g}}[i] = I_0$

We also write $\overline{\sigma} \xrightarrow{\overline{r}} \overline{\sigma}'$ instead of $(\overline{\sigma}, \overline{r}, \overline{\sigma}') \in \overline{\mathcal{T}}$.

In contrast to prior work [40], the domain of counters is not abstracted in ACS.

Paths of ACS. A sequence $\overline{\sigma}_0, \overline{r}_0, \overline{\sigma}_1, \ldots, \overline{\sigma}_{k-1}, \overline{r}_{k-1}, \overline{\sigma}_k$ of alternating abstract configurations and rules is called a *path* of $\mathsf{ACS}(\overline{A}) = (\overline{\Sigma}, \overline{\Sigma}_0, \overline{\mathcal{T}})$, if $\overline{\sigma}_0 \in \overline{\Sigma}_0$ and $(\overline{\sigma}_i, \overline{r}_i, \overline{\sigma}_{i+1}) \in \overline{\mathcal{T}}$ for $0 \leq i \leq k$. In this case we also write $\overline{\sigma}_0 \rightarrow^* \overline{\sigma}_k$. We denote by $Paths(\mathsf{ACS}(\overline{A}))$ the set of all paths of $\mathsf{ACS}(\overline{A})$.

Example 4. Let $I_0 = [0, 1[, I_1 = [1, t[, I_2 = [t, n - t[, I_3 = [n - t, \infty[$. The following is a valid path of the abstract counter system of the TA in Fig. 1:
$[(4, 0, 0, 0, 0)(I_0, I_0)], \overline{r}_0, [(3, 0, 1, 0, 0)(I_1, I_0)], \overline{r}_0, [(2, 0, 2, 0, 0)(I_2, I_0)], \overline{r}_0,$
$[(1, 0, 3, 0, 0)(I_3, I_0)], \overline{r}_2, [(1, 0, 2, 1, 0)(I_3, I_0)]$.

Relation Between $\mathsf{ACS}(\overline{A})$ **and** $\mathsf{CS}(A)$. In comparison to CS, in ACS we drop the resilience condition, as well as the function N that determines the number of processes to be modeled. Moreover, a transition in ACS may jump from one interval to the next too early and may stay in the same interval although it had to move. We will formalize the relation between the two models in Sect. 4.

3   Specifications

We consider three kinds of specifications: *general coverability*, which refers to the notion of coverability that is widely used in parameterized verification, e.g., Petri nets [31] or VASS [51], (non-general) *coverability* and *reachability*. The latter two are specifications used in prior work on threshold automata [8,43,47]. Note that general coverability can express mutual exclusion, e.g., that there cannot be two leaders at the same time, while coverability cannot.

Definition 5. *The* general parameterized coverability problem *is: Given* $\mathsf{CS}(\mathsf{A})$ *and a* general coverability specification $\Sigma_{spec} \subseteq \Sigma$, *decide if there is a path in* $\mathsf{CS}(\mathsf{A})$ *that covers* Σ_{spec} *(i.e., decide if there is some configuration* $\sigma_r \in \Sigma$ *reachable from* $\sigma_0 \in \Sigma_0$ *and* $\exists \sigma_{spec} \in \Sigma_{spec}$ *where* $\forall i \; \sigma_{spec}.\boldsymbol{k}[i] \leq \sigma_r.\boldsymbol{k}[i]$).

Definition 6. *The* parameterized coverability problem *is: Given a TA and coverability specification* $L_{spec} = L_{>0}$, *decide if there is a path of its* $\mathsf{CS}(\mathsf{A})$ *that satisfies* L_{spec} *(i.e., decide if there is some configuration* $\sigma_r \in \Sigma$ *reachable from* $\sigma_0 \in \Sigma_0$ *and* σ_r *satisfies* $\forall i \in L_{>0} \; \sigma_r.\boldsymbol{k}[i] > 0$).

Definition 7. *The* parameterized reachability problem *is: Given a TA and a* reachability specification $L_{spec} = (L_{=0}, L_{>0})$, *decide if there is a path of* $\mathsf{CS}(\mathsf{A})$ *that satisfies* L_{spec} *(i.e., decide if there is some configuration* $\sigma_r \in \Sigma$ *reachable from* $\sigma_0 \in \Sigma_0$ *and* σ_r *satisfies* $\forall i \in L_{=0} \; \sigma_r.\boldsymbol{k}[i] = 0$ *and* $\forall i \in L_{>0} \; \sigma_r.\boldsymbol{k}[i] > 0$).

We define similarly all three types of problems for an abstract TA and its abstract counter system. Usually, our specifications are definitions of error configurations, and therefore paths that satisfy them, are called *error paths*.

4 CS vs ACS

We now show that the abstraction from CS to ACS is complete with respect to the specifications introduced in the previous section.

A path $\bar{\pi} = \bar{\sigma}_0, \bar{r}_0, \ldots, \bar{r}_{m-1}, \bar{\sigma}_m$ in $\mathsf{ACS}(\overline{\mathsf{A}}) = (\overline{\Sigma}, \overline{\Sigma}_0, \overline{\mathcal{T}})$ *corresponds to the* paths $\pi = \sigma_0, r_0^{c_0}, \ldots, r_{m-1}^{c_{m-1}}, \sigma_m$ (where $r_i^{c_i}$ simulates applying r_i c_i times) of $\mathsf{CS}(\mathsf{A}) = (\Sigma, \Sigma_0, \mathcal{T})$ that satisfy the following conditions:

- $RC \wedge (\sum_{j \in \mathcal{I}} \sigma_0.\boldsymbol{k}[j] = N(n, t, f))$
- $\forall i < m \; \sigma_i.\boldsymbol{k}[r_i.from] = c_i + \sigma_{i+1}.\boldsymbol{k}[r_i.from] \wedge \sigma_{i+1}.\boldsymbol{k}[r_i. \to] = c_i + \sigma_i.\boldsymbol{k}[r_i. \to]$
- $\forall i < m \; \forall x_j \in \Gamma \; x_j \notin r_i.\tau \implies \sigma_{i+1}.\boldsymbol{g}[j] = \sigma_i.\boldsymbol{g}[j] + c_i \cdot r_i.\boldsymbol{uv}[j]$
- $\forall i < m \; \forall x_j \in r_i.\tau \; \sigma_{i+1}.\boldsymbol{g}[j] = 0$
- $\forall i < m \; \forall x_j \in \Gamma \; \sigma_i.\boldsymbol{g}[j] \in \overline{\sigma}_i.\overline{\boldsymbol{g}}[j] \wedge \sigma_{i+1}.\boldsymbol{g}[j] \in \overline{\sigma}_{i+1}.\overline{\boldsymbol{g}}[j]$
- $\forall i < m \; c_i > 1 \implies ((\sigma_{i+1}.\boldsymbol{g} - r_i.\boldsymbol{uv}) \models r_i.\varphi)^1$

Let $Concretize(\bar{\pi})$ be the conjunction of the constraints above, where quantified formulas are instantiated to a finite conjunction of quantifier-free formulas. Note that $Concretize(\bar{\pi})$ is a quantifier-free formula in linear integer arithmetic, and a satisfying assignment for $Concretize(\bar{\pi})$ (that can be computed by an SMT solver) represents a path of $\mathsf{CS}(\mathsf{A})$ that corresponds to $\bar{\pi}$. We say that a path $\bar{\pi} \in Paths(\mathsf{ACS}(\overline{\mathsf{A}}))$ is *spurious* if $Concretize(\bar{\pi})$ is unsatisfiable.

For a given $\bar{\pi} \in Paths(\mathsf{ACS}(\overline{\mathsf{A}}))$, let $Cover(\bar{\pi}) = \forall l \in L \; \sigma_m.\boldsymbol{k}[l] \geq \overline{\sigma}_m.\boldsymbol{k}[l]$. We can show[2] the following connection between error paths in $\mathsf{CS}(\mathsf{A})$ and $\mathsf{ACS}(\overline{\mathsf{A}})$:

---

[1] This is needed only in cases where an update affects any of the guards of $r_i.\varphi$.

[2] Formal proofs of all our results can be found in the extended version of the paper [10].

Lemma 1. ACS($\overline{A}$) *has a non-spurious path that covers a set of configurations* $\Sigma_{spec} \subseteq \Sigma$ *iff* CS(A) *has a path that covers* Σ_{spec}.

Note that Lemma 1 subsumes the case of non-general coverability.

Similarly, if $\overline{\pi}$ is a non-spurious path of ACS($\overline{A}$) that satisfies a reachability specification L_{spec}, let $Reach(\overline{\pi}) = \forall l \in L\ \sigma_m.k[l] > 0 \iff \overline{\sigma}_m.k[l] > 0$. Then we can show the following with a similar proof as above, where we replace $Cover(\overline{\pi})$ with $Reach(\overline{\pi})$ and reason accordingly.

Lemma 2. ACS($\overline{A}$) *has a non-spurious path that satisfies a reachability specification* L_{spec} *iff* CS(A) *has a path that satisfies* L_{spec}.

5   Checking General Parameterized Coverability

In this section, we show how abstract counter systems (including ours) can be framed as well-structured transition systems. We also introduce a parameterized model checking algorithm for checking general parameterized coverability in ACS.

5.1   Well-Structured Transition Systems

Well-structured transition systems [32] (WSTS) are a class of infinite-state systems for which the general parameterized coverability problem is decidable [1,39]. In the following, we recap the standard definitions of WSTS.

Well-Quasi-Order. Given a set S, a binary relation $\preceq\ \subseteq S \times S$ is a *well-quasi-order* (wqo) if $\preceq$ is reflexive, transitive, and if any infinite sequence $s_0, s_1, \dots \in S^\omega$ contains a pair $s_i \preceq s_j$ with $i < j$. A subset $R \subseteq S$ is an *anti-chain* if any two distinct elements of R are incomparable wrt. $\preceq$. Therefore, $\preceq$ is a wqo on S if and only if it is reflexive, transitive, and has no infinite anti-chains. The *upward closure* of a set $R \subseteq S$, denoted $\uparrow R$, is the set $\{s \in S \mid \exists s' \in R : s' \preceq s\}$. We say that R is *upward-closed* if $\uparrow R = R$, and we call $B \subseteq S$ a *basis* of R if $\uparrow B = R$. If $\preceq$ is also anti-symmetric, then any basis of R has a unique subset of minimal elements. We call this set the *minimal basis* of R, denoted $minBasis(R)$.

Compatibility. Given a transition system $M = (S, S_0, \mathcal{T})$, we say that a wqo $\preceq\ \subseteq S \times S$ is *compatible* with the transition relation $\mathcal{T}$ if the following holds:

$$\forall s, s', s_x \in S : \text{ if } s \to s' \text{ and } s \preceq s_x \text{ then } \exists s'_x \text{ with } s' \preceq s'_x \text{ and } s_x \to^* s'_x,$$

where $s \to s'$ is a transition in $\mathcal{T}$, and $s_x \to^* s'_x$ is a path in M.

WSTS. We say that $(M, \preceq)$ with $M = (S, S_0, \mathcal{T})$ is a *well-structured transition system* if $\preceq$ is a wqo on S that is compatible with $\mathcal{T}$. The set of *immediate predecessors* of a set $R \subseteq S$ is $pred(R) = \{s \in S \mid \exists s' \in R : s \to s'\}$. We say that a WSTS $(M, \preceq)$ *has effective pred-basis* if there exists an algorithm that takes as input any finite set $R \subseteq S$ and returns a finite basis of $pred(\uparrow R)$.

5.2   Abstract Counter Systems as WSTS

To prove that the general parameterized coverability problem is decidable for abstract TAs, we show that an ACS can be framed as WSTS. Here, for a given set $E' \subseteq \overline{\Sigma}$ we define $pred(E') = \{\overline{\sigma} \in \overline{\Sigma} \mid \overline{\sigma}' \in E' \wedge \exists \overline{r} \in \overline{\mathcal{R}} \text{ s.t. } (\overline{\sigma}, \overline{r}, \overline{\sigma}') \in \overline{\mathcal{T}}\}$.

Lemma 3. *Given an abstract counter system* $\mathsf{ACS}(\overline{A}) = (\overline{\Sigma}, \overline{\Sigma}_0, \overline{\mathcal{T}})$ *let* $\lesssim \subseteq \overline{\Sigma} \times \overline{\Sigma}$ *be the binary relation defined by:*

$$(\boldsymbol{k}, \overline{\boldsymbol{g}}) \lesssim (\boldsymbol{k}', \overline{\boldsymbol{g}}') \iff \boldsymbol{k} \le \boldsymbol{k}' \wedge \overline{\boldsymbol{g}} = \overline{\boldsymbol{g}}'$$

where $\le$ *is the component-wise ordering of vectors. Then* $(\mathsf{ACS}(\overline{A}), \lesssim)$ *is a WSTS.*

Note also that the order $\lesssim$ is anti-symmetric, and therefore every upward-closed set of configurations has a unique minimal basis.

Lemma 4. *Given an abstract counter system* $\mathsf{ACS}(\overline{A}) = (\overline{\Sigma}, \overline{\Sigma}_0, \overline{\mathcal{T}})$, *the WSTS* $((\overline{\Sigma}, \overline{\Sigma}_0, \overline{\mathcal{T}}), \lesssim)$ *has effective pred-basis.*

Let *BasisTrans* be the transitions from which we computed *CPredBasis* in the proof of Lemma 4. Concretely, let $\boldsymbol{u}_j$ be the unit vector with $\boldsymbol{u}_j(j) = 1$ and $\boldsymbol{u}_j(i) = 0$ for $i \ne j$ then *BasisTrans*(E') is the set

$$\left\{ ((\boldsymbol{k}, \overline{\boldsymbol{g}}), \overline{r}, (\boldsymbol{k}', \overline{\boldsymbol{g}}')) \in \overline{\mathcal{T}} \,\middle|\, \begin{matrix} (\boldsymbol{k}', \overline{\boldsymbol{g}}') \in E' \wedge \overline{r} = (l_i, l_j, \overline{\varphi}, \boldsymbol{uv}, \tau) \wedge \\ \left[(\boldsymbol{k}, \overline{\boldsymbol{g}}) \xrightarrow{\overline{r}} (\boldsymbol{k}', \overline{\boldsymbol{g}}') \vee ((\boldsymbol{k}, \overline{\boldsymbol{g}}) \xrightarrow{\overline{r}} (\boldsymbol{k}' + \boldsymbol{u}_j, \overline{\boldsymbol{g}}') \wedge \boldsymbol{k}'[j] = 0) \right] \end{matrix} \right\}.$$

The following corollary, derived from the aforementioned definitions, will be instrumental in establishing the correctness of our algorithms.

Corollary 1. *Given* $\overline{\sigma}'_1, \overline{\sigma}'_2 \in \overline{\Sigma}$, *if* $\overline{\sigma}'_1 \lesssim \overline{\sigma}'_2$ *then* $\{\overline{r} \in \overline{\mathcal{R}} \mid (\overline{\sigma}_1, \overline{r}, \overline{\sigma}'_1) \in BasisTrans(\overline{\sigma}'_1)\} = \{\overline{r} \in \overline{\mathcal{R}} \mid (\overline{\sigma}_2, \overline{r}, \overline{\sigma}'_2) \in BasisTrans(\overline{\sigma}'_2)\}$.

5.3   WSTS-Based General Parameterized Coverability Checking

In this section, we present our algorithm for solving the general parameterized coverability problem (see Definition 5). Given an abstract counter system $\mathsf{ACS}(\overline{A})$ and a finite set of error configurations $ERR \subseteq \overline{\Sigma}$, we say that a path of $\mathsf{ACS}(\overline{A})$ is an *error path* if it starts in $\overline{\Sigma}_0$ and ends in the upward closure of ERR. Lemma 4 enables us to use the transitive closure of $CPredBasis(ERR)$ to compute a set of error paths in $\mathsf{ACS}(\overline{A})$ or a fixed-point in which no initial configuration occurs. As defined in Sect. 4, we can examine whether any of these abstract error paths corresponds to error paths in $\mathsf{CS}(A)$. The detailed algorithm is given in Algorithm 1, which we explain in the following.

Procedure CHECKCOVERABILITY takes as argument an $\mathsf{ACS}(\overline{A})$ and a basis for a set of error configurations ERR. After initializing local variables, the procedure enters a while loop that, given E_{i-1}, invokes COMPUTEPREDBASIS (Line 5), a sub-procedure to compute $E_i \supseteq minBasis(pred(\uparrow E_{i-1}))$ such that $\forall \overline{\sigma} \in$

Algorithm 1 General Parameterized Coverability Checking

1: **procedure** CHECKCOVERABILITY(*Abstract Counter System ACS,ERR*)
2:     $E_0 \leftarrow ERR, i \leftarrow 1, errGraph \leftarrow \emptyset$
3:     $visitedTrans \leftarrow \emptyset$ //set of visited transitions
4:     **while** $E_{i-1} \neq \emptyset$ **do** //has a fixed-point been reached?
5:         $E_i, visitedTrans \leftarrow$ COMPUTEPREDBASIS($E_{i-1}, visitedTrans$)
6:         $i \leftarrow i+1$
7:     $visitedInitialConfigs \leftarrow \bigcup_{j<i}(E_j \cap \Sigma_0)$
8:     **if** $visitedInitialConfigs \neq \emptyset$ **then**   //intersects with initial configurations?
9:         $errGraph \leftarrow$ CONSTRUCTERRGRAPH($visitedInitialConfigs, visitedTrans$)
10:        $nonSpuriousCE = CheckforNonSpuriousCEs(errGraph)$
11:        **if** $nonSpuriousCE \neq \emptyset$ **then** //at least one CE is non-spurious
12:            **return** $nonSpuriousCE$ //an error is found!
13:    **return** " The system is safe! "
14: **procedure** COMPUTEPREDBASIS($E_{i-1}, visitedTrans$)
15:    Compute $BasisTrans(E_{i-1})$ as explained at the end of Section 5.2
16:    $E_i = \{\overline{\sigma} \in \overline{\Sigma} \mid \exists (\overline{\sigma}, \overline{r}, \overline{\sigma}') \in BasisTrans(E_{i-1})\}$
17:    $visitedTrans.add(BasisTrans(E_{i-1}))$
18:    $finalE_i \leftarrow \emptyset$
19:    **for all** $\overline{\sigma} \in E_i$ **do** //remove visited bigger configurations to ensure termination
20:        **if** $\exists j \leq i, \overline{\sigma}_s \in E_j$ s.t. $\overline{\sigma}_s \lesssim \overline{\sigma}$ **then** //smaller configurations, maybe ≥ 1
21:            $visitedTrans.add(\{(\overline{\sigma}_s, \overline{r}, \overline{\sigma}') \mid (\overline{\sigma}, \overline{r}, \overline{\sigma}') \in BasisTrans(E_{i-1})\})$
22:        **else**
23:            $finalE_i.add(\overline{\sigma})$
24:            **if** $\exists \overline{\sigma}_b \in finalE_i$ s.t. $\overline{\sigma} \lesssim \overline{\sigma}_b$ **then** //bigger configurations, maybe > 1
25:                $visitedTrans.add(\{(\overline{\sigma}, \overline{r}, \overline{\sigma}') \mid (\overline{\sigma}_b, \overline{r}, \overline{\sigma}') \in BasisTrans(E_{i-1})\})$
26:                $finalE_i.remove(\overline{\sigma}_b)$
27:    **return** $finalE_i, visitedTrans$

$\uparrow E_i \ \forall j < i \ \overline{\sigma} \notin \uparrow E_j$. COMPUTEPREDBASIS also updates *visitedTrans* which represents the set of transitions explored so far. The loop breaks once a fixed-point has been reached. Line 7 computes the visited set of initial configurations *visitedInitialConfigs*. If *visitedInitialConfigs* is not empty then the procedure extracts all computed error paths (Line 9). CONSTRUCTERRGRAPH starts from the discovered initial configuration(s) and uses *visitedTrans* to construct the error graph *errGraph* which encodes all error paths. In a breadth-first fashion, the procedure CHECKFORNONSPURIOUSCEs then unfolds *errGraph* and evaluates the spuriousness of uncovered error paths that starts in $\overline{\Sigma}_0$ and ends in *ERR* (Line 10). A path $\overline{\pi} = \overline{\sigma}_0, \overline{r}_0, \ldots, \overline{r}_{j-1}, \overline{\sigma}_j$ in *errGraph* is spurious if $Concretize(\overline{\pi}) \wedge Cover(\overline{\pi})$ is unsatisfiable (see Sect. 4). In the presence of cycles[3], unfolding may not terminate in the presence of shared-variable decrements and/or resets (see Theorem 1). If all error paths are spurious, we conclude that the system is safe. Otherwise a concrete path is returned as a witness of the buggy system (Line 12).

---

[3] A *cycle* is a sub-sequence of a path that starts and ends in the same configuration.

Procedure COMPUTEPREDBASIS takes as argument the current set E_{i-1}, and the set of visited transitions *visitedTrans*. We compute E_i as the predecessors of E_{i-1} as explained at the end of Sect. 5.2 (Line 16). At this point, E_i may contain configurations larger than those we have already explored. To ensure termination, they must be removed. However, before removing these configurations, we collect their visited transitions since these may introduce new, unexplored behaviors. The computation of a comprehensive set of visited transitions, denoted as *visitedTrans* in this context, is crucial for the correctness of our algorithm. The importance of this lies in the necessity to address spurious counterexamples, which mandates retrieving all paths from an initial configuration to an error configuration. This is in contrast to ordinary backward model checking, where a single counterexample suffices. After adding all computed transitions to *visitedTrans* (Line 17), we check for each configuration $\overline{\sigma}$ in E_i the following:

- For every configuration $\overline{\sigma}_s$ with $\overline{\sigma}_s \lesssim \overline{\sigma}$, we add from $BasisTrans(E_{i-1})$ transitions that start in $\overline{\sigma}$ to *visitedTrans* after replacing $\overline{\sigma}$ with $\overline{\sigma}_s$.
- Otherwise, we add $\overline{\sigma}$ to $finalE_i$. Also, for every $\overline{\sigma}_b \in finalE_i$ with $\overline{\sigma} \lesssim \overline{\sigma}_b$, we add from $BasisTrans(E_{i-1})$ transitions that start in $\overline{\sigma}_b$ to *visitedTrans* after replacing $\overline{\sigma}_b$ with $\overline{\sigma}$, and we remove $\overline{\sigma}_b$ from $finalE_i$.

5.4   Correctness

Algorithm 1 is sound, complete, and terminates when the TA is restricted as in [8,43,44,46,47]. Soundness follows directly from encoding non-spuriousness into the constraint $Concretize(\overline{\pi}) \wedge Cover(\overline{\pi})$, as defined in Sect. 4.

Corollary 2 (Soundness). *Algorithm 1 is sound. That is, if the algorithm computes a non-spurious error path, then there is a configuration in $\uparrow ERR$ that is reachable in* $\mathsf{CS(A)}$.

With Lemma 1, the following lemma proves the algorithm's completeness.

Lemma 5 (Completeness). *If* $\mathsf{ACS(\overline{A})}$ *has a non-spurious error path* $\overline{\pi}$*, then Algorithm 1 will find it.*

Termination. Since Algorithm 1 is sound and complete, it will terminate whenever CS has a path that covers Σ_{spec}. However, Lines 21 and 25 of the algorithm could create cycles in *errGraph*. In the presence of cycles however, the algorithm could compute an infinite sequence of error paths. Therefore, we proved the following theorem.

Theorem 1. *If* $\forall \overline{r} \in \overline{\mathcal{R}} : \overline{r}.\boldsymbol{uv} \in |\mathbb{N}_0|^{|\Gamma|} \wedge \overline{r}.\tau = \emptyset$*, then Algorithm 1 terminates.*

It is important to note that if *errGraph* is acyclic, the algorithm is also guaranteed to terminate. This includes the case when *errGraph* is empty, i.e., the corresponding ACS has neither spurious nor non-spurious error paths. The algorithm also terminates if no cycle in *errGraph* has decrements or resets.

6   Reachability via $(0, 1)$-Abstraction

Two configurations σ, σ' may be comparable with respect to order $\precsim$ even if some location l is occupied in σ while it is not occupied in σ'. This implies that an algorithm based on upward-closed sets wrt. $\precsim$ cannot be used to decide reachability properties. Furthermore, note that coverability and reachability specifications (Definition 6 and 7) are agnostic to the precise number of processes in each location, i.e., they require only to distinguish between locations that are occupied by one or more processes and those that are not occupied.

To enable reachability checking and to enhance the performance of our algorithm for (non-general) coverability checking, we introduce a second, similar abstraction of our system model as in [39], where each counter can only assume one of two values: 1 to indicate that the location is currently occupied by at least one process; and 0 to indicate that it is not occupied.

$(0, 1)$-**Configuration.** Given an abstract threshold automaton $\overline{A} = (L, \mathcal{I}, \overline{\Gamma}, \Pi,$ $\overline{\mathcal{R}})$, a $(0, 1)$-*configuration* is a tuple $\sigma^z = (\boldsymbol{k}^z, \overline{\boldsymbol{g}})$, where $\boldsymbol{k}^z \in \mathbb{B}^{|L|}$, and $\overline{\boldsymbol{g}}$ is defined as before. That is $\boldsymbol{k}^z[i]$ indicates the presence (1) or absence (0) of at least one process at location i.

Definition 8. *A $(0, 1)$-counter system (or ZCS) of $\overline{A} = (L, \mathcal{I}, \overline{\Gamma}, \Pi, \overline{\mathcal{R}})$, is a transition system $\mathsf{ZCS}(\overline{A}) = (\Sigma^z, \Sigma_0^z, \mathcal{T}^z)$, where:*

- $\Sigma^z = \mathbb{B}^{|L|} \times \mathcal{D}^{|\overline{\Gamma}|}$, *is the set of $(0, 1)$-configurations*
- $\Sigma_0^z \subseteq \Sigma^z$ *is the set of $(0, 1)$-configurations σ^z that satisfy the following:*
  - $\forall i \in \Gamma : \sigma^z.\overline{\boldsymbol{g}}[i] = I_0$
  - $\forall i \in L : \sigma^z.\boldsymbol{k}^z[i] = 1 \implies i \in \mathcal{I}$
- *the transition relation $\mathcal{T}^z$ is the set of transitions $(\sigma^z, \overline{r}, \sigma^{z'})$ with:*
  - $\overline{r} = \{from, \rightarrow, \overline{\varphi}, \boldsymbol{uv}\} \in \overline{\mathcal{R}}$
  - $\sigma^z.\overline{\boldsymbol{g}} \models \overline{r}.\overline{\varphi}$
  - $\sigma^z.\boldsymbol{k}^z[\overline{r}.from] = 1$ *and* $(\sigma^{z'}.\boldsymbol{k}^z[\overline{r}.from] = 0$ *or* $\sigma^{z'}.\boldsymbol{k}^z[\overline{r}.from] = 1)$
  - $\sigma^{z'}.\boldsymbol{k}^z[\overline{r}. \rightarrow] = 1$
  - $\sigma^{z'}.\overline{\boldsymbol{g}} = \sigma^z.\overline{\boldsymbol{g}} \dotplus \boldsymbol{uv}$
  - $\forall x_i \in \overline{r}.\tau : \sigma^{z'}.\overline{\boldsymbol{g}}[i] = I_0$

Paths. A sequence $\sigma^z{}_0, \overline{r}_0, \sigma^z{}_1, \ldots, \sigma^z{}_{k-1}, \overline{r}_{k-1}, \sigma^z{}_k$ of alternating $(0, 1)$-configur-ations and abstract rules is a *path* of $\mathsf{ZCS}(\overline{A})$ if $\forall i < k$ we have $(\sigma^z{}_i, \overline{r}_i, \sigma^z{}_{i+1}) \in \mathcal{T}^z$. We denote by $Paths(\mathsf{ZCS}(\overline{A}))$ the set of all paths of $\mathsf{ZCS}(\overline{A})$.

We say that a 01-configuration σ^z satisfies a reachability specification L_{spec}, denoted $\sigma^z \models L_{spec}$, if for all $i \in L_{=0}$, $\sigma^z.\boldsymbol{k}^z[i] = 0$, and for all $i \in L_{>0}$, $\sigma^z.\boldsymbol{k}^z[i] > 0$. We say that $\mathsf{ZCS}(\overline{A})$ satisfies L_{spec}, denoted $\mathsf{ZCS}(\overline{A}) \models L_{spec}$, if there is a non-spurious path of $\mathsf{ZCS}(\overline{A})$ that ends in σ^z with $\sigma^z \models L_{spec}$.

Together with Lemma 2, the following lemma shows that our $(0,1)$-abstraction is precise for reachability and coverability specifications. In other words, we have $\mathsf{ZCS}(\overline{A}) \models L_{spec}$ if and only if $\mathsf{CS}(A) \models L_{spec}$, given that L_{spec} is a reachability or coverability specification.

Lemma 6. *Let* $\overline{A} = (L, \mathcal{I}, \overline{\Gamma}, \Pi, \overline{\mathcal{R}})$ *be an abstract TA, and* L_{spec} *a reachability or coverability specification. We assume w.l.o.g. that* $\mathcal{I} = \{l_0\}$.

Then, there exists a path $\sigma^z{}_0, \overline{r}_0, \sigma^z{}_1, \ldots, \overline{r}_{n-1}, \sigma^z{}_n \in Paths(\mathsf{ZCS}(\overline{A}))$ *such that* $\sigma^z{}_n \models L_{spec}$ *if and only if there exists a path* $\overline{\sigma}_0, \overline{r}_0, \overline{\sigma}_1, \ldots, \overline{r}_{m-1}, \overline{\sigma}_m \in Paths(\mathsf{ACS}(\overline{A}))$ *such that* $\overline{\sigma}_m \models L_{spec}$.

6.1   Parameterized Reachability Algorithm (PRA)

Our algorithm PRA for solving the parameterized reachability problem accepts two input parameters: a 01-counter system $\mathsf{ZCS}(\overline{A})$ and a finite set of error configurations $ERR \subseteq \Sigma^z$. It outputs either "The system is safe" to indicate that no $(0,1)$-configuration in ERR is reachable, or an error path of $\mathsf{ZCS}(\overline{A})$. PRA is very similar to Algorithm 1, differing primarily in the approach to computing the predecessor set. Instead of checking if two configurations are comparable, we look for equality. Moreover, in contrast to Algorithm 1, checking whether an error path π^z in $\mathsf{ZCS}(\overline{A})$ is spurious is based on constraint $Reach(\pi^z)$ instead of $Cover(\pi^z)$, as described in Sect. 4. More details on PRA can be found in [10].

Just like Algorithm 1, we have demonstrated soundness and completeness of PRA in a general context, along with termination, subject to the restrictions outlined in Theorem 1. Moreover, with minimal adjustments to the reachability algorithm, we can also check coverability within a ZCS (see again [10]).

7   Implementation and Experimental Evaluation

We implemented Algorithm 1 with explicit, unbounded integer counters and PRA symbolically, leveraging CUDD Decision Diagrams [55] as BDD package. Both use Z3 [25] as SMT solver back-end. We evaluated our implementations on an AMD Ryzen 7 5800X CPU, running at 3.8 GHz with 32 GiB memory of system memory. For comparisons with ByMC [46], the state-of-the-art model checker for threshold automata, we executed the tool in the VM provided by the authors on the same machine, with 6 out of 8 cores and 25GiB of the total system memory. To ensure an equal environment, we also executed our tool in a virtual machine with the same restrictions.[4]

---

[4] The benchmark files and a container image with our tool are available on Zenodo [9].

As benchmarks in our decidable fragment, we used the following threshold-based algorithms from the literature [42]: folklore reliable broadcast (frb) [20], one-step consensus with zero-degradation (cf1s) [18], consensus in one communication step (c1cs) [19], consistent broadcast (strb), asynchronous byzantine agreement (aba) [17], non-blocking atomic commit (nbacr [53] and nbacg [34]), condition-based consensus (cc) [50], and byzantine one step consensus (bosco) [56]. Moreover, we considered the following parts of the Red Belly blockchain [22], which have already been modeled as TA in [12]: the broadcast protocol (RB-bc), the one-round consensus protocol (RB), and a simplified one-round consensus protocol (RB-Simpl).

We verified interesting safety specifications: *agreement* (consistent decisions among correct processes), *validity*

Table 1. Comparison of execution time (in s) between ByMC [46] and our symbolic implementation of PRA. In the Prop. column, A denotes agreement, V denotes validity, and U denotes unforgeability. *TO* denotes a timeout after 1.5 h.

Benchmark	Prop.	ByMC	PRA
aba	U	0.52	**0.12**
bcrb	U	0.30	**0.06**
bosco	V	42.22	**0.73**
c1cs	V	*TO*	**0.23**
cc	A, V	0.24	0.24
cf1s	V	380.81	**0.42**
frb	U	0.19	**0.07**
nbacg	A	**0.18**	0.36
nbacr	V	0.19	**0.14**
strb	U	0.17	**0.12**
RB-bc	A,V	**0.32**	0.49
RB	V	*TO*	1.03
RB-Simpl	V	*TO*	61.77

(the value that has been decided must have been proposed by some process), and *unforgeability* (if all correct processes have an initial value of 0, then no correct process ever accepts).

Table 1 compares execution times of ByMC and our implementation of PRA. It shows that PRA significantly outperforms ByMC on all benchmarks except two. Except for Red Belly protocols, our non-symbolic implementation can verify all the benchmarks above in less than 2 min.

For the undecidable fragment, we used our extended model of TA to model the following FTDAs from the literature: reliable broadcast [57], k-set agreement [21], multi-round simplified Red Belly blockchain consensus [22], multi-round full Red Belly blockchain consensus [22], and phase king consensus [11]. Note that, in [12], only the one-round protocols were modeled, and only the simple version was verified. In contrast, we can model the multi-round versions, and were able to verify all (single- and multi-round) versions except one.

For the aforementioned TAs, we conducted our experiments on a machine with 2x AMD EPYC 7773x - 128 Cores, 256 Threads and 2TB RAM. Table 2 presents execution for running our symbolic implementation on all the aforementioned multi-round protocols. For the phase-king protocol, PRA was able to locate a bug in an incorrect model of the algorithm within 2 minutes, and was also able to prove partial correctness properties, for example that consensus is actually reachable, in around 5 min. We verified *validity* for all the remaining benchmarks, and for floodmin we verified additionally *agreement*. During benchmarking, memory usage peaked at 73 GB.

Table 2. Execution time (in s) for PRA on multi-round protocols. *TO* denotes a timeout after 2 h.

Benchmark	PRA
multiR-floodMin	0.3
multiR-RelBrd	0.1
multiR-RB-Simpl	6859
multiR-RB	*TO*
phase-king-buggy	120
phase-king-partial	300

8 Related Work

After presenting an approach for verifying FTDAs based on abstraction [40], Konnov et al. [43–46] developed several approaches and algorithms specifically tailored for verifying the safety and liveness properties of threshold automata. Starting from an acyclic CFA (control flow automaton), they construct in [40] a finite counter system using parametric interval abstraction for variables and counters. To refine the abstraction, they detect spurious transitions using ordinary model checking and user-defined invariants. Subsequent works [43,45] improve on the efficiency when verifying reachability properties in TAs. In [45], they showed the existence of an upper bound on the distance between states within counter systems of TAs, hence, demonstrating the completeness of bounded model checking. In [43], the authors use partial order reduction to generate a finite set of sequences comprising sets of guards and rules. Each of these sequences represents a possibly infinite set of error traces. An SMT solver is employed to validate the existence of concrete error traces. Extending [43], Konnov et al. presented an approach capable of detecting lasso-shaped traces that violate a given liveness property [44]. The latter two approaches have been implemented in the tool ByMC [46]. To enable the functionality of all aforementioned approaches, the authors found it necessary to impose constraints on threshold automata. This involved explicitly prohibiting cycles and variable decrements.

A verification tool for parameterized distributed algorithms has been introduced in [59]. The tool relies on layered threshold automata [14] as a system model, which can be seen as an infinitely repeating threshold automata. However, the tool requires users to identify layers (rounds) in the model, their sequence (infinite interleaving or lasso-shaped sequences), and to provide predicates.

Decidability and the complexity of verification and synthesis of threshold automata have also been studied in [8]. Their decision procedure is based on an SMT encoding of potential error paths, where in general the size of the SMT formula grows exponentially with the length of the paths. While having achieved good results with some heuristics that avoid this exponential blow-up in practice, we believe that these heuristics would not work for threshold automata with decrements and/or resets[5]. Moreover, their method requires a bound on the number of changes in the valuation of thresholds. However, such a constraint does not apply in the presence of decrements and/or resets.

9   Conclusion

In this paper, we have introduced an extension of the computational model known as threshold automata, to support decrements and resets of shared variables. This extension in general comes at the cost of decidability, even for simple state-reachability properties. We developed a semi-decision procedure for this extended notion of TA, supporting not only the simple coverability properties from the TA literature, but also general coverability properties as known from Petri nets or well-structured systems. To support also reachability properties, we presented an additional abstraction, called $(0, 1)$-abstraction, which is the basis for a semi-decision procedure for reachability properties of extended TAs.

We have implemented our techniques and evaluated them on examples from the literature, and on several round-based algorithms that cannot be modeled with canonical TAs. We show that our semi-decision procedure can find bugs in a faulty protocol and prove correctness of protocols, even outside the known decidable fragment. Moreover, on a set of benchmarks in the decidable fragment, it matches or outperforms the TA model checker ByMC [46].

Acknowledgments. T. Baumeister and P. Eichler carried out this work as members of the Saarbrücken Graduate School of Computer Science. This research was funded in whole or in part by the German Research Foundation (DFG) grant 513487900 and the Luxembourg National Research Fund (FNR) grant C22/IS/17432184. For the purpose of open access, and in fulfilment of the obligations arising from the grant agreement, the author has applied a Creative Commons Attribution 4.0 International (CC BY 4.0) license to any Author Accepted Manuscript version arising from this submission.

Data Availability. The program, benchmark scripts and the benchmark files as evaluated in Sect. 7 are available at https://doi.org/10.5281/zenodo.12527556.

References

1. Abdulla, P.A., Cerans, K., Jonsson, B., Tsay, Y.K.: General decidability theorems for infinite-state systems. In: Proceedings 11th Annual IEEE Symposium on Logic in Computer Science, pp. 313–321. IEEE (1996)
2. Abdulla, P.A., Haziza, F., Holík, L.: Parameterized verification through view abstraction. Int. J. Softw. Tools Technol. Transf. **18**(5), 495–516 (2016). https://doi.org/10.1007/S10009-015-0406-X

---

[5] We could not verify this conjecture since their code is not publicly available.

3. Aminof, B., Jacobs, S., Khalimov, A., Rubin, S.: Parameterized model checking of token-passing systems. In: McMillan, K.L., Rival, X. (eds.) VMCAI 2014. LNCS, vol. 8318, pp. 262–281. Springer, Heidelberg (2014). https://doi.org/10.1007/978-3-642-54013-4_15

4. Aminof, B., Kotek, T., Rubin, S., Spegni, F., Veith, H.: Parameterized model checking of rendezvous systems. In: Baldan, P., Gorla, D. (eds.) CONCUR 2014. LNCS, vol. 8704, pp. 109–124. Springer, Heidelberg (2014). https://doi.org/10.1007/978-3-662-44584-6_9

5. Außerlechner, S., Jacobs, S., Khalimov, A.: Tight cutoffs for guarded protocols with fairness. In: Jobstmann, B., Leino, K.R.M. (eds.) VMCAI 2016. LNCS, vol. 9583, pp. 476–494. Springer, Heidelberg (2016). https://doi.org/10.1007/978-3-662-49122-5_23

6. Balasubramanian, A.R., Bertrand, N., Markey, N.: Parameterized verification of synchronization in constrained reconfigurable broadcast networks. In: Beyer, D., Huisman, M. (eds.) TACAS 2018. LNCS, vol. 10806, pp. 38–54. Springer, Cham (2018). https://doi.org/10.1007/978-3-319-89963-3_3

7. Balasubramanian, A.R., Guillou, L., Weil-Kennedy, C.: Parameterized analysis of reconfigurable broadcast networks. In: FoSSaCS 2022. LNCS, vol. 13242, pp. 61–80. Springer, Cham (2022). https://doi.org/10.1007/978-3-030-99253-8_4

8. Balasubramanian, A.R., Esparza, J., Lazić, M.: Complexity of verification and synthesis of threshold automata. In: Hung, D.V., Sokolsky, O. (eds.) ATVA 2020. LNCS, vol. 12302, pp. 144–160. Springer, Cham (2020). https://doi.org/10.1007/978-3-030-59152-6_8

9. Baumeister, T., Eichler, P., Jacobs, S., Sakr, M., Völp, M.: Parameterized verification of round-based distributed algorithms via extended threshold automata -. Artifact (2024). https://doi.org/10.5281/zenodo.12513748

10. Baumeister, T., Eichler, P., Jacobs, S., Sakr, M., Völp, M.: Parameterized verification of round-based distributed algorithms via extended threshold automata (2024). https://arxiv.org/abs/2406.19880

11. Berman, P., Garay, J.A., Perry, K.J., et al.: Towards optimal distributed consensus. In: FOCS, vol. 89, pp. 410–415 (1989)

12. Bertrand, N., Gramoli, V., Konnov, I., Lazic, M., Tholoniat, P., Widder, J.: Holistic verification of blockchain consensus. In: DISC. LIPIcs, vol. 246, pp. 10:1–10:24. Schloss Dagstuhl - Leibniz-Zentrum für Informatik (2022)

13. Bertrand, N., Thomas, B., Widder, J.: Guard automata for the verification of safety and liveness of distributed algorithms. In: Haddad, S., Varacca, D. (eds.) 32nd International Conference on Concurrency Theory, CONCUR 2021, August 24–27, 2021, Virtual Conference. LIPIcs, vol. 203, pp. 15:1–15:17. Schloss Dagstuhl - Leibniz-Zentrum für Informatik (2021). https://doi.org/10.4230/LIPICS.CONCUR.2021.15

14. Bertrand, N., Thomas, B., Widder, J.: Guard automata for the verification of safety and liveness of distributed algorithms. In: Concur 2021-International Conference on Concurrency Theory, pp. 1–17 (2021)

15. Bloem, R., et al.: Decidability of Parameterized Verification. Synthesis Lectures on Distributed Computing Theory, Morgan & Claypool Publishers (2015). https://doi.org/10.2200/S00658ED1V01Y201508DCT013

16. Bouajjani, A., Jonsson, B., Nilsson, M., Touili, T.: Regular model checking. In: Emerson, E.A., Sistla, A.P. (eds.) CAV 2000. LNCS, vol. 1855, pp. 403–418. Springer, Heidelberg (2000). https://doi.org/10.1007/10722167_31

17. Bracha, G., Toueg, S.: Asynchronous consensus and broadcast protocols. J. ACM (JACM) 32(4), 824–840 (1985)

18. Brasileiro, F., Greve, F., Mostefaoui, A., Raynal, M.: Consensus in one communication step. In: Malyshkin, V. (ed.) PaCT 2001. LNCS, vol. 2127, pp. 42–50. Springer, Heidelberg (2001). https://doi.org/10.1007/3-540-44743-1_4

19. Brasileiro, F., Greve, F., Mostefaoui, A., Raynal, M.: Consensus in one communication step. In: Malyshkin, V. (ed.) PaCT 2001. LNCS, vol. 2127, pp. 42–50. Springer, Heidelberg (2001). https://doi.org/10.1007/3-540-44743-1_4

20. Chandra, T.D., Toueg, S.: Unreliable failure detectors for reliable distributed systems. J. ACM (JACM) 43(2), 225–267 (1996)

21. Chaudhuri, S., Erlihy, M., Lynch, N.A., Tuttle, M.R.: Tight bounds for k-set agreement. J. ACM (JACM) 47(5), 912–943 (2000)

22. Crain, T., Gramoli, V., Larrea, M., Raynal, M.: DBFT: efficient leaderless byzantine consensus and its application to blockchains. In: 2018 IEEE 17th International Symposium on Network Computing and Applications (NCA), pp. 1–8. IEEE (2018)

23. Crain, T., Natoli, C., Gramoli, V.: Red belly: a secure, fair and scalable open blockchain. In: SP, pp. 466–483. IEEE (2021)

24. Czerwinski, W., Orlikowski, L.: Reachability in vector addition systems is Ackermann-complete. In: 62nd IEEE Annual Symposium on Foundations of Computer Science, FOCS 2021, Denver, CO, USA, February 7-10, 2022. pp. 1229–1240. IEEE (2021). https://doi.org/10.1109/FOCS52979.2021.00120

25. de Moura, L., Bjørner, N.: Z3: an efficient SMT solver. In: Ramakrishnan, C.R., Rehof, J. (eds.) TACAS 2008. LNCS, vol. 4963, pp. 337–340. Springer, Heidelberg (2008). https://doi.org/10.1007/978-3-540-78800-3_24

26. Delzanno, G., Sangnier, A., Zavattaro, G.: Parameterized verification of ad hoc networks. In: Gastin, P., Laroussinie, F. (eds.) CONCUR 2010. LNCS, vol. 6269, pp. 313–327. Springer, Heidelberg (2010). https://doi.org/10.1007/978-3-642-15375-4_22

27. Emerson, E.A., Kahlon, V.: Model checking guarded protocols. In: LICS, pp. 361–370. IEEE Computer Society (2003). https://doi.org/10.1109/LICS.2003.1210076

28. Emerson, E.A., Namjoshi, K.S.: On reasoning about rings. Found. Comput. Sci. 14(4), 527–549 (2003). https://doi.org/10.1142/S0129054103001881

29. Emerson, E.A., Kahlon, V.: Reducing model checking of the many to the few. In: McAllester, D. (ed.) CADE 2000. LNCS (LNAI), vol. 1831, pp. 236–254. Springer, Heidelberg (2000). https://doi.org/10.1007/10721959_19

30. Esparza, J., Finkel, A., Mayr, R.: On the verification of broadcast protocols. In: LICS, pp. 352–359. IEEE Computer Society (1999). https://doi.org/10.1109/LICS.1999.782630

31. Finkel, A.: The minimal coverability graph for Petri nets. In: Rozenberg, G. (ed.) ICATPN 1991. LNCS, vol. 674, pp. 210–243. Springer, Heidelberg (1993). https://doi.org/10.1007/3-540-56689-9_45

32. Finkel, A., Schnoebelen, P.: Well-structured transition systems everywhere! Theoret. Comput. Sci. 256(1–2), 63–92 (2001)

33. German, S.M., Sistla, A.P.: Reasoning about systems with many processes. J. ACM 39(3), 675–735 (1992). https://doi.org/10.1145/146637.146681

34. Guerraoui, R.: Non-blocking atomic commit in asynchronous distributed systems with failure detectors. Distrib. Comput. 15(1), 17–25 (2002)

35. Hawblitzel, C., et al.: Ironfleet: proving safety and liveness of practical distributed systems. Commun. ACM 60(7), 83–92 (2017). https://doi.org/10.1145/3068608

36. Jaber, N., Jacobs, S., Wagner, C., Kulkarni, M., Samanta, R.: Parameterized verification of systems with global synchronization and guards. In: Lahiri, S.K., Wang, C. (eds.) CAV 2020. LNCS, vol. 12224, pp. 299–323. Springer, Cham (2020). https://doi.org/10.1007/978-3-030-53288-8_15

37. Jaber, N., Wagner, C., Jacobs, S., Kulkarni, M., Samanta, R.: Quicksilver: modeling and parameterized verification for distributed agreement-based systems. Proc. ACM Program. Lang. **5**(OOPSLA), 1–31 (2021). https://doi.org/10.1145/3485534

38. Jacobs, S., Sakr, M.: Analyzing guarded protocols: better cutoffs, more systems, more expressivity. In: VMCAI 2018. LNCS, vol. 10747, pp. 247–268. Springer, Cham (2018). https://doi.org/10.1007/978-3-319-73721-8_12

39. Jacobs, S., Sakr, M., Völp, M.: Automatic repair and deadlock detection for parameterized systems. In: Conference on Formal Methods in Computer-Aided Design– FMCAD 2022, p. 225 (2022)

40. John, A., Konnov, I., Schmid, U., Veith, H., Widder, J.: Parameterized model checking of fault-tolerant distributed algorithms by abstraction. In: 2013 Formal Methods in Computer-Aided Design. pp. 201–209. IEEE (2013)

41. Kaiser, A., Kroening, D., Wahl, T.: Dynamic cutoff detection in parameterized concurrent programs. In: Touili, T., Cook, B., Jackson, P. (eds.) CAV 2010. LNCS, vol. 6174, pp. 645–659. Springer, Heidelberg (2010). https://doi.org/10.1007/978-3-642-14295-6_55

42. Konnov, I.: Fault-tolerant benchmarks. https://github.com/konnov/fault-tolerant-benchmarks/tree/master/cav15

43. Konnov, I., Lazić, M., Veith, H., Widder, J.: Para 2: parameterized path reduction, acceleration, and SMT for reachability in threshold-guarded distributed algorithms. Formal Meth. Syst. Des. **51**(2), 270–307 (2017)

44. Konnov, I., Lazić, M., Veith, H., Widder, J.: A short counterexample property for safety and liveness verification of fault-tolerant distributed algorithms. In: Proceedings of the 44th ACM SIGPLAN Symposium on Principles of Programming Languages, pp. 719–734 (2017)

45. Konnov, I., Veith, H., Widder, J.: On the completeness of bounded model checking for threshold-based distributed algorithms: reachability. Inf. Comput. **252**, 95–109 (2017)

46. Konnov, I., Widder, J.: ByMC: byzantine model checker. In: Margaria, T., Steffen, B. (eds.) ISoLA 2018. LNCS, vol. 11246, pp. 327–342. Springer, Cham (2018). https://doi.org/10.1007/978-3-030-03424-5_22

47. Kukovec, J., Konnov, I., Widder, J.: Reachability in parameterized systems: all flavors of threshold automata. In: CONCUR 2018-29th International Conference on Concurrency Theory (2018)

48. Marić, O., Sprenger, C., Basin, D.: Cutoff bounds for consensus algorithms. In: Majumdar, R., Kunčak, V. (eds.) CAV 2017. LNCS, vol. 10427, pp. 217–237. Springer, Cham (2017). https://doi.org/10.1007/978-3-319-63390-9_12

49. McMillan, K.L., Padon, O.: Ivy: a multi-modal verification tool for distributed algorithms. In: Lahiri, S.K., Wang, C. (eds.) CAV 2020. LNCS, vol. 12225, pp. 190–202. Springer, Cham (2020). https://doi.org/10.1007/978-3-030-53291-8_12

50. Mostéfaoui, A., Mourgaya, E., Parvédy, P.R., Raynal, M.: Evaluating the condition-based approach to solve consensus. In: 2003 International Conference on Dependable Systems and Networks, 2003. Proceedings, pp. 541–541. IEEE Computer Society (2003)

51. Rackoff, C.: The covering and boundedness problems for vector addition systems. Theoret. Comput. Sci. **6**(2), 223–231 (1978)

52. Rahli, V., Guaspari, D., Bickford, M., Constable, R.L.: Formal specification, verification, and implementation of fault-tolerant systems using eventml. Electron. Commun. Eur. Assoc. Softw. Sci. Technol. **72** (2015). https://doi.org/10.14279/TUJ.ECEASST.72.1013

53. Raynal, M.: A case study of agreement problems in distributed systems: non-blocking atomic commitment. In: Proceedings 1997 High-Assurance Engineering Workshop, pp. 209–214. IEEE (1997)

54. Schmitz, S., Schnoebelen, P.: The power of well-structured systems. In: D'Argenio, P.R., Melgratti, H. (eds.) CONCUR 2013. LNCS, vol. 8052, pp. 5–24. Springer, Heidelberg (2013). https://doi.org/10.1007/978-3-642-40184-8_2

55. Somenzi, F.: CUDD: cu decision diagram package release 2.3. 0. University of Colorado at Boulder **621** (1998)

56. Song, Y.J., van Renesse, R.: Bosco: one-step byzantine asynchronous consensus. In: Taubenfeld, G. (ed.) DISC 2008. LNCS, vol. 5218, pp. 438–450. Springer, Heidelberg (2008). https://doi.org/10.1007/978-3-540-87779-0_30

57. Srikanth, T., Toueg, S.: Simulating authenticated broadcasts to derive simple fault-tolerant algorithms. Distrib. Comput. **2**(2), 80–94 (1987)

58. Suzuki, I.: Proving properties of a ring of finite-state machines. Inf. Process. Lett. **28**(4), 213–214 (1988). https://doi.org/10.1016/0020-0190(88)90211-6

59. Thomas, B., Sankur, O.: Pylta: a verification tool for parameterized distributed algorithms. In: International Conference on Tools and Algorithms for the Construction and Analysis of Systems, pp. 28–35. Springer, Cham (2023). https://doi.org/10.1007/978-3-031-30820-8_4

60. Wilcox, J.R., et al.: Verdi: a framework for implementing and formally verifying distributed systems. In: Grove, D., Blackburn, S.M. (eds.) Proceedings of the 36th ACM SIGPLAN Conference on Programming Language Design and Implementation, Portland, OR, USA, June 15–17, 2015, pp. 357–368. ACM (2015). https://doi.org/10.1145/2737924.2737958

The Nonexistence of Unicorns and Many-Sorted Löwenheim–Skolem Theorems

Benjamin Przybocki[1]($\boxtimes$)(iD), Guilherme Toledo[2](iD), Yoni Zohar[2](iD), and Clark Barrett[1](iD)

[1] Stanford University, Stanford, USA
benjamin.przybocki@gmail.com, barrett@cs.stanford.edu
[2] Bar-Ilan University, Ramat Gan, Israel

Abstract. Stable infiniteness, strong finite witnessability, and smoothness are model-theoretic properties relevant to theory combination in satisfiability modulo theories. Theories that are strongly finitely witnessable and smooth are called *strongly polite* and can be effectively combined with other theories. Toledo, Zohar, and Barrett conjectured that stably infinite and strongly finitely witnessable theories are smooth and therefore strongly polite. They called counterexamples to this conjecture *unicorn theories*, as their existence seemed unlikely. We prove that, indeed, unicorns do not exist. We also prove versions of the Löwenheim–Skolem theorem and the Łoś–Vaught test for many-sorted logic.

1   Introduction

Given decision procedures for theories T_1 and T_2 with disjoint signatures, is there a decision procedure for $T_1 \cup T_2$? In general, the answer is "not necessarily", but a central question in Satisfiability Modulo Theories (SMT) [3] is: what assumptions on T_1 and T_2 suffice for theory combination? This line of research began with Nelson and Oppen's theory combination procedure [15], which applies when T_1 and T_2 are stably infinite, roughly meaning that every T_i-satisfiable quantifier-free formula is satisfied by an infinite T_i-interpretation for $i \in \{1, 2\}$.

The Nelson–Oppen procedure is quite useful, but requires *both* theories to be stably infinite, which is not always the case (e.g., the theories of bit-vectors and finite datatypes are not stably infinite). Thus, sufficient properties of only one of the theories were identified, such as gentleness [7], shininess [20], and flexibility [9]. The most relevant property for our purposes is strong politeness [4,8,18,19]. It is essential to the functioning of the SMT solver cvc5 [1], which is called billions of times per day in industrial production code. A theory is *strongly polite* if it is smooth and strongly finitely witnessable, which are model-theoretic properties we will define later. These properties are more involved than stable infiniteness, so proving a theory to be strongly polite is more difficult. But the advantage of strongly polite theories is that they can be combined with any other decidable theory, including theories that are not stably infinite.

© The Author(s) 2025
A. Platzer et al. (Eds.): FM 2024, LNCS 14933, pp. 658–675, 2025.
https://doi.org/10.1007/978-3-031-71162-6_34

Given the abundance of model-theoretic properties relevant to theory combination, some of which interact in subtle ways, it behooves us to understand the logical relations between them. Recent papers [21, 22] have sought to understand the relations between seven model-theoretic properties—including stable infiniteness, smoothness, and strong finite witnessability—by determining which combinations of properties are possible in various signatures. In most cases, a theory with the desired combination of properties was constructed, or it was proved that none exists. The sole exception was theories that are stably infinite and strongly finitely witnessable but not smooth, dubbed *unicorn theories* and conjectured not to exist. Our main result, Theorem 2, confirms this conjecture.

Besides completing the taxonomy of properties from [21, 22], our result has practical consequences. The nonexistence of unicorns implies that strongly polite theories can be equivalently defined as those that are stably infinite and strongly finitely witnessable. Since it is easier to prove that a theory is stably infinite than to prove that it is smooth, this streamlines the process of proving that a theory is strongly polite. Thus, each time a new theory is introduced, proving that it can be combined with other theories becomes easier.[1] Similarly, our results give a new characterization of shiny theories, which makes it easier to prove that a theory is amenable to the shiny combination procedure (see Corollary 2).

We also believe that our result is of theoretical interest. Theorem 3, which is the main ingredient in the proof of Theorem 2, can be seen as a variant of the upward Löwenheim–Skolem theorem for many-sorted logic, since proving that a theory is smooth amounts to proving that cardinalities of sorts can be increased arbitrarily, including to uncountable cardinals. This result may be of independent interest to logicians studying the model theory of many-sorted logic, and we hope the proof techniques are useful to them as well.

Speaking of proof techniques, our proof is curious in that it uses Ramsey's theorem from finite combinatorics. This is not the first time Ramsey's theorem has been used in logic. Ramsey proved his theorem in the course of solving a special case of the decision problem for first-order logic [17]. Ramsey's theorem also shows up in the Ehrenfeucht–Mostowski construction in model theory [5]. Our proof actually requires a generalization of Ramsey's theorem, which we prove using the standard version of Ramsey's theorem.

A major component of the proof of Theorem 2 amounts to proving a many-sorted version of the Löwenheim–Skolem theorem. On the course to proving this, we realized that a proper understanding of this theorem for many-sorted logic appears to be missing from the literature, despite the fact that the SMT-LIB standard [2] is based on many-sorted logic. To fill this gap, we prove generalizations of the Löwenheim–Skolem theorem for many-sorted logic, and use them to prove a many-sorted Łoś–Vaught test, useful for proving theory completeness.

The remainder of this paper is structured as follows. Section 2 provides background and definitions on many-sorted logic and SMT. Section 3 proves the main

---

[1] [21] already proved that stably infinite and strongly finitely witnessable theories can be combined with other theories. Our result gives a new proof (see Corollary 1), and shows that their procedure is not more general than polite combination.

result of this paper, namely the nonexistence of unicorn theories. Section 4 proves new many-sorted variants of the Löwenheim–Skolem theorem. Section 5 concludes and presents directions for future work.[2]

2 Preliminaries

2.1 Many-Sorted First-Order Logic

We work in many-sorted first-order logic [14]. A *signature* Σ consists of a nonempty set $\mathcal{S}_\Sigma$ of sorts, a set $\mathcal{F}_\Sigma$ of function symbols, and a set $\mathcal{P}_\Sigma$ of predicate symbols containing an equality symbol $=_\sigma$ for every sort $\sigma \in \mathcal{S}_\Sigma$.[3] Every function symbol has an arity $(\sigma_1, \ldots, \sigma_n, \sigma)$ and every predicate symbol an arity $(\sigma_1, \ldots, \sigma_n)$, where $\sigma_1, \ldots, \sigma_n, \sigma \in \mathcal{S}_\Sigma$ and $n \geq 0$. Every equality symbol $=_\sigma$ has arity (σ, σ). To quantify a variable x of sort σ, we write $\forall x : \sigma.$ and $\exists x : \sigma.$ for the universal and existential quantifiers respectively. Let $|\Sigma| = |\mathcal{S}_\Sigma| + |\mathcal{F}_\Sigma| + |\mathcal{P}_\Sigma|$. If a signature contains only sorts and equalities, we say it is *empty*. Two signatures are said to be *disjoint* if they share at most sorts and equality symbols.

We define Σ-terms and Σ-formulas as usual. The set of free variables of sort σ in φ is denoted $vars_\sigma(\varphi)$. For $S \subseteq \mathcal{S}_\Sigma$, let $vars_S(\varphi) = \bigcup_{\sigma \in S} vars_\sigma(\varphi)$. We also let $vars(\varphi) = vars_{\mathcal{S}_\Sigma}(\varphi)$. A Σ-sentence is a Σ-formula with no free variables.

A Σ-*structure* $\mathbb{A}$ interprets each sort $\sigma \in \mathcal{S}_\Sigma$ as a nonempty set $\sigma^\mathbb{A}$, each function symbol $f \in \mathcal{F}_\Sigma$ as a function $f^\mathbb{A}$ with the appropriate domain and codomain, and each predicate symbol $P \in \mathcal{P}_\Sigma$ as a relation $P^\mathbb{A}$ over the appropriate set, such that $=_\sigma^\mathbb{A}$ is the identity on $\sigma^\mathbb{A}$. A Σ-*interpretation* $\mathcal{A}$ is a pair $(\mathbb{A}, \nu)$, where $\mathbb{A}$ is a Σ-structure and ν is a function, called an *assignment*, mapping each variable x of sort σ to an element $\nu(x) \in \sigma^\mathbb{A}$, denoted $x^\mathcal{A}$. We write $t^\mathcal{A}$ for the interpretation of the Σ-term t under $\mathcal{A}$, which is defined in the usual way. The entailment relation, denoted $\vDash$, is defined as usual.

Two structures are *elementarily equivalent* if they satisfy the same sentences. We say that $\mathbb{A}$ is an *elementary substructure* of $\mathbb{B}$ if $\mathbb{A}$ is a substructure of $\mathbb{B}$ and, for all formulas φ and all assignments ν on $\mathbb{A}$, we have $(\mathbb{A}, \nu) \vDash \varphi$ if and only if $(\mathbb{B}, \nu) \vDash \varphi$. Note that if $\mathbb{A}$ is an elementary substructure of $\mathbb{B}$, then they are elementarily equivalent. $\mathcal{A}$ is an elementary subinterpretation of $\mathcal{B}$ if $\mathbb{A}$ is an elementary substructure of $\mathbb{B}$ and $\mathcal{A}$'s assignment is the same as $\mathcal{B}$'s assignment.

Given a Σ-structure $\mathbb{A}$, let $\mathcal{S}_{\geq \aleph_0}^\mathbb{A} = \{\sigma \in \mathcal{S}_\Sigma : |\sigma^\mathbb{A}| \geq \aleph_0\}$ and $\mathcal{S}_{< \aleph_0}^\mathbb{A} = \mathcal{S}_\Sigma \setminus \mathcal{S}_{\geq \aleph_0}^\mathbb{A}$. We similarly define $\mathcal{S}_{\geq \aleph_0}^\mathcal{A}$ and $\mathcal{S}_{< \aleph_0}^\mathcal{A}$ for a Σ-interpretation $\mathcal{A}$.

A Σ-*theory* $\mathcal{T}$ is a set of Σ-sentences, called the *axioms* of $\mathcal{T}$. We write $\vdash_\mathcal{T} \varphi$ instead of $\mathcal{T} \vDash \varphi$. Structures satisfying $\mathcal{T}$ are called $\mathcal{T}$-*models*, and interpretations satisfying $\mathcal{T}$ are called $\mathcal{T}$-*interpretations*. We say a Σ-formula is $\mathcal{T}$-*satisfiable* if it is satisfied by some $\mathcal{T}$-interpretation, and we say two Σ-formulas are $\mathcal{T}$-*equivalent* if every $\mathcal{T}$-interpretation satisfies one if and only if it satisfies the other. $\mathcal{T}$ is

---

[2] Due to lack of space, some proofs are omitted. They can be found in the arXiv version of this paper [16].

[3] When specifying a signature, we often omit the equality symbols, and include them implicitly. We also omit σ from $=_\sigma$ when it does not cause confusion.

complete if for every sentence φ, we have $\vdash_{\mathcal{T}} \varphi$ or $\vdash_{\mathcal{T}} \neg\varphi$. $\mathcal{T}$ is *consistent* if there is no formula φ such that $\vdash_{\mathcal{T}} \varphi$ and $\vdash_{\mathcal{T}} \neg\varphi$. If Σ_1 and Σ_2 are disjoint, let $\Sigma_1 \cup \Sigma_2$ be the signature with the union of their sorts, function symbols, and predicate symbols. Given a Σ_1-theory $\mathcal{T}_1$ and a Σ_2-theory $\mathcal{T}_2$, the $(\Sigma_1 \cup \Sigma_2)$-theory $\mathcal{T}_1 \cup \mathcal{T}_2$ is the theory whose axioms are the union of the axioms of $\mathcal{T}_1$ and $\mathcal{T}_2$.

The following theorem, proved in [14], is a many-sorted variant of the first-order compactness theorem.

Theorem 1 (Compactness Theorem [14]). *A set of Σ-formulas Γ is satisfiable if and only if every finite subset of Γ is satisfiable.*

We say that a Σ-theory $\mathcal{T}$ has *built-in Skolem functions* if for all formulas $\psi(\overrightarrow{x}, y)$, there is $f \in \mathcal{F}_\Sigma$ such that $\vdash_{\mathcal{T}} \forall \overrightarrow{x}. (\exists y. (\psi(\overrightarrow{x}, y)) \rightarrow \psi(\overrightarrow{x}, f(\overrightarrow{x}))).$[4] The following is a many-sorted variant of Lemma 2.3.6 of [12]. The proof is almost identical to that of the single-sorted case from [12].

Lemma 1. *If $\mathcal{T}$ is a Σ-theory for a countable Σ, then there is a countable signature $\Sigma^* \supseteq \Sigma$ and Σ^*-theory $\mathcal{T}^* \supseteq \mathcal{T}$ with built-in Skolem functions.*

We state a many-sorted generalization of the Tarski–Vaught test, whose proof is also similar to the single-sorted case [12, Proposition 2.3.5].

Lemma 2 (The Tarski–Vaught Test). *Suppose $\mathbb{A}$ is a substructure of $\mathbb{B}$. Then, $\mathbb{A}$ is an elementary substructure of $\mathbb{B}$ if and only if $(\mathbb{B}, \nu) \vDash \exists v. \varphi(\overrightarrow{x}, v)$ implies $(\mathbb{A}, \nu) \vDash \exists v. \varphi(\overrightarrow{x}, v)$ for every formula $\varphi(\overrightarrow{x}, v)$ and assignment ν over $\mathbb{A}$.*

2.2 Model-Theoretic Properties

Definition 1. *Let Σ be a many-sorted signature, $S \subseteq \mathcal{S}_\Sigma$, and $\mathcal{T}$ a Σ-theory.*

- $\mathcal{T}$ *is* stably infinite *with respect to S if for every $\mathcal{T}$-satisfiable quantifier-free formula φ, there is a $\mathcal{T}$-interpretation $\mathcal{A}$ satisfying φ with $|\sigma^{\mathcal{A}}| \geq \aleph_0$ for every $\sigma \in S$.*
- $\mathcal{T}$ *is* stably finite *with respect to S if for every quantifier-free Σ-formula φ and $\mathcal{T}$-interpretation $\mathcal{A}$ satisfying φ, there is a $\mathcal{T}$-interpretation $\mathcal{B}$ satisfying φ such that $|\sigma^{\mathcal{B}}| \leq |\sigma^{\mathcal{A}}|$ and $|\sigma^{\mathcal{B}}| < \aleph_0$ for every $\sigma \in S$.*
- $\mathcal{T}$ *is* smooth *with respect to S if for every quantifier-free formula φ, $\mathcal{T}$-interpretation $\mathcal{A}$ satisfying φ, and function κ from S to the class of cardinals such that $\kappa(\sigma) \geq |\sigma^{\mathcal{A}}|$ for every $\sigma \in S$, there is a $\mathcal{T}$-interpretation $\mathcal{B}$ satisfying φ with $|\sigma^{\mathcal{B}}| = \kappa(\sigma)$ for every $\sigma \in S$.*

Next, we define *arrangements*. Given a set of sorts $S \subseteq \mathcal{S}_\Sigma$, finite sets of variables V_σ of sort σ for each $\sigma \in S$, and equivalence relations E_σ on V_σ, the *arrangement* δ_V on $V = \bigcup_{\sigma \in S} V_\sigma$ induced by $E = \bigcup_{\sigma \in S} E_\sigma$ is

$$\bigwedge_{\sigma \in S} \left[\bigwedge_{x E_\sigma y} (x = y) \wedge \bigwedge_{x \overline{E_\sigma} y} \neg(x = y) \right],$$

---

[4] Intuitively: $\mathcal{T}$ has enough function symbols to witness all existential formulas.

where $\overline{E_\sigma}$ is the complement of E_σ.

Definition 2. *Let Σ be a many-sorted signature, $S \subseteq S_\Sigma$ a finite set, and T a Σ-theory. Then T is strongly finitely witnessable with respect to S if there is a computable function wit from the quantifier-free formulas into themselves such that for every quantifier-free formula φ:*

(i) φ and $\exists \overrightarrow{w}. \, wit(\varphi)$ are T-equivalent, where $\overrightarrow{w} = vars(wit(\varphi)) \setminus vars(\varphi)$; and

(ii) given a finite set of variables V and an arrangement δ_V on V, if $wit(\varphi) \wedge \delta_V$ is T-satisfiable, then there is a T-interpretation $\mathcal{A}$ satisfying $wit(\varphi) \wedge \delta_V$ such that $\sigma^{\mathcal{A}} = vars_\sigma(wit(\varphi) \wedge \delta_V)^{\mathcal{A}}$ for every $\sigma \in S$.

2.3   Notation

$\mathbb{N}$ denotes the set of non-negative integers. Given $m, n \in \mathbb{N}$, let $[m, n] := \{\ell \in \mathbb{N} : m \leq \ell \leq n\}$ and $[n] := [1, n]$. Given a set X, let $P_n(X) := \{Y \subseteq X : |Y| = n\}$, $X^n := \{(x_1, \ldots, x_n) : x_i \in X \text{ for all } i \in [n]\}$, and $X^* := \bigcup_{n \in \mathbb{N}} X^n$. For any x, we denote $(x, \ldots, x)$ by $(x)^{\oplus n}$. Given a tuple of tuples $(\overrightarrow{x_1}, \ldots, \overrightarrow{x_n})$, where $\overrightarrow{x_i} \in X^*$ for all i, we will often treat it as an element of X^* by flattening the tuple.

3   The Nonexistence of Unicorns

We now state our main theorem, which implies that unicorn theories do not exist. Note that since we are motivated by applications to SMT, we hereafter assume all signatures are countable.[5]

Theorem 2. *Assume that T is a Σ-theory, where Σ is countable. If T is stably infinite and strongly finitely witnessable, both with respect to $S \subseteq S_\Sigma$, then T is smooth with respect to S.*

For our proof, we define a weaker variant of smoothness, that focuses the requirements only for finite cardinals.

Definition 3. *A Σ-theory T is finitely smooth with respect to $S \subseteq S_\Sigma$ if for every quantifier-free formula φ, T-interpretation $\mathcal{A}$ with $\mathcal{A} \models \varphi$, and function κ from $S_{<\aleph_0}^{\mathcal{A}} \cap S$ to the class of cardinals with $|\sigma^{\mathcal{A}}| \leq \kappa(\sigma) < \aleph_0$ for every $\sigma \in S_{<\aleph_0}^{\mathcal{A}} \cap S$, there is a T-interpretation $\mathcal{B}$ with $\mathcal{B} \models \varphi$ with $|\sigma^{\mathcal{B}}| = \kappa(\sigma)$ for every $\sigma \in S_{<\aleph_0}^{\mathcal{A}} \cap S$.*

We make use of the following two lemmas.

Lemma 3. *If T is stably infinite and strongly finitely witnessable, both with respect to some set of sorts $S \subseteq S_\Sigma$, then T is finitely smooth with respect to S.*

Lemma 4 ([22, Theorem 3]). *If T is strongly finitely witnessable with respect to some set of sorts $S \subseteq S_\Sigma$, then T is stably finite with respect to S.*

---

[5] The paper that introduced unicorn theories [21] also made this assumption.

In light of the above two lemmas, the following theorem implies Theorem 2.

Theorem 3. *Assume that T is a Σ-theory, where Σ is countable. If T is stably finite and finitely smooth, both with respect to some set of sorts $S \subseteq S_\Sigma$, then T is smooth with respect to S.*

The remainder of this section is thus dedicated to the proof of Theorem 3.

3.1   Motivating the Proof

In this section, we illustrate the proof technique with a simple example. The goal is to motivate the proof of Theorem 3 before delving into the details.

Suppose T is a Σ-theory, where $S_\Sigma = \{\sigma_1, \sigma_2\}$, $\mathcal{F}_\Sigma = \{f\}$, f has arity (σ_2, σ_1), and the only predicate symbols are equalities. Suppose that T is also stably finite and finitely smooth, both with respect to $S = S_\Sigma$. Let φ be a T-satisfiable quantifier-free formula and $\mathcal{A}$ a T-interpretation satisfying φ. Let κ be a function from S to the class of cardinals such that $\kappa(\sigma) \geq |\sigma^{\mathcal{A}}|$ for both $\sigma \in S$. For concreteness, suppose $|\sigma_1^{\mathcal{A}}| = |\sigma_2^{\mathcal{A}}| = 10$, $\kappa(\sigma_1) = \aleph_0$, and $\kappa(\sigma_2) = \aleph_1$. Our goal is to show that there is a T-interpretation $\mathcal{B}^-$ satisfying φ with $|\sigma_1^{\mathcal{B}^-}| = \aleph_0$ and $|\sigma_2^{\mathcal{B}^-}| = \aleph_1$.[6]

A natural thought is to apply some variant of the upward Löwenheim–Skolem theorem, but this doesn't quite work. As will be seen in Sect. 4, generalizations of the Löwenheim–Skolem theorem to many-sorted logic do not let us control the cardinalities of σ_1 and σ_2 independently. Nevertheless, let us emulate the standard proof technique for the upward Löwenheim–Skolem theorem.

Here is the most natural way of generalizing the proof of the upward Löwenheim–Skolem theorem to our setting. For simplicity, assume that T already has built-in Skolem functions. We introduce $\aleph_0$ new constants $\{c_{1,\alpha}\}_{\alpha<\omega}$ and $\aleph_1$ new constants $\{c_{2,\alpha}\}_{\alpha<\omega_1}$. We define a set of formulas $\Gamma = \{\varphi\} \cup \Gamma_1$, where

$$\Gamma_1 = \{\neg(c_{i,\alpha} = c_{i,\beta}) : i \in \{1,2\}; \ \alpha, \beta < \kappa(\sigma_i); \ \alpha \neq \beta\}.$$

By Theorem 1 and finite smoothness, there is a T-interpretation $\mathcal{B}$ satisfying Γ: indeed, were that not true, Theorem 1 would guarantee that some finite subset of Γ is unsatisfiable; yet such a set would only demand the existence of finitely many new elements, which can be achieved by making use of finite smoothness. Since $\mathcal{B} \vDash \Gamma_1$, we have $|\sigma_1^{\mathcal{B}}| \geq \aleph_0$ and $|\sigma_2^{\mathcal{B}}| \geq \aleph_1$.

Since $\mathcal{B}$ may be too large, we construct a subinterpretation $\mathcal{B}^-$ with

$$\sigma_1^{\mathcal{B}^-} = \{c_{1,\alpha}^{\mathcal{B}}\}_{\alpha<\omega} \cup \{f^{\mathcal{B}}(c_{2,\alpha}^{\mathcal{B}})\}_{\alpha<\omega_1}$$
$$\sigma_2^{\mathcal{B}^-} = \{c_{2,\alpha}^{\mathcal{B}}\}_{\alpha<\omega_1}.$$

And using the assumption that T has built-in Skolem functions, we can prove that $\mathcal{B}^-$ is an elementary subinterpretation of $\mathcal{B}$, so $\mathcal{B}^- \vDash \Gamma$; we can then prove

---

[6] The reason for the $-$ superscript in $\mathcal{B}^-$ will be clear presently.

that $|\sigma_2^{\mathcal{B}^-}| = \aleph_1$, but we unfortunately cannot guarantee that $|\sigma_1^{\mathcal{B}^-}| = \aleph_0$. This is because $\mathcal{B}^-$ has not only the $\aleph_1$ elements $\{c_{2,\alpha}^{\mathcal{B}}\}_{\alpha<\omega_1}$ of sort σ_2, but also the elements $\{f^{\mathcal{B}}(c_{2,\alpha}^{\mathcal{B}})\}_{\alpha<\omega_1}$ of sort σ_1. The function symbol f has created a "spillover" of elements from σ_2 to σ_1.

To fix this, we need to ensure that $|\{f^{\mathcal{B}}(c_{2,\alpha}^{\mathcal{B}})\}_{\alpha<\omega_1}| \leq \aleph_0$. To that end, define Γ to instead be $\{\varphi\} \cup \Gamma_1 \cup \Gamma_2$, where

$$\Gamma_2 = \{f(b) = f(d) : b, d \in \{c_{2,\alpha}\}_{\alpha<\omega_1}\}.$$

Then, if there is a model $\mathcal{B}$ satisfying Γ, we have $|\{f^{\mathcal{B}}(c_{2,\alpha}^{\mathcal{B}})\}_{\alpha<\omega_1}| = 1 \leq \aleph_0$. To show Γ is $\mathcal{T}$-satisfiable, it suffices by the compactness theorem to show that $\mathcal{T}\cup\Gamma'$ is satisfiable for every finite subset $\Gamma' \subseteq \Gamma$. So let $\Gamma_1' \subseteq \Gamma_1$ and $\Gamma_2' \subseteq \Gamma_2$ be finite subsets. We will construct a $\mathcal{T}$-interpretation $\mathcal{B}'$ such that $\mathcal{B}' \vDash \{\varphi\} \cup \Gamma_1' \cup \Gamma_2'$. For concreteness, suppose that $\{c_{1,0}, c_{1,1}, \ldots, c_{1,99}\}$ and $\{c_{2,0}, c_{2,1}, \ldots, c_{2,9}\}$ are the new constants that appear in $\Gamma_1' \cup \Gamma_2'$. By finite smoothness, there is a $\mathcal{T}$-interpretation $\mathcal{B}'$ satisfying φ such that $|\sigma_1^{\mathcal{B}'}| = 100$ and $|\sigma_2^{\mathcal{B}'}| = 901$. By the pigeonhole principle, there is a subset $Y \subseteq \sigma_2^{\mathcal{B}'}$ with $|Y| \geq 10$ such that $f^{\mathcal{B}'}$ is constant on Y; if 901 pigeons are put in 100 holes, then some hole has at least 10 pigeons (although this is not true for 900 pigeons). Then, $\mathcal{B}'$ can interpret the constants $\{c_{1,0}, c_{1,1}, \ldots, c_{1,99}\}$ as distinct elements of $\sigma_1^{\mathcal{B}'}$ and the constants $\{c_{2,0}, c_{2,1}, \ldots, c_{2,9}\}$ as distinct elements of Y. This proves that Γ is $\mathcal{T}$-satisfiable.

We illustrate the top level structure of the proof idea in Fig. 1, applied to the working example. The x axis represents cardinalities of interpretations of σ_1, and the y axis does the same for σ_2. Starting from the interpretation $\mathcal{A}$ with $|\sigma_1^{\mathcal{A}}| = |\sigma_2^{\mathcal{A}}| = 10$, we construct some interpretation $\mathcal{B}$, represented by the array of red dots as there is some degree of uncertainty regarding the precise cardinalities of its domains, with $|\sigma_1^{\mathcal{B}}| \geq \aleph_0$ and $|\sigma_2^{\mathcal{B}}| \geq \aleph_1$. From $\mathcal{B}$ we hope to construct $\mathcal{B}^-$, which has $|\sigma_1^{\mathcal{B}^-}| = \aleph_0$ and $|\sigma_2^{\mathcal{B}^-}| = \aleph_1$: the latter can be achieved using techniques similar to the many-sorted Löwenheim-Skolem theorems (see Sect. 4 below), while the former requires the aforementioned pigeonhole principle arguments.

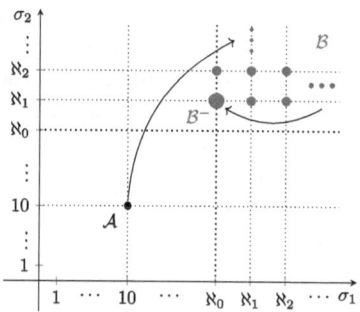

Fig. 1. How we move from interpretation to interpretation

The above proof sketch illustrates the main ideas behind the proof of Theorem 3. The generalization to more sorts and function symbols requires some extra bookkeeping. More interestingly, the generalization to functions of arity greater than one requires a version of Ramsey's theorem, which is a generalization of the pigeonhole principle.

3.2 Ramsey's Theorem and Generalizations

In this section, we state Ramsey's theorem and a generalization of it.

Ramsey's theorem is sometimes stated in terms of coloring the edges of hypergraphs, but for our purposes it is more convenient to state it as follows. In the following lemma, the notations $P_n(X)$ and $[k]$ are defined as in Sect. 2.3.

Lemma 5 (Ramsey's theorem [17, Theorem B]). *For any $k, n, m \in \mathbb{N}$, there is an $R(k, n, m) \in \mathbb{N}$ such that for any set X with $|X| \geq R(k, n, m)$ and function $f : P_n(X) \to [k]$, there is a subset $Y \subseteq X$ with $|Y| \geq m$ such that f is constant on $P_n(Y)$.*

Note that in Ramsey's theorem, the set $[k]$ can be replaced by any set of cardinality k.

We want to generalize Ramsey's theorem to functions $f : X^n \to [k]$. The most natural generalization would state that there is a large subset $Y \subseteq X$ such that f is constant on Y^n. But this generalization is false, as the following example shows.

Example 1. Let $X = \mathbb{Z}$, and let $f : X^2 \to [2]$ be given by

$$f(m, n) = \begin{cases} 1 & \text{if } m < n \\ 2 & \text{otherwise.} \end{cases}$$

Then, $f(m, n) \neq f(n, m)$ for all $m, n \in X$ with $m \neq n$. Thus, there is no subset $Y \subseteq X$ with $|Y| \geq 2$ such that f is constant on Y^2.

To avoid counterexamples like this, our generalization needs to consider the order of the arguments of f. This motivates the following definition.

Definition 4. *Let $(X, <)$ be a totally ordered set, and let $\vec{x} = (x_1, \ldots, x_n)$ and $\vec{y} = (y_1, \ldots, y_n)$ be elements of X^n. We write $\vec{x} \sim \vec{y}$ if for every $1 \leq i < j \leq n$ we have*

$$x_i < x_j \iff y_i < y_j \quad \text{and}$$
$$x_i = x_j \iff y_i = y_j.$$

Observe that $\sim$ is an equivalence relation on X^n with finitely many equivalence classes.[7]

Now we can state our first generalization of Ramsey's theorem.

Lemma 6. *For any $k, n, m \in \mathbb{N}$, there is an $R^*(k, n, m) \in \mathbb{N}$ such that for any totally ordered set $(X, <)$ with $|X| \geq R^*(k, n, m)$ and function $f : X^n \to [k]$, there is a subset $Y \subseteq X$ with $|Y| \geq m$ such that f is constant on each $\sim$-equivalence class of Y^n.*

Next, we further generalize Ramsey's theorem to multiple functions $f_1, \ldots, f_r$.

---

[7] The number of equivalence classes is given by the ordered Bell numbers (https://oeis.org/A000670).

Lemma 7. *For any $k, m \in \mathbb{N}$ and $\overrightarrow{n} = (n_1, \ldots, n_r) \in \mathbb{N}^r$, there is a number $R^{**}(k, \overrightarrow{n}, m) \in \mathbb{N}$, such that for any totally ordered set $(X, <)$ with $|X| \geq R^{**}(k, \overrightarrow{n}, m)$ and functions $f_i : X^{n_i} \to [k]$ for $i \in [r]$, there is a subset $Y \subseteq X$ with $|Y| \geq m$, such that f_i is constant on each $\sim$-equivalence class of Y^{n_i} for all $i \in [r]$.*

3.3   The Proof of Theorem 3

Fix a Σ-theory $\mathcal{T}$ and a set of sorts $S \subseteq \mathcal{S}_\Sigma$. Assume that Σ is countable. Suppose that $\mathcal{T}$ is stably finite and finitely smooth, both with respect to S. Let φ be a $\mathcal{T}$-satisfiable quantifier-free formula and $\mathcal{A}$ a $\mathcal{T}$-interpretation satisfying φ. Let κ be a function from S to the class of cardinals such that $\kappa(\sigma) \geq |\sigma^\mathcal{A}|$ for every $\sigma \in S$.

Write $S = \{\sigma_1, \sigma_2, \ldots\}$ and, without loss of generality, assume $\kappa(\sigma_1) \leq \kappa(\sigma_2) \leq \cdots$. For notational convenience, we write all Σ-terms in the form $t(\overrightarrow{x_1}, \overrightarrow{x_2}, \ldots),$[8] where $\overrightarrow{x_i}$ is a tuple of variables of sort σ_i. If $\kappa(\sigma_i) < \aleph_0$ for all i, then we are done by the fact $\mathcal{T}$ is finitely smooth. Otherwise, let ℓ be the largest natural number such that $\kappa(\sigma_\ell) < \aleph_0$ if there is such a number, and let $\ell = 0$ otherwise.

The proof of Theorem 3 proceeds in two steps. First, we construct a set of formulas Γ such that $\varphi \in \Gamma$ and prove that there is a $\mathcal{T}$-interpretation $\mathcal{B}$ satisfying Γ. Second, we prove that $\mathcal{B}$ has an elementary subinterpretation $\mathcal{B}^-$ such that $|\sigma_i^{\mathcal{B}^-}| = \kappa(\sigma_i)$ for all i. Since $\varphi \in \Gamma$, it will follow that $\mathcal{T}$ is smooth.

The assumption that $\mathcal{T}$ is stably finite and finitely smooth is used to construct $\mathcal{T}$-interpretations of the following form, which will be useful for a compactness argument.

Lemma 8. *There is a $\mathcal{T}$-interpretation $\mathcal{B}$ satisfying φ such that $|\sigma_i^\mathcal{B}| = \kappa(\sigma_i)$ for all $i \leq \ell$, and $|\sigma_i^\mathcal{B}|$ is arbitrarily large but finite for all $i > \ell$.*

Proof. First, apply stable finiteness to get a $\mathcal{T}$-interpretation $\mathcal{A}'$ satisfying φ such that $|\sigma_i^{\mathcal{A}'}| \leq |\sigma_i^\mathcal{A}|$ and $|\sigma_i^{\mathcal{A}'}| < \aleph_0$ for all i. Then, apply finite smoothness to $\mathcal{A}'$ with κ' given by $\kappa'(\sigma_i) = \kappa(\sigma_i)$ for all $i \leq \ell$ and $\kappa'(\sigma_i)$ arbitrarily large but finite for all $i > \ell$. $\qquad\square$

It will be convenient to work with a theory with built-in Skolem functions, so we use Lemma 1 to get a Σ^*-theory $\mathcal{T}^* \supseteq \mathcal{T}$, where $\Sigma^* \supseteq \Sigma$ and Σ^* is countable. To construct our set of formulas Γ, we introduce $\kappa(\sigma_i)$ new constants $\{c_{i,\alpha}\}_{\alpha < \kappa(\sigma_i)}$ of sort σ_i for each i. We consider these constants to be part of an even larger signature $\Sigma' \supseteq \Sigma^*$. In what follows, we construct sentences and interpretations over Σ'. Impose an arbitrary total order on each $\{c_{i,\alpha}\}_{\alpha < \kappa(\sigma_i)}$ to be used for the $\sim$ relation. For the definition below, recall that given a set X, we define $X^* = \bigcup_{n \in \mathbb{N}} X^n$.

---

[8] Even if S is infinite, the denoted term is still finite since each term only has a finite number of variables occurring in it.

Definition 5. *We define a set of formulas* $\Gamma = \{\varphi\} \cup \Gamma_1 \cup \Gamma_2 \cup \Gamma_3$, *where*

$$\Gamma_1 = \{\neg(c_{i,\alpha} = c_{i,\beta}) : 1 \le i \le |S|; \ \alpha, \beta < \kappa(\sigma_i); \ \alpha \ne \beta\}$$

$$\Gamma_2 = \left\{ t\left(\overrightarrow{c_1}, \ldots, \overrightarrow{c_i}, \overrightarrow{b_{i+1}}, \overrightarrow{b_{i+2}}, \ldots\right) = t\left(\overrightarrow{c_1}, \ldots, \overrightarrow{c_i}, \overrightarrow{d_{i+1}}, \overrightarrow{d_{i+2}}, \ldots\right) : \right.$$
$$t \text{ is a } \Sigma^* - term \text{ of sort } \sigma_i; \ i > \ell; \ \overrightarrow{c_k}, \overrightarrow{b_k}, \overrightarrow{d_k} \in (\{c_{k,\alpha}\}_{\alpha<\kappa(\sigma_k)})^*$$
$$\left. \text{for all } k; \ \overrightarrow{b_j} \sim \overrightarrow{d_j} \text{ for all } j > i \right\}$$

$$\Gamma_3 = \left\{ \forall x : \sigma_i. \bigvee_{\alpha<\kappa(\sigma_i)} x = c_{i,\alpha} : i \le \ell \right\}.$$

Note that the disjunctions in Γ_3 are finite given the condition $i \le \ell$.

Lemma 9. *There is a* T^**-interpretation* $\mathcal{B}$ *such that* $\mathcal{B} \vDash \Gamma$.

This lemma forms the core of the argument. By the compactness theorem, it suffices to prove that for any finite subset $\Gamma' \subseteq \Gamma$, there is a T^*-interpretation $\mathcal{B}'$ such that $\mathcal{B}' \vDash \Gamma'$. The tricky part is making $\mathcal{B}'$ satisfy $\Gamma' \cap \Gamma_2$. The strategy is to use Lemma 8 to construct a model $\mathcal{B}'$ in which $|\sigma_{i+1}^{\mathcal{B}'}|$ is very large in terms of $|\sigma_i^{\mathcal{B}'}|$ for each $i > \ell$. Lemma 7 will ensure that there is some way of interpreting the constants $\{c_{i,\alpha}\}_{\alpha<\kappa(\sigma_i)}$ so that $\mathcal{B}' \vDash \Gamma' \cap \Gamma_2$.

We are now ready to prove Theorem 3.

Proof (Theorem 3). By Lemma 9, there is a T^*-interpretation $\mathcal{B}$ such that $\mathcal{B} \vDash \Gamma$. Let

$$B = \left\{ t^{\mathcal{B}}\left((\overrightarrow{c_1})^{\mathcal{B}}, (\overrightarrow{c_2})^{\mathcal{B}}, \ldots\right) : t \text{ is a } \Sigma^*\text{-term}; \ \overrightarrow{c_i} \in (\{c_{i,\alpha}\}_{\alpha<\kappa(\sigma_i)})^* \text{ for all } i \right\}.$$

For every $f \in \mathcal{F}_\Sigma$, the set B is closed under $f^{\mathcal{B}}$. Thus, we can define $\mathcal{B}^-$ to be the subinterpretation of $\mathcal{B}$ obtained by restricting the sorts, functions, and predicates to B.[9] Since the Σ^*-theory T^* has built-in Skolem functions, $\mathcal{B}^-$ is an elementary subinterpretation of $\mathcal{B}$ by Lemma 2. We claim $|\sigma_i^{\mathcal{B}^-}| = \kappa(\sigma_i)$ for all i.

First, $\{c_{i,\alpha}^{\mathcal{B}^-}\}_{\alpha<\kappa(\sigma_i)}$ is a set of $\kappa(\sigma_i)$ distinct elements in $\sigma_i^{\mathcal{B}^-}$, because $\mathcal{B}^- \vDash \Gamma_1$. Thus, $|\sigma_i^{\mathcal{B}^-}| \ge \kappa(\sigma_i)$ for all i.

Second, $|\sigma_i^{\mathcal{B}^-}| \le |\{c_{i,\alpha}\}_{\alpha<\kappa(\sigma_i)}| = \kappa(\sigma_i)$ for all $i \in [\ell]$, as $\mathcal{B}^- \vDash \Gamma_3$.

Finally, it remains to show that $|\sigma_i^{\mathcal{B}^-}| \le \kappa(\sigma_i)$ for all $i > \ell$. Inductively suppose that $|\sigma_j^{\mathcal{B}^-}| \le \kappa(\sigma_j)$ for all $j < i$. Now, every element of $\sigma_i^{\mathcal{B}^-}$ is of the form

$$t^{\mathcal{B}}\left((\overrightarrow{c_1})^{\mathcal{B}}, \ldots, (\overrightarrow{c_i})^{\mathcal{B}}, (\overrightarrow{c_{i+1}})^{\mathcal{B}}, (\overrightarrow{c_{i+2}})^{\mathcal{B}}, \ldots\right),$$

where t is a Σ^*-term of sort σ_i. Since Σ^* is countable, there are at most $\aleph_0$ choices for t. We have at most $\kappa(\sigma_i)$ choices for $(\overrightarrow{c_1})^{\mathcal{B}}, \ldots, (\overrightarrow{c_i})^{\mathcal{B}}$. Finally, we have finitely many choices for $(\overrightarrow{c_{i+1}})^{\mathcal{B}}, (\overrightarrow{c_{i+2}})^{\mathcal{B}}, \ldots$ up to $\sim$-equivalence. Since

---

[9] In other words, $\mathcal{B}^-$ is the Skolem hull of $\bigcup_i \{c_{i,\alpha}^{\mathcal{B}}\}_{\alpha<\kappa(\sigma_i)}$ in $\mathcal{B}$ [12, p. 180].

$\mathcal{B}^- \vDash \Gamma_2$, it follows that there are at most $\kappa(\sigma_i)$ elements of $\sigma_i^{\mathcal{B}^-}$. Therefore, $\mathcal{B}^-$ is a $\mathcal{T}^*$-interpretation satisfying φ with $|\sigma_i^{\mathcal{B}^-}| = \kappa(\sigma_i)$ for all i. Taking the reduct of $\mathcal{B}^-$ to Σ gives the desired $\mathcal{T}$-interpretation.   □

3.4   Applications to Theory Combination

Since Theorem 2 implies that stably infinite and strongly finitely witnessable theories are strongly polite, we can restate the theorem on strongly polite theory combination with weaker hypotheses. This was already proved in [21] via a different method, but is now obtained as an immediate corollary of Theorem 2.

Corollary 1. *Let Σ_1 and Σ_2 be disjoint countable signatures. Let $\mathcal{T}_1$ and $\mathcal{T}_2$ be Σ_1- and Σ_2-theories respectively, and let φ_1 and φ_2 be quantifier-free Σ_1- and Σ_2-formulas respectively. Suppose $\mathcal{T}_1$ is stably infinite and strongly finitely witnessable, both with respect to $\mathcal{S}_{\Sigma_1} \cap \mathcal{S}_{\Sigma_2}$, and let $V = vars_{\mathcal{S}_{\Sigma_1} \cap \mathcal{S}_{\Sigma_2}}(wit(\varphi_1))$. Then, $\varphi_1 \wedge \varphi_2$ is $(\mathcal{T}_1 \cup \mathcal{T}_2)$-satisfiable if and only if there is an arrangement δ_V on V such that $wit(\varphi_1) \wedge \delta_V$ is $\mathcal{T}_1$-satisfiable and $\varphi_2 \wedge \delta_V$ is $\mathcal{T}_2$-satisfiable.*

We can also use our results to give a new characterization of shiny theories, which allows us to restate shiny combination theorem with weaker hypotheses.

To define shininess, we first need a few other notions. Let Σ be a signature with $\mathcal{S}_\Sigma$ finite, and let $S \subseteq \mathcal{S}_\Sigma$. Write $S = \{\sigma_1, \ldots, \sigma_n\}$. Then, the S-*size* of a Σ-interpretation $\mathcal{A}$ is given by the tuple $(|\sigma_1^{\mathcal{A}}|, \ldots, |\sigma_n^{\mathcal{A}}|)$. Such n-tuples are partially ordered by the product order: $(x_1, \ldots, x_n) \preceq (y_1, \ldots, y_n)$ if and only if $x_i \leq y_i$ for all $i \in [n]$. Given a quantifier-free formula φ, let $minmods_{\mathcal{T},S}(\varphi)$ be the set of minimal S-sizes of $\mathcal{T}$-interpretations satisfying φ. It follows from results in [10] that $minmods_{\mathcal{T},S}(\varphi)$ is a finite set of tuples.[10]

Then, we say a Σ-theory $\mathcal{T}$ is *shiny* with respect to some subset of sorts $S \subseteq \mathcal{S}_\Sigma$ if $\mathcal{S}_\Sigma$ is finite, $\mathcal{T}$ is stably finite and smooth, both with respect to S, and $minmods_{\mathcal{T},S}$ is computable. Theorem 3 implies that we can replace smoothness by finite smoothness, which may make it easier to prove that some theories are shiny. We can therefore improve the shiny theory combination theorem from [4, Theorem 2] as an immediate corollary of Theorem 3.

Corollary 2. *Let Σ_1 and Σ_2 be disjoint countable signatures, where $\mathcal{S}_{\Sigma_1}$ and $\mathcal{S}_{\Sigma_2}$ are finite. Let $\mathcal{T}_1$ and $\mathcal{T}_2$ be Σ_1- and Σ_2-theories respectively, and assume the satisfiability problems for quantifier-free formulas of both $\mathcal{T}_1$ and $\mathcal{T}_2$ are decidable. Suppose $\mathcal{T}_1$ is stably finite and finitely smooth, both with respect to $\mathcal{S}_{\Sigma_1} \cap \mathcal{S}_{\Sigma_2}$, and $minmods_{\mathcal{T}_1, \mathcal{S}_{\Sigma_1} \cap \mathcal{S}_{\Sigma_2}}$ is computable. Then, the satisfiability problem for quantifier-free formulas of $\mathcal{T}_1 \cup \mathcal{T}_2$ is decidable.*

---

[10] [4] proves this assuming that $\mathcal{T}$ is stably finite, using Hilbert's basis theorem. This assumption can be dropped by using the fact that if $(X, \leq)$ is a well-quasi-order, then so is $(X^n, \prec)$, where $\prec$ is the product order. Here X is the class of cardinals.

4   Many-Sorted Löwenheim–Skolem Theorems

In this section, we state many-sorted generalizations of the Löwenheim–Skolem theorem. Our first results, in Sect. 4.2, hold with no assumptions on the signature. Later, in Sect. 4.3, we state stronger results for restricted signatures, which we then use for a many-sorted variant of the Łoś–Vaught test in Sect. 4.4. But first, in Sect. 4.1, we explain the limitations of relying solely on translations to single-sorted first-order logic.

4.1   Lost in Translation

We may transform a many-sorted signature into a single-sorted signature by adding unary predicates signifying the sorts; of course, some restrictions are necessary, distinctness of sorts, etc. This procedure [6,13,24] is often used to lift results from single-sorted to many-sorted logic. As one example, standard versions of the downward Löwenheim–Skolem theorem for many-sorted logic, found in [14], are proven using this translation; we can, however, strengthen these results while still using only translations:

Theorem 4 (Downward). *Let Σ be a many-sorted signature with $|\mathcal{S}_\Sigma| < \aleph_0$. Suppose we have a Σ-structure $\mathbb{A}$ with $\max\{|\sigma^{\mathbb{A}}| : \sigma \in \mathcal{S}_\Sigma\} \geq \aleph_0$, a cardinal κ satisfying $\max\{|\Sigma|, \aleph_0\} \leq \kappa \leq \min\{|\sigma^{\mathbb{A}}| : \sigma \in \mathcal{S}^{\mathbb{A}}_{\geq \aleph_0}\}$, and sets $A_\sigma \subseteq \sigma^{\mathbb{A}}$ with $|A_\sigma| \leq \kappa$ for each $\sigma \in \mathcal{S}_\Sigma$. Then, there is an elementary substructure $\mathbb{B}$ of $\mathbb{A}$ such that $\sigma^{\mathbb{B}} = \sigma^{\mathbb{A}}$ for every $\sigma \in \mathcal{S}^{\mathbb{A}}_{<\aleph_0}$, $\aleph_0 \leq |\sigma^{\mathbb{B}}| \leq \kappa$ for all $\sigma \in \mathcal{S}^{\mathbb{A}}_{\geq \aleph_0}$, $|\sigma^{\mathbb{B}}| = \kappa$ for some $\sigma \in \mathcal{S}_\Sigma$, and $A_\sigma \subseteq \sigma^{\mathbb{B}}$ for all $\sigma \in \mathcal{S}_\Sigma$.*

Theorem 5 (Upward). *Let Σ be a many-sorted signature with $|\mathcal{S}_\Sigma| < \aleph_0$. Suppose we have a Σ-structure $\mathbb{A}$ with $\max\{|\sigma^{\mathbb{A}}| : \sigma \in \mathcal{S}_\Sigma\} \geq \aleph_0$ and a cardinal $\kappa \geq \max\{|\Sigma|, \max\{|\sigma^{\mathbb{A}}| : \sigma \in \mathcal{S}_\Sigma\}\}$. Then, there is a Σ-structure $\mathbb{B}$ containing $\mathbb{A}$ as an elementary substructure such that $\sigma^{\mathbb{B}} = \sigma^{\mathbb{A}}$ for all $\sigma \in \mathcal{S}^{\mathbb{A}}_{<\aleph_0}$, $\aleph_0 \leq |\sigma^{\mathbb{B}}| \leq \kappa$ for all $\sigma \in \mathcal{S}^{\mathbb{A}}_{\geq \aleph_0}$, and $|\sigma^{\mathbb{B}}| = \kappa$ for some sort $\sigma \in \mathcal{S}_\Sigma$.*

As convenient as translation arguments are, the above Löwenheim–Skolem theorems seem unsatisfactory, as they only allow us to choose a single cardinal, rather than one for each sort.

4.2   Downward, Upward, and Combined Versions

The following are generalizations of the downward and upward Löwenheim–Skolem theorems to many-sorted logic, which are proved by adapting the proofs of the single-sorted case. Notice that we set all infinite domains to the same cardinality, while finite domains preserve their cardinalities.

Theorem 6 (Downward). *Fix a first-order many-sorted signature Σ. Suppose we have a Σ-structure $\mathbb{A}$, a cardinal κ such that $\max\{\aleph_0, |\Sigma|\} \leq \kappa \leq \min\{|\sigma^{\mathbb{A}}| : \sigma \in \mathcal{S}^{\mathbb{A}}_{\geq \aleph_0}\}$, and sets $A_\sigma \subseteq \sigma^{\mathbb{A}}$ with $|A_\sigma| \leq \kappa$ for each $\sigma \in \mathcal{S}^{\mathbb{A}}_{\geq \aleph_0}$. Then, there is an elementary substructure $\mathbb{B}$ of $\mathbb{A}$ that satisfies $|\sigma^{\mathbb{B}}| = \kappa$ and $\sigma^{\mathbb{B}} \supseteq A_\sigma$ for every $\sigma \in \mathcal{S}^{\mathbb{A}}_{\geq \aleph_0}$, and also $\sigma^{\mathbb{B}} = \sigma^{\mathbb{A}}$ for every $\sigma \in \mathcal{S}^{\mathbb{A}}_{<\aleph_0}$.*

Theorem 7 (Upward). *Fix a first-order many-sorted signature Σ. Given a Σ-structure $\mathbb{A}$, pick a cardinal $\kappa \geq \max\{|\Sigma|, \aleph_0, \sup\{|\sigma^{\mathbb{A}}| : \sigma \in \mathcal{S}_{\geq\aleph_0}^{\mathbb{A}}\}\}$. Then, there is a Σ-structure $\mathbb{B}$ containing $\mathbb{A}$ as an elementary substructure that satisfies $|\sigma^{\mathbb{B}}| = \kappa$ for every $\sigma \in \mathcal{S}_{\geq\aleph_0}^{\mathbb{A}}$, and also $\sigma^{\mathbb{B}} = \sigma^{\mathbb{A}}$ for every $\sigma \in \mathcal{S}_{<\aleph_0}^{\mathbb{A}}$.*

Theorems 6 and 7 can be combined to yield yet another variant of the Löwenheim–Skolem theorem, which may be called the combined version.

Corollary 3 (Combined). *Fix a many-sorted signature Σ. Given a Σ-structure $\mathbb{A}$, pick a cardinal $\kappa \geq \max\{|\Sigma|, \aleph_0\}$. Then, there is a Σ-structure $\mathbb{B}$ elementarily equivalent to $\mathbb{A}$ with $|\sigma^{\mathbb{B}}| = \kappa$ for every $\sigma \in \mathcal{S}_{\geq\aleph_0}^{\mathbb{A}}$, and $\sigma^{\mathbb{B}} = \sigma^{\mathbb{A}}$ for $\sigma \in \mathcal{S}_{<\aleph_0}^{\mathbb{A}}$.*

We illustrate Corollary 3 in Fig. 2. In black, we represent the cardinalities of the resulting structure, and in red, those of the original one. When they coincide, we use marks split between the two colors. This representation shows a set of sorts in the horizontal axis, and the heights of the marks represent the cardinalities of the respective domains. We clearly separate cardinals larger and smaller than $\aleph_0$ with a rule. Assume, without

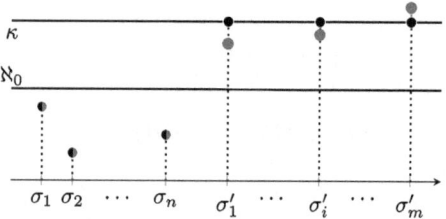

Fig. 2. Illustration of Corollary 3.

loss of generality, that initially $\sigma_1 \ldots \sigma_n$ have finite cardinalities and σ_1' has the least and σ_m' the greatest infinite cardinality.[11] Corollary 3 allows us to pick an infinite cardinal κ in between the least and greatest infinite cardinalities, and set all infinite cardinalities in the interpretation to κ.

The above theorems require that the desired cardinalities of the infinite sorts are all equal. The following example shows that this limitation is necessary.

Example 2. Take the signature Σ with sorts $S = \{\sigma_1, \sigma_2\}$, no predicates, and only one function f of arity (σ_1, σ_2). Take the Σ-structure $\mathbb{A}$ with: $\sigma_1^{\mathbb{A}}$ and $\sigma_2^{\mathbb{A}}$ of cardinality $\aleph_1$, and $f^{\mathbb{A}}$ a bijection. It is then true that $\mathbb{A} \vDash \varphi_{inj} \wedge \varphi_{sur}$, where $\varphi_{inj} = \forall x : \sigma_1. \forall y : \sigma_1. [[f(x) = f(y)] \rightarrow [x = y]]$ and $\varphi_{sur} = \forall u : \sigma_2. \exists x : \sigma_1. [f(x) = u]$, codifying that f is injective and surjective respectively. Notice then that, although $\max\{|\Sigma|, \aleph_0\} = \aleph_0$, there cannot be an elementary substructure $\mathbb{B}$ of $\mathbb{A}$ with $|\sigma_1^{\mathbb{B}}| = \aleph_0$ and $|\sigma_2^{\mathbb{B}}| = \aleph_1$: for if $\mathbb{B} \vDash \varphi_{inj} \wedge \varphi_{sur}$, $f^{\mathbb{B}}$ must be a bijection between $\sigma_1^{\mathbb{B}}$ and $\sigma_2^{\mathbb{B}}$. A similar argument shows that the corresponding generalization of the upwards theorem fails as well.

---

[11] For greater clarity, the diagram only depicts the cases where there are finitely many sorts and the signature is countable.

4.3   A Stronger Result for Split Signatures

Example 2 relies on "mixing sorts" by using a function symbol with arities spanning different sorts. We can state stronger versions of the many-sorted Löwenheim–Skolem theorems when such mixing of sorts is restricted.

Definition 6. *A signature Σ is said to be* split *by Λ into a family of signatures $\{\Sigma_\lambda : \lambda \in \Lambda\}$ if Λ is a partition of $\mathcal{S}_\Sigma$, $\mathcal{S}_{\Sigma_\lambda} = \lambda$ for each $\lambda \in \Lambda$, $\mathcal{F}_\Sigma = \bigcup_{\lambda \in \Lambda} \mathcal{F}_{\Sigma_\lambda}$, and $\mathcal{P}_\Sigma = \bigcup_{\lambda \in \Lambda} \mathcal{P}_{\Sigma_\lambda}$. If Σ is split by Λ and each $\lambda \in \Lambda$ is a singleton, then we say that Σ is* completely split *by Λ.*

If Σ is split by Λ, then the function/predicate symbols of Σ_λ must be disjoint from $\Sigma_{\lambda'}$ for $\lambda \neq \lambda'$. Given a partition Λ of $\mathcal{S}_\Sigma$ and $\lambda \in \Lambda$, let $\mathcal{S}^{\mathbb{A}}_{\geq \aleph_0}(\lambda) = \mathcal{S}^{\mathbb{A}}_{\geq \aleph_0} \cap \lambda$. We state the downward, upward, and combined theorems for split signatures.

Theorem 8 (Downward). *Fix a first-order many-sorted signature Σ split by Λ. Suppose we have a Σ-structure $\mathbb{A}$, a cardinal κ_λ such that $\max\{\aleph_0, |\Sigma_\lambda|\} \leq \kappa_\lambda \leq \min\{|\sigma^{\mathbb{A}}| : \sigma \in \mathcal{S}^{\mathbb{A}}_{\geq \aleph_0}(\lambda)\}$ for each $\lambda \in \Lambda$, and sets $A_\sigma \subseteq \sigma^{\mathbb{A}}$ with $|A_\sigma| \leq \kappa_\lambda$ for each $\sigma \in \mathcal{S}^{\mathbb{A}}_{\geq \aleph_0}(\lambda)$. Then, there is an elementary substructure $\mathbb{B}$ of $\mathbb{A}$ that satisfies $|\sigma^{\mathbb{B}}| = \kappa_\lambda$ and $\sigma^{\mathbb{B}} \supseteq A_\sigma$ for $\sigma \in \mathcal{S}^{\mathbb{A}}_{\geq \aleph_0}(\lambda)$, and $\sigma^{\mathbb{B}} = \sigma^{\mathbb{A}}$ for $\sigma \in \mathcal{S}^{\mathbb{A}}_{< \aleph_0}$.*

Theorem 9 (Upward). *Suppose Σ is split by Λ. Given a Σ-structure $\mathbb{A}$, pick a cardinal $\kappa_\lambda \geq \max\{|\Sigma_\lambda|, \aleph_0, \sup\{|\sigma^{\mathbb{A}}| : \sigma \in \mathcal{S}^{\mathbb{A}}_{\geq \aleph_0}(\lambda)\}\}$ for each $\lambda \in \Lambda$. Then, there is a Σ-structure $\mathbb{B}$ containing $\mathbb{A}$ as an elementary substructure that satisfies $|\sigma^{\mathbb{B}}| = \kappa_\lambda$ for $\sigma \in \mathcal{S}^{\mathbb{A}}_{\geq \aleph_0}(\lambda)$, and $\sigma^{\mathbb{B}} = \sigma^{\mathbb{A}}$ for $\sigma \in \mathcal{S}^{\mathbb{A}}_{< \aleph_0}$.*

Corollary 4 (Combined). *Suppose Σ is split by Λ. Given a Σ-structure $\mathbb{A}$, pick a cardinal $\kappa_\lambda \geq \max\{|\Sigma_\lambda|, \aleph_0\}$ for each $\lambda \in \Lambda$. Then, there is a Σ-structure $\mathbb{B}$ elementarily equivalent to $\mathbb{A}$ with $|\sigma^{\mathbb{B}}| = \kappa_\lambda$ for every $\sigma \in \mathcal{S}^{\mathbb{A}}_{\geq \aleph_0}(\lambda)$, and also $\sigma^{\mathbb{B}} = \sigma^{\mathbb{A}}$ for every $\sigma \in \mathcal{S}^{\mathbb{A}}_{< \aleph_0}$.*

Corollary 4 is illustrated in Fig. 3. We add sorts $S'' = \{\sigma''_1, \ldots, \sigma''_m\}$, and assume our signature is split into Σ_{λ_1} and Σ_{λ_2}, where $\mathcal{S}^{\mathbb{A}}_{\geq \aleph_0}(\lambda_1) = \{\sigma'_1, \ldots, \sigma'_m\}$ and $\mathcal{S}^{\mathbb{A}}_{\geq \aleph_0}(\lambda_2) = S''$ (the sorts with finite cardinalities can belong to either). Then, κ' is the cardinal associated with Σ_{λ_1}, and κ'' with Σ_{λ_2}. Thus, we are able to choose a cardinality for each class of sorts.

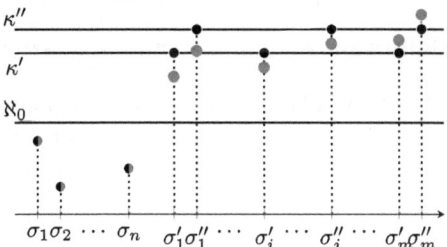

Fig. 3. Illustration of Corollary 4.

4.4   An Application: The Łoś–Vaught Test

We describe an application of our Löwenheim–Skolem theorems for theory-completeness: the Łoś–Vaught test. This is particularly relevant to SMT, as if a complete theory $\mathcal{T}$ has a decidable set of axioms, then it is decidable whether $\vdash_\mathcal{T} \varphi$ [12, Lemma 2.2.8]. The single-sorted Łoś–Vaught is the following.

Definition 7. *Let Σ be a signature and κ a function from $\mathcal{S}_\Sigma$ to the class of cardinals. A Σ-theory $\mathcal{T}$ is κ-categorical if it has exactly one model $\mathbb{A}$ (up to isomorphism) with the property that $|\sigma^\mathbb{A}| = \kappa(\sigma)$ for every $\sigma \in \mathcal{S}_\Sigma$. If there is only one sort $\sigma \in \mathcal{S}_\Sigma$, we abuse notation by using κ to denote the cardinal $\kappa(\sigma)$.*

Theorem 10 ([11,23]). *Suppose Σ is single-sorted and $\mathcal{T}$ is a Σ-theory with only infinite models. If $\mathcal{T}$ is κ-categorical for some $\kappa \geq |\Sigma|$, then $\mathcal{T}$ is complete.*

The Łoś–Vaught test is quite useful, e.g., for the completeness of dense linear orders without endpoints and algebraically closed fields. We generalize it to many sorts. Translating to one-sorted logic and using Theorem 10 gives us:

Corollary 5. *Let Σ be a signature with $|\mathcal{S}_\Sigma| < \aleph_0$. Suppose $\mathcal{T}$ is a Σ-theory, all of whose models $\mathbb{A}$ satisfy $\max\{|\sigma^\mathbb{A}| : \sigma \in \mathcal{S}_\Sigma\} \geq \aleph_0$. Suppose further that for some cardinal $\kappa \geq |\Sigma|$, $\mathcal{T}$ has exactly one model $\mathbb{A}$ (up to isomorphism) such that $\max\{|\sigma^\mathbb{A}| : \sigma \in \mathcal{S}_\Sigma\} = \kappa$. Then, $\mathcal{T}$ is complete.*

This is not the result one would hope for, because it excludes some many-sorted κ-categorical theories, as the following example demonstrates.

Example 3. Suppose Σ has $S = \{\sigma_1, \sigma_2\}$, no predicate symbols, and function symbols 0, 1, $+$, and $\times$, of the expected arities. Let $\mathcal{T} = \mathsf{ACF}_0 \cup \{\psi^{\sigma_2}_{\geq n} : n \in \mathbb{N}\}$, where ACF_0 is the theory of algebraically closed fields of characteristic zero (with respect to σ_1) and $\psi^\sigma_{\geq n} = \exists x_1 : \sigma. \cdots \exists x_n : \sigma. \bigwedge_{1 \leq i < j \leq n} \neg(x_i = x_j)$, which asserts that there are at least n elements of sort σ. $\mathcal{T}$ is κ-categorical, where $\kappa(\sigma_1) = \aleph_1$ and $\kappa(\sigma_2) = \aleph_0$. But $\mathcal{T}$ is also κ'-categorical, where $\kappa'(\sigma_1) = \kappa'(\sigma_2) = \aleph_1$. Thus, $\mathcal{T}$ has multiple models $\mathbb{A}$ satisfying $\max\{|\sigma^\mathbb{A}| : \sigma \in \mathcal{S}_\Sigma\} = \aleph_1$. Similar reasoning holds for other infinite cardinals, so Corollary 5 does not apply.

For completely split signatures, we prove a more natural Łoś–Vaught test:

Definition 8. *A Σ-structure $\mathbb{A}$ is strongly infinite if $|\sigma^\mathbb{A}| \geq \aleph_0$ for all $\sigma \in \mathcal{S}_\Sigma$.*

Theorem 11. *Suppose Σ is completely split into $\{\Sigma_\sigma : \sigma \in \mathcal{S}_\Sigma\}$, $\mathcal{T}$ is a Σ-theory all of whose models are strongly infinite, and $\mathcal{T}$ is κ-categorical for some function κ such that $\kappa(\sigma) \geq |\Sigma_\sigma|$ for every $\sigma \in \mathcal{S}_\Sigma$. Then, $\mathcal{T}$ is complete.*

The assumption that Σ is completely split is necessary for Theorem 11:

Example 4. Let Σ have sorts σ_1, σ_2, and function symbol f of arity (σ_1, σ_2). Let $\mathcal{T} = \{\psi^{\sigma_1}_{\geq n} : n \in \mathbb{N}\} \cup \{\psi^{\sigma_2}_{\geq n} : n \in \mathbb{N}\} \cup \{\varphi_{inj} \vee \forall x : \sigma_1. \forall y : \sigma_1. [f(x) = f(y)]\}$. In $\mathcal{T}$, σ_1, σ_2 are infinite, and f is injective or constant. $\mathcal{T}$ is κ-categorical for $\kappa(\sigma_1) = \aleph_1, \kappa(\sigma_2) = \aleph_0$, but not complete, due to the sentence $\forall x, y : \sigma_1. f(x) = f(y)$. This does not contradict Theorem 11, as Σ is not completely split.

5 Conclusion

We closed the problem of the existence of unicorn theories and discussed applications to SMT. This included a result similar to the Löwenheim–Skolem theorem, which inspired us to investigate the adaptation of this theorem to many-sorted logic. We also obtained a many-sorted version of the Łoś–Vaught test.

In future work, we plan to investigate whether Theorem 3 can be extended to uncountable signatures. More broadly, we intend to continue studying the relationships among many-sorted model-theoretic properties related to SMT.

Acknowledgments. This work was supported in part by the Stanford Center for Automated Reasoning, NSF-BSF grant numbers 2110397 (NSF) and 2020704 (BSF), ISF grant 619/21, and the Colman-Soref fellowship. The first author thanks the organizers of the CURIS research program.

References

1. Barbosa, H., et al.: cvc5: a versatile and industrial-strength SMT solver. In: TACAS (1). Lecture Notes in Computer Science, vol. 13243, pp. 415–442. Springer, Munich (2022)
2. Barrett, C., Fontaine, P., Tinelli, C.: The SMT-LIB Standard: Version 2.6. Tech. rep., Department of Computer Science, The University of Iowa (2017).http://smt-lib.org
3. Barrett, C., Tinelli, C.: Satisfiability modulo theories. In: Clarke, E.M., Henzinger, T.A., Veith, H., Bloem, R. (eds.) Handbook of Model Checking, pp. 305–343. Springer, New York (2018). https://doi.org/10.1007/978-3-319-10575-8_11, http://theory.stanford.edu/~barrett/pubs/BT18.pdf
4. Casal, F., Rasga, J.a.: Many-sorted equivalence of shiny and strongly polite theories. J. Automat. Reason. **60**(2), 221–236 (2018)
5. Ehrenfeucht, A., Mostowski, A.: Models of axiomatic theories admitting automorphisms. Fund. Math. **43**, 50–68 (1956)
6. Enderton, H.B.: A Mathematical Introduction to Logic. Academic Press, New York (1972)
7. Fontaine, P.: Combinations of theories for decidable fragments of first-order logic. In: Ghilardi, S., Sebastiani, R. (eds.) Frontiers of Combining Systems, pp. 263–278. Springer, Berlin Heidelberg, Berlin, Heidelberg (2009)
8. Jovanović, D., Barrett, C.: Polite theories revisited. Tech. Rep. TR2010-922, Department of Computer Science, New York University (Jan 2010). http://www.cs.stanford.edu/~barrett/pubs/JB10-TR.pdf
9. Krstić, S., Goel, A., Grundy, J., Tinelli, C.: Combined satisfiability modulo parametric theories. In: Grumberg, O., Huth, M. (eds.) Tools and Algorithms for the Construction and Analysis of Systems, pp. 602–617. Springer Berlin Heidelberg, Berlin, Heidelberg (2007). https://doi.org/10.1007/978-3-540-71209-1_47
10. Kruskal, J.B.: The theory of well-quasi-ordering: a frequently discovered concept. J. Comb. Theory Ser. A **13**, 297–305 (1972). https://doi.org/10.1016/0097-3165(72)90063-5
11. Ł oś, J.: On the categoricity in power of elementary deductive systems and some related problems. Colloquium Mathematicum **3**, 58–62 (1954)

12. Marker, D.: Model theory: an introduction, Graduate Texts in Mathematics, vol. 217. Springer-Verlag, New York (2002). https://doi.org/10.1007/b98860

13. Monk, J.D.: Mathematical Logic. Springer, New York (1976).https://doi.org/10. 1007/978-1-4684-9452-5

14. Monzano, M.: Introduction to many-sorted logic. In: Meinke, K., Tucker, J.V. (eds.) Many-sorted Logic and its Applications. Wiley professional computing, Wiley, New York (1993)

15. Nelson, G., Oppen, D.C.: Simplification by cooperating decision procedures. ACM Trans. Program. Lang. Syst. **1**(2), 245–257 (oct 1979).https://doi.org/10.1145/357073.357079

16. Przybocki, B., Toledo, G., Zohar, Y., Barrett, C.: The nonexistence of unicorns and many-sorted Löwenheim–Skolem theorems (2024). https://arxiv.org/abs/2406.18912

17. Ramsey, F.P.: On a problem of formal logic. Proc. London Math. Soc. (2) **30**(4), 264–286 (1929)

18. Ranise, S., Ringeissen, C., Zarba, C.G.: Combining data structures with nonstably infinite theories using many-sorted logic. In: Gramlich, B. (ed.) 5th International Workshop on Frontiers of Combining Systems - FroCoS'05. Lecture Notes in Artificial Intelligence, vol. 3717, pp. 48–64. Springer, Vienna/Austria (Sep 2005https://doi.org/10.1007/11559306, https://hal.inria.fr/inria-00000570

19. Sheng, Y., Zohar, Y., Ringeissen, C., Lange, J., Fontaine, P., Barrett, C.: Polite combination of algebraic datatypes. J. Autom. Reasoning **66**(3), 331–355 (2022). https://doi.org/10.1007/s10817-022-09625-3

20. Tinelli, C., Zarba, C.G.: Combining decision procedures for sorted theories. Tech. rep., Berlin, Heidelberg (2004).https://doi.org/10.1007/978-3-540-30227-8_53

21. de Toledo, G.V., Zohar, Y., Barrett, C.W.: Combining combination properties: an analysis of stable infiniteness, convexity, and politeness. In: CADE, Lecture Notes in Computer Science, vol. 14132, pp. 522–541. Springer, Rome (2023). https://doi.org/10.1007/978-3-031-38499-8_30

22. de Toledo, G.V., Zohar, Y., Barrett, C.W.: Combining finite combination properties: finite models and busy beavers. In: FroCoS, Lecture Notes in Computer Science, vol. 14279, pp. 159–175. Springer, Prague (2023). https://doi.org/10.1007/978-3-031-43369-6_9

23. Vaught, R.L.: Applications of the Löwenheim-Skolem-Tarski theorem to problems of completeness and decidability. Nederl. Akad. Wetensch. Proc. **57**, 467–472 (1954)

24. Wang, H.: Logic of many-sorted theories. J. Symbolic Logic **17**(2), 105–116 (1952). http://www.jstor.org/stable/2266241

Author Index

A

Ábrahám, Erika I-131
Adelt, Julius II-208
Akshay, S. I-111
Aldinucci, Marco I-226
Ammar, Nejib II-267
An, Jie I-620, II-286
Arcaini, Paolo II-286

B

Bae, Kyungmin I-425
Baier, Daniel II-543
Baldauf, Jake Brandon I-381
Barbosa, Haniel II-573
Bargmann, Lara I-519
Barrett, Clark I-658, II-573
Barros, Ana II-104
Basin, David I-29
Baumeister, Jan II-626
Baumeister, Tom I-638
Beckert, Bernhard II-599
Bergersen, Gunnar R. II-167
Beutner, Raven II-67
Beyer, Dirk II-39, II-543
Blicha, Martin I-558
Bombarda, Andrea II-492
Bonfanti, Silvia II-492
Bono, Viviana I-226
Bordais, Benjamin I-304
Bordis, Tabea I-151
Brain, Martin II-393
Britikov, Konstantin I-558
Bubel, Richard II-599
Bury, Guillaume II-76
Busany, Nimrod I-245

C

Cai, Shaowei I-55
Calinescu, Radu II-356
Chakraborty, Supratik I-111
Chambart, Pierre II-76
Chatterjee, Krishnendu I-600

C (cont.)

Chen, Guangke I-343
Chen, Mingshuai I-538
Chen, Taolue II-189
Chien, Po-Chun II-543
Chin, Wei-Ngan I-501
Colonnelli, Iacopo I-226
Coopmans, Tim II-420
Coughlin, Nicholas I-482
Courant, Nathanaëlle II-76
Cunha, Alcino II-104

D

De Giacomo, Giuseppe I-579
Dedden, Frank II-469
Dell'Erba, Daniele II-48
Deng, Weilin II-338
Di Stasio, Antonio I-579
Ding, Jianqiang II-140
Dong, Jin Song I-343
Dong, Zhen I-285
Dongol, Brijesh I-519
Drodt, Daniel II-599
Dutta, Souradeep I-381

E

Ehlers, Rüdiger I-170
Eichler, Paul I-638

F

Fang, Jian I-538
Fang, Wang I-403
Fedyukovich, Grigory I-558
Feliu, Marco A. II-20
Feng, Shenghua II-229, II-248
Finkbeiner, Bernd II-67, II-626
Foo, Darius I-501
Frohn, Florian I-73
Fu, Yubao II-325
Furia, Carlo A. I-285

G

Gan, Ting I-92, II-248
Ganlath, Akila II-267

X

Xia, Bican   I-92, II-248
Xiong, Yingfei   I-538
Xue, Bai   II-140
Xue, Jingling   II-307

Y

Yan, Pengbo   I-188
Yan, Rui   I-363
Yang, Xi   II-189
Yang, Zhibin   II-338
Ying, Mingsheng   I-403

Z

Zhan, Naijun   I-92, I-620, II-229, II-248
Zhan, Sinong   II-229
Zhang, Changjian   II-267
Zhang, Yedi   I-343
Zhang, Zhenya   II-286
Zhao, Mengyu   I-55
Zhou, Yong   II-338
Zhu, Shufang   I-579
Zi, Yuan   II-307
Žikelić, Đorđe   I-600
Zizyte, Milda   I-579
Zohar, Yoni   I-658, II-573